Handbook on Session Initiation Protocol

Networked Multimedia Communications for IP Telephony

OTHER COMMUNICATIONS BOOKS FROM CRC PRESS

Advances in Communications-Based Train Control Systems
Edited by F. Richard Yu
ISBN 978-1-4822-5743-4

Advances in Mobile Cloud Computing Systems
Edited by F. Richard Yu and Victor Leung
ISBN 978-1-4987-1509-6

Analytical Evaluation of Nonlinear Distortion Effects on Multicarrier Signals
Theresa Araújo and Rui Dinis
ISBN 978-1-4822-1594-6

Cognitive Radio Networks: Efficient Resource Allocation in Cooperative Sensing, Cellular Communications, High-Speed Vehicles, and Smart Grid
Tao Jiang, Zhiqiang Wang, and Yang Cao
ISBN 978-1-4987-2113-4

Cyber Physical Systems: Architectures, Protocols and Applications
Edited by Chi (Harold) Liu and Yan Zhang
ISBN 978-1-4822-0897-9

Cyber-Physical Systems: From Theory to Practice
Edited by Danda B. Rawat, Joel J.P.C. Rodrigues, and Ivan Stojmenovic
ISBN 978-1-4822-6332-9

Embedded Software Development for Safety-Critical Systems
Chris Hobbs
ISBN 978-1-4987-26702

Honeypots and Routers: Collecting Internet Attacks
Mohssen Mohammed and Habib-ur Rehman
ISBN 978-1-4987-0219-5

Introduction to Communications Technologies: A Guide for Non-Engineers, Third Edition
Stephan Jones, Ronald J. Kovac, and Frank M. Groom
ISBN 978-1-4987-0293-5

Introduction to Theory of Control in Organizations
Vladimir N. Burkov, Mikhail Goubko, Nikolay Korgin, and Dmitry Novikov
ISBN 978-1-4987-1423-5

Just Ordinary Robots: Automation from Love to War
Lamber Royakkers and Rinie van Est
ISBN 978-1-4822-6014-4

Managing the PSTN Transformation: A Blueprint for a Successful Migration to IP-Based Networks
Sandra Dornheim
ISBN 978-1-4987-0103-7

Micro- and Nano-Scale Sensors and Transducers
Ezzat G. Bakhoum
ISBN 978-1-4822-5090-9

Mobile Evolution: Insights on Connectivity and Service
Sebastian Thalanany
ISBN 978-1-4822-2480-1

Multi-Carrier Communication Systems with Examples in MATLAB®: A New Perspective
Emad Hassan
ISBN 978-1-4987-3532-2

Securing Cyber-Physical Systems
Edited by Al-Sakib Khan Pathan
ISBN 978-1-4987-0098-6

Systematic Strategic Planning: A Comprehensive Framework for Implementation, Control, and Evaluation
Hakan Butuner
ISBN 978-1-4987-2481-4

The Future of Wireless Networks: Architectures, Protocols, and Services
Edited by Mohesen Guizani, Hsiao-Hwa Chen, and Chonggang Wang
ISBN 978-1-4822-2094-0

The Future X Network: A Bell Labs Perspective
Marcus K. Weldon
ISBN 978-1-4987-5926-7

Understanding Spectrum Liberalisation
Martin Sims, Toby Youell, and Richard Womersley
ISBN 978-1-4987-0502-8

Wireless Sensor Multimedia Networks: Architectures, Protocols, and Applications
Edited by Mohamed Mostafa A. Azim and Xiaohong Jiang
ISBN 978-1-4822-5311-5

Wireless Network Performance Enhancement via Directional Antennas: Models, Protocols, and Systems
Edited by John D. Matyjas, Fei Hu, and Sunil Kumar
ISBN 978-1-4987-0753-4

Handbook on Session Initiation Protocol

Networked Multimedia Communications for IP Telephony

Radhika Ranjan Roy

CRC Press
Taylor & Francis Group
Boca Raton London New York

CRC Press is an imprint of the
Taylor & Francis Group, an **informa** business

CRC Press
Taylor & Francis Group
6000 Broken Sound Parkway NW, Suite 300
Boca Raton, FL 33487-2742

First issued in paperback 2020

Version Date: 20151124

ISBN 13: 978-0-367-57498-7 (pbk)
ISBN 13: 978-1-4987-4770-7 (hbk)

Visit the Taylor & Francis Web site at
http://www.taylorandfrancis.com

and the CRC Press Web site at
http://www.crcpress.com

To our dearest son, Debasri Roy, *Medicinae Doctoris* (MD) (January 20, 1988–October 31, 2014), who had a brilliant career (summa cum laude, undergraduate) and had so much more to contribute to this country and to the world as a whole. He had been so eager to see this book published, saying, "Daddy, you are my hero." Observing the deep relationship between Debasri and his fiancée, their friends exclaimed with wonder: "Love is forever." He wrote as his lifelong wishes: "I am ready for my life, I'd like to see the whole world, I will read spiritual scriptures to find the mystery of life, and I want to make a difference in the world." He loved all of us from the deepest part of his kindest heart, including his longtime fiancée, who is also an MD and was his classmate, and to whom he was engaged to be married on October 30, 2015, in front of relatives, friends, colleagues, and neighbors who, until his last breath, he had inspired in so many ways to love God, along with his prophetic words: "Mom, I am extremely happy that you are with me and I want to be happy in life." May God let his soul live in peace in His abode.

To my grandma for her causeless love; my parents Rakesh Chandra Roy and Sneholota Roy whose spiritual inspiration remains vividly alive within all of us; my late sisters GitaSree Roy, Anjali Roy, and Aparna Roy and their spouses; my brother Raghunath Roy and his wife Nupur for their inspiration; my daughter Elora and my son-in-law Nick; my son Ajanta; and finally my beloved wife, Jharna. I thank them all for their love.

And my heartfelt thanks go to my son Ajanta, for inspiring me with his wonderful creativity since his first major thoughtful invention of a multimedia telephony model using cupboard papers along with a vivid description written on a piece of paper detailing how the phone would work. I had been the technical lead of AT&T Vision 2001 Multimedia Architecture project at AT&T Bell Laboratories in 1993, when Ajanta was only in the fifth grade. Immediately I took the model to AT&T Bell Labs, and all of my colleagues were surprised to see his wonderful creativity in multimedia telephony. I wish I could patent his wonderful idea. Since then, I have been so inspired that I have worked on VoIP/multimedia telephony. Today, Ajanta is an energetic electrical engineer progressing toward a bright future in his own right, keeping his colleagues and all of us amazed. This book is a culmination of the vivid inspiration that he has embedded in me.

Contents

List of Figures

List of Tables

Preface

I have worked on networked multimedia communications, including in my present position at the US Army Research, Development and Engineering Command (RDECOM), Communications–Electronics Research, Development, and Engineering Center (CERDEC), Space and Terrestrial Communications Directorate (S&TCD) Laboratories, for large-scale global Session Initiation Protocol (SIP)-based Voice-over-Internet Protocol (VoIP)/multimedia networks since 1993 when I was at AT&T Bell Laboratories. I was the editor of the Multimedia Communications Forum (MMCF) when it was created by many participating companies worldwide, including AT&T, to promote technical standards for networked multimedia communications to fill an important gap at a time when no standard bodies came forward to do so. Later, I had the opportunity to participate in International Telecommunication Union–Telecommunication (ITU-T) on behalf of AT&T for the standardization of H.323. H.323 was the first successful technical standard for VoIP/multimedia telephony. However, SIP, which was standardized by the Internet Engineering Task Force (IETF) much later than H.323, and emulated the simplicity of the protocol architecture of Hypertext Transfer Protocol (HTTP), has been popularized for VoIP over the Internet because of the ease with which it can be meshed with web services.

After so many years of working on SIP to build large-scale VoIP networks, I found that it was an urgent requirement to have a complete book that integrates all SIP-related Requests for Comment (RFCs) in a systematic way—a book that network designers, software developers, product manufacturers, implementers, interoperability testers, professionals, professors, and researchers can use like a super-SIP RFC since the publication of SIP RFC 3261 in 2002. No one knows exactly how many RFCs, or even just those related to the base SIP specification, have been published over the last two decades or how they are interrelated after so many extensions and enhancements with new features and capabilities, corrections, and modifications with the latest consensus based on implementation and interoperability test experiences. Future studies are expected to break new ground in the current knowledge of SIP. This book on SIP is the first of its kind in an attempt to put together all SIP-related RFCs, with their mandatory and optional texts, in a chronological and systematic way for use as a single super-SIP RFC with an almost one-to-one integrity from beginning to end. It aims to show the big picture of SIP for the basic SIP functionalities.

It should be noted that the text of each RFC from the IETF has been reviewed by all members of a given working group composed of worldwide experts, and a rough consensus was made on which parts of the drafts needed to be *mandatory* or *optional*, including whether an RFC needed to be Standards Track, Informational, or Experimental. Trying to put all SIP-related RFCs together to make a textbook has serious challenges because the key point is not simply putting one RFC after another chronologically. The text of each RFC needs to be put together for each particular functionality, capability, and feature while retaining its integrity. Since this book is planned to serve as a single-SIP RFC specification, I had very limited freedom to change the text of the original RFCs aside from some editorial changes. I have used texts, figures, tables, and references from the original RFCs as much as necessary so that readers can use them in their original form. All RFCs, along with their authors, are provided as references, and all credit goes primarily to the authors of these RFCs and the many IETF working group members who shaped the final RFCs with their invaluable comments and input. In this connection, I also extend my sincere thanks to Paul Brigner, IETF Secretariat, for his kind consent to reproduce text, figures, and tables with IETF copyright notification. My only credit, as I mentioned earlier, is to put all those RFCs together in such a way that will make one complete SIP RFC.

I have organized this book into 20 chapters based on the major functionalities, features, and capabilities of SIP, as follows:

- Chapter 1: Networked Multimedia Services
- Chapter 2: Basic Session Initiation Protocol
- Chapter 3: SIP Message Elements
- Chapter 4: Addressing in SIP
- Chapter 5: SIP Event Framework and Packages
- Chapter 6: Presence and Instant Messaging in SIP
- Chapter 7: Media Transport Protocol and Media Negotiation

- Chapter 8: DNS and ENUM in SIP
- Chapter 9: Routing in SIP
- Chapter 10: User and Network-Asserted Identity in SIP
- Chapter 11: Early Media in SIP
- Chapter 12: Service and Served-User Identity in SIP
- Chapter 13: Connections Management and Overload Control in SIP
- Chapter 14: Interworking Services in SIP
- Chapter 15: Resource Priority and Quality of Service in SIP
- Chapter 16: Call Services in SIP
- Chapter 17: Media Server Interfaces in SIP
- Chapter 18: Multiparty Conferencing in SIP
- Chapter 19: Security Mechanisms in SIP
- Chapter 20: Privacy and Anonymity in SIP

However, presenting the SIP RFCs chronologically is not the only way to group them. My best intellectual instinct has guided me in arranging these RFCs according to basic SIP functionalities; however, the much more complex intelligent capabilities of SIP are yet to be included. I am looking forward to see whether readers will validate my judgment. In addition, I am providing a general statement for the IETF copyright information, as follows:

> IETF RFCs have texts that are mandatory and optional including the use of words like *shall*, *must*, *may*, *should*, and *recommended*. These texts are very critical for providing interoperability for implementation in using products from different vendors as well as for intercarrier communications. The main objective of this book is, as explained earlier, to create a single integrated SIP RFC. The text has been reproduced from the IETF RFCs for providing interoperability, with permission from the IETF, in Chapters 2 through 20. The copyright for the text that is being reproduced (with permission) in the different sections and subsections of this book belongs to the IETF. It is recommended that readers consult the original RFCs posted in the IETF website.

I am greatly indebted to many researchers, professionals, software and product developers, network designers, professors, intellectuals, and individual authors and contributors of technical standard documents, drafts, and RFCs worldwide for learning from their high-quality technical papers and discussions in group meetings, conferences, and e-mails in working groups for more than two decades. In addition, I had the privilege to meet many of those great souls in person during the MMCF, ITU-T, IETF, and other technical standard conferences held in different countries of the world. Their unforgettable personal touch has enriched my heart very deeply as well.

I admire Richard O'Hanley, publisher, ICT, Business, and Security, CRC Press, for his appreciative approach in publishing this book. I am thankful to Adel Rosario, project manager, for her sincere proofing of this book and helping in a variety of ways, and to Tara Nieuwesteeg, CRC project editor, for overseeing the production process.

Author

Radhika Ranjan Roy has been an electronics engineer, US Army Research, Development and Engineering Command (RDECOM), Communications–Electronics Research, Development, and Engineering Center (CERDEC), Space and Terrestrial Communications Directorate (S&TCD) Laboratories, Aberdeen Proving Ground (APG), Maryland, since 2009. Dr. Roy leads his research and development efforts in the development of scalable large-scale SIP-based VoIP/multimedia networks and services, mobile ad hoc networks (MANETs), peer-to-peer (P2P) networks, cyber security detection application software and network vulnerability, jamming detection, and supporting array of US Army/Department of Defense's Nationwide and Worldwide Warfighter Networking Architectures and participating in technical standards development in multimedia/real-time services collaboration, IPv6, radio communications, enterprise services management, and information transfer of Department of Defense (DoD) technical working groups. He earned his PhD in electrical engineering with a major in computer communications from the City University of New York, New York, in 1984, and his MS in electrical engineering from Northeastern University, Boston, Massachusetts, in 1978. He earned his BS in electrical engineering from the Bangladesh University of Engineering and Technology, Dhaka, Bangladesh, in 1967.

Prior to joining CERDEC, Dr. Roy worked as the lead systems engineer at CACI, Eatontown, New Jersey, from 2007 to 2009, and developed the Army Technical Resource Model (TRM), Army Enterprise Architecture (AEA), DoD Architecture Framework (DoDAF), and Army LandWarNet (LWN) Capability Sets, as well as technical standards for the Joint Tactical Radio System (JTRS), Mobile IPv6, MANET, and Session Initiation Protocol (SIP) supporting Army Chief Information Officer (CIO)/G-6. Dr. Roy worked as a senior systems engineer, SAIC, Abingdon, Maryland, from 2004 to 2007, supporting modeling, simulations, architectures, and system engineering of many Army projects: WIN-T, FCS, and JNN.

During his career, Dr. Roy worked at AT&T/Bell Laboratories, Middletown, New Jersey, as senior consultant from 1990 to 2004, and led a team of engineers in designing AT&T's worldwide SIP-based VoIP/multimedia communications network architecture, which consisted of wired and wireless parts, from the preparation of Requests for Information (RFI), evaluation of vendor RFI responses, and interactions with all selected major vendors related to their products. He participated and contributed in the development of VoIP/H.323/SIP multimedia standards in ITU-T, IETF, ATM, and Frame Relay standard organizations.

Dr. Roy worked as a senior principal engineer in CSC, Falls Church, Virginia, from 1984 to 1990, and worked in the design and performance analysis of the US Treasury nationwide X.25 packet-switching network. In addition, he designed the network architectures of many proposed US government and commercial worldwide and nationwide networks: Department of State Telecommunications Network (DOSTN), US Secret Service Satellite Network, Veteran Communications Network, and Ford Company's Dealership Network. Prior to CSC, he worked from 1967 to 1977 as deputy director (design) in PDP, Dhaka, Bangladesh.

Dr. Roy's research interests include the areas of mobile ad hoc networks, multimedia communications, peer-to-peer networking, and quality of service. He has published more than 50 technical papers and either holds or has pending more than 30 patents. He is a life member of IEEE and is a member of the Eta Kappa Nu honor society. He is also a member of many IETF working groups. Dr. Roy authored a book, *Handbook of Mobile Ad Hoc Networks for Mobility Models*, Springer, in 2010.

Chapter 1

Networked Multimedia Services

Abstract

Networked multimedia services have some key technical characteristics that need to be satisfied by any multimedia signaling and media protocols that deal with multimedia services over the networks. The characteristics of real-time, near-real-time, and non-real-time services, especially focusing on their performances, are described.

1.1 Introduction

Multimedia applications consisting of audio, video, and/or data that provide communications services at a distance, connected over networks, are termed *networked multimedia services.* These applications can be distributed across networks, and the communication connectivity can be one-to-one, many-to-many, many-to-one, and one-to-many over the networks. The networking function embedded into multimedia applications makes them networked multimedia services. The network architecture that facilitates networked multimedia services can be termed the *networked multimedia services architecture.*

1.2 Functional Characteristics

The functional characteristics of networked multimedia applications can be very complex. Multimedia communications for conversation applications will not only need to be in real-time, meeting the stringent performance requirements, but also a simple point-to-point audio call may evolve, at users' discretion, to become a multimedia call, or a multipoint multimedia call if more participants are added into the call [1,2]. If the data-sharing application is added into the same call, the situation becomes more complicated as it is expected to be the usual case for real-time multimedia collaboration. The connectivity of the communications between the participants can vary from point-to-point to many-to-many, usually with symmetric traffic flows. In the case of video-on-demand (VOD) applications, the connectivity will primarily be from one-to-many with highly asymmetric traffic flows because the video applications are usually distributed from the centralized multimedia servers to multiple users, although the performance constraints may be a little less stringent from those of the conversational applications. The functional characteristics of some multimedia applications, such as multimedia messaging, can be both one-to-many and many-to-many with respect to connectivity, while the traffic flows can also be symmetric and asymmetric depending on the needs of the participants. In general, the functional characteristics of all other multimedia applications may typically fall within these three categories explained here.

1.3 Performance Characteristics

The audio and video of multimedia applications can be continuous, while data consisting of text, still images, and/or graphics can be discrete. However, animation that is also considered as a part of data is continuous, consisting of audio, video, still images, graphics, and/or texts, and needs inter-/intramedia synchronization. Audio, video, and still images are usually captured from the real world, while text, graphics, and animation are synthesized by computers.

On the basis of the performance characteristics of communications, multimedia applications can be categorized as follows: real-time (RT), near-real-time (near-RT), and non-real-time (non-RT). RT applications will have strict bounds on packet loss, packet delay, and delay jitter, while near-RT applications will have less strict bounds on those performance parameters than those of the RT applications. For example, teleconferencing (TC) and video teleconferencing (VTC)/

videoconferencing (VC) are considered RT services because of real-time two-way, point-to-point/multipoint conversations between users and, the audio and video performance requirements can be stated as follows [1]:

- One-way end-to-end delay (including propagation, network, and equipment) for audio or video should be between 100 and 150 ms.
- Mean-opinion-score (MOS) level for audio should be between 4.0 and 5.0.
- MOS level for video should be between 3.5 and 5.0.
- End-to-end delay jitter should be very short, less than 250 μs in some cases.
- Bit error rate (BER) should be very low for good quality audio or video, although some BER can be tolerated.
- Intermedia and intramedia synchronization need to be maintained using suitable algorithms.
- Differential delay between audio and video transmission should be between no more than –20 ms to +40 ms for maintaining proper intermedia synchronization.

One-way VOD [2], which is considered a near-RT communication, can have much less stringent performances than those of TC or VTC. The text or graphics are non-RT applications, and the one-way delay requirement can be of the order of a few seconds; however, unlike audio or video, it cannot tolerate any BER.

The synchronization requirements between different media of multimedia applications impose a heavy burden on the multimedia transport networks, especially for the packet networks such as the Internet Protocol (IP). RT applications are also considered live multimedia applications with the generation of live audio, video, and/or data from live sources of microphones, video cameras, and/or application sharing by human/machine, while near-RT applications are usually retrieved from databases and can be considered as retrieval multimedia applications. Consequently, the synchronization requirements between RT and near-RT applications are also significantly different. The transmission side of the RT applications does not require much control, while near-RT applications must have some defined relationships between

Table 1.1 Intermedia Time Skew/Jitter Tolerance

Intermedia		*Media Communication Mode in Different Applications*	*Tolerable Time Skew/Jitter*[a]
Audio	Audio	Tightly coupled (e.g., stereo)	±11 microseconds
		Loosely coupled (e.g., teleconferencing)	±80 to ±150 milliseconds
		Loosely coupled (e.g., background music)	±500 milliseconds
	Animation	Event correlation (e.g., dancing)	±80 milliseconds
	Image	Tightly coupled (e.g., music with notes)	±5 milliseconds
		Loosely coupled (e.g., slide show)	±500 milliseconds
	Text	Text annotation	±240 milliseconds
	Pointer	Audio relates to shown item	–500 milliseconds to +750 milliseconds
Video	Audio	Lip synchronization (e.g., video conferencing, video streaming)	±80 to ±150 milliseconds[b]
	Animation	Correlated	±120 milliseconds
	Image	Overlay	±240 milliseconds
		Nonoverlay	±500 milliseconds
	Text	Overlay	±240 milliseconds
		Nonoverlay	±500 milliseconds

[a] Some variations of the following figures are also reported [1–7].

[b] The out-of-sync region spans somewhat at –160 milliseconds and +160 milliseconds.

media and require some scheduling mechanisms for guaranteed synchronization between the retrieved and transmitted media. The end-to-end delay requirements for RT applications are more stringent than for near-RT applications. RT applications require synchronization between media generated by different live sources, although it may not be so common. However, near-RT applications are commonly retrieved from different multimedia servers and are presented to users synchronously.

In general, multimedia synchronization can deal with many aspects: temporal, spatial, or even a logical relationship between objects, data entities, or media streams [3]. In the context of multimedia computing and communications, the synchronization accuracy is critical for high-quality multimedia applications and can be measured by the following performance parameters: delay, delay jitter, intermedia skew, and tolerable error rate. In RT applications, delay is measured in end-to-end delay from the live source to the destination, while in near-RT applications, delay is measured in retrieval time, i.e., the delay from the time a request is made to the time the application is retrieved from the server and reaches the destination. It implies that excessive buffering should not be used in RT applications. Delay jitter measures the deviation of presentation time of the continuous media samples from their fixed or desired presentation time. Intermedia skew measures the time shift between related media from the desired temporal relationship. The acceptable value for intermedia skew is determined by the media types concerned. Table 1.1 shows some examples of intermedia skew tolerance [1–7].

However, the implementation of multimedia synchronization services can be done using a variety of techniques depending on different mode of applications. Each synchronization implementation model can be quite complex [8]. As mentioned earlier, continuous media can tolerate some errors and error-free transmission is not essential to achieve acceptable good quality; moreover, the tolerable error rate measures the allowable BER and packet error rate (PER) for a particular media in a specific application. Multimedia traffic can be very bursty, and the burstiness can vary from 0.1 to 1. If constant bit rate (CBR) audio or video codec is used, there will be no variation in bit rates of the codec and the burstiness will be 1. The multimedia call duration can vary from a few seconds to few hours.

1.4 Summary

The signaling (e.g., session initiation protocol/session description protocol) and media (e.g., real-time transport protocol) protocols dealing with the networked multimedia services need to be carefully designed and developed to meet these performance requirements. In this context, the characteristics of RT, near-RT, and non-RT services, especially focusing on their performances, are described. In the subsequent chapters, we will describe all the multimedia signaling and media protocols, and how the technical challenges of multimedia communications services are met.

PROBLEMS

1. What are the key differences in performances between networked and non-networked multimedia applications?
2. What are intramedia and intermedia synchronization? Why are they important for each category of multimedia services?
3. What is lip synchronization? What are the key technical challenges in maintaining lip synchronization in VTC/VC?
4. What are the performance differences between RT, near-RT, and non-RT multimedia services?
5. What are the problems caused by packet losses in TC, VTC/VC, and file transfer services?
6. What are the problems caused by delay jitters in TC and VTC/VC applications?

References

1. Roy, R.R., "Networking constraints in multimedia conferencing and the role of ATM networks," *AT&T Technical Journal*, vol. 73, no. 4, 1994.
2. Roy, R.R. et al., "An analysis of universal multimedia switching architectures," *AT&T Technical Journal*, vol. 73, no. 6, 1994.
3. Georganas, N.D. et al., Editors, "Synchronization issues in multimedia communications," *IEEE SAC*, vol. 14, no. 1, 1996.
4. Fluckinger, F., *Understanding Networked Multimedia—Applications and Technology*, Prentice Hall, Hertfordshire, UK.
5. Steinmetz, R. et al., "Multimedia synchronization techniques: Experience based on different system structures," *Computer Communication Review*, vol. 22, no. 1, 1992.
6. Hehmann, D. et al., "Transport services for multimedia applications on broadband networks," *Computer Communications*, vol. 13, no. 4, 1990.
7. Ghinea, G. et al., "Perceived synchronization of olfactory multimedia," *IEEE Transactions on Systems Man and Cybernetics—Part A: Systems and Humans*, vol. 40, no. 4, 2010.
8. Blakowski, G. and Steinmetz, R., "A media synchronization survey: Reference model, specification, and case studies," *IEEE SAC*, vol. 14, no. 1, 1996.

Chapter 2

Basic Session Initiation Protocol

Abstract

The Session Initiation Protocol (SIP) is designed for networked multimedia communications. The basic SIP signaling protocol consists of request and response messages, message headers, message body, and message format. In addition, the SIP network functional entities consist of user agent, back-to-back user agent, proxy server, redirect server, register server, and application server. The location server that is not a SIP entity is also important for SIP address resolutions. The Augmented Backus–Naur Form syntax is used for the SIP. These key functional features of the networked multimedia SIP signaling protocol are described. This part is particularly taken from Request for Comment (RFC) 3261 and its enhancements by other RFCs as mentioned throughout the book.

2.1 Introduction

The Session Initiation Protocol (SIP) is a signaling protocol to set up, modify, and tear down networked multimedia sessions consisting of audio, video, or data applications. The International Engineering Task Force's (IETF) Request for Comment (RFC) 3261 is the first stable specification that defines SIP in a comprehensive manner. However, RFC 3261 obsoleted the initial SIP RFC 2543 soon after its publication. Eventually, many other RFCs have been published, extending the base capabilities of SIP described in RFC 3261 to meet the requirements of the complexities of network-based multimedia session ranging from point-to-point to multipoint calls, including media (audio, video, or data) bridging and feature-rich application sharing in real time. In fact, the enhancements are still going on even today as more sophisticated multimedia-rich requirements are being demanded for standardization for large-scale interoperable implementations.

The simplicity, flexibility, and versatility of SIP has made it one of the most popular signaling protocols, exceeding its initial mandate perceived in the beginning of its inception. For example, the interactive communications among the application servers for invoking and creating complex services for sharing among the real-time conferencing users whose multimedia sessions are established by SIP also find it convenient to use SIP. Primarily, we have used all SIP-related RFCs in describing the SIP, although there are many other companion RFCs and technical standards in this context. The real-time multimedia sessions of SIP can be so feature rich that they may need to use a huge amount of the capabilities of many other protocols especially in the application layer, including Session Description Protocol (SDP), Real-Time Transport Protocol (RTP), and many others. However, SDP and RTP are the two essential protocols that are needed by SIP as a minimum for multimedia sessions. We will describe these two protocols briefly later.

2.2 Terminology

The SIP has defined many terminologies, and it would be easier to understand SIP if those terminologies are known. Table 2.1 provides the definition of those terminologies that are primarily applicable to SIP described in different RFCs.

2.3 Multimedia Session

A multimedia conversational communications session can be very feature-rich with many very complex functionalities. Multimedia session control is an application-layer control protocol and is designed to provide services to multimedia

Table 2.1 Terminologies and Their Definitions

Terminology	*Definition*
Address of record (AOR)	A Session Initiation Protocol (SIP) or SIP Security (SIPS) Uniform Resource Identifier (URI) that points to a domain with a location service that can map the URI to another URI where the user might be available. Typically, the location service is populated through registrations. An AOR is frequently thought of as the *public address* of the user (RFC 3261: Standards Track).
Advertised address	The address that occurs in the Via header field's sent-by production rule, including the port number and transport (RFC 5923: Standards Track).
Agent	The protocol implementation involved in the offer–answer exchange. There are two agents involved in an offer–answer exchange (RFC 3264: Standards Track).
Alias	Reusing an existing connection to send requests in the backwards direction; that is, A opens a connection to B to send a request, and B uses that connection to send requests in the backwards direction to A. This is also known as *connection reuse* (RFC 5923: Standards Track).
Answer	An SDP message sent by an answerer in response to an offer received from an offerer (RFC 3264: Standards Track).
Answerer	An agent that receives a session description from another agent describing aspects of desired media communication, and then responds to that with its own session description.
Appearance number	A positive integer associated with one or more dialogs of an AOR. Appearance numbers are managed by an appearance agent, and displayed and rendered to the user by UAs that support this specification. When an appearance number is assigned or requested, generally the assigned number is the smallest positive integer that is not currently assigned as an appearance number to a dialog for this AOR. This specification does not define an upper limit on appearance numbers; however, using appearance numbers that are not easily represented using common integer representations is likely to cause failures (RFC 7463: Standards Track).
Authoritative proxy	A proxy that handles non-REGISTER requests for a specific AOR, performs the logical location server lookup described in RFC 3261, and forwards those requests to specific Contact URIs. In RFC 3261, the role that is authoritative for REGISTER requests for a specific AOR is a registration server (RFC 5626: Standards Track).
Back-to-back user agent (B2BUA)	A logical entity that receives a request and processes it as a user agent server (UAS). To determine how the request should be answered, it acts as a user agent client (UAC) and generates requests. Unlike a proxy server, it maintains the dialog state and must participate in all requests sent on the dialogs it has established. Since it is a concatenation of a UAC and UAS, no explicit definitions are needed for its behavior (RFC 3261: Standards Track).
Call	An informal term that refers to some communication between peers, generally set up for the purposes of a multimedia conversation (RFC 3261: Standards Track).
Call leg	Another name for a dialog (see below, this table) specified in RFC 2543, but is no longer used in RFC 3261 specification (RFC 3261: Standards Track).
Call stateful	A proxy is call stateful if it retains the state for a dialog from the initiating INVITE to the terminating BYE request. A call stateful proxy is always transaction stateful, but the converse is not necessarily true (RFC 3261: Standards Track).
Callee	A destination of the original call, and a target of the Completion of Call (CC call) (RFC 6910: Standards Track).

(Continued)

Table 2.1 (Continued) Terminologies and Their Definitions

Terminology	*Definition*
Callee's monitor	A logical component that implements the CC queue for destination user(s)/UA(s) and performs the associated tasks, including sending CC recall events, analogous to the destination local exchange's role in Signaling System 7 (SS7) CC (RFC 6910: Standards Track).
Caller	Within the context of this specification, a caller refers to the user on whose behalf a UAC is operating. It is not limited to a user whose UAC sends an INVITE request (RFC 3841: Standards Track). The initiator of the original call and the CC request. The user on whose behalf the CC call is made (RFC 6910: Standards Track).
Caller's agent	A logical component that makes CC requests and responds to CC recall events on behalf of originating user(s)/UA(s), analogous to the originating local exchange's role in SS7 CC (RFC 6910: Standards Track).
CC call	A call from the caller to the callee, triggered by the CC service when it has determined that the callee is available (RFC 6910: Standards Track).
Certificate	A public key infrastructure using X.509 (PKIX) (RFC 5280) style certificate containing a public key and a list of identities in the SubjectAltName that are bound to this key. The certificates discussed in this document are generally self-signed and use the mechanisms in the SIP Identity (RFC 4474, see Section 19.4.8) specification to vouch for their validity. Certificates that are signed by a certification authority can also be used with all the mechanisms in this document; however, they need not be validated by the receiver (although the receiver can validate them for extra assurance) (RFC 6072: Standards Track).
Client	Any network element that sends SIP requests and receives SIP responses. Clients may or may not interact directly with a human user. UACs and proxies are clients (RFC 3261: Standards Track).
Completion of Call (CC) activation	The indication by the caller to the caller's agent that the caller desires CC for a failed original call; this implies an indication transmitted from the caller's agent to the callee's monitor of the desire for CC processing (RFC 6910: Standards Track).
Completion of Call (CC) indicator	An indication in the CC call INVITE used to prioritize the call at the destination (RFC 6910: Standards Track).
Completion of Call (CC) possible indication	The data in responses to the INVITE of the original call that indicate that CC is available for the call (RFC 6910: Standards Track).
Completion of Call (CC) queue	A buffer at the callee's monitor that stores incoming calls that are targets for CC. Note: This buffer may or may not be organized as a queue. The use of the term *queue* is analogous to SS7 usage. CCE, or CC Entity: the representation of a CC request, or, equivalently, an existing CC subscription within the queue of a callee's monitor (RFC 6910: Standards Track).
Completion of Call (CC) recall	The action of the callee's monitor selecting a particular CC request for initiation of a CC call, resulting in an indication from the caller's agent to the caller that it is now possible to initiate a CC call (RFC 6910: Standards Track).
Completion of Call (CC) recall events	Event notifications of event package *call-completion*, sent by the callee's monitor to the caller's agent to inform it of the status of its CC request (RFC 6910: Standards Track).
Completion of Call (CC) request	Recall timer: the maximum time the callee's monitor will wait for the caller's response to a CC recall (RFC 6910: Standards Track).

(*Continued*)

Table 2.1 (Continued) Terminologies and Their Definitions

Terminology	*Definition*
Completion of Call (CC) request	The entry in the callee's monitor queue representing the caller's request for CC processing, that is, the caller's CC subscription (RFC 6910: Standards Track). CC service duration timer: maximum time a CC request may remain active within the network (RFC 6910: Standards Track).
Completion of Calls (CC)	A service that allows a caller who failed to reach a desired callee to be notified when the callee becomes available to receive a call (RFC 6910: Standards Track).
Completion of Calls on No Reply (CCNR)	A CC service provided when the initial failure was that the destination UA did not answer (RFC 6910: Standards Track).
Completion of Calls on Not Logged-in (CCNL)	A CC service provided when the initial failure was that the destination UA was not registered (RFC 6910: Standards Track).
Completion of Calls to Busy Subscriber (CCBS)	A CC service provided when the initial failure was that the destination UA was busy (RFC 6910: Standards Track).
Conference	A multimedia session (see below, this table) that contains multiple participants.
Core	Designates the functions specific to a particular type of SIP entity, that is, specific to either a stateful or a stateless proxy, a user agent (UA), or registrar. All cores, except those for the stateless proxy, are transaction users (RFC 3261: Standards Track).
Credential	The combination of a certificate and the associated private key. Password phrase: a password used to encrypt and decrypt a Public Key Cryptographic System #8 (PKCS #8) private key (RFC 6072: Standards Track).
Dialog	A peer-to-peer SIP relationship between two UAs that persists for some time. A dialog is established by SIP messages, such as a 2xx response to an INVITE request. A dialog is identified by a call identifier, local tag, and a remote tag. A dialog was formerly known as a call leg in RFC 2543 (RFC 3261: Standards Track).
Downstream	A direction of message forwarding within a transaction that refers to the direction that requests flow from the UAC to UAS (RFC 3261: Standards Track).
Edge proxy	Any proxy that is located topologically between the registering UA and the authoritative proxy. The *first* edge proxy refers to the first edge proxy encountered when a UA sends a request (RFC 5626: Standards Track).
Event hard state	The steady-state or default event state of a resource, which the ESC may use in the absence of, or in addition to, soft-state publications (RFC 3903: Standards Track).
Event package	An additional specification that defines a set of state information to be reported by a notifier to a subscriber. Event packages also define further syntax and semantics that are based on the framework defined by this document and are required to convey such state information (RFC 6665: Standards Track).
Event Publication Agent (EPA)	The UAC that issues PUBLISH requests to publish event state (RFC 3903: Standards Track).
Event Soft State	Event state published by an EPA using the PUBLISH mechanism. A protocol element (i.e., an entity-tag) is used to identify a specific soft-state entity at the event state compositor. Soft state has a defined lifetime and will expire after a negotiated amount of time (RFC 3903: Standards Track).

(*Continued*)

Table 2.1 (Continued) Terminologies and Their Definitions

Terminology	*Definition*
Event State	State information for a resource, associated with an event package and an AOR (RFC 3903: Standards Track).
Event State Compositor (ESC)	The UAS that processes PUBLISH requests, and is responsible for compositing event state into a complete, composite event state of a resource (RFC 3903: Standards Track).
Event Template-Package	A special kind of event package that defines a set of states that may be applied to all possible event packages, including itself (RFC 6665: Standards Track).
Explicit preference	A caller preference indicated explicitly in the Accept-Contact or Reject-Contact header fields (RFC 3841: Standards Track).
Failed call	A call that does not reach a desired callee, from the caller's point of view. Note that a failed call may be successful from the SIP point of view, for example, if the call reached the callee's voice mail but the caller desired to speak to the callee in real time, the INVITE receives a 200 response, but the caller considers the call to have failed (RFC 6910: Standards Track).
Feature preferences	Caller preferences that describe desired properties of a UA to which the request is to be routed. Feature preferences can be made explicit with the Accept-Contact and Reject-Contact header fields (RFC 3841: Standards Track).
Final response	A response that terminates a SIP transaction, as opposed to a provisional response that does not. All 2xx, 3xx, 4xx, 5xx, and 6xx responses are final (RFC 3261: Standards Track).
Flow	A transport-layer association between two hosts that is represented by the network address and port number of both ends and by the transport protocol. For Transmission Control Protocol (TCP), a flow is equivalent to a TCP connection. For User Datagram Protocol (UDP), a flow is a bidirectional stream of datagrams between a single pair of IP addresses and ports of both peers. With TCP, a flow often has a one-to-one correspondence with a single file descriptor in the operating system (RFC 5626: Standards Track).
Flow token	An identifier that uniquely identifies a flow that can be included in a SIP URI defined in RFC 3986 (RFC 5626: Standards Track).
Focus/conference focus	The focus is defined in RFC 4579 that hosts a SIP conference and maintains a SIP signaling relationship with each participant in the conference. RFC 4579 also defines that an isfocus feature tag (see Section 2.11) in a Contact header field will not cause interoperability issues between a focus and a conference-unaware UA since it will be treated as an unknown header parameter and ignored, as per standard SIP behavior. **General** The main design guidelines for the development of SIP extensions and conventions for conferencing are to define the minimum number of extensions and to have seamless backward compatibility with conference-unaware SIP UAs. The minimal requirement for SIP is being able to express that a dialog is a part of a certain conference referenced to by a URI. As a result of these extensions, it is possible to do the following using SIP: • Create a conference • Join a conference • Invite a user to a conference • Expel a user by third party • Discover if a URI is a conference URI • Delete a conference

(*Continued*)

Table 2.1 (Continued) Terminologies and Their Definitions

Terminology	*Definition*
	The approach taken is to use the feature parameter isfocus to express that a SIP dialog belongs to a conference. The use of feature parameters in Contact header fields to describe the characteristics and capabilities of a UA is described in the User Agent Capabilities document in RFC 3840 (see Section 2.11), which includes the definition of the isfocus feature parameter. **Session Establishment** In session establishment, a focus must include the isfocus feature parameter in the Contact header field unless the focus wishes to hide the fact that it is a focus. To a participant, the feature parameter will be associated with the remote target URI of the dialog. It is an indication to a conference-aware UA that the resulting dialog belongs to a conference, identified by the URI in the Contact header field, and that the call control conventions defined in this document can be applied. By their nature, the conferences supported by this specification are centralized. Therefore, typically, a conferencing system needs to allocate a SIP conference URI such that SIP requests to this URI are not forked and are routed to a dedicated conference focus. For example, a globally accessible SIP conference could be well constructed with a conference URI using a Globally Routable User Agent URI (GRUU) defined in RFC 5627 (see Section 4.3), because of its ability to support the nonforking and global routability requirements. **Discovery** Using the mechanism described in this section, it is possible, given an opaque URI, to determine if it belongs to a certain conference (i.e., meaning that it is a conference URI) or not. This discovery function can be implemented in SIP using an OPTIONS request, and can be done either inside an active dialog or outside a dialog. A focus must include the isfocus feature parameter in a 200 OK response to an OPTIONS unless the focus wishes to hide the fact that it is a focus (RFC 4579: Best Current Practice).
Header	A component of a SIP message that conveys information about the message. It is structured as a sequence of header fields.
Header field	A component of the SIP message header. A header field can appear as one or more header field rows. Header field rows consist of a header field name and zero or more header field values. Multiple header field values on a given header field row are separated by commas. Some header fields can only have a single header field value, and as a result, always appear as a single header field row (RFC 3261: Standards Track).
Header field value	A single value; a header field consists of zero or more header field values (RFC 3261: Standards Track).
Home domain	The domain providing service to a SIP user. Typically, this is the domain present in the URI in the AOR of a registration (RFC 3261: Standards Track).
Identity	An Identity, for the purposes of this document, is a sip:, sips:, or tel: URI, and optionally a Display Name. The URI must be meaningful to the domain identified in the URI (in the case of sip: or sips: URIs) or the owner of the E.164 number (in the case of tel: URIs), in the sense that when used as a SIP Request-URI in a request sent to that domain/number range owner, it would cause the request to be routed to the user/line that is associated with the identity, or to be processed by service logic running on that user's behalf. If the URI is a sip: or sips: URI, then depending on the local policy of the domain identified in the URI, the URI may identify some specific entity, such as a person. If the URI is a tel: URI, then depending on the local policy of the owner of the number range within which the telephone number remains, the number may identify some specific entity, such as a telephone line. However, it should be noted that identifying the owner of the number range is a less straightforward process than identifying the domain that owns a sip: or sips: URI (RFC 3324: Informational).

(*Continued*)

Table 2.1 (Continued) Terminologies and Their Definitions

Terminology	*Definition*
Implicit preference	A caller preference that is implied through the presence of other aspects of a request. For example, if the request method is INVITE, it represents an implicit caller preference to route the request to a UA that supports the INVITE method.
Informational response	Same as a provisional response (see below, this table) (RFC 3261: Standards Track).
Initial session refresh request	The first session refresh request sent with a particular Call-ID value (RFC 4028: Standards Track).
Initiator, calling party, caller	The party initiating a session (and dialog) with an INVITE request. A caller retains this role from the time it sends the initial INVITE that established a dialog until the termination of that dialog (RFC 3261: Standards Track).
Instance-id	This specification uses the word instance-id to refer to the value of the *sip.instance* media feature tag that appears as a +sip.instance Contact header field parameter. This is a Uniform Resource Name (URN) that uniquely identifies this specific UA instance (RFC 5626: Standards Track).
Invitee, invited user, called party, callee	The party that receives an INVITE request for the purpose of establishing a new session. A callee retains this role from the time it receives the INVITE until the termination of the dialog established by that INVITE (RFC 3261: Standards Track).
Location service	A location service is used by a SIP redirect or proxy server to obtain information about a callee's possible location(s). It contains a list of bindings of AOR keys to zero or more contact addresses. The bindings can be created and removed in many ways; this specification defines a REGISTER method that updates the bindings (RFC 3261: Standards Track).
Loop	A request that arrives at a proxy, is forwarded, and later arrives back at the same proxy. When it arrives the second time, its Request-URI is identical to the first time, and other header fields that affect proxy operation are unchanged, so that the proxy would make the same processing decision on the request it made the first time. Looped requests are errors, and the procedures for detecting them and handling them are described by the protocol (RFC 3261: Standards Track).
Loose routing	A proxy is said to be loose routing if it follows the procedures defined in RFC 3261 specification for processing of the Route header field. These procedures separate the destination of the request (present in the Request-URI) from the set of proxies that need to be visited along the way (present in the Route header field). A proxy compliant to these mechanisms is also known as a loose router (RFC 3261: Standards Track).
Media stream	From RTSP specified in RFC 2336 (see Section 7.5), a media stream is a single media instance, for example, an audio stream or a video stream as well as a single whiteboard or shared application group. In SDP, a media stream is described by an *m=* line and its associated attributes (RFC 3264: Standards Track).
Message	Data sent between SIP elements as part of the protocol. SIP messages are either requests or responses (RFC 3261: Standards Track).
Method	The method is the primary function that a request is meant to invoke on a server. The method is carried in the request message itself. Example methods are INVITE and BYE (RFC 3261: Standards Track).
Minimum Timer	Because of the processing load of mid-dialog requests, all elements (proxy, UAC, UAS) can have a configured minimum value for the session interval that they are willing to accept. This value is called the minimum timer (RFC 4028: Standards Track).

(*Continued*)

Table 2.1 (Continued) Terminologies and Their Definitions

Terminology	*Definition*
Network Asserted Identity	An identity derived by a SIP network entity as a result of an authentication process, which identifies the authenticated entity in the sense defined in *Identity*. In the case of a sip: or sips: URI, the domain included in the URI must be within the *Trust Domain*. In the case of a tel: URI, the owner of the E.164 number in the URI must be within the Trust Domain. The authentication process used, or at least its reliability/strength, is a known feature of the Trust Domain using the Network Asserted Identity mechanism, that is, in the language described in the Trust Domain, as defined in Spec(T) (RFC 3324: Informational).
Notification	The act of a notifier sending a NOTIFY request to a subscriber to inform the subscriber of the state of a resource (RFC 6665: Standards Track).
Notifier	A UA that generates NOTIFY requests for the purpose of notifying subscribers of the state of a resource. Notifiers typically also accept SUBSCRIBE requests to create subscriptions (RFC 6665: Standards Track). The UA that generates NOTIFY requests for the purpose of notifying subscribers of the callee's availability; for the CC service, this is the task of the callee's monitor (RFC 6910: Standards Track).
ob Parameter	A SIP URI parameter that has a different meaning depending on context. In a Path header field value, it is used by the first edge proxy to indicate that a flow token was added to the URI. In a Contact or Route header field value, it indicates that the UA would like other requests in the same dialog to be routed over the same flow (RFC 5626: Standards Track).
Offer	An SDP message sent by an offerer (RFC 3264: Standards Track).
Offerer	An agent that generates a session description to create or modify a session (RFC 3264: Standards Track).
Original call	The initial call that failed to reach a desired destination (RFC 6910: Standards Track).
Outbound proxy	A proxy that receives requests from a client, even though it may not be the server resolved by the Request-URI. Typically, a UA is manually configured with an outbound proxy, or can learn about one through autoconfiguration protocols (RFC 3261: Standards Track).
Outbound-proxy-set	A set of SIP URIs that represent each of the outbound proxies (often edge proxies) with which the UA will attempt to maintain a direct flow. The first URI in the set is often referred to as the primary outbound proxy, and the second as the secondary outbound proxy. There is no difference between any of the URIs in this set, nor does the primary/secondary terminology imply that one is preferred over the other (RFC 5626: Standards Track).
Parallel search	In a parallel search, a proxy issues several requests to possible user locations upon receiving an incoming request. Rather than issuing one request and then waiting for the final response before issuing the next request as in a sequential search, a parallel search issues requests without waiting for the result of previous requests (RFC 3261: Standards Track).
Persistent connection	The process of sending multiple, possibly unrelated requests on the same connection, and receiving responses on that connection as well. More succinctly, A opens a connection to B to send a request, and later reuses the same connection to send other requests, possibly unrelated to the dialog established by the first request. Responses will arrive over the same connection. Persistent connection behavior is specified in RFC 3261 (see Section 3.13). Persistent connections do not imply connection reuse. The persistent connection is also termed as the *shared connection* (RFC 5923: Standards Track).
Presence compositor	A type of ESC that is responsible for compositing presence state for a presentity (RFC 3903: Standards Track).

(*Continued*)

Table 2.1 (Continued) Terminologies and Their Definitions

Terminology	*Definition*
Provisional response	A response used by the server to indicate progress, but that does not terminate a SIP transaction. 1xx responses are provisional; other responses are considered final (RFC 3261: Standards Track).
Proxy, proxy server	An intermediary entity that acts as both a server and a client for the purpose of making requests on behalf of other clients. A proxy server primarily plays the role of routing, which means that its job is to ensure that a request is sent to another entity *closer* to the targeted user. Proxies are also useful for enforcing policy (e.g., making sure a user is allowed to make a call). A proxy interprets, and, if necessary, rewrites specific parts of a request message before forwarding it (RFC 3261: Standards Track).
Public Service Identity	A SIP URI that refers to a service instead of a user (RFC 5002: Informational).
Publication	The act of an EPA sending a PUBLISH request to an ESC to publish event state (RFC 3903: Standards Track).
Recipient URI	The Request-URI of an outgoing request sent by an entity (e.g., a user agent or a proxy). The sending of such a request may have been the result of a translation operation (RFC: 5360: Standards Track).
Recursion	A client recurses on a 3xx response when it generates a new request to one or more of the URIs in the Contact header field in the response (RFC 3261: Standards Track).
Redirect server	A UAS that generates 3xx responses to requests it receives, directing the client to contact an alternate set of URIs (RFC 3261: Standards Track).
REFER-Issuer	The UA issuing the REFER request (RFC 4488: Standards Track).
REFER-Recipient	The UA receiving the REFER request (RFC 4488: Standards Track).
REFER-Target	The UA designated in the Refer-To Uniform Resource Identifier (URI).
Refresh	Same as a session refresh request (RFC 4028: Standards Track).
Reg-id	The value of a new header field parameter for the Contact header field. When a UA registers multiple times, each for a different flow, each concurrent registration gets a unique reg-id value (RFC 5626: Standards Track).
Registrar	A server that accepts REGISTER requests and places the information it receives in those requests into the location service for the domain it handles (RFC 3261: Standards Track).
Regular transaction	Any transaction with a method other than INVITE, ACK, or CANCEL (RFC 3261: Standards Track).
Relay	Any SIP server, be it a proxy, B2BUA, or some hybrid, that receives a request, translates its Request-URI into one or more next-hop URIs (i.e., recipient URIs), and delivers the request to those URIs (RFC: 5360: Standards Track).
Request	A SIP message sent from a client to a server, for the purpose of invoking a particular operation (RFC 3261: Standards Track).
Request handling preferences	Caller preferences that describe desired request treatment at a server. These preferences are carried in the Request-Disposition header field (RFC 3841: Standards Track).
Resolved address	The network identifiers (IP address, port, transport) associated with a UA as a result of executing RFC 3263 (see Section 8.2.4) on a URI (RFC 5923: Standards Track).
Response	A SIP message sent from a server to a client, for indicating the status of a request sent from the client to the server (RFC 3261: Standards Track).

(Continued)

Table 2.1 (Continued) Terminologies and Their Definitions

Terminology	*Definition*
Retain option	A characteristic of the CC service; if supported, CC calls that again encounter a busy callee will not be queued again, but the position of the caller's entry in the queue is retained. Note that SIP CC always operates with the retain option active; a failed CC call does not cause the CC request to lose its position in the queue (RFC 6910: Standards Track).
Ringback	The signaling tone produced by the calling party's application indicating that a called party is being alerted (ringing) (RFC 3261: Standards Track).
Route set	A collection of ordered SIP or SIPS URI that represent a list of proxies that must be traversed when sending a particular request. A route set can be learned, through headers like Record-Route, or it can be configured (RFC 3261: Standards Track).
Seizing	An appearance can be reserved before a call being placed by seizing the appearance. An appearance can be seized by communicating an artificial state of *trying* before actually initiating a dialog (i.e., sending the INVITE), in order to appear as if it were already initiating a dialog (RFC 7463: Standards Track).
Selecting (or not seizing)	An appearance is merely selected (i.e., not seized) if there is no such communication of artificial state of trying before initiating a dialog; that is, the state is communicated when the dialog is actually initiated. The appearance number is learned after the INVITE is sent (RFC 7463: Standards Track).
Sequential search	In a sequential search, a proxy server attempts each contact address in sequence, proceeding to the next only after the previous one has generated a final response. A 2xx or 6xx class final response always terminates a sequential search (RFC 3261: Standards Track).
Server	A network element that receives requests in order to service them and sends back responses to those requests. Examples of servers are proxies, UASs, redirect servers, and registrars (RFC 3261: Standards Track).
Session	From the SDP specification (RFC 2327): "A multimedia session is a set of multimedia senders and receivers and the data streams flowing from senders to receivers. A multimedia conference is an example of a multimedia session." (A session as defined for SDP can comprise one or more RTP sessions.) As defined, a callee can be invited several times, by different calls, to the same session. If SDP is used, a session is defined by the concatenation of the SDP user name, session id, network type, address type, and address elements in the origin field (RFC 3261: Standards Track).
Session expiration	The time at which an element will consider the session timed out, if no successful session refresh transaction occurs beforehand (RFC 4028: Standards Track).
Session interval	The maximum amount of time that can occur between session refresh requests in a dialog before the session will be considered timed out. The session interval is conveyed in the Session-Expires header field, which is defined here. The UAS obtains this value from the Session-Expires header field in a 2xx response to a session refresh request that it sends. Proxies and UACs determine this value from the Session-Expires header field in a 2xx response to a session refresh request that they receive (RFC 4028: Standards Track).
Session refresh request	An INVITE or UPDATE request processed according to the rules of this specification. If the request generates a 2xx response, the session expiration is increased to the current time plus the session interval obtained from the response. A session refresh request is not to be confused with a *target refresh request* defined in 3261 (see below, this table), which is a request that can update the remote target of a dialog (RFC 4028: Standards Track).
Signaling System 7 (SS7)	The signaling protocol of the public switched telephone network, defined by ITU-T Recommendations Q.700 through Q.849 (RFC 6910: Standards Track).

(Continued)

Table 2.1 (Continued) Terminologies and Their Definitions

Terminology	*Definition*
SIP domain identity	An identity of a domain (e.g., sip:example.com) that is contained in an X.509 certificate bound to a subject that identifies the subject as an authoritative SIP server for a domain (RFC 5922: Standards Track).
SIP transaction	A SIP transaction occurs between a client and a server and comprises all messages from the first request sent from the client to the server up to a final (non-1xx) response sent from the server to the client. If the request is INVITE and the final response is a non-2xx, the transaction also includes an ACK to the response. The ACK for a 2xx response to an INVITE request is a separate transaction (RFC 3261: Standards Track).
Spec(T)	An aspect of the definition of a Trust Domain is that all the elements in that domain are compliant to a set of configurations and specifications generally referred to as Spec(T). Spec(T) is not a specification in the sense of a written document; rather, it is an agreed-upon set of information that all elements are aware of. Proper processing of the asserted identities requires that the elements know what is actually being asserted, how it was determined, and what the privacy policies are. All of that information is characterized by Spec(T) (RFC 3324: Informational).
Spiral	A spiral is a SIP request that is routed to a proxy, forwarded onwards, and arrives once again at that proxy, but this time differs in a way that will result in a different processing decision than the original request. Typically, this means that the request's Request-URI differs from its previous arrival. A spiral is not an error condition, unlike a loop. A typical cause for this is call forwarding. A user calls joe@example.com. The example.com proxy forwards it to Joe's personal computer (PC), which in turn, forwards it to bob@example.com. This request is proxied back to the example.com proxy. However, this is not a loop. Since the request is targeted at a different user, it is considered a spiral, and is a valid condition (RFC 3261: Standards Track).
Stateful proxy	A logical entity that maintains the client and server transaction state machines defined by this specification during the processing of a request, also known as a transaction stateful proxy. A (transaction) stateful proxy is not the same as a call stateful proxy (RFC 3261: Standards Track).
Stateless proxy	A logical entity that does not maintain the client or server transaction state machines defined in this specification when it processes requests. A stateless proxy forwards every request it receives downstream and every response it receives upstream (RFC 3261: Standards Track).
Strict routing	A proxy is said to be strict routing if it follows the Route processing rules of RFC 2543. That rule caused proxies to destroy the contents of the Request-URI when a Route header field was present. Strict routing behavior is not used in RFC 3261, in favor of a loose routing behavior. Proxies that perform strict routing are also known as strict routers (RFC 3261: Standards Track).
Subscriber	A UA that receives NOTIFY requests from notifiers; these NOTIFY requests contain information about the state of a resource in which the subscriber is interested. Subscribers typically also generate SUBSCRIBE requests and send them to notifiers to create subscriptions (RFC 6665: Standards Track). The UA that receives NOTIFY requests with information of the callee's availability; for the Completion of Call (CC) service, this is the task of the caller's agent. Suspended CC request: a CC request that is temporarily not to be selected for CC recall (RFC 6910: Standards Track).
Subscription	A set of application state associated with a dialog. This application state includes a pointer to the associated dialog, the event package name, and possibly identification token. Event packages will define additional subscription state information. By definition, subscriptions exist in both a subscriber and a notifier (RFC 6665: Standards Track).

(Continued)

Table 2.1 (Continued) Terminologies and Their Definitions

Terminology	*Definition*
Subscription migration	The act of moving a subscription from one notifier to another notifier (RFC 6665: Standards Track).
Subsequent session refresh request	Any session refresh request sent with a particular Call-ID after the initial session refresh request (RFC 4028: Standards Track).
Target refresh request	A target refresh request sent within a dialog is defined as a request that can modify the remote target of the dialog (RFC 3261: Standards Track).
Target set	A set of candidate URIs to which a proxy or redirect server can send or redirect a request. Frequently, target sets are obtained from a registration, but they need not be (RFC 3841: Standards Track).
Target URI	The Request-URI of an incoming request that arrives to a relay that will perform a translation operation (RFC: 5360: Standards Track).
Transaction user (TU)	The layer of protocol processing that resides above the transaction layer. TUs include the UAC core, UAS core, and proxy core (RFC 3261: Standards Track).
Translation logic	The logic that defines a translation operation at a relay. This logic includes the translation's target and recipient URIs (RFC: 5360: Standards Track).
Translation operation	Operation by which a relay translates the Request-URI of an incoming request (i.e., the target URI) into one or more URIs (i.e., recipient URIs) that are used as the Request-URIs of one or more outgoing requests (RFC: 5360: Standards Track).
Trust Domains	A Trust Domain for the purposes of Network Asserted Identity is a set of SIP nodes (UAC, UAS, proxies, or other network intermediaries) that are trusted to exchange Network Asserted Identity information in the sense described below. A node can be a member of a Trust Domain, T, only if the node is known to be compliant to a certain set of specifications, Spec(T), which characterize the handling of Network Asserted Identity within the Trust Domain, T. Trust Domains are constructed by human beings who know the properties of the equipment they are using/deploying. In the simplest case, a Trust Domain is a set of devices with a single owner/operator who can accurately know the behavior of those devices. Such simple Trust Domains may be joined into larger Trust Domains by bilateral agreements between the owners/operators of the devices. A node is *trusted* (with respect to a given Trust Domain) if and only if it is a member of that domain. We say that a node, A, in the domain is trusted by a node, B, (or "B trusts A") if and only if • There is a secure connection between the nodes. • B has configuration information indicating that A is a member of the Trust Domain. Note that B may or may not be a member of the Trust Domain. For example, B may be a UA that trusts a given network intermediary, A (e.g., its home proxy). A *secure connection* in this context means that messages cannot be read by third parties, cannot be modified by third parties without detection, and that B can be sure that the message really did come from A. The level of security required is a feature of the Trust Domain; that is, it is defined in Spec(T). Within this context, SIP signaling information received by one node from a node that it trusts is known to have been generated and passed through the network according to the procedures of the particular specification set Spec(T), and therefore can be known to be valid, or at least as valid as specified in the specifications Spec(T).

(Continued)

Table 2.1 (Continued) Terminologies and Their Definitions

Terminology	*Definition*
	Equally, a node can be sure that signaling information passed to a node that it trusts will be handled according to the procedures of Spec(T). For these capabilities to be useful, Spec(T) must contain requirements as to how the Network Asserted Identity is generated, how its privacy is protected, and how its integrity is maintained as it is passed around the network. A reader of Spec(T) can then make an informed judgment about the authenticity and reliability of Network Asserted Information received from the Trust Domain T. The term trusted (with respect to a given Trust Domain) can be applied to a given node in an absolute sense—it is just equivalent to saying the node is a member of the Trust Domain. However, the node itself does not know whether another arbitrary node is trusted, even within the Trust Domain. It does know about certain nodes with which it has secure connections as described above (RFC 3324: Informational).
UAC core	The set of processing functions required of a UAC that reside above the transaction and transport layers (RFC 3261: Standards Track).
UAS core	The set of processing functions required at a UAS that resides above the transaction and transport layers (RFC 3261: Standards Track).
Upstream	A direction of message forwarding within a transaction that refers to the direction that responses flow from the UAS back to the UAC (RFC 3261: Standards Track).
URL-encoded	Universal Resource Locator (URL)-encoded is a character string encoded according to Section 2.4 of RFC 2396 (RFC 3261: Standards Track).
User agent (UA)	A logical entity that can act as both a UAC and UAS (RFC 3261: Standards Track)
User agent client (UAC)	A logical entity that creates a new request, and then uses the client transaction state machinery to send it. The role of UAC lasts only for the duration of that transaction. In other words, if a piece of software initiates a request, it acts as a UAC for the duration of that transaction. If it receives a request later, it assumes the role of a user agent server for the processing of that transaction (RFC 3261: Standards Track).
User agent server (UAS)	A logical entity that generates a response to a SIP request. The response accepts, rejects, or redirects the request. This role lasts only for the duration of that transaction. In other words, if a piece of software responds to a request, it acts as a UAS for the duration of that transaction. If it generates a request later, it assumes the role of a UAC for the processing of that transaction (RFC 3261: Standards Track).
Wildcarded Public Service Identity	A set of Public Service Identities that match a regular expression and share the same profile (RFC 5002: Informational).

applications, as shown in Figure 2.1. The establishment of a real-time multimedia communications session, especially with humans, needs a lot of intelligence.

Even an automat can be a conference participant. Multiple users located in different geographical locations may participate in the same session. Each participant may play a different role in the conference based on the conference policy. Multimedia communications may consist of different kinds of media, and each media needs to be negotiated with each participant before the establishment of the call. Different codecs may be used for audio or video by each participant, and negotiations may require agreeing on a common codec, or transcoding services may need to be offered for dissimilar codecs. Application sharing may require a variety of control methods among the call participants. Even multimedia files may be shared or created through a collaboration among conference participants. In addition, each media has its own quality of service (QOS) requirements, and the QOS for each media needs to be guaranteed during the call setup if that is what the conference participants expect per service level agreement (SLA). Multimedia session security, which includes authentication, integrity, confidentiality, nonrepudiation, and authorization, is paramount for conference participants in relation to both signaling and media (audio, video, and data/application sharing).

Early media (e.g., audio, video) is another feature that is used to indicate the progress of the multimedia session before the call is accepted by the called party. It may

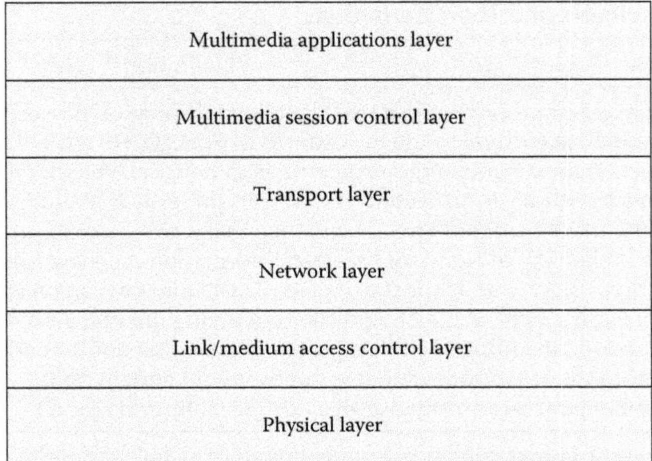

Figure 2.1 Relationship of multimedia session control layer to other layers.

be unidirectional or bidirectional, and can be generated by the calling party, the called party, or both. For example, early media generated by the caller can be ringing tone and announcements (e.g., queuing status). Early media typically may consist of voice commands or dual-tone multifrequency (DTMF) tones to drive interactive voice response (IVR) systems. Early media cannot be declined, modified, or identified. Consequently, it becomes very problematic to accommodate all complex functionalities of the early media in the call setup.

If more than two participants join in the conference call, media bridging is required. Although audio bridging is straightforward, video bridging can be from simple functionalities like video switching of the loudest speaker to the composition of very complex composite video of the conference participants maintaining audio and video intermedia synchronization so that lip synchronization can be maintained. It may so happen that the multipoint multimedia conference can be set up dynamically. For example, two participants are on a point-to-point conference call, and then a third party or more conference participants need to be added in the same conference call. In this situation, the call needs to be diverted to a conference bridge for bridging of audio, video, or data dynamically without tearing down the two-party conference call.

More complex functionalities like a virtual meeting room may be introduced to make the multimedia conferencing more resourceful and powerful. For example, there may be opportunities to join in a virtual meeting room for conferencing, while there may be many virtual meeting rooms available where many other conferences can be going on simultaneously, each of which being separate and independent. A participant may even have the option to be a part of multiple conferences simultaneously while coming in and out of each conference at each different instant of time. Even a conference participant joining late may also dial-in a conference recording server to listen to and may see what already had happened while the participant was not in the conference. Even high-quality video with an eye-contact feature during the meeting may be needed in case human personal interactions need to be known among the conference participants as if they are in a face-to-face meeting.

The multimedia session establishment and tear down also needs to support both user and terminal mobility. In case of user mobility, the session establishment mechanisms will have to deal with the recent address where a user has moved, and it is the user who will work proactively to update one's recent address. The conferencing system and the session establishment mechanisms should have in-built schemes to deal with this. In the case of terminal mobility, the terminal itself may break and reestablish the network point of attachment as it moves from one place to another while the session is going on. However, a session object resides in the application layer in Open Standard International (OSI) terminology and may not be aware of the lower network layer's change in point of attachment. It is expected that it is the lower-layer protocols, such as the transport layer, network layer, and media access control layer, and the physical-layer protocols that will work transparently mitigating any changes in the network point of attachment. However, multimedia service portability that demands the end user's ability to obtain subscribed services in a transparent manner regardless of the end user's point of attachment to the network needs the transparent support in the application-layer session establishment.

A host of new services features related to the same call may also need to be satisfied even after the session establishment. Subconferencing, side bars, call transfer, call consultation transfer, call conference out of consultation, call diversion, call hold, call parking, call completion services for unsuccessful calls, prepaid call services, invoking of new applications, and many others, are some example of this category of services. The signaling protocol for the session establishment needs to have all the intelligence to satisfy the variety of requirements of the conference participants, such as how each media/application will be sent, received, and shared. In addition, the multimedia signaling protocol needs to have the ability to offer many other services to the conference participants within the same session even long after the establishment of the call. Because of the complexity of the real-time multimedia conversational services, the session establishment signaling messages have to be separated from the media (audio, video, and data/application sharing). The path transferring of signaling messages, audio, video, and data/application sharing can be completely independent.

The emergence of a new kind of feature-rich web-based communications for application visualization and sharing has enriched users' experiences over the Internet. It implies that the Internet Protocol (IP) has not only emerged as the choice universal communications protocol over which audio, video, and data will be transferred having a single network; the users also want to keep the same experiences of communications over the Internet even for the audio and videoconferencing services for application sharing. These criteria have made the web service applications as an integral part of the application sharing for audio and video conferencing. A secondary consequence of this has been the popularity among the developers of using text encoding for multimedia conferencing services because text encoding has been used for web services for its simplicity to debug, modify, and integrate with many existing applications.

The SIP has been standardized in the IETF as the call control protocol for the establishment of multimedia conversational session between conference participants. The SIP has embraced the simplicity of web-based communications protocol architecture as well as of text encoding. The SIP is a very attractive protocol for multimedia session establishment for time- and mission-critical point-to-point conference calls because of its human-understandable text encoding of signaling messages and use of the Hypertext Transfer Protocol (HTTP)/Hypertext Markup Language (HTML)-based web services like a protocol architecture separating the signaling messages into two parts: header and body. This inherent inbuilt capability of SIP has been used to create an enormous amount of new application services not only for time- and mission-critical conversational audio and video services but also for integration of the non-time-critical web services defined within the framework of service-oriented architecture (SOA) primarily as a part of the application sharing under the same audio and video-conferencing session.

The building of multipoint multimedia conferencing services dynamically using SIP is very difficult, if not impossible, unless the presence of the SIP architecture is drastically changed. One of the observations is that the SIP architecture is very weak in its conference negotiation capabilities in multipoint multimedia communications environments that require much more embedded intelligence in the signaling protocol architecture. For example, initially set up as a point-to-point two-party conference call, the SIP cannot be used to construct a multipoint conference call dynamically when a third party or more users join in the same conference call that needs media bridging. As a result, knowing the address of the conference server *a priori*, a centralized multipoint conferencing with star-like connectivity architecture is set up where the conference is established between each user of the multipoint conference participants and the conference server in a point-to-point fashion. In this respect, the SIP is an application-layer protocol that has the capability for establishing and tearing down point-to-point and multipoint-to-multipoint sessions using unicast or multicast communication environments. Being an application-layer protocol, the SIP can support both user and terminal mobility because the application-layer mobility does not require any changes to the operating system of any of the participants, and thus can be deployed widely to other lower-layer protocols, including mobile IP, and can take care of mobility-like changes in network point of attachments transparently.

2.4 Session Initiation Protocol

The SIP, as described earlier, is an application-layer multimedia signaling protocol that supports the establishment, management, and tear down of multimedia session between the conference participants, but does not provide services. SIP only performs these specific functions and relies heavily on other protocols to describe the media sessions, transport the media, and provide the QOS. Figure 2.2 shows the relationship between SIP and other protocols.

The SIP message consists of two parts: header and message body. The header is primarily used to route the signaling messages from the caller to the called party and contains a request line composed of the request type, the SIP Uniform Resource Identifier (URI) of the destination or next hop, and the version of SIP being used. The message body is optional depending on the type of message and where it falls within the establishment process. A blank line is used separating the header and the message-body part. If SIP invitations used to create sessions carry session descriptions that allow participants to agree on a set of compatible media types and compatible codecs, the message-body part will include all this information as described in the SDP.

It should be noted that the SIP application-layer protocol provides services in setting up the sessions between conference participants as directed by multimedia applications like teleconferencing, video teleconferencing (VTC), video conferencing (VC), application sharing, and web conferencing. Only audio is used in TC; both audio and video are used in VTC; while audio, video, and application(s) sharing are

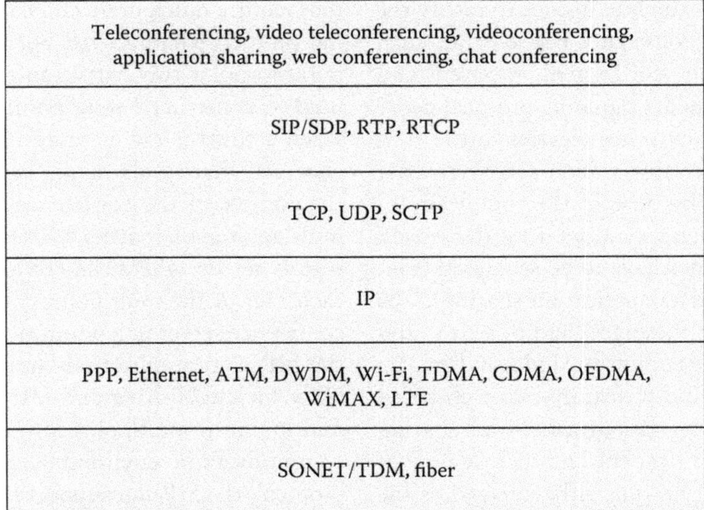

Figure 2.2 SIP and its relationship to other protocols.

used in VC. Sometimes, application sharing may be used as a part of web services integrated (or decoupling) with audio/video, and can be termed as web conferencing. Chat conferencing deals with real-time text messaging between two or more parties.

SIP signaling messages can be sent using any transport protocol such as Transmission Control Protocol (TCP), User Datagram Protocol (UDP), or Stream Control Transmission Protocol (SCTP). Of course, IP can run over Point-to-Point Protocol (PPP), Ethernet, asynchronous transfer mode (ATM), dense wavelength division multiplexing (DWDM), Wi-Fi, time division multiple access (TDMA), code division multiple access (CDMA), orthogonal frequency division multiple access (OFDMA), worldwide interoperability for microwave access (WiMAX), or long-term evolution (LTE) wireless networking protocol. It may be worthwhile to mention that ATM can run over synchronous optical network (SONET)/time division multiplexing (TDM) network that runs over fiber, and DWDM running over fiber increases the bandwidth by combining and transmitting multiple signals simultaneously at different wavelengths on the same fiber.

Different audio (e.g., International Telegraph Union—Telecommunication [ITU-T] G-series) and video (e.g., Moving Picture Expert Group [MPEG], Joint Photographic Expert Group [JPEG], and ITU-T H-series) codecs are used in multimedia sessions by conference participants. The bit streams of each codec are transferred over the RTP for transferring over UDP/IP. However, the common codec type either for audio or for video is negotiated by the SIP signaling messages that contain the information for each codec type that is proposed by the conference participants. SIP does not mandate any audio codec for any media that should be used by each participant if there is no common codec supported among the conferees. In this situation, the conferees may use the transcoding services for preventing failures of the session establishment. Real-Time Transport Control Protocol (RTCP) is based on the periodic transmission of control packets to all participants in the session and provides feedback on the quality of the data (e.g., RTP packets of audio/video) distribution. This is an integral part of RTP's role as a transport protocol and is related to the flow and congestion control functions of other transport protocols.

The Domain Name System (DNS) and Dynamic Host Configuration Protocol (DHCP) are the integral tools for IP address resolution and allocation, respectively, for routing of the SIP messages between the conference participants over the IP network. For example, a host can discover and contact a DHCP server to provide it with an IP address as well as the addresses of the DNS server and default router that can be used to route SIP messages over the IP network.

2.4.1 Augmented Backus–Naur Form for the SIP

The SIP uses augmented Backus–Naur Form (ABNF) for its messages. However, the syntaxes that are described here contain the SIP messages from the base SIP RFC 3261 and RFCs that extend and update this SIP RFC. Certain basic rules are in uppercase, such as SP (space), LWS (linear white space), HTAB (horizontal tab), CRLF (control return line feed), DIGIT, ALPHA, etc. Angle brackets are used within definitions to clarify the use of rule names. The use of square brackets is redundant syntactically. It is used as a semantic hint that the specific parameter is optional to use.

2.4.1.1 Basic Rules

The following rules are used throughout this specification to describe basic parsing constructs. The US American Standard Code for Information Interchange (US-ASCII) coded character set is defined by American National Standards Institute (ANSI) X3.4-1986.

```
alphanum = ALPHA/DIGIT
OCTET = <any 8-bit sequence of data>
CHAR = <any US-ASCII character (octets
0-127)>
UPALPHA = <any US-ASCII uppercase letter
"A".."Z">
ALPHA = UPALPHA | LOALPHA
DIGIT = <any US-ASCII digit "0".."9">
CTL = <any US-ASCII control character
      (octets 0 - 31) and DEL (127)>
CR = <US-ASCII CR, carriage return (13)>
LF = <US-ASCII LF, linefeed (10)>
SP = <US-ASCII SP, space (32)>
HT = <US-ASCII HT, horizontal-tab (9)>
<"> = <US-ASCII double-quote mark (34)>
```

Per RFC 3261, several rules are incorporated from RFC 2396 but are updated to make them compliant with RFC 2234. These include

```
reserved = ";"/"/"/"?"/":"/"@"/"&"/" = "/"+"
           /"$"/","
unreserved = alphanum/mark
mark = "-"/"ff"/"."/"!"/"~"/"*"/"'"
       /"("/")"
escaped = "%" HEXDIG HEXDIG
```

SIP header field values can be folded onto multiple lines if the continuation line begins with a space or horizontal tab. All linear white spaces, including folding, have the same semantics as SP. A recipient may replace any linear white space with a single SP before interpreting the field value or forwarding the message downstream. This is intended to behave exactly as HTTP/1.1 as described in RFC 2616. The SWS construct is used when linear white space is optional, generally between tokens and separators.

```
LWS = [*WSP CRLF] 1*WSP; linear white space
SWS = [LWS]; sep white space
```

To separate the header name from the rest of the value, a colon is used, which, by the above rule, allows white space before, but no line break, and white space after, including a line break. The HCOLON defines this construct.

```
HCOLON = *(SP/HTAB) ":" SWS
```

The TEXT-Unicode Transformation Format 8-bit (UTF-8) (TEXT-UTF-8) rule is only used for descriptive field contents and values that are not intended to be interpreted by the message parser. Words of *TEXT-UTF8 contain characters from the UTF-8 standard defined in RFC 2279. The TEXT-UTF8-TRIM rule is used for descriptive field contents that are not quoted strings, where the leading and trailing LWS is not meaningful. In this regard, SIP differs from HTTP, which uses the International Organization for Standardization (ISO) 8859-1 character set.

```
TEXT-UTF8-TRIM    =   1*TEXT-UTF8char *(*LWS
TEXT-UTF8char)
TEXT-UTF8char     =   %x21-7E/UTF8-NONASCII
UTF8-NONASCII     =   %xC0-DF 1UTF8-CONT
                      /%xE0-EF 2UTF8-CONT
                      /%xF0-F7 3UTF8-CONT
                      /%xF8-Fb 4UTF8-CONT
                      /%xFC-FD 5UTF8-CONT
UTF8-CONT         =   %x80-BF
```

A CRLF is allowed in the definition of TEXT-UTF8-TRIM only as part of a header field continuation. It is expected that the folding LWS will be replaced with a single SP before interpretation of the TEXT-UTF8-TRIM value. Hexadecimal numeric characters are used in several protocol elements. Some elements (authentication) force hex alphas to be lowercase.

```
LHEX = DIGIT/%x61-66;lowercase a-f
```

Many SIP header field values consist of words separated by LWS or special characters. Unless otherwise stated, tokens are case insensitive. These special characters must be in a quoted string to be used within a parameter value. The word construct is used in Call-ID to allow most separators to be used.

```
token = 1*(alphanum/"-"/"."/"!"/"%"/"*"
        /"ff"/"+"/"`"/"'"/"~")
separators = "("/")"/"<"/">"/"@"/
             ","/";"/":"/"\"/DQUOTE/
             "/"/"["/"]"/"?"/" = "/
             "{"/"}"/SP/HTAB
word = 1*(alphanum/"-"/"."/"!"/"%"/"*"/
       "ff"/"+"/"`"/"'"/"~"/
       "("/")"/"<"/">"/
       ":"/"\"/DQUOTE/
       "/"/"["/"]"/"?"/
       "{"/"}")
```

When tokens are used or separators are used between elements, white space is often allowed before or after these characters:

```
STAR = SWS "*" SWS; asterisk
SLASH = SWS "/" SWS; slash
EQUAL = SWS " = " SWS; equal
LPAREN = SWS "(" SWS; left parenthesis
RPAREN = SWS ")" SWS; right parenthesis
RAQUOT = ">" SWS; right angle quote
```

```
LAQUOT = SWS "<"; left angle quote
COMMA = SWS "," SWS; comma
SEMI = SWS ";" SWS; semicolon
COLON = SWS ":" SWS; colon
LDQUOT = SWS DQUOTE; open double quotation
mark
RDQUOT = DQUOTE SWS; close double quotation
mark
```

Comments can be included in some SIP header fields by surrounding the comment text with parentheses. Comments are only allowed in fields containing *comment* as part of their field value definition. In all other fields, parentheses are considered part of the field value.

```
comment = LPAREN *(ctext/quoted-pair/comment)
RPAREN
ctext = %x21-27/%x2A-5B/%x5D-7E/UTF8-NONASCII
/LWS
```

ctext includes all characters except left and right parentheses and backslash. A string of text is parsed as a single word if it is quoted using double-quote marks. In quoted strings, quotation marks (") and backslashes (\) need to be escaped.

```
quoted-string = SWS DQUOTE *(qdtext/quoted-
pair) DQUOTE
qdtext = LWS/%x21/%x23-5B/%x5D-7E
         /UTF8-NONASCII
```

The backslash character ("\") may be used as a single-character quoting mechanism only within quoted-string and comment constructs. Unlike HTTP/1.1, the characters CR and LF cannot be escaped by this mechanism to avoid conflict with line folding and header separation.

2.4.1.2 ABNF for SIP Messages

The methods and headers of SIP messages are described in subsequent sections. However, the ABNF syntaxes for SIP messages that are described in RFC 3261 are described below as per rules described above. However, RFC 3261 has been updated and extended following many RFCs. We have shown the ABNF syntaxes for those new messages here of the updated/extended SIP. Readers are reminded that RFC 5234 obsoletes RFC 4434, which again obsoletes RFC 2234 for ABNF standards. We describe the ABNF syntaxes and rules from RFC 5234 in Appendix A. All ABNF syntaxes are defined from RFC 3261 unless mentioned otherwise. Some parameters have been repeated for the sake of convenience.

```
quoted-pair  =  "\" (%x00-09/%x0B-0C
               /%x0E-7F)
SIP-URI   =  "sip:" [userinfo] hostport
             uri-parameters [headers]
SIPS-URI   = "sips:" [userinfo] hostport
             uri-parameters [headers]
userinfo = (user/telephone-subscriber)
             [":" password] "@"
user = 1*(unreserved/escaped/user-unreserved)
       user-unreserved = "&"/" = "/"+"/"$"/","/
                          ";"/"?"/"/"
password   =   *(unreserved/escaped/"&"/" =
               "/"+"/"$"/",")
hostport   =   host [":" port]
host   =   hostname/IPv4address/IPv6reference
hostname   =   *(domainlabel ".") toplabel
               ["."]
domainlabel    =   alphanum
               /alphanum *(alphanum/"-")
               alphanum
toplabel   =   ALPHA/ALPHA *(alphanum/"-")
               alphanum
```

RFC 5954 corrects the ABNF production rule associated with generating IPv6 literals in RFC 3261. It also clarifies the rule for URI comparison when the URIs contain textual representation of IP addresses. The ABNF (RFC 5234) for generating IPv6 literals in RFC 3261 is incorrect because of "extra colon in IPv4-mapped IPv6 address." When generating IPv4-mapped IPv6 addresses, the production rule may actually generate the following construct: [2001:db8:::192.0.2.1]—note the extra colon before the IPv4 address. The correct construct, of course, would only include two colons before the IPv4 address.

Historically, the ABNF pertaining to IPv6 references in RFC 3261 was derived from Appendix B of RFC 2373, which was flawed to begin with (see errata for RFC 2373). RFC 2373 has been subsequently obsoleted by RFC 4291.

The ABNF for IPv6 reference is reproduced from RFC 3261, as shown below:

```
IPv6reference   =   "[" IPv6address "]"
IPv6address   =   hexpart [":" IPv4address]
IPv4address   =   1*3DIGIT "." 1*3DIGIT "."
1*3DIGIT "." 1*3DIGIT
hexpart   =   hexseq/hexseq "::" [hexseq]/"::"
[hexseq]
hexseq   =   hex4 *(":" hex4)
hex4   =   1*4HEXDIG
```

Note that the ambiguity occurs in the <IPv6address> production rule where the <IPv4address> nonterminal is prefixed by the ":" token. Because the <hexpart> production rule is defined such that two of its alternatives already include the "::" token, this may yield to the faulty construction of an IPv6-mapped IPv4 address with an extra colon when expanding those alternatives.

The resolution to this ambiguity of extra colon in IPv4-mapped IPv6 address is simply to use the correct ABNF for the <IPv6address> production rule from Appendix A of RFC 3986. For the sake of completeness, it is reproduced below:

```
IPv6address =                        6(h16 ":")
                                     ls32
            /             "::" 5(h16 ":")
                          ls32
            /      [h16] "::" 4(h16 ":")
                   ls32
            /[*1(h16 ":") h16] "::" 3(h16
            ":") ls32
            /[*2(h16 ":") h16] "::" 2(h16
            ":") ls32
            /[*3(h16 ":") h16] "::" h16 ":"
            ls32
            /[*4(h16 ":") h16] "::"
            ls32
            /[*5(h16 ":") h16] "::" h16
            /[*6(h16 ":") h16] "::"

h16  =  1*4HEXDIG
ls32  = (h16 ":" h16)/IPv4address
IPv4address  = dec-octet "." dec-octet "."
               dec-octet "." dec-octet
dec-octet  =  DIGIT; 0-9
              /%x31-39 DIGIT; 10-99
              /"1" 2DIGIT; 100-199
              /"2"%x30-34 DIGIT; 200-249
              /"25"%x30-35; 250-255
```

Accordingly, this book updates RFC 3261 as follows: the <IPv6address> and <IPv4address> production rules from RFC 3261 must not be used and, instead, the production rules of the same name in RFC 3986 (and reproduced above) must be used as stated above. This will render <hexpart>, <hexseq>, and <hex4> production rules in RFC 3261 obsolete; as such, these three production rules—namely, <hexpart>, <hexseq>, and <hex4>—from RFC 3261 must not be used. The use of the <IPv4address> production rule from RFC 3986 no longer allows syntactically valid—though semantically invalid—SIP URIs of the form sip:bob@444.555.666.777, for example.

```
port          =      1*DIGIT
```

The BNF for telephone-subscriber can be found in RFCs 2806/4434/5234. Note, however, that any characters allowed there that are not allowed in the user part of the SIP URI must be escaped.

```
uri-parameters =  *(";" uri-parameter)
uri-parameter  =  transport-param/user-param/
                  method-param
                  /ttl-param/maddr-param/
                  lr-param/other-param
transport-param = "transport = "
                  ("udp"/"tcp"/"sctp"/"tls"
                  /other-transport)
other-transport = token
user-param = "user = " ("phone"/"ip"/
             other-user)
other-user = token
method-param =  "method = " Method
ttl-param  =  "ttl = " ttl
maddr-param  =  "maddr = " host
                lr-param = "lr"
other-param  =  pname [" = " pvalue]
pname  =  1*paramchar
pvalue  =  1*paramchar
paramchar  =  param-unreserved/unreserved/
              escaped
param-unreserved =  "["/"]"/"/"/":"/"&"/
                    "+"/"$"
headers  =  "?" header *("&" header)
header  =  hname " = " hvalue
hname  =  1*(hnv-unreserved/unreserved/
          escaped)
hvalue  =  *(hnv-unreserved/unreserved/
           escaped)
hnv-unreserved =  "["/"]"/"/"/"?"/":"/"+"/"$"
SIP-message  =  Request/Response
Request  =  Request-Line
            *(message-header)
            CRLF
            [message-body]
Request-Line  =  Method SP Request-URI SP
                 SIP-Version CRLF
Request-URI  =  SIP-URI/SIPS-URI/absoluteURI
absoluteURI  =  scheme ":" (hier-part/
                opaque-part)
hier-part  =  (net-path/abs-path) ["?" query]
net-path  =  "//" authority [abs-path]
abs-path  =  "/" path-segments
opaque-part  =  uric-no-slash *uric
uric  =  reserved/unreserved/escaped
uric-no-slash  =  unreserved/escaped/";"/
                  "?"/":"/"@"  /"&"/" =
                  "/"+"/"$"/","
path-segments =  segment *("/" segment)
segment  =  *pchar *(";" param)
param  =  *pchar
pchar  =  unreserved/escaped/":"/"@"/"&"/" =
          "/"+"/"$"/","
scheme  =  ALPHA *(ALPHA/DIGIT/"+"/"-"/".")
authority  =  srvr/reg-name
srvr  =  [[userinfo "@"] hostport]
reg-name  =  1*(unreserved/esca
             ped/"$"/","/";"/":"/"@"/"&"/" =
             "/"+")
query  =  *uric
SIP-Version  =  "SIP" "/" 1*DIGIT "." 1*DIGIT
message-header =  (Accept
                  /Accept-Contact
                  ;from RFC 3841
                  /Accept-Encoding
                  /Accept-Language
                  /Accept-Resource-Priority
                  ;from RFC 4412
                  /Alert-Info
                  /Allow
                  /Allow-Events
                  ;from RFC 6665
```

/Answer-Mode; from RFC 5373
/Authentication-Info
/Authorization
/Call-ID
/Call-Info
/Contact
/Content-Disposition
/Content-Encoding
/Content-Language
/Content-Length
/Content-Type
/CSeq
/Date
/Encryption; from RFC 2543 obsoleted by 3261
/Error-Info
/Event; from RFC 6665
/Expires
/Flow-Timer; from RFC 5626
/From
/Geolocation; from RFC 6442
/Geolocation-Error; from RFC 6442
/Geolocation-Routing; from RFC 6442
/Hide; from RFC 2543 obsoleted by RFC 3261
/History-Info; from RFC 4244
/Identity; from RFC 4474
/Identity-Info; from RFC 4474
/Info-Package; from RFC 6086
/In-Reply-To
/Join; from RFC 3911
/Max-Breadth; from RFC 5393
/Max-Forwards
/MIME-Version
/Min-Expires
/Min-SE; from RFC 4028
/Organization
/P-Access-Network-Info; from RFC 7315
/P-Asserted-Identity; from RFC 3325
/P-Asserted-Service; from RFC 6050
/P-Associated-URI; from RFC 7315
/Path; from RFC 3327
/P-Called-Party-ID; from RFC 7315
/P-Charging-Function-Addresses; from RFC 7315
/P-Charging-Vector; from RFC 7315
/P-Early-Media; from RFC 5009
/Permission-Missing; from RFC 5360
/P-Preferred-Identity; from RFC 3325
/P-Preferred-Service; from RFC 6050
/P-Profile-Key; from RFC 5002
/Priority
/Priv-Answer-Mode; from RFC 5373
/Privacy; from RFC 3323
/Proxy-Authenticate
/Proxy-Authorization
/Proxy-Require
/P-Refused-URI-List; from RFC 5318
/P-Served-User; from RFC 5502
/P-User-Database; from RFC 4457
/P-Visited-Network-ID; from RFC 7315
/RAck; from RFC 3262
/Reason; from RFC 3326
/Record-Route
/Recv-Info; from RFC 6086
/Referred-By; from RFC 3892
/Refer-Sub; from RFC 4488
/Refer-To; from RFC 3515
/Reject-Contact; from RFC 3841
/Replaces; from RFC 3891
/Reply-To
/Request-Disposition; from RFC 3841
/Require
/Resource-Priority; from RFC 4412
/Response-Key; from RFC 2543 obsoleted by RFC 3261
/Retry-After
/Route
/RSeq; from RFC 3262
/Security-Client; from RFC 3329
/Security-Server; from RFC 3329
/Security-Verify; from RFC 3329
/Server
/Service-Route; from RFC 3608
/Session-Expires; from RFC 4028
/SIP-ETag; from RFC 4028
/SIP-If-Match; from RFC 4028
/Subject
/Subscription-State; from RFC 6665
/Supported

```
                    /Suppress-If-Match; from
                    RFC 5839
                    /Target-Dialog; from RFC
                    4538
                    /Timestamp
                    /To
                    /Trigger-Consent; from RFC
                    5360
                    /Unsupported
                    /User-Agent
                    /User-to-User; from RFC
                    7433
                    /Via
                    /Warning
                    /WWW-Authenticate
                    /extension-header) CRLF
INVITEm  =  %x49.4E.56.49.54.45; INVITE in
            caps
ACKm  =  %x41.43.4B; ACK in caps
OPTIONSm  =  %x4F.50.54.49.4F.4E.53; OPTIONS
             in caps
BYEm  =  %x42.59.45; BYE in caps
CANCELm  =  %x43.41.4E.43.45.4C; CANCEL in
            caps
REGISTERm  =  %x52.45.47.49.53.54.45.52;
              REGISTER in caps
SUBSCRIBEm =  %x53.55.42.53.43.52.49.42.45;
              SUBSCRIBE in caps
              ; from RFC 6665
NOTIFYm  =  %x4E.4F.54.49.46.59; NOTIFY in
            caps
            ; from RFC 6665
PUBLISHm  =  %x50.55.42.4C.49.53.48; PUBLISH
             in caps
             ; from RFC 3903
MESSAGEm  =  %x4D.45.53.53.41.47.45; MESSAGE
             in caps
             ; from RFC 3428
UPDATEm  =  %x55.50.44.41.54.45; UPDATE in
            caps; from RFC 3311
PRACKm  =  %x50.52.41.43.4B; PRACK in caps
           ; from RFC 3262
INFOm  =  %x49.4E.46.4F; INFO in caps
          ; from RFC 6086
Method  =  INVITEm/ACKm/OPTIONSm/BYEm/
           CANCELm/REGISTERm/REFERm; from RFC
           3525/SUBSCRIBEm; from RFC 6665/
           NORIFYm; from RFC 6665/PUBLISHm;
           from RFC 3903/MESSAGEm; from RFC
           3428/UPDATEm; from RFC 3311/
           PRACKm;  from RFC 3262/INFOm; from
           RFC 6086
           /extension-method
           extension-method = token
           Response = Status-Line
           *(message-header)
           CRLF
           [message-body]
Status-Line  =  SIP-Version SP Status-Code SP
                Reason-Phrase CRLF
Status-Code  =  Informational
                /Redirection
                /Success
                /Client-Error
                /Server-Error
                /Global-Failure
                /extension-code
extension-code  =  3DIGIT
Reason-Phrase =  *(reserved/unreserved/
                 escaped
                 /UTF8-NONASCII/UTF8-CONT/SP/
                 HTAB)
Informational  =  "100"; Trying
                  /"180"; Ringing
                  /"181"; Call Is Being
                  Forwarded
                  /"182"; Call Queued
                  /"183"; Session Progress
Success  =  "200"; OK
          /"202"; Accepted; from RFC 6665
          /"204"; No Notification; from RFC
          5839
Redirection  =  "300"; Multiple Choices
                /"301"; Moved Permanently
                /"302"; Moved Temporarily
                /"305"; Use Proxy
                /"380"; Alternative Service
Client-Error  =  "400"; Bad Request
                 /"401"; Unauthorized
                 /"402"; Payment Required
                 /"403"; Forbidden
                 /"404"; Not Found
                 /"405"; Method Not Allowed
                 /"406"; Not Acceptable
                 /"407"; Proxy Authentication
                 Required
                 /"408"; Request Timeout
                 /"409"; Conflict; from RFC
                 2543 obsoleted by RFC 3261
                 /"410"; Gone
                 /"411"; Length Required;
                 from RFC 2543 obsoleted by
                 RFC; 3261
                 /"412"; Conditional Request
                 Failed; from RFC 3903
                 /"413"; Request Entity Too
                 Large
                 /"414"; Request-URI Too
                 Large
                 /"415"; Unsupported Media
                 Type
                 /"416"; Unsupported URI
                 Scheme
                 /"417"; Unknown Resource
                 Priority; from RFC 4412
                 /"420"; Bad Extension
                 /"421"; Extension Required
                 /"422"; Session Timer
                 Interval; from RFC 4028
                 /"423"; Interval Too Brief
```

```
                /"424"; Bad Location
                Information; "424" from RFC
                6442
                /"428"; User Identity
                Header; from RFC 4474
                /"429"; Provide Referror
                Identity; from RFC 3892
                /"433"; Anonymity
                Disallowed; from RFC 5079
                /"436"; Bad Identity-Info;
                from RFC 4474
                /"437"; Unsupported
                Certificate; from RFC 4474
                /"438"; Invalid Identity
                Header; form RFC 4474
                /"439"; First Hop Lacks
                Outbound Support
                ; from RFC 5626
                /"440"; Max-Breadth
                Exceeded; from RFC 5393
                /"469"; Bad Info Package;
                from RFC 6086
                /"470"; Consent Needed; from
                RFC 5360
                /"480"; Temporarily not
                available
                /"481"; Call Leg/Transaction
                Does Not Exist
                /"482"; Loop Detected
                /"483"; Too Many Hops
                /"484"; Address Incomplete
                /"485"; Ambiguous
                /"486"; Busy Here
                /"487"; Request Terminated
                /"488"; Not Acceptable Here
                /"489"; Bad Event; from 6665
                /"491"; Request Pending
                /"493"; Undecipherable
                /"494"; Security Agreement
                Required; from RFC 3329
Server-Error =  "500"; Internal Server Error
                /"501"; Not Implemented
                /"502"; Bad Gateway
                /"503"; Service Unavailable
                /"504"; Server Time-out
                /"505"; SIP Version not
                supported
                /"513"; Message Too Large
                /"508"; Precondition Failure;
                from RFC 3312
Global-Failure  =  "600"; Busy Everywhere
                   /"603"; Decline
                   /"604"; Does not exist
                   anywhere
                   /"606"; Not Acceptable
Accept  =  "Accept" HCOLON
           [accept-range *(COMMA
           accept-range)]
accept-range  =  media-range *(SEMI
                 accept-param)
media-range  =  ("*/*"
                /(m-type SLASH "*")
                /(m-type SLASH m-subtype)
                ) *(SEMI m-parameter)
accept-param  =  ("q" EQUAL qvalue)/
                 generic-param
                 qvalue = ("0" ["."
                 0*3DIGIT])
                 /("1" ["." 0*3("0")])
generic-param  =  token [EQUAL gen-value]
gen-value  =  via-params token/host/
              quoted-string
Accept-Encoding  =  "Accept-Encoding"
HCOLON
                    [encoding *(COMMA
                    encoding)]
encoding  =  codings *(SEMI accept-param)
codings  =  content-coding/"*"
content-coding  =  token
Accept-Language  =  "Accept-Language" HCOLON
                    [language *(COMMA
                    language)]
language  =  language-range *(SEMI
             accept-param)
language-range  =  ((1*8ALPHA *("-"
                   1*8ALPHA))/"*")
Alert-Info  =  "Alert-Info" HCOLON
               alert-param
               *(COMMA alert-param)
alert-param  =  LAQUOT absoluteURI RAQUOT
                *(SEMI generic-param)

; RFC 7463 extends RFC 3261 to add an
appearance parameter to the Alert-Info
header
; field and also to allow proxies to modify
or delete the Alert-Info header field. The
changes
; to the ABNF in RFC 3261 are

alert-param  =  LAQUOT absoluteURI RAQUOT
                *(SEMI(generic-param/
                appearance-param))
appearance-param  =  "appearance" EQUAL
                     1*DIGIT

; from RFC 7463
; A proxy inserting an appearance Alert-Info
parameter follows normal Alert-Info
; policies.

Allow  =  "Allow" HCOLON [Method *(COMMA
          Method)]
Authorization  =  "Authorization" HCOLON
                  credentials
credentials  =  ("Digest" LWS
                digest-response)
                /other-response
digest-response  =  dig-resp *(COMMA
                    dig-resp)
dig-resp  =  username/realm/nonce/digest-uri
             /dresponse/algorithm/cnonce
             /opaque/message-qop
             /nonce-count/auth-param
```

```
username  =  "username" EQUAL username-value
username-value  =  quoted-string
digest-uri  =  "uri" EQUAL LDQUOT digest-uri-
               value RDQUOT
digest-uri-value  =  rquest-uri; Equal to
                     request-uri as
                     specified
                     by HTTP/1.1
message-qop  =  "qop" EQUAL qop-value
cnonce  =  "cnonce" EQUAL cnonce-value
cnonce-value  =  nonce-value
nonce-count  =  "nc" EQUAL nc-value
nc-value  =  8LHEX
dresponse  =  "response" EQUAL
              request-digest
request-digest  =  LDQUOT 32LHEX RDQUOT
auth-param  =  auth-param-name EQUAL
               (token/quoted-string)
               auth-param-name = token
               other-response = auth-scheme
               LWS auth-param
               *(COMMA auth-param)
auth-scheme  =  token
Authentication-Info  =  "Authentication-Info"
                        HCOLON ainfo
                        *(COMMA ainfo)
                        ainfo = nextnonce/
                        message-qop
                        /response-auth/
                        cnonce/nonce-count
nextnonce  =  "nextnonce" EQUAL nonce-value
response-auth  =  "rspauth" EQUAL
                  response-digest
response-digest  =  LDQUOT *LHEX RDQUOT
Call-ID  =  ("Call-ID"/"i") HCOLON callid
callid  =  word ["@" word]
Call-Info  =  "Call-Info" HCOLON info *(COMMA
              info)
info     =  LAQUOT absoluteURI RAQUOT *(SEMI
            info-param)
info-param  =  ("purpose" EQUAL
               ("icon"/"info"
               /"card"/token))/generic-param
Contact  =  ("Contact"/"m") HCOLON
            (STAR/(contact-param *(COMMA
            contact-param)))
contact-param  =  (name-addr/addr-spec)
                  *(SEMI contact-params)
contact-params  =  c-p-q/c-p-expires/
                   feature-param
                   /contact-extension
; contact-params especially for feature-param
extensions from RFC 3840

feature-param  =  enc-feature-tag [EQUAL
                  LDQUOT (tag-value-list
                  /string-value) RDQUOT]
enc-feature-tag  =  base-tags/other-tags
base-tags  =  "audio"/"automata"/"class"/
              "duplex"/"data"/
              "control"/"mobility"/"description"/
              "events"/"priority"/"methods"/
              "schemes"/"application"/"vi
              deo"/
              "language"/"type"/
              "isfocus"/"actor"/"text"/"exten
              sions"
other-tags  =  "+" ftag-name
ftag-name  =  ALPHA *(ALPHA/DIGIT/
              "!"/"'"/"."/"-"/"%")
tag-value-list  =  tag-value *("," tag-value)
tag-value  =  ["!"] (token-nobang/boolean/
              numeric)
token-nobang  =  1*(alphanum/"-"/"."/"%"/"*"/
                 "ff"/"+"/"'"/"'"/"~")
boolean  =  "TRUE"/"FALSE"
numeric  =  "#" numeric-relation number
numeric-relation  =  "> = "/"< = "/" = "/
                     (number ":")
number  =  ["+"/"-"] 1*DIGIT ["." 0*DIGIT]
string-value  =  "<" *(qdtext-no-abkt/quoted-
                 pair) ">"
qdtext-no-abkt  =  LWS/%x21/%x23-3B/%x3D
                   /%x3F-5B/%x5D-7E/
                   UTF8-NONASCII
name-addr  =  [display-name] LAQUOT addr-spec
              RAQUOT
addr-spec  =  SIP-URI/SIPS-URI/absoluteURI
display-name  =  *(token LWS)/quoted-string
c-p-q  =  "q" EQUAL qvalue
c-p-expires  =  "expires" EQUAL
                delta-seconds
contact-extension  =  generic-param
delta-seconds  =  1*DIGIT
Content-Disposition  =  "Content-Disposition"
                        HCOLON
                        disp-type *(SEMI
                        disp-param)
disp-type  =  "render"/"session"/"icon"/
              "alert"/disp-extension-token

; The ABNF for the alert URNs is shown below
defined by RFC 7462:

alert-URN  =  "urn:alert:" alert-identifier
alert-identifier  =  alert-category ":"
                     alert-indication
alert-category  =  alert-name
alert-indication  =  alert-ind-part *(":"
                     alert-ind-part)
alert-ind-part  =  alert-name
alert-name  =  alert-label/private-name
private-name  =  alert-label "@" provider
provider  =  alert-label
alert-label  =  let-dig [*let-dig-hyp
                let-dig]
let-dig-hyp  =  let-dig/"-"
let-dig  =  ALPHA/DIGIT
ALPHA  =  %x41-5A/%x61-7A; A-Z/a-z
DIGIT  =  %x30-39; 0-9

; <alert-label>s must comply with the syntax
for Non-Reserved LDH labels (RFC
; 5890).
```

```
Registered URNs and components thereof must
be transmitted as registered
; (including case).
disp-param  =  handling-param/generic-param
handling-param  =  "handling" EQUAL
                   ("optional"/"required"/
                   other-handling)
other-handling  =  token
disp-extension-token  =  token
Content-Encoding  =  ("Content-Encoding"/"e")
                     HCOLON
                     content-coding *(COMMA
                     content-coding)
Content-Language  =  "Content-Language"
                     HCOLON
                     language-tag *(COMMA
                     language-tag)
language-tag  =  primary-tag *("-" subtag)
primary-tag  =  1*8ALPHA
subtag  =  1*8ALPHA
Content-Length  =  ("Content-Length"/"l")
                   HCOLON 1*DIGIT
Content-Type  =  ("Content-Type"/"c") HCOLON
                 media-type
media-type  =  m-type SLASH m-subtype *(SEMI
               m-parameter)
m-type  =  discrete-type/composite-type/
           access-type
; access-type from RFC 4483

access-type  =  "URL"; URL from RFC 3986
discrete-type  =  "text"/"image"/"audio"
                  /"video"
                  /"application"/
                  extension-token
composite-type  =  "message"/"multipart"/
                   extension-token
extension-token  =  ietf-token/x-token
ietf-token  =  token
x-token  =  "x-" token
m-subtype  =  extension-token/iana-token
iana-token  =  token
m-parameter  =  m-attribute EQUAL m-value
m-attribute  =  token
m-value  =  token/quoted-string
CSeq     =  "CSeq" HCOLON 1*DIGIT LWS
            Method
Date     =  "Date" HCOLON SIP-date
SIP-date  =  rfc1123-date
rfc1123-date  =  wkday "," SP date1 SP time
                 SP "GMT"
date1  =  2DIGIT SP month SP 4DIGIT
          ; day month year (e.g., 02 Jun
          1982)
time  =  2DIGIT ":" 2DIGIT ":" 2DIGIT
         ; 00:00:00 - 23:59:59
wkday  =  "Mon"/"Tue"/"Wed"
          /"Thu"/"Fri"/"Sat"/"Sun"
month  =  "Jan"/"Feb"/"Mar"/"Apr"
          /"May"/"Jun"/"Jul"/"Aug"
          /"Sep"/"Oct"/"Nov"/"Dec"
Error-Info  =  "Error-Info" HCOLON error-uri
               *(COMMA error-uri)
error-uri  =  LAQUOT absoluteURI RAQUOT
              *(SEMI generic-param)
Expires  =  "Expires" HCOLON delta-seconds
CRLF     =  CR LF
; CRLF from RFC 5626

double-CRLF = CR LF CR LF
; double-CRLF from RFC 5626

CR  =  %x0D
LF  =  %x0A
Flow-Timer  =  "Flow-Timer" HCOLON 1*DIGIT
; Flow-Timer; from RFC 5626

contact-params  =  /c-p-reg/c-p-instance
c-p-reg  =  "reg-id" EQUAL 1*DIGIT; 1 to (2^31
            - 1)
; The value of the reg-id must not be 0 and
must be less than 2^31 (from RFC 5626)

c-p-instance  =  "+sip.instance" EQUAL
                 DQUOTE "<" instance-val ">"
                 DQUOTE
instance-val  =  1*uric; defined in RFC 3261
From  =  ("From"/"f") HCOLON from-spec
from-spec  =  (name-addr/addr-spec)
              *(SEMI from-param)
from-param  =  tag-param/generic-param
tag-param  =  "tag" EQUAL token
In-Reply-To  =  "In-Reply-To" HCOLON callid
                *(COMMA callid)
Max-Forwards  =  "Max-Forwards" HCOLON
                 1*DIGIT
MIME-Version  =  "MIME-Version" HCOLON
                 1*DIGIT "." 1*DIGIT
Min-Expires  =  "Min-Expires" HCOLON
                delta-seconds
Organization  =  "Organization" HCOLON
                 [TEXT-UTF8-TRIM]
Priority  =  "Priority" HCOLON priority-value
priority-value  =  "emergency"/"urgent"
                   /"normal"
                   /"non-urgent"/
                   other-priority
other-priority  =  token
Proxy-Authenticate  =  "Proxy-Authenticate"
                       HCOLON challenge
challenge  =  ("Digest" LWS digest-cln
              *(COMMA digest-cln))
              /other-challenge
other-challenge  =  auth-scheme LWS
                    auth-param
                    *(COMMA auth-param)
                    digest-cln = realm/
                    domain/nonce
                    /opaque/stale/algorithm
                    /qop-options/auth-param
realm  =  "realm" EQUAL realm-value
realm-value  =  quoted-string
```

```
domain  =  "domain" EQUAL LDQUOT URI
           *(1*SP URI) RDQUOT
URI  =  absoluteURI/abs-path
nonce  =  "nonce" EQUAL nonce-value
nonce-value  =  quoted-string
opaque  =  "opaque" EQUAL quoted-string
stale  =  "stale" EQUAL ("true"/"false")
algorithm  =  "algorithm" EQUAL
              ("MD5"/"MD5-sess"
              /token)
qop-options  =  "qop" EQUAL LDQUOT qop-value
                *("," qop-value) RDQUOT
qop-value  =  "auth"/"auth-int"/token
Proxy-Authorization  =  "Proxy-Authorization"
                        HCOLON credentials
Proxy-Require  =  "Proxy-Require" HCOLON
                  option-tag
                  *(COMMA option-tag)
                  option-tag = token
Record-Route =      "Record-Route" HCOLON
                    rec-route *(COMMA
                    rec-route)
rec-route  =  name-addr *(SEMI rr-param)
rr-param  =  generic-param
Reply-To  =  "Reply-To" HCOLON rplyto-spec
rplyto-spec  =  (name-addr/addr-spec)
                *(SEMI rplyto-param)
rplyto-param  =  generic-param
Require  =  "Require" HCOLON option-tag
            *(COMMA option-tag)
Retry-After  =  "Retry-After" HCOLON
                delta-seconds
                [comment] *(SEMI
                retry-param)
retry-param  =  ("duration" EQUAL
                delta-seconds)
                /generic-param
Route  =  "Route" HCOLON route-param *(COMMA
          route-param)
route-param  =  name-addr *(SEMI rr-param)
Server  =  "Server" HCOLON server-val *(LWS
           server-val)
server-val  =  product/comment
product  =  token [SLASH product-version]
product-version  =  token
Subject  =  ("Subject"/"s") HCOLON
            [TEXT-UTF8-TRIM]
Supported  =  ("Supported"/"k") HCOLON
              [option-tag *(COMMA
              option-tag)]
Timestamp  =  "Timestamp" HCOLON 1*(DIGIT)
              ["." *(DIGIT)] [LWS delay]
delay  =  *(DIGIT) ["." *(DIGIT)]
To  =  ("To"/"t") HCOLON (name-addr
       /addr-spec) *(SEMI to-param)
to-param  =  tag-param/generic-param

Trigger-Consent  =  "Trigger-Consent" HCOLON
                    trigger-cons-spec*(COMMA
                    trigger-cons-spec)
; Trigger-Consent; from RFC 5360
trigger-cons-spec  =  (SIP-URI/SIPS-
                      URI)*(SEMI
                      trigger-param)
trigger-param  =  target-uri/generic-param
target-uri  =  "target-uri" EQUAL LDQUOT
               *(qdtext/quoted-pair) RDQUOT
; The target-uri header field parameter MUST
contain a URI

Unsupported  =  "Unsupported" HCOLON option-
                tag *(COMMA option-tag)
User-Agent  =  "User-Agent" HCOLON server-val
               *(LWS server-val)
Via  =  ("Via"/"v") HCOLON via-parm *(COMMA
        via-parm)
via-parm  =  sent-protocol LWS sent-by *(SEMI
             via-params)
via-params  =  via-ttl/via-maddr
               /via-received/via-branch
               /via-extension

; This (RFC 3581) extends the existing
definition of the Via header field parameters,
; so that its BNF now looks like

via-params  =  via-ttl/via-maddr/via-
               received/via-branch/response-
               port/via-extension

; RFC 5923 extends the via-params to include
a new via-alias defined below:

via-params  =  /via-alias
via-alias  =  "alias"

via-ttlvia-ttl"ttl" EQUAL ttl
via-maddr  =  "maddr" EQUAL host
via-received  =  "received" EQUAL
                 (IPv4address/IPv6address)
via-branch  =  "branch" EQUAL token
via-extension  =  generic-param
sent-protocol  =  protocol-name SLASH
                  protocol-version SLASH
                  transport
protocol-name  =  "SIP"/token
protocol-version  =  token
transport  =  "UDP"/"TCP"/"TLS"/"SCTP"
              /other-transport
sent-by  =  host [COLON port]
ttl  =  1*3DIGIT; 0 to 255
Warning  =  "Warning" HCOLON warning-value
            *(COMMA warning-value)
warning-value  =  warn-code SP warn-agent SP
                  warn-text
warn-code  =  DIGIT
warn-agent  =  hostport/pseudonym; the name
               or pseudonym of the server
               adding; the Warning header,
               for use in debugging
warn-text  =  quoted-string
pseudonym  =  token
```

```
WWW-Authenticate  =  "WWW-Authenticate"
                     HCOLON challenge
extension-header  =  header-name HCOLON
                     header-value
header-name  =  token
header-value  =  *(TEXT-UTF8char/UTF8-CONT/
                 LWS)
message-body  =  *OCTET
Accept-Contact  =  ("Accept-Contact"/"a")
                   HCOLON ac-value *(COMMA
                   ac-value); Accept-Contact
                   from RFC 3841 (see
                   Sections; 2.8 and 9.9)
Reject-Contact  =  ("Reject-Contact"/"j")
                   HCOLON rc-value*(COMMA
                   rc-value)
ac-value  =  "*" *(SEMI ac-params)
rc-value  =  "*" *(SEMI rc-params)
ac-params  =  feature-param/req-param/
              explicit-param/generic-param
              feature-param =    enc-feature-
              tag [EQUAL LDQUOT (tag-value-
              list/string-value) RDQUOT];
              feature-param from RFC 3840

enc-feature-tag  =  base-tags/other-tags
base-tags  =   "audio"/"automata"/"class"/
               "duplex"/"data"/
               "control"/"mobility"/"descript
               ion"/
               "events"/"priority"/"methods"/
               "schemes"/"application"/"vi
               deo"/
               "language"/"type"/"isfocus"/
               "actor"/"text"/"extensions"
other-tags  =  "+" ftag-name
ftag-name  =  ALPHA *(ALPHA/
              DIGIT/"!"/"'"/"."/"-"/"%")
tag-value-list  =  tag-value *(","
                   tag-value)
tag-value  =  ["!"] (token-nobang/boolean/
              numeric)
token-nobang = 1*(alphanum/"-"/"."/"%" /"*"/"
               ff"/"+"/"'"/"'"/"~")
boolean  =  "TRUE"/"FALSE"
numeric  =  "#" numeric-relation number
numeric-relation  =  "> = "/"< = "/" = "/
                     (number ":")
number  =  ["+"/"-"] 1*DIGIT ["." 0*DIGIT]
string-value  =  "<" *(qdtext-no-abkt/quoted-
                 pair) ">"
qdtext-no-abkt  =  LWS/%x21/%x23-3B/%x3D
                   /%x3F-5B/%x5D-7E/
                   UTF8-NONASCII
rc-params  =  feature-param/generic-param
req-param  =  "require"
explicit-param  =  "explicit"

; Despite the ABNF, there must not be more
than one req-param or explicit-param; in an
ac-;params. Furthermore, there can only be
one instance of any feature tag; in
feature-;param.

Accept-Resource-Priority  =  "Accept-Resource
                             -Priority"
HCOLON [r-value *(COMMA r-value)]
; Accept-Resource-Priority from RFC 4412

Event  =  ("Event"/"o") HCOLON event-type
          *(SEMI event-param)
; Event from RFC 6665
event-type  =  event-package *("."
               event-template)
event-package  =  token-nodot
event-template  =  token-nodot
token-nodot  =  1*(alphanum/"-"/"!"/"%"/"*"
                /"_"/"+"/"'"/"'"/"~")
; The use of the "id" parameter is
deprecated; it is included for backwards-
; compatibility purposes only.

event-param  =  generic-param/("id" EQUAL
                token)
Allow-Events  =  ("Allow-Events"/"u") HCOLON
                 event-type *(COMMA event-
                 type);Allow-Events from RFC
                 6665
Subscription-State  =  "Subscription-State"
                       HCOLON substate-value
                       *(SEMI subexp-params);
                       Subscription-State
                       from RFC 6665
substate-value  =  "active"/"pending"/
                   "terminated"/extension-
                   substate
extension-substatee  =  token
subexp-params  =  ("reason" EQUAL
                  event-reason-value)
                  /("expires" EQUAL
                  delta-seconds)
                  /("retry-after" EQUAL
                  delta-seconds)
                  /generic-param
event-reason-value  =  "deactivated"
                       /"probation"/"rejected"
                       /"timeout"/"giveup"
                       /"noresource"/"invariant"
                       /event-reason-extension
event-reason-extension  =  token
message-header  =  /Geolocation-header
Geolocation-header  =  "Geolocation" HCOLON
                       locationValue
                       *(COMMA locationValue)
; Geolocation and locationValue parameter
from RFC 6442
locationValue  =  LAQUOT locationURI RAQUOT *
                  (SEMI geoloc-param)
locationURI  =  sip-URI/sips-URI/pres-URI/
                http-URI/https-URI/cid-url;
                (from RFC 2392)/absoluteURI
geoloc-param  =  generic-param
```

```
; The pres-URI is defined in RFC 3859. http-
URI and https-URI are defined
; according to RFC 2616 and RFC 2818,
respectively. The cid-url is     defined in
; RFC 2392 to locate message-body parts. This
URI type is present in a   SIP request
; when location is conveyed as a MIME body in
the SIP message. GEO-URIs
; defined in RFC 5870 are not appropriate for
usage in the SIP    Geolocation header
; because it does not include retention and
retransmission flags as part     of the
; location information. Other URI schemes
used in the location URI must    be
; reviewed against the criteria defined in
RFC 3693 for a Using Protocol    that uses
; the location object (LO).

message-headere  =  /Georouting-header
Georouting-headere  =  "Geolocation-Routing"
                       HCOLON ("yes"/"no"/
                       generic-value)
generic-valuee  =  generic-param
message-headere  =  /Geolocation-Error
Geolocation-Errore  =  "Geolocation-Error"
                       HCOLON
                       locationErrorValue
; Geolocation-Error from RFC 6642

locationErrorValuee  =  location-error-code
                        *(SEMI location-
                        error-   params)
location-error-code  =  1*3DIGIT
location-error-params  =  location-error-
                          code-text/
                          generic-param
History-Info  =  "History-Info" HCOLON
                 hi-entry *(COMMA hi-entry)
; History-Info from RFC 4244

hi-entry  =  hi-targeted-to-uri *(SEMI
             hi-param)
hi-targeted-to-uri  =  name-addr
hi-param  =  hi-index/hi-extension
hi-index  =  "index" EQUAL 1*DIGIT *(DOT
             1*DIGIT)
hi-extension  =  generic-param:
Identity  =  "Identity" HCOLON
             signed-identity-digest
; Identity from RFC 4474

signed-identity-digest  =  LDQUOT 32LHEX
                           RDQUOT
Identity-Info  =  "Identity-Info" HCOLON
                  ident-info *(SEMI
                  ident-info-params)
ident-info  =  LAQUOT absoluteURI RAQUOT
ident-info-params  =  ident-info-alg/
                      ident-info-extension
ident-info-alg  =  "alg" EQUAL token
ident-info-extension  =  generic-param
```

```
digest-string   =  addr-spec "|" addr-spec
                   "|" callid "|"1*DIGIT SP
                   Method "|" SIP-date "|"
                   [addr-spec] "|"
                   message-body
Info-Package  =  "Info-Package" HCOLON
Info-package-type
; Info-Package from RFC 6086

Recv-Info  =  "Recv-Info" HCOLON
[Info-package-list]
; Recv-Info from RFC 6086

Info-package-list  =  Info-package-type
                      *(COMMA
                      Info-package-type)
Info-package-type  =  Info-package-name
                      *(SEMI
                      Info-package-param)
Info-package-name  =  token
Info-package-param  =  generic-param
Join  =  "Join" HCOLON callid *(SEMI
         join-param)
; Join from RFC 3911

join-param  =  to-tag/from-tag/generic-param
to-tag  =  "to-tag" EQUAL token
from-tag  =  "from-tag" EQUAL token
Max-Breadth  =  "Max-Breadth" HCOLON 1*DIGIT;
                Max-Breadth from RFC 5393
Session-Expires  =  ("Session-Expires"/"x")
                    HCOLON delta-seconds
                    *(SEMI se-params);
                    Session-Expires from RFC
                    5393
se-params  =  refresher-param/generic-param
refresher-param  =  "refresher" EQUAL
                    ("uas"/"uac")
Min-SE  =  "Min-SE" HCOLON delta-seconds
           *(SEMI generic-param)
; Min-SE from RFC 4028

P-Access-Network-Info  =  "P-Access-Network-
                          Info" HCOLON
                          access-net-spec
                          *(COMMA
                          access-net-spec)
; P-Access-Network-Info from RFC 7315

access-net-spec  =  (access-type/access-
                    class) *(SEMI
                    access-info)
access-type  =  "IEEE-802.11"/"IEEE-802.11a"/
                "IEEE-802.11b"/"IEEE-802.11g"/
                "IEEE-802.11n"/
                "IEEE-802.3"/"IEEE-802.3a"/
                "IEEE-802.3ab"/"IEEE-802.3ae"/
                "IEEE-802.3ak"/"IEEE-802.3ah"/
                "IEEE-802.3aq"/"IEEE-802.3an"/
                "IEEE-802.3e"/"IEEE-802.3i"/
```

```
                  "IEEE-802.3j"/"IEEE-802.3u"/
                  "IEEE-802.3y"/"IEEE-802.3z"/
                  "3GPP-GERAN"/
                  "3GPP-UTRAN-FDD"/"3GPP-
                  UTRAN-TDD"/
                  "3GPP-E-UTRAN-FDD"/"3GPP-E-
                  UTRAN-TDD"/
                  "3GPP2-1X-Femto"/"3GPP2-UMB"/
                  "3GPP2-1X-HRPD"/"3GPP2-1X"/
                  "ADSL"/"ADSL2"/"ADSL2+"/
                  "RADSL"/
                  "SDSL"/"HDSL"/"HDSL2"/
                  "G.SHDSL"/
                  "VDSL"/"IDSL"/
                  "DOCSIS"/"GSTN"/"GPON"/
                  "XGPON1"/
                  "DVB-RCS2"/token
access-class   =  "3GPP-GERAN"/"3GPP-UTRAN"/
                  "3GPP-E-UTRAN"/"3GPP-WLAN"/
                  "3GPP-GAN"/"3GPP-HSPA"/
                  "3GPP2"/token
access-info   =  cgi-3gpp/utran-cell-id-3gpp/
                  dsl-location/i-wlan-node-id/
                  ci-3gpp2/eth-location/
                  ci-3gpp2-femto/
                  fiber-location/
                  np/gstn-location/
                  local-time-zone/
                  dvb-rcs2-node-id/
extension-access-info
np  =  "network-provided"
extension-access-info  =  gen-value
cgi-3gpp  =  "cgi-3gpp" EQUAL (token/
             quoted-string)
utran-cell-id-3gpp  =  "utran-cell-id-3gpp"
                       EQUAL (token/
                       quoted-string)
i-wlan-node-id  =  "i-wlan-node-id" EQUAL
                   (token/quoted-string)
dsl-location  =  "dsl-location" EQUAL (token/
                 quoted-string)
eth-location  =  "eth-location" EQUAL (token/
                 quoted-string)
fiber-location  =  "fiber-location" EQUAL
                   (token/quoted-string)
ci-3gpp2  =  "ci-3gpp2" EQUAL (token/
             quoted-string)
ci-3gpp2-femto  =  "ci-3gpp2-femto" EQUAL
                   (token/quoted-string)
gstn-location  =  "gstn-location" EQUAL
                  (token/quoted-string)
dvb-rcs2-node-id  =  "dvb-rcs2-node-id" EQUAL
                     quoted-string
local-time-zone  =  "local-time-zone" EQUAL
                    quoted-string
operator-specific-GI  =  "operator-
                         specific-GI" EQUAL
                         (token/
                         quoted-string)
utran-sai-3gpp  =  "utran-sai-3gpp" EQUAL
                   (token/quoted-string)

; The access-info may contain additional
information relating to the
; access network. The values for cgi-3gpp,
utran-cell-id-3gpp,
; i-wlan-node-id, dsl-location, ci-3gpp2,
ci-3gpp2-femto, and
; gstn-location are defined in 3GPP TS 24.229
[1].
; 3GPP, "IP multimedia call control protocol
based on
; Session Initiation Protocol (SIP) and
Session
; Description Protocol (SDP); Stage 3," 3GPP
TS 24.229
; 12.4.0, March 2014.

; The syntax for the Answer-Mode and Priv-
Answer-Mode header fields defined by
; RFC 5373 is as follows:

Answer-Mode  =  "Answer-Mode" HCOLON answer-
                mode- value*(SEMI
                answer-mode-param)
Priv-Answer-Mode  =  "Priv-Answer-Mode"
                     HCOLON answer-mode-value
                     *(SEMI
                     answer-mode-param)
answer-mode-value  =  "Manual"/"Auto"/token
answer-mode-param  =  "require"/
                      generic-param

PAssertedID  =  "P-Asserted-Identity" HCOLON
                PAssertedID-value *(COMMA
                PAssertedID-value)
;PAssertedID and P-Asserted-Identity from RFC
3325

PAssertedID-value  =  name-addr/addr-spec

; The access-info may contain additional
information relating to the      access
network.
; The values for cgi-3gpp and utran-cell-id-
3gpp are defined in 3GPP
; TS 24.229 [1].

PAssertedService  =  "P-Asserted-Service"
                     HCOLON
                     PAssertedService-value
; PAssertedService and P-Asserted-Service
from RFC 6050

PAssertedService-value  =  Service-ID *(COMMA
                           Service-ID)
Service-ID  =  "urn:urn-7:" urn-service-id
urn-service-id  =  top-level *("."
                   sub-service-id)
top-level  =  let-dig [*26let-dig]
sub-service-id  =  let-dig [*let-dig]
let-diglet-digALPHA/DIGIT/"-"
```

```
P-Associated-URI  =  "P-Associated-URI"
                     HCOLON (p-aso-uri-spec)
                     *(COMMA p-aso-uri-spec)
; P-Associated-URI from RFC 7315

p-aso-uri-spec  =  name-addr *(SEMI ai-param)
ai-param  =  generic-param

Path  =  "Path" HCOLON path-value *(COMMA
         path-value)
; Path from RFC 3327

path-value  =  name-addr *(SEMI rr-param)

P-Called-Party-ID  =  "P-Called-Party-ID"
                      HCOLON
                      called-pty-id-spec
; P-Called-Party-ID from RFC 7315

called-pty-id-spec  =  name-addr *(SEMI
                       cpid-param)
cpid-param  =  generic-param

P-Charging-Addresses  =  "P-Charging-
                         Function-Addresses"
                         HCOLON

charge-addr-params

*(COMMA charge-addr-params)

; P-Charging-Addresses from RFC 7315

charge-addr-params  =  charge-addr-param
                       *(SEMI
                       charge-addr-param)
charge-addr-param  =  ccf/ecf/ccf-2/ecf-2/
                      generic-param
ccf  =  "ccf" EQUAL gen-value
ecf  =  "ecf" EQUAL gen-value
ccf-2  =  "ccf-2" EQUAL gen-value
ecf-2  =  "ecf-2" EQUAL gen-value

; The P-Charging-Function-Addresses header
field contains one or two
; addresses of the ECF (ecf and ecf-2) or CCF
(ccf and ccf-2). The
; first address of the sequence is ccf or
ecf. If the first address of
; the sequence is not available, then the
next address (ccf-2 or ecf-2)
; must be used if available.

P-Charging-Vector  =  "P-Charging-Vector"
                      HCOLON icid-value
                      *(SEMI charge-params)

; P-Charging-Vector from RFC 7315

charge-params  =  icid-gen-addr/orig-ioi/
                  term-ioi/
                  transit-ioi/related-icid/
                  related-icid-gen-addr/
                  generic-param
icid-value  =  "icid-value" EQUAL gen-value
icid-gen-addr  =  "icid-generated-at" EQUAL
                  host
orig-ioi  =  "orig-ioi" EQUAL gen-value
term-ioi  =  "term-ioi" EQUAL gen-value
transit-ioi  =  "transit-ioi" EQUAL
                transit-ioi-list
transit-ioi-list  =  DQUOTE transit-ioi-param
                     *(COMMA transit-ioi-
                     param) DQUOTE
transit-ioi-param  =  transit-ioi-indexed-
                      value/transit-
                      ioi-void-value
transit-ioi-indexed-value  =  transit-ioi-
                              name "."transit-
                              ioi-index
transit-ioi-name  =  ALPHA *(ALPHA/DIGIT)
transit-ioi-index  =  1*DIGIT
transit-ioi-void-value  =  "void"
related-icid  =  "related-icid" EQUAL
                 gen-value
related-icid-gen-addr  =  "related-icid-
                          generated-at" EQUAL
                          host

; The P-Charging-Vector header field contains
icid-value as a mandatory
; parameter. The icid-value represents the
IMS charging ID, and
; contains an identifier used for correlating
charging records and
; events. The first proxy that receives the
request generates this value.
; The icid-gen-addr parameter contains the
host name or IP address of
; the proxy that generated the icid-value.
; The orig-ioi and term-ioi parameters
contain originating and
; terminating interoperator identifiers. They
are used to correlate
; charging records between different
operators. The originating IOI
; represents the network responsible for the
charging records in the
; originating part of the session or stand-
alone request. Similarly,
; the terminating IOI represents the network
responsible for the
; charging records in the terminating part of
the session or stand-alone
; request. The transit-ioi parameter contains
values with each of them,
; respectively, representing a transit
interoperator identifier. It is
; used to correlate charging records between
different networks. The
; transit-ioi represents the network
responsible for the records in the
```

```
; transit part of the session or stand-alone
request.
; The related-icid parameter contains the
icid-value of a related
; charging record when more than one call leg
is associated with one
; session. This optional parameter is used
for correlation of charging
; information between two or more call legs
related to the same remote end
; dialog. The related-icid-gen-addr parameter
contains the host name or IP
; address of the proxy that generated the
related-icid.
; Applications using the P-Charging-Vector
header field within their
; own applicability are allowed to define
generic-param extensions
; without further reference to the IETF
specification process.

P-Early-Media  =  "P-Early-Media" HCOLON
                  [em-param*(COMMA em-param)]
;P-Early-Media from RFC 5009

em-param  =  "sendrecv"/"sendonly"/"recvonly"
             /"inactive"/"gated"/"supported"/
             token
Permission-Missing  =  "Permission-Missing"
                       HCOLON per-miss-spec
                       *(COMMA per-miss-spec)
; Permission-Missing from RFC 5360

per-miss-spec  =  (name-addr/addr-spec)
                  *(SEMI generic-param)

PPreferredID  =  "P-Preferred-Identity"
                 HCOLON PPreferredID-value
                 *(COMMA PPreferredID-value)
; PPreferredID and P-Preferred-Identity are
from RFC 3325

PPreferredID-value  =  name-addr/addr-spec
PPreferredService  =  "P-Preferred-Service"
                      HCOLONPPreferredService-
                      value
; PPreferredService and P-Preferred-Service
are from RFC 6050

PPreferredService-value  =  Service-ID
                            *(COMMA
                            Service-ID)
P-Profile-Key  =  "P-Profile-Key" HCOLON
                  (name-addr/ addr-
                  spec)*(SEMI generic-param)
      ; P-Profile-Key from RFC 5002

; The format of Wildcarded Public Service
Identities is defined in 3GPP TS 23.003
; [2]. They take the form of Extended Regular
Expressions (ERE) as defined
; in Chapter 9 of IEEE 1003.1-2004 Part 1
[3].

; The following is the ABNF syntax of the
P-Refused-URI-List P-Header (RFC 5318):

P-Refused-URI-List  =  "P-Refused-URI-List"
                       HCOLON uri-list-entry*
                       (COMMA uri-list-entry)

uri-list-entry  =  (name-addr/addr-
                   spec)*(SEMI refused-param)
refused-param  =  members-param/generic-param
members-param  =  "members" EQUAL LDQUOT *
                  (qdtext/quoted-pair) RDQUOT

; The members P-Header parameter must contain
a cid-url, which is defined in RFC 2392.
; The HCOLON, SEMI, EQUAL, LDQUOT, RDQUOT,
and generic-param are defined in
; RFC 3261.

P-Served-User  =  "P-Served-User" HCOLON
                  PServedUser-value *(SEMI
                  served-user-param)
; P-Served-User from RFC 5234

served-user-param  =  sessioncase-param/
                      registration-state
                      param/generic-param
PServedUser-value  =  name-addr/addr-spec
sessioncase-param  =  "sescase" EQUAL
                      "orig"/"term"
registration-state-param  =  "regstate" EQUAL
                             "unreg"/"reg"
P-User-Database  =  "P-User-Database" HCOLON
                    database *(SEMI
                    generic-param)
; P-User-Database from RFC 4452

database  =  LAQUOT DiameterURI RAQUOT

; The DiameterURI specified in RFC 6733 must
follow the Uniform Resource
; Identifiers syntax defined in RFC 3986
rules specified below.

"aaa://" FQDN [port] [transport] [protocol]
; No transport security
"aaas://" FQDN [port] [transport] [protocol]
; Transport security used

FQDN  =  < Fully Qualified Domain Name >
port  =  ":" 1*DIGIT

; One of the ports used to listen for
incoming connections. If absent, the default
; Diameter port (3868) is assumed if no
transport security is used and  port 5658
; when transport security (TLS/TCP and DTLS/
SCTP) is used.
```

```
transport  =  ";transport = "
transport-protocol

; One of the transports used to listen for
incoming connections. If the     transport is
; absent, the default protocol is assumed to
be TCP. UDP must not be used     when
; the aaa-protocol field is set to diameter.

transport-protocol  =  ("tcp"/"sctp"/"udp")
protocol  =  ";protocol = " aaa-protocol
; If absent, the default AAA protocol is
Diameter.

aaa-protocol  =  ("diameter"/"radius"
                 /"tacacs+")

Privacy-hdr  =  "Privacy" HCOLON priv-value
                                  *(";"
priv-value)
; Privacy-hdr and Privacy from RFC 3323

priv-value  =  "header"/"session"/"user"/"non
             e"/"critical"/token
P-Visited-Network-ID  =  "P-Visited-Network-
                         ID" HCOLON vnetwork-
                         spec *(COMMA
                         vnetwork-spec)
; P-Visited-Network-ID from RFC 7315

vnetwork-spec  =  (token/quoted-string)
                  *(SEMI vnetwork-param)
vnetwork-param  =  generic-param

RAck  =  "RAck" HCOLON response-num LWS
         CSeq-num LWS Method
; Rack from RFC 3262

response-num  =  1*DIGIT
CSeq-num  =  1*DIGIT
Reason  =  "Reason" HCOLON reason-value
           *(COMMA reason-value)
; Reason from RFC 3326

reason-value  =  protocol *(SEMI
                 reason-params)
protocol  =  "SIP"/"Q.850"/token
reason-params  =  protocol-cause/reason-text/
                  reason-extension
protocol-cause  =  "cause" EQUAL cause
cause  =  1*DIGIT
reason-text  =  "text" EQUAL quoted-string
reason-extension  =  generic-param
Refer-Sub  =  "Refer-Sub" HCOLON refer-sub-
              value *(SEMI exten)
; Refer-Sub from RFC 4488

refer-sub-value  =  "true"/"false"
exten  =  generic-param

Refer-To  =  ("Refer-To"/"r") HCOLON (name-
             addr/addr-spec) *(SEMI
             generic-param)
; Refer-To from RFC 3515

Referred-By  =  ("Referred-By"/"b") HCOLON
                referrer-uri *(SEMI
                (referredby-id- param/
                generic-param))
; Referred-By from RFC 3892

referrer-uri  =  (name-addr/addr-spec)
referredby-id-param  =  "cid" EQUAL
                        sip-clean-msg-id
sip-clean-msg-id  =  LDQUOT dot-atom "@"
                     (dot-atom/host) RDQUOT
dot-atom  =  atom *("." atom) atom =
             1*(alphanum/"-"/"!"/"%"/"*"/
             "_"/"+"/"'"/"'"/"~")
Replaces  =  "Replaces" HCOLON callid *(SEMI
             replaces-param)
; Replaces from RFC 3891

replaces-param  =  to-tag/from-tag/early-
                   flag/generic-param
to-tag  =  "to-tag" EQUAL token
from-tag  =  "from-tag" EQUAL token
early-flag  =  "early-only"

; A Replaces header field must contain
exactly one to-tag and exactly one
from-tag,
; as they are required for unique dialog
matching.

Request-Disposition  =  ("Request-
                        Disposition"/"d")
                        HCOLON directive
                        *(COMMA directive)
; Request-Disposition from RFC 3841

Directive  =  proxy-directive/cancel-
              directive/fork-directive/
              recurse-directive/parallel-
              directive/queue-directive
proxy-directive  =  "proxy"/"redirect"
cancel-directive  =  "cancel"/"no-cancel"
fork-directive  =  "fork"/"no-fork"
recurse-directive  =  "recurse"/"no-recurse"
parallel-directive  =  "parallel"/"sequential"
queue-directive  =  "queue"/"no-queue"
Resource-Priority  =  "Resource-Priority"
                      HCOLON r-value *(COMMA
                      r-value)
; Resource-Priority from RFC 4412

r-value  =  namespace "." r-priority
namespace  =  token-nodot
r-priority  =  token-nodot
token-nodot  =  1*(alphanum/"-"/"!"/"%"/"*"
                /"_"/"+"/"'"/"'"/"~")
```

```
; The syntax for the rport parameter (RFC
3581) is

response-port  =  "rport" [EQUAL 1*DIGIT]

; RFC 3581
RSeq  =  "RSeq" HCOLON response-num
; RSeq from RFC 3262

security-client  =  "Security-Client" HCOLON
                    sec-mechanism *(COMMA
                    sec-mechanism)
; security-client and Security-Client from
RFC 3329

security-server  =  "Security-Server" HCOLON
                    sec-mechanism *(COMMA
                    sec-mechanism)
; security-server and Security-Server from
RFC 3329

security-verify  =  "Security-Verify" HCOLON
                    sec-mechanism *(COMMA
                    sec-mechanism)
; security-verify and Security-Verify from
RFC 3329

sec-mechanism  =  mechanism-name *(SEMI
                  mech-parameters)
mechanism-name  =  ("digest"/"tls"/"ipsec-
                   ike"/"ipsec-man"/token)
mech-parameters  =  (preference/digest-
                    algorithm/digest-qop/
                    digest-verify/extension)
preference  =  "q" EQUAL qvalue
qvalue  =  ("0" ["." 0*3DIGIT])/("1" ["."
           0*3("0")])
digest-algorithm  =  "d-alg" EQUAL token
digest-qop  =  "d-qop" EQUAL token
digest-verify  =  "d-ver" EQUAL LDQUOT 32LHEX
                  RDQUOT
extension  =  generic-param
Service-Route  =  "Service-Route" HCOLON
                  sr-value * (COMMA sr-value)
; Service-Route from RFC 3608

sr-value  =  name-addr *(SEMI rr-param)
Session-Expires  =  ("Session-Expires"/"x")
                    HCOLON delta-seconds
                    *(SEMI se-params)
; Session-Expires from RFC 4028

se-params  =  refresher-param/generic-param
refresher-param  =  "refresher" EQUAL
                    ("uas"/"uac")
SIP-ETag  =  "SIP-ETag" HCOLON entity-tag
; SIP-ETag from RFC 3903

SIP-If-Match  =  "SIP-If-Match" HCOLON
                 entity-tag
; SIP-If-Match from RFC 3903

entity-tagSIP-If-Match from RFC 3903token

Suppress-If-MatchSIP-If-Match from RFC
3903"Suppress-If-Match" HCOLON
(entity-tag/"*")
; Suppress-If-Match from RFC 5839

Target-Dialog  =  "Target-Dialog" HCOLON
                  callid *(SEMI td-param)
; Target-Dialog from RFC 4538

td-param  =  remote-param/local-param/
             generic-param
remote-param  =  "remote-tag" EQUAL token
local-param  =  "local-tag" EQUAL token

current-status  =  "a = curr:" precondition-
                   type; from RFC 3312 SP
                   status-type SP
                   direction-tag
desired-status  =  "a = des:" precondition-
                   type SP strength-tag SP
                   status-type SP
                   direction-tag
confirm-status  =  "a = conf:" precondition-
                   type SP status-type SP
                   direction-tag
precondition-type  =  "qos"/token
strength-tag = ("mandatory" | "optional" |
               "none"
             = | "failure" |"unknown")
status-type  =  ("e2e" | "local" | "remote")
direction-tag  =  ("none" | "send" | "recv" |
                  "sendrecv")

UUI  =  "User-to-User" HCOLON uui-value
        *(COMMA uui-value)
UUI/User-to-User from RFC 7433
uui-value  =  uui-data *(SEMI uui-param)
uui-data  =  token/quoted-string
uui-param  =  pkg-param/cont-param/enc-param/
              generic-param
pkg-param  =  "purpose" EQUAL pkg-param-value
pkg-param-value  =  token
cont-param  =  "content" EQUAL
               cont-param-value
cont-param-value  =  token
enc-param  =  "encoding" EQUAL
              enc-param-value
enc-param-value  =  token/"hex
```

2.4.2 SIP Messages

SIP is designed in RFC 3261/2543 as a client–server protocol in an almost identical syntax to HTTP/1.1, although SIP is not HTTP or its extensions. Accordingly, a SIP message is either a request from a client to a server for invoking a particular operation, or a response from a server to a client to indicate the status of the request. Both types of messages consist of a start line, one or more header fields, an empty line indicating the end of the header fields, and an optional message body.

```
generic-message   =   start-line
                      *message-header
                      CRLF
                      [message-body]
start-line   =   Request-Line/Status-Line
```

The request message is also known as method. The start line, each message-header line, and the empty line must be terminated by a control return line feed (CRLF) sequence. However, the empty line must be present even if the message body is not.

2.4.2.1 Requests

SIP requests are sent for the purpose of invoking a particular operation by a client to a server. SIP requests are distinguished by having a Request-Line for a start line. A Request-Line contains a method name, a Request-URI, and the protocol version separated by a single space character. The Request-Line ends with CRLF. No CR or LF is allowed except in the end-of-line CRLF sequence. No LWS is allowed in any of the elements.

```
Request-Line   =   Method SP Request-URI SP
                   SIP-Version CRLF
```

SIP has defined the following methods:

- REGISTER for registration of contact information of the user
- INVITE, ACK, and CANCEL for setting up sessions
- BYE for terminating sessions
- OPTIONS for querying servers about their capabilities
- MESSAGE for chat sessions
- REFER for call transfer
- SUBSCRIBE and NOTIFY for SIP session-related event management
- PUBLISH for publication of SIP-specific event state
- UPDATE for updating the session parameters
- INFO for mid-session information transfer
- PRACK for acknowledgement of provisional requests

The most important method in SIP is the INVITE method, which is used to establish a session between participants. A session is a collection of participants, and streams of media between them, for the purposes of communication. SIP extensions, documented in Standards Track RFCs, may define additional methods for accommodating more feature-rich multimedia sessions especially for the multipoint multimedia conferencing services.

2.4.2.2 Responses

SIP responses sent from the server to the client indicate the status of the request and are distinguished from requests by having a Status-Line as their start line. A Status-Line consists of the protocol version followed by a numeric Status-Code and its associated textual phrase, with each element separated by a single SP character. No CR or LF is allowed except in the final CRLF sequence.

```
Request-Line = Method SP Request-
URI SP SIP-Version CRLF
```

The Status-Code is a three-digit integer result code that indicates the outcome of an attempt to understand and satisfy a request. The Reason-Phrase is intended to give a short textual description of the Status-Code. The Status-Code is intended for use by automata, whereas the Reason-Phrase is intended for the human user. SIP response classes are similar to those of HTTP, but have been defined in the context of SIP. The first digit of the Status-Code defines the class of response. The last two digits do not have any categorization role. For this reason, any response with a status code between 100 and 199 is referred to as a *1xx response*, any response with a status code between 200 and 299 as a *2xx response*, and so on. SIP/2.0 allows six values for the first digit shown in Table 2.2 (RFC 3261).

2.4.2.3 Headers

SIP header fields are similar to HTTP header fields in both syntax and semantics, each carrying its own well-defined information. Each header field is terminated by a CRLF at the end of the header. SIP specifies that multiple header fields of the same field name whose value is a comma-separated list can be combined into one header field whose grammar is of the form

```
header = "header-name" HCOLON header-value
*(COMMA header-value)
```

It allows for combining header fields of the same name into a comma-separated list. The Contact header field allows a comma-separated list unless the header field value is "*."

2.4.2.4 Message Body

The message body in SIP messages is an optional component. SIP request messages may contain a message body, unless otherwise noted, that can be read, created, processed, modified, or removed as necessary only by the SIP user agent (UA). The SIP message body shall always be opaque to the SIP proxy/redirect/registrar server. Requests, including new requests defined in extensions to this specification, may contain

Table 2.2 SIP Response Classes, Descriptions, and Actions

Response Class	*Response Description*	*Action Taken or to Be Taken*
1xx	Provisional	Request received, continuing to process the request.
2xx	Success	The action was successfully received, understood, and accepted.
3xx	Redirection	Further action needs to be taken in order to complete the request.
4xx	Client Error	The request contains bad syntax or cannot be fulfilled at this server.
5xx	Server Error	The server failed to fulfill an apparently valid request.
6xx	Global Failure	The request cannot be fulfilled at any server.

message bodies unless otherwise noted. The interpretation of the body depends on the request method. For response messages, the request method and the response status code determine the type and interpretation of any message body. Regardless of the type of body that a request contains, certain header fields must be formulated to characterize the contents of the body, such as (see Section 2.2) Allow, Allow-Events, Content-Disposition, Content-Encoding, Content-Language, Content-Length, and Content-Type. All responses may include a body.

2.4.2.5 Framing SIP Messages

Unlike HTTP, SIP implementations can use UDP or other unreliable datagram protocols. Each such datagram carries one request or response. See Section 3.12 on constraints on usage of unreliable transports. Implementations processing SIP messages over stream-oriented transports MUST ignore any CRLF appearing before the start line. The Content-Length header field value is used to locate the end of each SIP message in a stream. It will always be present when SIP messages are sent over stream-oriented transports.

2.4.3 SIP Message Structure

SIP is described with some independent processing stages with only a loose coupling between each stage. This protocol is structured in a way to be compliant with a set of rules for operations in different stages of the protocol that provides an appearance of a layered protocol. However, it does not dictate an implementation in any way. Not every element specified by the protocol contains every layer. Furthermore, the elements specified by SIP are logical elements, not physical ones. A physical realization can choose to act as different logical elements, perhaps even on a transaction-by-transaction basis. The SIP layer can be defined as follows: syntax and encoding, transport, transaction, and transaction user (TU). In addition, SIP also defines dialog between the two UAs. In syntax and encoding layer, SIP's encoding is specified using ABNF described earlier. The transport layer defines how a client sends requests and receives responses and how a server receives requests and sends responses over the network. All SIP elements contain a transport layer. As explained, TCP, UDP, or SCTP can be used as the transport protocol in SIP, while TLS can be used as the security transport protocol over TCP.

In the transaction layer, transactions are a fundamental component of SIP. A transaction is a request sent by a client transaction (using the transport layer) to a server transaction, along with all responses to that request sent from the server transaction back to the client. The transaction layer has a client component (referred to as a client transaction) and a server component (referred to as a server transaction), each of which are represented by a finite state machine that is constructed to process a particular request. The transaction layer handles application-layer retransmissions, matching of responses to requests, and application-layer timeouts. Any task that a UA client (UAC) accomplishes takes place using a series of transactions with the user agent server (UAS) or the SIP server. UAs and stateful proxy servers of SIP contain a transaction layer, while a stateless proxy does not contain one. The TU layer is above the transaction layer. All SIP entities, except the stateless proxy, are transaction users (TUs). The TU creates a client transaction instance and passes the request along with the destination IP address, port, and transport to which to send the request, and the TU that creates a transaction can also cancel it by sending a CANCEL request. At this, a server stops further processing the request and reverts to the state that existed before the transaction was initiated, and generates a specific error response to that transaction.

The SIP network also defines the core functional elements that consist of UACs and UASs, stateless and stateful proxies, and registrars. Cores, except for the stateless proxy, are TUs. Clearly, these processing functions reside above the transaction and transport layer. A dialog represents a context in which a peer-to-peer SIP relationship is established between two UAs that persists for some time to interpret SIP messages. It is another important concept in SIP. The dialog facilitates sequencing of messages and proper routing of requests between the UAs. The INVITE method is the only way to establish a dialog. When a UAC sends a request that is within the context of a dialog, it follows the common UAC rules.

2.4.3.1 *Request Message Format*

The SIP request message format consists of three important parts: request line, header, and message body. Figure 2.3 depicts an example of SIP INVITE method message format. The request line consists of the request type, SIP URI of the destination or next hop, and SIP version being used.

The SIP header part contains a set of headers, and each header carries its own well-defined information. However, each header is terminated by a CRLF at the end of the header. SIP message body of the request method is optional depending on the type of message and where it falls within the call establishment scheme. A blank line defines the boundary between the header part and the message body.

2.4.3.2 *Response Message Format*

SIP response message format has three major sections: status line, header, and message body. Of course, an empty line is present to separate the headers and the message body. Figure 2.4 shows an example of SIP 200 OK response message format. The response message contains the reason header indicating why this response has been sent. As a result, the response message can be quite large, explaining all the reasons.

The status line contains the protocol version, the status code, and the reason phrase. The reason phrase makes it easy for the human users to understand it, while the protocol version and the status code are processed by the SIP network. For example, status code 200 is a part of the 2xx response class (success), and specifically 200 responses are sent. At this point, a dialog transitions to a confirmed state. When a UAC does not want to continue with this dialog, it shall terminate the dialog sending a BYE request. Again, a header part will contain different headers and each header, like response message, will have its own specific information and each header is terminated by a CRLF at the end of the header. Like the request message, the message body is optional and is separated by a blank line from the header part. Figure 2.4 shows the IP address and audio code type and its characteristics are provided in response to the request message.

2.4.4 *SIP Network Functional Elements*

The networked multimedia services use SIP to establish, manage sessions, and tear down the multimedia sessions. As a result, the capabilities of SIP need to be used in the context of multimedia service networking context. SIP, being in the session control layer, is also a part of the application layer in OSI terminology. SIP has application-layer functional entities such as SIP UAs and SIP servers that are described

Request Line	INVITE sip:bob@biloxi.example.com SIP/2.0
Headers	Via: SIP/2.0/TCP
	client.atlanta.example.com:5060;branch=z9hG4bK74bf9
	Max-Forwards: 70
	From: Alice <sip:alice@atlanta.example.com>;tag=9fxced76sl
	To: Bob <sip:bob@biloxi.example.com>
	Call-ID: 3848276298220188511@atlanta.example.com
	CSeq: 1 INVITE
	Contact: <sip:alice@client.atlanta.example.com;transport=tcp>
	Content-Type: application/sdp
	Content-Length: 151
Empty Line	
Message Body	v=0
	o=alice2890844526 2890844526 IN IP4 client.atlanta.example.com
	s= -
	c=IN IP4 192.0.2.101
	t=0 0
	m=audio 49172 RTP/AVP 0
	a=rtpmap:0 PCMU/8000

Figure 2.3 Example SIP request message format.

Status Line	SIP/2.0 200 OK
Headers	Via: SIP/2.0/TCP client.atlanta.example.com:5060;branch=z9hG4bK74bf9;received=192.0.2.101
	From: Alice <sip:alice@atlanta.example.com>;tag=9fxced76sl
	To: Bob <sip:bob@biloxi.example.com>;tag=8321234356
	Call-ID: 3848276298220188511@atlanta.example.com
	CSeq: 1 INVITE
	Contact: <sip:bob@client.biloxi.example.com;transport=tcp>
	Content-Type: application/sdp
	Content-Length: 147
Empty Line	
Message Body	v=0
	o=bob 2890844527 2890844527 IN IP4 client.biloxi.example.com
	s=-
	c=IN IP4 192.0.2.201
	t=0 0
	m=audio 3456 RTP/AVP 0
	a=rtpmap:0 PCMU/8000

Figure 2.4 Example SIP response message format.

later. These entities communicate among themselves using SIP application-/session-layer protocol termed as the SIP network. Figure 2.5 depicts the logical view of the SIP network and its functional entities.

The functional elements of the SIP network are as follows: SIP UAs and SIP servers. SIP has defined three servers: SIP proxy, SIP registrar, and SIP redirect. However, the location servers and the different categories of application servers, not shown in Figure 2.5, do not belong to SIP. In this context, SIP; media sessions using RTP/RTCP controlled by SIP; SIP security protocols such as Transport Layer Security (TLS) protocol; and SIP transport protocols such as TCP, UDP, and SCTP are carried over the IP network. IP network

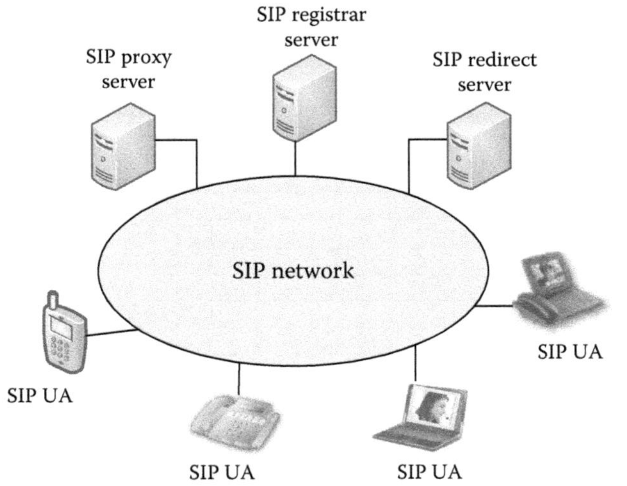

Figure 2.5 Logical view of a SIP network and its functional entities.

and SIP application servers such TC/VTC/VC server, location server, web conferencing server, media bridging server, chat server, and application sharing server are not shown here but are addressed later.

2.4.4.1 *SIP User Agent*

SIP has defined some functional entities that can be categorized broadly into two categories: SIP UAs and SIP servers. A UA works in a client server mode on behalf of the user: UAS and UAC. UAC generates the SIP request and sends to the UAS directly if the address is known or sends to the SIP server that routes the request to UAS. UAS receives the request, operates on them, and sends the responses back to the UAC either directly if the address is known or via the SIP server that sends the responses to the UAC. From a conferencing perspective, a number of possible different SIP components such as conference-unaware participant, conference-aware participant, and focus is specified by RFC 4579. We describe those kinds of SIP UAs in the next section.

2.4.4.1.1 Focus UA

A focus, as defined in the framework (RFC 4579), hosts a SIP conference and maintains a SIP signaling relationship with each participant in the conference. A focus contains a conference-aware UA that supports the conferencing call control conventions as defined in RFC 4579. A focus should support the conference package RFC 4575, behave as a notifier for that package, and indicate its support in the Allow-Events header fields in requests and responses. A focus may include information about the conference in SDP bodies sent as part of normal SIP signaling by populating the Session Information, URI, Email Address, and Phone Number SDP fields. In order to support advanced features, where a session established between two end points can migrate to a centralized conference, a focus should support the Replaces header field. A UA with focus capabilities could be implemented in end-user equipment and would be used for the creation of ad hoc conferences. A dedicated conferencing server, whose primary task is to simultaneously host conferences of arbitrary type and size, may allocate and publish a conference factory URI (as defined in Section 4.2) for creating an arbitrary number of ad hoc conferences (and subsequently their focuses) using SIP call control means.

2.4.4.1.2 Conference-Unaware UA

The simplest UA can participate in a conference ignoring all SIP conferencing-related information. The simplest UA is able to dial in to a conference and to be invited to a conference. Any conferencing information is optionally conveyed to/from it using non-SIP means. Such a UA would not usually host a conference (at least, not using SIP explicitly). A conference-unaware UA needs only to support basic SIP capabilities specified in RFC 3261. Call flows for conference-unaware UAs would be identical to those in the SIP call flows per specifications of RFC 3261. Note that the presence of an *isfocus* feature tag in a Contact header field will not cause interoperability issues between a focus and a conference-unaware UA since it will be treated as an unknown header parameter and ignored, as per standard SIP behavior.

2.4.4.1.3 Conference-Aware UA

A conference-aware UA supports SIP conferencing call control conventions defined in this document as a conference participant, in addition to support of RFC 3261. A conference-aware UA should be able to process SIP redirections such as described in RFC 3261 (see Section 3.1.2.3). A conference-aware UA must recognize the isfocus feature parameter. A conference-aware UA should support SIP REFER method (see Section 2.5), SIP events (see Section 5.2), and the conferencing package (RFC 4575) A conference-aware UA should subscribe to the conference package if the isfocus parameter is in the remote target URI of a dialog and if the conference package is listed by a focus in an Allow-Events header field. The SUBSCRIBE to the conference package should be sent outside any INVITE-initiated dialog. A termination of the INVITE dialog with a BYE does not necessarily terminate the SUBSCRIBE dialog. A conference-aware UA may render to the user any information about the conference obtained from the SIP header fields and SDP fields from the focus. A conference-aware UA should render to the user any information about the conference obtained from the SIP conference package.

2.4.4.2 SIP Back-to-Back User Agent

A back-to-back UA is a concatenation of a UAC and UAS functional entity in SIP. That is, it is a logical entity that receives a request and processes it as a UAS. It also acts as a UAC and generates requests in order to determine how the request should be answered. Unlike a proxy server, it maintains dialog state and must participate in all requests sent on the dialogs it has established.

However, SIP is being designed as the end-to-end model following principles of the Internet, and the use of B2BUA in SIP breaks this model, making it less scalable as SIP intermediaries implementing B2BUA need to keep track of the transactional states for the duration of the transaction as well as for the entire duration of the call. The integrity of SIP messages is also being protected using encryption, and these messages are subject to rejection because of integrity failures.

In many situations, the B2BUA capability is being deployed over the SIP network in many intermediaries for providing some services that may or may not directly relate to the session establishment: service control by SIP application servers, topology hiding, anonymization of call parties, crossing of network address translator (NAT) by SIP signaling messages and media traffic using application-level gateway (ALG), and generation of call detail record (CDR). For example, session border controller (SBC) defined in RFC 5853 (see Section 14.3) and SIP privacy service defined in RFC 3323 (see Section 20.2) employ B2BUAs.

2.4.4.3 SIP Servers

A SIP server uses the SIP to manage real-time communication among SIP clients. In fact, SIP servers are the key entities that enable communications among SIP clients by routing SIP messages though resolution of addresses, and are the core of the SIP network. SIP servers act on requests sent by SIP clients and process SIP messages and operate on rules per technical standards defined in the call control protocol SIP. SIP has defined SIP proxy server, SIP registration server, and SIP redirect server.

2.4.4.3.1 Proxy Server

A SIP proxy server receives all SIP request and response messages from UAs or other SIP servers such as proxies. It may use registrars/location servers, DNS, or database servers for routing of SIP messages for resolving addresses to other UAs or proxies. A proxy is only allowed to forward SIP messages except the generation of CANCEL and ACK message described later. It should be noted that the proxy may have access to a database server that will not use SIP. In this case, it is expected that a proxy may use a host of different protocols other than SIP in its backend servers for address resolution or other purposes. These protocols are outside the scope of SIP. A proxy can be stateful or stateless; a stateless proxy does not keep any state information of the call or transaction, while a stateful proxy keeps all state information of a call or a transaction for the duration of the call or transaction.

2.4.4.3.2 Redirect Server

A SIP redirect server receives a SIP request and, unlike a proxy server, responds back to it. It usually provides a 3xx (redirection class) response, described later, to a UA or proxy indicating that the call should be tried at a different location. The main purpose has been to deal with the temporary or permanent location change of a user.

2.4.4.3.3 Registrar Server

A SIP registration server keeps the contact and other information of UAs sent using REGISTER message. Registration creates bindings in a location service for a particular domain that associates an address-of-record (AOR) URI with one or more contact addresses. A proxy for that domain receives a request whose Request-URI matches the AOR; then, the proxy will forward the request to the contact addresses registered to that AOR. It is the usual case to register an AOR at a domain's location service when requests for that AOR would be routed to that domain. In most cases, this means that the domain of the registration will need to match the domain in the URI of the AOR. A registrar may store all the information including the contact sent via REGISTER message in a location server. The protocol between the SIP registrar and the location server is outside the scope of SIP.

The registrar server along with location server offers a discovery capability in SIP. If a user wants to initiate a session with another user, SIP must discover the current host(s) at which the destination user is reachable. This discovery process is frequently accomplished by SIP network elements such as proxy servers and redirect servers, which are responsible for receiving a request, determining where to send it based on knowledge of the location of the user, and then sending it there. To do this, SIP network elements consult the location service, which provides address bindings for a particular domain.

2.4.4.3.4 Location Server

A location server is envisioned in a SIP network that keeps the SIP contacts and other information in a database. The SIP registrar stores contacts and other information of users in the location server. The SIP servers communicate with the location server for address resolutions in order to route SIP messages to users or other servers such as proxies. However, the communication protocol between the location server and the SIP servers is not a part of SIP.

2.4.4.3.5 Application Server

A SIP application server acting as the SIP UA can send SIP request and receive SIP response messages. In fact, SIP application servers have emerged as the most important areas for the creation and offering of multimedia services using SIP. With the inception of SIP, new feature-rich multimedia services integrated with other services like web services have been enabled by SIP, and have opened up a new frontier for creating real-time multimedia services that are yet to come.

2.5 SIP Request Messages

SIP request messages are known as methods that specify the purpose of SIP messages for taking actions by SIP UA or server: REGISTER, INVITE, BYE, ACK, CANCEL, OPTIONS, REFER, SUBSCRIBE, NOTIFY, PUBLISH, MESSAGE, UPDATE, PRACK, and INFO. Table 2.3 describes each method briefly. The SIP method (or request message) names are case sensitive, and all uppercase letters are used for distinguishing from the header fields, which can be both a mixture of uppercase and lowercase letters. The SIP UAs are required to understand the SIP methods, while proxy servers are required to know the relevant header fields for routing of SIP request messages keeping the intermediaries of the SIP network simple, thereby making the SIP-based multimedia communications network more scalable. Note that, in addition to RFC 3261, all SIP methods are discussed throughout the whole book as appropriate, although we have provided a brief description for each method in Table 2.3.

2.6 SIP Response Messages

The SIP response message is generated by a SIP UAS or a SIP server in response to a SIP UAC carrying the result of the request. The response message may contain the reason phrases that are also usually understandable by humans. The response status code determines the type and interpretation of the message body sent by the request message, and all responses may include a body. Some warning codes also provide information supplemental to the status code in SIP response messages when the failure of the transaction results from an SDP specified in RFC 4566 (see Section 7.7). Table 2.4 provides the list of six SIP response classes:

Table 2.3 SIP Request Messages

SIP Method	*Description*
ACK	The ACK method is sent for the final acknowledgment of INVITEs. ACK is end-to-end for 2xx final responses, but is hop-by-hop for all other final responses such as 3xx, 4xx, 5xx, or 6xx. ACK may contain the message body if the initial INVITE does not contain a SDP message body. ACK also may not modify the message body containing the media description containing in initial INVITE because a re-INVITE must be used to modify the media description provided in SDP. In some exceptional cases, such as interworking between H.323 and SIP where the media description may not be known priory, ACK may contain SDP. The sequence number, CSeq, is never incremented in an ACK because a UAS needs to match the CSeq number of the ACK with the number of the corresponding INVITE request. The mandatory header fields in an ACK are Via, To, From, Call-ID, CSeq, and Max-Forwards (RFC 3261: Standards Track).
BYE	The BYE method is used to tear down an already established session and can be sent only by the UAs, never by any proxies or by third parties. It is an end-to-end method and can only be generated by participant UAs of the session. It is not recommended that a BYE be used to cancel pending INVITEs because it will not be forked like an INVITE and may not reach the same set of UAs as the INVITE. The mandatory header fields in a BYE are Via, To, From, Call-ID, CSeq, and Max-Forwards (RFC 3261: Standards Track).
CANCEL	The CANCEL method is used for termination of the pending SIP calls and can be generated by SIP UAs or proxy servers provided that only 1xx like provisional responses containing a tag is received. CANCEL is a hop-by-hop request and cannot be generated if final responses have been received. The mandatory header fields in a CANCEL are Via, To, From, Call-ID, CSeq, and Max-Forwards (RFC 3261: Standards Track).
INFO	The INFO method is used by a SIP UA to carry application-level information between end points, using the SIP dialog signaling path. For example, DTMF tones can be conveyed during the established session using the INFO message. It neither updates the characteristics of the SIP dialog or session nor constitutes a separate dialog usage. It only allows the applications that use the SIP session to exchange information that might update the state of those applications. INFO messages cannot be sent as part of other dialog usages, or outside an existing dialog. The mandatory header fields in an INFO are Allow, Call-ID, CSeq, Info-Package, From, Max-Forwards, Proxy-Authenticate, To, Via, and WWW-Authenticate (RFC 6086: Standards Track).
INVITE	The INVITE method is used for establishment of single media or multimedia sessions between UAs. It may include SDP bodies that describe what type and the characteristics of each media that the caller is prepared to receive. It may also carry more bodies describing other features (e.g., tunneled Integrated Services Digital Network [ISDN] User Part [ISUP]/Q Signaling [QSIG] Public Branch Exchange [PBX] signaling information) of the session. Every INVITE is confirmed by sending an ACK for reliability. If the call is in progress and has not been established yet, the caller may cancel it using CANCEL method. The CANCEL and ACK methods are only used in association with the INVITE request. If INVITE does not contain the media information, the ACK contains the media information of the UAC. A media session is considered established when the INVITE, 200 OK, and ACK messages have been exchanged between the UAC and UAS. Multiple INVITEs can be sent within a session to change its status. The mandatory header fields in an INVITE are Via, To, From, Call-ID, CSeq, Contact, and Max-Forwards (RFC 3261: Standards Track).
MESSAGE	The MESSAGE method that is described in Section 6.3.1 is used by SIP UA for transferring instant messaging (IM) that is often used in conversational mode for fast transfer of messages in near real-time using SIP. MESSAGE requests carry the content in the form of MIME body parts. MESSAGE requests do not themselves initiate a SIP dialog; under normal usage, each IM stands alone, much like pager messages. MESSAGE requests may be sent in the context of a dialog initiated by some other SIP request. It may be noted that an IM session can also be established in an alternative way using INVITE/200 OK/ACK with SDP body that describes that IM protocol will be used directly between the SIP UAs and then sending the IM as a part of media (data) between UAs. However, it takes longer time to set up the IM session. The mandatory header fields in a MESSAGE are Accept, Accept-Encoding, Accept-Language, Allow, Call-ID, CSeq, From, Max-Forwards, Proxy-Authenticate, To, Via, and WWW-Authenticate (RFC 3428: Standards Track).

(*Continued*)

Table 2.3 (Continued) SIP Request Messages

SIP Method	*Description*
NOTIFY	NOTIFY, which is described in more detail in Section 5.2, is a method used by a SIP UA to inform about the occurrence of a particular SIP-specific event asynchronously if the user subscribes to that specific event. The notification occurs within a dialog while a subscription exists between the SIP UAs (subscriber and notifier). The SIP request type REFER and other non-SIP means can also be used to establish an implicit subscription for getting the notifications of the event with the NOTIFY method without sending the SUBSCRIBE message. For example, the message store in a voice-mail server and the status of the voice server can be notified if those service events are subscribed. The mandatory header fields in a NOTIFY are Allow, Allow-Events, Call-ID, Contact, CSeq, Event, From, Max-Forwards, Proxy-Authenticate, Subscription-Sate, To, Via, and WWW-Authenticate (RFC 6665: Standards Track).
OPTIONS	The OPTIONS method allows a UA to query another UA or a proxy server as to its capabilities. The response of the request lists the capabilities of the UA or server. As a result, this allows a client to discover information about the supported methods, content types, extensions, codecs, etc. without ringing the other party. For example, before a client inserts a Require header field into an INVITE listing an option that it is not certain the destination UAS supports, the client can query the destination UAS with an OPTIONS to see if this option is returned in a Supported header field. All UAs must support the OPTIONS method. The OPTIONS method is an important mechanism of SIP for discovering of the capabilities of SIP entities. The mandatory header fields in an OPTIONS are Via, To, From, Call-ID, CSeq, and Max-Forwards.
PRACK	The SIP (RFC 3261) is a request/response protocol for initiating and managing communication sessions. SIP defines two types of responses: provisional and final. Final responses convey the result of the request processing, and are sent reliably. Provisional responses provide information on the progress of the request processing, but are not sent reliably in RFC 3261. It was later observed that reliability was important in several cases, including interoperability scenarios with the PSTN. Therefore, an optional capability was needed to support reliable transmission of provisional responses. That capability is provided in this specification. The reliability mechanism works by mirroring the current reliability mechanisms for 2xx final responses to INVITE. Those requests are transmitted periodically by the transaction user (TU) until a separate transaction, ACK, is received that indicates reception of the 2xx by the UAC. The reliability for the 2xx responses to INVITE and ACK messages are end-to-end. To achieve reliability for provisional responses, we do nearly the same thing. Reliable provisional responses are retransmitted by the TU with an exponential backoff. Those retransmissions cease when a PRACK message, which is defined in RFC 3262 and described here, is received. The PRACK request plays the same role as ACK, but for provisional responses. There is an important difference, however. PRACK is a normal SIP message, like BYE. As such, its own reliability is ensured hop-by-hop through each stateful proxy. Also like BYE, but unlike ACK, PRACK has its own response. If this were not the case, the PRACK message could not traverse proxy servers compliant to RFC 2543 (obsoleted by RFC 3261). Each provisional response is given a sequence number, carried in the RSeq header field in the response. The PRACK messages contain an RAck header field, which indicates the sequence number of the provisional response that is being acknowledged. The acknowledgments are not cumulative, and the specifications recommend a single outstanding provisional response at a time, for purposes of congestion control. **UAS Behavior** A UAS MAY send any non-100 provisional response to INVITE reliably, so long as the initial INVITE request (the request whose provisional response is being sent reliably) contained a Supported header field with the option tag 100rel. While this specification does not allow reliable provisional responses for any method but INVITE, extensions that define new methods that can establish dialogs may make use of the mechanism. The UAS must send any non-100 provisional response reliably if the initial request contained a Require header field with the option tag 100rel. If the UAS is unwilling to do so, it must reject the initial request with a 420 Bad Extension and include an Unsupported header field containing the option tag 100rel. A UAS must not attempt to send a 100 Trying response reliably. Only provisional responses numbered 101 to 199 responses may be sent reliably. If the request did not include either a Supported or Require header field indicating this feature, the UAS must not send the provisional response reliably. 100 Trying responses are hop-by-hop only. For this reason, the reliability mechanisms described here, which are end-to-end, cannot be used.

(*Continued*)

Table 2.3 (Continued) SIP Request Messages

SIP Method	*Description*
	An element that can act as a proxy can also send reliable provisional responses. In this case, it acts as a UAS for purposes of that transaction. However, it must not attempt to do so for any request that contains a tag in the To field. That is, a proxy cannot generate reliable provisional responses to requests sent within the context of a dialog. Of course, unlike a UAS, when the proxy element receives a PRACK that does not match any outstanding reliable provisional response, the PRACK must be proxied. There are several reasons why a UAS might want to send a reliable provisional response. One reason is if the INVITE transaction will take some time to generate a final response. As discussed in RFC 3261 (see Section 3.7.3.1.1), the UAS will need to send periodic provisional responses to request an *extension* of the transaction at proxies. The requirement is that a proxy receive them every 3 minutes, but the UAS needs to send those more frequently (once a minute is recommended) because of the possibility of packet loss. As a more efficient alternative, the UAS can send the response reliably, in which case the UAS should send provisional responses once every 2.5 minutes. Use of reliable provisional responses for extending transactions is recommended. The rest of this discussion assumes that the initial request contained a Supported or Require header field listing 100rel, and that there is a provisional response to be sent reliably. The provisional response to be sent reliably is constructed by the UAS core according to the procedures of RFC 3261 (see Section 3.1.3.6). In addition, it must contain a Require header field containing the option tag 100rel, and must include an RSeq header field. The value of the header field for the first reliable provisional response in a transaction must be between 1 and 2^{31-1}. It is recommended that it be chosen uniformly in this range. The RSeq numbering space is within a single transaction. This means that provisional responses for different requests may use the same values for the RSeq number. The reliable provisional response may contain a body. The usage of session descriptions is described later in the context offer–answer. The reliable provisional response is passed to the transaction layer periodically with an interval that starts at T1 seconds and doubles for each retransmission (T1 is defined in RFC 3261; see Section 3.12). Once passed to the server transaction, it is added to an internal list of unacknowledged reliable provisional responses. The transaction layer will forward each retransmission passed from the UAS core. This differs from retransmissions of 2xx responses, whose intervals cap at T2 seconds. This is because retransmissions of ACK are triggered on receipt of a 2xx, but retransmissions of PRACK take place independently of reception of 1xx. Retransmissions of the reliable provisional response cease when a matching PRACK is received by the UA core. PRACK is like any other request within a dialog, and the UAS core processes it according to the procedures of RFC 3261 (see Sections 3.1.3 and 3.6.2.1). A matching PRACK is defined as one within the same dialog as the response, and whose method, CSeq-num, and response-num in the RAck header field match, respectively, the method from the CSeq, the sequence number from the CSeq, and the sequence number from the RSeq of the reliable provisional response. If a PRACK request is received by the UA core that does not match any unacknowledged reliable provisional response, the UAS must respond to the PRACK with a 481 Dialog/Transaction Does Not Exist response. If the PRACK does match an unacknowledged reliable provisional response, it must be responded to with a 2xx response. The UAS can be certain at this point that the provisional response has been received in order. It should cease retransmissions of the reliable provisional response, and must remove it from the list of unacknowledged provisional responses.

(*Continued*)

Table 2.3 (Continued) SIP Request Messages

SIP Method	*Description*
	If a reliable provisional response is retransmitted for 64*T1 seconds without reception of a corresponding PRACK, the UAS should reject the original request with a 5xx response. If the PRACK contained a session description, it is processed as described in Section 2.1 of this document. If the PRACK instead contained any other type of body, the body is treated in the same way that body in an ACK would be treated. After the first reliable provisional response for a request has been acknowledged, the UAS may send additional reliable provisional responses. The UAS must not send a second reliable provisional response until the first is acknowledged. After the first, it is recommended that the UAS not send an additional reliable provisional response until the previous one is acknowledged. The first reliable provisional response receives special treatment because it conveys the initial sequence number. If additional reliable provisional responses were sent before the first was acknowledged, the UAS could not be certain these were received in order. The value of the RSeq in each subsequent reliable provisional response for the same request must be greater by exactly 1. RSeq numbers must not wrap around. Because the initial one is chosen to be less than 2^{31-1}, but the maximum is 2^{31-1}, there can be up to 2^{31} reliable provisional responses per request, which is more than sufficient. The UAS MAY send a final response to the initial request before having received PRACKs for all unacknowledged reliable provisional responses, unless the final response is 2xx and any of the unacknowledged reliable provisional responses contained a session description. In that case, it must not send a final response until those provisional responses are acknowledged. If the UAS does send a final response when reliable responses are still unacknowledged, it should not continue to retransmit the unacknowledged reliable provisional responses, but it must be prepared to process PRACK requests for those outstanding responses. A UAS must not send new reliable provisional responses (as opposed to retransmissions of unacknowledged ones) after sending a final response to a request. **UAC Behavior** When the UAC creates a new request, it can insist on a reliable delivery of provisional responses for that request. To do that, it inserts a Require header field with the option tag 100rel into the request. A Require header with the value 100rel must not be present in any requests excepting INVITE, although extensions to SIP may allow its usage with other request methods. If the UAC does not wish to insist on usage of reliable provisional responses, but merely indicate that it supports them if the UAS needs to send one, a Supported header must be included in the request with the option tag 100rel. The UAC should include this in all INVITE requests. If a provisional response is received for an initial request, and that response contains a Require header field containing the option tag 100rel, the response is to be sent reliably. If the response is a 100 Trying (as opposed to 101 to 199), this option tag must be ignored, and the procedures below must not be used. The provisional response must establish a dialog if one is not yet created. Assuming the response is to be transmitted reliably, the UAC must create a new request with the PRACK method. This request is sent within the dialog associated with the provisional response (indeed, the provisional response may have created the dialog). PRACK requests may contain bodies, which are interpreted according to their type and disposition. Note that the PRACK is like any other non-INVITE request within a dialog. In particular, a UAC should not retransmit the PRACK request when it receives a retransmission of the provisional response being acknowledged, although doing so does not create a protocol error.
	Once a reliable provisional response is received, retransmissions of that response must be discarded. A response is a retransmission when its dialog ID, CSeq, and RSeq match the original response. The UAC must maintain a sequence number that indicates the most recently received in-order reliable provisional response for the initial request. This sequence number must be maintained until a final response is received for the initial request. Its value must be initialized to the RSeq header field in the first reliable provisional response received for the initial request. Handling of subsequent reliable provisional responses for the same initial request follows the same rules as above, with the following difference: reliable provisional responses are guaranteed to be in order. As a result, if the UAC receives another reliable provisional response to the same request, and its RSeq value is not one higher than the value of the sequence number, that response must not be acknowledged with a PRACK, and must not be processed further by the UAC. An implementation may discard the response, or may cache the response in the hopes of receiving the missing responses. The UAC may acknowledge reliable provisional responses received after the final response or may discard them.

(Continued)

Table 2.3 (Continued) SIP Request Messages

SIP Method	*Description*
	Offer–Answer Model and PRACK RFC 3261 describes guidelines for the sets of messages in which offers and answers (RFC 3264, see Section 3.8.4) can appear. On the basis of those guidelines, this extension provides additional opportunities for offer–answer exchanges. If the INVITE contained an offer, the UAS may generate an answer in a reliable provisional response (assuming these are supported by the UAC). That results in the establishment of the session before completion of the call. Similarly, if a reliable provisional response is the first reliable message sent back to the UAC, and the INVITE did not contain an offer, one must appear in that reliable provisional response. If the UAC receives a reliable provisional response with an offer (this would occur if the UAC sent an INVITE without an offer, in which case the first reliable provisional response will contain the offer), it MUST generate an answer in the PRACK. If the UAC receives a reliable provisional response with an answer, it may generate an additional offer in the PRACK. If the UAS receives a PRACK with an offer, it must place the answer in the 2xx to the PRACK. Once an answer has been sent or received, the UA should establish the session based on the parameters of the offer and answer, even if the original INVITE itself has not been responded to. If the UAS had placed a session description in any reliable provisional response that is unacknowledged when the INVITE is accepted, the UAS must delay sending the 2xx until the provisional response is acknowledged. Otherwise, the reliability of the 1xx cannot be guaranteed, and reliability is needed for proper operation of the offer–answer exchange. All UAs that support this extension must support all offer–answer exchanges that are possible based on the rules in RFC 3261 (see Section 3.7.2), based on the existence of INVITE and PRACK as requests, and 2xx and reliable 1xx as nonfailure reliable responses. **Definition of the PRACK Method** The semantics of the PRACK method are described above. See PRACK method, explained above in this table, which provides details for this method. The mandatory header fields in a PRACK are Allow, Call-ID, CSeq, From, Max-Forwards, Proxy-Authenticate, RAck, To, Unsupported, Via, and WWW-Authenticate (RFC 3262: Standards Track).
PUBLISH	The PUBLISH method (RFC 3903, see Section 5.2) is used by a SIP UA that is responsible for compositing the SIP-specific event state for publication with an intention for distributing it to interested parties through the SIP event mechanisms (SUBSCRIBE/NOTIFY). For instance, an application of SIP events for message waiting indications might choose to collect the statuses of voice-mail boxes across a set of UAs using the PUBLISH mechanism. Similarly, a presence UA may also PUBLISH the presence states for distribution to the interested parties. The mandatory header fields in a PUBLISH are Accept, Accept-Encoding, Accept-Language, Allow, Allow-Events, Event, Call-ID, CSeq, From, Max-Forwards, Min-Expires, Proxy-Authenticate, SIP-ETag, To, Via, and WWW-Authenticate (RFC 3903: Standards Track).
REFER	RFC 3415 defines the REFER method that extends the basic SIP defined in RFC 3261. It is a new request message that the recipient REFER to a resource provided in the request. It provides a mechanism allowing the party sending the REFER to be notified of the outcome of the referenced request. In addition to the REFER method, RFC 3515 defines the refer event package and the Refer-To request header (see Section 2.8). This can be used to enable many applications, including Call Transfer. For instance, if Alice is in a call with Bob, and decides Bob needs to talk to Carol, Alice can instruct her SIP UA to send a SIP REFER request to Bob's UA providing Carol's SIP Contact information. Assuming Bob has given it permission, Bob's UA will attempt to call Carol using that contact. Bob's UA will then report whether it succeeded in reaching the contact to Alice's UA.

(Continued)

Table 2.3 (Continued) SIP Request Messages

SIP Method	*Description*
	REFER Method The REFER method indicates that the recipient (identified by the Request-URI) should contact a third party using the contact information provided in the request. Unless stated otherwise, the protocol for emitting and responding to a REFER request are identical to those for a BYE request in RFC 3261. The behavior of SIP entities not implementing the REFER (or any other unknown) method is explicitly defined in RFC 3261. A REFER request implicitly establishes a subscription to the refer event. Event subscriptions are defined in RFC 6665 (see Section 5.2). A REFER request may be placed outside the scope of a dialog created with an INVITE. REFER creates a dialog, and may be Record-Routed; hence, it must contain a single Contact header field value. REFERs occurring inside an existing dialog must follow the Route/Record-Route logic of that dialog. The mandatory header fields in a REFER are Allow, Call-ID, Contact, CSeq, From, Max-Forwards, Proxy-Authenticate, Refer-To To, Via, and WWW-Authenticate (see Section 2.8). **Message-Body Inclusion** A REFER method may contain a body. This specification assigns no meaning to such a body. A receiving agent may choose to process the body according to its Content-Type. **Behavior of SIP User Agents** ***Forming a REFER Request*** REFER is a SIP request and is constructed as defined in RFC 3261 (see Section 16.2). A REFER request must contain exactly one Refer-To header field value. ***Processing a REFER Request*** A UA accepting a well-formed REFER request should request approval from the user to proceed (this request could be satisfied with an interactive query or through accessing configured policy). If approval is granted, the UA must contact the resource identified by the URI in the Refer-To header field value, as discussed below. If the approval sought above for a well-formed REFER request is immediately denied, the UA may decline the request. An agent responding to a REFER method MUST return a 400 Bad Request if the request contained zero or more than one Refer-To header field values. An agent (including proxies generating local responses) may return a 100 Trying or any appropriate 4xx-6xx class response as prescribed by RFC 3261. Care should be taken when implementing the logic that determines whether or not to accept the REFER request. A UA not capable of accessing non-SIP URIs should not accept REFER requests to them. If no final response has been generated according to the rules above, the UA must return a 202 Accepted response before the REFER transaction expires. If a REFER request is accepted (i.e., a 2xx class response is returned), the recipient MUST create a subscription and send notifications of the status of the refer as described below. ***Accessing the Referred-to Resource*** The resource identified by the Refer-To URI is contacted using the normal mechanisms for that URI type. For example, if the URI is a SIP URI indicating INVITE (e.g., using a method=INVITE URI parameter), the UA would issue a new INVITE using all of the normal rules for sending an INVITE defined in RFC 3261. ***Using SIP Events to Report the Results of the Reference*** The NOTIFY mechanism defined in RFC 6665 (see Section 5.2) must be used to inform the agent sending the REFER of the status of the reference. The dialog identifiers (To, From, and Call-ID) of each NOTIFY must match those of the REFER as they would if the REFER had been a SUBSCRIBE request. Each NOTIFY must contain an Event header field with a value of refer and possibly an id parameter described below. Each NOTIFY must contain a body of type *message/sipfrag* defined in RFC 3420 (see Section 2.8.2). The creation of a subscription as defined by RFC 6665 (see Section 5.2) always results in an immediate NOTIFY. Analogous to the case for SUBSCRIBE described in that document, the agent that issued the REFER must be prepared to receive a NOTIFY before the REFER transaction completes.

(*Continued*)

Table 2.3 (Continued) SIP Request Messages

SIP Method	*Description*
	The implicit subscription created by a REFER is the same as a subscription created with a SUBSCRIBE request. The agent issuing the REFER can terminate this subscription prematurely by unsubscribing using the mechanisms described in RFC 6665 (see Section 5.2). Terminating a subscription, either by explicitly unsubscribing or rejecting NOTIFY, is not an indication that the referenced request should be withdrawn or abandoned. In particular, an agent acting on a REFER request should not issue a CANCEL to any referenced SIP requests because the agent sending the REFER terminated its subscription to the refer event before the referenced request completes. The agent issuing the REFER may extend its subscription using the subscription refresh mechanisms described in RFC 6665 (see Section 5.2). REFER is the only mechanism that can create a subscription to event refer. If a SUBSCRIBE request for event refer is received for a subscription that does not already exist, it must be rejected with a 403 Forbidden. Notice that unlike SUBSCRIBE, the REFER transaction does not contain a duration for the subscription in either the request or the response. The lifetime of the state being subscribed to is determined by the progress of the referenced request. The duration of the subscription is chosen by the agent accepting the REFER, and is communicated to the agent sending the REFER in the subscription's initial NOTIFY (using the Subscription-State expires header parameter). Note that agents accepting REFER and not wishing to hold subscription state can terminate the subscription with this initial NOTIFY. ***Body of NOTIFY*** Each NOTIFY must contain a body of type message/sipfrag defined in RFC 3420 (see Section 2.8.2). The body of a NOTIFY must begin with a SIP Response Status-Line as defined in RFC 3261. The response class in this status line indicates the status of the referred action. The body may contain other SIP header fields to provide information about the outcome of the referenced action. This body provides a complete statement of the status of the referred action. The refer event package does not support state deltas. If a NOTIFY is generated when the subscription state is pending, its body should consist only of a status line containing a response code of 100 Trying. A minimal, but complete, implementation can respond with a single NOTIFY containing either the body SIP/2.0 100 Trying if the subscription is pending, the body SIP/2.0 200 OK if the reference was successful, the body SIP/2.0 503 Service Unavailable if the reference failed, or the body SIP/2.0 603 Declined if the REFER request was accepted before approval to follow if the reference could be obtained and that approval was subsequently denied as described below. An implementation may include more of a SIP message in that body to convey more information. Warning header field values received in responses to the referred action are good candidates. In fact, if the reference was to a SIP URI, the entire response to the referenced action could be returned (perhaps to assist with debugging). However, doing so could have grave security repercussions (see Section 19.2). Implementers must carefully consider what they choose to include. Note that if the reference was to a non-SIP URI, status in any NOTIFY to the referrer must still be in the form of SIP Response Status-Lines. The minimal implementation discussed above is sufficient to provide a basic indication of success or failure. For example, if a client receives a REFER to a HTTP URL, and is successful in accessing the resource, its NOTIFY to the referrer can contain the message/sipfrag body of *SIP/2.0 200 OK*. If the notifier wishes to return additional non-SIP-specific information about the status of the request, it may place it in the body of the sipfrag message.

(*Continued*)

Table 2.3 (Continued) SIP Request Messages

SIP Method	*Description*
	Multiple REFER Requests in a Dialog A REFER creates an implicit subscription sharing the dialog identifiers in the REFER request. If more than one REFER is issued in the same dialog (e.g., a second attempt at transferring a call), the dialog identifiers do not provide enough information to associate the resulting NOTIFYs with the proper REFER. Thus, for the second and subsequent REFER requests a UA receives in a given dialog, it must include an id parameter defined in RFC 6665 (see Section 5.2) in the Event header field of each NOTIFY containing the sequence number (the number from the CSeq header field value) of the REFER this NOTIFY is associated with. This id parameter may be included in NOTIFYs to the first REFER a UA receives in a given dialog. A SUBSCRIBE sent to refresh or terminate this subscription must contain this id parameter. ***Using the Subscription-State Header Field with Event Refer*** Each NOTIFY must contain a Subscription-State header field as defined in RFC 6665 (see Section 2.8). The final NOTIFY sent in response to a REFER must indicate the subscription has been *terminated* with a reason of *noresource*. (The resource being subscribed to is the state of the referenced request.) If a NOTIFY states a reason that indicates a resubscribe is appropriate according to RFC 6665 (see Section 5.2), the agent sending the REFER is not obligated to resubscribe. In the case where a REFER was accepted with a 202 Accepted, but approval to follow the reference was subsequently denied, the reason and retry after elements of the Subscription-State header field can be used to indicate if and when the REFER can be reattempted as described for SUBSCRIBE in RFC 6665 (see Section 5.2). **Behavior of SIP Registrars/Redirect Servers** A registrar that is unaware of the definition of the REFER method will return a 501 Not Implemented response as defined in RFC 3261. A registrar aware of the definition of REFER should return a 405 Method Not Allowed response. This specification places no requirements on redirect server behavior beyond those specified in RFC 3261. Thus, it is possible for REFER requests to be redirected. **Behavior of SIP Proxies** SIP proxies do not require modification to support the REFER method. Specifically, as required by RFC 3261, a proxy should process a REFER request the same way it processes an OPTIONS request. **Package Details: Event Refer** RFC 3515 defines an event package as defined in RFC 6665 (see Section 5.2). ***Event Package Name*** The name of this event package is *refer*. ***Event Package Parameters*** This package uses the *id* parameter defined in RFC 6665 (see Section 5.2). Its use in package is described earlier. ***SUBSCRIBE Bodies*** SUBSCRIBE bodies have no special meaning for this event package. ***Subscription Duration*** The duration of an implicit subscription created by a REFER request is initially determined by the agent accepting the REFER and communicated to the subscribing agent in the Subscription-State header field's expire parameter in the first NOTIFY sent in the subscription. Reasonable choices for this initial duration depend on the type of request indicated in the Refer-To URI. The duration should be chosen to be longer than the time the referenced request will be given to complete. For example, if the Refer-To URI is a SIP INVITE URI, the subscription interval should be longer than the Expire value in the INVITE. Additional time may be included to account for the time needed to authorize the subscription. The subscribing agent may extend the subscription by refreshing it, or terminate it by unsubscribing. As described earlier, the agent accepting the REFER will terminate the subscription when it reports the final result of the reference, indicating that termination in the Subscription-State header field. ***NOTIFY Bodies*** The bodies of NOTIFY requests for event refer are discussed earlier.

(*Continued*)

Table 2.3 (Continued) SIP Request Messages

SIP Method	*Description*
	Notifier Processing of SUBSCRIBE Requests Notifier processing of SUBSCRIBE requests is discussed earlier. ***Notifier Generation of NOTIFY Requests*** Notifier generation of NOTIFY requests is discussed earlier. ***Subscriber Processing of NOTIFY Requests*** Subscriber processing of NOTIFY requests is discussed earlier. ***Handling of Forked Requests*** A REFER sent within the scope of an existing dialog will not fork. A REFER sent outside the context of a dialog MAY fork, and if it is accepted by multiple agents, may create multiple subscriptions. These subscriptions are created and managed as per "Handling of Forked Requests" in RFC 6665 (see Section 5.2) as if the REFER had been a SUBSCRIBE. The agent sending the REFER manages the state associated with each subscription separately. It does not merge the state from the separate subscriptions. The state is the status of the referenced request at each of the accepting agents. ***Rate of Notifications*** An event refer NOTIFY might be generated each time new knowledge of the status of a referenced requests becomes available. For instance, if the REFER was to a SIP INVITE, NOTIFYs might be generated with each provisional response and the final response to the INVITE. Alternatively, the subscription might only result in two NOTIFY requests: the immediate NOTIFY and the NOTIFY carrying the final result of the reference. NOTIFYs to event refer should not be sent more frequently than once per second. ***State Agents*** Separate state agents are not defined for event refer (RFC 3515: Standards Track).
REGISTER	The REGISTER method is used to register the Contact URI information with the AOR of the user by the UA to notify the SIP network where the user can be reached for a given period of time. In addition to the self-registration by the user, a third-party registration of the user can also be done. For security, the challenge and response can be used for authentication of the registration. The mandatory header fields in a REGISTER are Via, To, From, Call-ID, CSeq, and Max-Forwards (RFC 3261: Standards Track).
SUBSCRIBE	The SUBSCRIBE method (RFC 6665, see Chapter 3) is used by a SIP UA for subscribing to an event specific to SIP to another SIP UA, for getting the notifications in an asynchronous fashion for a certain period of time. A successful subscription establishes a dialog between UAC and UAS. The mandatory header fields in a SUBSCRIBE are Allow, Allow-Events, Call-ID, Contact, CSeq, Expires, Event, From, Max-Forwards, Min-Expires, Proxy-Authenticate, To, Via, and WWW-Authenticate (RFC 6665: Standards Track).
UPDATE	The UPDATE method (RFC 3311, see Chapter 3) is used by a SIP UA to update parameters of a session (such as the set of media streams and their codecs) but has no impact on the state of a dialog. It is like re-INVITE, but unlike re-INVITE, UPDATE can be sent before the initial INVITE has been completed. This makes it very useful for updating session parameters within early dialogs where re-INVITE cannot be sent because the session establishment has not been completed yet with sending of the initial INVITE. The mandatory header fields in an UPDATE are Allow, Call-ID, Contact, CSeq, From, Max-Forwards, Proxy-Authenticate, To, Unsupported, Via, and WWW-Authenticate (RFC 3311: Standards Track).

Provisional (1xx), Success (2xx), Redirection (3xx), Client Error (4xx), Server Error (5xx), and Global Failure (6xx). Table 2.4 describes the SIP response messages briefly.

2.7 SIP Call and Media Trapezoid Operation

We like to briefly introduce here the SIP operation at a high level, although the actual protocol details are provided in the subsequent chapters. We will provide a review of SIP in a nutshell—how registration is performed, and how a session is created, updated, and terminated between the participants. Figure 2.6a illustrates a SIP network with two SIP UAs known as Alice and Bob, and two SIP proxies designated as outgoing proxy and incoming proxy.

SIP signaling flows between the UAs and the proxies, and media flows directly between the UAs as shown in Figure 2.6a are frequently referred to as the SIP trapezoid. We are assuming that Alice being in the atlanta.com domain is trying to

Table 2.4 SIP Response Messages

Response Message	*Description*
Provisional (1xx): The provisional response classes indicate that the server contacted is performing some further action and does not yet have a definitive response considering the fact the final response will take more time (say, around 200 ms). This class of responses is not transmitted reliably. They never cause the client to send an ACK. These responses may contain message bodies, including session descriptions. However, if the reliability of the provisional responses is desired, a client may send PRACK to the server.	
100 Trying	This response indicates that the request has been received by the next-hop server and that some unspecified action is being taken on behalf of this call (e.g., a database is being consulted). This response, like all other provisional responses, stops retransmissions of an INVITE by a UAC. This response is different from other provisional responses, in that it is never forwarded upstream by a stateful proxy (RFC 3261: Standards Track).
180 Ringing	The UA receiving the INVITE is trying to alert the user. This response may be used to initiate local ringback (RFC 3261: Standards Track).
181 Call Is Being Forwarded	A server may use this status code to indicate that the call is being forwarded to a different set of destinations (RFC 3261: Standards Track).
182 Call Queued	The called party is temporarily unavailable, but the server has decided to queue the call rather than reject it. When the callee becomes available, it will return the appropriate final status response. The reason phrase MAY give further details about the status of the call, for example, "five calls queued; expected waiting time is 15 minutes." The server may issue several 182 Queued responses to update the caller about the status of the queued call (RFC 3261: Standards Track).
183 Session Progress	The 183 Session Progress response is used to convey information about the progress of the call that is not otherwise classified. The reason phrase, header fields, or message body MAY be used to convey more details about the call progress (RFC 3261: Standards Track).
199 Early Dialog Terminated	RFC 6228 (see Section 3.6.6 for more details) defines a new SIP response code, 199 Early Dialog Terminated, that a SIP forking proxy and a UAS can use to indicate to upstream SIP entities, including the UAC that an early dialog has been terminated, before a final response is sent toward the SIP entities. A UAS can send a 199 response code, before sending a non-2xx final response, for the same purpose. SIP entities that receive the 199 response can use it to trigger the release of resources associated with the terminated early dialog. In addition, SIP entities might also use the 199 response to make policy decisions related to early dialogs. For example, a media gate controlling a SIP entity might use the 199 response when deciding for which early dialogs media will be passed (RFC 6228: Standards Track).
Success (2xx): The Success class of responses is sent by a server to indicate that the request has been succeeded.	
200 OK	The request has succeeded. The information returned with the response depends on the method used in the request (RFC 3261: Standards Track).
202 Accepted	This response indicates that the request has been accepted and understood by the server, but the request may have not been authorized or processed yet by the server (RFC 6665: Standards Track).
204 No Notification	The 204 No Notification response code indicates that the request was successful, but the notification associated with the request will not be sent. It is valid only in response to a SUBSCRIBE message sent within an established dialog (RFC 5839: Standards Track).

(Continued)

Table 2.4 (Continued) SIP Response Messages

Response Message	*Description*
Redirection (3xx): The Redirection class of responses gives information about the user's new location, or about alternative services that might be able to satisfy the call.	
300 Multiple Choices	The address in the request resolved to several choices, each with its own specific location, and the user (or UA) can select a preferred communication end point and redirect its request to that location. The response may include a message body containing a list of resource characteristics and location(s) from which the user or UA can choose the one most appropriate, if allowed by the Accept request header field. However, no Multipurpose Internet Mail Extensions (MIME) types have been defined for this message body. The choices should also be listed as Contact fields in RFC 3261 (see Section 2.8). Unlike HTTP, the SIP response may contain several Contact fields or a list of addresses in a Contact field. UAs may use the Contact header field value for automatic redirection or may ask the user to confirm a choice. However, this specification does not define any standard for such automatic selection. This status response is appropriate if the callee can be reached at several different locations, and the server cannot or prefers not to proxy the request (RFC 3261: Standards Track).
301 Moved Permanently	The user can no longer be found at the address in the Request-URI, and the requesting client should retry at the new address given by the Contact header field. The requestor should update any local directories, address books, and user location caches with this new value and redirect future requests to the address (or addresses) listed (RFC 3261: Standards Track).
302 Moved Temporarily	The requesting client should retry the request at the new address (or addresses) given by the Contact header field. The Request-URI of the new request uses the value of the Contact header field in the response. The duration of the validity of the Contact URI can be indicated through an Expires header field or an Expires parameter in the Contact header field. Both proxies and UAs may cache this URI for the duration of the expiration time. If there is no explicit expiration time, the address is only valid once for recurring, and must not be cached for future transactions. If the URI cached from the Contact header field fails, the Request-URI from the redirected request may be tried again a single time. The temporary URI may have become out of date sooner than the expiration time, and a new temporary URI may be available (RFC 3261: Standards Track).
305 Use Proxy	The requested resource must be accessed through the proxy given by the Contact field. The Contact field gives the URI of the proxy. The recipient is expected to repeat this single request via the proxy. The 305 Use Proxy responses must only be generated by UASs (RFC 3261: Standards Track).
380 Alternative Service	380 Alternative Service: The call was not successful, but alternative services are possible. The alternative services are described in the message body of the response. Formats for such bodies are not defined here, and may be the subject of future standardization (RFC 3261: Standards Track).
Client Error (4xx): The Client Error class of responses are definite failure responses from a particular server. The client should not retry the same request without modification (e.g., adding appropriate authorization). However, the same request to a different server might be successful.	
400 Bad Request	The request could not be understood because of malformed syntax. The Reason-Phrase should identify the syntax problem in more detail, for example, *Missing Call-ID* header field (RFC 3261: Standards Track).
401 Unauthorized	The request requires user authentication. This response is issued by UASs and registrars, while 407 Proxy Authentication Required is used by proxy servers (RFC 3261: Standards Track).
402 Payment Required	This response is reserved for future use of SIP calls such as call completion charges (RFC 3261: Standards Track).

(*Continued*)

Table 2.4 (Continued) SIP Response Messages

Response Message	*Description*
403 Forbidden	The server understood the request but is refusing to fulfill it. Authorization will not help, and the request should not be repeated (RFC 3261: Standards Track).
404 Not Found	The server has definitive information that the user does not exist at the domain specified in the Request-URI. This status is also returned if the domain in the Request-URI does not match any of the domains handled by the recipient of the request (RFC 3261: Standards Track).
405 Method Not Allowed	The method specified in the Request-Line is understood but not allowed for the address identified by the Request-URI. The response must include an Allow header field containing a list of valid methods for the indicated address (RFC 3261: Standards Track).
406 Not Acceptable	The resource identified by the request is only capable of generating response entities that have content characteristics not acceptable according to the Accept header field sent in the request (RFC 3261: Standards Track).
407 Proxy Authentication Required	This code is similar to 401 Unauthorized, but indicates that the client must first authenticate itself with the proxy. This status code can be used for applications where access to the communication channel (e.g., a telephony gateway) rather than the callee requires authentication (RFC 3261: Standards Track).
408 Request Timeout	The server could not produce a response within a suitable amount of time, for example, if it could not determine the location of the user in time. The client may repeat the request without modifications at any later time (RFC 3261: Standards Track).
409 Conflict	This response code indicates that the request has created a conflict and cannot be processed. However, RFC 3261 that supersedes RFC 2543 has removed this response code (RFC 3261: Standards Track).
410 Gone	The requested resource is no longer available at the server, and no forwarding address is known. This condition is expected to be considered permanent. If the server does not know, or has no facility to determine, whether or not the condition is permanent, the status code 404 Not Found should be used instead (RFC 3261: Standards Track).
411 Length Required	This response code can be generated by a SIP proxy that switches the transport protocol from UDP to TCP if a request message contains a message body but not the Content-Length header because the Content-Length is more critical to TCP requests. However, RFC 3261 that supersedes RFC 2543 has removed this response code (RFC 3261: Standards Track).
412 Conditional Request Failed	The 412 Conditional Request Failed response code is added to the *Client-Error* header field definition. 412 Conditional Request Failed is used to indicate that the precondition given for the request has failed. That is, if there is no matching event state, for example, the event state to be refreshed has already expired, the Event Publication Agent, acting as a SIP UAC in issuing the PUBLISH request, receives a 412 Conditional Request Failed response to the PUBLISH request (RFC 3903: Standards Track).
413 Request Entity Too Large	The server is refusing to process a request because the request entity-body is larger than the server is willing or able to process. The server may close the connection to prevent the client from continuing the request. If the condition is temporary, the server should include a Retry-After header field to indicate that it is temporary and after what time the client may try again (RFC 3261: Standards Track).
414 Request-URI Too Long	The server is refusing to service the request because the Request-URI is longer than the server is willing to interpret (RFC 3261: Standards Track).

(Continued)

Table 2.4 (Continued) SIP Response Messages

Response Message	*Description*
415 Unsupported Media Type	The server is refusing to service the request because the message body of the request is in a format not supported by the server for the requested method. The server must return a list of acceptable formats using the Accept, Accept-Encoding, or Accept-Language header field, depending on the specific problem with the content (RFC 3261: Standards Track).
416 Unsupported URI Scheme	The server cannot process the request because the scheme of the URI in the Request-URI is unknown to the server (RFC 3261: Standards Track).
417 Unknown Resource-Priority	This response code is used by a SIP functional entity that acts as a resource-priority (RP) actor when it does not understand any of the resource values in the request. However, the treatment depends on the presence of the *Require resource-priority* option tag: 1. Without the option tag, the RP actor treats the request as if it contained no Resource-Priority header field and processes it with default priority. Resource values that are not understood must not be modified or deleted. 2. With the option tag, it must reject the request with a 417 Unknown Resource-Priority response code. Making case 1 the default is necessary since otherwise, there would be no way to successfully complete any calls in the case where a proxy on the way to the UAS shares no common namespaces with the UAC, but the UAC and UAS do have such a namespace in common. In general, as noted, a SIP request can contain more than one Resource-Priority header field. This is necessary if a request needs to traverse different administrative domains, each with its own set of valid resource values. For example, the ETS namespace might be enabled for US government networks that also support the Defense Switched Network (DSN) or Defense Switched Network RED (DRSN) namespaces for most individuals in those domains. A 417 Unknown Resource-Priority response may, according to local policy, include an *Accept-Resource-Priority* header field enumerating the acceptable resource values. SIP UACs supporting RFC 4412 must be able to generate the Resource-Priority header field for requests that require elevated resource access priority. The UAC should be able to generate more than one resource value in a single SIP request. Upon receiving a 417 Unknown Resource-Priority response, the UAC may attempt a subsequent request with the same or different resource value. If available, it should choose authorized resource values from the set of values returned in the Accept-Resource-Priority header field (RFC 4412: Standards Track).
420 Bad Extension	The server did not understand the protocol extension specified in a Proxy-Require or Require header field. The server must include a list of the unsupported extensions in an Unsupported header field in the response (RFC 3261: Standards Track).
421 Extension Required	The UAS needs a particular extension to process the request; however, this extension is not listed in a Supported header field in the request. Responses with this status code must contain a Require header field listing the required extensions. A UAS should not use this response unless it truly cannot provide any useful service to the client. Instead, if a desirable extension is not listed in the Supported header field, servers should process the request using baseline SIP capabilities and any extensions supported by the client (RFC 3261: Standards Track).
422 Session Timer Interval Too Small	This response code is used by a server to reject a request containing the Session-Expires header field that is too short an interval in order to prevent excess traffic of SIP signaling messages, especially by re-INVITE and UPDATE. If the session duration needs to be updated frequently due to the short time, it will create excessive traffic (RFC 4028: Standards Track).
423 Interval Too Brief	The server is rejecting the request because the expiration time of the resource refreshed by the request is too short. This response can be used by a registrar to reject a registration whose Contact header field expiration time was too small (RFC 3261: Standards Track).

(Continued)

Table 2.4 (Continued) SIP Response Messages

Response Message	*Description*
424 Bad Location Information	The 424 Bad Location Information response code is a rejection of the request due to its location contents, indicating location information that was malformed or not satisfactory for the recipient's purpose, or could not be dereferenced. The 424 response message should be included in the response as a MIME message body (i.e., a location value) rather than as a URI; however, in cases where the intermediary is willing to share location with recipients but not with a UA, a reference might be necessary. A SIP intermediary can also reject a location it receives from a Target when it understands the Target to be in a different location. SIP intermediaries that are forwarding (as opposed to generating) a 424 response must not add, modify, or delete any location appearing in that response. This specifically applies to intermediaries that are between the 424 response generator and the original UAC. The Geolocation and Geolocation-Error header fields and Presence Information Data Format (PIDF)–Location Object (LO) (PIDF–LO) body parts must remain unchanged, never added to, or deleted. The Geolocation-Error header field must be included in the 424 response. It is only appropriate to generate a 424 response when the responding entity needs a locationValue and there are no values in the request that are usable by the responder, or when the responder has additional location information to provide. A 424 response must not be sent in response to a request that lacks a Geolocation header entirely, as the UA in that case may not support this extension at all. If a SIP intermediary inserted a locationValue into a SIP request where one was not previously present, it must take any and all responsibility for the corrective action if it receives a 424 response to a SIP request it sent. A 424 (Bad Location Information) response is a final response within a transaction and must not terminate an existing dialog (RFC 6442: Standards Track).
428 Use Identity Header	This response is sent when a verifier receives a SIP request that lacks an Identity header to indicate that the request should be re-sent with an Identity header (RFC 4474: Standards Track).
429 Provide Referror Identity	This response is used by a server to indicate that a Referred-By header field is to be re-sent with a valid Referred-By security token and the security token is carried by S/MIME message body (RFC 3892: Standards Track).
430 Flow Failed	This response code is used by an edge proxy to indicate to the authoritative proxy that a specific flow to a UA instance has failed. Other flows to the same instance could still succeed. The authoritative proxy should attempt to forward to another target (flow) with the same instance-id and AOR. End points should never receive a 430 Flow Failed response. If an end point receives a 430 Flow Failed response, it should treat it as a 400 Bad Request per normal procedures, as in of RFC 3261 (RFC 5626: Standards Track).
433 Anonymity Disallowed	This response indicates that the server refused to fulfill the request because the requestor was anonymous. Its default reason phrase is *Anonymity Disallowed* (RFC 5079: Standards Track).
436 Bad Identity-Info	This response is sent when the Identity-Info header contains a URI that cannot be dereferenced by the verifier (either the URI scheme is unsupported by the verifier, or the resource designated by the URI is otherwise unavailable) (RFC 4474: Standards Track).
437 Unsupported Certificate	This response is sent when the verifier cannot validate the certificate referenced by the URI of the Identity-Info header, because, for example, the certificate is self-signed, or signed by a root certificate authority for which the verifier does not possess a root certificate (RFC 4474: Standards Track).
438 Invalid Identity Header	This response is sent when the verifier receives a message with an Identity signature that does not correspond to the digest-string calculated by the verifier (RFC 4474: Standards Track).

(*Continued*)

Table 2.4 (Continued) SIP Response Messages

Response Message	*Description*
439 First Hop Lacks Outbound Support	This response code is used by a registrar to indicate that it supports the *outbound* feature described in this specification, but that the first outbound proxy that the user is attempting to register through does not. It should be noted that this response code is only appropriate in the case that the registering UA advertises support for outbound processing by including the outbound option tag in a Supported header field. Proxies must not send a 439 response to any requests that do not contain a *reg-id* parameter and an outbound option tag in a Supported header field (RFC 5626: Standards Track).
440 Max-Breadth Exceeded	If there is insufficient value set in the Max-Breadth header field to carry out a desired parallel forking, a proxy sends this response code. A client receiving a 440 Max-Breadth Exceeded response can infer that its request did not reach all possible destinations (RFC 5393: Standards Track).
469 Bad Info Package	If a UA receives an INFO request associated with an Info Package that the UA has not indicated willingness to receive, the UA must send a 469 Bad Info Package response, which contains a Recv-Info header field with Info Packages for which the UA is willing to receive INFO requests. The UA must not use the response to update the set of Info Packages, but simply to indicate the current set. In the terminology of multiple dialog usages defined in RFC 5057 (see Sections 3.6.6 and 16.2), this represents a Transaction-Only failure, and does not terminate the invite dialog usage. If a UA receives an INFO request associated with an Info Package, and the message-body part with Content-Disposition *Info-Package* has a MIME type that the UA supports but not in the context of that Info Package, it is recommended that the UA send a 415 Unsupported Media Type response. The UA may send other error responses, such as Request Failure (4xx), Server Failure (5xx), and Global Failure (6xx), in accordance with the error-handling procedures defined in RFC 3261. Otherwise, if the INFO request is syntactically correct and well structured, the UA must send a 200 OK response. It should be noted that if the application needs to reject the information that it received in an INFO request, it needs to be done on the application level. That is, the application needs to trigger a new INFO request that contains information that the previously received application data was not accepted. Individual Info Package specifications need to describe the details for such procedures (RFC 6086: Standards Track).
480 Temporarily Unavailable	The callee's end system was contacted successfully but the callee is currently unavailable (e.g., is not logged in, logged in but in a state that precludes communication with the callee, or has activated the *do not disturb* feature). The response may indicate a better time to call in the Retry-After header field. The user could also be available elsewhere (unbeknownst to this server). The reason phrase should indicate a more precise cause as to why the callee is unavailable. This value should be settable by the UA. Status 486 (Busy Here) may be used to more precisely indicate a particular reason for the call failure. This status is also returned by a redirect or proxy server that recognizes the user identified by the Request-URI, but does not currently have a valid forwarding location for that user (RFC 3261: Standards Track).
481 Dialog/ Transaction Does Not Exist	This status indicates that the UAS received a request that does not match any existing dialog or transaction (RFC 3261: Standards Track).
482 Loop Detected	The server has detected a loop. It means that the request has been routed back to the server that previously forwarded the same request message (RFC 3261: Standards Track).
483 Too Many Hops	The server received a request that contains a Max-Forwards header field with the value zero (RFC 3261: Standards Track).
484 Address Incomplete	The server received a request with a Request-URI that was incomplete. Additional information should be provided in the reason phrase. This status code allows overlapped dialing. With overlapped dialing, the client does not know the length of the dialing string. It sends strings of increasing lengths, prompting the user for more input, until it no longer receives a 484 Address Incomplete status response (RFC 3261: Standards Track).

(*Continued*)

Table 2.4 (Continued) SIP Response Messages

Response Message	*Description*
485 Ambiguous	The Request-URI was ambiguous. The response may contain a listing of possible unambiguous addresses in Contact header fields. Revealing alternatives can infringe on the privacy of the user or the organization. It must be possible to configure a server to respond with status 404 Not Found or to suppress the listing of possible choices for ambiguous Request-URIs. Example response to a request with the Request-URI: sip:lee@example.com:SIP/2.0 485 Ambiguous Contact: Carol Lee <sip:carol.lee@example.com> Contact: Ping Lee <sip:p.lee@example.com> Contact: Lee M. Foote <sips:lee.foote@example.com> The e-mail and voice-mail systems provide this functionality. A status code separate from 3xx is used since the semantics are different: for 300, it is assumed that the same person or service will be reached by the choices provided. While an automated choice or sequential search makes sense for a 3xx response, user intervention is required for a 485 Ambiguous response (RFC 3261: Standards Track).
486 Busy Here	The callee's end system was contacted successfully, but the callee is currently not willing or able to take additional calls at this end system. The response may indicate a better time to call in the Retry-After header field. The user could also be available elsewhere, such as through a voice-mail service. Status 600 Busy Everywhere should be used if the client knows that no other end system will be able to accept this call (RFC 3261: Standards Track).
470 Consent Needed Response	A 470 Consent Needed response indicates that the request that triggered the response contained a URI list with at least one URI for which the relay had no permissions. A UAS generating a 470 Consent Needed response should include a Permission-Missing header field in it. This header field carries the URI or URIs for which the relay had no permissions. A UAC receiving a 470 Consent Needed response without a Permission-Missing header field needs to use an alternative mechanism, for example, eXtension Markup Language (XML) Configuration Access Protocol (XCAP), to discover for which URI or URIs there were no permissions. A client receiving a 470 Consent Needed response uses a manipulation mechanism (e.g., XCAP) to add those URIs to the relay's list of URIs. The relay will obtain permissions for those URIs as usual (RFC 5360: Standards Track).
487 Request Terminated	The request was terminated by a BYE or CANCEL request. This response is never returned for a CANCEL request itself (RFC 3261: Standards Track).
488 Not Acceptable	The response has the same meaning as 606 Not Acceptable, but only applies to the specific resource addressed by the Request-URI and the request may succeed elsewhere. A message body containing a description of media capabilities may be present in the response, which is formatted according to the Accept header field in the INVITE (or application/SDP if not present), the same as a message body in a 200 OK response to an OPTIONS request (RFC 3261: Standards Track).
489 Bad Event	This response is used by a server to reject a subscription request or notification containing a Event package that is unknown or not supported by the server (RFC 6665: Standards Track).
491 Request Pending	The request was received by a UAS that had a pending request within the same dialog. This response can be used to resolve the *glare* situations (RFC 3261: Standards Track).
493 Request Undecipherable	The request was received by a UAS that contained an encrypted MIME body for which the recipient does not possess or will not provide an appropriate decryption key. This response may have a single body containing an appropriate public key that should be used to encrypt MIME bodies sent to this UA (RFC 3261: Standards Track).

(*Continued*)

Table 2.4 (Continued) SIP Response Messages

Response Message	*Description*
494 Security Agreement Required	A server receiving an unprotected request that contains a Require or Proxy-Require header field with the value *sec-agree* must respond to the client with a 494 Security Agreement Required response. The server must add a Security-Server header field to this response listing the security mechanisms that the server supports. The server must add its list to the response even if there are no common security mechanisms in the client's and server's lists. The server's list must not depend on the contents of the client's list. If *digest* is chosen, the 494 Security Agreement Required response will contain an HTTP Digest authentication challenge. The client must use the algorithm and quality-of-protection (qop) parameters in the Security-Server header field to replace the same parameters in the HTTP Digest challenge. The client must also use the digest-verify parameter in the Security-Verify header field to protect the Security-Server header field as specified in RFC 3329 (see Section 19.3) (RFC 3329: Standards Track).
Server Error (5xx): The Server Error (5xx) class of responses consists of sent failure responses given when a server itself has erred. The Retry-After header may be used with this class of response, indicating that the request may be sent after a certain period of time.	
500 Server Internal Error	The server encountered an unexpected condition that prevented it from fulfilling the request. The client may display the specific error condition and may retry the request after several seconds. If the condition is temporary, the server may indicate when the client may retry the request using the Retry-After header field (RFC 3261: Standards Track).
501 Not Implemented	The server does not support the functionality required to fulfill the request. This is the appropriate response when a UAS does not recognize the request method and is not capable of supporting it for any user. However, proxies forward all requests regardless of method. Note that a 405 Method Not Allowed is sent when the server recognizes the request method, but that method is not allowed or supported (RFC 3261: Standards Track).
502 Bad Gateway	The server, while acting as a gateway or proxy, received an invalid response from the downstream server it accessed in attempting to fulfill the request (RFC 3261: Standards Track).
503 Service Unavailable	The server is temporarily unable to process the request due to a temporary overloading or maintenance of the server. The server may indicate when the client should retry the request in a Retry-After header field. If no Retry-After is given, the client must act as if it had received a 500 Server Internal Error response. A client (proxy or UAC) receiving a 503 Service Unavailable should attempt to forward the request to an alternate server. It should not forward any other requests to that server for the duration specified in the Retry-After header field, if present. Servers may refuse the connection or drop the request instead of responding with 503 Service Unavailable (RFC 3261: Standards Track).
504 Gateway Timeout	The server did not receive a timely response from an external server it accessed in attempting to process the request. 408 Request Timeout should be used instead if there was no response within the period specified in the Expires header field from the upstream server (RFC 3261: Standards Track).
505 Version Not Supported	The server does not support, or refuses to support, the SIP version that was used in the request. The server is indicating that it is unable or unwilling to complete the request using the same major version as the client, other than with this error message (RFC 3261: Standards Track).
513 Message Too Long	The server was unable to process the request since the message length exceeded its capabilities (RFC 3261: Standards Track).
580 Precondition Failure	When a UAS acting as an answerer cannot or is not willing to meet the preconditions in the offer, it should reject the offer by returning a 580 Precondition-Failure response (RFC 3312: Standards Track).

(Continued)

Table 2.4 (Continued) SIP Response Messages

Response Message	*Description*
Global Failure (6xx): The Global Failure (6xx) class of responses indicates that a server has definitive information about a particular user, not just the particular instance indicated in the Request-URI.	
600 Busy Everywhere	The callee's end system was contacted successfully but the callee is busy and does not wish to take the call at this time. The response may indicate a better time to call in the Retry-After header field. If the callee does not wish to reveal the reason for declining the call, the callee uses status code 603 Decline instead. This status response is returned only if the client knows that no other end point (such as a voice-mail system) will answer the request. Otherwise, 486 Busy Here should be returned (RFC 3261: Standards Track).
603 Decline	The callee's machine was successfully contacted but the user explicitly does not wish to or cannot participate. The response may indicate a better time to call in the Retry-After header field. This status response is returned only if the client knows that no other end point will answer the request (RFC 3261: Standards Track).
604 Does Not Exist Anywhere	The server has authoritative information that the user indicated in the Request-URI does not exist anywhere (RFC 3261: Standards Track).

606 Not Acceptable	The UA was contacted successfully but some aspects of the session description such as the requested media, bandwidth, or addressing style were not acceptable. A 606 Not Acceptable response means that the user wishes to communicate, but cannot adequately support the session described. The 606 Not Acceptable response may contain a list of reasons in a Warning header field describing why the session described cannot be supported.
	A message body containing a description of media capabilities may be present in the response, which is formatted according to the Accept header field in the INVITE (or application/sap if not present), the same as a message body in a 200 OK response to an OPTIONS request.
	It is hoped that negotiation will not frequently be needed, and when a new user is being invited to join an already existing conference, negotiation may not be possible. It is up to the invitation initiator to decide whether or not to act on a 606 Not Acceptable response.
	This status response is returned only if the client knows that no other end point will answer the request. Received requests must adhere to the following guidelines for creation of a realm string for their server:
	• Realm strings must be globally unique. It is recommended that a realm string contain a host name or domain name, following the recommendation in RFC 2617 (see Section 19.4.5).
	• Realm strings should present a human-readable identifier that can be rendered to a user.
	For example:
	`INVITE sip:bob@biloxi.com SIP/2.0`
	`Authorization: Digest realm="biloxi.com", <...>`
	Generally, SIP authentication is meaningful for a specific realm, a protection domain. Thus, for Digest authentication, each such protection domain has its own set of user names and passwords. If a server does not require authentication for a particular request, it may accept a default user name, *anonymous*, which has no password (password of ""). Similarly, UACs representing many users, such as PSTN gateways, may have their own device-specific user name and password, rather than accounts for particular users, for their realm.
	While a server can legitimately challenge most SIP requests, there are two requests defined by this document that require special handling for authentication: ACK and CANCEL (RFC 3261: Standards Track).

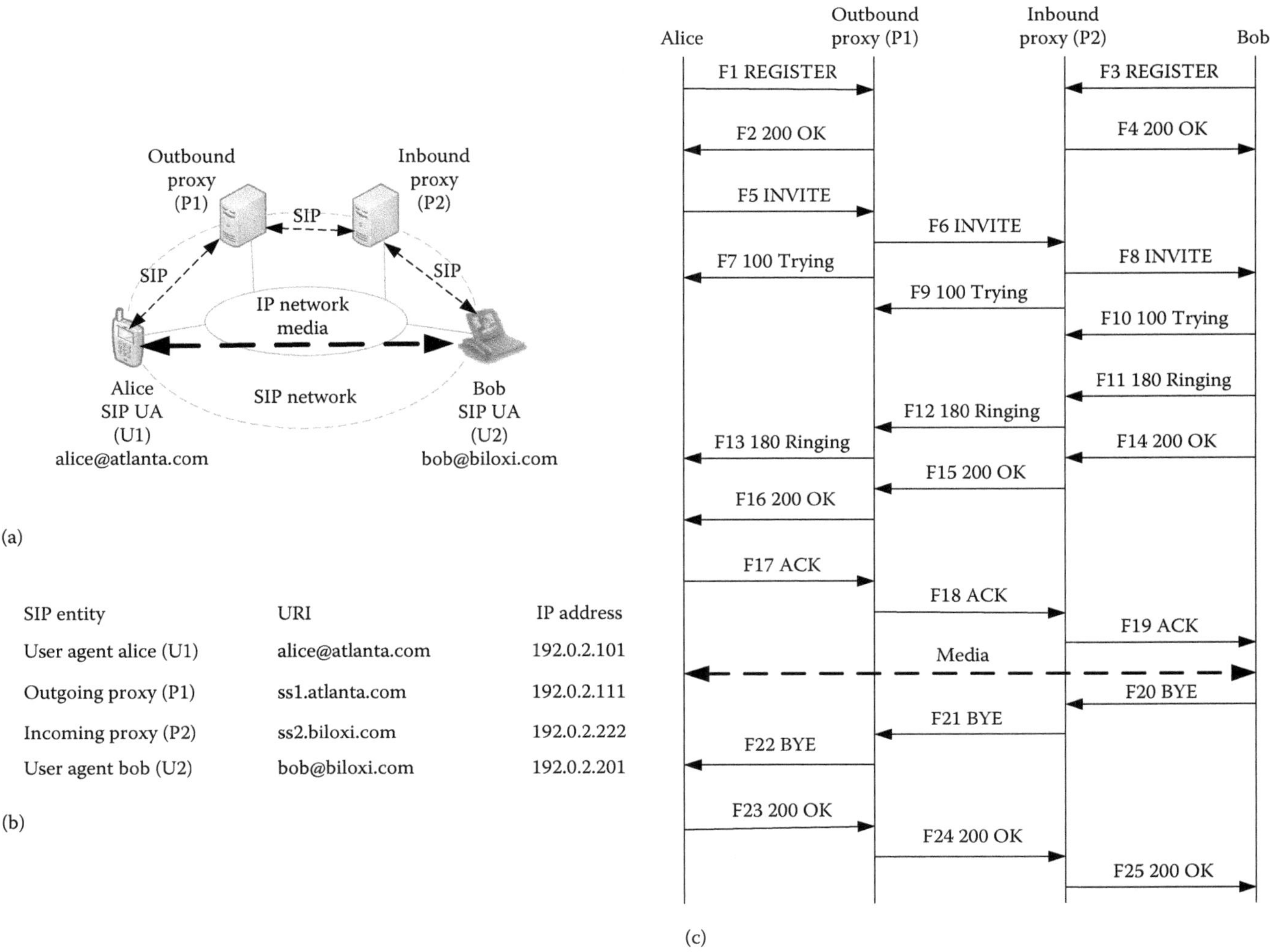

SIP entity	URI	IP address
User agent alice (U1)	alice@atlanta.com	192.0.2.101
Outgoing proxy (P1)	ss1.atlanta.com	192.0.2.111
Incoming proxy (P2)	ss2.biloxi.com	192.0.2.222
User agent bob (U2)	bob@biloxi.com	192.0.2.201

(b)

Figure 2.6 SIP network with trapezoid operation with signaling and media: (a) SIP network with two UAs and two proxies with SIP trapezoid operation, (b) URIs and IP addresses for SIP entities, and (c) SIP session establishment and termination.

establish the call via the proxy (P1) residing in its own administrative domain with Bob who is residing in the biloxi.com administrative domain. Consequently, we designate the proxy server of the atlanta.com domain as the outgoing proxy (P1) and the proxy of the biloxi.com as the incoming proxy (P2). First, the SIP signaling path is created between Alice's phone, outgoing proxy, incoming proxy, and Bob's phone for establishment of the session. Then, the media is passed between the phones directly and the human users, Alice and Bob, communicate among themselves using their phones. We are assuming that the proxy servers will also act as the registration servers for their users in the respective domains. Figure 2.6b shows the URIs and IP addresses of the SIP entities over the network.

Figure 2.6c shows an example of SIP call flows for registration of users along with establishment and termination of a session between two SIP UAs using an outgoing and incoming proxy. In the beginning, Alice registers with the proxy of her administrative domain sending a REGISTER (F1) request, and SIP server (P1) confirms the request with positive response of 200 OK (F2). In this way, the SIP server (P1) knows about the addresses of all phones in its administrative domain through registration of all users. Similarly, Bob also registers his phone with the proxy server (P2) of his administrative domain sending the REGISTER (F3) request and the servers confirms his registration sending 200 OK (F4) response. We have discussed about the location server in Section 2.4.4.3.4; however, this is not shown in Figure 2.6 for simplicity. It is quite logical that the SIP servers of both administrative domains can store all addresses of the phones in the location server that acts as the global database for all addresses of the phones if a business relationship between these domains exists. In this way, both P1 and P2 proxy servers can resolve the addresses of the cross-domain phone numbers when calls need to be routed between different administrative domains.

In the SIP signaling protocol, if Alice needs to place a call to Bob, she has to send an INVITE (F5) request that contains Bob's phone URI among other information to her outgoing proxy (P2). The proxy server (P2) examines the destination address after querying the location server database, as the destination address does not reside in its local registration database (not shown in Figure 2.6 for simplicity), and finds that the callee (Bob) remains in a separate atlanta.com administrative domain. Thus, the proxy server (P1) forwards the INVITE (F6) to the incoming proxy server (P2), and it also confirms the receipt of the INVITE (F5) sending a provisional 100 Trying (F7) hop-by-hop response to the caller (Alice). Receiving the INVITE (F6) message, the incoming proxy (P2) consults its local registration database and finds that the callee (Bob) remains in its administrative domain and forwards the INVITE (F8) to the callee (Bob), and also sends a provisional 100 Trying (F9) hop-by-hop response to the incoming proxy (P1).

Receiving the INVITE (F8) message, the callee (Bob) immediately sends a provisional 100 Trying (F10) hop-by-hop response to the incoming proxy (P2). If 100 Trying responses (F7, F9, and F10) are not sent, the senders will continue to retransmit the request after certain time intervals when timers expire, as the process of an INVITE message usually takes a substantial amount of time. In the meantime, the phone of the callee (Bob) generates the ringtone for altering the callee (Bob) and sends the 180 Ringing (F11) message to the incoming proxy (P2). In turn, P2 forwards the 180 Ringing (F12) message to P1; P1 then sends the 180 Ringing (F13) message to the caller (Alice); and the caller (Alice) starts to hear that the phone of the callee (Bob) is ringing.

In this example, we have shown that the callee (Bob) has accepted the call without further negotiations with respect to audio/video codecs or data applications and their corresponding performances, and the callee (Bob) answers the call. The callee (Bob) chooses the audio/video codec or data application parameter used in the call by the caller (Alice) and sends a final 200 OK (F14) response back to the incoming proxy (P2), and then P2 forwards the 200 OK (F15) response to P1, and P1 forwards the 200 OK (F16) response to the caller (Alice). The caller (Alice) acknowledges this for reliability purposes by sending the ACK (F17) message to P1, and P1 forwards the ACK (F18) to P2, and P2 forwards the ACK (19) to the callee (Bob). It should be noted that the ACK message can be sent directly end-to-end between the UAs without going via the proxies. At this point in time, the session is established and both phones begin to exchange media (audio/video over RTP or data applications using respective application protocols).

At the end of the session, either party can decide to terminate the session by sending the BYE request. In this example, the callee (Bob) sends the BYE (F20) request to P2, and P2 forwards the BYE (F21) request to P1, and then P1 forwards the BYE (F22) request to the caller (Alice). Like ACK, the BYE message can also be sent directly end-to-end between the UAs without going via the proxies. In turn, the caller (Alice) sends the confirmation with the 200 OK (F23) response to P1, and P1 forwards the 200 OK (F24) response to P2, and finally P2 forwards it to the callee (Bob). Now the session has been terminated and media does not flow anymore. The call flows containing the SIP signaling message path and media path complete as the logical trapezoid path, as shown in Figure 2.6a.

The SIP session establishment and termination shown here is a simple one. We have not shown how a session can be modified and updated, nor the many other features for each of these audio, video, or data applications that a rich multimedia session can have. We have not dealt with any security features or QOS issues in this example. A call may fail due to failures in the network during the call setup or after establishment of the session, and the paths may be shaped differently than a trapezoid. Moreover, this is only a point-to-point call where only two users are involved. A multipoint conference call with multiple users and with multiple media of audio, video, or data applications will be much more complex. In the real world, even a point-to-point call is much more complicated, where a call may traverse over many more administrative domains with their different security and QOS features, a host of different administrative security policies, and middle boxes like network address translators, not to speak about different kinds of networks with different call control protocols. In the subsequent chapters, we will be describing many of those functional features.

2.8 SIP Header Fields

2.8.1 Overview

SIP header fields are mostly constructed following the HTTP/1.1 specifications in RFC 2616, although not all headers are used in SIP. We have described the general syntax for header fields in Section 2.4.1.2. Table 2.5 lists the full set of header fields along with notes on syntax, meaning, and usage.

The *Where* column of Table 2.5 describes the request and response types in which the header field can be used. Values in this column are given in Table 2.6.

The *Proxy* column of Table 2.5 describes the operations a proxy may perform on a header field shown in Table 2.7.

The next six columns of Table 2.5 relate to the presence of a header field in a method shown in Table 2.8.

Table 2.5 SIP Header Fields

Header Field	*Where*	*Proxy*	*ACK*	*BYE*	*CANCEL*	*INVITE*	*OPTIONS*	*REGISTER*	*REFER*	*UPDATE*	*SUBSCRIBE*	*NOTIFY*	*PUBLISH*	*MESSAGE*	*PRACK*	*INFO*
Accept	R	ar	–	o	–	o	m*	o	o	o	o	o	o	–	o	o
Accept	2xx		–	–	–	o	m*	o	–	o	–	–	–	–	–	–
Accept	415		–	c	–	c	c	c	c	c	o	o	m*	m*	c	o
Accept-Contact	R	ar	o	o	o	o	o	–		o	o	o		o	o	o
Accept-Encoding	R		–	o	–	o	o	o	o	o	o	o	o	–	o	o
Accept-Encoding	2xx		–	–	–	o	m*	o	–	o	–	–	–	–	–	o
Accept-Encoding	415		–	c	–	c	c	c	c	c	o	o	m*	m*	c	c
Accept-Language	R		–	o	–	o	o	o	o	o	o	o		–	o	o
Accept-Language	2xx		–	–	–	o	m*	o	–	o	–	–	–	–	–	o
Accept-Language	415		–	c	–	c	c	c	c	c	o	o	m*	m*	c	o
Accept-Resource-Priority	200	admr	–	o	o	o	o	o	o	o	o	o	o	o	o	o
Accept-Resource-Priority	417	admr	–	o	o	o	o	o	o	o	o	o	o	o	o	o
Alert-Info	R	ar	–	–	–	o	–	–	–	–	–	–		–	–	–
Alert-Info	180	ar	–	–	–	o	–	–	–	–	–	–		–	–	–
Alert-Info													–			
Allow	R		–	o	–	o	o	o	o	o	o	o	o	o	o	o
Allow	2xx		–	o	–	m*	m*	m*		o	o	o		o	o	–
Allow	r		–	o	–	o	o	o	o	o	o	o	o	o	o	o

(Continued)

Table 2.5 (Continued) SIP Header Fields

Header Field	*Where*	*Proxy*	*ACK*	*BYE*	*CANCEL*	*INVITE*	*OPTIONS*	*REGISTER*	*REFER*	*UPDATE*	*SUBSCRIBE*	*NOTIFY*	*PUBLISH*	*MESSAGE*	*PRACK*	*INFO*
Allow	405		–	m	–	m	m	m	m	m	m	m	m	m	m	m
Allow-Events	R		o	o	–	o	o	o	o	o	o	o	o			
Allow-Events	2xx		–	o	–	o	o	o	o	o	o	o				
Allow-Events	489		–	–	–	–	–	–	–	–	m	m	m			
Allow-Events	(1)									–						
Authentication-Info	2xx		–	o	–	o	o	o	o	o	o	o	o	o	o	o
Authorization	R		o	o	o	o	o	o	o	o	o	o	o	o	o	o
Call-ID	c	r	m	m	m	m	m	m	m	m	m	m	m	m	m	m
Call-Info		ar	–	–	–	o	o	o	–	o			o	o	–	o
Contact	R		o	–	–	m	o	o	m	m	m	m	–	–	–	–
Contact	1xx		–	–	–	o	–	–	–	o	o	o	–	–	–	
Contact	2xx		–	–	–	m	o	o	m	m	m	o	–	–	–	
Contact	3xx	d	–	o	–	o	o	o		o	m	m	o	o	o	
Contact	3xx–6xx								o							
Contact	485		–	o	–	o	o	o		o	o	o	o	o	o	
Content-Disposition			o	o	–	o	o	o	o	o	o	o	o	o	o	o
Content-Encoding			o	o	–	o	o	o	o	o	o	o	o	o	o	o
Content-Language			o	o	–	o	o	o	o	o	o	o	o	o	o	o
Content-Length		ar	t	t	t	t	t	t	o	t	t	t	t	t	t	o
Content-Type			*	*	–	*	*	*	*	*	*	*	*	*	*	*
CSeq	c	c	m	m	m	m	m	m	m	m	m	m	m	m	m	m

(Continued)

Table 2.5 (Continued) SIP Header Fields

Header Field	*Where*	*Proxy*	*ACK*	*BYE*	*CANCEL*	*INVITE*	*OPTIONS*	*REGISTER*	*REFER*	*UPDATE*	*SUBSCRIBE*	*NOTIFY*	*PUBLISH*	*MESSAGE*	*PRACK*	*INFO*
Date		a	o	o	o	o	o	o	o	o	o	o	o	o	o	o
Encryption (+)								o								
Error-Info	300-699	a	–	o	o	o	o	o	o		o	o	o	o	o	o
Event	R		–	–	–	–	–	–	–	–	m	m	m			
Expires			–	–	–	o	–	o		–	o	–	o		–	–
Expires	R								o					o		
Expires	2xx										m	–				
Flow-Timer	r							o								
From	c	r	m	m	m	m	m	m	m	m	m	m	m	m	m	m
Geolocation	R		o	o	o	o	o	o	o	o	o	o	o	o	o	o
Geolocation-Routing			o	o	o	o	o	o	o	o	o	o	o	o	o	
Geolocation-Error	r		o	o	o	o	o	o	o	o	o	o	o	o	o	o
Hide (+)	R		o	o	o	o	o	o								
History-Info		admr	–	–	–	o	o	o	o	–	o	o	–	o	–	
Identity	R	a	o	o	o	–	o	o	o	o	o	o	o			
Identity-Info	R	a	o	o	o	–	o	o	o	o	o	o	o			
Info-Package	R	–	–	–	–	–	–	–	–	–	–	–	–	–	–	m1
In-Reply-To	R		–	–	–	o	–	–		–	–	–	–	o	–	
In-Reply-To									–							
Join	R		–	–	–	o	–	–	–	–	–	–	–	–	–	–
Max-Breadth	R															–
Max-Forwards	R	amr	m	m	m	m	m	m	m	m	m	m	m	m	m	m

(Continued)

Table 2.5 (Continued) SIP Header Fields

Header Field	*Where*	*Proxy*	*ACK*	*BYE*	*CANCEL*	*INVITE*	*OPTIONS*	*REGISTER*	*REFER*	*UPDATE*	*SUBSCRIBE*	*NOTIFY*	*PUBLISH*	*MESSAGE*	*PRACK*	*INFO*
Min-Expires	423		–	–	–	–	–	m	–	–	m	–	m		–	–
Min-SE	R	amr	–	–	–	o	–	–	–	o	–	–	–	–	–	
Min-SE	422		–	–	–	m	–	–	–	m	–	–	–	–	–	
MIME-Version			o	o	–	o	o	o		o	o	o	o		o	o
Organization		ar	–	–	–	o	o	o	o	o	o	–	o	o	–	–
P-Access-Network-Info		ad	–	–	o	–	o	o	o	o	o	o		o	o	
P-Asserted-Identity		adr	–	o	–	o	o	–	o	–	o	o			–	
P-Asserted-Service	R	admr	–	–	–	o	o	–	o	–	o	–	o	o	–	
P-Associated-URI	2xx		–	–	–	–	–	o	–	–	–	–		–	–	
Path	R	ar	–	–	–	–	–	o								
Path	2xx		–	–	–	–	–	o								
P-Called-Party-ID	R	amr	–	–	–	o	o	–	o	–	o	–		o	–	
P-Charging-Function-Addresses		adr	–	o	–	o	o	o	o	o	o	o		o	o	
P-Charging-Vector		admr	–	o	–	o	o	o	o	o	o	o		o	o	
P-Early-Media	R	amr	–	–	–	o	–	–		o					o	
P-Early-Media	18x	amr	–	–	–	o	–	–		–					–	
P-Early-Media	2xx	amr	–	–	–	–	–	–		o					o	
Permission-Missing	470	amr				o			o		o		o	o		

(Continued)

Table 2.5 (Continued) SIP Header Fields

Header Field	*Where*	*Proxy*	*ACK*	*BYE*	*CANCEL*	*INVITE*	*OPTIONS*	*REGISTER*	*REFER*	*UPDATE*	*SUBSCRIBE*	*NOTIFY*	*PUBLISH*	*MESSAGE*	*PRACK*	*INFO*
P-Preferred-Identity		adr	–	o	–	o	o	–	o	–	o	o			–	
P-Preferred-Service	R	dr	–	–	–	o	o	–	o	–	o	–	o	o	–	
P-Profile-Key	R	admr						o								
P-Served-User	R	admr						o								
P-User-Database	R	admr						o								
Priority	R	ar	–	–	–	o	–	–	–	–	o	–	o	o	–	–
Privacy		admr	o	o	o	o	o	o	o	o	o	o	o	o	o	o
Proxy-Authenticate	407	ar	–	m	–	m	m	m	m	m	m	m	m	m	m	m
Proxy-Authenticate	401	ar	–	o	o	o	o	o	o	o			o	o	o	o
Proxy-Authorization	R	dr	o	o	–	o	o	o	o	o	o	o	o	o	o	o
Proxy-Require	R	ar	–	o	–	o	o	o	o	o	o	o	o	o	o	o
P-Visited-Network-ID	R	ad	–	–	–	o	o	o	o	–	o	–		o	–	
RAck	R		–	–	–	–	–	–	–	–	–	–			m	
Reason	R	a		o	o											o
Recv-Info	R	–	–	–	–	m	–	o	–	o	–	–	–	–	o	–
Recv-Info	2xx	–	–	–	–	o2	–	–	–	o2	–	–	–	–	o3	–
Recv-Info	1xx	–	–	–	–	o2	–	–		–	–	–	–	–	–	–
Recv-Info	469	–	–	–	–	–	–	–	–	–	–	–	–	–	–	m1
Recv-Info	r	–	–	–	–	o	–	–	–	o	–	–	–	–	o	–

(Continued)

Table 2.5 (Continued) SIP Header Fields

Header Field	*Where*	*Proxy*	*ACK*	*BYE*	*CANCEL*	*INVITE*	*OPTIONS*	*REGISTER*	*REFER*	*UPDATE*	*SUBSCRIBE*	*NOTIFY*	*PUBLISH*	*MESSAGE*	*PRACK*	*INFO*
Record-Route	R	ar	o	o	o	o	o	–	o	o	o	o			o	o
Record-Route	2xx, 18x	mr	–	o	o	o	o	–	o	o	o	o			o	
Record-Route													–			
Record-Route		ar												–		
Refer-Sub	R, 2xx		–	–	–	–	–		o	–	–	–	–	–	–	
Refer-To	R		–	–	–	–	–	–	m	–				o	–	
Referred-By	R	ar	–	o	–	o	o	o								o
Reject-Contact	R		o	o	o	o	o	–		o	o	o		o	o	
Replaces	R		–	–	–	o	–	–	–	–	–	–	–	–	–	–
Reply-To			–	–	–	o	–	–	–		–	–	–		–	
Request-Disposition	R	ar	o	o	o	o	o	o		o	o	o		o	o	o
Require		ar	–	c	–	c	c	c	c	c	o	o	o	c	c	o
Resource-Priority	R	admr	o	o	o	o	o	o	o	o	o	o	o	o	o	o
Response-Key																
Retry-After	404, 413, 480, 486		–	o	o	o	o	o	o	o	o	o	o	o	o	o
	500, 503		–	o	o	o	o	o	o	o	o	o	o	o	o	o
	600, 603		–	o	o	o	o	o	o	o	o	o	o	o	o	o

(Continued)

Table 2.5 (Continued) SIP Header Fields

Header Field	*Where*	*Proxy*	*ACK*	*BYE*	*CANCEL*	*INVITE*	*OPTIONS*	*REGISTER*	*REFER*	*UPDATE*	*SUBSCRIBE*	*NOTIFY*	*PUBLISH*	*MESSAGE*	*PRACK*	*INFO*
Route	R	adr	c	c	c	c	c	c	c	c	c	c	c	o		o
RSeq			–	–	–	o	–	–	–	–	o	o				
Security-Client	R	adr		o		o	o	o		o	o	o		o		o
Security-Server	421, 494			o		o	o	o		o	o	o		o		o
Security-Verify	R	adr		o		o	o	o		o	o	o		o		o
Server	r		–	o	o	o	o	o		o	o	o	o	o		o
Service-Route	2xx	ar						o								
Session-Expires	R	amr	–	–	–	o	–	–	–	o	–	–	–	–	–	
Session-Expires	2xx	ar	–	–	–	o	–	–	–	o	–	–	–	–	–	
SIP-ETag	2xx		–	–	–	–	–	–	–	–	–	–	m	–	–	–
SIP-If-Match	R		–	–	–	–	–	–	–	–	–	–	o	–	–	–
Subject	R		–	–	–	o	–	–	–	–	–	–	o	o	–	o
Subscription-State	R		–	–	–	–	–	–	–	–	–	m				
Supported	R		–	o	o	m*	o	o	o	o	o	o	o		o	o
Supported	2xx		–	o	o	m*	m*	o	o	o	o	o	o		o	o
Suppress-If-Match	R										o					
Target-Dialog	R	–	–	–	–	o	–	–	o	–	o	–	–	–	–	
Timestamp				o	o	o	o	o	o	o	o	o	o	o	o	o
To	c(1)	r	m	m	m	m	m	m	m	m	m	m	m	m	m	m

(Continued)

Table 2.5 (Continued) SIP Header Fields

Header Field	*Where*	*Proxy*	*ACK*	*BYE*	*CANCEL*	*INVITE*	*OPTIONS*	*REGISTER*	*REFER*	*UPDATE*	*SUBSCRIBE*	*NOTIFY*	*PUBLISH*	*MESSAGE*	*PRACK*	*INFO*
Trigger-Consent	R	amr				o			o		o		o	o		
Unsupported	420		–	m	–	m	m	m	o	m	o	o	o		m	o
User-Agent			o	o	o	o	o	o	o	o	o	o	o		o	o
Via	c								m	m	m	m			m	
Via	c(2)								m							
Via	R	amr	m	m	m	m	m	m		m			m	m		m
Via	rc	dr	m	m	m	m	m	m		m			m	m		
Warning	r		–	o	o	o	o	o	o	o	o	o	o	o	o	o
WWW-Authenticate	401	ar	–	m	–	m	m	m	m	m	m	m	m	m	m	m
WWW-Authenticate	407	ar	–	o	–	o	o	o	o	o			o	o		o

Table 2.6 Notation and Description of the *Where* Column of Table 2.5

Notation	*Description*
R	Header field may only appear in requests.
r	Header field may only appear in responses.
2xx, 4xx, etc.	A numerical value or range indicating response codes with which the header field can be used.
c	Header field is copied from the request to the response.

Note: An empty cell in the Where column indicates that the header field may be present in all requests and responses.

Table 2.7 Notation and Description of the *Proxy* Column of Table 2.5

Notation	*Description*
a	A proxy can add or concatenate the header field if not present.
m	A proxy can modify an existing header field value.
d	A proxy can delete a header field value.
r	A proxy must be able to read the header field, and thus this header field cannot be encrypted.

Table 2.8 Notation and Description (ACK/BYE/CANCEL/INVITE/OPTIONS/REGISTER/REFER/UPDATE/SUBSCRIBE/NOTIFY/PUBLISH/MESSAGE/PRACK/INFO) Column of Table 2.5

Notation	*Description*
c	Conditional; requirements on the header field depend on the context of the message.
m	The header field is mandatory.
m*	The header field should be sent, but clients/servers need to be prepared to receive messages without that header field.
o	The header field is optional.
t	The header field should be sent, but clients/servers need to be prepared to receive messages without that header field.
1	Not applicable to INFO requests and responses associated with legacy INFO usages.
2	Mandatory in at least one reliable 18x/2xx response, if sent, to the INVITE request, if the associated INVITE request contained a Recv-Info header field.
3	Mandatory if the associated request contained a Recv-Info header field.

If a stream-based protocol (such as TCP) is used as a transport, then the header field must be sent. Some special notations used in Table 2.5 are described in Table 2.9.

Optional means that an element may include the header field in a request or response, and a UA may ignore the header field if present in the request or response. The exception to this rule is the Require header field. A *mandatory* header field must be present in a request, and must be understood by the UAS receiving the request. A mandatory response header field must be present in the response, and the header field must be understood by the UAC processing the response. *Not applicable* means that the header field must not be present in a request. If one is placed in a request by mistake, it must be ignored by the UAS receiving the request. Similarly, a header field labeled not applicable for a response means that the UAS must not place the header field in the response, and the UAC must ignore the header field in the response.

Table 2.9 Special Notation and Description of All Columns of Table 2.5

Notation	Description
*	The header field is required if the message body is not empty.
–	The header field is not applicable.
(1)	Copied with possible addition of tag.
(+)	Used by RFC 2543 but not supported by RFC 3261 that obsoletes RFC 2543.

A UA should ignore extension header parameters that are not understood.

A compact form of some common header field names is also defined for use when overall message size is an issue.

The Contact, From, and To header fields contain a URI. If the URI contains a comma, question mark, or semicolon, the URI must be enclosed in angle brackets (< and >). Any URI parameters are contained within these brackets. If the URI is not enclosed in angle brackets, any semicolon-delimited parameters are header parameters, not URI parameters.

2.8.2 Header-Field Descriptions

SIP header fields that are used in different SIP methods that may or may not contain message bodies can be categorized on the basis of their usages as follows:

1. Request and Response
2. Request
3. Response
4. Message Body

In addition, some of the header fields can be modified including insertion by the SIP proxy. Table 2.10 describes the SIP header fields briefly. However, ABNF syntaxes of these headers are defined earlier in Section 2.4.1.2.

2.9 SIP Tags

The *tag* parameter is used in the To and From header fields of SIP messages. It serves as a general mechanism to identify a dialog, which is the combination of the Call-ID along with two tags, one from each participant in the dialog. When a UA sends a request outside of a dialog, it contains a From tag only, providing half of the dialog ID. The dialog is completed from the response(s), each of which contributes the second half in the To header field. The forking of SIP requests means that multiple dialogs can be established from a single request. This also explains the need for the two-sided dialog identifier; without a contribution from the recipients, the originator could not disambiguate the multiple dialogs established from a single request. When a tag is generated by a UA for insertion into a request or response, it must be globally unique and cryptographically random with at least 32 bits of randomness. A property of this selection requirement is that a UA will place a different tag into the From header of an INVITE than it would place into the To header of the response to the same INVITE. This is needed in order for a UA to invite itself to a session, a common case for *hairpinning* of calls in public switched telephone network (PSTN) gateways. Similarly, two INVITEs for different calls will have different From tags, and two responses for different calls will have different To tags.

Besides the requirement for global uniqueness, the algorithm for generating a tag is implementation specific. Tags are helpful in fault-tolerant systems, where a dialog is to be recovered on an alternate server after a failure. A UAS can select the tag in such a way that a backup can recognize a request as part of a dialog on the failed server, and therefore determine that it should attempt to recover the dialog and any other state associated with it. SIP has some support for expression of capabilities. The Allow, Accept, Accept-Language, and Supported header fields convey some information about the capabilities of a UA. However, these header fields convey only a small part of the information that is needed. They do not provide a general framework for expression of capabilities. Furthermore, they only specify capabilities indirectly; the header fields really indicate the capabilities of the UA as they apply to this request. SIP also has no ability to convey characteristics, that is, information that describes a UA.

2.10 SIP Option Tags

Option tags are unique identifiers used to designate new options (extensions) in SIP. These tags are used in the Require, Proxy-Require, Supported, and Unsupported header fields defined in RFC 3261 (see Section 2.8). Note that these options appear as parameters in those header fields in an option-tag = token form for the definition of token defined in RFC 3261 (see Section 2.4.1). Option tags are defined in Standards Track RFCs. This is a change from past practice, and is instituted to ensure continuing multivendor

Table 2.10 SIP Header Field Descriptions

Header Field/RFC/Header Field Type	*Description*
Accept/RFC 3261 (Standards Track)/Request and Response	The Accept header field follows the syntax defined in Section 2.4.1.2. The semantics are also identical, with the exception that if no Accept header field is present, the server should assume a default value of application/SDP. An empty Accept header field means that no formats are acceptable. Accept: application/sdp;level=1, application/x-private, text/html

Accept-Contact/RFC 3841 (Standards Track)/Request	The Accept-Contact header field allows the UAC to specify that a UA should be contacted if it matches some or all of the values of the header field. Each value of the Accept-Contact header field contains a *, and is parameterized by a set of feature parameters. Any UA whose capabilities match the feature set described by the feature parameters matches the value. In fact, it defines some additional parameters for Contact header fields such as media, duplex, and language, indicating some preferences of the caller. Despite the ABNF, there must not be more than one req-param or explicit-param in an ac-params. Furthermore, there can only be one instance of any feature tag in feature-param. Example:
	
	`Accept-Contact: *;audio;require`
	`Accept-Contact: *;video;explicit`
	`Accept-Contact: *;methods="BYE";class="business";q=1.0`

Accept-Encoding/RFC 3261 (Standards Track)/Request and Response	The Accept-Encoding header field is similar to Accept, but restricts the content-codings defined in Section 3.5 of RFC 2616 (obsoleted by RFCs 7230–7235) that are acceptable in the response. See Section 14.3 of RFC 2616. The semantics in SIP are identical to those defined in Section 14.3 of RFC 2616. An empty Accept-Encoding header field is permissible. It is equivalent to Accept-Encoding: identity, that is, only the identity encoding, meaning no encoding, is permissible. If no Accept-Encoding header field is present, the server should assume a default value of identity. This differs slightly from the HTTP definition, which indicates that when not present, any encoding can be used, but the identity encoding is preferred. Example: `Accept-Encoding: gzip`
Accept-Language/RFC 3261 (Standards Track)/Request and Response	The Accept-Language header field is used in requests to indicate the preferred languages for reason phrases, session descriptions, or status responses carried as message bodies in the response. If no Accept-Language header field is present, the server should assume all languages are acceptable to the client. The Accept-Language header field follows the syntax defined in Section 14.4 of RFC 2616 (obsoleted by RFCs 7230–7235). The rules for ordering the languages based on the *q* parameter apply to SIP as well. Example: `Accept-Language: da, en-gb;q=0.8, en;q=0.7`
Accept-Resource-Priority/RFC 4412 (Standards Track)/Response	The Accept-Resource-Priority response header field enumerates the resource values (r-values) a SIP UAS is willing to process. (This does not imply that a call with such values will find sufficient resources and succeed.) Some administrative domains may choose to disable the use of the Accept-Resource-Priority header for revealing too much information about that domain in responses. However, this behavior is not recommended, as this header field aids in troubleshooting.

(Continued)

Table 2.10 (Continued) SIP Header Field Descriptions

<table>
<tr><th>Header Field/RFC/Header Field Type</th><th>Description</th></tr>
<tr><td>Alert-Info/RFC 3261 (Standards Track)/Request and Response</td><td>
When present in an INVITE request, the Alert-Info header field specifies an alternative ringtone to the UAS. When present in a 180 Ringing response, the Alert-Info header field specifies an alternative ringback tone to the UAC. A typical usage is for a proxy to insert this header field to provide a distinctive ring feature. The Alert-Info header field can introduce security risks. These risks and the ways to handle them are discussed in Section 19.6.4, which discusses the Call-Info header field since the risks are identical. In addition, a user should be able to disable this feature selectively. This helps prevent disruptions that could result from the use of this header field by untrusted elements. Example:
<pre>Alert-Info: http://www.example.com/sounds/moo.wav</pre>
RFC 7463 registers the SIP header field defining a new parameter as shown below through IANA registration:
<table>
<tr><th>Header Field</th><th>Parameter Name</th><th>Predefined Values</th><th>Reference</th></tr>
<tr><td>Alert-Info</td><td>appearance</td><td>No</td><td>RFC 7463</td></tr>
</table>
RFC 7462: URNs for the SIP Alert-Info Header Field.
SIP RFC 3261 supports the capability to provide a reference to a specific rendering to be used by the UA as an alerting signal (e.g., a ringtone or ringback tone) when the user is alerted. This is done using the Alert-Info header field. However, the reference (typically a URL) addresses only a specific network resource with specific rendering properties. However, RFC 3261 currently has no support for standard identifiers for describing the semantics of the alerting situation or the characteristics of the alerting signal, without being tied to a particular rendering. RFC 7462 that is described here overcomes these limitations and supports new applications, a new family of URNs for use in Alert-Info header fields (and situations with similar requirements) normatively updating RFC 3261. This specification changes the usage of the Alert-Info header field defined in RFC 3261 by additionally allowing its use in any non-100 provisional response to INVITE. RFC 7462 also permits proxies to add or remove an Alert-Info header field and to add or remove Alert-Info header field values.
1. Updates to RFC 3261
1.1. Allow Alert-Info in Provisional Responses
This specification changes the usage of the Alert-Info header field defined in RFC 3261 by additionally allowing its use in any non-100 provisional response to INVITE. Previously, the Alert-Info header field was only permitted in 180 Ringing responses. However, in telephony, other situations indicated by SIP provisional responses, such as 181 Call Is Being Forwarded and 182 Call Is Being Queued, are often indicated by tones. Extending the applicability of the Alert-Info header field allows the telephony practice to be implemented in SIP. To support this change, the following paragraph replaces the first paragraph of RFC 3261 (see above):
<blockquote>When present in an INVITE request, the Alert-Info header field specifies an alternative ringtone to the UAS. When present in a non-100 provisional response, the Alert-Info header field specifies an alternative ringback tone to the UAC. A typical usage is for a proxy to insert this header field to provide a distinctive ring feature.</blockquote>
</td></tr>
</table>

(Continued)

Table 2.10 (Continued) SIP Header Field Descriptions

Header Field/RFC/Header Field Type	*Description*
	1.2. Proxies May Alter Alert-Info Header Fields A SIP proxy MAY add or remove an Alert-Info header field, and it may add or remove Alert-Info header field values, in a SIP request or a non-100 provisional response. 2. Use Cases This section describes some use cases for which the alert URN mechanism is needed today. 2.1. PBX Ringtones This section defines some commonly encountered ringtones on PBX or business phones. They are as listed in the following subsections. 2.1.1. Normal This tone indicates that the default or normal ringtone should be rendered. This is essentially a no-operation alert URN and should be treated by the UA as if no alert URN is present. This is most useful when Alert-Info header field parameters are being used. For example, in RFC 7463 (see Section 16.2.11), an Alert-Info header field needs to be present containing the appearance parameter, but no special ringtone needs to be specified. 2.1.2. External This tone is used to indicate that the caller is external to the enterprise or PBX system. This could be a call from the PSTN or from a SIP trunk. 2.1.3. Internal This tone is used to indicate that the caller is internal to the enterprise or PBX system. The call could have been originated from another user on this PBX or on another PBX within the enterprise. 2.1.4. Priority A PBX tone needs to indicate that a priority level alert should be applied for the type of alerting specified (e.g., internal alerting). 2.1.5. Short In this case, the alerting type specified (e.g., internal alerting) should be rendered shorter than normal. In contact centers, this is sometimes referred to as *abbreviated ringing* or a *zip tone*. 2.1.6. Delayed In this case, the alerting type specified should be rendered after a short delay. In some bridged-line/shared-line-appearance implementations, this is used so that the bridged line does not ring at exactly the same time as the main line but is delayed a few seconds. 2.2. Service Tones These tones are used to indicate specific PBX and public network telephony services. 2.2.1. Call Waiting The call-waiting service [TS24.615] permits a callee to be notified of an incoming call while the callee is engaged in an active or held call. Subsequently, the callee can either accept, reject, or ignore the incoming call. There is an interest on the caller side to be informed about the call-waiting situation on the callee side. Having this information, the caller can decide whether to continue waiting for callee to pick up or better to call some time later when it is estimated that the callee could have finished the ongoing conversation. To provide this information, a callee's UA (or proxy) that is aware of the call-waiting condition can add the call-waiting indication to the Alert-Info header field in the 180 Ringing response.

(*Continued*)

Table 2.10 (Continued) SIP Header Field Descriptions

Header Field/RFC/Header Field Type	*Description*
	2.2.2. Forward This feature is used in a 180 (Ringing) response when a call-forwarding feature has been initiated on an INVITE. Many PBX systems implement a forwarding *beep* followed by normal ringing to indicate this. Note that a 181 response can be used in place of this URN. 2.2.3. Transfer Recall This feature is used when a blind transfer (RFC 5589, see Section 16.2) has been performed by a server on behalf of the transferor and fails. Instead of failing the call, the server calls back the transferor, giving them another chance to transfer or otherwise deal with the call. This service tone is used to distinguish this INVITE from a normal incoming call. 2.2.4. Auto Callback This feature is used when a user has utilized a server to implement an automatic callback service (RFC 6910, see Section 16.2.12). When the user is available, the server calls back the user and utilizes this service tone to distinguish this INVITE from a normal incoming call. 2.2.5. Hold Recall This feature is used when a server implements a call hold timer on behalf of an end point. After a certain period of time of being on hold, the user who placed the call on hold is alerted to either retrieve the call or otherwise dispose of the call. This service tone is used to distinguish this case from a normal incoming call. 2.3. Country-Specific Ringback Tone Indications for the PSTN In the PSTN, different tones are used in different countries. End users are accustomed to hear the callee's country ringback tone and would like to have this feature for SIP. 3. URN Specification for the alert Namespace Identifier This section provides the registration template for the alert URN namespace identifier (NID) according to RFCs 2141 and 3406. Namespace ID: alert Registration Information: Registration version: 1 Registration date: 2014-12-10 Declared registrant of the namespace: Registering organization: Real-Time Applications and Infrastructure Area, IETF Designated contact: RAI Area Director Designated contact e-mail: rai-ads@ietf.org Declaration of syntactic structure: The Namespace Specific String (NSS) for the alert URNs is called an <alert-identifier> and has a hierarchical structure. The first colon-separated part after alert is called the <alert-category>; the parts to the right of that are <alert-ind-part>s, and together form the <alert-indication>. The general form is urn:alert:<alert-category>:<alert-indication>. The following <alert-category> identifiers are defined in this document: service, priority, source, duration, delay, and locale. The <alert-category> set can be extended in the future, either by standardization or by private action. The <alert-category>s describe distinct features of alerting signals. Any alert URN defined in this specification is syntactically valid for ring and ringback tones, and can be used in SIP INVITE requests or in provisional 1xx responses excepting the 100 response.

(Continued)

Table 2.10 (Continued) SIP Header Field Descriptions

Header Field/RFC/Header Field Type	*Description*

	The ABNF for the alert URNs is shown below defined by RFC 7462:
	`alert-URN = "urn:alert:" alert-identifier`
	`alert-identifier = alert-category ":" alert-indication`
	`alert-category = alert-name`
	`alert-indication = alert-ind-part *(":" alert-ind-part)`
	`alert-ind-part = alert-name`
	`alert-name = alert-label/private-name`
	`private-name = alert-label "@" provider`
	`provider = alert-label`
	`alert-label = let-dig [*let-dig-hyp let-dig]`
	`let-dig-hyp = let-dig/"-"`
	`let-dig = ALPHA/DIGIT`
	`ALPHA =%x41-5A/%x61-7A; A-Z/a-z`
	`DIGIT =%x30-39; 0-9`
	<alert-label>s must comply with the syntax for Non-reserved LDH labels (RFC 5890). Registered URNs and components thereof must be transmitted as registered (including case).
	Relevant ancillary documentation: RFC 7462
	Namespace considerations:
	This specification defines a URN namespace alert for URNs representing signals or renderings that are presented to users to inform them of events and actions. The initial usage is to specify ringtones and ringback tones when dialogs are established in SIP, but they can also be used for other communication-initiation protocols (e.g., H.323), and more generally, in any situation (e.g., web pages or end-point device software configurations) to describe how a user should be signaled.
	An alert URN does not describe a complete signal, but rather it describes a particular characteristic of the event it is signaling or a feature of the signal to be presented. The complete specification of the signal is a sequence of alert URNs specifying the desired characteristics/significance of the signal in priority order, with the most important aspects specified by the earlier URNs. This allows the sender of a sequence of URNs to compose very detailed specifications from a restricted set of URNs, and to clearly specify which aspects of the specification it considers most important.
	The initial scope of usage is in the Alert-Info header field, in initial INVITE requests (to indicate how the called user should be alerted regarding the call) and non-100 provisional (1xx) responses to those INVITE requests (to indicate the ringback, how the calling user should be alerted regarding the progress of the call).
	To ensure widespread adoption of these URNs for indicating ringtones and ringback tones, the scheme must allow replication of the current diversity of these tones. Currently, these tones vary between the PSTNs of different nations and between equipment supplied by different vendors. Thus, the scheme must accommodate national variations and proprietary extensions in a way that minimizes the information that is lost during interoperation between systems that follow different national variations or that are supplied by different vendors.
	The scheme allows definition of private-extension URNs that refine and extend the information provided by standard URNs. Private-extension URNs can also refine and extend the information provided by other private-extension URNs. Private extensions can also define entirely new categories of information about calls. We expect these extensions to be used extensively when existing PBX products are converted to support SIP operation.

(*Continued*)

Table 2.10 (Continued) SIP Header Field Descriptions

Header Field/RFC/Header Field Type	*Description*
	The device that receives an Alert-Info header field containing a sequence of alert URNs provides to the user a rendering that represents the semantic content of the URNs. The device is given great leeway in choosing the rendering, but it is constrained by rules that maximize interoperability between systems that support different sets of private extensions. In particular, earlier URNs in the sequence have priority of expression over later URNs in the sequence, and URNs that are not usable in their entirety (because they contain unknown extensions or are incompatible with previous URNs) are successively truncated in attempt to construct a URN that retains some information and is renderable in the context. Owing to the practical importance of private extensions for the adoption of URNs for alerting calls, and the very specific rules for private extensions and the corresponding processing rules that allow quality interoperation in the face of private extensions, the requirements of the alert URN scheme cannot be met by a fixed enumeration of URNs and corresponding meanings. In particular, the existing namespace *urn:ietf:params* does not suffice (unless the private-extension apparatus is applied to that namespace). There do not appear to be other URN namespaces that uniquely identify the semantic of a signal or rendering feature. Unlike most other currently registered URN namespaces, the alert URN does not identify documents and protocol objects (e.g., RFCs 3044, 3120, 3187, 3188, 4179, 4195, and 4198), types of telecommunications equipment (RFC 4152), people, or organizations (RFC 3043). The <alert-URN>s are hierarchical identifiers. An <alert-URN> asserts some fact or feature of the offered SIP dialog, or some fact or feature of how it should be presented to a user, or of how it is being presented to a user. Removing an <alert-ind-part> from the end of an <alert-URN> (which has more than one <alertind-part>) creates a shorter <alert-URN> with a less specific meaning; the set of dialogs to which the longer <alert-URN> applies is necessarily a subset of the set of dialogs to which the shorter <alert-URN> applies. (If the starting <alert-URN> contains only one <alert-ind-part>, and thus the <alert-ind-part> cannot be removed to make a shorter <alert-URN>, we can consider the set of dialogs to which the <alert-URN> applies to be a subset of the set of all dialogs.) The specific criteria defining the subset to which the longer <alert-URN> applies, within the larger set of dialogs, is considered to be the meaning of the final <alert-ind-part>. This meaning is relative to and depends on the preceding <alert- category> and <alert-ind-part>s (if any). The meanings of two <alert-ind-part>s that are textually the same but are preceded by different <alert-category>s or <alert-ind-part>s have no necessary connection. (An <alert-category> considered alone has no meaning in this sense.) The organization owning the <provider> within a <private-name> specifies the meaning of that <private-name> when it is used as an <alert-ind-part>. (The organization owning a <provider> is specified by the IANA registry.) The organization owning the <provider> within a <private-name> (in either an <alert-category> or an <alert-ind-part>) specifies the meaning of each <alert-ind-part>, which is an <alert-label> that follows that <private-name> and that precedes the next <alert-indpart>, which is a <private-name> (if any). The meaning of all other <alert-ind-part>s (i.e., those that are not <private-name>s and do not follow a <private-name>) is defined by standardization.

(Continued)

Table 2.10 (Continued) SIP Header Field Descriptions

Header Field/RFC/Header Field Type	*Description*
	Community considerations: The alert URNs are relevant to a large cross section of Internet users, namely those that initiate and receive communication connections via the SIP. These users include both technical and nontechnical users, on a variety of devices and with a variety of perception capabilities. The alert URNs will allow Internet users to receive more information about offered calls and enable them to better make decisions about accepting an offered call, and to get better feedback on the progress of a call they have made. User interfaces that utilize alternative sensory modes can better render the ring and ringback tones based on the alert URNs because the URNs provide more detailed information regarding the intention of communications than is provided by current SIP mechanisms. *Process of identifier assignment*: The assignment of standardized alert URNs is by insertion into the IANA registry. This process defines the meanings of <alert-ind-part>s that have standardized meanings, as described in "Namespace Considerations." A new URN must not be registered if it is equal by the comparison rules to an already registered URN. Private extensions are alert URNs that include <alert-ind-part>s that are <private-name>s and <alert-label>s that appear after a <private-name> (either as an <alert-category> or an <alertindication>). If such an <alert-ind-part> is a <private-name>, its meaning is defined by the organization that owns the <provider> that appears in the <private-name>. If the <alert-indpart> is an <alert-label>, its meaning is defined by the organization that owns the <provider> that appears in the closest <private-name> preceding the <alert-label>. The organization owning a <provider> is specified by the IANA registry. *Identifier uniqueness and persistence considerations*: An alert URN identifies a semantic feature of a call or a sensory feature of how the call alerting should be a rendered at the caller's or callee's end device. For standardized <alert-ind-part>s in URNs, uniqueness and persistence of their meanings is guaranteed by the fact that they are registered with IANA; the feature identified by a particular alert URN is distinct from the feature identified by any other standardized alert URN. Assuring uniqueness and persistence of the meanings of private extensions is delegated to the organizations that define private extension <alert-ind-part>s. The organization responsible for a particular <alert-ind-part> in a particular alert URN is the owner of a syntactically determined <provider> part within the URN. An organization should use only one <provider> value for all of the <private-name>s it defines. *Process for identifier resolution*: The process of identifier resolution is the process by which a rendering device chooses a rendering to represent a sequence of alert URNs. The device is allowed great leeway in making this choice, but the process must obey the rules defined this specification (RFC 7462). The device is expected to provide renderings that users associate with the meanings assigned to the URNs within their cultural context. A nonnormative example resolution algorithm is given in RFC 7462. Rules for lexical equivalence: alert URNs are compared according to case-insensitive string equality.

(Continued)

Table 2.10 (Continued) SIP Header Field Descriptions

Header Field/RFC/Header Field Type	*Description*
	Conformance with URN syntax: All alert URNs must conform to the ABNF in the "Declaration of Syntactic Structure" described earlier (also see Section 2.4.1). That ABNF is a subset of the generic URN syntax (RFC 2141). <alert-label>s are constrained to be Non-reserved LDH labels (RFC 5890), that is, ordinary ASCII labels. Future standardization may allow <alert-label>s that are A-labels (RFC 5890), and so interpreters of alert URNs must operate correctly (per RFC 7462) when given such URNs as input. *Validation mechanism*: An alert URN containing no private extensions can be validated on the basis of the IANA registry of standardized alert URNs. Validating an alert URN containing private extensions requires obtaining information regarding the private extensions defined by the organization that owns the <provider> in the relevant <private-name>. The identity of the organization can be determined from the IANA registry. However, if an alert URN contains at least one <alert-identifier> that precedes the first <private-name>, the portion of the alert URN that precedes the first <private-name> must itself be a valid standardized alert URN, which may be validated as above. Scope: The scope for this URN is public and global. 4. alert URN Values 4.1. <alert-category> Values The following <alert-category> values are defined in this document: service, source, priority, duration, delay, and locale. 4.2. <alert-indication> Values This section describes the alert URN indication values for the<alert-category>s defined in this document. For each <alert-category>, a default <alert-indication> is defined, which is essentially a no-operation alert URN and should be treated by the UA as if no alert URN for the respective category is present. alert URN default indications are most useful when Alert-Info header field parameters are being used. For example, in RFC 7463 (see Section 16.2.11), an Alert-Info header field needs to be present containing the appearance parameter; however, no special ringtone needs to be specified. The <private-name> syntax is used for extensions defined by independent organizations, as specified in RFC 7462. 4.2.1. <alert-indication> Values for the <alert-category> *service*: normal (default), call-waiting, forward, recall:callback, recall:hold, recall:transfer, and <private-name>. Examples: `<urn:alert:service:call-waiting> or <urn:alert:service:recall:transfer>.` 4.2.2. <alert-indication> Values for the <alert-category> *source*: –unclassified (default)–internal–external–friend–family, and <private-name>. (These <alert-indication>s will rarely be provided by the sending UA; rather, they will usually be inserted by a proxy acting on behalf of the recipient UA to inform the recipient UA about the origins of a call.) Examples: `<urn:alert:source:external>.` 4.2.3. <alert-indication> Values for the <alert-category> *priority*: normal (default), low-high, and <private-name> Examples: `<urn:alert:priority:high>.` 4.2.4. <alert-Indication> Values for the <alert-category> *duration*: normal (default), short–long, and <private-name>

(*Continued*)

Table 2.10 (Continued) SIP Header Field Descriptions

Header Field/RFC/Header Field Type	*Description*
	Examples: `<urn:alert:duration:short>`. 4.2.5. <alert-indication> Values for the <alert-category> *delay*: none (default), yes, and <private-name> Examples: `<urn:alert:delay:yes>`. 4.2.6. <alert-indication> Values for the <alert-category> *locale*: default (default), country:<ISO 3166-1 country code>, and <private-name>
	The ISO 3166-1 country code [ISO3166-1] is used to inform the renderer on the other side of the call that a country-specific rendering should be used. For example, to indicate ringback tones from South Africa, the following URN would be used: <urn:alert:locale:country:za>. [ISO3166-1] ISO, "English country names and code elements," ISO 3166-1. Available at http://www.iso.org/iso/english_country_names_and_code_elements. [TS24.615] 3GPP, "Communication Waiting (CW) using IP Multimedia (IM) Core Network (CN) subsystem; Protocol Specification," 3GPP TS 24.615, September 2015.
Allow/RFC 3261 (Standards Track)/Message-Body	The Allow header field lists the set of methods supported by the UA generating the message. All methods, including ACK and CANCEL, understood by the UA MUST be included in the list of methods in the Allow header field, when present. The absence of an Allow header field must not be interpreted to mean that the UA sending the message supports no methods. Rather, it implies that the UA is not providing any information on what methods it supports. Supplying an Allow header field in responses to methods other than OPTIONS reduces the number of messages needed. Example: `Allow: INVITE, ACK, OPTIONS, CANCEL, BYE`
Allow-Events/RFC 6665 (Standards Track)/Request and Response	The Allow-Events header field indicates a list of SIP event packages supported by a SIP UA that can be subscribed. SIP SUBSCRIBE/NOTIFY messages are used by SIP UAs for subscriptions and then notifications of those SIP events.
Answer-Mode and Priv-Answer-Mode/RFC 5373 (Standards Track)/Request and Response	RFC 5373 extends SIP with two header fields and associated option tags that can be used in INVITE requests to convey the requester's preference for user-interface handling related to answering of that request. The first header, *Answer-Mode*, expresses a preference as to whether the target node's user interface waits for user input before accepting the request or, instead, accepts the request without waiting on user input. The second header, *Priv-Answer-Mode*, is similar to the first, except that it requests administrative-level access and has consequent additional authentication and authorization requirements. These behaviors have applicability to applications such as push-to-talk and to diagnostics like loop-back. Usage of each header field in a response to indicate how the request was handled is also defined. The conventional model for session establishment using SIP involves (i) sending a request for a session (a SIP INVITE) and notifying the user receiving the request, (ii) acceptance of the request and of the session by that user, and (iii) the sending of a response (SIP 200 OK) back to the requester before the session is established. Some usage scenarios deviate from this model, specifically with respect to the notification and acceptance phase. While it has always been possible for the node receiving the request to skip the notification and acceptance phases, there has been no standard mechanism for the party sending the request to specifically indicate a desire (or requirement) for this sort of treatment. This document defines a SIP extension header field that can be used to request specific treatment related to the notification and acceptance phase.

(*Continued*)

Table 2.10 (Continued) SIP Header Field Descriptions

Header Field/RFC/Header Field Type	*Description*
	The first usage scenario is the requirement for diagnostic loop-back calls. In this sort of scenario, a testing service sends an INVITE to a node being tested. The tested node accepts and a dialog is established. However, rather than establishing a two-way media flow, the tested node loops back or *echoes* media received from the testing service back toward the testing service. The testing service can then analyze the media flow for quality and timing characteristics. Session Description Protocol (SDP) usage for this sort of flow is described in [LOOPBACK]. In this sort of application, it might not be necessary that the human using the tested node interact with the node in any way for the test to be satisfactorily executed. In some cases, it might be appropriate to alert the user to the ongoing test, and in other cases it might not be.
	The second scenario is that of push-to-talk applications, which have been specified by the Open Mobile Alliance. In this sort of environment, SIP is used to establish a dialog supporting asynchronous delivery of unidirectional media flow, providing a user experience like that of a traditional two-way radio. It is conventional for the INVITES used to be automatically accepted by the called UA, and the media is commonly played out on a loudspeaker. The called party's UA's microphone is not engaged until the user presses the local *talk* button to respond. A third scenario is the Private Branch Exchange (PBX) attendant. Traditional office PBX systems often include intercom functionality. A typical use for the intercom function is to allow a receptionist to activate a loudspeaker on a desk telephone in order to announce a visitor. Not every caller can access the loudspeaker, only the receptionist or operator, and it is not expected that these callers will always want *intercom* functionality—they might instead want to make an ordinary call. There are presumably many more use cases for the extensions defined in this specification; however, this document was developed to specifically meet the requirements of these scenarios, or others with essentially similar properties. These sorts of mechanisms are not required to provide the functionality of an *answering machine* or *voice-mail recorder*. Such a device knows that it is expected to answer and does not require a SIP extension to support its behavior. Much of the discussion of this topic in working group meetings and on the mailing list dealt with differentiating *answering mode* from *alerting mode*. Some early work did not make this distinction. We therefore proceed with the following definitions: • Answering Mode includes behaviors in a SIP UA relating to acceptance or rejection of a request that are contingent on interaction between the UA and the user of that UA after the UA has received the request. We are principally concerned with the user interaction involved in accepting the request and initiating an active session. An example of this might be pressing the *yes* button on a mobile phone. • Alerting Mode includes behaviors in a SIP UA relating to informing the user of the UA that a request to initiate a session has been received. An example of this might be activating the ringtone of a mobile phone.

(*Continued*)

Table 2.10 (Continued) SIP Header Field Descriptions

Header Field/RFC/Header Field Type	*Description*

	RFC 5373 deals only with Answering Mode. Issues relating to Alerting Mode are outside its scope. This document defines two SIP extension header fields: Answer-Mode and Priv-Answer-Mode. These two extensions take the same parameters and operate in the same general way. The distinction between Answer-Mode and Priv-Answer-Mode relates to the level of authorization claimed by the UAC and verified and policed by the UAS. Requests are usually made using Answer-Mode. Requests made using Priv-Answer-Mode request *privileged* treatment from the UAS. Priv-Answer-Mode is not an assertion of privilege. Instead, it is a request for privileged treatment. This is similar to the UNIX model, where a user might run a command normally or use *sudo* to request administrative privilege for the command. Including *Priv-* is equivalent to prefixing a UNIX command with sudo. In other words, a separate policy table (like */etc/sudoers*) is consulted to determine whether the user may receive the requested treatment.
	Option Tags:
	This option tag is for support of the Answer-Mode and Priv-Answer-Mode extensions used to negotiate automatic or manual answering of a request (see Section 2.10).
	Usage of the Answer-Mode and Priv-Answer-Mode Header Fields:
	RFC 5373 defines usage of the Answer-Mode and Priv-Answer-Mode header fields in initial (dialog-forming) SIP INVITE requests and in 200 OK responses to those requests. This document specifically does not define usage in any other sort of request or response, including but not limited to ACK, CANCEL, or any mid-dialog usage. This limitation stems from the intended usage of this extension, which is to affect the way that users interact with communications devices when requesting new communications sessions and when responding to such requests. This sort of interaction occurs only during the formation of a dialog and its initial usage, not during subsequent operations such as re-INVITE. However, the security aspects of the session initiation must be applied to changes in media description introduced by re-INVITES or similar requests.
	Examples of Usage:
	The following examples show Bob registering a contact that supports the negotiation of answering mode. Alice then calls Bob with an INVITE request, asking for automatic answering and explicitly asking that the request not be routed to contacts that have not indicated support for this extension. Furthermore, Alice requires that the request be rejected if Bob's UA does not support the negotiation of answering mode. Bob replies with a 200 OK response indicating that the call was answered automatically. The Content-Length header field shown in the examples contains a placeholder "..." instead of a valid Content-Length. Furthermore, the SDP bodies that would be expected in the INVITE requests and 200 OK responses are not shown.
	
	`REGISTER Request:`
	
	In the following example, Bob's UA is registering and indicating that it supports the answermode extension.
	
	`REGISTER sip:example.com SIP/2.0`
	`From: Bob<sip:bob@example.com>`
	`To: Bob <sip:bob@example.com>`
	`CallID: hh89as0d-asd88jkk@cell-phone.example.com`
	`CSeq: 1 REGISTER`
	`Contact: sip:cell-phone.example.com;`
	`;audio`
	`;+sip.extensions="answermode"`
	`;methods="INVITE,BYE,OPTIONS,CANCEL,ACK"`

(*Continued*)

Table 2.10 (Continued) SIP Header Field Descriptions

Header Field/RFC/Header Field Type	*Description*
	;schemes="sip" INVITE Request: In this example, Alice is calling Bob and asking Bob's UA to answer automatically. However, Alice is willing for Bob to answer manually if Bob's policy is to prefer manual answer, so Alice does not include a *;require* modifier on *Answer-Mode: Auto*. INVITE sip:bob@example.com SIP/2.0 Via: SIP/2.0/TCP client-alice.example.com:5060; branch=z9hG4bK74b43 Max-Forwards: 70 From: Alice <sip:alice@atlanta.example.com>;tag=9fxced76sl To: Bob <sip:bob@example.com> Call-ID:3848276298220188511@client-alice.example.com CSeq: 1 INVITE Contact: <sip:alice@client.atlanta.example.com;transport=tcp> Require: answermode Accept-contact:*;require;explicit;extensions="answermode" Answer-Mode: Auto Content-Type: application/sdp Content-Length:... 200 OK Response: Here, Bob has accepted the call and his UA has answered automatically, which it indicates in the 200 OK response. SIP/2.0 200 OK Via: SIP/2.0/TCP client-alice.example.com:5060; branch= z9hG4bK74b43 From: Alice <sip:alice@example.com>;tag=9fxced76sl To: Bob <sip:bob@example.com>;tag=8321234356 Call-ID: 3848276298220188511@client-alice.example.com CSeq: 1 INVITE Contact: <sip:bob@client.biloxi.example.com;transport=tcp> Answer-Mode: Auto Content-Type: application/sdp Content-Length:... The extensions described in this document provide mechanisms by which a UAC can request that a UAS not deploy two of the five defensive mechanisms listed below: user alerting and user acceptance. For this not to produce undue risk of insertion attacks or increased risk of interception attacks, we are therefore forced to rely on the remaining defensive mechanisms. This document defines a minimum threshold for satisfactory security. Certainly, more restrictive policies might reasonably be used; however, any policy less restrictive than the approach described below is very likely to result in significant security issues. From the previous discussion of risks, attacks, and vulnerabilities, we can derive five defensive mechanisms available at the application level:

(*Continued*)

Table 2.10 (Continued) SIP Header Field Descriptions

Header Field/RFC/Header Field Type	*Description*
	• Identity—Know who the request came from. • Alerting—Let the called user know what is happening. Some applications might use inbound media as an alert. • Acceptance—Require called user to make run-time decision. Asking the user to make a run-time decision without alerting the user to the need to make a decision is generally infeasible. This will have implications for possible alerting options that are outside the scope of this document. • Limit the Input/Output (I/O)—Turn off loudspeakers or microphone. This could be used to convert a bidirectional media session (very risky, possible *bug my phone*) into a unidirectional, inbound-only (less risky, possible *spam* or *rundown*, etc.) session while waiting for user acceptance. • Policy—Rules about other factors, such as black- and whitelisting based on identity, disallowing acceptance without alerting, etc. Since SIP and related work already provide several mechanisms (including SIP Digest Authentication [see Section 19.4], the SIP Identity mechanism [see Section 19.4.8], and the SIP mechanism for asserted identity within private networks [see Section 20.3], in networks for which they are suitable) for establishing the identity of the originator of a request, we presume that an appropriately selected mechanism is available for UAs implementing the extensions described in this document. In short, UAs implementing these extensions must be equipped with and must exercise a request-identity mechanism. The analysis below proceeds from an assumption that the identity of the sender of each request is either known or is known to be unknown, and can therefore be considered in related policy considerations. Failure to meet this identity requirement either opens the door to a wide range of attacks or requires operational policy so tight as to make these extensions useless. We previously established a class distinction between inbound and outbound media flows, and can model bidirectional flows as *worst-case* sums of the risks of the other two classes. Given this distinction, it seems reasonable to provide separate directionality policy classes for • Inbound media flows • Outbound media flows For each directionality policy class, we can divide the set of request identities into three classes: • Identities explicitly authorized for the class • Identities explicitly denied for the class • Identities for which we have no explicit policy and need the user to make a decision Note that not all combinations of policies possible in this decomposition are generally useful. Specifically, a policy of *inbound media denied, outbound media allowed* equates to a *bug my phone* attack, and is disallowed by the minimal policy described below, which as written excludes all cases of *outbound media explicitly authorized.*

(*Continued*)

Table 2.10 (Continued) SIP Header Field Descriptions

<table>
<tr><th>Header Field/RFC/Header Field Type</th><th>Description</th></tr>
<tr><td></td><td>Minimal Policy Requirement:
User agents implementing this specification should not establish a session providing inbound media without explicit user acceptance where the requesting user is unknown, or is known and has not been granted authorization for such a session. This requirement is intended to prevent SPAM broadcast attacks where unexpected and unwanted media is played out at a UAS. UAs implementing this specification must not establish a session providing outbound or bidirectional media sourced from the UA without explicit user acceptance. Loop-back media used for connectivity testing is not constrained by this requirement. This requirement is intended to assure that this extension cannot be used to turn a UAS into a remote-controlled microphone (or bug) without the knowledge of its user. Since SIP allows for a session to be initially established with inbound-only media and then transitioned (via re-INVITE or UPDATE) to an outbound or bidirectional session, enforcing this policy requires dialog-stateful inspection in the SIP UAS. In other words, if a session was initiated with automatic answering, the UAS MUST NOT transition to a mode that sends outbound media without explicit acceptance by the user of the UAS.
IANA Registration of Header Field Parameters:
RFC 5373 defines parameters for the header fields defined in the preceding section. The header fields Answer-Mode and Priv-Answer-Mode can take the values Manual or Auto. The following rows have been added to the "Header Field Parameters and Parameter Values" section of the SIP parameter registry:
<table>
<tr><th>Header Field</th><th>Parameter Name</th><th>Predefined Values</th><th>Reference</th></tr>
<tr><td>Answer-Mode</td><td>require</td><td>No</td><td rowspan="2">RFC 5373</td></tr>
<tr><td>Priv-Answer-Mode</td><td>require</td><td>No</td></tr>
</table></td></tr>
<tr><td>Authentication-Info/RFC 3261 (Standards Track)/ Response</td><td>The Authentication-Info header field provides for mutual authentication with HTTP Digest. A UAS may include this header field in a 2xx response to a request that was successfully authenticated using digest based on the Authorization header field. Syntax and semantics follow those specified in RFC 2617. Example:
Authentication-Info: nextnonce="47364c23432d2e131a5fb210812c"</td></tr>
<tr><td>Authorization/RFC 3261 (Standards Track)/Response</td><td>The Authorization header field contains authentication credentials of a UA. Section 2.4.1 describes the syntax and semantics when used with HTTP authentication. This header field, along with Proxy-Authorization, breaks the general rules about multiple header field values. Although not a comma-separated list, this header field name may be present multiple times, and must not be combined into a single header line using the usual rules. In the example below, there are no quotes around the Digest parameter:
Authorization: Digest username="Alice", realm="atlanta.com",
nonce="84a4cc6f3082121f32b42a2187831a9e",
response="7587245234b3434cc3412213e5f113a5432"</td></tr>
</table>

(*Continued*)

Table 2.10 (Continued) SIP Header Field Descriptions

Header Field/RFC/Header Field Type	*Description*
Call-ID/RFC 3261 (Standards Track)/Request and Response	The Call-ID header field uniquely identifies a particular invitation or all registrations of a particular client. A single multimedia conference can give rise to several calls with different Call-IDs, for example, if a user invites a single individual several times to the same (long-running) conference. Call-IDs are case sensitive and are simply compared byte by byte. The compact form of the Call-ID header field is i. Examples: Call-ID: f81d4fae-7dec-11d0-a765-00a0c91e6bf6@biloxi.com i:f81d4fae-7dec-11d0-a765-00a0c91e6bf6@192.0.2.4
Call-Info/RFC 3261 (Standards Track)/Request	The Call-Info header field provides additional information about the caller or callee, depending on whether it is found in a request or response. The purpose of the URI is described by the *purpose* parameter. The *icon* parameter designates an image suitable as an iconic representation of the caller or callee. The *info* parameter describes the caller or callee in general, for example, through a web page. The *card* parameter provides a business card, for example, in vCard specified in RFC 6350 or Lightweight Directory Access (LDAP) Data Interchange Format (LDIF) described in RFC 2849 formats. Additional tokens can be registered using IANA. Use of the Call-Info header field can pose a security risk. If a callee fetches the URIs provided by a malicious caller, the callee may be at risk for displaying inappropriate or offensive content, dangerous or illegal content, and so on. Therefore, it is recommended that a UA only render the information in the Call-Info header field if it can verify the authenticity of the element that originated the header field and trusts that element. This need not be the peer UA; a proxy can insert this header field into requests. Example: Call-Info: <http://wwww.example.com/alice/photo.jpg>; purpose=icon, <http://www.example.com/alice/>;purpose=info
Contact/RFC 3261 (Standards Track)/Request and Response	A Contact header field value provides a URI whose meaning depends on the type of request or response it is in. A Contact header field value can contain a display name, a URI with URI parameters, and header parameters. This document defines the Contact parameters *q* and *expires*. These parameters are only used when the Contact is present in a REGISTER request or response, or in a 3xx response. Additional parameters may be defined in other specifications. When the header field value contains a display name, the URI including all URI parameters is enclosed in < and >. If no < and > are present, all parameters after the URI are header parameters, not URI parameters. The display name can be tokens, or a quoted string, if a larger character set is desired. Even if the *display-name* is empty, the *name-addr* form MUST be used if the *addr-spec* contains a comma, semicolon, or question mark. There may or may not be LWS between the display-name and the <. These rules for parsing a display name, URI and URI parameters, and header parameters also apply for the header fields To and From. The Contact header field has a role similar to the Location header field in HTTP. However, the HTTP header field only allows one address, unquoted. Since URIs can contain commas and semicolons as reserved characters, they can be mistaken for header or parameter delimiters, respectively. The compact form of the Contact header field is m (for *moved*). Examples: Contact: "Mr. Watson" <sip:watson@worcester.bell- telephone.com>;q=0.7; expires=3600, "Mr. Watson" <mailto:watson@bell-telephone.com>;q=0.1 m: <sips:bob@192.0.2.4>;expires=60

(*Continued*)

Table 2.10 (Continued) SIP Header Field Descriptions

<table>
<tr><th>Header Field/RFC/Header Field Type</th><th>Description</th></tr>
<tr><td>Content-Disposition/RFC 3261 (Standards Track)/ Message-Body</td><td>The Content-Disposition header field describes how the message body or, for multipart messages, a message-body part is to be interpreted by the UAC or UAS. This SIP header field extends the MIME Content-Type defined in RFC 2183. Several new disposition-types of the Content-Disposition header are defined by SIP. The value session indicates that the body part describes a session, for either calls or early (precall) media. The value render indicates that the body part should be displayed or otherwise rendered to the user. Note that the value render is used rather than inline to avoid the connotation that the MIME body is displayed as a part of the rendering of the entire message (since the MIME bodies of SIP messages oftentimes are not displayed to users). For backward compatibility, if the Content-Disposition header field is missing, the server should assume bodies of Content-Type application/SDP are the disposition session, while other content types are render.
The disposition type icon indicates that the body part contains an image suitable as an iconic representation of the caller or callee that could be rendered for information by a UA when a message has been received, or persistently while a dialog takes place. The value alert indicates that the body part contains information, such as an audio clip, that should be rendered by the UA in an attempt to alert the user to the receipt of a request, generally a request that initiates a dialog; this alerting body could, for example, be rendered as a ringtone for a phone call after a 180 Ringing provisional response has been sent.
Any MIME body with a disposition-type that renders content to the user should only be processed when a message has been properly authenticated. The handling parameter, handling-param, describes how the UAS should react if it receives a message body whose content type or disposition type it does not understand. The parameter has defined values of optional and required. If the handling parameter is missing, the value required should be assumed. The handling parameter is described in MIME Media Type RFC 3204. If this header field is missing, the MIME type determines the default content disposition. If there is none, render is assumed. Example:

<code>Content-Disposition: session</code>

RFC 3873 defines a new MIME Content-Disposition disposition-type value of aib. This value is reserved for MIME bodies that contain an authenticated identity. Example:

<code>Content-Disposition: aib; handling=optional</code>

RFC 5621 defines a new Content-Disposition header field disposition type: by-reference. This value has been registered in the IANA registry for Mail Content Disposition Values with the following description:
by-reference: The body needs to be handled according to a reference to the body that is located in the same SIP message as the body.
IANA references this specification to RFCs 3204 and 3459. These updates have been added to the entry for the Content-Disposition handling parameter in the Header Field Parameters and Parameter Values registry. The following is the resulting entry:

<table>
<tr><th>Header Field</th><th>Parameter Name</th><th>Predefined Values</th><th>Reference</th></tr>
<tr><td>Content-Disposition</td><td>handling</td><td>Yes</td><td>RFCs 3204, 3261, 3459, and 5621</td></tr>
</table>
</td></tr>
</table>

(*Continued*)

Table 2.10 (Continued) SIP Header Field Descriptions

Header Field/RFC/Header Field Type	*Description*

Content-Encoding/RFC 3261 (Standards Track)/ Message-Body	The Content-Encoding header field is used as a modifier to the *media-type*. When present, its value indicates what additional content codings have been applied to the entity body, and thus what decoding mechanisms MUST be applied in order to obtain the media-type referenced by the Content-Type header field. Content-Encoding is primarily used to allow a body to be compressed without losing the identity of its underlying media type. If multiple encodings have been applied to an entity body, the content codings must be listed in the order in which they were applied.
	All content-coding values are case insensitive. IANA acts as a registry for content-coding value tokens. RFC 2616 that is obsoleted by RFCs 7230–7235 (see Section 2.4.1) provides the definition of the syntax for content coding. Clients may apply content encodings to the body in requests. A server may apply content encodings to the bodies in responses. The server must only use encodings listed in the Accept-Encoding header field in the request. The compact form of the Content-Encoding header field is e. Examples:
	`Content-Encoding: gzip`
	`e: tar`
	RFC 6140 defined a new parameter for the Contact header with no predefined value as follows:
	Parameter name: temp-gruu-cookie
	Predefined values: No

Content-Language/RFC 3261 (Standards Track)/ Message-Body	This header field is defined per Section 14.12 of RFC 2616 (obsoleted by RFCs 7230–7235). The Content-Language entity-header field describes the natural language(s) of the intended audience for the enclosed entity. Note that this might not be equivalent to all the languages used within the entity body. The primary purpose of Content-Language is to allow a user to identify and differentiate entities according to the user's own preferred language. Thus, if the body content is intended only for a Danish-literate audience, the appropriate field is
	`Content-Language: da`
	If no Content-Language is specified, the default is that the content is intended for all language audiences. This might mean that the sender does not consider it to be specific to any natural language, or that the sender does not know for which language it is intended. Multiple languages may be listed for content that is intended for multiple audiences. For example, a rendition of the "Treaty of Waitangi," presented simultaneously in the original Maori and English versions, would call for
	`Content-Language: mi, en`
	However, just because multiple languages are present within an entity does not mean that it is intended for multiple linguistic audiences. An example would be a beginner's language primer, such as "A First Lesson in Latin," which is clearly intended to be used by an English-literate audience. In this case, the Content-Language would properly only include *en*. Content-Language may be applied to any media type—it is not limited to textual documents.

(Continued)

Table 2.10 (Continued) SIP Header Field Descriptions

Header Field/RFC/Header Field Type	*Description*

Content-Length/RFC 3261 (Standards Track)/ Message-Body	The Content-Length header field indicates the size of the message body, in decimal number of octets, sent to the recipient. Applications should use this field to indicate the size of the message body to be transferred, regardless of the media type of the entity. If a stream-based protocol (such as TCP) is used as transport, the header field must be used. The size of the message body does not include the CRLF separating header fields and body. Any Content-Length greater than or equal to zero is a valid value. If no message body is present in a message, then the Content-Length header field value must be set to zero. The ability to omit Content-Length simplifies the creation of cgi-like scripts that dynamically generate responses. The compact form of the header field is l. Examples:
	`Content-Length: 349`
	`l: 173`

Content-Type/RFC 3261 (Standards Track)/ Message-Body	The Content-Type header field indicates the media type of the message body sent to the recipient. If the body has undergone any encoding such as compression, then this must be indicated by the Content-Encoding header field; otherwise, Content-Encoding must be omitted. If applicable, the character set of the message body is indicated as part of the Content-Type header-field value. The *multipart* MIME type defined in RFC 2046 may be used within the body of the message. Implementations that send requests containing multipart message bodies must send a session description as a non-multipart message body if the remote implementation requests this through an Accept header field that does not contain multipart. SIP messages may contain binary bodies or body parts. When no explicit charset parameter is provided by the sender, media subtypes of the *text* type are defined to have a default charset value of UTF-8. If the Content-Disposition header field is missing, bodies of Content-Type application/sdp imply the disposition session, while other content types imply render. The presence or absence of a parameter might be significant to the processing of a media-type, depending on its definition within the media-type registry. The Content-Type header field must be present if the body is not empty. If the body is empty, and a Content-Type header field is present, it indicates that the body of the specific type has zero length (e.g., an empty audio file). RFC 4483 defines an extension to the URL MIME External-Body access-type to satisfy the content indirection requirements for the SIP, while the access-type parameter is specified in the syntax of the Content-Type header field (see Section 2.4.1). These extensions are aimed at allowing any MIME part in a SIP message to be referred to indirectly via a URI. There are numerous reasons why it might be desirable to specify the content of the SIP message body indirectly. For bandwidth-limited applications such as cellular wireless, indirection provides a means to annotate the (indirect) content with meta-data, which may be used by the recipient to determine whether or not to retrieve the content over a resource-limited link. Similarly, there are many other reasons for relieving the SIP signaling entities not to be overwhelmed with media contents. A UAC/UAS indicates support for content indirection by including the message/external-body MIME type in the Accept header. The UAC/UAS may supply additional values in the Accept header to indicate the content types that it is willing to accept, either directly or through content indirection. UAs supporting content indirection must support content indirection of the application/sdp MIME type. Applications that use this content indirection mechanism must support the HTTP URI scheme. Additional URI schemes may be used, but a UAC/UAS must support receiving a HTTP URI for indirect content if it advertises support for content indirection. The UAS may advertise alternate access schemes in the schemes parameter of the Contact header in the UAS response to the UAC's session establishment request (e.g., INVITE, SUBSCRIBE), as described in RFC 3840 (see Section 3.4).

(*Continued*)

Table 2.10 (Continued) SIP Header Field Descriptions

Header Field/RFC/Header Field Type	*Description*

	If a UAS receives a SIP request that contains a content indirection payload and the UAS cannot or does not wish to support such a content type, it must reject the request with a 415 Unsupported Media Type response. In particular, the UAC should note the absence of the message/external-body MIME type in the Accept header of this response to indicate that the UAS does not support content indirection, or the absence of the particular MIME type of the requested comment to indicate that the UAS does not support the particular media type. Applications that use this content indirection mechanism MUST support the HTTP URI scheme. Additional URI schemes may be used, but a UAC/UAS must support receiving a HTTP URI for indirect content if it advertises support for content indirection. The UAS may advertise alternate access schemes in the schemes parameter of the Contact header in the UAS response to the UAC's session establishment request (e.g., INVITE, SUBSCRIBE), as described in RFC 3840 (see Section 3.4).
	Some content is not critical to the context of the communication if there is a fetch or conversion failure. The content indirection mechanism uses the Critical-Content mechanism described in RFC 5389 (see Section 14.3).
	In particular, if the UAS is unable to fetch or render an optional body part, then the server must not return an error to the UAC. To determine whether the content indirectly referenced by the URI has changed, a Content-ID entity header is used. The Content-ID and Message-ID syntax for the URLs specified in RFC 2392 are as follows:
	`content-id = url-addr-spec`
	`message-id = url-addr-spec`
	`url-addr-spec = addr-spec`
	`; URL encoding of RFC 5322 addr-spec`
	`cid-url = "cid" ":" content-id`
	`mid-url = "mid" ":" message-id ["/" content-id]`
	Note that in Internet mail messages, the addr-spec in a Content-ID defined in RFC 2045 or Message-ID specified in RFC 5322 header is enclosed in angle brackets (<>). Since addr-spec in a Message-ID or Content-ID might contain characters not allowed within a URL, any such character (including /, which is reserved within the *mid* scheme) must be hex-encoded using the %hh escape mechanism in RFCs 4248 and 4266.
	A mid URL with only a message-id refers to an entire message. With the appended content-id, it refers to a body part within a message, as does a *cid* URL. The Content-ID of a MIME body part is required to be globally unique. However, in many systems that store messages, body parts are not indexed independently according to their content (message). The mid URL long form was designed to supply the context needed to support interoperability with such systems.
	Content-ID values must be generated to be world-unique. The Content-ID value may be used for uniquely identifying MIME entities in several contexts, particularly for caching data referenced by the message/external-body mechanism. Changes in the underlying content referred to by a URI must result in a change in the Content-ID associated with that URI. Multiple SIP messages carrying URIs that refer to the same content should reuse the same Content-ID, to allow the receiver to cache this content and to avoid unnecessary retrievals. The Content-ID is intended to be globally unique and should be temporally unique across SIP dialogs. For example:
	`Content-ID: <4232423424@www.example.com>`

(*Continued*)

Table 2.10 (Continued) SIP Header Field Descriptions

Header Field/RFC/Header Field Type	*Description*

	The URI supplied by the Content-Type header is not required to be accessible or valid for an indefinite period of time. Rather, the supplier of the URI must specify the time period for which this URI is valid and accessible. This is done through an EXPIRATION parameter of the Content-Type. The format of this expiration parameter is an RFC 1123 date–time value. This is further restricted in this application to use only GMT time, consistent with the Date: header in SIP. This is a mandatory parameter. Note that the date–time value can range from minutes to days or even years.
	If the sender knows the specific content being referenced by the indirection, and if the sender wishes the recipient to be able to validate that this content has not been altered from that intended by the sender, the sender includes a SHA-1 specified in RFC 3174 hash of the content. If it is included, the hash is encoded by extending the MIME syntax defined in RFC 2046 to include a *hash* parameter for the content type *message/external-body*, whose value is a hexadecimal encoding of the hash. One may use the Content-Description entity header to provide optional, freeform text to comment on the indirect content. This text may be displayed to the end user but must not be used by other elements to determine the disposition of the body. One may also see the Content-Description entity header to provide optional, freeform text to comment on the indirect content. This text may be displayed to the end user but must not be used by other elements to determine the disposition of the body.
	SIP defines Call-Info, Error-Info, and Alert-Info headers that supply additional information with regard to a session, a particular error response, or alerting. All three of these headers allow the UAC or UAS to indicate additional information through a URI. They may be considered a form of content indirection. The content indirection mechanism defined in this document is not intended as a replacement for these headers. Rather, the headers defined in SIP must be used in preference to this mechanism, where applicable, because of the well-defined semantics of those headers.
	The compact form of the header field is c. Examples:
	
	`Content-Type: application/SDP`
	`c: text/html; charset=ISO-8859-4`
	`Content-Type: message/external-body;`
	`access-type="URL";`
	`expiration="Mon, 24 June 2002 09:00:00 GMT";`
	`URL="http://www.example.com/the-indirect-content .au";`
	`size=52723;`
	`hash=10AB568E91245681AC1B`
	`<CRLF>`
	`Content-Description: Multicast Gaming`
	`Content-Disposition: render`
	
	The *message/sip* MIME Message-Body Type:
	RFC 3261 registers the message/sip MIME media type in order to allow SIP messages to be tunneled as bodies within SIP, primarily for end-to-end security purposes. This media type is defined by the following information:
	
	• Media type name: message.
	• Media subtype name: sip.
	• Required parameters: none.
	• Optional parameters: version.
	• version: The SIP-Version number of the enclosed message (e.g., 2.0). If not present, the version defaults to 2.0.

(*Continued*)

Table 2.10 (Continued) SIP Header Field Descriptions

Header Field/RFC/Header Field Type	*Description*

- Encoding scheme: SIP messages consist of an 8-bit header optionally followed by a binary MIME data object. As such, SIP messages must be treated as binary. Under normal circumstances, SIP messages are transported over binary-capable transports; no special encodings are needed.
- Security considerations: Motivation and examples of this usage as a security mechanism in concert with S/MIME are given in Section 23.4 of RFC 3261 (see Section 19.6).

The message/sipfrag MIME Message-Body Type:
Similarly, RFC 3420 registers the message/sipfrag MIME media type. This type is similar to message/sip, but allows certain subsets of well-formed SIP messages to be represented instead of requiring a complete SIP message. In addition to end-to-end security uses, message/sipfrag is used with the REFER method to convey information about the status of a referenced request. A valid message/sipfrag part is one that could be obtained by starting with some valid SIP message and deleting any of the following:

- The entire start line
- One or more entire header fields
- The body

The following ABNF rule describes a message/sipfrag part using the SIP grammar elements defined in RFC 3261 (see Section 2.4.1). The expansion of any element is subject to the restrictions on valid SIP messages defined there.

```
sipfrag =      [start-line]
                 *message-header
                 [CRLF [message-body]]
```

If the message/sipfrag part contains a body, it must also contain the appropriate header fields describing that body (such as Content-Length) and the null-line separating the header from the body. We are providing some valid message/sipfrag message-body examples using a vertical bar and a space to the left of each example to illustrate the example's extent. Each line of the message/sipfrag element begins with the first character after the "|" pair. The first two examples show that a message/sipfrag part can consist of only a start line.

```
| INVITE sip:alice@atlanta.com SIP/2.0
```

or

```
| SIP/2.0 603 Declined
```

The next two show that Subsets of a full SIP message may be represented.

```
| REGISTER sip:atlanta.com SIP/2.0
| To: sip:alice@atlanta.com
| Contact: <sip:alicepc@atlanta.com>;q=0.9,
| <sip:alicemobile@atlanta.com>;q=0.1
| SIP/2.0 400 Bad Request
| Warning: 399 atlanta.com Your Event header field was malformed
```

A message/sipfrag part does not have to contain a start line. This example shows a part that might be signed to make assertions about a particular message.

```
| From: Alice <sip:alice@atlanta.com>
| To: Bob <sip:bob@biloxi.com>
| Contact: <sip:alice@pc33.atlanta.com>
```

(*Continued*)

Table 2.10 (Continued) SIP Header Field Descriptions

Header Field/RFC/Header Field Type	*Description*
	| Date: Thu, 21 Feb 2002 13:02:03 GMT | Call-ID: a84b4c76e66710 | Cseq: 314159 INVITE The next two examples show message/sipfrag parts that contain bodies. | SIP/2.0 200 OK | Content-Type: application/sdp | Content-Length: 247 | | v=0 | o=alice 2890844526 2890844526 IN IP4 host.anywhere.com | s= | c=IN IP4 host.anywhere.com | t=0 0 | m=audio 49170 RTP/AVP 0 | a=rtpmap:0 PCMU/8000 | m=video 51372 RTP/AVP 31 | a=rtpmap:31 H261/90000 | m=video 53000 RTP/AVP 32 | a=rtpmap:32 MPV/90000 | Content-Type: text/plain | Content-Length: 11 | Hi There!
CSeq/RFC 3261 (Standards Track)/Request and Response	A CSeq header field in a request contains a single decimal sequence number and the request method. The sequence number MUST be expressible as a 32-bit unsigned integer. The method part of CSeq is case sensitive. The CSeq header field serves to order transactions within a dialog, to provide a means to uniquely identify transactions, and to differentiate between new requests and request retransmissions. Two CSeq header fields are considered equal if the sequence number and the request method are identical. Example: CSeq: 4711 INVITE
Date/RFC 3261 (Standards Track)/Request and Response	The Date header field contains the date and time. Unlike HTTP/1.1, SIP only supports the most recent RFC 1123 format for dates. However, SIP restricts the time zone in SIP-date to GMT, while RFC 1123 allows any time zone. An RFC 1123 date is case sensitive. The Date header field reflects the time when the request or response is first sent. The Date header field can be used by simple end systems without a battery-backed clock to acquire a notion of current time. However, in its GMT form, it requires clients to know their offset from GMT. Example: Date: Sat, 13 Nov 2010 23:29:00 GMT
Encryption/RFC 2543 (Standards Track)/Request and Response	The Encryption header field defined in RFC 2543 obsoleted by RFC 3261 indicates that the content has been encrypted, but is not included in RFC 3261 that obsoletes RFC 2543. Instead, RFC 3261 defined encryption using S/MIME.

(*Continued*)

Table 2.10 (Continued) SIP Header Field Descriptions

<table>
<tr><th>Header Field/RFC/Header Field Type</th><th>Description</th></tr>
<tr><td>Error-Info/RFC 3261 (Standards Track)/Response</td><td>The Error-Info header field provides a pointer to additional information about the error status response. SIP UACs have user interface capabilities ranging from pop-up windows and audio on PC soft clients to audio-only on black phones or end points connected via gateways. Rather than forcing a server generating an error to choose between sending an error status code with a detailed reason phrase and playing an audio recording, the Error-Info header field allows both to be sent.
The UAC then has the choice of which error indicator to render to the caller. A UAC may treat a SIP or SIPS URI in an Error-Info header field as if it were a Contact in a redirect and generate a new INVITE, resulting in a recorded announcement session being established. A non-SIP URI may be rendered to the user. Examples:
SIP/2.0 404 The number you have dialed is not in service

<code>Error-Info: <sip:not-in-service-recording@atlanta.com></code></td></tr>
<tr><td>Event/RFC 6665 (Standards Track)/Request</td><td>The Event header field is used by SIP UAs in SUBSCRIBE (or NOTIFY) method indicating to which event or class of events they are subscribing. The Event header will contain a token that indicates the type of state for which a subscription is being requested. This token will be registered with the IANA and will correspond to an event package that further describes the semantics of the event or event class. The Event header may also contain an id parameter. This id parameter, if present, contains an opaque token that identifies the specific subscription within a dialog. An id parameter is only valid within the scope of a single dialog.
For the purposes of matching responses and NOTIFY messages with SUBSCRIBE messages, the event-type portion of the Event header is compared byte by byte, and the id parameter token (if present) is compared byte by byte. An Event header containing an id parameter never matches an Event header without an id parameter. No other parameters are considered when performing a comparison.
RFC 7463 registers the SIP header field defining a new parameter as shown below through IANA registration:

<table>
<tr><th>Header Field</th><th>Parameter Name</th><th>Predefined Values</th><th>Reference</th></tr>
<tr><td>Event</td><td>shared</td><td>No</td><td>RFC 7463</td></tr>
</table></td></tr>
<tr><td>Expires/RFC 3261 (Standards Track)/Request and Response</td><td>The Expires header field gives the relative time after which the message (or content) expires. The precise meaning of this is method dependent. The expiration time in an INVITE does not affect the duration of the actual session that may result from the invitation. Session description protocols may offer the ability to express time limits on the session duration, however. The value of this field is an integral number of seconds (in decimal) between 0 and ($2^{32} - 1$), measured from the receipt of the request. Example:

<code>Expires: 5</code></td></tr>
</table>

(Continued)

Table 2.10 (Continued) SIP Header Field Descriptions

Header Field/RFC/Header Field Type	*Description*
Flow-Timer/RFC 5626 (Standards Track)/Response	The Flow-Timer header field defined in RFC 5626 (see Section 13.2) indicates the amount of time remaining for a registered flow with the registration server before considering it dead if no keep-alive message is sent by the UA to the registrar. This header field is very important for maintaining the outbound connections, which are usually considered of long duration especially for real-time teleconferencing or video conferencing, managed by SIP proxies for the SIP request messages that may frequently be disconnected or disturbed by middle boxes like NATs and firewalls. A UA may not have any clue if those outbound connections are disconnected. The Flow-Timer header field contains parameters like reg-id and instance-id that are used to identify the uniqueness of flow even if a UA or proxy fails and reboots. The same is also used by the REGISTER message in the Contact header field if a UA and registrar supports the outbound connection management specified in RFC 5626. To set up connections between the clients by an outbound proxy or outbound-proxy-set, a lot of processing and communications are done, which can easily make the SIP connection setup nonscalable even for a moderately large network. RFC 3263 (see Section 8.2.4) has mandated some IP connection setup procedures to make the SIP network scalable where millions of calls need to be handled for the large-scale network. In view of the disconnections by middle boxes like NATs and firewalls that remain in the path, the connection setup in the SIP network needs to be further scaled. The client-initiated connection management defined by RFC 5626 that uses reg-id and instance-id parameters in REGISTER message and Time-Flow header field has optimized the connection and setup, and hence the management, further making the SIP network connection highly scalable. The detail of the registration using RFC 5626 is described in Section 13.2. Example: `Flow-Timer: 3600`

From/RFC 3261 (Standards Track)/Request and Response	The From header field indicates the initiator of the request. This may be different from the initiator of the dialog. Requests sent by the callee to the caller use the callee's address in the From header field. The optional display-name is meant to be rendered by a human user interface. A system should use the display name Anonymous if the identity of the client is to remain hidden. Even if the *displayname* is empty, the name-addr form must be used if the addr-spec contains a comma, question mark, or semicolon. Syntax issues are discussed in Section 2.4.1.2.
	Two From header fields are equivalent if their URIs match, and their parameters match. Extension parameters in one header field, not present in the other, are ignored for the purposes of comparison. This means that the display name and presence or absence of angle brackets do not affect matching. See Section 4.2 (RFC 3261) for the rules for parsing a display name, URI and URI parameters, and header field parameters. The compact form of the From header field is f. Examples:
	
	`From: "A. G. Bell" <sip:agb@bell-telephone.com>;tag=a48s`
	`From: sip:+12125551212@server.phone2net.com;tag=887s`
	`f: Anonymous <sip:c8oqz84zk7z@privacy.org>;tag=hyh8`

(*Continued*)

Table 2.10 (Continued) SIP Header Field Descriptions

Header Field/RFC/Header Field Type	*Description*
Geolocation/RFC 6442 (Standards Track)/Request	The Geolocation header field in SIP conveys the location information of the SIP functional entities on end-to-end, and SIP entities in the SIP network may use this location information for making routing decisions. pres-URI is defined in RFC 3859 (see Section 6.2.2). http-URI and https-URI are defined according to RFC 2616 (obsoleted by RFCs 7230–7235) and RFC 2818, respectively. The cid-url is defined in RFC 2392 to locate message-body parts. This URI type is present in a SIP request when location is conveyed as a MIME body in the SIP message. GEO-URIs defined in RFC 5870 are not appropriate for usage in the SIP Geolocation header because it does not include retention and retransmission flags as part of the location information. Other URI schemes used in the location URI must be reviewed against the criteria defined in RFC 3693 for a Using Protocol that uses the location object (LO). The generic-param in the definition of locationValue is included as a mechanism for future extensions that might require parameters. This document defines no parameters for use with locationValue. If a Geolocation header field is received that contains generic-params, each parameter should be ignored and should not be removed when forwarding the locationValue. If a need arises to define parameters for use with locationValue, a revision/extension to this document is required. The Geolocation header field must have at least one locationValue. A SIP intermediary should not add location to a SIP request that already contains location. This will quite often lead to confusion within location recipients (LRs). However, if a SIP intermediary adds location, even if location was not previously present in a SIP request, that SIP intermediary is fully responsible for addressing the concerns of any 424 Bad Location Information SIP response it receives about this location addition and must not pass on (upstream) the 424 Bad Location Information response. A SIP intermediary that adds a locationValue must position the new locationValue as the last locationValue within the Geolocation header field of the SIP request. The Geolocation header field is valid in the following SIP requests: INVITE, REGISTER, OPTIONS, BYE, UPDATE, INFO, MESSAGE, REFER, SUBSCRIBE, NOTIFY, and PUBLISH. The Geolocation header field may be included in any one of the above-listed requests by a UA and a 424 response to any one of the requests sent above. Fully appreciating the caveats/warnings mentioned above, a SIP intermediary may add the Geolocation header field. A SIP intermediary may add a Geolocation header field if one is not present, for example, when a UA does not support the Geolocation mechanism but their outbound proxy does and knows the Target's location, or any of a number of other use cases. The Geolocation header field may be present in a SIP request or response without the presence of a Geolocation-Routing header. The default value of Geolocation-Routing header-value is *no*, meaning SIP intermediaries must not view (i.e., process, inspect, or actively dereference) any direct or indirect location within this SIP message. This is for at least two fundamental reasons: • To make the possibility of retention of the Target's location moot (because it was not viewed in the first place). • To prevent a different treatment of this SIP request based on the contents of the Location Information in the SIP request.

(*Continued*)

Table 2.10 (Continued) SIP Header Field Descriptions

Header Field/RFC/Header Field Type	*Description*
	Any locationValue must be related to the original Target. This is equally true for the location information in a SIP response, that is, from a SIP intermediary back to the Target. SIP intermediaries should not modify or delete any existing locationValue(s). A use case in which this would not apply would be where the SIP intermediary is an anonymizer. The problem with this scenario is that the geolocation included by the Target then becomes useless for the purpose or service for which they wanted to use (include) it. For example, 911 (emergency calling) or finding the nearest (towing company/pizza delivery/dry cleaning) service(s) will not yield the intended results if the Location Information were to be modified or deleted from the SIP request. Example: `Geolocation: <cid:target123@atlanta.example.com>`
Geolocation-Error/RFC 6442 (Standards Track)/Response	The Geolocation-Error header field is used for providing more granular error notifications specific to location errors within a received SIP request message that carries the location information if the location inserting entity is to know what was wrong within the original request. That is, the Geolocation-Error header field is used to convey location-specific errors within a response. The Geolocation-Error header field must contain only one locationErrorValue to indicate what was wrong with the locationValue the Location Recipient determined was bad. The locationErrorValue contains a three-digit error code indicating what was wrong with the location in the request. This error code has a corresponding quoted error text string that is human understandable. The text string is optional, but recommended for human readability, similar to the string phrase used for SIP response codes. The strings are complete enough for rendering to the user, if so desired. The strings in this document are recommendations, and are not standardized—meaning an operator can change the strings but must not change the meaning of the error code. Similar to RFC 3261 specification, there must not be more than one string per error code. The Geolocation-Error header field may be included in any response to one of the SIP methods mentioned in the case of Geolocation header field, so long as a locationValue was in the request part of the same transaction. For example, Alice includes her location in an INVITE to Bob. Bob can accept this INVITE, thus creating a dialog, even though his UA determined the location contained in the INVITE was bad. Bob merely includes a Geolocation-Error header value in the 200 OK responses to the INVITE informing Alice the INVITE was accepted but the location provided was bad. If, on the other hand, Bob cannot accept Alice's INVITE without a suitable location, a 424 Bad Location Information response is sent. If Alice is deliberately leaving location information out of the location object because she does not want Bob to have this additional information, implementations should be aware that Bob could have made the error repeatedly in order to receive more location information about Alice in a subsequent SIP request. Implementations must be on guard for this, by not allowing continually more information to be revealed unless it is clear that any LR is permitted by Alice to know all that Alice knows about her location. A limit on the number of such rejections to learn more location information should be configurable, with a recommended maximum of three times for each related transaction. A SIP intermediary that requires Alice's location in order to properly process Alice's INVITE also sends a 424 Bad Location Information response with a Geolocation-Error code. If more than one locationValue is present in a SIP request and at least one locationValue is determined to be valid by the LR, the location in that SIP request must be considered good as far as location is concerned, and no Geolocation-Error is to be sent.

(Continued)

Table 2.10 (Continued) SIP Header Field Descriptions

Header Field/RFC/Header Field Type	*Description*

	Here is an initial list of location-based error code ranges for any SIP response, including provisional responses (other than 100 Trying) and the new 424 Bad Location Information response. These error codes are divided into three categories, based on how the response receiver should react to these errors. There must be no more than one Geolocation-Error code in a SIP response, regardless of how many locationValues there are in the correlating SIP request. When more than one locationValue is present in a SIP request, this mechanism provides no indication to which one the Geolocation-Error code corresponds. If multiple errors are present, the LR applies local policy to select one.
	
	• 1xx errors mean the LR cannot process the location within the request: A nonexclusive list of reasons for returning a 1xx is as follows:
	– The location was not present or could not be found in the SIP request.
	– There was not enough location information to determine where the Target was.
	– The location information was corrupted or known to be inaccurate.
	• 2xx errors mean some specific permission is necessary to process the included location information.
	• 3xx errors mean there was trouble dereferencing the Location URI sent.
	
	Dereference attempts to the same request should be limited to 10 attempts within a few minutes. This number should be configurable, but result in a Geolocation-Error: 300 error once reached.
	It should be noted that for non-INVITE transactions, the SIP response will likely be sent before the dereference response has been received. This document does not alter that SIP reality. This means the receiver of any non-INVITE response to a request containing location should not consider a 200 OK response to mean that the act of dereferencing has concluded, and the dereferencer (i.e., the LR) has successfully received and parsed the Presence Information Data Format–Location Object (PIDF–LO) defined in RFC 4119 for errors and found none considering the transaction timing requirement.
	Additionally, if an LR cannot or chooses not to process location from a SIP request, a 500 Server Internal Error should be used with or without a configurable Retry-After header field. There is no special location error code for what already exists within SIP today. Within each of these ranges, there is a top-level error as follows:
	
	`Geolocation-Error: 100; code = "Cannot Process Location"`
	`Geolocation-Error: 200; code = "Permission to Use Location Information"`
	`Geolocation-Error: 300; code = "Dereference Failure"`
	
	If an error recipient cannot process a specific error code (such as the 201 or 202 below), perhaps because it does not understand that specific error code, the error recipient should process the error code as if it originally were a top-level error code where the X in X00 matches the specific error code. If the error recipient cannot process a non-100 error code, for whatever reason, then the error code 100 must be processed.
	There are two specific Geolocation-Error codes necessary to include in this document; both have to do with permissions necessary to process the SIP request; they are Geolocation-Error: 201; code = "Permission to Retransmit Location Information to a Third Party"

(*Continued*)

Table 2.10 (Continued) SIP Header Field Descriptions

Header Field/RFC/Header Field Type	*Description*
	This location error is specific to having the PIDF–LO <retransmission-allowed> defined in RFC 4119 element set to *no*. This location error is stating it requires permission (i.e., PIDF–LO <retransmission-allowed> element set to "yes") to process this SIP request further. If the location server (LS), a server that keeps location information in the SIP network, sending the location information does not want to give this permission, it will not change this permission in a new request. If the LS wants this message processed with the <retransmission-allowed> element set to *yes*, it must choose another logical path (if one exists) for this SIP request. `Geolocation-Error: 202; code = "Permission to Route Based on Location Information"` This location error is specific to having the Geolocation-Routing header value set to *no*. This location error is stating it requires permission (i.e., the Geolocation-Routing header value set to *yes*) to process this SIP request further. If the LS sending the location information does not want to give this permission, it will not change this permission in a new request. If the LS wants this message processed with the <retransmission-allowed> element set to *yes*, it must choose another logical path (if one exists) for this SIP request.
Geolocation-Routing/RFC 6442 (Standards Track)/ Request	The Geolocation-Routing header field used in SIP request messages to indicate whether or not SIP functional entities can route the messages within the SIP network based on the information provided in the location object. The only defined values for the Geolocation-Routing header field are *yes* or *no*. When the value is *yes*, the locationValue can be used for routing decisions along the downstream signaling path by intermediaries. Values other than *yes* or *no* are left for future extensions. Implementations not aware of an extension must treat any other received value the same as *no*. If no Geolocation-Routing header field is present in a SIP request, a SIP intermediary may insert this header. Without knowledge from a Rule Maker, the SIP intermediary inserting this header-value should not set the value to *yes*, as this may be more permissive than the originating party intends. An easy way around this is to have the Target always insert this header-value as *no*. When this Geolocation-Routing header-value is set to *no*, this means no locationValue (inserted by the originating UAC or any intermediary along the signaling path) can be used by any SIP intermediary to make routing decisions. Intermediaries that attempt to use the location information for routing purposes in spite of this counter indication could end up routing the request improperly as a result. The practical implication is that when the Geolocation-Routing header-value is set to *no*, if a cid:url is present in the SIP request, intermediaries must not view the location (because it is not for intermediaries to consider when processing the request); if a location URI is present, intermediaries must not dereference it. UAs are allowed to view location in the SIP request even when the Geolocation-Routing header-value is set to *no*. An LR must by default consider the Geolocation-Routing header-value as set to *no*, with no exceptions, unless the header field value is set to *yes* security properties. At most, it is a request for behavior within SIP intermediaries. That said, if the Geolocation-Routing header-value is set to *no*, SIP intermediaries are still to process the SIP request and send it further downstream within the signaling path if there are no errors present in this SIP request.

(*Continued*)

Table 2.10 (Continued) SIP Header Field Descriptions

<table>
<tr><th>Header Field/RFC/Header Field Type</th><th>Description</th></tr>
<tr><td></td><td>
The Geolocation-Routing header field satisfies the recommendations made in Section 3.5 of RFC 5606 regarding indication of permission to use location-based routing in SIP. SIP implementations are advised to pay special attention to the policy elements for location retransmission and retention described in RFC 4119. The Geolocation-Routing header field cannot appear without a header-value in a SIP request or response; that is, a null value is not allowed. The absence of a Geolocation-Routing header-value in a SIP request is always the same as the following header field: Geolocation-Routing: no.
The Geolocation-Routing header field may be present without a Geolocation header field in the same SIP request. The Geolocation header field contains a Target's location, and it must not be present if there is no location information in this SIP request. The location information is contained in one or more locationValues. These locationValues may be contained in a single Geolocation header field or distributed among multiple Geolocation header fields as indicated in RFC 3261.
The Geolocation-Routing header field indicates whether or not SIP intermediaries can view and then route this SIP request based on the included (directly or indirectly) location information. The Geolocation-Routing header field must not appear more than once in any SIP request, and must not lack a header-value. The default or implied policy of a SIP request that does not have a Geolocation-Routing header field is the same as if one were present and the header-value were set to no.
There are only three possible states regarding the Geolocation-Routing header field: No, Yes, or No header-field present in this SIP request. The expected results in each state are as shown below:
<table>
<tr><th>If Geolocation-Routing Is</th><th>Only Possible Interpretations</th></tr>
<tr><td>No</td><td>SIP intermediaries must not process the included geolocation information within this SIP request. SIP intermediaries inserting a locationValue into a Geolocation header field (whether adding to an existing header-value or inserting the Geolocation header field for the first time) must not modify or delete the received no header-value.</td></tr>
<tr><td>Yes</td><td>SIP intermediaries can process the included geolocation information within this SIP request and can change the policy to no for intermediaries further downstream.</td></tr>
<tr><td>Geolocation-Routing absent</td><td>If a Geolocation header field exists (meaning a locationValue is already present), a SIP intermediary MUST interpret the lack of a Geolocation-Routing header field as if there were one present and the header-value is set to no.
If there is no Geolocation header field in this SIP request, the default Geolocation-Routing is open and can be set by a SIP intermediary or not at all.</td></tr>
</table>
Example:
<code>Geolocation-Routing: no</code>
<code>Geolocation-Routing: yes</code>
<code>Geolocation-Routing: Geolocation-Routing absent</code>
</td></tr>
</table>

(*Continued*)

Table 2.10 (Continued) SIP Header Field Descriptions

Header Field/RFC/Header Field Type	*Description*
Hide/RFC 2543 (Standards Track)/Request	The Hide header field defined in RFC 2543 (obsoleted by RFC 3261) is used by UAs or proxies to request that the next hop proxy encrypts the Via header fields to hide message route information. However, RFC 3261 has deprecated this header field. RFC 3261 that supersedes RFC 2543 has deprecated the use of this header.
History-Info/RFC 4244 (Standards Track)/Request and Response	The History-Info header field used in the SIP request and response messages to inform proxies and UAs involved in processing a request about the history or progress of that request. This header field captures the history of a request that would be lost with the normal SIP processing involved in the subsequent forwarding of the request. The support of the History-Info header field requires no changes in the fundamental determination of request targets or in the request forwarding as defined in RFC 3261 (see Section 3.11). The History-Info header can appear in any request not associated with an established dialog, for example, INVITE, REGISTER, MESSAGE, REFER, OPTIONS, PUBLISH, and SUBSCRIBE request messages and any valid response to these requests. This capability enables many enhanced services by providing the information as to how and why a call arrives at a specific application or user. The History-Info header is added to a Request when a new request is created by a UAC or forwarded by a proxy, or when the target of a request is changed. That is, the History-Info header provides the useful information especially to application servers, proxies, and UAs when the request/response messages are retargeted. The term retarget refers to the changing of the target of a request and the subsequent forwarding of that request. It should be noted that retargeting only occurs when the Request-URI indicates a domain for which the processing entity is responsible. In terms of the SIP, the processing associated with retargeting, as described in RFC 3261 (see Section 3.11), is possible for the target of a request to be changed by the same proxy multiple times referred to as *internal retargeting*, as the proxy may add targets to the target set after beginning Request Forwarding. RFC 3261 (see Section 3.11) describes Request Forwarding. It is during this process of Request Forwarding that the History Information is captured as an optional, additional header field. Thus, the addition of the History-Info header does not affect fundamental SIP Request Forwarding. An entity (UA or proxy) changing the target of a request in response to a redirect or REFER should also propagate any History-Info header from the initial Request in the new request. The History-Info header is optional in that neither UAs nor proxies are required to support it. A new Supported header, *histinfo*, is included in the Request to indicate whether the History-Info header is returned in Responses. In addition to the histinfo Supported header, local policy determines whether or not the header is added to any request, or for a specific Request-URI, being retargeted. It is possible that this could restrict the applicability of services that make use of the Request History Information to be limited to retargeting within domain(s) controlled by the same local policy, or between domain(s) that negotiate policies with other domains to ensure support of the given policy, or services for which complete History Information is not required to provide the service. All applications making use of the History-Info header must clearly define the impact of the information not being available, and specify the processing of such a request.

(Continued)

Table 2.10 (Continued) SIP Header Field Descriptions

Header Field/RFC/Header Field Type	*Description*

	The History-Info header can reveal the detailed information on how a request or response message has been targeted and retargeted. The History-Info header should not be used where the Privacy header described in RFC 3323 (see Section 20.2) indicated that the general routing information should not be viewed by any intermediaries. In general, the Privacy header should be used to determine whether an intermediary can include the History-Info header in a Request that it receives and forwards or that it retargets. Thus, the History-Info header should not be included in Requests where the requestor has indicated a priv-value of Session-level or Header-level privacy.
	The local policy may also be used to determine whether to include the History-Info header at all, whether to capture a specific Request-URI in the header, or whether it be included only in the Request as it is retargeted within a specific domain. In the latter case, this is accomplished by adding a new priv-value, history, to the Privacy header of RFC 3323, indicating whether any or a specific History-Info header(s) should be forwarded.
	It is recognized that satisfying the privacy requirements can influence the functionality of this solution by overriding the request to generate the information. The applications making use of History-Info should address any impact on security and privacy this header may have, or must explain why it does not have an impact on security and privacy. The History-Info header carries the following information, with the mandatory parameters required when the header is included in a request or response:
	
	• Targeted-to-URI (hi-targeted-to-uri): A mandatory parameter for capturing the Request-URI for the specific Request as it is forwarded.
	• Index (hi-index): A mandatory parameter for History-Info reflecting the chronological order of the information, indexed to also reflect the forking and nesting of requests. The format for this parameter is a string of digits, separated by dots to indicate the number of forward hops and retargets. This results in a tree representation of the history of the request, with the lowest-level index reflecting a branch of the tree. By adding the new entries in order, including the index and securing the header, the ordering of the History-Info headers in the request is assured. In addition, applications may extract a variety of metrics (total number of retargets, total number of retargets from a specific branch, etc.) based on the index values.
	• Reason: An optional parameter for History-Info, reflected in the History-Info header by including the Reason header escaped in the hi-targeted-to-uri. A reason is not included for a hi-targeted-to-uri when it is first added in a History-Info header, but rather is added when the retargeting actually occurs.
	• Note that this does appear to complicate the security problem; however, retargeting only occurs when the hi-targeted-to-uri indicates a domain for which the processing entity is responsible. Thus, it would be the same processing entity that initially added the hi-targeted-to-URI to the header that would be updating it with the Reason.
	• Privacy: An optional parameter for History-Info, reflected in the History-Info header field values by including the Privacy header with a priv-value of *history* escaped in the hi-targeted- to-uri or by adding the Privacy header with a priv-value of history to the Request. The use of the Privacy Header with a priv-value of history indicates whether a specific or all History-Info headers should not be forwarded.
	• Extension (hi-extension): An optional parameter to allow for future optional extensions. As per RFC 3261, any implementation not understanding an extension should ignore it.
	
	Example:
	
	`History-Info: <sip:Bob@P1.example.com>;index=1,`
	`<sip:Bob@P2.example.com>; index=1.1,`
	`<sip:User3@UA3.example.com>; index=1.2`

(*Continued*)

Table 2.10 (Continued) SIP Header Field Descriptions

Header Field/RFC/Header Field Type	*Description*
Identity/RFC 4474 (Standards Track)/Request	The Identity header field defines a mechanism for securely identifying originators of SIP messages that can be used for both intra- and interdomain through conveying a signature used for validating the identity. SIP UAs or SIP servers can provide the authentication service over the SIP network. The Identity string is constructed with different parts of the SIP message that are separated by a "|" character. In fact, the Identity header is the signed hash of a canonical identity string consisting of caller's AOR expressed in the form of SIP URI, SIPS URI, Tel URI, or any other URI that is included in the caller's From and callee's To header fields; information from the Call-Id, CSeq, Date, and Contact header fields; and all the body content that contains the SDP part. However, the Date header field may not be present in the request and Contact header field may be empty. If the Date field is not present, the authentication service adds one. If the Contact header field is empty, then the corresponding field in the string is left empty as well. Using the private key of the service provider, the authentication service signs the hash calculated over the identity string and adds the Identity header to the SIP request. The signed-identity-digest is a signed hash of a canonical string generated from certain components of a SIP request. To create the contents of the signed-identity-digest, the following elements of a SIP message must be placed in a bit-exact string in the order specified here, separated by a vertical line, "|" or %x7C character: • The AOR of the UA sending the message, or addr-spec of the From header field (referred to occasionally here as the identity field). • The addr-spec component of the To header field, which is the AoR to which the request is being sent. • The callid from Call-Id header field. • The digit (1*DIGIT) and method (method) portions from CSeq header field, separated by a single space (ABNF SP, or %x20). Note that the CSeq header field allows LWS rather than SP to separate the digit and method portions, and thus the CSeq header field may need to be transformed to be canonicalized. The authentication service must strip leading zeros from the *digit* portion of the Cseq before generating the digest-string. • The Date header field, with exactly one space each for each SP, and the weekday and month items case set as shown in ABNF in RFC 3261 (see Section 2.4.1.2). RFC 3261 specifies that the ABNF for weekday and month is a choice among a set of tokens. The RFC 2234 (obsoleted by RFC 5234) rules for the ABNF specify that tokens are case sensitive. However, when used to construct the canonical string defined here, the first letter of each week and month must be capitalized, and the remaining two letters must be lowercase. This matches the capitalization provided in the definition of each token. All requests that use the Identity mechanism must contain a Date header. • The addr-spec component of the Contact header field value. If the request does not contain a Contact header, this field must be empty (i.e., there will be no white space between the fourth and fifth "|" characters in the canonical string). • The body content of the message with the bits exactly as they are in the Message (in the ABNF for SIP, the message body). This includes all components of multipart message bodies. Note that the message body does NOT include the CRLF separating the SIP headers from the message body, but does include everything that follows that CRLF. If the message has no body, then message body will be empty, and the final "|" will not be followed by any additional characters.

(*Continued*)

Table 2.10 (Continued) SIP Header Field Descriptions

Header Field/RFC/Header Field Type	*Description*
	Note again that the first addr-spec must be taken from the From header field value, the second addr-spec must be taken from the To header field value, and the third addr-spec must be taken from the Contact header field value, provided the Contact header is present in the request. After the digest-string is formed, it must be hashed and signed with the certificate for the domain. The hashing and signing algorithm is specified by the *alg* parameter of the Identity-Info header (see below this table for more information on Identity-Info header parameters). This document defines only one value for the alg parameter: *rsa-sha1*; further values must be defined in a Standards Track RFC. All implementations of this specification must support rsa-sha1. When the rsa-sha1 algorithm is specified in the alg parameter of Identity-Info, the hash and signature must be generated as follows: compute the results of signing this string with sha1WithRSAEncryption as described in RFC 3370 (obsoleted by RFC 5730) and base64 encode the results as specified in RFC 3548 (obsoleted by RFC 4648). A 1024-bit or longer RSA key must be used. The result is placed in the Identity header field. For detailed examples of the usage of this algorithm, see Section 2.6. The *absoluteURI* portion of the Identity-Info header must contain a URI that dereferences to a resource containing the certificate of the authentication service. All implementations of this specification must support the use of HTTP and HTTPS URIs in the Identity-Info header. Such HTTP and HTTPS URIs must follow the conventions of RFC 2585, and for those URIs the indicated resource must be of the form *application/pkix-cert* described in that specification. Note that this introduces key life-cycle management concerns; were a domain to change the key available at the Identity-Info URI before a verifier evaluates a request signed by an authentication service, this would cause obvious verifier failures. When a rollover occurs, authentication services should thus provide new Identity-Info URIs for each new certificate, and should continue to make older key acquisition URIs available for duration longer than the plausible lifetime of a SIP message (an hour would most likely suffice). The Identity-Info header field must contain an alg parameter. No other parameters are defined for the Identity-Info header in this document. Future Standards Track RFCs may define additional Identity-Info header parameters. An example is shown below: Identity:"ZYNBbHC00VMZr2kZt6VmCvPonWJMGvQTBDqghoWeLxJfzB2a1pxAr3VgrB0 SsSAaifsRdiOPoQZYOy2wrVghuhcsMbHWUSFxl6p6q5TOQXHMmz6uEo3svJsSH49thy GnFVcnyaZ++yRlBYYQTLqWzJ+KVhPKbfU/pryhVn9Yc6U=" In the same way, the caller might also want to know whether the call has reached to the callee is actually the one with whom he/she wants to communicate. In theory, the same approach can be used for authenticating the identity of the callee. In this case, the authentication service can add an Identity header in the response to assert the identity included in the To header. However, the responses cannot be authenticated unless either the authentication service is located in the callee's device or the communication between the callee and the authentication service is secured. Even then, there can be some problems if the call is retargeted to reach the callee, and as a result, the URI used in the To header used by the caller will be different than that of the retargeted URI where the callee has been reached. Since it is mandatory that the From and To headers of the SIP request messages and their responses cannot be changed, the authentication service of the retargeted domain cannot authenticate the callee of the retargeted URI.

(Continued)

Table 2.10 (Continued) SIP Header Field Descriptions

Header Field/RFC/Header Field Type	*Description*
	This problem of retargeting the callee has been solved in RFC 4919 (see Section 10.4.3.1) through deprecating mandatory reflection of the original To and From URIs in mid-dialog requests and their responses, which constitutes a change to RFC 3261. RFC 4919 makes no provision for proxies that are unable to tolerate a change of URI, since changing the URI has been expected for a considerable time. To cater for any UAs that are not able to tolerate a change of URI, a new option tag *from-change* is introduced for providing a positive indication of support in the Supported header field. By sending a request with a changed From header field URI only to targets that have indicated support for this option, there is no need to send this option tag in a Require header field. The retargeted callee with whom the call has finally been established is defined as the connected identity, and the callee sends a request UPDATE or re-INVITE to the caller once the session is established using as the From header the connected identity. This identity is asserted by the authentication service of the retargeted URI domain and is then verified at the caller side. However, the caller must be willing to accept the deviation from the SIP specifications defined in RFC 3261 and accept the in-dialog request with the From header that differs from the To header that the caller has used for setting up the dialog as stated earlier. The Identity defined in RFC 4474 (see Section 19.4.8) and the connected identity mechanisms specified in RFC 4916 allow an authenticated indemnity. However, it cannot prevent itself from the man-in-the-middle attack. Identity and Identity-Info headers from the request can be stripped by the attacker, and the request can still be valid. In this case, the callee cannot be able to verify the identity of the caller, and the caller would reject the call in the worst-case scenario.
Identity-Info/RFC 4474 (Standards Track)/Request	The Identity-Info header field conveys a reference to the certificate of the signer of the authentication service that signs the hash calculated over the identity string and adds the Identity header to the SIP message. It contains a URI of a resource that contains the certificate of the authentication service as well as the names of the algorithms used for generating the Identity header. The syntax of this header is defined in the Identify header of this table. Example: `Identity-Info: <https://atlanta.example.com/atlanta.cer>;alg=rsa-sha1`
Info-Package/RFC 6086 (Standards Track)/Request	The Info-Package header field is used by a UA to indicate which Info Package is associated with the request usually with the INFO method. One particular INFO request can only be associated with a single Info Package. RFC 6086 of the INFO method (see Section 16.8) defines an Info Package mechanism. An Info Package specification defines the content and semantics of the information carried in an INFO message associated with the Info Package. The Info Package mechanism also provides a way for UAs to indicate for which Info Packages they are willing to receive INFO requests, and which Info Package a specific INFO request is associated with.
In-Reply-To/RFC 3261 (Standards Track)/Request	The In-Reply-To header field enumerates the Call-IDs that this call references or returns. These Call-IDs may have been cached by the client, then included in this header field in a return call. This allows automatic call distribution systems to route return calls to the originator of the first call. This also allows callees to filter calls, so that only return calls for calls they originated will be accepted. This field is not a substitute for request authentication. Example: `In-Reply-To: 70710@saturn.bell-tel.com, 17320@saturn.bell-tel.com`

(Continued)

Table 2.10 (Continued) SIP Header Field Descriptions

Header Field/RFC/Header Field Type	*Description*

Join/RFC 3911 (Standards Track)/Request	The Join header field is used to logically join an existing SIP dialog with a new SIP dialog. The one consequence of this insertion of a new participant to an existing two-party multimedia call will essentially make the call a three-way multiparty conference call where media bridging may be required. Use of an explicit Join header is needed in some cases instead of addressing an INVITE to a conference URI for the following reasons:
	• A conference may not yet exist—the new invitation may be trying to join an ordinary two-party call.
	• The party joining may not know if the dialog it wants to join is part of a conference.
	• The party joining may not know the conference URI.
	This primitive can be used to enable a variety of features, for example: Barge-In, answering-machine-style Message Screening, Call Center Monitoring, and other multiparty conferencing services. A Join header must contain exactly one to-tag and exactly one from-tag, as they are required for unique dialog matching. For compatibility with dialogs initiated by RFC 2543-compliant UAs, which is superseded by RFC 3261, a to-tag of zero matches both a to-tag value of zero and a null to-tag. Likewise, a from-tag of zero matches both a to-tag value of zero and a null from-tag. Examples:
	`Join: 98732@sip.example.com`
	`      ;from-tag=r33th4x0r`
	`      ;to-tag=ff87ff`
	`Join: 12adf2f34456gs5;to-tag=12345;from-tag=54321`
	`Join: 87134@192.0.2.23;to-tag=24796;from-tag=0`
	`Join: joe@howell.network.com;to-tag=xyz;from-tag=pdq`

Max-Breadth/RFC 5393 (Standards Track)/Request	The Max-Breadth mechanism (RFC 5393, see Section 19.9) limits the total number of concurrent branches caused by a forked SIP request. With this mechanism, all proxyable requests are assigned a positive integral Max-Breadth value, which denotes the maximum number of concurrent branches this request may spawn through parallel forking as it is forwarded from its current point. When a proxy forwards a request, its Max-Breadth value is divided among the outgoing requests. In turn, each of the forwarded requests has a limit on how many concurrent branches it may spawn. As branches complete, their portion of the Max-Breadth value becomes available for subsequent branches, if needed. If there is insufficient Max-Breadth to carry out a desired parallel fork, a proxy can return the 440 Max-Breadth Exceeded response defined in this document. Max-Breadth does not prevent forking. It only limits the number of concurrent parallel forked branches. In particular, a Max-Breadth of 1 restricts a request to pure serial forking rather than restricting it from being forked at all. A client receiving a 440 Max-Breadth Exceeded response can infer that its request did not reach all possible destinations. The Max-Breadth header field value takes no parameters. For each response context defined in Section 16 of RFC 3261 in a proxy, this mechanism defines two positive integral values: Incoming Max-Breadth and Outgoing Max-Breadth. Incoming Max-Breadth is the value in the Max-Breadth header field in the request that formed the response context. Outgoing Max-Breadth is the sum of the Max-Breadth header field values in all forwarded requests in the response context that have not received a final response.

(Continued)

Table 2.10 (Continued) SIP Header Field Descriptions

Header Field/RFC/Header Field Type	*Description*
Max-Forwards/RFC 3261 (Standards Track)/Request	The Max-Forwards header field must be used with any SIP method to limit the number of proxies or gateways that can forward the request to the next downstream server. This can also be useful when the client is attempting to trace a request chain that appears to be failing or looping in mid-chain. The Max-Forwards value is an integer in the range 0–255 indicating the remaining number of times this request message is allowed to be forwarded. This count is decremented by each server that forwards the request. The recommended initial value is 70. This header field should be inserted by elements that cannot otherwise guarantee loop detection. For example, a B2BUA should insert a Max-Forwards header field. Example: `Max-Forwards: 6`

MIME-Version/RFC 3261 (Standards Track)/Response	This SIP header is adopted from HTTP/1.1 of RFC 2616 (obsoleted by RFCs 7230–7235). According to this RFC, SIP RFC 3261 messages may include a single MIME-Version general-header field to indicate what version of the MIME protocol was used to construct the message. Use of the MIME-Version header field indicates that the message is in full compliance with the MIME protocol as defined in RFC 2045. Proxies/gateways are responsible for ensuring full compliance (where possible) when exporting SIP messages to strict MIME environments.
	`MIME-Version = "MIME-Version" ":" 1*DIGIT "." 1*DIGIT`
	MIME version 1.0 is the default for use in SIP. However, SIP message parsing and semantics are defined by RFC 2616 (obsoleted by RFCs 7230–7235) and not the MIME specification. Example:
	`MIME-Version: 1.0`

Min-Expires/RFC 3261 (Standards Track)/Response	The Min-Expires header field conveys the minimum refresh interval supported for soft-state elements managed by that server. This includes Contact header fields that are stored by a registrar. The header field contains a decimal integer number of seconds from 0 to $(2^{32} - 1)$. The use of the header field in a 423 (Interval Too Brief) response is described in RFC 3261 (see Section 3.3). Example: `Min-Expires: 60`
Min-SE/RFC 4028 (Standards Track)/Request and Response	The Min-SE header field indicates the minimum value for the session interval, in units of delta-seconds. When used in an INVITE or UPDATE request, it indicates the smallest value of the session interval that can be used for that session. When present in a request or response, its value must not be less than 90 seconds. When the header field is not present, its default value for is 90 seconds. The Min-SE header field must not be used in responses except for those with a 422 response code. It indicates the minimum value of the session interval that the server is willing to accept. Example: `Min-SE: 360`
Organization/RFC 3261 (Standards Track)/Request and Response	The Organization header field conveys the name of the organization to which the SIP element issuing the request or response belongs. The field may be used by client software to filter calls. Example: Organization: Boxes by Bob

(Continued)

Table 2.10 (Continued) SIP Header Field Descriptions

Header Field/RFC/Header Field Type	*Description*
P-Access-Network-Info/RFC 7315 (Informational)/ Request and Response	The P-Access-Network-Info header field can appear in all SIP methods except ACK and CANCEL. This header field is useful in SIP-based networks that also provide OSI Layer 2 (L2)/OSI Layer 3 (L3) connectivity through different access technologies. SIP UAs may use this header field to relay information about the access technology to proxies that are providing services. The serving proxy may then use this information to optimize services for the UA. For example, a 3GPP (Third Generation Partnership Project) UA may use this header field to pass information about the access network, such as radio access technology and radio cell identity, to its home service provider. For the purpose of this extension, we define an access network as the network providing the L2/L3 IP connectivity, which, in turn, provides a user with access to the SIP capabilities and services provided. In some cases, the SIP server that provides the user with services may wish to know information about the type of access network that the UA is currently using. Some services are more suitable or less suitable depending on the access type, and some services are of more value to subscribers if the access network details are known by the SIP proxy that provides the user with services. In other cases, the SIP server that provides the user with services may simply wish to know crude location information in order to provide certain services to the user. For example, many of the location-based services available in wireless networks today require the home network to know the identity of the cell the user is being served by. Some regulatory requirements exist mandating that for cellular radio systems, the identity of the cell where an emergency call is established is made available to the emergency authorities. The SIP server that provides services to the user may desire to have knowledge about the access network. This is achieved by defining a new private SIP extension header field: P-Access-Network-Info. This header field carries information relating to the access network between the UAC and its serving proxy in the home network. A proxy providing services based on the P-Access-Network-Info header field must consider the trust relationship to the UA or outbound proxy including the P-Access-Network-Info header field. **Applicability Statement for the P-Access-Network-Info Header Field:** This mechanism is appropriate in environments where SIP services are dependent on SIP elements knowing details about the IP and lower-layer technologies used by a UA to connect to the SIP network. Specifically, the extension requires that the UA know the access technology it is using, and that a proxy desires such information to provide services. Generally, SIP is built on the everything-over-IP and IP-over-everything principles, where the access technology is not relevant for the operation of SIP. Since SIP systems generally should not care or even know about the access technology, this SIP extension is not for general SIP usage. The information revealed in the P-Access-Network-Info header field is potentially very sensitive. Proper protection of this information depends on the existence of specific business and security relationships among the proxies that will see SIP messages containing this header field. It also depends on explicit knowledge of the UA of the existence of those relationships. Therefore, this mechanism is only suitable in environments where the appropriate relationships are in place, and the UA has explicit knowledge that they exist.

(Continued)

Table 2.10 (Continued) SIP Header Field Descriptions

Header Field/RFC/Header Field Type	*Description*
	Usage of the P-Access-Network-Info Header: When a UA generates a SIP request or response that it knows is going to be securely sent to its SIP proxy that is providing services, the UA inserts a P-Access-Network-Info header field into field the SIP message. This header contains information on the access network that the UA is using to get IP connectivity. The header is typically ignored by intermediate proxies between the UA and the SIP proxy that is providing services. The proxy providing services can inspect the header and make use of the information contained there to provide appropriate services, depending on the value of the header. Before proxying the request onwards to an untrusted administrative network domain, this proxy strips the header from the message. Additionally, the first outbound proxy, if in possession of appropriate information, can also add a P-Access-Network-Info header field with its own information. *UA Behavior*: A UA that supports this extension and is willing to disclose the related parameters may insert the P-Access-Network-Info header field in any SIP request or response. The UA inserting this information MUST have a trust relationship with the proxy that is providing services to protect its privacy by deleting the header before forwarding the message outside of the proxy's domain. This proxy is typically located in the home network. To avoid the deletion of the header, there must also be a transitive trust in intermediate proxies between the UA and the proxy that provides the services. This trust is established by business agreements between the home network and the access network, and generally supported by the use of standard security mechanisms, for example, IPsec, AKA, and TLS. *Proxy Behavior*: A proxy must not modify the value of the P-Access-Network-Info header field. A proxy in possession of appropriate information about the access technology may insert a P-Access-Network-Info header field with its own values. A proxy sending toward an untrusted entity must remove any P-Access-Network-Info header field containing a *network-provided* value. A proxy that is providing services to the UA can act upon any information present in the P-Access-Network-Info header field value, to provide a different service depending on the network or the location through which the UA is accessing the server. For example, for cellular radio access networks, the SIP proxy located in the home network may use the cell ID to provide basic localized services. A proxy that provides services to the user is typically located in the home network and is therefore trusted. It must delete the header when the SIP signaling is forwarded to a SIP server located in an untrusted administrative network domain. The SIP server providing services to the UA uses the access network information that is of no interest to other proxies located in different administrative domains.

P-Asserted-Identity/RFC 3325 (Informational)/Request	The P-Asserted-Identity header field is used among trusted SIP entities (typically intermediaries) to carry the identity of the user sending a SIP message as it was verified by authentication. It contains a URI (commonly a SIP URI) and an optional display-name. There may be one or two P-Asserted-Identity values. If there is one value, it must be a sip, sips, or tel URI. If there are two values, one value must be a sip or sips URI and the other must be a tel URI. It is worth noting that proxies can (and will) add and remove this header field. Example:
	
	`P-Asserted-Identity: "John Williams"`
	`sip:john@network.com`
	`P-Asserted-Identity: tel:+14085264000`

(*Continued*)

Table 2.10 (Continued) SIP Header Field Descriptions

Header Field/RFC/Header Field Type	*Description*
P-Asserted-Service/RFC 6050 (Informational)/Request	The private P-Asserted-Service header field enables a network of trusted SIP servers to assert the service of authenticated users. This header carries the service information of the user sending a SIP message. The use of this header is only applicable inside an administrative domain with previously agreed-upon policies for generation, transport, and usage of such information. However, this header does not offer a general service identification model suitable for use between different Trust Domains or for use in the Internet at large. The P-Asserted-Service header field carries information that is derived service identification. While declarative service identification can assist in deriving the value transferred in this header field, this should be in the form of streamlining the correct derived service identification. By providing a mechanism to compute and store the results of the domain-specific service calculation, that is, the derived service identification, this optimization allows a single trusted proxy to perform an analysis of the request and authorize the requestor's permission to request such a service. The proxy may then include a service identifier that relieves other trusted proxies and trusted UAs from performing further duplicate analysis of the request for their service identification purposes. In addition, this header allows UACs outside the Trust Domain to provide a hint of the requested service. This header does not provide for the dialog or transaction to be rejected if the service is not supported end-to-end. SIP provides other mechanisms, such as the option tag and use of the Require and Proxy-Require header fields, where such functionality is required. No explicitly signaled service identification exists, and the session proceeds for each node's definition of the service in use, on the basis of information contained in the SDP and in other SIP header fields. This mechanism is specifically for managing the information needs of intermediate routing devices between the calling user and the user represented by the Request-URI. In support of this mechanism, an informal URN is defined to identify the services. This provides a hierarchical structure for defining services and subservices, and provides an address that can be resolvable for various purposes. It should be noted that how a service can be uniquely resolved has not been addressed by this header or URN. A proxy server that handles a request can, after authenticating the originating user in some way (e.g., digest authentication) to ensure that the user is entitled to that service, insert a header field such as a P-Asserted-Service into the request and forward it. However it is not sufficient to uniquely identify a service, and the remedy of this is to extend the SIP signaling to capture the missing element. A proxy server or UA that it does not trust removes all the P-Asserted-Service header field values. Syntactically, there may be multiple P-Preferred-Service header fields in a request. The semantics of multiple P-Preferred-Service header fields appearing in the same request is not defined at this time. Implementations of this specification must only provide one P-Preferred-Service header field value.

(Continued)

Table 2.10 (Continued) SIP Header Field Descriptions

Header Field/RFC/Header Field Type	*Description*

	The naming convention described above uses the term *service*; however, all the constructs are equally applicable to identifying applications within the UA. The URN consists of a hierarchical service identifier or application identifier, with a sequence of labels separated by periods. The leftmost label is the most significant one and is called *top-level service identifier*, while names to the right are called *subservices* or *subapplications*. The set of allowable characters is the same as that for domain names and a subset of the labels allowed in RFC 3958. Labels are case insensitive and MUST be specified in all lowercase. For any given service identifier, labels can be removed right-to-left and the resulting URN is still valid, referring a more generic service, with the exception of the top-level service identifier and possibly the first subservice or subapplication identifier. Labels cannot be removed beyond a defined basic service; for example, the label w.x may define a service, but the label w may only define an assignment authority for assigning subsequent values and not define a service in its own right. In other words, if a service identifier *w.x.y.z* exists, the URNs *w.x* and *w.x.y* are also valid service identifiers, but w may not be a valid service identifier if it merely defines who is responsible for defining x. Example:
	`P-Asserted-Service:`
	`urn:urn-7:3gpp-service.exampletelephony.version1`

P-Associated-URI/RFC 7315 (Informational)/Response	The P-Associated-URI header field can appear in the SIP REGISTER method and 2xx responses. This extension allows a registrar to return a set of associated URIs for a registered SIP AOR. We define the P-Associated- URI header field, used in the 200 OK response to a REGISTER request. The P-Associated-URI header field contains the set of URIs that are associated with the registered AOR. In addition to the AOR, an associated URI is a URI that the service provider has allocated to a user. A registrar contains information that allows zero or more URIs to be associated with an AOR. Usually, all these URIs (the AOR and the associated URIs) are allocated for the usage of a particular user. This extension to SIP allows the UAC to know, upon a successful authenticated registration, which other URIs, if any, the service provider has associated with an AOR URI. Note that, in standard SIP usage (RFC 3261), the registrar does not register the associated URIs on behalf of the user. Only the AOR that is present in the To header field of the REGISTER is registered and bound to the contact address. The only information conveyed is that the registrar is aware of other URIs that can be used by the same user. A situation may be possible, however, in which an application server (or even the registrar itself) registers any of the associated URIs on behalf of the user by means of a third-party registration. However, this third-party registration is beyond the scope of this document. A UAC must not assume that the associated URIs are registered. If a UAC wants to check whether any of the associated URIs is registered, it can do so by mechanisms specified outside this document; for example, the UA may send a REGISTER request with the To header field value set to any of the associated URIs and without a Contact header field. The 200 OK response will include a Contact header field with the list of AORs that have been registered with contact addresses. If the associated URI is not registered, the UA may register it before its utilization.

(Continued)

Table 2.10 (Continued) SIP Header Field Descriptions

Header Field/RFC/Header Field Type	*Description*
	Applicability Statement for the P-Associated-URI Header Field: The P-Associated-URI header field is applicable in SIP networks where the SIP provider allows a set of identities that a user can claim (in header fields like the From header field) in requests that the UA generates. Furthermore, it assumes that the provider knows the entire set of identities that a user can legitimately claim and that the user is willing to restrict its claimed identities to that set. This is in contrast to normal SIP usage, where the From header field is explicitly an end-user-specified field. **Usage of the P-Associated-URI Header Field:** The registrar inserts the P-Associated-URI header field into the 200 OK response to a REGISTER request. The header field value is populated with a list of URIs that are associated to the AOR. If the registrar supports the P-Associated-URI header field extension and there is at least one associated URI, then the registrar must insert the P-Associated-URI header field in all the 200 OK responses to a REGISTER request. The absence of a P-Associated-URI header field indicates that there are no associated URIs for the registered AOR. ***Procedures at the UA:*** A UAC may receive a P-Associated-URI header field in the 200 OK response for a REGISTER request. The presence of a header field in the 200 OK response for a REGISTER request implies that the extension is supported at the registrar. The header field value contains a list of one or more URIs associated to the AOR. The UAC may use any of the associated URIs to populate the From header field value, or any other SIP header field value that provides information of the identity of the calling party, in a subsequent request. The UAC may check whether or not the associated URI is registered. This check can be done, for example, by populating the To header field value in a REGISTER request sent to the registrar and without a Contact header field. The 200 OK response will include a Contact header field with the list of AORs that have been registered with contact addresses. As described in SIP (RFC 3261), the 200 OK response may contain a Contact header field with zero or more values (zero meaning the AOR is not registered). ***Procedures at the Registrar:*** A registrar that receives and authorizes a REGISTER request may associate zero or more URIs with the registered AOR. If the AOR under registration does not have any associated URIs, the P-Associated-URI header field shall not be included. Otherwise, a registrar that supports this specification MUST include a P-Associated-URI header field in the 200 OK response to a REGISTER request that contains a contact header. The header field must be populated with a comma-separated list of URIs that are associated to the AOR under registration. ***Procedures at the Proxy:*** This header is not intended to be used by proxies—a proxy does not add, read, modify, or delete the header field; therefore, any proxy MUST relay this header field unchanged.

(*Continued*)

Table 2.10 (Continued) SIP Header Field Descriptions

Header Field/RFC/Header Field Type	*Description*
Path/RFC 3327 (Standards Track)/Request and Response	The SIP Path header field is very similar to the Record-Route header and is used in conjunction with SIP REGISTER requests and with 200 class messages in response to REGISTER (REGISTER responses). A preloaded Path header field may be inserted into a REGISTER by any SIP node traversed by that request. Like the Route header field, sequential Path header fields are evaluated in the sequence in which they are present in the request, and Path header fields may be combined into compound Path header in a single Path header field. The registrar reflects the accumulated Path back into the REGISTER response, and intermediate nodes propagate this back toward the originating UA. The difference between Path and Record-Route is that Path applies to REGISTER and 200 class responses to REGISTER. Record-Route does not, and cannot, be defined in REGISTER for reasons of backward compatibility. Furthermore, the vector established by Record-Route applies only to requests within the dialog that established that Record-Route, whereas the vector established by Path applies to future dialogs. Note that the Path header field values conform to the syntax of a Route element as defined in RFC 3261. As suggested therein, such values must include the loose-routing indicator parameter *;lr* for full compliance with RFC 3261. Support for the Path header field may be indicated by a UA by including the option tag *path* in a Supported header field. Example: `Path: <sip:P3.EXAMPLEHOME.COM;lr>,<sip:P1.EXAMPLEVISITED.COM;lr>`
P-Called-Party-ID/RFC 7315 (Informational)/Request	The P-Called-Party-ID header field can appear in SIP INVITE, OPTIONS, PUBLISH, SUBSCRIBE, and MESSAGE methods and all responses. A proxy server inserts a P-Called-Party-ID header field, typically in an INVITE request, en route to its destination. The header is populated with the Request-URI received by the proxy in the request. The UAS identifies to which AOR, out of several registered AORs, the invitation was sent (e.g., the user may be simultaneously using one personal SIP URI and one business SIP URI to receive invitation to sessions). The UAS can use the information to render different distinctive audiovisual alerting tones, depending on the URI used to receive the invitation to the session. Users in the 3GPP IP Multimedia Subsystem (IMS) may get one or several SIP URIs (AOR) to identify the user. For example, a user may get one business SIP URI and one personal SIP URI. As an example of utilization, the user may make available the business SIP URI to coworkers and may make available the personal SIP URI to members of the family. At a certain point in time, both the business SIP URI and the personal SIP URI are registered in the SIP registrar, so both URIs can receive invitations to new sessions. When the user receives an invitation to join a session, he/she should be aware of which of the registered SIP URIs this session was sent to. This requirement is stated in the 3GPP Release 5 requirements on SIP (RFC 4083). The problem arises during the terminating side of a session establishment. At that time, the SIP proxy that is serving a UA gets an INVITE request, and the SIP server retargets the SIP URI that is present in the Request-URI, and replaces that SIP URI with the SIP URI published by the user in the Contact header field of the REGISTER request at registration time. One can argue that the To header field conveys the semantics of the called user, and therefore, this extension to SIP is not needed. Although the To header field in SIP may convey the called party ID in most situations, there are two particular cases when the above assumption is not correct:

(Continued)

Table 2.10 (Continued) SIP Header Field Descriptions

Header Field/RFC/Header Field Type	*Description*

	1. The session has been forwarded, redirected, etc., by previous SIP proxies, before arriving to the proxy that is serving the called user.
	2. The UAC builds an INVITE request and the To header field is not the same as the Request-URI. The problem of using the To header field is that this field is populated by the UAC and not modified by proxies in the path. If the UAC, for any reason, did not populate the To header field with the AOR of the destination user, then the destination user is not able to distinguish to which AOR the session was destined.
	
	Another possible solution to the problem is built upon the differentiation of the Contact header field value between different AOR at registration time. The UA can differentiate each AOR it registers by assigning a different Contact header field value. For example, when the UA registers the AOR sip:id1, the Contact header field value can be sip:id1@ua, while the registration of the AOR sip:id2 can be bound to the Contact header field value sip:id2@ua. The solution described above assumes that the UA explicitly registers each of its AORs, and therefore, it has full control over the contact address values assigned to each registration.
	However, if the UA does not have full control of its registered AORs, because of, for example, a third-party registration, the solution does not work. This may be the case of the 3GPP registration, where the UA may have previously indicated to the network, by means outside of SIP, that some other AORs may be automatically registered when the UA registers a particular AOR. The requirement is covered in the 3GPP Release 5 requirements on SIP (RFC 4083). In the next paragraphs, we show an example of the problem, in the case in which there has been some sort of call forwarding in the session, so that the UAC is not aware of the intended destination URI in the current INVITE request. We assume that a UA is registering to its proxy (P1).
	Scenario UA–P1
	F1 Register UA -> P1
	
	`REGISTER sip:example.com SIP/2.0`
	`Via: SIP/2.0/UDP 192.0.2.4:5060;branch=z9hG4bKnashds7`
	`To: sip:user1-business@example.com`
	`From: sip:user1-business@example.com;tag=456248`
	`Call-ID: 843817637684230998sdasdh09`
	`CSeq: 1826 REGISTER`
	`Contact: <sip:user1@192.0.2.4>`
	
	The user also registers his personal URI to his/her registrar.
	F2 Register UA -> P1
	
	`REGISTER sip:example.com SIP/2.0`
	`Via: SIP/2.0/UDP 192.0.2.4:5060;branch=z9hG4bKnashdt8`
	`To: sip:user1-personal@example.com`
	`From: sip:user1-personal@example.com;tag=346249`
	`Call-ID: 2Q3817637684230998sdasdh10`
	`CSeq: 1827 REGISTER`
	`Contact: <sip:user1@192.0.2.4>`

(Continued)

Table 2.10 (Continued) SIP Header Field Descriptions

<table>
<tr><th>Header Field/RFC/Header Field Type</th><th>Description</th></tr>
<tr><td></td><td>Later, the proxy/registrar (P1) receives an INVITE request from another proxy (P2) destined to the user's business SIP AOR. We assume that this INVITE request has undergone some sort of forwarding in the past, and as such, the To header field is not populated with the SIP URI of the user. In this case, we assume that the session was initially addressed to sip:other-user@othernetwork.com. The SIP server at othernetwork.com has forwarded this session to sip:user1-business@example.com.
Scenario UA–P1–P2
F3 Invite P2 -> P1

INVITE sip:user1-business@example.com SIP/2.0
Via: SIP/2.0/UDP 192.0.2.20:5060;branch=z9hG4bK03djaoe1
To: sip:other-user@othernetwork.com
From: sip:another-user@anothernetwork.com;tag=938s0
Call-ID: 843817637684230998sdasdh09
CSeq: 101 INVITE

The proxy P1 retargets the user and replaces the Request-URI with the SIP URI published during registration time in the Contact header field value.
F4 Invite P1 -> UA

INVITE sip:user1@192.0.2.4 SIP/2.0
Via: SIP/2.0/UDP 192.0.2.10:5060;branch=z9hG4bKg48sh128
Via: SIP/2.0/UDP 192.0.2.20:5060;branch=z9hG4bK03djaoe1
To: sip:other-user@othernetwork.com
From: sip:another-user@anothernetwork.com;tag=938s0
Call-ID: 843817637684230998sdasdh09
CSeq: 101 INVITE

When the UAS receives the INVITE request, it cannot determine whether it got the session invitation due to the user's registration of the business or personal AOR. Neither the UAS nor proxies/application servers can provide this user a service based on the destination AOR of the session. We solve this problem by allowing the proxy that is responsible for the home domain (as defined in SIP) of the user to insert a P-Called-Party-ID header field that identifies the AOR to which this session is destined.
If this SIP extension is used, the proxy serving the called user will get the message flow F5; it will populate the P-Called-Party-ID header field in message flow F6 with the contents of the Request-URI in F4. This is shown in flows F5 and F6, as follows:
F5 Invite P2 -> P1

INVITE sip:user1-business@example.com SIP/2.0
Via: SIP/2.0/UDP 192.0.2.20:5060;branch=z9hG4bK03djaoe1
To: sip:other-user@othernetwork.com
From: sip:another-user@anothernetwork.com;tag=938s0
Call-ID: 843817637684230998sdasdh09
CSeq: 101 INVITE
F6 Invite P1 -> UA
INVITE sip:user1@192.0.2.4 SIP/2.0
Via: SIP/2.0/UDP 192.0.2.10:5060;branch=z9hG4bKg48sh128
Via: SIP/2.0/UDP 192.0.2.20:5060;branch=z9hG4bK03djaoe1
To: sip:other-user@othernetwork.com
From: sip:another-user@anothernetwork.com;tag=938s0
Call-ID: 843817637684230998sdasdh09
P-Called-Party-ID: <sip:user1-business@example.com>
CSeq: 101 INVITE</td></tr>
</table>

(Continued)

Table 2.10 (Continued) SIP Header Field Descriptions

Header Field/RFC/Header Field Type	*Description*
	When the UA receives the INVITE request F6, it can determine the intended AOR of the session and apply whatever service is needed for that AOR. **Applicability Statement for the P-Called-Party-ID Header Field:** The P-Called-Party-ID header field is applicable when the UAS needs to be aware of the intended AOR that was present in the Request-URI of the request, before the proxy retargets to the contact address. The UAS may be interested in applying different audiovisual alerting effects or other filtering services, depending on the intended destination of the request. It is especially valuable when the UAS has registered several AORs to his registrar, and therefore, the UAS is not aware of the AOR that was present in the INVITE request when it hit his proxy/registrar, unless this extension is used. It is acknowledged that the History-Info header field will provide equivalent coverage to that of the P-Called-Party-ID header field. However, the P-Called-Party-ID header field is used entirely within the 3GPP system and does not appear to SIP entities outside that of a single 3GPP operator. **Usage of the P-Called-Party-ID Header Field:** The P-Called-Party-ID header field provides proxies and the UAS with the AOR that was present in the Request-URI of the request, before a proxy retargets the request. This information is intended to be used by subsequent proxies in the path or by the UAS. Typically, a SIP proxy inserts the P-Called-Party-ID header field before retargeting the Request-URI in the SIP request. The header field value is populated with the contents of the Request-URI, before replacing it with the contact address. ***Procedures at the UA:*** A UAC must not insert a P-Called-Party-ID header field in any SIP request or response. A UAS may receive a SIP request that contains a P-Called-Party-ID header field. The header field will be populated with the AOR received by the proxy in the Request-URI of the request, before its forwarding to the UAS. The UAS may use the value in the P-Called-Party-ID header field to provide services based on the called party URI, such as, for example, filtering of calls depending on the date and time, distinctive presentation services, distinctive alerting tones, and others. ***Procedures at the Proxy:*** A proxy that has access to the contact information of the user can insert a P-Called-Party-ID header field in any of the SIP INVITE, OPTIONS, PUBLISH, SUBSCRIBE, and MESSAGE requests. When included, the proxy must populate the header field value with the contents of the Request-URI present in the SIP request that the proxy received. It is necessary that the proxy that inserts the P-Called-Party-ID header field has information about the user, in order to prevent a wrong delivery of the called party ID. This information may, for example, have been learned through a registration process. A proxy or application server that receives a request containing a P-Called-Party-ID header field may use the contents of the header field to provide a service to the user based on the URI of that header field value. A SIP proxy must not insert a P-Called-Party-ID header field in REGISTER requests.

(*Continued*)

Table 2.10 (Continued) SIP Header Field Descriptions

Header Field/RFC/Header Field Type	*Description*
P-Charging-Function-Addresses/RFC 7315 (Informational)/Request	3GPP has defined a distributed architecture that results in multiple network entities becoming involved in providing access and services. There is a need to inform each SIP proxy involved in a transaction about the common charging functional entities to receive the generated charging records or charging events. The solution provided by 3GPP is to define two types of charging functional entities: Charging Collection Function (CCF) and Event Charging Function (ECF). CCF is used for offline charging (e.g., for postpaid account charging). ECF is used for online charging (e.g., for prepaid account charging). There may be more than a single instance of CCF and ECF in a network, in order to provide redundancy in the network. In case there are more than a single instance of either the CCF or the ECF addresses, implementations should attempt sending the charging data to the ECF or CCF address, starting with the first address of the sequence (if any) in the P-Charging-Function-Addresses header field. If the first address of the sequence is not available, then the next address (ccf-2 or ecf-2) must be used if available. The CCF and ECF addresses may be passed during the establishment of a dialog or in a stand-alone transaction. More detailed information about charging can be found in 3GPP TS 32.240 [4] and 3GPP TS 32.260 [5]. We define the SIP private header field P-Charging-Function-Addresses header field. The P-Charging-Function-Addresses header field can appear in all SIP methods except ACK and CANCEL. A proxy may include this header field, if not already present, in either the initial request or response for a dialog or in the request and response of a stand-alone transaction outside a dialog. When present, only one instance of the header must be present in a particular request or response. The mechanisms by which a SIP proxy collects the values to populate the P-Charging-Function-Addresses header field values are outside the scope of this document. However, as an example, a SIP proxy may have preconfigured these addresses or may obtain them from a subscriber database. **Applicability Statement for the P-Charging-Function-Addresses Header Field:** The P-Charging-Function-Addresses header field is applicable within a single private administrative domain where coordination of charging is required, for example, according to the architecture specified in 3GPP TS 32.240 [4]. The P-Charging-Function-Addresses header field is not included in a SIP message sent outside of the own administrative domain. The header is not applicable if the administrative domain does not provide a charging function. The P-Charging-Function-Addresses header field is applicable whenever the following circumstances are met: 1. A UA sends a REGISTER or dialog-initiating request (e.g., INVITE request) or a stand-alone transaction request outside a dialog to a proxy located in the administrative domain of a private network. 2. A registrar, proxy, or UA that is located in the administrative domain of the private network wants to generate charging records. 3. A registrar, proxy, or UA that is located in the private network has access to the addresses of the charging function entities for that network. 4. There are other proxies that are located in the same administrative domain of the private network and that generate charging records or charging events. The proxies want to send, by means outside SIP, the charging information to the same charging collecting entities than the first proxy.

(Continued)

Table 2.10 (Continued) SIP Header Field Descriptions

Header Field/RFC/Header Field Type	*Description*
	Usage of the P-Charging-Function-Addresses Header Field: A SIP proxy that receives a SIP request may insert a P-Charging-Function-Addresses header field before forwarding the request, if the header was not already present in the SIP request. The header field contains one or more parameters that contain the host names or IP addresses of the nodes that are willing to receive charging information. A SIP proxy that receives a SIP request that includes a P-Charging-Function-Addresses header field can use the host names or IP addresses included in the value, as the destination of charging information or charging events. The means to send those charging information or events are outside the scope of this document, and usually, do not use SIP for that purpose. ***Procedures at the UA:*** This document does not specify any procedure at the UA located outside the administrative domain of a private network, with regard to the P-Charging-Function-Addresses header field. Such UAs need not understand this header. However, it might be possible that a UA is located within the administrative domain of a private network (e.g., PSTN gateway or conference mixer), and it may have access to the addresses of the charging entities. In this case, a UA may insert the P-Charging-Function-Addresses header field in a SIP request or response when the next hop for the message is a proxy or UA located in the same administrative domain. Similarly, such a UA may use the contents of the P-Charging-Function-Addresses header field in communicating with the charging entities. ***Procedures at the Proxy:*** A SIP proxy that supports this extension and receives a request or response without the P-Charging-Function-Addresses header field may insert a P-Charging-Function-Addresses header field before forwarding the message. The header is populated with a list of the addresses of one or more charging entities where the proxy should send charging-related information. If a proxy that supports this extension receives a request or response with the P-Charging-Function-Addresses header field, it may retrieve the information from the header field to use with application-specific logic, that is, charging. If the next hop for the message is within the administrative domain of the proxy, then the proxy should include the P-Charging-Function-Addresses header field in the outbound message. However, if the next hop for the message is outside the administrative domain of the proxy, then the proxy must remove the P-Charging-Function-Addresses header field. ***Examples of Usage:*** We present an example in the context of the scenario shown in the following network diagram: Scenario UA1–P1–P2–UA2 In this scenario, we assume that P1 and P2 belong to the same administrative domain. The example below shows the message sequence for an INVITE transaction originating from UA1 and eventually arriving at UA2. P1 is an outbound proxy for UA1. In this case, P1 inserts charging information. Then, P1 routes the request via P2 to UA2. Message sequence for INVITE using P-Charging-Function-Addresses header field:

(Continued)

Table 2.10 (Continued) SIP Header Field Descriptions

Header Field/RFC/Header Field Type	*Description*

	F1 Invite UA1 -> P1
	
	`INVITE sip:ua2@home1.net SIP/2.0`
	`Via: SIP/2.0/UDP 192.0.2.4:5060;branch=z9hG4bKnashds7`
	`To: sip:ua2@home1.net`
	`From: sip:ua1@home1.net;tag=456248`
	`Call-ID: 843817637684230998sdasdh09`
	`CSeq: 18 INVITE`
	`Contact: sip:ua1@192.0.2.4`
	
	F2 Invite P1 -> P2
	
	`INVITE sip:ua2@home1.net SIP/2.0`
	`Via: SIP/2.0/UDP p1@home1.net:5060;branch=z9hG4bK34ghi7ab04`
	`Via: SIP/2.0/UDP 192.0.2.4:5060;branch=z9hG4bKnashds7`
	`To: sip:ua2@home1.net`
	`From: sip:ua1@home1.net;tag=456248`
	`Call-ID: 843817637684230998sdasdh09`
	`CSeq: 18 INVITE`
	`Contact: sip:ua1@192.0.2.4`
	`P-Charging-Function-Addresses:`
	`ccf=192.0.8.1; ecf=192.0.8.3,`
	`ccf-2=192.0.8.2; ecf-2=192.0.8.4`
	
	Now both P1 and P2 are aware of the IP addresses of the entities that collect charging record or charging events. Both proxies can send the charging information to the same entities.

P-Charging-Vector/RFC 7315 (Informational)/Request	3GPP has defined a distributed architecture that results in multiple network entities becoming involved in providing access and services. Operators need the ability and flexibility to charge for the access and services as they see fit. This requires coordination among the network entities (e.g., SIP proxies), which includes correlating charging records generated from different entities that are related to the same session. The correlation information includes, but is not limited to, a globally unique charging identifier that makes the billing effort easy. A charging vector is defined as a collection of charging information. The charging vector may be filled in during the establishment of a dialog or stand-alone transaction outside a dialog. The information inside the charging vector may be filled in by multiple network entities (including SIP proxies) and retrieved by multiple network entities. There are three types of correlation information to be transferred: the IMS Charging Identity (ICID) value, the address of the SIP proxy that creates the ICID value, and the Inter-operator Identifier (IOI). ICID is a charging value that identifies a dialog or a transaction outside a dialog. It is used to correlate charging records. ICID must be a globally unique value. One way to achieve globally uniqueness is to generate the ICID using two components: a locally unique value and the host name or IP address of the SIP proxy that generated the locally unique value. The IOI identifies both the originating and terminating networks involved in a SIP dialog or transaction outside a dialog. There may be an IOI generated from each side of the dialog to identify the network associated with each side.

(Continued)

Table 2.10 (Continued) SIP Header Field Descriptions

Header Field/RFC/Header Field Type	*Description*
	Additionally, in a multinetwork environment, one or more transit IOI identifiers may be included along the path of the SIP dialog or transaction outside a dialog. Owing to network policy, a void value may be included instead of the transit network name. The void value is used to indicate that a transit network appeared but due to operator policy the network name is not shown. Furthermore, in a multiservice provider environment, one or more transit IOIs may be included along the path of the SIP dialog or transaction outside a dialog. Owing to service provider policy, a void value may be included instead of the transit service provider. The void value is used to indicate that a transit appeared but due to service provider policy the service provider name is not shown. There is also expected to be access network charging information, which consists of network-specific identifiers for the access level, for example, Universal Mobile Telecommunications System (UMTS) radio access network or IEEE 802.11b. The details of the information for each type of network are not described in this memo. We define the SIP private header P-Charging-Vector header field. The P-Charging-Vector header field can appear in all SIP methods except CANCEL. A proxy may include this header, if not already present, in either the initial request or response for a dialog, or in the request and response of a stand-alone transaction outside a dialog. When present, only one instance of the header must be present in a particular request or response. The mechanisms by which a SIP proxy collects the values to populate the P-Charging-Vector header field are outside the scope of this document. **Applicability Statement for the P-Charging-Vector Header Field:** The P-Charging-Vector header field is applicable within a single private administrative domain or between different administrative domains where there is a trust relationship between the domains. The P-Charging-Vector header field is not included in a SIP message sent to another network if there is no trust relationship. The header is not applicable if the administrative domain manages charging in a way that does not require correlation of records from multiple network entities (e.g., SIP proxies). The P-Charging-Vector header field is applicable whenever the following circumstances are met: 1. A UA sends a REGISTER or dialog-initiating request (e.g., INVITE) or mid-dialog request (e.g., UPDATE) or a stand-alone transaction request outside a dialog to a proxy located in the administrative domain of a private network. 2. A registrar, proxy, or UA that is located in the administrative domain of the private network wants to generate charging records. 3. A proxy or UA that is located in the administrative domain of the private network has access to the charging correlation information for that network. 4. Optionally, a registrar, proxy, or UA that is part of a second administrative domain in another private network, whose SIP requests and responses are traversed through, en route to/from the first private network, wants to generate charging records and correlate those records with those of the first private network. This assumes that there is a trust relationship between both private networks.

(*Continued*)

Table 2.10 (Continued) SIP Header Field Descriptions

Header Field/RFC/Header Field Type	*Description*

	Usage of the P-Charging-Vector Header Field:
	The P-Charging-Vector header field is used to convey charging-related information, such as the globally unique ICID value. Typically, a SIP proxy that receives a SIP request that does not contain a P-Charging-Vector header field may insert it, with those parameters that are available at the SIP proxy. A SIP proxy that receives a SIP request that contains a P-Charging-Vector header field can use the values, such as the globally unique ICID, to produce charging records.
	Procedures at the UA:
	This document does not specify any procedure at a UA located outside the administrative domain of a private network (e.g., PSTN gateway or conference mixer), with regard to the P-Charging-Vector header field. UAs need not understand this header. However, it might be possible that a UA be located within the administrative domain of a private network (e.g., a PSTN gateway or conference mixer), and it may interact with the charging entities. In this case, a UA may insert the P-Charging-Vector header field in a SIP request or response when the next hop for the message is a proxy or UA located in the same administrative domain. Similarly, such a UA may use the contents of the P-Charging-Vector header field in communicating with the charging entities.
	Procedures at the Proxy:
	A SIP proxy that supports this extension and receives a request or response without the P-Charging-Vector header field may insert a P-Charging-Vector header field before forwarding the message. The header is populated with one or more parameters, as described in the syntax, including but not limited to, a globally unique charging identifier. If a proxy that supports this extension receives a request or response with the P-Charging-Vector header field, it may retrieve the information from the header value to use with application-specific logic, that is, charging. If the next hop for the message is within the trusted domain, then the proxy should include the P-Charging-Vector header field in the outbound message. If the next hop for the message is outside the trusted domain, then the proxy may remove the P-Charging-Function-Addresses header field. Per local application-specific logic, the proxy may modify the contents of the P-Charging-Vector header field before sending the message.
	Examples of Usage:
	We present an example in the context of the scenario shown in the following network diagram:
	Scenario UA1–P1–P2–UA2
	This example shows the message sequence for an INVITE transaction originating from UA1 and eventually arriving at UA2. P1 is an outbound proxy for UA1. In this case, P1 inserts charging information. Then, P1 routes the call via P2 to UA2. Message sequence for INVITE using P-Charging-Vector header field:
	F1 Invite UA1 -> P1
	`INVITE sip:joe@example.com SIP/2.0`
	`Via: SIP/2.0/UDP 192.0.2.4:5060;branch=z9hG4bKnashds7`
	`To: sip:joe@example.com`
	`From: sip:ua1@home1.net;tag=456248`
	`Call-ID: 843817637684230998sdasdh09`
	`CSeq: 18 INVITE`
	`Contact: sip:ua1@192.0.2.4`
	`F2 Invite P1 -> P2`
	`INVITE sip:joe@example.com SIP/2.0`

(*Continued*)

Table 2.10 (Continued) SIP Header Field Descriptions

Header Field/RFC/Header Field Type	*Description*
	Via: SIP/2.0/UDP P1@home1.net:5060;branch=z9hG4bK34ghi7a Via: SIP/2.0/UDP 192.0.2.4:5060;branch=z9hG4bKnashds7 To: sip:joe@example.com From: sip:ua1@home1.net;tag=456248 Call-ID: 843817637684230998sdasdh09 CSeq: 18 INVITE Contact: sip:ua1@192.0.2.4 P-Charging-Vector: icid-value=1234bc9876e; icid-generated-at=192.0.6.8; orig-ioi=home1.net **Usage of the transit-ioi:** The transit-ioi is added to the P-Charging-Vector header field when traversing transit networks. It is allowed to have multiple transit-ioi values within one SIP message or response. The values within the response are independent from the values set up within the request. The element could be added either by a transit network itself or by the succeeding network at the entry point where the preceding network is known. On the basis of network policy, a void value can be used. Depending on the call scenario, each transit network can add either a transit network name or a void value. However, it cannot be guaranteed that all the values that are added will appear within the P-Charging-Vector header field. Some networks can screen the P-Charging-Vector header field and delete transit-ioi values, e.g., networks not supporting this value. There are scenarios where the appearance of the transit-ioi values of all networks is needed to have a correct end-to-end view. The policies of adding, modifying, and deleting transit-ioi values are out of the scope of this document. The transit-ioi contains an indexed value that MUST be incremented with each value added to the P-Charging-Vector header field. A void value has no index. By adding the next value, the index has to be incremented by the number of void entries +1. ***Procedures at the Proxy:*** A SIP proxy that supports this extension and receives a request or response without the P-Charging-Function-Addresses header field may insert a P-Charging-Function-Addresses header field before forwarding the message. The header is populated with a list of the addresses of one or more charging entities where the proxy should send charging-related information. If a proxy that supports this extension receives a request or response with the P-Charging-Function-Addresses header field, it may retrieve the information from the header field to use with application-specific logic, that is, charging. If the next hop for the message is within the administrative domain of the proxy, then the proxy should include the P-Charging-Function-Addresses header field in the outbound message. However, if the next hop for the message is outside the administrative domain of the proxy, then the proxy must remove the P-Charging-Function-Addresses header field. A transit-ioi may be added or modified by a proxy. A deletion of the transit-ioi or an entry within the tranist-ioi could appear depending on the network policy and trust rules. This is also valid by replacing the transit-ioi with a void value.

(Continued)

Table 2.10 (Continued) SIP Header Field Descriptions

Header Field/RFC/Header Field Type	*Description*
	Usage of the related-icid: ***Procedures at the UA:*** The UAS acting as a B2BUA may add the related-icid into the P-Charging-Vector header field into SIP request or SIP responses. For example, the UAS can include the related-icid in a response to an INVITE request when the received INVITE request creates a new call leg toward the same remote end. The value of the related-icid is the icid value of the original dialog toward the remote end. ***Procedures at the Proxy:*** A SIP proxy that supports this extension and receives a request or response without the P-Charging-Function-Addresses header field may insert a P-Charging-Function-Addresses header field before forwarding the message. The header is populated with a list of the addresses of one or more charging entities where the proxy should send charging-related information. If a proxy that supports this extension receives a request or response with the P-Charging-Function-Addresses header field, it may retrieve the information from the header field to use with application-specific logic, that is, charging. If the next hop for the message is within the administrative domain of the proxy, then the proxy should include the P-Charging-Function-Addresses header field in the outbound message. However, if the next hop for the message is outside the administrative domain of the proxy, then the proxy must remove the P-Charging-Function-Addresses header field. A related-icid and *related-icid-generated-at* may be added or modified by a proxy. A deletion of the elements could appear depending on the network policy and trust rules.
P-Early-Media/RFC 5009 (Informational)/Request and Response	The private P-Early-Media header field with the *supported* parameter may be included in an INVITE request to indicate that the UAC or a proxy on the path recognizes the header field. This header is not used in the Internet. A network entity may request the authorization of early media or change a request for authorization of early media by including the P-Early-Media header field in any message allowed by Table 2.5 (Section 2.8), within the dialog toward the sender of the INVITE request. The P-Early-Media header field includes one or more direction parameters where each has one of the values *sendrecv*, *sendonly*, *recvonly*, or *inactive*, following the convention used for SDP stream directionality. Each parameter applies, in order, to the media lines in the corresponding SDP messages establishing session media. Unrecognized parameters shall be silently discarded. Nondirection parameters are ignored for purposes of early-media authorization. If there are more direction parameters than media lines, the excess shall be silently discarded. If there are fewer direction parameters than media lines, the value of the last direction parameter shall apply to all remaining media lines. A message directed toward the UAC containing a P-Early-Media header field with no recognized direction parameters shall not be interpreted as an early-media authorization request. The parameter value sendrecv indicates a request for authorization of early media associated with the corresponding media line, both from the UAS toward the UAC and from the UAC toward the UAS (both backward and forward early media). The value sendonly indicates a request for authorization of early media from the UAS toward the UAC (backward early media), and not in the other direction. The value recvonly indicates a request for authorization of early media from the UAC toward the UAS (forward early media), and not in the other direction. The value inactive indicates either a request that no early media associated with the corresponding media line be authorized, or a request for revocation of authorization of previously authorized early media.

(Continued)

Table 2.10 (Continued) SIP Header Field Descriptions

Header Field/RFC/Header Field Type	*Description*
	The P-Early-Media header field in any message within a dialog toward the sender of the INVITE request may also include the nondirection parameter gated to indicate that a network entity on the path toward the UAS is already gating the early media, according to the direction parameter(s). When included in the P-Early-Media header field, the gated parameter shall come after all direction parameters in the parameter list. When receiving a message directed toward the UAC without the P-Early-Media header field and no previous early-media authorization request has been received within the dialog, the default early-media authorization depends on local policy and may depend on whether the header field was included in the INVITE request. After an early-media authorization request has been received within a dialog, and a subsequent message is received without the P-Early-Media header field, the previous early-media authorization remains unchanged. The P-Early-Media header field in any message within a dialog toward the UAS may be ignored or interpreted according to local policy. The P-Early-Media header field does not interact with SDP offer–answer procedures in any way. Early-media authorization is not influenced by the state of the SDP offer–answer procedures (including preconditions and directionality) and does not influence the state of the SDP offer–answer procedures. The P-Early-Media header field may or may not be present in messages containing SDP. The most recently received early-media authorization applies to the corresponding media line in the session established for the dialog until receipt of the 200 OK response to the INVITE request, at which point all media lines in the session are implicitly authorized. Early-media flow in a particular direction requires that early media in that direction is authorized, that media flow in that direction is enabled by the SDP direction attribute for the stream, and that any applicable preconditions for resources management described in RFC 3312 (see Section 15.4) are met. Early-media authorization does not override the SDP direction attribute or preconditions state, and the SDP direction attribute does not override early-media authorization. The syntax of the P-Early-Media header field is described below in ABNF as an extension to the ABNF for SIP in RFC 3261. Note that not all combinations of em-param elements are semantically valid.
Permission-Missing/RFC 5360 (Standards Track)/Response	The Permission-Missing header field is provided in the SIP response message for the consent-based communications with 470 Consent Needed response code defined in RFC 5360 (see Section 19.8). It indicates that the sender of the message has not taken permission before communications with the called party. In the consent-based communications defined in RFC 5360, a relay that can be any SIP server, be it a proxy, B2BUA, or some hybrid is used for facilitating to obtain the consent of the users before sending request messages. The triggering of communications without explicit consent can cause a number of problems. These include amplification and DoS (denial of service) attacks. These problems are described in more detail in the consent-based communications requirements (RFC 4453, see Section 19.8.1).

(Continued)

Table 2.10 (Continued) SIP Header Field Descriptions

Header Field/RFC/Header Field Type	*Description*
	On receiving a request-contained URI list, the relay checks whether or not it has permissions for all the URIs contained in the incoming URI list. If it does, the relay performs the translation. If it lacks permissions for one or more URIs, the relay must not perform the translation and should return an error response. A relay that receives a request-contained URI list with a URI for which the relay has no permissions should return a 470 Consent Needed response. The relay should add a Permission-Missing header field with the URIs for which the relay has no permissions. For example, a relay receives an INVITE that contains URIs for which the relay does not have permission (the INVITE carries the recipient URIs in its message body). The relay rejects the request with a 470 Consent Needed response. That response contains a Permission-Missing header field with the URIs for which there was no permission. RFC 5360 also defines the format of the permission document that the user needs to send to the relay for taking permission. Relays implementing this framework obtain and store permissions associated to their translation logic. These permissions indicate whether or not a particular recipient has agreed to receive traffic at any given time. Recipients that have not given the relay permission to send them traffic are simply ignored by the relay when performing a translation. In principle, permissions are valid as long as the context where they were granted is valid or until they are revoked. For example, the permissions obtained by a URI-list SIP service that distributes MESSAGE requests to a set of recipients will be valid as long as the URI-list SIP service exists or until the permissions are revoked. Additionally, if a recipient is removed from a relay's translation logic, the relay should delete the permissions related to that recipient. For example, if the registration of a Contact URI expires or is otherwise terminated, the registrar deletes the permissions related to that contact address. It is also recommended that relays request recipients to refresh their permissions periodically. If a recipient fails to refresh its permissions for a given period of time, the relay should delete the permissions related to that recipient. This framework does not provide any guidance for the values of the refreshment intervals because different applications can have different requirements to set those values. For example, a relay dealing with recipients that do not implement this framework may choose to use longer intervals between refreshes. The refresh process in such recipients has to be performed manually by their users (since the recipients do not implement this framework), and having too short refresh intervals may become too heavy a burden for those users. Example: `Permission-Missing: sip:C@example.com`
P-Preferred-Identity/RFC 3325 (Informational)/ Request	The P-Preferred-Identity header field is used from a UA to a trusted proxy to carry the identity the user sending the SIP message wishes to be used for the P-Asserted-Header field value that the trusted element will insert. Like P-Asserted-Identity, there may also be one or two P-Preferred-Identity values. If there is one value, it must be a sip, sips, or tel URI. If there are two values, one value must be a sip or sips URI and the other must be a tel URI. It is worth noting that proxies can (and will) remove this header field. Example: `P-Preferred-Identity: "John Williams" <sip:john@network.com>`
P-Preferred-Service/RFC 6050 (Informational)/Request	The P-Preferred-Service header field is used by a UA sending the SIP request to provide a hint to a trusted proxy of the preferred service that the user wishes to be used for the P-Asserted-Service header field value that the trusted element will insert. The use and applicability of this header is similar, which has been explained in the case of the P-Asserted-Service header field.

(Continued)

Table 2.10 (Continued) SIP Header Field Descriptions

Header Field/RFC/Header Field Type	*Description*
P-Profile-Key/RFC 5002 (Informational)/Request	The private P-Profile-Key P-header field contains the key to be used by a proxy to query the user database for a given profile. This header field carries the key of a service profile that is stored in a user database used by SIP proxies that belong to the same administrative domain and share a common frame of reference to the use database. Typically, when SIP is used on the Internet, there are no multiple proxies with a trust relationship between them querying the same user database. Consequently, the P-Profile-Key header field does not seem useful in a general Internet environment. There can be scenarios where a set of proxies handling a request need to consult the same user database for providing services to the users through using a variety of service features. That is, they address a specific application in an application server. Those proxies typically use the destination SIP URI of the request as the key for their database queries where service identities are SIP URIs that refer to services instead of users. There can be wildcarded service identities that are a set of service identities that match a regular expression and share the same profile. For example, the service identities sip:chatroom-12@example.com and sip:chatroom-657@example.com would match the wildcarded service identity sip:chatroom-!.*!@example.com. Nevertheless, when a proxy handles a wildcarded service identity, the key to be used in its database query is not the destination SIP URI of the request, but a regular expression instead. When a proxy queries the user database for a service identity for which there is no profile in the user database, the user database needs to find its matching wildcarded service identity. For example, if the user database receives a query for sip:chatroom-657@example.com, the user database needs to go through all the wildcarded service identity it has until it finds a matching one; in this case, sip:chatroom-!.*!@example.com. The process to find a matching wildcarded service identity can be computationally expensive, time consuming, or both. When two proxies query the user database for the same service identity, which matches a wildcarded service identity, the user database needs to perform the matching process twice. Having to perform that process twice can be avoided by having the first proxy obtain the wildcarded service identity from the user database and transfer it, piggy-backed in the SIP message, to the second proxy. This way, the second proxy can query the user database using the wildcarded service identity directly. An alternative, but undesirable, solution would consist of having the user database store every service identity and its matching wildcarded service identity. The scalability and manageability properties of this approach are considerably worse than those of the approach described earlier. We, therefore, can derive the usefulness of the P-Profile-Key header field from the above analysis as follows: • It allows optimizing the response time for session establishment. • It facilitates keeping the user database's size and maintenance manageable (e.g., storing individual service identities matching a wildcarded service identity in the user database is not believed to be an acceptable solution). P-Profile-Key: <sip:chatroom-!.*!@example.com>

(Continued)

Table 2.10 (Continued) SIP Header Field Descriptions

Header Field/RFC/Header Field Type	*Description*
Priority/RFC 3261 (Standards Track)/Request	The Priority header field indicates the urgency of the request as perceived by the client. The Priority header field describes the priority that the SIP request should have to the receiving human or its agent. For example, it may be factored into decisions about call routing and acceptance. For these decisions, a message containing no Priority header field should be treated as if it specified a Priority of *normal*. The Priority header field does not influence the use of communications resources such as packet forwarding priority in routers or access to circuits in PSTN gateways. The header field can have the values *non-urgent*, *normal*, *urgent*, and *emergency*, but additional values can be defined elsewhere. It is recommended that the value of emergency only be used when life, limb, or property are in imminent danger. Otherwise, there are no semantics defined for this header field. These are the values of RFC 2076, with the addition of *emergency*. Example: Subject: A tornado is heading our way! Priority: emergency or Subject: Weekend plans Priority: nonurgent
Privacy/RFC 3323 (Standards Track)/Request	The Privacy header field allows a SIP UA to request a certain degree of privacy for a message. There are some headers that a UA cannot conceal itself, because they are used in routing, which could be concealed by an intermediary that subsequently takes responsibility for directing messages to and from the anonymous user. The UA must have some way to request such privacy services from the network. For that purpose, this document defines a new SIP header, Privacy, that can be used to specify privacy handling for requests and responses. UAs should include a Privacy header when network-provided privacy is required. Note that some intermediaries may also add the Privacy header to messages, including privacy services. However, such intermediaries should only do so if they are operating at a user's behest, for example, if a user has an administrative arrangement with the operator of the intermediary that it will add such a Privacy header. An intermediary must not modify the Privacy header in any way if the *none* priv-value is already specified. The values of priv-value today are restricted to the above options, although further options can be defined as appropriate. Each legitimate priv-value can appear zero or one time in a Privacy header. The current values are • header: The user requests that a privacy service obscure those headers that cannot be completely expunged of identifying information without the assistance of intermediaries (such as Via and Contact). Also, no unnecessary headers should be added by the service that might reveal personal information about the originator of the request. • session: The user requests that a privacy service provide anonymization for the session(s) (described, for example, in an SDP body defined in RFC 4566, see Section 7.7) initiated by this message. This will mask the IP address from which the session traffic would ordinarily appear to originate. When session privacy is requested, UAs must not encrypt SDP bodies in messages. • user: This privacy level is usually set only by intermediaries, in order to communicate that user-level privacy functions must be provided by the network, presumably because the UA is unable to provide them. UAs may, however, set this privacy level for REGISTER requests, but should not set *user*-level privacy for other requests.

(Continued)

Table 2.10 (Continued) SIP Header Field Descriptions

Header Field/RFC/Header Field Type	*Description*

	• none: The user requests that a privacy service apply no privacy functions to this message, regardless of any preprovisioned profile for the user or default behavior of the service. UAs can specify this option when they are forced to route a message through a privacy service that will, if no Privacy header is present, apply some privacy functions that the user does not desire for this message. Intermediaries must not remove or alter a Privacy header whose priv-value is *none*. UAs must not populate any other priv-values (including critical) in a Privacy header that contains a value of *none*.
	• critical: The user asserts that the privacy services requested for this message are critical, and that, therefore, if these privacy services cannot be provided by the network, this request should be rejected. Criticality cannot be managed appropriately for responses. When a Privacy header is constructed, it must consist of either the value *none*, or one or more of the values *user*, *header*, and *session* (each of which must appear at most once), which may, in turn, be followed by the *critical* indicator.
	
	IANA registration for the Privacy header field values is required along with the RFC publication. RFC 6050 (see Section 12.3) adds a new privacy type (priv-value) to the Privacy header, defined in RFC 3323 (see Section 20.2). The presence of this privacy type in a Privacy header field indicates that the user would like the Network Asserted Identity to be kept private with respect to SIP entities outside the Trust Domain with which the user authenticated. Note that a user requesting multiple types of privacy must include all of the requested privacy types in its Privacy header field value.
	
	`priv-value = "id"`
	
	Example:
	
	`Privacy: id`

Proxy-Authenticate/RFC 3261 (Standards Track)/Response	A Proxy-Authenticate header field value contains an authentication challenge. The use of this header field is defined in Section 14.33 of RFC 2616 (obsoleted by RFCs 7230–7235). See Section 22.3 of RFC 2616 for further details on its usage. Example:
	
	`Proxy-Authenticate: Digest realm="atlanta.com",`
	`domain="sip:ss1.carrier.com", qop="auth",`
	`nonce="f84f1cec41e6cbe5aea9c8e88d359",`
	`opaque="", stale=FALSE, algorithm=MD5`

Proxy-Authorization/RFC 3261 (Standards Track)/ Request	The Proxy-Authorization header field allows the client to identify itself (or its user) to a proxy that requires authentication. A Proxy-Authorization field value consists of credentials containing the authentication information of the UA for the proxy or realm of the resource being requested. See Section 3.6.3 for a definition of the usage of this header field. This header field, along with Authorization, breaks the general rules about multiple header field names. Although not a comma-separated list, this header field name may be present multiple times, and must not be combined into a single header line using the usual rules described in RFC 3261. Example:
	
	`Proxy-Authorization: Digest username="Alice", realm="atlanta.com",`
	`nonce="c60f3082ee1212b402a21831ae",`
	`response="245f23415f11432b3434341c022"`

(Continued)

Table 2.10 (Continued) SIP Header Field Descriptions

Header Field/RFC/Header Field Type	*Description*
P-Refused-URI-List/RFC 5318 (Informational)/Request and Response	RFC 5318 specifies the SIP P-Refused-URI-List Private-Header (P-Header). This P-Header is used in the Open Mobile Alliance's (OMA) Push to talk over Cellular (PoC) system. It enables URI-list servers to refuse the handling of incoming URI lists that have embedded URI lists. This P-Header also makes it possible for the URI-list server to inform the client about the embedded URI list that caused the rejection and the individual URIs that form such a URI list. **Usage Scenario:** An ad hoc PoC group session is a type of multiparty PoC session. The originator of a particular ad hoc PoC group session chooses in an ad hoc manner (e.g., selecting from an address book) the set of desired participants. To establish the ad hoc PoC group session, the originator sends an INVITE request with a URI list that contains the URIs of those participants. The PoC network, following the procedures defined in RFC 5366, receives such an INVITE request and generates an individual INVITE request toward each of the URIs in the URI list. In previous versions of the OMA PoC service, the originator of an ad hoc PoC group session was only allowed to populate the initial URI list with URIs identifying individual PoC users. Later versions of the service allow the originator to also include URI lists whose entries represent URI lists. That is, the initial URI list contains entries that are URI lists themselves. The expected service behavior then is that the members of the embedded URI lists are invited to join the ad hoc PoC group session. Figure 2.7a illustrates the expected behavior of the PoC. The originator (not shown) places the URI list friends@example.org, along with the URI alice@ example.com, in the initial URI list. The PoC network resolves friends@example.org into its members, bob@example.org and carol@example.net, and sends INVITE requests to all the recipients. The PoC network in Figure 2.7a consists of PoC servers, which are SIP entities that can behave as proxies or B2BUAs. There are two types of logical PoC servers: controlling and participating. In an ad hoc PoC group session, there is always exactly one controlling PoC server. The controlling PoC server of an ad hoc PoC group session resolves an incoming URI list and sends INVITEs to the members of the list. The controlling PoC server also functions as the focus of the session. Every participant in an ad hoc PoC group has an associated participating PoC server, which resides in the home domain of the participant. Figure 2.7b shows how the PoC servers of the PoC network behave in the scenario shown in Figure 2.7a. An originating PoC UA sends an INVITE request (F1) with a URI list to its participating PoC server. The participating PoC server of the originator receives the INVITE request, assumes the role of controlling PoC server for the ad hoc PoC group session, and sends an INVITE request to the recipient.

(Continued)

Table 2.10 (Continued) SIP Header Field Descriptions

Header Field/RFC/Header Field Type	*Description*
	The first URI of the list, alice@example.com, identifies a single user. The second URI of the URI list, friends@example.org, identifies a URI list. In PoC terminology, friends@ example.com identifies a prearranged PoC group. The PoC server at example.org, which knows the membership of friends@example.com, cannot send INVITE requests to the members of friends@example.org because that PoC server does not act as a controlling PoC server for the ad hoc PoC group session being established. Instead, it informs the controlling PoC server that friends@example.org is a list whose members are bob@example.org and carol@example.net. Upon receiving this information, the controlling PoC server generates INVITE requests toward bob@example.org and carol@example.net. Although not shown in the above example, the participating PoC server (example.org) can include—based on policy, presence of the members, etc.—just a partial list of URIs of the URI list. Furthermore, a URI that the participating PoC server returns can be a URI list. At present, there is no mechanism for a participating PoC server to inform a controlling PoC server that a URI identifies a list and the members of that list, nor is there a mechanism to indicate the URIs contained in the list. This document defines such a mechanism: the P-Refused-URI-List P-Header. **Overview of Operation:** When a URI-list server receives an INVITE request with a URI list containing entries that are URI lists themselves, and the server cannot handle the request, it returns a 403 Forbidden response with a P-Refused-URI-List P-Header, as shown in Figure 2.7c. The P-Refused-URI-List P-Header contains the members of the URI list or lists that caused the rejection of the request. This way, the client can send requests directly to those member URIs. **Response Generation:** A 403 Forbidden response can contain more than one P-Refused-URI-List entries. The P-Refused-URI-List header field MUST NOT be used with any other response. The P-Refused-URI-List P-Header contains one or more URIs, which were present in the URI list in the incoming request and could not be handled by the server. Additionally, the P-Refused-URI-List can optionally carry some or all of the members of the URI lists identified by those URIs. The 403 (Forbidden) response may contain body parts that contain URI lists. Those body parts can be referenced by the P-Refused-URI-List entries through their Content-IDs (RFC 2392). If there is a Content-ID defined in the P-Refused-URI-List, one of the body parts must have an equivalent Content-ID. The format of a URI list is service specific. This kind of message structure enables clients to determine which URI relates to which URI list, if the URI-list server is willing to disclose that information. Furthermore, the information enclosed in the URI lists enable clients to take further actions to remedy the rejection situation (e.g., send individual requests to the members of the URI list). **Message Sequence Example:** In the following message sequence example, a controlling PoC server sends an INVITE request to a participating PoC server. The participating PoC server rejects the request with a 403 Forbidden response. The 403 response has a P-Refused-URI-List P-Header that carries the members of the rejected URI lists that the participating PoC server determines to disclose to this controlling PoC server in the body of the message. The INVITE request shown in Figure 2.7c is as follows (Via header fields are not shown for simplicity):

(Continued)

Table 2.10 (Continued) SIP Header Field Descriptions

<table>
<tr><th>Header Field/RFC/Header Field Type</th><th>Description</th></tr>
<tr><td></td><td>
<pre>
INVITE sip:poc-service@example.net SIP/2.0
Max-Forwards: 70
From: PoC service <sip:poc-service@example.com>;tag=4fxaed73sl
To: PoC service <sip:poc-service@example.net>
Call-ID: 7xTn9vxNit65XU7p4@example.com
CSeq: 1 INVITE
Contact: <sip:poc-service@poc-as.example.com>
Require: recipient-list-invite
Content-Type: multipart/mixed;boundary="boundary1"
Content-Length: 538

---boundary1
Content-Type: application/sdp
(SDP not shown)

---boundary1
Content-Type: application/resource-lists+xml
Content-Disposition: recipient-list
<?xml version="1.0" encoding="UTF-8"?>
  <resource-lists xmlns="urn:ietf:params:xml:ns:resource-
  lists">
    <list>
      <entry uri="sip:bob@example.net"/>
      <entry uri="sip:friends-list@example.net"/>
      <entry uri="sip:colleagues-list@example.net"/>
    </list>
  </resource-lists>
  ---boundary1---
</pre>
The URIs sip:friends-list@example.net and sip:colleagues-list@example.net in the example above are actually references to URI lists (i.e., prearranged PoC groups). In the following response, the URI lists are in the XML resource list format (RFC 4826). The content of the 403 (Forbidden) response in Figure 2.7c is as follows (Via header fields are not shown for simplicity):
<pre>
SIP/2.0 403 Forbidden
From: PoC service <sip:poc-service@example.com>;tag=4fxaed73sl
To: PoC service <sip:poc-service@example.net>;tag=814254
Call-ID: 7xTn9vxNit65XU7p4@example.com
CSeq: 1 INVITE
P-Refused-URI-List: sip:friends-list@example.net;
members=<cid:an3bt8jf03@example.net>
P-Refused-URI-List: sip:colleagues-list@example.net;
members=<cid:bn35n8jf04@example.net>
Content-Type: multipart/mixed;boundary="boundary1"
Content-Length: 745
</pre>
</td></tr>
</table>

(Continued)

Table 2.10 (Continued) SIP Header Field Descriptions

Header Field/RFC/Header Field Type	*Description*

	`---boundary1`
	`Content-Type: application/resource-lists+xml`
	`Content-Disposition: recipient-list`
	`Content-ID: <an3bt8jf03@example.net>`
	`<?xml version="1.0" encoding="UTF-8"?>`
	`<resource-lists xmlns="urn:ietf:params:xml:ns:resource-lists">`
	`<list>`
	`<entry uri="sip:bill@example.org"/>`
	`<entry uri="sip:randy@example.com"/>`
	`<entry uri="sip:eddy@example.com"/>`
	`</list>`
	`</resource-lists>`
	`---boundary1`
	`Content-Type: application/resource-lists+xml`
	`Content-Disposition: recipient-list`
	`Content-ID: <bn35n8jf04@example.net>`
	`<?xml version="1.0" encoding="UTF-8"?>`
	`<resource-lists xmlns="urn:ietf:params:xml:ns:resource-lists">`
	`<list>`
	`<entry uri="sip:joe@example.org"/>`
	`<entry uri="sip:carol@example.com"/>`
	`</list>`
	`</resource-lists>`
	`---boundary1---`
	
	Using the message body of the 403 Forbidden response above, the controlling PoC server can determine the members of sip:friend-list@example.net and sip:colleagues-list@example.net that the participating PoC server determines to disclose to this controlling PoC server. Furthermore, the controlling PoC server can deduce that the participating PoC server has not sent any outgoing requests, per regular URI-list server procedures.
	Applicability:
	The P-Refused-URI-List header field is intended to be used in OMA PoC networks. This header field is used between PoC servers and carries information about those URI lists that were rejected by the server receiving the request. The OMA PoC services is designed so that, in a given session, only one PoC server can resolve incoming URI lists and send INVITEs to members of these lists. This restriction is not present on services developed to be used on the public Internet. Therefore, the P-Refused-URI-List P-Header does not seem to have general applicability outside the OMA PoC service. Additionally, the use of the P-Refused-URI-List P-Header requires special trust relationships between servers that do not typically exist on the public Internet. It is important to note that the P-Refused-URI-List is optional and does not change the basic behavior of a SIP URI-list service. The P-Refused-URI-List only provides clients with additional information about the refusal of the request.

Proxy-Require/RFC 3261 (Standards Track)/Request	The Proxy-Require header field is used to indicate proxy-sensitive features that must be supported by the proxy. See Section 3.11 (RFC 3261) for more details on the mechanics of proxy behavior and a usage example. Example: `Proxy-Require: foo`

(*Continued*)

Table 2.10 (Continued) SIP Header Field Descriptions

Header Field/RFC/Header Field Type	*Description*
P-Served-User/RFC 5502 (Informational)/Request	The private P-Served-User header field conveys the identity of the served user and the session case parameter that applies to this particular communication session and application invocation. The header is not used in the Internet in general. The session case parameter is used to indicate the category of the served user: Originating served user or Terminating served user and Registered user or Unregistered user. Note that there can be many kinds of ASs in the farm for providing a variety of services to the SIP users based on different subscription types. This header field can be added to initial requests for a dialog or stand-alone requests, which are routed between nodes in a Trust Domain for P-Served-User. The P-Served-User header field contains an identity of the user that represents the served user. The *sescase* parameter may be used to convey whether the initial request is originated by the served user or destined for the served user. The *regstate* parameter may be used to indicate whether the initial request is for a registered or unregistered user. The following is an example of a P-Served-User header field: `P-Served-User: <sip:user@example.com>; sescase=orig; regstate=reg`

P-User-Database/RFC 4457 (Informational)/Request	A distributed SIP network architecture results in multiple network entities, and the SIP registrar database that keeps the users' profiles may be distributed across the network. The SIP REGISTER sent by a UA may have to traverse through multiple SIP proxies before reaching the SIP registrar database. The private P-User-Database header field is designed to meet this requirement. This header is a private extension of the SIP header and is not used in the Internet. This header field can be added to requests routed from one SIP proxy to another one to convey the address of the database that contains the user profiles. The P-User-Database P-header contains the address of the Home Subscriber Server (HSS) handling the user that generated the request. The key benefit of using this SIP header field is to reduce the time and the traffic handling it takes for a UA to register to the distributed SIP network with multiple registrar databases in a given administrative domain. Because Diameter URIs are used by this header, the following examples of valid Diameter host identities are provided:
	`aaa://host.example.com;transport=tcp`
	`aaa://host.example.com:6666;transport=tcp`
	`aaa://host.example.com;protocol=diameter`
	`aaa://host.example.com:6666;protocol=diameter`
	`aaa://host.example.com:6666;transport=tcp;protocol=diameter`
	`aaa://host.example.com:1813;transport=udp;protocol=radius`
	Example:
	`P-User-Database: <aaa://host.example.com;transport=tcp>`

(*Continued*)

Table 2.10 (Continued) SIP Header Field Descriptions

Header Field/RFC/Header Field Type	*Description*
P-Visited-Network-ID/RFC 7315 (Informational)/ Request	3GPP networks are composed of a collection of so-called home networks, visited networks, and subscribers. A particular home network may have roaming agreements with one or more visited networks. The effect of this is that when a mobile terminal is roaming, it can use resources provided by the visited network in a transparent fashion. One of the conditions for a home network to accept the registration of a UA roaming to a particular visited network is the existence of a roaming agreement between the home and the visited network. There is a need to indicate to the home network which network is the visited network that is providing services to the roaming UA. 3GPP UAs always register to the home network. The REGISTER request is proxied by one or more proxies located in the visited network toward the home network. For the sake of a simple approach, it seems sensible that the visited network includes an identification that is known to the home network. This identification should be globally unique, and it takes the form of a quoted-text string or a token. The home network may use this identification to verify the existence of a roaming agreement with the visited network, and to authorize the registration through that visited network. Note that P-Visited-Network-ID information reveals the location of the user, to the level of the coverage area of the visited network. For a national network, for example, P-Visited-Network-ID would reveal that the user is in the country in question. **Applicability Statement for the P-Visited-Network-ID Header Field:** The P-Visited-Network-ID header field is applicable whenever the following circumstances are met: 1. There is transitive trust in intermediate proxies between the UA and the home network proxy via established relationships between the home network and the visited network, supported by the use of standard security mechanisms, e.g., IPsec, Authentication and Key Agreement (AKA), or Transport Layer Security (TLS). 2. An end point is using resources provided by one or more visited networks (a network to which the user does not have a direct business relationship). 3. A proxy that is located in one of the visited networks wants to be identified at the user's home network. 4. There is no requirement that every visited network need be identified at the home network. Those networks that want to be identified make use of this extension. Those networks that do not want to be identified do nothing. 5. A commonly pre-agreed text string or token identifies the visited network at the home network. 6. The UAC sends a REGISTER request or dialog-initiating request (e.g., INVITE request) or a stand-alone request outside a dialog (e.g., OPTIONS request) to a proxy in a visited network. 7. The request traverses, en route to its destination, a first proxy located in the visited network and a second proxy located in the home network or its destination is the registrar in the home network. 8. The registrar or home proxy verifies and authorizes the usage of resources (e.g., proxies) in the visited network.

(*Continued*)

Table 2.10 (Continued) SIP Header Field Descriptions

Header Field/RFC/Header Field Type	*Description*
	The P-Visited-Network-ID header field assumes that there is trust relationship between a home network and one or more transited visited networks. It is possible for other proxies between the proxy in the visited network that inserts the header, and the registrar and the home proxy, to modify the value of P-Visited-Network-ID header field. Therefore, intermediaries participating in this mechanism must apply a hop-by-hop integrity-protection mechanism such as IPsec or other available mechanisms in order to prevent such attacks. **Usage of the P-Visited-Network-ID Header Field:** The P-Visited-Network-ID header field is used to convey to the registrar or home proxy in the home network the identifier of a visited network. The identifier is a text string or token that is known by both the registrar or the home proxy at the home network and the proxies in the visited network. Typically, the home network authorizes the UA to roam to a particular visited network. This action requires an existing roaming agreement between the home and the visited network. While it is possible for a home network to identify one or more visited networks by inspecting the domain name in the Via header fields, this approach has a heavy dependency on DNS. It is an option for a proxy to populate the Via header field with an IP address, for example, and in the absence of a reverse DNS entry, the IP address will not convey the desired information. The P-Visited-Network-ID header field can appear in all SIP methods except ACK, BYE, and CANCEL and all responses. Any SIP proxy in the visited network that receives any of these requests may insert a P-Visited-Network-ID header field when it forwards the request. In case a REGISTER request or other request is traversing different administrative domains (e.g., different visited networks), a SIP proxy may insert a new P-Visited-Network-ID header field if the request does not contain a P-Visited-Network-ID header field with the same network identifier as its own network identifier (e.g., if the request has traversed other different administrative domains). Note also that there is no requirement for this header field value to be readable in the proxies. Therefore, a first proxy may insert an encrypted header field that only the registrar can decrypt. If the request traverses a second proxy located in the same administrative domain as the first proxy, the second proxy may not be able to read the contents of the P-Visited-Network-ID header field. In this situation, the second proxy will consider that its visited network identifier is not already present in the value of the header field, and therefore, it will insert a new P-Visited-Network-ID header field value (hopefully with the same identifier that the first proxy inserted, although perhaps, not encrypted). When the request arrives at the registrar or proxy in the home network, it will notice that the header field value is repeated (both the first and the second proxy inserted it). The decrypted values should be the same because both proxies were part of the same administrative domain.

(Continued)

Table 2.10 (Continued) SIP Header Field Descriptions

Header Field/RFC/Header Field Type	*Description*
	While this situation is not desirable, it does not create any harm at the registrar or proxy in the home network. The P-Visited-Network-ID header field is normally used at registration. However, this extension does not preclude other usages. For example, a proxy located in a visited network that does not maintain registration state may insert a P-Visited-Network-ID header field into any stand-alone request outside a dialog or a request that creates a dialog. At the time of writing this document, the only requests that create dialogs are INVITE requests, SUBSCRIBE requests, and REFER requests. To avoid conflicts with identifiers, especially when the number of roaming agreements between networks increase, care must be taken when selecting the value of the P-Visited-Network-ID header field. The identifier must be globally unique to avoid duplications. Although there are many mechanisms to create globally unique identifiers across networks, one such mechanism is already in operation, and that is DNS. The P-Visited-Network-ID header field does not have any connection to DNS, but the values in the header field can be chosen from the DNS entry representing the domain name of the network. This guarantees the uniqueness of the value. ***Procedures at the UA:*** In the context of the network to which the header fields defined in this document apply, a UA has no knowledge of the P-Visited-Network-ID when sending the REGISTER request. Therefore, UACs must not insert a P-Visited-Network-ID header field in any SIP message. ***Procedures at the Registrar and Proxy:*** A SIP proxy that is located in a visited network may insert a P-Visited-Network-ID header field in any of the requests in all SIP methods except ACK, BYE, and CANCEL and all responses. The header field must be populated with the contents of a text string or a token that identifies the administrative domain of the network where the proxy is operating toward the user's home network. A SIP proxy or registrar that is located in the home network can use the contents of the P-Visited-Network-ID header field as an identifier of one or more visited networks that the request traversed. The proxy or registrar in the home network may take local-policy-driven actions based on the existence (or nonexistence) of a roaming agreement between the home and the visited networks. This means, for instance, that the authorization of the actions of the request is based on the contents of the P-Visited-Network-ID header field. A SIP proxy that is located in the home network MUST delete this header field when forwarding the message outside the home network administrative domain, in order to retain the user's privacy. A SIP proxy that is located in the home network should delete this header field when the home proxy has used the contents of the header field or the request is routed based on the called party's identification, even when the request is not forwarded outside the home network administrative domain. Note that a received P-Visited-Network-ID from a UA is not allowed and must be deleted when the request is forwarded. ***Examples of Usage:*** We present an example in the context of the scenario shown in the following network diagram: Scenario UA–P1–P2–REGISTRAR This example shows the message sequence for a REGISTER transaction originating from the UA eventually arriving at the REGISTRAR. P1 is an outbound proxy in the visited network for UA. In this case, P1 inserts the P-Visited-Network-ID header field. Then, P1 routes the REGISTER request to REGISTRAR via P2. Message sequence for REGISTER using P-Visited-Network-ID header field:

(*Continued*)

Table 2.10 (Continued) SIP Header Field Descriptions

<table>
<tr><th>Header Field/RFC/Header Field Type</th><th>Description</th></tr>
<tr><td></td><td>F1 Register UA -> P1
<pre>REGISTER sip:example.com SIP/2.0
Via: SIP/2.0/UDP 192.0.2.4:5060;branch=z9hG4bKnashds7
To: sip:user1-business@example.com
From: sip:user1-business@example.com;tag=456248
Call-ID: 843817637684230998sdasdh09
CSeq: 1826 REGISTER
Contact: <sip:user1@192.0.2.4></pre>In flow F2, proxy P1 adds its own identifier in a quoted string to the P-Visited-Network-ID header field.
F2 Register P1 -> P2
<pre>REGISTER sip:example.com SIP/2.0
Via: SIP/2.0/UDP p1@visited.net;branch=z9hG4bK203igld
Via: SIP/2.0/UDP 192.0.2.4:5060;branch=z9hG4bKnashd8
To: sip:user1-personal@example.com
From: sip:user1-personal@example.com;tag=346249
Call-ID: 2Q3817637684230998sdasdh10
CSeq: 1826 REGISTER
Contact: <sip:user1@192.0.2.4>
P-Visited-Network-ID: "Visited network number 1"</pre>Finally, in flow F3, proxy P2 decides to insert its own identifier, derived from its own domain name to the P-Visited-Network-ID header field.
F3 Register P2 -> REGISTRAR
<pre>REGISTER sip:example.com SIP/2.0
Via: SIP/2.0/UDP p2@other.net;branch=z9hG4bK2bndnvk
Via: SIP/2.0/UDP p1@visited.net;branch=z9hG4bK203igld
Via: SIP/2.0/UDP 192.0.2.4:5060;branch=z9hG4bKnashd8
To: sip:user1-personal@example.com
From: sip:user1-personal@example.com;tag=346249
Call-ID: 2Q3817637684230998sdasdh10
CSeq: 1826 REGISTER
Contact: <sip:user1@192.0.2.4>
P-Visited-Network-ID: other.net,"Visited network number 1"</pre></td></tr>
<tr><td>RAck/RFC 3262 (Standards Track)/Request</td><td>The RAck header is sent in a PRACK request to support the reliability of provisional (1xx class) responses. It contains two numbers and a method tag. The first number is the value from the RSeq header in the provisional response that is being acknowledged. The next number, and the method, are copied from the CSeq in the response that is being acknowledged. The method name in the RAck header is case sensitive. Example:
<pre>RAck: 776656 1 INVITE</pre></td></tr>
</table>

(Continued)

Table 2.10 (Continued) SIP Header Field Descriptions

<table>
<tr><th>Header Field/RFC/Header Field Type</th><th>Description</th></tr>
<tr><td>Reason/RFC 3326 (Standards Track)/Request</td><td>
The Reason header field is also intended to be used to encapsulate a final status code in a provisional response. This functionality is needed to resolve the heterogeneous error response forking problem (HEREP) to know the reason why SIP request is used for creation of services. The Reason header field may appear in any request within a dialog, in any CANCEL request, and in any response whose status code explicitly allows the presence of this header field. A SIP message may contain more than one Reason value (i.e., multiple Reason lines), but all of them must have different protocol values (e.g., one SIP and another Q.850). The following values for the protocol field have been defined for SIP and Q.850 [ITU-T Q.850] for interworking between SIP and ISUP over the IP and PSTN network, respectively:
<table>
<tr><th>Protocol Value</th><th>Protocol Cause</th><th>Reference</th></tr>
<tr><td>SIP</td><td>Status Code</td><td>RFC 3261</td></tr>
<tr><td>Q.850</td><td>Cause value in decimal representation</td><td>ITU-T Q.850</td></tr>
</table>
Example:
<pre>Reason: SIP;cause=200;text="Call completed elsewhere"
Reason: Q.850;cause=16;text="Terminated"
Reason: SIP;cause=600;text="Busy Everywhere"
Reason: SIP;cause=580;text="Precondition Failure"</pre>
RFC 4411 (see Section 15.3) defines two use cases in which new preemption Reason values are necessary:
<ul>
<li>Access Preemption Event: This is when a UA receives a new SIP session request message with a valid RP (Resource-Priority) value that is higher than the one associated with the currently active session at that UA. The UA must discontinue the existing session in order to accept the new one (according to local policy of some domains).</li>
<li>Network Preemption Event: This is when a network element—such as a router—reaches capacity on a particular interface and has the ability to statefully choose which session(s) will remain active when a new session/reservation is signaled for under the parameters outlined in SIP Preconditions per RFC 3312 (see Section 15.4) that would otherwise overload that interface (perhaps adversely affecting all sessions). In this case, the router must terminate one or more reservations of lower priority in order to allow this higher-priority reservation access to the requested amount of bandwidth (according to local policy of some domains).</li>
</ul>
RFC 3312 has also registered Precondition Type with IANA as follows:
</td></tr>
</table>

(Continued)

Table 2.10 (Continued) SIP Header Field Descriptions

<table>
<tr><th>Header Field/RFC/Header Field Type</th><th>Description</th></tr>
<tr><td></td><td>Precondition Type: qos
The semantics for these two cases are registered with IANA by RFC 4411 for the new protocol value Preemption for the Reason Header field, with four cause values for the above preemption conditions. Additionally, this RFC has created a new IANA Registry for reason-text strings that are not currently defined through existing SIP Response codes or Q.850 [ITU-Q.850] cause codes. This new Registry will be useful for future protocols used by the SIP Reason header. RFC 4411 defines the following new protocol value for the protocol field of the Reason header field:
Preemption: The cause parameter contains a preemption cause code shown as follows:
Preemption Cause Code
<table>
<tr><th>Value</th><th>Default Text</th><th>Description</th></tr>
<tr><td>1</td><td>UA Preemption</td><td>The session has been preempted by a UA.</td></tr>
<tr><td>2</td><td>Reserved Resources</td><td>The session preemption has been Preempted, initiated within the network via a purposeful RSVP preemption occurrence, and not a link error.</td></tr>
<tr><td>3</td><td>Generic Preemption</td><td>This is a limited-use preemption indication to be used on the final leg to the preempted UA to generalize the event.</td></tr>
<tr><td>4</td><td>Non-IP Preemption</td><td>The session preemption has occurred in a non-IP portion of the infrastructure, and this is the Reason cause code given by the SIP Gateway.</td></tr>
</table>
Example syntax for the above preemption types are as follows:
<code>Reason: preemption ;cause=1 ;text="UA Preemption"</code>
<code>Reason: preemption ;cause=2 ;text="Reserved Resources Preempted"</code>
<code>Reason: preemption ;cause=3 ;text="Generic Preemption"</code>
<code>Reason: preemption ;cause=4 ;text="Non-IP Preemption"</code></td></tr>
<tr><td>Record-Route/RFC 3261 (Standards Track)/Request and Response</td><td>The Record-Route header field is inserted by proxies in a request to force future requests in the dialog to be routed through the proxy. Examples of its use with the Route header field are described in Section 3.11 (RFC 3261). Example:
<code>Record-Route: <sip:server10.biloxi.com;lr>,</code>
<code><sip:bigbox3.site3.atlanta.com;lr></code></td></tr>
<tr><td>Recv-Info/RFC 6086 (Standards Track)/Request and Response</td><td>A UA uses the Recv-Info header field, on a per-dialog basis, to indicate for which Info Packages it is willing to receive usually with INFO requests. A UA can indicate an initial set of Info Packages during dialog establishment and can indicate a new set during the lifetime of the invite dialog usage. A UA can also use an empty Recv-Info header field (a header field without a value) to indicate that it is not willing to receive INFO requests for any Info Package, while still informing other UAs that it supports the Info Package mechanism.</td></tr>
</table>

(*Continued*)

Table 2.10 (Continued) SIP Header Field Descriptions

Header Field/RFC/Header Field Type	*Description*
Referred-By/RFC 3892 (Standards Track)/Request	The Referred-By request header field is a request header field used by the REFER method. It can appear in any request. It carries a SIP URI representing the identity of the referrer and, optionally, the Content-ID of a body part (the Referred-By token) that provides a more secure statement of that identity. The Referred-By header field may appear in any SIP request, but is meaningless for ACK and CANCEL. Proxies do not need to be able to read Referred-By header field values and must not remove or modify them. Example (indicates the token is in the body part with Content-ID: <2UWQFN309shb3@ref.example>): Referred-By: sip:r@ref.example;cid="2UWQFN309shb3@ref.example"
Refer-Sub/RFC 4488 (Standards Track)/Request and Response	The Refer-Sub header field that is only meaningful within a REFER transaction indicates whether or not an implicit/explicit subscription has been created by issuing a REFER request. This header field may be used with a REFER request and the corresponding 2xx response only. When this header field is set to *false*, it specifies that a REFER-Issuer requests that the REFER-Recipient does not establish an implicit subscription and the resultant dialog. However, when Refer-Sub field is set *true*, only then it specifies that a subscription has been established with the issuing of the REFER request. This header field clarifies the SIP REFER extension as defined in RFC 3515 that automatically establishes a typically short-lived implicit event subscription used to notify the party sending a REFER request about the receiver's status in executing the transaction requested by the REFER. The fact of the matter is that these notifications are not needed in all cases. This header field provides a way to prevent the automatic establishment of an event subscription and subsequent notifications using a new SIP extension header field that may be included in a REFER request. It should be noted that the *Refer-Sub* header field set to *false* may be used by the REFER-Issuer only when the REFER-Issuer can be certain that the REFER request will not be forked. If the REFER-Recipient supports the extension and is willing to process the REFER transaction without establishing an implicit subscription, it must insert the Refer-Sub header field set to false in the 2xx response to the REFER-Issuer. In this case, no implicit subscription is created. Consequently, no new dialog is created if this REFER was issued outside any existing dialog. If the REFER-Issuer inserts the Refer-Sub header field set to false, but the REFER-Recipient does not grant the suggestion (i.e., either does not include the Refer-Sub header field or includes the Refer-Sub header field set to *true* in the 2xx response), an implicit subscription is created as in the default case. The Refer-Sub header field may be encrypted as part of end-to-end encryption. The REFER specification allows for the possibility of forking a REFER request that is sent outside of an existing dialog. In addition, a proxy may fork an unknown method type. Should forking occur, the sender of the REFER with Refer-Sub will not be aware as only a single 2xx response will be forwarded by the forking proxy. As a result, the responsibility is on the issuer of the REFER with Refer-Sub to ensure that no forking will result. If a REFER request to a given Request-URI might fork, the REFER-Issuer should not include the Refer-Sub header field. The REFER-Issuer should use standardized mechanisms for ensuring the REFER request does not fork. In the absence of any other mechanism, the Request-URI of the REFER request should have Globally Routable User Agent URI (GRUU) properties according to the definitions of RFC 5627 (see Section 4.3) as those properties ensure the request will not fork.

(*Continued*)

Table 2.10 (Continued) SIP Header Field Descriptions

Header Field/RFC/Header Field Type	*Description*
Refer-To/RFC 3515 (Standards Track)/Request	The Refer-To header field is a request header field (request-header) used in the REFER method. It provides a URL to reference. The Refer-To header field may be encrypted as part of end-to-end encryption. Example: Refer-To: sip:alice@atlanta.example.com Refer-To: <sip:carol@cleveland.example.org;method=SUBSCRIBE>
Reject-Contact/RFC 3841 (Standards Track)/Request	The Reject-Contact header field allows the UAC to specify that a UA should not be contacted if it matches any of the values of the header field. Each value of the Reject-Contact header field contains a "*," and is parameterized by a set of feature parameters. Some additional parameters are also defined for Contact header field, such as media, duplex, and language, when used in the header field. Any UA whose capabilities match the feature set described by the feature parameters matches the value. For each contact predicate, each Reject-Contact predicate (i.e., each predicate associated with the Reject-Contact header field) is examined. If that Reject-Contact predicate contains a filter for a feature tag, and that feature tag is not present anywhere in the contact predicate, that Reject-Contact predicate is discarded for the processing of that contact predicate. If the Reject-Contact predicate is not discarded, it is matched with the contact predicate using the matching operation of RFC 2533 (see Section 3.4.3). If the result is a match, the URI corresponding to that contact predicate is discarded from the target set. The ABNF syntax of the Reject-Contact header is provided in the Accept-Header described in this table. Example: Reject-Contact: *;actor="msg-taker";video
Replaces/RFC 3891 (Standards Track)/Request	The Replaces header field indicates that a single dialog identified by the header field is to be shut down and logically replaced by the incoming INVITE in which it is contained. It is a request header only, and defined only for INVITE requests. The Replaces header field may be encrypted as part of end-to-end encryption. Only a single Replaces header field value may be present in a SIP request. A Replaces header field must contain exactly one to-tag and exactly one from-tag, as they are required for unique dialog matching. For compatibility with dialogs initiated by RFC 2543 that is obsoleted by RFC 3261-compliant UAs, a tag of zero matches both tags of zero and null. A Replaces header field may contain the early-flag. Examples: Replaces: 98732@sip.example.com;from-tag=r33th4x0r;to-tag=ff87ff Replaces: 12adf2f34456gs5;to-tag=12345;from-tag=54321 Replaces: 87134@171.161.34.23;to-tag=24796;from-tag=0
Reply-To/RFC 3261 (Standards Track)/Request	The Reply-To header field contains a logical return URI that may be different from the From header field. For example, the URI may be used to return missed calls or unestablished sessions. If the user wishes to remain anonymous, the header field should either be omitted from the request or populated in such a way that does not reveal any private information. Even if the display-name is empty, the name-addr form must be used if the addr-spec contains a comma, question mark, or semicolon. Syntax issues are discussed in Section 2.4.1 RFC 3261. Example: Reply-To: Bob <sip:bob@biloxi.com>

(*Continued*)

Table 2.10 (Continued) SIP Header Field Descriptions

Header Field/RFC/Header Field Type	*Description*

Request-Disposition/RFC 3841 (Standards Track)/ Request	The Request-Disposition header field specifies caller preferences for how a server should process a request. Its value is a list of tokens, each of which specifies a particular directive. The directives are grouped into types. There can only be one directive of each type per request (e.g., both proxy and redirect cannot be put in the same Request-Disposition header field). Note that a compact form, using the letter d, has been defined. Example:
	`Request-Disposition: proxy, recurse, parallel`
	`d: redirect`

Require/RFC 3261 (Standards Track)/Request	The Require header field is used by UACs to tell UASs about options that the UAC expects the UAS to support in order to process the request. Although an optional header field, the Require must not be ignored if it is present. The Require header field contains a list of option tags, described in Section 2.10 (RFC 3261). Each option tag defines a SIP extension that must be understood to process the request. Frequently, this is used to indicate that a specific set of extension header fields need to be understood. A UAC compliant to this specification MUST only include option tags corresponding to Standards Track RFCs. Example: `Require: 100rel`

Resource-Priority/RFC 4412 (Standards Track)/Request	The Resource-Priority request header field marks a SIP request as desiring prioritized access to resources. There is no protocol requirement that all requests within a SIP dialog or session use the Resource-Priority header field. Local administrative policy may mandate the inclusion of the Resource-Priority header field in all requests. Implementations of this specification must allow inclusion to be either by explicit user request or automatic for all requests. The syntax of the Resource-Priority header field is described below. An example Resource-Priority header field is shown below:
	`Resource-Priority: dsn.flash`
	The *r*-value parameter in the Resource-Priority header field indicates the resource priority desired by the request originator. Each resource value (r-value) is formatted as *namespace . priority value*. The value is drawn from the namespace identified by the namespace token. Namespaces and priorities are case-insensitive ASCII tokens that do not contain periods. Thus, *dsn.flash* and *DSN.Flash*, for example, are equivalent. Each namespace has at least one priority value. Namespaces and priority values within each namespace must be registered with the IANA. Initial six registered namespaces are as follows: dsn, drsn 6, q735, ets, and wps. Since a request may traverse multiple administrative domains with multiple different namespaces, it is necessary to be able to enumerate several different namespaces within the same message.
	However, a particular namespace must not appear more than once in the same SIP message. These may be expressed equivalently as either comma-separated lists within a single header field, as multiple header fields, or as some combination. The ordering of *r*-values within the header field has no significance. Thus, for example, the following three header snippets are equivalent:
	`Resource-Priority: dsn.flash, wps.3`
	`Resource-Priority: wps.3, dsn.flash`
	`Resource-Priority: wps.3`
	`Resource-Priority: dsn.flash`

Response-Key/RFC 2543 (Standards Track)/Request	The Response-Key request-header field defined in RFC 2543 is used by a client to request the key that the called UA should use to encrypt the response with; however, it has been deprecated in RFC 3261.

(*Continued*)

Table 2.10 (Continued) SIP Header Field Descriptions

Header Field/RFC/Header Field Type	*Description*

Retry-After/RFC 3261 (Standards Track)/Response	The Retry-After header field can be used with a 500 Server Internal Error or 503 Service Unavailable response to indicate how long the service is expected to be unavailable to the requesting client and with a 404 Not Found, 413 Request Entity Too Large, 480 Temporarily Unavailable, 486 Busy Here, 600 Busy, or 603 Decline response to indicate when the called party anticipates being available again. The value of this field is a positive integer number of seconds (in decimal) after the time of the response.
	An optional comment can be used to indicate additional information about the time of callback. An optional *duration* parameter indicates how long the called party will be reachable starting at the initial time of availability. If no duration parameter is given, the service is assumed to be available indefinitely. Examples:
	`Retry-After: 18000;duration=3600`
	`Retry-After: 120 (I'm in a meeting)`

Route/RFC 3261 (Standards Track)/Request	The Route header field is used to force routing for a request through the listed set of proxies. Examples of the use of the Route header field are in Section 3.11 (RFC 3261). Example:
	`Route: <sip:bigbox3.site3.atlanta.com;lr>,`
	`<sip:server10.biloxi.com;lr>`

RSeq/RFC 3262 (Standards Track)/Response	The RSeq header is used in provisional (1xx class) responses in order to transmit them reliably. This header field may only be sent if the INVITE request contains the Supported: rel100 header field. If RSeq is present in a provisional response, the UAC should acknowledge the receipt of the response with a PRACK method. It contains a single numeric value from 1 to (2^{32} – 1). Each provisional response is given a sequence number, carried in the RSeq header field in the response. The RSeq numbering space is within a single transaction. This means that provisional responses for different requests may use the same values for the RSeq number. The value of the RSeq in each subsequent reliable provisional response for the same request must be greater by exactly 1. RSeq numbers must not wrap around. Because the initial one is chosen to be less than (2^{31} – 1), but the maximum is (2^{32} – 1), there can be up to 2^{31} reliable provisional responses per request, which is more than sufficient. Example: `RSeq: 7859254`
Security-Client/RFC 3329 (Standards Track)/Request	The Security-Client header field with non-TLS connections must be used by a SIP UAC that wishes to use the security agreement specified in RFC 3329 (see Section 19.3) to a SIP request message addressed to its first-hop server/proxy (i.e., the destination of the request is the first-hop proxy). This header field contains a list of all the security mechanisms that the client supports. The client should not add preference parameters to this list. The client must add both a Require and Proxy-Require header field with the value *sec-agree* in the option tag to its request. The contents of the Security-Client header field may be used by the server to include any necessary information in its response. The parameters described by the ABNF syntaxes described in Section 2.4.1.2 have the following semantics: • **Mechanism-name:** This token identifies the security mechanism supported by the client, when it appears in a Security-Client header field; or by the server, when it appears in a Security-Server or in a Security-Verify header field. The mechanism-name tokens are registered with the IANA. This specification defines four values: – *tls* for TLS – *digest* for HTTP Digest – *ipsec-ike* for IPsec with IKE – *ipsec-man* for manually keyed IPsec without IKE

(*Continued*)

Table 2.10 (Continued) SIP Header Field Descriptions

Header Field/RFC/Header Field Type	*Description*
	• **Preference:** The *q*-value indicates a relative preference for the particular mechanism. The higher the value, the more preferred the mechanism is. All the security mechanisms must have different *q*-values. It is an error to provide two mechanisms with the same *q*-value. • **Digest-algorithm:** This optional parameter is defined here only for HTTP Digest in RFC 2617 (see Sections 19.4.5 and 19.12.2.3) in order to prevent the bidding-down attack for the HTTP Digest algorithm parameter. The content of the field may have same values as defined in RFC 2617 for the *algorithm* field. • **Digest-qop:** This optional parameter is defined here only for HTTP Digest RFC 2617 in order to prevent the bidding-down attack for the HTTP Digest qop parameter. The content of the field may have same values as defined in RFC 2617 for the *qop* field. • **Digest-verify:** This optional parameter is defined here only for HTTP Digest RFC 2617 to prevent the bidding-down attack for the SIP security mechanism agreement (this document). The content of the field is counted exactly the same way as request-digest in RFC 2617 except that the Security-Server header field is included in the A2 parameter. If the *qop* directive's value is *auth* or is unspecified, then A2 is A2 = Method ":" digest-uri-value ":" security-server If the *qop* value is auth-int, then A2 is A2 = Method ":" digest-uri-value ":" H(entity-body) ":" security-server All linear white spaces in the Security-Server header field must be replaced by a single SP before calculating or interpreting the digest-verify parameter. Method, digest-uri-value, entity-body, and any other HTTP Digest parameter are as specified in RFC 2617. Note that this specification does not introduce any extension or change to HTTP Digest RFC 2617. RFC 3329 (see Section 19.3) only reuses the existing HTTP Digest mechanisms to protect the negotiation of security mechanisms between SIP entities.
Security-Server/RFC 3329 (Standards Track)/Response	The Security-Server header field provides a list of security capabilities of the server. A server that by policy requires the use of this specification and receives a request that does not have the sec-agree option tag in a Require, Proxy-Require, or Supported header field must return a 421 Extension Required response. If the request had the sec-agree option tag in a Supported header field, it must return a 494 Security Agreement Required response. In both situations, the server must also include in the response a Security-Server header field listing its capabilities and a Require header field with an option tag sec-agree in it. The server must also add necessary information so that the client can initiate the preferred security mechanism (e.g., a Proxy-Authenticate header field for HTTP Digest).
Security-Verify/RFC 3329 (Standards Track)/Request	The Security-Verify header field is used to protect the Security-Server header field of SIP messages. For example, the client must also use the digest-verify parameter in the Security-Verify header field to protect the Security-Server header field as specified in RFC 3329 (see Section 19.3). When the client receives a response with a Security-Server header field, it must choose the security mechanism in the server's list with the highest *q*-value among all the mechanisms that are known to the client. Then, it must initiate that particular security mechanism as described in RFC 3329. This initiation may be carried out without involving any SIP message exchange (e.g., establishing a TLS connection). If an attacker modified the Security-Client header field in the request, the server may not include in its response the information needed to establish the common security mechanism with the highest preference value (e.g., the Proxy-Authenticate header field is missing).

(*Continued*)

Table 2.10 (Continued) SIP Header Field Descriptions

Header Field/RFC/Header Field Type	*Description*
	A client detecting such a lack of information in the response must consider the current security agreement specified in RFC 3329 (see Section 19.3) process aborted, and may try to start it again by sending a new request with a Security-Client header field. All the subsequent SIP requests sent by the client to that server should make use of the security mechanism initiated in the previous step. These requests must contain a Security-Verify header field that mirrors the server's list received previously in the Security-Server header field. These requests must also have both a Require and Proxy-Require header fields with the value sec-agree. The server must check that the security mechanisms listed in the Security-Verify header field of incoming requests correspond to its static list of supported security mechanisms.
Server/RFC 3261 (Standards Track)/Response	The Server header field contains information about the software used by the UAS to handle the request. Revealing the specific software version of the server might allow the server to become more vulnerable to attacks against software that is known to contain security holes. Implementers should make the Server header field a configurable option. Example: `Server: HomeServer v2`
Service-Route/RFC 3608 (Standards Track)/Response	The SIP Service-Route header field contains a route vector that will direct requests through a specific sequence of proxies. A registrar may use a Service-Route header field to inform a UA of a service route that, if used by the UA, will provide services from a proxy or set of proxies associated with that registrar. The Service-Route header field may be included by a registrar in the response to a REGISTER request. Consequently, a registering UA learns of a service route that may be used to request services from the system it just registered with. The routing established by the Service-Route mechanism applies only to requests originating in the UA. That is, it applies only to UA-originated requests, and not to requests terminated by that UA. The registrar generates a service route for the registering UA and returns it in the response to each successful REGISTER request. This service route has the form of a Route header field that the registering UA may use to send requests through the service proxy selected by the registrar. The UA would use this route by inserting it as a preloaded Route header field in requests originated by the UA intended for routing through the service proxy. Note that the Service-Route header field values MUST conform to the syntax of a Route element as defined in RFC 3261. As suggested therein, such values must include the loose-routing indicator parameter ;lr for full compliance with RFC 3261. Example: `Service-Route: <sip:P2.HOME.EXAMPLE.COM;lr>,` `<sip:HSP.HOME.EXAMPLE.COM;lr>`
Session-Expires/RFC 4028 (Standards Track)/Request	The Session-Expires header field conveys the session interval for a SIP session. It is placed only in INVITE or UPDATE requests, as well as in any 2xx response to an INVITE or UPDATE. Like the SIP Expires header field, it contains a delta-time. The absolute minimum for the Session-Expires header field is 90 seconds. This value represents a bit more than twice the duration that a SIP transaction can take in the event of a timeout. This allows sufficient time for a UA to attempt a refresh at the half point of the session interval, and for that transaction to complete normally before the session expires. However, 1800 seconds (30 minutes) is recommended as the value for the Session-Expires header field. In other words, SIP entities must be prepared to handle Session-Expires header field values of any duration greater than 90 seconds, but entities that insert the Session-Expires header field should not choose values of less than 30 minutes. Example: `Session-Expires: 4800`

(Continued)

Table 2.10 (Continued) SIP Header Field Descriptions

Header Field/RFC/Header Field Type	*Description*
SIP-ETag/RFC 3903 (Standards Track)/Response	The SIP-ETag header field must be used in the response code of the PUBLISH request message by the Event State Compositor, acting as a SIP UAS for processing the PUBLISH request, indicating the type of published event state. In fact, the Event Publication Agent, acting as a SIP UAC representing a SIP UAC in issuing the PUBLISH request, must include a single Event header field in PUBLISH requests for determining the type of the published event state. The value of this header field indicates the event package for which this request is publishing event state. For each successful PUBLISH request, the ESC will generate and assign an entity-tag and return it in the SIP-ETag header field of the 2xx response.
SIP-If-Match/RFC 3903 (Standards Track)/Request	The If-Match header field must be used for updating previously published event state by the EPA, acting as a SIP UAC representing a SIP UAC in issuing the PUBLISH request. In other words, when updating a previously published event state, PUBLISH requests must contain a single SIP-If-Match header field identifying the specific event state that the request is refreshing, modifying, or removing. This header field must contain a single entity-tag that was returned by the ESC in the SIP-ETag header field of the response to a previous publication. The PUBLISH request may contain a body, which contains event state that the client wishes to publish. The content format and semantics are dependent on the event package identified in the Event header field. The presence of a body and the SIP-If-Match header field determine the specific operation that the request is performing, as described below: *Operation* / *Body?* / *SIP-If-Match* / *Expires Value* Initial / Yes / No / >0 Refresh / No / Yes / >0 Modify / Yes / No / >0 Remove / No / Yes / 0 An *Initial* publication sets the initial event state for a particular EPA. There may, of course, already be event state published by other EPAs (for the same AOR). Note that this state is unaffected by an initial publication. A *Refresh* publication refreshes the lifetime of a previous publication, whereas a *Modify* publication modifies the event state of a previous publication. A *Remove* publication requests immediate removal of event state. These operations are described in more detail in the following chapters. An EPA is responsible for refreshing its previously established publications before their expiration interval has elapsed. To refresh a publication, the EPA must create a PUBLISH request that includes in a SIP-If-Match header field the entity-tag of the publication to be refreshed. The SIP-If-Match header field containing an entity-tag conditions the PUBLISH request to refresh a specific event state established by a prior publication. If the entity-tag matches the previously published event state at the ESC, the refresh succeeds, and the EPA receives a 2xx response. Like the 2xx response to an initial PUBLISH request, the 2xx response to a refresh PUBLISH request will contain a SIP-ETag header field with an entity-tag. The EPA must store this entity-tag, replacing any existing entity-tag for the refreshed event state.

(*Continued*)

Table 2.10 (Continued) SIP Header Field Descriptions

Header Field/RFC/Header Field Type	*Description*
Subject/RFC 3261 (Standards Track)/Request	The Subject header field provides a summary or indicates the nature of the call, allowing call filtering without having to parse the session description. The session description does not have to use the same subject indication as the invitation. The compact form of the Subject header field is s. Example: Subject: Need more boxes s: Tech Support
Subscription-State/RFC 6665 (Standards Track)/Request	The Subscription-State header is used by a SIP UA to know the current state of the subscription and is a required header field in the NOTIFY method. The values defined in this header are active, pending, or terminated. Additional parameters like Expires, Reason, and Retry-After are also included. Values in the Reason parameter can include deactivated, giveup, probation, noresource, rejected, or timeout. The ABNF syntaxes of this header are provided with the Event header described in this table. Example: `Subscription: pending; reason=probation`
Supported/RFC 3261 (Standards Track)/Request and Response	The Supported header field enumerates all the extensions supported by the UAC or UAS. The Supported header field contains a list of option tags, described in Section 2.10 (RFC 3261), that are understood by the UAC or UAS. A UA compliant to this specification must only include option tags corresponding to Standards Track RFCs. If empty, it means that no extensions are supported. The compact form of the Supported header field is *k*. Example: `Supported: 100rel`
Suppress-If-Match/RFC 5839 (Standards Track)/Request	The SUBSCRIBE request may include the conditional Suppress-If-Match header field including an entity tag specified in RFC 5839 for reduction of the number of NOTIFY requests the subscriber can expect to receive. The subscriber must include a single conditional header field including an entity-tag in the request when generating a conditional SUBSCRIBE request. The condition is evaluated by comparing the entity-tag (see Section 2.9) of the subscribed resource with the entity-tag carried in the conditional header field. If they match, the condition evaluates to true. Unlike the condition introduced for the PUBLISH method specified in RFC 3903 (see Section 5.2.2.2), these conditions do not apply to the SUBSCRIBE request itself; however, they result in changes in the behavior of NOTIFY requests with regard to sending the notifications to the subscriber after sending the SUBSCRIBE request provided the condition is true. If the condition is true, it instructs the notifier either to omit the body of the resulting NOTIFY message (if the SUBSCRIBE is not sent within an existing dialog) or to suppress (i.e., block) the NOTIFY request that would otherwise be triggered by the SUBSCRIBE (for an established dialog). In the latter case, the SUBSCRIBE message will be answered with a 204 No Notification response. If the condition is false, the notifier follows its default behavior specified in RFCs 6665 and 5839. If the subscriber receives a 204 No Notification response to an in-dialog SUBSCRIBE, the subscriber must consider the event state and the subscription state unchanged. The value of the Suppress-If-Match header field is an entity-tag, which is an opaque token that the subscriber simply copies (byte-wise) from a previously received NOTIFY request. The inclusion of an entity-tag in a Suppress-If-Match header field of a SUBSCRIBE request indicates that the client has a copy of, or is capable of recreating a copy of, the entity associated with that entity-tag (see Section 2.9 for more detail).

(Continued)

Table 2.10 (Continued) SIP Header Field Descriptions

Header Field/RFC/Header Field Type	*Description*
	Example: `Suppress-If-Match: b4cf7` The header field can also be wildcarded using the special "*" entity-tag value. Such a condition always evaluates to true regardless of the value of the current entity-tag for the resource. Example: `Suppress-If-Match: *`
Target-Dialog/RFC 4538 (Standards Track)	The Target-Dialog header field is used in requests that create SIP dialogs facilitating secured communications authenticating out-of-dialog SIP requests. It indicates to the recipient that the sender is aware of an existing dialog with the recipient, either because the sender is on the other side of that dialog or because it has access to the dialog identifiers. The recipient can then authorize the request based on this awareness. The SIP option tag tdialog can be used in a Supported header field implying that the sender of the message supports it. This header field contains the dialog identifier of the other dialog that includes Call-ID, local tag, and remote tag. One such example is call transfer, accomplished through REFER. If UAs A and B are in an INVITE dialog, and UA A wishes to transfer UA B to UA C, UA A needs to send a REFER request to UA B, asking UA B to send an INVITE request to UA C. UA B needs to authorize this REFER. The proper authorization decision is that UA B should accept the request if it came from a user with whom B currently has an INVITE dialog relationship. In this case, the better approach is for UA A to send the REFER request to UA B outside of the dialog. In that case, UA B can authorize the REFER request through using the Target-Dialog header field. Another example is the application interaction framework specified in RFC 5629. In that framework, proxy servers on the path of a SIP INVITE request can place user interface components on the UA that generated or received the request. To do this, the proxy server needs to send a REFER request to the UA, targeted to its GRUU specified in RFC 5627 (see Section 4.3), asking the UA to fetch an HTTP resource containing the user interface component. In such a case, the Target-Dialog header will provide a means for the UA to authorize the REFER because the application interaction framework recommends that the request be authorized if it was sent from an entity on the path of the original dialog. Another example is if two UAs share an INVITE dialog, and an element on the path of the INVITE request wishes to track the state of the INVITE. In such a case, it sends a SUBSCRIBE request to the GRUU of the UA, asking for a subscription to the dialog event package. If the SUBSCRIBE request came from an element on the INVITE request path, it can be authorized using the Target-Dialog header. In addition, the use of the Target-Dialog header should not be confused with the In-Reply-To header. Target-Dialog is similar, in that it also references a previous session like In-Reply-To header. Because of their similarities, it is important to understand the differences, as these two header fields are not substitutes for each other. • First, In-Reply-To is meant for consumption by a human or a user interface widget, for providing the users with a context that allows them to decide what a call is about and whether they should take it. Target-Dialog, on the other hand, is meant for consumption by the UA itself, to facilitate authorization of session requests in specific cases where authorization is not a function of the user, but rather the underlying protocols. A UA will authorize a call containing Target-Dialog based on a correct value of the Target-Dialog header field. • Second, Target-Dialog references a specific dialog that must be currently in progress. In-Reply-To references a previous call attempt, most likely one that did not result in a dialog. This is why In-Reply-To uses a Call-ID, and Target-Dialog uses a set of dialog identifiers.

(Continued)

Table 2.10 (Continued) SIP Header Field Descriptions

Header Field/RFC/Header Field Type	*Description*
	Finally, In-Reply-To implies cause and effect. When In-Reply-To is present, it means that the request is being sent because of the previous request that was delivered. Target-Dialog does not imply cause and effect, merely awareness for the purposes of authorization. Example: `Target-Dialog: fa77as7dad8-sd98ajzz@host.example.com; local-tag=kkaz-; remote-tag=6544`
Timestamp/RFC 3261 (Standards Track)/Request and Response	The Timestamp header field describes when the UAC sent the request to the UAS. See Section 3.1 (RFC 3261) for details on how to generate a response to a request that contains the header field. Although there is no normative behavior defined here that makes use of the header, it allows for extensions or SIP applications to obtain round trip time (RTT) estimates. Example: `Timestamp: 54`

To/RFC 3261 (Standards Track)/Request and Response	The To header field specifies the logical recipient of the request. The optional display-name is meant to be rendered by a human-user interface. The tag parameter serves as a general mechanism for dialog identification. See Section 2.9 (RFC 3261) for details of the tag parameter. Comparison of To header fields for equality is identical to comparison of From header fields. RFC 3261 (see Section 4.2) defines the rules for parsing a display name, URI and URI parameters, and header field parameters.
	The compact form of the To header field is t. The following are examples of valid To header fields:
	`To: The Operator`
	`<sip:operator@cs.columbia.edu>;tag=287447`
	`t: sip:+12125551212@server.phone2net.com`

Trigger-Consent/RFC 5360 (Standards Track)/Request	The Trigger-Consent header field specified in RFC 5360 (see Section 19.8) facilitates the consent-based communications between the users providing the resource lists in SIP request messages to trigger consent lookups. Receipt of these requests without explicit consent can cause a number of problems. These include amplification and DoS attacks. These problems are described in more detail in RFC 4453. RFC 5360 conceptualizes that a relay that can be any SIP server, be it a proxy, B2BUA, or some hybrid, that receives a request, translates its Request-URI into one or more next-hop URIs, and delivers the request to those URIs. The Request-URI of the incoming request is referred to as *target URI*, while the destination URIs of the outgoing requests are referred to as *recipient URIs*. Thus, an essential aspect of a relay is that of translation. When a relay receives a request, it translates the Request-URI (target URI) into one or more additional URIs (recipient URIs). Through this translation operation, the relay can create outgoing requests to one or more additional recipient URIs, thus creating the consent problem. The consent problem is created by two types of translations: translations based on local data and translations that involve amplifications. Translation operations based on local policy or local data (such as registrations) are the vehicle by which a request is delivered directly to an end point, when it would not otherwise be possible to. In other words, if a spammer has the address of a user, sip:user@example.com, it cannot deliver a MESSAGE request to the UA of that user without having access to the registration data that maps sip:user@example.com to the UA on which that user is present. Thus, it is the usage of this registration data, and more generally, the translation logic, that is expected to be authorized in order to prevent undesired communications. Of course, if the spammer knows the address of the UA, it will be able to deliver requests directly to it.

(*Continued*)

Table 2.10 (Continued) SIP Header Field Descriptions

Header Field/RFC/Header Field Type	*Description*

	Translation operations that result in more than one recipient URI are a source of amplification. Servers that do not perform translations, such as outbound proxy servers, do not cause amplification. On the other hand, servers that perform translations (e.g., inbound proxies authoritatively responsible for a SIP domain) may cause amplification if the user can be reached at multiple end points (thereby resulting in multiple recipient URIs). The Trigger-Consent header field allows potential recipients of a translation to agree to be actual recipients by giving the relay performing the translation permission to send them traffic. Example:
	`Trigger-Consent: sip:123@relay.example.com;`
	`target-uri=sip:friends@relay.example.com`

Unsupported/RFC 3261 (Standards Track)/Response	The Unsupported header field lists the features not supported by the UAS. See Section 3.4.32 of RFC 3261 for motivation. Example: `Unsupported: foo`
User-Agent/RFC 3261 (Standards Track)/Request and Response	The User-Agent header field contains information about the UAC originating the request. The semantics of this header field are defined in Section 14.43 of RFC 2616 (obsoleted by RFCs 7230–7235). Revealing the specific software version of the UA might allow the UA to become more vulnerable to attacks against software that is known to contain security holes. Implementers should make the User-Agent header field a configurable option. Example: `User-Agent: Softphone Beta1.5`
User-to-User/RFC 7433 (Standards Track)/ Message-Body	RFC 7433 (see Section 16.9) defines a new SIP header field *User-to-User* to transport call control UUI data to meet the requirements specified in RFC 6567. To help tag and identify the UUI data used with this header field, *purpose*, *content*, and *encoding* header field parameters are defined. The purpose header field parameter identifies the package that defines the generation and usage of the UUI data for a particular application. The value of the purpose parameter is the package name, as registered in the UUI Packages subregistry defined in Section 6.3 of RFC 7344. For the case of interworking with the ISDN UUI service, the ISDN UUI service interworking package is used. The default value for the purpose header field is *isdn-uui* as defined in RFC 7434. If the purpose header field parameter is not present, the ISDN UUI must be used. The *content* header field parameter identifies the actual content of the UUI data. If not present, the default content defined for the package must be used. Newly defined UUI packages must define or reference at least a default content value. The encoding header field parameter indicates the method of encoding the information in the UUI data associated with a particular content value. This specification only defines *encoding=hex*. If the encoding header field parameter is not present, the default encoding defined for the package MUST be used. UUI data is considered an opaque series of octets. This mechanism must not be used to convey a URL or URI, since the Call-Info header field already supports this use case. Example: `User-to-User: 342342ef34;encoding=hex`

(Continued)

Table 2.10 (Continued) SIP Header Field Descriptions

<table>
<tr><th>Header Field/RFC/Header Field Type</th><th>Description</th></tr>
<tr><td></td><td>RFC 7433 has also registered the UUI header field parameters with the IANA. The following rows .have been added to the "Header Field Parameters and Parameter Values" section of the SIP parameter registry:

<table>
<tr><th>Header Field</th><th>Parameter Name</th><th>Predefined Values</th><th>Reference</th></tr>
<tr><td>User-to-User</td><td>encoding</td><td>Yes</td><td>RFC 7433</td></tr>
<tr><td>User-to-User</td><td>content</td><td>No</td><td>RFC 7433</td></tr>
<tr><td>User-to-User</td><td>purpose</td><td>No</td><td>RFC 7433</td></tr>
</table></td></tr>
<tr><td>Via/RFC 3261 (Standards Track)/Request and Response</td><td>The Via header field indicates the path taken by the request thus far and indicates the path that should be followed in routing responses. The branch ID parameter in the Via header field values serves as a transaction identifier, and is used by proxies to detect loops. A Via header field value contains the transport protocol used to send the message, the client's host name or network address, and possibly the port number at which it wishes to receive responses. A Via header field value can also contain parameters such as maddr, ttl, received, and branch, whose meaning and use are described in other sections. For implementations compliant to this specification, the value of the branch parameter must start with the magic cookie z9hG4bK, as discussed in Section 3.1 (RFC 3261). Transport protocols defined here are UDP, TCP, TLS, and SCTP. TLS means TLS over TCP. When a request is sent to a SIPS URI, the protocol still indicates SIP, and the transport protocol is TLS.

<code>Via: SIP/2.0/UDP erlang.bell-telephone.com:5060;branch=z9hG4bK87asdks7</code>
<code>Via: SIP/2.0/UDP 192.0.2.1:5060;received=192.0.2.207 ;branch = z9hG4bK77asjd</code>

The compact form of the Via header field is v. In this example, the message originated from a multihomed host with two addresses, 192.0.2.1 and 192.0.2.207. The sender guessed wrong as to which network interface would be used. erlang.belltelephone.com noticed the mismatch and added a parameter to the previous hop's Via header field value, containing the address that the packet actually came from. The host or network address and port number are not required to follow the SIP URI syntax. Specifically, LWS on either side of the ":" or "/" is allowed, as shown here:

<code>Via: SIP/2.0/UDP first.example.com: 4000;ttl=16;maddr=224.2.0.1 ;branch=z9hG4bKa7c6a8dlze.1</code>

Even though this specification mandates that the branch parameter be present in all requests, the ABNF for the header field indicates that it is optional. This allows interoperation with RFC 2543 (obsoleted by RFC 3261) elements, which did not have to insert the branch parameter. Two Via header fields are equal if their sent-protocol and sent-by fields are equal, both have the same set of parameters, and the values of all parameters are equal.</td></tr>
</table>

(Continued)

Table 2.10 (Continued) SIP Header Field Descriptions

<table>
<tr><th>Header Field/RFC/Header Field Type</th><th>Description</th></tr>
<tr><td></td><td>RFC 7339 (see Section 13.3) specification defines four new Via header parameters as detailed below in the "Header Field Parameter and Parameter Values" subregistry as per the registry created by RFC 3968. The required information is
<table>
<tr><th>Header Field</th><th>Parameter Name</th><th>Predefined Values</th><th>Reference</th></tr>
<tr><td>Via</td><td>oc</td><td>Yes</td><td>RFC 7339</td></tr>
<tr><td>Via</td><td>oc-validity</td><td>Yes</td><td>RFC 7339</td></tr>
<tr><td>Via</td><td>oc-seq</td><td>Yes</td><td>RFC 7339</td></tr>
<tr><td>Via</td><td>oc-algo</td><td>Yes</td><td>RFC 7339</td></tr>
</table></td></tr>
<tr><td>Warning/RFC 3261 (Standards Track)/Response</td><td>The Warning header field is used to carry additional information about the status of a response. Warning header field values are sent with responses and contain a three-digit warning code, host name, and warning text. The warn-text should be in a natural language that is most likely to be intelligible to the human user receiving the response. This decision can be based on any available knowledge, such as the location of the user, the Accept-Language field in a request, or the Content-Language field in a response. The default language is i-default as defined in RFC 2277.
The currently defined warn-codes are listed below, with a recommended warn-text in English and a description of their meaning. These warnings describe failures induced by the session description. The first digit of warning codes beginning with "3" indicates warnings specific to SIP. Warnings 300 through 329 are reserved for indicating problems with keywords in the session description, 330 through 339 are warnings related to basic network services requested in the session description, 370 through 379 are warnings related to quantitative QOS parameters requested in the session description, and 390 through 399 are miscellaneous warnings that do not fall into one of the above categories.

• 300 Incompatible network protocol: One or more network protocols contained in the session description are not available.
• 301 Incompatible network address formats: One or more network address formats contained in the session description are not available.
• 302 Incompatible transport protocol: One or more transport protocols described in the session description are not available.
• 303 Incompatible bandwidth units: One or more bandwidth measurement units contained in the session description were not understood.
• 304 Media type not available: One or more media types contained in the session description are not available.
• 305 Incompatible media format: One or more media formats contained in the session description are not available.
• 306 Attribute not understood: One or more of the media attributes in the session description are not supported.
• 307 Session description parameter not understood: A parameter other than those listed above was not understood.
• 330 Multicast not available: The site where the user is located does not support multicast.
• 331 Unicast not available: The site where the user is located does not support unicast communication (usually due to the presence of a firewall).</td></tr>
</table>

(*Continued*)

Table 2.10 (Continued) SIP Header Field Descriptions

Header Field/RFC/Header Field Type	*Description*

	• 370 Insufficient bandwidth: The bandwidth specified in the session description or defined by the media exceeds that known to be available.
	• 399 Miscellaneous warning: The warning text can include arbitrary information to be presented to a human user or logged. A system receiving this warning must not take any automated action.
	• 380 SIPS Not Allowed: The UAS or proxy cannot process the request because the SIPS scheme is not allowed (e.g., because there are currently no registered SIPS contacts) (RFC 5630, Standards Track).
	• 381 SIPS Required: The UAS or proxy cannot process the request because the SIPS scheme is required (RFC 5630, Standards Track).
	
	1xx and 2xx have been taken from HTTP/1.1. Additional warn-codes can be defined through IANA. Examples:
	
	`Warning: 307 isi.edu "Session parameter foo not understood"`
	`Warning: 301 isi.edu "Incompatible network address type 'E.164'"`

WWW-Authenticate/RFC 3261 (Standards Track)/ Response	A WWW-Authenticate header field value contains an authentication challenge. See Section 19.4.3 (RFC 3261) for further details on its usage. Example:
	
	`WWW-Authenticate: Digest realm="atlanta.com",`
	`domain="sip:boxesbybob.com", qop="auth",`
	`nonce="f84f1cec41e6cbe5aea9c8e88d359",`
	`opaque="", stale=FALSE, algorithm=MD5`

interoperability. An Internet Assigned Numbers Authority (IANA) registry of option tags is used to ensure easy reference. The option tags defined in SIP are shown in Table 2.11.

2.11 SIP Media Feature Tags

RFC 3840 (also see Section 3.4) that is described here provides a more general framework for an indication of capabilities and characteristics in SIP. Capability and characteristic information about a UA is carried as parameters of the Contact header field. These parameters can be used within REGISTER requests and responses, OPTIONS responses, and requests and responses that create dialogs such as INVITE.

2.11.1 Contact Header Field

RFC 3840 (also see Section 3.4) extends the Contact header field. In particular, it allows for the Contact header field parameters to include feature-param. Feature-param is a feature parameter that describes a feature of the UA associated with the URI in the Contact header field. Feature parameters are identifiable because they either belong to the well-known set of base feature tags, or they begin with a plus sign. It should be noted that the tag-value-list uses an actual comma instead of the comma construction because it appears within a quoted string, where line folding cannot take place. The production for qdtext can be found in RFC 3261. There are additional constraints on the usage of feature-param that cannot be represented in an ABNF. There must only be one instance of any feature tag in feature-param. Any numbers present in a feature parameter must be representable using an ANSI C double. Following these rules, RFC 3840 updates the one in RFC 3261 for contact-params (see detail ABNF syntax in Section 2.4.1.2):

```
contact-params      =      c-p-q/c-p-expires/
                           feature-param
                           /contact-extension
```

In addition, RFC 5626 has extended the contact parameters using reg-id and instance-id as described earlier. The detail of all ABNF syntaxes can be seen in Section 2.4.1.2.

2.11.2 Feature Tag Name, Description, and Usage

RFC 3840 (also see Section 3.4) defines an initial set of SIP media feature tags for use registered with IANA as depicted in Table 2.12. If any new media type is defined in the future, the name of the feature tag must equal *sip.* concatenated with the name of the media type, unless there is an unlikely naming collision between the new media type and an existing feature tag registration. For example, if a new feature tag *sip.gruu* is

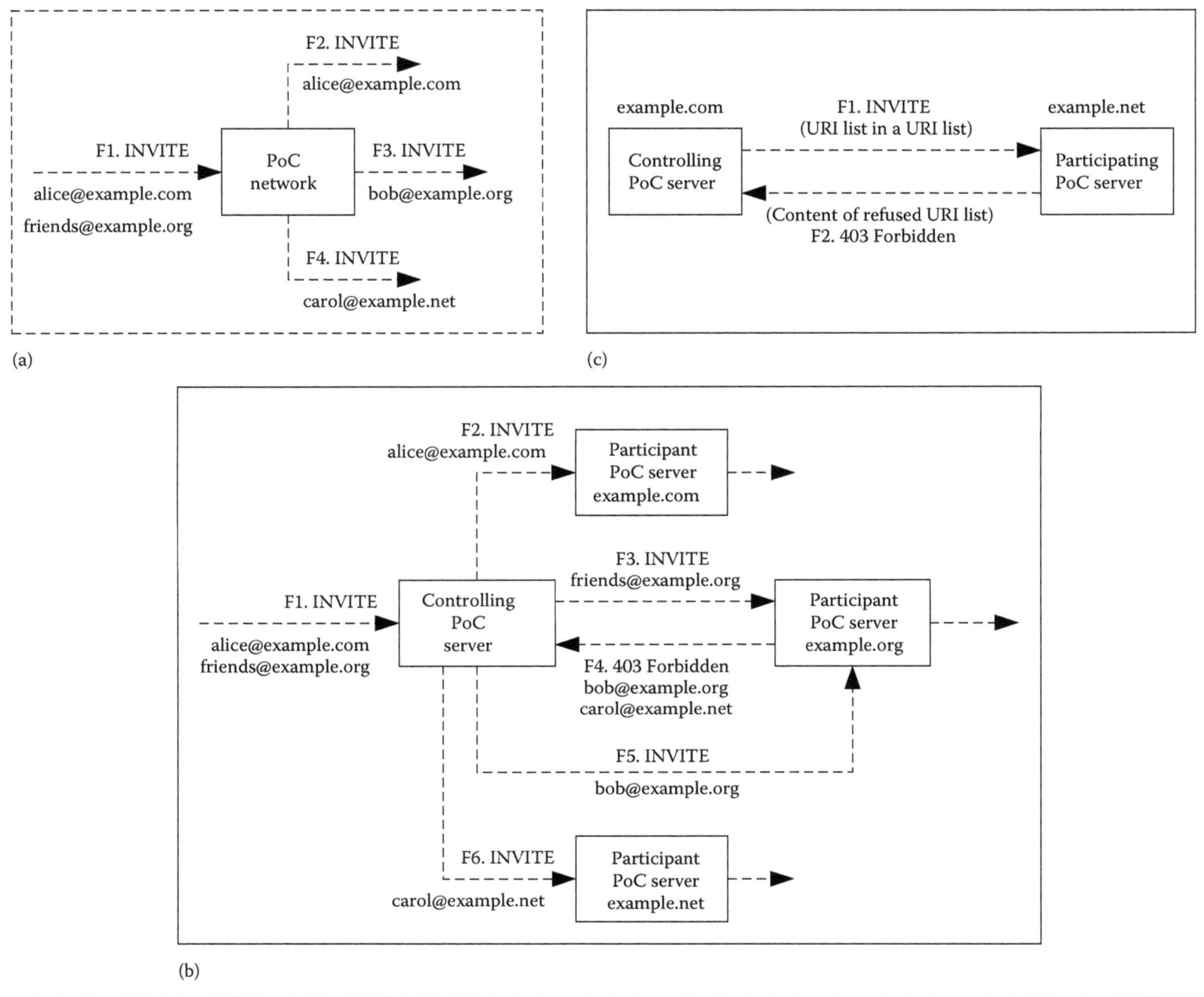

Figure 2.7 PoC behavior and operation—(a) expected behavior, (b) network behavior, and (c) operational view. (Copyright IETF. Reproduced with permission.)

registered in the SIP tree, the IANA registration would be for the tag sip.gruu and not +sip.gruu or gruu. As such, all registrations into the SIP tree will have the sip. prefix.

2.11.3 Conveying Feature Tags with REFER

2.11.3.1 Overview

The SIP Caller Preferences extension defined in RFC 3840 provides a mechanism that allows a SIP request to convey information relating to the originator's capabilities and preferences for the handling of that request. The SIP REFER method defined in RFC 3515 (see Section 2.5) provides a mechanism that allows one party to induce another to initiate a SIP request. This document extends the REFER method to use the mechanism of RFC 3840. By doing so, the originator of a REFER may inform the recipient about the characteristics of the target that the induced request is expected to reach.

RFC 4508 extends the SIP REFER method to be used with feature parameters defined in RFC 3840. Feature tags are used by a UA to convey to another UA information about capabilities and features. This information can be shared by a UA using a number of mechanisms, including REGISTER requests and responses, and OPTIONS responses. This information can also be shared in the context of a dialog by inclusion with a remote target URI (Contact URI). Feature tag information can be very useful to another UA. It is especially useful before the establishment of a session. For example, if a UA knows (e.g., through an OPTIONS query) that the remote UA supports both video and audio, the calling

Table 2.11 SIP Option Tags Description

Option Tag/ Standards Track RFC	*Description*
199/RFC 6228	This option tag is for indicating support of the 199 Early Dialog Terminated provisional response code. When present in a Supported header of a request, it indicates that the UAC supports the 199 response code. When present in a Require or Proxy-Require header field of a request, it indicates that the UAS, or proxies, must support the 199 response code. It does not require the UAS, or proxies, to actually send 199 responses.
100rel/RFC 3262	This option tag is for reliability of provisional responses. When present in a Supported header, it indicates that the UA can send or receive reliable provisional responses. When present in a Require header in a request, it indicates that the UAS must send all provisional responses reliably. When present in a Require header in a reliable provisional response, it indicates that the response is to be sent reliably.
answermode/RFC 5373	This *answermode* option tag is for support of the Answer-Mode and Priv-Answer-Mode extensions used to negotiate automatic or manual answering of a request. The SIP option tag indicating support for this extension is answermode. For implementers: SIP header field names and values are always compared in a case-insensitive manner. The pretty capitalization is just for readability. This syntax includes extension hooks (*token* for answer-mode values and *generic-param* for optional parameters) that could be defined in the future. This specification defines only the behavior for the values given explicitly above. To provide forward compatibility, implementations must ignore unknown values.
early-session/RFC 3959	A UA adding the early-session option tag to a message indicates that it understands the early-session disposition type. Content-Disposition: early-session
eventlist/RFC 4662	The eventlist option tag allows subscriptions to lists of resources.
from-change/RFC 4916	This option tag is used to indicate that a UA supports changes to URIs in From and To header fields during a dialog.
gin/RFC 6140	This option tag is used to identify the extension that provides registration for Multiple Phone Numbers in SIP. When present in a Require or Proxy-Require header field of a REGISTER request, it indicates that support for this extension is required of registrars and proxies, respectively, which are a party to the registration transaction.
Join/RFC 3911	RFC 3911 defines a Require/Supported header option tag *join*. UAs that support the Join header must include the join option tag in a Supported header field. UAs that want explicit failure notification if Join is not supported may include the join option in a Require header field. Example: `Require: join, 100rel`
multiple-refer/RFC 5368	The multiple-refer option tag indicates support for REFER requests that contain a resource list document describing multiple REFER targets.

(*Continued*)

Table 2.11 (Continued) SIP Option Tags Description

Option Tag/ Standards Track RFC	*Description*
norefersub/RFC 4486	This option tag specifies a UA ability of accepting a REFER request without establishing an implicit subscription (compared with the default case defined in RFC 3515). This option tag, when included in the Supported header field, specifies that a UA is capable of accepting a REFER request without creating an implicit subscription when acting as a REFER-Recipient. The REFER-Issuer can know the capabilities of the REFER-Recipient from the presence of the option tags in the Supported header field of the dialog initiating request or response. Another way of learning the capabilities would be by using presence, such as defined in RFC 5196. However, if the capabilities of the REFER-Recipient are not known, using the *norefersub* tag with the Require header field is not recommended. This is because in the event the REFER-Recipient does not support the extension, in order to fall back to the normal REFER, the REFER-Issuer will need to issue a new REFER transaction, thus resulting in additional round trips. A REFER-Recipient will reject a REFER request containing a Require: norefersub header field with a 420 Bad Extension response unless it supports this extension. Note that Require: norefersub can be present with a Refer-Sub: false header field.
outbound/RFC 5626	The outbound option tag is used to identify UAs and registrars that support extensions for Client-Initiated Connections. A UA places this option in a Supported header to communicate its support for this extension. A registrar places this option tag in a Require header to indicate to the registering UA that the registrar used registrations using the binding rules defined in this extension.
resource-priority/ RFC 4412	The resource-priority option tag indicates or requests support for the resource priority mechanism. 417 Unknown Resource-Priority response code (see Section 2.6) defines its behavior.
sec-agree/RFC 3329	The sec-agree option tag indicates support for the Security Agreement mechanism. When used in the Require, or Proxy-Require headers, it indicates that proxy servers are required to use the Security Agreement mechanism. When used in the Supported header, it indicates that the UA Client supports the Security Agreement mechanism. When used in the Require header in the 494 Security Agreement Required or 421 Extension Required responses, it indicates that the UAC must use the Security Agreement Mechanism.
tdialog/RFC 4538	This option tag is used to identify the target dialog header field extension. When used in a Require header field, it implies that the recipient needs to support the Target-Dialog header field. When used in a Supported header field, it implies that the sender of the message supports it.
uui/RFC 7433	This option tag is used to indicate that a UA supports and understands the Use-to-User header field.

UA might call, offering video in the SDP. Another example is when a UA knows that a remote UA is acting as a focus and hosting a conference. In this case, the UA might first subscribe to the conference URI and find out details about the conference before sending an INVITE to join. This extension to the REFER method provides a mechanism by which the REFER-Issuer can provide this useful information about the REFER-Target capabilities and functionality to the REFER-Recipient by including feature tags in the Refer-To header field in a REFER request.

2.11.3.2 Syntax and Semantics

The Refer-To ABNF from RFC 3515 (see Section 2.5) is repeated here for convenience, although all ABNF syntaxes for SIP are provided in Section 2.4.1.2:

```
Refer-To       =      ("Refer-To"/"r") HCOLON
                      (name-addr/addr-spec)
                      *(SEMI generic-param)
```

is extended to

```
Refer-To       =      ("Refer-To"/"r") HCOLON
                      (name-addr/addr-spec)
                      *(SEMI refer-param)
refer-param    =      generic-param/
                      feature-param
where feature-param is defined in Section 9 of
RFC 3840 [4].
```

Note that if any URI parameters are present, the entire URI must be enclosed in < and >. If the < and > are not present, all parameters after the URI are header parameters, not URI parameters.

Table 2.12 SIP Media Feature Tag Defined in RFC 3840 and Other RFCs

Media Feature/Media Feature Tag Name/ASN.1 Identifier	*Description*	*Value*	*Primary Usage*	*Example of Typical Usage*
Audio/sip. audio/1.3.6.1.8.4.1	It indicates that the device supports audio as a streaming media type.	Boolean	It is most useful in a communications application for describing the capabilities of a device, such as a phone or PDA.	Routing a call to a phone that can support audio
Application/sip. application/1.3.6.1.8.4.2	It indicates that the device supports application as a streaming media type.	Boolean	It is most useful in a communications application, for describing the capabilities of a device, such as a phone or PDA.	Routing a call to a phone that can support a media control application
Data/sip.data/1.3.6.1.8.4.3	It indicates that the device supports data as a streaming media type.	Boolean	It is most useful in a communications application, for describing the capabilities of a device, such as a phone or PDA.	Routing a call to a phone that can support a data streaming application
Control/sip. control/1.3.6.1.8.4.4	It indicates that the device supports control as a streaming media type.	Boolean	It is most useful in a communications application for describing the capabilities of a device, such as a phone or PDA.	Routing a call to a phone that can support a floor control application
Video/sip. video/1.3.6.1.8.4.5	It indicates that the device supports video as a streaming media type.	Boolean	It is most useful in a communications application for describing the capabilities of a device, such as a phone or PDA.	Routing a call to a phone that can support video
Text/sip.text/1.3.6.1.8.4.6	It indicates that the device supports text as a streaming media type.	Boolean	It is most useful in a communications application for describing the capabilities of a device, such as a phone or PDA.	Routing a call to a phone that can support text

(Continued)

Table 2.12 (Continued) SIP Media Feature Tag Defined in RFC 3840 and Other RFCs

Media Feature/Media Feature Tag Name/ASN.1 Identifier	*Description*	*Value*	*Primary Usage*	*Example of Typical Usage*
Automata/sip. automata/1.3.6.1.8.4.7	It indicates whether the UA represents an automata (such as a voice-mail server, conference server, IVR, or recording device) or a human.	Boolean. TRUE indicates that the UA represents an automata.	It is most useful in a communications application for describing the capabilities of a device, such as a phone or PDA.	Refusing to communicate with the automata when it is known that automated services are unacceptable
Class/sip.class/1.3.6.1.8.4.8	It indicates the setting, business or personal, in which a communications device is used.	Token with an equality relationship. Typical values include business (the device is used for business communications) and personal (the device is used for personal communications).	It is most useful in a communications application, for describing the capabilities of a device, such as a phone or PDA.	Choosing between a business phone and a home phone
Duples/sip. duplex/1.3.6.1.8.4.9	It indicates whether a communications device can simultaneously send and receive media (full), alternate between sending and receiving (half), can only receive (receive-only) or only send (send-only).	Token with an equality relationship. Typical values include *full* (the device can simultaneously send and receive media), *half* (the device can alternate between sending and receiving media), receive-only (the device can only receive media), and send-only (the device can only send media).	It is most useful in a communications application for describing the capabilities of a device, such as a phone or PDA.	Choosing to communicate with a broadcast server, as opposed to a regular phone, when making a call to hear an announcement
Mobility/sip. mobility/1.3.6.1.8.4.10	It indicates whether the device is fixed (meaning that it is associated with a fixed point of contact with the network), or mobile (meaning that it is not associated with a fixed point of contact). Note that cordless phones are fixed, not mobile, based on this definition.	Token with an equality relationship. Typical values include *fixed* (the device is stationary) and *mobile* (the device can move around with the user).	It is most useful in a communications application for describing the capabilities of a device, such as a phone or PDA.	Choosing to communicate with a wireless phone instead of a desktop phone

(Continued)

Table 2.12 (Continued) SIP Media Feature Tag Defined in RFC 3840 and Other RFCs

Media Feature/Media Feature Tag Name/ASN.1 Identifier	*Description*	*Value*	*Primary Usage*	*Example of Typical Usage*
Description/sip. description/1.3.6.1.8.4.11	It provides a textual description of the device.	String with an equality relationship	It is most useful in a communications application for describing the capabilities of a device, such as a phone or PDA.	Indicating that a device is of a certain make and model
Events/sip. events/1.3.6.1.8.4.12	It indicates a SIP event package, defined in RFC 6665, supported by a SIP UA. The values for this tag equal the event package names that are registered by each event package.	Token with an equality relationship. Values are taken from the IANA SIP Event type namespace registry.	It is most useful in a communications application for describing the capabilities of a device, such as a phone or PDA.	Choosing to communicate with a server that supports the message waiting event package, such as a voice-mail server defined in RFC 3842
Priority/sip. priority/1.3.6.1.8.4.13	It indicates the call priorities the device is willing to handle. A value of X means that the device is willing to take requests with priority X and higher. This does not imply that a phone has to reject calls of lower priority. As always, the decision on handling of such calls is a matter of local policy.	An integer. Each integral value corresponds to one of the possible values of the Priority header field as specified in SIP of RFC 3261. The mapping is defined as *nonurgent* (integral value of 10; the device supports non-urgent calls), *normal* (integral value of 20; the device supports normal calls), *urgent* (integral value of 30; the device supports urgent calls), and *emergency* (integral value of 40; the device supports calls in the case of an emergency situation).	It is most useful in a communications application for describing the capabilities of a device, such as a phone or PDA.	Choosing to communicate with the emergency cell phone of a user

(*Continued*)

Table 2.12 (Continued) SIP Media Feature Tag Defined in RFC 3840 and Other RFCs

Media Feature/Media Feature Tag Name/ASN.1 Identifier	*Description*	*Value*	*Primary Usage*	*Example of Typical Usage*
Methods/sip. methods/1.3.6.1.8.4.14	It indicates a SIP method supported by this UA. In this case, *supported* means that the UA can receive requests with this method. In that sense, it has the same connotation as the Allow header field.	Token with an equality relationship. Values are taken from the Methods table defined in the IANA SIP parameters registry.	It is most useful in a communications application for describing the capabilities of a device, such as a phone or PDA.	Choosing to communicate with a presence application on a PC, instead of a PC phone application
Extensions/sip. extensions/1.3.6.1.8.4.15	It is a SIP extension (each of which is defined by an option tag registered with IANA) that is understood by the UA. Understood, in this context, means that the option tag would be included in a Supported header field in a request.	Token with an equality relationship. Values are taken from the option tags table in the IANA SIP parameters registry.	It is most useful in a communications application for describing the capabilities of a device, such as a phone or PDA.	Choosing to communicate with a phone that supports QOS preconditions instead of one that does not
Schemes/sip. schemes/1.3.6.1.8.4.16	It indicates a URI scheme, defined in RFC 2396, that is supported by a UA. Supported implies, for example, that the UA would know how to handle a URI of that scheme in the Contact header field of a redirect response.	Token with an equality relationship. Values are taken from the IANA URI scheme registry.	It is most useful in a communications application for describing the capabilities of a device, such as a phone or PDA.	Choosing to get redirected to a phone number when a called party is busy, rather than a web page

(*Continued*)

Table 2.12 (Continued) SIP Media Feature Tag Defined in RFC 3840 and Other RFCs

Media Feature/Media Feature Tag Name/ASN.1 Identifier	*Description*	*Value*	*Primary Usage*	*Example of Typical Usage*
Actor/sip. actor/1.3.6.1.8.4.17	It indicates the type of entity that is available at this URI.	Token with an equality relationship. The following values are defined: Principal—the device provides communication with the principal that is associated with the device. Often this will be a specific human being, but it can be an automata (e.g., when calling a voice portal); Attendant—the device provides communication with an automaton or person that will act as an intermediary in contacting the principal associated with the device, or a substitute; and Msg-Taker—the device provides communication with an automaton or person that will take messages and deliver them to the principal; Information—the device provides communication with an automaton or person that will provide information about the principal.	It is most useful in a communications application for describing the capabilities of a device, such as a phone or PDA.	Requesting that a call not be routed to voice mail

(Continued)

Table 2.12 (Continued) SIP Media Feature Tag Defined in RFC 3840 and Other RFCs

Media Feature/Media Feature Tag Name/ASN.1 Identifier	*Description*	*Value*	*Primary Usage*	*Example of Typical Usage*
isfocus/sip. isfocus/1.3.6.1.8.4.18	It indicates that the UA is a conference server, also known as a focus, and will mix together the media for all calls to the same URI defined in RFC 4353.	Boolean	It is most useful in a communications application for describing the capabilities of a device, such as a phone or PDA.	Indicating to a UA that the server to which it has connected is a conference server
sip.uui-isdn/1.3.6.1.8.4.x	This media feature tag when used in a Contact header field of a SIP request or a SIP response indicates that the entity sending the SIP message supports the package uui-isdn specified in RFC 7434.	None	It is most useful for interworking and transporting User-to-User Information (UUI) from the ITU-T Digital Subscriber Signaling System No. 1 (DSS1). User-user information elements within SIP are described in RFC 6567.	Indicating that a mobile phone supports Single Radio Voice call Continuity (SRVCC) for calls in the alerting phase.

2.11.3.3 Feature Tag Usage Examples

2.11.3.3.1 isfocus

The example below shows how the isfocus feature tag can be used by REFER-Issuer to tell the REFER-Recipient that the REFER-Target is a conference focus and, consequently, that sending an INVITE will bring the REFER-Recipient into the conference:

```
Refer-To: sip:conf44@example.com;isfocus
```

2.11.3.3.2 Voice and Video

The example below shows how a REFER-Issuer can tell the REFER-Recipient that the REFER-Target supports audio and video and, consequently, that a video and audio session can be established by sending an INVITE to the REFER-Target:

```
Refer-To: "Alice's Videophone" <sip:alice@
videophone.example.com>;audio;video
```

2.11.3.3.3 URI and Multiple Feature Tags

The example below shows how the REFER-Issuer can tell the REFER-Recipient that the REFER-Target is a voice-mail server. Note that the transport URI parameter is enclosed within the < and > so that it is not interpreted as a header parameter.

```
Refer-To: <sip:alice-vm@example.com;
transport=tcp>;actor="msg-taker";
automata;audio
```

2.12 Summary

We have described the key characteristics of the networked multimedia session for both point-to-point and multipoint communications. A multimedia session may consist of audio, video, or data applications. Each user may have many audio codecs, video codecs, or data applications. It is natural that negotiations between users for using audio codecs, video codecs, or data applications for setting up the session will take place along with meeting the requirements of QOS for audio/video codecs and data-sharing applications. For multimedia communications between more than two users, media bridging is an essential requirement. The SIP signaling protocol is designed in meeting many of those requirements for the networked multimedia communications.

We explained the trapezoidal model of the SIP session setup for the point-to-point call between two users with signaling and media. In addition, the characteristics of the SIP network functional entities such as UA, Back-to-Back UA, Proxy Server, Redirect Server, Register Server, and Application Server are described, including the Location Server that is not a SIP entity. The ABNF syntax that is used for SIP signaling messages are also provided. We have described the details of the terminologies, request and response messages, message headers, message body, option tag, tag, and message format of the basic SIP.

PROBLEMS

1. What are the differences between networked and stand-alone multimedia communications?
2. Describe the key functional features of the point-to-point and multipoint-to-multipoint networked multimedia communications. What are their major differences?
3. Describe the media bridging characteristic of audio, video, and data applications. What are their major differences?
4. What are the fundamental differences between the circuit-switching and the IP packet-switching communication networks? What are the challenges in developing the multimedia call signaling protocol over these two fundamentally different kinds of networks?
5. What are the challenges in meeting the QOS requirements of multimedia communications over the IP packet-switching network? How can a multimedia call control signaling protocol deal with solving the QOS problems? How does the QOS solution differ in solving the QOS problems between the private IP network and the public Internet?
6. Describe the rules of ABNF. Describe the key differences between RFCs 2806, 4434, and 5234. What are the exceptions in SIP ABNF syntaxes adopted for SIP messages described in RFC 3261?
7. Describe the major features of the SIP call signaling protocol. Describe request, response, header, and body of SIP messages.
8. What are the request messages of SIP? Describe the characteristics of each SIP method. What are the key differences between all the SIP methods? Why is the INVITE method so special in SIP?
9. What are the key differences between SIP and HTTP? What are the pros and cons of SIP that is targeted for setting up the sessions for the real-time conversational networked multimedia communications because of adopting messaging structures similar to those of HTTP?
10. Describe in detail why SIP needs to use a host of protocols under its umbrella to set up the multimedia session?
11. Describe the concept of the SIP network. Describe the characteristics of each SIP server that is used over the SIP network. Why is a location server not a SIP functional entity?

12. Why is a SIP proxy server so important that it is termed as the call controller in the SIP network? Compare the functional/capability differences between each server of the SIP network.
13. Describe the call flows of SIP signaling for the point-to-point call using only a proxy server assuming both users are in the same administrative domain. Populate the headers of SIP request and response messages with the key features that may be needed conceptually. Develop a conceptual call model for a three-party conference call assuming that a centralized conference server is used where a user sets up the point-to-call with the conference server.
14. What will be the modifications of the conceptual call flow of the three-party call flow of Q.11 if the media bridging server is separated from the conference application server?
15. Why is SIP so popular as a signaling protocol even for communications between application servers for the creation and invoking of services that go far beyond the primary objectives in designing SIP?

References

1. 3GPP, "TS 24.229: IP Multimedia Call Control Protocol based on SIP and SDP; Stage 3 (Release 5)," 3GPP 24.229, September 2002. Available at ftp://ftp.3gpp.org/Specs/archive /24_series/24.229/.
2. 3GPP, "Numbering, addressing and identification," 3GPP TS 23.003 3.15.0, October 2006.
3. IEEE, "Standard for information technology—Portable operating system interface (POSIX). Base definitions," IEEE 1003.1-2004, 2004.
4. 3GPP, "Telecommunication management; Charging management; Charging architecture and principles," 3GPP TS 32.240 12.3.0, March 2013.
5. 3GPP, "Multimedia Subsystem (IMS) Charging," 3GPP TS 32.260 V13.2.0 IP Release 13, June 2015.

Chapter 3

SIP Message Elements

Abstract

The core Session Initiation Protocol (SIP) (RFC 3261) and the SIP network infrastructure that provide end-to-end communications between the SIP functional entities are described. The SIP request messages that have some uniqueness in creating, modifying, and tearing down of sessions are described in detail. The request and response message processing, forwarding, and handling of transport errors are explained in great length. The SIP transaction handling by clients and server is articulated. Sending requests and receiving responses of messages by SIP clients are specified. In addition, receiving requests and sending responses by SIP servers are also explained. Specifically, SIP message elements contain framing, error handling, common message components, method names, header fields, request and status line structures and manipulation, message request and response structure and operations, multipart message bodies, parsing of message and message elements, Uniform Resource Identifier types and manipulations, and other related functional features of the core SIP. The core material of this part also includes many other Requests for Comment (RFCs) that have enhanced RFC 3261.

3.1 Introduction

The Session Initiation Protocol (SIP) message elements contain many functional features of request and response messages. The knowledge of using these functional features is important in creating, modifying, and terminating multimedia sessions. The SIP user registration sending REGISTER, setting up a session sending INVITE, cancellation of a request sending CANCEL, modifying a session sending UPDATE, SIP client and server transaction, transport, framing, error handling, and other capabilities of the basic SIP service are described in subsequent sections. Before discussing SIP message elements, we describe the method-independent general behavior (Request for Comment [RFC] 3261) of the SIP user agent (UA), UA client (UAC), UA server (UAS), and redirect server.

3.1.1 SIP UA General Behavior

A UA represents an end system. It contains a UAC, which generates requests, and a UAS, which responds to them. A UAC is capable of generating a request based on some external stimulus (the user clicking a button, or a signal on a public switched telephone network [PSTN] line) and processing a response. A UAS is capable of receiving a request and generating a response based on user input, external stimulus, the result of a program execution, or some other mechanism.

When a UAC sends a request, the request passes through some number of proxy servers, which forward the request toward the UAS. When the UAS generates a response, the response is forwarded toward the UAC. UAC and UAS procedures depend strongly on two factors. First, based on whether the request or response is inside or outside of a dialog, and second, based on the method of a request. Dialogs are discussed thoroughly in Section 2.8; they represent a peer-to-peer relationship between UAs and are established by specific SIP methods, such as INVITE.

In this section, we discuss the method-independent rules for UAC and UAS behavior when processing requests that are outside of a dialog. This includes, of course, the requests that themselves establish a dialog. Security procedures for requests and responses outside of a dialog are described in Sections 19.1 through 20.7. Specifically, mechanisms exist for the UAS and UAC to mutually authenticate. A limited set of privacy features are also supported through encryption of bodies using Secure/Multipurpose Internet Mail Extensions (S/MIME; see Section 19.6).

3.1.2 UAC General Behavior

This section covers UAC behavior outside of a dialog.

3.1.2.1 Generating the Request

A valid SIP request formulated by a UAC must, at a minimum, contain the following header fields: To, From, CSeq, Call-ID, Max-Forwards, and Via; all of these header fields are mandatory in all SIP requests. These six header fields are the fundamental building blocks of a SIP message, as they jointly provide for most of the critical message routing services, including the addressing of messages, the routing of responses, limiting message propagation, ordering of messages, and the unique identification of transactions. These header fields are in addition to the mandatory request line, which contains the method, Request-URI, and SIP version. Examples of requests sent outside of a dialog include an INVITE to establish a session (Section 3.7) and an OPTIONS request to query for capabilities (Section 3.4).

3.1.2.1.1 Request-URI

The initial Request-URI of the message should be set to the value of the Uniform Resource Identifier (URI) in the To field. One notable exception is the REGISTER method; the behavior for setting the Request-URI of REGISTER is given in Section 3.3. It may also be undesirable for privacy reasons or convenience to set these fields to the same value (especially if the originating UA expects that the Request-URI will be changed during transit). In some special circumstances, the presence of a preexisting route set can affect the Request-URI of the message. A preexisting route set is an ordered set of URIs that identify a chain of servers to which a UAC will send outgoing requests that are outside of a dialog. Commonly, they are configured on the UA by a user or service provider manually, or through some other non-SIP mechanism. When a provider wishes to configure a UA with an outbound proxy, it is recommended that this be done by providing it with a preexisting route set with a single URI, that of the outbound proxy. When a preexisting route set is present, the procedures for populating the Request-URI and Route header field detailed in Section 3.6.2.1.1 must be followed (even though there is no dialog), using the desired Request-URI as the remote target URI.

3.1.2.1.2 To

The To header field first and foremost specifies the desired *logical* recipient of the request, or the address of record (AOR) of the user or resource that is the target of this request. This may or may not be the ultimate recipient of the request. The To header field may contain a SIP or SIP Security (SIPS) URI, but it may also make use of other URI schemes (e.g., the tel URL; RFC 3966, see Section 4.2.2) when appropriate. All SIP implementations MUST support the SIP URI scheme. Any implementation that supports Transport Layer Security (TLS) MUST support the SIPS URI scheme. The To header field allows for a display name. A UAC may learn how to populate the To header field for a particular request in a number of ways. Usually, the user will suggest the To header field through a human interface, perhaps inputting the URI manually or selecting it from some sort of address book. Frequently, the user will not enter a complete URI, but rather a string of digits or letters (e.g., *bob*). It is at the discretion of the UA to choose how to interpret this input. Using the string to form the user part of a SIP URI implies that the UA wishes the name to be resolved in the domain to the right-hand side (RHS) of the at-sign in the SIP URI (e.g., sip:bob@example.com).

Using the string to form the user part of a SIPS URI implies that the UA wishes to communicate securely, and that the name is to be resolved in the domain to the RHS of the at-sign. The RHS will frequently be the home domain of the requestor, which allows for the home domain to process the outgoing request. This is useful for features like *speed dial* that require interpretation of the user part in the home domain. The tel URL may be used when the UA does not wish to specify the domain that should interpret a telephone number that has been input by the user. Rather, each domain through which the request passes would be given that opportunity. As an example, a user in an airport might log in and send requests through an outbound proxy in the airport. If they enter 411 (this is the phone number for local directory assistance in the United States), that needs to be interpreted and processed by the outbound proxy in the airport, not the user's home domain. In this case, tel:411 would be the right choice. A request outside of a dialog must not contain a To tag; the tag in the To field of a request identifies the peer of the dialog. Since no dialog is established, no tag is present. For further information on the To header field, see Section 2.8.2 (Table 2.10). The following is an example of a valid To header field:

```
To: Carol <sip:carol@chicago.com>
```

3.1.2.1.3 From

The From header field indicates the logical identity of the initiator of the request, possibly the user's AOR. Like the To header field, it contains a URI and optionally a display name. It is used by SIP elements to determine which processing rules to apply to a request (e.g., automatic call rejection).

As such, it is very important that the From URI not contain Internet Protocol (IP) addresses or the fully qualified domain name (FQDN) of the host on which the UA is running, since these are not logical names. The From header field allows for a display name. A UAC should use the display name *Anonymous*, along with a syntactically correct, but otherwise meaningless, URI (like sip:thisis@anonymous.invalid), if the identity of the client is to remain hidden.

Usually, the value that populates the From header field in requests generated by a particular UA is preprovisioned by the user or by the administrators of the user's local domain. If a particular UA is used by multiple users, it might have switchable profiles that include a URI corresponding to the identity of the profiled user. Recipients of requests can authenticate the originator of a request in order to ascertain that they are who their From header field claims they are (see Sections 19.4.5 and 19.4.9 for more details on authentication). The From field MUST contain a new *tag* parameter, chosen by the UAC. See Section 2.9 for details on choosing a tag. For further information on the From header field, see Section 2.8.2. Examples:

```
From: "Bob" <sips:bob@biloxi.com>;tag=a48s
From: sip:+12125551212@phone2net.com;tag=887s
From: Anonymous <sip:c8oqz84zk7z@privacy
.org>;tag=hyh8
```

3.1.2.1.4 Call-ID

The Call-ID header field acts as a unique identifier to group together a series of messages. It must be the same for all requests and responses sent by either UA in a dialog. It should be the same in each registration from a UA. In a new request created by a UAC outside of any dialog, the Call-ID header field must be selected by the UAC as a globally unique identifier over space and time unless overridden by method-specific behavior. All SIP UAs must have a means to guarantee that the Call-ID header fields they produce will not be inadvertently generated by any other UA. Note that when requests are retried after certain failure responses that solicit an amendment to a request (e.g., a challenge for authentication), these retried requests are not considered new requests, and therefore do not need new Call-ID header fields (see Section 2.8.2).

Use of cryptographically random identifiers (RFC 4086) in the generation of Call-IDs is recommended. Implementations may use the form *localid@host*. Call-IDs are case sensitive and are simply compared byte by byte. Using cryptographically random identifiers provides some protection against session hijacking and reduces the likelihood of unintentional Call-ID collisions. No provisioning or human interface is required for the selection of the Call-ID header field value for a request. For further information on the Call-ID header field, see Section 2.8.2. Example:

```
Call-ID: f81d4fae-7dec-11d0-a765
-00a0c91e6bf6@foo.bar.com
```

3.1.2.1.5 CSeq

The CSeq header field serves as a way to identify and order transactions. It consists of a sequence number and a method. The method must match that of the request. For non-REGISTER requests outside of a dialog, the sequence number value is arbitrary. The sequence number value must be expressible as a 32-bit unsigned integer and MUST be less than 2**31. As long as it follows the above guidelines, a client may use any mechanism it would like to select CSeq header field values. Section 3.6.2.1.1 discusses construction of the CSeq for requests within a dialog. Example:

```
CSeq: 4711 INVITE
```

3.1.2.1.6 Max-Forwards

The Max-Forwards header field serves to limit the number of hops a request can transit on the way to its destination. It consists of an integer that is decremented by one at each hop. If the Max-Forwards value reaches 0 before the request reaches its destination, it will be rejected with a 483 Too Many Hops error response. A UAC must insert a Max-Forwards header field into each request it originates with a value that should be 70. This number was chosen to be sufficiently large to guarantee that a request would not be dropped in any SIP network when there are no loops, but not so large as to consume proxy resources when a loop does occur. Lower values should be used with caution and only in networks where topologies are known by the UA.

3.1.2.1.7 Via

The Via header field indicates the transport used for the transaction and identifies the location where the response is to be sent. A Via header field value is added only after the transport that will be used to reach the next hop has been selected (which may involve the usage of the procedures in RFC 3263, see Section 8.2.4). When the UAC creates a request, it must insert a Via into that request. The protocol name and protocol version in the header field must be SIP and 2.0, respectively. The Via header field value must contain a branch parameter. This parameter is used to identify the transaction created by that request. This parameter is used by both the client and the server.

The branch parameter value must be unique across space and time for all requests sent by the UA. The exceptions to this rule are CANCEL and ACK for non-2xx responses. As discussed below, a CANCEL request will have the same value of the branch parameter as the request it cancels. As discussed in Section 3.12.1.1.3, an ACK for a non-2xx response will also have the same branch ID as the INVITE whose response it acknowledges. The uniqueness property of the branch ID parameter, to facilitate its use as a transaction ID, was not part of RFC 2543 obsoleted by RFC 3261. The branch ID inserted by an element compliant with this specification MUST always begin with the characters *z9hG4bK*. These seven characters are used as a magic cookie (seven is deemed sufficient to ensure that an older RFC 2543 implementation would not pick such a value), so that servers receiving the request can determine that the branch ID was constructed in the fashion described by this specification (i.e., globally unique). Beyond this requirement, the precise format of the branch token is implementation defined. The Via header maddr, ttl, and sent-by components will be set when the request is processed by the transport layer (Section 3.13). Via processing for proxies is described in Sections 3.11.6 and 3.11.7.

3.1.2.1.8 Contact

The Contact header field provides a SIP or SIPS URI that can be used to contact that specific instance of the UA for subsequent requests. The Contact header field MUST be present and contain exactly one SIP or SIPS URI in any request that can result in the establishment of a dialog. For the methods defined in this specification, that includes only the INVITE request. For these requests, the scope of the Contact header field is global. That is, the Contact header field value contains the URI at which the UA would like to receive requests, and this URI must be valid even if used in subsequent requests outside of any dialogs. If the Request-URI or top Route header field value contains a SIPS URI, the Contact header field must contain a SIPS URI as well. For further information on the Contact header field, see Section 2.8.2.

3.1.2.1.9 Supported and Require

If the UAC supports extensions to SIP that can be applied by the server to the response, the UAC should include a Supported header field in the request listing the option tags (Section 2.10) for those extensions. The option tags listed must only refer to extensions defined in Standards Track RFCs. This is to prevent servers from insisting that clients implement nonstandard, vendor-defined features in order to receive service. Extensions defined by experimental and informational RFCs are explicitly excluded from usage with the Supported header field in a request, since they too are often used to document vendor-defined extensions.

If the UAC wishes to insist that a UAS understand an extension that the UAC will apply to the request in order to process the request, it must insert a Require header field into the request listing the option tag for that extension. If the UAC wishes to apply an extension to the request and insist that any proxies that are traversed understand that extension, it must insert a Proxy-Require header field into the request listing the option tag for that extension. As with the Supported header field, the option tags in the Require and Proxy-Require header fields must only refer to extensions defined in Standards Track RFCs.

3.1.2.1.10 Additional Message Components

After a new request has been created, and the header fields described above have been properly constructed, any additional optional header fields are added, as are any header fields specific to the method. SIP requests may contain a MIME-encoded message body. Regardless of the type of body that a request contains, certain header fields must be formulated to characterize the contents of the body. For further information on these header fields, see Section 2.8.2.

3.1.2.2 Sending the Request

The destination for the request is then computed. Unless there is local policy specifying otherwise, the destination must be determined by applying the Domain Name System (DNS) procedures described in RFC 3263 (see Section 8.2.4) as follows. If the first element in the route set indicated a strict router (resulting in forming the request as described in Section 3.6.2.1.1), the procedures MUST be applied to the Request-URI of the request. Otherwise, the procedures are applied to the first Route header field value in the request (if one exists), or to the request's Request-URI if there is no Route header field present. These procedures yield an ordered set of address, port, and transports to attempt. Independent of which URI is used as input to the procedures of RFC 3263 (see Section 8.2.4), if the Request-URI specifies a SIPS resource, the UAC must follow the procedures of RFC 3263 (see Section 8.2.4) as if the input URI were a SIPS URI.

Local policy may specify an alternate set of destinations to attempt. If the Request-URI contains a SIPS URI, any alternate destinations must be contacted with TLS. Beyond that, there are no restrictions on the alternate destinations if the request contains no Route header field. This provides a simple alternative to a preexisting route set as a way to specify an outbound proxy. However, that approach for configuring an outbound proxy is not recommended; a preexisting route set with a single URI should be used instead. If the request contains a Route header field, the request should be sent to the locations derived from its topmost value, but maybe sent to any server that the UA is certain will honor the Route and Request-URI policies specified in this document (as opposed to those in RFC 2543 obsoleted by RFC 3261). In particular, a UAC configured with an outbound proxy should attempt to send the request to the location indicated in the first Route header field value instead of adopting the policy of sending all messages to the outbound proxy.

This ensures that outbound proxies that do not add Record-Route header field values will drop out of the path of subsequent requests. It allows end points that cannot resolve the first Route URI to delegate that task to an outbound proxy. The UAC should follow the procedures defined in RFC 3263 (see Section 8.2.4) for stateful elements, trying each address until a server is contacted. Each try constitutes a new transaction, and therefore each carries a different top-most Via header field value with a new branch parameter. Furthermore, the transport value in the Via header field is set to whatever transport was determined for the target server.

3.1.2.3 Processing Responses

Responses are first processed by the transport layer and then passed to the transaction layer. The transaction layer performs its processing and then passes the response to the transaction user (TU). The majority of response processing in the TU is method specific. However, there are some general behaviors independent of the method.

3.1.2.3.1 Transaction Layer Errors

In some cases, the response returned by the transaction layer will not be a SIP message, but rather a transaction layer error. When a timeout error is received from the transaction layer, it must be treated as if a 408 Request Timeout status code has been received. If a fatal transport error is reported by the transport layer (generally, due to fatal Internet Control Message Protocol [ICMP] errors in User Datagram Protocol [UDP] or connection failures in Transmission Control Protocol [TCP]), the condition must be treated as a 503 Service Unavailable status code.

3.1.2.3.2 Unrecognized Responses

A UAC must treat any final response it does not recognize as being equivalent to the x00 response code of that class, and must be able to process the x00 response code for all classes. For example, if a UAC receives an unrecognized response code of 431, it can safely assume that there was something wrong with its request and treat the response as if it had received a 400 Bad Request response code. A UAC must treat any provisional response different than 100 that it does not recognize as 183 Session Progress. A UAC must be able to process 100 and 183 responses.

3.1.2.3.3 Via

If more than one Via header field value is present in a response, the UAC should discard the message. The presence of additional Via header field values that precede the originator of the request suggests that the message was misrouted or possibly corrupted.

3.1.2.3.4 Processing 3xx Responses

Upon receipt of a redirection response (e.g., a 301 response status code), clients should use the URI(s) in the Contact header field to formulate one or more new requests based on the redirected request. This process is similar to that of a proxy recursing on a 3xx class response as detailed in Sections 3.11.5 and 3.11.6. A client starts with an initial target set containing exactly one URI, the Request-URI of the original request. If a client wishes to formulate new requests based on a 3xx class response to that request, it places the URIs to try into the target set. Subject to the restrictions in this specification, a client can choose which Contact URIs it places into the target set. As with proxy recursion, a client processing 3xx class responses must not add any given URI to the target set more than once. If the original request had a SIPS URI in the Request-URI, the client may choose to recurse to a non-SIPS URI, but should inform the user of the redirection to an insecure URI.

Any new request may receive 3xx responses themselves containing the original URI as a contact. Two locations can be configured to redirect to each other. Placing any given URI in the target set only once prevents infinite redirection loops. As the target set grows, the client may generate new requests to the URIs in any order. A common mechanism is to order the set by the *q* parameter value from the Contact header field value. Requests to the URIs may be generated serially or in parallel. One approach is to process groups of decreasing *q*-values serially and process the URIs in each *q*-value group in parallel. Another is to perform only serial processing in decreasing *q*-value order, arbitrarily choosing between contacts of equal *q*-value.

If contacting an address in the list results in a failure, as defined in the next paragraph, the element moves to the next address in the list, until the list is exhausted. If the list is exhausted, then the request has failed. Failures should be detected through failure response codes (codes greater than 399); for network errors, the client transaction will report any transport layer failures to the TU. Note that some response codes (detailed in Section 3.1.2.3.5) indicate that the request can be retried; requests that are reattempted should not be considered failures. When a failure for a particular contact address is received, the client should try the next contact address. This will involve creating a new client transaction to deliver a new request. To create a request based on a contact address in a 3xx response, a UAC must copy the entire URI from the target set into the Request-URI, except for the *method-param* and *header* URI parameters (see Section 4.2.1 for a definition of these parameters).

It uses the header parameters to create header field values for the new request, overwriting header field values associated with the redirected request in accordance with the guidelines in Section 4.2.1.5. Note that in some instances, header fields that have been communicated in the contact address may instead append to existing request header fields in the original redirected request. As a general rule, if the header field can accept a comma-separated list of values, then the new header field value may be appended to any existing values in the original redirected request. If the header field does not accept multiple values, the value in the original redirected request may be overwritten by the header field value communicated in the contact address. For example, if a contact address is returned with the following value:

```
sip:user@host?Subject=foo&Call-Info=<http://
www.foo.com>
```

Then, any Subject header field in the original redirected request is overwritten, but the HTTP URL is merely appended to any existing Call-Info header field values. It is recommended that the UAC reuse the same To, From, and Call-ID used in the original redirected request; however, the UAC may also choose to update the Call-ID header field value for new requests, for example. Finally, once the new request has been constructed, it is sent using a new client transaction, and therefore must have a new branch ID in the top Via field as discussed in Section 3.1.2.1.7. In all other respects, requests sent upon receipt of a redirect response should reuse the header fields and bodies of the original request. In some instances, Contact header field values may be cached at UAC temporarily or permanently depending on the status code received and the presence of an expiration interval (see Section 2.6).

3.1.2.3.5 Processing 4xx Responses

Certain 4xx response codes require specific UA processing, independent of the method. If a 401 Unauthorized or 407 Proxy Authentication Required response is received, the UAC should follow the authorization procedures of Sections 19.4.5 and 19.4.9 to retry the request with credentials. If a 413 Request Entity Too Large response is received (Section 2.6), the request contained a body that was longer than the UAS was willing to accept. If possible, the UAC should retry the request, either omitting the body or using one of a smaller length. If a 415 Unsupported Media Type response is received (Section 2.6), the request contained media types not supported by the UAS. The UAC should retry sending the request, this time only using content with types listed in the Accept header field in the response, with encodings listed in the Accept-Encoding header field in the response, and with languages listed in the Accept-Language in the response. If a 416 Unsupported URI Scheme response is received (Section 2.6), the Request-URI used a URI scheme not supported by the server. The client should retry the request, this time using a SIP URI. If a 420 Bad Extension response is received (Section 2.6), the request contained a Require or Proxy-Require header field listing an option tag for a feature not supported by a proxy or UAS. The UAC should retry the request, this time omitting any extensions listed in the Unsupported header field in the response. In all of the above cases, the request is retried by creating a new request with the appropriate modifications. This new request constitutes a new transaction and should have the same value as the Call-ID, To, and From of the previous request, but the CSeq should contain a new sequence number that is one higher than the previous one. With other 4xx responses, including those yet to be defined, a retry may or may not be possible depending on the method and the use case.

3.1.3 UAS General Behavior

When a request outside of a dialog is processed by a UAS, there is a set of processing rules that are followed, independent of the method. Section 3.6 gives guidance on how a UAS can tell whether a request is inside or outside of a dialog. Note that request processing is atomic. If a request is accepted, all state changes associated with it must be performed. If it is rejected, all state changes must not be performed. UASs should process the requests in the order of the steps that follow in this section (i.e., starting with authentication, then inspecting the method, the header fields, and so on, throughout the remainder of this section).

3.1.3.1 Method Inspection

Once a request is authenticated (or authentication is skipped), the UAS must inspect the method of the request. If the UAS recognizes but does not support the method of a request, it must generate a 405 Method Not Allowed response. Procedures for generating responses are described in Section 3.1.3.6. The UAS must also add an Allow header field to the 405 Method Not Allowed response. The Allow header field must list the set of methods supported by the UAS generating the message. The Allow header field is presented in Section 2.8.2. If the method is one supported by the server, processing continues.

3.1.3.2 Header Inspection

If a UAS does not understand a header field in a request (i.e., the header field is not defined in this specification or in any supported extension), the server must ignore that header field and continue processing the message. A UAS should ignore any malformed header fields that are not necessary for processing requests.

3.1.3.2.1 To and Request-URI

The To header field identifies the original recipient of the request designated by the user identified in the From field. The original recipient may or may not be the UAS processing the request, due to call forwarding or other proxy operations. A UAS may apply any policy it wishes to determine whether to accept requests when the To header field is not the identity of the UAS. However, it is recommended that a UAS accept requests even if they do not recognize the URI scheme (e.g., a tel: URI) in the To header field, or if the To header field does not address a known or current user of this UAS. If, on the other hand, the UAS decides to reject the request, it should generate a response with a 403 Forbidden status code and pass it to the server transaction for transmission.

However, the Request-URI identifies the UAS that is to process the request. If the Request-URI uses a scheme not supported by the UAS, it should reject the request with a 416 Unsupported URI Scheme response. If the Request-URI does not identify an address that the UAS is willing to accept requests for, it should reject the request with a 404 (Not Found) response. Typically, a UA that uses the REGISTER method to bind its AOR to a specific contact address will see requests whose Request-URI equals that contact address. Other potential sources of received Request-URIs include the Contact header fields of requests and responses sent by the UA that establish or refresh dialogs.

3.1.3.2.2 Merged Requests

If the request has no tag in the To header field, the UAS core must check the request against ongoing transactions. If the From tag, Call-ID, and CSeq exactly match those associated with an ongoing transaction, but the request does not match that transaction (based on the matching rules in Section 3.12.1.3), the UAS core should generate a 482 Loop Detected response and pass it to the server transaction. The same request has arrived at the UAS more than once, following different paths, most likely due to forking. The UAS processes the first such request received and responds with a 482 Loop Detected to the rest of them.

3.1.3.2.3 Require

Assuming the UAS decides that it is the proper element to process the request, it examines the Require header field, if present. The Require header field is used by a UAC to tell a UAS about SIP extensions that the UAC expects the UAS to support in order to process the request properly. Its format is described in Section 2.8.2. If a UAS does not understand an option tag listed in a Require header field, it must respond by generating a response with status code 420 Bad Extension. The UAS must add an Unsupported header field, and list in it those options it does not understand among those in the Require header field of the request. Note that Require and Proxy-Require must not be used in a SIP CANCEL request, or in an ACK request sent for a non-2xx response. These header fields must be ignored if they are present in these requests. An ACK request for a 2xx response must contain only those Require and Proxy-Require values that were present in the initial request. Example:

UAC->UAS:

```
INVITE sip:watson@bell-telephone.com SIP/2.0
Require: 100rel
```

UAS->UAC:

```
SIP/2.0 420 Bad Extension
Unsupported: 100rel
```

This behavior ensures that the client–server interaction will proceed without delay when all options are understood by both sides, and only slow down if options are not understood (as in the example above). For a well-matched client–server pair, the interaction proceeds quickly, saving a round trip often required by negotiation mechanisms. In addition, it also removes ambiguity when the client requires features that the server does not understand. Some features, such as call handling fields, are only of interest to end systems.

3.1.3.3 Content Processing

Assuming the UAS understands any extensions required by the client, the UAS examines the body of the message, and the header fields that describe it. If there are any bodies whose type (indicated by the Content-Type), language (indicated by the Content-Language), or encoding (indicated by the Content-Encoding) are not understood, and that body part is not optional (as indicated by the Content-Disposition header field), the UAS must reject the request with a 415 Unsupported Media Type response. The response must contain an Accept header field listing the types of all bodies it understands, in the event the request contained bodies of types not supported by the UAS. If the request contained content encodings not understood by the UAS, the response must contain an Accept-Encoding header field listing the encodings understood by the UAS. If the request contained content with languages not understood by the UAS, the response must contain an Accept-Language header field indicating the languages understood by the UAS. Beyond these checks, body handling depends on the method and type. For further information on the processing of content-specific header fields, see Sections 2.4.2.4, 3.9, and 16.6.

3.1.3.4 Applying Extensions

A UAS that wishes to apply some extension when generating the response must not do so unless support for that extension is indicated in the Supported header field in the request. If the desired extension is not supported, the server should rely only on baseline SIP and any other extensions supported by the client. In rare circumstances, where the server cannot process the request without the extension, the server may send a 421 Extension Required response. This response indicates that the proper response cannot be generated without the support of a specific extension. The needed extension(s) must be included in a Require header field in the response. This behavior is not recommended, as it will generally break interoperability. Any extensions applied to a non-421 response must be listed in a Require header field included in the response. Of course, the server must not apply extensions not listed in the Supported header field in the request. As a result of this, the Require header field in a response will only ever contain option tags defined in Standards Track RFCs.

3.1.3.5 Processing the Request

Assuming all of the checks in the previous subsections are passed, the UAS processing becomes method specific. Section 3.3 covers the REGISTER request, Section 3.4 covers the OPTIONS request, Section 3.7 covers the INVITE request, and Section 2.12 covers the BYE request.

3.1.3.6 Generating the Response

When a UAS wishes to construct a response to a request, it follows the general procedures detailed in the following subsections. Additional behaviors specific to the response code in question, which are not detailed in this section, may also be required. Once all procedures associated with the creation of a response have been completed, the UAS hands the response back to the server transaction from which it received the request.

3.1.3.6.1 Sending a Provisional Response

One largely non-method-specific guideline for the generation of responses is that UASs should not issue a provisional response for a non-INVITE request. Rather, UASs should generate a final response to a non-INVITE request as soon as possible. When a 100 Trying response is generated, any Time-stamp header field present in the request must be copied into this 100 Trying response. If there is a delay in generating the response, the UAS should add a delay value into the Time-stamp value in the response. This value must contain the difference between the time of sending of the response and receipt of the request, measured in seconds.

3.1.3.6.2 Headers and Tags

The From field of the response must equal the From header field of the request. The Call-ID header field of the response must equal the Call-ID header field of the request. The CSeq header field of the response must equal the CSeq field of the request. The Via header field values in the response must equal the Via header field values in the request, and must maintain the same ordering. If a request contained a To tag in the request, the To header field in the response must equal that of the request. However, if the To header field in the request did not contain a tag, the URI in the To header field in the response must equal the URI in the To header field; additionally, the UAS must add a tag to the To header field in the response (with the exception of the 100 [Trying] response, in which a tag may be present). This serves to identify the UAS that is responding, possibly resulting in a component of a dialog ID. The same tag must be used for all responses to that request, both final and provisional (again excepting the 100 Trying). Procedures for the generation of tags are defined in Section 2.9.

3.1.3.7 Stateless UAS Behavior

A stateless UAS is a UAS that does not maintain transaction state. It replies to requests normally but discards any state that would ordinarily be retained by a UAS after a response has been sent. If a stateless UAS receives a retransmission of a request, it regenerates the response and resends it, just as if it were replying to the first instance of the request. A UAS cannot be stateless unless the request processing for that method would always result in the same response if the requests are identical. This rules out stateless registrars, for example. Stateless UASs do not use a transaction layer; they receive requests directly from the transport layer and send responses directly to the transport layer. The stateless UAS role is needed primarily to handle unauthenticated requests for which a challenge response is issued. If unauthenticated requests were handled statefully, then malicious floods of unauthenticated requests could create massive amounts of transaction state that might slow or completely halt call processing in a UAS, effectively creating a denial of service condition; for more information, see Section 19.12.1.5. The most important behaviors of a stateless UAS are the following:

- A stateless UAS must NOT send provisional (1xx) responses.
- A stateless UAS MUST NOT retransmit responses.
- A stateless UAS MUST ignore ACK requests.
- A stateless UAS MUST ignore CANCEL requests.
- To header tags MUST be generated for responses in a stateless manner—in a manner that will generate the same tag for the same request consistently. For information on tag construction, see Section 2.9.

In all other respects, a stateless UAS behaves in the same manner as a stateful UAS. A UAS can operate in either a stateful or stateless mode for each new request.

3.1.4 Redirect Server General Behavior

In some architectures, it may be desirable to reduce the processing load on proxy servers that are responsible for routing requests, and improve signaling path robustness, by relying on redirection. Redirection allows servers to push routing information for a request back in a response to the client, thereby taking themselves out of the loop of further messaging for this transaction while still aiding in locating the target of the request. When the originator of the request receives the redirection, it will send a new request based on the URI(s) it has received. By propagating URIs from the core of the network to its edges, redirection allows for considerable network scalability.

A redirect server is logically constituted of a server transaction layer and a TU that has access to a location service of some kind (see Section 2.6 for more information on registrars and location services). This location service is effectively a database containing mappings between a single URI and a set of one or more alternative locations at which the target of that URI can be found.

A redirect server does not issue any SIP requests of its own. After receiving a request other than CANCEL, the server either refuses the request or gathers the list of alternative locations from the location service and returns a final response of class 3xx. For well-formed CANCEL requests, it should return a 2xx response. This response ends the SIP transaction. The redirect server maintains transaction state for an entire SIP transaction. It is the responsibility of clients to detect forwarding loops between redirect servers. When a redirect server returns a 3xx response to a request, it populates the list of (one or more) alternative locations into the Contact header field. An *expires* parameter to the Contact header field values may also be supplied to indicate the lifetime of the Contact data.

The Contact header field contains URIs giving the new locations or user names to try, or may simply specify additional transport parameters. A 301 Moved Permanently or 302 Moved Temporarily response may also give the same location and user name that was targeted by the initial request, but specify additional transport parameters such as a different server or multicast address to try, or a change of SIP transport from UDP to TCP or vice versa. However, redirect servers must not redirect a request to a URI equal to the one in the Request-URI; instead, provided that the URI does not point to itself, the server may proxy the request to the destination URI, or may reject it with a 404. If a client is using an outbound proxy, and that proxy actually redirects requests, a potential arises for infinite redirection loops.

Note that a Contact header field value may also refer to a different resource than the one originally called. For example, a SIP call connected to a PSTN gateway may need to deliver a special informational announcement such as, "The number you have dialed has been changed." A Contact response header field can contain any suitable URI indicating where the called party can be reached, not limited to SIP URIs. For example, it could contain URIs for phones, fax [1–3], or irc (if they were defined) or a mailto: (RFC 6068) URL. Section 19.12.2.2 discusses implications and limitations of redirecting a SIPS URI to a non-SIPS URI.

The expires parameter of a Contact header field value indicates how long the URI is valid. The value of the parameter is a number indicating seconds. If this parameter is not provided, the value of the Expires header field determines how long the URI is valid. Malformed values should be treated as equivalent to 3600. This provides a modest level of backwards compatibility with RFC 2543 obsoleted by RFC 3261, which allowed absolute times in this header field. If an absolute time is received, it will be treated as malformed, and then default to 3600. Redirect servers must ignore features that are not understood (including unrecognized header fields, any unknown option tags in Require, or even method names) and proceed with the redirection of the request in question.

3.2 Canceling a Request

The CANCEL request is a hop-by-hop message and is designed to be used to cancel a previous request sent by a client for the message like INVITE that may take a long time to respond and where a UAS has not sent a final response yet. Specifically, it asks the UAS to cease processing the request and to generate an error response to that request. For this reason, CANCEL is best for INVITE requests, which can take a long time to generate a response. In that usage, a UAS that receives a CANCEL request for an INVITE, but has not yet sent a final response, would stop ringing, and then respond to the INVITE with a specific error response (e.g., 487 Request Terminated). CANCEL requests can be constructed and sent by both proxies and UACs.

A CANCEL request should not be sent by a client to cancel a request other than INVITE. Since requests other than INVITE are responded to immediately, sending a CANCEL for a non-INVITE request would always create a race condition. The Request-URI, Call-ID, To, the numeric part of CSeq, and From header fields in the CANCEL request must be identical to those in the request being cancelled, including tags. A CANCEL constructed by a client must have only a single Via header field value matching the top Via value in the request being cancelled. Using the same values for these header fields allows the CANCEL to be matched with the request it cancels. However, the method part of the CSeq header field must have a value of CANCEL. This allows CANCEL to be identified and processed as a transaction, as a distinct SIP method. If the request being cancelled contains a Route header field, the CANCEL request must include that Route header field's values. This is needed so that stateless proxies are able to route CANCEL requests properly. If no provisional response has been received, the CANCEL request must not be sent by the client; rather, the client must wait for the arrival of a provisional response before sending the request.

For a server, the CANCEL method requests that the TU at the server side cancel a pending transaction. A stateless proxy will forward it, a stateful proxy might respond to it and generate some CANCEL requests of its own, and a UAS will respond to it. This request cannot be challenged by the server in order to get proper credentials in an Authorization header field as it is a hop-by-hop request and cannot be resubmitted. If the UAS does not find a matching transaction for the CANCEL as described, it should respond to the CANCEL with a 481 Call Leg/Transaction Does Not Exist. If the UAS has not issued a final response for the original request, its behavior depends on the method of the original request. If the original request was an INVITE, the UAS should immediately respond to the INVITE with a 487 Request Terminated. A CANCEL request has no impact on the processing of transactions with any other method. Regardless of the method of the original request, as long as the CANCEL matched an existing transaction, the UAS answers the CANCEL request itself with a 200 OK response. An example of CANCEL method is as follows:

```
CANCEL sip:bob@biloxi.example.com SIP/2.0
Via: SIP/2.0/UDP client.atlanta.example.
com:5060;branch=z9hG4bK74bf9
Max-Forwards: 70
From: Alice <sip:alice@atlanta.example.
com>;tag=9fxced76sl
To: Bob <sip:bob@biloxi.example.com>
Route: <sip:ss1.atlanta.example.com;lr>
Call-ID: 2xTb9vxSit55XU7p8@atlanta.example.
com
CSeq: 1 CANCEL
Content-Length: 0
```

3.3 Registration

Registration creates bindings in a location service for a particular domain that associates an AOR URI with one or more contact addresses. Thus, when a proxy for that domain receives a request whose Request-URI matches the AOR, the proxy will forward the request to the contact addresses registered to that AOR. Generally, it only makes sense to register an AOR at a domain's location service when requests for that AOR would be routed to that domain. In most cases, this means that the domain of the registration will need to match the domain in the URI of the AOR. The registration scheme indicated above using RFC 3261 procedures does not manage the outbound connection of the SIP requests. As a result, if the outbound connection of the REGISTER request are disconnected, as it happens frequently by middle boxes like network address translators (NATs) or firewalls, the client will have no clue that it needs to refresh its binding with the registration server. RFC 5626 has devised a registration with Client-Initiated Connection Management described in Section 13.2 to take care of this problem, thereby making the client-initiated connection management much more scalable in the large-scale SIP network. Registration of UA's contacts information for SIPS URI is provided in Section 4.2.3. In view of multiple UAs registering using the same AOR, RFC 5627 describes the Globally Routable UA URI (GRUU)-based registration using an instant-id so that the call can be routed to that particular UA. The detail of GRUU registration is provided in Section 4.3. However, GRUU SIPS URI registration is described in Section 4.2.3.

3.3.1 Registration without Managing Client-Initiated Connection

Figure 3.1a illustrates a SIP trapezoidal network with two UAs, an outbound proxy server, and an inbound proxy server where each proxy is acting as a registration server as well. Earlier, we described all of these entities including the discovery of the registrar server briefly that the location server is not a part of SIP, but a registrar for some domain must be able to read and write data to the location service, and a proxy or a redirect server for that domain must be capable of reading that same data. A registrar may be colocated with a particular SIP proxy server for the same domain.

Registration entails sending a REGISTER request to a special type of UAS known as a registrar. A registrar acts as the front end to the location service for a domain, reading and writing mappings based on the contents of REGISTER requests. This location service is then typically consulted by a proxy server that is responsible for routing requests for that domain. Here, we will describe about REGISTER method in detail.

3.3.1.1 Constructing the REGISTER Request

REGISTER requests add, remove, and query bindings. A REGISTER request can add a new binding between an AOR and one or more contact addresses. Registration on behalf of a particular AOR can be performed by a suitably authorized third party. A client can also remove previous bindings or query to determine which bindings are currently in place for

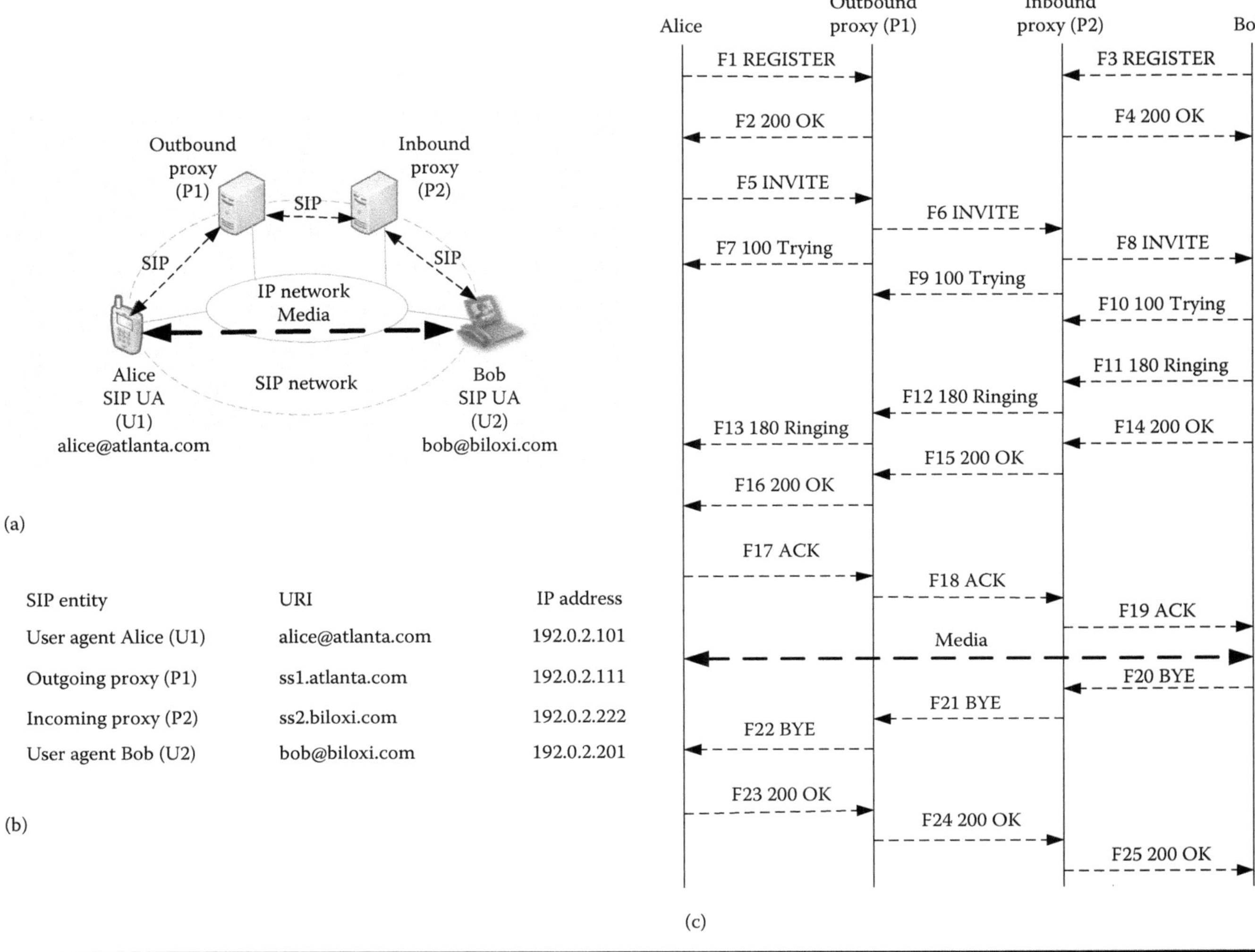

SIP entity	URI	IP address
User agent Alice (U1)	alice@atlanta.com	192.0.2.101
Outgoing proxy (P1)	ss1.atlanta.com	192.0.2.111
Incoming proxy (P2)	ss2.biloxi.com	192.0.2.222
User agent Bob (U2)	bob@biloxi.com	192.0.2.201

Figure 3.1 SIP registration: (a) SIP trapezoidal network, (b) SIP URIs and IP addresses of functional entities, and (c) registration call flows. (Copyright IETF. Reproduced with permission.)

an AOR. A REGISTER request does not establish a dialog. A UAC may include a Route header field in a REGISTER request based on a preexisting route set, as described in a separate section. The Record-Route header field has no meaning in REGISTER requests or responses, and must be ignored if present. In particular, the UAC must not create a new route set based on the presence or absence of a Record-Route header field in any response to a REGISTER request. The following header fields, except Contact, must be included in a REGISTER request. A Contact header field may be included:

- **Request-URI:** The Request-URI names the domain of the location service for which the registration is meant. The *userinfo* and @ components of the SIP URI must not be present.
- **To:** The To header field contains the AOR whose registration is to be created, queried, or modified. The To header field and the Request-URI field typically differ, as the former contains a user name. This AOR must be a SIP URI or SIPS URI.
- **From:** The From header field contains the AOR of the person responsible for the registration. The value is the same as the To header field unless the request is a third-party registration.
- **Call-ID:** All registrations from a UAC should use the same Call-ID header field value for registrations sent to a particular registrar. If the same client were to use different Call-ID values, a registrar could not detect whether a delayed REGISTER request might have arrived out of order.
- **CSeq:** The CSeq value guarantees proper ordering of REGISTER requests. A UA must increment the CSeq value by one for each REGISTER request with the same Call-ID.
- **Contact:** REGISTER requests may contain a Contact header field with zero or more values containing

address bindings. UAs must not send a new registration (i.e., containing new Contact header field values, as opposed to a retransmission) until they have received a final response from the registrar for the previous one, or the previous REGISTER request has timed out.

An example of the REGISTER method:

```
REGISTER sips:ss2.biloxi.example.com SIP/2.0
Via: SIP/2.0/TLS client.biloxi.example.
com:5061;branch=z9hG4bKnashds7
Max-Forwards: 70
From: Bob <sips:bob@biloxi.example.
com>;tag=a73kszlfl
To: Bob <sips:bob@biloxi.example.com>
Call-ID: 1j9FpLxk3uxtm8tn@biloxi.example.com
CSeq: 1 REGISTER
Authorization: Digest user name="bob",
realm="atlanta.example.com",
   nonce="df84f1cec4341ae6cbe5ap359a9c8e88",
   opaque="",
       uri="sips:ss2.biloxi.example.com",
   response="aa7ab4678258377c6f7d4be6087e2f60"
Content-Length: 0
```

3.3.1.2 *Adding Bindings*

The REGISTER request sent to a registrar includes the contact address(es) to which SIP requests for the AOR should be forwarded. The AOR is included in the To header field of the REGISTER request. The Contact header field values of the request typically consist of SIP or SIPS URIs that identify particular SIP end points; however, they may use any URI scheme. A SIP UA can choose to register telephone numbers (with the tel URL; RFC 3966, see Section 4.2.2) or e-mail addresses (with a mailto URL, RFC 2368) as Contacts for an AOR. Once a client has established bindings at a registrar, it may send subsequent registrations containing new bindings or modifications to existing bindings as necessary. The 2xx response to the REGISTER request will contain, in a Contact header field, a complete list of bindings that have been registered for this AOR at this registrar.

If the AOR in the To header field of a REGISTER request is a SIPS URI, then any Contact header field values in the request should also be SIPS URIs. Clients should only register non-SIPS URIs under a SIPS AOR when the security of the resource represented by the contact address is guaranteed by other means. This may be applicable to URIs that invoke protocols other than SIP, or SIP devices secured by protocols other than TLS. Registrations do not need to update all bindings. Typically, a UA only updates its own contact addresses.

3.3.1.3 *Setting the Expiration Interval of Contact Addresses*

When a client sends a REGISTER request, it may suggest an expiration interval that indicates how long the client would like the registration to be valid. There are two ways in which a client can suggest an expiration interval for a binding: through an Expires header field or an expires Contact header parameter. The latter allows expiration intervals to be suggested on a per-binding basis when more than one binding is given in a single REGISTER request, whereas the former suggests an expiration interval for all Contact header field values that do not contain the expires parameter. If neither mechanism for expressing a suggested expiration time is present in a REGISTER, the client is indicating its desire for the server to choose.

3.3.1.3.1 Preferences among Contact Addresses

If more than one Contact is sent in a REGISTER request, the registering UA intends to associate all of the URIs in these Contact header field values with the AOR present in the To field. This list can be prioritized with the *q* parameter in the Contact header field. The *q* parameter indicates a relative preference for the particular Contact header field value compared with other bindings for this AOR.

3.3.1.3.2 Removing Bindings

Registrations are soft state and expire unless refreshed, but can also be explicitly removed. A client can attempt to influence the expiration interval selected by the registrar. A UA requests the immediate removal of a binding by specifying an expiration interval of 0 for that contact address in a REGISTER request. UAs should support this mechanism so that bindings can be removed before their expiration interval has passed. The REGISTER-specific Contact header field value of "*" applies to all registrations; however, it must not be used unless the Expires header field is present with a value of 0. Use of the "*" Contact header field value allows a registering UA to remove all bindings associated with an AOR without knowing their precise values.

3.3.1.3.3 Fetching Bindings

A success response to any REGISTER request contains the complete list of existing bindings, regardless of whether the request contained a Contact header field. If no Contact header field is present in a REGISTER request, the list of bindings is left unchanged.

3.3.1.3.4 Refreshing Bindings

Each UA is responsible for refreshing the bindings that it has previously established. A UA should not refresh bindings set up by other UAs.

3.3.2 Discovering a SIP Registrar

UAs can use three ways to determine the address to which to send registrations (RFC 3261): by configuration, using the AOR, and multicast. A UA can be configured, in ways beyond the scope of this specification, with a registrar address. If there is no configured registrar address, the UA should use the host part of the AOR as the Request-URI and address the request there, using the normal SIP server location mechanisms described in RFC 3263 (see Section 8.2.4). For example, the UA for the user sip:carol@chicago .com addresses the REGISTER request to sip:chicago.com.

Finally, a UA can be configured to use multicast. Multicast registrations are addressed to the well-known *all SIP servers* multicast address sip.mcast.net (224.0.1.75 for IPv4). No well-known IPv6 multicast address has been allocated; such an allocation will be documented separately when needed. SIP UAs may listen to that address and use it to become aware of the location of other local users; however, they do not respond to the request. Multicast registration may be inappropriate in some environments, for example, if multiple businesses share the same local area network.

3.3.3 Multiple-AOR Registration

The present REGISTER method does not allow registering multiple AORs because it uses only the single AOR for each registration. In some situations, the registration of multiple AORs may be useful as articulated in RFC 5947. For example, a SIP Private Branch Exchange (PBX) needs to provide the registration for all AORs of all SIP UAs behind it, while each AOR may have different requirements for Contact (e.g., SIP URI, tel URI), security (e.g., P-Associated-URI, P-Asserted Identity, P-Preferred Identity), and policy (e.g., quality of service [QOS], security). Owing to lack of multiple-AOR registration in SIP, the benefits such as reduction in registration response growth, proper handling of SIP-aware middle boxes, use of wildcard syntax, correct routing of the incoming requests to the SIP middle boxes with the target-URI, and proper matching of security and QOS policies cannot be obtained. To meet these requirements, a private extension in SIP header known as the P-Associated-URI header specified in RFC 7315 (see Section 2.8.2) is made, and is not used in the Internet. The P-Associated-URI header field transports a set of associated URIs to the registered AOR, and allows a registrar to return a set of associated URIs for a registered AOR. The P-Associated-URI header field is used in 200 OK responses to a REGISTER request. A more detailed discussion of this header can be seen in the SIP header section (see Section 2.8.2).

In case of the GRUU defined in RFC 5627 (see Section 4.3), if a UA has a multiplicity of AORs, either in different domains or within the same domain, additional considerations apply. When a UA sends a request, the request will be sent *using* one of its AORs. This AOR will typically show up in the From header field of the request, and credentials unique to that AOR will be used to authenticate the request. The GRUU placed into the Contact header field of such a request should be one that is associated with the AOR used to send the request. In cases where the UA uses a tel URI to populate the From header field, the UA typically has a SIP AOR that is treated as an alias for the tel URI. The GRUU associated with that SIP AOR should be used in the Contact header field. When a UA receives a request, the GRUU placed into the Contact header field of a 2xx response should be the one associated with the AOR or GRUU to which the request was most recently targeted. There are several ways to determine the AOR or GRUU to which a request was sent. For example, if a UA registered a different contact to each AOR by using a different user part of the URI, the Request-URI (which contains that contact) will indicate the AOR.

3.3.4 Registration Call Flows

We have taken the registration call flows example for explaining most of the features of SIP registration defined in RFC 3261.

3.3.4.1 Successful New Registration

We have taken an example shown in Figure 3.1c. Bob sends a SIP REGISTER request to the SIP server. The request includes the user's contact list. This flow shows the use of HTTP Digest for authentication using TLS transport. TLS transport is used because of the lack of integrity protection in HTTP Digest and the danger of registration hijacking without it, as described in RFC 3261. The SIP server provides a challenge to Bob. Bob enters his valid user ID and password. Bob's SIP client encrypts the user information according to the challenge issued by the SIP server and sends the response to the SIP server. The SIP server validates the user's credentials. It registers the user in its contact database and returns a response (200 OK) to Bob's SIP client. The response includes the user's current contact list in Contact headers. The format of the authentication shown is HTTP digest. It is assumed that Bob has not previously registered with this server. The message details are shown below:

F1 REGISTER Bob -> SIP Registration Server

```
REGISTER sips:ss2.biloxi.example.com SIP/2.0
Via: SIP/2.0/TLS client.biloxi.example.
com:5061;branch=z9hG4bKnashds7
Max-Forwards: 70
From: Bob <sips:bob@biloxi.example.com>;
tag=a73kszlfl
To: Bob <sips:bob@biloxi.example.com>
Call-ID: 1j9FpLxk3uxtm8tn@biloxi.example.com
```

```
CSeq: 1 REGISTER
Contact: <sips:bob@client.biloxi.example.com>
Content-Length: 0
```

F2 401 Unauthorized SIP Registration Server -> Bob

```
SIP/2.0 401 Unauthorized
Via: SIP/2.0/TLS client.biloxi.example.
com:5061;branch=z9hG4bKnashds7;
      received=192.0.2.201
From: Bob <sips:bob@biloxi.example.com>;
tag=a73kszlfl
To: Bob <sips:bob@biloxi.example.com>;
tag=1410948204
Call-ID: 1j9FpLxk3uxtm8tn@biloxi.example.com
CSeq: 1 REGISTER
WWW-Authenticate: Digest realm="atlanta.
example.com", qop="auth",
      nonce="ea9c8e88df84f1cec4341ae6cb
      e5a359",
      opaque="", stale=FALSE, algorithm=MD5
Content-Length: 0
```

F3 REGISTER Bob -> SIP Registration Server

```
REGISTER sips:ss2.biloxi.example.com SIP/2.0
Via: SIP/2.0/TLS client.biloxi.example.
com:5061;branch=z9hG4bKnashd92
Max-Forwards: 70
From: Bob <sips:bob@biloxi.example.
com>;tag=ja743ks76zlflH
To: Bob <sips:bob@biloxi.example.com>
Call-ID: 1j9FpLxk3uxtm8tn@biloxi.example.com
CSeq: 2 REGISTER
Contact: <sips:bob@client.biloxi.example.com>
Authorization: Digest username="bob",
realm="atlanta.example.com"
      nonce="ea9c8e88df84f1cec4341ae6cb
      e5a359", opaque="",
      uri="sips:ss2.biloxi.example.com",
      response="dfe56131d1958046689d83306477
      ecc"
Content-Length: 0
```

F4 200 OK SIP Registration Server -> Bob

```
SIP/2.0 200 OK
Via: SIP/2.0/TLS client.biloxi.example.
com:5061;branch=z9hG4bKnashd92
      ;received=192.0.2.201
From: Bob <sips:bob@biloxi.example.com>;
tag=ja743ks76zlflH
To: Bob <sips:bob@biloxi.example.com>;
tag=37GkEhwl6
Call-ID: 1j9FpLxk3uxtm8tn@biloxi.example.com
CSeq: 2 REGISTER
Contact: <sips:bob@client.biloxi.example.
com>;expires=3600
Content-Length: 0
```

3.3.4.2 Update of Contact List

Continuing the same example of Figure 3.1c, Bob wishes to update the list of addresses where the SIP server will redirect or forward INVITE requests. Bob sends a SIP REGISTER request to the SIP server. Bob's request includes an updated contact list. We know that the user already has authenticated with the server; the user supplies authentication credentials with the request and is not challenged by the server. The SIP server validates the user's credentials. It registers the user in its contact database, updates the user's contact list, and returns a response (200 OK) to Bob's SIP client. The response includes the user's current contact list in Contact headers. The message details are as follows:

F1 REGISTER Bob -> SIP Registration Server

```
REGISTER sips:ss2.biloxi.example.com SIP/2.0
Via: SIP/2.0/TLS client.biloxi.example.
com:5061;branch=z9hG4bKnashds7
Max-Forwards: 70
From: Bob <sips:bob@biloxi.example.
com>;tag=a73kszlfl
To: Bob <sips:bob@biloxi.example.com>
Call-ID: 1j9FpLxk3uxtm8tn@biloxi.example.com
CSeq: 1 REGISTER
Contact: mailto:bob@biloxi.example.com
Authorization: Digest user name="bob",
realm="atlanta.example.com",
      qop="auth", nonce="1cec4341ae6cbe5a359
      ea9c8e88df84f", opaque="",
      uri="sips:ss2.biloxi.example.com",
      response="71ba27c64bd01de719686aa45
      90d5824"
Content-Length: 0
```

F2 200 OK SIP Registration Server -> Bob

```
SIP/2.0 200 OK
Via: SIP/2.0/TLS client.biloxi.example.
com:5061;branch=z9hG4bKnashds7;
      received=192.0.2.201
From: Bob <sips:bob@biloxi.example.com>;
tag=a73kszlfl
To: Bob <sips:bob@biloxi.example.com>;
tag=34095828jh
Call-ID: 1j9FpLxk3uxtm8tn@biloxi.example.com
CSeq: 1 REGISTER
Contact: <sips:bob@client.biloxi.example.
com>;expires=3600
Contact: <mailto:bob@biloxi.example.com>;
expires=4294967295
Content-Length: 0
```

3.3.4.2.1 Request for Current Contact List

Bob sends a register request to the proxy server containing no Contact headers extending the same example of Figure 3.1c, indicating that the user wishes to query the server for the user's current contact list. It is known that the user already has authenticated with the server; the user supplies authentication credentials with the request and is not challenged by the server. The SIP server validates the user's credentials. The server returns a response (200 OK) that includes the user's current registration list in Contact headers. The message details are as follows:

F1 REGISTER Bob -> SIP Registration Server

```
REGISTER sips:ss2.biloxi.example.com SIP/2.0
Via: SIP/2.0/TLS client.biloxi.example.
com:5061;branch=z9hG4bKnashds7
Max-Forwards: 70
From: Bob <sips:bob@biloxi.example.com>;
tag=a73kszlfl
To: Bob <sips:bob@biloxi.example.com>
Call-ID: 1j9FpLxk3uxtm8tn@biloxi.example.com
CSeq: 1 REGISTER
Authorization: Digest user name="bob",
realm="atlanta.example.com",
       nonce="df84f1cec4341ae6cbe5ap359a9
       c8e88", opaque="",
       uri="sips:ss2.biloxi.example.com",
       response="aa7ab4678258377c6f7d4be6087
       e2f60"
Content-Length: 0
```

F2 200 OK SIP Registration Server -> Bob

```
SIP/2.0 200 OK
Via: SIP/2.0/TLS client.biloxi.example.com:50
61;branch=z9hG4bKnashds7;received=192.0.2.
201
From: Bob <sips:bob@biloxi.example.com>;
tag=a73kszlfl
To: Bob <sips:bob@biloxi.example.com>;
tag=jqoiweu75
Call-ID: 1j9FpLxk3uxtm8tn@biloxi.example.com
CSeq: 1 REGISTER
Contact: <sips:bob@client.biloxi.example.
com>;expires=3600
Contact: <mailto:bob@biloxi.example.com>;
expires=4294967295
Content-Length: 0
```

3.3.4.3 Cancellation of Registration

In the final example using Figure 3.1c, Bob wishes to cancel their registration with the SIP server. Bob sends a SIP REGISTER request to the SIP server. The request has an expiration period of 0 and applies to all existing contact locations. As explained earlier, the user already has authenticated with the server; the user supplies authentication credentials with the request and is not challenged by the server. The SIP server validates the user's credentials. It clears the user's contact list, and returns a response (200 OK) to Bob's SIP client. The message details are as follows:

F1 REGISTER Bob -> SIP Registration Server

```
REGISTER sips:ss2.biloxi.example.com SIP/2.0
Via: SIP/2.0/TLS client.biloxi.example.
com:5061;branch=z9hG4bKnashds7
Max-Forwards: 70
From: Bob <sips:bob@biloxi.example.com>;
tag=a73kszlfl
To: Bob <sips:bob@biloxi.example.com>
Call-ID: 1j9FpLxk3uxtm8tn@biloxi.example.com
CSeq: 1 REGISTER
Expires: 0
Contact: *
Authorization: Digest username="bob",
realm="atlanta.example.com",
nonce="88df84f1cac4341aea9c8ee6cbe5a359",
opaque="",
uri="sips:ss2.biloxi.example.com",
response="ff0437c51696f9a76244f0cf1dbabbea"
Content-Length: 0
```

F2 200 OK SIP Registration Server -> Bob

```
SIP/2.0 200 OK
Via: SIP/2.0/TLS client.biloxi.example.
com:5061;branch=z9hG4bKnashds7
;received=192.0.2.201
From: Bob <sips:bob@biloxi.example.com>;
tag=a73kszlfl
To: Bob <sips:bob@biloxi.example.com>;
tag=1418nmdsrf
Call-ID: 1j9FpLxk3uxtm8tn@biloxi.example.com
CSeq: 1 REGISTER
Content-Length: 0
```

3.3.5 Registration for Multiple Phone Numbers in SIP

RFC 6140 that is described here defines a mechanism by which a SIP server acting as a traditional PBX can register with a SIP Service Provider (SSP) to receive phone calls for SIP UAs. To function properly, this mechanism requires that each of the AORs registered in bulk maps to a unique set of contacts. This requirement is satisfied by AORs representing phone numbers regardless of the domain, since phone numbers are fully qualified and globally unique. This specification (RFC 6140) therefore focuses on the use case of the fully qualified and globally identifiable phone number that can be used for routing. Note that the security of this mechanism is described in Section 19.2.2.

In actual deployments, some SIP servers have been deployed in architectures that, for various reasons, have requirements to provide dynamic routing information for large blocks of AORs, where all of the AORs in the block were to be handled by the same server. For purposes of efficiency, many of these deployments (Figure 3.2) do not wish to maintain separate registrations for each of the AORs in the block. For example, in virtually all models, the SIP–PBX generates a SIP REGISTER request using a mutually agreed-upon SIP AOR—typically based on the SIP–PBX's main attendant-/reception-desk number.

The AOR is often in the domain of the SSP, and both the To and From URIs used for the REGISTER request identify that AOR. In all respects, it appears on the wire as a *normal* SIP REGISTER request, as if from a typical user's UA. However, it generally implicitly registers other AORs associated with the SIP–PBX. Thus, an alternate mechanism to provide dynamic routing information for blocks of AORs is desirable. However, the following two constraints have the most profound effect in addressing this multiple AORs registration: the SIP–PBX cannot be assumed to be assigned a static IP address and no DNS entry can be relied upon to consistently resolve to the IP address of the SIP–PBX.

Although the use of SIP REGISTER request messages to update reachability information for multiple users simultaneously is somewhat beyond the original semantics defined for REGISTER requests by RFC 3261 (see Section 3.3.1), this approach has seen significant deployment in certain environments. In particular, deployments in which small to medium SIP–PBX servers are addressed using E.164 numbers have used this mechanism to avoid the need to maintain DNS entries or static IP addresses for the SIP–PBX servers. In recognition of the momentum that REGISTER-based approaches have seen in deployments, this document defines a REGISTER-based approach. Since E.164-addressed UAs are very common today in SIP–PBX environments, and since SIP URIs in which the user portion is an E.164 number are always globally unique, regardless of the domain, this document focuses on registration of SIP URIs in which the user portion is an E.164 number.

Before describing the detail about the multiple AORs of global routable telephone numbers, we summarize the fact that this specification (RFC 6140) satisfies the following mandatory requirements described in RFC 5947:

- The mechanism allows a SIP–PBX to enter into a trunking arrangement with an SSP, whereby the two parties have agreed on a set of telephone numbers assigned to the SIP–PBX.
- The mechanism allows a set of assigned telephone numbers to comprise E.164 numbers, which can be in contiguous ranges, discrete, or in any combination of the two. However, the Direct Inward Dialing (DID) numbers associated with a registration are established by a bilateral agreement between the SSP and the SIP–PBX; they are not part of the mechanism described in this specification (RFC 6140).
- The mechanism allows a SIP–PBX to register reachability information with its SSP, to enable the SSP to route to the SIP–PBX inbound requests targeted at assigned telephone numbers.
- The mechanism allows UAs attached to a SIP–PBX to register with the SIP–PBX for AORs based on assigned telephone numbers, to receive requests targeted at those telephone numbers, without needing to involve the SSP in the registration process; in the presumed architecture, SIP–PBX UAs register with the SIP–PBX and requires no interaction with the SSP.

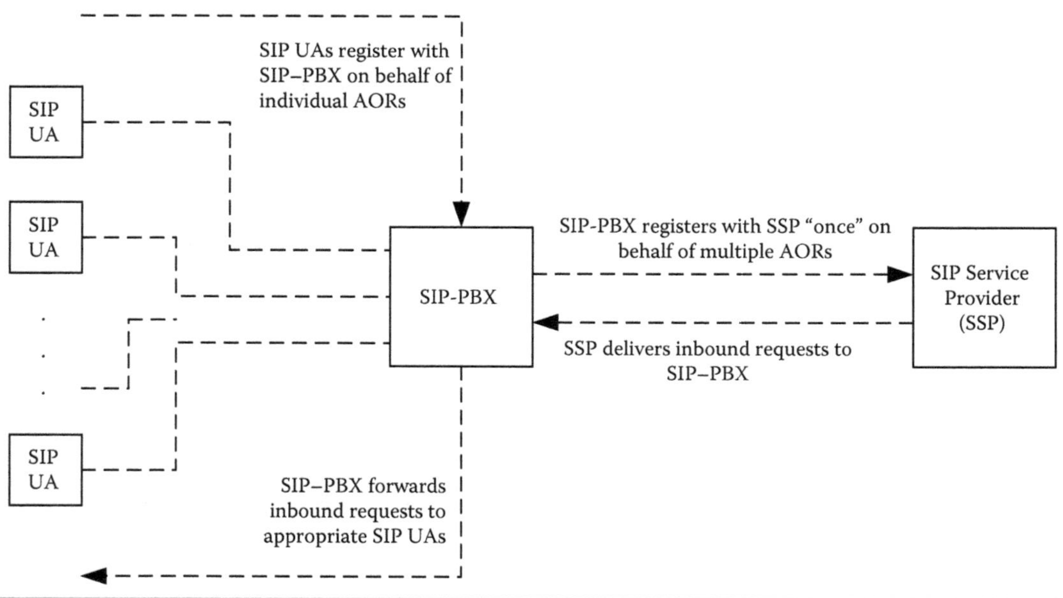

Figure 3.2 Multiple-AOR registration by SIP–PBX with SSP. (Copyright IETF. Reproduced with permission.)

- The mechanism allows a SIP–PBX to handle requests originating at its own UAs and targeted at its assigned telephone numbers, without routing those requests to the SSP; SIP–PBXs may recognize their own DID numbers and GRUUs, and perform on-SIP–PBX routing without sending the requests to the SSP.
- The mechanism allows a SIP–PBX to receive requests to its assigned telephone numbers originating outside the SIP–PBX and arriving via the SSP, so that the SIP–PBX can route those requests onwards to its UAs, as it would for internal requests to those telephone numbers.
- The mechanism provides a means whereby a SIP–PBX knows which of its assigned telephone numbers an inbound request from its SSP is targeted at. The requirement is satisfied. For ordinary calls and calls using public GRUUs, the DID number is indicated in the user portion of the Request-URI. For calls using Temp GRUUs constructed with the mechanism described here, the *gr* parameter provides a correlation token the SIP–PBX can use to identify to which UA the call should be routed.
- The mechanism provides a means of avoiding problems due to one side using the mechanism and the other side not using the mechanism: the *gin* option tag and the *bnc* Contact URI parameter.
- The mechanism observes SIP backwards compatibility principles through using the gin option tag.
- The mechanism works in the presence of a sequence of intermediate SIP entities on the SIP–PBX-to-SSP interface (i.e., between the SIP–PBX and the SSP's domain proxy), where those intermediate SIP entities indicated during registration need to be on the path of inbound requests to the SIP–PBX. It is accomplished through the use of the path mechanism defined in RFC 3327 (see Section 2.8).
- The mechanism works when a SIP–PBX obtains its IP address dynamically. It is done by allowing the SIP–PBX to use an IP address in the bulk number contact (bnc) URI contained in a REGISTER Contact header field.
- The mechanism works without requiring the SIP–PBX to have a domain name or the ability to publish its domain name in the DNS. It is performed by allowing the SIP–PBX to use an IP address in the bnc URI contained in a REGISTER Contact header field.
- For a given SIP–PBX and its SSP, there is no impact on other domains, which are expected to be able to use normal RFC 3263 (see Section 8.2.4) procedures to route requests, including requests needing to be routed via the SSP in order to reach the SIP–PBX. It is accomplished by allowing the domain name in the Request-URI used by external entities to resolve to the SSP's servers via normal RFC 3263 resolution procedures.
- The mechanism is able to operate over a transport that provides end-to-end integrity protection and confidentiality between the SIP–PBX and the SSP, for example, using TLS as specified in RFC 3261 (see Section 3.13); nothing in the proposed mechanism prevents the use of TLS between the SSP and the SIP–PBX.
- The mechanism supports authentication of the SIP–PBX by the SSP and vice versa, for example, using SIP digest authentication plus TLS server authentication as specified in RFC 3261 (see Section 19.4); SIP–PBXs may employ either SIP digest authentication or mutually authenticated TLS for authentication purposes.
- The mechanism allows the SIP–PBX to provide its UAs with public or temporary GRUUs (see Section 4.3). It is performed via the mechanisms described here.
- The mechanism works over any existing transport specified for SIP, including UDP. It is accomplished to the extent that UDP can be used for REGISTER requests in general. The application of certain extensions or network topologies may exceed UDP maximum transmission unit (MTU) sizes; however, such issues arise both with and without the mechanism described here. This specification (RFC 6140) does not exacerbate such issues.
- This specification (RFC 6140) provides guidance or warnings about how authorization policies may be affected by the mechanism, to address the problems described in RFC 5947.
- The mechanism is extensible to allow a set of assigned telephone numbers to comprise local numbers as specified in RFC 3966 (see Section 4.2.3), which can be in contiguous ranges, discrete, or in any combination of the two. Assignment of telephone numbers to a registration is performed by the SSP's registrar, which is not precluded from assigning local numbers in any combination it desires.
- The mechanism is also extensible to allow a set of arbitrarily assigned SIP URIs as specified in RFC 3261 (see Section 4.2), as opposed to just telephone numbers, without requiring a complete change of mechanism as compared with that used for telephone numbers. The mechanism is extensible in such a fashion, as demonstrated by the document "GIN with Literal AORs for SIP in SSPs (GLASS)" [4].

The following desirable requirements described in RFC 5947 are also met by this specification (RFC 6140):

- The mechanism allows an SSP to exploit its mechanisms for providing SIP service to normal UAs in order to provide a SIP trunking service to SIP–PBXs; the routing mechanism described in this document is identical to the routing performed for singly registered AORs.

- The mechanism scales to SIP–PBXs of several thousand assigned telephone numbers. The desired property is satisfied; nothing in this specification (RFC 6140) precludes DID number pools of arbitrary size.
- The mechanism also scales to support several thousand SIP–PBXs on a single SSP. The desired property is satisfied; nothing in this specification (RFC 6140) precludes an arbitrary number of SIP–PBXs from attaching to a single SSP.

3.3.5.1 Mechanism Overview

The overall mechanism is achieved using a REGISTER request with a specially formatted Contact URI. This document also defines an option tag that can be used to ensure that a registrar and any intermediaries understand the mechanism described herein. The Contact URI itself is tagged with a URI parameter to indicate that it actually represents multiple phone-number-associated contacts. We also define some lightweight extensions to the GRUU mechanism defined by RFC 5627 (see Section 4.3) to allow the use of public and temporary GRUUs assigned by the SSP. Aside from these extensions, the REGISTER request itself is processed by a registrar in the same way as normal registrations: by updating its location service with additional AOR-to-Contact bindings. Note that the list of AORs associated with a SIP–PBX is a matter of local provisioning at the SSP and the SIP–PBX. The mechanism defined in this document does not provide any means to detect or recover from provisioning mismatches (although the registration event package can be used as a standardized means for auditing such AORs).

3.3.5.2 Registering for Multiple Phone Numbers

3.3.5.2.1 SIP–PBX Behavior

To register for multiple AORs, the SIP–PBX sends a REGISTER request to the SSP. This REGISTER request varies from a typical REGISTER request in two important ways. First, it must contain an option tag of gin in both a Require header field and a Proxy-Require header field. (The option tag gin is an acronym for *generate implicit numbers*.) Second, in at least one Contact header field, it must include a Contact URI that contains the URI parameter bnc (which stands for *bulk number contact*) and has no user portion (hence, no "@" symbol). A URI with a bnc parameter must not contain a user portion. Except for the SIP URI *user* parameter, this URI may contain any other parameters that the SIP–PBX desires. These parameters will be echoed back by the SSP in any requests bound for the SIP–PBX. Because of the constraints discussed earlier, the host portion of the Contact URI will generally contain an IP address, although nothing in this mechanism enforces or relies upon that fact.

If the SIP–PBX operator chooses to maintain DNS entries that resolve to the IP address of this SIP–PBX via RFC 3263 (see Section 8.2.4) resolution procedures, then this mechanism works just fine with domain names in the Contact header field. The bnc URI parameter indicates that special interpretation of the Contact URI is necessary: instead of indicating the insertion of a single Contact URI into the location service, it indicates that multiple URIs (one for each associated AOR) should be inserted. Any SIP–PBX implementing the registration mechanism defined in this document MUST also support the path mechanism defined by RFC 3327 (see Section 2.8), and MUST include a *path* option tag in the Supported header field of the REGISTER request (which is a stronger requirement than imposed by the path mechanism itself). This behavior is necessary because proxies between the SIP–PBX and the registrar may need to insert Path header field values in the REGISTER request for this document's mechanism to function properly, and, per RFC 3327 (see Section 2.8), they can only do so if the UAC inserted the option tag in the Supported header field. In accordance with the procedures defined in RFC 3327, the SIP–PBX is allowed to ignore the Path header fields returned in the REGISTER response.

3.3.5.2.2 Registrar Behavior

The registrar, upon receipt of a REGISTER request containing at least one Contact header field with a bnc parameter, will use the value in the To header field to identify the SIP–PBX for which registration is being requested. It then authenticates the SIP–PBX (e.g., using SIP digest authentication, mutual TLS [RFC 5246], or some other authentication mechanism). After the SIP–PBX is authenticated, the registrar updates its location service with a unique AOR-to-Contact mapping for each of the AORs associated with the SIP–PBX. Semantically, each of these mappings will be treated as a unique row in the location service. The actual implementation may, of course, perform internal optimizations to reduce the amount of memory used to store such information.

For each of these unique rows, the AOR will be in the format that the SSP expects to receive from external parties (e.g., sip:+12145550102@ssp.example.com). The corresponding contact will be formed by adding to the REGISTER request's Contact URI a user portion containing the fully qualified, E.164-formatted number (including the preceding "+" symbol) and removing the bnc parameter. Aside from the initial + symbol, this E.164-formatted number must consist exclusively of digits from 0 through 9, and explicitly must not contain any visual separator symbols (e.g., "–," ".," "(," or ")"). For example, if the Contact header field contains the

URI <sip:198.51.100.3:5060;bnc>, then the contact value associated with the aforementioned AOR will be <sip:+12145550102@198.51.100.3:5060>.

Although the SSP treats this registration as a number of discrete rows for the purpose of retargeting incoming requests, the renewal, expiration, and removal of these rows is bound to the registered contact. In particular, this means that REGISTER requests that attempt to deregister a single AOR that has been implicitly registered must not remove that AOR from the bulk registration. In this circumstance, the registrar simply acts as if the UA attempted to unregister a contact that was not actually registered (e.g., return the list of presently registered contacts in a success response). A further implication of this property is that an individual extension that is implicitly registered may also be explicitly registered using a normal, nonbulk registration (subject to SSP policy). If such a registration exists, it is refreshed independently of the bulk registration and is not removed when the bulk registration is removed.

A registrar that receives a REGISTER request containing a Contact URI with both a bnc parameter and a user portion MUST NOT send a 200-class (Success) response. If no other error is applicable, the registrar can use a 400 Bad Request response to indicate this error condition. Note that the preceding paragraph is talking about the user portion of a URI:

```
sip:+12145550100@example.com
    ^^^^^^^^^^^^
```

A registrar compliant with this document MUST support the path mechanism defined in RFC 3327 (see Section 2.8). The rationale for the support of this mechanism is given earlier. Aside from the bnc parameter, all URI parameters present on the Contact URI in the REGISTER request must be copied to the contact value stored in the location service. If the SSP servers perform processing based on UA capabilities (as defined in RFC 3840, see Sections 2.11 and 3.4), they will treat any feature tags present on a Contact header field with a bnc parameter in its URI as applicable to all of the resulting AOR-to-Contact mappings. Similarly, any option tags present on the REGISTER request that indicate special handling for any subsequent requests are also applicable to all of the AOR-to-Contact mappings.

3.3.5.2.3 SIP URI User Parameter Handling

This specification (RFC 6140) does not modify the behavior specified in RFC 3261 (see Section 3.3.1) for inclusion of the user parameter on Request-URIs. However, to avoid any ambiguity in handling at the SIP–PBX, the following normative behavior is imposed on its interactions with the SSP. When a SIP–PBX registers with an SSP using a Contact URI containing a bnc parameter, that Contact URI must not include a user parameter. A registrar that receives a REGISTER request containing a Contact URI with both a bnc parameter and a user parameter must not send a 200-class (success) response. If no other error is applicable, the registrar can use a 400 Bad Request response to indicate this error condition. Note that the preceding paragraph is talking about the user parameter of a URI:

```
sip:+12145550100@example.com;user=phone
                             ^^^^^^^^^^
```

When a SIP–PBX receives a request from an SSP, and the Request-URI contains a user portion corresponding to an AOR registered using a Contact URI containing a bnc parameter, then the SIP–PBX must not reject the request (or otherwise cause the request to fail) due to the absence, presence, or value of a user parameter on the Request-URI.

3.3.5.3 SSP Processing of Inbound Requests

In general, after processing the AOR-to-Contact mapping described in the preceding section, the SSP proxy/registrar (or equivalent entity) performs traditional proxy/registrar behavior, based on the mapping. For any inbound SIP requests whose AOR indicates an E.164 number assigned to one of the SSP's customers, this will generally involve setting the target set to the registered contacts associated with that AOR, and performing request forwarding as described in RFC 3261 (see Section 3.11.6). An SSP using the mechanism defined in this document must perform such processing for inbound INVITE requests and SUBSCRIBE requests to the reg event package, and should perform such processing for all other method types, including unrecognized SIP methods.

3.3.5.4 Interaction with Other Mechanisms

The following sections describe the means by which this mechanism interacts with relevant REGISTER-related extensions currently defined by the International Engineering Task Force (IETF). To enable advanced services to work with UAs behind a SIP–PBX, it is important that the GRUU mechanism defined by RFC 5627 (see Section 4.3) work correctly with the mechanism defined by this document—that is, UAs served by the SIP–PBX can acquire and use GRUUs for their own use. Neither the SSP nor the SIP–PBX is required to support the registration event package defined by RFC 3680. However, if they do support the registration event package, they must conform to the behavior described in this section and its subsections. As this mechanism inherently deals with REGISTER transaction behavior, it is imperative to consider its impact on the registration event package defined by RFC 3680. In practice, there will be two main use cases for subscribing to registration data: learning about the overall registration state for the SIP–PBX and learning about the registration state for a single SIP–PBX AOR.

3.3.5.5 Interaction with Public GRUUs

Support of public GRUUs is optional in SSPs and SIP–PBXs. When a SIP–PBX registers a bulk number contact (a contact with a bnc parameter), and also invokes GRUU procedures for that contact during registration, then the SSP will assign a public GRUU to the SIP–PBX in the normal fashion. Because the URI being registered contains a bnc parameter, the GRUU will also contain a bnc parameter. In particular, this means that the GRUU will not contain a user portion. When a UA registers a contact with the SIP–PBX using GRUU procedures, the SIP–PBX provides to the UA a public GRUU formed by adding an *sg* parameter to the GRUU parameter it received from the SSP. This sg parameter contains a disambiguation token that the SIP–PBX can use to route inbound requests to the proper UA. Thus, for example, when the SIP–PBX registers with the following Contact header field

```
Contact: <sip:198.51.100.3;bnc>;
+sip.instance="<urn:uuid:
f81d4fae-7dec-11d0-a765-00a0c91e6bf6>"
```

the SSP may choose to respond with a Contact header field that looks like this (<allOneLine> definition per RFC 4475):

```
<allOneLine>
       Contact: <sip:198.51.100.3;bnc>;
       pub-gruu="sip:ssp.example.
       com;bnc;gr=urn:

uuid:f81d4fae-7dec-11d0-a765-00a0c91e6bf6";
       +sip.instance="<urn:uuid:
f81d4fae-7dec-11d0-a765-00a0c91e6bf6>"
       ;expires=7200
</allOneLine>
```

When its own UAs register using GRUU procedures, the SIP–PBX can then add whatever device identifier it feels appropriate in an sg parameter, and present this value to its own UAs. For example, assume the UA associated with the AOR +12145550102 sent the following Contact header field in its REGISTER request:

```
Contact: <sip:line-1@10.20.1.17>;
+sip.instance="<urn:uuid:
d0e2f290-104b-11df-8a39-0800200c9a66>"
```

The SIP–PBX will add an sg parameter to the pub-gruu it received from the SSP with a token that uniquely identifies the device (possibly the URN itself, or possibly some other identifier), insert a user portion containing the fully qualified E.164 number associated with the UA, and return the result to the UA as its public GRUU. The resulting Contact header field sent from the SIP–PBX to the registering UA would look something like this:

```
<allOneLine>
       Contact: <sip:line-1@10.20.1.17>;
       pub-gruu="sip:+12145550102@ssp.
       example.com;gr=urn:
       uuid:f81d4fae-7dec-11d0-a765-00a0c91e6
       bf6;sg=00:05:03:5e:70:a6";
       +sip.
instance="<urn:uuid:d0e2f290-104b-11df-8a39-
0800200c9a66>"
       ;expires=3600
</allOneLine>
```

When an incoming request arrives at the SSP for a GRUU corresponding to a bnc, the SSP performs slightly different processing for the GRUU than it would for a URI without a bnc parameter. When the GRUU is retargeted to the registered bnc, the SSP must copy the sg parameter from the GRUU to the new target. The SIP–PBX can then use this sg parameter to determine to which UA the request should be routed. For example, the first line of an INVITE request that has been retargeted to the SIP–PBX for the UA shown above would look like this:

```
INVITE sip:+12145550102@198.51.100.3;sg=00:05
:03:5e:70:a6 SIP/2.0
```

3.3.5.6 Interaction with Temporary GRUUs

To provide support for privacy, the SSP should implement the temporary GRUU mechanism described in this section. Reasons for not doing so would include systems with an alternative privacy mechanism that maintains the integrity of public GRUUs (i.e., if public GRUUs are anonymized, then the anonymizer function would need to be capable of providing—as the anonymized URI—a globally routable URI that routes back only to the target identified by the original public GRUU). Temporary GRUUs are used to provide anonymity for the party creating and sharing the GRUU. Being able to correlate two temporary GRUUs as having originated from behind the same SIP–PBX violates this principle of anonymity. Consequently, rather than relying upon a single, invariant identifier for the SIP–PBX in its UA's temporary GRUUs, we define a mechanism whereby the SSP provides the SIP–PBX with sufficient information for the SIP–PBX to mint unique temporary GRUUs. These GRUUs have the property that the SSP can correlate them to the proper SIP–PBX, but no other party can do so. To achieve this goal, we use a slight modification of the procedure described in RFC 5627 (see Section 4.3).

The SIP–PBX needs to be able to construct a temp-gruu in a way that the SSP can decode. To ensure that the SSP can decode GRUUs, we need to standardize the algorithm for creation of temp-gruus at the SIP–PBX. This allows the SSP to reverse the algorithm in order to identify the registration entry that corresponds to the GRUU. It is equally important that no party other than the SSP be capable of decoding a temporary GRUU, including other SIP–PBXs serviced by the SSP. To achieve this property, an SSP that supports temporary GRUUs MUST create and store an asymmetric key pair: {K_e1,K_e2}. K_e1 is kept secret by the SSP, while K_e2 is shared with the SIP–PBXs via provisioning. All base64 encoding discussed in the following sections must use the character set and encoding defined in RFC 4648, except that any trailing "=" characters are discarded on encoding and added as necessary to decode. The following sections make use of the term *HMAC-SHA256-80* to describe a particular Hashed Message Authentication Code (HMAC) algorithm. In this specification (RFC 6140), HMAC-SHA256-80 is defined as the application of the SHA-256 [5] secure hashing algorithm, truncating the results to 80 bits by discarding the trailing (least-significant) bits.

3.3.5.6.1 Generation of Temp-gruu-cookie by the SSP

An SSP that supports temporary GRUUs must include a *temp-gruu-cookie* parameter on all Contact header fields containing a bnc parameter in a 200-class REGISTER response. This temp-gruu-cookie must have the following properties:

- It can be used by the SSP to uniquely identify the registration to which it corresponds.
- It is encoded using base64. This allows the SIP–PBX to decode it in as compact a form as possible for use in its calculations.
- It is of a fixed length. This allows for its extraction once the SIP–PBX has concatenated a distinguisher onto it.
- The temp-gruu-cookie must not be forgeable by any party. In other words, the SSP needs to be able to examine the cookie and validate that it was generated by the SSP.
- The temp-gruu-cookie must be invariant during the course of a registration, including any refreshes to that registration. This property is important, as it allows the SIP–PBX to examine the temp-gruu-cookie to determine whether the temp-gruus it has issued to its UAs are still valid.

The above properties can be met using the following algorithm, which is nonnormative. Implementers may chose to implement any algorithm of their choosing for generation of the temp-gruu-cookie, as long as it fulfills the five properties listed above. The registrar maintains a counter, I. This counter is 48 bits long and initialized to zero. This counter is persistently stored, using a back-end database or similar technique. When the registrar creates the first temporary GRUU for a particular SIP–PBX and instance ID (as defined by RFC 5627, see Section 4.3), the registrar notes the current value of the counter, I_i, and increments the counter in the database. The registrar then maps I_i to the contact and instance ID using the database, a persistent hash map, or similar technology. If the registration expires such that there are no longer any contacts with that particular instance ID bound to the GRUU, the registrar removes the mapping.

Similarly, if the temporary GRUUs are invalidated due to a change in Call-ID, the registrar removes the current mapping from I_i to the AOR and instance ID, notes the current value of the counter I_j, and stores a mapping from I_j to the contact containing a bnc parameter and instance ID. On the basis of these rules, the hash map will contain a single mapping for each contact containing a bnc parameter and instance ID for which there is a currently valid registration. The registrar maintains a symmetric key SK_a, which is regenerated every time the counter rolls over or is reset. When the counter rolls over or is reset, the registrar remembers the old value of SK_a for a while. To generate a temp-gruu-cookie, the registrar computes

```
SA                  =    HMAC(SK_a, I_i)
temp-gruu-cookie    =    base64enc(I_i || SA)
```

where || denotes concatenation. *HMAC* represents any suitably strong HMAC algorithm (see RFC 2104 for a discussion of HMAC algorithms). One suitable HMAC algorithm for this purpose is HMACSHA256-80.

3.3.5.6.2 Generation of Temp-gruu by the SIP–PBX

According to RFC 5627 (see Section 4.3), every registration refresh generates a new temp-gruu that is valid for as long as the contact remains registered. This property is both critical for the privacy properties of temp-gruu and is expected by UAs that implement the temp-gruu procedures. Nothing in this document should be construed as changing this fundamental temp-gruu property in any way. SIP–PBXs that implement temporary GRUUs must generate a new temp-gruu according to the procedures in this section for every registration or registration refresh from GRUU-supporting UAs attached to the SIP–PBX. Similarly, if the registration that a SIP–PBX has with its SSP expires or is terminated, then the temp-gruu cookie it maintains with the SSP will change. This change will invalidate all the temp-gruus the SIP–PBX has issued to its UAs. If the SIP–PBX tracks this information (e.g., to include <temp-gruu> elements in registration event bodies, as described in RFC 5628), it can determine that previously issued temp-gruus are invalid by observing a change in the temp-gruu-cookie provided to it by the SSP. A SIP–PBX that issues temporary GRUUs to its UAs must maintain an HMAC key: PK_a. This value is used to validate that incoming GRUUs were generated by the SIP–PBX.

To generate a new temporary GRUU for use by its own UAs, the SIP–PBX must generate a random distinguisher value: D. The length of this value is up to implementers, but it must be long enough to prevent collisions among all the temporary GRUUs issued by the SIP–PBX. A size of 80 bits or longer is recommended. RFC 4086 describes in detail considerations on the generation of random numbers in a security context. After generating the distinguisher D, the SIP–PBX must calculate

```
M       =       base64dec(SSP-cookie) || D
E       =       RSA-Encrypt(K_e2, M)
PA      =       HMAC(PK_a, E)
Temp-Gruu-userpart  =      "tgruu." ||
base64(E) || "." || base64(PA)
```

where || denotes concatenation. HMAC represents any suitably strong HMAC algorithm (see RFC 2104 for a discussion of HMAC algorithms). One suitable HMAC algorithm for this purpose is HMACSHA256-80.

Finally, the SIP–PBX adds a gr parameter to the temporary GRUU that can be used to uniquely identify the UA registration record to which the GRUU corresponds. The means of generation of the gr parameter are left to the implementer, as long as they satisfy the properties of a GRUU as described in RFC 5627 (see Section 4.3). One valid approach for generation of the gr parameter is calculation of E and A as described in RFC 5627 and forming the gr parameter as

```
gr      =       base64enc(E) || base64enc(A)
```

Using this procedure may result in a temporary GRUU returned to the registering UA by the SIP–PBX that looks similar to this:

```
<allOneLine>
       Contact: <sip:line-1@10.20.1.17>
       ;temp-gruu="sip:tgruu.MQyaRiLEd78RtaWk
       cP7N8Q.5qVbsasdo2pkKw@
       ssp.example.com;gr=YZGSCjKD42ccxO08pA7
       HwAM4XNDIlMSLOHlA"
       ;+sip.instance="<urn:uuid:d0e2f290
       -104b-11df-8a39-0800200c9a66>"
       ;expires=3600
</allOneLine>
```

3.3.5.6.3 Decoding of Temp-gruu by the SSP

When the SSP proxy receives a request in which the user part begins with *tgruu.*, it extracts the remaining portion and splits it at the "." character into E and PA. It discards PA. It then computes E by performing a base64 decode of E. Next, it computes

```
M       =       RSA-Decrypt(K_e1, E)
```

The SSP proxy extracts the fixed-length temp-gruu-cookie information from the beginning of this M and discards the remainder (which will be the distinguisher added by the SIP–PBX). It then validates this temp-gruu-cookie. If valid, it uses it to locate the corresponding SIP–PBX registration record and routes the message appropriately. If the nonnormative, exemplary algorithm described earlier is used to generate the temp-gruu-cookie, then this identification is performed by splitting the temp-gruu-cookie information into its 48-bit counter I and 80-bit HMAC. It validates that the HMAC matches the counter I and then uses counter I to locate the SIP–PBX registration record in its map. If the counter has rolled over or reset, this computation is performed with the current and previous SK_a.

3.3.5.6.4 Decoding of Temp-gruu by the SIP–PBX

When the SIP–PBX receives a request in which the user part begins with tgruu, it extracts the remaining portion and splits it at the "." character into E and PA. It then computes E and PA by performing a base64 decode of E and PA, respectively. Next, it computes

```
PAc     =       HMAC(PK_a, E)
```

where HMAC is the HMAC algorithm used for the steps described earlier. If this computed value for PAc does not match the value of PA extracted from the GRUU, then the GRUU is rejected as invalid. The SIP–PBX then uses the value of the gr parameter to locate the UA registration to which the GRUU corresponds, and routes the message accordingly.

3.3.5.7 Interaction with SIP–PBX Aggregate Registration State

If the SIP–PBX (or another interested and authorized party) wishes to monitor or audit the registration state for all of the AORs currently registered to that SIP–PBX, it can subscribe to the SIP registration event package at the SIP–PBX's main URI—that is, the URI used in the To header field of the REGISTER request. The NOTIFY messages for such a subscription will contain a body that contains one record for each AOR associated with the SIP–PBX. The AORs will be in the format expected to be received by the SSP (e.g., sip:+12145550105@ssp.example.com), and the contacts will correspond to the mapped contact created by the registration (e.g., sip:+12145550105@98.51.100.3). In particular, the bnc parameter is forbidden from appearing in the body of a reg-event NOTIFY request unless the subscriber has indicated knowledge of the semantics of the bnc parameter. The means for indicating this support are beyond the scope of this document. Because the SSP does not necessarily know which GRUUs have been issued by the SIP–PBX to its associated UAs, these records will not generally contain the <temp-gruu> or <pub-gruu> elements defined in RFC 5628. This information can be learned, if necessary, by subscribing to the individual AOR registration state, as described below.

3.3.5.8 Interaction with Individual AOR Registration State

As described in Section 2.2, the SSP will generally retarget all requests addressed to an AOR owned by a SIP–PBX to that SIP–PBX according to the mapping established at registration time. Although policy at the SSP may override this generally expected behavior, proper behavior of the registration event package requires that all *reg* event SUBSCRIBE requests are processed by the SIP–PBX. As a consequence, the requirements on an SSP for processing registration event package SUBSCRIBE requests are not left to policy. If the SSP receives a SUBSCRIBE request for the registration event package with a Request-URI that indicates an AOR registered via the bnc mechanism defined in this document, then the SSP must proxy that SUBSCRIBE to the SIP–PBX in the same way that it would proxy an INVITE bound for that AOR, unless the SSP has and can maintain a copy of complete, accurate, and up-to-date information from the SIP–PBX (e.g., through an active back-end subscription).

If the Request-URI in a SUBSCRIBE request for the registration event package indicates a contact that is registered by more than one SIP–PBX, then the SSP proxy will fork the SUBSCRIBE request to all the applicable SIP–PBXs. Similarly, if the Request-URI corresponds to a contact that is both implicitly registered by a SIP–PBX and explicitly registered directly with the SSP proxy, then the SSP proxy will semantically fork the SUBSCRIBE request to the applicable SIP–PBX or SIP–PBXs and to the registrar function (which will respond with registration data corresponding to the explicit registrations at the SSP). The forking in both of these cases can be avoided if the SSP has and can maintain a copy of up-to-date information from the PBXs. RFC 3680 indicates that "a subscriber must not create multiple dialogs as a result of a single registration event subscription request." Consequently, subscribers who are not aware of the extension described by this document will accept only one dialog in response to such requests.

In the case described in the preceding paragraph, this behavior will result in such clients receiving accurate but incomplete information about the registration state of an AOR. As an explicit change to the normative behavior of RFC 3680, this document stipulates that subscribers to the registration event package may create multiple dialogs as the result of a single subscription request. This will allow subscribers to create a complete view of an AOR's registration state. Defining the behavior as described above is important, since the reg-event subscriber is interested in finding out about the comprehensive list of devices associated with the AOR. Only the SIP–PBX will have authoritative access to this information. For example, if the user has registered multiple UAs with differing capabilities, the SSP will not know about the devices or their capabilities. By contrast, the SIP–PBX will. If the SIP–PBX is not registered with the SSP when a registration event subscription for a contact that would be implicitly registered if the SIP–PBX were registered is received, then the SSP should accept the subscription and indicate that the user is not currently registered. Once the associated SIP–PBX is registered, the SSP should use the subscription migration mechanism defined in RFC 6665 (see Section 4.5) to migrate the subscription to the SIP–PBX.

When a SIP–PBX receives a registration event subscription addressed to an AOR that has been registered using the bulk registration mechanism described in this document, then each resulting registration information document SHOULD contain an *aor* attribute in its <registration/> element that corresponds to the AOR at the SSP. For example, consider a SIP–PBX that has registered with an SSP that has a domain of ssp.example.com. The SIP–PBX used a Contact URI of sip:198.51.100.3:5060;bnc. After such registration is complete, a registration event subscription arriving at the SSP with a Request-URI of sip:+12145550102@ssp.example.com will be retargeted to the SIP–PBX, with a Request-URI of sip:+12145550102@198.51.100.3:5060. The resulting registration document created by the SIP–PBX would contain a <registration/> element with an aor attribute of sip:+12145550102@ssp.example.com. This behavior ensures that subscribers external to the system (and unaware of GIN [generate implicit numbers] procedures) will be able to find the relevant information in the registration document (since they will be looking for the publicly visible AOR, not the address used for sending information from the SSP to the SIP–PBX). A SIP–PBX that supports both GRUU procedures and the registration event packages should implement the extension defined in RFC 5628.

3.3.5.9 Interaction with Client-Initiated (Outbound) Connections

RFC 5626 (see Section 13.2) defines a mechanism that allows UAs to establish long-lived TCP connections or UDP associations with a proxy in a way that allows bidirectional traffic between the proxy and the UA. This behavior is particularly important in the presence of NATs, and whenever TLS (RFC 5246) security is required. Neither the SSP nor the SIP–PBX is required to support client-initiated connections. Generally, the outbound mechanism works with the solution defined in this document, without any modifications. Implementers should note that the instance ID used between the SIP–PBX and the SSP's registrar identifies the SIP–PBX itself, and not any of the UAs registered with the SIP–PBX. As a consequence, any attempts to use caller preferences (defined in RFC 3841, see Section 9.9) to target a specific instance are likely to fail. This should not be an issue, as the preferred mechanism for targeting specific instances of a UA is GRUU.

3.3.5.10 Interaction with Nonadjacent Contact Registration (Path) and Service-Route Discovery

RFC 3327 (see Section 2.8) defines a means by which a registrar and its associated proxy can be informed of a route that is to be used between the proxy and the registered UA. The scope of the route created by a Path header field is contact specific; if an AOR has multiple contacts associated with it, the routes associated with each contact may be different from each other. Support for nonadjacent contact registration is required in all SSPs and SIP–PBXs implementing the multiple-AOR-registration protocol described in this document. At registration time, any proxies between the UA and the registrar may add themselves to the Path header field. By doing so, they request that any requests destined to the UA as a result of the associated registration include them as part of the Route toward the UA. Although the path mechanism does deliver the final path value to the registering UA, UAs typically ignore the value of the path. To provide similar functionality in the opposite direction—that is, to establish a route for requests sent by a registering UA—RFC 3608 (see Section 2.8) defines a means by which a UA can be informed of a route that is to be used by the UA to route all outbound requests associated with the AOR used in the registration.

This information is scoped to the AOR within the UA, and is not specific to the contact (or contacts) in the REGISTER request. Support of service route discovery is optional in SSPs and SIP–PBXs. The registrar unilaterally generates the values of the service route using whatever local policy it wishes to apply. Although it is common to use the Path or Route header field information in the request in composing the service route, registrar behavior is not constrained in any way that requires it to do so. In considering the interaction between these mechanisms and the registration of multiple AORs in a single request, implementers of proxies, registrars, and intermediaries must keep in mind the following issues, which stem from the fact that GIN effectively registers multiple AORs and multiple contacts.

First, all location service records that result from expanding a single Contact URI containing a bnc parameter will necessarily share a single path. Proxies will be unable to make policy decisions on a contact-by-contact basis regarding whether to include themselves in the path. Second, and similarly, all AORs on the SIP–PBX that are registered with a common REGISTER request will be forced to share a common service route. One interesting technique that the path and service route mechanisms enable is the inclusion of a token or cookie in the user portion of the service route or path entries. This token or cookie may convey information to proxies about the identity, capabilities, or policies associated with the user. Since this information will be shared among several AORs and several contacts when multiple AOR registration is employed, care should be taken to ensure that doing so is acceptable for all AORs and all contacts registered in a single REGISTER request.

3.3.5.11 Examples

Note that the following examples elide any steps related to authentication. This is done for the sake of clarity. Actual deployments will need to provide a level of authentication appropriate to their system.

3.3.5.11.1 Usage Scenario: Basic Registration

This example shows the message flows for a basic bulk REGISTER transaction (Figure 3.3), followed by an INVITE addressed to one of the registered UAs. Example messages are shown after the sequence diagram (Figure 3.3).

F1: The SIP–PBX registers with the SSP for a range of AORs.

```
REGISTER sip:ssp.example.com SIP/2.0
Via: SIP/2.0/UDP 198.51.100.3:5060;branch=z9h
G4bKnashds7
Max-Forwards: 70
To: <sip:pbx@ssp.example.com>
From: <sip:pbx@ssp.example.com>;tag=a23589
Call-ID: 843817637684230@998sdasdh09
CSeq: 1826 REGISTER
Proxy-Require: gin
Require: gin
Supported: path
Contact: <sip:198.51.100.3:5060;bnc>
Expires: 7200
Content-Length: 0
```

F3: The SSP receives a request for an AOR assigned to the SIP–PBX.

```
INVITE sip:+12145550105@ssp.example.com
SIP/2.0
```

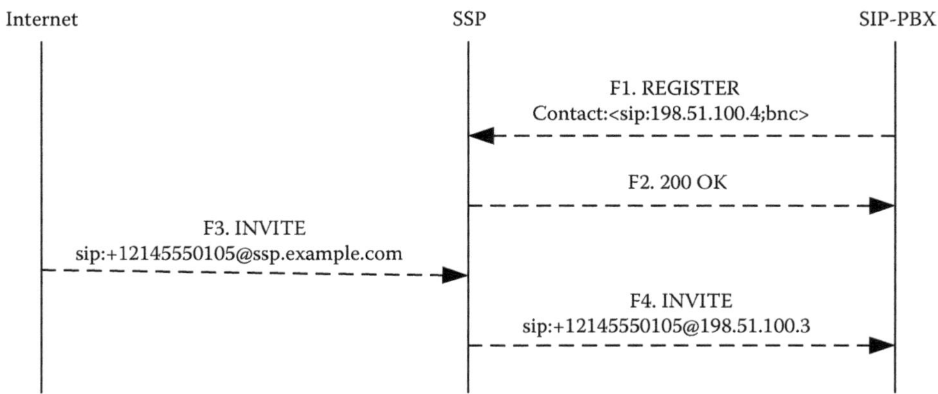

Figure 3.3 Basic bulk SIP REGISTER transaction. (Copyright IETF. Reproduced with permission.)

```
Via: SIP/2.0/UDP foo.example;branch=z9hG4bKa0
bc7a0131f0ad
Max-Forwards: 69
To: <sip:2145550105@some-other-place.example.
net>
From: <sip:gsmith@example.org>;tag=456248
Call-ID: f7aecbfc374d557baf72d6352e1fbcd4
CSeq: 24762 INVITE
Contact: <sip:line-1@192.0.2.178:2081>
Content-Type: application/sdp
Content-Length:...
<sdp body here>
```

F4: The SSP retargets the incoming request according to the information received from the SIP–PBX at registration time.

```
INVITE sip:+12145550105@198.51.100.3 SIP/2.0
Via: SIP/2.0/UDP ssp.example.com;branch=
z9hG4bKa45cd5c52a6dd50
Via: SIP/2.0/UDP foo.example;branch=
z9hG4bKa0bc7a0131f0ad
Max-Forwards: 68
To: <sip:2145550105@some-other-place.example.
net>
From: <sip:gsmith@example.org>;tag=456248
Call-ID: f7aecbfc374d557baf72d6352e1fbcd4
CSeq: 24762 INVITE
Contact: <sip:line-1@192.0.2.178:2081>
Content-Type: application/sdp
Content-Length:...
<sdp body here>
```

3.3.5.11.2 Usage Scenario: Using Path to Control Request-URI

This example shows a bulk REGISTER transaction with the SSP making use of the Path header field (Figure 3.4) extension (RFC 3327, see Section 2.8). This allows the SSP to designate a domain on the incoming Request-URI that does not necessarily resolve to the SIP–PBX when the SSP applies RFC 3263 (see Section 8.2.4) procedures to it.

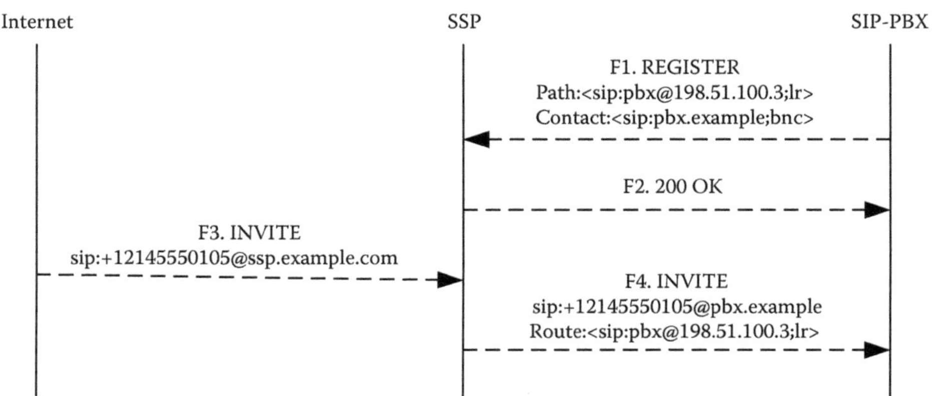

Figure 3.4 Bulk REGISTER transaction with SSP making use of path header.

F1: The SIP–PBX registers with the SSP for a range of AORs. It includes the form of the URI it expects to receive in the Request-URI in its Contact header field, and it includes information that routes to the SIP–PBX in the Path header field.

```
REGISTER sip:ssp.example.com SIP/2.0
Via: SIP/2.0/UDP 198.51.100.3:5060;branch=
z9hG4bKnashds7
Max-Forwards: 70
To: <sip:pbx@ssp.example.com>
From: <sip:pbx@ssp.example.com>;tag=a23589
Call-ID: 326983936836068@998sdasdh09
CSeq: 1826 REGISTER
Proxy-Require: gin
Require: gin
Supported: path
Path: <sip:pbx@198.51.100.3:5060;lr>
Contact: <sip:pbx.example;bnc>
Expires: 7200
Content-Length: 0
```

F3: The SSP receives a request for an AOR assigned to the SIP–PBX.

```
INVITE sip:+12145550105@ssp.example.com
SIP/2.0
Via: SIP/2.0/UDP foo.example;branch=
z9hG4bKa0bc7a0131f0ad
Max-Forwards: 69
To: <sip:2145550105@some-other-place.example.
net>
From: <sip:gsmith@example.org>;tag=456248
Call-ID: 7ca24b9679ffe9aff87036a105e30d9b
CSeq: 24762 INVITE
Contact: <sip:line-1@192.0.2.178:2081>
Content-Type: application/sdp
Content-Length:...
<sdp body here>
```

F4: The SSP retargets the incoming request according to the information received from the SIP–PBX at registration time. Per the normal processing associated with Path, it will insert the Path value indicated by the SIP–PBX at registration time in a Route header field, and set the Request-URI to the registered contact.

```
INVITE sip:+12145550105@pbx.example SIP/2.0
Via: SIP/2.0/UDP ssp.example.com;branch=
z9hG4bKa45cd5c52a6dd50
Via: SIP/2.0/UDP foo.example;branch=
z9hG4bKa0bc7a0131f0ad
Route: <sip:pbx@198.51.100.3:5060;lr>
Max-Forwards: 68
To: <sip:2145550105@some-other-place.example.
net>
From: <sip:gsmith@example.org>;tag=456248
Call-ID: 7ca24b9679ffe9aff87036a105e30d9b
CSeq: 24762 INVITE
Contact: <sip:line-1@192.0.2.178:2081>
Content-Type: application/sdp
Content-Length:...
<sdp body here>
```

3.4 Indicating UA Capabilities

SIP has some support for expression of capabilities. The Allow, Accept, Accept-Language, and Supported header fields convey some information about the capabilities of a UA. However, these header fields convey only a small part of the information that is needed. They do not provide a general framework for expression of capabilities. Furthermore, they only specify capabilities indirectly; the header fields really indicate the capabilities of the UA as they apply to this request. SIP also has no ability to convey characteristics, that is, information that describes a UA.

As a result, RFC 3840 (also see Section 2.11) provides a more general framework for an indication of capabilities and characteristics in SIP. Capability and characteristic information about a UA is carried as parameters of the Contact header field. These parameters can be used within REGISTER requests and responses, OPTIONS responses, and requests and responses that create dialogs such as INVITE.

3.4.1 Contact Header Field

RFC 3840 (also see Section 2.11) and other RFCs extend the Contact header field. In particular, it allows for the Contact header field parameters to include feature-param. Feature-param is a feature parameter that describes a feature of the UA associated with the URI in the Contact header field. Feature parameters are identifiable because they either belong to the well-known set of base feature tags, or they begin with a plus sign. It should be noted that the tag-value-list uses an actual comma instead of the comma construction because it appears within a quoted string, where line folding cannot take place. The production for qdtext can be found in RFC 3261. There are additional constraints on the usage of feature-param that cannot be represented in an augmented Backus–Naur Form (ABNF; see Section 2.4.1.2). There must only be one instance of any feature tag in feature-param. Any numbers present in a feature parameter must be representable using an ANSI C double. The following production updates the one in RFC 3261 for contact-params (see detail ABNF syntax in Section 2.4.1.2):

```
contact-params   =   c-p-q/c-p-expires/
                     feature-param
                     /contact-extension
```

In addition, RFC 5626 (see Section 13.2) has extended the contact parameters using reg-id and instance-id as described earlier. The detail of all ABNF syntaxes can be seen in Section 2.4.1.2.

3.4.2 Capability Expression Using Media Feature Tag

The UA capabilities that are used in the Contact header field using the URI for supporting different media are specified in RFC 3840 (see Section 2.11) and other RFCs. Table 2.12 (Section 2.11) shows those SIP media feature tags, their description, and example usage.

3.4.3 Usage of the Content Negotiation Framework

RFC 3840 (also see Section 2.11) makes heavy use of the terminology and concepts in the content negotiation work carried out within the IETF, and documented in several RFCs, such as RFC 2506 (which provides a template for registering media feature tags), RFC 2533 (which presents a syntax and matching algorithm for media feature sets), RFC 2738 (which provides a minor update to RFC 2533), and RFC 2703 (which provides a general framework for content negotiation). A feature collection represents a single point in this space. It represents a particular rendering or instance of an entity (in our case, a UA). For example, a *rendering* of a UA would define an instantaneous mode of operation that it can support. One such rendering would be processing the INVITE method, which carried the application/Session Description Protocol (SDP) MIME type, sent to a UA for a user that is speaking English.

RFC 2533 describes syntax for writing down these *N*-dimensional Boolean functions, borrowed from LDAP defined in RFC 4515. It uses a prolog-style syntax that is fairly self-explanatory. This representation is called a feature set predicate. The base unit of the predicate is a filter, which is a Boolean expression encased in round brackets. A filter can be complex, where it contains conjunctions and disjunctions of other filters, or it can be simple. A simple filter is one that expresses a comparison operation on a single media feature tag. For example, consider the feature set predicate:

```
(& (foo=A)
(bar=B)
(| (baz=C) (& (baz=D) (bif=E))))
```

This defines a function over four media features—foo, bar, baz, and bif. Any point in feature space with foo equal to A, bar equal to B, and baz equal to either C or D, and bif equal to E, is in the feature set defined by this feature set predicate. Note that the predicate does not say anything about the number of dimensions in feature space. The predicate operates on a feature space of any number of dimensions, but only those dimensions labeled foo, bar, baz, and bif matter. The result is that values of other media features do not matter. The feature collection {foo=A,bar=B,baz=C,bop=F} is in the feature set described by the predicate, even though the media feature tag *bop* is not mentioned.

Feature set predicates are therefore inclusive by default. A feature collection is present unless the Boolean predicate rules it out. This was a conscious design choice in RFC 2533. RFC 2533 also talks about matching a preference with a capability set. This is accomplished by representing both with a feature set. A preference is a feature set—it is a specification of a number of feature collections, any one of which would satisfy the requirements of the sender. A capability is also a feature set—it is a specification of the feature collections that the recipient supports. There is a match when the spaces defined by both feature sets overlap. When there is overlap, there exists at least one feature collection that exists in both feature sets, and therefore a modality or rendering desired by the sender that is supported by the recipient. This leads directly to the definition of a match. Two feature sets match if there exists at least one feature collection present in both feature sets.

Computing a match for two general feature set predicates is not easy. RFC 2533 presents an algorithm for doing it by expanding an arbitrary expression into disjunctive normal form. However, the feature set predicates used by this specification are constrained. They are always in conjunctive normal form, with each term in the conjunction describing values for different media features. This makes computation of a match easy. It is computed independently for each media feature, and then the feature sets overlap if media features specified in both sets overlap. Computing the overlap of a single media feature is very straightforward, and is a simple matter of computing whether two finite sets overlap. Since the content negotiation work was primarily meant to apply to documents or other resources with a set of possible renderings, it is not immediately apparent how it is used to model SIP UAs.

A feature set is composed of a set of feature collections, each of which represents a specific rendering supported by the entity described by the feature set. In the context of a SIP UA, a feature collection represents an instantaneous modality. That is, if we look at the run time processing of a SIP UA and take a snapshot in time, the feature collection describes what it is doing at that very instant. This model is important, since it provides guidance on how to determine whether something is a value for a particular feature tag, or a feature tag by itself. If two properties can be exhibited by a UA simultaneously so that both are present in an instantaneous modality, they need to be represented by separate media feature tags.

For example, a UA may be able to support some number of media types—audio, video, and control. Should each of these be different values for a single *media-types* feature tag, or should each of them be a separate Boolean feature tag? The model provides the answer. Since, at any instance in time, a UA could be handling both audio and video, they need to be separate media feature tags. However, the SIP methods supported by a UA can each be represented as different values for the same media feature tag (the *sip.methods* tag), because fundamentally, a UA processes a single request at a time. It may be multithreading, so that it appears that this is not so, but at a purely functional level, it is true. Clearly, there are weaknesses in this model; however, it serves as a useful guideline for applying the concepts of RFC 2533 to the problem at hand.

To construct a set of Contact header field parameters that indicate capabilities, a UA constructs a feature predicate for that contact. This process is described in terms of RFC 2533 and its minor update (RFC 2738), syntax and constructs, followed by a conversion to the syntax used in this specification. However, this represents a logical flow of processing. There is no requirement that an implementation actually use RFC 2533 syntax as an intermediate step. When using the sip.methods feature tag, a UA must not include values that correspond to methods not standardized in IETF Standards Track RFCs. When using the *sip.events* feature tag, a UA must not include values that correspond to event packages not standardized in IETF Standards Track RFCs. When using the *sip.schemes* feature tag, a UA must not include values that correspond to schemes not standardized in IETF Standards Track RFCs. When using the *sip.extensions* feature tag, a UA must not include values that correspond to option tags not standardized in IETF Standards Track RFCs.

Note that the sip.schemes feature tag does not indicate the scheme of the registered URI. Rather, it indicates schemes that a UA is capable of sending requests to, should such a URI be received in a web page or Contact header field of a redirect response. It is recommended that a UA provide complete information in its contact predicate. That is, it should provide information on as many feature tags as possible. The mechanisms in this specification work best when UAs register complete feature sets. Furthermore, when a UA registers values for a particular feature tag, it MUST list all values that it supports. For example, when including the sip. methods feature tag, a UA must list all methods it supports.

The contact predicate constructed by a UA must be an AND of terms (called a conjunction). Each term is either an OR (called a disjunction) of simple filters or negations of simple filters, or a single simple filter or negation of a single filter. In the case of a disjunction, each filter in the disjunction must indicate feature values for the same feature tag (i.e., the disjunction represents a set of values for a particular feature tag), while each element of the conjunction must be for a different feature tag. Each simple filter can be an equality, or in the case of numeric feature tags, an inequality or range. If a string (as defined in RFC 2533) is used as the value of a simple filter, that value must not include the < or > characters, the simple filter must not be negated, and it must be the only simple filter for that particular feature tag. This contact predicate is then converted to a list of feature parameters, following the procedure outlined below.

The contact predicate is a conjunction of terms. Each term indicates constraints on a single feature tag, and each term is represented by a separate feature parameter that will be present in the Contact header field. The syntax of this parameter depends on the feature tag. Each forward slash in the feature tag is converted to a single quote, and each colon is converted to an exclamation point. For the base tags—that is, those feature tags documented in this specification (sip.audio, sip.automata, sip.class, sip.duplex, sip.data, sip. control, sip.mobility, sip.description, sip.events, sip.priority, sip.methods, sip.extensions, sip.schemes, sip.application, sip. video, language, type, sip.isfocus, sip.actor, and sip.text), the leading sip., if present, is stripped. For feature tags not in this list, the leading sip. must not be stripped if present, and indeed, a plus sign ("+") must be added as the first character of the Contact header field parameter. The result is the feature parameter name. As a result of these rules, the base tags appear *naked* in the Contact header field—they have neither a + nor a sip. prefix. All other tags will always have a leading + when present in the Contact header field, and will additionally have a sip. if the tag is in the SIP tree.

The value of the feature parameter depends on the term of the conjunction. If the term is a Boolean expression with a value of true, that is, (sip.audio=TRUE), the contact parameter has no value. If the term of the conjunction is a disjunction, the value of the contact parameter is a quoted string. The quoted string is a comma-separated list of strings, each one derived from one of the terms in the disjunction. If the term of the conjunction is a negation, the value of the contact parameter is a quoted string. The quoted string begins with an exclamation point (!), and the remainder is constructed from the expression being negated.

The remaining operation is to compute a string from a primitive filter. If the filter is a simple filter that is performing a numeric comparison, the string starts with an octothorpe (#), followed by the comparator in the filter (=, >=, or <=), followed by the value from the filter. If the value from the filter is expressed in rational form (X/Y), then X and Y are divided, yielding a decimal number, and this decimal number is output to the string. RFC 2533 uses a fractional notation to describe rational numbers. This specification uses a decimal form. The above text merely converts between the two representations. Practically speaking, this conversion is not needed since the numbers are the same in either case. However, it is described in case implementations wish to directly plug the predicates generated by the rules in this section into an RFC 2533 implementation.

If the filter is a range (foo=X...Y), the string is equal to X:Y, where X and Y have been converted from fractional numbers (A/B) to their decimal equivalent. If the filter is an equality over a token or Boolean, then that token or Boolean value (TRUE or FALSE) is output to the string. If the filter is an equality over a quoted string, the output is a less than (<), followed by the quoted string, followed by a greater than (>). As an example, this feature predicate:

```
(& (sip.mobility=fixed)
(| (! (sip.events=presence)) (sip.
events=message-summary))
(| (language=en) (language=de))
(sip.description="PC")
(sip.newparam=TRUE)
(rangeparam=-4..5125/1000))
```

would be converted into the following feature parameters:

```
mobility="fixed";events="!presence,message
-summary";language="en,de";
description="<PC>";+sip.newparam;+rangepa
ram="#-4:+5.125"
```

These feature tags would then appear as part of the Contact header field:

```
Contact: <sip:user@pc.example.com>;
mobility="fixed";events="!presence,message
-summary";
language="en,de";description="<PC>";
+sip.newparam;+rangeparam="#-4:+5.125"
```

Notice how the leading sip. was stripped from the sip.mobility, sip.events, and sip.description feature tags before encoding them in the Contact header field. This is because these feature tags are among the base tags listed above. It is for this reason that these feature tags were not encoded with a leading + either. However, the sip.newparam feature tag was encoded with both the + and its leading sip., and the rangeparam was also encoded with a leading +. This is because neither of these feature tags is defined in this specification. As such, the leading sip. is not stripped off, and a + is added.

3.4.3.1 Expressing Capabilities in a Registration

When a UA registers, it can choose to indicate a feature set associated with a registered contact. Whether or not a UA does so depends on what the registered URI represents. If the registered URI represents a UA instance (the common case in registrations), a UA compliant to this specification should indicate a feature set using the mechanisms described here. If, however, the registered URI represents an AOR, or some other resource that is not representable by a single feature set, it should not include a feature set. As an example, if a user wishes to forward calls from sip:user1@example.com to sip:user2@example.org, it could generate a registration that looks like, in part

```
REGISTER sip:example.com SIP/2.0
To: sip:user1@example.com
Contact: sip:user2@example.org
```

In this case, the registered contact is not identifying a UA, but rather, another AOR. In such a case, the registered contact would not indicate a feature set. However, in some cases, a UA may wish to express feature parameters for an AOR. One example is an AOR that represents a multiplicity of devices in a home network, and routes to a proxy server in the user's home. Since all devices in the home are for personal use, the AOR itself can be described with the ;class="personal" feature parameter. A registration that forwards calls to this home AOR could make use of that feature parameter.

Generally speaking, a feature parameter can only be associated with an AOR if all devices bound to that AOR share the exact same set of values for that feature parameter. Similarly, in some cases, a UA can exhibit one characteristic or another; however, the characteristic is not known in advance. For example, a UA could represent a device that is a phone with an embedded answering machine. The ideal way to treat such devices is to model them as if they were actually a proxy fronting two devices—a phone (which is never an answering machine) and an answering machine (which is never a phone). The registration from this device would be constructed as if it were an AOR, as per the procedures above. Generally, this means that, unless the characteristic is identical between the logical devices, that characteristic will not be present in any registration generated by the actual device.

This feature set that a UA would like to associate with a contact that it is registering is constructed and converted to a series of Contact header field parameters, as described earlier, and those feature parameters are added to the Contact header field value containing the URI to which the parameters apply. The Allow, Accept, Accept-Language, and Allow-Events (defined in RFC 6665, see Sections 5.1 and 2.8.2) header fields are allowed in REGISTER requests, and also indicate capabilities. However, their semantic in REGISTER is different, indicating capabilities, used by the registrar, for generation of the response. As such, they are not a substitute or an alternate for the Contact feature parameters, which indicate the capabilities of the UA generally speaking.

The REGISTER request may contain a Require header field with the value *pref* if the client wants to be sure that the registrar understands the extensions defined in this specification. This means that the registrar will store the feature parameters, and make them available to elements accessing the location service within the domain. In the absence of the Require header field, a registrar that does not understand this extension will simply ignore the Contact header field parameters. If a UA registers against multiple separate AORs, and the contacts registered for each have different capabilities, a UA must use different URIs in each registration. This allows the UA to uniquely determine the feature set that is associated with the Request-URI of an incoming request. As an example, a voice-mail server that is a UA that supports audio and video media types and is not mobile would construct a feature predicate like this:

```
(& (sip.audio=TRUE)
(sip.video=TRUE)
(sip.actor=msg-taker)
(sip.automata=TRUE)
(sip.mobility=fixed)
(| (sip.methods=INVITE) (sip.methods=BYE)
(sip.methods=OPTIONS)
(sip.methods=ACK) (sip.methods=CANCEL)))
```

These would be converted into feature parameters and included in the REGISTER request:

```
REGISTER sip:example.com SIP/2.0
From: sip:user@example.com;tag=asd98
To: sip:user@example.com
Call-ID: hh89as0d-asd88jkk@host.example.com
CSeq: 9987 REGISTER
Max-Forwards: 70
Via: SIP/2.0/UDP host.example.com;
branch=z9hG4bKnashds8
Contact: <sip:user@host.example.com>;
audio;video;
actor="msg-taker";automata;mobility="fixed";
methods="INVITE,BYE,OPTIONS,ACK,CANCEL"
Content-Length: 0
```

Note that a voice-mail server is usually an automata and a message taker. When a UAC refreshes its registration, it must include its feature parameters in that refresh if it wishes for them to remain active. Furthermore, when a registrar returns a 200 OK response to a REGISTER request, each Contact header field value must include all the feature parameters associated with that URI.

3.4.4 Indicating Feature Sets in Remote Target URIs

Target refresh requests and responses are used to establish and modify the remote target URI in a dialog. The remote target URI is conveyed in the Contact header field. A UAC or UAS may add feature parameters to the Contact header field value in target refresh requests and responses for the purpose of indicating the capabilities of the UA. To do that, it constructs a set of feature parameters according to the description provided earlier. These are then added as Contact header field parameters in the request or response. The feature parameters can be included in both initial requests and mid-dialog requests, and may change mid-dialog to signal a change in UA capabilities.

There is overlap in the callee capabilities mechanism with the Allow, Accept, Accept-Language, and Allow-Events (defined in RFC 6665, see Section 2.8.2) header fields, which can also be used in target refresh requests. Specifically, the Allow header field and sip.methods feature tag indicate the same information. The Accept header field and the *type* feature tag indicate the same information. The Accept-Language header field and the *language* feature tag indicate the same information. The Allow-Events header field and the sip.events feature tag indicate the same information. It is possible that other header fields and feature tags defined in the future may also overlap. When there exists a feature tag that describes a capability that can also be represented with a SIP header field, a UA must use the header field to describe the capability. A UA receiving a message that contains both the header field and the feature tag must use the header field, and not the feature tag.

3.4.5 OPTIONS Processing

When a UAS compliant to this specification receives an OPTIONS request, it may add feature parameters to the Contact header field in the OPTIONS response for the purpose of indicating the capabilities of the UA. To do that, it constructs a set of feature parameters according to the description provided earlier. These are then added as Contact header field parameters in OPTIONS response. Indeed, if feature parameters were included in the registration generated by that UA, those same parameters should be used in the OPTIONS response. The guidelines regarding the overlap of the various callee capabilities feature tags with SIP header fields described earlier apply to the generation of OPTIONS responses as well. In particular, they apply when a Contact header field is describing the UA that generated the OPTIONS response. When a Contact header field in the OPTIONS response is identifying a different UA, there is no overlap.

3.5 Discovering UA and Proxy Capabilities

The SIP method OPTIONS allows a UA to query another UA or a proxy server as to its capabilities. This allows a client to discover information about the supported methods, content types, extensions, codecs, and other capabilities before sending a request message such as INVITE to the other party, as all UAs must support the OPTIONS method. The target of the OPTIONS request is identified by the Request-URI, which could identify another UA or a SIP server. If the OPTIONS method is addressed to a proxy server, the Request-URI is set without a user part, similar to the way a Request-URI is set for a REGISTER request.

Alternatively, a server receiving an OPTIONS request with a Max-Forwards header field value of 0 may respond to the request regardless of the Request-URI. This behavior is common with HTTP/1.1. This behavior can be used as a *traceroute* functionality to check the capabilities of individual hop servers by sending a series of OPTIONS requests with incremented Max-Forwards values. As is the case for general UA behavior, the transaction layer can return a timeout error if the OPTIONS yields no response. This may indicate that the target is unreachable and hence unavailable. An OPTIONS request may be sent as part of an established dialog to query the peer on capabilities that may be utilized later in the dialog.

3.5.1 OPTIONS Request

A Contact header field may be present in an OPTIONS method. An Accept header field should be included to indicate the type of message body the UAC wishes to receive in the response. Typically, this is set to a format that is used to describe the media capabilities of a UA, such as SDP (*application/SDP*). The response to an OPTIONS request is assumed to be scoped to the Request-URI in the original request. However, only when an OPTIONS method is sent as part of an established dialog is it guaranteed that future requests will be received by the server that generated the OPTIONS response. An example OPTIONS request is shown below:

```
OPTIONS sip:carol@chicago.com SIP/2.0
Via: SIP/2.0/UDP pc33.atlanta.com;
branch=z9hG4bKhjhs8ass877
Max-Forwards: 70
To: <sip:carol@chicago.com>
From: Alice <sip:alice@atlanta.com>;
tag=1928301774
Call-ID: a84b4c76e66710
CSeq: 63104 OPTIONS
Contact: <sip:alice@pc33.atlanta.com>
Accept: application/SDP
Content-Length: 0
```

3.5.2 Response to OPTIONS Request

The response code chosen to an OPTIONS method must be the same as that which would have been chosen had the request been an INVITE. For example, a 200 OK would be returned if the UAS is ready to accept a call, and a 486 Busy Here would be returned if the UAS is busy. This allows an OPTIONS request to be used to determine the basic state of a UAS, which can be an indication of whether the UAS will accept an INVITE request. An OPTIONS request received within a dialog generates a 200 OK response that is identical to one constructed outside a dialog and does not have any impact on the dialog. This use of OPTIONS has limitations due to the differences in proxy handling of OPTIONS and INVITE requests. While a forked INVITE can result in multiple 200 OK responses being returned, a forked OPTIONS method will only result in a single 200 OK response, since it is treated by proxies using the non-INVITE handling.

If the response to an OPTIONS method is generated by a proxy server, the proxy returns a 200 OK, listing the capabilities of the server. The response does not contain a message body. Allow, Accept, Accept-Encoding, Accept-Language, and Supported header fields should be present in a 200 OK response to an OPTIONS request. If the response is generated by a proxy, the Allow header field should be omitted as it is ambiguous since a proxy is method agnostic. Contact header fields may be present in a 200 OK response and have the same semantics as in a 3xx response. That is, they may list a set of alternative names and methods of reaching the user. A Warning header field may be present.

A message body may be sent, the type of which is determined by the Accept header field in the OPTIONS request (application/SDP is the default if the Accept header field is not present). If the types include one that can describe media capabilities, the UAS should include a body in the response for that purpose. Details on the construction of such a body in the case of application/SDP are described in RFC 3264 (see Section 3.8.4).

```
SIP/2.0 200 OK
Via: SIP/2.0/UDP pc33.atlanta.com;
branch=z9hG4bKhjhs8ass877;
received=192.0.2.4
To: <sip:carol@chicago.com>;tag=93810874
From: Alice <sip:alice@atlanta.com>;
tag=1928301774
Call-ID: a84b4c76e66710
CSeq: 63104 OPTIONS
Contact: <sip:carol@chicago.com>
Contact: <mailto:carol@chicago.com>
Allow: INVITE, ACK, CANCEL, OPTIONS, BYE
Accept: application/SDP
Accept-Encoding: gzip
Accept-Language: en
Supported: foo
Content-Type: application/SDP
Content-Length: 274
(SDP not shown)
```

3.6 Dialogs

A dialog represents a peer-to-peer SIP relationship between two UAs that persists for some time. The dialog facilitates sequencing of messages between the UAs and proper routing of requests between both of them. The dialog represents a context in which to interpret SIP messages. We will describe how the SIP requests and responses are used to construct a dialog, and then how subsequent requests and responses are sent within a dialog. A dialog is identified at each UA with a dialog ID, which consists of a Call-ID value, a local tag, and a remote tag. The dialog ID at each UA involved in the dialog is not the same. Specifically, the local tag at one UA is identical to the remote tag at the peer UA. The tags are opaque tokens that facilitate the generation of cryptographically random unique dialog IDs.

A dialog ID is also associated with all responses and with any request that contains a tag in the To field. The rules for computing the dialog ID of a message depend on whether the SIP element is a UAC or UAS. For a UAC, the Call-ID value of the dialog ID is set to the Call-ID of the message, the remote tag is set to the tag in the To field of the message, and the local tag is set to the tag in the From field of the message (these rules apply to both requests and responses). As one would expect for a UAS, the Call-ID value of the dialog ID is set to the Call-ID of the message, the remote tag is set to the tag in the From field of the message, and the local tag is set to the tag in the To field of the message.

A dialog contains certain pieces of state needed for further message transmissions within the dialog. This state consists of the dialog ID, a local sequence number (used to order requests from the UA to its peer), a remote sequence number (used to order requests from its peer to the UA), a local URI, a remote URI, remote target, a Boolean flag called *secure*, and a route set, which is an ordered list of URIs. The route set is the list of servers that need to be traversed to send a request to the peer. A dialog can also be in the *early* state, which occurs when it is created with a provisional response and then transition to the *confirmed* state when a 2xx final response arrives. For other responses, or if no response arrives at all on that dialog, the early dialog terminates.

3.6.1 Creation of a Dialog

Dialogs are created through the generation of nonfailure responses to requests with specific methods. Within this specification, only 2xx and 101–199 responses with a To tag, where the request was INVITE, will establish a dialog. A dialog established by a nonfinal response to a request is in the early state, and it is called an early dialog. Here, we describe the process for the creation of a dialog state that is not dependent on the method. UAs must assign values to the dialog ID components as described below.

3.6.1.1 UAS Behavior

When a UAS responds to a request with a response that establishes a dialog (such as a 2xx to INVITE), the UAS must copy all Record-Route header field values from the request into the response (including the URIs, URI parameters, and any Record-Route header field parameters, whether they are known or unknown to the UAS) and must maintain the order of those values. The UAS must add a Contact header field to the response. The Contact header field contains an address where the UAS would like to be contacted for subsequent requests in the dialog (which includes the ACK for a 2xx response in the case of an INVITE).

Generally, the host portion of this URI is the IP address or FQDN of the host. The URI provided in the Contact header field must be a SIP or SIPS URI. If the request that initiated the dialog contained a SIPS URI in the Request-URI or in the top Record-Route header field value, if there was any, or the Contact header field if there was no Record-Route header field, the Contact header field in the response must be a SIPS URI. The URI should have global scope (i.e., the same URI can be used in messages outside this dialog). The same way, the scope of the URI in the Contact header field of the INVITE is not limited to this dialog either. It can therefore be used in messages to the UAC even outside this dialog.

The UAS then constructs the state of the dialog. This state must be maintained for the duration of the dialog. If the request arrived over TLS, and the Request-URI contained a SIPS URI, the *secure* flag is set to TRUE. The route set must be set to the list of URIs in the Record-Route header field from the request, taken in order and preserving all URI parameters. If no Record-Route header field is present in the request, the route set must be set to the empty set. This route set, even if empty, overrides any preexisting route set for future requests in this dialog. The remote target must be set to the URI from the Contact header field of the request.

The remote sequence number must be set to the value of the sequence number in the CSeq header field of the request. The local sequence number must be empty. The call identifier component of the dialog ID must be set to the value of the Call-ID in the request. The local tag component of the dialog ID must be set to the tag in the To field in the response to the request (which always includes a tag), and the remote tag component of the dialog ID must be set to the tag from the From field in the request. A UAS must be prepared to receive a request without a tag in the From field, in which case the tag is considered to have a value of null. This is to maintain backwards compatibility with RFC 2543 (obsoleted by RFC 3261), which did not mandate From tags. The remote URI must be set to the URI in the From field, and the local URI must be set to the URI in the To field.

3.6.1.2 UAC Behavior

When a UAC sends a request that can establish a dialog (such as an INVITE), it must provide a SIP or SIPS URI with global scope (i.e., the same SIP URI can be used in messages outside this dialog) in the Contact header field of the request. If the request has a Request-URI or a topmost Route header field value with a SIPS URI, the Contact header field must contain a SIPS URI. When a UAC receives a response that establishes a dialog, it constructs the state of the dialog. This state MUST be maintained for the duration of the dialog. If the request was sent over TLS, and the Request-URI contained a SIPS URI, the secure flag is set to TRUE. The route set must be set to the list of URIs in the Record-Route header field from the response, taken in reverse order and preserving all URI parameters. If no Record-Route header field is present in the response, the route set must be set to the empty set. This route set, even if empty, overrides any preexisting route set for future requests in this dialog. The remote target must be set to the URI from the Contact header field of the response.

The local sequence number must be set to the value of the sequence number in the CSeq header field of the request. The remote sequence number must be empty (it is established when the remote UA sends a request within the dialog). The call identifier component of the dialog ID MUST be set to the value of the Call-ID in the request. The local tag component of the dialog ID MUST be set to the tag in the From field in the request, and the remote tag component of the dialog ID must be set to the tag in the To field of the response. A UAC must be prepared to receive a response without a tag in the To field, in which case the tag is considered to have a value of null. This is to maintain backwards compatibility with RFC 2543 (obsoleted by RFC 3261), which did not mandate To tags. The remote URI must be set to the URI in the To field, and the local URI must be set to the URI in the From field.

3.6.2 Requests within a Dialog

Once a dialog has been established between two UAs, either of them may initiate new transactions as needed within the dialog. The UA sending the request will take the UAC role for the transaction. The UA receiving the request will take the UAS role. Note that these may be different roles than the UAs held during the transaction that established the dialog. Requests within a dialog may contain Record-Route and Contact header fields. However, these requests do not cause the dialog's route set to be modified, although they may modify the remote target URI.

Specifically, requests that are not target refresh requests do not modify the dialog's remote target URI, and requests that are target refresh requests do. For dialogs that have been established with an INVITE, the only target refresh request defined is re-INVITE. Other extensions may define different target refresh requests for dialogs established in other ways. Note that an ACK is not a target refresh request. Target refresh requests only update the dialog's remote target URI, and not the route set formed from the Record-Route. Updating the latter would introduce severe backwards compatibility problems with RFC 2543 (obsoleted by RFC 3261)-compliant systems.

3.6.2.1 UAC Behavior

3.6.2.1.1 Generating the Request

A request within a dialog is constructed by using many of the components of the state stored as part of the dialog. The URI in the To field of the request must be set to the remote URI from the dialog state. The tag in the To header field of the request must be set to the remote tag of the dialog ID. The From URI of the request must be set to the local URI from the dialog state. The tag in the From header field of the request must be set to the local tag of the dialog ID. If the value of the remote or local tags is null, the tag parameter must be omitted from the To or From header fields, respectively.

Usage of the URI from the To and From fields in the original request within subsequent requests is done for backwards compatibility with RFC 2543 (obsoleted by RFC 3261), which used the URI for dialog identification. In this specification, only the tags are used for dialog identification. It is expected that mandatory reflection of the original To and From URI in mid-dialog requests will be deprecated in a subsequent revision of this specification. The Call-ID of the request MUST be set to the Call-ID of the dialog. Requests within a dialog must contain strictly monotonically increasing and contiguous CSeq sequence numbers (increasing by one) in each direction (expecting ACK and CANCEL of course, whose numbers equal the requests being acknowledged or cancelled). Therefore, if the local sequence number is not empty, the value of the local sequence number must be incremented by one, and this value must be placed into the CSeq header field. The method field in the CSeq header field value must match the method of the request.

With a length of 32 bits, a client could generate, within a single call, one request a second for about 136 years before needing to wrap around. The initial value of the sequence number is chosen so that subsequent requests within the same call will not wrap around. A nonzero initial value allows clients to use a time-based initial sequence number. A client could, for example, choose the 31 most significant bits of a 32-bit second clock as an initial sequence number. The UAC uses the remote target and route set to build the Request-URI and Route header field of the request. If the route set is empty, the UAC must place the remote target URI into the Request-URI. The UAC must not add a Route header field to the request.

If the route set is not empty, and the first URI in the route set contains the lr parameter, the UAC must place the remote target URI into the Request-URI and must include a Route header field containing the route set values in order, including all parameters. If the route set is not empty, and its first URI does not contain the lr parameter, the UAC must place the first URI from the route set into the Request-URI, stripping any parameters that are not allowed in a Request-URI. The UAC must add a Route header field containing the remainder of the route set values in order, including all parameters. The UAC must then place the remote target URI into the Route header field as the last value. For example, if the remote target is sip:user@remoteua and the route set contains

```
<sip:proxy1>,<sip:proxy2>,<sip:proxy3;lr>,
<sip:proxy4>
```

the request will be formed with the following Request-URI and Route header field:

```
METHOD sip:proxy1
Route: <sip:proxy2>,<sip:proxy3;lr>,
<sip:proxy4>,<sip:user@remoteua>
```

If the first URI of the route set does not contain the lr parameter, the proxy indicated does not understand the routing mechanisms described in this document and will act as specified in RFC 2543 (obsoleted by RFC 3261), replacing the Request-URI with the first Route header field value it receives while forwarding the message. Placing the Request-URI at the end of the Route header field preserves the information in that Request-URI across the strict router (it will be returned to the Request-URI when the request reaches a loose router).

A UAC should include a Contact header field in any target refresh requests within a dialog, and unless there is a need to change it, the URI should be the same as used in previous requests within the dialog. If the secure flag is true, that URI must be a SIPS URI. A Contact header field in a target refresh request updates the remote target URI. This allows a UA to provide a new contact address, should its address change during the duration of the dialog. However, requests that are not target refresh requests do not affect the remote target URI for the dialog.

Once the request has been constructed, the address of the server is computed and the request is sent, using the same procedures for requests outside of a dialog. The procedures will normally result in the request being sent to the address indicated by the topmost Route header field value or the Request-URI if no Route header field is present. Subject to certain restrictions, they allow the request to be sent to an alternate address (such as a default outbound proxy not represented in the route set).

3.6.2.1.2 Processing the Responses

The UAC will receive responses to the request from the transaction layer. If the client transaction returns a timeout, this is treated as a 408 Request Timeout response. The behavior of a UAC that receives a 3xx response for a request sent within a dialog is the same as if the request had been sent outside a dialog. Note, however, that when the UAC tries alternative locations, it still uses the route set for the dialog to build the Route header of the request. When a UAC receives a 2xx response to a target refresh request, it must replace the dialog's remote target URI with the URI from the Contact header field in that response, if present. If the response for a request within a dialog is a 481 Call/Transaction Does Not Exist or a 408 Request Timeout, the UAC should terminate the dialog. A UAC should also terminate a dialog if no response at all is received for the request (the client transaction would inform the TU about the timeout). For INVITE-initiated dialogs, terminating the dialog consists of sending a BYE.

3.6.2.2 UAS Behavior

Requests sent within a dialog, as any other requests, are atomic. If a particular request is accepted by the UAS, all the state changes associated with it are performed. If the request is rejected, none of the state changes are performed. Note that some requests, such as INVITEs, affect several pieces of state. The UAS will receive the request from the transaction layer. If the request has a tag in the To header field, the UAS core computes the dialog identifier corresponding to the request and compares it with existing dialogs. If there is a match, this is a mid-dialog request. If the request has a tag in the To header field, but the dialog identifier does not match any existing dialogs, the UAS may have crashed and restarted, or it may have received a request for a different (possibly failed) UAS (the UASs can construct the To tags so that a UAS can identify that the tag was for a UAS for which it is providing recovery).

Another possibility is that the incoming request has been simply misrouted. On the basis of the To tag, the UAS may either accept or reject the request. Accepting the request for acceptable To tags provides robustness, so that dialogs can persist even through crashes. UAs wishing to support this capability must take into consideration some issues such as choosing monotonically increasing CSeq sequence numbers even across reboots, reconstructing the route set, and accepting out-of-range Real-Time Transport Protocol (RTP) time stamps and sequence numbers. If the UAS wishes to reject the request because it does not wish to recreate the dialog, it must respond to the request with a 481 Call/Transaction Does Not Exist status code and pass that to the server transaction. Requests that do not change in any way the state of a dialog may be received within a dialog (e.g., an OPTIONS request). They are processed as if they had been received outside the dialog.

If the remote sequence number is empty, it must be set to the value of the sequence number in the CSeq header field value in the request. If the remote sequence number was not empty, but the sequence number of the request is lower than the remote sequence number, the request is out of order and must be rejected with a 500 Server Internal Error response. If the remote sequence number was not empty, and the sequence number of the request is greater than the remote sequence number, the request is in order. It is possible for the CSeq sequence number to be higher than the remote sequence number by more than one. This is not an error condition, and a UAS should be prepared to receive and process requests with CSeq values more than one higher than the previous received request. The UAS must then set the remote sequence number to the value of the sequence number in the CSeq header field value in the request. If a proxy challenges a request generated by the UAC, the UAC has to resubmit the request with credentials. The resubmitted request will have a new CSeq number. The UAS will never see the first request, and thus, it will notice a gap in the CSeq number space. Such a gap does not represent any error condition. When a UAS receives a target refresh request, it must replace the dialog's remote target URI with the URI from the Contact header field in that request, if present.

3.6.3 Termination of a Dialog

Independent of the method, if a request outside of a dialog generates a non-2xx final response, any early dialogs created through provisional responses to that request are terminated. The mechanism for terminating confirmed dialogs is method specific. In this specification, the BYE method terminates a session and the dialog associated with it.

3.6.4 Example of Dialog State

We are going back to an earlier example shown in Figure 3.1a of SIP trapezoid operations. It shows that Bob's UA is sending the 180 Ringing (F11) message to proxy 2, and proxy 2 sends 180 Ringing (F12) to proxy 1, and proxy 1 forwards the 180 Ringing message to Alice's UA. The early dialog state of Alice's and Bob's UA is shown in Figure 3.5.

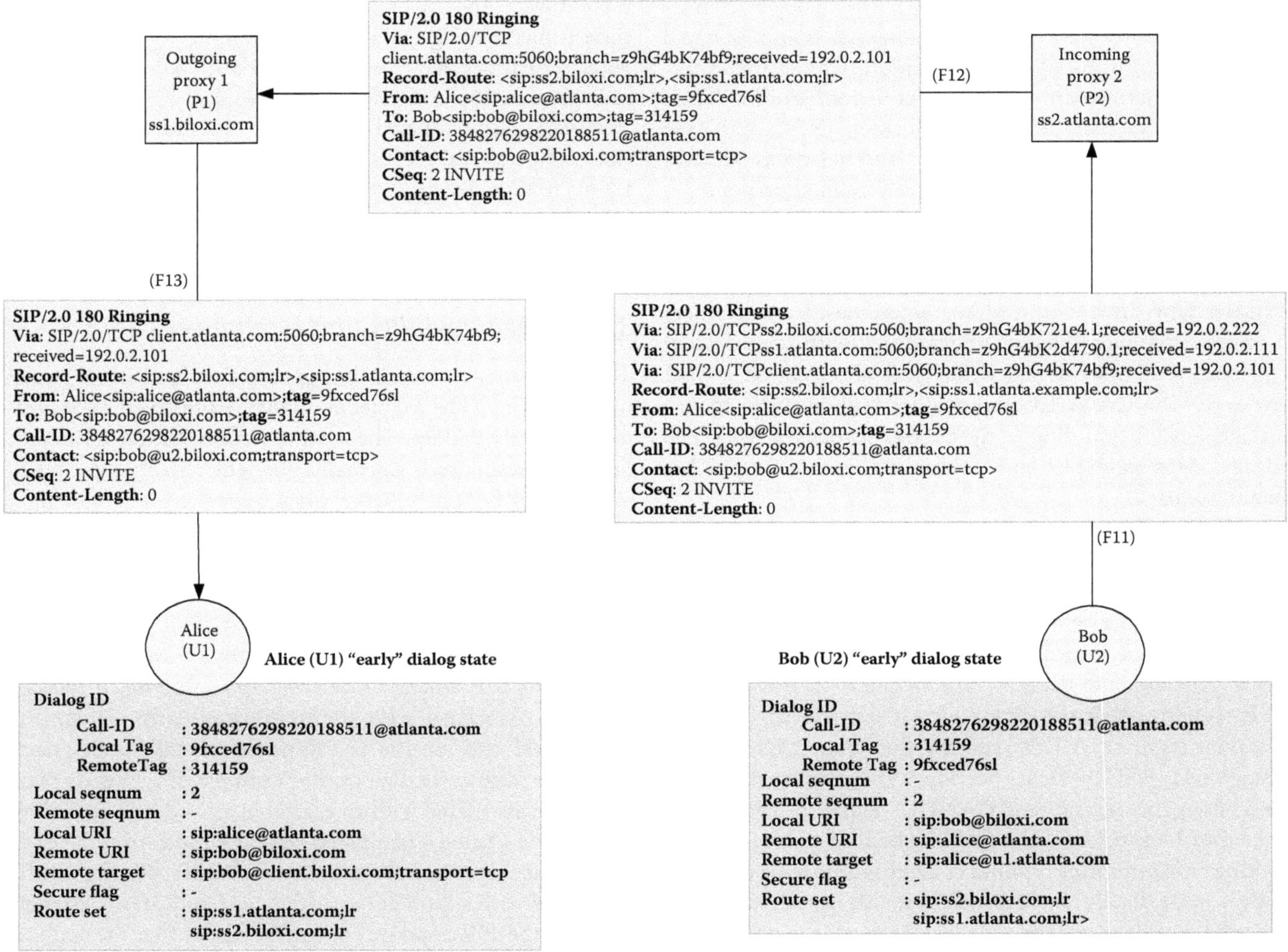

Figure 3.5 Example of early dialog state in UAs.

3.6.5 Multiple Dialogs

RFC 5057 explains in great detail that handling multiple usages within a single dialog is complex and introduces scenarios where the right thing to do is not clear. Implementations should avoid entering into multiple usages whenever possible. New applications should be designed to never introduce multiple usages. There are some accepted SIP practices, including transfer, that currently require multiple usages. Recent work, most notably GRUU (see Section 4.3), makes those practices unnecessary. The standardization of those practices and the implementations should be revised as soon as possible to use only single-usage dialogs. More about multiple dialogs is discussed in Section 16.2 with respect to call transfer using REFER method.

3.6.6 Early Dialog Termination Indication

A SIP early dialog is created when a non-100 provisional response is sent to the initial dialog initiation request (e.g., INVITE, outside an existing dialog). The dialog is considered to be in early state until a final response is sent. When a proxy receives an initial dialog initiation request, it can forward the request toward multiple remote destinations. When the proxy does that, it performs forking (RFC 3261; see Sections 2.2, 2.8, and 3.7). When a forking proxy receives a non-100 provisional response, or a 2xx final response, it forwards the response upstream toward the sender of the associated request. After a forking proxy has forwarded a 2xx final response, it normally generates and sends CANCEL requests downstream toward all remote destinations where it previously forked the request associated with the 2xx final response, and from which it has still not received a final response. The CANCEL requests are sent in order to terminate any outstanding early dialogs associated with the request. Upstream SIP entities might receive multiple 2xx final responses.

When a SIP entity receives the first 2xx final response, and it does not intend to accept any subsequent 2xx final responses, it will automatically terminate any other outstanding early dialog associated with the request. If the SIP entity receives a subsequent 2xx final response, it will normally generate and send an ACK request, followed with a BYE request, using the dialog identifier retrieved from the 2xx final response. A UAC can use the Request-Disposition header field (RFC 3841, see Section 9.9) to request that proxies do not generate and send CANCEL requests downstream once they have received the first 2xx final response. When a forking proxy receives a non-2xx final response, it does not always immediately forward the response upstream toward the sender of the associated request. Instead, the proxy *stores* the response and waits for subsequent final responses from other remote destinations where the associated request was forked. At some point, the proxy uses a specified mechanism to determine the *best* final response code, and forwards a final response using that response code upstream toward the sender of the associated request. When an upstream SIP entity receives the non-2xx final response, it will release resources associated with the session. The UAC will terminate, or retry, the session setup.

Since the forking proxy does not always immediately forward non-2xx final responses, upstream SIP entities (including the UAC that initiated the request) are not immediately informed that an early dialog has been terminated, and will therefore maintain resources associated with the early dialog reserved until a final response is sent by the proxy, even if the early dialog has already been terminated. A SIP entity could use the resources for other things, for example, to accept subsequent early dialogs that it otherwise would reject. RFC 6228 that is described here defines a new SIP response code, 199 Early Dialog Terminated, that a SIP forking proxy and a UAS can use to indicate to upstream SIP entities including the UAC that an early dialog has been terminated, before a final response is sent toward the SIP entities. A UAS can send a 199 response code, before sending a non-2xx final response, for the same purpose. SIP entities that receive the 199 Early Dialog Terminated response can use it to trigger the release of resources associated with the terminated early dialog. In addition, SIP entities might also use the 199 response to make policy decisions related to early dialogs. For example, a media gate controlling a SIP entity might use the 199 Early Dialog Terminated response when deciding for which early dialogs media will be passed.

3.6.6.1 Applicability and Limitation

The 199 response code is an optimization, and it only optimizes how quickly recipients might be informed about terminated early dialogs. The achieved optimization is limited. Since the response is normally not sent reliably by a UAS, and cannot be sent reliably when generated and sent by a proxy, it is possible that some or all of the 199 Early Dialog Terminated responses will get lost before they reach the recipients. In such cases, recipients will behave the same as if the 199 response code were not used at all. One example for which a UAC could use the 199 Early Dialog Terminated response is that when it receives a 199 response, it releases resources associated with the terminated early dialog. The UAC could also use the 199 response to make policy decisions related to early dialogs. For example, if a UAC is playing media associated with an early dialog, and it then receives a 199 Early Dialog Terminated response indicating the early dialog has been terminated; it could start playing media associated with a different early dialog. Application designers utilizing the 199 response code must ensure that the application's user experience is acceptable if all 199 responses are lost and not delivered to the recipients.

3.6.6.2 UAC Behavior

When a UAC sends an initial dialog initiation request, and if it is willing to receive 199 responses, it must insert a 199 option tag in the Supported header field (RFC 3261, see Section 2.8) of the request. The option tag indicates that the UAC supports, and is willing to receive, 199 responses. A UAC should not insert a 199 option tag in the Require or the Proxy-Require header field (RFC 3261, see Section 2.8) of the request, since in many cases it would result in unnecessary session establishment failures. The UAC always needs to insert a 199 option tag in the Supported header field, in order to indicate that it supports, and is willing to receive, 199 responses, even if it also inserts the option tag in the Require or Proxy-Require header field. It is recommended that a UAC not insert a 100rel option tag (RFC 3262, see Section 2.8) in the Require header field when it also indicates support for 199 responses, unless the UAC also uses some other SIP extension or procedure that mandates it to do so. The reason is that proxies are not allowed to generate and send 199 responses when the UAC has required provisional responses to be sent reliably.

When a UAC receives a 199 response, it might release resources associated with the terminated early dialog. A UAC might also use the 199 response to make policy decisions related to early dialogs. The 199 response indicates that the early dialog has been terminated, so there is no need for the UAC to send a BYE request in order to terminate the early dialog when it receives the 199 response. The 199 response does not affect other early dialogs associated with the session establishment. For those dialogs, the normal SIP rules regarding transaction timeout, etc., still apply. Once a UAC has received and accepted a 199 Early Dialog Terminated response, it must not send any media associated with the early dialog. In addition, if the UAC is able to associate received media with early dialogs, it must not process any received media associated with the early dialog that was terminated. If multiple usages (RFC 5057, see Sections 3.6.5 and 16.2) are used within an early dialog, and it is not clear which dialog usage the 199 response terminates, SIP entities that keep dialog state shall not release resources associated with the early dialog when they receive the 199 response.

If a UAC receives an unreliably sent 199 response on a dialog that has not previously been established (this can happen if a 199 response reaches the client before the 18x response that would establish the early dialog), it shall discard the 199 response. If a UAC receives a reliably sent 199 response on a dialog that has not previously been created, it must acknowledge the 199 response, as described in RFC 3262 (see Section 2.8). If a UAC has received a 199 response for all early dialogs, and no early dialogs associated with the session establishment remain, it maintains the Proceeding state (RFC 3261, Section 3.6.2) and waits for possible subsequent early dialogs to be established, and eventually for a final response to be received.

3.6.6.3 UAS Behavior

If a UAS receives an initial dialog initiation request with a Supported header field that contains a 199 option tag, it should not send a 199 response on an early dialog associated with the request before it sends a non-2xx final response. Cases where a UAS might send a 199 response are if it has been configured to do so due to lack of support for the 199 response code by forking proxies or other intermediate SIP entities, or if it is used in an environment that specifies that it shall send a 199 response before sending a non-2xx response. If a UAS has created multiple early dialogs associated with an initial dialog initiation request (the UAS is acting similarly to a forking proxy), it does not always intend to send a final response on all of those early dialogs. If the Require header field of an initial dialog initiation request contains a 100rel option tag, proxies will not be able to generate and send 199 responses. In such cases, the UAS might choose to send a 199 response on an early dialog before it sends a non-2xx final response, even if it would not do so in other cases. If the Supported header field of an initial dialog initiation request does not contain a 199 option tag, the UAC must not send a 199 response on any early dialog associated with the request. When a UAS generates a 199 response, the response must contain a To header field tag parameter (RFC 3261, see Section 2.9), in order for other entities to identify the early dialog that has been terminated.

The UAS must also insert a Reason header field (RFC 3326, see Section 2.8) that contains a response code describing the reason why the early dialog was terminated. The UAS must not insert a 199 option tag in the Supported, Require, or Proxy-Require header field of the 199 response. If a UAS intends to send 199 responses, and if it supports the procedures defined in RFC 3840 (see Section 2.11 and 3.4), it may, during the registration procedure, use the sip.extensions feature tag (RFC 3840, see Section 2.11) to indicate support for the 199 response code. A 199 response should not contain a SDP offer–answer message body, unless required by the rules in RFC 3264. According to RFC 3264, if an INVITE request does not contain an SDP offer, and the 199 response is the first reliably sent response associated with the request, the 199 response is required to contain an SDP offer. In this case, the UAS should send the 199 response unreliably, or send the 199 response reliably and include an SDP offer with no *m*= lines in the response. Since a 199 response is only used for information purposes, the UAS should send it unreliably, unless the 100rel option tag is present in the Require header field of the associated request.

3.6.6.4 Proxy Behavior

When a proxy receives a 199 response to an initial dialog initiation request, it MUST process the response as any other non-100 provisional response. The proxy will forward the response upstream toward the sender of the associated request. The proxy may release resources it has reserved associated with the early dialog that is terminated. If a proxy receives a 199 response out of dialog, it must process it as other non-100 provisional responses received out of dialog. When a forking proxy receives a non-2xx final response to an initial dialog initiation request that it recognizes as terminating one or more early dialogs associated with the request, it must generate and send a 199 response upstream for each of the terminated early dialogs that satisfy each of the following conditions:

- The forking proxy does not intend to forward the final response immediately (in accordance with rules for a forking proxy).
- The UAC has indicated support (by inserting the 199 option tag in a Supported header field) for the 199 response code in the associated request.
- The UAC has not required provisional responses to be sent reliably, that is, has not inserted the 100rel option tag in a Require or Proxy-Require header field, in the associated request.
- The forking proxy has not already received and forwarded a 199 response for the early dialog.
- The forking proxy has not already sent a final response for any of the early dialogs.

As a consequence, once a final response to an initial dialog initiation request has been issued by the proxy, no further 199 responses associated with the request will be generated or forwarded by the proxy. When a forking proxy forks an initial dialog initiation request, it generates a unique Via header branch parameter value for each forked leg. A proxy can determine whether additional forking has occurred downstream of the proxy by storing the top Via branch value from each response that creates an early dialog. If the same top Via branch value is received for multiple early dialogs, the proxy knows that additional forking has occurred downstream of the proxy. A non-2xx final response received for a specific early dialog also terminates all other early dialogs for which the same top Via branch value was received in the responses that created those early dialogs.

On the basis of the implementation policy, a forking proxy may wait before sending the 199 response, for example, if it expects to receive a 2xx final response on another dialog shortly after it received the non-2xx final response that triggered the 199 response. When a forking proxy generates a 199 response, the response must contain a To header field tag parameter that identifies the terminated early dialog. A proxy must also insert a Reason header field that contains the SIP response code of the response that triggered the 199 response. The SIP response code in the Reason header field informs the receiver of the 199 response about the SIP response code that was used by the UAS to terminate the early dialog, and the receiver might use that information for triggering different types of actions and procedures. The proxy must not insert a 199 option tag in the Supported, Require, or Proxy-Require header field of the 199 response.

A forking proxy that supports the generation of 199 responses must keep track of early dialogs, in order to determine whether to generate a 199 response when the proxy receives a non-2xx final response. In addition, a proxy must keep track on which early dialogs it has received and forwarded 199 responses, in order to not generate additional 199 responses for those early dialogs. If a forking proxy receives a reliably sent 199 response for a dialog for which it has previously generated and sent a 199 response, it must forward the 199 response. If a proxy receives an unreliably sent 199 response for which it has previously generated and sent a 199 response, it may forward the response, or it may discard it. When a forking proxy generates and sends a 199 response, the response should not contain a Contact header field or a Record-Route header field (RFC 3261, see Section 2.8). If the Require header field of an initial dialog initiation request contains a 100rel option tag, a proxy must not generate and send 199 responses associated with that request. The reason is that a proxy is not allowed to generate and send 199 responses reliably.

3.6.6.5 Backwards Compatibility

Since all SIP entities involved in a session setup do not necessarily support the specific meaning of the 199 Early Dialog Terminated provisional response, the sender of the response must be prepared to receive SIP requests and responses associated with the dialog for which the 199 response was sent (a proxy can receive SIP messages from either direction). If such a request is received by a UA, it must act in the same way as if it had received the request after sending the final non-2xx response to the INVITE request, as specified in RFC 3261. A UAC that receives a 199 response for an early dialog must not send any further requests on that dialog, except for requests that acknowledge reliable responses. A proxy must forward requests according to RFC 3261, even if the proxy has knowledge that the early dialog has been terminated. A 199 response does not *replace* a final response. RFC 3261 specifies when a final response is sent.

3.6.6.6 Usage with SDP Offer–Answer

A 199 response should not contain an SDP offer–answer (RFC 3264, see Section 3.8.4) message body, unless required by the rules in RFC 3264. If an INVITE request does not contain an SDP offer, and the 199 response is the first reliably sent response, the 199 response is required to contain an SDP offer. In this case, the UAS should send the 199 response unreliably, or include an SDP offer with no m= lines in a reliable 199 response.

3.6.6.7 Message Flow Examples

3.6.6.7.1 Example with a Forking Proxy that Generates 199

Figure 3.6 shows an example where a proxy P1 forks an INVITE received from a UAC. The forked INVITE reaches UAS 2, UAS 3, and UAS 4, which send 18x provisional responses in order to establish early dialogs between themselves and the UAC. UAS 2 and UAS 3 each reject the INVITE by sending a 4xx error response. When P1 receives the 4xx responses, it immediately sends 199 Early Dialog Terminated responses toward the UAC, to indicate that the early dialogs for which it received the 4xx responses have been terminated. The early dialog leg is shown in parentheses.

3.6.6.7.2 Example with a Forking Proxy that Receives 200 OK

Figure 3.7 shows an example where a proxy P1 forks an INVITE request received from a UAC. The forked request

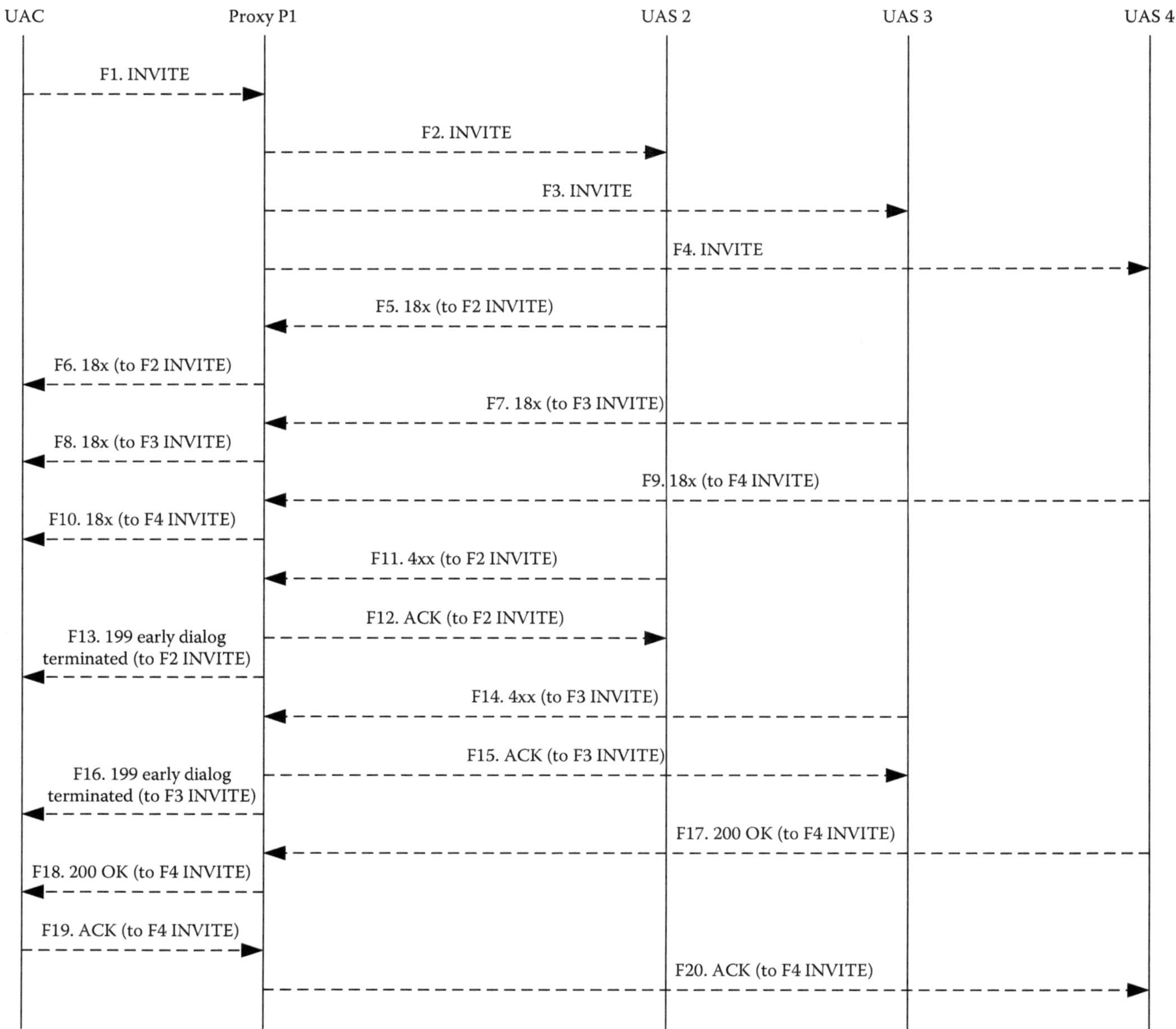

Figure 3.6 Forking proxy generating 199 Early Dialog Terminated. (Copyright IETF. Reproduced with permission.)

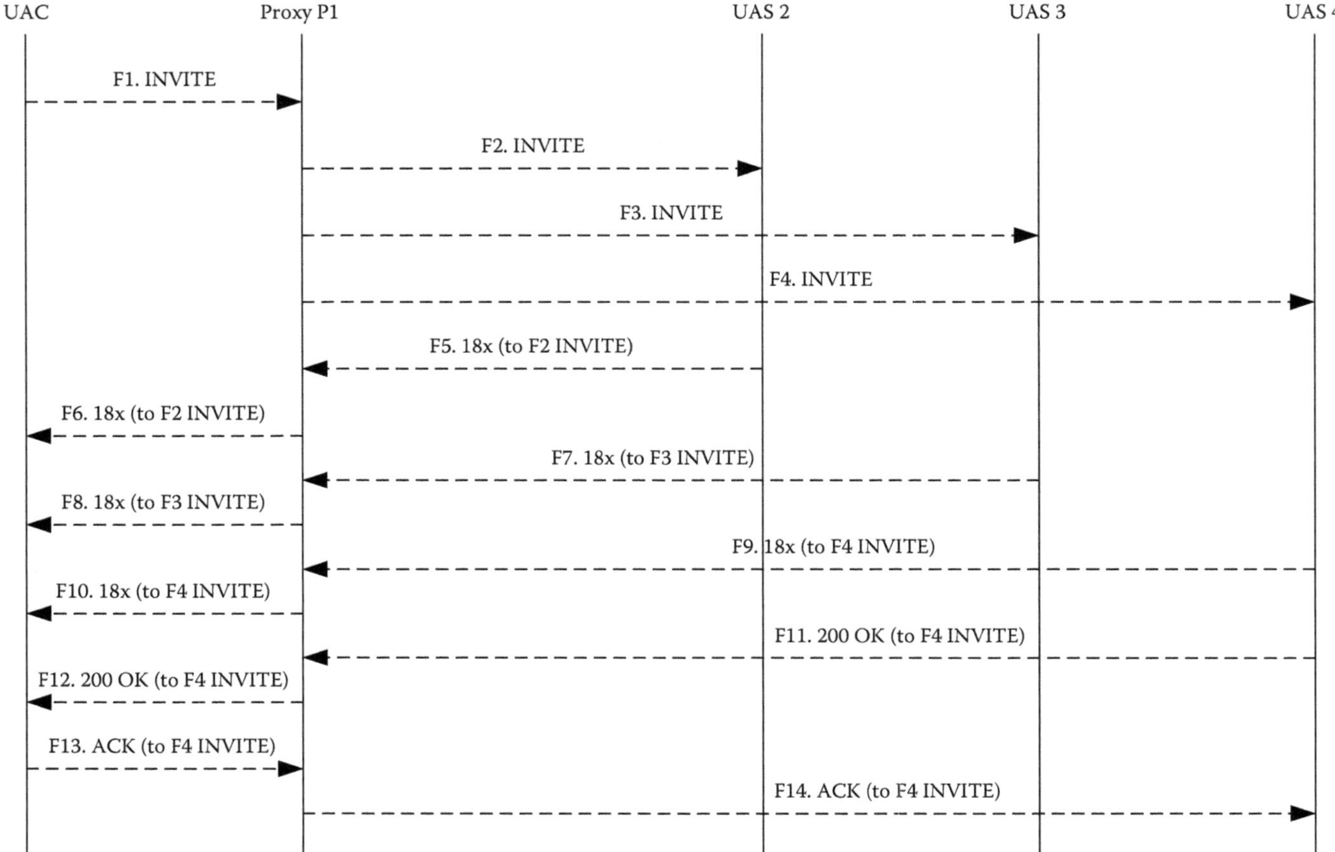

Figure 3.7 Forking proxy receiving 200 OK. (Copyright IETF. Reproduced with permission.)

reaches UAS 2, UAS 3, and UAS 4, all of which send 18x provisional responses in order to establish early dialogs between themselves and the UAC. Later, UAS 4 accepts the session and sends a 200 OK final response. When P1 receives the 200 OK response, it immediately forwards it toward the UAC. Proxy P1 does not send 199 responses for the early dialogs from UAS 2 and UAS 3, since P1 has still not received any final responses on those early dialogs (even if proxy P1 sends CANCEL requests to UAS 2 and UAS 3, proxy P1 may still receive a 200 OK final response from UAS 2 or UAS 3, which proxy P1 would have to forward toward the UAC). The early dialog leg is shown in parentheses.

3.6.6.7.3 Example with Two Forking Proxies, of which One Generates 199

Figure 3.8 shows an example where a proxy P1 forks an INVITE request received from a UAC. One of the forked requests reaches UAS 2. The other requests reach another proxy P2, which forks the request to UAS 3 and UAS 4. UAS 3 and UAS 4 send 18x provisional responses in order to establish early dialogs between themselves and the UAC.

Later, UAS 3 and UAS 4 each reject the INVITE request by sending a 4xx error response. Proxy P2 does not support the 199 response code and forwards a single 4xx response. Proxy P1 supports the 199 response code, and when it receives the 4xx response from proxy P2, it also manages to associate the early dialogs from both UAS 3 and UAS 4 with the response. Therefore, proxy P1 generates and sends two 199 responses to indicate that the early dialogs from UAS 3 and UAS 4 have been terminated. The early dialog leg is shown in parentheses.

3.7 Initiating a Session

3.7.1 Overview of Operation

When a UAC desires to initiate a session (e.g., audio, video, or a game), it formulates an INVITE request. The INVITE request asks a server to establish a session as shown in Figure 3.9 (RFC 3261).

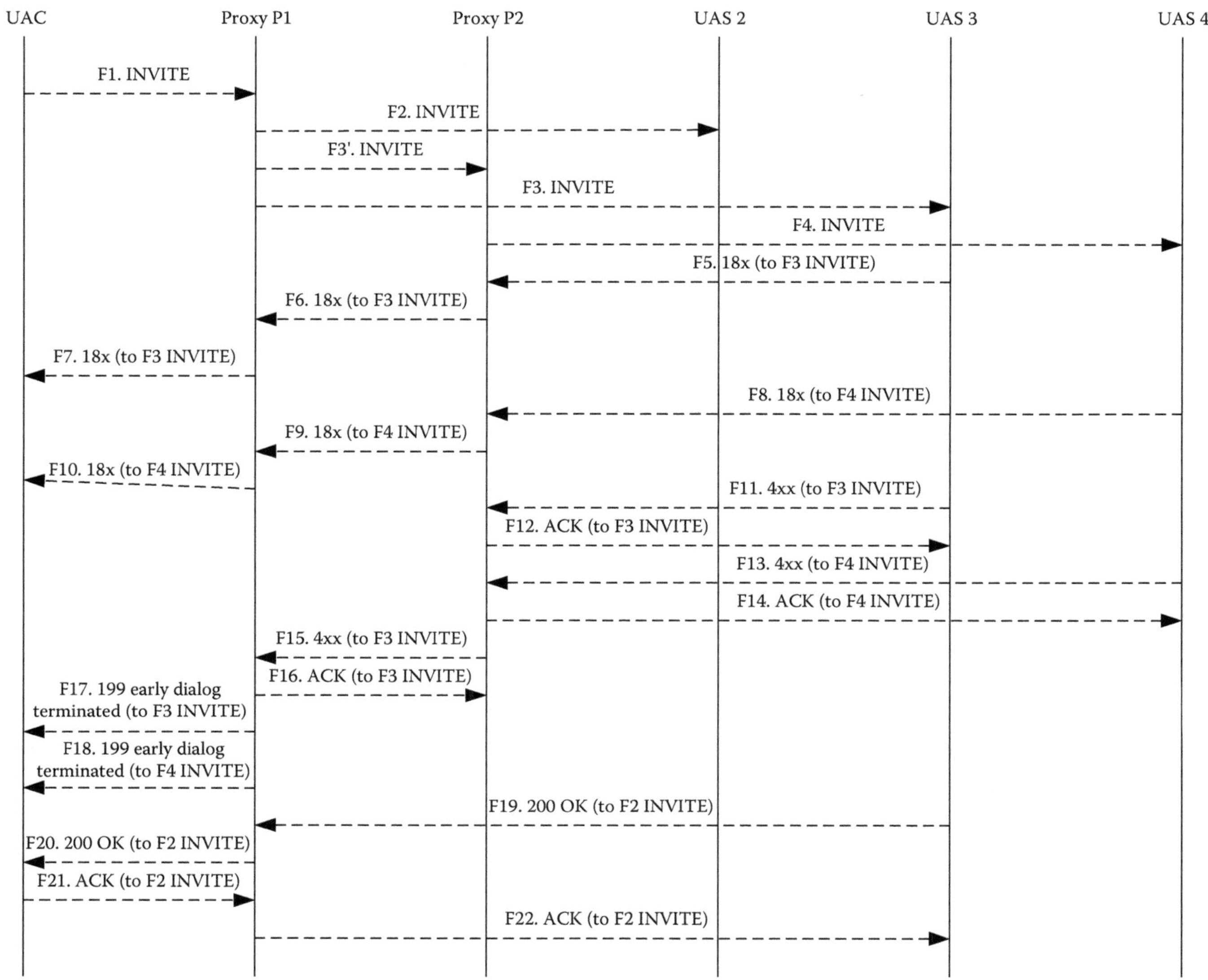

Figure 3.8 Two forking proxies, one of them generating 199. (Copyright IETF. Reproduced with permission.)

```
INVITE sip:bob@biloxi.com SIP/2.0
Via: SIP/2.0/UDP pc33.atlanta.com;
branch=z9hG4bK776asdhds
Max-Forwards: 70
To: Bob <sip:bob@biloxi.com>
From: Alice <sip:alice@atlanta.com>;
tag=1928301774
Call-ID: a84b4c76e66710@pc33.atlanta.com
CSeq: 314159 INVITE
Contact: <sip:alice@pc33.atlanta.com>
Content-Type: application/sdp
Content-Length: 142

(Alice's SDP not shown)
```

This request may be forwarded by proxies, eventually arriving at one or more UAS that can potentially accept the invitation. These UASs will frequently need to query the user about whether to accept the invitation. After some time, those UASs can accept the invitation (meaning the session is to be established) by sending a 2xx response. If the invitation is not accepted, a 3xx, 4xx, 5xx, or 6xx response is sent, depending on the reason for the rejection. Before sending a final response, the UAS can also send provisional responses (1xx) to advise the UAC of progress in contacting the called user. After possibly receiving one or more provisional responses, the UAC will get one or more 2xx responses or one non-2xx final response. Because of the protracted amount of time it can take to receive final responses to INVITE, the reliability mechanisms for INVITE transactions differ from those of other requests (like OPTIONS).

Once it receives a final response, the UAC needs to send an ACK for every final response it receives. The procedure

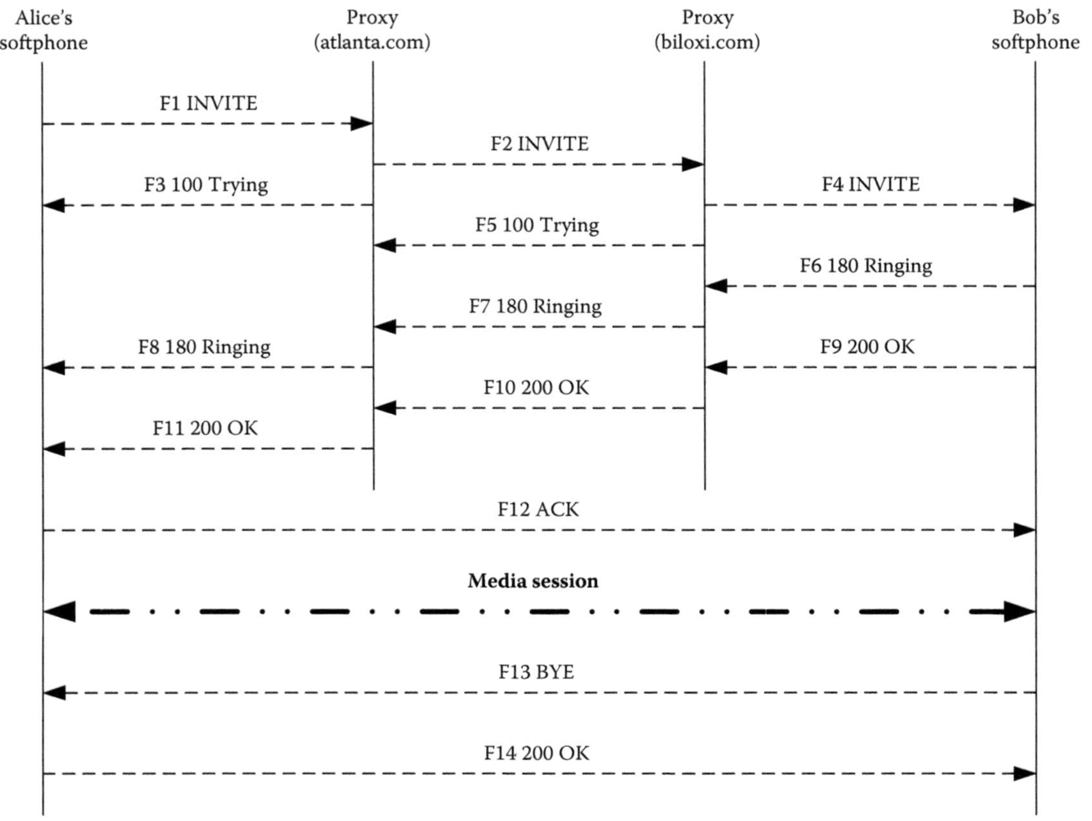

Figure 3.9 SIP session setup. (Copyright IETF. Reproduced with permission.)

for sending this ACK depends on the type of response. For final responses between 300 and 699, the ACK processing is done in the transaction layer and follows one set of rules (see Section 3.12). For 2xx responses, the ACK is generated by the UAC core. A 2xx response to an INVITE establishes a session, and it also creates a dialog between the UA that issued the INVITE and the UA that generated the 2xx response. Therefore, when multiple 2xx responses are received from different remote UAs (because the INVITE forked), each 2xx establishes a different dialog. All these dialogs are part of the same call. This section provides details on the establishment of a session using INVITE. A UA that supports INVITE must also support ACK, CANCEL, and BYE.

3.7.2 UAC Processing

3.7.2.1 Creating the Initial INVITE

Since the initial INVITE represents a request outside of a dialog, its construction follows the procedures of Section 3.6.2.1.1. Additional processing is required for the specific case of INVITE. An Allow header field (see Section 2.8.2) should be present in the INVITE. It indicates what methods can be invoked within a dialog, on the UA sending the INVITE, for the duration of the dialog. For example, a UA capable of receiving INFO requests within a dialog described in RFC 6086 (see Section 16.8) should include an Allow header field listing the INFO method. A Supported header field (Section 2.8.2) should be present in the INVITE. It enumerates all the extensions understood by the UAC. An Accept (see Section 2.8.2) header field may be present in the INVITE. It indicates which Content-Types are acceptable to the UA, in both the response received by it, and in any subsequent requests sent to it within dialogs established by the INVITE. The Accept header field is especially useful for indicating support of various session description formats. The UAC may add an Expires header field (see Section 2.8.2) to limit the validity of the invitation. If the time indicated in the Expires header field is reached and no final answer for the INVITE has been received, the UAC core should generate a CANCEL request for the INVITE, as per Section 3.2.

A UAC may also find it useful to add, among others, Subject (see Section 2.8.2), Organization (see Section 2.8.2), and User-Agent (Section 2.8.2) header fields. They all contain information related to the INVITE. The UAC may choose to add a message body to the INVITE. We have described earlier how to construct the header fields—Content-Type among others—needed to describe the message body. There are special rules for message bodies that contain a session description—their corresponding Content-Disposition is *session*. SIP uses an offer–answer model where one UA sends a session description, called the offer, which contains a proposed description of the session. The offer indicates the desired communications means (audio, video, games), parameters of those means (such as codec types), and addresses for receiving media from the answerer. The other UA responds with another session description, called the answer, which indicates which communications means are accepted, the parameters that apply to those means, and addresses for receiving media from the offerer.

An offer–answer exchange is within the context of a dialog, so that if a SIP INVITE results in multiple dialogs, each is a separate offer–answer exchange. The offer–answer model defines restrictions on when offers and answers can be made (e.g., you cannot make a new offer while one is in progress). This results in restrictions on where the offers and answers can appear in SIP messages. In this specification, offers and answers can only appear in INVITE requests and responses, and ACK. The usage of offers and answers is further restricted. For the initial INVITE transaction, the rules are as follows:

- The initial offer must be in either an INVITE or, if not there, in the first reliable nonfailure message from the UAS back to the UAC. In this specification, that is the final 2xx response.
- If the initial offer is in an INVITE, the answer must be in a reliable nonfailure message from the UAS back to the UAC that is correlated to that INVITE. For this specification, that is only the final 2xx response to that INVITE. That same exact answer may also be placed in any provisional responses sent before the answer. The UAC must treat the first session description it receives as the answer, and must ignore any session descriptions in subsequent responses to the initial INVITE.
- If the initial offer is in the first reliable nonfailure message from the UAS back to the UAC, the answer must be in the acknowledgement for that message (in this specification, ACK for a 2xx response).
- After having sent or received an answer to the first offer, the UAC may generate subsequent offers in requests based on rules specified for that method, but only if it has received answers to any previous offers and has not sent any offers to which it has not gotten an answer.
- Once the UAS has sent or received an answer to the initial offer, it must not generate subsequent offers in any responses to the initial INVITE. This means that a UAS based on this specification alone can never generate subsequent offers until completion of the initial transaction.

Concretely, the above rules specify two exchanges for UAs compliant to this specification alone—the offer is in the INVITE, and the answer in the 2xx (and possibly in a 1xx as well, with the same value), or the offer is in the 2xx, and the answer is in the ACK. All UAs that support INVITE must support these two exchanges. The SDP described in RFC 4566 (see Section 7.7) must be supported by all UAs as a means to describe sessions, and its usage for constructing offers and answers must follow the procedures defined in RFC 3264 (see Section 3.8.4). The restrictions of the offer–answer model just described only apply to bodies whose Content-Disposition header field value is session. Therefore, it is possible that both the INVITE and the ACK contain a message body (e.g., the INVITE carries a photo [Content-Disposition: render] and the ACK a session description [Content-Disposition: session]). If the Content-Disposition header field is missing, bodies of Content-Type application/SDP imply the disposition session, while other content types imply *render*. Once the INVITE has been created, the UAC follows the procedures defined for sending requests outside of a dialog (Sections 3.6 and 3.7.2). This results in the construction of a client transaction that will ultimately send the request and deliver responses to the UAC.

3.7.2.2 Processing INVITE Responses

Once the INVITE has been passed to the INVITE client transaction, the UAC waits for responses for the INVITE. If the INVITE client transaction returns a timeout rather than a response, the TU acts as if a 408 Request Timeout response had been received.

3.7.2.2.1 1xx Responses

Zero, one, or multiple provisional responses may arrive before one or more final responses are received. Provisional responses for an INVITE request can create early dialogs. If a provisional response has a tag in the To field, and if the dialog ID of the response does not match an existing dialog, one is constructed using the procedures defined in Section 3.6. The early dialog will only be needed if the UAC needs to send a request to its peer within the dialog before the initial INVITE transaction completes. Header fields present in a provisional response are applicable as long as the dialog is in the early state (e.g., an Allow header field in a provisional response contains the methods that can be used in the dialog while this is in the early state).

3.7.2.2.2 3xx Responses

A 3xx response may contain one or more Contact header field values providing new addresses where the callee might be reachable. Depending on the status code of the 3xx response (see Section 2.6), the UAC may choose to try those new addresses.

3.7.2.2.3 4xx, 5xx, and 6xx Responses

A single non-2xx final response may be received for the INVITE. 4xx, 5xx, and 6xx responses may contain a Contact header field value indicating the location where additional information about the error can be found. Subsequent final responses (which would only arrive under error conditions) must be ignored. All early dialogs are considered terminated upon reception of the non-2xx final response. After having received the non-2xx final response, the UAC core considers the INVITE transaction completed. The INVITE client transaction handles the generation of ACKs for the response (see Section 3.12).

3.7.2.2.4 2xx Responses

Multiple 2xx responses may arrive at the UAC for a single INVITE request due to a forking proxy. Each response is distinguished by the tag parameter in the To header field, and each represents a distinct dialog, with a distinct dialog identifier. If the dialog identifier in the 2xx response matches the dialog identifier of an existing dialog, the dialog must be transitioned to the *confirmed* state, and the route set for the dialog must be recomputed on the basis of the 2xx response using the procedures of Section 3.6.2.1.2. Otherwise, a new dialog in the confirmed state must be constructed using the procedures of Section 3.6.2.1. Note that the only piece of state that is recomputed is the route set. Other pieces of state, such as the highest sequence numbers (remote and local) sent within the dialog, are not recomputed. The route set is only recomputed for backwards compatibility. RFC 2543 did not mandate mirroring of the Record-Route header field in a 1xx, only 2xx. However, we cannot update the entire state of the dialog, since mid-dialog requests may have been sent within the early dialog, modifying the sequence numbers, for example.

The UAC core must generate an ACK request for each 2xx received from the transaction layer. The header fields of the ACK are constructed in the same way as for any request sent within a dialog (see Section 3.6), with the exception of the CSeq and the header fields related to authentication. The sequence number of the CSeq header field must be the same as the INVITE being acknowledged; however, the CSeq method must be ACK. The ACK must contain the same credentials as the INVITE. If the 2xx contains an offer (based on the rules above), the ACK must carry an answer in its body. If the offer in the 2xx response is not acceptable, the UAC core must generate a valid answer in the ACK and then send a BYE immediately. Once the ACK has been constructed, the procedures defined in RFC 3263 (see Section 8.2.4) are used to determine the destination address, port, and transport. However, the request is passed to the transport layer directly for transmission, rather than a client transaction.

This is because the UAC core handles retransmissions of the ACK, not the transaction layer. The ACK must be passed to the client transport every time a retransmission of the 2xx final response that triggered the ACK arrives. The UAC core considers the INVITE transaction completed 64*T1 seconds after the reception of the first 2xx response. At this point, all the early dialogs that have not transitioned to established dialogs are terminated. Once the INVITE transaction is considered completed by the UAC core, no more new 2xx responses are expected to arrive. If, after acknowledging any 2xx response to an INVITE, the UAC does not want to continue with that dialog, then the UAC must terminate the dialog by sending a BYE request as described in Section 3.10.

3.7.3 UAS Processing

3.7.3.1 Processing of the INVITE

The UAS core will receive INVITE requests from the transaction layer. It first performs the request processing procedures of Section 3.1.3, which are applied for both requests inside and outside of a dialog. Assuming these processing states are completed without generating a response, the UAS core performs the additional processing steps:

1. If the request is an INVITE that contains an Expires header field, the UAS core sets a timer for the number of seconds indicated in the header field value. When the timer fires, the invitation is considered to be expired. If the invitation expires before the UAS has generated a final response, a 487 Request Terminated response should be generated.
2. If the request is a mid-dialog request, the method-independent processing described in Section 3.6.2.2 is first applied. It might also modify the session; Section 3.8 provides details.
3. If the request has a tag in the To header field but the dialog identifier does not match any of the existing dialogs, the UAS may have crashed and restarted, or may have received a request for a different (possibly failed) UAS. Section 3.6.2.2 provides guidelines to achieve a robust behavior under such a situation.

Processing from here forward assumes that the INVITE is outside of a dialog, and is thus for the purposes of establishing a new session. The INVITE may contain a session description, in which case the UAS is being presented with an offer for that session. It is possible that the user is already a participant in that session, even though the INVITE is outside of a dialog. This can occur when a user is invited to the same multicast conference by multiple other participants. If desired, the UAS may use identifiers within the session description to detect this duplication. For example, SDP contains a session id and version number in the origin (o) field. If the user is already a member of the session, and the session parameters contained in the session description have not changed, the UAS may silently accept the INVITE (i.e., send a 2xx response without prompting the user). If the INVITE does not contain a session description, the UAS is being asked to participate in a session, and the UAC has asked that the UAS provide the offer of the session. It must provide the offer in its first nonfailure reliable message back to the UAC. In this specification, that is a 2xx response to the INVITE. The UAS can indicate progress, accept, redirect, or reject the invitation. In all of these cases, it formulates a response using the procedures described in Section 3.1.3.6.

3.7.3.1.1 Progress

If the UAS is not able to answer the invitation immediately, it can choose to indicate some kind of progress to the UAC (e.g., an indication that a phone is ringing). This is accomplished with a provisional response between 101 and 199. These provisional responses establish early dialogs and therefore follow the procedures of Section 3.6.1.1 in addition to those of Section 3.1.3.6. A UAS may send as many provisional responses as it likes. Each of these must indicate the same dialog ID. However, these will not be delivered reliably. If the UAS desires an extended period of time to answer the INVITE, it will need to ask for an *extension* in order to prevent proxies from canceling the transaction. A proxy has the option of canceling a transaction when there is a gap of 3 minutes between responses in a transaction. To prevent cancellation, the UAS must send a non-100 provisional response at every minute, to handle the possibility of lost provisional responses. An INVITE transaction can go on for extended durations when the user is placed on hold, or when interworking with PSTN systems that allow communications to take place without answering the call. The latter is common in Interactive Voice Response systems.

3.7.3.1.2 INVITE Is Redirected

If the UAS decides to redirect the call, a 3xx response is sent. A 300 Multiple Choices, 301 Moved Permanently, or 302 Moved Temporarily response should contain a Contact header field containing one or more URIs of new addresses to be tried. The response is passed to the INVITE server transaction, which will deal with its retransmissions.

3.7.3.1.3 INVITE Is Rejected

A common scenario occurs when the callee is currently not willing or able to take additional calls at this end system. A 486 Busy Here should be returned in such a scenario. If the UAS knows that no other end system will be able to accept this call, a 600 Busy Everywhere response should be sent instead. However, it is unlikely that a UAS will be able to know this in general, and thus this response will not usually be used. The response is passed to the INVITE server transaction, which will deal with its retransmissions. A UAS rejecting an offer contained in an INVITE should return a 488 Not Acceptable Here response. Such a response should include a Warning header field value explaining why the offer was rejected.

3.7.3.1.4 INVITE Is Accepted

The UAS core generates a 2xx response. This response establishes a dialog, and therefore follows the procedures of Section 3.6.1.1 in addition to those of Section 3.1.3.6. A 2xx response to an INVITE should contain the Allow header field and the Supported header field, and may contain the Accept header field. Including these header fields allows the UAC to determine the features and extensions supported by the UAS for the duration of the call, without probing. If the INVITE request contained an offer, and the UAS had not yet sent an answer, the 2xx must contain an answer. If the INVITE did not contain an offer, the 2xx must contain an offer if the UAS had not yet sent an offer.

Once the response has been constructed, it is passed to the INVITE server transaction. To ensure reliable end-to-end transport of the response, it is necessary to periodically pass the response directly to the transport until the ACK arrives. The 2xx response is passed to the transport with an interval that starts at T1 seconds and doubles for each retransmission until it reaches T2 seconds (T1 and T2 are defined in Section 3.12). Response retransmissions cease when an ACK request for the response is received. This is independent of whatever transport protocols are used to send the response. (Note that this paragraph has been updated/modified per RFC 6026.)

Since 2xx is retransmitted end-to-end, there may be hops between UAS and UAC that are UDP. To ensure reliable delivery across these hops, the response is retransmitted periodically even if the transport at the UAS is reliable. If the server retransmits the 2xx response for 64*T1 seconds without receiving an ACK, the dialog is confirmed, but the session should be terminated.

3.8 Modifying an Existing Session

A successful INVITE request (see Section 3.7) establishes both a dialog between two UAs and a session using the offer–answer model. Section 3.6 explains how to modify an existing dialog using a target refresh request (e.g., changing the remote target URI of the dialog). This section describes how to modify the actual session. This modification can involve changing addresses or ports, adding a media stream, deleting a media stream, and so on. This is accomplished by sending a new INVITE request within the same dialog that established the session. An INVITE request sent within an existing dialog is known as a re-INVITE. Note that a single re-INVITE can modify the dialog and the parameters of the session at the same time. Either the caller or callee can modify an existing session. The behavior of a UA on detection of media failure is a matter of local policy. However, automated generation of re-INVITE or BYE is not recommended to avoid flooding the network with traffic when there is congestion. In any case, if these messages are sent automatically, they should be sent after some randomized interval. Note that the paragraph above refers to automatically generated BYEs and re-INVITEs. If the user hangs up upon media failure, the UA would send a BYE request as usual.

3.8.1 UAC Behavior

The same offer–answer model that applies to session descriptions in INVITEs (Section 3.7.2.1) applies to re-INVITEs. As a result, a UAC that wants to add a media stream, for example, will create a new offer that contains this media stream, and send that in an INVITE request to its peer. It is important to note that the full description of the session, not just the change, is sent. This supports stateless session processing in various elements, and supports failover and recovery capabilities. Of course, a UAC may send a re-INVITE with no session description, in which case the first reliable nonfailure response to the re-INVITE will contain the offer (in this specification, that is a 2xx response). If the session description format has the capability for version numbers, the offerer should indicate that the version of the session description has changed. The To, From, Call-ID, CSeq, and Request-URI of a re-INVITE are set following the same rules as for regular requests within an existing dialog, described in Section 3.6.

A UAC may choose not to add an Alert-Info header field or a body with Content-Disposition *alert* to re-INVITEs because UASs do not typically alert the user upon reception of a re-INVITE. Unlike an INVITE, which can fork, a re-INVITE will never fork, and therefore, only ever generate a single final response. The reason a re-INVITE will never fork is that the Request-URI identifies the target as the UA instance it established the dialog with, rather than identifying an AOR for the user. Note that a UAC must not initiate a new INVITE transaction within a dialog while another INVITE transaction is in progress in either direction.

1. If there is an ongoing INVITE client transaction, the TU must wait until the transaction reaches the completed or terminated state before initiating the new INVITE.
2. If there is an ongoing INVITE server transaction, the TU must wait until the transaction reaches the confirmed or terminated state before initiating the new INVITE.

However, a UA may initiate a regular transaction while an INVITE transaction is in progress. A UA MAY also initiate an INVITE transaction while a regular transaction is in progress. If a UA receives a non-2xx final response to a re-INVITE, the session parameters must remain unchanged, as if no re-INVITE had been issued. Note that, as stated in Section 3.6.2.1.2, if the non-2xx final response is a 481 Call/Transaction Does Not Exist, or a 408 (Request Timeout), or no response at all is received for the re-INVITE (i.e., a timeout is returned by the INVITE client transaction), the UAC will terminate the dialog. If a UAC receives a 491 response to a re-INVITE, it should start a timer with a value *T* chosen as follows:

1. If the UAC is the owner of the Call-ID of the dialog ID (meaning it generated the value), *T* has a randomly chosen value between 2.1 and 4 seconds in units of 10 milliseconds.
2. If the UAC is not the owner of the Call-ID of the dialog ID, T has a randomly chosen value of between 0 and 2 seconds in units of 10 milliseconds.

When the timer fires, the UAC should attempt the re-INVITE once more, if it still desires for that session modification to take place. For example, if the call was already hung up with a BYE, the re-INVITE would not take place. The rules for transmitting a re-INVITE and for generating an ACK for a 2xx response to re-INVITE are the same as for the initial INVITE (Section 3.7.2.1).

3.8.2 UAS Behavior

Section 3.7.3.1 describes the procedure for distinguishing incoming re-INVITEs from incoming initial INVITEs and handling a re-INVITE for an existing dialog. A UAS that receives a second INVITE before it sends the final response to a first INVITE with a lower CSeq sequence number on the same dialog must return a 500 Server Internal Error response to the second INVITE and must include a Retry-After header field with a randomly chosen value of between 0 and 10 seconds. A UAS that receives an INVITE on a dialog while an INVITE it had sent on that dialog is in progress MUST return a 491 Request Pending response to the received INVITE. If a UA receives a re-INVITE for an existing dialog, it must check any version identifiers in the session description or, if there are no version identifiers, the content of the session description to see if it has changed. If the session description has changed, the UAS must adjust the session parameters accordingly, possibly after asking the user for confirmation. Versioning of the session description can be used to accommodate the capabilities of new arrivals to a conference, add or delete media, or change from a unicast to a multicast conference.

If the new session description is not acceptable, the UAS can reject it by returning a 488 Not Acceptable Here response for the re-INVITE. This response should include a Warning header field. If a UAS generates a 2xx response and never receives an ACK, it should generate a BYE to terminate the dialog. A UAS may choose not to generate 180 Ringing responses for a re-INVITE because UACs do not typically render this information to the user. For the same reason, UASs may choose not to use an Alert-Info header field or a body with Content-Disposition alert in responses to a re-INVITE. A UAS providing an offer in a 2xx (because the INVITE did not contain an offer) should construct the offer as if the UAS was making a brand new call, subject to the constraints of sending an offer that updates an existing session, as described in RFC 3264 (see Section 3.8.4) in the case of SDP. Specifically, this means that it should include as many media formats and media types that the UA is willing to support. The UAS must ensure that the session description overlaps with its previous session description in media formats, transports, or other parameters that require support from the peer. This is to avoid the need for the peer to reject the session description. If, however, it is unacceptable to the UAC, the UAC should generate an answer with a valid session description, and then send a BYE to terminate the session.

3.8.3 UPDATE

3.8.3.1 Overview

The SIP specified in RFC 3261 defines the INVITE method for the initiation and modification of sessions. However, this method actually affects two important pieces of state. It affects the session (the media streams SIP sets up) and also the dialog (the state that SIP itself defines). While this is reasonable in many cases, there are important scenarios in which this coupling causes complications. The primary difficulty is when aspects of the session need to be modified before the initial INVITE has been answered. An example of this situation is *early media*, a condition where the session is established, for the purpose of conveying the progress of the call, but before the INVITE itself is accepted. It is important that either caller or callee be able to modify the characteristics of that session (e.g., putting the early media on hold), before the call is answered. However, a re-INVITE cannot be used for this purpose because the re-INVITE has an impact on the state of the dialog, in addition to the session.

As a result, a solution is needed that allows the caller or callee to provide updated session information before a final response to the initial INVITE request is generated. The UPDATE method, defined in RFC 3311, fulfills that need. It can be sent by a UA within a dialog (early or confirmed) to update session parameters without affecting the dialog state itself. UPDATE allows a client to update parameters of a session (such as the set of media streams and their codecs) but has no impact on the state of a dialog. In that sense, it is like a re-INVITE, but unlike re-INVITE, it can be sent before the initial INVITE has been completed. This makes it very useful for updating session parameters within early dialogs.

3.8.3.2 Overview of Operation

The operation of this extension is straightforward. The caller begins with an INVITE transaction, which proceeds normally. Once a dialog is established, either early or confirmed, the caller can generate an UPDATE method that contains an SDP offer defined in RFC 3264 (see Section 3.8.4) for the purposes of updating the session. The response to the UPDATE method contains the answer. Similarly, once a dialog is established, the callee can send an UPDATE with an offer, and the caller places its answer in the 2xx to the UPDATE. The Allow header field is used to indicate support for the UPDATE method. There are additional constraints on when UPDATE can be used, based on the restrictions of the offer–answer model.

3.8.3.3 Determining Support for This Extension

A UAC compliant to this specification should also include an Allow header field in the INVITE request, listing the method UPDATE, to indicate its ability to receive an UPDATE request. When a UAS compliant to this specification receives an INVITE request for a new dialog, and generates a reliable provisional response containing SDP, that response should contain an Allow header field that lists the UPDATE method. This informs the caller that the callee is capable of receiving an UPDATE request at any time. An unreliable provisional response may contain an Allow header field listing the UPDATE method, and a 2xx response should contain an Allow header field listing the UPDATE method. Responses are processed normally as per RFC 3261, and in the case of reliable provisional responses, according to RFC 3262 (see Sections 9, 2.8.2, and 14). It is important to note that a reliable provisional response will always create an early dialog at the UAC. Creation of this dialog is necessary in order to receive UPDATE requests from the callee. If the response contains an Allow header field containing the value UPDATE, the UAC knows that the callee supports UPDATE, and the UAC is allowed to follow the procedures described in the next section.

3.8.3.4 UPDATE Handling

3.8.3.4.1 Sending an UPDATE

The UPDATE request is constructed as would any other request within an existing dialog, as described in Section 3.6.2.1. It may be sent for both early and confirmed dialogs, and may be sent by either caller or callee. Although UPDATE can be used on confirmed dialogs, it is recommended that a re-INVITE be used instead. This is because an UPDATE needs to be answered immediately, ruling out the possibility of user approval. Such approval will frequently be needed, and is possible with a re-INVITE.

The UAC may add optional headers for the UPDATE request. UPDATE is a target refresh request. This means that it can update the remote target of a dialog. If a UA uses an UPDATE request or response to modify the remote target while an INVITE transaction is in progress, and it is a UAS for that INVITE transaction, it must place the same value into the Contact header field of the 2xx to the INVITE that it placed into the UPDATE request or response. The rules for inclusion of offers and answers in SIP messages as defined in Section 3.7.2.1 still apply. These rules exist to guarantee a consistent view of the session state. This means that, for the caller:

- If the UPDATE is being sent before completion of the initial INVITE transaction, and the initial INVITE contained an offer, the UPDATE can contain an offer if the callee generated an answer in a reliable provisional response, and the caller has received answers to any other offers it sent in either PRACK or UPDATE, and has generated answers for any offers it received in an UPDATE from the callee.
- If the UPDATE is being sent before completion of the initial INVITE transaction, and the initial INVITE did not contain an offer, the UPDATE can contain an offer if the callee generated an offer in a reliable provisional response, and the UAC generated an answer in the corresponding PRACK. Of course, it cannot send an UPDATE if it has not received answers to any other offers it sent in either PRACK or UPDATE, or has not generated answers for any other offers it received in an UPDATE from the callee.
- If the UPDATE is being sent after the completion of the initial INVITE transaction, it cannot contain an offer if the caller has generated or received offers in a re-INVITE or UPDATE that has not been answered.

For the callee:

- If the UPDATE is being sent before the completion of the INVITE transaction, and the initial INVITE contained an offer, the UPDATE cannot be sent with an offer unless the callee has generated an answer in a reliable provisional response, has received a PRACK for that reliable provisional response, has not received any requests (PRACK or UPDATE) with offers that it has not answered, and has not sent any UPDATE requests containing offers that have not been answered.
- If the UPDATE is being sent before completion of the INVITE transaction, and the initial INVITE did not contain an offer, the UPDATE cannot be sent with an offer unless the callee has sent an offer in a reliable provisional response, received an answer in a PRACK, and has not received any UPDATE requests with offers that it has not answered, and has not sent any UPDATE requests containing offers that have not been answered.
- If the UPDATE is being sent after the completion of the initial INVITE transaction, it cannot be sent with an offer if the callee has generated or received offers in a re-INVITE or UPDATE that has not been answered.

3.8.3.4.2 Receiving an UPDATE

The UPDATE is processed as any other mid-dialog target refresh request, as described in Section 3.6.2.2. If the request is generally acceptable, processing continues as described below. This processing is nearly identical to that of Section 3.8.2, but generalized for the case of UPDATE. A UAS that receives an UPDATE before it has generated a final response to a previous UPDATE on the same dialog must return a 500 response to the new UPDATE, and must include a Retry-After header field with a randomly chosen value between 0 and 10 seconds. If an UPDATE is received that contains an offer, and the UAS has generated an offer (in an UPDATE, PRACK, or INVITE) to which it has not yet received an answer, the UAS must reject the UPDATE with a 491 response. Similarly, if an UPDATE is received that contains an offer, and the UAS has received an offer (in an UPDATE, PRACK, or INVITE) to which it has not yet generated an answer, the UAS must reject the UPDATE with a 500 response, and must include a Retry-After header field with a randomly chosen value between 0 and 10 seconds.

If a UA receives an UPDATE for an existing dialog, it must check any version identifiers in the session description or, if there are no version identifiers, the content of the session description to see if it has changed. If the session description has changed, the UAS must adjust the session parameters accordingly and generate an answer in the 2xx response. However, unlike a re-INVITE, the UPDATE must be responded to promptly, and therefore the user cannot generally be prompted to approve the session changes. If the UAS cannot change the session parameters without prompting the user, it should reject the request with a 504 response. If the new session description is not acceptable, the UAS can reject it by returning a 488 Not Acceptable Here response for the UPDATE. This response should include a Warning header field.

3.8.3.4.3 Processing the UPDATE Response

Processing of the UPDATE response at the UAC follows the rules in Section 3.6.2.1.2 for a target refresh request. Once that processing is complete, it continues as specified below. This processing is nearly identical to the processing of Section 3.8.1, but generalized for UPDATE. If a UA receives a non-2xx final response to a UPDATE, the session parameters must remain unchanged, as if no UPDATE had been issued. Note that, as stated in Section 3.6.2.1, if the non-2xx final response is a 481 Call/Transaction Does Not Exist, or a 408 Request Timeout, or no response at all is received for the UPDATE (i.e., a timeout is returned by the UPDATE client transaction), the UAC will terminate the dialog. If a UAC receives a 491 Request Pending response to a UPDATE, it should start a timer with a value *T* chosen as follows:

- If the UAC is the owner of the Call-ID of the dialog ID (meaning it generated the value), *T* has a randomly chosen value between 2.1 and 4 seconds in units of 10 milliseconds.
- If the UAC is not the owner of the Call-ID of the dialog ID, *T* has a randomly chosen value between 0 and 2 seconds in units of 10 milliseconds.

When the timer fires, the UAC should attempt the UPDATE once more, if it still desires for that session modification to take place. For example, if the call was already hung up with a BYE, the UPDATE would not take place.

3.8.3.5 Proxy Behavior

Proxy processing of the UPDATE request is identical to any other non-INVITE request.

3.8.3.6 Example Call Flow

This section presents an example call flow using the UPDATE method. The flow is shown in Figure 3.10. The caller sends an initial INVITE (F1) that contains an offer. The callee generates a 180 response (F2) with an answer to that offer. With the completion of an offer–answer exchange, the session is established, although the dialog is still in the early state. The caller generates a PRACK (F3) to acknowledge the 180, and the PRACK is answered with a 200 OK (F4). The caller decides to update some aspect of the session—to put it on hold, for example. Thus, they generate an UPDATE request (F5) with a new offer.

This offer is answered in the 200 response to the UPDATE (F6). Shortly thereafter, the callee decides to update some aspect

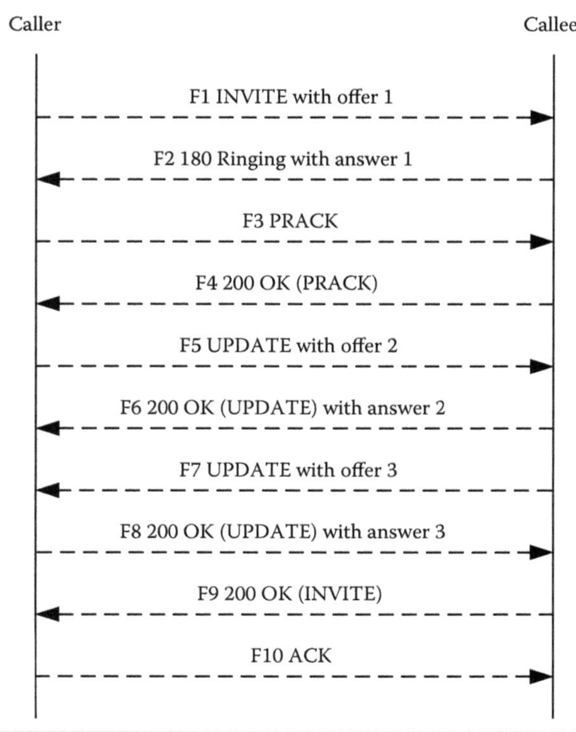

Figure 3.10 UPDATE call flow. (Copyright IETF. Reproduced with permission.)

of the session, so it generates an UPDATE request (F7) with an offer, and the answer is sent in the 200 response (F8). Finally, the callee answers the call, resulting in a 200 OK response to the INVITE (F9), and then an ACK (F10). Neither the 200 OK to the INVITE, nor the ACK, will contain SDP.

3.8.4 SDP Offer and Answer

3.8.4.1 Overview

The SDP specified in RFC 4566 (see Section 7.7) was originally conceived as a way to describe multicast sessions carried on the Mbone. The Session Announcement Protocol (SAP) defined in RFC 2974 was devised as a multicast mechanism to carry SDP messages. Although the SDP specification allows for unicast operation, it is not complete. Unlike multicast, where there is a global view of the session that is used by all participants, unicast sessions involve two participants, and a complete view of the session requires information from both participants, and agreement on parameters between them. As an example, a multicast session requires conveying a single multicast address for a particular media stream. However, for a unicast session, two addresses are needed—one for each participant. As another example, a multicast session requires an indication of which codecs will be used in the session. However, for unicast, the set of codecs needs to be determined by finding an overlap in the set supported by each participant. As a result, even though SDP has the expressiveness to describe unicast sessions, it is missing the semantics and operational details of how it is actually done.

RFC 3264 that is described here defines a mechanism by which two entities can make use of SDP to arrive at a common view of a multimedia session between them. In this model, one participant offers the other a description of the desired session from their perspective, and the other participant answers with the desired session from their perspective. This offer–answer model is most useful in unicast sessions where information from both participants is needed for the complete view of the session. The offer–answer model is used by protocols like SIP. More specifically, one participant in the session generates an SDP message that constitutes the offer—the set of media streams and codecs the offerer wishes to use, along with the IP addresses and ports the offerer would like to use to receive the media. The offer is conveyed to the other participant, called the answerer.

The answerer generates an answer, which is an SDP message that responds to the offer provided by the offerer. The answer has a matching media stream for each stream in the offer, indicating whether the stream is accepted or not, along with the codecs that will be used and the IP addresses and ports that the answerer wants to use to receive media. It is also possible for a multicast session to work similar to a unicast one; its parameters are negotiated between a pair of users as in the unicast case, but both sides send packets to the same multicast address, rather than unicast ones. This document also discusses the application of the offer–answer model to multicast streams. We also define guidelines for how the offer–answer model is used to update a session after an initial offer–answer exchange. The means by which the offers and answers are conveyed are outside the scope of this document. The offer–answer model defined here is the mandatory baseline mechanism used by SIP.

3.8.4.2 Protocol Operation

The offer–answer exchange assumes the existence of a higher-layer protocol (such as SIP) that is capable of exchanging SDP for the purposes of session establishment between agents. Protocol operation begins when one agent sends an initial offer to another agent. An offer is initial if it is outside of any context that may have already been established through the higher-layer protocol. It is assumed that the higher-layer protocol provides maintenance of some kind of context that allows the various SDP exchanges to be associated together. The agent receiving the offer may generate an answer, or it may reject the offer. The means for rejecting an offer are dependent on the higher-layer protocol. The offer–answer exchange is atomic; if the answer is rejected, the session reverts to the state before the offer (which may be absence of a session).

At any time, either agent may generate a new offer that updates the session. However, it must not generate a new offer if it has received an offer that it has not yet answered or rejected. Furthermore, it must not generate a new offer if it has generated a prior offer for which it has not yet received an answer or a rejection. If an agent receives an offer after having sent one, but before receiving an answer to it, this is considered a *glare* condition. The term glare was originally used in circuit switched telecommunications networks to describe the condition where two switches both attempt to seize the same available circuit on the same trunk at the same time. Here, it means both agents have attempted to send an updated offer at the same time. The higher-layer protocol needs to provide a means for resolving such conditions. The higher-layer protocol will need to provide a means for ordering of messages in each direction and SIP meets these requirements.

3.8.4.3 Generating the Initial Offer

The offer (and answer) must be a valid SDP message, as defined by RFC 4566 (see Section 7.7), with one exception. RFC 4566 mandates that either an e or a p line is present in the SDP message. This specification relaxes that constraint; an SDP formulated for an offer–answer application may omit both the e and p lines. The numeric value of the session id and version in the o line must be representable with a 64-bit signed integer. The initial value of the version must be less than (2**62) – 1, to avoid rollovers. Although the SDP specification allows for multiple session descriptions to be concatenated together into a large SDP message, an SDP message used in the offer–answer model must contain exactly one session description. The SDP *s=* line conveys the subject of the session, which is reasonably defined for multicast but ill defined for unicast. For unicast sessions, it is recommended that it consist of a single space character (0×20) or a dash (–).

Unfortunately, SDP does not allow the *s=* line to be empty. The SDP *t=* line conveys the time of the session. Generally, streams for unicast sessions are created and destroyed through external signaling means, such as SIP. In that case, the *t=* line should have a value of 0 0. The offer will contain zero or more media streams (each media stream is described by an *m=* line and its associated attributes). Zero media streams implies that the offerer wishes to communicate, but that the streams for the session will be added at a later time through a modified offer. The streams may be for a mix of unicast and multicast; the latter obviously implies a multicast address in the relevant *c=* line(s). Construction of each offered stream depends on whether the stream is multicast or unicast.

3.8.4.3.1 Unicast Streams

If the offerer wishes to only send media on a stream to its peer, it must mark the stream as sendonly with the *a=sendonly* attribute. We refer to a stream as being marked with a certain direction if a direction attribute was present as either a media stream attribute or a session attribute. If the offerer wishes to only receive media from its peer, it must mark the stream as recvonly. If the offerer wishes to communicate, but wishes to neither send nor receive media at this time, it must mark the stream with an *a=inactive* attribute. The inactive direction attribute is specified in RFC 3108. Note that in the case of RTP specified in RFC 3550 (see Section 7.2), Real-Time Transport Control Protocol (RTCP) is still sent and received for sendonly, recvonly, and inactive streams. That is, the directionality of the media stream has no impact on the RTCP usage. If the offerer wishes to both send and receive media with its peer, it may include an *a=sendrecv* attribute, or it may omit it, since sendrecv is the default. For recvonly and sendrecv streams, the port number and address in the offer indicate where the offerer would like to receive the media stream. For sendonly RTP streams, the address and port number indirectly indicate where the offerer wants to receive RTCP reports.

Unless there is an explicit indication otherwise, reports are sent to the port number one higher than the number indicated. The IP address and port present in the offer indicate nothing about the source IP address and source port of RTP and RTCP packets that will be sent by the offerer. A port number of zero in the offer indicates that the stream is offered but must not be used. This has no useful semantics in an initial offer, but is allowed for reasons of completeness, since the answer can contain a zero port indicating a rejected stream. Furthermore, existing streams can be terminated by setting the port to zero. In general, a port number of zero indicates that the media stream is not wanted.

The list of media formats for each media stream conveys two pieces of information, namely the set of formats (codecs and any parameters associated with the codec, in the case of RTP) that the offerer is capable of sending and/or receiving (depending on the direction attributes), and, in the case of RTP, the RTP payload type numbers used to identify those formats. If multiple formats are listed, it means that the offerer is capable of making use of any of those formats during the session. In other words, the answerer may change formats in the middle of the session, making use of any of the formats listed, without sending a new offer. For a sendonly stream, the offer should indicate those formats the offerer is willing to send for this stream. For a recvonly stream, the offer should indicate those formats the offerer is willing to receive for this stream. For a sendrecv stream, the offer should indicate those codecs that the offerer is willing to send and receive with.

For recvonly RTP streams, the payload type numbers indicate the value of the payload type field in RTP packets the offerer is expecting to receive for that codec. For sendonly RTP streams, the payload type numbers indicate the value of the payload type field in RTP packets the offerer is planning to send for that codec. For sendrecv RTP streams, the payload type numbers indicate the value of the payload type field the offerer expects to receive, and would prefer to send. However, for sendonly and sendrecv streams, the answer might indicate different payload type numbers for the same codecs, in which case, the offerer MUST send with the payload type numbers from the answer. Different payload type numbers may be needed in each direction because of interoperability concerns with H.323. As per RFC 4566 (see Section 7.7), fmtp parameters may be present to provide additional parameters of the media format. In the case of RTP streams, all media descriptions should contain *a=rtpmap* mappings from RTP payload types to encodings. If there is no a=rtpmap, the default payload type mapping, as defined by the current profile in use, for example, RFC 3551, is to be used. This allows easier migration away from static payload types.

In all cases, the formats in the *m=* line must be listed in order of preference, with the first format listed being preferred. In this case, preferred means that the recipient of the offer should use the format with the highest preference that is acceptable to it. If the ptime attribute is present for a stream, it indicates the desired packetization interval that the offerer would like to receive. The ptime attribute must be greater than zero. If the bandwidth attribute is present for a stream, it indicates the desired bandwidth that the offerer would like to receive. A value of zero is allowed, but discouraged. It indicates that no media should be sent. In the case of RTP, it would also disable all RTCP. If multiple media streams of different types are present, it means that the offerer wishes to use those streams at the same time. A typical case is an audio and a video stream as part of a videoconference. If multiple media streams of the same type are present in an offer, it means that the offerer wishes to send (and/or receive) multiple streams of that type at the same time. When sending multiple streams of the same type, it is a matter of local policy as to how each media source of that type (e.g., a video camera and VCR in the case of video) is mapped to each stream.

When a user has a single source for a particular media type, only one policy makes sense: the source is sent to each stream of the same type. Each stream may use different encodings. When receiving multiple streams of the same type, it is a matter of local policy as to how each stream is mapped to the various media sinks for that particular type (e.g., speakers or a recording device in the case of audio). There are a few constraints on the policies, however. First, when receiving multiple streams of the same type, each stream must be mapped to at least one sink for the purpose of presentation to the user. In other words, the intent of receiving multiple streams of the same type is that they should all be presented in parallel, rather than choosing just one. Another constraint is that when multiple streams are received and sent to the same sink, they must be combined in some media-specific way. For example, in the case of two audio streams, the received media from each might be mapped to the speakers. In that case, the combining operation would be to mix them. In the case of multiple instant messaging streams, where the sink is the screen, the combining operation would be to present all of them to the user interface. The third constraint is that if multiple sources are mapped to the same stream, those sources must be combined in some media-specific way before they are sent on the stream.

Although policies beyond these constraints are flexible, an agent would not generally want a policy that will copy media from its sinks to its sources unless it is a conference server (i.e., do not copy received media on one stream to another stream). A typical usage example for multiple media streams of the same type is a prepaid calling card application, where the user can press and hold the pound (#) key at any time during a call to hang up and make a new call on the same card. This requires media from the user to two destinations—the remote gateway and the DTMF processing application that looks for the pound. This could be accomplished with two media streams, one sendrecv to the gateway, and the other sendonly (from the perspective of the user) to the DTMF application. Once the offerer has sent the offer, it must be prepared to receive media for any recvonly streams described by that offer. It must be prepared to send and receive media for any sendrecv streams in the offer, and send media for any sendonly streams in the offer (of course, it cannot actually send until the peer provides an answer with the needed address and port information). In the case of RTP, even though it may receive media before the answer arrives, it will not be able to send RTCP receiver reports until the answer arrives.

3.8.4.3.2 Multicast Streams

If a session description contains a multicast media stream that is listed as receive (send) only, it means that the participants, including the offerer and answerer, can only receive (send) on that stream. This differs from the unicast view, where the directionality refers to the flow of media between offerer and answerer. Beyond that clarification, the semantics of an offered multicast stream are exactly as described in RFC 4566 (see Section 7.7).

3.8.4.4 Generating the Answer

The answer to an offered session description is based on the offered session description. If the answer is different from the offer in any way (different IP addresses, ports, etc.), the origin line must be different in the answer, since the answer is generated by a different entity. In that case, the version number in the o= line of the answer is unrelated to the version number in the o= line of the offer. For each m= line in the offer, there must be a corresponding m= line in the answer. The answer must contain exactly the same number of m= lines as the offer. This allows for streams to be matched up on the basis of their order. This implies that if the offer contained zero m= lines, the answer must contain zero m= lines. The t= line in the answer MUST equal that of the offer. The time of the session cannot be negotiated. An offered stream may be rejected in the answer, for any reason. If a stream is rejected, the offerer and answerer must not generate media (or RTCP packets) for that stream. To reject an offered stream, the port number in the corresponding stream in the answer must be set to zero. Any media formats listed are ignored. At least one must be present, as specified by SDP. Constructing an answer for each offered stream differs for unicast and multicast.

3.8.4.4.1 Unicast Streams

If a stream is offered with a unicast address, the answer for that stream must contain a unicast address. The media type of the stream in the answer must match that of the offer. If a stream is offered as sendonly, the corresponding stream must be marked as recvonly or inactive in the answer. If a media stream is listed as recvonly in the offer, the answer must be marked as sendonly or inactive in the answer. If an offered media stream is listed as sendrecv (or if there is no direction attribute at the media or session level, in which case the stream is sendrecv by default), the corresponding stream in the answer may be marked as sendonly, recvonly, sendrecv, or inactive. If an offered media stream is listed as inactive, it must be marked as inactive in the answer. For streams marked as recvonly in the answer, the m= line must contain at least one media format the answerer is willing to receive with from among those listed in the offer. The stream may indicate additional media formats, not listed in the corresponding stream in the offer, that the answerer is willing to receive. For streams marked as sendonly in the answer, the m= line must contain at least one media format the answerer is willing to send from among those listed in the offer. For streams marked as sendrecv in the answer, the m= line must contain at least one codec the answerer is willing to both send and receive, from among those listed in the offer.

The stream may indicate additional media formats, not listed in the corresponding stream in the offer, that the answerer is willing to send or receive (of course, it will not be able to send them at this time, since it was not listed in the offer). For streams marked as inactive in the answer, the list of media formats is constructed on the basis of the offer. If the offer was sendonly, the list is constructed as if the answer was recvonly. Similarly, if the offer was recvonly, the list is constructed as if the answer was sendonly, and if the offer was sendrecv, the list is constructed as if the answer was sendrecv. If the offer was inactive, the list is constructed as if the offer was actually sendrecv and the answer was sendrecv. The connection address and port in the answer indicate the address where the answerer wishes to receive media (in the case of RTP, RTCP will be received on the port that is one higher unless there is an explicit indication otherwise). This address and port MUST be present even for sendonly streams; in the case of RTP, the port one higher is still used to receive RTCP. In the case of RTP, if a particular codec was referenced with a specific payload type number in the offer, that same payload type number should be used for that codec in the answer. Even if the same payload type number is used, the answer must contain rtpmap attributes to define the payload type mappings for dynamic payload types, and should contain mappings for static payload types.

The media formats in the m= line must be listed in order of preference, with the first format listed being preferred. In this case, *preferred* means that the offerer should use the format with the highest preference from the answer. Although the answerer may list the formats in their desired order of preference, it is recommended that unless there is a specific reason, the answerer lists formats in the same relative order they were present in the offer. In other words, if a stream in the offer lists audio codecs 8, 22, and 48 (see Section 7.2.2.4), in that order, and the answerer only supports codecs 8 and 48, it is recommended that, if the answerer has no reason to change it, the ordering of codecs in the answer should be 8, 48, and not 48, 8 (see Section 7.2.2.4). This helps assure that the same codec is used in both directions.

The interpretation of fmtp parameters in an offer depends on the parameters. In many cases, those parameters describe specific configurations of the media format, and should therefore be processed as the media format value itself would be. This means that the same fmtp parameters with the same values must be present in the answer if the media format they describe is present in the answer. Other fmtp parameters are more like parameters, for which it is perfectly acceptable for each agent to use different values. In that case, the answer may contain fmtp parameters, and those may have the same values as those in the offer, or they may be different. SDP extensions that define new parameters should specify the proper interpretation in offer–answer. The answerer may include a nonzero ptime attribute for any media stream; this indicates the packetization interval that the answerer would like to receive. There is no requirement that the packetization interval be the same in each direction for a particular stream. The answerer may include a bandwidth attribute for any media stream; this indicates the bandwidth that the answerer would like the offerer to use when sending media.

The value of zero is allowed, interpreted as described earlier. If the answerer has no media formats in common for a particular offered stream, the answerer must reject that media stream by setting the port to zero. If there are no media formats in common for all streams, the entire offered session is rejected. Once the answerer has sent the answer, it must be prepared to receive media for any recvonly streams described by that answer. It must be prepared to send and receive media for any sendrecv streams in the answer, and it may send media immediately. The answerer must be prepared to receive media for recvonly or sendrecv streams using any media formats listed for those streams in the answer, and it may send media immediately. When sending media, it should use a packetization interval equal to the value of the ptime attribute in the offer, if any was present. It should send media using a bandwidth no higher than the value of the bandwidth attribute in the offer, if any was present. The answerer must send using a media format in the offer that is also listed in the answer, and should send using the most preferred media format in the offer that is also listed in the answer. In the case of RTP, it must use the payload type numbers from the offer, even if they differ from those in the answer.

3.8.4.4.2 Multicast Streams

Unlike unicast, where there is a two-sided view of the stream, there is only a single view of the stream for multicast. As such, generating an answer to a multicast offer generally involves modifying a limited set of aspects of the stream. If a multicast stream is accepted, the address and port information in the answer must match that of the offer. Similarly, the directionality information in the answer (sendonly, recvonly, or sendrecv) must equal that of the offer. This is because all participants in a multicast session need to have equivalent views of the parameters of the session, an underlying assumption of the multicast bias of RFC 4566 (see Section 7.7). The set of media formats in the answer must be equal to or be a subset of those in the offer. Removing a format is a way for the answerer to indicate that the format is not supported. The ptime and bandwidth attributes in the answer must equal the ones in the offer, if present. If not present, a nonzero ptime may be added to the answer.

3.8.4.5 Offerer Processing of the Answer

When the offerer receives the answer, it may send media on the accepted stream(s) (assuming it is listed as sendrecv or recvonly in the answer). It must send using a media format listed in the answer, and it should use the first media format listed in the answer when it does send. The reason this is a SHOULD, and not a MUST (its also a SHOULD, and not a MUST, for the answerer), is because there will oftentimes be a need to change codecs on the fly. For example, during silence periods, an agent might like to switch to a comfort noise codec. Or, if the user presses a number on the keypad, the agent might like to send that using RFCs 4733, 4734, and 5244 (see Section 16.10). Congestion control might necessitate changing to a lower rate codec based on feedback. The offerer should send media according to the value of any ptime and bandwidth attribute in the answer. The offerer may immediately cease listening for media formats that were listed in the initial offer, but not present in the answer.

3.8.4.6 Modifying the Session

At any point during the session, either participant may issue a new offer to modify the characteristics of the session. It is fundamental to the operation of the offer–answer model that the exact same offer–answer procedure defined above is used for modifying the parameters of an existing session. The offer may be identical to the last SDP provided to the other party (which may have been provided in an offer or an answer), or it may be different. We refer to the last SDP provided as the previous SDP. If the offer is the same, the answer may be the same as the previous SDP from the answerer, or it may be different. If the offered SDP is different from the previous SDP, some constraints are placed on its construction, discussed below. Note that nearly all characteristics of a media stream can be modified. Nearly all aspects of the session can be modified. New streams can be added, existing streams can be deleted, and parameters of existing streams can change. When issuing an offer that modifies the session, the o= line of the new SDP must be identical to that in the previous SDP, except that the version in the origin field must increment by one from the previous SDP.

If the version in the origin line does not increment, the SDP must be identical to the SDP with that version number. The answerer must be prepared to receive an offer that contains SDP with a version that has not changed; this is effectively a no-op. However, the answerer must generate a valid answer (which may be the same as the previous SDP from the answerer, or may be different), according to the procedures defined here. If an SDP is offered, which is different from the previous SDP, the new SDP must have a matching media stream for each media stream in the previous SDP. In other words, if the previous SDP had N m= lines, the new SDP must have at least N m= lines. The i-th media stream in the previous SDP, counting from the top, matches the i-th media stream in the new SDP, counting from the top. This matching is necessary in order for the answerer to determine which stream in the new SDP corresponds to a stream in the previous SDP. Because of these requirements, the number of m= lines in a stream never decreases, but either stays the same or increases. Deleted media streams from a previous SDP must not be removed in a new SDP; however, attributes for these streams need not be present.

3.8.4.6.1 Adding a Media Stream

New media streams are created by new additional media descriptions below the existing ones, or by reusing the *slot* used by an old media stream that had been disabled by setting its port to zero. Reusing its slot means that the new media description replaces the old one, but retains its positioning relative to other media descriptions in the SDP. New media descriptions must appear below any existing media sections. The rules for formatting these media descriptions are identical to those described earlier. When the answerer receives an SDP with more media descriptions than the previous SDP from the offerer, or it receives an SDP with a media stream in a slot where the port was previously zero, the answerer knows that new media streams are being added. These can be rejected or accepted by placing an appropriately structured media description in the answer. The procedures for constructing the new media description in the answer are described here.

3.8.4.6.2 Removing a Media Stream

Existing media streams are removed by creating a new SDP with the port number for that stream set to zero. The stream description may omit all attributes present previously, and may list just a single media format. A stream that is offered with a port of zero must be marked with port zero in the answer. Like the offer, the answer may omit all attributes present previously, and may list just a single media format from among those in the offer. Removal of a media stream implies that media is no longer sent for that stream, and any media that is received is discarded. In the case of RTP, RTCP transmission also ceases, as does processing of any received RTCP packets. Any resources associated with it can be released. The user interface might indicate that the stream has terminated, by closing the associated window on a personal computer (PC), for example.

3.8.4.6.3 Modifying Address, Port, or Transport of Media

The port number for a stream may be changed. To do this, the offerer creates a new media description, with the port number in the m= line different from the corresponding stream in the previous SDP. If only the port number is to be changed, the rest of the media stream description should remain unchanged. The offerer must be prepared to receive media on both the old and new ports as soon as the offer is sent. The offerer should not cease listening for media on the old port until the answer is received and media arrives on the new port. Doing so could result in loss of media during the transition. Received, in this case, means that the media is passed to a media sink. This means that if there is a playout buffer, the agent would continue to listen on the old port until the media on the new port reached the top of the playout buffer. At that time, it may cease listening for media on the old port. The corresponding media stream in the answer may be the same as the stream in the previous SDP from the answerer, or it may be different. If the updated stream is accepted by the answerer, the answerer should begin sending traffic for that stream to the new port immediately.

If the answerer changes the port from the previous SDP, it must be prepared to receive media on both the old and new ports as soon as the answer is sent. The answerer must not cease listening for media on the old port until media arrives on the new port. At that time, it may cease listening for media on the old port. The same is true for an offerer that sends an updated offer with a new port; it must not cease listening for media on the old port until media arrives on the new port. Of course, if the offered stream is rejected, the offerer can cease being prepared to receive using the new port as soon as the rejection is received. To change the IP address where media is sent, the same procedure is followed for changing the port number. The only difference is that the connection line is updated, not the port number. The transport for a stream may be changed. The process for doing this is identical to changing the port, except the transport is updated, not the port.

3.8.4.6.4 Changing the Set of Media Formats

The list of media formats used in the session may be changed. To do this, the offerer creates a new media description, with the list of media formats in the m= line different from the corresponding media stream in the previous SDP. This list may include new formats, and may remove formats present from the previous SDP. However, in the case of RTP, the mapping from a particular dynamic payload type number to a particular codec within that media stream must not change for the duration of a session. For example, if A generates an offer with G.711 [6] assigned to dynamic payload type number 46, payload type number 46 must refer to G.711 from that point forward in any offers or answers for that media stream within the session. However, it is acceptable for multiple payload type numbers to be mapped to the same codec, so that an updated offer could also use payload type number 72 for G.711. The mappings need to remain fixed for the duration of the session because of the loose synchronization between signaling exchanges of SDP and the media stream. The corresponding media stream in the answer is formulated as described here, and may result in a change in media formats as well.

Similarly, as described here, as soon as it sends its answer, the answerer must begin sending media using any formats in the offer that were also present in the answer, and should use the most preferred format in the offer that was also listed in the answer (assuming the stream allows for sending), and must not send using any formats that are not in the offer, even if they were present in a previous SDP from the peer. Similarly, when the offerer receives the answer, it must begin sending media using any formats in the answer, and should use the most preferred one (assuming the stream allows for sending), and must not send using any formats that are not in the answer, even if they were present in a previous SDP from the peer. When an agent ceases using a media format (by not listing that format in an offer or answer, even though it was in a previous SDP), the agent will still need to be prepared to receive media with that format for a brief time. How does it know when it can be prepared to stop receiving with that format? If it needs to know, there are three techniques that can be applied. First, the agent can change ports in addition to changing formats.

When media arrives on the new port, it knows that the peer has ceased sending with the old format, and it can cease being prepared to receive with it. This approach has the benefit of being media format independent. However, changes in ports may require changes in resource reservation or rekeying of security protocols. The second approach is to use a totally new set of dynamic payload types for all codecs when one is discarded. When media is received with one of the new payload types, the agent knows that the peer has ceased sending with the old format. This approach does not affect reservations or security contexts, but it is RTP specific and wasteful of a very small payload type space. A third approach is to use a timer. When the SDP from the peer is received, the timer is set. When it fires, the agent can cease being prepared to receive with the old format. A value of 1 minute would typically be more than sufficient. In some cases, an agent may not care and thus continually be prepared to receive with the old formats. Nothing needs to be done in this case. Of course, if the offered stream is rejected, the offer can cease being prepared to receive using any new formats as soon as the rejection is received.

3.8.4.6.5 Changing Media Types

The media type (audio, video, etc.) for a stream may be changed. It is recommended that the media type be changed (as opposed to adding a new stream), when the same logical data is being conveyed, but just in a different media format. This is particularly useful for changing between voiceband fax and fax in a single stream, which are both separate media types [7]. To do this, the offerer creates a new media description, with a new media type, in place of the description in the previous SDP that is to be changed. The corresponding media stream in the answer is formulated as described here. Assuming the stream is acceptable, the answerer should begin sending with the new media type and formats as soon as it receives the offer. The offerer must be prepared to receive media with both the old and new types until the answer is received, and media with the new type is received and reaches the top of the playout buffer.

3.8.4.6.6 Changing Media Attributes

Any other attributes in a media description may be updated in an offer or answer. Generally, an agent must send media (if the directionality of the stream allows) using the new parameters once the SDP with the change is received.

3.8.4.6.7 Putting a Unicast Media Stream on Hold

If a party in a call wants to put the other party *on hold*, that is, request that it temporarily stops sending one or more unicast media streams, a party offers the other an updated SDP. If the stream to be placed on hold was previously a sendrecv media stream, it is placed on hold by marking it as sendonly. If the stream to be placed on hold was previously a recvonly media stream, it is placed on hold by marking it inactive. This means that a stream is placed on hold separately in each direction. Each stream is placed on hold independently. The recipient of an offer for a stream on hold should not automatically return an answer with the corresponding stream on hold. An SDP with all streams on hold is referred to as held SDP.

Certain third-party call control scenarios do not work when an answerer responds to held SDP with held SDP. Typically, when a user presses hold, the agent will generate an offer with all streams in the SDP indicating a direction of sendonly, and it will also locally mute, so that no media is sent to the far end, and no media is played out. RFC 2543 (obsoleted by RFC 3261) specified that placing a user on hold was accomplished by setting the connection address to 0.0.0.0. Its usage for putting a call on hold is no longer recommended, since it does not allow for RTCP to be used with held streams, does not work with IPv6, and breaks with connection oriented media. However, it can be useful in an initial offer when the offerer knows it wants to use a particular set of media streams and formats, but does not know the addresses and ports at the time of the offer. Of course, when used, the port number must not be zero, which would specify that the stream has been disabled. An agent must be capable of receiving SDP with a connection address of 0.0.0.0, in which case it means that neither RTP nor RTCP should be sent to the peer.

3.8.4.7 Indicating Capabilities

Before an agent sends an offer, it is helpful to know if the media formats in that offer would be acceptable to the answerer. Certain protocols, like SIP, provide a means to query for such capabilities. SDP can be used in responses to such queries to indicate capabilities. This section describes how such an SDP message is formatted. Since SDP has no way to indicate that the message is for the purpose of capability indication, this is determined from the context of the higher-layer protocol. The ability of baseline SDP to indicate capabilities is very limited. It cannot express allowed parameter ranges or values, and cannot be done in parallel with an offer–answer itself. Extensions might address such limitations in the future. An SDP constructed to indicate media capabilities is structured as follows. It must be a valid SDP, except that it may omit both e= and p= lines. The t= line must be equal to 0 0. For each media type supported by the agent, there must be a corresponding media description of that type. The session ID in the origin field must be unique for each SDP constructed to indicate media capabilities.

The port must be set to zero, but the connection address is arbitrary. The usage of port zero makes sure that an SDP formatted for capabilities does not cause media streams to be established if it is interpreted as an offer or answer. The transport component of the m= line indicates the transport for that media type. For each media format of that type supported by the agent, there should be a media format listed in the m= line. In the case of RTP, if dynamic payload types are used, an rtpmap attribute must be present to bind the type to a specific format. There is no way to indicate constraints, such as how many simultaneous streams can be supported for a particular codec, and so on.

The SDP of Figure 3.11 indicates that the agent can support three audio codecs (PCMU, 1016, and GSM) and two video codecs (H.261 and H.263).

```
v=0
o=carol 28908764872 28908764872 IN IP4 100.3.6.6
s=-
t=0 0
c=IN IP4 192.0.2.4
m=audio 0 RTP/AVP 0 1 3
a=rtpmap:0 PCMU/8000
a=rtpmap:1 1016/8000
a=rtpmap:3 GSM/8000
m=video 0 RTP/AVP 31 34
a=rtpmap:31 H261/90000
a=rtpmap:34 H263/90000
```

Figure 3.11 SDP indicating capabilities.

3.8.4.8 Example Offer–Answer Exchanges

This section provides example offer–answer exchanges.

3.8.4.8.1 Basic Exchange

Assume that the caller, Alice, has included the following description in her offer. It includes a bidirectional audio stream and two bidirectional video streams, using H.261

(payload type 31) and MPEG (payload type 32). The offered SDP is

```
v=0
o=alice 2890844526 2890844526 IN IP4 host.
anywhere.com
s=
c=IN IP4 host.anywhere.com
t=0 0
m=audio 49170 RTP/AVP 0
a=rtpmap:0 PCMU/8000
m=video 51372 RTP/AVP 31
a=rtpmap:31 H261/90000
m=video 53000 RTP/AVP 32
a=rtpmap:32 MPV/90000
```

The callee, Bob, does not want to receive or send the first video stream, so he returns the SDP below as the answer:

```
v=0
o=bob 2890844730 2890844730 IN IP4 host.
example.com
s=
c=IN IP4 host.example.com
t=0 0
m=audio 49920 RTP/AVP 0
a=rtpmap:0 PCMU/8000
m=video 0 RTP/AVP 31
m=video 53000 RTP/AVP 32
a=rtpmap:32 MPV/90000
```

At some point later, Bob decides to change the port where he will receive the audio stream (from 49920 to 65422), and at the same time, add an additional audio stream as receive only, using the RTP payload format for events (RFC 4733). Bob offers the following SDP in the offer:

```
v=0
o=bob 2890844730 2890844731 IN IP4 host.
example.com
s=
c=IN IP4 host.example.com
t=0 0
m=audio 65422 RTP/AVP 0
a=rtpmap:0 PCMU/8000
m=video 0 RTP/AVP 31
m=video 53000 RTP/AVP 32
a=rtpmap:32 MPV/90000
m=audio 51434 RTP/AVP 110
a=rtpmap:110 telephone-events/8000
a=recvonly
```

Alice accepts the additional media stream, and so generates the following answer:

```
v=0
o=alice 2890844526 2890844527 IN IP4 host.
anywhere.com
s=
c=IN IP4 host.anywhere.com
t=0 0
m=audio 49170 RTP/AVP 0
a=rtpmap:0 PCMU/8000
m=video 0 RTP/AVP 31
a=rtpmap:31 H261/90000
m=video 53000 RTP/AVP 32
a=rtpmap:32 MPV/90000
m=audio 53122 RTP/AVP 110
a=rtpmap:110 telephone-events/8000
a=sendonly
```

3.8.4.9 One of N Codec Selection

A common occurrence in embedded phones is that the Digital Signal Processor (DSP) used for compression can support multiple codecs at a time; however, once that codec is selected, it cannot be readily changed on the fly. This example shows how a session can be set up using an initial offer–answer exchange, followed immediately by a second one to lock down the set of codecs. The initial offer from Alice to Bob indicates a single audio stream with the three audio codecs that are available in the DSP. The stream is marked as inactive, since media cannot be received until a codec is locked down:

```
v=0
o=alice 2890844526 2890844526 IN IP4 host.
anywhere.com
s=
c=IN IP4 host.anywhere.com
t=0 0
m=audio 62986 RTP/AVP 0 4 18
a=rtpmap:0 PCMU/8000
a=rtpmap:4 G723/8000
a=rtpmap:18 G729/8000
a=inactive
```

Bob can support dynamic switching between PCMU and G.723. So, he sends the following answer:

```
v=0
o=bob 2890844730 2890844731 IN IP4 host.
example.com
s=
c=IN IP4 host.example.com
t=0 0
m=audio 54344 RTP/AVP 0 4
a=rtpmap:0 PCMU/8000
a=rtpmap:4 G723/8000
a=inactive
```

Alice can then select any one of these two codecs. So, she sends an updated offer with a sendrecv stream:

```
v=0
o=alice 2890844526 2890844527 IN IP4 host.
anywhere.com
s=
```

```
c=IN IP4 host.anywhere.com
t=0 0
m=audio 62986 RTP/AVP 4
a=rtpmap:4 G723/8000
a=sendrecv
```

Bob accepts the single codec:

```
v=0
o=bob 2890844730 2890844732 IN IP4 host.
example.com
s=
c=IN IP4 host.example.com
t=0 0
m=audio 54344 RTP/AVP 4
a=rtpmap:4 G723/8000
a=sendrecv
```

If the answerer (Bob) was only capable of supporting one-of-*N* codecs, Bob would select one of the codecs from the offer, and place that in his answer. In this case, Alice would do a re-INVITE to activate that stream with that codec. As an alternative to using a=inactive in the first exchange, Alice can list all codecs, and as soon as she receives media from Bob, generate an updated offer locking down the codec to the one just received. Of course, if Bob only supports one-of-*N* codecs, there would only be one codec in his answer, and in this case, there is no need for a re-INVITE to lock down to a single codec.

3.8.4.10 Current Offer–Answer Model Usage Summary

The description of the offer–answer model in SIP is dispersed across multiple RFCs. RFC 6337 summarizes all the current usages of the offer–answer model in SIP communication. We have not provided all those usage examples of the offer–answer model in SIP for the sake of brevity.

3.8.5 Re-INVITE and Target Refresh Request Handling in SIP

The procedures for handling SIP re-INVITEs are described in RFC 3261 (see Section 3.8). Implementation and deployment experience has uncovered a number of issues with the original documentation, and this specification (RFC 6141) that is described here provides additional procedures that update the original specification to address those issues. In particular, this document defines in which situations a UAS should generate a success response and in which situations a UAS should generate an error response to a re-INVITE. Additionally, this document defines further details of procedures related to target refresh requests. As discussed in RFC 3261 (see Section 3.8), an INVITE request sent within an existing dialog is known as a re-INVITE. A re-INVITE is used to modify session parameters, dialog parameters, or both. That is, a single re-INVITE can change both the parameters of its associated session (e.g., changing the IP address where a media stream is received) and the parameters of its associated dialog (e.g., changing the remote target of the dialog). A re-INVITE can change the remote target of a dialog because it is a target refresh request, as defined in RFC 3261 (see Section 2.2).

A re-INVITE transaction has an offer–answer (RFC 3264, see Section 3.8.4) exchange associated with it. The UAC generating a given re-INVITE can act as the offerer or as the answerer. A UAC willing to act as the offerer includes an offer in the re-INVITE. The UAS then provides an answer in a response to the re-INVITE. A UAC willing to act as answerer does not include an offer in the re-INVITE. The UAS then provides an offer in a response to the re-INVITE becoming, thus, the offerer. Certain transactions within a re-INVITE (e.g., UPDATE, see Section 3.8.3) can also have offer–answer exchanges associated to them. A UA can act as the offerer or the answerer in any of these transactions regardless of whether the UA was the offerer or the answerer in the umbrella re-INVITE transaction. There has been some confusion among implementers regarding how a UAS should handle re-INVITEs. In particular, implementers requested clarification on which type of response a UAS should generate in different situations. In this document, we clarify these issues. Additionally, there has also been some confusion among implementers regarding target refresh requests, which include but are not limited to re-INVITEs. In this document, we also clarify the process by which remote targets are refreshed. Indented passages such as this one are used in this document to provide additional information and clarifying text. They do not contain normative protocol behavior.

3.8.5.1 Changing the Session State during a Re-INVITE

The following subsections discuss how to change the state of the session during a re-INVITE transaction.

3.8.5.1.1 Background on Re-INVITE Handling by UASs

Eventually, a UAS receiving a re-INVITE will need to generate a response to it. Some re-INVITEs can be responded to immediately because their handling does not require user interaction (e.g., changing the IP address where a media stream is received). The handling of other re-INVITEs requires user interaction (e.g., adding a video stream to an audio-only session). Therefore, these re-INVITEs cannot be responded to immediately. An error response to a re-INVITE has the following semantics. As specified in RFC

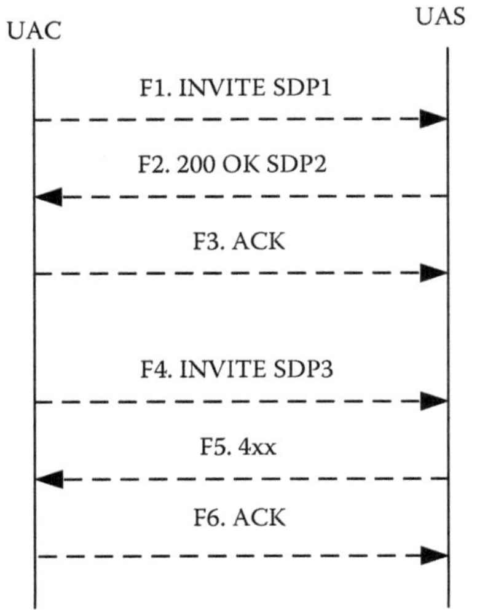

Figure 3.12 Rejection of a re-INVITE. (Copyright IETF. Reproduced with permission.)

3261 (see Section 3.3.1.3), if a re-INVITE is rejected, no state changes are performed. These state changes include state changes associated to the re-INVITE transaction and all other transactions within the re-INVITE (this section deals with changes to the session state; target refreshes are discussed in the next section). That is, the session state is the same as before the re-INVITE was received. The example in Figure 3.12 illustrates this point.

The UAs perform an offer–answer exchange to establish an audio-only session:

SDP1:

```
m=audio 30000 RTP/AVP 0
```

SDP2:

```
m=audio 31000 RTP/AVP 0
```

At a later point, the UAC sends a re-INVITE (4) in order to add a video stream to the session.

SDP3:

```
m=audio 30000 RTP/AVP 0
m=video 30002 RTP/AVP 31
```

The UAS is configured to automatically reject video streams. Consequently, the UAS returns an error response (F5). At that point, the session parameters in use are still those resulting from the initial offer–answer exchange, which are described by SDP1 and SDP2. That is, the session state is the same as before the re-INVITE was received. In the previous example, the UAS rejected all the changes requested in the re-INVITE by returning an error response. However, there are situations where a UAS wants to accept some but not all the changes requested in a re-INVITE. In these cases, the UAS generates a 200 OK response with a SDP indicating which changes were accepted and which were not. The example in Figure 3.13 illustrates this point.

The UAs perform an offer–answer exchange to establish an audio-only session:

SDP1:

```
m=audio 30000 RTP/AVP 0
c=IN IP4 192.0.2.1
```

SDP2:

```
m=audio 31000 RTP/AVP 0
c=IN IP4 192.0.2.5
```

At a later point, the UAC moves to an access that provides a higher bandwidth. Therefore, the UAC sends a re-INVITE (F4) in order to change the IP address where it receives the audio stream to its new IP address and add a video stream to the session.

SDP3:

```
m=audio 30000 RTP/AVP 0
c=IN IP4 192.0.2.2
m=video 30002 RTP/AVP 31
c=IN IP4 192.0.2.2
```

The UAS is automatically configured to reject video streams. However, the UAS needs to accept the change of the audio stream's remote IP address. Consequently, the UAS returns a 200 OK response and sets the port of the video stream to zero in its SDP.

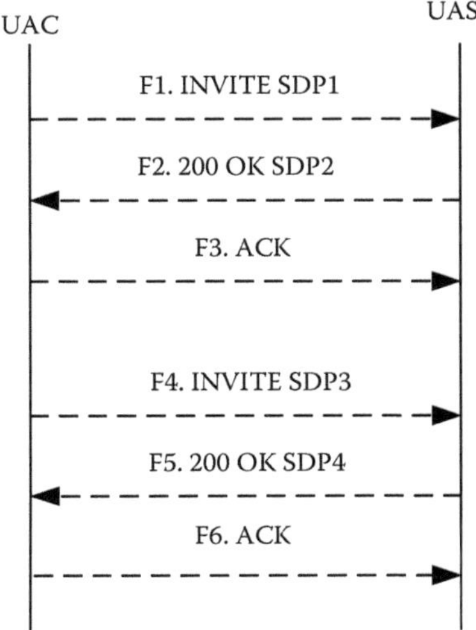

Figure 3.13 Automatic rejection of a video stream. (Copyright IETF. Reproduced with permission.)

SDP4:

```
m=audio 31000 RTP/AVP 0
c=IN IP4 192.0.2.5
m=video 0 RTP/AVP 31
```

In the previous example, the UAS was configured to automatically reject the addition of video streams. The example in Figure 3.14 assumes that the UAS requires its user's input in order to accept or reject the addition of a video stream and uses reliable provisional responses (RFC 3262, see Section 2.8) (PRACK transactions are not shown for clarity).

Everything up to (F4) is identical to the previous example. In (F5), the UAS accepts the change of the audio stream's remote IP address but does not accept the video stream yet (it provides a null IP address instead of setting the stream to inactive because inactive streams still need to exchange RTCP traffic).

SDP4:

```
m=audio 31000 RTP/AVP 0
c=IN IP4 192.0.2.5
m=video 31002 RTP/AVP 31
c=IN IP4 0.0.0.0
```

At a later point, the UAS's user rejects the addition of the video stream. Consequently, the UAS sends an UPDATE request (F6) setting the port of the video stream to zero in its offer.

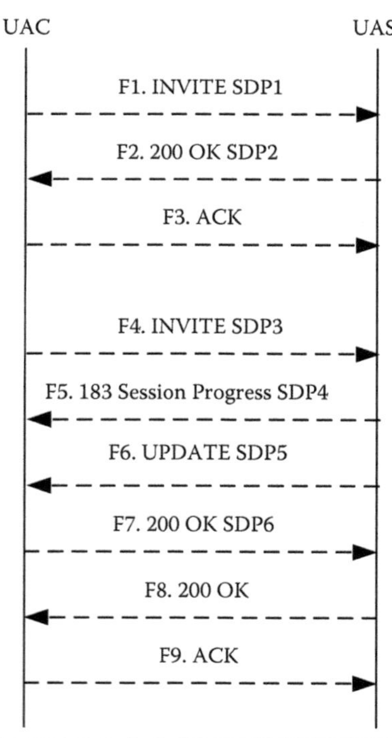

Figure 3.14 Manual rejection of a video stream by user. (Copyright IETF. Reproduced with permission.)

SDP5:

```
m=audio 31000 RTP/AVP 0
c=IN IP4 192.0.2.5
m=video 0 RTP/AVP 31
c=IN IP4 0.0.0.0
```

The UAC returns a 200 OK response (F7) to the UPDATE with the following answer:

SDP6:

```
m=audio 30000 RTP/AVP 0
c=IN IP4 192.0.2.2
m=video 0 RTP/AVP 31
```

The UAS now returns a 200 OK response (F8) to the re-INVITE. In all the previous examples, the UAC of the re-INVITE transaction was the offerer. Examples with UACs acting as the answerers would be similar.

3.8.5.1.2 Problems with Error Responses and Already Executed Changes

The earlier section contains examples on how a UAS rejects all the changes requested in a re-INVITE without executing any of them by returning an error response (Figure 3.12), and how a UAS executes some of the changes requested in a re-INVITE and rejects some of them by returning a 2xx response (Figures 3.13 and 3.14). A UAS can accept and reject different sets of changes simultaneously (Figure 3.13) or at different times (Figure 3.14). The scenario that created confusion among implementers consists of a UAS that receives a re-INVITE, executes some of the changes requested in it, and then wants to reject all those already executed changes and revert to the pre-re-INVITE state. Such a UAS may consider returning an error response to the re-INVITE (the message flow would be similar to the one in Figure 3.12), or using an UPDATE request to revert to the pre-re-INVITE state and then returning a 2xx response to the re-INVITE (the message flow would be similar to the one in Figure 24.5).

This section explains the problems associated with returning an error response in these circumstances. To avoid these problems, the UAS should use the latter option (UPDATE request plus a 2xx response). The next two sections contain the normative statements needed to avoid these problems. The reason for not using an error response to undo already executed changes is that an error response to a re-INVITE for which changes have already been executed (e.g., as a result of UPDATE transactions or reliable provisional responses) is effectively requesting a change in the session state. However, the UAC has no means to reject that change if it is unable to execute them. That is, if the UAC is unable to revert to the pre-re-INVITE state, it will not be able to communicate this fact to the UAS.

3.8.5.1.3 UAS Behavior

UASs should only return an error response to a re-INVITE if no changes to the session state have been executed since the re-INVITE was received. Such an error response indicates that no changes have been executed as a result of the re-INVITE or any other transaction within it. If any of the changes requested in a re-INVITE or in any transaction within it have already been executed, the UAS should return a 2xx response. A change to the session state is considered to have been executed if an offer–answer without preconditions (RFC 4032, see Sections 3.8.3 and 15.4.12) for the stream has completed successfully, or the UA has sent or received media using the new parameters. Connection establishment messages (e.g., TCP SYN), connectivity checks, for example, when using Interactive Connectivity Establishment (ICE) (RFC 5245, see Section 14.3), and any other messages used in the process of meeting the preconditions for a stream are not considered media. Normally, a UA receiving media can easily detect when the new parameters for the media stream are used (e.g., media is received on a new port). However, in some scenarios, the UA will have to process incoming media packets to detect whether they use the old or new parameters.

The successful completion of an offer–answer exchange without preconditions indicates that the new parameters for the media stream are already considered to be in use. The successful completion of an offer–answer exchange with preconditions means something different. The fact that all mandatory preconditions for the stream are met indicates that the new parameters for the media stream are ready to be used. However, they will not actually be used until the UAS decides to use them. During a session establishment, the UAS can wait before using the media parameters until the callee starts being alerted or until the callee accepts the session. During a session modification, the UAS can wait until its user accepts the changes to the session. When dealing with streams where the UAS sends media more or less continuously, the UAC notices that the new parameters are in use because the UAC receives media that uses the new parameters. However, this mechanism does not work with other types of streams. Therefore, it is recommended that when a UAS decides to start using the new parameters for a stream for which all mandatory preconditions have been met, the UAS either sends media using the new parameters or sends a new offer where the precondition-related attributes for the stream have been removed. As indicated above, the successful completion of an offer–answer exchange without preconditions indicates that the new parameters for the media stream are already considered to be in use.

3.8.5.1.4 UAC Behavior

A UAC that receives an error response to a re-INVITE that undoes already executed changes within the re-INVITE may be facing a legacy UAS that does not support this specification (i.e., a UAS that does not follow the guidelines described earlier). There are also certain race condition situations that get both UAs out of synchronization. To cope with these race condition situations, a UAC that receives an error response to a re-INVITE for which changes have been already executed should generate a new re-INVITE or UPDATE request in order to make sure that both UAs have a common view of the state of the session (the UAC uses the criteria described in the earlier section in order to decide whether or not changes have been executed for a particular stream). The purpose of this new offer–answer exchange is to synchronize both UAs, not to request changes that the UAS may choose to reject. Therefore, session parameters in the offer–answer exchange should be as close to those in the pre-re-INVITE state as possible.

3.8.5.1.5 Glare Situations

RFC 3264 (see Section 3.8.4) defines glare conditions as a UA receiving an offer after having sent one but before having received an answer to it. That section specifies rules to avoid glare situations in most cases. When, despite following those rules, a glare condition occurs (as a result of a race condition), it is handled as specified in RFC 3261 (see Sections 3.8.1 and 3.8.2). The UAS returns a 491 Request Pending response and the UAC retries the offer after a randomly selected time, which depends on which UA is the owner of the Call-ID of the dialog. The rules in RFC 3261 not only cover collisions between re-INVITEs that contain offers, but they also cover collisions between two re-INVITEs in general, even if they do not contain offers. RFC 3311 (see Section 3.8.3) extends those rules to also cover collisions between an UPDATE request carrying an offer and another message (UPDATE, PRACK, or INVITE) also carrying an offer. The rules in RFC 3261 do not cover collisions between an UPDATE request and a non-2xx final response to a re-INVITE. Since both the UPDATE request and the reliable response could be requesting changes to the session state, it would not be clear which changes would need to be executed first. However, the procedures discussed in the earlier section already cover this type of situation. Therefore, there is no need to specify further rules here.

3.8.5.1.6 Example of UAS Behavior

This section contains an example of a UAS that implements this specification using an UPDATE request and a 2xx response to a re-INVITE in order to revert to the pre-re-INVITE state. The example shown in Figure 3.15 assumes that the UAS requires its user's input in order to accept or reject the addition of a video stream and uses reliable provisional responses (RFC 3262, see Sections 2.5, 2.8, and 2.10) (PRACK transactions are not shown for clarity).

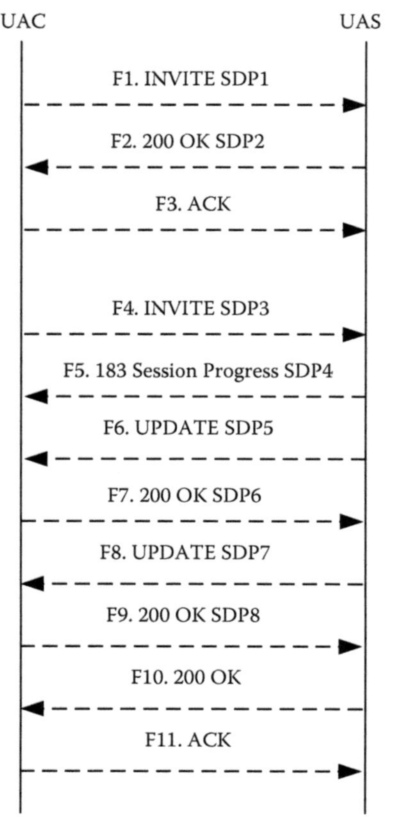

Figure 3.15 Rejection of a video stream by user. (Copyright IETF. Reproduced with permission.)

The UAs perform an offer–answer exchange to establish an audio-only session:

SDP1:

```
m=audio 30000 RTP/AVP 0
c=IN IP4 192.0.2.1
SDP2:
m=audio 31000 RTP/AVP 0
c=IN IP4 192.0.2.5
```

At a later point, the UAC sends a re-INVITE (4) in order to add a new codec to the audio stream and to add a video stream to the session.

SDP3:

```
m=audio 30000 RTP/AVP 0 3
c=IN IP4 192.0.2.1
m=video 30002 RTP/AVP 31
c=IN IP4 192.0.2.1
```

In (F5), the UAS accepts the addition of the audio codec but does not accept the video stream yet (it provides a null IP address instead of setting the stream to inactive because inactive streams still need to exchange RTCP traffic).

SDP4:

```
m=audio 31000 RTP/AVP 0 3
c=IN IP4 192.0.2.5
m=video 31002 RTP/AVP 31
c=IN IP4 0.0.0.0
```

At a later point, the UAC sends an UPDATE request (F6) to remove the original audio codec from the audio stream (the UAC could have also used the PRACK to (F5) to request this change).

SDP5:

```
m=audio 30000 RTP/AVP 3
c=IN IP4 192.0.2.1
m=video 30002 RTP/AVP 31
c=IN IP4 192.0.2.1
```

SDP6:

```
m=audio 31000 RTP/AVP 3
c=IN IP4 192.0.2.5
m=video 31002 RTP/AVP 31
c=IN IP4 0.0.0.0
```

Yet, at a later point, the UAS's user rejects the addition of the video stream. Additionally, the UAS decides to revert to the original audio codec. Consequently, the UAS sends an UPDATE request (F8) setting the port of the video stream to zero and offering the original audio codec in its SDP.

SDP7:

```
m=audio 31000 RTP/AVP 0
c=IN IP4 192.0.2.5
m=video 0 RTP/AVP 31
c=IN IP4 0.0.0.0
```

The UAC accepts the change in the audio codec in its 200 OK response (F9) to the UPDATE request.

SDP8:

```
m=audio 30000 RTP/AVP 0
c=IN IP4 192.0.2.1
m=video 0 RTP/AVP 31
c=IN IP4 192.0.2.1
```

The UAS now returns a 200 OK response (F10) to the re-INVITE. Note that the media state after this 200 (OK) response is the same as the pre-re-INVITE media state.

3.8.5.1.7 Example of UAC Behavior

Figure 3.16 shows an example of a race condition situation in which the UAs end up with different views of the state of the session.

The UAs in Figure 3.16 are involved in a session that, just before the message flows in the figures starts, includes a sendrecv audio stream and an inactive video stream. UA1 sends a re-INVITE (F1) requesting to make the video stream sendrecv.

SDP1:

```
m=audio 20000 RTP/AVP 0
a=sendrecv
m=video 20002 RTP/AVP 31
a=sendrecv
```

UA2 is configured to automatically accept incoming video streams but to ask for user input before generating an outgoing video stream. Therefore, UAS2 makes the video stream recvonly by returning a 183 Session Progress response (F2).

SDP2:

```
m=audio 30000 RTP/AVP 0
a=sendrecv
m=video 30002 RTP/AVP 31
a=recvonly
```

When asked for input, UA2's user chooses not to have either incoming or outgoing video. To make the video stream inactive, UA2 returns a 4xx error response (F5) to the re-INVITE. The ACK request (F6) for this error response is generated by the proxy between both UAs. Note that this error response undoes already executed changes. Thus, UA2 is a legacy UA that does not support this specification. The proxy relays the 4xx response (F7) toward UA1. However, the 4xx response (F7) takes time to arrive to UA1 (e.g., the response may have been sent over UDP and the first few retransmissions were lost). In the meantime, UA2's user decides to put the audio stream on hold. UA2 sends an UPDATE request (F8) making the audio stream recvonly. The video stream, which is inactive, is not modified and, thus, continues being inactive.

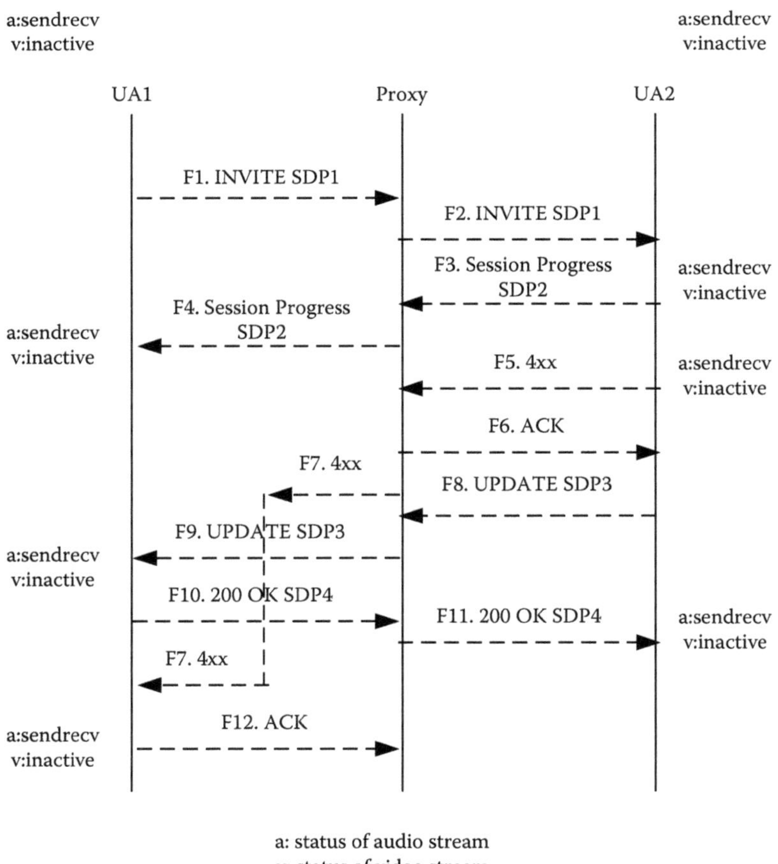

Figure 3.16 Message flow with race condition. (Copyright IETF. Reproduced with permission.)

SDP3:

```
m=audio 30000 RTP/AVP 0
a=recvonly
m=video 30002 RTP/AVP 31
a=inactive
```

The proxy relays the UPDATE request (F9) to UA1. The UPDATE request (F9) arrives at UA1 before the 4xx response (F7) that had been previously sent. UA1 accepts the changes in the UPDATE request and returns a 200 OK response (F10) to it.

SDP4:

```
m=audio 20000 RTP/AVP 0
a=sendonly
m=video 30002 RTP/AVP 31
a=inactive
```

At a later point, the 4xx response (F7) finally arrives at UA1. This response makes the session return to its pre-re-INVITE state. Therefore, for UA1, the audio stream is sendrecv and the video stream is inactive. However, for UA2, the audio stream is recvonly (the video stream is also inactive). After the message flow in Figure 3.16, following the recommendations in this section, when UA1 received an error response (F7) that undid already executed changes, UA1 would generate an UPDATE request with an SDP reflecting the pre-re-INVITE state (i.e., sendrecv audio and inactive video). UA2 could then return a 200 OK response to the UPDATE request making the audio stream recvonly, which is the state UA2's user had requested. Such an UPDATE transaction would get the UAs back into synchronization.

3.8.5.1.8 Clarifications on Canceling Re-INVITEs

RFC 3261 (see Section 3.2) specifies the behavior of a UAS responding to a CANCEL request. Such a UAS responds to the INVITE request with a 487 Request Terminated at the SHOULD level. Per the rules specified in the earlier section, if the INVITE request was a re-INVITE and some of its requested changes had already been executed, the UAS would return a 2xx response instead.

3.8.5.2 Refreshing a Dialog's Targets

The following sections discuss how to refresh the targets of a dialog.

3.8.5.2.1 Background and Terminology on a Dialog's Targets

As described in RFC 3261 (see Section 3.6), a UA involved in a dialog keeps a record of the SIP or SIPS URI at which it can communicate with a specific instance of its peer (this is called the *dialog's remote target URI* and is equal to the URI contained in the Contact header of requests and responses it receives from the peer). This document introduces the complementary concept of the *dialog's local target URI*, defined as a UA's record of the SIP or SIPS URI at which the peer can communicate with it (equal to the URI contained in the Contact header of requests and responses it sends to the peer). These terms are complementary because the dialog's remote target URI according to one UA is the dialog's local target URI according to the other UA, and vice versa.

3.8.5.2.2 Background on Target Refresh Requests

A target refresh request is defined as follows in RFC 3261 (see Section 2.2): a target refresh request sent within a dialog is defined as a request that can modify the remote target of the dialog. Additionally, 2xx responses to target refresh requests can also update the remote target of the dialog. As discussed in RFC 3261 (see Section 3.6), re-INVITEs are target refresh requests. RFC 3261 specifies the behavior of UASs receiving target refresh requests and of UACs receiving a 2xx response for a target refresh request.

> RFC 3261 (see Section 3.6.2.2) says:
>
> When a UAS receives a target-refresh request, it must replace the dialog's remote target URI with the URI from the Contact header field in that request, if present.
>
> RFC 3261 (see Section 3.6.2.1.2) says:
>
> When a UAC receives a 2xx response to a target refresh request, it must replace the dialog's remote target URI with the URI from the Contact header field in that response, if present.

The fact that re-INVITEs can be long-lived transactions and can have other transactions within them makes it necessary to revise these rules. The next section specifies new rules for the handling of target refresh requests. Note that the new rules apply to any target refresh request, not only to re-INVITEs.

3.8.5.2.3 Clarification on the Atomicity of Target Refresh Requests

The local and remote targets of a dialog are special types of state information because of their essential role in the exchange of SIP messages between UAs in a dialog. A UA involved in a dialog receives the remote target of the dialog from the remote UA. The UA uses the received remote target to send SIP requests to the remote UA. The dialog's local target is a piece of state information that is not meant to be negotiated. When a UA changes its local target (i.e., the UA changes its IP address), the UA simply communicates its new local target to the remote UA (e.g., the UA communicates its new IP address to the remote UA to remain reachable by the remote UA). UAs need to follow the behavior specified in the next few sections of this specification (RFC 6141) instead of that specified in RFC 3261, which was discussed in the earlier section. The new behavior regarding target refresh requests implies that a target refresh request can, in some cases, update the remote target even if the request is responded to with a final error response. This means that target refresh requests are not atomic.

3.8.5.2.4 UA Updating the Dialog's Local Target in a Request

To update its local target, a UA can send a target refresh request. If the UA receives an error response to the target refresh request, the remote UA has not updated its remote target. This allows UASs to authenticate target refresh requests (RFC 3261, see Section 19.4). If the UA receives a reliable provisional response or a 2xx response to the target refresh request, or the UA receives an in-dialog request on the new local target, the remote UA has updated its remote target. The UA can consider the target refresh operation completed. Even if the target request was a re-INVITE and the final response to the re-INVITE was an error response, the UAS would not revert to the pre-re-INVITE remote target.

A UA should not use the same target refresh request to refresh the target and to make session changes unless the session changes can be trivially accepted by the remote UA (e.g., an IP address change). Piggybacking a target refresh with more complicated session changes would make it unnecessarily complicated for the remote UA to accept the target refresh while rejecting the session changes. Only in case the target refresh request is a re-INVITE and the UAS supports reliable provisional response or UPDATE requests, the UAC may piggyback session changes and a target refresh in the same re-INVITE.

3.8.5.2.5 UA Updating the Dialog's Local Target in a Response

A UA processing an incoming target refresh request can update its local target by returning a reliable provisional response or a 2xx response to the target refresh request. The response needs to contain the updated local target URI in its Contact header field. On sending the response, the UA can consider the target refresh operation completed.

3.8.5.2.6 Request Updating the Dialog's Remote Target

The behavior of a UA after having received a target refresh request updating the remote target is as follows: if the UA receives a target refresh request that has been properly authenticated (RFC 3261, see Section 19.4), the UA should generate a reliable provisional response or a 2xx response to the target refresh request. If generating such responses is not possible (e.g., the UA does not support reliable provisional responses and needs user input before generating a final response), the UA should send an in-dialog request to the remote UA using the new remote target (if the UA does not need to send a request for other reasons, the UAS can send an UPDATE request). On sending a reliable provisional response or a 2xx response to the target refresh request, or a request to the new remote target, the UA must replace the dialog's remote target URI with the URI from the Contact header field in the target refresh request.

Reliable provisional responses in SIP are specified in RFC 3262 (see Sections 2.5, 2.8, and 2.10). In this document, reliable provisional responses are those that use the mechanism defined in RFC 3262. Other specifications may define ways to send provisional responses reliably using non-SIP mechanisms (e.g., using media-level messages to acknowledge the reception of the SIP response). For the purposes of this document, provisional responses using those non-SIP mechanisms are considered unreliable responses. Note that non-100 provisional responses are only applicable to INVITE transactions (RFC4320, see Section 3.12.2.5). If instead of sending a reliable provisional response or a 2xx response to the target refresh request, or a request to the new target, the UA generates an error response to the target refresh request, the UA must not update its dialog's remote target.

3.8.5.2.7 Response Updating the Dialog's Remote Target

If a UA receives a reliable provisional response or a 2xx response to a target refresh request, the UA must replace the dialog's remote target URI with the URI from the Contact header field in that response, if present. If a UA receives an unreliable provisional response to a target refresh request, the UA must not refresh the dialog's remote target.

3.8.5.2.8 Race Conditions and Target Refreshes

SIP provides request ordering by using the Cseq header field. That is, a UA that receives two requests at roughly the same time can know which one is newer. However, SIP does not provide ordering between responses and requests. For example, if a UA receives a 200 OK response to an UPDATE request and an UPDATE request at roughly the same time, the UA cannot know which one was sent last. Since both messages can refresh the remote target, the UA needs to know which message was sent last in order to know which remote target needs to be used.

RFC 6141 specifies the following rule to avoid the situation just described. If the protocol allows a UA to use a target refresh request at the point in time that the UA wishes to refresh its local target, the UA must use a target refresh request instead of a response to refresh its local target. This rule implies that a UA only uses a response (i.e., a reliable provisional response or a 2xx response to a target refresh request) to refresh its local target if the UA is unable to use a target refresh request at that point in time (e.g., the UAS of an ongoing re-INVITE without support for UPDATE).

3.8.5.2.9 Early Dialogs

The rules given in this section about which messages can refresh the target of a dialog also apply to early dialogs created by an initial INVITE transaction. Additionally, as specified in RFC 3261 (see Section 3.7.2.2.4), on receiving a 2xx response to the initial INVITE, the UAC recomputes the whole route set of the dialog, which transitions from the early state to the confirmed state. RFC 3261 (see Section 3.6.1) allows unreliable provisional responses to create early dialogs. However, per the rules given in this section, unreliable provisional responses cannot refresh the target of a dialog. Therefore, the UAC of an initial INVITE transaction will not perform any target refresh as a result of the reception of an unreliable provisional response with an updated Contact value on an (already established) early dialog. Note also that a given UAS can establish additional early dialogs, which can have different targets, by returning additional unreliable provisional responses with different To tags.

3.8.5.3 A UA Losing Its Contact

The following sections discuss the case where a UA loses its transport address during an ongoing re-INVITE transaction. Such a UA will refresh the dialog's local target so that it reflects its new transport address. Note that target refreshes that do not involve changes in the UA's transport address are beyond the scope of this section. Also, UAs losing their transport address during a non-re-INVITE transaction (e.g., a UA losing its transport address right after having sent an UPDATE request before having received a response to it) are beyond the scope as well. The rules given in this section are also applicable to initial INVITE requests that have established early dialogs.

3.8.5.3.1 Background on Re-INVITE Transaction Routing

Re-INVITEs are routed using the dialog's route set, which contains all the proxy servers that need to be traversed by requests sent within the dialog. Responses to the re-INVITE are routed using the Via entries in the re-INVITE. ACK requests for 2xx responses and for non-2xx final responses are generated in different ways. As specified in RFC 3261 (see Sections 3.8.1 and 3.7.2.1), ACK requests for 2xx responses are generated by the UAC core and are routed using the dialog's route set. As specified in RFC 3261 (see Section 3.12), ACK requests for non-2xx final responses are generated by the INVITE client transaction (i.e., they are generated in a hop-by-hop fashion by the proxy servers in the path) and are sent to the same transport address as the re-INVITE.

3.8.5.3.2 Problems with UAs Losing Their Contact

Refreshing the dialog's remote target during a re-INVITE transaction as described earlier presents some issues because of the fact that re-INVITE transactions can be long lived. As described in the previous section, the way responses to the re-INVITE and ACKs for non-2xx final responses are routed is fixed once the re-INVITE is sent. The routing of these messages does not depend on the dialog's route set and, thus, target refreshes within an ongoing re-INVITE do not affect their routing. A UA that changes its location (i.e., performs a target refresh) but is still reachable at its old location will be able to receive those messages (which will be sent to the old location). However, a UA that cannot be reachable at its old location any longer will not be able to receive them.

The following sections describe the errors UAs face when they lose their transport address during a re-INVITE. On detecting some of these errors, UAs following the rules specified in RFC 3261 will terminate the dialog. When the dialog is terminated, the only option for the UAs is to establish a new dialog. The following sections change the requirements RFC 3261 places on UAs when certain errors occur so that the UAs can recover from those errors. In short, the UAs generate a new re-INVITE transaction to synchronize both UAs. Note that there are existing UA implementations deployed that already implement this behavior.

3.8.5.3.3 UAS Losing Its Contact: UAC Behavior

When a UAS that moves to a new contact and loses its old contact generates a non-2xx final response to the re-INVITE, it will not be able to receive the ACK request. The entity receiving the response, and thus generating the ACK request, will either get a transport error or a timeout error, which, as described in Section 8.1.3.1 of RFC 3261 (see Section 3.1.2.3.1), will be treated as a 503 (Service Unavailable) response and as a 408 Request Timeout response, respectively. If the sender of the ACK request is a proxy server, it will typically ignore this error. If the sender of the ACK request is the UAC, according to RFC 3261 (see Section 3.6.2.1.2), it is supposed to (at the should level) terminate the dialog by sending a BYE request.

However, because of the special properties of ACK requests for non-2xx final responses, most existing UACs do not terminate the dialog when an ACK request fails, which is fortunate. A UAC that accepts a target refresh within a re-INVITE MUST ignore transport and timeout errors when generating an ACK request for a non-2xx final response. Additionally, the UAC should generate a new re-INVITE in order to make sure that both UAs have a common view of the state of the session. It is possible that the errors ignored by the UAC were not related to the target refresh operation. If that was the case, the second re-INVITE would fail and the UAC would terminate the dialog because, per the rules above, UACs only ignore errors when they accept a target refresh within the re-INVITE.

3.8.5.3.4 UAC Losing Its Contact: UAS Behavior

When a UAC moves to a new contact and loses its old contact, it will not be able to receive responses to the re-INVITE. Consequently, it will never generate an ACK request. As described in RFC 3261 (see Section 3.11.9), a proxy server that gets an error when forwarding a response does not take any measures. Consequently, proxy servers relaying responses will effectively ignore the error. If there are no proxy servers in the dialog's route set, the UAS will get an error when sending a non-2xx final response. The UAS core will be notified of the transaction failure, as described in RFC 3261 (see Section 3.12). Most existing UASs do not terminate the dialog on encountering this failure, which is fortunate. Regardless of the presence or absence of proxy servers in the dialog's route set, a UAS generating a 2xx response to the re-INVITE will never receive an ACK request for it. According to RFC 3261 (see Section 3.8.2), such a UAS is supposed to (at the SHOULD level) terminate the dialog by sending a BYE request. A UAS that accepts a target refresh within a re-INVITE and never receives an ACK request after having sent a final response to the re-INVITE should not terminate the dialog if the UA has received a new re-INVITE with a higher CSeq sequence number than the original one.

3.8.5.3.5 UAC Losing Its Contact: UAC Behavior

When a UAC moves to a new contact and loses its old contact, it will not be able to receive responses to the re-INVITE. Consequently, it will never generate an ACK request. Such a UAC should generate a CANCEL request to cancel the re-INVITE and cause the INVITE client transaction corresponding to the re-INVITE to enter the Terminated state. The UAC should also send a new re-INVITE in order to make sure that both UAs have a common view of the state of the session. Per RFC 3261 (see Section 3.8.2), the UAS will accept new incoming re-INVITEs as soon as it has generated a final response to the previous INVITE request, which had a lower CSeq sequence number.

3.9 Handling Message Body

3.9.1 Objective

Message-body handling in SIP was originally specified in RFC 3261, which relied on earlier specifications (e.g., MIME) to describe some areas. RFC 5621 that is described here contains background material on how bodies are handled in SIP, and normative material on areas that had not been specified before or whose specifications needed to be completed. Sections containing background material are clearly identified as such by their titles. The material on the normative sections is based on experience gained since RFC 3261 was written. Implementers need to implement what is specified in RFC 3261 and its references in addition to what is specified in this RFC 5621.

3.9.2 Message-Body Encoding

This section deals with the encoding of message bodies in SIP.

3.9.2.1 Background on Message-Body Encoding

SIP (RFC 3261, see Section 2.4.2.4) messages consist of an initial line (request line in requests and status line in responses), a set of header fields, and an optional message body. The message body is described using header fields such as Content-Disposition, Content-Encoding, and Content-Type, which provide information on its contents. Figure 3.17 shows a SIP message that carries a body. Some of the header fields are not shown for simplicity:

The message body of a SIP message can be divided into various body parts. Multipart message bodies are encoded using the MIME (RFC 2045) format. Body parts are also described using header fields such as Content-Disposition, Content-Encoding, and Content-Type, which provide information on the contents of a particular body part. Figure 3.18

```
INVITE sip:conf-fact@example.com SIP/2.0
Content-Type: application/sdp
Content-Length: 192
v=0
o=alice 2890844526 2890842807 IN IP4 atlanta.example.com
s=-
c=IN IP4 192.0.2.1
t=0 0
m=audio 20000 RTP/AVP 0
a=rtpmap:0 PCMU/8000
m=video 20002 RTP/AVP 31
a=rtpmap:31 H261/90000
```

Figure 3.17 SIP message carrying a body.

```
INVITE sip:conf-fact@example.com SIP/2.0
Content-Type: multipart/mixed;boundary="boundary1"
Content-Length: 619

--boundary1

Content-Type: application/sdp
v=0
o=alice 2890844526 2890842807 IN IP4 atlanta.example.com
s=-
c=IN IP4 192.0.2.1
t=0 0
m=audio 20000 RTP/AVP 0
a=rtpmap:0 PCMU/8000
m=video 20002 RTP/AVP 31
a=rtpmap:31 H261/90000

--boundary1

Content-Type: application/resource-lists+xml
Content-Disposition: recipient-list
<?xml version="1.0" encoding="UTF-8"?>
<resource-lists xmlns="urn:ietf:params:xml:ns:resource-lists">
<list>
<entry uri="sip:bill@example.com"/>
<entry uri="sip:randy@example.net"/>
<entry uri="sip:joe@example.org"/>
</list>
</resource-lists>

--boundary1--
```

Figure 3.18 SIP message carrying two bodies.

shows a SIP message that carries two body parts. Some of the header fields are not shown for simplicity:

SIP uses S/MIME (see Section 19.6) to protect message bodies. As specified in RFC 3261, UASs that cannot decrypt a message body or a body part can use the 493 Undecipherable response to report the error.

3.9.2.2 UA Behavior to Encode Binary Message Bodies

SIP messages can carry binary message bodies such as legacy signaling objects (RFC 3204). SIP proxy servers are 8-bit safe. That is, they are able to handle binary bodies. Therefore, there is no need to use encodings such as base64 to transport binary bodies in SIP messages. Consequently, UAs should use the binary transfer encoding (RFC 4289) for all payloads in SIP, including binary payloads. The only case where a UA may use a different encoding is when transferring application data between applications that only handle a different encoding (e.g., base64).

3.9.3 Message Bodies: Multipart

This section deals with *multipart* message bodies and their handling.

3.9.3.1 Background on Multipart Message Bodies

RFC 3261 did not mandate support for multipart message bodies in MIME format (RFC 2046). However, since RFC 3261 was written, many SIP extensions rely on them. The use of *multipart/mixed* MIME bodies is a useful tool to build SIP extensions. An example of such an extension could be the inclusion of location information in an INVITE request. Such an INVITE request would use the multipart/mixed MIME type (RFC 2046) to carry two body parts: a session description and a location object. An example of an existing extension that uses multipart/mixed to send a session description and a legacy-signaling object is defined in RFC 3204.

Another MIME type that is useful to build SIP extensions is *multipart/alternative* (RFC 2046). Each body part within a multipart/alternative carries an alternative version of the same information. The transition from SDP to new SDPs could be implemented using multipart/alternative bodies. SIP messages (e.g., INVITE requests) could carry a multipart/alternative body with two body parts: a session description written in SDP and a session description written in a newer session description format.

Legacy recipient UAs would use the session description written in SDP. New recipient UAs would use the one written in the newer format. Nested MIME bodies are yet another useful tool to build and combine SIP extensions. Using the extensions in the previous examples, a UA that supported a new session description format and that needed to include a location object in an INVITE request would include a multipart/mixed body with two body parts: a location object and a multipart/alternative. The multipart/alternative body part would, in turn, have two body parts: a session description written in SDP and a session description written in the newer session description format.

3.9.3.2 Mandatory Support for Multipart Message Bodies

For all MIME-based extensions to work, the recipient needs to be able to decode the multipart bodies. Therefore, SIP UAs must support parsing multipart MIME bodies, including nested body parts. Additionally, UAs must support the multipart/mixed and multipart/alternative MIME types. Support for other MIME types such as *multipart/related* is optional. Note that, by default, unknown multipart subtypes are treated as multipart/mixed. Also note that SIP extensions can also include multipart MIME bodies in responses. That is why both UACs and UASs need to support multipart bodies. Legacy SIP UAs without support for multipart bodies generate a 415 Unsupported Media Type response when they receive a multipart body in a request. A UAC sending a multipart body can receive such an error response when communicating with a legacy SIP UA that predates this specification. It has been observed in the field that a number of legacy SIP UAs without support for multipart bodies simply ignored those bodies when they were received. These UAs did not return any error response. Unsurprisingly, SIP UAs not being able to report this type of error have caused serious interoperability problems in the past.

3.9.3.3 UA Behavior to Generate Multipart Message Bodies

UAs should avoid unnecessarily nesting body parts because doing so would, unnecessarily, make processing the body more laborious for the receiver. However, RFC 2046 states that a multipart media type with a single body part is useful in some circumstances (e.g., for sending nontext media types). In any case, UAs should not nest one multipart/mixed within another unless there is a need to reference the nested one (i.e., using the Content-ID of the nested body part). Moreover, UAs should not nest one multipart/alternative within another. Note that UAs receiving unnecessarily nested body parts treat them as if they were not nested.

3.9.4 Message Bodies: Multipart/Mixed

This section does not specify any additional behavior regarding how to generate and process multipart/mixed bodies. This section is simply included for completeness.

3.9.5 Message Bodies: Multipart/Alternative

This section deals with multipart/alternative message bodies and their handling.

3.9.5.1 Background on Multipart/Alternative Message Bodies

Each body part within a multipart/alternative carries an alternative version of the same information. The body parts are ordered so that the last one is the richest representation of the information. The recipient of a multipart/alternative body chooses the last body part it understands. Note that within a body part encoded in a given format (i.e., of a given content type), there can be optional elements that can provide richer information to the recipient in case the recipient supports them. For example, in SDP (RFC 4566, see Section 7.7), those optional elements are encoded in "a" lines.

These types of optional elements are internal to a body part and are not visible at the MIME level. That is, a body part is understood if the recipient understands its content type, regardless of whether or not the body part's optional elements are understood. Note as well that each part of a multipart/alternative body represents the same data, but the mapping between any two parts is not necessarily without information loss. For example, information can be lost when translating text/html to text/plain. RFC 2046 recommends that each part should have a different Content-ID value in the case where the information content of the two parts is not identical.

3.9.5.2 UA Behavior to Generate Multipart/Alternative Message Bodies

RFC 5621 mandates all the top-level body parts within a multipart/alternative to have the same disposition type. The session and early-session (RFC 3959, see Section 11.4) disposition types require that all the body parts of a multipart/alternative body have different content types. Consequently, for the session and early-session disposition types, UAs must not place more than one body part with a given content type in a multipart/alternative body. That is, for session and early-session, no body part within a multipart/alternative can have the same content type as another body part within the same multipart/alternative.

3.9.5.3 UA Behavior to Process Multipart/Alternative Message Bodies

RFC 5621 does not specify any additional behavior regarding how to process multipart/alternative bodies. We have included this section simply for completeness.

3.9.6 Message Bodies: Multipart/Related

This section deals with multipart/related message bodies and their handling.

3.9.6.1 Background on Multipart/Related Message Bodies

Compound objects in MIME are represented using the multipart/related content type (RFC 2387). The body parts within a particular multipart/related body are all part of a compound object and are processed as such. The body part within a multipart/related body that needs to be processed first is referred to as the *root* body part. The root body part of a multipart/related body is identified by the *start* parameter, which is a Content-Type header field parameter and contains a Content-ID URL pointing to the root body part. If the start parameter is not present, the root body part is, by default, the first part of the multipart/related body. An example of a compound object is a web page that contains images. The html body part would be the root. The remaining body parts would contain the images. An example of a SIP extension using multipart/related is specified in RFC 4662.

3.9.6.2 UA Behavior to Generate Multipart/Related Message Bodies

RFC 5621 does not specify any additional behavior regarding how to generate multipart/related bodies. We have included this section simply for completeness.

3.9.6.3 UA Behavior to Process Multipart/Related Message Bodies

Per RFC 2387, a UA processing a multipart/related body processes the body as a compound object ignoring the disposition types of the body parts within it. Ignoring the disposition types of the individual body parts makes sense in the context in which multipart/related was originally specified. For instance, in the example of the web page, the implicit disposition type for the images would be *inline*, since the images are displayed as indicated by the root html file. However, in SIP, the disposition types of the individual body parts within a multipart/related play an important role and, thus, need to be considered by the UA processing the multipart/related.

Different SIP extensions that use the same disposition type for the multipart/related body can be distinguished by the disposition types of the individual body parts within the multipart/related. Consequently, SIP UAs processing a multipart/related body with a given disposition type must process the disposition types of the body parts within it according to the SIP extension making use the disposition type of the multipart/related body. Note that UAs that do not understand multipart/related will treat multipart/related bodies as multipart/mixed bodies. These UAs will not be able to process a given body as a compound object. Instead, they will process the body parts according to their disposition type as if each body part was independent from each other.

3.9.7 Disposition Types

This section deals with disposition types in message bodies.

3.9.7.1 Background on Content and Disposition Types in SIP

The Content-Disposition header field (see Section 2.8.2), defined in RFC 2183 and extended by RFC 3261, describes how to handle a SIP message's body or an individual body part. Examples of disposition types used in SIP in the Content-Disposition header field are *session* and *render*. RFCs 3204 and 3459 define the *handling* parameter for the Content-Disposition header field. This parameter describes how a UAS reacts if it receives a message body whose content type or disposition type it does not understand. If the parameter has the value *optional*, the UAS ignores the message body; if the parameter has the value *required*, the UAS returns a 415 Unsupported Media Type response. The default value for the handling parameter is *required*. The following is an example of a Content-Disposition header field:

```
Content-Disposition: signal; handling=optional
```

RFC 3204 identifies two situations where a UAS needs to reject a request with a body part whose handling is required:

- If it has an unknown content type
- If it has an unknown disposition type

If the UAS did not understand the content type of the body part, the UAS can add an Accept header field to its 415 Unsupported Media Type response listing the content types that the UAS does understand. Nevertheless, there is no mechanism for a UAS that does not understand the disposition type of a body part to inform the UAC about which disposition type was not understood or about the disposition types that are understood by the UAS. The reason for not having such a mechanism is that disposition types are typically supported within a context. Outside that context, a UA need not support the disposition type. For example, a UA can support the session disposition type for body parts in INVITE and UPDATE requests and their responses. However, the same UA would not support the session disposition type in MESSAGE requests.

In another example, a UA can support the render disposition type for text/plain and text/html body parts in MESSAGE requests. In addition, the UA can support the session disposition type for application/sdp body parts in INVITE and UPDATE requests and their responses. However, the UA might not support the render disposition type for application/sdp body parts in MESSAGE requests, even if, in different contexts, the UA supported all of the following: the render disposition type, the application/sdp content type, and the MESSAGE method.

A given context is generally (but not necessarily) defined by a method, a disposition type, and a content type. Support for a specific context is usually defined within an extension. For example, the extension for instant messaging in SIP RFC 3428 (see Sections 2.5 and 6.3.1) mandates support for the MESSAGE method, the render disposition type, and the text/plain content type. Note that, effectively, content types are also supported within a context. Therefore, the use of the Accept header field in a 415 Unsupported Media Type response is not enough to describe in which contexts a particular content type is supported. Therefore, support for a particular disposition type within a given context is typically signaled by the use of a particular method or an option tag in a Supported or a Require header field. When support for a particular disposition type within a context is mandated, support for a default content type is also mandated (e.g., a UA that supports the session disposition type in an INVITE request needs to support the application/sdp content type).

3.9.7.2 UA Behavior to Set the Handling Parameter

As stated earlier, the handling Content-Disposition parameter can take two values: required or optional. While it is typically easy for a UA to decide which type of handling an individual body part requires, setting the handling parameter of multipart bodies requires extra considerations. If the handling of a multipart/mixed body as a whole is required for processing its enclosing body part or message, the UA must set the handling parameter of the multipart/mixed body to required. Otherwise, the UA must set it to optional. The handling parameters of the top-level body parts within the multipart/mixed body are set independently from the handling parameter of the multipart/mixed body. If the handling of a particular top-level body part is required, the UA must set the handling parameter of that body part to required. Otherwise, the UA must set it to optional.

Per the previous rules, a multipart/mixed body whose handling is optional can contain body parts whose handling is required. In such a case, the receiver is required to process the body parts whose handling is required if and only if the receiver decides to process the optional multipart/mixed body. Also per the previous rules, a multipart/mixed body whose handling is required can contain only body parts whose handling is optional. In such a case, the receiver is required to process the body as a whole; however, when processing it, the receiver may decide (on the basis of its local policy) not to process any of the body parts. The handling parameter is a Content-Disposition parameter.

Therefore, to set this parameter, it is necessary to provide the multipart/mixed body with a disposition type. Per RFC 3261, the default disposition type for application/sdp is *session* and for other bodies, it is *render*. UAs should assign multipart/mixed bodies a disposition type of render. Note that the fact that multipart/mixed bodies have a default disposition type of render does not imply that they will be rendered to the user. The way the body parts within the multipart/mixed are handled depends on the disposition types of the individual body parts. The actual disposition type of the whole multipart/mixed is irrelevant. The render disposition type has been chosen for multipart/mixed bodies simply because render is the default disposition type in SIP.

If the handling of a multipart/alternative body as a whole is required for processing its enclosing body part or message, the UA must set the handling parameter of the multipart/alternative body to required. Otherwise, the UA must set it to optional. The UA should also set the handling parameter of all the top-level body part within the multipart/alternative to optional. The receiver will process the body parts based on the handling parameter of the multipart/alternative body. The receiver will ignore the handling parameters of the body parts. That is why setting them to optional is at the SHOULD level and not at the MUST level—their value is irrelevant.

The UA must use the same disposition type for the multipart/alternative body and all its top-level body parts. If the handling of a multipart/related body as a whole is required for processing its enclosing body part or message, the UA must set the handling parameter of the multipart/related body to required. Otherwise, the UA must set it to optional. The handling parameters of the top-level body parts within the multipart/related body are set independently from the handling parameter of the multipart/related body. If the handling of a particular top-level body part is required, the UA must set the handling parameter of that body part to required. Otherwise, the UA must set it to optional. If at least one top-level body part within a multipart/related body has a handling parameter of required, the UA should set the handling parameter of the root body part to required.

3.9.7.3 UA Behavior to Process Multipart/Alternative

The receiver of a multipart/alternative body must process the body based on its handling parameter. The receiver should ignore the handling parameters of the body parts within the multipart/alternative.

3.9.7.4 UAS Behavior to Report Unsupported Message Bodies

If a UAS cannot process a request because, in the given context, the UAS does not support the content type or the disposition type of a body part whose handling is required, the UAS should return a 415 Unsupported Media Type response even if the UAS supported the content type, the disposition type, or both in a different context. Consequently, it is possible to receive a 415 Unsupported Media Type response with an Accept header field containing all the content types used in the request. If a UAS receives a request with a body part whose disposition type is not compatible with the way the body part is supposed to be handled according to other parts of the SIP message (e.g., a Refer-To header field with a Content-ID URL pointing to a body part whose disposition type is *session*), the UAS should return a 415 Unsupported Media Type response.

3.9.8 Message-Body Processing

This section deals with the processing of message bodies and how that processing is influenced by the presence of references to them.

3.9.8.1 Background on References to Message-Body Parts

Content-ID URLs allow creating references to body parts. A given Content-ID URL (RFC 2392, see Section 2.8.2), which can appear in a header field or within a body part (e.g., in an SDP attribute), points to a particular body part. The way to handle that body part is defined by the field where the Content-ID URL appears. For example, the extension to refer to multiple resources in SIP (RFC 5368, see Section 16.4) places a Content-ID URL in a Refer-To header field. Such a Content-ID URL points to a body part that carries a URI list. In another example, the extension for file transfer in SDP (RFC 5547) places a Content-ID URL in a *fileicon* SDP attribute. This Content-ID URL points to a body part that carries a (typically small) picture.

3.9.8.2 UA Behavior to Generate References to Message Bodies

UAs must only include forward references in the SIP messages they generate. That is, an element in a SIP message can reference a body part only if the body part appears after the element. Consequently, a given body part can only be referenced by another body part that appears before it or by a header field. Having only forward references allows recipients to process body parts as they parse them. They do not need to parse the remainder of the message in order to process a body part. It was considered to only allow (forward) references among body parts that belonged to the same multipart/related (RFC 2387) wrapper. However, it was finally decided that this extra constraint was not necessary.

3.9.8.3 UA Behavior to Process Message Bodies

To process a message body or a body part, a UA needs to know whether a SIP header field or another body part contains a reference to the message body or body part (e.g., a Content-ID URL pointing to it). If the body part is not referenced in any way (e.g., there are no header fields or other body parts with a Content-ID URL pointing to it), the UA processes the body part as indicated by its disposition type and the context in which the body part was received. If the SIP message contains a reference to the body part, the UA processes the body part according to the reference.

If the SIP message contains more than one reference to the body part (e.g., two header fields contain Content-ID URLs pointing to the body part), the UA processes the body part as many times as the number of references. Note that, following the rules in RFC 3204, if a UA does not understand a body part whose handling is optional, the UA ignores it. Also note that the content indirection mechanism in SIP (RFC 4483, see Section 16.6) allows UAs to point to external bodies. Therefore, a UA receiving a SIP message that uses content indirection could need to fetch a body part (e.g., using HTTP (RFCs 7230–7235) in order to process it.

3.9.8.4 Disposition Type: By-Reference

Per the rules described above, if a SIP message contains a reference to a body part, the UA processes the body part according to the reference. Since the reference provides the context in which the body part needs to be processed, the disposition type of the body part is irrelevant. However, a UA that missed a reference to a body part (e.g., because the reference was in a header field the UA did not support) would attempt to process the body part according to its disposition type alone. To keep this from happening, we define a new disposition type for the Content-Disposition header field: by-reference.

A body part whose disposition type is *by-reference* needs to be handled according to a reference to the body part that is located in the same SIP message as the body part (given that SIP only allows forward references, the reference will appear in the same SIP message before the body part). A recipient of a body part whose disposition type is by-reference that cannot find any reference to the body part (e.g., the reference was in a header field the recipient does not support and, thus, did not process) must not process the body part. Consequently, if the handling of the body part was required, the UA needs to report an error. Note that extensions that predate this specification use references to body parts whose disposition type is not by-reference. Those extensions use option tags to make sure the recipient understands the whole extension and, thus, cannot miss the reference and attempt to process the body part according to its disposition type alone.

3.9.9 Future SIP Extensions

These guidelines are intended for authors of SIP extensions that involve, in some way, message bodies or body parts. These guidelines discuss aspects that authors of such extensions need to consider when designing them. This specification mandates support for multipart/mixed and multipart/alternative. At present, there are no SIP extensions that use different multipart subtypes such as parallel (RFC 2046) or digest (RFC 2046). If such extensions were to be defined in the future, their authors would need to make sure (e.g., by using an option tag or by other means) that entities receiving those multipart subtypes were able to process them. As stated earlier, UAs treat unknown multipart subtypes as multipart/mixed.

Authors of SIP extensions making use of multipart/related bodies have to explicitly address the handling of the disposition types of the body parts within the multipart/related body. Authors wishing to make use of multipart/related bodies should keep in mind that UAs that do not understand multipart/related will treat it as multipart/mixed. If such treatment by a recipient is not acceptable for a particular extension, the authors of such extension would need to make sure (e.g., by using an option tag or by other means) that entities receiving the multipart/related body were able to correctly process them.

As stated earlier, SIP extensions can also include multipart MIME bodies in responses. Hence, a response can be extremely complex and the UAC receiving the response might not be able to process it correctly. Because UACs receiving a response cannot report errors to the UAS that generated the response (i.e., error responses can only be generated for requests), authors of SIP extensions need to make sure that requests clearly indicate (e.g., by using an option tag or by other means) the capabilities of the UAC so that UASs can decide what to include in their responses.

3.10 Terminating a Session

This section describes the procedures for terminating a session established by SIP. The state of the session and the state of the dialog are very closely related. When a session is initiated with an INVITE, each 1xx or 2xx response from a distinct UAS creates a dialog, and if that response completes the offer–answer exchange, it also creates a session. As a result, each session is associated with a single dialog—the one that resulted in its creation. If an initial INVITE generates a non-2xx final response, that terminates all sessions (if any) and all dialogs (if any) that were created through responses to the request. By virtue of completing the transaction, a non-2xx final response also prevents further sessions from being created as a result of the INVITE. The BYE request is used to terminate a specific session or attempted session. In this case, the specific session is the one with the peer UA on the other side of the dialog. When a BYE is received on a dialog, any session associated with that dialog should terminate. A UA must not send a BYE outside of a dialog. The caller's UA may send a BYE for either confirmed or early dialogs, and the callee's UA may send a BYE on confirmed dialogs, but must not send a BYE on early dialogs.

However, the callee's UA must not send a BYE on a confirmed dialog until it has received an ACK for its 2xx response or until the server transaction times out. If no SIP extensions have defined other application layer states associated with the dialog, the BYE also terminates the dialog. The impact of a non-2xx final response to INVITE on dialogs and sessions makes the use of CANCEL attractive. The CANCEL attempts to force a non-2xx response to the INVITE (in particular, a 487).

Therefore, if a UAC wishes to give up on its call attempt entirely, it can send a CANCEL. If the INVITE results in 2xx final response(s) to the INVITE, this means that a UAS accepted the invitation while the CANCEL was in progress. The UAC may continue with the sessions established by any 2xx responses, or may terminate them with BYE. The notion of *hanging up* is not well defined within SIP. It is specific to a particular, albeit common, user interface. Typically, when the user hangs up, it indicates a desire to terminate the attempt to establish a session, and to terminate any sessions already created. For the caller's UA, this would imply a CANCEL request if the initial INVITE has not generated a final response and a BYE to all confirmed dialogs after a final response. For the callee's UA, it would typically imply a BYE; presumably, when the user picked up the phone, a 2xx was generated, and so hanging up would result in a BYE after the ACK is received. This does not mean a user cannot hang up before receipt of the ACK; it just means that the software in his phone needs to maintain state for a short while in order to clean up properly. If the particular user interface allows for the user to reject a call before it is answered, a 403 Forbidden is a good way to express that. As per the rules above, a BYE cannot be sent.

3.10.1 Terminating a Session with a BYE Request

3.10.1.1 UAC Behavior

A BYE request is constructed as would any other request within a dialog, as described in Section 3.6. Once the BYE is constructed, the UAC core creates a new non-INVITE client transaction, and passes it the BYE request. The UAC must consider the session terminated (and therefore stop sending or listening for media) as soon as the BYE request is passed to the client transaction. If the response for the BYE is a 481 Call/Transaction Does Not Exist or a 408 Request Timeout, or no response at all is received for the BYE (i.e., a timeout is returned by the client transaction), the UAC must consider the session and the dialog terminated.

3.10.1.2 UAS Behavior

A UAS first processes the BYE request according to the general UAS processing described in Section 3.1.3. A UAS core receiving a BYE request checks if it matches an existing dialog. If the BYE does not match an existing dialog, the

UAS core should generate a 481 Call/Transaction Does Not Exist response and pass that to the server transaction. This rule means that a BYE sent without tags by a UAC will be rejected. This is a change from RFC 2543, which allowed BYE without tags.

A UAS core receiving a BYE request for an existing dialog must follow the procedures of Section 3.6.2.2 to process the request. Once done, the UAS should terminate the session (and therefore stop sending and listening for media). The only case where it can elect not to are multicast sessions, where participation is possible even if the other participant in the dialog has terminated its involvement in the session. Whether or not it ends its participation on the session, the UAS core must generate a 2xx response to the BYE, and must pass that to the server transaction for transmission. The UAS must still respond to any pending requests received for that dialog. It is recommended that a 487 Request Terminated response be generated to those pending requests.

3.11 Proxy Behavior

3.11.1 Overview

SIP proxies are elements that route SIP requests to UASs and SIP responses to UACs. A request may traverse several proxies on its way to a UAS. Each will make routing decisions, modifying the request before forwarding it to the next element. Responses will route through the same set of proxies traversed by the request in the reverse order. Being a proxy is a logical role for a SIP element. When a request arrives, an element that can play the role of a proxy first decides if it needs to respond to the request on its own. For instance, the request may be malformed or the element may need credentials from the client before acting as a proxy. The element may respond with any appropriate error code. When responding directly to a request, the element is playing the role of a UAS and must behave as described in Section 3.1.3.

A proxy can operate in either a stateful or stateless mode for each new request. When stateless, a proxy acts as a simple forwarding element. It forwards each request downstream to a single element determined by making a targeting and routing decision based on the request. It simply forwards every response it receives upstream. A stateless proxy discards information about a message once the message has been forwarded. A stateful proxy remembers information (specifically, transaction state) about each incoming request and any requests it sends as a result of processing the incoming request. It uses this information to affect the processing of future messages associated with that request. A stateful proxy may choose to *fork* a request, routing it to multiple destinations. Any request that is forwarded to more than one location must be handled statefully.

In some circumstances, a proxy may forward requests using stateful transports (such as TCP) without being transaction stateful. For instance, a proxy may forward a request from one TCP connection to another transaction statelessly as long as it places enough information in the message to be able to forward the response down the same connection the request arrived on. Requests forwarded between different types of transports where the proxy's TU must take an active role in ensuring reliable delivery on one of the transports must be forwarded transaction statefully.

A stateful proxy may transition to stateless operation at any time during the processing of a request, so long as it did not do anything that would otherwise prevent it from being stateless initially (forking, for example, or generation of a 100 response). When performing such a transition, all state is simply discarded. The proxy should not initiate a CANCEL request. Much of the processing involved when acting statelessly or statefully for a request is identical. The next several subsections are written from the point of view of a stateful proxy. The last section calls out those places where a stateless proxy behaves differently.

3.11.2 Stateful Proxy

When stateful, a proxy is purely a SIP transaction-processing engine. Its behavior is modeled here in terms of the server and client transactions defined in Section 3.12. A stateful proxy has a server transaction associated with one or more client transactions by a higher-layer proxy-processing component (see Figure 3.19), known as a proxy core. An incoming request is processed by a server transaction. Requests from the server transaction are passed to a proxy core. The proxy core determines where to route the request, choosing one or more next-hop locations. An outgoing request for each next-hop location is processed by its own associated client transaction. The proxy core collects the responses from the client transactions and uses them to send responses to the server transaction.

A stateful proxy creates a new server transaction for each new request received. Any retransmissions of the request will then be handled by that server transaction

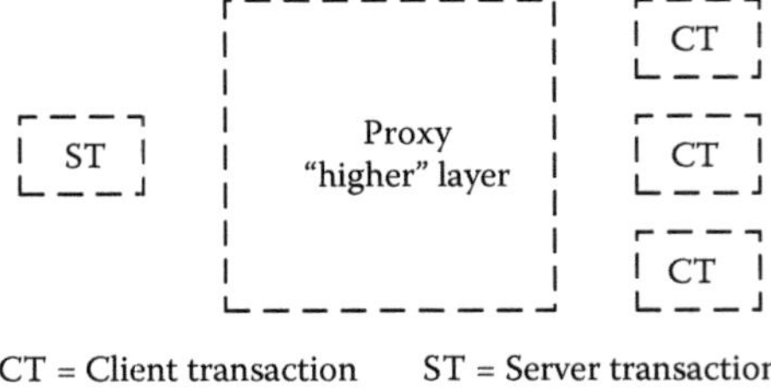

Figure 3.19 Stateful proxy model. (Copyright IETF. Reproduced with permission.)

per Section 3.12. The proxy core must behave as a UAS with respect to sending an immediate provisional on that server transaction (such as 100 Trying), as described in Section 3.1.3.6. Thus, a stateful proxy should not generate 100 Trying responses to non-INVITE requests. This is a model of proxy behavior, not of software. An implementation is free to take any approach that replicates the external behavior this model defines. For all new requests, including any with unknown methods, an element intending to proxy the request must

1. Validate the request (Section 3.11.3)
2. Preprocess routing information (Section 3.11.4)
3. Determine target(s) for the request (Section 3.11.5)
4. Forward the request to each target (Section 3.11.6)
5. Process all responses (Section 3.11.7)

3.11.3 Request Validation

Before elements can proxy a request, it must verify the message's validity. A valid message must pass the following checks:

1. Reasonable syntax
2. URI scheme
3. Max-Forwards
4. (Optional) loop detection
5. Proxy-Require
6. Proxy-Authorization

If any of these checks fail, the element must behave as a UAS (see Section 3.1.3) and respond with an error code. Notice that a proxy is not required to detect merged requests and must not treat merged requests as an error condition. The end points receiving the requests will resolve the merge as described in Section 3.1.3.2.2.

3.11.3.1 Reasonable Syntax Check

The request must be well formed enough to be handled with a server transaction. Any components involved in the remainder of these Request Validation steps or the Request Forwarding section must be well formed. Any other components, well formed or not, should be ignored and remain unchanged when the message is forwarded. For instance, an element would not reject a request because of a malformed Date header field. Likewise, a proxy would not remove a malformed Date header field before forwarding a request. This protocol is designed to be extended. Future extensions may define new methods and header fields at any time. An element must not refuse to proxy a request because it contains a method or header field it does not know about.

3.11.3.2 URI Scheme Check

If the Request-URI has a URI whose scheme is not understood by the proxy, the proxy should reject the request with a 416 Unsupported URI Scheme response.

3.11.3.3 Max-Forwards Check

The Max-Forwards header field (Section 2.8.2) is used to limit the number of elements a SIP request can traverse. If the request does not contain a Max-Forwards header field, this check is passed. If the request contains a Max-Forwards header field with a field value greater than zero, the check is passed. If the request contains a Max-Forwards header field with a field value of zero (0), the element must not forward the request. If the request was for OPTIONS, the element may act as the final recipient and respond per Section 3.5. Otherwise, the element must return a 483 Too Many Hops response.

3.11.3.4 Optional Loop-Detection Check

3.11.3.4.1 Per RFC 3261

An element may check for forwarding loops before forwarding a request. If the request contains a Via header field with a sent-by value that equals a value placed into previous requests by the proxy, the request has been forwarded by this element before. The request has either looped or is legitimately spiraling through the element. To determine if the request has looped, the element may perform the branch parameter calculation described in Section 3.11.6 on this message and compare it with the parameter received in that Via header field. If the parameters match, the request has looped. If they differ, the request is spiraling, and processing continues. If a loop is detected, the element may return a 482 Loop Detected response.

3.11.3.4.2 Per 5393

Section 4.2.2 of RFC 5393: Update to Section 16.3 of RFC 3261:

> This section replaces all of item 4 in Section 16.3 (see Section 3.11.3.4.1) of RFC 3261 (item 4 appears on page 95 of RFC 3261).
>
> 4. Loop-Detection Check
>
> Proxies required to perform loop detection by RFC 5393 (see Section 9.11) must perform the following loop-detection test before forwarding a request. Each Via header field value in the request whose sent-by value matches a value placed into previous requests by this proxy must be inspected for the second part defined

in Section 4.2.1 of RFC 5393 (see Section 9.11). This second part will not be present if the message was not forked when that Via header field value was added. If the second field is present, the proxy must perform the second-part calculation described in Section 4.2.1 of RFC 5393 (see Section 9.11) on this request and compare the result to the value from the Via header field. If these values are equal, the request has looped and the proxy must reject the request with a 482 Loop Detected response. If the values differ, the request is spiraling and processing continues to the next step.

3.11.3.5 Proxy-Require Check

Future extensions to this protocol may introduce features that require special handling by proxies. End points will include a Proxy-Require header field in requests that use these features, telling the proxy not to process the request unless the feature is understood. If the request contains a Proxy-Require header field (Section 2.8.2) with one or more option tags this element does not understand, the element must return a 420 Bad Extension response. The response must include an Unsupported (Section 2.8.2) header field listing those option tags the element did not understand.

3.11.3.6 Proxy-Authorization Check

If an element requires credentials before forwarding a request, the request must be inspected as described in Section 19.6.3. That section also defines what the element must do if the inspection fails.

3.11.4 Route Information Preprocessing

The proxy must inspect the Request-URI of the request. If the Request-URI of the request contains a value this proxy previously placed into a Record-Route header field (see Section 3.11.6), the proxy must replace the Request-URI in the request with the last value from the Route header field, and remove that value from the Route header field. The proxy must then proceed as if it received this modified request. This will only happen when the element sending the request to the proxy (which may have been an end point) is a strict router. This rewrite on receive is necessary to enable backwards compatibility with those elements. It also allows elements following this specification to preserve the Request-URI through strict-routing proxies (see Section 3.6.2.1.1). This requirement does not obligate a proxy to keep state in order to detect URIs it previously placed in Record-Route header fields.

Instead, a proxy need only place enough information in those URIs to recognize them as values it provided when they later appear. If the Request-URI contains a maddr parameter, the proxy must check to see if its value is in the set of addresses or domains the proxy is configured to be responsible for. If the Request-URI has a maddr parameter with a value the proxy is responsible for, and the request was received using the port and transport indicated (explicitly or by default) in the Request-URI, the proxy must strip the maddr and any nondefault port or transport parameter and continue processing as if those values had not been present in the request. A request may arrive with a maddr matching the proxy, but on a port or transport different from that indicated in the URI. Such a request needs to be forwarded to the proxy using the indicated port and transport. If the first value in the Route header field indicates this proxy, the proxy must remove that value from the request.

3.11.5 Determining Request Targets

Next, the proxy calculates the target(s) of the request. The set of targets will either be predetermined by the contents of the request or will be obtained from an abstract location service. Each target in the set is represented as a URI. If the Request-URI of the request contains a maddr parameter, the Request-URI must be placed into the target set as the only target URI, and the proxy must proceed to Section 3.11.6. If the domain of the Request-URI indicates a domain this element is not responsible for, the Request-URI must be placed into the target set as the only target, and the element must proceed to the task of Request Forwarding (Section 3.11.6). There are many circumstances in which a proxy might receive a request for a domain it is not responsible for. A firewall proxy handling outgoing calls (the way HTTP proxies handle outgoing requests) is an example of where this is likely to occur. If the target set for the request has not been predetermined as described above, this implies that the element is responsible for the domain in the Request-URI, and the element may use whatever mechanism it desires to determine where to send the request. Any of these mechanisms can be modeled as accessing an abstract location service.

This may consist of obtaining information from a location service created by a SIP Registrar, reading a database, consulting a presence server, utilizing other protocols, or simply performing an algorithmic substitution on the Request-URI. When accessing the location service constructed by a registrar, the Request-URI must first be canonicalized as described in Section 3.3 before being used as an index. The output of these mechanisms is used to construct the target set. If the Request-URI does not provide sufficient information for the proxy to determine the target set, it should return a 485 Ambiguous response. This response should contain a Contact header field containing URIs of new addresses to be tried. For example, an INVITE to sip:John.Smith@company.com may be ambiguous at a proxy whose location service has multiple John Smiths listed. See Section 2.8.2 for details.

Any information in or about the request or the current environment of the element may be used in the construction of the target set. For instance, different sets may be constructed depending on contents or the presence of header fields and bodies, the time of day of the request's arrival, the interface on which the request arrived, failure of previous requests, or even the element's current level of utilization. As potential targets are located through these services, their URIs are added to the target set. Targets can only be placed in the target set once. If a target URI is already present in the set (based on the definition of equality for the URI type), it must not be added again. A proxy must not add additional targets to the target set if the Request-URI of the original request does not indicate a resource this proxy is responsible for. A proxy can only change the Request-URI of a request during forwarding if it is responsible for that URI. If the proxy is not responsible for that URI, it will not recurse on 3xx or 416 responses as described below. If the Request-URI of the original request indicates a resource this proxy is responsible for, the proxy may continue to add targets to the set after beginning Request Forwarding. It may use any information obtained during that processing to determine new targets.

For instance, a proxy may choose to incorporate contacts obtained in a redirect response (3xx) into the target set. If a proxy uses a dynamic source of information while building the target set (for instance, if it consults a SIP Registrar), it should monitor that source for the duration of processing the request. New locations should be added to the target set as they become available. As above, any given URI must not be added to the set more than once. Allowing a URI to be added to the set only once reduces unnecessary network traffic, and, in the case of incorporating contacts from redirect requests, prevents infinite recursion. For example, a trivial location service is a *no-op*, where the target URI is equal to the incoming Request-URI. The request is sent to a specific next-hop proxy for further processing. During request forwarding of Section 3.11.6, the identity of that next hop, expressed as a SIP or SIPS URI, is inserted as the topmost Route header field value into the request. If the Request-URI indicates a resource at this proxy that does not exist, the proxy must return a 404 Not Found response. If the target set remains empty after applying all of the above, the proxy must return an error response, which should be the 480 Temporarily Unavailable responses.

3.11.6 Request Forwarding

As soon as the target set is nonempty, a proxy may begin forwarding the request. A stateful proxy may process the set in any order. It may process multiple targets serially, allowing each client transaction to complete before starting the next. It may start client transactions with every target in parallel. It also may arbitrarily divide the set into groups, processing the groups serially and processing the targets in each group in parallel. A common ordering mechanism is to use the *q*-value parameter of targets obtained from Contact header fields (see Section 2.8.2). Targets are processed from the highest *q*-value to the lowest. Targets with equal *q*-values may be processed in parallel.

A stateful proxy must have a mechanism to maintain the target set as responses are received and associate the responses to each forwarded request with the original request. For the purposes of this model, this mechanism is a *response context* created by the proxy layer before forwarding the first request. For each target, the proxy forwards the request following these steps:

1. Make a copy of the received request.
2. Update the Request-URI.
3. Update the Max-Forwards header field.
4. Optionally add a Record-route header field value.
5. Optionally add additional header fields.
6. Postprocess routing information.
7. Determine the next-hop address, port, and transport.
8. Add a Via header field value.
9. Add a Content-Length header field if necessary.
10. Forward the new request.
11. Set timer C.

Each of these steps is detailed in the following sections.

3.11.6.1 Copy Request

The proxy starts with a copy of the received request. The copy must initially contain all of the header fields from the received request. Fields not detailed in the processing described below must not be removed. The copy should maintain the ordering of the header fields as in the received request. The proxy must not reorder field values with a common field name (see Section 2.8). The proxy must not add to, modify, or remove the message body. An actual implementation need not perform a copy; the primary requirement is that the processing for each next hop begins with the same request.

3.11.6.2 Request-URI

The Request-URI in the copy's start line must be replaced with the URI for this target. If the URI contains any parameters not allowed in a Request-URI, they must be removed. This is the essence of a proxy's role. This is the mechanism through which a proxy routes a request toward its destination. In some circumstances, the received Request-URI is placed into the target set without being modified. For that target, the replacement above is effectively a no-op.

3.11.6.3 Max-Forwards

If the copy contains a Max-Forwards header field, the proxy must decrement its value by 1. If the copy does not contain a Max-Forwards header field, the proxy must add one with a field value, which should be 70. Some existing UAs will not provide a Max-Forwards header field in a request.

3.11.6.4 Record-Route

If this proxy wishes to remain on the path of future requests in a dialog created by this request (assuming the request creates a dialog), it must insert a Record-Route header field value into the copy before any existing Record-Route header field values, even if a Route header field is already present. Requests establishing a dialog may contain a preloaded Route header field. If this request is already part of a dialog, the proxy should insert a Record-Route header field value if it wishes to remain on the path of future requests in the dialog. In normal end-point operation as described in Section 3.6, these Record-Route header field values will not have any effect on the route sets used by the end points.

The proxy will remain on the path if it chooses to not insert a Record-Route header field value into requests that are already part of a dialog. However, it would be removed from the path when an end point that has failed reconstitutes the dialog. A proxy may insert a Record-Route header field value into any request. If the request does not initiate a dialog, the end points will ignore the value. See Section 3.6 for details on how end points use the Record-Route header field values to construct Route header fields. Each proxy in the path of a request chooses whether to add a Record-Route header field value independently—the presence of a Record-Route header field in a request does not obligate this proxy to add a value.

The URI placed in the Record-Route header field value must be a SIP or SIPS URI. This URI must contain an lr parameter (see Section 4.2.1). This URI may be different for each destination the request is forwarded to. The URI should not contain the transport parameter unless the proxy has knowledge (such as in a private network) that the next downstream element that will be in the path of subsequent requests supports that transport. The URI this proxy provides will be used by some other element to make a routing decision. This proxy, in general, has no way of knowing the capabilities of that element, so it must restrict itself to the mandatory elements of a SIP implementation: SIP URIs and either the TCP or UDP transports.

The URI placed in the Record-Route header field MUST resolve to the element inserting it (or a suitable stand-in) when the server location procedures of RFC 3263 (see Section 8.2.4) are applied to it, so that subsequent requests reach the same SIP element. If the Request-URI contains a SIPS URI, or the topmost Route header field value contains a SIPS URI, the URI placed into the Record-Route header field must be a SIPS URI. Furthermore, if the request was not received over TLS, the proxy must insert a Record-Route header field. In a similar fashion, a proxy that receives a request over TLS, but generates a request without a SIPS URI in the Request-URI or topmost Route header field, must insert a Record-Route header field that is not a SIPS URI.

A proxy at a security perimeter must remain on the perimeter throughout the dialog. If the URI placed in the Record-Route header field needs to be rewritten when it passes back through in a response, the URI must be distinct enough to locate at that time. (The request may spiral through this proxy, resulting in more than one Record-Route header field value being added.) Section 3.11.7 recommends a mechanism to make the URI sufficiently distinct. The proxy may include parameters in the Record-Route header field value. These will be echoed in some responses to the request such as the 200 OK responses to INVITE. Such parameters may be useful for keeping state in the message rather than the proxy.

If a proxy needs to be in the path of any type of dialog (such as one straddling a firewall), it should add a Record-Route header field value to every request with a method it does not understand since that method may have dialog semantics. The URI a proxy places into a Record-Route header field is only valid for the lifetime of any dialog created by the transaction in which it occurs. A dialog-stateful proxy, for example, may refuse to accept future requests with that value in the Request-URI after the dialog has terminated. Nondialog stateful proxies, of course, have no concept of when the dialog has terminated; however, they may encode enough information in the value to compare it against the dialog identifier of future requests and may reject requests not matching that information.

End points must not use a URI obtained from a Record-Route header field outside the dialog in which it was provided. See Section 3.6 for more information on an end point's use of Record-Route header fields. Record-routing may be required by certain services where the proxy needs to observe all messages in a dialog. However, it slows down processing and impairs scalability, and thus proxies should only Record-Route if required for a particular service. The Record-Route process is designed to work for any SIP request that initiates a dialog. INVITE is the only such request in this specification, but extensions to the protocol may define others.

3.11.6.5 Add Additional Header Fields

The proxy may add any other appropriate header fields to the copy at this point.

3.11.6.6 Postprocessing Routing Information

A proxy may have a local policy that mandates that a request visit a specific set of proxies before being delivered to the destination. A proxy must ensure that all such proxies are loose routers. Generally, this can only be known with certainty if the proxies are within the same administrative domain. This set of proxies is represented by a set of URIs (each of which contains the lr parameter). This set must be pushed into the Route header field of the copy ahead of any existing values, if present. If the Route header field is absent, it must be added, containing that list of URIs.

If the proxy has a local policy that mandates that the request visit one specific proxy, an alternative to pushing a Route value into the Route header field is to bypass the forwarding logic of item 10 below, and instead just send the request to the address, port, and transport for that specific proxy. If the request has a Route header field, this alternative must not be used unless it is known that next-hop proxy is a loose router. Otherwise, this approach may be used; however, the Route insertion mechanism above is preferred for its robustness, flexibility, generality, and consistency of operation.

Furthermore, if the Request-URI contains a SIPS URI, TLS must be used to communicate with that proxy. If the copy contains a Route header field, the proxy must inspect the URI in its first value. If that URI does not contain an lr parameter, the proxy must modify the copy as follows:

- The proxy must place the Request-URI into the Route header field as the last value.
- The proxy must then place the first Route header field value into the Request-URI and remove that value from the Route header field.

Appending the Request-URI to the Route header field is part of a mechanism used to pass the information in that Request-URI through strict-routing elements. *Popping* the first Route header field value into the Request-URI formats the message the way a strict-routing element expects to receive it (with its own URI in the Request-URI and the next location to visit in the first Route header field value).

3.11.6.7 Determine Next-Hop Address, Port, and Transport

The proxy may have a local policy to send the request to a specific IP address, port, and transport, independent of the values of the Route and Request-URI. Such a policy must not be used if the proxy is not certain that the IP address, port, and transport correspond to a server that is a loose router. However, this mechanism for sending the request through a specific next hop is not recommended; instead, a Route header field should be used for that purpose as described above. In the absence of such an overriding mechanism, the proxy applies the procedures listed in RFC 3263 (see Section 8.2.4) as follows to determine where to send the request. If the proxy has reformatted the request to send to a strict-routing element, the proxy must apply those procedures to the Request-URI of the request. Otherwise, the proxy must apply the procedures to the first value in the Route header field, if present, else the Request-URI. The procedures will produce an ordered set of (address, port, and transport) tuple.

Independently of which URI is being used as input to the procedures of RFC 3263 (see Section 8.2.4), if the Request-URI specifies a SIPS resource, the proxy must follow the procedures of RFC 3263 as if the input URI were a SIPS URI. As described in RFC 3263 (see Section 8.2.4), the proxy must attempt to deliver the message to the first tuple in that set, and proceed through the set in order until the delivery attempt succeeds. For each tuple attempted, the proxy must format the message as appropriate for the tuple and send the request using a new client transaction. Since each attempt uses a new client transaction, it represents a new branch. Thus, the branch parameter provided with the Via header field must be different for each attempt. If the client transaction reports failure to send the request or a timeout from its state machine, the proxy continues to the next address in that ordered set. If the ordered set is exhausted, the request cannot be forwarded to this element in the target set. The proxy does not need to place anything in the response context, but otherwise acts as if this element of the target set returned a 408 Request Timeout final response.

3.11.6.8 Add a Via Header Field Value

3.11.6.8.1 Per RFC 3261

The proxy must insert a Via header field value into the copy before the existing Via header field values. The construction of this value follows the same guidelines of Section 3.1.2.1.7. This implies that the proxy will compute its own branch parameter, which will be globally unique for that branch, and contain the requisite magic cookie. Note that this implies that the branch parameter will be different for different instances of a spiraled or looped request through a proxy. Proxies choosing to detect loops have an additional constraint in the value they use for construction of the branch parameter. A proxy choosing to detect loops should create a branch parameter separable into two parts by the implementation. The first part must satisfy the constraints of Section 3.1.2.1.7 as described above. The second is used to perform loop detection and distinguish loops from spirals.

Loop detection is performed by verifying that, when a request returns to a proxy, those fields having an impact on the processing of the request have not changed. The value placed in this part of the branch parameter should reflect all of those fields (including any Route, Proxy-Require, and Proxy-Authorization header fields). This is to ensure that if the request is routed back to the proxy and one of those fields changes, it is treated as a spiral and not a loop (see Section 3.11.3). A common way to create this value is to compute a cryptographic hash of the To tag, From tag, Call-ID header field, the Request-URI of the request received (before translation), the topmost Via header, and the sequence number from the CSeq header field, in addition to any Proxy-Require and Proxy-Authorization header fields that may be present. The algorithm used to compute the hash is implementation dependent; however, MD5, defined in RFCs 1321 and 6151 expressed in hexadecimal, is a reasonable choice. (Base64 is not permissible for a token.)

If a proxy wishes to detect loops, the *branch* parameter it supplies must depend on all information affecting processing of a request, including the incoming Request-URI and any header fields affecting the request's admission or routing. This is necessary to distinguish looped requests from requests whose routing parameters have changed before returning to this server. The request method must not be included in the calculation of the branch parameter. In particular, CANCEL and ACK requests (for non-2xx responses) must have the same branch value as the corresponding request they cancel or acknowledge. The branch parameter is used in correlating those requests at the server handling them (see Sections 3.2 and 3.12.2.3).

3.11.6.8.2 Per RFC 5393

Section 4.2.1 of RFC 5393: Update to Section 16.6 of RFC 3261:

> This section replaces all of item 8 in Section 16.6 (see Section 3.11.6.8.1) of RFC 3261 (item 8 begins on page 105 and ends on page 106 of RFC 3261).
>
> 8. Add a Via Header Field Value
>
> The proxy must insert a Via header field value into the copy before the existing Via header field values. The construction of this value follows the same guidelines of Section 8.1.1.7 (see Section 3.1.2.1.7) of RFC 3261. This implies that the proxy will compute its own branch parameter, which will be globally unique for that branch, and will contain the requisite magic cookie. Note that following only the guidelines in Section 8.1.1.7 (see Section 3.1.2.1.7) of RFC 3261 will result in a branch parameter that will be different for different instances of a spiraled or looped request through a proxy. Proxies required to perform loop detection by RFC 5393 (see Section 9.11.1.2) have an additional constraint on the value they place in the Via header field. Such proxies create a branch value separable into two parts in any implementation-dependent way.
>
> The remainder of this section's description assumes the existence of these two parts. If a proxy chooses to employ some other mechanism, it is the implementer's responsibility to verify that the detection properties defined by the requirements placed on these two parts are achieved.
>
> The first part of the branch value must satisfy the constraints of Section 8.1.1.7 (see Section 3.1.2.1.7) of RFC 3261. The second part is used to perform loop detection and distinguish loops from spirals. This second part must vary with any field used by the location service logic in determining where to retarget or forward this request. This is necessary to distinguish looped requests from spirals by allowing the proxy to recognize if none of the values affecting the processing of the request have changed. Hence, the second part must depend at least on the received Request-URI and any Route header field values used when processing the received request. Implementers need to take care to include all fields used by the location service logic in that particular implementation. This second part must not vary with the request method. CANCEL and non-200 ACK requests must have the same branch parameter value as the corresponding request they cancel or acknowledge. This branch parameter value is used in correlating those requests.

3.11.6.9 Add a Content-Length Header Field if Necessary

If the request will be sent to the next hop using a stream-based transport and the copy contains no Content-Length header field, the proxy must insert one with the correct value for the body of the request (see Section 2.8).

3.11.6.10 Forward Request

A stateful proxy must create a new client transaction for this request as described in Section 3.12.1 and instruct the transaction to send the request using the address, port, and transport.

3.11.6.11 Set Timer C

To handle the case where an INVITE request never generates a final response, the TU uses a timer, called timer C. Timer C must be set for each client transaction when an

INVITE request is proxied. The timer MUST be larger than 3 minutes. Section 3.11.7 discusses how this timer is updated with provisional responses, and Section 3.11.8 discusses processing when it fires.

3.11.7 Response Processing

When a response is received by an element, it first tries to locate a client transaction (Section 3.12.1.3) matching the response. If a transaction is found, the response is handed to the client transaction. If none is found, the element must not forward the response. (Note that these two sentences have been updated/modified per RFC 6026.) As client transactions pass responses to the proxy layer, the following processing must take place:

1. Find the appropriate response context.
2. Update timer C for provisional responses.
3. Remove the topmost Via.
4. Add the response to the response context.
5. Check to see if this response should be forwarded immediately.
6. When necessary, choose the best final response from the response context.

If no final response has been forwarded after every client transaction associated with the response context has been terminated, the proxy must choose and forward the *best* response from those it has seen thus far. The following processing must be performed on each response that is forwarded. It is likely that more than one response to each request will be forwarded: at least each provisional and one final response.

7. Aggregate authorization header field values if necessary.
8. Optionally rewrite Record-Route header field values.
9. Forward the response.
10. Generate any necessary CANCEL requests.

Each of the above steps is detailed in the following sections.

3.11.7.1 Find Context

The proxy locates the response context it created before forwarding the original request using the key described in Section 3.11.6. The remaining processing steps take place in this context.

3.11.7.2 Update Timer C for Provisional Responses

For an INVITE transaction, if the response is a provisional response with status codes 101 to 199 inclusive (i.e., anything but 100), the proxy must reset timer C for that client transaction. The timer MAY be reset to a different value, but this value must be greater than 3 minutes.

3.11.7.3 Via

The proxy removes the topmost Via header field value from the response. If no Via header field values remain in the response, the response was meant for this element and must not be forwarded. The remainder of the processing described in this section is not performed on this message, the UAC processing rules described in Section 3.1.2 are followed instead (transport layer processing has already occurred). This will happen, for instance, when the element generates CANCEL requests as described in Section 3.3.

3.11.7.4 Add Response to Context

Final responses received are stored in the response context until a final response is generated on the server transaction associated with this context. The response may be a candidate for the best final response to be returned on that server transaction. Information from this response may be needed in forming the best response, even if this response is not chosen. If the proxy chooses to recurse on any contacts in a 3xx response by adding them to the target set, it must remove them from the response before adding the response to the response context. However, a proxy should not recurse to a non-SIPS URI if the Request-URI of the original request was a SIPS URI. If the proxy recurses on all of the contacts in a 3xx response, the proxy should not add the resulting contactless response to the response context.

Removing the contact before adding the response to the response context prevents the next element upstream from retrying a location this proxy has already attempted. 3xx responses may contain a mixture of SIP, SIPS, and non-SIP URIs. A proxy may choose to recurse on the SIP and SIPS URIs and place the remainder into the response context to be returned, potentially in the final response. If a proxy receives a 416 Unsupported URI Scheme response to a request whose Request-URI scheme was not SIP, but the scheme in the original received request was SIP or SIPS (i.e., the proxy changed the scheme from SIP or SIPS to something else when it proxied a request), the proxy should add a new URI to the target set. This URI should be a SIP URI version of the non-SIP URI that was just tried. In the case of the tel URL, this is accomplished by placing the telephone-subscriber part of the tel URL into the user part of the SIP URI, and setting the host part to the domain where the prior request was sent. See Section 4.2.2.1 for more detail on forming SIP URIs from tel URLs. As with a 3xx response, if a proxy *recurses* on the 416 by trying a SIP or SIPS URI instead, the 416 response should not be added to the response context.

3.11.7.5 Check Response for Forwarding

Until a final response has been sent on the server transaction, the following responses must be forwarded immediately:

- Any provisional response other than 100 Trying
- Any 2xx response

If a 6xx response is received, it is not immediately forwarded, but the stateful proxy should cancel all client pending transactions as described in Section 3.3, and it MUST NOT create any new branches in this context. This is a change from RFC 2543 obsoleted by RFC 3261, which mandated that the proxy was to forward the 6xx response immediately. For an INVITE transaction, this approach had the problem that a 2xx response could arrive on another branch, in which case the proxy would have to forward the 2xx. The result was that the UAC could receive a 6xx response followed by a 2xx response, which should never be allowed to occur. Under the new rules, upon receiving a 6xx, a proxy will issue a CANCEL request, which will generally result in 487 responses from all outstanding client transactions, and then at that point the 6xx is forwarded upstream. After a final response has been sent on the server transaction, the following responses must be forwarded immediately:

- Any 2xx response to an INVITE request

A stateful proxy must not immediately forward any other responses. In particular, a stateful proxy must not forward any 100 Trying response. Those responses that are candidates for forwarding later as the best response have been gathered as described in step Add Response to Context. Any response chosen for immediate forwarding must be processed as described in steps Aggregate Authorization Header Field Values through Record-Route. This step, combined with the next, ensures that a stateful proxy will forward exactly one final response to a non-INVITE request, and either exactly one non-2xx response or one or more 2xx responses to an INVITE request.

3.11.7.6 Choosing the Best Response

A stateful proxy must send a final response to a response context's server transaction if no final responses have been immediately forwarded by the above rules and all client transactions in this response context have been terminated. The stateful proxy must choose the best final response among those received and stored in the response context. If there are no final responses in the context, the proxy must send a 408 Request Timeout response to the server transaction. Otherwise, the proxy must forward a response from the responses stored in the response context. It must choose from the 6xx class responses if any exist in the context. If no 6xx class responses are present, the proxy should choose from the lowest response class stored in the response context. The proxy may select any response within that chosen class. The proxy should give preference to responses that provide information affecting resubmission of this request, such as 401, 407, 415, 420, and 484 if the 4xx class is chosen. A proxy that receives a 503 Service Unavailable response should not forward it upstream unless it can determine that any subsequent requests it might proxy will also generate a 503. In other words, forwarding a 503 means that the proxy knows it cannot service any requests, not just the one for the Request-URI in the request that generated the 503.

If the only response that was received is a 503, the proxy should generate a 500 response and forward that upstream. The forwarded response must be processed as described in steps Aggregate Authorization Header Field Values through Record-Route. For example, if a proxy forwarded a request to four locations, and received 503, 407, 501, and 404 responses, it may choose to forward the 407 Proxy Authentication Required responses. 1xx and 2xx responses may be involved in the establishment of dialogs. When a request does not contain a To tag, the To tag in the response is used by the UAC to distinguish multiple responses to a dialog creating request. A proxy must not insert a tag into the To header field of a 1xx or 2xx response if the request did not contain one. A proxy must not modify the tag in the To header field of a 1xx or 2xx response. Since a proxy may not insert a tag into the To header field of a 1xx response to a request that did not contain one, it cannot issue non-100 provisional responses on its own. However, it can branch the request to a UAS sharing the same element as the proxy.

This UAS can return its own provisional responses, entering into an early dialog with the initiator of the request. The UAS does not have to be a discreet process from the proxy. It could be a virtual UAS implemented in the same code space as the proxy. 3-6xx responses are delivered hop by hop. When issuing a 3-6xx response, the element is effectively acting as a UAS, issuing its own response, usually based on the responses received from downstream elements. An element should preserve the To tag when simply forwarding a 3-6xx response to a request that did not contain a To tag. A proxy must not modify the To tag in any forwarded response to a request that contains a To tag. While it makes no difference to the upstream elements if the proxy replaced the To tag in a forwarded 3-6xx response, preserving the original tag may assist with debugging. When the proxy is aggregating information from several responses, choosing a To tag from among them is arbitrary, and generating a new To tag may make debugging easier. This happens, for instance, when combining 401 Unauthorized and 407 Proxy Authentication Required challenges, or combining Contact values from unencrypted and unauthenticated 3xx responses.

3.11.7.7 Aggregate Authorization Header Field Values

If the selected response is a 401 Unauthorized or 407 Proxy Authentication Required, the proxy must collect any WWWAuthenticate and Proxy-Authenticate header field values from all other 401 Unauthorized and 407 Proxy Authentication Required responses received thus far in this response context, and add them to this response without modification before forwarding. The resulting 401 (Unauthorized) or 407 Proxy Authentication Required response could have several WWWAuthenticate and Proxy-Authenticate header field values. This is necessary because any or all of the destinations the request was forwarded to may have requested credentials. The client needs to receive all of those challenges and supply credentials for each of them when it retries the request. Motivation for this behavior is provided in Section 19.12.

3.11.7.8 Record-Route

If the selected response contains a Record-Route header field value originally provided by this proxy, the proxy may choose to rewrite the value before forwarding the response. This allows the proxy to provide different URIs for itself to the next upstream and downstream elements. A proxy may choose to use this mechanism for any reason. For instance, it is useful for multihomed hosts. If the proxy received the request over TLS, and sent it out over a non-TLS connection, the proxy must rewrite the URI in the Record-Route header field to be a SIPS URI. If the proxy received the request over a non-TLS connection, and sent it out over TLS, the proxy must rewrite the URI in the Record-Route header field to be a SIP URI. The new URI provided by the proxy must satisfy the same constraints on URIs placed in Record-Route header fields in requests (see Section 3.11.6) with the following modifications: the URI should not contain the transport parameter unless the proxy has knowledge that the next upstream (as opposed to downstream) element that will be in the path of subsequent requests supports that transport. When a proxy does decide to modify the Record-Route header field in the response, one of the operations it performs is locating the Record-Route value that it had inserted.

If the request spiraled, and the proxy inserted a Record-Route value in each iteration of the spiral, locating the correct value in the response (which must be the proper iteration in the reverse direction) is tricky. The rules above recommend that a proxy wishing to rewrite Record-Route header field values insert sufficiently distinct URIs into the Record-Route header field so that the right one may be selected for rewriting. A recommended mechanism to achieve this is for the proxy to append a unique identifier for the proxy instance to the user portion of the URI. When the response arrives, the proxy modifies the first Record-Route whose identifier matches the proxy instance. The modification results in a URI without this piece of data appended to the user portion of the URI. Upon the next iteration, the same algorithm (find the topmost Record-Route header field value with the parameter) will correctly extract the next Record-Route header field value inserted by that proxy. Not every response to a request to which a proxy adds a Record-Route header field value will contain a Record-Route header field. If the response does contain a Record-Route header field, it will contain the value the proxy added.

3.11.7.9 Forward Response

After performing the processing described in steps Aggregate Authorization Header Field Values through Record-Route, the proxy may perform any feature-specific manipulations on the selected response. The proxy must not add to, modify, or remove the message body. Unless otherwise specified, the proxy must not remove any header field values other than the Via header field value discussed in Section 3.11.7. In particular, the proxy must not remove any *received* parameter it may have added to the next Via header field value while processing the request associated with this response. The proxy must pass the response to the server transaction associated with the response context. This will result in the response being sent to the location now indicated in the topmost Via header field value. If the server transaction is no longer available to handle the transmission, the element must forward the response statelessly by sending it to the server transport. The server transaction might indicate failure to send the response or signal a timeout in its state machine. These errors would be logged for diagnostic purposes as appropriate; however, the protocol requires no remedial action from the proxy. The proxy must maintain the response context until all of its associated transactions have been terminated, even after forwarding a final response.

3.11.7.10 Generate CANCELs

If the forwarded response was a final response, the proxy must generate a CANCEL request for all pending client transactions associated with this response context. A proxy should also generate a CANCEL request for all pending client transactions associated with this response context when it receives a 6xx response. A pending client transaction is one that has received a provisional response, but no final response (it is in the proceeding state), and has not had an associated CANCEL generated for it. Generating CANCEL requests is described in Section 3.2. The requirement to CANCEL pending client transactions upon forwarding a final response does not guarantee that an end point will not receive multiple 200 OK responses to an INVITE. 200 OK responses on more than one branch may be generated before the CANCEL requests can be sent and processed. Furthermore, it is reasonable to expect that a future extension may override this requirement to issue CANCEL requests.

3.11.8 Processing Timer C

If timer C should fire, the proxy must either reset the timer with any value it chooses, or terminate the client transaction. If the client transaction has received a provisional response, the proxy must generate a CANCEL request matching that transaction. If the client transaction has not received a provisional response, the proxy must behave as if the transaction received a 408 Request Timeout response. Allowing the proxy to reset the timer allows the proxy to dynamically extend the transaction's lifetime based on current conditions (such as utilization) when the timer fires.

3.11.9 Handling Transport Errors

If the transport layer notifies a proxy of an error when it tries to forward a request (see Section 3.13.4), the proxy must behave as if the forwarded request received a 503 Service Unavailable response. If the proxy is notified of an error when forwarding a response, it drops the response. The proxy should not cancel any outstanding client transactions associated with this response context due to this notification. If a proxy cancels its outstanding client transactions, a single malicious or misbehaving client can cause all transactions to fail through its Via header field.

3.11.10 CANCEL Processing

A stateful proxy may generate a CANCEL to any other request it has generated at any time (subject to receiving a provisional response to that request as described in Section 3.2). A proxy MUST cancel any pending client transactions associated with a response context when it receives a matching CANCEL request. A stateful proxy may generate CANCEL requests for pending INVITE client transactions based on the period specified in the INVITE's Expires header field elapsing. However, this is generally unnecessary since the end points involved will take care of signaling the end of the transaction.

While a CANCEL request is handled in a stateful proxy by its own server transaction, a new response context is not created for it. Instead, the proxy layer searches its existing response contexts for the server transaction handling the request associated with this CANCEL. If a matching response context is found, the element must immediately return a 200 OK response to the CANCEL request. In this case, the element is acting as a UAS as defined in Section 3.1.3. Furthermore, the element must generate CANCEL requests for all pending client transactions in the context as described in Section 3.11.7. If a response context is not found, the element does not have any knowledge of the request to apply the CANCEL to. It must statelessly forward the CANCEL request (it may have statelessly forwarded the associated request previously).

3.11.11 Stateless Proxy

When acting statelessly, a proxy is a simple message forwarder. Much of the processing performed when acting statelessly is the same as when behaving statefully. The differences are detailed here. A stateless proxy does not have any notion of a transaction, or of the response context used to describe stateful proxy behavior. Instead, the stateless proxy takes messages, both requests and responses, directly from the transport layer (see Section 3.13). As a result, stateless proxies do not retransmit messages on their own. They do, however, forward all retransmissions they receive (they do not have the ability to distinguish a retransmission from the original message). Furthermore, when handling a request statelessly, an element must not generate its own 100 Trying or any other provisional response. A stateless proxy must validate a request as described in Section 3.11.3.

A stateless proxy must follow the request processing steps described in Sections 3.11.4 and 3.11.5 with the following exception:

- A stateless proxy must choose one and only one target from the target set. This choice must only rely on fields in the message and time-invariant properties of the server. In particular, a retransmitted request must be forwarded to the same destination each time it is processed. Furthermore, CANCEL and non-Routed ACK requests must generate the same choice as their associated INVITE.

A stateless proxy must follow the request processing steps described in Section 2.12.6 with the following exceptions:

- The requirement for unique branch IDs across space and time applies to stateless proxies as well. However, a stateless proxy cannot simply use a random number generator to compute the first component of the branch ID, as described in Section 3.11.6. This is because retransmissions of a request need to have the same value, and a stateless proxy cannot tell a retransmission from the original request. Therefore, the component of the branch parameter that makes it unique must be the same each time a retransmitted request is forwarded. Thus, for a stateless proxy, the branch parameter must be computed as a combinatoric function of message parameters that are invariant on retransmission.

The stateless proxy may use any technique it likes to guarantee the uniqueness of its branch IDs across transactions. However, the following procedure is recommended. The proxy examines the branch ID in the topmost Via header field of the received request. If it begins with the magic cookie, the first component of the branch ID of the outgoing request is computed as a hash of the received branch ID. Otherwise, the first component of the branch ID is computed as a hash of the topmost Via, the tag in the To header field, the tag in the From header field, the Call-ID header field, the CSeq number (but not method), and the Request-URI from the received request. One of these fields will always vary across two different transactions.

- All other message transformations specified in Section 3.11.6 must result in the same transformation of a retransmitted request. In particular, if the proxy inserts a Record-Route value or pushes URIs into the Route header field, it must place the same values in retransmissions of the request. As for the Via branch parameter, this implies that the transformations must be based on time-invariant configuration or retransmission-invariant properties of the request.
- A stateless proxy determines where to forward the request as described for stateful proxies in Section 3.11.2. The request is sent directly to the transport layer instead of through a client transaction. Since a stateless proxy must forward retransmitted requests to the same destination and add identical branch parameters to each of them, it can only use information from the message itself and time-invariant configuration data for those calculations. If the configuration state is not time invariant (e.g., if a routing table is updated), any requests that could be affected by the change may not be forwarded statelessly during an interval equal to the transaction timeout window before or after the change. The method of processing the affected requests in that interval is an implementation decision.

A common solution is to forward the transaction statefully. Stateless proxies must not perform special processing for CANCEL requests. They are processed by the above rules as any other requests. In particular, a stateless proxy applies the same Route header field processing to CANCEL requests that it applies to any other request. Response processing as described in Section 3.11.7 does not apply to a proxy behaving statelessly. When a response arrives at a stateless proxy, the proxy must inspect the sent-by value in the first (topmost) Via header field value. If that address matches the proxy (it equals a value this proxy has inserted into previous requests), the proxy must remove that header field value from the response and forward the result to the location indicated in the next Via header field value. The proxy must not add to, modify, or remove the message body. Unless specified otherwise, the proxy must not remove any other header field values. If the address does not match the proxy, the message must be silently discarded.

3.11.12 Summary of Proxy Route Processing

In the absence of local policy to the contrary, the processing that a proxy performs on a request containing a Route header field can be summarized in the following steps:

1. The proxy will inspect the Request-URI. If it indicates a resource owned by this proxy, the proxy will replace it with the results of running a location service. Otherwise, the proxy will not change the Request-URI.
2. The proxy will inspect the URI in the topmost Route header field value. If it indicates this proxy, the proxy removes it from the Route header field (this route node has been reached).
3. The proxy will forward the request to the resource indicated by the URI in the topmost Route header field value or in the Request-URI if no Route header field is present. The proxy determines the address, port, and transport to use when forwarding the request by applying the procedures in RFC 3263 (see Section 8.2.4) to that URI. If no strict-routing elements are encountered on the path of the request, the Request-URI will always indicate the target of the request.

3.11.12.1 Examples

3.11.12.1.1 Basic SIP Trapezoid

This scenario is the basic SIP trapezoid, U1 -> P1 -> P2 -> U2, with both proxies record-routing. Here is the flow.

U1 sends

```
INVITE sip:callee@domain.com SIP/2.0
Contact: sip:caller@u1.example.com to P1. P1
is an outbound proxy. P1 is not responsible
for domain.com, so it looks it up in DNS and
sends it there. It also adds a Record-Route
header field value: INVITE sip:callee@domain.
com SIP/2.0 Contact: sip:caller@u1.example.
com Record-Route: <sip:p1.example.com;lr>
```

P2 gets this. It is responsible for domain.com, so it runs a location service and rewrites the Request-URI. It also adds a Record-Route header field value. There is no Route header field, so it resolves the new Request-URI to determine where to send the request:

```
INVITE sip:callee@u2.domain.com SIP/2.0
Contact: sip:caller@u1.example.com
Record-Route: <sip:p2.domain.com;lr>
Record-Route: <sip:p1.example.com;lr>
The callee at u2.domain.com gets this and
responds with a 200 OK:
SIP/2.0 200 OK
Contact: sip:callee@u2.domain.com
Record-Route: <sip:p2.domain.com;lr>
Record-Route: <sip:p1.example.com;lr>
```

The callee at u2 also sets its dialog state's remote target URI to sip:caller@u1.example.com and its route set to (<sip:p2.domain.com;lr>,<sip:p1.example.com;lr>). This is forwarded by P2 to P1 to U1 as normal. Now, U1 sets its dialog state's remote target URI to sip:callee@u2.domain.com and its route set to (<sip:p1.example.com;lr>,<sip:p2.domain.com;lr>). Since all the route set elements contain the lr parameter, U1 constructs the following BYE request:

```
BYE sip:callee@u2.domain.com SIP/2.0
Route: <sip:p1.example.com;lr>,<sip:p2.
domain.com;lr>
```

As any other element (including proxies) would do, it resolves the URI in the topmost Route header field value using DNS to determine where to send the request. This goes to P1. P1 notices that it is not responsible for the resource indicated in the Request-URI so it does not change it. It does see that it is the first value in the Route header field; thus, it removes that value and forwards the request to P2:

```
BYE sip:callee@u2.domain.com SIP/2.0
Route: <sip:p2.domain.com;lr>
```

P2 also notices it is not responsible for the resource indicated by the Request-URI (it is responsible for domain.com, not u2.domain.com), so it does not change it. It does see itself in the first Route header field value, so it removes it and forwards the following to u2.domain.com based on a DNS lookup against the Request-URI:

```
BYE sip:callee@u2.domain.com SIP/2.0
```

3.11.12.1.2 Traversing a Strict-Routing Proxy

In this scenario, a dialog is established across four proxies, each of which adds Record-Route header field values. The third proxy implements the strict-routing procedures specified in RFC 2543 and many works in progress.

```
U1->P1->P2->P3->P4->U2
```

The INVITE arriving at U2 contains

```
INVITE sip:callee@u2.domain.com SIP/2.0
Contact: sip:caller@u1.example.com
Record-Route: <sip:p4.domain.com;lr>
Record-Route: <sip:p3.middle.com>
Record-Route: <sip:p2.example.com;lr>
Record-Route: <sip:p1.example.com;lr>
```

which U2 responds to with a 200 OK. Later, U2 sends the following BYE request to P4 based on the first Route header field value:

```
BYE sip:caller@u1.example.com SIP/2.0
Route: <sip:p4.domain.com;lr>
Route: <sip:p3.middle.com>
Route: <sip:p2.example.com;lr>
Route: <sip:p1.example.com;lr>
```

P4 is not responsible for the resource indicated in the Request-URI, so it will leave it alone. It notices that it is the element in the first Route header field value, so it removes it. It then prepares to send the request based on the now first Route header field value of sip:p3.middle.com; however, it notices that this URI does not contain the lr parameter, so before sending, it reformats the request to be

```
BYE sip:p3.middle.com SIP/2.0
Route: <sip:p2.example.com;lr>
Route: <sip:p1.example.com;lr>
Route: <sip:caller@u1.example.com>
P3 is a strict router, so it forwards the
following to P2:
BYE sip:p2.example.com;lr SIP/2.0
Route: <sip:p1.example.com;lr>
Route: <sip:caller@u1.example.com>
```

P2 sees that the request-URI is a value it placed into a Record-Route header field, so before further processing, it rewrites the request to be

```
BYE sip:caller@u1.example.com SIP/2.0
Route: <sip:p1.example.com;lr>
```

P2 is not responsible for u1.example.com, so it sends the request to P1 based on the resolution of the Route header field value. P1 notices itself in the topmost Route header field value, so it removes it, resulting in

```
BYE sip:caller@u1.example.com SIP/2.0
```

Since P1 is not responsible for u1.example.com and there is no Route header field, P1 will forward the request to u1.example.com based on the Request-URI.

3.11.12.1.3 Rewriting Record-Route Header Field Values

In this scenario, U1 and U2 are in different private namespaces and they enter a dialog through a proxy P1, which acts as a gateway between the namespaces.

```
U1->P1->U2
```

U1 sends

```
INVITE sip:callee@gateway.leftprivatespace.
com SIP/2.0
Contact: <sip:caller@u1.leftprivatespace.com>
P1 uses its location service and sends the
following to U2:
INVITE sip:callee@rightprivatespace.com
SIP/2.0
Contact: <sip:caller@u1.leftprivatespace.com>
Record-Route: <sip:gateway.rightprivatespace.
com;lr>
U2 sends this 200 (OK) back to P1:
SIP/2.0 200 OK
Contact: <sip:callee@u2.rightprivatespace.
com>
Record-Route: <sip:gateway.rightprivatespace.
com;lr>
```

P1 rewrites its Record-Route header parameter to provide a value that U1 will find useful, and sends the following to U1:

```
SIP/2.0 200 OK
Contact: <sip:callee@u2.rightprivatespace.
com>
Record-Route: <sip:gateway.leftprivatespace.
com;lr>
Later, U1 sends the following BYE request to
P1:
```

```
BYE sip:callee@u2.rightprivatespace.com
SIP/2.0
Route: <sip:gateway.leftprivatespace.com;lr>
```

which P1 forwards to U2 as

```
BYE sip:callee@u2.rightprivatespace.com
SIP/2.0
```

3.12 Transactions

SIP is a transactional protocol, and its transactions have a client side and a server side. The client side is known as a client transaction, and the server side as a server transaction. The client transaction sends the request, and the server transaction sends the response. In SIP transaction, a single request may follow with zero or more provisional responses and one or more final responses. The client and server transactions are logical functions that are embedded in any number of elements. Specifically, they exist within UAs and stateful proxy servers. Per RFC 3261, in the INVITE transaction where the request is an INVITE, it should be noted that the transaction also includes the ACK only if the final response is not a 2xx response. If the response is a 2xx, the ACK is not considered part of the transaction. The reason for this separation is

REASON FOR CHANGE OF RFC 3261 MANDATED BY RFC 6026

One use of the INVITE method in SIP is to establish new sessions. These *initial* INVITEs may fork at intermediaries, and more than one receiving end point may choose to accept the request. SIP is designed such that the requester receives all of these success responses. Two sets of requirements in RFC 3261 work together to allow multiple 2xx responses to be processed correctly by the requester. First, all elements are required to immediately destroy any INVITE client transaction state upon forwarding a matching 2xx class response. This requirement applies to both UAs and proxies (proxies forward the response upstream, the transaction layer at UAs forwards the response to its *UA core*). Second, all proxies are required to statelessly forward upstream any 2xx class responses that do not match an existing transaction, also called stray responses. The transaction layer at UAs is required to forward these responses to its UA core. Logic in the UA core deals with acknowledging each of these responses. This technique for specifying the behavior was chosen over adjusting INVITE client transaction state machines as a simpler way to specify the correct behavior. Over time, implementation experience demonstrated the existing text is in error.

Once any element with a server transaction (say, a proxy in the path of the INVITE) deletes that transaction state, any retransmission of the INVITE will be treated as a new request, potentially forwarded to different locations than the original. Many implementations in the field have made proprietary adjustments to their transaction logic to avoid this error. The requirement to statelessly forward stray responses has also been identified as a security risk. Through it, elements compliant to RFC 3261 are compelled to do work (forward packets) that is not protected by the admission policies applied to requests. This can be leveraged to, for instance, use a SIP proxy as an anonymizing forwarder of packets in a distributed denial-of-service attack. General Internet end points can also collude to tunnel non-SIP content through such proxies by wrapping them in a SIP response envelope. Additionally, RFC 3261 requires that if an unrecoverable transport error is encountered while sending a response in a client transaction, that transaction moves immediately into the Terminated state. This will result in any retransmitted INVITE requests received after such an error was encountered to be processed as a new request instead of being absorbed as a retransmission.

rooted in the importance of delivering all 200 OK responses to an INVITE to the UAC. To deliver them all to the UAC, the UAS alone takes responsibility for retransmitting them, and the UAC alone takes responsibility for acknowledging them with ACK. Since this ACK is retransmitted only by the UAC, it is effectively considered its own transaction.

However, RFC 6026 normatively updates RFC 3261, the SIP, to address an error in the specified handling of success (2xx class) responses to INVITE requests. Elements following RFC 3261 (see Sections 2.5 and 2.6) exactly will misidentify retransmissions of the request as a new, unassociated request. The correction involves modifying the INVITE transaction state machines. The correction also changes the way responses that cannot be matched to an existing transaction are handled to address a security risk. This specification (RFC 6026) describes an essential correction to the SIP, defined in RFC 3261. The change addresses an error in the handling of 2xx class responses to INVITE requests that leads to retransmissions of the INVITE being treated as new requests and forbids forwarding stray INVITE responses.

SUMMARY OF CHANGE IN RFC 3261

This correction specification (RFC 6026) updates RFC 3261, adding a state and changing the transitions in the INVITE client state machine such that the INVITE client transaction remains in place to receive multiple 2xx responses. It adds a state to the INVITE server state machine to absorb retransmissions of the INVITE after a 2xx response has been sent. It modifies state transitions in the INVITE server state machine to absorb retransmissions of the INVITE request after encountering an unrecoverable transport error when sending a response. It also forbids forwarding stray responses to INVITE requests (not just 2xx responses), which RFC 3261 requires.

CONSEQUENCES IF NOT IMPLEMENTED MANDATED BY RFC 6026

Implementations strictly conformant to RFC 3261 will process retransmitted initial INVITE requests as new requests. Proxies may forward them to different locations than the original. Proxies may also be used as anonymizing forwarders of bulk traffic. Implementations will process any retransmitted INVITE request as a new request after an attempt to send a response results in an unrecoverable error.

Let us consider an example as shown in Figure 3.20b taken from RFC 3261. In this example, the UAC executes the client transaction, and its outbound proxy executes the server transaction.

The outbound proxy also executes a client transaction, which sends the request to a server transaction in the inbound proxy. That proxy also executes a client transaction, which in turn sends the request to a server transaction in the UAS. A stateless proxy does not contain a client or server transaction. The transaction exists between the UA or stateful proxy on one side, and the UA or stateful proxy on the other side. The purpose of the client transaction is to receive a request from the element in which the client is embedded, and this element is called the transaction user (TU); it can be a UA or a stateful proxy, and reliably deliver the request to a server transaction. The client transaction is also responsible for receiving responses and delivering them to the TU, filtering out any response retransmissions or disallowed responses. Similarly, the purpose of the server transaction is to receive requests from the transport layer and deliver them to the TU. The server transaction filters any request retransmissions from the network. The server transaction accepts responses from the TU and delivers them to the transport layer for transmission over the network. SIP transactions and the corresponding state machines are timer dependent. Table 3.1 provides the values and meaning of different SIP transaction timers.

In the case of an INVITE transaction, it absorbs the ACK request for any final response excepting a 2xx response. The 2xx response and its ACK receive special treatment. This response is retransmitted only by a UAS, and its ACK generated only by the UAC. This end-to-end treatment is needed so that a caller knows the entire set of users that have accepted the call. Because of this special handling, retransmissions of the 2xx response are handled by the UA core, not the transaction layer. Similarly, generation of the ACK for the 2xx is handled by the UA core. Each proxy along the path merely forwards each 2xx response to INVITE and its corresponding ACK. However, the non-INVITE transactions do not make use of ACK and are simple request–response interactions. In this respect, the characteristics of SIP request message transactions can be divided primarily into two groups: INVITE and ACK Client/Server Transaction and Non-INVITE Client/Server Transaction.

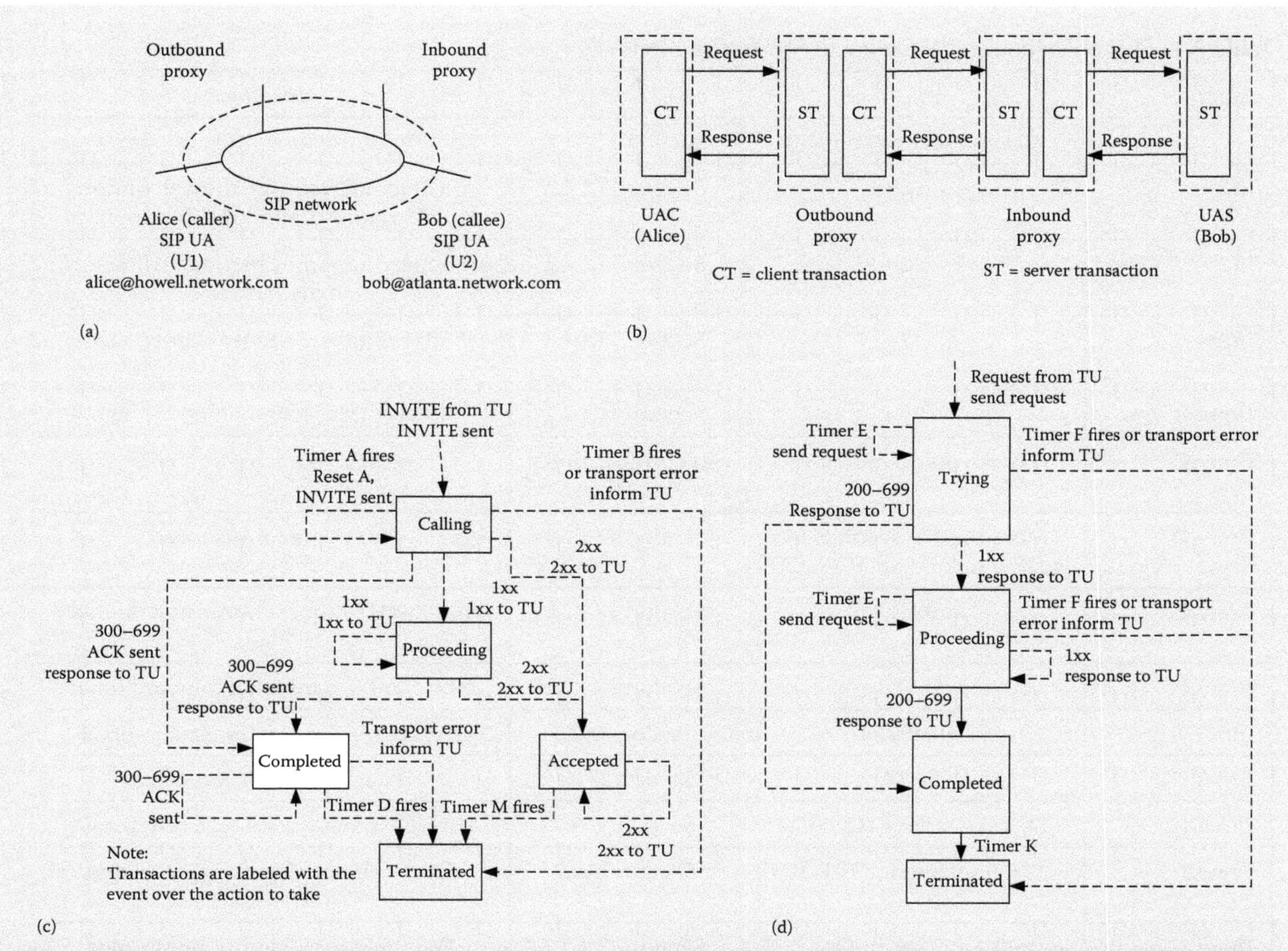

Figure 3.20 SIP transaction: (a) SIP network, (b) SIP transaction relationships, (c) INVITE client transaction state machine (including updates from RFC 6026), and (d) non-INVITE client transaction state machine. (Copyright IETF. Reproduced with permission.)

Table 3.1 Timer Values and Meaning of SIP Transactions

Timer	*Value*	*RFC 3261*	*Meaning*
T1	500 milliseconds default	Section 17.1.1.1	Round-trip time (RTT) estimate
T2	4 seconds	Section 17.1.2.2	Maximum retransmit interval for non-INVITE requests and INVITE responses
T4	5 seconds	Section 17.1.2.2	Maximum duration a message will remain in the network
Timer A	Initially T1	Section 17.1.1.2	INVITE request retransmit interval, for UDP only
Timer B	64*T1	Section 17.1.1.2	INVITE transaction timeout timer
Timer C	More than 3 minutes	Section 16.6, bullet 11	Proxy INVITE transaction timeout
Timer D	More than 32 seconds for UDP, 0 second for TCP/SCTP	Section 17.1.1.2	Wait time for response
Timer E	Initially T1	Section 17.1.2.2	Non-INVITE request retransmit interval, UDP only
Timer F	64*T1	Section 17.1.2.2	Non-INVITE transaction timeout timer
Timer G	Initially T1	Section 17.2.1	INVITE response retransmit interval
Timer H	64*T1	Section 17.2.1	Wait time for ACK receipt
Timer I	T4, 0 second for TCP/SCTP	Section 17.2.1	For UDP wait time for ACK retransmits
Timer J	64*T1, 0 second for TCP/SCTP	Section 17.2.2	For UDP wait time for non-INVITE request retransmits
Timer K	T4 for UDP, 0 second for TCP/SCTP	Section 17.1.2.2	Wait time for response retransmits
Timer L	64*T1	Section 17.2.1	Wait time for accepted INVITE request retransmits
Timer M	64*T1	Section 17.1.1	Wait time for retransmission of 2xx to INVITE or additional 2xx from other branches of a forked INVITE

Source: Copyright IETF. Reproduced with permission.

3.12.1 Client Transaction

The client transaction provides its functionality through the maintenance of a state machine. The TU communicates with the client transaction through a simple interface. When the TU wishes to initiate a new transaction, it creates a client transaction and passes it the SIP request to send, and an IP address, port, and transport to which to send it. The client transaction begins the execution of its state machine. Valid responses are passed up to the TU from the client transaction. There are two types of client transaction state machines, depending on the method of the request passed by the TU. One handles client transactions for INVITE requests. This type of machine is referred to as an INVITE client transaction. Another type handles client transactions for all requests except INVITE and ACK. This is referred to as a non-INVITE client transaction. There is no client transaction for ACK. If the TU wishes to send an ACK, it passes one directly to the transport layer for transmission. The INVITE transaction is different from those of other methods because of its extended duration. Normally, human input is required in order to respond to an INVITE. The long delays expected for sending a response argue for a three-way handshake. On the other hand, requests of other methods are expected to complete rapidly. Because of the non-INVITE transaction's reliance on a two-way handshake, TUs should respond immediately to non-INVITE requests.

3.12.1.1 INVITE Client Transaction

3.12.1.1.1 Overview

The INVITE transaction consists of a three-way handshake. The client transaction sends an INVITE, the server transaction sends responses, and the client transaction sends an ACK. For unreliable transports (such as UDP), the client transaction retransmits requests at an interval that starts at T1 seconds and doubles after every retransmission. T1 is an estimate of the round-trip time (RTT), and it defaults to 500 milliseconds. Nearly all of the transaction timers described here scale with T1, and changing T1 adjusts their values. The request is not retransmitted over reliable transports. After receiving a 1xx response, any retransmissions cease altogether, and the client waits for further responses. The server transaction can send additional 1xx responses, which are not transmitted reliably by the server transaction. Eventually, the server transaction decides to send a final response. For unreliable transports, that response is retransmitted periodically, and for reliable transports, it is sent once. For each final response that is received at the client transaction, the client transaction sends an ACK, the purpose of which is to quench retransmissions of the response.

3.12.1.1.2 Description

The state machine for the INVITE client transaction is shown in Figure 3.20c. The initial state, calling, must be entered when the TU initiates a new client transaction with an INVITE request. The client transaction must pass the request to the transport layer for transmission. If an unreliable transport is being used, the client transaction must start timer A with a value of T1. If a reliable transport is being used, the client transaction should not start timer A (timer A controls request retransmissions). For any transport, the client transaction must start timer B with a value of 64*T1 seconds (timer B controls transaction timeouts). When timer A fires, the client transaction must retransmit the request by passing it to the transport layer. It then must reset the timer with a value of 2*T1. The formal definition of retransmit within the context of the transaction layer is to take the message previously sent to the transport layer and pass it to the transport layer once more. When timer A fires 2*T1 seconds later, the request must be retransmitted again (assuming the client transaction is still in this state). This process must continue so that the request is retransmitted with intervals that double after each transmission. These retransmissions should only be done while the client transaction is in the calling state.

The default value for T1 is 500 milliseconds. T1 is an estimate of the RTT between the client and server transactions. Elements may (though it is not recommended) use smaller values of T1 within closed, private networks that do not permit general Internet connection. T1 may be chosen larger, and this is recommended if it is known in advance (such as on high latency access links) that the RTT is larger. Whatever the value of T1, the exponential back-offs on retransmissions described in this section must be used. When timer B fires and if the client transaction is still in the Calling state, the client transaction should inform the TU that a timeout has occurred. The client transaction must not generate an ACK. The value of 64*T1 is equal to the amount of time required to send seven requests in the case of an unreliable transport. If the client transaction receives a provisional response while in the Calling state, it transitions to the Proceeding state. In the Proceeding state, the client transaction should not retransmit the request any longer. Furthermore, the provisional response must be passed to the TU. Any further provisional responses must be passed up to the TU while in the Proceeding state. (Note that the next three paragraphs have been updated/modified in accordance to RFC 6926.)

When in either the Calling or Proceeding states, reception of a response with status code from 300 to 699 must cause the client transaction to transition to Completed. The client transaction MUST pass the received response up to the TU, and the client transaction must generate an ACK request, even if the transport is reliable (guidelines for constructing the ACK from the response are given in the next section), and then pass the ACK to the transport layer for transmission. The ACK must be sent to the same address, port, and transport to which the original request was sent. The client transaction must start Timer D when it enters the Completed state for any reason, with a value of at least 32 seconds for unreliable transports, and a value of 0 seconds for reliable transports. Timer D reflects the amount of time that the server transaction can remain in the Completed state when unreliable transports are used. This is equal to timer H in the INVITE server transaction, whose default is 64*T1, and is also equal to the time a UAS core will wait for an ACK once it sends a 2xx response.

However, the client transaction does not know the value of T1 in use by the server transaction or any downstream UAS cores, so an absolute minimum of 32 seconds is used instead of basing timer D on T1. Any retransmissions of a response with status code 300–699 that are received while in the Completed state must cause the ACK to be repassed to the transport layer for retransmission; however, the newly received response must not be passed up to the TU. A retransmission of the response is defined as any response that would match the same client transaction based on the rules of matching responses described later. If timer D fires while the client transaction is in the Completed state, the client transaction MUST move to the Terminated state. When a 2xx response is received while in either the Calling or Proceeding states, the client transaction must transition to the Accepted state, and timer M must be started with a value of 64*T1. The 2xx response MUST be passed up to the TU.

The client transaction must not generate an ACK to the 2xx response—its handling is delegated to the TU. A UAC core will send an ACK to the 2xx response using a new transaction. A proxy core will always forward the 2xx response upstream. The purpose of the Accepted state is to allow the client transaction to continue to exist to receive, and pass to the TU, any retransmissions of the 2xx response and any additional 2xx responses from other branches of the INVITE if it forked downstream. Timer M reflects the amount of time that the TU will wait for such messages. Any 2xx responses that match this client transaction and that are received while in the Accepted state MUST be passed up to the TU. The client transaction must not generate an ACK to the 2xx response. The client transaction takes no further action. If timer M fires while the client transaction is in the Accepted state, the client transaction must move to the Terminated state. The client transaction must be destroyed the instant it enters the Terminated state.

If timer D fires while the client transaction is in the Completed state, the client transaction must move to the terminated state. When in either the Calling or Proceeding states, reception of a 2xx response must cause the client transaction to enter the Terminated state, and the response must be passed up to the TU. The handling of this response depends on whether the TU is a proxy core or a UAC core. A UAC core will handle generation of the ACK for this response, while a proxy core will always forward the 200 OK upstream. The differing treatment of 200 OK between proxy and UAC is the reason that handling of it does not take place in the transaction layer. The client transaction must be destroyed the instant it enters the Terminated state. This is actually necessary to guarantee correct operation. The reason is that 2xx responses to an INVITE are treated differently; each one is forwarded by proxies, and the ACK handling in a UAC is different. Thus, each 2xx needs to be passed to a proxy core (so that it can be forwarded) and to a UAC core (so it can be acknowledged). No transaction layer processing takes place. Whenever a response is received by the transport, if the transport layer finds no matching client transaction, the response is passed directly to the core. Since the matching client transaction is destroyed by the first 2xx, subsequent 2xx will find no match and therefore be passed to the core.

3.12.1.1.3 Construction of the ACK Request

This section specifies the construction of ACK requests sent within the client transaction (Figure 3.20c). A UAC core that generates an ACK for 2xx must instead follow the rules as follows:

- The ACK must be passed to the client transport every time a retransmission of the 2xx final response that triggered the ACK arrives.
- Response retransmissions cease when an ACK request for the response is received. This is independent of whatever transport protocols are used to send the response.

The ACK request constructed by the client transaction must contain values for the Call-ID, From, and Request-URI that are equal to the values of those header fields in the request passed to the transport by the client transaction (let us call this the original request). The To header field in the ACK must equal the To header field in the response being acknowledged, and therefore will usually differ from the To header field in the original request by the addition of the tag parameter. The ACK must contain a single Via header field, and this must be equal to the top Via header field of the original request. The CSeq header field in the ACK must contain the same value for the sequence number as was present in the original request, but the method parameter must be equal to ACK. If the INVITE request whose response is being acknowledged had Route header fields, those header fields must appear in the ACK. This is to ensure that the ACK can be routed properly through any downstream stateless proxies. Although any request may contain a body, a body in an ACK is special since the request cannot be rejected if the body is not understood. Therefore, placement of bodies in ACK for non-2xx is not recommended, but if done, the body types are restricted to any that appeared in the INVITE, assuming that the response to the INVITE was not 415. If it was, the body in the ACK may be any type listed in the Accept header field in the 415.

For example, consider the following request:

```
INVITE sip:bob@biloxi.com SIP/2.0
Via: SIP/2.0/UDP pc33.atlanta.com;
branch=z9hG4bKkjshdyff
To: Bob <sip:bob@biloxi.com>
From: Alice <sip:alice@atlanta.com>;
tag=88sja8x
Max-Forwards: 70
Call-ID: 987asjd97y7atg
CSeq: 986759 INVITE
```

The ACK request for a non-2xx final response to this request would look like this:

```
ACK sip:bob@biloxi.com SIP/2.0
Via: SIP/2.0/UDP pc33.atlanta.com;
branch=z9hG4bKkjshdyff
To: Bob <sip:bob@biloxi.com>;tag=99sa0xk
```

```
From: Alice <sip:alice@atlanta.com>;
tag=88sja8x
Max-Forwards: 70
Call-ID: 987asjd97y7atg
CSeq: 986759 ACK
```

3.12.1.2 Non-INVITE Client Transaction

The non-INVITE client transaction is depicted in Figure 3.20d. Non-INVITE transactions do not make use of ACK. They are simple request–response interactions. For unreliable transports, requests are retransmitted at an interval that starts at T1 and doubles until it hits T2. If a provisional response is received, retransmissions continue for unreliable transports, but at an interval of T2. The state machine for the non-INVITE client transaction is shown in Figure 3.10. It is very similar to the state machine for INVITE. The Trying state is entered when the TU initiates a new client transaction with a request. When entering this state, the client transaction should set timer F to fire in 64*T1 seconds. The request must be passed to the transport layer for transmission. If an unreliable transport is in use, the client transaction must set timer E to fire in T1 seconds. If timer E fires while still in this state, the timer is reset. However, it is with a reset time value of MIN(2*T1, T2).

When the timer fires again, it is reset to a MIN(4*T1, T2). This process continues so that retransmissions occur with an exponentially increasing interval that caps at T2. The default value of T2 is 4 seconds, and it represents the amount of time a non-INVITE server transaction will take to respond to a request, if it does not respond immediately. For the default values of T1 and T2, this results in intervals of 500 milliseconds, 1 second, 2 seconds, 3 seconds, 4 seconds, 4 seconds, etc. If timer F fires while the client transaction is still in the Trying state, the client transaction should inform the TU about the timeout, and then it should enter the Terminated state. If a provisional response is received while in the Trying state, the response must be passed to the TU, and then the client transaction should move to the Proceeding state. If a final response (status codes 200–699) is received while in the Trying state, the response must be passed to the TU, and the client transaction must transition to the Completed state.

If timer E fires while in the Proceeding state, the request must be passed to the transport layer for retransmission and timer E must be reset with a value of T2 seconds. If timer F fires while in the Proceeding state, the TU must be informed of a timeout, and the client transaction must transition to the terminated state. If a final response (status codes 200–699) is received while in the Proceeding state, the response must be passed to the TU, and the client transaction must transition to the Completed state. Once the client transaction enters the Completed state, it must set timer K to fire in T4 seconds for unreliable transports, and 0 seconds for reliable transports. The Completed state exists to buffer any additional response retransmission that may be received (which is why the client transaction remains there only for unreliable transports). T4 represents the amount of time the network will take to clear messages between client and server transactions. The default value of T4 is 5 seconds. A response is a retransmission when it matches the same transaction, using the rules specified earlier. If timer K fires while in this state, the client transaction must transition to the Terminated state. Once the transaction is in the terminated state, it must be destroyed immediately.

3.12.1.3 Matching Responses to Client Transactions

When the transport layer in the client receives a response, it has to determine which client transaction will handle the response, so that the processing described earlier can take place. The branch parameter in the top Via header field is used for this purpose. A response matches a client transaction under two conditions:

- If the response has the same value of the branch parameter in the top Via header field as the branch parameter in the top Via header field of the request that created the transaction.
- If the method parameter in the CSeq header field matches the method of the request that created the transaction. The method is needed since a CANCEL request constitutes a different transaction, but shares the same value of the branch parameter.

If a request is sent via multicast, it is possible that it will generate multiple responses from different servers. These responses will all have the same branch parameter in the topmost Via, but vary in the To tag. The first response received, based on the rules above, will be used, and others will be viewed as retransmissions. That is not an error; multicast SIP provides only a rudimentary single-hop-discovery-like service that is limited to processing a single response.

3.12.1.4 Handling Transport Errors

When the client transaction sends a request to the transport layer to be sent, the following procedures are followed if the transport layer indicates a failure. The client transaction should inform the TU that a transport failure has occurred, and the client transaction should transition directly to the Terminated state. The TU will handle the failover mechanisms described in RFC 3263.

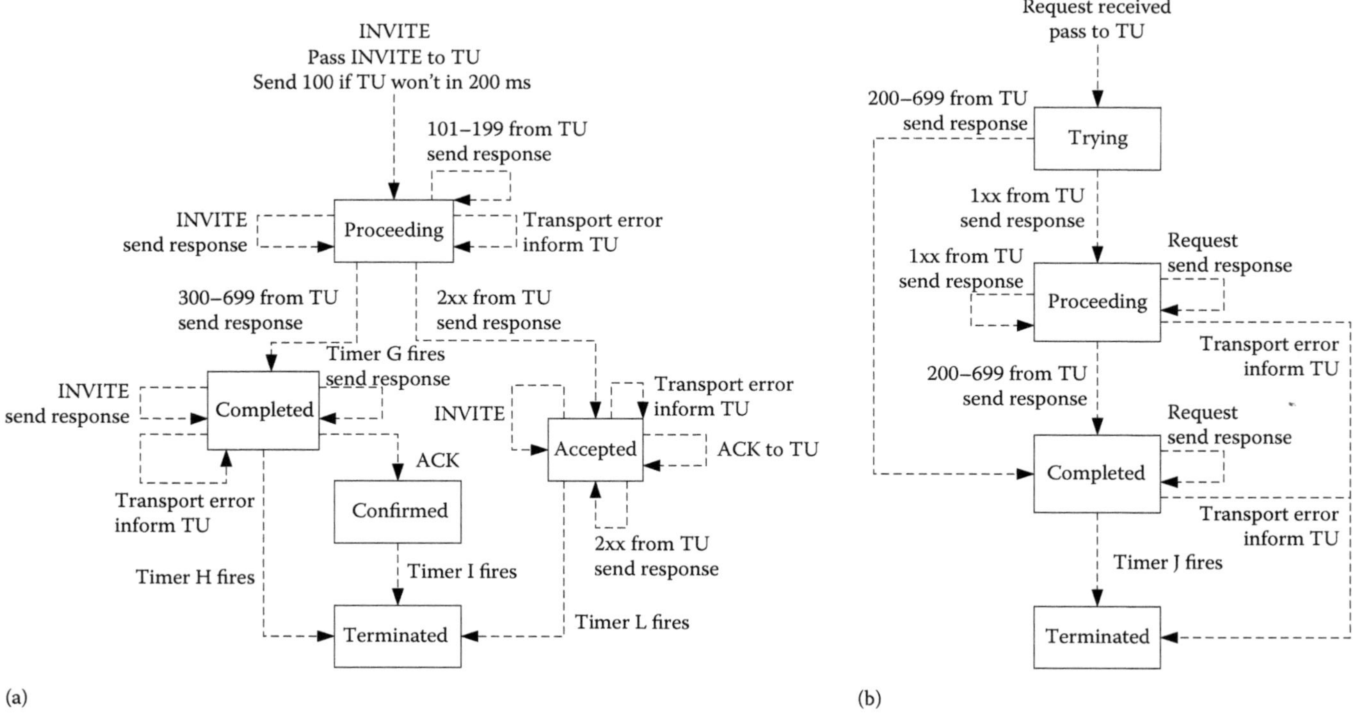

Figure 3.21 State machines for server transactions: (a) INVITE server transaction (including updates from RFC 6026) and (b) non-INVITE server transaction. (Copyright IETF. Reproduced with permission.)

3.12.2 Server Transaction

The server transaction is responsible for the delivery of requests to the TU and the reliable transmission of responses. It accomplishes this through a state machine. Server transactions are created by the core when a request is received, and transaction handling is desired for that request (this is not always the case). As with the client transactions, the state machine depends on whether the received request is an INVITE request.

3.12.2.1 INVITE Server Transaction

The state diagram for the INVITE server transaction is shown in Figure 3.21a. When a server transaction is constructed for a request, it enters the Proceeding state. The server transaction must generate a 100 Trying response unless it knows that the TU will generate a provisional or final response within 200 milliseconds, in which case it may generate a 100 Trying response. This provisional response is needed to quench request retransmissions rapidly in order to avoid network congestion.

The request must be passed to the TU. The TU passes any number of provisional responses to the server transaction. So long as the server transaction is in the Proceeding state, each of these must be passed to the transport layer for transmission. They are not sent reliably by the transaction layer (they are not retransmitted by it) and do not cause a change in the state of the server transaction. If a request retransmission is received while in the Proceeding state, the most recent provisional response that was received from the TU must be passed to the transport layer for retransmission. A request is a retransmission if it matches the same server transaction based on the rules described earlier.

If, while in the Proceeding state, the TU passes a 2xx response to the server transaction, the server transaction must pass this response to the transport layer for transmission. It is not retransmitted by the server transaction; retransmissions of 2xx responses are handled by the TU. The server transaction must then transition to the Accepted state. (Note that these two sentences have been updated/modified per RFC 6026).

While in the Proceeding state, if the TU passes a response with status code from 300 to 699 to the server transaction, the response must be passed to the transport layer for transmission, and the state machine must enter the Completed state. For unreliable transports, timer G is set to fire in T1 seconds, and is not set to fire for reliable transports. This is a change from RFC 2543, where responses were always retransmitted, even over reliable transports.

When the Completed state is entered, timer H must be set to fire in 64*T1 seconds for all transports. Timer H determines when the server transaction abandons retransmitting the response. Its value is chosen to equal timer B, the amount of time a client transaction will continue to retry sending a request. If timer G fires, the response is passed to the transport layer once more for retransmission, and timer G is set to fire in min(2*T1, T2) seconds. From then on, when timer G fires, the response is passed to the transport again for transmission, and timer G is reset with a value that doubles, unless that value exceeds T2, in which case it is reset with the value of T2. This is identical to the retransmit behavior for requests in the Trying state of the non-INVITE client transaction. Furthermore, while in the Completed state, if a request retransmission is received, the server should pass the response to the transport for retransmission.

If an ACK is received while the server transaction is in the Completed state, the server transaction must transition to the Confirmed state. As timer G is ignored in this state, any retransmissions of the response will cease. If timer H fires while in the Completed state, it implies that the ACK was never received. In this case, the server transaction must transition to the Terminated state, and must indicate to the TU that a transaction failure has occurred. The purpose of the Confirmed state is to absorb any additional ACK messages that arrive, triggered from retransmissions of the final response. When this state is entered, timer I is set to fire in T4 seconds for unreliable transports, and 0 seconds for reliable transports. Once timer I fires, the server must transition to the Terminated state. (Note that the next two paragraphs have been updated/modified per RFC 6026.)

The purpose of the Accepted state is to absorb retransmissions of an accepted INVITE request. Any such retransmissions are absorbed entirely within the server transaction. They are not passed up to the TU since any downstream UAS cores that accepted the request have taken responsibility for reliability and will already retransmit their 2xx responses if necessary. While in the Accepted state, if the TU passes a 2xx response, the server transaction must pass the response to the transport layer for transmission.

When the INVITE server transaction enters the Accepted state, timer L must be set to fire in 64*T1 for all transports. This value matches both timer B in the next upstream client state machine (the amount of time the previous hop will wait for a response when no provisionals have been sent) and the amount of time this (or any downstream) UAS core might be retransmitting the 2xx while waiting for an ACK. If an ACK is received while the INVITE server transaction is in the Accepted state, then the ACK must be passed up to the TU. If timer L fires while the INVITE server transaction is in the Accepted state, the transaction must transition to the Terminated state. Once the transaction is in the Terminated state, it must be destroyed immediately.

3.12.2.2 Non-INVITE Server Transaction

The state machine for the non-INVITE server transaction is shown in Figure 3.21b. The state machine is initialized in the Trying state and is passed a request other than INVITE or ACK when initialized. This request is passed up to the TU. Once in the Trying state, any further request retransmissions are discarded. A request is a retransmission if it matches the same server transaction, using the rules specified earlier. While in the Trying state, if the TU passes a provisional response to the server transaction, the server transaction must enter the Proceeding state. The response must be passed to the transport layer for transmission. Any further provisional responses that are received from the TU while in the Proceeding state must be passed to the transport layer for transmission. If a retransmission of the request is received while in the Proceeding state, the most recently sent provisional response must be passed to the transport layer for retransmission.

If the TU passes a final response (status codes 200–699) to the server while in the Proceeding state, the transaction must enter the Completed state, and the response must be passed to the transport layer for transmission. When the server transaction enters the Completed state, it must set timer J to fire in 64*T1 seconds for unreliable transports, and 0 seconds for reliable transports. While in the Completed state, the server transaction must pass the final response to the transport layer for retransmission whenever a retransmission of the request is received. Any other final responses passed by the TU to the server transaction must be discarded while in the Completed state. The server transaction remains in this state until timer J fires, at which point it must transition to the Terminated state. The server transaction must be destroyed the instant it enters the Terminated state.

3.12.2.3 Matching Requests to Server Transactions

When a request is received from the network by the server, it has to be matched to an existing transaction. This is accomplished in the following manner. The branch parameter in the topmost Via header field of the request is examined. If it is present and begins with the magic cookie *z9hG4bK*, the request was generated by a client transaction compliant to this specification. Therefore, the branch parameter will be unique across all transactions sent by that client. The request matches a transaction if

- The branch parameter in the request is equal to the one in the top Via header field of the request that created the transaction.
- The sent-by value in the top Via of the request is equal to the one in the request that created the transaction.
- The method of the request matches the one that created the transaction, except for ACK, where the method of the request that created the transaction is INVITE.

This matching rule applies to both INVITE and non-INVITE transactions alike. The sent-by value is used as part of the matching process because there could be accidental or malicious duplication of branch parameters from different clients. If the branch parameter in the top Via header field is not present, or does not contain the magic cookie, the following procedures are used. These exist to handle backwards compatibility with RFC 2543 obsoleted by RFC 3261–compliant implementations. The INVITE request matches a transaction if the Request-URI, To tag, From tag, Call-ID, CSeq, and top Via header field match those of the INVITE request that created the transaction. In this case, the INVITE is a retransmission of the original one that created the transaction. The ACK request matches a transaction if the Request-URI, From tag, Call-ID, CSeq number (not the method), and top Via header field match those of the INVITE request that created the transaction, and the To tag of the ACK matches the To tag of the response sent by the server transaction. Matching is done based on the matching rules defined for each of those header fields.

Inclusion of the tag in the To header field in the ACK matching process helps disambiguate ACK for 2xx from ACK for other responses at a proxy, which may have forwarded both responses. This can occur in unusual conditions. Specifically, when a proxy forked a request, and then crashes, the responses may be delivered to another proxy, which might end up forwarding multiple responses upstream. An ACK request that matches an INVITE transaction matched by a previous ACK is considered a retransmission of that previous ACK. For all other request methods, a request is matched to a transaction if the Request-URI, To tag, From tag, Call-ID, CSeq (including the method), and top Via header field match those of the request that created the transaction. Matching is done on the basis of the matching rules defined for each of those header fields. When a non-INVITE request matches an existing transaction, it is a retransmission of the request that created that transaction. Because the matching rules include the Request-URI, the server cannot match a response to a transaction. When the TU passes a response to the server transaction, it must pass it to the specific server transaction for which the response is targeted.

3.12.2.4 Handling Transport Errors

When the server transaction sends a response to the transport layer to be sent, the following procedures are followed if the transport layer indicates a failure. First, the procedures in RFC 3263 (see Section 8.2.4) are followed, which attempt to deliver the response to a backup. If those should all fail, based on the definition of failure in RFC 3263 (see Section 8.2.4), the server transaction should inform the TU that a failure has occurred, and must remain in the current state. (Note that the last two sentences have been updated/modified per RFC 6026.)

First, the procedures in RFC 3263 (see Section 8.2.4) are followed, which attempt to deliver the response to a backup. If those should all fail, based on the definition of failure in RFC 3263 (see Section 8.2.4), the server transaction should inform the TU that a failure has occurred, and should transition to the terminated state.

3.12.2.5 Non-INVITE Transactions

The procedures described in RFC 3261 may have the high probability of messages losing the race condition inherent in the non-INVITE transactions, and may create unnecessary network traffic storm as documented in RFC 4321. To take care of this problem, RFC 4320 provides the normative updates of RFC 3261 for the SIP non-INVITE transactions as follows:

- Make the best use of provisional responses
  - A SIP element must not send any provisional response with a Status-Code other than 100 to a non-INVITE request.
  - A SIP element must not respond to a non-INVITE request with a Status-Code of 100 over any unreliable transport, such as UDP, before the amount of time it takes a client transaction's timer E to be reset to T2.
  - A SIP element may respond to a non-INVITE request with a Status-Code of 100 over a reliable transport at any time.
  - Without regard to transport, an SIP element must respond to a non-INVITE request with a Status-Code of 100 if it has not otherwise responded after the amount of time it takes a client transaction's timer E to be reset to T2.
- Remove the useless late-response storm
  - A transaction-stateful SIP element must not send a response with Status-Code of 408 to a non-INVITE request. As a consequence, an element that cannot respond before the transaction expires will not send a final response at all.
  - A transaction-stateful SIP proxy must not send any response to a non-INVITE request unless it has a matching server transaction that is not in the Terminated state. As a consequence, this proxy will not forward any late non-INVITE responses.

3.13 Transport

The transport layer is responsible for the actual transmission of requests and responses over network transports. This includes determination of the connection to use for a request or response in the case of connection-oriented transports. The transport layer is responsible for managing persistent connections for transport protocols like TCP and SCTP, or TLS over those, including ones opened to the transport layer. This includes connections opened by the client or server transports, so that connections are shared between client and server transport functions. These connections are indexed by the tuple formed from the address, port, and transport protocol at the far end of the connection. When a connection is opened by the transport layer, this index is set to the destination IP, port, and transport. When the connection is accepted by the transport layer, this index is set to the source IP address, port number, and transport. Note that, because the source port is often ephemeral, but it cannot be known whether it is ephemeral or selected through procedures in RFC 3263 (see Section 8.2.4), connections accepted by the transport layer will frequently not be reused. The result is that two proxies in a *peering* relationship using a connection-oriented transport frequently will have two connections in use, one for transactions initiated in each direction.

It is recommended that connections be kept open for some implementation-defined duration after the last message was sent or received over that connection. This duration should at least equal the longest amount of time the element would need in order to bring a transaction from instantiation to the terminated state. This is to make it likely that transactions are completed over the same connection on which they are initiated (e.g., request, response, and in the case of INVITE, ACK for non-2xx responses). This usually means at least 64*T1 (see Section 3.12.1.1.1 for a definition of T1). However, it could be larger in an element that has a TU using a large value for timer C (Section 3.11.6), for example. All SIP elements must implement UDP and TCP. SIP elements may implement other protocols. Making TCP mandatory for the UA is a substantial change from RFC 2543 obsoleted by RFC 3261. It has arisen out of the need to handle larger messages, which must use TCP, as discussed below. Thus, even if an element never sends large messages, it may receive one and needs to be able to handle them.

3.13.1 Clients

3.13.1.1 Sending Requests

The client side of the transport layer is responsible for sending the request and receiving responses. The user of the transport layer passes the client transport the request, an IP address, port, transport, and possibly time to live (TTL) for multicast destinations. If a request is within 200 bytes of the path MTU, or if it is larger than 1300 bytes and the path MTU is unknown, the request must be sent using an RFC 2914 congestion controlled transport protocol, such as TCP. If this causes a change in the transport protocol from the one indicated in the top Via, the value in the top Via must be changed. This prevents fragmentation of messages over UDP and provides congestion control for larger messages. However, implementations must be able to handle messages up to the maximum datagram packet size. For UDP, this size is 65,535 bytes, including IP and UDP headers. The 200 byte *buffer* between the message size and the MTU accommodates the fact that the response in SIP can be larger than the request. This happens due to the addition of Record-Route header field values to the responses to INVITE, for example. With the extra buffer, the response can be about 170 bytes larger than the request, and still not be fragmented on IPv4 (about 30 bytes is consumed by IP/UDP, assuming no IPSec). 1300 is chosen when path MTU is not known based on the assumption of a 1500 byte Ethernet MTU.

If an element sends a request over TCP because of these message size constraints, and that request would have otherwise been sent over UDP, if the attempt to establish the connection generates either an ICMP Protocol Not Supported, or results in a TCP reset, the element should retry the request, using UDP. This is only to provide backwards compatibility with RFC 2543 (obsoleted by RFC 3261)–compliant implementations that do not support TCP. It is anticipated that this behavior will be deprecated in a future revision of this specification. A client that sends a request to a multicast address must add the *maddr* parameter to its Via header field value containing the destination multicast address, and for IPv4, should add the *ttl* parameter with a value of 1. Usage of IPv6 multicast is not defined in this specification, and will be a subject of future standardization when the need arises. These rules result in a purposeful limitation of multicast in SIP. Its primary function is to provide a *single-hop-discovery-like* service, delivering a request to a group of homogeneous servers, where it is only required to process the response from any one of them. This functionality is most useful for registrations. In fact, based on the transaction processing rules in Section 3.12.1.3, the client transaction will accept the first response, and view any others as retransmissions because they all contain the same Via branch identifier.

Before a request is sent, the client transport must insert a value of the *sent-by* field into the Via header field. This field contains an IP address or host name, and port. The usage of an FQDN is recommended. This field is used for sending responses under certain conditions, described below. If the port is absent, the default value depends on the transport. It is 5060 for UDP, TCP, and SCTP, and 5061 for TLS. For reliable transports, the response is normally sent on the connection on which the request was received. Therefore, the client transport must be prepared to receive the response on the same connection used to send the request. Under error conditions, the server may attempt to open a new connection to send the response. To handle this case, the transport layer must also be prepared to receive an incoming connection on the source IP address from which the request was sent and port number in the sent-by field. It also MUST be prepared to receive incoming connections on any address and port that would be selected by a server based on the procedures described in RFC 3263 (see Section 8.2.4).

For unreliable unicast transports, the client transport must be prepared to receive responses on the source IP address from which the request is sent (as responses are sent back to the source address) and the port number in the sent-by field. Furthermore, as with reliable transports, in certain cases the response will be sent elsewhere. The client must be prepared to receive responses on any address and port that would be selected by a server based on the procedures described in RFC 3263 (see Section 8.2.4). For multicast, the client transport must be prepared to receive responses on the same multicast group and port to which the request is sent (i.e., it needs to be a member of the multicast group it sent the request to.) If a request is destined to an IP address, port, and transport to which an existing connection is open, it is recommended that this connection be used to send the request, but another connection may be opened and used. If a request is sent using multicast, it is sent to the group address, port, and TTL provided by the transport user. If a request is sent using unicast unreliable transports, it is sent to the IP address and port provided by the transport user.

3.13.1.2 Receiving Responses

When a response is received, the client transport examines the top Via header field value. If the value of the sent-by parameter in that header field value does not correspond to a value that the client transport is configured to insert into requests, the response must be silently discarded. The client transport uses the matching procedures of Section 3.12.1.3 to attempt to match the response to an existing transaction. If there is a match, the response must be passed to that transaction. Otherwise, any element other than a stateless proxy must silently discard the response. (Note that the last three sentences have been updated/modified per RFC 6026.)

3.13.2 Servers

3.13.2.1 Receiving Requests

A server should be prepared to receive requests on any IP address, port, and transport combination that can be the result of a DNS lookup on a SIP or SIPS URI specified in RFC 3263 (see Section 8.2.4) that is handed out for the purposes of communicating with that server. In this context, *handing out* includes placing a URI in a Contact header field in a REGISTER request or a redirect response, or in a Record-Route header field in a request or response. A URI can also be handed out by placing it on a web page or business card. It is also recommended that a server listen for requests on the default SIP ports (5060 for TCP and UDP, 5061 for TLS over TCP) on all public interfaces. The typical exception would be private networks, or when multiple server instances are running on the same host. For any port and interface that a server listens on for UDP, it MUST listen on that same port and interface for TCP. This is because a message may need to be sent using TCP, rather than UDP, if it is too large. As a result, the converse is not true. A server need not listen for UDP on a particular address and port just because it is listening on that same address and port for TCP. There may, of course, be other reasons why a server needs to listen for UDP on a particular address and port.

When the server transport receives a request over any transport, it must examine the value of the sent-by parameter in the top Via header field value. If the host portion of the sent-by parameter contains a domain name, or if it contains an IP address that differs from the packet source address, the server must add a *received* parameter to that Via header field value. This parameter MUST contain the source address from which the packet was received. This is to assist the server transport layer in sending the response, since it must be sent to the source IP address from which the request came. Consider a request received by the server transport that looks like, in part:

```
INVITE sip:bob@Biloxi.com SIP/2.0
Via: SIP/2.0/UDP bobspc.biloxi.com:5060
```

The request is received with a source IP address of 192.0.2.4. Before passing the request up, the transport adds a received parameter, so that the request would look like, in part:

```
INVITE sip:bob@Biloxi.com SIP/2.0
Via: SIP/2.0/UDP bobspc.biloxi.
com:5060;received=192.0.2.4
```

Next, the server transport attempts to match the request to a server transaction. It does so using the matching rules described in Section 3.12.2.3. If a matching server transaction is found, the request is passed to that transaction for processing. If no match is found, the request is passed to the core, which may decide to construct a new server transaction for that request. (Note that the last three sentences have been updated/modified per RFC 6026.)

3.13.2.2 Sending Responses

The server transport uses the value of the top Via header field in order to determine where to send a response. It must follow the following process:

- If the *sent-protocol* is a reliable transport protocol such as TCP or SCTP, or TLS over those, the response must be sent using the existing connection to the source of the original request that created the transaction, if that connection is still open. This requires the server transport to maintain an association between server transactions and transport connections. If that connection is no longer open, the server should open a connection to the IP address in the received parameter, if present, using the port in the sent-by value, or the default port for that transport, if no port is specified. If that connection attempt fails, the server should use the procedures in RFC 3263 (see Section 8.2.4) for servers in order to determine the IP address and port to open the connection and send the response to.
- Otherwise, if the Via header field value contains a maddr parameter, the response must be forwarded to the address listed there, using the port indicated in sent-by, or port 5060 if none is present. If the address is a multicast address, the response should be sent using the TTL indicated in the ttl parameter, or with a TTL of 1 if that parameter is not present.
- Otherwise (for unreliable unicast transports), if the top Via has a received parameter, the response must be sent to the address in the received parameter, using the port indicated in the sent-by value, or using port 5060 if none is specified explicitly. If this fails, for example, elicits an ICMP *port unreachable* response, the procedures of RFC 3263 (see Section 8.2.4) should be used to determine where to send the response.
- Otherwise, if it is not receiver tagged, the response must be sent to the address indicated by the sent-by value, using the procedures in RFC 3263 (see Section 8.2.4).

3.13.3 Framing

In the case of message-oriented transports (such as UDP), if the message has a Content-Length header field, the message body is assumed to contain that many bytes. If there are additional bytes in the transport packet beyond the end of the body, they must be discarded. If the transport packet ends before the end of the message body, this is considered an error. If the message is a response, it must be discarded. If the message is a request, the element should generate a 400 Bad Request response. If the message has no Content-Length header field, the message body is assumed to end at the end of the transport packet. In the case of stream-oriented transports such as TCP, the Content-Length header field indicates the size of the body. The Content-Length header field must be used with stream-oriented transports.

3.13.4 Error Handling

Error handling is independent of whether the message was a request or response. If the transport user asks for a message to be sent over an unreliable transport, and the result is an ICMP error, the behavior depends on the type of ICMP error. Host, network, port or protocol unreachable errors, or parameter problem errors should cause the transport layer to inform the transport user of a failure in sending. Source quench and TTL exceeded ICMP errors should be ignored. If the transport user asks for a request to be sent over a reliable transport, and the result is a connection failure, the transport layer should inform the transport user of a failure in sending.

3.14 Summary

We have described the core SIP message elements in detail for canceling a request, registration, UA capabilities indication, use of OPTION method for discovery, and creation, termination, requests within a dialog. The initiation of a session, modification of an existing session using the UPDATE message, along with SDP offer and answer for negotiations between the conferencing parties are also articulated. The UA behavior is explained for termination of the session using the BYE message. Both stateful and stateless SIP proxy behaviors are explained in detail for processing and routing of SIP messages, including the CANCEL method among SIP entities over the SIP network. Client and server transactions for both INVITE and non-INVITE SIP messages are elaborately discussed. The transport protocols used by SIP entities, SIP request and response messages processing by client and server, framing, error handling, and common message components that are an important part of the SIP message elements are also highlighted. SIP, SIPS, and tel URI that are newly introduced in SIP are discussed in great detail using examples. The call flows that provide more insights in dealing with the SIP message elements for session establishment, modifications, capability negotiations, and termination over the network are included in great detail.

PROBLEMS

1. Why is the CANCEL message designated as the hop-by-by message in SIP? Can a CANCEL message be sent after sending the final response? If not, what are the problems?
2. Why does a user need to register in a SIP network? What are the fields used in the REGISTER method? Provide SIP registration call flows that show user did not use the correct credential in the first attempt. How do the CSeq and Call-ID field play the role for a successful registration in view of incorrect credential?

When does a registration expire? How does a user refresh and cancel the registration?

3. What are the benefits of doing SIP Registration with GRUU and managing client-initiated connection?
4. Which field can a UA use to indicate its capabilities in a SIP message? What are the specific capabilities that a UA can indicate per RFC 3840?
5. What is SIP media feature tag? Describe SIP media tags that are being registered by IANA. Explain briefly what the sip.isfocus media feature tag is.
6. Describe briefly how UA capabilities can be registered in SIP using the detailed call flows. Explain briefly how content can be negotiated in SIP. How does the OPTION method help in discovering UA capabilities?
7. Show the detailed call flows of how a SIP entity can discover UA and proxy capabilities.
8. What is a SIP dialog? Describe UA behaviors for the creation of a dialog, requests, and responses within a dialog after establishment of the dialog and termination of a dialog.
9. What is the remote target URI? Show an example with call flows of how target request and responses are used to establish and modify the remote target URI that includes feature sets in a dialog.
10. Explain with detailed call flows how a session can be created with SIP. Describe in detail how each SIP functional entity process the SIP INVITE and the response message in establishing the session, including other methods, if applicable.
11. How can the existing SIP session can be modified using the SIP UPDATE method? How does each functional entity of the source–destination path handle the UPDATE method? Explain in detail using the call flows.
12. How does the SDP offer and answer play a role in modifying the existing session using SDP along with the UPDATE method?
13. Describe in detail how the SDP is used in generating the answer for the unicast and multicast streams in view of offer and answer. How does the offerer process the answer?
14. Explain using examples how an existing session can be modified using SDP offer and answer for the following: adding and removing a media stream, and putting a unicast media stream on hold.
15. Explain briefly how capabilities are expressed in SDP. Explain with call flows how the basic SDP offer–answer can be exchanged.
16. How can a SIP message body be encoded? How does a UA behave with a message body using the binary encoding scheme? Explain the following types of SIP message body: multipart, multipart/mixed, multipart/alternative, and multipart-related. How does a UA process each kind of SIP message body?
17. What are different Content and Disposition types in SIP? Explain in detail including UA behavior. How are different kinds message-bodies processed in SIP specified by RFC 5621?
18. How can an existing SIP session be terminated? Explain the behavior of SIP UAC, UAS, stateful proxy, and stateless proxy. Explain in detail how the route information is handled by both the stateful and stateless proxies in the context of the terminating the session including the processing of the Record-Route field. How does SIP timer C play a role in terminating the session?
19. What constitutes a transaction in SIP? Explain the INVITE and non-INVITE client transaction including their differences. How can the matching requests be created for the existing transaction by the client?
20. What is the SIP server transaction? Explain the INVITE and non-INVITE server transaction including their differences. How can the matching requests be created for the existing transaction by the server?
21. How are the transport errors handled by the SIP client and server?
22. Explain in detail how RFC 4320 updates RFC 3261 in handling the non-INVITE transactions?
23. Explain how the SIP timers and transport protocols' (TCP, UDP, SCTP, and TLS) timers complement one another?
24. Describe in detail how the SIP client handles transport protocols (TCP, UDP, SCTP, and TLS) in sending SIP requests and receiving SIP responses?
25. Describe in detail how the SIP sever handle transports protocols (TCP, UDP, SCTP, and TLS) in receiving SIP requests and sending SIP responses?
26. How do the SIP client and server handle framing and errors for transport protocols (TCP, UDP, SCTP, and TLS)?

References

1. International Telecommunication Union, "Procedures for real-time Group 3 facsimile communication over IP Networks," ITU-T Recommendation T.38, October 2010.
2. International Telecommunication Union, "Procedures for document facsimile transmission in the general switched telephone network," ITU-T Recommendation T.30, September 2005.
3. International Telecommunication Union, "Standardization of Group 3 facsimile terminals for document transmission," ITU-T Recommendation T.4, July 2003.

4. Kaplan, H., "GIN with Literal AORs for SIP in SSPs (GLASS)," IETF draft, Work in Progress, 2014.
5. National Institute of Standards and Technology, "Secure Hash Standard (SHS)," FIPS PUB 180-3, October 2008. Available at http://csrc.nist.gov/publications/fips/fips180-3/fips180-3_final.pdf.
6. International Telephone and Telegraph Consultative Committee, "Pulse code modulation (PCM) of voice frequencies," CCITT Recommendation G.711, 1972.
7. International Telecommunication Union, "Procedures for supporting voice-band data over IP networks," ITU-T Recommendation V.152, September 2010.

Chapter 4

Addressing in SIP

Abstract

The Request-Uniform Resource Identifier (Request-URI) of the Session Initiation Protocol (SIP) carries the logical public address for reachability in establishing the session between the communicating parties. The different kinds of URIs, such as SIP, SIP Security, and telephone (tel) URI, that the SIP messages can use are described here. The rules for the formation of SIP Request-URI with different kinds of URIs, the relationship between these different URI types, and their mapping among themselves are explained. The creation and registration of the unique globally routable user agent (UA) URI out of multiple URIs for the same SIP address-of-record for reaching the SIP UA is also described in detail. Finally, some service URIs that are created using informational Requests for Comment (RFC) and may be useful for using or offering SIP-related specific services are discussed. In addition to RFC 3261, the material from many other RFCs that have enhanced SIP is included here.

4.1 Introduction

Session Initiation Protocol (SIP) addresses are used for uniquely identifying SIP entities such as SIP user agents (UAs) and SIP servers. The users, services, and automata that want to communicate either as SIP UAs or SIP servers need to use the SIP address (Uniform Resource Identifier [URI]). However, the SIP also has a formally defined user's public address known as address-of-record (AOR), expressed in terms of SIP or SIP Security (SIPS) URI. Like the telephone number and e-mail address, the AOR can be used by a user publicly in the business card, web page, and pocketbook for calling the user in a variety of ways. The E.164 telephone address defined by ITU-T can also be used in SIP by using tel-URI; however, a mapping is needed between E.194 and SIP AOR. As a result, the E.164 number (ENUM) and domain name system (DNS) are used for address resolution. Some SIP service URIs have also been defined for invoking multimedia services such as voice mail, multimedia mail, and media services using SIP.

4.2 SIP Public Address

The SIP public address, as explained, is an AOR expressed in SIP or SIPS URI to be used publicly for calling the user. Thus, an AOR is also thought of as the *public address* of the user. An example of SIP AOR can be as follows: sip:smith @food.net. However, an AOR points to a domain with a location service that can map the URI to another URI where the user might be available. In SIP, a location service is assumed to be populated through registrations; however, location services are not required to provide a SIPS binding for a SIPS Request-URI. As location services are out of scope in SIP, various other protocols and interfaces could conceivably supply contact addresses for an AOR, and these tools are free to map SIPS URIs to SIP URIs as appropriate. It is envisioned that a location service returns its contact addresses without regard for whether it received a request with a SIPS Request-URI when queries are made for bindings by SIP servers such as proxies and redirect servers. If a redirect server is accessing the location service, it is up to the entity that processes the Contact header field of a redirection to determine the propriety of the contact addresses.

4.2.1 SIP and SIPS Uniform Resource Indicators

A SIP or SIPS URI identifies a communications resource. Like all URIs, SIP and SIPS URIs may be placed in web pages, e-mail messages, or printed literature. They contain sufficient information to initiate and maintain a communication session with the resource. Examples of communications resources include the following:

- A user of an online service
- An appearance on a multiline phone
- A mailbox on a messaging system
- A public switched telephone network (PSTN) number at a gateway service
- A group (such as *sales* or *helpdesk*) in an organization

A SIPS URI specifies that the resource be contacted securely. This means, in particular, that Transport Layer Security (TLS) is to be used between the UA client (UAC) and the domain that owns the URI. From there, secure communications are used to reach the user, where the specific security mechanism depends on the policy of the domain. Any resource described by a SIP URI can be upgraded to a SIPS URI by just changing the scheme, if it is desired to communicate with that resource securely.

4.2.1.1 SIP and SIPS URI Components

The *sip:* and *sips:* schemes follow the guidelines in RFC 3986. They use a form similar to the mailto Universal Resource Locator (URL), allowing the specification of SIP request-header fields and the SIP message body. This makes it possible to specify the subject, media type, or urgency of sessions initiated by using a URI on a web page or in an e-mail message. The formal syntax for a SIP or SIPS URI is presented in Section 2.4.1.2. Its general form, in the case of a SIP URI, is

```
sip:user:password@host:port;
uri-parameters?headers
```

The format for a SIPS URI is the same, except that the scheme is sips instead of sip. These tokens, and some of the tokens in their expansions, have the following meanings—user: The identifier of a particular resource at the host being addressed. The term *host* in this context frequently refers to a domain. The *userinfo* of a URI consists of this user field, the password field, and the @ sign following them. The userinfo part of a URI is optional and may be absent when the destination host does not have a notion of users or when the host itself is the resource being identified. If the @ sign is present in a SIP or SIPS URI, the user field must not be empty.

If the host being addressed can process telephone numbers, for instance, an Internet telephony gateway, a telephone subscriber field defined in RFC 3966 may be used to populate the user field. There are special escaping rules for encoding telephone-subscriber fields in SIP and SIPS URIs.

- **Password:** A password associated with the user. While the SIP and SIPS URI syntax allows this field to be present, its use is not recommended because the passing of authentication information in clear text (such as URIs) has proven to be a security risk in almost every case where it has been used. For instance, transporting a personal identification number (PIN) in this field exposes the PIN. Note that the password field is just an extension of the user portion. Implementations not wishing to give special significance to the password portion of the field may simply treat *user:password* as a single string.
- **Host:** The host providing the SIP resource. The host part contains either a fully qualified domain name or numeric IPv4 or IPv6 address. Using the fully qualified domain name form is recommended whenever possible.
- **Port:** The port number where the request is to be sent. URI parameters: parameters affecting a request constructed from the URI. URI parameters are added after the hostport component and are separated by semicolons.
- **URI:** URI parameters take the form parameter name "=" parameter value.

Although an arbitrary number of URI parameters may be included in a URI, any given parameter name must not appear more than once. This extensible mechanism includes the transport, maddr, ttl, user, method, and lr parameters. The transport parameter determines the transport mechanism to be used for sending SIP messages, as specified in RFC 3263 (see Section 8.2.4). SIP can use any network transport protocol. Parameter names are defined for the user datagram protocol (UDP) specified in RFC 768, transmission control protocol (TCP) described in RFC 761, and stream control transmission protocol (SCTP) defined in RFC 2960. For a SIPS URI, the transport parameter must indicate a reliable transport.

The maddr parameter indicates the server address to be contacted for this user, overriding any address derived from the host field. When an maddr parameter is present, the port and transport components of the URI apply to the address indicated in the maddr parameter value. RFC 3263 (see Section 8.2.4) describes the proper interpretation of the transport, maddr, and hostport in order to obtain the destination address, port, and transport for sending a request. The maddr field has been used as a simple form of loose source routing. It allows a URI to specify a proxy that must be traversed en route to the destination. Continuing to use the maddr parameter this way is strongly discouraged (the mechanisms that enable it are deprecated). Implementations should instead use the Route mechanism described in this document, establishing a preexisting route set if necessary (see Section 3.1.2.1.1). This provides a full URI to describe the node to be traversed.

The ttl parameter determines the time-to-live value of the UDP multicast packet and MUST only be used if maddr is a multicast address and the transport protocol is UDP. For example, to specify a call to alice@atlanta.com using multicast to 239.255.255.1 with a ttl of 15, the following URI would be used:

```
sip:alice@atlanta.com;
maddr=239.255.255.1;ttl=15
```

The set of valid telephone-subscriber strings is a subset of valid user strings. The user URI parameter exists to distinguish telephone numbers from user names that happen to look like telephone numbers. If the user string contains a telephone number formatted as a telephone-subscriber, the user parameter value *phone* should be present. Even without this parameter, recipients of SIP and SIPS URIs may interpret the pre-@ part as a telephone number if local restrictions on the namespace for user name allow it. The method of the SIP request constructed from the URI can be specified with the method parameter.

The lr parameter, when present, indicates that the element responsible for this resource implements the routing mechanisms specified in this document. This parameter will be used in the URI proxies placed into Record-Route header field values, and may appear in the URIs in a preexisting route set. This parameter is used to achieve backwards compatibility with systems implementing the strict-routing mechanisms of RFC 2543 (obsoleted by RFC 3261). An element preparing to send a request based on a URI not containing this parameter can assume that the receiving element implements strict routing and reformats the message to preserve the information in the Request-URI. Since the uri-parameter mechanism is extensible, SIP elements must silently ignore any uri-parameters that they do not understand.

- Headers: Header fields to be included in a request constructed from the URI. Headers fields in the SIP request can be specified with the "?" mechanism within a URI. The header names and values are encoded in ampersand separated hname = hvalue pairs. The special hname *body* indicates that the associated hvalue is the message body of the SIP request.

Table 4.1 summarizes the use of SIP and SIPS URI components based on the context in which the URI appears. The external column describes URIs appearing anywhere outside of a SIP message, for instance, on a web page or business card. Entries marked "m" are mandatory; those marked "o" are optional; and those marked "-" are not allowed.

Elements processing URIs should ignore any disallowed components if they are present. The second column indicates the default value of an optional element if it is not present. "--" indicates that the element is either not optional, or has no default value. URIs in Contact header fields have different restrictions depending on the context in which the header field appears. One set applies to messages that establish and maintain dialogs (INVITE and its 200 OK response). The other applies to registration and redirection messages (REGISTER, its 200 OK response, and 3xx class responses to any method).

4.2.1.2 Character Escaping Requirements

SIP follows the requirements and guidelines of RFC 2396 (obsoleted by RFC 3986) when defining the set of characters that must be escaped in a SIP URI, and uses its *% HEX HEX* mechanism for escaping. From RFC 2396: The set of characters actually reserved within any given URI component is defined by that component. In general, a character is reserved if the semantics of the URI changes if the character is replaced with its escaped US-ASCII encoding specified in RFC 2396. Excluded US-ASCII characters defined in RFC 2396, such as space and control characters and characters used as URI delimiters, also must be escaped. URIs must not contain unescaped space and control characters.

For each component, the set of valid augmented Backus–Naur Form (ABNF) expansions defines exactly which characters may appear unescaped. All other characters must be escaped. For example, @ is not in the set of characters in the user component, so the user *j@s0n* must have at least the @ sign encoded, as in *j%40s0n*. Expanding the hname and hvalue tokens in Section 3.9 show that all URI reserved characters in header field names and values must be escaped. The telephone-subscriber subset of the user component has special escaping considerations. The set of characters not reserved in the RFC 3966 (obsoleted by RFC 3986) description of telephone-subscriber contains a number of characters in various syntax elements that need to be escaped when used in SIP URIs. Any characters occurring in a telephone-subscriber that do not appear in an expansion of the ABNF for the user rule must be escaped.

Note that character escaping is not allowed in the host component of a SIP or SIPS URI (the % character is not valid in its expansion). This is likely to change in the future as requirements for Internationalized Domain Names (IDNs) are finalized. Current implementations must not attempt to improve robustness by treating received escaped characters in the host component as literally equivalent to their unescaped counterpart. The behavior required to meet the requirements of IDN may be significantly different.

Table 4.1 Summary of SIP and SIPS URI Components

	Default	Request-URI	To	From	Registration/ Redirection/ Contact	Dialog/ Contact/ R-R/ Route	External	Remarks
user	–	o	o	o	o	o	o	Identifier of a resource of a host being addressed
password	–	o	o	o	o	o	o	Password associated with the user (use not recommended as it might have security risk)
host	–	m	m	m	m	m	m	Host providing the SIP resource (fully qualified domain name of IPv4 or IPv6 address)
port	*	o	-	-	o	o	o	Port number where the request to be sent
user-param	ip	o	o	o	o	o	o	User parameters can be "phone," "ip," or other-user parameters ("ip" is default)
method	INVITE	-	-	-	-	-	o	All SIP methods, but INVITE method is default
maddr-param	–	o	-	-	o	o	o	Server address to be contacted for the user overriding any address derived from host field
ttl-param	1	o	-	-	o	-	o	Time-to-live value of UDP multicast packet
transport-param	**	o	-	-	o	o	o	UDP, TCP, or SCTP transport protocol
lr-param	–	o	-	-	-	o	o	Element that is responsible for resource implements routing mechanisms in SIP
other-param	–	o	o	o	o	o	o	Any parameters as wished
headers	–	-	-	-	o	-	o	To be included in a request constructed from URI

Note: "-", not allowed; "–", the element is either not optional, or has no default value; m, mandatory; o, optional; R-R, Record-Route.

* The default port value is transport and scheme dependent. The default is 5060 for sip: using UDP, TCP, or SCTP. The default is 5061 for sip: using TLS over TCP and sips: over TCP.

** The default transport is scheme dependent. For sip:, it is UDP. For sips:, it is TCP.

4.2.1.3 Example SIP and SIPS URIs

We are providing some examples of SIP and SIPS URIs as follows from RFC 3261:

```
sip:alice@atlanta.com
sip:alice:secretword@atlanta.com;
transport=tcp
sips:alice@atlanta.com?subject=project%20
x&priority=urgent
sip:+1-212-555-1212:1234@gateway.com;
user=phone
sips:1212@gateway.com
sip:alice@192.0.2.4
sip:atlanta.com;method=REGISTER?to=alice%40
atlanta.com
sip:alice;day=tuesday@atlanta.com
```

The last sample URI above has a user field value of *alice;day=tuesday*. The escaping rules defined above allow a semicolon to appear unescaped in this field. For the purposes of this protocol, the field is opaque. The structure of that value is only useful to the SIP element responsible for the resource.

4.2.1.4 URI Comparison

Some operations in this specification require determining whether two SIP or SIPS URIs are equivalent. In this specification, registrars need to compare bindings in Contact URIs in REGISTER requests (see Section 3.3). SIP and SIPS URIs are compared for equality according to the following rules:

- A SIP and SIPS URI are never equivalent.
- Comparison of the userinfo of SIP and SIPS URIs is case sensitive. This includes userinfo containing passwords or formatted as telephone-subscribers. Comparison of all other components of the URI is case-insensitive unless explicitly defined otherwise.

- The ordering of parameters and header fields is not significant in comparing SIP and SIPS URIs.
- Characters other than those in the *reserved* set defined in RFC 2396 (obsoleted by RFC 3986) are equivalent to their % HEX HEX encoding.
- An Internet Protocol (IP) address that is the result of a DNS lookup of a host name does not match that host name.
- RFC 5954 updates RFC 3261 for rules for matching of two URIs. According to RFC 5954, for two URIs to be equal, the user, password, host, and port components must match. If the host component contains a textual representation of IP addresses, then the representation of those IP addresses may vary. If so, the host components are considered to match if the different textual representations yield the same binary IP address. RFC 5954 also recommends that implementers should generate IPv6 text representation as defined in RFC 5952.

According to the modified rule of RFC 5954 (updates Section 19.1.4 of RFC 3261), the following URIs are equivalent because the underlying binary representation of the IP addresses are the same although their textual representations vary:

```
sip:bob@[::ffff:192.0.2.128]
sip:bob@[::ffff:c000:280]
sip:bob@[2001:db8::9:1]
sip:bob@[2001:db8::9:01]
sip:bob@[0:0:0:0:0:FFFF:129.144.52.38]
sip:bob@[::FFFF:129.144.52.38]
```

A URI omitting the user component will not match a URI that includes one. A URI omitting the password component will not match a URI that includes one. A URI omitting any component with a default value will not match a URI explicitly containing that component with its default value. For instance, a URI omitting the optional port component will not match a URI explicitly declaring port 5060. The same is true for the transport-parameter, ttl-parameter, user-parameter, and method components. Defining sip:user @host to not be equivalent to sip:user@host:5060 is a change from RFC 2543 (obsoleted by RFC 3261). When deriving addresses from URIs, equivalent addresses are expected from equivalent URIs. The URI sip:user@host:5060 will always resolve to port 5060. The URI sip:user@host may resolve to other ports through the DNS SRV mechanisms detailed in RFC 3263 (see Section 8.2.4).

- URI uri-parameter components are compared as follows:
  - Any uri-parameter appearing in both URIs must match.
  - A user, ttl, or method uri-parameter appearing in only one URI never matches, even if it contains the default value.
  - A URI that includes an maddr parameter will not match a URI that contains no maddr parameter.
  - All other uri-parameters appearing in only one URI are ignored when comparing the URIs.
- URI header components are never ignored. Any present header component must be present in both URIs and match for the URIs to match.

The URIs within each of the following sets are equivalent:

```
sip:%61lice@atlanta.com;transport=TCP
sip:alice@AtLanTa.CoM;Transport=tcp
sip:carol@chicago.com
sip:carol@chicago.com;newparam=5
sip:carol@chicago.com;security=on
sip:biloxi.com;transport=tcp;method=REGISTER?
to=sip:bob%40biloxi.com
sip:biloxi.com;method=REGISTER;transport=tcp?
to=sip:bob%40biloxi.com
sip:alice@atlanta.com?subject=project%20
x&priority=urgent
sip:alice@atlanta.com?priority=urgent&subject
=project%20x
```

The URIs within each of the following sets are not equivalent:

```
SIP:ALICE@AtLanTa.CoM;Transport=udp
(different usernames)
sip:alice@AtLanTa.CoM;Transport=UDP
sip:bob@biloxi.com (can resolve to different
ports)
sip:bob@biloxi.com:5060
sip:bob@biloxi.com (can resolve to different
transports)
sip:bob@biloxi.com;transport=udp
sip:bob@biloxi.com (can resolve to different
port and transports)
sip:bob@biloxi.com:6000;transport=tcp
sip:carol@chicago.com (different header
component)
sip:carol@chicago.com?Subject=next%20meeting
sip:bob@phone21.boxesbybob.com (even though
that is what
sip:bob@192.0.2.4 phone21.boxesbybob.com
resolves to)
```

Note that equality is not transitive:

- sip:carol@chicago.com and sip:carol@chicago.com; security=on are equivalent.
- sip:carol@chicago.com and sip:carol@chicago.com; security=off are equivalent.
- sip:carol@chicago.com;security=on and sip:carol @chicago.com;security=off are not equivalent.

4.2.1.5 Forming Requests from a URI

An implementation needs to take care when forming requests directly from a URI. URIs from business cards, web pages, and even from sources inside the protocol such as registered contacts may contain inappropriate header fields or body parts. An implementation must include any provided transport, maddr, ttl, or user parameter in the Request-URI of the formed request. If the URI contains a method parameter, its value must be used as the method of the request. The method parameter must not be placed in the Request-URI. Unknown URI parameters must be placed in the message's Request-URI. An implementation should treat the presence of any headers or body parts in the URI as a desire to include them in the message, and choose to honor the request on a per-component basis. An implementation should not honor these obviously dangerous header fields: From, Call-ID, CSeq, Via, and Record-Route. An implementation should not honor any requested Route header field values in order to not be used as an unwitting agent in malicious attacks. An implementation should not honor requests to include header fields that may cause it to falsely advertise its location or capabilities. These include Accept, Accept-Encoding, Accept-Language, Allow, Contact (in its dialog usage), Organization, Supported, and User-Agent.

An implementation should verify the accuracy of any requested descriptive header fields, including Content-Disposition, Content-Encoding, Content-Language, Content-Length, Content-Type, Date, Mime-Version, and Timestamp. If the request formed from constructing a message from a given URI is not a valid SIP request, the URI is invalid. An implementation must not proceed with transmitting the request. It should instead pursue the course of action due an invalid URI in the context it occurs. The constructed request can be invalid in many ways. These include, but are not limited to, syntax error in header fields, invalid combinations of URI parameters, or an incorrect description of the message body. Sending a request formed from a given URI may require capabilities unavailable to the implementation. The URI might indicate use of an unimplemented transport or extension, for example. An implementation should refuse to send these requests rather than modifying them to match their capabilities. An implementation must not send a request requiring an extension that it does not support. For example, such a request can be formed through the presence of a Require header parameter or a method URI parameter with an unknown or explicitly unsupported value.

4.2.1.6 Conference Factory URI

According to RFC 4579 (see Sections 2.2 and 2.4.4.1) that defines conferencing call control features for SIP, there are many ways in which a conference can be created. A conferencing server implementation is free to choose from these methods, which include nonautomated means such as an Interactive Voice Response system, SIP, or any conference control protocol. To automatically create an arbitrary number of ad hoc conferences (and subsequently their focuses) using SIP call control means, a globally routable Conference Factory URI can be allocated and published. A successful attempt to establish a call to this URI would result in the automatic creation of a new conference and its focus. As a result, note that the Conference Factory URI and the newly created focus URI may resolve to different physical devices, and some examples are provided in RFC 4579.

4.2.2 Telephone URI

The tel URI (RFC 3966) scheme describes resources identified by telephone numbers. A telephone number is a string of decimal digits that uniquely indicates the network termination point. The number contains the information necessary to route the call to this point. SIP also uses the tel URI in its requests as the SIP specification inherits the *subscriber* part of the syntax as part of the *user element* in the SIP URI. The tel URI can also be used by other protocols in their URI schemes. However, the tel URI does not specify the call type, such as voice, fax, or data call, and does not provide the connection parameters for a data call. The type and parameters are assumed to be negotiated either in-band by the telephone device or through a signaling protocol such as SIP. More important, the tel URI scheme facilitates interworking between the PSTN/Integrated Services Digital Network (ISDN) and IP network. The tel URI is expressed as follows:

```
telephone-uri = "tel:" telephone-subscriber
```

The telephone-subscriber parameter can be a global number or a local number. The tel URL telephone number is not restricted and can be in any kinds of networks such as the public telephone network, a private telephone network, or the Internet. Some examples of tel URI can be stated as follows:

- tel:+1-908-752-5123: This tel URI indicates to a phone number in the United States.
- tel:8209;phone-context=example.com: The tel URI describes a local phone number valid within the context *example.com*.
- tel:582-5679;phone-context=+1-201-3756: The tel URI describes a local phone number that is valid within a particular phone prefix.

Telephone numbers comprise two related but distinct concepts: a canonical AOR and a dial string. Although both approaches can be expressed as a URI, the dial string approach is beyond the scope of the tel URI. The telephone number used as the canonical AOR or identifier indicates a termination point within a specific network. E.164 rules are followed by these telephone numbers for the public network. However, the private numbers will follow the rules of the private network. Subscribers publish these identifiers so that they can be reached, regardless of the location of the caller. As result, not all telephone numbers can be reachable from any other numbers globally as the private network rules are proprietary, although they may use the telephone digits. The tel URI specifies the telephone number as an AOR or identifier, which can be either globally unique or only valid within a local context. The dialing application is aware of the local context, knowing, for example, whether special digits need to be dialed to seize an outside line; whether network, pulse, or tone dialing is needed; and what tones indicate call progress.

The dialing application then converts the telephone number into a dial sequence and performs the necessary signaling actions. The dialer does not have to be a user application as found in traditional desktop operating systems but could well be part of an IP-to-PSTN gateway. To reach a telephone number from a phone on a Private Branch Exchange (PBX), for example, the user of that phone has to know how to convert the telephone number identifier into a dial string appropriate for that phone. The telephone number itself does not convey what needs to be done for a particular terminal. Instructions may include dialing 9 before placing a call or prepending 00 to reach a number in a foreign country. The phone may also need to strip area and country codes. The identifier approach described in this document has the disadvantage that certain services, such as electronic banking or voice mail, cannot be specified in a tel URI. In the SIP network, the routing is made based on the domain name and a call reaches to the destination domain; the SIP server that is responsible for that domain will route the call to the user. However, unlike other URIs, the tel URI does not have the domain name or user part. As a result, there is no mechanism on how a tel URI will be routed over the SIP network.

4.2.2.1 Relating SIP URIs and Tel URLs

When a tel URL defined in RFC 3966 is converted to a SIP or SIPS URI, the entire telephone-subscriber portion of the tel URL, including any parameters, is placed into the userinfo part of the SIP or SIPS URI. Thus,

```
tel:+358-555-1234567;postd=pp22 becomes
sip:+358-555-1234567;postd=pp22@foo.com;
user=phone or
sips:+358-555-1234567;postd=pp22@foo.com;
user=phone not
sip:+358-555-1234567@foo.com;
postd=pp22;user=phone or
sips:+358-555-1234567@foo.com;
postd=pp22;user=phone
```

In general, equivalent tel URLs converted to SIP or SIPS URIs in this fashion may not produce equivalent SIP or SIPS URIs. The userinfo of SIP and SIPS URIs are compared as a case-sensitive string. Variance in case-insensitive portions of tel URLs and reordering of tel URL parameters do not affect tel URL equivalence, but do affect the equivalence of SIP URIs formed from them.

For example,

```
tel:+358-555-1234567;postd=pp22
tel:+358-555-1234567;POSTD=PP22
```

are equivalent, while

```
sip:+358-555-1234567;postd=pp22@foo.com;
user=phone
sip:+358-555-1234567;POSTD=PP22@foo.com;
user=phone
```

are not.

Likewise,

```
tel:+358-555-1234567;postd=pp22;isub=1411
tel:+358-555-1234567;isub=1411;postd=pp22
```

are equivalent, while

```
sip:+358-555-1234567;postd=pp22;isub=1411@
foo.com;user=phone
sip:+358-555-1234567;isub=1411;postd=pp22@
foo.com;user=phone
```

are not.

To mitigate this problem, elements constructing telephone-subscriber fields to place in the userinfo part of a SIP or SIPS URI should fold any case-insensitive portion of telephone-subscriber to lowercase, and order the telephone-subscriber parameters lexically by parameter name, excepting isdn-subaddress and post-dial, which occur first and in that order. (All components of a tel URL except for future extension parameters are defined to be compared case insensitive.)

Following this suggestion, both

```
tel:+358-555-1234567;postd=pp22
tel:+358-555-1234567;POSTD=PP22
```

become

```
sip:+358-555-1234567;postd=pp22@foo.com;
user=phone
```

and both

```
tel:+358-555-1234567;tsp=a.b;phone-context=5
tel:+358-555-1234567;phone-context=5;tsp=a.b
```

become

```
sip:+358-555-1234567;phone-context=5;tsp=a.b@
foo.com;user=phone
```

4.2.3 Use of SIPS URI Scheme in SIP

RFC 5630 that is described here provides clarifications and guidelines concerning the use of the SIPS URI scheme in the SIP. The meaning and usage of the SIPS URI scheme and of TLS (RFC 5246) are underspecified in SIP (RFC 3261, see Section 4.2) and have been a source of confusion for implementers. RFC 5630 provides clarifications and guidelines concerning the use of the SIPS URI scheme in SIP. It also makes normative changes to SIP including both RFC 3261 (see Section 4.2) and RFC 3608 (see Section 2.8 and Chapter 9).

4.2.3.1 TLS Server-Provided Certificate

In this model, only the TLS server provides a certificate during the TLS handshake. This is applicable only between the UA and a proxy, where the UA is the TLS client and the proxy is the TLS server, and hence the UA uses TLS to authenticate the proxy but the proxy does not use TLS to authenticate the UA. If the proxy needs to authenticate the UA, this can be achieved by SIP HTTP digest authentication. This directionality implies that the TLS connection always needs to be set up by the UA (e.g., during the registration phase). Since SIP allows for requests in both directions (e.g., an incoming call), the UA is expected to keep the TLS connection alive, and that connection is expected to be reused for both incoming and outgoing requests. This solution of having the UA always initiate and keep alive the connection also solves the network address translation (NAT) and firewall problem as it ensures that responses and further requests will always be deliverable on the existing connection. RFC 5626 (see Section 13.2) provides the mechanism for initiating and maintaining outbound connections in a standard interoperable way.

4.2.3.2 Mutual Authentication Using TLS

In this model, both the TLS client and the TLS server provide a certificate in the TLS handshake phase. When used between a UA and a proxy (or between two UAs), this implies that a UA is in possession of a certificate. When sending a SIP request when there is not already a suitable TLS connection in place, a UAC takes on the role of TLS client in establishing a new TLS connection. When establishing a TLS connection for receipt of a SIP request, a UA server (UAS) takes on the role of TLS server. Because in SIP, a UA or a proxy acts both as UAC and UAS depending on if it is sending or receiving requests, the symmetrical nature of mutual TLS is very convenient. This allows for TLS connections to be set up or torn down at will and does not rely on keeping the TLS connection alive for further requests. However, there are some significant limitations. The first obvious limitation is not with mutual authentication per se, but with the model where the underlying TCP connection can be established by either side, interchangeably, which is not possible in many environments.

For example, NATs and firewalls will often allow TCP connections to be established in one direction only. This includes most residential SIP deployments, for example. Mutual authentication can be used in those environments, but only if the connection is always started by the same side, for example, by using RFC 5626 (see Section 13.2). Having to rely on RFC 5626 in this case negates many of the advantages of mutual authentication. The second significant limitation is that mutual authentication requires both sides to exchange a certificate. This has proven to be impractical in many environments, in particular for SIP UAs, because of the difficulties of setting up a certificate infrastructure for a wide population of users. For these reasons, mutual authentication is mostly used in server-to-server communications (e.g., between SIP proxies, or between proxies and gateways or media servers), and in environments where using certificates on both sides is possible (e.g., high-security devices used within an enterprise).

4.2.3.3 Using TLS with SIP instead of SIPS

Because a SIPS URI implies that requests sent to the resource identified by it be sent over each SIP hop over TLS, SIPS URIs are not suitable for *best-effort TLS*: they are only suitable for *TLS only* requests. This is recognized in RFC 3261 (see Section 19.12.2.2). Users that distribute a SIPS URI as an AOR may elect to operate devices that refuse requests over insecure transports. If one wants to use best-effort TLS for SIP, one just needs to use a SIP URI, and send the request over TLS. Using SIP over TLS is very simple. A UA opens a TLS connection and uses SIP URIs instead of SIPS URIs for all the header fields in a SIP message (From, To, Request-URI, Contact header field, Route, etc.). When TLS is used, the Via header field indicates TLS. RFC 3261 (see Section 19.12.3.2.1) states: When a UA comes online and registers with its local administrative domain, it should establish a TLS connection with its registrar.

Once the registration has been accepted by the registrar, the UA should leave this TLS connection open provided that the registrar also acts as the proxy server to which requests are sent for users in this administrative domain. The existing TLS connection will be reused to deliver incoming requests to the UA that had just completed registration. RFC 5626 (see Section 13.2) describes how to establish and maintain a TLS connection in environments where it can only be initiated by the UA. Similarly, proxies can forward requests using

TLS if they can open a TLS connection, even if the route set used SIP URIs instead of SIPS URIs. The proxies can insert Record-Route header fields using SIP URIs even if it uses TLS transport. RFC 3261 Section 19.12.3.2.2 explains how interdomain requests can use TLS. Some UAs, redirect servers, and proxies might have local policies that enforce TLS on all connections, independently of whether or not SIPS is used.

4.2.3.4 Usage of Transport=tls URI Parameter and TLS via Parameter

RFC 3261 (Section 19.12.2.2) deprecated the transport=tls URI transport parameter in SIPS or SIP URIs: Note that in the SIPS URI scheme, transport is independent of TLS, and thus sips:alice@atlanta.com;transport=TCP and sips:alice@atlanta.com;transport=sctp are both valid (although note that UDP is not a valid transport for SIPS). The use of transport=tls has consequently been deprecated, partly because it was specific to a single hop of the request. This is a change since RFC 2543 (obsoleted by RFC 3261). The tls parameter has not been eliminated from the ABNF in RFC 3261 (Section 3.9) since the parameter needs to remain in the ABNF for backward compatibility in order for parsers to be able to process the parameter correctly. The transport=tls parameter has never been defined in an RFC, but only in some of the Internet drafts between RFC 2543 and RFC 3261. This specification does not make use of the transport=tls parameter. The reinstatement of the transport=tls parameter, or an alternative mechanism for indicating the use of the TLS on a single hop in a URI, is outside the scope of this specification. For Via header fields, the following transport protocols are defined in RFC 3261 (see Section 3.13): UDP, TCP, TLS, SCTP, and in RFC 4168, TLSSCTP.

4.2.3.5 Detection of Hop-by-Hop Security

The presence of a SIPS Request-URI does not necessarily indicate that the request was sent securely on each hop. So how does a UAS know if SIPS was used for the entire request path to secure the request end-to-end? Effectively, the UAS cannot know for sure. However, RFC 3261 (Section 19.12.4.4) recommends how a UAS can make some checks to validate the security. Additionally, the History-Info header field (RFC 4244, see Section 2.8) could be inspected for detecting retargeting from SIP and SIPS. Retargeting from SIP to SIPS by a proxy is an issue because it can leave the receiver of the request with the impression that the request was delivered securely on each hop, while in fact, it was not.

To emphasize, all the checking can be circumvented by any proxies or B2BUAs on the path that do not follow the rules and recommendations of this specification and of RFC 3261 (see Section 4.2.1). Proxies can have their own policies regarding routing of requests to SIP or SIPS URIs. For example, some proxies in some environments can be configured to only route SIPS URIs. Some proxies can be configured to detect noncompliances and reject unsecure requests. For example, proxies could inspect Request-URIs, Path, Record-Route, To, From, Contact header fields, and Via header fields to enforce SIPS. RFC 3261 (Section 19.12.4.4) explains that S/MIME can also be used by the originating UAC to ensure that the original form of the To header field is carried end-to-end. While not specifically mentioned in RFC 3261 (Section 19.12.4.4), this is meant to imply that RFC 3893 (see Section 19.4.7) would be used to *tunnel* important header fields (such as To and From) in an encrypted and signed S/MIME body, replicating the information in the SIP message, and allowing the UAS to validate the content of those important header fields. While this approach is certainly legal, a preferable approach is to use the SIP Identity mechanism defined in RFC 4474 (see Sections 2.8 and 19.4.8). SIP Identity creates a signed identity digest, which includes, among other things, the AOR of the sender (from the From header field) and the AOR of the original target (from the To header field).

4.2.3.6 Problems with Meaning of SIPS in RFC 3261

RFC 3261 (Section 4.2.1) describes a SIPS URI as follows: a SIPS URI specifies that the resource be contacted securely. This means, in particular, that TLS is to be used between the UAC and the domain that owns the URI. From there, secure communications are used to reach the user, where the specific security mechanism depends on the policy of the domain. RFC 3261 (Section 19.12.2.2) reiterates it, with regards to Request-URIs: when used as the Request-URI of a request, the SIPS scheme signifies that each hop over which the request is forwarded, until the request reaches the SIP entity responsible for the domain portion of the Request-URI, must be secured with TLS; once it reaches the domain in question, it is handled in accordance with local security and routing policy, quite possibly using TLS for any last hop to a UAS. When used by the originator of a request (as would be the case if they employed a SIPS URI as the AOR of the target), SIPS dictates that the entire request path to the target domain be so secured. Let us take the classic SIP trapezoid (Figure 4.1) to explain the meaning of a sips:b@B URI. Instead of using real domain names like example.com and example.net, logical names like A and B are used, for clarity.

According to RFC 3261, if a@A is sending a request to sips:b@B, the following applies:

- TLS is required between UA a@A and proxy A.
- TLS is required between proxy A and proxy B.
- TLS is required between proxy B and UA b@B, depending on local policy.

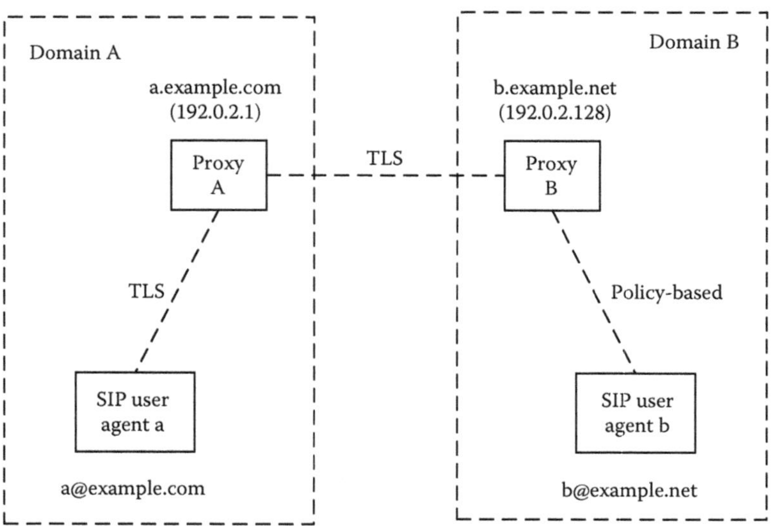

Figure 4.1 SIP trapezoid with last-hop exception. (Copyright IETF. Reproduced with permission.)

One can then wonder why TLS is mandatory between UA a@A and proxy A but not between proxy B and UA b@B. The main reason is that RFC 3261 was written before RFC 5626 (see Section 13.2). At that time, it was recognized that in many practical deployments, proxy B might not be able to establish a TLS connection with UA b because only proxy B would have a certificate to provide and UA b would not. Since UA b would be the TLS server, it would then not be able to accept the incoming TLS connection. The consequence is that an RFC 3261 compliant UAS b, while it might not need to support TLS for incoming requests, will nevertheless have to support TLS for outgoing requests as it takes the UAC role. Contrary to what many believed, the last-hop exception was not created to allow for using a SIPS URI to address a UAS that does not support TLS: the last-hop exception was an attempt to allow for incoming requests to not be transported over TLS when a SIPS URI is used, and it does not apply to outgoing requests.

The rationale for this was somewhat flawed, and since then, RFC 5626 (see Section 13.2) has provided a more satisfactory solution to this problem. RFC 5626 also solves the problem that if UA b is behind a NAT or firewall, proxy B would not even be able to establish a TCP session in the first place. Furthermore, consider the problem of using SIPS inside a dialog. If a@A sends a request to b@B using a SIPS Request-URI, then, according to RFC 3261 (Section 3.1.2.1.8), "the Contact header field must contain a SIPS URI as well." This means that b@B, upon sending a new Request within the dialog (e.g., a BYE or re-INVITE), will have to use a SIPS URI. If there is no Record-Route entry, or if the last Record-Route entry consists of a SIPS URI, this implies that b@B is expected to understand SIPS in the first place, and is required to also support TLS. If the last Record-Route entry, however, is a sip URI, then b would be able to send requests without using TLS (but b would still have to be able to handle SIPS schemes when parsing the message). In either case, the Request-URI in the request from b@B to B would be a SIPS URI.

4.2.3.7 Overview of Operations

Because of all the problems described earlier, this specification deprecates the last-hop exception when forwarding a request to the last hop (Figure 4.2). This will ensure that TLS is used on all hops all the way up to the remote target.

The SIPS scheme implies transitive trust. Obviously, there is nothing that prevents proxies from cheating (RFC 3261, see Section 19.12.4.4). While SIPS is useful to request that a resource be contacted securely, it is not useful as an indication that a resource was in fact contacted securely. Therefore, it is not appropriate to infer that because an incoming request had a Request-URI (or even a To header field) containing a SIPS URI, it necessarily guarantees that the request was in fact transmitted securely on each hop. Some have been tempted to believe that the SIPS scheme was equivalent to an HTTPS scheme in the sense that one could provide a visual indication to a user (e.g., a padlock icon) to the effect that the session is secured. This is obviously not the case, and therefore the meaning of a SIPS URI is not to be oversold. There is currently no mechanism to provide an indication of end-to-end security for SIP. Other mechanisms can provide a more concrete indication of some level of security. For example, SIP Identity (RFC 4474, see Sections 2.8 and 19.4.8) provides an authenticated identity mechanism and a domain-to-domain integrity

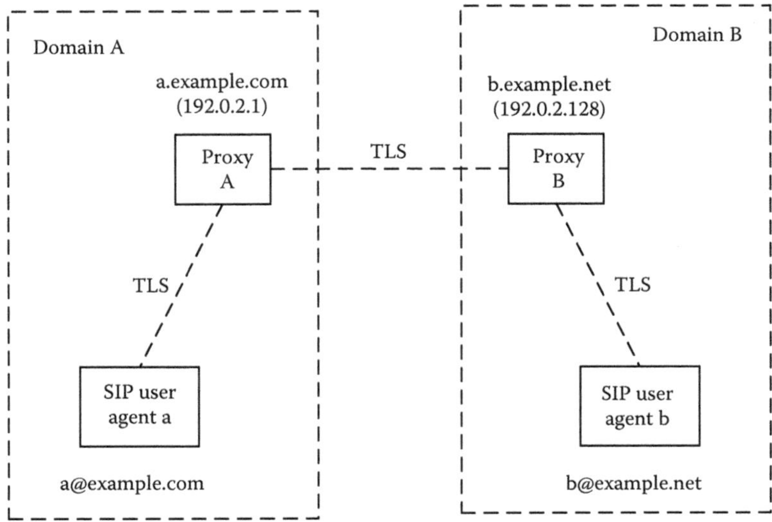

Figure 4.2 SIP trapezoid without last-hop exception. (Copyright IETF. Reproduced with permission.)

protection mechanism. Some have asked, why is SIPS useful in a global open environment such as the Internet, if (when used in a Request-URI) it is not an absolute guarantee that the request will in fact be delivered over TLS on each hop? Why is SIPS any different from just using TLS transport with SIP?

The difference is that using a SIPS URI in a Request-URI means that if you are instructing the network to use TLS over each hop and if it is not possible to reject the request, you would rather have the request fail than have the request delivered without TLS. Just using TLS with a SIP Request-URI instead of a SIPS Request-URI implies a *best-effort* service: the request can but need not be delivered over the TLS on each hop. Another common question is, why not have a Proxy-Require and a Require option tag forcing the use of TLS instead? The answer is that it would only be functionally equivalent to using SIPS in a Request-URI. SIPS URIs, however, can be used in many other header fields: in Contact for registration, Contact in dialog-creating requests, Route, Record-Route, Path, From, To, Refer-To, Referred-By, etc. SIPS URIs can also be used in human-usable format (e.g., business cards and user interface). SIPS URIs can even be used in other protocols or document formats that allow for including SIPS URIs (e.g., HTML). This document (RFC 5630) specifies that SIPS means that the SIP resource designated by the target SIPS URI is to be contacted securely, using TLS on each hop between the UAC and the remote UAS (as opposed to only to the proxy responsible for the target domain of the Request-URI). It is beyond the scope of this document to specify what happens when a SIPS URI identifies a UAS resource that *maps* outside the SIP network, for example, to other networks such as the PSTN.

4.2.3.7.1 Routing

SIP and SIPS URIs that are identical except for the scheme itself (e.g., sip:alice@example.com and sips:alice@example.com) refer to the same resource. This requirement is implicit in RFC 3261 (see Section 4.2.1), which states that "any resource described by a SIP URI can be 'upgraded' to a SIPS URI by just changing the scheme, if it is desired to communicate with that resource securely." This does not mean that the SIPS URI will necessarily be reachable, in particular, if the proxy cannot establish a secure connection to a client or another proxy. This does not suggest either that proxies would arbitrarily *upgrade* SIP URIs to SIPS URIs when forwarding a request. Rather, it means that when a resource is addressable with SIP, it will also be addressable with SIPS.

For example, consider the case of a UA that has registered with a SIPS Contact header field. If a UAC later addresses a request using a SIP Request-URI, the proxy will forward the request addressed to a SIP Request-URI to the UAS. The proxy forwards the request to the UA using a SIP Request-URI and not the SIPS Request-URI used in registration. The proxy does this by replacing the SIPS scheme that was used in the registered Contact header field binding with a SIP scheme while leaving the rest of the URI as is, and then by using this new URI as the Request-URI. If the proxy did not do this, and instead used a SIPS Request-URI, then the response (e.g., a 200 to an INVITE) would have to include a SIPS Contact header field. That SIPS Contact header field would then force the other UA to use a SIPS Contact header field in any mid-dialog request, including the ACK (which would not be possible if that UA did not support SIPS).

This specification (RFC 5630) mandates that when a proxy is forwarding a request, a resource described by a SIPS Request-URI cannot be *downgraded* to a SIP URI by changing the scheme, or by sending the associated request over a nonsecure link. If a request needs to be rejected because otherwise it would be a downgrade, the request would be rejected with a 480 (Temporarily Unavailable) response (potentially with a Warning header with warn-code 380 SIPS Not Allowed). Similarly, this specification mandates that when a proxy is forwarding a request, a resource described by a SIP Request-URI cannot be upgraded to a SIPS URI by changing the scheme (otherwise, it would be an upgrade only for that hop onwards rather than on all hops, and would therefore mislead the UAS). If a request needs to be rejected because otherwise it would be a misleading upgrade, the request would be rejected with a 480 Temporarily Unavailable response (potentially with a Warning header field with warn-code 381 SIPS Required).

For example, the sip:bob@example.com and sips:bob@example.com AORs refer to the same user Bob in the domain example.com: the first URI is the SIP version, and the second one is the SIPS version. From the point of view of routing, requests to either sip:bob@example.com or sips:bob@example.com are treated the same way. When Bob registers, it therefore does not really matter if he is using a SIP or a SIPS AOR, since they both refer to the same user. At first glance, RFC 3261 (see Section 4.2.1) seems to contradict this idea by stating that a SIP and a SIPS URI are never equivalent. Specifically, it says that they are never equivalent for the purpose of comparing bindings in Contact header field URIs in REGISTER requests. The key point is that this statement applies to the Contact header field bindings in a registration: it is the association of the Contact header field with the AOR that will determine whether or not the user is reachable with a SIPS URI.

Consider this example: if Bob (AOR bob@example.com) registers with a SIPS Contact header field (e.g., sips:bob@bobphone.example.com), the registrar and the location service then know that Bob is reachable at sips:bob@bobphone.example.com and at sip:bob@bobphone.example.com. If a request is sent to AOR sips:bob@example.com, Bob's proxy will route it to Bob at Request-URI sips:bob@bobphone.example.com. If a request is sent to AOR sip:bob@example.com, Bob's proxy will route it to Bob at Request-URI sip:bob@bobphone.example.com. If Bob wants to ensure that every request delivered to him will always be transported over the TLS, Bob can use RFC 5626 (see Section 13.2) when registering. However, if Bob had registered with a SIP Contact header field instead of a SIPS Contact header field (e.g., sip:bob@bobphone.example.com), then a request to AOR sips:bob@example.com would not be routed to Bob, since there is no SIPS Contact header field for Bob, and downgrades from SIPS to SIP are not allowed. See Section 2.2 for illustrative call flows.

4.2.3.8 UAC Normative Behavior

When presented with a SIPS URI, a UAC must not change it to a SIP URI. For example, if a directory entry includes a SIPS AOR, the UAC is not expected to send requests to that AOR using a SIP Request-URI. Similarly, if a user reads a business card with a SIPS URI, it is not possible to infer a SIP URI. If a 3xx response includes a SIPS Contact header field, the UAC does not replace it with a SIP Request-URI (e.g., by replacing the SIPS scheme with a SIP scheme) when sending a request as a result of the redirection. As mandated by RFC 3261 (see Section 3.1.2.1.8) in a request, "if the Request-URI or top Route header field value contains a SIPS URI, the Contact header field must contain a SIPS URI as well." Upon receiving a 416 response or a 480 Temporarily Unavailable response with a Warning header with warn-code 380 SIPS Not Allowed, a UAC must not reattempt the request by automatically replacing the SIPS scheme with a SIP scheme as described in RFC 3261 (see Section 3.1.2.3.5), as it would be a security vulnerability. If the UAC does reattempt the call with a SIP URI, the UAC should get a confirmation from the user to authorize reinitiating the session with a SIP Request-URI instead of a SIPS Request-URI.

When the route set is not empty (e.g., when a service route RFC 3608 [see Section 2.8] is returned by the registrar), it is the responsibility of the UAC to use a Route header field consisting of all SIPS URIs when using a SIPS Request-URI. Specifically, if the route set included any SIP URI, the UAC must change the SIP URIs to SIPS URIs simply by changing the scheme from sip to sips before sending the request. This allows for configuring or discovering one service route with all SIP URIs and allowing sending requests to both SIP and SIPS URIs. When the UAC is using a SIP Request-URI, if the route set is not empty and the topmost Route header field entry is a SIPS URI with the lr parameter, the UAC must send the request over the TLS (using a SIP Request-URI). If the route is not empty and the Route header field entry is a SIPS URI without the lr parameter, the UAC MUST send the request over the TLS using a SIPS Request-URI corresponding to the topmost entry in the route set. To emphasize what is already defined in RFC 3261, UAs must not use the transport=tls parameter.

4.2.3.8.1 Registration

The UAC registers Contact header fields to either a SIPS or a SIP AOR. If a UA wishes to be reachable with a SIPS URI, the UA must register with a SIPS Contact header field. Requests addressed to that UA's AOR using either a SIP or SIPS Request-URI will be routed to that UA. This includes UAs that support both SIP and SIPS. This specification does not provide any SIP-based mechanism for a UA to provision its proxy to only forward requests using a SIPS

Request-URI. A non-SIP mechanism such as a web interface could be used to provision such a preference. A SIP mechanism for provisioning such a preference is outside the scope of this specification. If a UA does not wish to be reached with a SIPS URI, it must register with a SIP Contact header field. Because registering with a SIPS Contact header field implies a binding of both a SIPS Contact and a corresponding SIP Contact to the AOR, a UA must not include both the SIPS and the SIP versions of the same Contact header field in a REGISTER request; the UA must only use the SIPS version in this case. Similarly, a UA should not register both a SIP Contact header field and a SIPS Contact header field in separate registrations as the SIP Contact header field would be superfluous.

If it does, the second registration replaces the first one (e.g., a UA could register first with a SIP Contact header field, meaning it does not support SIPS, and later register with a SIPS Contact header field, meaning it now supports SIPS). Similarly, if a UA registers first with a SIPS Contact header field and later registers with a SIP Contact header field, that SIP Contact header field replaces the SIPS Contact header field. RFC 5626 (see Section 13.2) can be used by a UA if it wants to ensure that no requests are delivered to it without using the TLS connection it used when registering. If all the Contact header fields in a REGISTER request are SIPS, the UAC must use SIPS AORs in the From and To header fields in the REGISTER request. If at least one of the Contact header fields is not SIPS (e.g., sip, mailto, tel, http, https), the UAC must use SIP AORs in the From and To header fields in the REGISTER request. To emphasize what is already defined in RFC 3261, UACs must not use the transport=tls parameter.

4.2.3.8.2 SIPS in a Dialog

If the Request-URI in a request that initiates a dialog is a SIP URI, then the UAC needs to be careful about what to use in the Contact header field (in case Record-Route is not used for this hop). If the Contact header field was a SIPS URI, it would mean that the UAS would only accept mid-dialog requests that are sent over secure transport on each hop. Since the Request-URI in this case is a SIP URI, it is quite possible that the UA sending a request to that URI might not be able to send requests to SIPS URIs. If the top Route header field does not contain a SIPS URI, the UAC MUST use a SIP URI in the Contact header field, even if the request is sent over a secure transport (e.g., the first hop could be reusing a TLS connection to the proxy as would be the case with RFC 5626; see Section 13.2). When a target refresh occurs within a dialog (e.g., re-INVITE request, UPDATE request), the UAC must include a Contact header field with a SIPS URI if the original request used a SIPS Request-URI.

4.2.3.8.3 Derived Dialogs and Transactions

Sessions, dialogs, and transactions can be *derived* from existing ones. A good example of a derived dialog is one that was established as a result of using the REFER method. As a general principle, derived dialogs and transactions cannot result in an effective downgrading of SIPS to SIP, without the explicit authorization of the entities involved. For example, when a REFER request is used to perform a call transfer, it results in an existing dialog being terminated and another one being created based on the Refer-To URI. If that initial dialog was established using SIPS, then the UAC must not establish a new one using SIP, unless there is an explicit authorization given by the recipient of the REFER request. This could be a warning provided to the user. Having such a warning could be useful, for example, for a secure directory service application, to warn a user that a request may be routed to a UA that does not support SIPS. A REFER request can also be used for referring to resources that do not result in dialogs being created. In fact, a REFER request can be used to point to resources that are of a different type than the original one (i.e., not SIP or SIPS). Other examples of derived dialogs and transactions include the use of Third-Party Call Control RFC 3725 (see Section 18.3), the Replaces header field (RFC 3891, see Section 2.8), and the Join header field (RFC 3911, see Section 2.8). Again, the general principle is that these mechanisms should not result in an effective downgrading of SIPS to SIP, without the proper authorization.

4.2.3.8.4 Globally Routable UA URI (GRUU)

When a Globally Routable UA URI (GRUU) (RFC 5627, see Section 4.3) is assigned to an instance ID/AOR pair, both SIP and SIPS GRUUs will be assigned. When a GRUU is obtained through registration, if the Contact header field in the REGISTER request contains a SIP URI, the SIP version of the GRUU is returned. If the Contact header field in the REGISTER request contains a SIPS URI, the SIPS version of the GRUU is returned. If the wrong scheme is received in the GRUU (which would be an error in the registrar), the UAC should treat it as if the proper scheme was used (i.e., it should replace the scheme with the proper scheme before using the GRUU).

4.2.3.9 UAS Normative Behavior

When presented with a SIPS URI, a UAS must not change it to a SIP URI. As mandated by RFC 3261 (see Section 3.6.1.1), if the request that initiated the dialog contained a SIPS URI in the Request-URI or in the top Record-Route header field value, if there was any, or the Contact header field if there was no Record-Route header field, the Contact header field in the response must be a SIPS URI. If a UAS does not wish to be reached with a SIPS URI but only with a SIP URI, the UAS must respond with a 480 Temporarily Unavailable response. The UAS should include a Warning header with warn-code 380 SIPS Not Allowed. RFC 3261 (see Section 3.1.3.2.1) states that UASs that do not support the SIPS URI scheme at all "should reject the request with a 416 Unsupported URI scheme response." If a UAS does not wish to be contacted with a SIP URI but instead by a SIPS URI, it must reject a request to a SIP Request-URI with a 480 Temporarily Unavailable response. The UAS should include a Warning header with warn-code 381 SIPS Required. It is a matter of local policy for a UAS to accept incoming requests addressed to a URI scheme that does not correspond to what it used for registration.

For example, a UA with a policy of *always SIPS* would address the registrar using a SIPS Request-URI over the TLS, would register with a SIPS Contact header field, and the UAS would reject requests using the SIP scheme with a 480 Temporarily Unavailable response with a Warning header with warn-code 381 SIPS Required. A UA with a policy of best-effort SIPS would address the registrar using a SIPS Request-URI over TLS, would register with a SIPS Contact header field, and the UAS would accept requests addressed to either SIP or SIPS Request-URIs. A UA with a policy of No SIPS would address the registrar using a SIP Request-URI, could use TLS or not, would register with a SIP AOR and a SIP Contact header field, and the UAS would accept requests addressed to a SIP Request-URI. If a UAS needs to reject a request because the URIs are used inconsistently (e.g., the Request-URI is a SIPS URI but the Contact header field is a SIP URI), the UAS must reject the request with a 400 Bad Request response. When a target refresh occurs within a dialog (e.g., re-INVITE request, UPDATE request), the UAS must include a Contact header field with a SIPS URI if the original request used a SIPS Request-URI. To emphasize what is already defined in RFC 3261, UASs must not use the transport=tls parameter.

4.2.3.10 Registrar Normative Behavior

The UAC registers Contacts header fields to either a SIPS or a SIP AOR. From a routing perspective, it does not matter which one is used for registration as they identify the same resource. The registrar must consider AORs that are identical except for one having the SIP scheme and the other having the SIPS scheme to be equivalent. A registrar MUST accept a binding to a SIPS Contact header field only if all the appropriate URIs are of the SIPS scheme; otherwise, there could be an inadvertent binding of a secure resource (SIPS) to an unsecured one (SIP). This includes the Request-URI and the Contacts and all the Path header fields, but does not include the From and To header fields. If the URIs are not of the proper SIPS scheme, the registrar must reject the REGISTER with a 400 Bad Request.

A registrar can return a service route (RFC 3608, see Section 2.8) and impose some constraints on whether or not TLS will be mandatory on specific hops. For example, if the topmost entry in the Path header field returned by the registrar is a SIPS URI, the registrar is telling the UAC that the TLS is to be used for the first hop, even if the Request-URI is SIP. If a UA is registered with a SIPS Contact header field, the registrar returning a service route (RFC 3608) must return a service route consisting of SIP URIs if the intent of the registrar is to allow both SIP and SIPS to be used in requests sent by that client. If a UA registers with a SIPS Contact header field, the registrar returning a service route must return a service route consisting of SIPS URIs if the intent of the registrar is to allow only SIPS URIs to be used in requests sent by that UA.

4.2.3.10.1 Globally Routable UA URI

When a GRUU (RFC 5627, see Section 4.3) is assigned to an instance ID/AOR pair through registration, the registrar MUST assign both a SIP GRUU and a SIPS GRUU. If the Contact header field in the REGISTER request contains a SIP URI, the registrar MUST return the SIP version of the GRUU. If the Contact header field in the REGISTER request contains a SIPS URI, the registrar must return the SIPS version of the GRUU.

4.2.3.11 Proxy Normative Behavior

Proxies must not use the last-hop exception of RFC 3261 when forwarding or retargeting a request to the last hop. Specifically, when a proxy receives a request with a SIPS Request-URI, the proxy must only forward or retarget the request to a SIPS Request-URI. If the target UAS had registered previously using a SIP Contact header field instead of a SIPS Contact header field, the proxy must not forward the request to the URI indicated in the Contact header field. If the proxy needs to reject the request for that reason, the proxy must reject it with a 480 Temporarily Unavailable response. In this case, the proxy should include a Warning header with warn-code 380 SIPS Not Allowed. Proxies should transport requests using a SIP URI over TLS when it is possible to set up a TLS connection, or reuse an existing one. RFC 5626 (see Section 13.2), for example, allows for reusing an existing TLS connection. Some proxies could have policies that prohibit sending any request over anything but the TLS. When a proxy receives a request with a SIP Request-URI, the proxy must not forward the request to a SIPS Request-URI.

If the target UAS had registered previously using a SIPS Contact header field, and the proxy decides to forward the request, the proxy must replace that SIPS scheme with a SIP scheme while leaving the rest of the URI as is, and use the resulting URI as the Request-URI of the forwarded request. The proxy must use the TLS to forward the request to the UAS. Some proxies could have a policy of not forwarding requests at all using a non-SIPS Request-URI if the UAS had registered using a SIPS Contact header field. If the proxy elects to reject the request because it has such a policy or because it is not capable of establishing a TLS connection, the proxy may reject it with a 480 Temporarily Unavailable response with a Warning header with warn-code 381 SIPS Required. If a proxy needs to reject a request because the URIs are used inconsistently (e.g., the Request-URI is a SIPS URI but the Contact header field is a SIP URI), the proxy should use response code 400 Bad Request. It is recommended that the proxy use the outbound proxy procedures defined in RFC 5626 (see Section 13.2) for supporting UACs that cannot provide a certificate for establishing a TLS connection (i.e., when server-side authentication is used).

When a proxy sends a request using a SIPS Request-URI and receives a 3xx response with a SIP Contact header field, or a 416 response, or a 480 Temporarily Unavailable response with a Warning header with warn-code 380 SIPS Not Allowed response, the proxy must not recurse on the response. In this case, the proxy should forward the best response instead of recursing, in order to allow for the UAC to take the appropriate action. When a proxy sends a request using a SIP Request-URI and receives a 3xx response with a SIPS Contact header field, or a 480 Temporarily Unavailable response with a Warning header with warn-code 381 SIPS Required, the proxy must not recurse on the response. In this case, the proxy should forward the best response instead of recursing, in order to allow for the UAC to take the appropriate action. To emphasize what is already defined in RFC 3261, proxies must not use the transport=tls parameter.

4.2.3.12 Redirect Server Normative Behavior

Using a redirect server with TLS instead of using a proxy has some limitations that have to be taken into account. Since there is no preestablished connection between the proxy and the UAS (such as with RFC 5626, see Section 13.2), it is only appropriate for scenarios where inbound connections are allowed. For example, it could be used in a server-to-server environment (redirect server or proxy server) where TLS mutual authentication is used, and where there are no NAT traversal issues. A redirect server would not be able to redirect to an entity that does not have a certificate. A redirect server might not be usable if there is a NAT between the server and the UAS. When a redirect server receives a request with a SIP Request-URI, the redirect server may redirect with a 3xx response to either a SIP or a SIPS Contact header field. If the target UAS had registered previously using a SIPS Contact header field, the redirect server should return a SIPS Contact header field if it is in an environment where TLS is usable (as described in the previous paragraph). If the target UAS had registered previously using a SIP Contact header field, the redirect server must return a SIP Contact header field in a 3xx response if it redirects the request.

When a redirect server receives a request with a SIPS Request-URI, the redirect server may redirect with a 3xx response to a SIP or a SIPS Contact header field. If the target UAS had registered previously using a SIPS Contact header field, the redirect server should return a SIPS Contact header field if it is in an environment where TLS is usable. If the target UAS had registered previously using a SIP Contact header field, the redirect server must return a SIP Contact header field in a 3xx response if it chooses to redirect; otherwise, the UAS may reject the request with a 480 Temporarily Unavailable response with a Warning header with warn-code 380 SIPS Not Allowed. If a redirect server redirects to a UAS that it has no knowledge of (e.g., an AOR in a different domain), the Contact header field could be of any scheme. If a redirect server needs to reject a request because the URIs are used inconsistently (e.g., the Request-URI is a SIPS URI but the Contact header field is a SIP URI), the redirect server should use response code 400 Bad Request. To emphasize what is already defined in RFC 3261, redirect servers must not use the transport=tls parameter.

4.2.3.13 Call Flows

RFC 5630 has also provided detailed call flows describing each of the SIP messages with their headers as follows: SIP UA's contacts registration using SIPS URI, calling between two SIP UAs using SIPS AOR, one SIP UA calling another SIP UA's SIP AOR using TCP, and one SIP UA calling another SIP UA's SIP AOR using TLS. We have left these call flows as exercises to the reader.

4.2.3.14 Further Considerations

RFC 3261 itself introduces some complications with using SIPS, for example, when Record-Route (see Sections 2.8 and 4.2.1 and Chapter 9) is not used. When a SIPS URI is used in a Contact header field in a dialog-initiating request and Record-Route is not used, that SIPS URI might not be usable by the other end. If the other end does not support SIPS or TLS, it will not be able to use it. The last-hop exception is an example of when this can occur. In this case, using Record-Route so that the requests are sent through proxies can help in making it work. Another example is that even in a case where the Contact header field is a SIPS URI, no Record-Route is used, and the far end supports SIPS and TLS, it might still not be possible for the far end to establish a TLS connection with the SIP originating end if the certificate cannot be validated by the far end. This could typically be the case if the originating end was using server-side authentication as described below, or if the originating end is not using a certificate that can be validated. TLS itself has a significant impact on how SIPS can be used. Server-side authentication (where the server side provides its certificate but the client side does not) is typically used between a SIP end-user device acting as the TLS client side (e.g., a phone or a personal computer) and its SIP server (proxy or registrar) acting as the TLS server side.

TLS mutual authentication (where both the client side and the server side provide their respective certificates) is typically used between SIP servers (proxies, registrars), or statically configured devices such as PSTN gateways or media servers. In the mutual authentication model, for two entities to be able to establish a TLS connection, it is required that both sides be able to validate each other's certificates, either by static configuration or by being able to recurse to a valid root certificate. With server-side authentication, only the client side is capable of validating the server side's certificate, as the client side does not provide a certificate. The consequences of all this are that whenever a SIPS URI is used to establish a TLS connection, it is expected to be possible for the entity establishing the connection (the client) to validate the certificate from the server side. For server-side authentication, RFC 5626 (see Section 13.2) is the recommended approach. For mutual authentication, one needs to ensure that the architecture of the network is such that connections are made between entities that have access to each other's certificates. Record-Route RFC 3261 (see Section 2.8 and Chapter 9) and Path (RFC 3327, Section 2.8) are very useful in ensuring that previously established TLS connections can be reused. Other mechanisms might also be used in certain circumstances: for example, using root certificates that are widely recognized allows for more easily created TLS connections.

4.3 Globally Routable UA URI

4.3.1 Overview

A single user in a SIP network can have a number of UAs for a host of devices for many functions such as handsets, softphones, voice-mail accounts, and others. All of those UAs of that particular use are referenced by the same AOR. There are a number of contexts in which it is desirable to have an identifier that addresses a single UA for reaching the user rather than the group of UAs indicated by an AOR. Many of the SIP applications require a UA to construct and distribute a URI that can be used by anyone on the Internet to route a call to that specific UA instance. A URI that routes to a specific UA instance is called a GRUU defined in RFC 5627 that is described here. Note that multiple telephone AORs register with GRUU in Section 3.3.5. In this context, RFC 5627 defines the following additional terms:

- **Contact:** The term *contact*, when used in all lowercase, refers to a URI that is bound to an AOR and GRUU by means of a registration. A contact is usually a SIP URI, and is bound to the AOR and GRUU through a REGISTER request by appearing as a value of the Contact header field. The contact URI identifies a specific UA.
- **Remote target:** The term *remote target* refers to a URI that a UA uses to identify itself for receipt of both mid-dialog and out-of-dialog requests. A remote target is established by placing a URI in the Contact header field of a dialog-forming request or response and is updated by target refresh requests or responses.
- **Contact header field:** The term *Contact header field*, with a capitalized C, refers to the header field that can appear in REGISTER requests and responses, redirects, or dialog-creating requests and responses. Depending on the semantics, the Contact header field sometimes conveys a contact, and sometimes conveys a remote target.

4.3.2 GRUU Grammar

RFC 5627 defines two new Contact header field parameters (temp-gruu and pub-gruu) by extending the grammar for *contactparams* as defined in RFC 3261. It also defines a new SIP URI parameter (gr) by extending the grammar for uri-parameter as defined in RFC 3261. The ABNF is provided here for convenience although detail SIP syntaxes are provided in Section 2.4.1.2 as follows:

```
contact-params =/ temp-gruu / pub-gruu
temp-gruu = "temp-gruu" EQUAL quoted-string
pub-gruu = "pub-gruu" EQUAL quoted-string
uri-parameter =/ gr-param
gr-param = "gr" ["=" pvalue]; defined in RFC
3261
```

The quoted strings for temp-gruu and pub-gruu must contain a SIP URI. However, they are encoded like all other quoted strings and can therefore contain quoted-pair escapes when represented this way.

4.3.3 Operation

GRUUs are issued by SIP domains and always route back to a proxy in that domain. In turn, the domain maintains the binding between the GRUU and the particular UA instance. When a GRUU is dereferenced while sending a SIP request, that request arrives at the proxy. It maps the GRUU to the contact for the particular UA instance, and sends the request there.

4.3.3.1 Structure of GRUUs

A GRUU is a SIP URI that has two properties:

- It routes to a specific UA instance.
- It can be successfully dereferenced by any UA on the Internet, not just ones in the same domain or IP network as the UA instance to which the GRUU points.

In principle, a GRUU can be constructed in any way the domain chooses, as long as it meets the criteria above. However, all GRUUs contain the gr URI parameter (either with or without a value), so that a recipient of a GRUU can tell that it has these two properties. In practice, there are two different types of GRUUs:

- GRUUs that expose the underlying AOR
- GRUUs that hide the underlying AOR

4.3.3.2 GRUUs That Expose the Underlying AOR

The GRUU that exposes the underlying AOR is called the public GRUU. It is constructed by taking the AOR, and adding the gr URI parameter with a value chosen by the registrar in the domain. The value of the gr URI parameter contains a representation of the UA instance. For instance, if the AOR was sip:alice@example.com, the GRUU might be

```
sip:alice@example.com;gr=kjh29x97us97d
```

For example, many UAs retain call logs, which keep track of incoming and outgoing call attempts. If the UA had made a call to a GRUU, the call log will contain the GRUU. Since the call log is rendered to the user, it would be useful to be able to present the user with the AOR instead, since the AOR is meaningful to users as an identifier. If a UA removes the gr URI parameter, the result is the AOR. Since many systems ignore unknown parameters anyway, a public GRUU will *look* like the AOR to those systems.

4.3.3.3 GRUUs That Hide the Underlying AOR

The GRUU that obfuscates the AOR such that it cannot be extracted by a recipient of the GRUU is called the temporary GRUU. The most obvious reason to do this is to protect the user's privacy. In such cases, the GRUU can have any content, provided that it meets the structural requirements described earlier and is created meeting the rules described later, and the AOR cannot be readily determined from the GRUU. The GRUU will have the gr URI parameter, either with or without a value. To avoid creating excessive state in the registrar, it is often desirable to construct cryptographically protected *stateless* GRUUs using an algorithm. An example of a temporary GRUU constructed using a stateful algorithm would be

```
sip:asd887f9dfkk76690@example.com;gr
```

The mechanism for constructing a GRUU or network design for GRUU is not subject to the specification of RFC 5627. We are providing some examples that can be used by a registrar to construct a public and a temporary GRUU and consideration of the network design for GRUU in the following subsections described in RFC 5627. Of course, others are permitted, as long as they meet the constraints defined for a GRUU.

4.3.3.3.1 Public GRUU Construction

The most basic approach for constructing a public GRUU is to take the AOR and place the actual value of the instance ID into the contents of the gr URI parameter.

4.3.3.3.2 Temporary GRUU Construction Algorithms

This specification requires a registrar to create a new temporary GRUU on each registration refresh. If a registration is very long lived, this can quickly result in hundreds or even thousands of temporary GRUUs being created and allocated to a UA. Consequently, it is important to have an algorithm for constructing temporary GRUUs that does not require additional storage that grows in size with the number of temporary GRUUs. The following algorithm meets this goal. The registrar maintains a counter, I_i. This counter is 48 bits and is initialized to zero. The counter is persistently stored, using a backend database or other similar technique. When the registrar creates the first temporary GRUU for a particular AOR and instance ID, the registrar notes the current value of the counter, I_i, and increments the counter in the database.

The registrar then maps I_i to the AOR and instance ID using the database, a persistent hashmap, or similar technology. If the registration expires such that there are no longer any contacts with that particular instance ID bound to the GRUU, the registrar removes the mapping. Similarly, if the temporary GRUUs are invalidated due to a change in Call-ID, the registrar removes the current mapping from I_i to the AOR and instance ID, notes the current value of the counter I_i, and stores a mapping from I_i to the AOR and instance ID. On the basis of these rules, the hashmap will contain a single mapping for each AOR and instance ID for which there is a currently valid registration.

The usage of a counter in a 48-bit space with sequential assignment allows for a compact representation of the hashmap key, which is important for generating GRUUs of reasonable size. The counter starts at zero when the system is initialized. Persistent and reliable storage of the counter is required to avoid misrouting of a GRUU to the wrong AOR and instance ID. Similarly, persistent storage of the hashmap is required, even though the proxy and registrar restart. If the hashmap is reset, all previous temporary GRUUs become invalidated. This might cause dialogs in progress to fail, or future requests toward a temporary GRUU to fail, when they normally would not. The same hashmap needs to be accessible by all proxies and registrars that can field requests for a particular AOR and instance ID.

The registrar maintains a pair of local symmetric keys K_e and K_a. These are regenerated every time the counter is reset. When the counter rolls over or is reset, the registrar remembers the old values of K_e and K_a for a time. Like the hashmap itself, these keys need to be shared across all proxy and registrars that can service requests for a particular AOR and instance ID. To generate a new temporary GRUU, the registrar generates a random 80-bit distinguisher value D. It then computes

$$M = D \,||\, I_i$$

$$E = \text{AES-ECB-Encrypt}(K_e, M)$$

$$A = \text{HMAC-SHA256-80}(K_a, E)$$

Temp-Gruu-userpart = "tgruu" || base64(E) || base64(A)

where || denotes concatenation, and AES-ECB-Encrypt represents AES encryption in electronic codebook mode. M will be 128 bits long, producing a value of E that is 128 bits and A that is 80 bits. This produces a user part that has 42 characters.

When a proxy receives a request whose user part begins with tgruu, it extracts the remaining portion and splits it into 22 characters (E') and the remaining 14 characters (A'). It then computes A and E by performing a base64 decode of A' and E', respectively. Next, it computes

$$A_c = \text{HMAC-SHA256-80}(K_a, E)$$

If the counter has rolled over or reset, this computation is performed with the current and previous K_a. If the A_c value(s) that are computed do not match the value of A extracted from the GRUU, the GRUU is rejected as invalid. Next, the proxy computes

$$M = \text{AES-ECB-Decrypt}(K_e, E)$$

If the counter has rolled over, this computation is done using the value of K_e that goes with the value of K_a, which produced a valid A_c in the previous HMAC validation. The leading 80 bits (the distinguisher D) are discarded, leaving an index I_i in the hashmap. This index is looked up. If it exists, the proxy now has the AOR and instance ID corresponding to this temporary GRUU. If there is nothing in the hashmap for the key I_i, the GRUU is no longer valid and the request is rejected. The usage of a 48-bit counter allows for the registrar to have as many as a billion AORs, with 10 instances per AOR, and cycle through 10,000 Call-ID changes for each instance through the duration of a single registration. These numbers reflect the average; the system works fine if a particular AOR has more than 10 instances or a particular instance cycles through more than 10,000 Call-IDs in its registration, as long as the average meets these constraints.

4.3.3.3.3 Network Design Considerations

The GRUU specification works properly based on logic implemented at the UAs and in the authoritative proxies on both sides of a call. Consequently, it is possible to construct network deployments in which GRUUs will not work properly. One important assumption made by the GRUU mechanism is that, if a request passes through any proxies in the originating domain before visiting the terminating domain, one of those proxies will be the authoritative proxy for the UAC. Administrators of SIP networks will need to make sure that this property is retained. There are several ways it can be accomplished:

- If the UAs support the service-route mechanism (RFC 3608, see Section 2.8.2), the registrar can implement it and return a service route that points to the authoritative proxy. This will cause requests originated by the UA to pass through the authoritative proxy.
- The UAs can be configured to never use an outbound proxy, and send requests directly to the domain of the terminating party. This configuration is not practical in many use cases, but it is a solution to this requirement.
- The UAs can be configured with an outbound proxy in the same domain as the authoritative proxy, and this outbound proxy forwards requests to the authoritative proxy by default. This works very well in cases where the clients are not roaming; in such cases, the outbound proxy in a visited network may be discovered dynamically through the Dynamic Host Configuration Protocol (DHCP) (RFC 3361).
- In cases where the client discovers a local outbound proxy via a mechanism such as DHCP, and is not implementing the service route mechanism, the UA can be configured to automatically add an additional

Route header field after the outbound proxy, which points to a proxy in the home network. This has the same net effect of the service route mechanism, but is accomplished through static configuration.

4.3.4 Obtaining a GRUU

A UA can obtain a GRUU in one of several ways:

- As part of its REGISTER transaction.
- By constructing one locally, using the IP address or host name of the UA instance as the domain part of the URI. These are called self-made GRUUs, and are only really GRUUs when constructed by UAs that know they are globally reachable using their IP address or host name.
- Via some locally specified administrative mechanism.

A UA that wants to obtain a GRUU via its REGISTER request does so by providing an instance ID in the +sip. instance Contact header field parameter, defined in RFC 5626 (see Section 13.2). For example:

```
Contact: <sip:callee@192.0.2.2>
;+sip.instance="<urn:uuid:f81d4fae-7dec-11d0
-a765-00a0c91e6bf6>"
```

The registrar detects this header field parameter and provides two GRUUs in the REGISTER response. One of these is a temporary GRUU, and the other is the public GRUU. These two GRUUs are returned in the temp-gruu and pub-gruu Contact header field parameters in the response, respectively. For example (<allOneLine> tag is used as defined in RFC 4475):

```
<allOneLine>
Contact: <sip:callee@192.0.2.2>
;pub-gruu="sip:callee@example.com;gr=urn:
uuid:f81d4fae-7dec-11d0-a765-00a0c91e6bf6"
;temp-gruu="sip:tgruu.7hs==
jd7vnzga5w7fajsc7-ajd6fabz0f8g5@example.com;
gr"
;+sip.instance="<urn:uuid:f81d4fae-7dec-11d0
-a765-00a0c91e6bf6>"
;expires=3600
</allOneLine>
```

When a UA refreshes this registration before its expiration, the registrar will return back the same public GRUU but will create a new temporary GRUU. Although each refresh provides the UA with a new temporary GRUU, all of the temporary GRUUs learned from previous REGISTER responses during the lifetime of a contact remain valid as long as the following conditions are met:

- A contact with that instance ID remains registered.
- The UA does not change the Call-ID in its REGISTER request compared with previous ones for the same reg-id (RFC 5626, see Section 13.2).

When the last contact for the instance expires, either through explicit deregistration or timeout, all of the temporary GRUUs become invalidated. Similarly, if a register refresh for a contact (or, if RFC 5626 is being used, for a reg-id) changes the Call-ID compared with previous register refreshes, all of the previous temporary GRUUs are invalidated. When the UA later creates a new registration with the same instance ID, the public GRUU is the same. The temporary GRUU will be new (as it is with refreshes), and it will be the only valid temporary GRUU for the instance until the next refresh, at which point a second one also becomes valid. Consequently, temporary GRUUs *accumulate* during the lifetime of a registration.

4.3.5 Using a GRUU

Once a UA obtains GRUUs from the registrar, it uses them in several ways. First, it uses them as the contents of the Contact header field in non-REGISTER requests and responses that it emits (e.g., an INVITE request and 200 OK response). According to RFC 3261 (see Section 2.8.2), the Contact header field is supposed to contain a URI that routes to that UA. Before this specification, there has not been a way to really meet that requirement. The UA would use one of its temporary GRUUs for anonymous calls, and use its public GRUU otherwise. Second, the UA can use the GRUU in any other place it needs to use a URI that resolves to itself, such as a web page.

4.3.6 Dereferencing a GRUU

Because a GRUU is simply a URI, a UA dereferences it in exactly the same way as it would any other URI. However, once the request has been routed to the appropriate proxy, the behavior is slightly different. The proxy will map the GRUU to the AOR and determine the set of contacts that the particular UA instance has registered. The GRUU is then mapped to those contacts, and the request is routed toward the UA.

4.3.7 UA Behavior

4.3.7.1 Generating a REGISTER Request

When a UA compliant to this specification generates a REGISTER request (initial or refresh), it must include the

Supported header field in the request. The value of that header field MUST include gruu as one of the option tags. This alerts the registrar for the domain that the UA supports the GRUU mechanism. Furthermore, for each contact for which the UA desires to obtain a GRUU, the UA must include a sip.instance media feature tag (see RFC 5626, Section 13.2) as a UA characteristic (see RFC 3840, Section 3.4, whose value must be the instance ID that identifies the UA instance being registered. Each such Contact header field should not contain a pub-gruu or tempgruu header field. The contact URI must not be equivalent, based on the URI equality rules in RFC 3261 (see Section 4.2), to the AOR in the To header field. If the contact URI is a GRUU, it must not be a GRUU for the AOR in the To header field.

As in RFC 3261 (see Section 3.3), the Call-ID in a REGISTER refresh should be identical to the Call-ID used to previously register a contact. With GRUU, an additional consideration applies. If the Call-ID changes in a register refresh, the server will invalidate all temporary GRUUs associated with that UA instance; the only valid one will be the new one returned in that REGISTER response. When RFC 5626 is in use, this rule applies to the reg-ids: if the Call-ID changes for the registration refresh for a particular reg-id, the server will invalidate all temporary GRUUs associated with that UA instance as a whole. Consequently, if a UA wishes its previously obtained temporary GRUUs to remain valid, it must utilize the same Call-ID in REGISTER refreshes. However, it may change the Call-ID in a refresh if invalidation is the desired objective.

Note that, if any dialogs are in progress that utilize a temporary GRUU as a remote target, and a UA performs a registration refresh with a change in Call-ID, those temporary GRUUs become invalid, and the UA will not be reachable for subsequent mid-dialog messages. If a UA instance is trying to register multiple contacts for the same instance for the purposes of redundancy, it MUST use the procedures defined in RFC 5626 (see Section 13.2). A UA utilizing GRUUs can still perform third-party registrations and can include contacts that omit the +sip.instance Contact header field parameter. If a UA wishes to guarantee that the REGISTER request is not processed unless the domain supports and uses this extension, it may include a Require header field in the request with a value that contains the gruu option tag. This is in addition to the presence of the Supported header field, also containing the gruu option tag. The use of Proxy-Require is not necessary and is not recommended.

4.3.7.2 Learning GRUUs from REGISTER Responses

If the REGISTER response is a 2xx, each Contact header field that contains the +sip.instance Contact header field parameter can also contain a pub-gruu and temp-gruu Contact header field parameters. These header field parameters convey the public and a temporary GRUU for the UA instance, respectively. A UA MUST be prepared for a Contact header field to contain just a pub-gruu, just a temp-gruu, neither, or both. The temporary GRUU will be valid for the duration of the registration (i.e., through refreshes), while the public GRUU persists across registrations. The UA will receive a new temporary GRUU in each successful REGISTER response, while the public GRUU will typically be the same. However, a UA must be prepared for the public GRUU to change from a previous one, since the persistence property is not guaranteed with complete certainty. If a UA changed its Call-ID in this REGISTER request compared with a previous REGISTER request for the same contact or reg-id, the UA MUST discard all temporary GRUUs learned through prior REGISTER responses. A UA may retain zero, one, some, or all of the temporary GRUUs that it is provided during the time over which at least one contact or reg-id remains continuously registered. If a UA stores any temporary GRUUs for use during its registration, it needs to be certain that the registration does not accidentally lapse due to clock skew between the UA and registrar.

Consequently, the UA must refresh its registration such that the REGISTER refresh transaction will either complete or timeout before the expiration of the registration. For default transaction timers, this would be at least 32 seconds before expiration, assuming the registration expiration is larger than 64 seconds. If the registration expiration is less than 64 seconds, the UA should refresh its registration halfway before expiration. Note that when RFC 5626 (see Section 13.2) is in use, and the UA is utilizing multiple flows for purposes of redundancy, the temporary GRUUs remain valid as long as at least one flow is registered. Thus, even if the registration of one flow expires, the temporary GRUUs learned previously remain valid. In cases where registrars forcefully shorten registration intervals, the registration event package, RFC 3680 (see Section 5.3), is used by UAs to learn of these changes. A UA implementing both RFC 3680 and GRUU must also implement the extensions to RFC 3680 for conveying information on GRUU, as defined in RFC 5628, as these are necessary to keep the set of temporary GRUUs synchronized between the UA and the registrar. More generally, the utility of temporary GRUUs depends on the UA and registrar being in sync on the set of valid temporary GRUUs at any time. Without the support of RFC 3680 and its extension for GRUU, the client will remain in sync only as long as it always reregisters well before the registration expiration. Besides forceful de-registrations, other events (e.g., network outages, connection failures, and short refresh intervals) can lead to potential inconsistencies in the set of valid temporary GRUUs. For this reason, it is recommended that a UA that utilizes temporary GRUUs implement RFC 3680 and RFC 5628.

A non-2xx response to the REGISTER request has no impact on any existing GRUUs previously provided to the UA. Specifically, if a previously successful REGISTER request provided the UA with a GRUU, a subsequent failed request does not remove, delete, or otherwise invalidate the GRUU. The user and host parts of the GRUU learned by the UA in the REGISTER response must be treated opaquely by the UA. That is, the UA must not modify them in any way. A UA must not modify or remove URI parameters it does not recognize. Furthermore, the UA must not add, remove, or modify URI parameters relevant for receipt and processing of request at the proxy, including the transport, lr, maddr, ttl, user, and comp (see RFC 3486, Section 15.7) URI parameters. The other URI parameter defined in RFC 3261 (see Section 4.2), method, would not typically be present in a GRUU delivered from a registrar, and a UA may add a method URI parameter to the GRUU before handing it out to another entity. Similarly, the URI parameters defined in RFCs 4240 and 4458 (see Section 4.4) are meant for consumption by the UA. These would not be included in the GRUU returned by a registrar and may be added by a UA wishing to provide services associated with those URI parameters. Note, however, that should another UA dereference the GRUU, the parameters will be lost at the proxy when the Request-URI is translated into the registered contact, unless some other means is provided for the attributes to be delivered to the UA.

4.3.7.3 Constructing a Self-Made GRUU

Many UAs (e.g., gateways to the PSTN, conferencing servers, and media servers) do not perform registrations and cannot obtain GRUUs through that mechanism. These types of UAs can be publicly reachable. This would mean that the policy of the domain is that requests can come from anywhere on the public Internet and be delivered to the UA without requiring processing by intervening proxies within the domain. Furthermore, firewall and NAT policies administered by the domain would allow such requests into the network. When a UA is certain that these conditions are met, a UA may construct a self-made GRUU. Of course, a UA that does REGISTER, but for whom these conditions are met regardless, may also construct a self-made GRUU. However, usage of GRUUs obtained by the registrar is recommended instead.

A self-made GRUU is one whose domain part equals the IP address or host name of the UA. The user part of the SIP URI is chosen arbitrarily by the UA. Like all other GRUUs, the URI must contain the gr URI parameter, with or without a value, indicating it is a GRUU. If a UA does not register, but is not publicly reachable, it would need to obtain a GRUU through some other means. Typically, the UA would be configured with a GRUU, the GRUU would be configured into the proxy, and the proxy will be configured with a mapping from the GRUU to the IP address (or host name) and port of the UA.

4.3.7.4 Using One's Own GRUUs

A UA should use a GRUU when populating the Contact header field of dialog-forming and target refresh requests and responses. In other words, a UA compliant to this specification should use one of its GRUUs as its remote target. This includes

- The INVITE request
- A2xx or 18x response to an INVITE that contains a To tag
- The SUBSCRIBE request
- A 2xx response to a SUBSCRIBE which contains a To tag
- The NOTIFY request
- The REFER request
- A 2xx response to NOTIFY
- The UPDATE request
- A 2xx response to NOTIFY

The only reason not to use a GRUU would be privacy considerations. When using a GRUU obtained through registrations, a UA must have an active registration before using a GRUU, and must use a GRUU learned through that registration. It must not reuse a GRUU learned through a previous registration that has lapsed (in other words, one obtained when registering a contact that has expired). The UA may use either the public or one of its temporary GRUUs provided by its registrar. A UA must not use a temporary GRUU learned in a REGISTER response whose Call-ID differs from the one in the most recent REGISTER request generated by the UA for the same AOR and instance ID (and, if RFC 5626, Section 13.2, is in use, reg-id). When a UA wishes to construct an anonymous request as described in RFC 3323 (see Section 20.2), it should use a temporary GRUU. As per RFC 3261 (see Section 2.8.2), a UA should include a Supported header with the option tag gruu in requests and responses it generates.

4.3.7.4.1 Considerations for Multiple AORs

These considerations are described in Section 3.3.3.

4.3.7.5 Dereferencing a GRUU

A GRUU is identified by the presence of the gr URI parameter, and this URI parameter might or might not have a value. A UA that wishes to send a request to a URI that contains a GRUU knows that the request will be delivered to a specific UA instance without further action on the part of the requestor. Some UAs implement nonstandard URI-handling mechanisms that compensate for the fact that heretofore many contact URIs have not been globally routable. Since any URI containing the gr URI parameter is known to be globally routable, a UA should not apply such mechanisms when a contact URI contains the gr URI parameter.

Because the instance ID is a callee capabilities parameter, a UA might be tempted to send a request to the AOR of a user, and include an Accept-Contact header field (see Section 2.8.2) that indicates a preference for routing the request to a UA with a specific instance ID. Although this would appear to have the same effect as sending a request to the GRUU, it does not. The caller preferences expressed in the Accept-Contact header field are just preferences. Their efficacy depends on a UA constructing an Accept-Contact header field that interacts with domain-processing logic for an AOR, to cause a request to route to a particular instance. Given the variability in routing logic in a domain (e.g., time-based routing to only selected contacts), this does not work for many domain-routing policies. However, this specification does not forbid a client from attempting such a request, as there can be cases where the desired operation truly is a preferential routing request.

4.3.7.6 Rendering GRUUs on a User Interface

When rendering a GRUU to a user through a user interface, it is recommended that the gr URI parameter be removed. For public GRUUs, this will produce the AOR, as desired. For temporary GRUUs, the resulting URI will be seemingly random. Future work might provide improved mechanisms that would allow an automaton to know that a URI is anonymized, and therefore inappropriate to render.

4.3.8 Registrar Behavior

4.3.8.1 Processing a REGISTER Request

A REGISTER request might contain a Require header field with the gruu option tag; this indicates that the registrar has to understand this extension to process the request. It does not require the registrar to create GRUUs, however. As the registrar is processing the contacts in the REGISTER request according to the procedures (see Section 3.3), the registrar checks whether each Contact header field in the REGISTER message contains a +sip.instance header field parameter. If present with a non-zero expiration, the contact is processed further based on the rules in the remainder of this section. Otherwise, the contact is processed based on normal RFC 3261 (see Section 3.3) rules.

Note that handling of a REGISTER request containing a Contact header field with value "*" and an expiration of zero still retains the meaning defined in RFC 3261 (see Section 3.3)—all contacts, not just those with a specific instance ID, are deleted. As described earlier, this removes the binding of each contact to the AOR and the binding of each contact to its GRUUs. If the contact URI is equivalent (based on URI equivalence in RFC 3261, Section 4.2.1) to the AOR, the registrar must reject the request with a 403 Forbidden, since this would cause a routing loop. If the contact URI is a GRUU for the AOR in the To header field of the REGISTER request, the registrar must reject the request with a 403 Forbidden, for the same reason.

If the contact is not a SIP URI, the REGISTER request must be rejected with a 403 Forbidden. Next, the registrar checks if there is already a valid public GRUU for the AOR (present in the To header field of the REGISTER request) and the instance ID (present as the content of the +sip.instance Contact header field parameter). If there is no valid public GRUU, the registrar should construct a public GRUU at this time according to the procedures described later. The public GRUU must be constructed by adding the gr URI parameter, with a value, to the AOR. If the contact contained a pub-gruu Contact header field parameter, the header field parameter must be ignored by the registrar. A UA cannot suggest or otherwise provide a public GRUU to the registrar.

Next, the registrar checks for any existing contacts registered to the same AOR, instance ID, and if the contact in the REGISTER request is registering a flow (RFC 5626, Section 13.2), reg-id. If there is at least one, the registrar finds the one that was most recently registered, and examines the Call-ID value associated with that registered contact. If it differs from the one in the REGISTER request, the registrar must invalidate all previously generated temporary GRUUs for the AOR and instance ID. A consequence of this invalidation is that requests addressed to those GRUUs will be rejected by the domain with a 404 from this point forward.

Next, the registrar should create a new temporary GRUU for the AOR and instance ID with the characteristics described later. The temporary GRUU construction algorithm must have the following two properties:

- The likelihood that the temporary GRUU is equal to another GRUU that the registrar has created MUST be vanishingly small.
- Given a pair of GRUUs, it must be computationally infeasible to determine whether they were issued for the same AOR or instance ID or for different AORs and instance IDs.

If the contact contained a temp-gruu Contact header field parameter, the header field parameter must be ignored by the registrar. A UA cannot suggest or otherwise provide a temporary GRUU to the registrar.

4.3.8.2 Generating a REGISTER Response

When generating the 200 OK response to the REGISTER request, the procedures of RFC 3261 (see Section 3.3) are followed. Furthermore, for each Contact header field value placed in the response, if the registrar has stored an instance ID associated with that contact, that instance ID is returned as a Contact header field parameter. If the REGISTER request contained a Supported header field that included the gruu option tag, and the registrar has at least one temporary GRUU assigned to the instance ID and AOR, the registrar must add a temp-gruu Contact header field parameter to that Contact header field. The value of the temp-gruu parameter is a quoted string, and must contain the most recently created temporary GRUU for that AOR and instance ID. In addition, if the registrar has a public GRUU assigned to the instance ID and AOR (and the client supports GRUUs), the registrar MUST add a pub-gruu Contact header field parameter to that Contact header field. The value of the pubgruu Contact header field parameter is the public GRUU. The registrar should not include the gruu option tag in the Require or Supported header field of the response.

4.3.8.3 Timing Out a Registration

When a registered contact expires (either due to timeout or explicit deregistration), its binding to the AOR is removed as usual. In addition, its binding to its GRUUs are removed at the same time, as a consequence of the relationships described earlier. If, as a consequence of the expiration of the contact, a particular GRUU no longer has any registered contacts bound to it, and the GRUU is a temporary GRUU, the GRUU must be invalidated. This means that all of the accumulated temporary GRUUs get invalidated once the last contact for a given instance ID expires.

If, however, the GRUU was a public GRUU, the registrar should continue to treat the GRUU as valid. Consequently, subsequent requests targeted to the GRUU, before reregistration of a contact to the GRUU, should return a 480 (Temporarily Unavailable) response. In addition, since the GRUU remains valid, the rules in Section 4.3.7.1 will cause it to be retained when a contact with that instance ID is once again registered to the AOR. These rules give a public GRUU a semipermanent property. The intent is that the registrar makes every attempt to retain the validity of the GRUU for as long as the AOR itself is known within the domain. The requirements for doing so are at *should* strength and not *must* strength because of the difficulty in meeting a must-strength requirement; registrar failures could cause the set of valid GRUUs to be lost, and this specification requires the UA to be robust against such cases. That said, it is possible for a public GRUU to be constructed such that a registrar does not need to retain any additional state for it, yet the GRUU still meets the requirements described here.

4.3.8.4 Creation of a GRUU

This section defines additional behaviors associated with the construction and maintenance of a GRUU that are specific to a registrar. These rules do not apply to self-made GRUUs or GRUUs not obtained through registrations. When a registrar creates a GRUU, it is required to maintain certain information associated with the GRUU, regardless of whether it is a public or temporary GRUU. Every GRUU is associated with a single AOR and a single instance ID. A registrar must be able to determine the instance ID and AOR when presented with a GRUU. In addition, the GRUU, like an AOR, resolves to zero or more contacts. While the AOR resolves to all registered contacts for an AOR, a GRUU resolves only to those contacts whose instance ID matches the one associated with the GRUU. For this reason, a contact with an instance ID is always bound to both a GRUU and its AOR, never just an AOR or just a GRUU.

This is shown pictorially in Figure 4.3a. The figure shows three contacts registered to a single AOR. One of the contacts has an instance ID of 1, and the other two have an instance ID of 2. There are two GRUUs for this AOR. One is associated with instance ID 1, and the other with instance ID 2. The first GRUU resolves only to contacts whose instance ID is 1, and the second resolves only to contacts whose instance ID is 2. There will typically be multiple contacts for a given instance ID if a UA has crashed, rebooted, and reregistered with the same instance ID, or is using the mechanisms of RFC 5626 (see Section 13.2) to have multiple registrations for redundancy. If the contact for instance ID 1 expires, the AOR would resolve to two contacts but the GRUU associated with instance ID 1 would resolve to zero.

There can be multiple GRUUs with the same instance ID and AOR. Indeed, this specification requires registrars to maintain many—one that is public and several that are temporary. However, if two GRUUs are associated with different AORs or different instance IDs or both, the GRUUs must be different based on URI equality comparison. A GRUU in a domain must not be equivalent, based on URI comparison (see Section 4.2.1.4), to any AOR in a domain except for the one associated with the GRUU. A public GRUU will always be equivalent to the AOR based on URI equality rules. The reason is that the rules in RFC 3261 (see Section 4.2.1) cause URI parameters that are in one URI, but not in the other, to be ignored for equality purposes. Since a public GRUU differs from an AOR only by the presence of the gr URI parameter, the two URIs are equivalent based on those rules.

Once a temporary GRUU is constructed, it must be considered valid by the registrar until invalidated based on the rules described previously. Once a public GRUU is constructed, it must be considered valid for the duration that the AOR itself is valid. Once an AOR is no longer valid within a domain, all of its GRUUs must be considered invalid as well. This specification

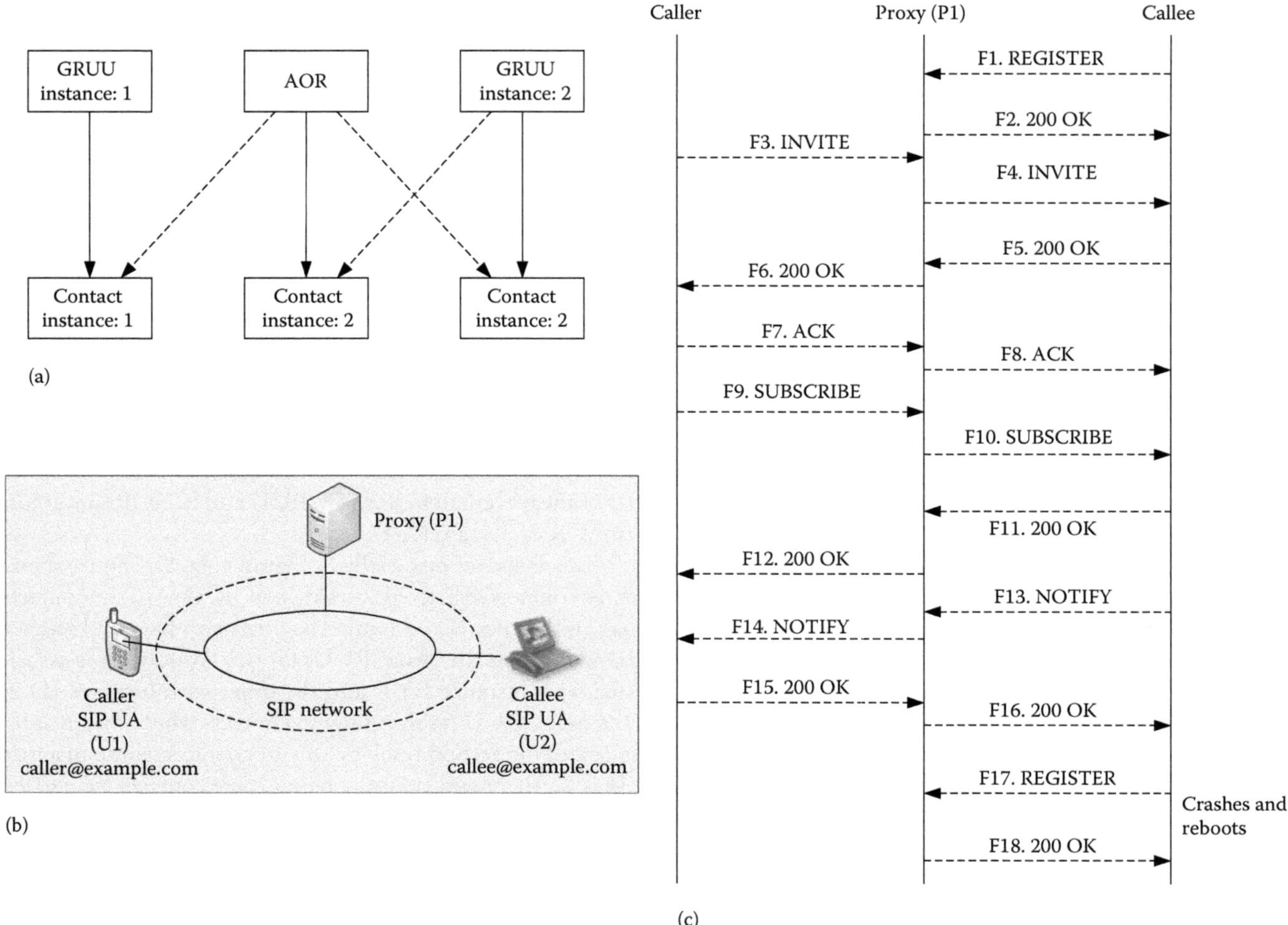

Figure 4.3 GRUU usage in a SIP network: (a) GRUU, AOR, Contact, and Instances; (b) SIP network; and (c) call flows using GRUU. (Copyright IETF. Reproduced with permission.)

does not mandate a particular mechanism for construction of the GRUU. Example algorithms for public and temporary GRUUs that work well are provided above. However, in addition to the properties described earlier, a GRUU constructed by a registrar must exhibit the following properties:

- The domain part of the URI is an IP address present on the public Internet, or, if it is a host name, the resolution procedures of RFC 3263 (see Section 8.2.4), once applied, result in an IP address on the public Internet.
- When a request is sent to the GRUU, it routes to a proxy that can access the registration data generated by the registrar. Such a proxy is called an authoritative proxy, defined in RFC 5626 (see Section 13.2).

4.3.8.5 Registration Event Support

RFC 3680 (see Section 5.3) defines an event package that allows a client to learn about registration events at the registrar. This package allows registrars to alter registrations forcefully (e.g., shortening them to force a reregistration). If a registrar is supporting RFC 3680 and GRUU, it must also support RFC 5628.

4.3.9 Proxy Behavior

Proxy behavior is fully defined in Section 3.11 (RFC 3261). GRUU processing influences that processing in two places—request targeting at the authoritative proxy and record-routing.

4.3.9.1 Request Targeting

When a proxy receives a request, owns the domain in the Request-URI, and is supposed to access a location service in order to compute request targets (as specified in RFC 3261, Section 3.11.5), the proxy examines the Request-URI. If it contains the gr URI parameter but is not equivalent, based on URI comparison (see Section 4.2.1.4), to a currently valid GRUU within the domain, it should be rejected with a 404 Not Found response; this is the same behavior a proxy would exhibit for any other URI within the domain that is not valid. If the Request-URI contains the gr URI parameter and is equivalent, based on URI comparison, to a GRUU that is currently valid within the domain, processing proceeds as it would for any other URI present in the location service, as defined in Section 3.11.5, except that the gr URI parameter is not removed as part of the canonicalization process. This is the case for both out-of-dialog requests targeted to the GRUU and mid-dialog requests targeted to the GRUU (in which case the incoming request would have a Route header field value containing the URI that the proxy used for record routing).

Note that the gr URI parameter is retained just for the purposes of finding the GRUU in the location service; if a match is found, the Request-URI will be rewritten with the registered contacts, replacing the GRUU and its gr URI parameter. The gr URI parameter is not carried forward into the rewritten Request-URI. If there are no registered contacts bound to the GRUU, the server must return a 480 Temporarily Unavailable response. If there are more than one, there are two cases:

- The client is using RFC 5626 (see Section 13.2) and registering multiple contacts for redundancy. In that case, these contacts contain reg-id Contact header field parameters, and the rules described in Section 13.2 for selecting a single registered contact apply.
- The client was not using RFC 5626, in which case there would only be multiple contacts with the same instance ID if the client had rebooted, restarted, and reregistered. In this case, these contacts would not contain the reg-id Contact header field parameter. The proxy MUST select the most recently refreshed contact. As with RFC 5626, if a request to this target fails with a 408 Request Timeout or 430 Flow Failed response, the proxy should retry with the next most recently refreshed contact.

Furthermore, if the request fails with any other response, the proxy must not retry on any other contacts for this instance. Any caller preferences in the request as defined in RFC 3841 (see Section 9.9) should be processed against the contacts bound to the GRUU. In essence, to select a registered contact, the GRUU is processed just like it was the AOR, but with only a subset of the contacts bound to the AOR.

Special considerations apply to the processing of any Path headers stored in the registration (see RFC 3327, Section 2.8.2). If the received request has Route header field values beyond the one pointing to the authoritative proxy itself (this will happen when the request is a mid-dialog request), the Path URI must be discarded. This is permitted by RFC 3327 as a matter of local policy; usage of GRUUs will require this policy in order to avoid call spirals and likely call failures.

A proxy may apply other processing to the request, such as execution of called party features, as it might do for requests targeted to an AOR. For requests that are outside of a dialog, it is recommended to apply screening types of functions, both automated (such as blacklist and whitelist screening) and interactive (such as interactive voice response) applications that confer with the user to determine whether to accept a call. In many cases, the new request is related to an existing dialog, and might be an attempt to join it (using the Join header field defined in RFC 3911, Section 2.8.2) or replace it (using the Replaces header field; RFC 3891, see Section 2.8.2). When the new request is related to an existing dialog, the UA will typically make its own authorization decisions; bypassing screening services at the authoritative proxy might make sense, but needs to be carefully considered by network designers, as the ability to do so depends on the specific type of screening service.

However, forwarding services, such as call forwarding, should not be provided for requests sent to a GRUU. The intent of the GRUU is to target a specific UA instance, and this is incompatible with forwarding operations. If the request is a mid-dialog request, a proxy should only apply services that are meaningful for mid-dialog requests, generally speaking. This excludes screening and forwarding functions. In addition, a request sent to a GRUU should not be redirected. In many instances, a GRUU is used by a UA in order to assist in the traversal of NATs and firewalls, and a redirection might prevent such a case from working.

4.3.9.2 Record-Routing

See Sections 9.5 and 9.6.

4.3.10 GRUU Example

We have considered a SIP network, shown in Figure 4.3b and c, that shows a basic registration and call setup, followed by a subscription directed to the GRUU. It then shows a failure of the callee, followed by a reregistration. The conventions of RFC 4475 are used to describe the representation of long message lines. The callee supports the GRUU extension. As such, its REGISTER (message F1) looks as follows:

```
REGISTER sip:example.com SIP/2.0
Via: SIP/2.0/UDP
192.0.2.1;branch=z9hG4bKnashds7
Max-Forwards: 70
From: Callee <sip:callee@example.com>;
tag=a73kszlfl
```

```
Supported: gruu
To: Callee <sip:callee@example.com>
Call-ID: 1j9FpLxk3uxtm8tn@192.0.2.1
CSeq: 1 REGISTER
Contact: <sip:callee@192.0.2.1>
;+sip.
instance="<urn:uuid:f81d4fae-7dec-11d0-a765-
00a0c91e6bf6>"
Content-Length: 0
```

The registrar assigns a temporary and a public GRUU. The REGISTER response (message F2) would look like

```
SIP/2.0 200 OK
Via: SIP/2.0/UDP
192.0.2.1;branch=z9hG4bKnashds7
From: Callee <sip:callee@example.com>;
tag=a73kszlfl
To: Callee <sip:callee@example.com>;tag=b88sn
Call-ID: 1j9FpLxk3uxtm8tn@192.0.2.1
CSeq: 1 REGISTER

<allOneLine>
       Contact: <sip:callee@192.0.2.1>
       ;pub-gruu="sip:callee@example.com
       ;gr=urn:uuid:f81d4fae-7dec-11d0-a765-
       00a0c91e6bf6"
       ;temp-gruu="sip:tgruu.7hs==
       jd7vnzga5w7fajsc7-ajd6fabz0f8g5@example
       .com;gr"
       ;+sip.
instance="<urn:uuid:f81d4fae-7dec-11d0-a765-
00a0c91e6bf6>"
       ;expires=3600
</allOneLine>

Content-Length: 0
```

The Contact header field in the REGISTER response contains the pubgruu Contact header field parameter with the public GRUU sip:callee@example.com;gr=urn:uuid:f81d4fae-7dec-11d0-a765-00a0c91e6bf6, and the temp-gruu header field parameter with the temporary GRUU sip:tgruu.7hs== jd7vnzga5w7fajsc7-ajd6fabz0f8g5@example.com;gr. Both are valid GRUUs for the AOR and instance ID, and both translate to the contact sip:callee@192.0.2.1. The INVITE from the caller (message F3) is a normal SIP INVITE. However, the 200 OK generated by the callee (message F5) now contains a GRUU as the remote target. The UA has chosen to use its public GRUU.

```
SIP/2.0 200 OK
Via: SIP/2.0/UDP proxy.example.com;
branch=z9hG4bKnaa8
Via: SIP/2.0/UDP host.example.com;
branch=z9hG4bK99a
From: Caller <sip:caller@example.com>;
tag=n88ah
To: Callee <sip:callee@example.com>;tag=a0z8
Call-ID: 1j9FpLxk3uxtma7@host.example.com
CSeq: 1 INVITE
Supported: gruu
Allow: INVITE, OPTIONS, CANCEL, BYE, ACK,
SUBSCRIBE

<allOneLine>
       Contact:
       <sip:callee@example.com
       ;gr=urn:uuid:f81d4fae-7dec-11d0-a765-
       00a0c91e6bf6>
       </allOneLine>

Content-Length: --
Content-Type: application/SDP
[SDP Not shown]
```

At some point later in the call, the caller decides to subscribe to the dialog event package (defined in RFC 4235) at that specific UA. To do that, it generates a SUBSCRIBE request (message F9), but directs it toward the remote target, which is a GRUU:

```
<allOneLine>
       SUBSCRIBE sip:callee@example.com;
       gr=urn:uuid:f8
       1d4fae-7dec-11d0-a765-00a0c91e6bf6
       SIP/2.0
</allOneLine>

Via: SIP/2.0/UDP host.example.com;
       branch=z9hG4bK9zz8
From: Caller <sip:caller@example.com>;tag=kkaz-

<allOneLine>
       To: <sip:callee@example.com;
       gr=urn:uuid:f8
       1d4fae-7dec-11d0-a765-00a0c91e6bf6>
</allOneLine>

Call-ID: faif9a@host.example.com
CSeq: 2 SUBSCRIBE
Supported: gruu
Event: dialog
Allow: INVITE, OPTIONS, CANCEL, BYE, ACK,
NOTIFY
Contact: <sip:caller@example.com;
gr=hdg7777ad7aflzig8sf7>
Content-Length: 0
```

In this example, the caller itself supports the GRUU extension and is using its own GRUU to populate its remote target. This request is routed to the proxy, which proceeds to perform a location lookup on the Request-URI. It is translated into the contact for that instance, and then proxied to that contact.

```
SUBSCRIBE sip:callee@192.0.2.1 SIP/2.0
Via: SIP/2.0/UDP proxy.example.com;
branch=z9hG4bK9555
```

```
Via: SIP/2.0/UDP host.example.com;
branch=z9hG4bK9zz8
From: Caller <sip:caller@example.com>;tag=kkaz-

<allOneLine>
      To: <sip:callee@example.com;
      gr=urn:uuid:f8
      1d4fae-7dec-11d0-a765-00a0c91e6bf6>
</allOneLine>

Call-ID: faif9a@host.example.com
CSeq: 2 SUBSCRIBE
Supported: gruu
Event: dialog
Allow: INVITE, OPTIONS, CANCEL, BYE, ACK,
NOTIFY
Contact: <sip:caller@example.com;
gr=hdg7777ad7aflzig8sf7>
Content-Length: 0
```

The SUBSCRIBE generates a 200 response (message F11), which is followed by a NOTIFY (messages F13 and F14) and its response (messages F15 and F16). At some point after message 16 is received, the callee's machine crashes and recovers. It obtains a new IP address, 192.0.2.2. Unaware that it had previously had an active registration, it creates a new one (message F17 below). Notice how the instance ID remains the same, as it persists across reboot cycles:

```
REGISTER sip:example.com SIP/2.0
Via: SIP/2.0/UDP
192.0.2.2;branch=z9hG4bKnasbba
Max-Forwards: 70
From: Callee <sip:callee@example.com>;
tag=ha8d777f0
Supported: gruu
To: Callee <sip:callee@example.com>
Call-ID: hf8asxzff8s7f@192.0.2.2
CSeq: 1 REGISTER

<allOneLine>
      Contact: <sip:callee@192.0.2.2>
      ;+sip.instance="<urn:uuid:
f81d4fae-7dec-11d0-a765-00a0c91e6bf6>"
</allOneLine>

Content-Length: 0
```

The registrar notices that a different contact, sip:callee@192.0.2.1, is already associated with the same instance ID. It registers the new one too and returns both in the REGISTER response. Both have the same public GRUUs, but the registrar has generated a second temporary GRUU for this AOR and instance ID combination. Both contacts are included in the REGISTER response, and the temporary GRUU for each is the same—the most recently created one for the instance ID and AOR. The registrar then generates the following response:

```
SIP/2.0 200 OK
Via: SIP/2.0/UDP
192.0.2.2;branch=z9hG4bKnasbba
From: Callee <sip:callee@example.com>;
tag=ha8d777f0
To: Callee <sip:callee@example.com>;
tag=99f8f7
Call-ID: hf8asxzff8s7f@192.0.2.2
CSeq: 1 REGISTER

<allOneLine>
      Contact: <sip:callee@192.0.2.2>
      ;pub-gruu="sip:callee@example.com;
      gr=urn:
      uuid:f81d4fae-7dec-11d0-a765-00a0c9
      1e6bf6"
      ;temp-gruu="sip:tgruu.7hatz6cn-098sh
      fyq193=
      ajfux8fyg7ajqqe7@example.com;gr"
      ;+sip.instance="<urn:uuid:f81d
4fae-7dec-11d0-a765-00a0c91e6bf6>"
      ;expires=3600
</allOneLine>

<allOneLine>
      Contact: <sip:callee@192.0.2.1>
      ;pub-gruu="sip:callee@example.com;
      gr=urn:
      uuid:f81d4fae-7dec-11d0-a765-00a0c9
      1e6bf6"
      ;temp-gruu="sip:tgruu.7hatz6cn-098sh
      fyq193=
      ajfux8fyg7ajqqe7@example.com;gr"
      ;+sip.instance="<urn:uuid:f81d4
fae-7dec-11d0-a765-00a0c91e6bf6>"
      ;expires=400
</allOneLine>

Content-Length: 0
```

There is no need for the UA to remove the stale registered contact; the request targeting rules described earlier will cause the request to be delivered to the most recent one.

4.4 Services URI

SIP signaling schemes or URIs are independent of any specific services and are not standardized for expressing any services. However, there are some nonstandard attempts in the form of informational IETF (International Engineering Task Force) RFCs to specify the SIP Request-URIs to have some sort of context-aware knowing which SIP UAs or SIP servers can invoke some specific services as configured during service provisioning. It requires that the SIP servers or application servers need to be configured a priori for invoking those services. The context-aware request-URIs can only be applied in a private SIP network in a single administrative domain and may even not be suitable for a large administrative domain.

4.4.1 Messaging Services

Real-time multimedia communications services, including multimedia messaging, are very complex because a huge number of feature-rich multimedia capabilities/services can be provided through manipulating each individual media consisting of a composite multimedia application or a single media of a given application. Some of those feature-rich multimedia services are already being offered or are emerging, but many more innovative complex multimedia services that are yet to imagine are left for the future. However, there are some simple real-time or near-real-time multimedia services that have to deal with some immediate information at hand that seems to be very important for the users for complementing primary call services.

For example, a user may need to retrieve the voice mail from the voice-mail server because the messages have been left in one's voice mailbox while the user has not been available to take the call. In addition, the phone of the called party needs to be able to store the voice message of the calling party in the called party's voice mailbox through transferring of the call. It is interesting to note that this simple voice-mail service can be offered with a variation of many features considering the overall communications such as announcement services by the voice-mail server, authentication services for the calling party for message retrieval, and call forwarding services to the mail server with no answer or on busy.

This simple voice-mail service shows that service context-awareness is needed in providing services. The key is that SIP is the protocol for the session establishment and cannot have any awareness of services. However, if the SIP URI itself is created in such a way that SIP devices interpret the URI as if it is context-aware, it will offer services based on the context being embedded.

4.4.1.1 Specific Context-Aware Approach

The concept of context-awareness has been captured in a service implementing SIP as defined in RFC 3261, without modification, through the standard use of that protocol's Request-URI. However, the concept is applicable to any SIP-based service where the initial application state is determined from context. This concept is a usage convention of standard SIP as defined in RFC 3261 and does not modify or extend that protocol in any way. It is important to note, in practical applications, that an application does not apply semantic rules to the various URIs. Instead, it should allow any arbitrary string to be provisioned, and map the string to the desired behavior. The private owner of the system may choose to provision mnemonic strings, but the application should not require it. In any large installation, the system owner is likely to have preexisting rules for mnemonic URIs, and any attempt by an application to define its own rules may create a conflict.

In this example, a voice-mail system should allow an arbitrary mix of URLs from these schemes, or any other scheme that renders valid SIP URIs to be provisioned, rather than enforce one particular scheme. The key limitations of these service URIs, such as for voice mail, are that they will only work within a given administrative domain, and SIP UAs and servers need to be provisioned with these rules and service configurations. Accordingly, some sample private service URIs have been defined per RFC 4240 in relation to the voice-mail services context shown in Table 4.2.

In addition to providing this set of URIs to the subscriber (to use as one sees fit), an integrated service provider could add these to the set of contacts in a find-me proxy. The proxy could then route calls to the appropriate URI based on the origin of the request, the subscriber's preferences, and current state. This simple example shows how a variety of voice-mail services can be created by adding some services context even in SIP Request-URI. The example call flows for different voice-mail services are shown in RFC 4240 in PSTN–IP networking environments. The cause codes for retargeting or history information of retargeting of multiple targets cannot be expressed or known in these specific context-aware request-URIs. A more general approach is needed for inclusion of causes for retargeting and information about multiple retargeting.

4.4.1.2 RFC 4458: Generalized Context-Aware Approach

Earlier, we have seen that the specific Request-URIs created for retargeting the services cannot provide the causes to the caller why the services have been retargeted or no information can be provided to the caller about the multiple retargeting of services. A more intelligent approach described in RFC 4458 that is described in this section can be taken for creation of services like voice mail, interactive voice recognition, and similar services using SIP URIs based on redirecting targets from these applications. Two key pieces of information are needed: first, the target application (e.g., mailbox) to use, and second, the indication of the desired service (e.g., cause for transferring the call to the target application). The userinfo and hostport parts of the Request-URI will identify the voice-mail service, the target mailbox can be put in the target parameter, and the reason can be put in the cause parameter. For example, if the proxy

Table 4.2 Example SIP Service URIs for Voice-Mail Services

URI Identity	Example Scheme 1	Example Scheme 2	Example Scheme 3
Deposit with standard greeting	sip:sub-rrr-deposit@vm.rnl.com	sip:677283@vm.rnl.com	sip:rrr@vm.rnl.com;mode=deposit
Deposit with phone greeting	sip:sub-rrr-deposit-busy.vm.rnl.com	sip:677372@vm.rnl.com	sip:rrr@vm.rnl.com;mode=3991243
Deposit with special greeting	sip:sub-rrr-deposit-sg@vm.rnl.com	sip:677384@vm.rnl.com	sip:rrr@vm.rnl.com;mode=sg
Retrieve through (SIP) authentication	sip:sub-rrr-retrieve@vm.rnl.com	sip:677405@vm.rnl.com	sip:rrr@vm.rnl.com;mode=retrieve
Retrieve through prompt for personal identification number (PIN) in-band	sip:sub-rrr-retrieve-inpin.vm.rnl.com	sip:677415@vm.rnl.com	sip:rrr@vm.rnl.com;mode=inpin
Deposit through identify target mailbox by To:	sip:deposit@vm.rnl.com	sip:670001@vm.rnl.com	sip:deposit@vm.rnl.com
Retrieve through identify target mailbox by SIP authentication	sip:retrieve@vm.rnl.com	sip:670002@vm.rnl.com	sip:retrieve@vm.rnl.com
Deposit through prompt target mailbox in-band	sip:deposit-in@vm.rnl.com	sip:670003@vm.rnl.com	sip:deposit@vm.rnl.com;mode=inband
Retrieve through prompt for target mailbox and PIN in-band	sip:retrieve-in@vm.rnl.com	sip:670004@vm.rnl.com	sip:retrieve@vm.rnl.com;mode=inband

wished to use Bob's mailbox because his phone was busy, the URI sent to the unified messaging (UM) system could be something like

```
sip:voicemail@example.com;
target=bill%40example.com;cause=408
```

- **Target:** Target is a URI parameter that indicates the address of the retargeting entity: in the context of UM, this can be the mailbox number. For example, in the case of a voice-mail system on the PSTN, the user portion will contain the phone number of the voice-mail system, while the target will contain the phone number of the subscriber's mailbox. The syntax for target parameter using ABNF grammar is shown below (pvalue defined in RFC 3261; Section 2.4.1.2):

```
target-param = "target" EQUAL pvalue
```

- **Cause:** Cause is a URI parameter that is used to indicate the service that the UAS receiving the message should perform. The ABNF grammar for the cause parameter is as follows (status-code defined in TFC 3261):

```
cause-param = "cause" EQUAL Status-Code
```

The values for the cause URI parameter are defined in Table 4.3 (RFC 4458).

Note that the ABNF requires some characters to be escaped if they occur in the value of the target parameters. For example, the "@" character needs to be escaped. These reason codes are chosen partly because of interworking between the IP network that uses SIP and PSTN network that uses Integrated Services Digital Network User Part signaling. If no appropriate mapping to a cause value defined in this specification exists in a network either IP or PSTN, it would be mapped to 302 Unconditional. If a new cause

Table 4.3 Defined Values for Cause Parameter

Redirecting Reason	*Value*
Unknown/not available	404
User busy	486
No reply	408
Unconditional	302
Deflection during alerting	487
Deflection immediate response	480
Mobile subscriber not reachable	503

parameter needs to be defined, this specification will have to be updated. The user portion of the URI should be used as the address of the voice-mail system on the PSTN, while the target should be mapped to the original redirecting number on the PSTN side. The redirection counters should be set to one unless additional information is available. Because of multiple retargeting through changing the caller's original Request-URI, it is not possible know any information about all those targets. The History-Info header field can be used to build up as the request progresses and, upon reaching the UAS, can be returned in certain responses.

All the messaging services described in the case of the specific context-aware Request-URIs can also be created using this more generalized approach. In addition, this approach can also provide the specific reason for retargeting, including the history of all targets through which the call has been retargeted. The limitations of this generalized context-aware Request-URI are that the service needs to understand whether the messaging system it is targeting supports the syntax defined in this specification. Today, this information is provided to the proxy by configuration. This implies that this approach is also unlikely to work in cases in which the proxy is not configured with information about the messaging system or in which the messaging system is not in the same administrative domain. Thereby, this scheme is not suitable for implementation in the large system because a proxy will not be able to do anything when the same target is being tried multiple times.

4.4.2 Media Services

The multifunction media server needs to provide some basic media services such as playing announcements, prompting and collecting of information with users, and audio, video, or data bridging/mixing services in the SIP network. These media services are a part of the application layer function and are offered with application server protocols with markup languages like voice extensible markup language (VoiceXML) and media server control markup language (MSCML). However, these media services are offered to the users after establishment of sessions between the users and the multifunction media server using SIP. The key is how to invoke media services when SIP Request-URIs are sent to the media server for the session establishments between the media server and users. RFC 3087 describes a client or a proxy can communicate context through the use of a distinctive Request-URI used in SIP and provides examples of how this mechanism could be used in a voice-mail application with reference to RFC 2543 that was obsoleted by RFC 3261. Similar to RFC 3087, RFC 4240 has also defined some generalized media service context-aware SIP Request-URIs, such as announcements to users by playing media, prompting and collecting services where the media server prompts users and collect information from users and media bridging/mixing (audio, video, or data) services during multipoint conferencing. The user part of each SIP Request-URI for media services has been created having the following properties:

- No change is made to core SIP.
- Only devices that choose to conform to this private standard (IETF Informational RFC 4240) have to implement it. Thereby, interoperability among these implementations can be facilitated for the media services.
- Media service SIP Request-URIs only apply to multifunction SIP-controlled media servers.
- Non-multifunction SIP-controlled media servers are not affected.
- SIP devices other than media servers will have no impact.

4.4.2.1 Announcement Services

The announcement services provide the delivery of multimedia services such as the prompt file and audio and/video prompt by a media server to a terminal or to a group of terminals. In SIP, a simple way of doing is to set up a call between the media server and the terminal sending an INVITE message, and then the announcement services will be offered by the media server. The key of RFC 4240 is to create the Request-URI of the INVITE message in such a way that the media server will be configured for providing the specific announcement services accordingly. That is, services are being created to offer by the announcement applications of the media server just by knowing the session level information provided in Request-URIs. In this case, the Request-URI fully describes the announcement service through the use of the user part of the address and additional URI parameters. The user portion of the address, *annc*, specifies the announcement service on the media server. The service has several associated URI parameters that control the content and delivery of the announcement. For example, the form of the SIP Request-URI for announcement services can be as follows:

```
sip:annc@ms2.example.net; \
             play=http://audio.example.net/
             allcircuitsbusy.g711
sip:annc@ms2.example.net; \
             play=file://fileserver.example.
             net//geminii/yourHoroscope.wav
```

The above example shows that service has several associated URI parameters that control the content and delivery of the announcement. All these parameters are described below:

- **Play:** Specifies the resource or announcement sequence to be played.

- **Repeat:** Specifies how many times the media server should repeat the announcement or sequence named by the *play=* parameter. The value *forever* means the repeat should be effectively unbounded. In this case, it is recommended the media server implements some local policy, such as limiting what forever means, to ensure errant clients do not create a denial of service attack.
- **Delay:** Specifies a delay interval between announcement repetitions. The delay is measured in milliseconds.
- **Duration:** Specifies the maximum duration of the announcement. The media server will discontinue the announcement and end the call if the maximum duration has been reached. The duration is measured in milliseconds.
- **Locale:** Specifies the language and optionally country variant of the announcement sequence named in the play= parameter. RFC 4646 specifies the locale tag. The locale tag is usually a two- or three-letter code per ISO 639-1. The country variant is also often a two-letter code per ISO 3166-1. These elements are concatenated with a single under bar (%x5F) character, such as *enffCA*. If only the language is specified, such as locale=en, the choice of country variant is an implementation matter. Implementations should provide the best possible match between the requested locale and the available languages in the event the media server cannot honor the locale request precisely. For example, if the request has locale=caffFR, but the media server only has frffFR available, the media server should use the frffFR variant. Implementations should provide a default locale to use if no language variants are available.
- **Param[n]:** Provides a mechanism for passing values that are to be substituted into an announcement sequence. Up to nine parameters (param1= through param9=) may be specified. The mechanics of announcement sequences are beyond the scope of this document.
- **Extension:** Provides a mechanism for extending the parameter set. If the media server receives an extension it does not understand, it must silently ignore the extension parameter and value.

The play= parameter is mandatory and must be present. All other parameters are optional. Some encodings are not self-describing. Thus, the implementation relies on filename extension conventions for determining the media type. It should be noted that RFC 3261 implies that proxies are supposed to pass parameters through unchanged. However, be aware that nonconforming proxies may strip Request-URI parameters. In this case, the implementation needs to take care of this. For example, the proxy inserting the parameters is the last proxy before the media server.

4.4.2.1.1 Formal Syntax

The following syntax specification uses the ABNF as described in RFC 4234:

```
ANNC-URL            = sip-ind annc-ind "@"
                      hostport annc-parameters
                    uri-parameters
sip-ind             = "sip:"/"sips:"
annc-ind            = "annc"
annc-parameters     = ";" play-param [";"
                    content-param]
                        [";" delay-param]
                        [";" duration-param]
                        [";" repeat-param]
                        [";" locale-param]
                        [";" variable-params]
                        [";" extension-params]
play-param          = "play = " prompt-url
content-param       = "content-type = " MIME-type
delay-param         = "delay = " delay-valudelay-
value               = 1*DIGIT
duration-param      = "duration = "duration-value
duration-value      = 1*DIGIT
repeat-param          = "repeat = "
repeat-value
repeat-value          = 1*DIGIT/"forever"
locale-param          = "locale = " token
                      ; per RFC 3066, usually
                      ; ISO639-1ffISO3166-1
                      ; e.g., en, enffUS,
                    enffUK, etc.
variable-params       = param-name " = "
                        variable-value
param-name            = "param" DIGIT; e.g.,
                        "param1"
variable-value        = 1*(ALPHA / DIGIT)
extension-params      = extension-param [";"
                        extension-params]
extension-param       = token "=" token
```

uri-parameters is the SIP Request-URI parameter list as described in RFC 3261 (see Section 2.8.2). All parameters of the Request-URI are part of the URI matching algorithm. The MIME-type is the MIME content type for the announcement, such as audio/basic, audio/G729, audio/mpeg, video/mpeg, and so on. A number of MIME registrations, which could be used here, have parameters, for instance, video/DV. To accommodate this, and retain compatibility with the SIP URI structure, the MIME-type parameter separator (semicolon, %3b) and value separator (equal, %d3) must be escaped. For example:

```
sip:annc@ms.example.net; \
      play=file://fs.example.net//clips/
      my-intro.dvi; \
      content-type=video/mpeg%3bencode%
      d3314M-25/625-50
```

The locale-value consists of a tag as specified in RFC 4646. The definition of hostport is as specified by RFC 3261. The syntax of prompt-url consists of a URL scheme as specified by RFC 3986 or a special token indicating a provisioned announcement sequence. For example, the URL scheme may include any of the following: http/https, ftp, file, referencing a local or Network File Transfer protocol (NFS) (RFC 3530), object and NRFS URL (RFC 2224). If a provisioned announcement sequence is to be played, the value of prompt-url will have the following form:

```
prompt-url         =   "/provisioned/"
                       announcement-id
announcement-id    =   1*(ALPHA/DIGIT)
```

Note that the scheme */provisioned/* was chosen because of a hesitation to register a *provisioned:* URI scheme. This document is strictly focused on the SIP interface for the announcement service and, as such, does not detail how announcement sequences are provisioned or defined. Note that the media type of the object the prompt-url refers to can be most anything, including audio file formats, text file formats, or URI lists.

4.4.2.2 Prompting and Collection Services

The prompt and collection services use voice communications and are also known as voice dialogs. It establishes an aural dialog with the user. The dialog service follows the model of the announcement service. However, the service indicator is *dialog*. The dialog service takes a parameter, voicexml=, indicating the URI of the VoiceXML script to execute, and the request URI may look like as follows:

```
sip:dialog@mediaserver.example.net; \
      voicexml=http://vxmlserver.example.
      net/cgi-bin/script.vxml
```

A Media Server may accept additional SIP Request-URI parameters and deliver them to the VoiceXML interpreter session as session variables. Although not good VoiceXML programming practice, VoiceXML scripts might contain sensitive information, such as a user's pass code in a DTMF grammar. Thus, the media server must support the https scheme for the voicexml parameter for secure fetching of scripts. Likewise, dynamic grammars often do have user-identifying information. As such, the VoiceXML browser implementation on the media server must support https fetching of grammars and subsequent documents. Returned information often is sensitive. For example, the information could be financial information or instructions. Thus, the media server must support https posting of results.

4.4.2.2.1 Syntax for Prompt and Collect Services

The following syntax specification uses the ABNF as described in RFC 4234.

```
DIALOG-URL           = sip-ind dialog-ind "@"
                       hostport
                       dialog-parameters
sip-ind              = "sip:"/"sips:"
dialog-ind           = "dialog"
dialog-parameters    = ";" dialog-param
                       [vxml-parameters]
                       [uri-parameters]
dialog-param         = "voicexml = " vxml-url
vxml-parameters      = vxml-param
                       [vxml-parameters]
vxml-param           = ";" vxml-keyword " = "
vxml-value
vxml-keyword         = token
vxml-value           = token
```

The vxml-url is the URI of the VoiceXML script. If present, other parameters get passed to the VoiceXML interpreter session with the assigned vxml-keyword vxml-value pairs. Note that all vxml-keywords must have values. If there is a vxml-keyword without a corresponding vxml-value, the media server must reject the request with a 400 Bad Request response code. In addition, the media server must state *Missing VXML Value* in the reason phrase. The media server presents the parameters as environment variables in the connection object. Specifically, the parameter appears in the connection.sip tree. If the Media Server does not support the passing of keyword-value pairs to the VoiceXML interpreter session, it must ignore the parameters. uri-parameters is the SIP Request-URI parameter list as described in RFC 3261. All parameters in the parameter list, whether they come from uri-parameters or from vxml-keyworks, are part of the URI matching algorithm.

4.4.2.3 Media Bridging/Mixing Services

The media bridging/mixing services are offered as a part of multimedia conferencing services. It is envisioned that a SIP session will be established with the media server sending the Request-URI before media bridging/mixing of the conference participants. It is these SIP Request-URIs from which the application residing in the media server can identify mixing sessions if the media mixing application is configured accordingly. To create a mixing session, one sends an INVITE to a Request-URI that represents the session. If the URI does not already exist on the media server and the requested resources are available, the media server creates a new mixing session. If there is an existing URI for the session, then the media server interprets it as a request for the new session to join the existing session. The form of the SIP

Request-URI for media mixing of the multimedia conference participants is

```
sip:conf=uniqueIdentifier@mediaserver.
example.net
```

The left-hand side of the Request-URI is actually the username of the request in the Request-URI and the To header. The host portion of the URI identifies a particular media server. The *conf* user name conveys to the media server that this is a request for the mixing service. The unique Identifier can be any value that is compliant with the SIP URI specification. It is the responsibility of the conference control application to ensure the identifier is unique within the scope of any potential conflict. In the terminology of the conferencing framework (RFC 4353), this URI convention tells the media server that the application server is requesting it to act as a Focus. The conf-id value identifies the particular focus instance. As a focus in the conferencing framework, the media server must support the *;isfocus* parameter in the Request-URI. Note, however, that the presence or absence of the ;isfocus parameter has no protocol impact at the media server.

It is worth noting that the conference URI shared between the application and media servers provides enhanced security, as the SIP control interface does not have to be exposed to participants. It also allows the assignment of a specific media server to be delayed as long as possible, thereby simplifying resource management. One can add additional legs to the conference by sending them INVITE messages to the above-mentioned Request-URI. Per the matching rules of RFC 3261 (see Section 4.2), the conf-id parameter is part of the matching string. Conversely, one can remove legs by issuing a BYE in the corresponding dialog. The mixing session, and thus the conference-specific Request-URI, remains active so long as there is at least one SIP dialog associated with the given Request-URI. If the Request-URI has conf as the user part, but does not have a conf-id parameter, the media server must respond with a 404 Not Found.

It should be noted that the media server could create a unique conference instance and return the conf-id string to the UAC if there is no conf-id present. However, such an operation may have other operational issues, such as permissions and billing. Thus, an application server or proxy is a better place to do such an operation. Moreover, such action would make the media server into a Conference Factory in the terminology of conference-framework (RFC 4353). That is not the appropriate behavior for a media server. Since some conference use cases, such as business conferencing, have billing implications, the media server should authenticate the application server or proxy. At a minimum, the media server MUST implement sips:. The multipoint multimedia conference is controlled by the conference application server. Using the terminology of conference-framework (RFC 4353), the application server is the Conference Factory, and the media server is the Conference Focus. Note that the conference application server is a server to the conference participants (i.e., UACs). However, the conference application server is a client for mixing services to the media server.

4.4.2.4 Formal Syntax for Media Bridging/Mixing

The following syntax specification uses the ABNF as described in RFC 4234.

```
CONF-URL      =  sip-ind conf-ind " = "
                 instance-id "@" hostport
                 [uri-parameters]
sip-ind       =  "sip:"/"sips:"
conf-ind      =  "conf"
instance-id   =  token
```

uri-parameters is the SIP Request-URI parameter list as described in RFC 3261 (see Section 2.8.2). All parameters in the parameter list are part of the URI matching algorithm.

4.4.2.5 Internet Assigned Numbers Authority (IANA) Registration: SIP/SIPS URI Parameter

RFC 4240 has registered the parameters in Table 4.4 in the SIP/SIPS URI Parameters registry of IANA, following the specification required policy of RFC 3969.

4.4.2.6 Limitations of Network Media Services

The network media service Request-URIs are also context-aware, and limitations remain the same as those of the other context-aware URIs. That is, the application servers need to be configured a priori for invocation of all media services for bridging knowing the contexts in the Request-URIs. In addition, names used in Request-URIs, although with a very low probability of occurrence, may collide.

Table 4.4 SIP/SIPS URI Parameter Registered in IANA

Parameter Name	*Predefined Values*	*Reference*
Play	No	RFC 4240
Repeat	No	RFC 4240
Delay	No	RFC 4240
Duration	No	RFC 4240
Locale	No	RFC 4240
Param[n]	No	RFC 4240
Extension	No	RFC 4240

4.5 Summary

The semantics, syntax, and rules for creation of SIP URI, SIPS URI, and tel URI that are used as the logical address in the SIP Request-URI are explained in great length. These addresses are publicly used by SIP users like e-mails for setting up the sessions. Each parameter of each URI type is described along with examples. The relationship and mapping rules among these URIs are articulated. However, a given AOR can be used by multiple UAs because a SIP may have many devices where each device will have a different UA. The GRUU that is unique for reaching a SIP user at a particular instance has been explained elaborately including its semantics, syntax, construction, registration, discovery, and operation.

PROBLEMS

1. What are SIP and SIPS URIs? Explain in detail the following common functions (with examples) that appear common in SIP signaling messages: (a) SIP and SIPS URI components; (b) character escaping requirements; (c) URI comparison, forming requests from a URI; and (d) relating SIP URIs and tel URLs.
2. What is GRUU? How does it operate related to the GRUUs that expose and hide the underlying AOR?
3. How do you do the following: obtaining a GRUU, using a GRUU, and dereferencing a GRUU?
4. How does a UA behave with GRUU for the following: generating a REGISTER request, learning GRUUs from REGISTER responses, connecting a self-made GRUU, using one's own GRUUs and considering for multiple AORs, dereferencing a GRUU, and rendering GRUUs on user interface.
5. How does a registrar behave with GRUU for the following: processing a REGISTER request, generating a REGISTER response, timing out on a registration, creating a GRUU, and supporting a registration event?
6. How does a proxy behave with GRUU for the following: request targeting and record-routing?
7. What is services URI? What are message service URIs in relation to the following: specific and generalized context-aware approach? What are media service URIs in relation to the following: announcement, prompting/collection, and media mixing/bridging services? What are limitations of network media service URIs?

Chapter 5

SIP Event Framework and Packages

Abstract

The Session Initiation Protocol (SIP) event framework extends SIP signaling for delivering of events only related to the session initiation, establishment, and termination between SIP entities over the SIP network, as opposed to the general-purpose event model. Initially, the event model specified in Request for Comment (RFC) 6665 extends SIP with two more methods: SUBSCRIBE and NOTIFY. A subscriber subscribes to know the states of events related to a SIP entity and, later on, the notification is sent to the subscriber if there are changes in the states of the said entity. However, it is also seen that the states of a SIP entity need to be published for subscription to inform the states of that SIP entity. Consequently, the PUBLISH method is defined in SIP (RFC 3903) to meet this requirement. We have described the SIP event framework on the basis of these three methods. However, the states of a given SIP entity that deals with real-time multimedia communications with two or multiple fixed or mobile parties located anywhere in the world, where each of the users may be using a variety of devices, can be huge ones. In addition, the time and condition of one's availability, preferred mode of communications using a particular device, preferred application(s) to share, preferred type of codec for audio or video to choose, privacy, security, and many conditions for each party need to be known before a successful session is established. As a result, the states of a given SIP entity to which a user will subscribe may need to be filtered, making a package that is only suitable to meet the specific requirement of the subscriber. To simplify the complexities of the subscription to the states of a SIP entity, many SIP event packages are standardized. We will only provide an outline about the SIP event package and will not describe any SIP event package for the sake of brevity.

5.1 Introduction

The Session Initiation Protocol (SIP) event framework consists of the following three methods: SUBSCRIBE, NOTIFY, and PUBLISH. We describe the event framework here based on Requests for Comment (RFCs) 3903 and 6665. In this context, we also briefly describe the relationship between the SIP event framework and the SIP presence, presentity, and watcher. We will describe the details of SIP presence, presentity, and watcher in a separate section (see Chapter 6). We describe the detailed operations of SUBSCRIBE, NOTIFY, and PUBLISH. Many SIP event packages are also defined in many RFCs, and we only provide an outline for the event package because all SIP event packages themselves need a separate detailed treatment.

5.2 Event Framework

5.2.1 Overview

The SIP event framework defined in RFC 6665 extends the usage of SIP toward an event delivery over the network between SIP functional entities. SIP events generally represent state information for a particular resource that is associated with the particular SIP event. In real-time multimedia communications, the states of the SIP user agents (UAs) can vary from a simple one to very complex ones where humans and automata may be involved for communications like audio, video, or data applications. A caller may place a call to another user, but the called party may be too busy to accept the call. If the busy state of the called party was known through some kind of notifications to the caller, the call would not even be tried. In another situation, if the availability of a called party in certain times is known in advance through a notification, the caller might try to place the call in those time intervals. With SIP being the call control signaling protocol for these highly complex networked multimedia communications, there must be some built-in mechanisms to know these event states through SIP functional entities such as SIP UAs.

For realizing the actual event delivery functionality, RFC 6665 introduces two new SIP methods, namely SUBSCRIBE and NOTIFY. A key requirement of the SIP event notification framework is the publication of the event states, and the PUBLISH method defined in RFC 3903 is used for this purpose. A subscriber subscribes to SIP resources to know a particular event's state, and the notification receives the latter for the initial notification and all subsequent ones that are related to this subscription. It is envisioned that the so-called SIP event server hosts the state information of the particular event. SIP functional entities route the subscription to the SIP event server from SIP UAs and route back the notification to the respective SIP UAs.

5.2.2 Subscription, Notification, and Publication Event Model

5.2.2.1 SUBSCRIBE and NOTIFY

Figure 5.1 depicts an overview of the general concept for the operation of a SIP event based on subscription and notification. Note that the subscription must be confirmed before expecting any notification. A notification is only sent when the state changes. The reception of the notification also needs to be acknowledged. Of course, for an initial subscription, a notification is due immediately because no state information was sent to the subscriber.

A more detailed logical implementation example of the SIP event framework over the SIP network is depicted in Figure 5.2. Here we show that a SIP event server that hosts the state information of events of the resources of SIP functional entities is placed behind a SIP proxy.

This logical SUBSCRIBE/NOTIFY event implementation model considers a separate SIP event server for providing scalability for the large-scale SIP network. The key is that the SIP event server acts on behalf of the SIP UAs in keeping updates on any changes of states of SIP resources on behalf of UAs. SIP has elaborate standards about creating, refreshing, removing, confirming, receiving and processing, and forking of subscriptions and notifications along with maintaining detailed security. For each recourse state of a UA, there may be a huge number of subscribers. In this situation, an individual SIP UA may not be efficient enough to deal with those notifications of the updated states to all its subscribers individually. Therefore, a separate SIP event server will be a natural choice. In addition, there can be many SIP proxies in a given administrative domain. Many separate administrative domains may also be involved where SIP UAs may be located. As a result, many more SIP event servers may be needed across single or multiple administrative domains. The details are beyond the scope of the current discussion.

5.2.2.2 PUBLISH

The PUBLISH method allows a user to create, modify, and remove the state in another entity that manages this state on behalf of the user that may have a single or multiple

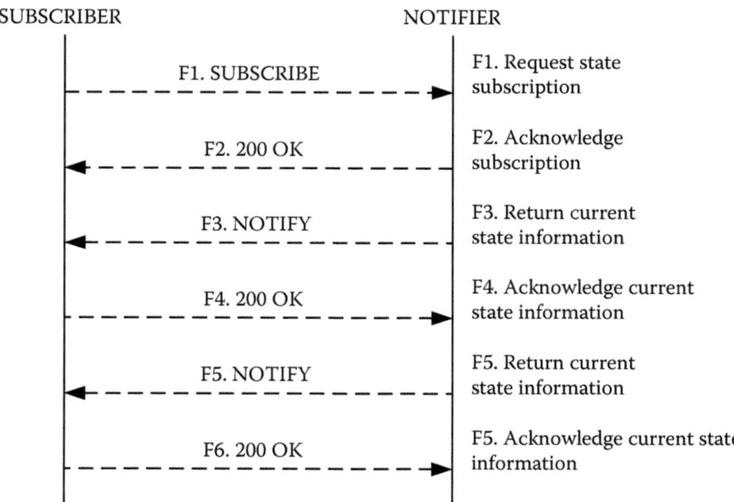

Figure 5.1 Typical operation of event subscription and notification. (Copyright IETF. Reproduced with permission.)

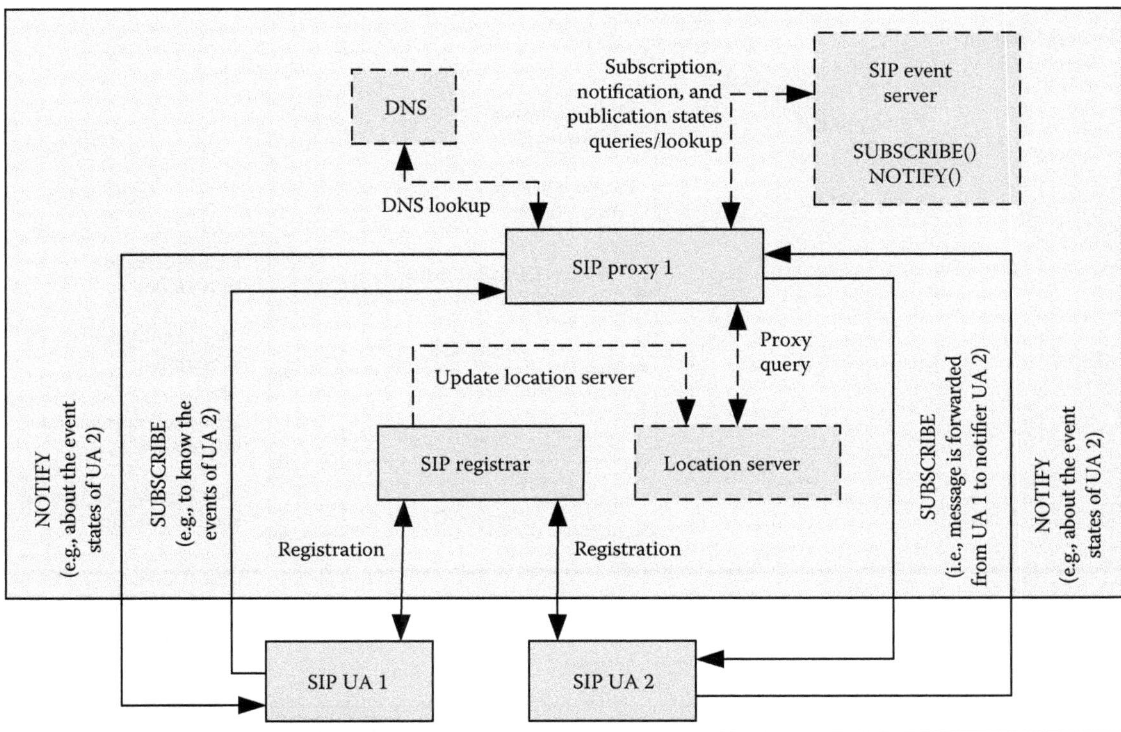

Figure 5.2 Logical view of SUBSCRIBE/NOTIFY event model implementation. (Copyright IETF. Reproduced with permission.)

publication UAs/endpoints. The PUBLISH request contains the Request Uniform Resource Identifier, which is a request populated with the address of the resource for which the user wishes to publish the event state. However, the event state compositor generates the composite event state of the resource, taking out the information from the unique state published by an individual user. In addition to a particular resource, all published event states are associated with a specific event package. The user is able to discover the composite event state of all of the active publications through a subscription to that particular event package as described in the SUBSCRIBE method. Moreover, RFC 3903 specifies that a UAC that publishes an event state is labeled an Event Publication Agent (EPA). For presence, this is the familiar presence user agent (PUA) role as defined in RFC 3856. The entity that processes the PUBLISH request is known as an event state compositor (ESC). For presence, this is the familiar presence agent (PA) role as defined in RFC 3856.

Unlike SUBSCRIBE, a PUBLISH request does not establish a dialog as specified in RFC 3903. A UA client may include a Route header field in a PUBLISH request based on a preexisting route. The Record–Route header field has no meaning in PUBLISH requests or responses, and must be ignored if present. In particular, the UAC must not create a new route set based on the presence or absence of a Record–Route header field in any response to a PUBLISH request. Similar to the subscription, a SIP EPA can publish its states to a SIP event state compositor that can also distribute the PUA's states as a notifier to all its subscribers. The general operation of the states' publication, subscription, and notification is shown in Figure 5.3.

Figure 5.4 shows an example of a logical view of the PUBLISH event implementation model. As before, we show a separate SIP event server that acts as an ESC for the PUBLISH method.

The key of the implementation example of the SIP event framework shows that a separate SIP event server is more scalable for implementation of the subscription, publication, and notification over the SIP network.

5.2.2.3 SIP Extensions

The SIP event framework and packages define the mechanisms by which SIP nodes can request notification from remote nodes indicating that certain events have occurred. The event notification framework needs some additional capabilities for which the base SIP specified in RFC 3261 has been extended in the following respects:

- Methods: SUBSCRIBE, NOTIFY, and PUBLISH
- Header fields: Event, Allow-Events, Subscription-State, and Suppress-If-Match

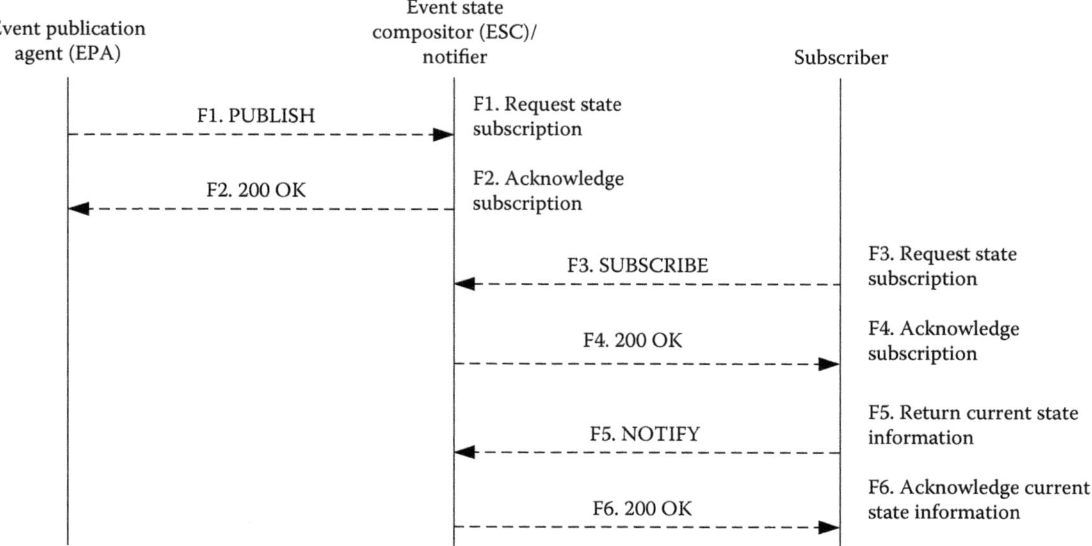

Figure 5.3 Typical operation of event publication, subscription, and notification. (Copyright IETF. Reproduced with permission.)

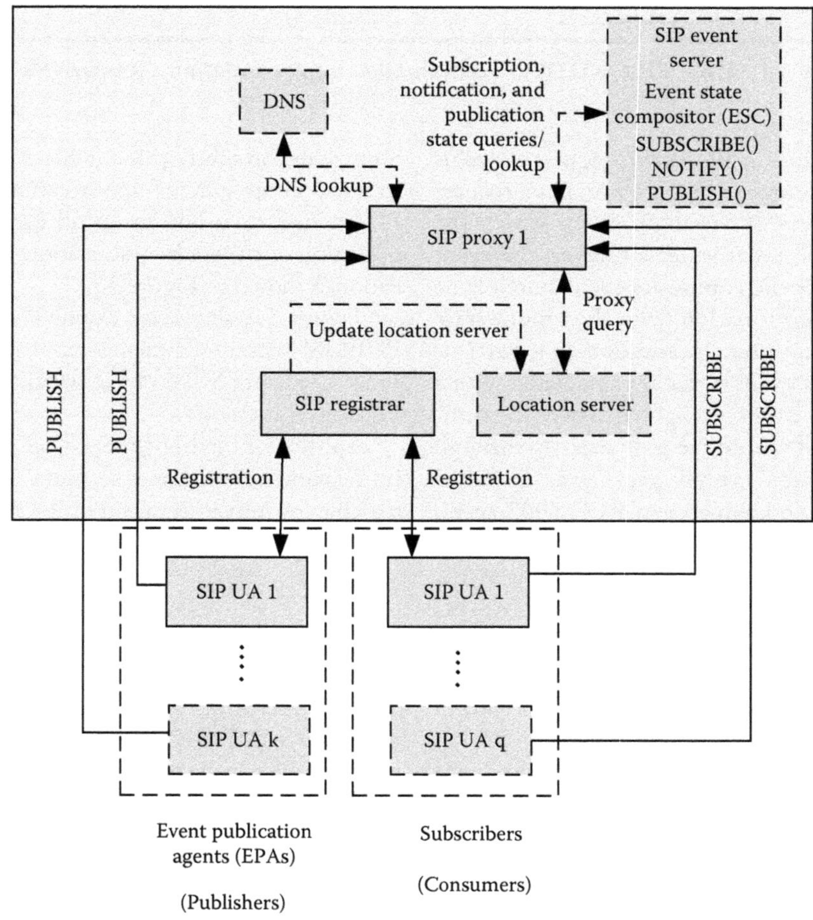

Figure 5.4 Logical view of PUBLISH event model implementation. (Copyright IETF. Reproduced with permission.)

- Respond codes: 202 Accepted, 204 No Notification, and 409 Bad Event
- Event header field parameters: max-rate, min-rate, and adaptive-min-rate
- Subscription-state header field reason codes (event–reason–value): deactivated, probation, rejected, timeout, giveup, noresource, invariant, and badfilter
- Option tag: eventlist
- Event notification filtering
- State aggregation

5.2.2.4 Presence, Presentity, and Watcher

The SIP event framework extended to other RFCs also defines a few more functional entities for optimizing the large-scale event services providing interoperability for building the scalable interoperable SIP system further: presence, presentity, and watcher. Presence indicates the willingness for communication while presentity is that which publishes one's presence information. However, the watcher uses the presence service through publications, subscriptions, and notifications, and the presentity information is displayed to the watcher on the UA as a *buddy* or *contact.* We describe these functionalities of SIP in Chapter 6, which specifies the presence protocol. The presence protocol is a not new protocol, but it consists of these three SIP methods along with some extensions of SIP UA functionalities for proving presence service in a more appropriate way.

5.3 Event Package

The SUBSCRIBE, NOTIFY, and PUBLISH method are used by SIP event packages as a mechanism for publication of the respective event packages. In accordance to the SIP event framework, it is required that notification needs to be sent to the subscriber when there are changes to the states of the resources that have been subscribed to. There can be many changes in the states of the resource(s), and a subscriber may be only interested about a certain kind of state change of the resource(s) instead of sending all the state changes. Thus, the event notification service will be efficient if there have been some defined rules for filtering the state changes of the resources and the subscriber can subscribe to those event changes described by specific filtering rules.

Thereby, the filtering mechanism can be used for controlling the content of event notifications, and RFC 4660 provides a mechanism for filtering whereby a subscriber describes its preference for when notifications are to be sent to it and what they are to contain. RFC 4661 defines a preferred format in the form of an XML document that is used to enable the subscriber to describe the state changes of a resource that cause notifications to be sent to it and what those notifications are to contain. The filter mechanisms and the document format can be used for many SIP event packages. Note that subscriptions are expired and must be refreshed by subsequent SUBSCRIBE requests before the expiration time. Detailed discussions on all SIP event packages are beyond the scope of this chapter.

5.4 Summary

We have described the SIP event framework that has extended SIP with three methods: SUBSCRIBE, PUBLISH, and NOTIFY. In addition, some additional SIP respond codes, event header field parameters, subscription reason codes, and others that have extended SIP are also mentioned. The call flows are provided to show the usage of these methods explaining the basic functionalities. A logical view of SIP event framework implementation architecture is also provided. It is explained that a separate SIP event server is needed for scalability. A brief outline for SIP event package is discussed. The presence, presentity, and watcher functional entities of the SIP event framework are briefly defined, and their functional capabilities will be further explained in Chapter 6.

PROBLEMS

1. What is the event framework needed in SIP? Explain the functionalities of SUBSCRIBE, NOTIFY, and PUBLISH.
2. Describe the detailed header fields of each message of each call flow of Figures 5.1 and 5.3 along with their message bodies with reasonable explanations for a given scenario of your choice.
3. How do the SUBSCRIBE, NOTIFY, and PUBLISH methods differ with respect to other SIP methods?
4. Develop the detailed call flows of Figures 5.2 and 5.4 using all relevant messages including the SIP event server. Explain why a separate SIP event server is scalable for the large-scale SIP network.
5. Extend the call flows of Figures 5.2 and 5.4 considering two separate administrative domains where the inter-domain communications are done only via SIP proxies while each domain has a separate SIP event server.
6. What constitutes the SIP event package? Is presence protocol a new protocol? Justify your answer.

Chapter 6

Presence and Instant Messaging in SIP

Abstract

This chapter describes Session Initiation Protocol (SIP) extensions for presence and instant messaging (IM) based on Requests for Comment 2778, 3856, 3857, 3859, 4975–76, and 5365. For providing IM capabilities, the SIP is extended using another method: MESSAGE. Both page and conferencing modes for IM are discussed. Earlier, we have provided very brief explanations about presence, presentity, and watcher in the context of the SIP event framework. However, we provide more detailed description of these functionalities, including presence user agent, presence agent, edge presence server, and presence Uniform Resource Identifier. However, a full treatment of SIP presence and IM needs a complete separate treatment, and we have not done this for brevity.

6.1 Introduction

We here describe Session Initiation Protocol (SIP) extensions for presence and instant messaging (IM) because both of them facilitate real-time communications for session initiation, establishment, and termination in SIP. Only a new MESSAGE method is created for enabling the presence and IM capabilities in SIP. The most important thing is that SIP has already developed the infrastructure for real-time communications that presence and IM require. We also provide the definitions of presence user agent, presence agent, edge presence server, and presence Uniform Resource Identifier. The presence operations and data format are described along with some examples. The IM pager mode with single and multiple recipients as well as two-party and multiparty session modes are described briefly as the detailed description of all aspects of presence and IM is beyond the scope of the present chapter.

6.2 SIP Presence

6.2.1 Overview

Presence is an important abstraction for real-time communications especially between humans. Real-time communications can only be made if both the caller and the called party are available. The SIP being the signaling protocol for real-time communications, it is a paramount need to know whether both parties are available. Even if both parties are available at the same time, the states, moods, policies, or other aspects of the communicating parties need to be known before a successful call is made at that particular time. Moreover, a given user may have many devices such as mobile cell phone, fixed wire-line phone, laptop, personal digital assistant (PDA), or others (Figure 6.1), while the user may be fixed in a location or mobile (moving from one place to another). It is a huge problem to communicate in real time with a user unless one knows which device needs to be dialed in to reach the user at a given time.

Presence is the key functionality that helps solve the above problems for real-time communications in SIP through publications, subscriptions, and notifications about the detailed information about the user, for example, how and when the user will be present for communications in real time. In this case, a user who publishes their presence information for willingness to communicate in real time is termed as the presentity. Presence, also known as presence information, conveys the ability and willingness of a user to communicate across a set of devices. Request for Comment (RFC) 2778 defines a model and terminology for describing systems that provide presence information. In that model, a presence service is a system that accepts, stores, and distributes presence

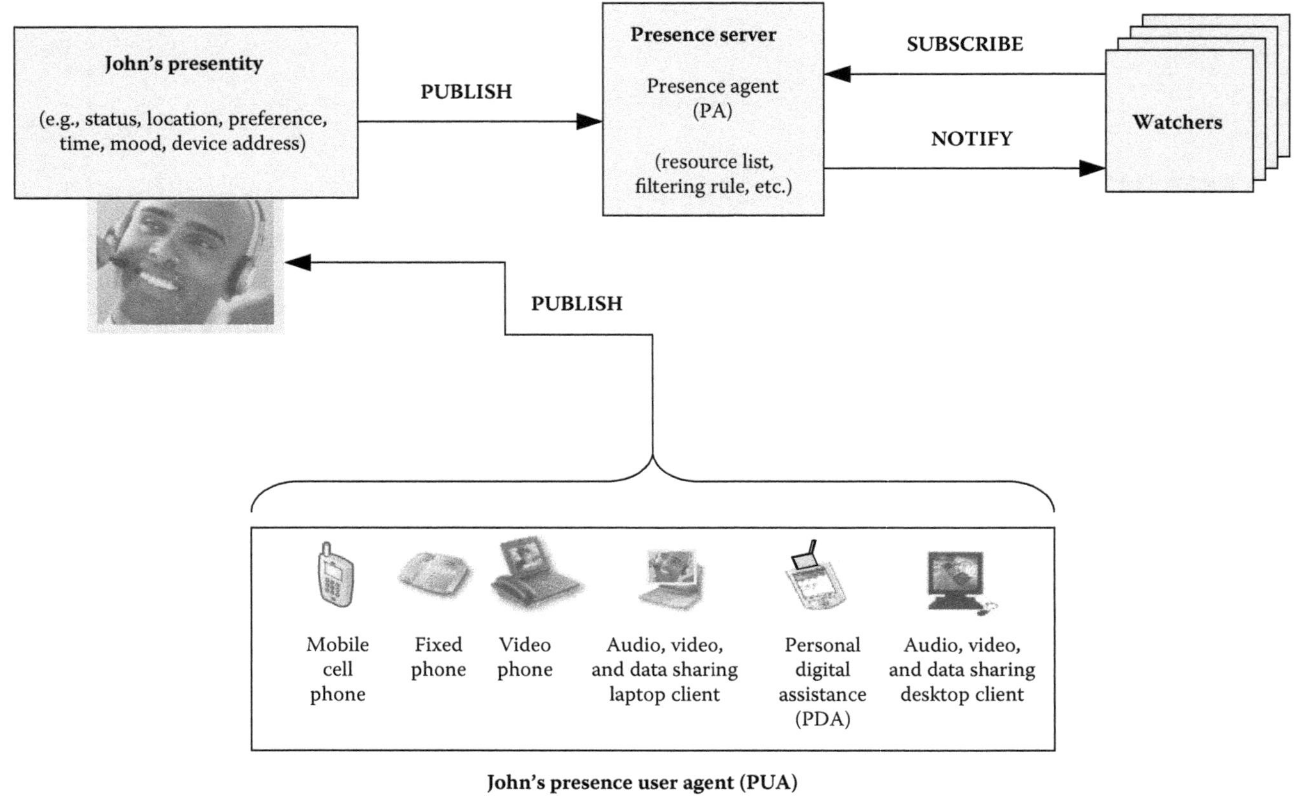

Figure 6.1 Publication, subscription, and notifications of presence/presentity for reachability in real time.

information to interested parties, called watchers. A presence protocol is a protocol for providing a presence service over the Internet or any Internet Protocol network. RFC 3856 extends SIP for proving the presence service, while RFC 3857 defines a SIP event package for the watcher.

6.2.2 SIP Extensions for Presence

RFC 3856 extends the SIP protocol through defining new functionalities of SIP especially the SIP UA. The new functionalities of SIP for providing presence services are defined as follows:

- **Presence:** It is defined as the willingness and ability of a user to communicate with other users on the network. Publications, subscriptions, and notifications of presence are supported by defining an event package within the general SIP event notification framework. There can be rules about how and what part of presence information can be accessed. The detailed information includes location, preferred communication mode, current mood, and activity.
- **Presentity:** It represents a user or a group of users or programs that are the source of presence information.
- **Presence user agent (PUA):** A PUA manipulates presence information for a presentity. This manipulation can be the side effect of some other action (such as sending a SIP REGISTER request to add a new Contact) or can be done explicitly through the publication of presence documents. We explicitly allow multiple PUAs per presentity. This means that a user can have many devices, such as a cell phone and PDA, each of which is independently generating a component of the overall presence information for a presentity. PUAs push data into the presence system, but are outside of it, in that they do not receive SUBSCRIBE messages or send NOTIFY messages.
- **Presence agent (PA):** A PA is a SIP user agent that is capable of receiving SUBSCRIBE requests, responding to them, and generating notifications of changes in the presence state. A PA must have knowledge of the presence state of a presentity. This means that it must have access to presence data manipulated by PUAs for the presentity. One way to do this is by colocating the PA with the proxy/registrar.

  Another way is to colocate it with the PUA of the presentity. However, these are not the only ways, and this specification makes no recommendations about where the PA function should be located. A PA is always addressable with a SIP Uniform Resource Identifier (URI) that uniquely identifies the presentity (i.e., sip:joe@example.com). There can be multiple PAs for a particular presentity, each of which handles some subset of the total subscriptions currently active for the presentity. A PA is also a notifier defined in RFC 3265 that supports the presence event package.

- **Presence server:** A presence server is a physical entity that can act as either a PA or as a proxy server for SUBSCRIBE requests. When acting as a PA, it is aware of the presence information of the presentity through some protocol means. When acting as a proxy, the SUBSCRIBE requests are proxied to another entity that may act as a PA.
- **Edge presence server:** An edge presence server is a PA that is colocated with a PUA. It is aware of the presence information of the presentity because it is colocated with the entity that manipulates this presence information.
- **Presence URI:** A presentity is identified in the most general way through a presence URI (RFC 3859), which is of the form pres:user@domain. These URIs are resolved to protocol-specific URIs, such as the SIP or secure SIP (SIPS) URI, through domain-specific mapping policies maintained on a server. It is very possible that a user will have both a SIP (or SIPS) URI and a presence URI to identify both themselves and other users. This leads to questions about how these URIs relate and which are to be used.
- **Watcher:** This represents (RFC 3857) the requester of presence information about a presentity. Watcher information refers to the set of users subscribed to a particular resource within a particular event package. Watcher information changes dynamically as users subscribe, unsubscribe, are approved, or are rejected. A user can subscribe to this information, and therefore learn about changes to it. This event package is a template package because it can be applied to any event package, including itself.

6.2.3 Presence Data Formats and Processing

The Presence Information Data Format (PIDF) defines a basic format for representing presence information for a presentity. This format defines a textual note, an indication of availability (open or closed), and a URI for communication. The Rich Presence Information Data described here is an extension that adds optional elements to the PIDF. These extensions provide additional information about the presentity and its contacts, such as "What is one's current activity?," "What is the mood?," and others. The information is designed so that much of it can be derived automatically, for example, from calendar files or user activity. The rate of presence notification, type of composition policies that need to be supported, size of the sent watcher filter sent by the watcher in the SUBSCRIBE message, and the partial notification used to conserve bandwidth by sending only the changes in the presence document to the watchers are among the things that affect the scalability of the presence implementation significantly. The detailed discussions are beyond the scope of this chapter.

6.2.4 Presence Operations

Figure 6.2 depicts a simple example (RFC 3863) of how the presence server can be responsible for sending notifications for a presentity. This flow assumes that the watcher has previously been authorized to subscribe to this resource at the server. In this flow, the PUA informs the server about the updated presence information through some non-SIP means. When the value of the Content-Length header field is "...," this means that the value should be whatever the computed length of the body is.

Each of the message details is provided below:

F1 SUBSCRIBE watcher -> example.com server

```
SUBSCRIBE sip:resource@example.com SIP/2.0
Via: SIP/2.0/TCP watcherhost.example.com;
branch=z9hG4bKnashds7
```

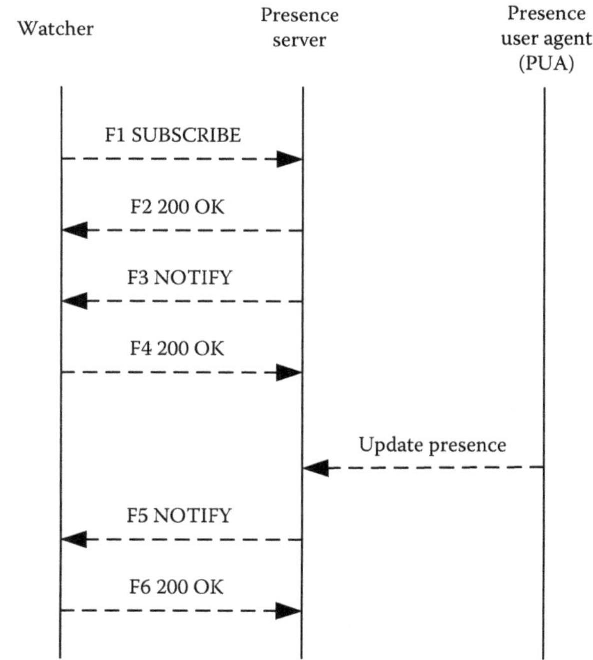

Figure 6.2 Example message flows for presence operations. (Copyright IETF. Reproduced with permission.)

```
To: <sip:resource@example.com>
From: <sip:user@example.com>;tag=xfg9
Call-ID: 2010@watcherhost.example.com
CSeq: 17766 SUBSCRIBE
Max-Forwards: 70
Event: presence
Accept: application/pidf+xml
Contact: <sip:user@watcherhost.example.com>
Expires: 600
Content-Length: 0
```

F2 200 OK example.com server -> watcher

```
SIP/2.0 200 OK
Via: SIP/2.0/TCP watcherhost.example.com;
branch=z9hG4bKnashds7
;received=192.0.2.1
To: <sip:resource@example.com>;tag=ffd2
From: <sip:user@example.com>;tag=xfg9
Call-ID: 2010@watcherhost.example.com
CSeq: 17766 SUBSCRIBE
Expires: 600
Contact: sip:server.example.com
Content-Length: 0
```

F3 NOTIFY example.com server -> watcher

```
NOTIFY sip:user@watcherhost.example.com SIP/2.0
Via: SIP/2.0/TCP server.example.com;branch
=z9hG4bKna998sk
From: <sip:resource@example.com>;tag=ffd2
To: <sip:user@example.com>;tag=xfg9
Call-ID: 2010@watcherhost.example.com
Event: presence
Subscription-State: active;expires=599
Max-Forwards: 70
CSeq: 8775 NOTIFY
Contact: sip:server.example.com
Content-Type: application/pidf+xml
Content-Length:...
[PIDF Document]
```

F4 200 OK watcher -> example.com server

```
SIP/2.0 200 OK
Via: SIP/2.0/TCP server.example.com;branch=
z9hG4bKna998sk
;received=192.0.2.2
From: <sip:resource@example.com>;tag=ffd2
To: <sip:user@example.com>;tag=xfg9
Call-ID: 2010@watcherhost.example.com
CSeq: 8775 NOTIFY
Content-Length: 0
```

F5 NOTIFY example.com server -> watcher

```
NOTIFY sip:user@watcherhost.example.com SIP/2.0
Via: SIP/2.0/TCP server.example.com;branch=
z9hG4bKna998sl
From: <sip:resource@example.com>;tag=ffd2
To: <sip:user@example.com>;tag=xfg9
Call-ID: 2010@watcherhost.example.com
CSeq: 8776 NOTIFY
Event: presence
Subscription-State: active;expires=543
Max-Forwards: 70
Contact: sip:server.example.com
Content-Type: application/pidf+xml
Content-Length:...
[New PIDF Document]
```

F6 200 OK Watcher -> example.com server

```
SIP/2.0 200 OK
Via: SIP/2.0/TCP server.example.com;branch
=z9hG4bKna998sl
;received=192.0.2.2
From: <sip:resource@example.com>;tag=ffd2
To: <sip:user@example.com>;tag=xfg9
Call-ID: 2010@watcherhost.example.com
CSeq: 8776 NOTIFY
Content-Length: 0
```

6.3 SIP Instant Messaging

IM is application that allows two-way or multiway communications among users in an interactive nature, where users exchange messages in near real time, engaging in conversations with a low latency of delivering messages. These messages are usually, but not required to be, short. SIP has been extended for carrying IM for communications for one-to-one or one-to-many conversation: pager mode and session mode. It has been very convenient for extensions of SIP for supporting IM with very minimal efforts because the underlying SIP infrastructure has already be standardized for authentication and routing of SIP messages. The pager mode is appropriate for brief message exchanges, while the session mode is similar to a conference hosted by a network where individual users join and leave the group conversation over time. These IM messages form a unidirectional communication at any given time. Participating users may respond to any of the IM messages that are sent; however, all responses and subsequent messages occur independently and are unrelated to the messages sent earlier.

6.3.1 Pager-Mode Single Recipient

RFC 3428 extends SIP with the MESSAGE method that allows the transfer of IMs. Since the MESSAGE request is an extension to the SIP, it inherits all the request routing and security features of that protocol. MESSAGE requests carry the content in the form of MIME body parts. MESSAGE requests do not themselves initiate a SIP dialog; under normal usage, each IM stands alone, much like pager messages. MESSAGE requests may be sent in the context of a dialog initiated by some other SIP request. The core SIP capabilities already defined in standards provide the routing between the IM servers and IM client without establishing a SIP session. However, the SIP MESSAGE method poses some limitations in IM message size that can be sent especially if the IM contents are multimedia in nature. This limitation has been taken care of by another extension in SIP (RFC 4975), known as the Message Session Relay Protocol (MSRP), described in the next section.

An example message flow (RFC 3428) is shown in Figure 6.3. The message flow shows an initial IM sent from user 1 to user 2, both users in the same domain—*domain* through a single proxy.

Message F1 looks like

```
MESSAGE sip:user2@domain.com SIP/2.0
Via: SIP/2.0/TCP user1pc.domain.com;branch=
z9hG4bK776sgdkse
Max-Forwards: 70
From: sip:user1@domain.com;tag=49583
To: sip:user2@domain.com
Call-ID: asd88asd77a@1.2.3.4
CSeq: 1 MESSAGE
Content-Type: text/plain
Content-Length: 18
Watson, come here.
```

User 1 forwards this message to the server for domain.com. The proxy receives this request and recognizes that it is the server for domain.com. It looks up user 2 in its database (built up through registrations), and finds a binding from sip:user2@domain.com to sip:user2@user2pc.domain.com. It forwards the request to user 2. The resulting message, F2, looks like

```
MESSAGE sip:user2@domain.com SIP/2.0
Via: SIP/2.0/TCP proxy.domain.com;branch=
z9hG4bK123dsghds
Via: SIP/2.0/TCP user1pc.domain.com;branch=
z9hG4bK776sgdkse;
received=1.2.3.4
Max-Forwards: 69
From: sip:user1@domain.com;tag=49394
To: sip:user2@domain.com
Call-ID: asd88asd77a@1.2.3.4
CSeq: 1 MESSAGE
Content-Type: text/plain
Content-Length: 18

Watson, come here.
```

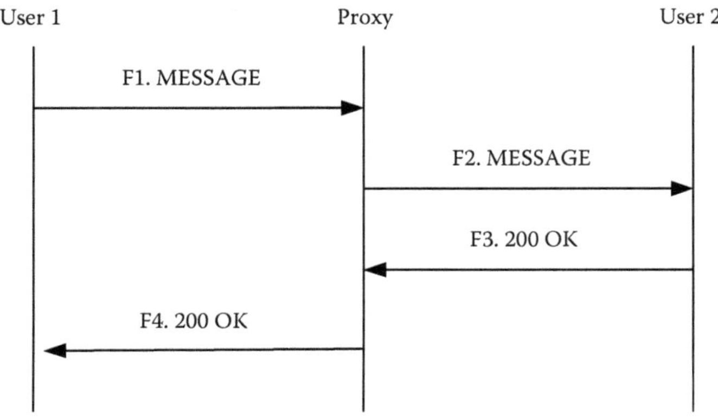

Figure 6.3 Example message flow. (Copyright IETF. Reproduced with permission.)

The message is received by user 2, displayed, and a response is generated, message F3, and sent to the proxy, as follows:

```
SIP/2.0 200 OK
Via: SIP/2.0/TCP proxy.domain.com;branch=
z9hG4bK123dsghds;
received=192.0.2.1
Via: SIP/2.0/TCP user1pc.domain.com;;branch=
z9hG4bK776sgdkse;
received=1.2.3.4
From: sip:user1@domain.com;tag=49394
To: sip:user2@domain.com;tag=ab8asdasd9
Call-ID: asd88asd77a@1.2.3.4
CSeq: 1 MESSAGE
```

6.3.2 Pager-Mode Multiple Recipients

RFC 5365 specifies a mechanism that allows a SIP UAC to send a SIP MESSAGE request to a set of destinations, by using a SIP URI-list service. The UAC sends a SIP MESSAGE request that includes the payload along with the URI list to the MESSAGE URI-list service, which sends a MESSAGE request including the payload to each of the URIs included in the list. Alternatively, a list of recipients may be carried as a MIME attachment in the body of the SIP message. An IM Group URI may be part of the recipient list. The IM server delivers the message to the whole group. The detailed discussion is beyond the scope of this chapter.

6.3.3 Two-Party Session Mode

In session mode, an IM session is created in contrast to the pager mode. The senders and receivers join together for a period of time in an IM session. The IM session is established at some moment in time, continues for a finite duration, and then is dissolved. RFC 4975 describes the MSRP, a protocol for transmitting a series of related IMs in the context of a session. However, MSRP sessions can be negotiated with an offer or answer described in RFC 3264 (see Section 3.8.4) using the session description protocol (SDP). The exchange is carried by some signaling protocol, such as SIP. This allows a communication user agent to offer a messaging session as one of the possible media types in a session. Message sessions are treated like any other media stream when set up

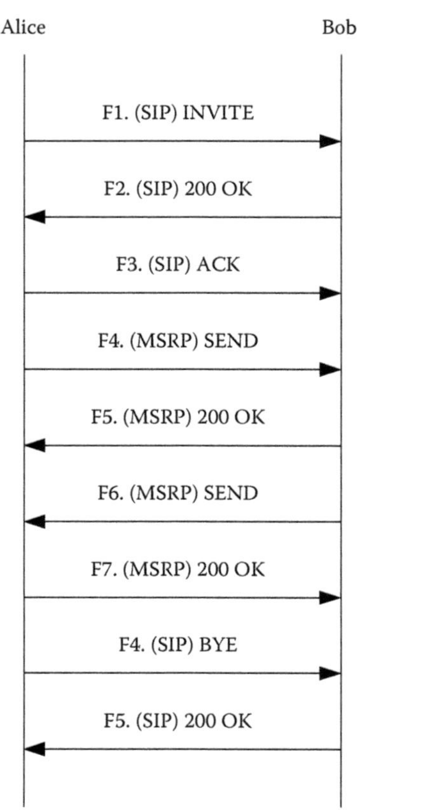

Figure 6.4 Basic IM session example. (Copyright IETF. Reproduced with permission.)

via a rendezvous or session creation protocol such as the SIP. Sometimes, the session mode communication is also termed as joining a chat session or chat room. The key is that, unlike pager mode, the exchanged messages are associated together in the context of this session.

A basic IM session (RFC 5365) shows an example flow for the most common scenario in Figure 6.4. The example assumes that SIP is used to transport the SDP exchange. Details of the SIP messages and SIP proxy infrastructure are omitted for the sake of brevity. In the example, assume that the offerer is sip:alice@example.com and the answerer is sip:bob@example.com.

F1. Alice constructs a local URI of msrp://alicepc.example.com:7777/iau39soe2843z;tcp.

```
Alice->Bob (SIP): INVITE sip:bob@example.com

v=0
o=alice 2890844557 2890844559 IN IP4 alicepc.
example.com
s=-
c=IN IP4 alicepc.example.com
t=0 0
m=message 7777 TCP/MSRP *
a=accept-types:text/plain
a=path:msrp://alicepc.example.com:7777/iau39
soe2843z;tcp
```

F2. Bob listens on port 8888, and sends the following response:

```
Bob->Alice (SIP): 200 OK

v=0
o=bob 2890844612 2890844616 IN IP4 bob.
example.com
s=-
c=IN IP4 bob.example.com
t=0 0
m=message 8888 TCP/MSRP *
a=accept-types:text/plain
a=path:msrp://bob.example.com:8888/9di4eae
923wzd;tcp
```

F3. Alice->Bob (SIP): ACK sip:bob@example.com
F4. (Alice opens connection to Bob.) Alice->Bob (MSRP):

```
MSRP d93kswow SEND
To-Path: msrp://bob.example.com:8888/9di4eae
923wzd;tcp
From-Path: msrp://alicepc.example.com:7777/
iau39soe2843z;tcp
Message-ID: 12339sdqwer
Byte-Range: 1-16/16
Content-Type: text/plain
Hi, I'm Alice!
-------d93kswow$
```

F5. Bob->Alice (MSRP):

```
MSRP d93kswow 200 OK
To-Path: msrp://alicepc.example.com:7777/iau
39soe2843z;tcp
From-Path: msrp://bob.example.com:8888/9di4eae
923wzd;tcp
-------d93kswow$
```

F6. Bob->Alice (MSRP):

```
MSRP dkei38sd SEND
To-Path: msrp://alicepc.example.com:7777/iau39
soe2843z;tcp
From-Path: msrp://bob.example.com:8888/9di4
eae923wzd;tcp
Message-ID: 456s9wlk3
Byte-Range: 1-21/21
Content-Type: text/plain
Hi, Alice! I'm Bob!
-------dkei38sd$
```

F7. Alice->Bob (MSRP):

```
MSRP dkei38sd 200 OK
To-Path: msrp://bob.example.com:8888/9di4eae
923wzd;tcp
From-Path: msrp://alicepc.example.com:7777/
iau39soe2843z;tcp
-------dkei38sd$
```

F8. Alice->Bob (SIP): BYE sip:bob@example.com

```
Alice invalidates local session state.
```

F9. Bob invalidates local state for the session.

```
Bob->Alice (SIP): 200 OK
```

6.3.4 Multiparty Session Mode

The MSRP protocol is being extended (IETF draft-ietf-simple-chat-18, January 2013) for providing multiparty IM conferencing. Participants in a chat room can be identified by a pseudonym, and decide if their real identifier is disclosed to other participants. It uses the SIP conferencing framework (RFC 4353) as a design basis. It also aims to be compatible with the centralized conferencing framework (RFC 5239). Before a chat room can be entered, it must be created. Users wishing to host a chat room themselves can of course do just that; their UA simply morphs from an ordinary UA into a special-purpose one called a focus UA. Another commonly used setup is one where a dedicated node in the network functions as a focus UA. Each chat room has an identifier of its own: a SIP URI that participants use to join the chat room, for example, by sending an INVITE request to it. The conference focus processes the invitations, and as such, maintains SIP dialogs with each participant. In a multiparty chat, or chat room, MSRP is one of the established media streams. Each chat-room participant establishes an MSRP session with the MSRP switch, which is a special-purpose MSRP application. The MSRP sessions can be relayed by one or more MSRP relays, which are specified in RFC 4976 (Figure 6.5).

The MSRP switch is similar to a conference mixer in that it handles media sessions with each of the participants and bridges these streams together. However, unlike a conference mixer, the MSRP switch merely forwards messages between participants but does not actually mix the streams in any way. The system is illustrated in Figure 6.6.

Typically, chat-room participants also subscribe to a conference event package to gather information about the conference roster in the form of conference state notifications. For example, participants can learn about other participants' identifiers, including their nicknames. All messages in the chat room use the Message/CPIM wrapper content type

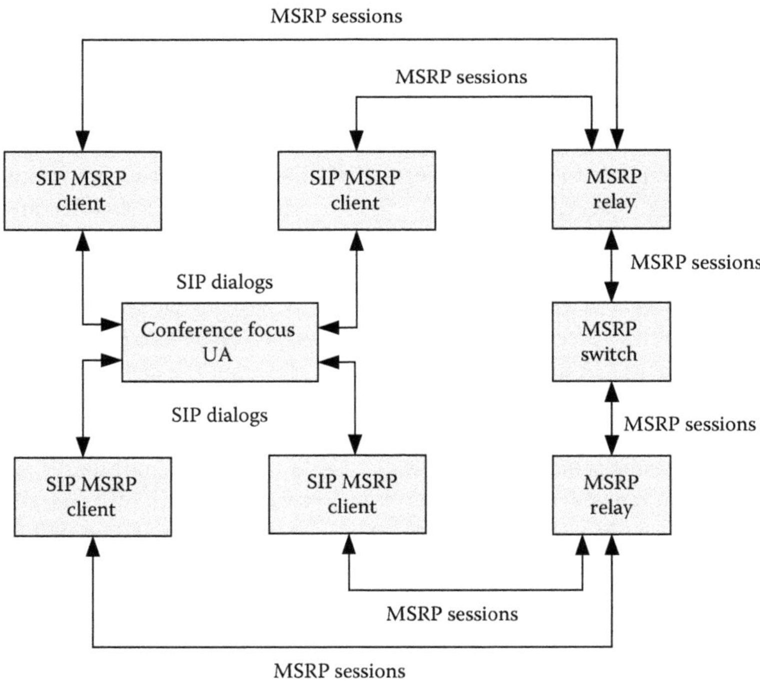

Figure 6.5 Multiparty chat overview shown with MSRP relays and a conference focus UA. (Copyright IETF. Reproduced with permission.)

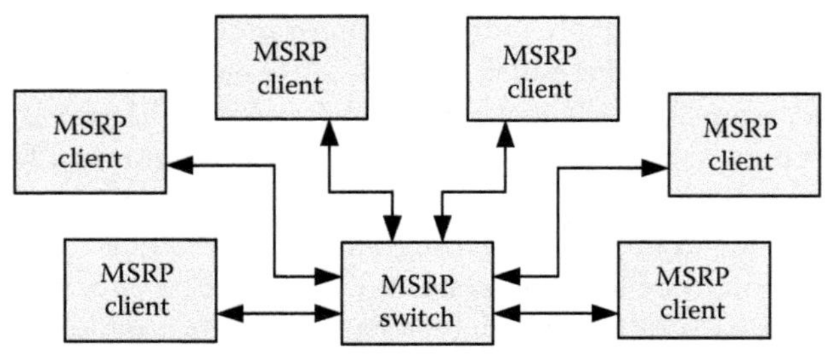

Figure 6.6 Multiparty chat in a centralized chat room. (Copyright IETF. Reproduced with permission.)

(RFC 3862), so that it is possible to distinguish between private and regular messages. When a participant wants to send an IM to the chat room, it constructs an MSRP SEND request and submits it to the MSRP switch including a regular payload (e.g., a Message/CPIM message that contains text, HTML, an image, etc.). The Message/CPIM To header is set to the chat-room URI. The switch then fans out the SEND request to all of the other participants using their existing MSRP sessions.

A participant can also send a private IM addressed to a participant whose identifier has been learned, for example, via a conference event package. In this case, the sender creates an MSRP SEND request with a Message/CPIM wrapper whose To header contains not the chat-room URI but the recipient's URI. The MSRP switch then forwards the SEND request to that recipient. This specification supports the sending of private messages to one and only one recipient. However, if the recipient is logged in from different end points, the MSRP switch will distribute the private message to each end point the recipient is logged in. We extend the current MSRP negotiation that takes place in SDP (RFC 4566, see Section 7.7) to allow participants to learn whether the chat room supports and is willing to accept (e.g., due to local policy restrictions) certain MSRP functions defined in this memo, such as nicknames or private messaging.

This is achieved by a new *chatroom* attribute in SDP. Naturally, when a participant wishes to leave a chat room, it sends a SIP BYE request to the focus UA and terminates the SIP dialog with the focus and MSRP sessions with the MSRP switch. We assume that each chat room is allocated its own SIP URI. A user joining a chat room sends an INVITE request to that SIP URI, and as a result, a new MSRP session is established between the user and the MSRP switch. It is assumed that an MSRP session is mapped to a chat room. If a user wants to join a second chat room, he creates a different INVITE request, through a different SIP dialog, which leads to the creation of a second MSRP session between the user and the MSRP switch. Notice that these two MSRP sessions can still be multiplexed over the same TCP connection as per regular MSRP procedures. However, each chat room is associated with a unique MSRP session and a unique SIP dialog. A detailed discussion about multiparty chat conferencing is out of scope of this chapter.

6.4 Summary

The SIP presence and IM that extend the SIP protocol are explained briefly. The importance of both presence and IM communications in SIP are discussed because of supporting real-time communications for which the SIP already provides the core infrastructure with minimal extensions. The basic call flows for both presence and IM are provided. IM in both pager mode and session mode are articulated. The initial aspect of multiparty chat in session mode for IM communications facilitating centralized conferencing is described.

PROBLEMS

1. What are presence, presentity, and watcher? Why is presence an important application for SIP? How does presence facilitate placing calls in real time in SIP?
2. Why is the SIP the correct protocol to support both present and IM with minimal extensions? Can presence be used in IM communications? If so, explain it.
3. Develop a scalable logical presence architecture along with call flows with all its functionalities in extending SIP in supporting communications including the existing SIP infrastructure that is used for presence communications between the presentity and the watcher.
4. Describe point-to-point and group communications in pager mode of IM. What are the pros and cons for pager mode communications in IM?
5. Explain the session mode communications in IM. Describe what aspects of functionalities differ between pager mode and session mode IM communications.
6. How can the capability between the parties be negotiated using the offer and answer of SDP in the IM session mode?
7. What is the multiparty session mode of communication in IM? Why is the multiparty conferencing framework in SIP needed for the multiparty chat conferencing as well?
8. Develop a scalable centralized multiparty chat conferencing architecture along with probable call flows and all functionalities that are needed for conferencing.

Chapter 7

Media Transport Protocol and Media Negotiation

Abstract

We are now concentrating our discussions focusing solely only on the media transport and negotiations in Session Initiation Protocol (SIP). The transfer of the real-time audio or video media needs a separate new protocol because they need sequence number, time stamp, synchronization, and content source identification and loss identification for the packetized media streams that are sent over the Internet Protocol (IP) network. Most of those functionalities, especially the synchronization capability, cannot be provided by Transmission Control Protocol (TCP), User Datagram Protocol (UDP), or other Non-Real-Time Transport Protocol. We describe the Real-Time Transmission Protocol (RTP), Secure RTP (SRTP), ZRTP, Real-Time Streaming Protocol (RTSP), and Media Resource Control Protocol (MRCP) that are used for transferring of the real-time audio and video media streams on the top of the existing transport protocols such as UDP or others for transferring over the IP network. Note that Real-Time Control Protocol (RTCP) and secure RTCP (SRTCP) are the companion protocols of RTP and SRTP, respectively, which are used for monitoring the quality of service (QOS) of the audio and video media streams sent using the RTP and SRTP. In addition, we describe the Session Description Protocol (SDP) that is carried by the SIP signaling message body for media negotiations along with their QOS parameters. Both real-time transport protocols and SDP require separate detail stand-alone discussion individually because of their own merits. We have only provided a summarized description for each of these topics here for brevity.

7.1 Introduction

The specifications of Real-Time Transmission Protocol/Real-Time Control Protocol (RTP/RTCP), secure RTP/secure RTCP (SRTP/SRTCP), ZRTP, RTSP, and Media Resource Control Protocol (MRCP) real-time transport protocol are described briefly because they require a complete stand-alone discussion should one need to cover all the real-time media transport protocols in detail. In addition, the Session Description Protocol (SDP) that is used in media negotiations is also explained quite comprehensively, if not in full detail. We explain the specification of RTP byte order, alignment and time format, header field, media payload type, multiplexing sessions, and media stream translators and mixers. The header format and specification of the RTCP that is a companion protocol of RTP for monitoring the quality of service (QOS) of RTP media streams are also provided. The SDP specification along with media descriptions; content-agnostic attribute descriptions that are opaque to applications; content attributes that are understandable to applications; bandwidth modifier and utilization; and interactions with RTSP, SIP, and Session Announcement Protocol (SAP) are explained. The SDP attributes for supporting Binary Floor Control Protocol (BFCP) are also specified in great detail. Finally, the security aspects of media negotiations in SDP are briefly explained although more on media security can be seen in Section 19.2.3.

7.2 Real-Time Transmission and Control Protocol

7.2.1 Overview

The RTP specified in Request for Comment (RFC) 3550 provides end-to-end network transport functions, such as sequence number, time stamp, synchronization and content source identification, and loss identification suitable for applications transmitting real-time data, such as audio, video, or simulation data that have strict real-time performance requirements including media stream synchronization, over multicast or unicast network services. A companion protocol known as RTCP, described in the next section, is also defined in RFC 3550 to augment the RTP to allow monitoring of the quality of data delivery in a manner scalable especially for large multicast networks, and to provide minimal control and identification functionality because RTP does not address resource reservation and does not guarantee QOS for real-time services.

Both RTP and RTCP are designed to be independent of the underlying transport and network layers. RTP is a transport protocol that usually runs over the UDP as the real-time applications like audio and video are quite suitable for error corrections via retransmissions. Moreover, multicasting of any applications is done using UDP. However, RTCP can be run over the reliable Transmission Control Protocol (TCP) protocol. The protocol supports the use of RTP-level translators and mixers of multimedia streams, which are also the essential requirements for multipoint real-time multimedia streams. RFC 3550 has been further enhanced by RFCs 5506, 5761, 6051, and 7022 for optimized operations of RTP and RTCP.

7.2.2 RTP Specification

7.2.2.1 RTP Header Description

- **RTP payload:** The data transported by RTP in a packet, for example, audio samples or compressed video data. The payload format and interpretation are beyond the scope of this document.
- **RTP packet:** A data packet consisting of the fixed RTP header, a possibly empty list of contributing sources, and the payload data. Some underlying protocols may require an encapsulation of the RTP packet to be defined. Typically one packet of the underlying protocol contains a single RTP packet, but several RTP packets may be contained if permitted by the encapsulation method.
- **RTCP packet:** A control packet consisting of a fixed header part similar to that of RTP data packets, followed by structured elements that vary depending on the RTCP packet type. Typically, multiple RTCP packets are sent together as a compound RTCP packet in a single packet of the underlying protocol; this is enabled by the length field in the fixed header of each RTCP packet.
- **Port:** The abstraction that transport protocols use to distinguish among multiple destinations within a given host computer. TCP/IP protocols identify ports using small positive integers. The transport selectors (TSEL) used by the Open Standard International transport layer are equivalent to ports. RTP depends on the lower-layer protocol to provide some mechanism such as ports to multiplex the RTP and RTCP packets of a session.
- **Transport address:** The combination of a network address and port that identifies a transport-level end point, for example, an IP address and a UDP port. Packets are transmitted from a source transport address to a destination transport address.
- **RTP media type:** An RTP media type is the collection of payload types that can be carried within a single RTP session. The RTP profile assigns RTP media types to RTP payload types.
- **Multimedia session:** A set of concurrent RTP sessions among a common group of participants. For example, a video conference (which is a multimedia session) may contain an audio RTP session and a video RTP session.
- **RTP session:** An association among a set of participants communicating with RTP. A participant may be involved in multiple RTP sessions at the same time. In a multimedia session, each medium is typically carried in a separate RTP session with its own RTCP packets unless the encoding itself multiplexes multiple media into a single data stream. A participant distinguishes multiple RTP sessions by reception of different sessions using different pairs of destination transport addresses, where a pair of transport addresses comprises one network address plus a pair of ports for RTP and RTCP.
- **Synchronization source (SSRC):** The source of a stream of RTP packets, identified by a 32-bit numeric SSRC identifier carried in the RTP header so as not to be dependent on the network address. All packets from a synchronization source form part of the same timing and sequence number space, so a receiver groups packets by synchronization source for playback. Examples of synchronization sources include the sender of a stream of packets derived from a signal source such as a microphone or a camera, or an RTP mixer. A synchronization source may change its data format, for example, audio encoding, over time. The SSRC identifier is a randomly chosen value meant to be globally unique within a particular RTP session. A participant need not use the same SSRC identifier for all the RTP

sessions in a multimedia session; the binding of the SSRC identifiers is provided through RTCP. If a participant generates multiple streams in one RTP session, for example, from separate video cameras, each must be identified as a different SSRC.

- **Contributing source (CSRC):** A source of a stream of RTP packets that has contributed to the combined stream produced by an RTP mixer. The mixer inserts a list of the SSRC identifiers of the sources that contributed to the generation of a particular packet into the RTP header of that packet. This list is called the CSRC list. An example application is audio conferencing where a mixer indicates all the talkers whose speech was combined to produce the outgoing packet, allowing the receiver to indicate the current talker, even though all the audio packets contain the same SSRC identifier (that of the mixer).
- **End system:** An application that generates the content to be sent in RTP packets or consumes the content of received RTP packets. An end system can act as one or more synchronization sources in a particular RTP session, but typically only one.
- **Mixer:** An intermediate system that receives RTP packets from one or more sources, possibly changes the data format, combines the packets in some manner, and then forwards a new RTP packet. Since the timing among multiple input sources will not generally be synchronized, the mixer will make timing adjustments among the streams and generate its own timing for the combined stream. Thus, all data packets originating from a mixer will be identified as having the mixer as their synchronization source.
- **Translator:** An intermediate system that forwards RTP packets with their synchronization source identifier intact. Examples of translators include devices that convert encodings without mixing, replicators from multicast to unicast, and application-level filters in firewalls.
- **Monitor:** An application that receives RTCP packets sent by participants in an RTP session, in particular the reception reports, and estimates the current QOS for distribution monitoring, fault diagnosis, and long-term statistics. The monitor function is likely to be built into the application(s) participating in the session, but may also be a separate application that does not otherwise participate and does not send or receive the RTP data packets (since they are on a separate port). These are called third-party monitors. It is also acceptable for a third-party monitor to receive the RTP data packets but not send RTCP packets or otherwise be counted in the session.
- **Non-RTP means:** Protocols and mechanisms that may be needed in addition to RTP to provide a usable service. In particular, for multimedia conferences, a control protocol may distribute multicast addresses and keys for encryption, negotiate the encryption algorithm to be used, and define dynamic mappings between RTP payload type values and the payload formats they represent for formats that do not have a predefined payload type value. Examples of such protocols include the SIP (RFC 3261), ITU Recommendation H.323, and applications using SDP (RFC 4566, see Section 7.7), such as RTSP (RFC 2326 to be obsoleted by the International Engineering Task Force [IETF] draft if approved: draft-ietf-mmusic-rfc2326bis-40, October 2014). For simple applications, electronic mail or a conference database may also be used. The specification of such protocols and mechanisms is beyond the scope of this document.

7.2.2.2 Byte Order, Alignment, and Time Format

All integer fields are carried in network byte order, that is, the most significant byte (octet) first. This byte order is commonly known as big endian. Unless otherwise noted, numeric constants are in decimal (base 10). All header data is aligned to its natural length, that is, 16-bit fields are aligned on even offsets, 32-bit fields are aligned at offsets divisible by four, and others. Octets designated as padding have the value zero. Wall clock time (absolute date and time) is represented using the time-stamp format of the Network Time Protocol (NTP), which is in seconds relative to 0h UTC on January 1, 1900 (RFC 1350).

7.2.2.3 RTP Fixed Header Fields

The RTP packet header format is shown in Figure 7.1. The first 12 octets are present in every RTP packet, while the list of CSRC identifiers is present only when inserted by a mixer. The fields have the following meaning:

- **Version (V):** 2 bits. This field identifies the version of RTP. The version defined by this specification is two (2). (The value 1 is used by the first draft version of RTP, and the value 0 is used by the protocol initially implemented in the vat audio tool.)
- **Padding (P):** 1 bit. If the padding bit is set, the packet contains one or more additional padding octets at the end that are not part of the payload. The last octet of the padding contains a count of how many padding octets should be ignored, including itself. Padding may be needed by some encryption algorithms with fixed block sizes or for carrying several RTP packets in a lower-layer protocol data unit.

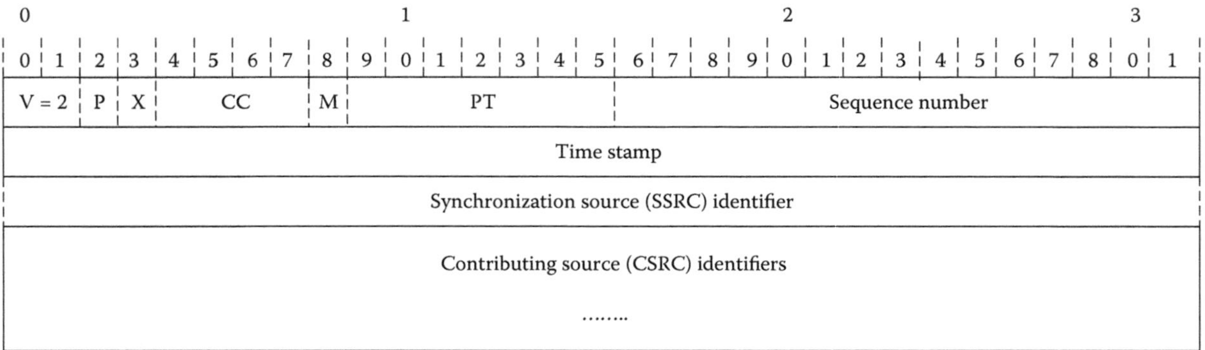

Figure 7.1 RTP packet header. (Copyright IETF. Reproduced with permission.)

- **Extension (X):** 1 bit. If the extension bit is set, the fixed header must be followed by exactly one header extension.
- **CSRC count (CC):** 4 bits. The CSRC count contains the number of CSRC identifiers that follow the fixed header.
- **Marker (M):** 1 bit. The interpretation of the marker is defined by a profile. It is intended to allow significant events such as frame boundaries to be marked in the packet stream. A profile may define additional marker bits or specify that there is no marker bit by changing the number of bits in the payload type field.
- **Payload type (PT):** 7 bits. This field identifies the format of the RTP payload and determines its interpretation by the application. A profile may specify a default static mapping of payload type codes to payload formats. Additional payload type codes may be defined dynamically through non-RTP means. A set of default mappings for audio and video is specified in the companion RFC 3551. An RTP source may change the payload type during a session, but this field should not be used for multiplexing separate media streams. A receiver must ignore packets with payload types that it does not understand.
- **Sequence number:** 16 bits. The sequence number increments by one for each RTP data packet sent, and may be used by the receiver to detect packet loss and to restore packet sequence. The initial value of the sequence number should be random (unpredictable) to make known-plaintext attacks on encryption more difficult. Techniques for choosing unpredictable numbers are discussed in RFC 4086.
- **Time stamp:** 32 bits. The time stamp reflects the sampling instant of the first octet in the RTP data packet. The sampling instant must be derived from a clock that increments monotonically and linearly in time to allow synchronization and jitter calculations. The resolution of the clock must be sufficient for the desired synchronization accuracy and for measuring packet arrival jitter (one tick per video frame is typically not sufficient).

7.2.2.4 Media Payload Type

The media payload type (PT) for different audio (A), video (V), and audio-video (AV) combined encodings are shown in Tables 7.1 and 7.2, as standardized by RFC 3551.

7.2.2.5 Multiplexing RTP Sessions

In RTP, multiplexing is provided by the destination transport address (network address and port number), which is different for each RTP session. For example, in a teleconference composed of audio and video media encoded separately, each medium should be carried in a separate RTP session with its own destination transport address. Separate audio and video streams should not be carried in a single RTP session and demultiplexed based on the payload type or SSRC fields. Using a different SSRC for each medium for multiplexing but sending them in the same RTP session would avoid several problems: interleaving media streams changing encodings, timing and sequence number space, and RTCP sender and receiver reports describing timing and sequence number. Note that RTP mixer may not be able to combine interleaved streams of incompatible media into one stream. Carrying multiple media in one RTP session over the network will force all streams to follow the same path.

7.2.2.6 RTP Translators and Mixers

RFC 3530 specifies some aspects of RTP translators and mixers at the RTP level. Although this support adds some complexity to the protocol, the need for these functions has been clearly established by experiments with multicast audio and video applications in the IP network. The details are beyond the scope of this section.

Table 7.1 Payload Types (PT) for Audio Encodings

PT	*Encoding Name*	*Media Type*	*Clock Rate (Hz)*	*Channels*	*PT*	*Encoding Name*	*Media Type*	*Clock Rate (Hz)*	*Channels*
0	PMCU	A	8000	1	17	DV14	A	22,050	1
1	Reserved	A		1	18	G729	A	8000	1
2	Reserved	A		1	19	Reserved	A		
3	GSM	A	8000	1	20	Unassigned	A		
4	G723	A	8000	1	21	Unassigned	A		
5	DV14	A	8000	1	22	Unassigned	A		
6	DV14	A	16,000	1	23	Unassigned	A		
7	LPC	A	8000	1	Dynamic	G726-40	A	8000	1
8	PCMA	A	8000	1	Dynamic	G726-32	A	8000	1
9	G722	A	8000	1	Dynamic	G726-12	A	8000	1
10	L16	A	44,100	2	Dynamic	G726-16	A	8000	1
11	L16	A	44,100	1	Dynamic	G729D	A	8000	1
12	QCELP	A	8000	1	Dynamic	G729E	A	8000	1
13	CN	A	8000	1	Dynamic	GSM-EFR	A	8000	1
14	MPA	A	90,000		Dynamic	L8	A	Variable	Variable
15	G728	A	8000	1	Dynamic	RED	A		
16	D14	A	11,025	1	Dynamic	VDVI	A	Variable	1

Source: Copyright IETF. Reproduced with permission.

7.2.3 RTCP Specification

The RTP control protocol is based on the periodic transmission of control packets to all participants in the session, using the same distribution mechanism as the data packets. The underlying protocol must provide multiplexing of the data and control packets, for example, using separate port numbers with UDP. RTCP performs four functions: providing feedback on the quality of the data distribution, keeping track of each participant using canonical name (CNAME), sending RTCP control packets so that each party can independently observe the number of participants, and providing session information including participant identification conveyed with minimal session control information.

7.2.3.1 RTCP Packet Format

This specification defines several RTCP packet types to carry a variety of control information:

- **SR:** sender report, for transmission and reception statistics from participants that are active senders
- **RR:** receiver report, for reception statistics from participants that are not active senders and in combination with SR for active senders reporting on more than 31 sources
- **SDES:** source description items, including CNAME
- **BYE:** indicates end of participation
- **APP:** application-specific functions

An example of RTCP compound packets is shown in Figure 7.2. However, all RTCP packets must be sent in a compound packet of at least two individual packets, with the following format:

- **Encryption prefix:** If and only if the compound packet is to be encrypted according to the method in RFC 3550, it must be prefixed by a random 32-bit quantity redrawn for every compound packet transmitted. If padding is required for the encryption, it must be added to the last packet of the compound packet.
- **SR or RR:** The first RTCP packet in the compound packet must always be a report packet to facilitate

Table 7.2 Payload Types (PT) for Video and Combined Encodings

PT	*Encoding Name*	*Media Type*	*Clock Rate (Hz)*
24	Unsigned	V	
25	CelB	V	90,000
26	JPEG	V	90,000
27	Unassigned	V	
28	nv	V	90,000
29	Unassigned	V	
30	Unassigned	V	
31	H261		90,000
32	MPV		90,000
33	MP2T	AV	90,000
34	H263	V	90,000
35–71	Unassigned		
72–76	Reserved	N/A	N/A
77–95	Unassigned	?	
96–127	Dynamic	?	
Dynamic	H263-1998	V	90,000

Source: Copyright IETF. Reproduced with permission.

header validation as described in RFC 3550. This is true even if no data has been sent or received, in which case an empty RR must be sent, and even if the only other RTCP packet in the compound packet is a BYE.

- **Additional RRs:** If the number of sources for which reception statistics are being reported exceeds 31, the number that will fit into one SR or RR packet, then additional RR packets should follow the initial report packet.
- **SDES:** An SDES packet containing a CNAME item must be included in each compound RTCP packet, however, there can be some exceptions as well. For example, SDES information might be encrypted while reception reports were sent in the clear to accommodate third-party monitors that are not privy to the encryption key. In those cases, the SDES information must be appended to an RR packet with no reports (and the random number) to satisfy the requirement that all compound RTCP packets begin with an SR or RR packet. The SDES CNAME item is required in either the encrypted or unencrypted packet, but not both. The same SDES information should not be carried in both packets as this may compromise the encryption. Other source description items may optionally be included if required by a particular application, subject to bandwidth constraints specified in RFC 3550.
- **BYE or APP:** Other RTCP packet types, including those yet to be defined, may follow in any order, except that BYE should be the last packet sent with a given SSRC/CSRC. Packet types may appear more than once.

7.2.3.2 Additional RTCP Functionalities

RFC 3530 specifies many other functionalities such as RTCP packet transmission interval along with maintaining the number of session members and RTCP packet send-and-receive rules. However, the packet send-and-receive rules have further been detailed, as follows: computing the RTCP transmission interval, initialization, receiving an RTP or non-BYE RTCP packet, receiving an RTCP BYE packet, timing out an SSRC, expiration of transmission timer, transmitting a BYE packet, updating we-sent, and allocation of source description bandwidth. More important, as RTCP is usually sent as a compound packet, the RTCP packet start with sender report (SR) or receiver report (RR), if necessary, then additional packets are sent. Moreover, RTCP reports such as extending the sender and receiver reports and analyzing sender and receiver reports are also specified. The BYE packet is used to leave a session. The APP packet is an application-specific packet that is used in RTCP extensions. With respect to RTP translators and mixers including cascaded

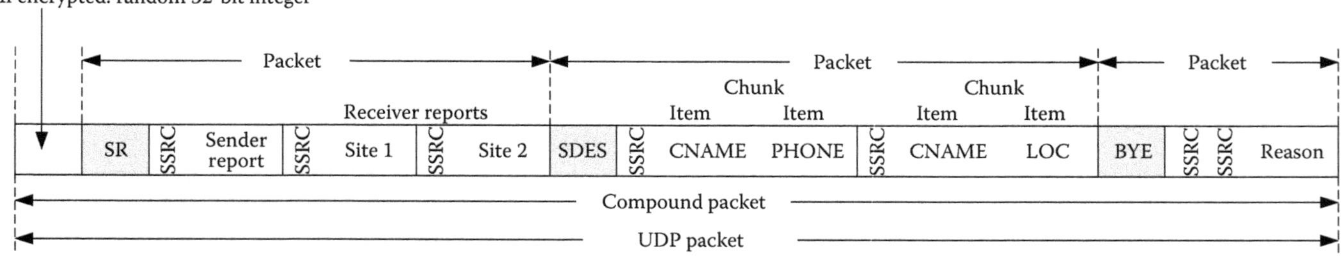

Figure 7.2 Example of an RTCP compound packet. (Copyright IETF. Reproduced with permission.)

ones, RTCP also has features describing the detailed operation and maintenance aspects of media translation and mixing properties.

7.3 Secure RTP (SRTP)

RFC 3371 specifies the Secure Real-Time Transport Protocol (SRTP) extending RTP to provide confidentiality of the RTP payload while leaving the RTP header in the clear so that link-level header compression algorithms can still operate. Figure 7.3 shows the SRTP packet format that extends the RTP for providing security.

Note that SRTP extends the RTP with only two parameters:

- **Master key identifier (MKI):** MKI is an optional parameter and its length is configurable. The MKI is defined, signaled, and used by key management. The MKI identifies the master key from which the session keys were derived that authenticate or encrypt the particular packet. Note that the MKI shall not identify the SRTP cryptographic context. The MKI may be used by key management for the purposes of rekeying, identifying a particular master key within the cryptographic context.
- **Authentication tag:** This parameter is recommended and its length is configurable. The authentication tag is used to carry message authentication data. The authenticated portion of an SRTP packet consists of the RTP header followed by the encrypted portion of the SRTP packet. Thus, if both encryption and authentication are applied, encryption shall be applied before authentication on the sender side and conversely on the receiver side. The authentication tag provides authentication of the RTP header and payload, and it indirectly provides replay protection by authenticating the sequence number. Note that the MKI is not integrity protected, as this does not provide any extra protection.

One or more SRTP crypto attributes, known as SDP security description (SDES), specified in RFC 4568 (see Sections 7.7.3 and 7.7.4), that are later used for media encryption are negotiated at the SIP session level using SDP offer–answer model. SDES is not an authenticated key mechanism as clear texts are used and communicated for the security parameters and the keys. A crypto parameter should not be specified at the session level unless SIP signaling is protected or encrypted by other means. SRTP is based on the Advanced Encryption Standard (AES) and provides stronger security. The new secure RTP for audio-video transport profile, designated as RTP/SAVP, offers confidentiality, integrity protection, data origin authentication in case of point-to-point communications, and replay protection to the RTP and RTCP media stream. In cryptographic context that are associated with the one RTP and RTCP stream, SRTP allows to negotiate the security parameters using a number of key management protocols such as multimedia key exchange (MIKEY) and others, and provides the end points with a pair of shared secret known as master key and master salt. This

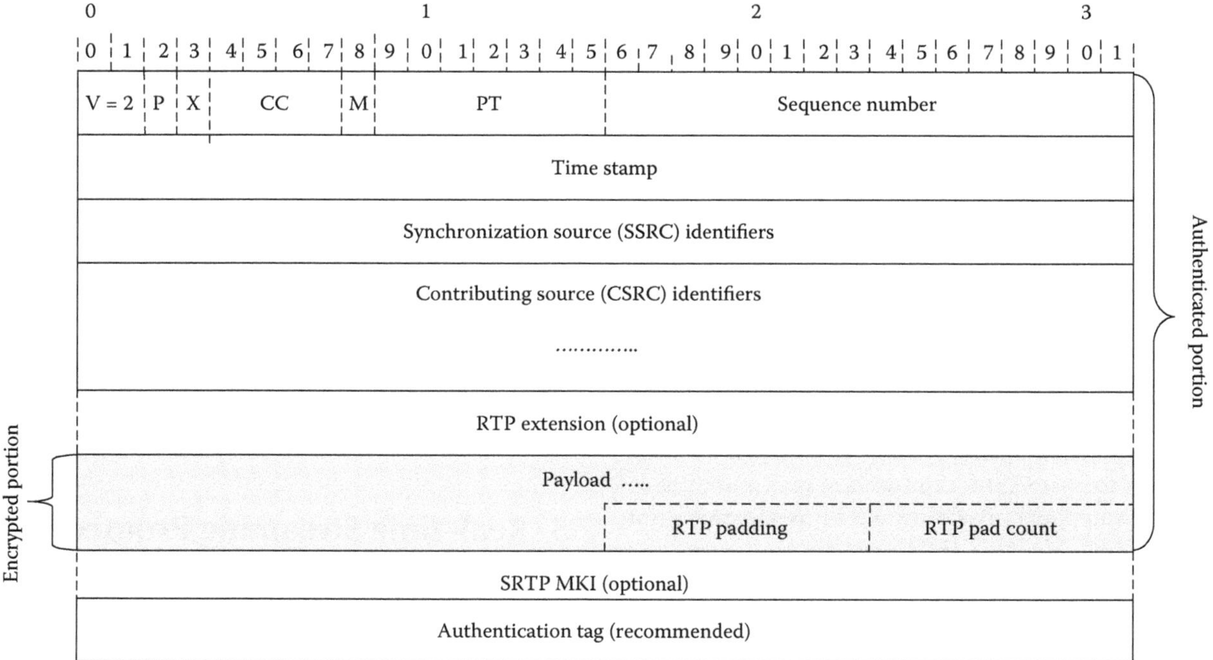

Figure 7.3 SRTP packet format. (Copyright IETF. Reproduced with permission.)

pair shared secret is then used as input into a key derivation mechanism to generate the session key for the SRTP cryptographic contexts. In addition, SRTP defines modification of the RTP payload that enables datagram enable datagrams containing encrypted media and media authentication code (MAC) field, and this is then transported between SRTP end points.

RFC 5669 standardizes the use of the SEED (RFC 4269) block cipher algorithm in the SRTP for providing confidentiality for RTP traffic and for the control traffic that is sent by RTCP. SEED is a symmetric encryption algorithm. The input/output block size of SEED is 128-bit, and the key length is also 128-bit. SEED has the 16-round Feistel structure. A 128-bit input is divided into two 64-bit blocks, and the right 64-bit block is an input to the round function with a 64-bit subkey generated from the key scheduling. It is easily implemented in various software and hardware because it is designed to increase the efficiency of memory storage and the simplicity of generating keys without degrading the security of the algorithm. In addition, the Datagram Transport Layer Security (DTLS) extension to establish keys for the SRTP and the Secure RTCP (SRTCP) flows is specified in RFC 5764. DTLS keying happens on the media path, independent of any out-of-band signaling channel present. RFC 6188 specifies the use of AES-192 and AES-256 for SRTP and SRTCP for much stronger security. The protocol architecture of the RTP and the associated RTCP is very flexible for a wide variety of scenarios with different security needs of multimedia applications where a single security mechanism will be applicable as explained in RFC 7203. As a result, it is recommended that the RTP/RTCP shall not be mandated for use as a single security mechanism.

7.4 ZRTP

The complexity of obtaining session keys/certificates by end points in SRTP using a central authority such as trusted their party or public key infrastructure are paramount. Moreover, SRTP is vulnerable to the man-in-the-middle attack. ZRTP specified in RFC 6189 is designed to obtain key exchanges without trusted third parties or certificate infrastructure while providing protection against man-in-the-middle attacks. The caller and callee can simply verify that there is no man-in-the-middle attacker by displaying a short authentication string (SAS) for the users to read and verbally compare over the phone. Basically, ZRTP is a protocol for media path Diffie–Hellman (DH) exchange to agree on a session key and parameters for establishing unicast SRTP sessions for real-time multimedia applications. The ZRTP is media path keying because it is multiplexed on the same port as RTP and does not require support in the signaling protocol. For the media session, ZRTP provides confidentiality, protection against man-in-the-middle attacks, and, in cases where the signaling protocol provides end-to-end integrity protection, authentication. ZRTP can utilize a SDP crypto attribute specified in RFC 4568 (see Sections 7.7.3 and 7.7.4) to provide discovery and authentication through the signaling channel.

ZRTP has Perfect Forward Secrecy, meaning the keys are destroyed at the end of the call, which precludes retroactively compromising the call by future disclosures of key material. However, even if the users are too lazy to bother with short authentication strings, we still get reasonable authentication against a man-in-the-middle attack, based on a form of key continuity. It does this by caching some key material to use in the next call, to be mixed in with the next call's DH shared secret, giving it key continuity properties. To provide best-effort SRTP, ZRTP utilizes normal RTP/AVP (audio-visual profile) profiles. ZRTP secures media sessions that include a voice media stream and can also secure media sessions that do not include voice by using an optional digital signature. In addition, ZRTP does not rely on SIP signaling for the key management, and in fact, it does not rely on any servers at all.

It performs its key agreements and key management in a purely peer-to-peer manner over the RTP packet stream. ZRTP can be used and discovered without being declared or indicated in the signaling path. This provides a best-effort SRTP capability. Also, this reduces the complexity of implementations and minimizes interdependency between the signaling and media layers. However, when ZRTP is indicated in the signaling via the zrtp-hash SDP attribute, ZRTP has additional useful properties. By sending a hash of the ZRTP Hello message in the signaling, ZRTP provides a useful binding between the signaling and media paths. When this is done through a signaling path that has end-to-end integrity protection, the DH exchange is automatically protected from a man-in-the-middle attack. ZRTP is designed for unicast media sessions in which there is a voice media stream. For multiparty secure conferencing, separate ZRTP sessions may be negotiated between each party and the conference bridge. For sessions lacking a voice media stream, man-in-the-middle protection may be provided by the mechanisms signing the SAS or integrity-protected signaling as described in RFC 6189. The detailed description of all capabilities of ZRTP is beyond the scope of this section.

7.5 Real-Time Streaming Protocol (RTSP)

Near-real-time (near-RT) media streaming like audio and video is usually a one-way distribution from a streaming server to multiple users. The near-RT streaming between the server and the users may persist for a long time until the viewer stops receiving the stream as if there is a connection between the server and each of these receivers persists although it does not have to be so in practice. As a result, a near-RT streaming is considered as stateful. Moreover, a near-RT streaming protocol may need to enable seeking random points in the media (e.g., audio or video) file, and adaptive streaming where multiple encoded files could be distributed to the receiver. From the commercial implementation point of view, the streaming server may need to stream out the flow of near-RT media flow to the receiver on a just time basis.

The Real-Time Streaming Protocol (RTSP), an application-level protocol, is being developed for control over the delivery of data with real-time properties of the near-RT media stream. RTSP (RFC 2326) provides an extensible framework to enable controlled, on-demand delivery of real-time data, such as audio and video. Sources of data can include both live data feeds and stored clips. This protocol is intended to control multiple data delivery sessions; provide a means for choosing delivery channels such as UDP, multicast UDP, and TCP; and to provide a means for choosing delivery mechanisms based on RTP (RFC 3550).

RTSP, as specified in RFC 2326, establishes and controls either a single or several time-synchronized streams of continuous media such as audio and video. It does not typically deliver the continuous streams itself per se, although interleaving of the continuous media stream with the control stream is possible. In other words, RTSP acts as a *network remote control* for multimedia servers. The set of streams to be controlled is defined by a presentation description. This memorandum does not define a format for a presentation description. There is no notion of an RTSP connection; instead, a server maintains a session labeled by an identifier. An RTSP session is in no way tied to a transport-level connection such as a TCP connection. During an RTSP session, an RTSP client may open and close many reliable transport connections to the server to issue RTSP requests. Alternatively, it may use a connectionless transport protocol such as UDP.

The streams controlled by RTSP may use RTP (RFC 3550), but the operation of RTSP does not depend on the transport mechanism used to carry continuous media. The protocol is intentionally similar in syntax and operation to HTTP/1.1 (RFCs 7230–7235) so that extension mechanisms to HTTP can, in most cases, also be added to RTSP. However, RTSP differs in a number of important aspects from HTTP:

- RTSP introduces a number of new methods and has a different protocol identifier.
- An RTSP server needs to maintain state by default in almost all cases, as opposed to the stateless nature of HTTP.
- Both an RTSP server and client can issue requests.
- Data is carried out-of-band by a different protocol. (There is an exception to this.)
- RTSP is defined to use ISO 10646 (UTF-8) rather than ISO 8859-1, consistent with current HTML internationalization efforts (RFC 2854).
- The Request-Uniform Resource Identifier (Request-URI) always contains the absolute URI. Because of backward compatibility with a historical blunder, HTTP/1.1 (RFs 7230–7235) carries only the absolute path in the request and puts the host name in a separate header field. This makes *virtual hosting* easier, where a single host with one IP address hosts several document trees.

The protocol supports the following operations:

- Retrieval of media from media server: The client can request a presentation description via HTTP or some other method. If the presentation is being multicast, the presentation description contains the multicast addresses and ports to be used for the continuous media. If the presentation is to be sent only to the client via unicast, the client provides the destination for security reasons.
- Invitation of a media server to a conference: A media server can be invited to join an existing conference, either to play back media into the presentation or to record all or a subset of the media in a presentation. This mode is useful for distributed teaching applications. Several parties in the conference may take turns pushing the remote control buttons.

Addition of media to an existing presentation:

- Particularly for live presentations, it is useful for the media server to indicate for adding of media, if the server can tell the client about additional media becoming available.
- RTSP requests that establish and control streams for continuous media may be handled by proxies, tunnels, and caches as in HTTP/1.1 (RFCs 7230–7235).

Table 7.3 describes the RSTP methods, their direction, objects on which they operate on, their requirement, and brief description of methods (RFC 2326).

In summary, the RTSP provides videocassette recorder (VCR)-like control operations, allows to choose delivery channels (e.g., UDP, TCP), supports the description of any session, and establishes and controls stream of continuous near-RT streaming media (e.g., audio stream, video stream) like retrieval of the requested media and adding media to an existing session. More important, the operation of RTSP is very HTTP friendly. The detailed description of RTSP is beyond the scope of this section.

Table 7.3 RSTP Methods, Their Direction, and Which Objects (P: Presentation, S: Stream) They Operate On

RTSP Method	*Direction*	*Object*	*Description*	*Requirement*
DESCRIBE	C->S	P,S	Get low-level description of media object	Recommended
ANNOUNCE	C->S, S->C	P,S	Change description of media object	Optional
GET_PARAMETER	C->S, S->C	P,S	Getting device or encoding control parameters	Optional
OPTIONS	C->S, S->C	P,S	Get available methods	Required (S->C: Optional)
PAUSE	C->S	P,S	Temporarily halts a stream	Recommended
PLAY	C->S	P,S	Starts data transmission on a stream	Recommended
RECORD	C->S	P,S	Server starts recording a stream	Optional
REDIRECT	S->C	P,S	Redirect client to new server	Optional
SETUP	C->S	S	Server allocates resources for a stream and starts an RTSP	Required
SET_PARAMETER	C->S, S->C	P,S	Setting device or encoding control parameters	Optional
TEARDOWN	C->S	P,S	Free resources of the stream, no RTSP session on server anymore	Required

Source: Copyright IETF. Reproduced with permission.

Note: PAUSE is recommended, but not required, in that a fully functional server can be built that does not support this method, for example, for live feeds. If a server does not support a particular method, it MUST return 501 Not Implemented and a client should not try this method again for this server.

7.6 Media Resource Control Protocol (MRCP)

The MRCP version 2 (MRCPv2) specified in RFC 6787 allows client hosts to control media service resources like speech synthesizers such as Text-to-Speech (TTS), recognizers such as Automatic-Speech-Recognition (ASR), fax, signal detection, verifiers, and identifiers residing in servers on the network. MRCP is built on the assumption that other protocols like SIP coordinate MRCP clients and servers and manage sessions between them, and the SDP describes, discovers, and exchanges capabilities as it itself is not a standalone protocol for providing all the infrastructures other than the above value-added features and functionalities. In addition, MRCP needs SIP and SDP to establish the media sessions and associated parameters between the media source or sink and the media server. Once this is done, the MRCP exchange operates over the control session established above, allowing the client to control the media-processing resources in the speech resource server. MRCP is, as it can be seen from the protocol architecture itself, inherently a client–server protocol as opposed to peer-to-peer (P2P) protocol. Client applications communicate requests for media resources to MRCP servers, which provide resources using MRCP signaling and commands. The MRCP servers respond and supply the media services requested.

MRCP enables the implementation of distributed interactive voice response platforms using VoiceXML browsers or other client applications, while maintaining separate back-end speech-processing capabilities on specialized speech-processing servers. The protocol requirements of Speech Services Control (SPEECHSC) (RFC 4313) include that the solution be capable of reaching a media-processing server, setting up communication channels to the media resources, and sending and receiving control messages and media streams to/from the server using SIP. In addition, the MRCP client can use a SIP re-INVITE method (an INVITE dialog sent within an existing SIP session) to change the characteristics of these media and control sessions while maintaining the SIP dialog between the client and server. As described, SDP is used to describe the parameters of the media sessions associated with that dialog. It is mandatory to support SIP as the session establishment protocol to ensure interoperability.

It is clearly seen that MRCP uses SIP and SDP to create the speech client–server dialog and set up the media channels to the server. It also uses SIP and SDP to establish MRCP control sessions between the client and the server for each media-processing resource required for that dialog. The MRCP commands are executed asynchronously, and the exchanges between the client and the media resource are carried on that control session. MRCP exchanges do not change the state of the SIP dialog, media sessions, or other parameters of the dialog initiated via SIP. It controls and affects the state of the media-processing resource associated with the MRCP session(s).

MRCP defines the messages to control the different media-processing resources and the state machines required to guide their operation. It also describes how these messages are carried over a transport layer protocol such as the TCP (RFC 0793) or the Transport Layer Security Protocol (RFC 5246). MRCP facilitates to build the client library commands for supporting automatic speech recognition, text-to-speech, verification, authentication, and recorder functions providing interoperability. The details of the MRCP and their implementations for providing value-added services are beyond the scope of this section.

7.7 Session Description Protocol (SDP)

7.7.1 Overview

The SDP is used for media negotiations in SIP. The original SDP was designed to be used to describe the session of the multicast session where media negotiations are not possible. In the course of time, SDP capabilities are modified and enhanced to be used for media negotiations for point-to-point and even to some extent for real-time networked multipoint multimedia conferencing. For example, RFC 3264 (see Section 3.8.4) provides the detailed description of how SDP can be used for media negotiations using the offer–answer model. However, SDP needs the help of a transport protocol like SIP as a part of its message body to be carried between the end points as it lacks capabilities to be transported all by itself as other protocols do. In this respect, SDP rather provides the syntax of media that is text encoding to be used in the session as opposed to be a protocol.

7.7.2 SDP Specification

RFC 4566 provides the core SDP specifications enhancing the previous versions, although many other RFCs have recently extended the capabilities of RFC 4566. We will briefly summarize SDP capabilities mainly centering on RFC 4566 in describing SDP. An SDP session description is denoted by the media type *application/sdp*, and the session description is entirely textual using the ISO 10646 character set in UTF-8 encoding. SDP field names and attribute names use only the US-ASCII subset of UTF-8, but textual fields and attribute values may use the full ISO 10646 character set. Field and attribute values that use the full UTF-8 character set are never directly compared, hence there is no requirement for UTF-8 normalization. The textual form, as opposed to a binary encoding such as ASN.1 or XDR, was chosen to enhance portability, to enable a variety of transports to be used, and to allow flexible, text-based toolkits to be used to generate and process session descriptions. However, since SDP may be used in environments where the maximum permissible size of a session description is limited, the encoding is deliberately compact. An SDP session description consists of a number of lines of text of the form:

```
<type>=<value>
```

where <type> must be exactly one case-significant character and <value> is structured text whose format depends on <type>. In general, <value> is either a number of fields delimited by a single space character or a free format string, and is case significant unless a specific field defines otherwise. White space must not be used on either side of the "=" sign.

An SDP session description consists of a session-level section followed by zero or more media-level sections. The session-level part starts with a v= line and continues to the first media-level section. Each media-level section starts with an m= line and continues to the next media-level section or end of the whole session description. In general, session-level values are the default for all media unless overridden by an equivalent media-level value. Some lines in each description are required and some are optional, but all must appear in exactly the order given here (the fixed order greatly enhances error detection and allows for a simple parser). SDP provides the media description as follows where optional items are marked as "*:"

- Session description

```
v= (protocol version)
o= (originator and session identifier)
s= (session name)
i=* (session information)
u=* (URI of description)
e=* (e-mail address)
p=* (phone number)
c=* (connection information—not required if
included in all media)
b=* (zero or more bandwidth information
lines)
```

One or more time descriptions (t= and r= lines; see below in Time Description)

```
z=* (time zone adjustments)
k=* (encryption key)
a=* (zero or more session attribute lines)
```

Zero or more media descriptions
- Time description

```
t= (time the session is active)
r=* (zero or more repeat times)
```

- Media description, if present

```
m= (media name and transport address)
i=* (media title)
c=* (connection information—optional if
included at session level)
b=* (zero or more bandwidth information
lines)
k=* (encryption key)
a=* (zero or more media attribute lines)
```

The set of type letters is deliberately small and not intended to be extensible. However, the attribute mechanism (a=, described in Section 7.7.3) is the primary means for extending SDP and tailoring it to particular applications or media. Some attributes that are already standardized and described here have a defined meaning; however, others may be added on an application-, media-, or session-specific basis. An SDP session description may contain URIs that reference external content in the u=, k=, and a= lines. These URIs may be dereferences in some cases, making the session description non-self-contained.

The connection (c=) and attribute (a=) information in the session-level section applies to all the media of that session unless overridden by connection information or an attribute of the same name in the media description. For instance, in the example below, each media behaves as if it were given a *recvonly* attribute. An example SDP description is as follows:

```
v=0
o=jdoe 2890844526 2890842807 IN IP4
10.47.16.5
s=SDP seminar
i=a seminar on the SDP
u=http://www.example.com/seminars/sdp.pdf
e=j.doe@example.com (Jane Doe)
c=IN IP4 224.2.17.12/127
t=2873397496 2873404696
a=recvonly
m=audio 49170 RTP/AVP 0
m=video 51372 RTP/AVP 99
a=rtpmap:99 h263-1998/90000
```

Text fields such as the session name and information are octet strings that may contain any octet with the exceptions of 0x00 (Nul), 0x0a (ASCII newline), and 0x0d (ASCII carriage return). The sequence CRLF (0x0d0a) is used to end a record, although parsers should be tolerant and also accept records terminated with a single newline character. If the a=charset attribute is not present, these octet strings must be interpreted as containing ISO-10646 characters in UTF-8 encoding (the presence of the a=charset attribute may force some fields to be interpreted differently).

A session description can contain domain names in the o=, u=, e=, c=, and a= lines. Any domain name used in SDP must comply with RFCs 1034 and 1035. Internationalized domain names (IDNs) must be represented using the ASCII Compatible Encoding (ACE) form defined in RFC 3490 and must not be directly represented in UTF-8 or any other encoding (this requirement is for compatibility with RFC 2327 and other SDP-related standards, which predate the development of IDNs).

7.7.3 SDP Field Description

7.7.3.1 Protocol Version

```
v=0
```

This indicates that the SDP protocol version is 0. There is no minor version number.

7.7.3.2 Origin

The v= field gives the version of the SDP.

```
o=<username> <sess-id> <sess-version>
<nettype> <addrtype>
<unicast-address>
```

The o= field gives the originator of the session (her user name and the address of the user's host) plus a session identifier and version number:

- <username> is the user's login on the originating host, or it is "-" if the originating host does not support the concept of user IDs. The <username> must not contain spaces.
- <sess-id> is a numeric string such that the tuple of <username>, <sess-id>, <nettype>, <addrtype>, and <unicast-address> forms a globally unique identifier for the session. The method of <sess-id> allocation is up to the creating tool, but it has been suggested that a NTP format time stamp be used to ensure uniqueness (RFC 1305).
- <sess-version> is a version number for this session description. Its usage is up to the creating tool, so long as <sess-version> is increased when a modification is

made to the session data. Again, it is recommended that an NTP format time stamp is used.

- <nettype> is a text string giving the type of network. Initially, IN is defined to have the meaning *Internet*; however, other values may be registered in the future.
- <addrtype> is a text string giving the type of the address that follows. Initially, *IP4* and *IP6* are defined; however, other values may be registered in the future.
- <unicast-address> is the address of the machine from which the session was created. For an address type of IP4, this is either the fully qualified domain name of the machine or the dotted decimal representation of the IP version 4 address of the machine. For an address type of IP6, this is either the fully qualified domain name of the machine or the compressed textual representation of the IP version 6 address of the machine. For both IP4 and IP6, the fully qualified domain name is the form that should be given unless this is unavailable, in which case the globally unique address may be substituted. A local IP address must not be used in any context where the SDP description might leave the scope in which the address is meaningful (e.g., a local address must not be included in an application-level referral that might leave the scope).

In general, the o= field serves as a globally unique identifier for this version of this session description, and the subfields excepting the version taken together identify the session irrespective of any modifications. For privacy reasons, it is sometimes desirable to obfuscate the user name and IP address of the session originator. If this is a concern, an arbitrary <username> and private <unicast-address> may be chosen to populate the o= field, provided that these are selected in a manner that does not affect the global uniqueness of the field.

7.7.3.3 Session Name

The s= field is the textual session name. There must be one and only one s= field per session description.

```
s=<session name>
```

The s= field must not be empty and should contain ISO 10646 characters (but see also the a=charset attribute). If a session has no meaningful name, the value s= should be used (i.e., a single space as the session name).

7.7.3.4 Session Information

The i= field provides textual information about the session. There must be at most one session-level i= field per session description, and at most one i= field per media.

```
i=<session description>
```

If the a=charset attribute is present, it specifies the character set used in the i= field. If the a=charset attribute is not present, the i= field must contain ISO 10646 characters in UTF-8 encoding.

A single i= field may also be used for each media definition. In media definitions, i= fields are primarily intended for labeling media streams. As such, they are most likely to be useful when a single session has more than one distinct media stream of the same media type. An example would be two different whiteboards, one for slides and one for feedback and questions. The i= field is intended to provide a free-form human-readable description of the session or the purpose of a media stream. It is not suitable for parsing by automata.

7.7.3.5 Uniform Resource Identifier (URI)

A URI is a Uniform Resource Identifier as used by WWW clients (RFC 3986). The URI should be a pointer to additional information about the session.

```
u=<uri>
```

This field is optional, but if it is present it must be specified before the first media field. No more than one URI field is allowed per session description.

7.7.3.6 E-mail Address and Phone Number

The e= and p= lines specify contact information for the person responsible for the conference. This is not necessarily the same person that created the conference announcement.

```
e=<email-address>
p=<phone-number>
```

Inclusion of an e-mail address or phone number is optional. Note that the previous version of SDP specified that either an e-mail field or a phone field must be specified, but this was widely ignored. The change brings the specification into line with common usage. If an e-mail address or phone number is present, it must be specified before the first media field. More than one e-mail or phone field can be given for a session description.

Phone numbers should be given in the form of an international public telecommunication number (see ITU-T Recommendation E.164) preceded by a "+." Spaces and hyphens may be used to split up a phone field to aid readability if desired. For example:

```
p=+1 617 555-6011
```

Both e-mail addresses and phone numbers can have an optional free text string associated with them, normally giving the name of the person who may be contacted. This must be enclosed in parentheses if it is present. For example:

```
e=j.doe@example.com (Jane Doe)
```

The alternative RFC 2822 name quoting convention is also allowed for both e-mail addresses and phone numbers. For example:

```
e=Jane Doe <j.doe@example.com>
```

The free text string should be in the ISO-10646 character set with UTF-8 encoding, or alternatively in ISO-8859-1 or other encodings if the appropriate session-level a=charset attribute is set.

7.7.3.7 Connection Data

The c= field contains connection data. A session description must contain either at least one c= field in each media description or a single c= field at the session level. It may contain a single-session-level c= field and additional c= field(s) per media description, in which case the per-media values override the session-level settings for the respective media.

```
c=<nettype> <addrtype> <connection-address>
```

The first subfield (<nettype>) is the network type, which is a text string giving the type of network. Initially, IN is defined to have the meaning *Internet*, but other values may be registered in the future (see Section 2.4). The second subfield (<addrtype>) is the address type. This allows SDP to be used for sessions that are not IP based. This memo only defines IP4 and IP6, but other values may be registered in the future.

The third subfield (<connection-address>) is the connection address. Optional subfields may be added after the connection address depending on the value of the <addrtype> field. When the <addrtype> is IP4 and IP6, the connection address is defined as follows:

- If the session is multicast, the connection address will be an IP multicast group address. If the session is not multicast, then the connection address contains the unicast IP address of the expected data source or data relay or data sink as determined by additional attribute fields. It is not expected that unicast addresses will be given in a session description that is communicated by a multicast announcement, though this is not prohibited.
- Sessions using an IPv4 multicast connection address must also have a time to live (TTL) value present in addition to the multicast address. The TTL and the address together define the scope with which multicast packets sent in this conference will be sent. TTL values must be in the range 0–255. Although the TTL must be specified, its use to scope multicast traffic is deprecated; applications should use an administratively scoped address instead.

The TTL for the session is appended to the address using a slash as a separator. An example is

```
c=IN IP4 224.2.36.42/127
```

IPv6 multicast does not use TTL scoping, and hence the TTL value must not be present for IPv6 multicast. It is expected that IPv6 scoped addresses will be used to limit the scope of conferences. Hierarchical or layered encoding schemes are data streams where the encoding from a single media source is split into a number of layers. The receiver can choose the desired quality (and hence bandwidth) by only subscribing to a subset of these layers. Such layered encodings are normally transmitted in multiple multicast groups to allow multicast pruning. This technique keeps unwanted traffic from sites only requiring certain levels of the hierarchy. For applications requiring multiple multicast groups, we allow the following notation to be used for the connection address:

```
<base multicast address>[/<ttl>]/<number of
addresses>
```

If the number of addresses is not given, it is assumed to be one. Multicast addresses so assigned are contiguously allocated above the base address, so that, for example:

```
c=IN IP4 224.2.1.1/127/3
```

would state that addresses 224.2.1.1, 224.2.1.2, and 224.2.1.3 are to be used at a TTL of 127. This is semantically identical to including multiple c= lines in a media description:

```
c=IN IP4 224.2.1.1/127
c=IN IP4 224.2.1.2/127
c=IN IP4 224.2.1.3/127
```

Similarly, an IPv6 example would be

```
c=IN IP6 FF15::101/3
```

which is semantically equivalent to

```
c=IN IP6 FF15::101
c=IN IP6 FF15::102
c=IN IP6 FF15::103
```

(remembering that the TTL field is not present in IPv6 multicast).

Multiple addresses or c= lines may be specified on a per-media basis only if they provide multicast addresses for different layers in a hierarchical or layered encoding scheme. They must not be specified for a session-level c= field. The slash notation for multiple addresses described above must not be used for IP unicast addresses.

7.7.3.8 Bandwidth

This optional field denotes the proposed bandwidth to be used by the session or media. The <bwtype> is an alphanumeric modifier giving the meaning of the <bandwidth> figure.

```
b=<bwtype>:<bandwidth>
```

Two values are defined in this specification, but other values may be registered in the future:

- **Conference total (CT):** If the bandwidth of a session or media in a session is different from the bandwidth implicit from the scope, a "b=CT:..." line should be supplied for the session giving the proposed upper limit to the bandwidth used (the *conference total* bandwidth). The primary purpose of this is to give an approximate idea as to whether two or more sessions can coexist simultaneously. When using the CT modifier with RTP, if several RTP sessions are part of the conference, the conference total refers to total bandwidth of all RTP sessions.
- **Application specific (AS):** The bandwidth is interpreted to be application specific (it will be the application's concept of maximum bandwidth). Normally, this will coincide with what is set on the application's *maximum bandwidth* control if applicable. For RTP-based applications, AS gives the RTP *session bandwidth* as defined in RFC 3550 (see Section 7.2).

Note that CT gives a total bandwidth figure for all the media at all sites. AS gives a bandwidth figure for a single media at a single site, although there may be many sites sending simultaneously. A prefix X- is defined for <bwtype> names. This is intended for experimental purposes only. For example:

```
b=X-YZ:128
```

Use of the X- prefix is not recommended: instead, new modifiers should be registered with the Internet Assigned Numbers Authority (IANA) in the standard namespace. SDP parsers must ignore bandwidth fields with unknown modifiers. Modifiers must be alphanumeric and, although no length limit is given, it is recommended that they be short. The <bandwidth> is interpreted as kilobits per second by default. The definition of a new <bwtype> modifier may specify that the bandwidth is to be interpreted in some alternative unit (the CT and AS modifiers defined in this memo use the default units).

7.7.3.9 Timing

The t= lines specify the start and stop times for a session. Multiple t= lines may be used if a session is active at multiple irregularly spaced times; each additional t= line specifies an additional period of time for which the session will be active.

```
t=<start-time> <stop-time>
```

If the session is active at regular times, an r= line (see below in the next section) should be used in addition to, and following, a t= line, in which case the t= line specifies the start and stop times of the repeat sequence.

The first and second subfields give the start and stop times, respectively, for the session. These values are the decimal representation of NTP time values in seconds since 1900 (RFC 1305). To convert these values to UNIX time, subtract decimal 2208988800. NTP time stamps are elsewhere represented by 64-bit values, which wrap sometime in the year 2036. Since SDP uses an arbitrary length decimal representation, this should not cause an issue (SDP time stamps must continue counting seconds since 1900, NTP will use the value modulo the 64-bit limit).

If the <stop-time> is set to zero, then the session is not bounded, though it will not become active until after the <start-time>. If the <start-time> is also zero, the session is regarded as permanent. User interfaces should strongly discourage the creation of unbounded and permanent sessions as they give no information about when the session is actually going to terminate, and so make scheduling difficult. The general assumption may be made, when displaying unbounded sessions that have not timed out to the user, that an unbounded session will only be active until half an hour from the current time or the session start time, whichever comes later. If behavior other than this is required, an end time should be given and modified as appropriate when new information becomes available about when the session should really end. Permanent sessions may be shown to the user as never being active unless there are associated repeat times that state precisely when the session will be active.

7.7.3.10 Repeat Times

r= fields specify repeat times for a session. For example, if a session is active at 10 am on Monday and 11 am on Tuesday for 1 hour each week for 3 months, then the <start-time> in the corresponding t= field would be the NTP representation of 10 am on the first Monday, the <repeat interval> would be 1 week, the <active duration> would be 1 hour, and the offsets would be 0 and 25 hours.

```
r=<repeat interval> <active duration>
<offsets from start-time>
```

The corresponding t= field stop time would be the NTP representation of the end of the last session 3 months later. By default, all fields are in seconds, so the r= and t= fields might be the following:

```
t=3034423619 3042462419
r=604800 3600 0 90000
```

To make the description more compact, times may also be given in units of days, hours, or minutes. The syntax for these is a number immediately followed by a single case-sensitive character. Fractional units are not allowed—a smaller unit should be used instead. The following unit specification characters are allowed:

```
d—days (86,400 seconds)
h—hours (3600 seconds)
m—minutes (60 seconds)
s—seconds (allowed for completeness)
```

Thus, the above session announcement could also have been written: r=7d 1h 0 25h. Monthly and yearly repeats cannot be directly specified with a single SDP repeat time; instead, separate t= fields should be used to explicitly list the session times.

7.7.3.11 Time Zones

To schedule a repeated session that spans a change from daylight saving time to standard time or vice versa, it is necessary to specify offsets from the base time.

```
z=<adjustment time> <offset> <adjustment
time> <offset>....
```

This is required because different time zones change time at different times of day, different countries change to or from daylight saving time on different dates, and some countries do not have daylight saving time at all.

Thus, in order to schedule a session that is at the same time winter and summer, it must be possible to specify unambiguously by whose time zone a session is scheduled. To simplify this task for receivers, we allow the sender to specify the NTP time that a time zone adjustment happens and the offset from the time when the session was first scheduled. The z= field allows the sender to specify a list of these adjustment times and offsets from the base time. An example might be the following:

```
z=2882844526 -1h 2898848070 0
```

This specifies that at time 2882844526, the time base by which the session's repeat times are calculated is shifted back by 1 hour, and that at time 2898848070, the session's original time base is restored. Adjustments are always relative to the specified start time—they are not cumulative. Adjustments apply to all t= and r= lines in a session description. If a session is likely to last several years, it is expected that the session announcement will be modified periodically rather than transmit several years' worth of adjustments in one session announcement.

7.7.3.12 Encryption Keys

If transported over a secure and trusted channel, the SDP may be used to convey encryption keys.

```
k=<method>
k=<method>:<encryption key>
```

A simple mechanism for key exchange is provided by the key field (k=), although this is primarily supported for compatibility with older implementations and its use is not recommended. Work is in progress to define new key exchange mechanisms for use with SDP (RFCs 4567 and 4568), and it is expected that new applications will use those mechanisms.

A key field is permitted before the first media entry (in which case it applies to all media in the session), or for each media entry as required. The format of keys and their usage are outside the scope of this document, and the key field provides no way to indicate the encryption algorithm to be used, key type, or other information about the key: this is assumed to be provided by the higher-level protocol using SDP. If there is a need to convey this information within SDP, the extensions mentioned previously should be used. Many security protocols require two keys: one for confidentiality, another for integrity. This specification does not support transfer of two keys.

The method indicates the mechanism to be used to obtain a usable key by external means, or from the encoded encryption key given. The following methods are defined:

```
k=clear:<encryption key>
```

The encryption key is included untransformed in this key field. This method must not be used unless it can be guaranteed that the SDP is conveyed over a secure channel. The encryption key is interpreted as text according to the charset attribute; use the k=base64: method to convey characters that are otherwise prohibited in SDP.

```
k=base64:<encoded encryption key>
```

The encryption key is included in this key field but has been base64 encoded (RFC 3548) because it includes characters that are prohibited in SDP. This method must not be used unless it can be guaranteed that the SDP is conveyed over a secure channel.

```
k=uri:<URI to obtain key>
```

A URI is included in the key field. The URI refers to the data containing the key, and may require additional authentication before the key can be returned. When a request is made to the given URI, the reply should specify the encoding for the key. The URI is often a Secure Socket Layer/Transport Layer Security (SSL/TLS)-protected HTTP URI (https:), although this is not required.

```
k=prompt
```

No key is included in this SDP description, but the session or media stream referred to by this key field is encrypted.

The user should be prompted for the key when attempting to join the session, and this user-supplied key should then be used to decrypt the media streams. The use of user-specified keys is not recommended, since such keys tend to have weak security properties. The key field must not be used unless it can be guaranteed that the SDP is conveyed over a secure and trusted channel. An example of such a channel might be SDP embedded inside an S/MIME message or a TLS-protected HTTP session. It is important to ensure that the secure channel is with the party that is authorized to join the session, not an intermediary: if a caching proxy server is used, it is important to ensure that the proxy is either trusted or unable to access the SDP.

7.7.4 SDP Media

7.7.4.1 Media Descriptions

A session description may contain a number of media descriptions. Each media description starts with an m= field and is terminated by either the next m= field or by the end of the session description.

```
m=<media> <port> <proto> <fmt>...
```

A media field has several subfields:

- <media> is the media type. Currently defined media are audio, video, text, application, and message, although this list may be extended in the future.
- <port> is the transport port to which the media stream is sent. The meaning of the transport port depends on the network being used as specified in the relevant c= field, and on the transport protocol defined in the <proto> subfield of the media field. Other ports used by the media application, such as the RTCP port defined in RFC 3550 (see Section 7.2), may be derived algorithmically from the base media port or may be specified in a separate attribute (e.g., a=rtcp: as defined in RFC 3605). If noncontiguous ports are used or if they do not follow the parity rule of even RTP ports and odd RTCP ports, the a=rtcp: attribute MUST be used. Applications that are requested to send media to a <port> that is odd and where the a=rtcp: is present must not subtract 1 from the RTP port: that is, they must send the RTP to the port indicated in <port> and send the RTCP to the port indicated in the a=rtcp attribute.

  For applications where hierarchically encoded streams are being sent to a unicast address, it may be necessary to specify multiple transport ports. This is done using a similar notation to that used for IP multicast addresses in the c= field:

  ```
  m=<media> <port>/<number of ports> <proto>
  <fmt>...
  ```

  In such a case, the ports used depend on the transport protocol. For RTP, the default is that only the even-numbered ports are used for data with the corresponding one-higher odd ports used for the RTCP belonging to the RTP session, and the <number of ports> denoting the number of RTP sessions.

- <proto> is the transport protocol. The meaning of the transport protocol is dependent on the address type field in the relevant c= field. Thus, a c= field of IP4 indicates that the transport protocol runs over IP4. The following transport protocols are defined (RFC 4566), but may be extended through registration of new protocols with IANA:
  - udp: denotes an unspecified protocol running over UDP
  - RTP/AVP: denotes RTP (RFC 3550, see Section 7.2) used under the RTP profile for audio and video conferences with minimal control (RFC 3551, see Section 7.2) running over UDP
  - RTP/SAVP: denotes the SRTP (RFC 3711, see Section 7.3) running over UDP

  The main reason to specify the transport protocol in addition to the media format is that the same standard media formats may be carried over different transport protocols even when the network protocol is the same—a historical example is vat Pulse Code Modulation (PCM) audio and RTP PCM audio; another might be TCP/RTP PCM audio. In addition, relays and monitoring tools that are transport protocol specific but format independent are possible.

- <fmt> is a media format description. The fourth and any subsequent subfields describe the format of the media. The interpretation of the media format depends on the value of the <proto> subfield.

  If the <proto> subfield is RTP/AVP or RTP/SAVP, the <fmt> subfields contain RTP payload type numbers. When a list of payload type numbers is given, this implies that all of these payload formats may be used in the session; however, the first of these formats should be used as the default format for the session. For dynamic payload type assignments, the a=rtpmap: attribute (see Section 7.7.4.2) should be used to map from an RTP payload type number to a media encoding name that identifies the payload format. The a=fmtp: attribute may be used to specify format parameters (see Section 7.7.4.2).

If the <proto> subfield is udp, the <fmt> subfields must reference a media type describing the format under the audio, video, text, application, or message top-level media types. The media type registration should define the packet format for use with UDP transport. For media using other transport protocols, the <fmt> field is protocol specific. Rules for interpretation of the <fmt> subfield must be defined when registering new protocols.

7.7.4.2 Standardized Media Types

The RTP used for audio and video conferencing is specified in RFC 3550 (see Section 7.2) while RFC 3711 (see Section 7.3) defines the secure RTP for audio and video conferencing. However, there can be different types of audio (or video) codecs that may transfer audio (or video) media streams that have specific payload format/types depending on which kinds of codecs are being used. RFC 3551 defines a specific payload format/type number (i.e., <fmt>) for each audio and video codec for differentiating the bit streams of all media transferred over the network, and the RTP transport protocol for audio and video is designated as RTP/AVP (i.e., <proto>). In the same token, the SRTP transport protocol for audio and video is designated as RTP/AVP (i.e., <proto>). In general, the SDP media description for audio or video can be expressed as follows depending on whether RTP or SRTP transport protocol is used:

```
m=audio<port>/<number of ports> RTP/AVP <fmt>
m=audio<port>/<number of ports> RTP/SAVP
<fmt>

m=video<port>/<number of ports> RTP/AVP <fmt>
m=video<port>/<number of ports> RTP/SAVP
<fmt>
```

Note that <port>/<number of ports> can provide dynamically or statically for each media while <fmt> is being standardized for each media in RFC 3551. The payload format/type number (<fmt>) that is not specified in RFC 3551 can be standardized with IANA in the future.

Let us consider the following example for video:

```
m=video 49170/2 RTP/AVP 31
```

would specify that ports 49170 and 49171 form one RTP/RTCP pair and 49172 and 49173 form the second RTP/RTCP pair. RTP/AVP is the transport protocol and 31 is the format. If noncontiguous ports are required, they must be signaled using a separate attribute (e.g., a=rtcp: as defined in RFC 3605). If multiple addresses are specified in the c= field and multiple ports are specified in the m= field, a one-to-one mapping from port to the corresponding address is implied. For example:

```
c=IN IP4 224.2.1.1/127/2
m=video 49170/2 RTP/AVP 31
```

would imply that address 224.2.1.1 is used with ports 49170 and 49171, and address 224.2.1.2 is used with ports 49172 and 49173. The semantics of multiple m= lines using the same transport address are undefined. This implies that, unlike limited past practice, there is no implicit grouping defined by such means and an explicit grouping framework (e.g., RFC 3388) should instead be used to express the intended semantics. Table 7.4 depicts some additional standardized SDP media types.

7.7.5 SDP Content-Agnostic Attributes

7.7.5.1 Attribute Descriptions

Attributes are the primary means for extending SDP. Attributes may be defined to be used as session-level attributes, media-level attributes, or both.

```
a=<attribute>
a=<attribute>:<value>
```

Table 7.4 SDP Media Types

Media Description	*Type*	*RFC*
m=image 50011 TCP t38	Real-Time Facsimile (T.38) over TCP transport protocol	RFC 3362
M=audio 51221 TCP t38	Real-Time Facsimile (T.38) over TCP transport protocol	RFC 4612
m=application 5000 TCP/TLS/BFCP*	Binary Floor Control Protocol (BFCP) application over TCP/TLS transport protocol	RFC 4583
m=message 7394 TCP/MSRP*	Message Session Relay Protocol (MSRP) message over TCP transport protocol	RFC 4975
m=text 11000 RTP/AVP 98	Real-Time Text (T.140) over RTP transport protocol	RFC 4103

Source: Copyright IETF. Reproduced with permission.

A media description may have any number of attributes (a= fields) that are media specific. These are referred to as media-level attributes and add information about the media stream. Attribute fields can also be added before the first media field; these session-level attributes convey additional information that applies to the conference as a whole rather than to individual media. Attribute fields may be of two forms:

- A property attribute is simply of the form a=<flag>. These are binary attributes, and the presence of the attribute conveys that the attribute is a property of the session. An example might be a=recvonly.
- A value attribute is of the form a=<attribute>:<value>. For example, a whiteboard could have the value attribute a=orient: landscape.

Attribute interpretation depends on the media tool being invoked. Thus, receivers of session descriptions should be configurable in their interpretation of session descriptions in general and of attributes in particular. Attribute names MUST use the US-ASCII subset of ISO-10646/UTF-8.

Attribute values are octet strings, and may use any octet value except 0x00 (Nul), 0x0A (LF), and 0x0D (CR). By default, attribute values are to be interpreted as in ISO-10646 character set with UTF-8 encoding. Unlike other text fields, attribute values are not normally affected by the charset attribute, as this would make comparisons against known values problematic. However, when an attribute is defined, it can be defined to be charset dependent, in which case its value should be interpreted in the session charset rather than in ISO-10646. Attributes must be registered with IANA. If an attribute is received that is not understood, it must be ignored by the receiver.

7.7.5.2 Standardized Attribute Values

The following attributes are defined in RFC 4566. Since application writers may add new attributes as they are required, this list is not exhaustive.

```
a=cat:<category>
```

This attribute gives the dot-separated hierarchical category of the session. This is to enable a receiver to filter unwanted sessions by category. There is no central registry of categories. It is a session-level attribute, and it is not dependent on charset.

```
a=keywds:<keywords>
```

Like the cat attribute, this is to assist identifying wanted sessions at the receiver. This allows a receiver to select interesting session based on keywords describing the purpose of the session; there is no central registry of keywords. It is a session-level attribute. It is a charset-dependent attribute, meaning that its value should be interpreted in the charset specified for the session description if one is specified, or by default in ISO 10646/UTF-8.

```
a=tool:<name and version of tool>
```

This gives the name and version number of the tool used to create the session description. It is a session-level attribute, and it is not dependent on charset.

```
a=ptime:<packet time>
```

This gives the length of time in milliseconds represented by the media in a packet. This is probably only meaningful for audio data, but may be used with other media types if it makes sense. It should not be necessary to know ptime to decode RTP or vat audio, and it is intended as a recommendation for the encoding/packetization of audio. It is a media-level attribute, and it is not dependent on charset.

```
a=maxptime:<maximum packet time>
```

This gives the maximum amount of media that can be encapsulated in each packet, expressed as time in milliseconds. The time shall be calculated as the sum of the time the media present in the packet represents. For frame-based codecs, the time should be an integer multiple of the frame size. This attribute is probably only meaningful for audio data, but may be used with other media types if it makes sense. It is a media-level attribute, and it is not dependent on charset. Note that this attribute was introduced after RFC 2327, and nonupdated implementations will ignore this attribute.

```
a=rtpmap:<payload type> <encoding
name>/<clock rate> [/<encoding
parameters>]
```

This attribute maps from an RTP payload type number (as used in an m= line) to an encoding name denoting the payload format to be used. It also provides information on the clock rate and encoding parameters. It is a media-level attribute that is not dependent on charset. Although an RTP profile may make static assignments of payload type numbers to payload formats, it is more common for that assignment to be done dynamically using a=rtpmap: attributes.

As an example of a static payload type, consider u-law PCM-coded single-channel audio sampled at 8 kHz. This is completely defined in the RTP audio/video profile as payload type 0, so there is no need for an a=rtpmap: attribute, and the media for such a stream sent to UDP port 49232 can be specified as

```
m=audio 49232 RTP/AVP 0
```

An example of a dynamic payload type is 16-bit linear encoded stereo audio sampled at 16 kHz. If we wish to use the dynamic RTP/AVP payload type 98 for this stream, additional information is required to decode it:

```
m=audio 49232 RTP/AVP 98
a=rtpmap:98 L16/16000/2
```

Up to one rtpmap attribute can be defined for each media format specified. Thus, we might have the following:

```
m=audio 49230 RTP/AVP 96 97 98
a=rtpmap:96 L8/8000
a=rtpmap:97 L16/8000
a=rtpmap:98 L16/11025/2
```

RTP profiles that specify the use of dynamic payload types must define the set of valid encoding names or a means to register encoding names if that profile is to be used with SDP. The RTP/AVP and RTP/SAVP profiles use media subtypes for encoding names, under the top-level media type denoted in the m= line. In the example above, the media types are audio/l8 and audio/l16.

For audio streams, <encoding parameters> indicates the number of audio channels. This parameter is optional and may be omitted if the number of channels is one, provided that no additional parameters are needed. For video streams, no encoding parameters are currently specified. Additional encoding parameters may be defined in the future, but codec-specific parameters should not be added. Parameters added to an a=rtpmap: attribute should only be those required for a session directory to make the choice of appropriate media to participate in a session. Codec-specific parameters should be added in other attributes (e.g., a=fmtp:).

Note that RTP audio formats typically do not include information about the number of samples per packet. If a nondefault (as defined in the RTP audio/video profile) packetization is required, the ptime attribute is used as given above.

```
a=recvonly
```

This specifies that the tools should be started in receive-only mode where applicable. It can be either a session- or media-level attribute, or it is not dependent on charset. Note that recvonly applies to the media only, not to any associated control protocol (e.g., an RTP-based system in recvonly mode SHOULD still send RTCP packets).

```
a=sendrecv
```

This specifies that the tools should be started in send and receive mode. This is necessary for interactive conferences with tools that default to receive-only mode. It can be either a session or media-level attribute, and it is not dependent on charset. If none of the attributes sendonly, recvonly, inactive, and sendrecv is present, sendrecv should be assumed as the default for sessions that are not of the conference type broadcast or H332 (see as shown below).

```
a=sendonly
```

This specifies that the tools should be started in send-only mode. An example may be where a different unicast address is to be used for a traffic destination than for a traffic source. In such a case, two media descriptions may be used, one sendonly and one recvonly. It can be either a session- or media-level attribute, but would normally only be used as a media attribute. It is not dependent on charset. Note that sendonly applies only to the media, and any associated control protocol (e.g., RTCP) should still be received and processed as normal.

```
a=inactive
```

This specifies that the tools should be started in inactive mode. This is necessary for interactive conferences where users can put other users on hold. No media is sent over an inactive media stream. Note that an RTP-based system should still send RTCP, even if started inactive. It can be either a session- or media-level attribute, and it is not dependent on charset.

```
a=orient:<orientation>
```

Normally this is only used for a whiteboard or presentation tool. It specifies the orientation of the workspace on the screen. It is a media-level attribute. Permitted values are portrait, landscape, and seascape (upside-down landscape). It is not dependent on charset.

```
a=type:<conference type>
```

This specifies the type of the conference. Suggested values are broadcast, meeting, moderated, test, and H332. recvonly should be the default for type:broadcast sessions, type:meeting should imply sendrecv, and type:moderated should indicate the use of a floor control tool and that the media tools are started so as to mute new sites joining the conference.

Specifying the attribute type:H332 indicates that this loosely coupled session is part of an H.332 session as defined in the ITU H.332 specification. Media tools should be started recvonly. Specifying the attribute type:test is suggested as a hint that, unless explicitly requested otherwise, receivers can safely avoid displaying this session description to users. The type attribute is a session-level attribute, and it is not dependent on charset.

```
a=charset:<character set>
```

This specifies the character set to be used to display the session name and information data. By default, the ISO-10646 character set in UTF-8 encoding is used. If a more compact representation is required, other character sets may be used. For example, the ISO 8859-1 is specified with the following SDP attribute:

```
a=charset:ISO-8859-1
```

This is a session-level attribute and is not dependent on charset. The charset specified must be one of those registered with IANA, such as ISO-8859-1. The character set identifier is a US-ASCII string and must be compared against the IANA identifiers using a case-insensitive comparison. If the identifier is not recognized or not supported, all strings that are affected by it should be regarded as octet strings.

Note that a character set specified must still prohibit the use of bytes 0x00 (Nul), 0x0A (LF), and 0x0d (CR). Character sets requiring the use of these characters must define a quoting mechanism that prevents these bytes from appearing within text fields.

```
a=sdplang:<language tag>
```

This can be a session-level attribute or a media-level attribute. As a session-level attribute, it specifies the language for the session description. As a media-level attribute, it specifies the language for any media-level SDP information field associated with that media. Multiple sdplang attributes can be provided either at session or media level if multiple languages in the session description or media use multiple languages, in which case the order of the attributes indicates the order of importance of the various languages in the session or media from most important to least important.

In general, sending session descriptions consisting of multiple languages is discouraged. Instead, multiple descriptions should be sent describing the session, one in each language. However, this is not possible with all transport mechanisms, and so multiple sdplang attributes are allowed although not recommended. The sdplang attribute value must be a single RFC 3066 language tag in US-ASCII. It is not dependent on the charset attribute. An sdplang attribute should be specified when a session is of sufficient scope to cross geographic boundaries where the language of recipients cannot be assumed, or where the session is in a different language from the locally assumed norm.

```
a=lang:<language tag>
```

This can be a session-level attribute or a media-level attribute. As a session-level attribute, it specifies the default language for the session being described. As a media-level attribute, it specifies the language for that media, overriding any session-level language specified. Multiple lang attributes can be provided either at session or media level if the session description or media use multiple languages, in which case the order of the attributes indicates the order of importance of the various languages in the session or media from most important to least important.

The lang attribute value must be a single RFC 3066 language tag in US-ASCII. It is not dependent on the charset attribute. A lang attribute should be specified when a session is of sufficient scope to cross geographic boundaries where the language of recipients cannot be assumed, or where the session is in a different language from the locally assumed norm.

```
a=framerate:<frame rate>
```

This gives the maximum video frame rate in frames per second. It is intended as a recommendation for the encoding of video data. Decimal representations of fractional values using the notation <integer>.<fraction> are allowed. It is a media-level attribute, defined only for video media, and it is not dependent on charset.

```
a=quality:<quality>
```

This gives a suggestion for the quality of the encoding as an integer value. The intention of the quality attribute for video is to specify a nondefault trade-off between frame-rate and still-image quality. For video, the value is in the range 0 to 10, with the following suggested meaning:

10—the best still-image quality the compression scheme can give
5—the default behavior given no quality suggestion
0—the worst still-image quality the codec designer thinks is still usable

It is a media-level attribute, and it is not dependent on charset.

```
a=fmtp:<format> <format specific parameters>
```

This attribute allows parameters that are specific to a particular format to be conveyed in a way that SDP does not have to understand them. The format must be one of the formats specified for the media. Format-specific parameters may be any set of parameters required to be conveyed by SDP and given unchanged to the media tool that will use this format. At most, one instance of this attribute is allowed for each format. It is a media-level attribute, and it is not dependent on charset. In addition, Table 7.5 shows more SDP attributes that are defined in different RFCs.

Table 7.5 SDP Attributes

Attribute	*RFC*
a=floorctrl:<floor control>	RFC 4583
a=confide:<conference id>	
a=userid:<user id>	
a=floorid:<floor id>	
a=accept-types:<acceptable media types>	RFC 4975
a=accept-wrapped-types:<acceptable media types within wrappers>	
a=max-size:<maximum message size>	
a=path:<MSRP URI path>	
a=rtcp:<RTCP port number and optional address>	RFC 3605
a=mid<media stream identification>	RFC 5888
a=group:<grouping together different media streams at session level>	
a=setup:<End-point TCP connection establishment at session level>	RFC 4145
a=connection:<End-point TCP connection value at media level>	
a=key-mgt:<key management attributes used at session level, media level, or at both levels, but when media level is present, it overrides an attribute defined at session level>	RFC 4567
a=crypto:<cryptographic suite, key parameters, and session parameters for the preceding unicast media line at the SDP media level (not at the session level)>	RFC 4568
a=fingerprint:<secure one-way hash of the DER (distinguished encoding rules) form of the certificate of fingerprint for media using TLS connection>	RFC 4572
a=label:<a media level pointer to a media stream in the context of an arbitrary network application that may even be external to the session setup>	RFC 4574
a=candidate:<ICE attribute that provides one of many possible candidate addresses for communication at media level>	RFC 5245
a=remote-candidates:<ICE attribute that provides the identity of the remote candidates that the offerer wishes the answerer to use in its answer at media level>	
a=ice-pwd:<ICE attributes that provides the password used to protect STUN (RFC 5389) connectivity checks at session or media level>	
a=ice-ufrag:<ICE attribute that provides the fragments used to construct the user name in STUN (RFC 5389) connectivity checks at session- or media-level>	
a=ice-light:<ICE attribute that indicates that an agent has the minimum functionality required to support ICE interoperation with a peer that has a full implementation at session level>	
a=ice-mismatch:<ICE attribute that indicates that an agent is ICE capable, but did not proceed with ICE due to a mismatch of candidates with the default destination for media signaled in the SDP at session level>	
a=ice-options:<ICE attribute that indicates the ICE options or extensions used by the agent at session level>	
a=chatroom:<A mere indication that the chat room capabilities are supported and allowed by the local policy and is not a negotiation subject to the SDP offer–answer model specified in RFC 3264, but instead a declaration.>	IETF Draft: draft-ietf-simple-chat-18, January 2013
a=msrp-cema:<attribute used by MSRP entities to indicate support of the Connection Establishment for Media Anchoring (CEMA) extension (RFC 6714)>	RFC 6714

7.7.6 SDP Transport-Independent Bandwidth Modifier

7.7.6.1 Overview

RFC 3890 defines an SDP Transport-Independent Application-Specific Maximum (TIAS) bandwidth modifier that does not include transport overhead; instead, an additional packet rate attribute is defined. The transport-independent bit-rate value together with the maximum packet rate can then be used to calculate the real bit-rate over the transport actually used. The existing SDP bandwidth modifiers and their values include the bandwidth needed for the transport and IP layers. When using SDP with protocols like SAP, SIP, and RTSP, and when the involved hosts have different transport overheads, for example due to different IP versions, the interpretation of what lower layer bandwidths are included is not clear.

7.7.6.2 Bandwidth Attribute

In SDP, as described earlier, there exists a bandwidth attribute, which has a modifier used to specify what type of bit rate the value refers to. The attribute has the following form:

```
b=<modifier>:<value>
```

Today, there are four defined modifiers used for different purposes.

7.7.6.2.1 Conference Total

The conference total is indicated by giving the modifier CT. Conference total gives a maximum bandwidth that a conference session will use. Its purpose is to decide if this session can coexist with any other sessions, defined in Section 7.7.5 (RFC 4566).

7.7.6.2.2 Application-Specific Maximum

The Application-Specific maximum bandwidth is indicated by the modifier AS. The interpretation of this attribute is dependent on the application's notion of maximum bandwidth. For an RTP application, this attribute is the RTP session bandwidth as defined in RFC 3550 (see Section 7.2). The session bandwidth includes the bandwidth that the RTP data traffic will consume, including the lower layers, down to the IP layer. Therefore, the bandwidth is, in most cases, calculated over RTP payload, RTP header, UDP, and IP, defined in Section 7.7.5 (RFC 4566).

7.7.6.2.3 RTCP Report Bandwidth

In RFC 3556, two bandwidth modifiers are defined. These modifiers, RS and RR, define the amount of bandwidth that is assigned for RTCP reports by active data senders and RTCP reports by other participants (receivers), respectively.

7.7.6.3 IPv6 and IPv4

Today, there are two IP version 4 (RFC 791) and IP version 6 (RFC 2460), used in parallel on the Internet, creating problems. However, there exist a number of possible transition mechanisms. The nodes that wish to communicate must share the IP version; typically, this is done by deploying dual-stack nodes. For example, an IPv4-only host cannot communicate with an IPv6-only host.

- If communication between nodes that do not share a protocol version is required, use of a translation or proxying mechanism would be required (Figure 7.4).
- IPv6 nodes belonging to different domains running IPv6, but lacking IPv6 connectivity between them, solve this by tunneling over the IPv4 net (Figure 7.5). Basically, the IPv6 packets are sent as payload in IPv4 packets between the tunneling end points at the edge of each IPv6 domain. The bandwidth required over the IPv4 domain will be different from IPv6 domains. However, as the tunneling is normally not performed by the application end point, this scenario cannot usually be taken into consideration.

IPv4 has a minimum header size of 20 bytes, while the fixed part of the IPv6 header is 40 bytes. The difference in header sizes means that the bit rate required for the two IP versions is different. The significance of the difference depends on the packet rate and payload size of each packet.

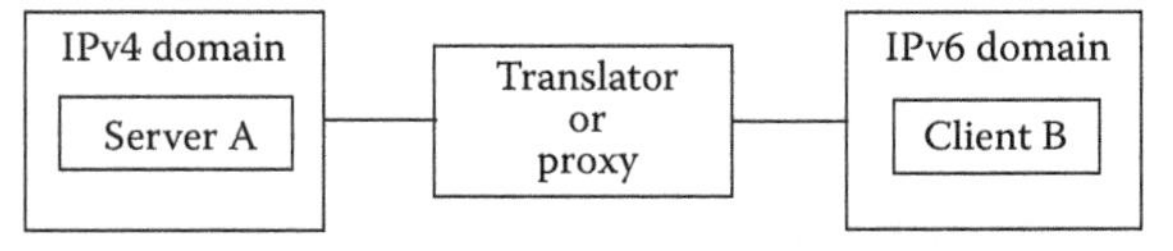

Figure 7.4 Translation or proxying between IPv6 and IPv4 addresses. (Copyright IETF. Reproduced with permission.)

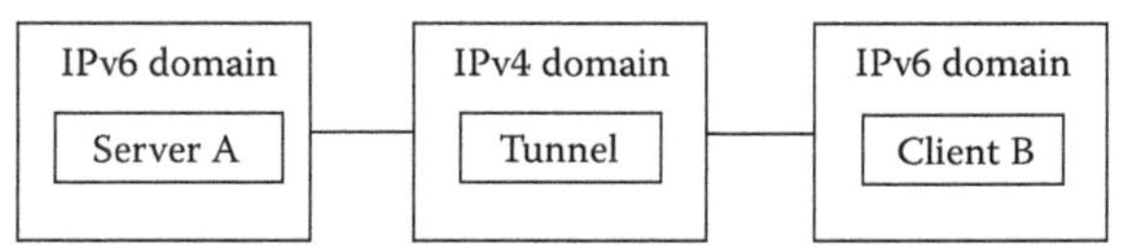

Figure 7.5 Tunneling through an IPv4 domain. (Copyright IETF. Reproduced with permission.)

7.7.6.4 *Further Mechanisms That Change the Bandwidth Utilization*

There exist a number of other mechanisms that also may change the overhead at layers below media transport. We will briefly cover a few of these here.

7.7.6.4.1 IPsec

IP security (IPsec) (RFC 4301) can be used between end points to provide confidentiality through the application of the IP Encapsulating Security Payload (ESP) (RFC 4303) or integrity protection using the IP Authentication Header (AH) (RFC 4302) of the media stream. The addition of the ESP and AH headers increases each packet's size. To provide virtual private networks, complete IP packets may be encapsulated between an end node and the private networks security gateway, thus providing a secure tunnel that ensures confidentiality, integrity, and authentication of the packet stream. In this case, the extra IP and ESP header will significantly increase the packet size.

7.7.6.4.2 Header Compression

Another mechanism that alters the actual overhead over links is header compression. Header compression uses the fact that most network protocol headers have either static or predictable values in their fields within a packet stream. Compression is normally only done on a per-hop basis, that is, on a single link. The normal reason for doing header compression is that the link has fairly limited bandwidth and significant gain in throughput is achieved. There exist several different header compression standards. For compressing IP headers only, there is RFC 2507. For compressing packets with IP/UDP/RTP headers, RFC 2508 was created at the same time. More recently, the Robust Header Compression (ROHC) working group has been developing a framework and profiles (RFC 3095) for compressing certain combinations of protocols, like IP/UDP and IP/UDP/RTP.

7.7.6.5 *Bandwidth Signaling Problems*

When an application wants to use SDP to signal the bandwidth required for this application, some problems become evident due to the inclusion of the lower layers in the bandwidth values.

7.7.6.5.1 IP Version

If one signals the bandwidth in SDP, for example, using b= S: as an RTP-based application, one cannot know if the overhead is calculated for IPv4 or IPv6. An indication of which protocol has been used when calculating the bandwidth values is given by the c= connection address line. This line contains either a multicast group address or a unicast address of the data source or sink. The c= line's address type may be assumed to be of the same type as the one used in the bandwidth calculation, although no document specifying this point seems to exist. In cases of SDP transported by RTSP, this is even less clear. The normal usage for a unicast on-demand streaming session is to set the connection data address to a null address. This null address does have an address type, which could be used as an indication. However, this is also not clarified anywhere. Figure 7.4 illustrates a connection scenario between a streaming server A and a client B over a translator. When B receives the SDP from A over RTSP, it will be very difficult for B to know what the bandwidth values in the SDP represent. The following possibilities exist:

1. The SDP is unchanged and the c= null address is of type IPv4. The bandwidth value represents the bandwidth needed in an IPv4 network.
2. The SDP has been changed by an Application Level Gateway (ALG). The c= address is changed to an IPv6 type. The bandwidth value is unchanged.
3. The SDP is changed and both c= address type and bandwidth value is converted. Unfortunately, this can seldom be done.

In case 1, the client can understand that the server is located in an IPv4 network and that it uses IPv4 overhead when calculating the bandwidth value. The client can almost never convert the bandwidth value described below. In case 2, the client does not know that the server is in an IPv4 network and that the bandwidth value is not calculated with IPv6 overhead. In cases where a client uses this value to determine if its end of the network has sufficient resources, the client will underestimate the required bit rate, potentially resulting in bad application performance very rare. If one tries to convert the bandwidth value without further information about the packet rate, significant errors may be introduced into the value.

7.7.6.5.2 Taking Other Mechanisms into Account

We have described earlier that there will be a number of reasons, like header compression and tunnels, that would change lower-layer header sizes. For these mechanisms, there exist different possibilities to take them into account. Using IPsec directly between end points should definitely be known to the application, thus enabling it to take the extra headers into account. However, the same problem also exists with the current SDP bandwidth modifiers where a receiver is not able to convert these values taking the IPsec headers into account. It is less likely that an application would be aware of the existence of a virtual private network. Thus, the generality of the mechanism to tunnel all traffic may prevent the application from even considering whether it would be possible to convert the values.

When using header compression, the actual overhead will be less deterministic; however, in most cases, an average overhead can be determined for a certain application. If a network node knows that some type of header compression is employed, this can be taken into consideration. For resources reservation protocol (RSVP) (RFC 2205), there exists an extension (RFC 3006) that allows the data sender to inform network nodes about the compressibility of the data flow. To be able to do this with any accuracy, the compression factor and packet rate or size is needed, as RFC 3006 provides.

7.7.6.5.3 Converting Bandwidth Values

If one would like to convert a bandwidth value calculated using IPv4 overhead to IPv6 overhead, the packet rate is required. The new bandwidth value for IPv6 is normally IPv4 bandwidth + packet rate * 20 bytes, where 20 bytes is the usual difference between IPv6 and IPv4 headers. The overhead difference may be some other value in cases when IPv4 options (RFC 791) or IPv6 extension headers (RFC 2460) are used. As converting requires the packet rate of the stream, this is not possible in the general case. Many codecs have either multiple possible packet/frame rates or can perform payload format aggregation, resulting in many possible rates. Therefore, some extra information in the SDP will be required. The a=ptime: parameter may be a possible candidate. However, this parameter is normally only used for audio codecs. Its definition as described earlier (RFC 4566) is that it is only a recommendation, which the sender may disregard. A better parameter is needed.

7.7.6.5.4 RTCP Problems

When RTCP is used between hosts in IPv4 and IPv6 networks over a translator, similar problems exist. The RTCP traffic going from the IPv4 domain will result in a higher RTCP bit rate than intended in the IPv6 domain due to the larger headers. This may result in up to a 25% increase in required bandwidth for the RTCP traffic. The largest increase will be for small RTCP packets when the number of IPv4 hosts is much larger than the number of IPv6 hosts. Fortunately, as RTCP has a limited bandwidth compared with RTP, it will only result in a maximum of 1.75% increase of the total session bandwidth when RTCP bandwidth is 5% of RTP bandwidth. The RTCP randomization may easily result in short-term effects of the same magnitude, so this increase may be considered tolerable. The increase in bandwidth will, in most cases, be less. At the same time, this results in unfairness in the reporting between an IPv4 and IPv6 node. In the worst-case scenario, the IPv6 node may report with 25% longer intervals. These problems have been considered insignificant enough to not be worth any complex solutions. Therefore, only a simple algorithm for deriving RTCP bandwidth is defined in this specification.

7.7.6.5.5 Problem Conclusion

A shortcoming of the current SDP bandwidth modifiers is that they also include the bandwidth needed for lower layers. It is, in many cases, difficult to determine which lower layers and their versions were included in the calculation, especially in the presence of translation or proxying between different domains. This prevents a receiver from determining if given bandwidth needs to be converted based on the actual lower layers being used. Second, an attribute to give the receiver an explicit determination of the maximum packet rate that will be used does not exist. This value is necessary for accurate conversion of any bandwidth values if the difference in overhead is known.

7.7.6.6 Problem Scope

The problems described earlier are common and effect application-level signaling using SDP, other signaling protocols, and also resource reservation protocols. However, this document targets the specific problem of signaling the bit rate in SDP. As SDP information is normally transported end-to-end by an application protocol, nodes between the end points will not have access to the bit-rate information. It will normally only be the end points that are able to take this information into account. An interior node will need to receive the information through a means other than SDP, and that is outside the scope of this specification. Nevertheless, the bit-rate information provided in this specification is sufficient for cases such as first-hop resource reservation and admission control. It also provides information about the maximum codec rate, which is independent of lower-level protocols. This specification does not try to solve the problem of detecting network address translators or other middle boxes.

7.7.6.7 Requirements

The problems outlined in the preceding sections and with the above applicability should meet the following requirement:

- The bandwidth value shall be given in a way such that it can be calculated for all possible combinations of transport overhead.

7.7.6.8 Solution

7.7.6.8.1 Overview

This chapter describes a solution for the problems outlined in this document for the AS bandwidth modifier, thus enabling the derivation of the required bit rate for an application, or RTP session's data and RTCP traffic. The solution is based on the definition of a new TIAS bandwidth modifier and a new SDP attribute for the maximum packet rate (maxprate). The CT is a session-level modifier and cannot easily be dealt with. To address the problems with different overhead, it is recommended that the CT value be calculated using reasonable worst-case overhead. An example of how to calculate a reasonable worst-case overhead is as follows:

- Take the overhead of the largest transport protocol (using average size if variable), then add that to the largest IP overhead that is expected for use, plus the data traffic rate. Do this for every individual media stream used in the conference and add them together. The RR and RS modifiers (RFC 3556) will be used as defined and include transport overhead, where RS indicates the RTCP bandwidth allocated to active data senders (as defined by the RTP spec) and RR indicates the RTCP bandwidth allocated to other participants in the RTP session (i.e., receivers). The small unfairness between hosts is deemed acceptable.

7.7.6.8.2 TIAS Bandwidth Modifier Usage

A new bandwidth modifier is defined to be used for the following purposes:

- **Resource reservation:** A single bit rate can be enough for use as a resource reservation. Some characteristics can be derived from the stream, codec type, etc. In cases where more information is needed, another SDP parameter will be required.
- **Maximum media codec rate:** With the definition below of TIAS, the given bit rate will mostly be from the media codec. Therefore, it gives a good indication of the maximum codec bit rate required to be supported by the decoder.
- **Communication bit rate required for the stream:** The TIAS value together with maxprate can be used to determine the maximum communication bit rate the stream will require. Using session-level values or by adding all maximum bit rates from the streams in a session together, a receiver can determine if its communication resources are sufficient to handle the stream. For example, a modem user can determine if the session fits his modem's capabilities and the established connection.
- Determine the RTP session bandwidth and derive the RTCP bandwidth. The derived transport-dependent attribute will be the RTP session bandwidth in case of RTP-based transport. The TIAS value can also be used to determine the RTCP bandwidth to use when using implicit allocation. RTP (RFC 3550, see Section 7.2) specifies that if not explicitly stated, additional bandwidth, equal to 5% of the RTP session bandwidth, shall be used by RTCP. The RTCP bandwidth can be explicitly allocated by using the RR and RS modifiers defined in RFC 3556.

7.7.6.8.3 Bandwidth Modifier Definition

A new session- and media-level bandwidth modifier is defined:

```
b=TIAS:<bandwidth-value>; ABNF definition is
provided later.
```

The TIAS bandwidth modifier has an integer bit-rate value in bits per second. A fractional bandwidth value shall always be rounded up to the next integer. The bandwidth value is the maximum needed by the application (SDP session level) or media stream (SDP media level) without counting IP or other transport layers like TCP or UDP. At the SDP session level, the TIAS value is the maximal amount of bandwidth needed when all declared media streams are used. This may be less than the sum of all the individual media streams values. This is due to the possibility that not all streams have their maximum at the same point in time. This can normally only be verified for stored media streams. For RTP transported media streams, TIAS at the SDP media level can be used to derive the RTP session bandwidth, defined in RFC 3550 (see Section 7.2). In the context of RTP transport, the TIAS value is defined as follows:

Only the RTP payload as defined in RFC 3550 SHALL be used in the calculation of the bit rate, that is, excluding the lower layers (IP/UDP) and RTP headers including RTP header, RTP header extensions, CSRC list, and other RTP profile-specific fields. Note that the RTP payload includes both the payload format header and the data. This may allow one to use the same value for RTP-based media transport, non-RTP transport, and stored media.

Note that the usage of bits per second is not in accordance with RFC 4566 as described earlier. This change has no implications on the parser; only the interpreter of the value must be aware. The change is done to allow for better resolution, and has also been used for the RR and RS bandwidth modifiers. RTCP bandwidth is not included in the bandwidth value. In applications using RTCP, the bandwidth used by RTCP is either 5% of the RTP session bandwidth including lower layers or as specified by the RR and

RS modifiers. A specification of how to derive the RTCP bit rate when using TIAS is presented later.

7.7.6.8.4 Bandwidth Modifier Usage Rules

TIAS is primarily intended to be used at the SDP media level. The TIAS bandwidth attribute MAY be present at the session level in SDP, if all media streams use the same transport. In cases where the sum of the media level values for all media streams is larger than the actual maximum bandwidth need for all streams, it should be included at session level. However, if present at the session level, it should be present also at the media level. TIAS shall not be present at the session level unless the same transport protocols are used for all media streams. The same transport is used as long as the same combination of protocols is used, like IPv6/UDP/RTP. To allow for backwards compatibility with applications of SDP that do not implement TIAS, it is recommended to also include the AS modifier when using TIAS. The presence of a value including lower-layer overhead, even with its problems, is better than none. However, an SDP application implementing TIAS should ignore the AS value and use TIAS instead when both are present. When using TIAS for an RTP-transported stream, the maxprate attribute, if possible to calculate, defined next, shall be included at the corresponding SDP level.

7.7.6.8.5 Packet Rate Parameter

To be able to calculate the bandwidth value including the lower layers actually used, a packet rate attribute is also defined. The SDP session and media level maximum packet rate attribute is defined as

```
a=maxprate:<packet-rate>; ABNF definition is
provided later.
```

The <packet-rate> is a floating-point value for the stream's maximum packet rate in packets per second. If the number of packets is variable, the given value shall be the maximum the application can produce in case of a live stream, or for stored on-demand streams, has produced. The packet rate is calculated by adding the number of packets sent within a 1-second window. The maxprate is the largest value produced when the window slides over the entire media stream. In cases when this cannot be calculated, that is, a live stream, an estimated value of the maximum packet rate the codec can produce for the given configuration and content shall be used. Note that the sliding window calculation will always yield an integer number. However, the attributes field is a floating-point value because the estimated or known maximum packet rate per second may be fractional.

At the SDP session level, the maxprate value is the maximum packet rate calculated over all the declared media streams. If this cannot be measured (stored media) or estimated (live), the sum of all media level values provides a ceiling value. Note that the value at session level can be less than the sum of the individual media streams due to temporal distribution of media stream's maximums. The maxprate attribute must not be present at the session level if the media streams use different transport. The attribute may be present if the media streams use the same transport. If the attribute is present at the session level, it should also be present at the media level for all media streams. The maxprate shall be included for all transports where a packet rate can be derived and TIAS is included. For example, if you use TIAS and a transport like IP/UDP/RTP, for which the max packet rate (actual or estimated) can be derived, then maxprate shall be included. However, if either (a) the packet rate for the transport cannot be derived, or (b) TIAS is not included, then maxprate is not required to be included.

7.7.6.8.6 Converting to Transport-Dependent Values

When converting the transport-independent bandwidth value (bw-value) into a transport-dependent value, including the lower layers, the following steps must be carried out:

1. Determine which lower layers will be used and calculate the sum of the sizes of the headers in bits (*h*-size). In cases of variable header sizes, the average size shall be used. For RTP-transported media, the lower layers shall include the RTP header with header extensions, if used, the CSRC list, and any profile-specific extensions.
2. Retrieve the maximum packet rate from the SDP (prate = maxprate).
3. Calculate the transport overhead by multiplying the header sizes by the packet rate (*t* over = *h*-size * prate).
4. Round the transport overhead up to nearest integer in bits (*t*-over = CEIL(*t*-over)).
5. Add the transport overhead to the transport-independent bandwidth value (total bit-rate = bw-value + *t*-over). When the above calculation is performed using the maxprate, the bit-rate value will be the absolute maximum the media stream may use over the transport assumed in the calculations.

7.7.6.8.7 Deriving RTCP Bandwidth

This chapter does not solve the fairness and possible bit-rate change introduced by IPv4 to IPv6 translation. These differences are considered small enough, and known solutions introduce code changes to the RTP/RTCP implementation. This section provides a consistent way of calculating the bit rate to assign to RTCP, if not explicitly given. First, the transport-dependent RTP session bit rate is calculated, in accordance with as described in the earlier section, using the actual transport layers used at the end point where the calculation is done. The RTCP bit rate is then derived as usual based on the RTP session bandwidth, that is, normally equal to 5% of the calculated value.

Giving the exact same RTCP bit-rate value to both the IPv4 and IPv6 hosts will result in the IPv4 host having a higher RTCP sending rate. The sending rate represents the number of RTCP packets sent during a given time interval. The sending of RTCP is limited according to rules defined in the RTP specification (RFC 3550, see Section 7.2). For a 100-byte RTCP packet (including UDP/IPv4), the IPv4 sender has an approximately 20% higher sending rate. This rate falls with larger RTCP packets. For example, 300-byte packets will only give the IPv4 host a 7% higher sending rate.

The above rule for deriving RTCP bandwidth gives the same behavior as fixed assignment when the RTP session has traffic parameters giving a large TIAS/maxprate ratio. The two hosts will be fair when the TIAS/maxprate ratio is approximately 40 bytes/packet, given 100-byte RTCP packets. For a TIAS/maxprate ratio of 5 bytes/packet, the IPv6 host will be allowed to send approximately 15–20% more RTCP packets.

The larger the RTCP packets become, the more it will favor the IPv6 host in its sending rate. The conclusions is that, within the normal useful combination of transport-independent bit rates and packet rates, the difference in fairness between hosts on different IP versions with different overhead is acceptable. For the 20-byte difference in overhead between IPv4 and IPv6 headers, the RTCP bandwidth actually used in a unicast connection case will not be larger than approximately 1% of the total session bandwidth.

7.7.6.8.8 Augmented Backus–Naur Form (ABNF) Syntax

The ABNF syntax for the bandwidth modifier and the packet rate attribute is provided as follows:

```
TIAS-bandwidth-def  =   "b" " = " "TIAS" ":"
bandwidth-value CRLF
bandwidth-value     =   1*DIGIT
```

The maximum packet rate attribute is

```
max-p-rate-def =   "a" "=" "maxprate" ":"
packet-rate CRLF
packet-rate    =   1*DIGIT ["." 1*DIGIT]
```

7.7.6.8.9 Example

```
v=0
o=Example_SERVER 3413526809 0 IN IP4 server.
example.com
s=Example of TIAS and maxprate in use
c=IN IP4 0.0.0.0
b=AS:60
b=TIAS:50780
t=0 0
a=control:rtsp://server.example.com/media.3gp
a=range:npt=0-150.0
a=maxprate:28.0
m=audio 0 RTP/AVP 97
b=AS:12
b=TIAS:8480
a=maxprate:10.0
a=rtpmap:97 AMR/8000
a=fmtp:97 octet-align;
a=control:rtsp://server.example.com/
media.3gp/trackID=1
m=video 0 RTP/AVP 99

b=AS:48
b=TIAS:42300
a=maxprate:18.0
a=rtpmap:99 MP4V-ES/90000
a=fmtp:99 profile-level-id=8;
config=000001B008000001B50900000101000001200O
884006682C2090A21F
a=control:rtsp://server.example.com/media.3gp/
trackID=3
```

In this SDP example of a streaming session's SDP, there are two media streams, one audio stream encoded with AMR and one video stream encoded with the MPEG-4 video encoder. AMR is used here to produce a constant rate media stream and uses a packetization resulting in 10 packets per second. This results in a TIAS bandwidth rate of 8480 bits per second, and the claimed 10 packets per second. The video stream is more variable. However, it has a measured maximum payload rate of 42,300 bits per second. The video stream also has a variable packet rate, despite the fact that the video is 15 frames per second, where at least one instance in a second-long window contains 18 packets.

7.7.6.9 Protocol Interaction

7.7.6.9.1 RTSP

The TIAS and maxprate parameters can be used with RTSP as currently specified. To be able to calculate the transport-dependent bandwidth, some of the transport header parameters will be required. There should be no problem for a client to calculate the required bandwidth(s) prior to an RTSP SETUP. The reason is that a client supports a limited number of transport setups. The one actually offered to a server in a SETUP request will be dependent on the contents of the SDP description. The m= line(s) will signal the desired transport profile(s) to the client.

7.7.6.9.2 SIP

The usage of TIAS together with maxprate should not be different from the handling of the AS modifier currently in use. The needed transport parameters will be available in the transport field in the m= line. The address class can be determined from the c= field and the client's connectivity.

7.7.6.9.3 SAP

In the case of SAP, all available information to calculate the transport-dependent bit rate should be present in the SDP. The c= information gives the address family used for the multicast. The transport layer, for example, RTP/UDP, for each media is evident in the media line (m=) and its transport field.

7.7.7 SDP Format for BFCP Streams

7.7.7.1 Overview

RFC 4583 specifies how to describe BFCP streams in SDP descriptions. User agents using the offer–answer model to establish BFCP streams use this format in their offers and answers. A given BFCP client needs a set of data in order to establish a BFCP connection to a floor control server. These data include the transport address of the server, the conference identifier, and the user identifier. One way for clients to obtain this information is to use an offer–answer (RFC 3264, see Section 3.8.4) exchange. This document specifies how to encode this information in the SDP session descriptions that are part of such an offer–answer exchange. User agents typically use the offer–answer model to establish a number of media streams of different types. Following this model, a BFCP connection is described as any other media stream by using an SDP m line, possibly followed by a number of attributes encoded in "a" lines.

7.7.7.2 Fields in the m Line

This section describes how to generate an m line for a BFCP stream. According to the SDP specification described earlier, the m line format is as follows:

```
m=<media> <port> <transport> <fmt>...
```

The media field must have a value of *application*. The port field is set following the rules in RFC 4145. Depending on the value of the *setup* attribute discussed later, the port field contains the port to which the remote end point will initiate its TCP connection or is irrelevant (i.e., the end point will initiate the connection toward the remote end point) and should be set to a value of 9, which is the discard port. Since BFCP only runs on top of TCP, the port is always a TCP port. A port field value of zero has the standard SDP meaning (i.e., rejection of the media stream). We define two new values for the transport field: TCP/BFCP and TCP/TLS/BFCP. The former is used when BFCP runs directly on top of TCP, and the latter is used when BFCP runs on top of TLS, which in turn runs on top of TCP. The fmt (format) list is ignored for BFCP. The fmt list of BFCP m lines should contain a single "*" character. The following is an example of an m line for a BFCP connection:

```
m=application 50000 TCP/TLS/BFCP *
```

7.7.7.3 Floor Control Server Determination

When two end points establish a BFCP stream, they need to determine which of them acts as a floor control server. In the most common scenario, a client establishes a BFCP stream with a conference server that acts as the floor control server. Floor control server determination is straightforward because one end point can only act as a client and the other can only act as a floor control server. However, there are scenarios where both end points could act as a floor control server. For example, in a two-party session that involves an audio stream and a shared whiteboard, the end points need to decide which party will be acting as the floor control server. Furthermore, there are situations where both the offerer and the answerer act as both clients and floor control servers in the same session. For example, in a two-party session that involves an audio stream and a shared whiteboard, one party acts as the floor control server for the audio stream and the other acts as the floor control server for the shared whiteboard. We define the floorctrl SDP media-level attribute to perform floor control determination. Its ABNF syntax is

```
floor-control-attribute = "a = floorctrl:"
role *(SP role)
role                    = "c-only"/"s-only"/"c-s"
```

The offerer includes this attribute to state all the roles it would be willing to perform:

c-only: The offerer would be willing to act as a floor control client only.
s-only: The offerer would be willing to act as a floor control server only.
c-s: The offerer would be willing to act both as a floor control client and as a floor control server.

If an m line in an offer contains a floorctrl attribute, the answerer must include one in the corresponding m line in the answer. The answerer includes this attribute to state which role the answerer will perform. That is, the answerer chooses one of the roles the offerer is willing to perform and generates an answer with the corresponding role for the answerer. The following table shows the corresponding roles for an answerer, depending on the offerer's role.

Offerer	*Answerer*
c-only	s-only
s-only	c-only
c-s	c-s

The following are the descriptions of the roles when they are chosen by an answerer:

c-only: The answerer will act as a floor control client. Consequently, the offerer will act as a floor control server.
s-only: The answerer will act as a floor control server. Consequently, the offerer will act as a floor control client.
c-s: The answerer will act both as a floor control client and as a floor control server. Consequently, the offerer will also act both as a floor control client and as a floor control server.

End points that use the offer–answer model to establish BFCP connections MUST support the floorctrl attribute. A floor control server acting as an offerer or as an answerer should include this attribute in its session descriptions. If the floorctrl attribute is not used in an offer–answer exchange, by default the offerer and the answerer will act as a floor control client and as a floor control server, respectively. The following is an example of a floorctrl attribute in an offer. When this attribute appears in an answer, it only carries one role:

```
a=floorctrl:c-only s-only c-s
```

7.7.7.4 SDP Attributes: Confid and Userid

We define the confid and the userid SDP media-level attributes. These attributes are used by a floor control server to provide a client with a conference ID and a user ID, respectively. Their ABNF syntax is

```
confid-attribute     =
"a=confid:" conference-id
conference-id        =       token
userid-attribute     =       "a=userid:" user-id
user-id              =       token
```

The confid and the userid attributes carry the integer representation of a conference ID and a user ID, respectively. End points that use the offer–answer model to establish BFCP connections MUST support the confid and the userid attributes. A floor control server acting as an offerer or as an answerer should include these attributes in its session descriptions.

7.7.7.5 Association between Streams and Floors

We define the floorid SDP media-level attribute. Its ABNF syntax is

```
floor-id-attribute    =       "a=floorid:" token
["mstrm:" token *(SP token)]
```

The floorid attribute is used in BFCP m lines. It defines a floor identifier and, possibly, associates it with one or more media streams. The token representing the floor ID is the integer representation of the Floor ID to be used in BFCP. The token representing the media stream is a pointer to the media stream, which is identified by an SDP label attribute RFC 4582. End points that use the offer–answer model to establish BFCP connections must support the floorid and the label attributes. A floor control server acting as an offerer or as an answerer should include these attributes in its session descriptions.

7.7.7.6 TCP Connection Management

The management of the TCP connection used to transport BFCP is performed using the setup and connection attributes, as defined in RFC 4145. The setup attribute indicates which of the end points (client or floor control server) initiates the TCP connection. The connection attribute handles TCP connection reestablishment. The BFCP specification (RFC 4582) describes a number of situations when the TCP connection between a client and the floor control server needs to be reestablished. However, that specification does not describe the reestablishment process because this process depends on how the connection was established in the first place. BFCP entities using the offer–answer model follow the following rules. When the existing TCP connection is reset following the rules in RFC 4145, the client should generate an offer toward the floor control server in order to reestablish the connection. If a TCP connection cannot deliver a BFCP message and times out, the entity that attempted to send the message (i.e., the one that detected the TCP timeout should generate an offer in order to reestablish the TCP connection. End points that use the offer–answer model to establish BFCP connections must support the setup and connection attributes.

7.7.7.7 Authentication

When a BFCP connection is established using the offer–answer model, it is assumed that the offerer and the answerer authenticate each other using some mechanism. Once this mutual authentication takes place, all the offerer and the answerer need to ensure is that the entity they are receiving the BFCP messages from is the same as the one that generated the previous offer or answer. When SIP is used to perform an offer–answer exchange, the initial mutual authentication takes place at the SIP level. Additionally, SIP uses S/MIME (see Section 19.6) to provide an integrity-protected channel with optional confidentiality for the offer–answer exchange. BFCP takes advantage of this integrity-protected offer–answer exchange to perform authentication. Within the offer–answer exchange, the offerer and answerer exchange the fingerprints of their self-signed certificates. These self-signed certificates are then used to establish the TLS connection that will carry BFCP traffic between the offerer and the answerer.

BFCP clients and floor control servers follow the rules in (RFC 4572) regarding certificate choice and presentation. This implies that unless a fingerprint attribute is included in the session description, the certificate provided at the TLS level must either be directly signed by one of the other party's trust anchors or be validated using a certification path that terminates at one of the other party's trust anchors (RFC 3280). End points that use the offer–answer model to establish BFCP connections must support the fingerprint attribute and should include it in their session descriptions. When TLS is used, once the underlying TCP connection is established, the answerer acts as the TLS server regardless of its role (passive or active) in the TCP establishment procedure.

7.7.7.8 Examples

For the purpose of brevity, the main portion of the session description is omitted in the examples, which only show m lines and their attributes. The following is an example of an offer sent by a conference server to a client.

```
m=application 50000 TCP/TLS/BFCP *
a=setup:passive
a=connection:new
a=fingerprint:SHA-1 \
       4A:AD:B9:B1:3F:82:18:3B:54:02:12:DF:3E
:5D:49:6B:19:E5:7C:AB
a=floorctrl:s-only
a=confid:4321
a=userid:1234
a=floorid:1 m-stream:10
a=floorid:2 m-stream:11
m=audio 50002 RTP/AVP 0
a=label:10
m=video 50004 RTP/AVP 31
a=label:11
```

Note that due to RFC formatting conventions, this document splits SDP across lines whose content would exceed 72 characters. A backslash character marks where this line folding has taken place. This backslash and its trailing CRLF and white space would not appear in actual SDP content. The following is the answer returned by the client.

```
m=application 9 TCP/TLS/BFCP *
a=setup:active
a=connection:new
a=fingerprint:SHA-1 \
       3D:B4:7B:E3:CC:FC:0D:1B:5D:31:33:9E:48
:9B:67:FE:68:40:E8:21
a=floorctrl:c-only
m=audio 55000 RTP/AVP 0
m=video 55002 RTP/AVP 31
```

7.7.8 SDP Content Attribute

7.7.8.1 Overview

There are situations where one application receives several similar media streams, which are described in an SDP session description. The media streams can be similar in the sense that their content cannot be distinguished just by examining their media description lines (e.g., two video streams). The content attribute is needed so that the receiving application can treat each media stream appropriately based on its content. RFC 4796 defines a new SDP media level attribute, content. The content attribute defines the content of the media stream to a more detailed level than the media description line. The SDP content media-level attribute provides more information about the media stream than the m line in an SDP session description. The sender of an SDP session description can attach the content attribute to one or more media streams. The receiving application can then treat each media stream differently (e.g., show it on a big or small screen) based on its content The main purpose of this specification is to allow applications to take automated actions based on the content attributes. However, this specification does not define those actions. Consequently, two implementations can behave completely differently when receiving the same content attribute.

7.7.8.2 Related Techniques

The label attribute defined in RFC 4574 enables a sender to attach a pointer to a particular media stream. The namespace of the label attribute itself is unrestricted; so, in principle, it could also be used to convey information about the content of a media stream. However, in practice, this is not possible because of the need for backward compatibility. Existing implementations of the label attribute already use values from that unrestricted namespace in an application-specific way. Thus, it is not possible to reserve portions of the label attribute's namespace without possible conflict with already used application-specific labels. It is possible to assign semantics to a media stream with an external document that uses the label attribute as a pointer. The downside of this approach is that it requires an external document. Therefore, this kind of mechanism is only applicable to special-use cases where such external documents are used (e.g., centralized conferencing). Yet another way to attach semantics to a media stream is to use the "i" SDP attribute, defined in RFC 4566 described earlier. However, values of the "i" attribute are intended for human users and not for automata.

7.7.8.3 Motivation for the New Content Attribute

Currently, SDP does not provide any means for describing the content of a media stream (e.g., speaker's image, slides, sign language) in a form that the application can understand. Of course, the end user can see the content of the media stream and read its title, but the application cannot understand what the media stream contains. The application that is receiving multiple similar (e.g., same type and format) media streams needs, in some cases, to know what the contents of those streams are. This kind of situation occurs, for example, in cases where presentation slides, the speaker's image, and sign language are transported as separate media streams. It would be desirable that the receiving application could distinguish them in a way that it could handle them automatically in an appropriate manner. Figure 7.6 shows a screen of a typical communication application. The content attribute makes it possible for the application to decide where to show each media stream. From an end user's perspective, it is desirable that the user does not need to arrange each media stream every time a new media session starts.

The content attribute could also be used in more complex situations. An example of such a situation is application controlling equipment in an auditorium. An auditorium can have many different output channels for video (e.g., main screen and two smaller screens) and audio (e.g., main speakers and headsets for the participants). In this kind of environment, a lot of interaction from the end user who operates the application would be required in the absence of cues from a controlling application. The content attribute would make it possible, for example, for an end user to specify, only once, which output each media stream of a given session should use. The application could automatically apply the same media layout for subsequent sessions. Therefore, the content attribute can help reduce the amount of required end-user interaction considerably.

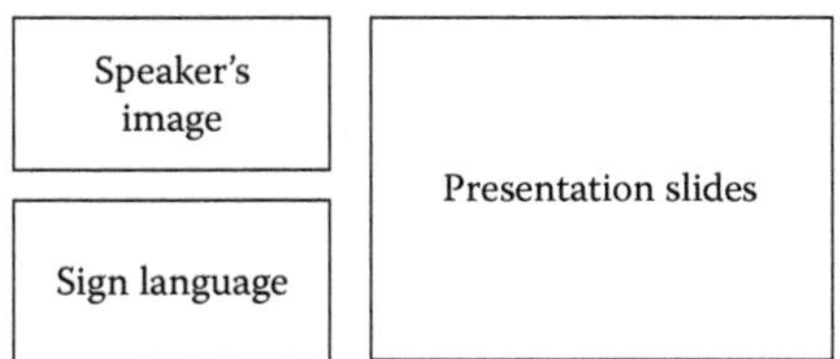

Figure 7.6 Application's screen. (Copyright IETF. Reproduced with permission.)

7.7.8.4 Content Attribute

This specification defines a new media-level value attribute, content. Its formatting in SDP is described by the following ABNF:

```
content-attribute = "a=content:" mediacnt-tag
mediacnt-tag =        mediacnt*("," mediacnt)
mediacnt      =       "slides"/"speaker"/"sl"/"
main"/"alt"/mediacnt-ext
mediacnt-ext =        token
```

The content attribute contains one or more tokens, which may be attached to a media stream by a sending application. An application may attach a content attribute to any media stream it describes. This document provides a set of predefined values for the content attribute. Other values can be defined in the future. The predefined values are as follows:

- **Slides:** the media stream includes presentation slides. The media type can be, for example, a video stream or a number of instant messages with pictures. Typical use cases for this are online seminars and courses. This is similar to the presentation role in H.239 [1].
- **Speaker:** the media stream contains the image of the speaker. The media can be, for example, a video stream or a still image. Typical use cases for this are online seminars and courses.
- **Sl:** the media stream contains sign language. A typical use case for this is an audio stream that is translated into sign language, which is sent over a video stream.
- **Main:** the media stream is taken from the main source. A typical use case for this is a concert where the camera is shooting the performer.
- **Alt:** the media stream is taken from the alternative source. A typical use case for this is an event where the ambient sound is separated from the main sound. The alternative audio stream could be, for example, the sound of a jungle. Another example is the video of a conference room, while the main stream carries the video of the speaker. This is similar to the *live* role in H.239.

All these values can be used with any media type. We chose not to restrict each value to a particular set of media types in order not to prevent applications from using innovative combinations of a given value with different media types. The application can make decisions on how to handle a single media stream based on both the media type and the value of the content attribute. If the application does not implement any special logic for the handling of a given media type and content value combination, it applies the application's default handling for the media type. Note that the same content attribute value can occur more than once in a single session description.

7.7.8.5 Content Attribute in the Offer–Answer Model

This specification does not define a means to discover whether the peer end point understands the content attribute because content values are just informative at the offer–answer model (RFC 3264, see Section 3.8.4) level. The fact that the peer end point does not understand the content attribute does not keep the media session from being established. The only consequence is that end-user interaction on the receiving side may be required to direct the individual media streams appropriately.

The content attribute describes the data that the application generating the SDP session description intends to send over a particular media stream. The content values for both directions of a media stream do not need to be the same. Therefore, an SDP answer may contain content attributes even if none were present in the offer. Similarly, the answer may contain no content attributes even if they were present in the offer. Furthermore, the values of content attributes do not need to match in an offer and an answer. The content attribute can also be used in scenarios where SDP is used in a declarative style. For example, content attributes can be used in SDP session descriptors that are distributed with SAP (RFC 2974).

7.7.8.6 Examples

There are two examples in this section. The first example, shown below, uses a single content attribute value per media stream:

```
v=0
o=Alice 292742730 29277831 IN IP4
131.163.72.4
s=Second lecture from information technology
c=IN IP4 131.164.74.2
t=0 0
m=video 52886 RTP/AVP 31
a=rtpmap:31 H261/9000
a=content:slides
m=video 53334 RTP/AVP 31
a=rtpmap:31 H261/9000
a=content:speaker
m=video 54132 RTP/AVP 31
a=rtpmap:31 H261/9000
a=content:sl
```

The second example, below, is a case where there is more than one content attribute value per media stream. The difference with the previous example is that now the conferencing system might automatically mix the video streams from the presenter and slides:

```
v=0
o=Alice 292742730 29277831 IN IP4
131.163.72.4
s=Second lecture from information technology
c=IN IP4 131.164.74.2
t=0 0
m=video 52886 RTP/AVP 31
a=rtpmap:31 H261/9000
a=content:slides,speaker
m=video 54132 RTP/AVP 31
a=rtpmap:31 H261/9000
a=content:sl
```

7.7.8.7 Operation with SMIL

The values of content attribute, defined in Section 2.1, can also be used with Synchronized Multimedia Integration Language (SMIL) [2]. SMIL contains a param element, which is used for describing the content of a media flow. However, this param element, like the content attribute, provides an application-specific description of the media content. Details on how to use the values of the content attribute with SMIL's param element are beyond the scope of this specification.

7.8 Summary

We have presented the new real-time media transport protocols and media negotiations in SIP. We briefly summarize the most important RTP and RTCP specifications that are used for media transport for multimedia applications including SIP. RTP and RTCP header format, multiple interleaving RTP stream multiplexing, RTP translator and mixer, RTCP reports, and other features and functionalities are described. In addition, the characteristics of real-time SRTP/SRTCP, ZRTP, RTSP, and MRCP are provided. All these media transport protocols require a complete separate treatment in order to discuss them in detail. We have explained the SDP and its content-agnostics and content-aware attributes, and media negotiation capabilities quite comprehensively although not so much in detail. Again, this also needs a separate stand-alone discussion for its own merit due to complexities of media negotiations in SIP and related protocols. Finally, the security aspects of both real-time transport protocols and SDP have specifically articulated although the entire security and privacy of both SIP signaling and media are specified in Sections 3.8.4 and 19.2.3.

PROBLEMS

1. Why is there a need to develop RTP specifically for transporting over the IP network for real-time multimedia applications like audio and video?
2. What are the specific functional characteristics of RTP that differ fundamentally with respect to those of the non-real-time application protocols?
3. Why does RTP need to be transferred over the connectionless transport protocols like UDP for real-time audio and video multimedia conferencing?
4. What are the problems for transmission through multiplexing of multiple interleaving media streams (say audio and video) over the single RTP session? How can these problems be avoided?
5. How does the RTCP report work? Describe all features and functionalities of RTCP reports and packets. How does the RTCP facilitate monitoring and operations of ongoing multimedia sessions?
6. How does the RTP and RTCP complement each other for the ongoing multimedia sessions in real-time? How do the operations and maintenance of multimedia sessions by RTCP differ from those of the non-real-time management applications such as Simple Network Management Protocol (SNMP)?
7. How do the RTP translators and mixers work? How is the RTCP report generated specific to the operations and maintenance of RTP translators and mixers?
8. Explain the salient functional and performance characteristics of SRTP/SRTCP, ZRTP, RTSP, and MRCP including security as applicable briefly. Compare their protocol functional capabilities in the context of SIP.
9. Explain the SDP briefly. Explain the characteristics of SDP content-agnostics and content-aware attributes.
10. How does the SDP transport–independent bandwidth modifier work for the following: conference total, application-specific maximum, RTCP report bandwidth, IPv6 and IPv4, and IPsec and header compression?
11. What are the problems of bandwidth signaling in SDP for the following: IP version, taking other mechanisms into account, converting bandwidth values, and future development? How do you scope all of those problems? Discuss the solution of these problems in SDP using examples.
12. Describe all SDP attributes for the BFCP streams.
13. Explain how the SDP offer–answer model is used for media negotiations mitigating security and privacy.

References

1. ITU-T, "Infrastructure of audiovisual services, Systems aspects; Role management and additional media channels for H.300-series terminals," Series H H.239, July 2003.
2. Michel, T. and Ayars, J., "Synchronized Multimedia Integration Language (SMIL 2.0) [Second Edition]," World Wide Web Consortium Recommendation REC-SMIL2-20050107, January 2005. Available at http://www.w3.org/TR/2005/REC-SMIL2-20050107.

Chapter 8

DNS and ENUM in SIP

Abstract

The use of the Domain Name System (DNS) for resolving of the domain host names (e.g., bob@example.com) to the Internet Protocol (IP) addresses and other attributes related to the Session Initiation Protocol (SIP) functional entities is essential for the client–server SIP protocol. Request for Comment 3263 that is also described here specifies the DNS procedures for locating/discovering the SIP entities. Before we describe the DNS usage in SIP, we describe the DNS architecture itself first because DNS has become almost a general-purpose distributed database for controlling accesses to resources for client–server applications over the IP network. In the beginning, public switched telephone network (PSTN) has been used for telecommunications administered by the International Telecommunication Union-Telephone (ITU-T). ITU-T Recommendation E.164 is used as the number system of the PSTN functional entities, including telephones throughout the world, and the assignment of number prefixes to each country code is also administered by the ITU-T. It implies that interoperability between the IP addresses and E.164 numbers is needed. In this context, the E.164 number (ENUM) technical standard facilitates the mapping using a DNS name parent of e164.arpa. This chapter exclusively discusses both DNS and ENUM address resolution mechanisms, as well as the mapping between the IP addresses and the E.164 telephone numbers in detail.

8.1 Introduction

The Domain Name System (DNS) resolves the human-readable host names (e.g., rrr@rnl.com) into Internet Protocol (IP) addresses. The DNS is a hierarchical, domain-based naming scheme distributed database system for implementing the naming scheme. Because of the distributed nature of the DNS architecture, the use of caching is highly scalable over a large network, as large as the public Internet, including any private networks. However, it can also be used for many other purposes, such as controlling access to resources, traffic management and load balancing, and network planning. As a result, it appears that DNS has become a general-purpose distributed database for controlling accesses to resources: virtually all applications including Session Initiation Protocol/Voice over IP (SIP/VoIP), e-mail, World Wide Web (WWW), instant messaging, File Transfer Protocol, Lightweight Directory Access Protocol, Network Time Protocol, Post Office Protocol (POP), Simple Mail Transfer Protocol (SMTP) mail, and peer-to-peer (P2P) applications.

Historically, circuit-switched-based public switched telephone network (PSTN) was used for telecommunications in the beginning. The PSTN network uses the numbering plan as administered by the ITU-T, and the plan, Recommendation E.164, involves the assignment of number prefixes to each country code administrator. This E.164 numbering plan has evolved today into a global numbering plan where every device connected to the telephone network is assigned a unique numerical address.

If the Internet telephony that is also the IP device with an IP address needs to interoperate seamlessly with the telephone network, it becomes urgent for supporting this E.164 numbering plain into the realm of the Internet. The seamless interworking between the IP and PSTN telephones requires a mapping between the IP address and the E.164 address. The Electronic Number (ENUM) technical standard facilitates this mapping using a DNS name parent of e164.arpa. It also implies that every Internet device that supports telephone operation needs to also have an alias in the form of a unique telephone address. In this way, the Internet telephony world is able to interface to the telephone network by allowing Internet-connected telephone devices to make and receive calls to any other telephone device, whether the other device is connected to the Internet, connected to the telephone network, or connected to any other network that seamlessly interoperates with the telephone network.

8.2 Domain Name System

8.2.1 Namespace

The hierarchical naming system with a distributed database for hosts of DNS makes it possible to assign domain names to groups of Internet resources and users in a meaningful way, independent of each entity's physical location. The DNS uses an application program known as the resolver passing the name as a parameter to map a name onto the IP address. Figure 8.1 shows the hierarchical naming system with domain names, with each domain having a name server. All of these domains are represented by a tree. The leaves of the tree represent domains that have no subdomains, and a leaf domain may contain a single host or thousands of hosts. Each domain is named by the path upward from it to the unnamed root, and domain names are case insensitive. The components are separated by periods (e.g., eng.llc.com). However, DNS names avoid specifics such as IP addresses and port numbers.

The decentralization of DNS administration is obtained through delegation of domain names, a given domain can be divided into subdomains, and each of the subdomains can be delegated to other organizations. It implies that the delegated organization becomes responsible for maintaining all the data responsible to that subdomain. For example, the engineering.llc domain (Figure 8.1) is delegated to the folks of engineering. The efficient caching scheme that is applied

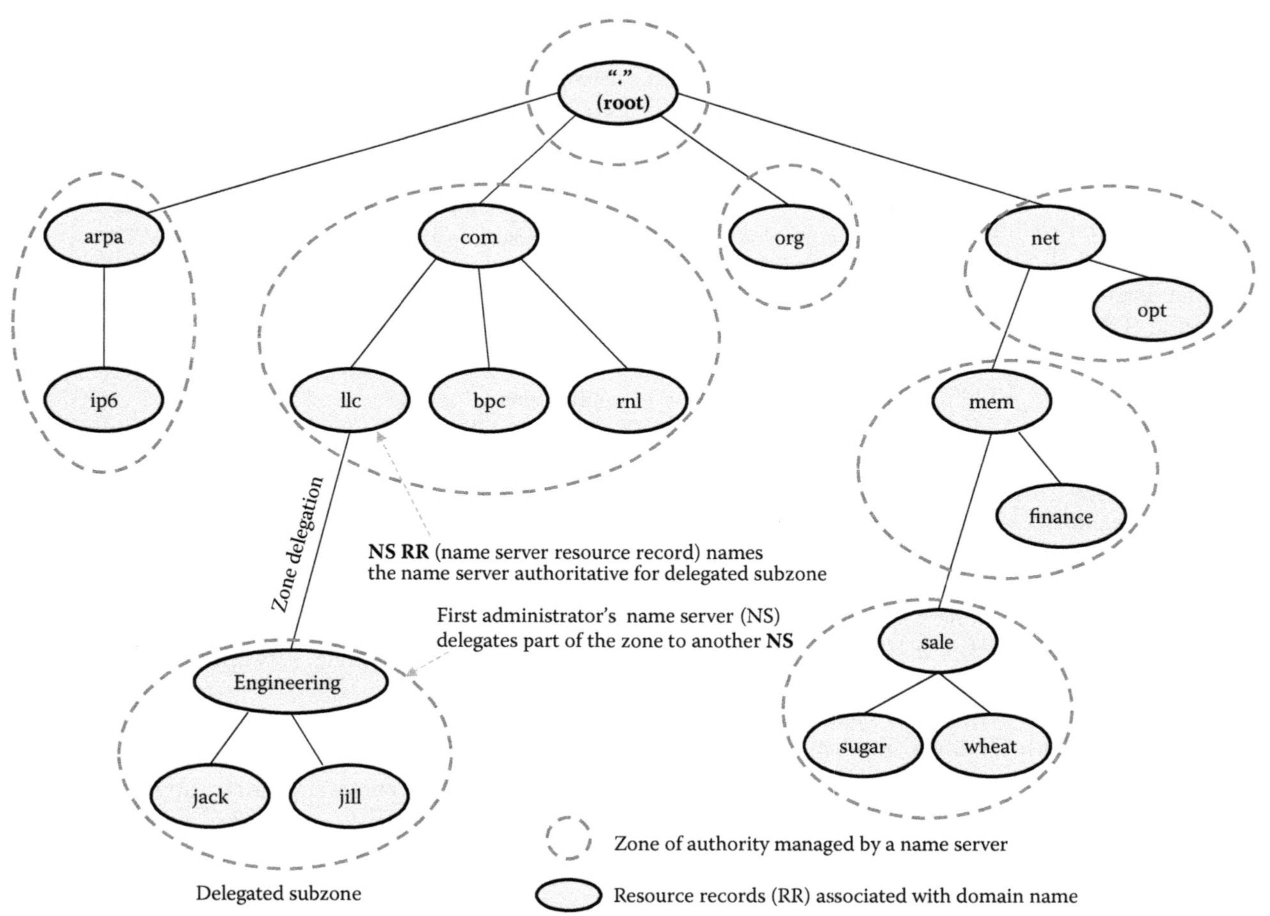

Figure 8.1 DNS naming system. (Copyright IETF. Reproduced with permission.)

in DNS allows most DNS queries to traverse only one or two DNS servers. As a result, DNS updates require significant time to propagate in the Internet. The mobility services that require IP addresses to be changed rapidly cannot use DNS services. However, a cached record may sometimes be out of date, and authoritative records need to be used to avoid this problem. An authoritative record is one that comes from the authority that manages the record, and is thus always correct.

8.2.2 Resource Records

Every domain can have a set of resource records (RRs) associated with it. The most common item of the RR is the IP address of the host; however, many other RRs can also exist as DNS and can be used for many other applications. Thus, when a resolver sends a query passing a namespace (i.e., domain name) to DNS, the DNS simply maps the domain name onto an RR associated with it and sends the query back to the resolver. An RR is five tuple, as shown in Table 8.1 (Request for Comment [RFC] 1035): NAME, TTL, CLASS, TYPE, RDLENGTH, and RDATA. Table 8.2 depicts the different types of RRs, the value for each RR type, and the description of each RR type.

Table 8.1 Resource Record Fields

Resource Record	*Length (in Octets)*	*Description*
Name	(Variable)	A domain in which an RR is applicable.
TTL	4	Time-to-live (TTL) is the length of time an RR will last.
Class	2	It indicates an RR's class. For Internet, it is IN; for non-Internet, other codes can be used.
Type	2	It indicates an RR's type assigned by IANA (DNS parameters). There are many types of RR as shown in Table 8.2. Each RR type has a value that is also assigned by IANA, as shown in Table 8.2.
RDLENGTH	2	Length of RDATA field.
RDATA	(Variable)	Additional RR-specific data.

- NAME is the fully qualified domain name (FQDN) of the node in the tree. The domain name may be compressed where ends of domain names in the packet can be substituted for the end of the current domain name.
- TTL is the time to live and is expressed in seconds so that the RR stays valid up to that duration. The maximum is $2^{31} - 1$ (~68 years).
- TYPE is the record type and indicates the format of the data. It provides a hint of its intended use. Table 8.2 shows different RR types and the value of each type as assigned by the Internet Assigned Numbers Authority (IANA) for DNS.
- RDATA is data of type-specific relevance, such as the IP address for address records, or the priority and host name for mail exchange (MX) records. Well-known record types may use label compression in the RDATA field, but *unknown* record types must not (RFC 3597).
- The CLASS of a record is set to IN (for Internet) for common DNS records involving Internet host names, servers, or IP addresses. In addition, the classes Chaos (CN) and Hesiod (HS) exist. Each class is an independent namespace with potentially different delegations of DNS zones.

In addition to RRs defined in a zone file, the domain name system also defines several request types that are used only in communication with other DNS nodes (on the wire), such as when performing full zone transfers (operation code, AXFR), incremental zone transfers (IXFR), or for extension mechanisms for DNS (EDNS) OPT RR (Table 8.2).

8.2.3 Name Servers

The name server that remains in a given domain keeps the namespace stored in its database using application programs. A name server that has the complete information about some part of a given domain namespace is called a zone because the DNS namespace is divided into nonoverlapping zones. For example, the mem.net name server (Figure 8.1) handles engineering.finance.mem.net but not sale.mem.net, which is a separate zone with its own name server. This is the way a name server is provisioned. For example, in Figure 8.1, we can say that the finance department does not wish to run its own name server, but the sales department does like to run one. Consequently, sale.mem.net is a separate zone, but finance.mem.net is not. If a resolver is used for address resolution, it passes the query containing the domain name to one of the local name servers starting from the root server (Figure 8.2) that knows where the authoritative name servers for all top-level domains are. If the domain being sought falls under the jurisdiction of the same name server (e.g., engineering.llc.com falling under llc.com in Figures 8.1 and 8.2), it returns the authoritative RRs with IP address (e.g., IPv6) to the resolver.

Table 8.2 DNS Resource Record Type, Value, and Description

RR Type	*RR Type Value*	*RFC*	*Description*
A	1	RFC 1035	IPv4 address record for a host.
AAAA	28	RFC 3596	IPv6 address record for a host (forward-mapped zones recommended by IETF).
A6	38	RFC 2874	Forward mapping of IPv6 addresses record for a host within the zone (experimental).
AFSDB	18	RFC 1183	Location record of AFS servers for special apps only (experimental).
CNAME	5	RFC 1035	An alias canonical name record for a host.
DNAME	39	RFC 2672	Delegation record of reverse addresses primarily for IPv6 (experimental).
DNSKEY	48	RFC 4034	DNS public key RR (DNS Security [DNSSEC]).
DS	43	RFC 4034	Delegated signer RR (DNS Security [DNSSEC]).
HINFO	13	RFC 1035	Host information/description record about a host (optional text data).
ISDN	20	RFC 1183	ISDN address record for special applications only (experimental).
KEY	25	RFC 2535	Public key record associated with a DNS name.
LOC	29	RFC 1876	GPS data record related to location information—widely used (experimental).
MX	15	RFC 1035	Mail exchanger record and RFC 974-defined valid names—a preference value and the host name for a mail server/exchanger that will service this zone.
NAPTR	35	RFC 3403	Naming Authority Pointer Record. General-purpose definition of rule set to be used by applications (e.g., SIP/VoIP).
NS	2	RFC 1035	Name Server record that defines the authoritative name server(s) for the domain (defined by the SOA record) or the subdomain.
NSEC	47	RFC 4034	Next Secure record used to provide proof of nonexistence of a name.
NXT	30	RFC 3755/2535	DNS Security (DNSSEC) Next Domain record type that obsoletes use of NSEC.
OPT	41	RFC 2671	Known as pseudo-RR because it pertains to a particular transport level message and not to any actual DNS data. OPT RRs shall never be cached, forwarded, or stored in or loaded from master files.
PTR	12	RFC 1035	Alias records for the IP address (IPv4 or IPv6) for the host used in reverse maps.
RP	17	RFC 1183	Information record about responsible person for special applications only (experimental).
RRSIG	46	RFC 4034	Signed RRset record (DNSSEC).
RT	21	RFC 1183	Through-route binding record for special applications only (experimental).
SIG	24	RFC 2931/2535	Signature record for DNS Security (DNSSEC) that obsoletes the use of RR signature (RRSIG) and SIG(0) is used as a special meta RR in Dynamic DNS (DDNS) and zone transfer security.
SOA	6	RFC 1035	Start of Authority record that defines the zone name, an e-mail contact and various time and refresh values applicable to the zone.

(Continued)

Table 8.2 (Continued) DNS Resource Record Type, Value, and Description

RR Type	*RR Type Value*	*RFC*	*Description*
SPF	99	RFC 4408	Sender Policy Framework (SPF) (v1) record that defines the servers that are authorized to send mail for a domain, and its primary function is to prevent identity theft by spammers.
SRV	33	RFC 2872	Service record that defines services available in the zone (e.g., SIP, IM, XMPP, LDAP, HTTP, SMTP).
TXT	16	RFC 1035	Text information record associated with a name. Note: The SPF record should be defined using TXT record and may be defined using an SPF RR. Domain Keys Identified Mail (DKIM) (RFC 487) (also makes use of the TXT RR for authenticating e-mail.
WKS	11	RFC 1035	Well-Known Services record deprecated in favor of SRV record.
X25	19	RFC 1183	X.25 addresses record for special applications only (experimental).

Source: IANA DNS Parameters: http://www.iana.org/assignments/dns-parameters. Copyright IETF. Reproduced with permission.

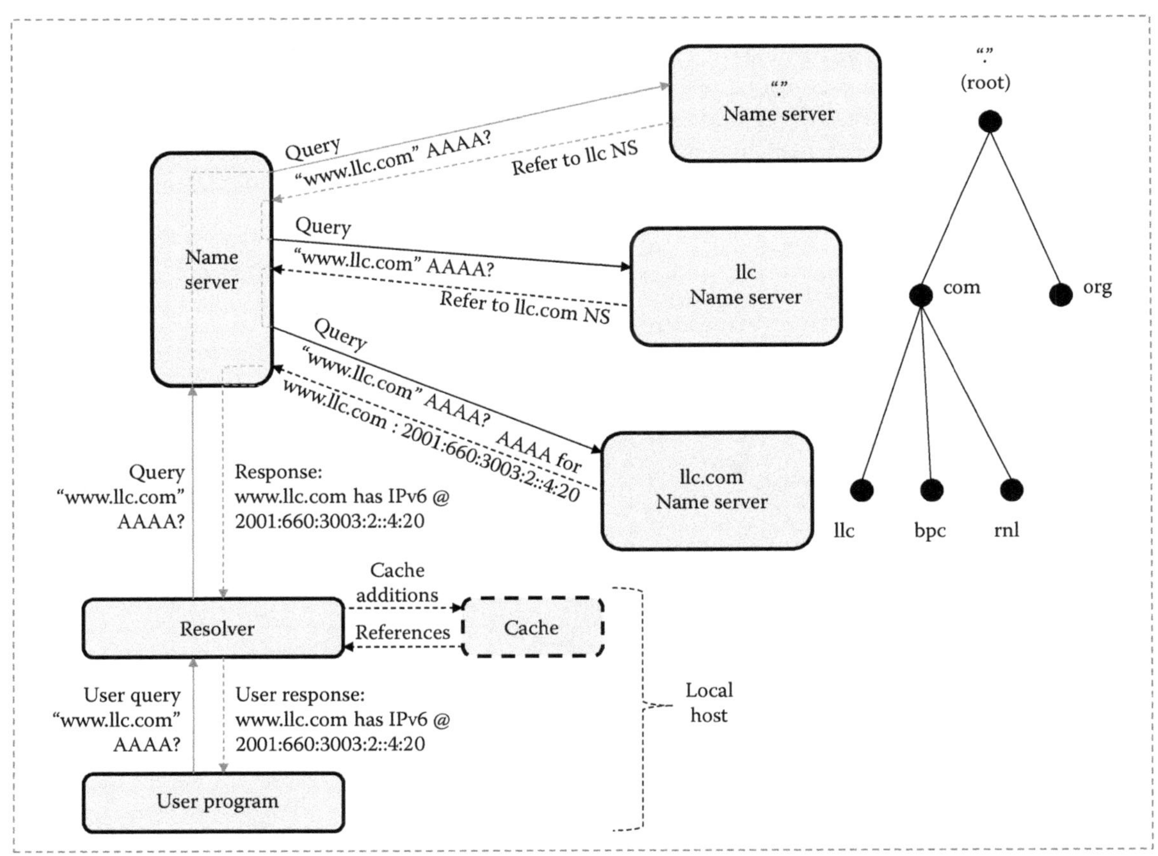

Figure 8.2 DNS address lookup.

Another scenario can be that the domain is remote and the local naming server does not have access to that domain directly. The local name server sends the query to the top domain server for the domain requested. For example, a resolver on finance.mem.net (Figure 8.1) wants to resolve the IP address of the host jack.engineering.llc.com. At first, the resolver will send the query to the local name server mem .net. The query will then be sent to com.server.net as the name server, mem.net or net, does not know the domain space. The com name server will then forward the query to its child, engineering.llc.com, name server as it does not know the domain space. In turn, it will send the query to the engineering.llc.com name server that must have the authoritative RRs. The query has formed a path from the client to the server, and the response from the engineering .llc.com name server will follow the same path and will come back to the originator. It is important to note that once these RRs are obtained by the engineering.llc.com name server, the server will keep these records into a cache in case they are used later. However, the TTL field of these RRs should not live long because cache data, as explained earlier, is not authoritative.

It should be noted that the Dynamic Host Configuration Protocol (DHCP) can be used to discover the IP addresses of local catching resolvers. The DHCP server manages a pool of IP addresses and information about client configuration parameters, such as domain names and name servers in local environments. The allocated IP addresses can be assigned to the local host dynamically (i.e., as if leasing IP addresses for a limited time), automatically (i.e., permanent assignment of IP addresses), and statically (i.e., allocation of IP addresses manually) depending on implementation. DHCP is useful because it automates the network parameter assignment to network devices from one or more DHCP servers. DHCP makes it easy to add new machines in the network locally and can complement work with DNS that resolves the IP addresses across the global Internet. The DNS and DHCP mechanisms described here are also equally applicable for the enterprise and private IP network.

8.2.4 Locating/Discovering SIP Entities

8.2.4.1 Overview

The SIP, being a client–server protocol, uses DNS procedures to allow a client to resolve a SIP Uniform Resource Identifier (URI) into the IP address, port, and transport protocol of the next hop to contact. It also uses DNS to allow a server to send a response to a backup client if the primary client has failed. RFC 3263 that is described here specifies those DNS procedures in detail. A typical SIP configuration, referred to as the SIP trapezoid with two administrative domains, is shown in Figure 8.3. In this diagram, a caller in domain A (UA 1) wishes to call Joe in domain B (joe@B). To do so, it communicates with proxy 1 in its domain (domain A). Proxy 1 forwards the request to the proxy for the domain of the called party (domain B), which is proxy 2. Proxy 2 forwards the call to the called party, UA 2. As part of this call flow, proxy 1 needs to determine a SIP server for domain B. To do this, proxy 1 makes use of DNS procedures, using both Service (SRV) (RFC 2782) and Naming Authority Pointer (NAPTR) (RFCs 3401–3404) records. We describe the

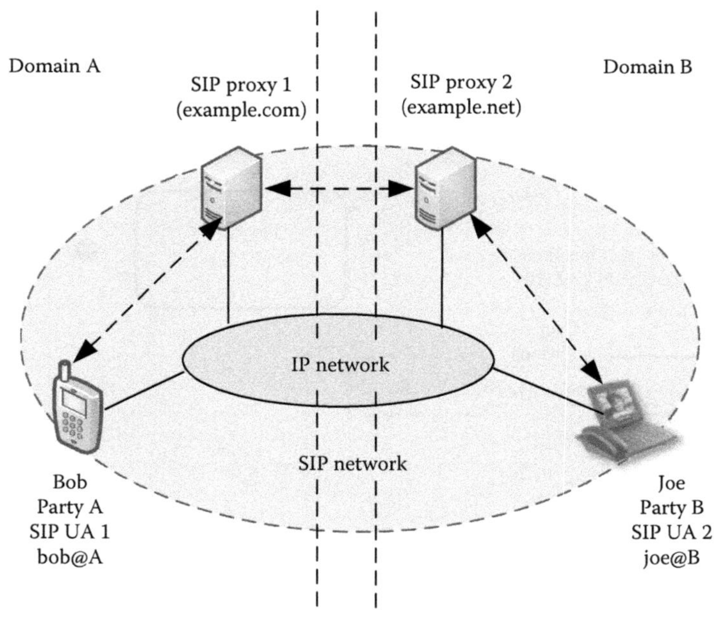

Figure 8.3 SIP trapezoid with two administrative domains. (Copyright IETF. Reproduced with permission.)

specific problems for which SIP uses DNS to help solve, and provides a solution. However, the use of DNS by the stateful client (stateful user client or stateful proxy) and stateless proxy differs slightly.

8.2.4.2 Problems DNS Needs to Solve

DNS is needed to help solve two aspects of the general call flow described in Section 8.1. The first is for proxy 1 to discover the SIP server in domain B, in order to forward the call for joe@B. The second is for proxy 2 to identify a backup for proxy 1 in the event that it fails after forwarding the request. For the first aspect, proxy 1 specifically needs to determine the IP address, port, and transport protocol for the server in domain B. The choice of transport protocol is particularly noteworthy. Unlike many other protocols, SIP can run over a variety of transport protocols, including Transmission Control Protocol (TCP), User Datagram Protocol, and Stream Control Transmission Protocol (SCTP). SIP can also use TLS. Currently, use of TLS is defined for TCP only. Thus, clients need to be able to automatically determine which transport protocols are available. The proxy sending the request has a particular set of transport protocols it supports and a preference for using those transport protocols. Proxy 2 has its own set of transport protocols it supports, and relative preferences for those transport protocols. All proxies must implement both UDP and TCP, along with TLS over TCP, so that there is always an intersection of capabilities. Some form of DNS procedures are needed for proxy 1 to discover the available transport protocols for SIP services at domain B, and the relative preferences of those transport protocols. Proxy 1 intersects its list of supported transport protocols with those of proxy 2, and then chooses the protocol preferred by proxy 2.

It is important to note that DNS lookups can be used multiple times throughout the processing of a call. In general, an element that wishes to send a request (called a client) may need to perform DNS processing to determine the IP address, port, and transport protocol of a next-hop element, called a server (it can be a proxy or a user agent). Such processing could, in principle, occur at every hop between elements. Since SIP is used for the establishment of interactive communications services, the time it takes to complete a transaction between a caller and the called party is important. Typically, the time from when the caller initiates a call until the time the called party is alerted should be no more than a few seconds. Given that there can be multiple hops, each of which is doing DNS lookups in addition to other potentially time-intensive operations, the amount of time available for DNS lookups at each hop is limited.

Scalability and high availability are important in SIP. SIP services scale up through clustering techniques. Typically, in a realistic version of the network in Figure 8.3, proxy 2 would be a cluster of homogeneously configured proxies. DNS needs to provide the ability for domain B to configure a set of servers, along with prioritization and weights, in order to provide a crude level of capacity-based load balancing. SIP assures high availability by having upstream elements detect failures. For example, assume that proxy 2 is implemented as a cluster of two proxies, proxy 2.1 and proxy 2.2. If proxy 1 sends a request to proxy 2.1 and the request fails, it retries the request by sending it to proxy 2.2. In many cases, proxy 1 will not know which domains it will ultimately communicate with. That information would be known when a user actually makes a call to another user in that domain. Proxy 1 may never communicate with that domain again after the call completes. Proxy 1 may communicate with thousands of different domains within a few minutes, and proxy 2 could receive requests from thousands of different domains within a few minutes. Because of this many-to-many relationship, and the possibly long intervals in communications between a pair of domains, it is not generally possible for an element to maintain a dynamic availability state for the proxies it will communicate with.

When a proxy gets its first call with a particular domain, it will try the servers in that domain in some order until it finds one that is available. The identity of the available server would ideally be cached for some amount of time in order to reduce call setup delays of subsequent calls. The client cannot query a failed server continuously to determine when it becomes available again, since this does not scale. Furthermore, the availability state must eventually be flushed in order to redistribute load to recovered elements when they come back online. It is possible for elements to fail in the middle of a transaction. For example, after proxy 2 forwards the request to UA 2, proxy 1 fails. UA 2 sends its response to proxy 2, which tries to forward it to proxy 1, which is no longer available. The second aspect of the flow in the introduction for which DNS is needed is for proxy 2 to identify a backup for proxy 1 that it can send the response to. This problem is more realistic in SIP than it is in other transactional protocols. The reason is that some SIP responses can take a long time to be generated, because a human user frequently needs to be consulted in order to generate that response. As such, it is not uncommon for tens of seconds to elapse between a call request and its acceptance.

8.2.4.3 Client Usage

Usage of DNS differs for clients and for servers. This section discusses client usage. We assume that the client is stateful (either a UAC [user agent client] or a stateful proxy). Stateless proxies are discussed later in this chapter. The procedures here are invoked when a client needs to send a request to a resource identified by a SIP or SIPS URI. This URI can identify the desired resource to which the request is targeted (in which case, the URI is found in the Request-URI), or it can identify an intermediate hop toward that resource (in which case, the URI is found in the Route header). The procedures defined here in no way affect this URI (i.e., the URI is not rewritten with the result of the DNS lookup); they only result in an IP address, port, and transport protocol where the request can be sent. RFC 3261 provides guidelines on determining which URI needs to be resolved in DNS to determine the host that the request needs to be sent to. In some cases, also documented in RFC 3261, the request can be sent to a specific intermediate proxy not identified by a SIP URI, but rather by a host name or numeric IP address. In that case, a temporary URI, used for purposes of this specification, is constructed. That URI is of the form sip:<proxy>, where <proxy> is the FQDN or numeric IP address of the next-hop proxy. As a result, in all cases, the problem boils down to resolution of a SIP or SIPS URI in DNS to determine the IP address, port, and transport of the host to which the request is to be sent.

The procedures here must be done exactly once per transaction, where transaction is as defined in RFC 3261. That is, once a SIP server has successfully been contacted (success is defined below), all retransmissions of the SIP request and the ACK for non-2xx SIP responses to INVITE must be sent to the same host. Furthermore, a CANCEL for a particular SIP request must be sent to the same SIP server that the SIP request was delivered to. Because the ACK request for 2xx responses to INVITE constitutes a different transaction, there is no requirement that it be delivered to the same server that received the original request (indeed, if that server did not record-route, it will not get the ACK). We define TARGET as the value of the maddr parameter of the URI, if present; otherwise, as the host value of the hostport component of the URI. It identifies the domain to be contacted. A description of the SIP and SIPS URIs and a definition of these parameters can be found in RFC 3261. We determine the transport protocol, port, and IP address of a suitable instance of TARGET described below.

8.2.4.3.1 Selecting a Transport Protocol

First, the client selects a transport protocol. If the URI specifies a transport protocol in the transport parameter, that transport protocol should be used. Otherwise, if no transport protocol is specified, but the TARGET is a numeric IP address, the client should use UDP for a SIP URI, and TCP for a SIPS URI. Similarly, if no transport protocol is specified, and the TARGET is not numeric, but an explicit port is provided, the client should use UDP for a SIP URI and TCP for a SIPS URI. This is because UDP is the only mandatory transport in RFC 2543 superseded by RFC 3261, and thus the only one guaranteed to be interoperable for a SIP URI. It was also specified as the default transport in RFC 2543 when no transport was present in the SIP URI. However, another transport, such as TCP, may be used if the guidelines of SIP mandate it for this particular request. That is the case, for example, for requests that exceed the path maximum transmission unit (MTU).

Otherwise, if no transport protocol or port is specified, and the target is not a numeric IP address, the client should perform a NAPTR query for the domain in the URI. The services relevant for the task of transport protocol selection are those with NAPTR service fields with values SIP+D2X and SIPS+D2X, where X is a letter that corresponds to a transport protocol supported by the domain. This specification defines D2U for UDP, D2T for TCP, and D2S for SCTP. We also establish an IANA registry for NAPTR service name to transport protocol mappings. These NAPTR records provide a mapping from a domain to the SRV record for contacting a server with the specific transport protocol in the NAPTR services field. The RR will contain an empty regular expression and a replacement value, which is the SRV record for that particular transport protocol. If the server supports multiple transport protocols, there will be multiple NAPTR records, each with a different service value. As per RFCs 3401–3404, the client discards any records whose service fields are not applicable. For the purposes of this specification, several rules are defined.

First, a client resolving a SIPS URI must discard any services that do not contain *SIPS* as the protocol in the service field. The converse is not true, however. A client resolving a SIP URI should retain records with SIPS as the protocol, if the client supports TLS. Second, a client must discard any service fields that identify a resolution service whose value is not *D2X*, for values of X that indicate transport protocols supported by the client. The NAPTR processing as described in RFCs 3401–3404 will result in the discovery of the most preferred transport protocol of the server that is supported by the client, as well as an SRV record for the server. It will also allow the client to discover if TLS is available and its preference for its usage.

As an example, consider a client that wishes to resolve sip:user@example.com. The client performs a NAPTR query for that domain, and the following NAPTR records are returned:

```
; order pref flags service regexp replacement
IN NAPTR 50 50 "s" "SIPS+D2T" "" _sips._tcp.
example.com.
IN NAPTR 90 50 "s" "SIP+D2T" ""  _sip._tcp.
example.com
IN NAPTR 100 50 "s" "SIP+D2U" "" _sip._udp.
example.com.
```

This indicates that the server supports TLS over TCP, TCP, and UDP, in that order of preference. Since the client supports TCP and UDP, TCP will be used, targeted to a host determined by an SRV lookup of _sip._tcp.example .com. That lookup would return

```
;;        Priority      Weight Port   Target
IN SRV  0            1   5060    server1.example.com
IN SRV  0            2   5060    server2.example.com
```

If a SIP proxy, redirect server, or registrar is to be contacted through the lookup of NAPTR records, there must be at least three records—one with a SIP+D2T service field, one with a SIP+D2U service field, and one with a SIPS+D2T service field. The records with SIPS as the protocol in the service field should be preferred (i.e., have a lower value of the order field) above records with SIP as the protocol in the service field. A record with a SIPS+D2U service field should not be placed into the DNS, since it is not possible to use TLS over UDP. It is not necessary for the domain suffixes in the NAPTR replacement field to match the domain of the original query (i.e., example.com above). However, for backwards compatibility with RFC 2543, a domain must maintain SRV records for the domain of the original query, even if the NAPTR record is in a different domain. As an example, even though the SRV record for TCP is _sip._tcp.school.edu, there must also be an SRV record at _sip._tcp.example.com. RFC 2543 will look up the SRV records for the domain directly. If these do not exist because the NAPTR replacement points to a different domain, the client will fail.

For NAPTR records with SIPS protocol fields (if the server is using a site certificate), the domain name in the query and the domain name in the replacement field must both be valid based on the site certificate handed out by the server in the TLS exchange. Similarly, the domain name in the SRV query and the domain name in the target in the SRV record must both be valid based on the same site certificate. Otherwise, an attacker could modify the DNS records to contain replacement values in a different domain, and the client could not validate that this was the desired behavior or the result of an attack. If no NAPTR records are found, the client constructs SRV queries for those transport protocols it supports, and does a query for each. Queries are done using the service identifier *_sip* for SIP URIs and *_sips* for SIPS URIs. A particular transport is supported if the query is successful. The client may use any transport protocol it desires that is supported by the server. This is a change from RFC 2543 (obsoleted by RFC 3261). It specifies that a client would look up SRV records for all transports it supported, and merge the priority values across those records. Then, it would choose the most preferred record. If no SRV records are found, the client should use TCP for a SIPS URI, and UDP for a SIP URI. However, another transport protocol, such as TCP, may be used if the guidelines of SIP mandate it for this particular request. That is the case, for example, for requests that exceed the path MTU.

8.2.4.3.2 Determining Port and IP Address

Once the transport protocol has been determined, the next step is to determine the IP address and port. If the TARGET is a numeric IP address, the client uses that address. If the URI also contains a port, it uses that port. If no port is specified, it uses the default port for the particular transport protocol. If the TARGET is not a numeric IP address, but a port is present in the URI, the client performs an A or AAAA record lookup of the domain name. The result will be a list of IP addresses, each of which can be contacted at the specific port from the URI and transport protocol determined previously. The client should try the first record. If an attempt should fail, based on the definition of failure described in the next section, the next should be tried, and if that should fail, the next SHOULD be tried, and so on. This is a change from RFC 2543 (obsoleted by RFC 3261). Previously, if the port was explicit, but with a value of 5060, SRV records were used. Now, A or AAAA records will be used. If the TARGET is not a numeric IP address, and no port is present in the URI, the client performs an SRV query on the record returned from the NAPTR processing described in the earlier section, if such processing was performed.

If it was not, because a transport was specified explicitly, the client performs an SRV query for that specific transport, using the service identifier _sips for SIPS URIs. For a SIP URI, if the client wishes to use TLS, it also uses the service identifier _sips for that specific transport; otherwise, it uses _sip. If the NAPTR processing was not done because no NAPTR records were found, but an SRV query for a supported transport protocol was successful, those SRV records are selected. Regardless of how the SRV records were determined, the procedures of RFC 2782, as described in the section titled "Usage Rules," are followed, augmented by the additional procedures described in the next section. If no SRV records were found, the client performs an A or AAAA record lookup of the domain name. The result will be a list of IP addresses, each of which can be contacted using the transport protocol determined previously, at the default port for that transport. Processing then proceeds as described above for an explicit port once the A or AAAA records have been looked up.

8.2.4.3.3 Details of RFC 2782 Process

RFC 2782 spells out the details of how a set of SRV records are sorted and then tried. However, it only states that the client should "try to connect to the (protocol, address, service)" without giving any details on what happens in the event of failure. Those details are described here for SIP. For SIP requests, failure occurs if the transaction layer reports a 503 Server Unavailable error response or a transport failure of some sort (generally, due to fatal Internet Control Message

Protocol errors in UDP or connection failures in TCP). Failure also occurs if the transaction layer times out without ever having received any response, provisional or final (i.e., timer B or timer F in RFC 3261 fires; see Section 3.12). If a failure occurs, the client should create a new request that is identical to the previous one but has a different value of the Via branch ID (and therefore constitutes a new SIP transaction). That request is sent to the next element in the list as specified by RFC 2782.

8.2.4.3.4 Consideration for Stateless Proxies

The process of the previous sections is highly stateful. When a server is contacted successfully, all retransmissions of the request for the transaction, as well as ACK for a non-2xx final response, and CANCEL requests for that transaction, must go to the same server. The identity of the successfully contacted server is a form of transaction state. This presents a challenge for stateless proxies, which still need to meet the requirement for sending all requests in the transaction to the same server. The problem is similar, but different, to the problem of HTTP transactions within a cookie session getting routed to different servers based on DNS randomization. There, such distribution is not a problem. Farms of servers generally have common back-end data stores, where the session data is stored. Whenever a server in the farm receives an HTTP request, it takes the session identifier, if present, and extracts the needed state to process the request. A request without a session identifier creates a new one. The problem with stateless proxies is at a lower layer; it is retransmitted requests within a transaction that are being potentially spread across servers.

Since none of these retransmissions carries a *session identifier* (a complete dialog identifier in SIP terms), a new dialog would be created identically at each server. This could, for example, result in multiple phone calls to be made to the same phone. Therefore, it is critical to prevent such a thing from happening in the first place. The requirement is not difficult to meet in the simple case where there were no failures when attempting to contact a server. Whenever the stateless proxy receives the request, it performs the appropriate DNS queries as described above. However, the procedures of RFC 2782 are not guaranteed to be deterministic. This is because records that contain the same priority have no specified order. The stateless proxy must define a deterministic order to the records in that case, using any algorithm at its disposal. One suggestion is to alphabetize them, or, more generally, sort them by ASCII-compatible encoding. To make processing easier for stateless proxies, it is recommended that domain administrators make the weights of SRV records with equal priority different (e.g., using weights of 1000 and 1001 if two servers are equivalent, rather than assigning both a weight of 1000), and similarly for NAPTR records.

If the first server is contacted successfully, the proxy can remain stateless. However, if the first server is not contacted successfully, and a subsequent server is, the proxy cannot remain stateless for this transaction. If it were stateless, a retransmission could very well go to a different server if the failed one recovers between retransmissions. As such, whenever a proxy does not successfully contact the first server, it should act as a stateful proxy. Unfortunately, it is still possible for a stateless proxy to deliver retransmissions to different servers, even if it follows the recommendations above. This can happen if the DNS TTLs expire in the middle of a transaction, and the entries had changed. This is unavoidable. Network implementers should be aware of this limitation and not use stateless proxies that access DNS if this error is deemed critical.

8.2.4.3.5 Server Usage

RFC 3261 (see Chapters 2 and 3) defines procedures for sending responses from a server back to the client. Typically, for unicast UDP requests, the response is sent back to the source IP address where the request came from, using the port contained in the Via header. For reliable transport protocols, the response is sent over the connection the request arrived on. However, it is important to provide failover support when the client element fails between sending the request and receiving the response. A server, according to RFC 3261, will send a response on the connection it arrived on (in the case of reliable transport protocols), and for unreliable transport protocols, to the source address of the request, and the port in the Via header field. The procedures here are invoked when a server attempts to send to that location and that response. *Fails* is defined as any closure of the transport connection the request came in on before the response can be sent, or communication of a fatal error from the transport layer. In these cases, the server examines the value of the sent-by construction in the topmost Via header.

If it contains a numeric IP address, the server attempts to send the response to that address, using the transport protocol from the Via header, and the port from sent-by, if present, else the default for that transport protocol. The transport protocol in the Via header can indicate *TLS*, which refers to TLS over TCP. When this value is present, the server must use TLS over TCP to send the response. If, however, the sent-by field contained a domain name and a port number, the server queries for A or AAAA records with that name. It tries to send the response to each element on the resulting list of IP addresses, using the port from the Via, and the transport protocol from the Via (again, a value of TLS refers to TLS over TCP). As in the client processing, the next entry in the list is tried if the one before it results in a failure. If, however, the sent-by field contains a domain name and no port, the server queries for SRV records at that domain name using the service identifier _sips if the Via transport is TLS, _sip otherwise, and the transport from the topmost Via header (TLS implies that the transport protocol in the SRV query is TCP). The resulting list is sorted as described in RFC 2782, and the response is sent to the topmost element on the new list described there. If that results in a failure, the next entry on the list is tried.

8.2.4.4 Constructing SIP URIs

In many cases, an element needs to construct a SIP URI for inclusion in a Contact header in a REGISTER, or in a Record-Route header in an INVITE. According to RFC 3261 (see Section 4.2), these URIs have to have the property that they resolve to the specific element that inserted them. However, if they are constructed with just an IP address, for example

```
sip:1.2.3.4
```

then should the element fail, there is no way to route the request or response through a backup. SRV provides a way to fix this. Instead of using an IP address, a domain name that resolves to an SRV record can be used:

```
sip:server23.provider.com
```

The SRV records for a particular target can be set up so that there is a single record with a low value for the priority field (indicating the preferred choice), and this record points to the specific element that constructed the URI. However, there are additional records with higher values of the priority field that point to backup elements that would be used in the event of failure. This allows the constraint of RFC 3261 to be met while allowing for robust operation.

8.2.4.5 Selecting the Transport Protocol

The SIP URI of a SIP entity that needs to be resolved may have the transport parameters specified. If the transport parameters are specified, those transport parameters should be used by the stateful client for communication with DNS. Otherwise, if no transport protocol is specified, but the target is a numeric IP address, the client should use UDP for a SIP URI and TCP for a SIPS URI. Similarly, if no transport protocol is specified, and the target is not numeric, but an explicit port is provided, the client should use UDP for a SIP URI and TCP for a SIPS URI.

If no transport protocol or port is specified, and the target is not a numeric IP address, the client should perform a NAPTR query for the domain in the URI. The services relevant for the task of transport protocol selection are those with NAPTR service fields with values SIP+D2X and SIPS+D2X, where X is a letter that corresponds to a transport protocol supported by the domain. This specification defines D2U for UDP, D2T for TCP, and D2S for SCTP.

8.2.4.6 Transport Determination Application

The Dynamic Delegation Discovery System (DDDS) represents the evolution of the NAPTR RR. DDDS defines applications that can make use of the NAPTR record for specific resolution services. This application is called the Transport Determination Application, and its goal is to map an incoming SIP or SIPS URI to a set of SRV records for the various servers that can handle the URI. The following are the details that the DDDS requests an application to provide:

- **Application Unique String (AUS):** The AUS is the input to the resolution service. For this application, it is the URI that is to be resolved.
- **First Well-Known Rule:** The First Well-Known Rule extracts a key from the AUS. For this application, the First Well-Known Rule extracts the host portion of the SIP or SIPS URI.
- **Valid Databases:** The key resulting from the First Well-Known Rule is looked up in a single database, the DNS. Expected output: the result of the application is an SRV record for the server to contact.

8.3 ENUM

ENUM is a protocol that has the capability to map ITU-T's E.164 numbers into URIs as described in RFCs 6116 and 6117 using DNS in the Internet and then to the IP addresses. It first transforms E.164 numbers into ENUM domain names and then uses the DNS-based architecture to access records from which the URIs are derived. As a result, ENUM allows the exiting telephone numbering plan or its administration to be kept without modifying it, bridging networks overseen by different standards bodies: ITU-T and IETF. ENUM is also used for many other services in addition to address translation. In fact, ENUM can be defined as a protocol that maps a telephone number to a domain name, maps the domain name to a group of service-specific URIs, and then looks up what services (e.g., e-mail address, web site, VoIP service address, or others) are available for a particular telephone number including the translation to the IP address. ENUM uses the DNS NAPTR RR type to store its DDDS rules into DNS domains. ENUM relies on DNS services and, thereby, it is also important for ENUM implementation to carry out a thorough analysis of all of the existing DNS standard documents to understand what services are provided to ENUM and what load ENUM provisioning and queries will place on the DNS. The ENUM implementation employs a DNS-based tiered architecture as shown in Figure 8.4.

The different ENUM's DNS-based tiered architecture is described as follows:

- **Tier 0:** It corresponds to the ENUM root level. At this level, the ENUM architecture contains only one domain (the ENUM root). The ITU-Telecommunication Standardization Bureau (TSB) is the ENUM Tier 0 Registrar for that domain. The ENUM Tier 0 Registry should be designated by the ENUM Tier 0 Manager. The Tier 0 name servers contain records that point to ENUM Tier 1 name servers.
- **Tier 1:** It corresponds to the E.164 country code (CC), or a portion of an integrated numbering plan that is assigned to an individual country. Delegations of the subdomains are made by the ITU-TSB to the entities designated by each country as administratively responsible for the domain corresponding to their country code. The ENUM Tier 1 Manager for a domain corresponding to a country code is the entity responsible for the management of the numbering plan in this country. The Registry of the domain may be chosen by this entity. The name servers of the domain contain records that indicate the authoritative name servers for individual E.164 numbers or blocks of numbers in the country code or portion thereof.
- **Tier 2:** It corresponds to the E.164 number. Which entity will act as the ENUM Tier 2 Manager for domains at the Tier 2 level is a national matter. The name servers will contain domain names corresponding to E.164 numbers and NAPTR RRs with information for specific communication services. Some entity must interact with E.164 number subscribers (i.e., the ENUM Registrant) to have records for their numbers provisioned into the ENUM DNS-based

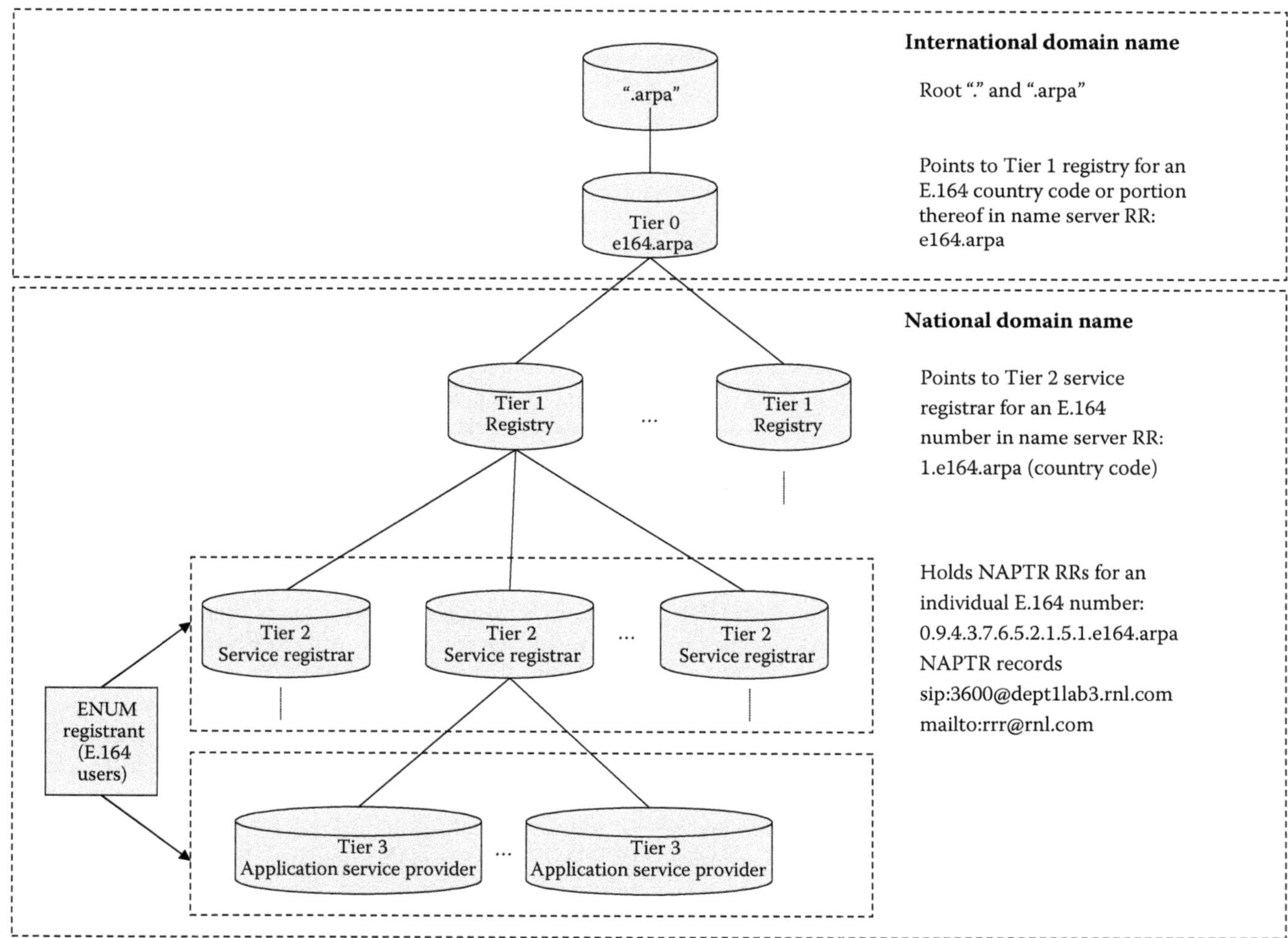

Figure 8.4 ENUM's DNS-based tiered architecture.

architecture. This entity, the ENUM Registrar, might in some implementations be the same as the ENUM Tier 2 Name Server Provider, which maintains the subscriber's NAPTR RRs, of the corresponding E.164 number.

- **Tier 3:** The functions described here have not been officially defined as Tier 3. The ENUM Registrar (and potentially other entities) may also have to interact with other parties such as Application Service Providers (ASPs) that provide services like telephony/VoIP/SIP, e-mail, web, fax, and others. The ASPs will have the knowledge of number assignments, including telephone service providers and, in some cases, number portability administrators of central reference databases.

It should be noted that the Internet Architecture Board (IAB) is responsible for the architectural and standards oversight of the Internet and DNS, while the ITU-T handles decisions about delegation requests. The several regional Internet registries manage and register public Internet number resources within their respective regions. Figure 8.5 depicts the hierarchical structure and functional architecture for North America with functional entities in different tiers employed within the framework as shown in Figure 8.4. ENUM relies on the DDDS for its operation, as it is an application of DDDS. Because the DDDS is designed to be flexible, this property of the DDDS opens the possibility of different interpretations. It requires that the international domain consists of the DNS root and Tier 0 for ENUM. Tier 0 has the domain name e164.arpa and contains the delegations for country codes. In this implementation, Tier 1 has further been divided into two parts: Tier 1A and Tier 1B. Tier 1A is for county code 1 with the domain name 1.e164.arpa and contains delegations for number planning areas (area codes) from North American countries. The individual E.164 zone (or zones) consists of the Tier 1B registry, registrars, and registrants. This layer

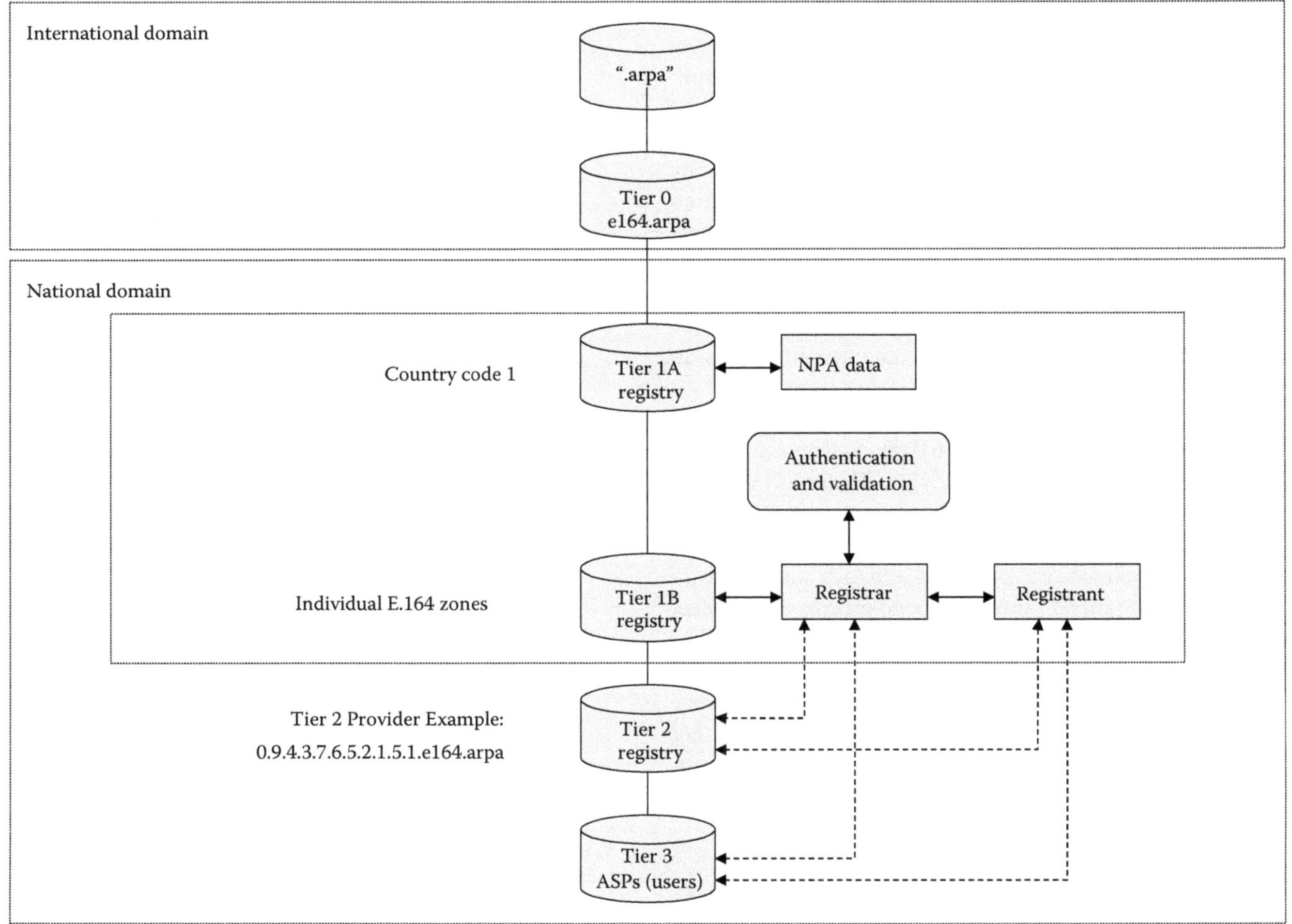

Figure 8.5 ENUM functional architecture for implementation in North America.

enables each numbering plan area to be managed as a DNS zone. It also includes authentication and verification entities and points to Tier 2 for an E.164 number. Below these are Tier 2 providers, which maintain the NAPTR records, and application service providers. However, in Tier 3, the ASPs will assign numbers for different services including number portability.

Because the DDDS is designed to be flexible, this property of the DDDS opens the possibility of different interpretations. It implies that ENUM relies on the DDDS for its operation. The ENUM-specific interpretation of text within the DDDS specifications should be done carefully. The goal should be to ensure interoperability between ENUM clients and provisioning systems used to populate domains with E2U NAPTRs. As part of ongoing development works on the ENUM specifications, RFC 5483 provides an analysis of the way in which ENUM client and provisioning system implementations behave and the interoperability issues that have arisen. ENUM has two constrains. First, the input is represented by a single telephone number in the form according to ITU-T E.164, although there are services that require processing of nondigit inputs such as password. Second, a single input can be processed, although there are services such as abbreviated dialing that require additional input parameters for converting the abbreviated number into called party identifier. DDDS application represents an abstract algorithm operating on a database with rewrite rules used by the application for string conversion. In order to design an alternative DDDS application to ENUM, several parameters need to be defined: algorithm, database, and application-specific parameters (e.g., Unique Inputs of E.164 numbers, First Well-Known Rule, Database Selection, and Outputs).

In addition, DDDS has used some terminologies in defining the algorithm as follows:

- **Application Unique String (AUS):** A string that is the initial input to a DDDS application. The lexical structure of this string must imply a unique delegation path, which is analyzed and traced by the repeated selection and application of Rewrite Rules. In ENUM, the AUS is a fully qualified E.164 number minus any nondigit characters except for the "+" character that appears at the beginning of the number. The + is kept to provide a well-understood anchor for the AUS in order to distinguish it from other telephone numbers that are not part of the E.164 namespace. For example, the E.164 number could start out as +44-1164-960348. All nondigits except + are removed, ensuring that no syntactic sugar is allowed into the AUS.
- **Rewrite Rule:** It is also simply known as Rule. A rule that is applied to an AUS to produce either a new key to select a new rewrite rule from the rule database, or a final result string that is returned to the calling application.
- **First Well-Known Rule:** This is a Rewrite Rule that is defined by the application and not actually in the Rule Database. It is used to produce the first valid key.
- **Terminal Rule:** A Rewrite Rule that, when used, yields a string that is the final result of the DDDS process, rather than another database key.
- **Application:** A set of protocols and specifications that specify actual values for the various generalized parts of the DDDS algorithm. An Application must define the syntax and semantics of the AUS, the First Well-Known Rule, and one or more Databases that are valid for the Application. In ENUM, it is the client application that uses ENUM services for conversion of E.164 numbers into URIs.
- **Services:** A common rule database may be used to associate different services with a given AUS, for example, different protocol functions, different operational characteristics, geographic segregation, backwards compatibility, etc. Possible service differences might be message receiving services for e-mail/fax/voice mail, load balancing over web servers, selection of a nearby mirror server, cost versus performance trade-offs, etc. These Services are included as part of a Rule to allow the Application to make branching decisions based on the applicability of one branch or the other from a Service standpoint. Service Parameters for this Application take the form of a string of characters that follow this Augmented Backus–Naur Form (ABNF):

```
servicefffield = [[protocol] *("+" rs)]
protocol       = ALPHA *31ALPHANUM
rs             = ALPHA *31ALPHANUM
; The protocol and rs fields are limited to 32
; characters and must start with an alphabetic.
```

In other words, an optional protocol specification followed by 0 or more resolution services. Each resolution service is indicated by an initial + character.

In ENUM, it is a <character-string> that specifies the service parameters applicable to this delegation path. It is up to the application specification to specify the values found in this field. Service parameters for this Application take the following ABNF (specified in RFC 5234) and are found in the Services field of the NAPTR record that holds a terminal Rule. Where the NAPTR holds a nonterminal rule, the Services field should be empty, and clients should ignore its content. The services fields are defined as follows:

```
service-field = "E2U" 1*(servicespec)
servicespec = "+" enumservice
enumservice = type 0*(subtypespec)
subtypespec = ":" subtype
type = 1*32(ALPHA/DIGIT/"-")
subtype = 1*32(ALPHA/DIGIT/"-")
```

In other words, a nonoptional E2U (used to denote ENUM only Rewrite Rules in order to mitigate record collisions) is followed by one or more ENUM services that indicate the class of functionality a given end point offers. Each ENUM service is indicated by an initial + character.

- **Flags:** Most Applications will require a way for a Rule to signal to the Application that some Rules provide particular outcomes that others do not, for example, different output formats, extensibility mechanisms, terminal rule signaling, etc. Most Databases will define a Flags field that an Application can use to encode various values that express these signals. In ENUM, it is a <character-string> containing flags to control aspects of the rewriting and interpretation of the fields in the record. Flags are single characters from the set A–Z and 0–9.
- **Rule:** A Rule is made of four functional components: Priority, Set of Flags, Description of Services, and Substitution of Expression.
  - **Priority:** A priority is simply a number used to show which of two otherwise equal rules may have precedence. This allows the database to express rules that may offer roughly the same results, but one delegation path may be faster, better, and cheaper than the other.
  - **Set of Flags:** Flags are used to specify attributes of the rule that determine if this rule is the last one to be applied. The last rule is called the terminal rule, and its output should be the intended result for the application. Flags are unique across Applications. An Application may specify that it is using a flag defined by yet another Application but it must use that other Application's definition. One Application cannot redefine a Flag used by another Application. This may mean that a registry of Flags will be needed in the future but at this time it is not a requirement.
  - **Description of Services:** Services are used to specify semantic attributes of a particular delegation branch. There are many cases where two delegation branches are identical except that one delegates down to a result that provides one set of features while another provides some other set. Features may include operational issues such as load balancing, geographically based traffic segregation, degraded but backwardly compatible functions for older clients, etc. For example, two rules may equally apply to a specific delegation decision for a string. One rule can lead to a terminal rule that produces information for use in high-availability environments, while another may lead to an archival service that may be slower but is more stable over long periods of time.
  - **Substitution Expression:** This is the actual string modification part of the rule. It is a combination of a POSIX Extended Regular Expression and a replacement string similar to Unix sed-style substitution expression. The syntax of the Substitution Expression part of the rule is a sed-style substitution expression. True sed-style substitution expressions are not appropriate for use in this application for a variety of reasons; therefore, the contents of the regexp field must follow this grammar:

```
subst-expr    = delim-char ere delim-char repl
delim-char *flags
delim-char    = "/"/"!"/<Any octet not in
"POS-DIGIT" or "flags">
              ; All occurrences of a
delimffchar in a substffexpr
              ; must be the same character.>
ere           = <POSIX Extended Regular
Expression>
repl          = *(string/backref)
string        = *(anychar/escapeddelim)
anychar       = <any character other than
delim-char>
escapeddelim  = "\" delim-char
backref       = "\" POS-DIGIT
flags         = "i"
POS-DIGIT = "1"/"2"/"3"/"4"/"5"/"6"/"7"/"8"/"9"
```

The result of applying the substitution expression to the String must result in a key that obeys the rules of the Database (unless of course it is a Terminal Rule in which case the output follows the rules of the application). Since it is possible for the regular expression to be improperly specified, such that a nonconforming key can be constructed, client software SHOULD verify that the result is a legal database key before using it.

Backref expressions in the repl portion of the substitution expression are replaced by the (possibly empty) string of characters enclosed by "(" and ")" in the ERE portion of the substitution expression. N is a single digit from 1 through 9, inclusive. It specifies the Nth backref expression, the one that begins with the Nth "(" and continues to the matching ")." For example, the ERE-(A(B(C)DE)(F)G) has backref expressions:

```
\1 = ABCDEFG
\2 = BCDE
\3 = C
\4 = F
\5..\9 = error—no matching subexpression
```

The "i" flag indicates that the ERE matching shall be performed in a case-insensitive fashion. Furthermore, any backref replacements may be normalized to lower case when the "i" flag is given. This flag has meaning only when both the Application and Database define a character set where case insensitivity is valid.

The first character in the substitution expression shall be used as the character that delimits the components of the substitution expression. There must be exactly three nonescaped occurrences of the delimiter character in a substitution expression. Since escaped occurrences of the delimiter character will be interpreted as occurrences of that character, digits MUST NOT be used as delimiters. Backrefs would be confused with literal digits were this allowed. Similarly, if flags are specified in the substitution expression, the delimiter character must not also be a flag character.

- **Rule Database:** Any store of Rules such that a unique key can identify a set of Rules that specify the delegation step used when that particular Key is used. In ENUM, the database contains rewrite rules for string conversion. DDDS specification does not imply any specific database; however, a DNS-based hierarchical system has been proposed in RFC 3403. Properties of well-known DNS and its scalability make it desirable storage for application rewrite rules. The rules are stored in the format of NAPTR RRs.

8.3.1 DDDS Algorithm

The general DDDS algorithm is specified in RFC 3402. The service is provided as a string processing defined by the algorithm depicted diagrammatically in Figure 8.6. In brief, the input is initially converted into a database search key used later to query the database. The key is then matched to database records in order to retrieve rewrite rules for input string conversion. In case a rule is not final, it is applied on the initial input and the search is repeated. Once the terminal rule is reached, it is applied on the input string to produce output string for further call processing.

8.3.2 DDDS Algorithm Application to ENUM

First, the AUS is the initial input to a DDDS application (Figure 8.6). AUS in the context of ENUM is explained earlier with an example. In a similar example, to address the E.164 number +44-3069-990038, a user might dial 03069990038 or 00443069990038 or 011443069990038. These dialed digit strings differ from one another, but none of them start with the + character. Finally, if these techniques are used for dialing plans or other digit strings, implementers and operators of systems using these techniques for such purpose must not describe these schemes as ENUM. The initial E in ENUM stands for E.164, and the term ENUM is used exclusively to describe application of these techniques to E.164 numbers according to this specification.

Second, the First Well-Known Rule for any ENUM query creates a key (an FQDN within the e164.arpa domain apex) from an E.164 number. This FQDN is queried for NAPTR records, and returned records are processed and interpreted according to this specification. The DDDS database used by the application is found in RFC 3403, which is the document that defines the NAPTR DNS RR type. The NAPTR RR packet format that has DNS type code 35 contains the fields namely Order, Preference, Flags, Services, Regexp, and Replacement. However, Flags and Services are explained earlier; Order, Preference, Regexp, and Replacement are described below:

- **Order:** It is a16-bit unsigned integer specifying the order in which the NAPTR records must be processed in order to accurately represent the ordered list of rules. The ordering is from lowest to highest. If two records have the same order value, then they are considered to be the same rule and should be selected on the basis of the combination of the Preference values and Services offered.
- **Preference:** It is a 16-bit unsigned integer that specifies the order in which NAPTR records with equal Order values should be processed, low numbers being processed before high numbers. Although it is called *preference* in deference to DNS terminology, this field is equivalent to the Priority value in the DDDS algorithm.
- **Regexp:** It is actually *regular expression* and is a <character-string> containing a substitution expression that is applied to the original string held by the client in order to construct the next domain name to look up. The only place where NAPTR field content is case sensitive is in any static text in the Repl subfield of the Regexp field (see RFCs 3402 and 6116 for Regexp field definitions). In that subfield, case must be preserved when generating the record output. Elsewhere, case sensitivity is not used.
- **Replacement:** It is a <domain-name> that is the next domain-name to query for depending on the potential values found in the Flags field. This field is used when the regular expression is a simple replacement operation. Any value in this field MUST be a fully qualified domain-name. Name compression is not to be used for this field. Note that this field and the Regexp field together make up the substitution expression in the DDDS algorithm.

In fact, ENUM uses the NAPTR to provide a URI and look up what services are available for a particular telephone number, mapping the ITU-T E.164 telephone number onto

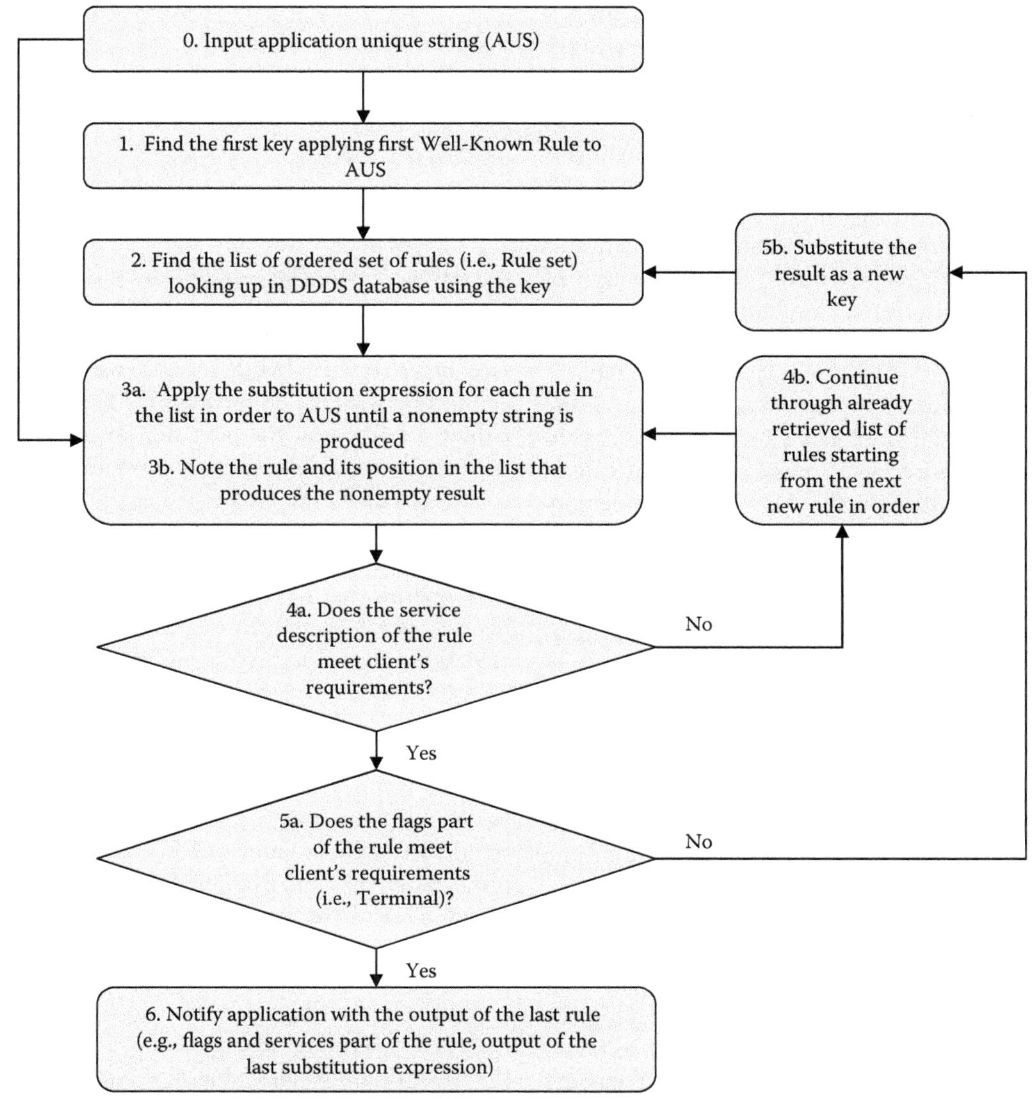

Figure 8.6 DDDS algorithm flow chart. (Copyright IETF. Reproduced with permission.)

the DNS. Once a phone number is mapped into a domain name, the ENUM protocol can query the DNS and provide a corresponding URI location or the locations of multiple URIs and their order of processing, and service preferences information it finds in the NAPTR record. ENUM then maps the telephone number to a group of service-specific URIs, making it possible to manage multiple services. To convert the AUS to a unique key in this database, the string is converted into a domain name according to this algorithm using the four-step process for mapping a telephone number onto DNS:

- Remove all characters with the exception of the digits. For example, given the E.164 number +44-20-7946-0148 (which would then have been converted into an AUS of +442079460148), this step would simply remove the leading +, producing 442079460148.
- Reverse the order of the digits. Example: 84106497 0244.
- Put dots (".") between each digit. Example: 8.4.1.0.6.4.9.7.0.2.4.4.
- Append the string *.e164.arpa.* to the end and interpret as a domain name. Example: 8.4.1.0.6.4.9.7.0.2.4.4.e164.arpa.

The e164.arpa domain provides the DNS infrastructure for storing qualified E.164 telephone numbers. The .arpa top-level domain's (TLD's) ability to reverse-map IP addresses to domain names is foundational, since ENUM looks up services by one-to-one reverse-mapping digits in the E.164

number into separate DNS zones, delineated by dots. In this example, the input telephone number has been +44-20-7946-0148, and the corresponding equivalent output domain name is 8.4.1.0.6.4.9.7.0.2.4.4.e164.arpa. The E.164 namespace and this application's database are organized in such a way that it is possible to go directly from the name to the smallest granularity of the namespace directly from the name itself, so no further processing is required to generate the initial key. This domain name is used to request NAPTR records. Each of these records may contain the end result or, if its Flags field is empty, produce a new key in the form of a domain name that is used to request further NAPTR records from the DNS.

Third, the DDDS database needs to be looked up using the initial first key obtained in step 2 using the First Well-Known Rule. The Substitution Expression for each Rule in the list is applied, in order, to the AUS until a nonempty string is produced. The position in the list is noted and the Rule that produced the nonempty string is used for the next step. If the next step rejects this rule and returns to this step, then the Substitution Expression application process continues at the point where it left off. If the list is exhausted without a valid match, then the application is notified that no valid output was available. However, only the DNS database (RFC 3403) that specifies a DDDS database that uses the NAPTR DNS RR contains the rewrite rules for the ENUM application. The keys for this database are encoded as domain names. The allowed input characters are all those characters that are allowed anywhere in an E.164 number. The characters allowed being in a key are those that are currently defined for DNS domain names. Some name server implementations attempt to be intelligent about items that are inserted into the additional information section of a given DNS response. For example, BIND will attempt to determine if it is authoritative for a domain whenever it encodes one into a packet. If it is, then it will insert any A-records it finds for that domain into the additional information section of the answer until the packet reaches the maximum length allowed. It is therefore potentially useful for a client to check for this additional information.

Fourth, if the Service description of the rule does not meet the client's requirements, the process will go back to step 3 and continue through the already retrieved list of rules. If it does match the client's requirements, then this Rule is used for the next step. If and only if the client is capable of handling it and if it is deemed safe to do so by the Application's specification, the client may make a note of the current Rule but still return to step 3 as though it had rejected it. In either case, the output of this step is one and only one Rule. Some examples of ENUM services are provided below to make further clarify things as follows:

```
$ORIGIN 3.8.0.0.6.9.2.3.6.1.4.4.e164.arpa.
NAPTR 100 50 "u" "E2U+sip"
       "!^(\\+441632960083)$!sip:\\1@example.
com!".
NAPTR 100 51 "u" "E2U+h323"
       "!^\\+441632960083$!h323:operator@
example.com!".
NAPTR 100 52 "u" "E2U+email:mailto"
       "!^.*$!mailto:info@example.com!".
```

This describes that the domain 3.8.0.0.6.9.2.3.6.1.4.4.e164.arpa. is preferably contacted by SIP, second via H.323 for voice, and third by SMTP for messaging. Note that the ENUM service tokens *sip*, *h323*, and *email* are ENUM service Types registered with IANA, and they have no implicit connection with the protocols or URI schemes with the same names. In all cases, the next step in the resolution process is to use the resolution mechanism for each of the protocols (specified by the URI schemes sip, h323, and mailto) to know what node to contact.

In each of the first two records, the ERE subfield matches only queries that have been made for the telephone number (+441632960083). In the last record, the ERE matches any AUS value. The first record also demonstrates how the matched pattern can be used in the generated URI. Note that where NAPTR RRs are shown in DNS master file syntax (as in this example above), each backslash must itself be escaped using a second backslash. The DNS on-the-wire packet will have only a single backslash in each case. Table 8.3 depicts some examples of ENUM services with service/protocol, service, and example URI schemes, while Table 8.4 shows a list of the registered IANA ENUM services type, subtype, and the URI scheme that specify client's application requirements.

Fifth, if the Flags part of the Rule designate that this Rule is not Terminal, the process will go back to step 2 with the substitution result as the new Key. As described earlier, ENUM Flags contain single characters from the set A–Z and

Table 8.3 Example Service/Protocol, Service Field, and Example URI Scheme for ENUM Services

Service/ Protocol	*Service Field*	*Example URI Scheme*
SIP	E2U+sip	sip:rrr@sip.nrl.com
H.323	E2U+h323	h323:sbr@h323.example.com
Internet fax	E2U+ifax	mailto:fax@fax.bou.com
Telephone	E2U+tel	Tel:+17364213923;srv=voice
Fax	E2U+fax:tel	Tel:+15933748693;srv=fax
E-mail	E2U+mailto	mailto:info@epu.mou.com
Web	E2U+http	http://www.mrl.com/

Table 8.4 Registered IANA ENUM Services

ENUM Service Type	*ENUM Service Subtype*	*URI Scheme(s)*	*ENUM Service Specification(s)*	
ems	mailto	mailto	RFC 4355	RFC 6188
ems	tel	tel	RFC 4355	RFC 6188
fax	tel	tel	RFC 4355	RFC 6188
ft	ftp	ftp	RFC 4002	RFC 6188
h323	N/A	h323	RFC 3762	RFC 6188
iax	N/A	iax	RFC 6315	–
ical-access	http	http	RFC 5333	RFC 6188
ical-access	https	https	RFC 5333	RFC 6188
ical-sched	mailto	mailto	RFC 5333	RFC 6188
ifax	mailto	mailto	RFC 4143	RFC 6188
im	N/A	im	RFC 5028	RFC 6188
mms	mailto	mailto	RFC 4355	RFC 6188
mms	tel	tel	RFC 4355	RFC 6188
pres	N/A	pres	RFC 3953	RFC 6188
pstn	sip	sip	RFC 4769	RFC 6188
pstn	tel	tel	RFC 4769	RFC 6188
sip	N/A	sip, sips	RFC 3764	RFC 6188
sms	mailto	mailto	RFC 4355	RFC 6188
sms	tel	tel	RFC 4355	RFC 6188
unifmsg	http	http	RFC 5278	RFC 6188
unifmsg	https	https	RFC 5278	RFC 6188
unifmsg	sip	sip	RFC 5278	RFC 6188
unifmsg	sips	sips	RFC 5278	RFC 6188
vcard	N/A	http, https	RFC 4969	RFC 6188
videomsg	http	http	RFC 5278	RFC 6188
videomsg	https	https	RFC 5278	RFC 6188
videomsg	sip	sip	RFC 5278	RFC 6188
videomsg	sips	sips	RFC 5278	RFC 6188
voice	tel	tel	RFC 4415	RFC 6188
voicemsg	http	http	RFC 5278	RFC 6188
voicemsg	https	https	RFC 5278	RFC 6188
voicemsg	sip	sip	RFC 5278	RFC 6188
voicemsg	sips	sips	RFC 5278	RFC 6188

(*Continued*)

Table 8.4 (Continued) Registered IANA ENUM Services

ENUM Service Type	*ENUM Service Subtype*	*URI Scheme(s)*	*ENUM Service Specification(s)*	
voicemsg	tel	tel	RFC 5278	RFC 6188
vpim	ldap	ldap	RFC 4238	RFC 6188
vpim	mailto	mailto	RFC 4238	RFC 6188
web	http	http	RFC 4002	RFC 6188
web	https	https	RFC 4002	RFC 6188
xmpp	N/A	xmpp	RFC 4979	RFC 6188

Source: http://www.iana.org/assignments/enum-services/enum-services.xml. Copyright IETF. Reproduced with permission.

0–9, and the Application defines the Flags specified in the DNS database. The case of the alphabetic characters is not significant. The field can be empty. It is up to the application (e.g., ENUM) specifying how it is using this database to define the Flags in this field. It must define which ones are terminal and which ones are not. In fact, the database's Flags field signals when the DDDS algorithm has finished. At this time, only one flag, U, is defined. This means that this rule is the last one and that the output of the rule is a URI (RFC 3986). If a client encounters an RR with an unknown flag, it must ignore it and move to the next rule. This test takes precedence over any ordering since flags can control the interpretation placed on fields.

A novel flag might change the interpretation of the Regexp or Replacement fields such that it is impossible to determine if an RR matched a given target. If this flag is not present, then this rule is nonterminal. If a rule is nonterminal, then the result produced by this rewrite rule must be an FQDN. Clients must use this result as the new key in the DDDS loop (i.e., the client will query for NAPTR RRs at this FQDN). Lastly, the process notifies the Application that the database search has been finished, and provides the Application with the Flags and Services part of the Rule along with the output of the last Substitution Expression.

8.3.2.1 Expected Output

The output of the last DDDS loop is a Uniform Resource Identifier in its absolute form according to the <absolute-URI> production in the Collected ABNF found in RFC 3986.

8.3.3 ENUM with Compound NAPTRs

It is possible to have more than one ENUM service associated with a single NAPTR. These ENUM services share the same Regexp field and so generate the same URI. Such a *compound* NAPTR could well be used to indicate a mobile phone that supports both voice:tel and sms:tel ENUM services. The Services field in that case would be E2U+voice:tel+sms:tel. A compound NAPTR can be treated as a set of NAPTRs that each holds a single ENUM service. These reconstructed NAPTRs share the same Order and Preference/Priority field values but should be treated as if each had a logically different priority. A left-to-right priority is assumed.

8.3.4 ENUM Operations

We are describing with a high-level example how the ENUM client interacts with the ENUM DNS server to obtain the NATAR record that, as explained earlier, contains six resource fields: Order, Preference, Flags, Services, Regexp, and Replacement. An example NAPTR record is as follows (Figure 8.7): 7.2.8.6.9.5.3.2.1.2.1.e164.arpa.IN NAPTR 110 10 "u" "E2U+sip" "!^.*$!sip:2123596827@rrr.rnl.com!". In this record, Order = 110, Preference = 10, Flags = u, Services = E2U+sip, and Regular Expression = !^.*$!sip:2123596827@rrr.rnl.com!. As described, ENUM specifies a method for storing information in the DNS server to URIs (e.g., SIP phone, SIP servers, cell phone,

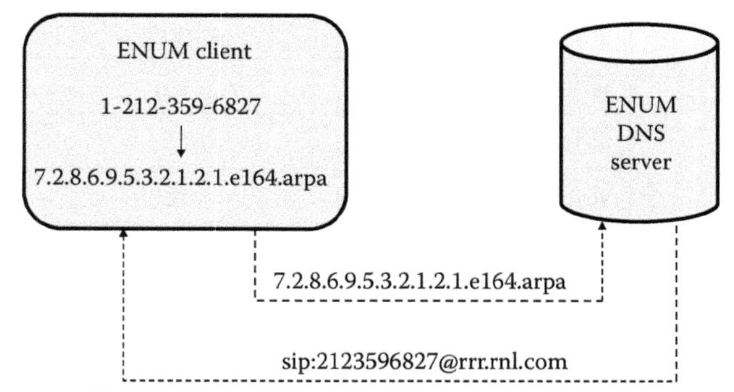

Figure 8.7 High-level example of ENUM operations.

and other entities) for associated services (e.g., SIP audio/video conferencing services, XMPP chat services, Fax services, e-mail services, and others). Each URI is stored in a DNS NAPTR record, which is in an E.164 domain. Figure 8.7 shows that an ENUM client is trying to resolve an E.164 telephone number into the corresponding URI of SIP telephony services.

The main steps of operations can be described as follows:

- An ENUM client needs to resolve the E.164 telephone number of the called party (e.g., 1-212-359-6827) to set up the call over the IP network.
- The ENUM client converts the E.164 number into a domain name (e.g., 7.2.8.6.9.5.3.2.1.2.1.e164.arpa) as described earlier.
- The client queries a DNS server with the domain name using a resolver as described earlier.
- The DNS server returns the NAPTR records that contain services and URIs (e.g., sip:2123596827@rrr.rnl.com) in the domain to the client after resolving this, running the DDDS algorithm specific to ENUM services as explained earlier.
- If the multiple NAPTR records are retuned, the ENUM client picks one to use based on the Order, Preference, and Services field values in the records.
- The ENUM client will do a second non-ENUM DNS query to determine the called party's IP address, if the URI in the selected NAPTR record contains the called party's name (e.g., rrr.rnl.com).

8.3.5 ENUM Service Registration for SIP Addresses of Record (AORs)

RFC 3764 that is described here registers an ENUM service focusing on provisioning SIP AORs, pursuant to the guidelines in RFC 3761. ENUM, as explained earlier, is a system that uses DNS to translate telephone numbers, like +12025332600, into URIs, like sip:egar@example.com. ENUM exists primarily to facilitate the interconnection of systems that rely on telephone numbers with those that use URIs to route transactions. RFC 3764 uses the text-based ENUM application protocol (RFC 6116) that allows end points on the Internet to discover one another in order to exchange context information about a session they would like to share. Common forms of communication that are set up by SIP include Internet telephony, instant messaging, video, Internet gaming, and other forms of real-time communications. SIP is a multiservice protocol capable of initiating sessions involving different forms of real-time communications simultaneously. SIP is a protocol that finds the best way for parties to communicate.

8.3.5.1 ENUM Service Registration

As defined in RFC 3761 (obsoleted by RFCs 6116 and 6117), the following is a template covering information needed for the registration of the ENUM service specified as follows:

```
Enumservice Name: "E2U+SIP"
Type(s): "SIP"
Subtype(s): N/A
URI Scheme(s): "sip:", "sips:"
```

8.3.5.2 AOR in SIP

RFC 3764 specifies an ENUM service field that is appropriate for SIP AOR URIs. Various other types of URIs can be present in SIP requests. A URI that is associated with a particular SIP user agent (e.g., a SIP phone) is commonly known as a SIP contact address. The difference between a contact address and an AOR is like the difference between a device and its user. While there is no formal distinction in the syntax of these two forms of addresses, contact addresses are associated with a particular device and may have a very device-specific form (like sip:10.0.0.1 or sip:edgar@ua21.example.com). An AOR, however, represents an identity of the user, generally a long-term identity, and it does not have a dependency on any device; users can move between devices or even be associated with multiple devices at one time while retaining the same AOR. A simple URI, generally of the form sip:egdar@example.com, is used for an AOR. When a SIP request is created by a user agent, it populates the AOR of its target in its To header field and (generally) Request-URI. The AOR of the user that is sending the request populates the From header field of the message; the contact address of the device from which the request is sent is listed in the Contact header field.

By sending a registration to a registrar on behalf of its user, a SIP device (i.e., a user agent) can temporarily associate its own contact address with the user's AOR. In so doing, the device becomes eligible to receive requests that are sent to the AOR. Upon receiving the registration request, the registrar modifies the provisioning data in a SIP location service to create a mapping between the AOR for the user and the device where the user can currently be reached. When future requests arrive at the administrative domain of this location service for the user in question, proxy servers ask the location service where to find the user, and will in turn discover the registered contact address(es). A SIP-based follow-me telephony service, for example, would rely on this real-time availability data in order to find the best place to reach the end user without having to cycle through numerous devices from which the user is not currently registered. Note that AORs can be registered with other AORs; for example, while at home, a user might elect to register the AOR they use as their personal identity under their work AOR in order to direct requests for their work identity to whatever devices they might have associated with their home AOR.

When a SIP entity (be it a user agent or proxy server) needs to make a forwarding decision for a Request-URI containing an AOR, it uses the mechanisms described in the SIP specification (RFC 3263, see Section 8.2.4) to locate the proper resource in the network. Ordinarily, this entails resolving the domain portion of the URI (example.com in the example above) in order to route the call to a proxy server that is responsible for that domain. SIP user agents have specific communications capabilities (such as the ability to initiate voice communications with particular codecs, or support for particular SIP protocol extensions). Because an AOR does not represent any particular device or set of devices, an AOR does not have capabilities as such.

When a SIP user agent sends a request to an AOR, it begins a phase of capability negotiation that will eventually discover the best way for the originator to communicate with the target. The originating user agent first expresses capabilities of its own in the request it sends (and preferences for the type of session it would like to initiate). The expression of these capabilities may entail the usage of SDP (see Section 7.7) to list acceptable types of media supported and favored by the client, the inclusion of Required/Supported headers to negotiate compatibility of extensions, and possibly the usage of optional SIP extensions, for example using callee capabilities (see Section 3.4) to communicate request handling dispositions. Proxy servers or end points subsequently return responses that allow a rich bidirectional capability negotiation process.

The process by which SIP end points negotiate capabilities can overlap with the primary service provided by NAPTR records: permitting the originating client to select a particular URI for communications based on an ordered list of ENUM services. However, ENUM's capability management mechanism is decidedly one way—the administrator of the telephone number expresses capabilities (in the form of protocol names) and preferences that the client must evaluate without negotiation. Moreover, listing available protocols is not comparable to agreement on session media (down to the codec/interval level) and protocol extension support—it would be difficult to express, in the level of detail necessary to arrange a desired session, the capabilities of a SIP device within a NAPTR service field. Provisioning contact addresses in ENUM rather than AORs would compromise the SIP capability negotiation and discovery process. Much of the benefit of using a URI comes from the fact that it represents a logical service associated with a user, rather than a device—indeed, if ENUM wished to target particular devices, E2IPv4 would be a more appropriate resolution service to define than E2U. SIP AORs may use the SIP URI scheme or the SIPS URI scheme. The SIPS URI scheme, when used in an AOR, indicates that the user it represents can only be reached over a secure connection (using TLS).

8.3.5.3 E2U+SIP ENUM Service

Traditionally, the services field of a NAPTR record (as defined in RFC 3403) contains a string that is composed of two subfields: a *protocol* subfield and a *resolution service* subfield. ENUM in particular defines an E2U (E.164 to URI) resolution service. This document defines an E2U+SIP ENUM services for SIP. The scheme of the URI that will appear in the regexp field of a NAPTR record using the E2U+SIP ENUM services may either be SIP or SIPS. This ENUM services is best suited to SIP AORs. When a SIP AOR appears in the regexp field of a NAPTR record, there is no need to further qualify the ENUM services field with any capability data, since AORs do not have capabilities. There is also generally no need to have more than one NAPTR record under a single telephone number that points to a SIP AOR. Note that the user portion of a SIP URI may contain a telephone number (e.g., sip:+1442079460148@example.com). Clients should be careful to avoid infinite loops when recursively performing ENUM queries on URIs that result from an ENUM lookup.

8.3.5.4 Example of E2U+SIP ENUM Service

The following is an example of the use of the ENUM services registered by this document in a NAPTR RR.

```
$ORIGIN 8.4.1.0.6.4.9.7.0.2.4.4.e164.arpa.
      IN NAPTR 10 100 "u" "E2U+sip"
"!^.*$!sip:edgar@example.com!".
```

8.3.6 ENUM Services Registration in XML Chunk

RFC 6117 has obsoleted the IANA registration section of RFC 3761. Since the IANA ENUM service registry contains various ENUM services registered under the regime of RFC 3761, those registrations do not conform to the new guidelines as specified in RFC 6117. To ensure consistency among all ENUM service registrations at IANA, this document adds the (nowadays) missing elements to those legacy registrations. Furthermore, all legacy ENUM service registrations are converted to the new XML-chunk format, and, where deemed necessary, minor editorial corrections are applied. However, this document only adds the missing elements to the XML chunks as specified in the IANA Considerations section of RFC 6117, but it does not complete the (nowadays) missing sections of the corresponding ENUM service Specifications. To conform to the new registration regime as specified in RFC 6117, those ENUM service specifications still have to be revised. Legacy Enumservice Registrations have been converted to XML Chunks for the following ENUM services whose details can be seen in RFC 6117:

```
email:mailto, ems:mailto, ems:tel, fax:tel,
ft:ftp, h323, ical-access:http, ical-
access:https, ical-sched:mailto, ifax:mailto,
im, mms:mailto, mms:tel, pres, pstn:sip,
pstn:tel, sip, sms:mailto, sms:tel,
unifmsg:http, unifmsg:https, unifmsg:sip,
unifmsg:sips, vcard, videomsg:http,
videomsg:https, videomsg:sip, videomsg:sips,
voice:tel, voicemsg:http, voicemsg:https,
voicemsg:sip, voicemsg:sips, voicemsg:tel,
vpim:ldap, vpim:mailto, web:http, web:https,
and xmpp.
```

8.3.7 Using E.164 Numbers with SIP

There are a number of contexts in which telephone numbers are employed by SIP applications, many of which can be addressed by ENUM. Although SIP was one of the primary applications for which ENUM was created, there is nevertheless a need to define procedures for integrating ENUM with SIP implementations. RFC 3824 that is described here illustrates how the two protocols might work in concert, and clarifies the authoring and processing of ENUM records for SIP applications. It also provides guidelines for instances in which ENUM, for whatever reason, cannot be used to resolve a telephone number. SIP is a text-based application protocol that allows two end points in the Internet to discover one another in order to exchange context information about a session they would like to share. Common applications for SIP include Internet telephony, instant messaging, video, Internet gaming, and other forms of real-time communications. SIP is a multiservice protocol capable of initiating sessions involving different forms of real-time communications simultaneously.

The most widespread application for SIP today is Voice over IP (VoIP). As such, there are a number of cases in which SIP applications are forced to contend with telephone numbers. Unfortunately, telephone numbers cannot be routing in accordance with the traditional DNS resolution procedures standardized for SIP (see Section 8.2.4), which rely on SIP URIs. ENUM provides a method for translating E.164 numbers into URIs, including potentially SIP URIs. This document therefore provides an account of how SIP can handle telephone numbers by making use of ENUM. Guidelines are proposed for the authoring of the DNS records used by ENUM, and for client-side processing once these DNS records have been received.

The guidelines in this document are oriented toward authoring and processing ENUM records specifically for SIP applications. These guidelines assume that the reader is familiar with NAPTR records (RFC 3403) and ENUM (RFC 6117). Only those aspects of NAPTR record authoring and processing that have special bearing on SIP, or that require general clarification, are covered in this document; these procedures do not update or override the NAPTR or ENUM core documents. Note that the ENUM specification has undergone a revision shortly before the publication of this document, driven by the update of the NAPTR system described in RFC 2915 (that is obsoleted by RFCs 3401–3404) to the DDDS family of specifications (including RFC 3403). This document therefore provides some guidance for handling records designed for the original RFC 2916 (obsoleted by RFCs 6116 and 6117).

8.3.7.1 Handling Telephone Numbers in SIP

There are a number of reasons why a user might want to initiate a SIP request that targets an E.164 number. One common reason is that the user is calling from the PSTN through a PSTN–SIP gateway; such gateways usually map routing information from the PSTN directly onto SIP signaling. Or a native SIP user might intentionally initiate a session addressed to an E.164 number—perhaps because the target user is canonically known by that number, or the originator's SIP user agent only supports a traditional numeric telephone keypad. A request initially targeting a conventional SIP URI might also be redirected to an E.164 number. In most cases, these are requests for a telephony session (voice communication), though numerous other services are also reached through telephone numbers (including instant messaging services). Unlike a URI, a telephone number does not contain a host name, or any hints as to where one might deliver a request targeting a telephone number on the Internet. While SIP user agents or proxy servers could be statically provisioned with a mapping of destinations corresponding to particular telephone numbers or telephone number ranges, considering the size and complexity of a complete mapping, it would be preferable for SIP user agents to be able to query as needed for a destination appropriate for a particular telephone number.

In such cases, a user agent might use ENUM to discover a URI associated with the E.164 number—including a SIP URI. URIs discovered through ENUM can then be used normally to route SIP requests to their destination. Note that support for the NAPTR DNS RR format is specified for ordinary SIP URI processing in RFC 3263 (see Section 8.2.4), and thus support for ENUM is not a significant departure from baseline SIP DNS routing. Most of the remainder of this document provides procedures for the use of ENUM, but a few guidelines are given in the remainder of this section for cases in which ENUM is not used, for whatever reason. If a user agent is unable to translate an E.164 number with ENUM, it can create a type of SIP Request-URI that contains a telephone number. Since one of the most common applications of SIP is telephony, a great deal of attention has already been devoted to the representation of telephone numbers in SIP. In particular, the tel URL RFC 3966 (see Section 4.2.2) has been identified as a way of carrying telephone routing information within SIP. A tel URL usually consists of the number in E.164 format preceded by a plus sign, for example, tel:+12025332600. This format is so useful that it has been incorporated into the baseline SIP specification; the user portion of a SIP URI can contain a tel URL (without the scheme string, like sip:+12025332600@carrier.com;user=phone). A SIP proxy server might therefore receive a request from a user agent with a tel URL in the Request-URI; one way in which the proxy server could handle this sort of request is by launching an ENUM query request in accordance with the returned ENUM records.

In the absence of support for ENUM, or if ENUM requests return no records corresponding to a telephone number, local policy can be used to determine how to forward SIP requests with an E.164 number in the Request-URI. Frequently, such calls are routed to gateways that interconnect SIP networks with the PSTN. These proxy server policies might be provisioned dynamically with routing information for telephone numbers by TRIP (RFC 3219). As a matter of precedence, SIP user agents should attempt to translate telephone numbers to URIs with ENUM, if implemented, before creating a tel URL, and deferring the routing of this request to a SIP proxy server.

8.3.7.2 Design Principles

Although the applicability of ENUM to SIP has always been clear, the exact way in which the two should cooperate has been a subject of some controversy. How many SIP URIs should appear in ENUM, what kind of URIs they are, whether or not the *service* field of NAPTR records should contain capability information—numerous questions have arisen around the authoring, and interpretation of ENUM records for SIP consumers. The following, then, is a statement of the particular philosophy that has motivated the recommendations in this document: AOR SIP URIs appear in ENUM, not contact address URIs. Roughly speaking, an AOR is the canonical identity of a SIP user—it usually appears in the From field of SIP requests sent by that user; a contact address is the URI of a device. The process of registration in SIP (using the REGISTER method), for example, temporarily binds the contact address of a device to the AOR of a user. A DNS record has a long time-to-live when compared with the time frame of SIP registrations. The availability of an AOR also transcends the availability of any single device. ENUM is more suitable for representing a long-term identity than the URI of any device with which a user is temporarily associated. If ENUM was purposed to map to specific devices, it would be better to translate telephone numbers to IPv4 addresses than to URIs (which express something richer).

SIP URIs in ENUM do not convey capability information. SIP has its own methods for negotiating capability information between user agents (see Sections 3.4 and 7.7); providing more limited capability information within ENUM is at best redundant and at worst potentially misleading to SIP's negotiation system. Also, AORs do not have capabilities (only devices registered under an AOR have actual capabilities), and putting contact addresses in ENUM is not recommended. Only one SIP URI, ideally, appears in an ENUM record set for a telephone number. While it may initially seem attractive to provide multiple SIP URIs that reach the same user within ENUM, if there are multiple addresses at which a user can be contacted, considerably greater flexibility is afforded if multiple URIs are managed by a SIP location service that is identified by a single record in ENUM. Behavior for parallel and sequential forking in SIP, for example, is better managed in SIP than in a set of ENUM records. User agents, rather than proxy servers, should process ENUM records. The assumptions underlying the processing of NAPTR records dictate that the ENUM client knows the set of ENUM services supported by the entity that is attempting to communicate. A SIP proxy server is unlikely to know the ENUM services supported by the originator of a SIP request.

8.3.7.3 Authoring NAPTR Records for SIP

This document makes no assumptions about who authors NAPTR records (service providers or end users), nor about any mechanisms by which a record, once it is authored, may be uploaded to the appropriate DNS servers. Authorship in the context of this document concerns only the processes by which the NAPTR records themselves are constructed. There are a few general guidelines that are applicable to the authoring of DNS records that should be considered by the authors of ENUM NAPTR record sets. The most important is that authors should keep record sets relatively small—DNS is not optimized for the transference of large files. Having five or six NAPTR records is quite reasonable; however, policies that encourage record sets of hundreds of NAPTR records are not appropriate. Also, DNS records are relatively permanent; authors SHOULD NOT use ENUM NAPTR records to express relationships between E.164 numbers and URIs that potentially exist for only a short time. DNS is most scalable when it can assume records will be valid for a reasonable length of time (at least several hours).

8.3.7.3.1 Service Field

The Service field of a NAPTR record (per RFC 3403) contains a string token that designates the protocol or service associated with a particular record (and which imparts some inkling of the sort of URI that will result from the use of the record). ENUM requires the IANA registration of service fields known as *ENUM services.* An ENUM Service for SIP has been described earlier, which uses the format E2U+sip to designate that a SIP AOR appears in the URI field of a NAPTR record. It is strongly recommended that authors of NAPTR records use the E2U+sip service field whenever the regexp contains a SIP AOR URI.

8.3.7.3.2 Creating the Regular Expression: Matching

The authorship of the regular expression (henceforth regexp) in a NAPTR record intended for use by ENUM is vastly simplified by the absence of an antecedent in the substitution (i.e., the section between the first two delimiters). It is recommended that implementations use an exclamation point as a delimiter, since this is the only delimiter used throughout the ENUM core specification. When a NAPTR record is processed, the expression in the antecedent is matched against the starting string (for ENUM, the telephone number) to assist in locating the proper record in a set; however, in ENUM applications, since the desired record set is located through a reverse resolution in the e164.arpa domain that is based on the starting string, further analysis of the starting string on the client side will usually be unnecessary. In such cases, the antecedent of the regular expression is commonly *greedy*—it uses the regexp ^.*$, which matches any starting string. Some authors of ENUM record sets may want to use the full power of regexps and create nongreedy antecedents; the DDDS standard requires that ENUM resolvers support these regexps when they are present. For providing a trivial mapping from a telephone number to a SIP URI, the use of a greedy regexp usually suffices.

```
Example: !^.*$!sip:user@example.com!
```

Note that when the antecedent of the regexp is greedy, this does not mean that the replacement field in NAPTR records provides a viable alternative to authoring with a regexp. Authors of NAPTR records for ENUM must not use the replacement field in records with an E2U+sip service field.

8.3.7.3.3 Creating the Regular Expression: URI

The consequent side of a regexp contains a URI; NAPTR records that are intended to be used for session initiation (including SIP telephony) should use a SIP URI. While this may not sound especially controversial at first sight, there are other sorts of URIs that might be considered appropriate for SIP applications: tel URIs, im or pres URIs, or others that describe specific services that might be invoked through SIP are all potentially candidates. While the use of these URIs might seem reasonable under some circumstances, including these in NAPTR records rather than SIP URIs could weaken the proper composition of services and negotiation of capabilities in SIP. It is recommended that authors of ENUM records should always use the SIP or SIPS URI scheme when the service field is E2U+sip, and the URIs in question MUST be AORs, not contact addresses. Users of SIP can register one or more contact addresses with a SIP registrar that will be consulted by the proxy infrastructure of an administrative domain to contact the end user when requests are received for their AOR. Much of the benefit of using a URI comes from the fact that it represents a logical service associated with a user rather than a device—indeed, if ENUM needs to target specific devices rather than URIs, then a hypothetical E2IPv4+sip ENUM service would be more appropriate.

8.3.7.3.4 Setting Order and Preference among Records

For maximal compatibility, authors of ENUM records for SIP SHOULD always use the same order value for all NAPTR records in an ENUM record set. If relative preference among NAPTR records is desirable, it should be expressed solely with the preference field.

8.3.7.3.5 Example

The following example shows a well-formed ENUM NAPTR Record Set for SIP:

```
$ORIGIN 0.0.6.2.3.3.5.2.0.2.1.e164.arpa.
        IN NAPTR 100 10 "u" "E2U+sip"
"!^.*$!sip:user@example.com!".
        IN NAPTR 100 20 "u" "E2U+mailto"
"!^.*$!mailto:info@example.com!".
```

8.3.7.4 Processing ENUM Records

These guidelines do not, by any means, exhaustively describe the NAPTR algorithm or the processing of NAPTR records; implementers should familiarize themselves with the DDDS algorithm and ENUM before reviewing this section. Although in some cases, ENUM record sets will consist only a single E2U+sip record, this section assumes that integrators of ENUM and SIP must be prepared for more complicated scenarios—however, just because we recommend that clients should be generous in what they receive, and try to make sense of potentially confusing NAPTR records, does not mean that we recommend any of the potentially troublesome authoring practices that make this generosity necessary.

8.3.7.4.1 Contending with Multiple SIP Records

If an ENUM query returns multiple NAPTR records that have a service field of E2U+sip, or other service field that may be used by SIP (such as E2U+pres; see RFC 3953), the ENUM client must first determine whether or not it should attempt to make use of multiple records or select a single one. The pitfalls of intentionally authoring ENUM record sets with multiple NAPTR records for SIP are detailed above. If the ENUM client is a user agent, then at some point a single NAPTR record must be selected to serve as the Request-URI of the desired SIP request. If the given NAPTR records have different preferences, the most preferred record should be used. If two or more records share the most preferred status, the ENUM client should randomly determine which record will be used, though it may defer to a local policy that employs some other means to select a record. If the ENUM client is a SIP intermediary that can act a redirect server, then it should return a 3xx response with more than one contact header field corresponding to the multiple selected NAPTR records in an ENUM record set. If the NAPTR records have different preferences, then *q*-values may be used in the Contact header fields to correspond to these preferences. Alternatively, the redirect server may select a single record in accordance with the NAPTR preference fields (or randomly when no preference is specified) and send this resulting URI in a Contact header field in a 3xx response. Otherwise, if the ENUM client is a SIP intermediary that can act as a proxy server, then it MAY fork the request when it receives multiple appropriate NAPTR records in an ENUM record set. Depending on the relative precedence values of the NAPTR records, the proxy may wish to fork sequentially or in parallel. However, the proxy must build a route set from these NAPTR records that consists exclusively of SIP or SIPS URIs, not other URI schemes. Alternatively, the proxy server may select a single record in accordance with the NAPTR preference fields (or randomly when no preference is specified, or in accordance with local policy) and proxy the request with a Request-URI corresponding to the URI field of this NAPTR record—though again, it must select a record that contains a SIP or SIPS URI. Note that there are significant limitations that arise if a proxy server processes ENUM record sets instead of a user agent, and that therefore it is recommended that SIP network elements act as redirect servers rather than proxy servers after performing an ENUM query.

8.3.7.4.2 Processing the Selected NAPTR Record

Obviously, when an appropriate NAPTR record has been selected, the URI should be extracted from the regexp field. The URI is between the second and third exclamation points in the string. Once a URI has been extracted from the NAPTR record, it should be used as the Request-URI of the SIP request for which the ENUM query was launched. SIP clients should perform some sanity checks on the URI, primarily to ensure that they support the scheme of the URI, but also to verify that the URI is well formed. Clients must at least verify that the Request-URI does not target themselves. Once an AOR has been extracted from the selected NAPTR record, clients follow the standard SIP mechanisms (RFC 3263, see Section 8.2.4) for determining how to forward the request. This may involve launching subsequent NAPTR or SRV queries in order to determine how best to route to the domain identified by an AOR; clients, however, must not make the same ENUM query recursively (if the URI returned by ENUM is a tel URL; see Section 4.2.2). Note that SIP requests based on the use of NAPTR records may fail for any number of reasons. If there are multiple NAPTR records relevant to SIP present in an ENUM record set, then after a failure has occurred on an initial attempt with one NAPTR record, SIP user agents may try their request again with a different NAPTR record from the ENUM record set.

8.3.7.5 Compatibility with RFC 2916

Note that both RFCs 2916 and 3716 are obsoleted by RFCs 6116 and 6117, and these newer RFCs were created before the publication of RFC 3824 that has been described above. As a result, we are also discussing the older RFCs 2916 and 3716 in this section as RFC 3824 has done. Note that RFC 6117, as described earlier, converts ENUM services into XML chunk only. RFC 3761 is based on the DDDS (RFC 3401) revision to the NAPTR RR specified in RFC 2915 (obsoleted by RFCs 3401–3404). For the most part, DDDS is an organizational revision that makes the algorithmic aspects of record processing separable from any underlying database format (such as the NAPTR DNS RR). The most important revision in RFC 3761 is the concept of ENUM services. The original ENUM specification, RFC 2916, specified a number of *service* values that could be used for ENUM, including the sip+E2U service field. RFC 3761 introduces an IANA registration system with new guidelines for the registration of ENUM services, which are no longer necessarily divided into discreet *service* and *protocol* fields, and which admit more complex structures. In order to differentiate ENUM services in RFC 3761 from those in RFC 2916, the string E2U is the leading element in an ENUM service field, whereas by RFC 2916 it was the trailing element.

An ENUM service for SIP AORs is described in RFC 5947. This ENUM service uses the ENUM service field E2U+sip. RFC 3761–compliant authors of ENUM records for SIP MUST therefore use the E2U+sip ENUM service field instead of the sip+E2U field. For backwards compatibility with existing legacy records, however, the sip+E2U field should be supported by an ENUM client that supports SIP. Also note that the terminology of DDDS differs in a number of respects from the initial NAPTR terminology in RFC 2916. DDDS introduces the concept of an Application, an Application-Specific String, a First Well-Known Rule, and so on. The terminology used in this document is a little looser (it refers to a *starting string*, e.g., where Application-Specific String would be used for DDDS). The new terminology is reflected in RFC 3761.

8.3.8 ENUM for SIP Services

The use of ENUM in the SIP network is straightforward. We are considering DNS and ENUM as a single server for illustration, although the DNS and ENUM servers are usually separate in most networks for simplification. We are also assuming that the called party remains in the calling party's home network. Also, although not shown, the following is done: the S-CSCF sends a SIP Invite message to the I-CSCF, and it queries the Home Subscriber Server (not shown) in the Called Party Home Network to determine the S-CSCF currently serving Client B.

The CSCFs handle all the SIP session signaling; however, they neither take part in transferring user media nor are they on the path of the application data. The IMS proxies are hierarchically divided in two categories: the proxies-CSCFs (P-CSCFs) are the IMS contact points for the SIP–user agents (SIP–UAs) and the serving-CSCF (S-CSCF) is the proxy server controlling the session. In some topologies, there is a third type of CSCF, the interrogating-CSCF (I-CSCF). The I-CSFC is an element used mainly for topology-hiding purposes between different operators and, also, in the case of having several S-CSCFs in the domain, to assist in selecting the appropriate one. In addition, there can be Breakout Gateway Control Function (BGCF) proxy that controls resources allocation to IP sessions, such as which IP-TDM network gateway needs to be used to reach the destination efficiently. We have taken two point-to-point high-level call-flow examples as follows: IMS subscriber over the IP network to the PSTN subscriber over the TDM network (Figure 8.8), and IMS subscriber to IMS subscriber over the IP network (Figure 8.9).

It should be noted that TDM network uses the ISDN User Part/Signaling System # 7 (SS7) for voice calls. Interestingly,

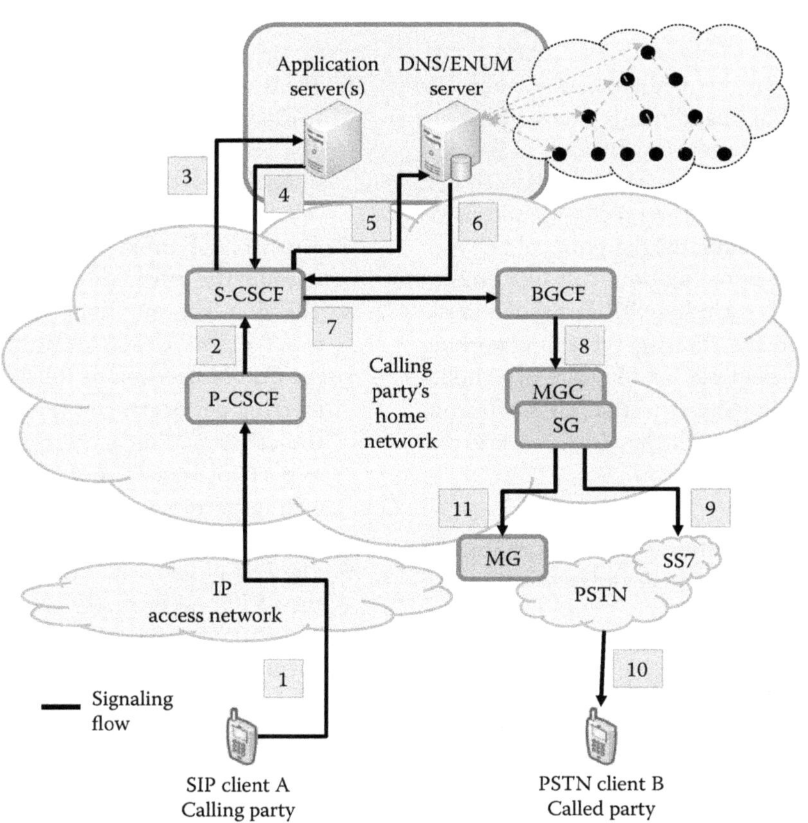

Figure 8.8 Point-to-point call flows from IP subscriber to the PSTN subscriber when both subscribers have the same home network. (Copyright IETF. Reproduced with permission.)

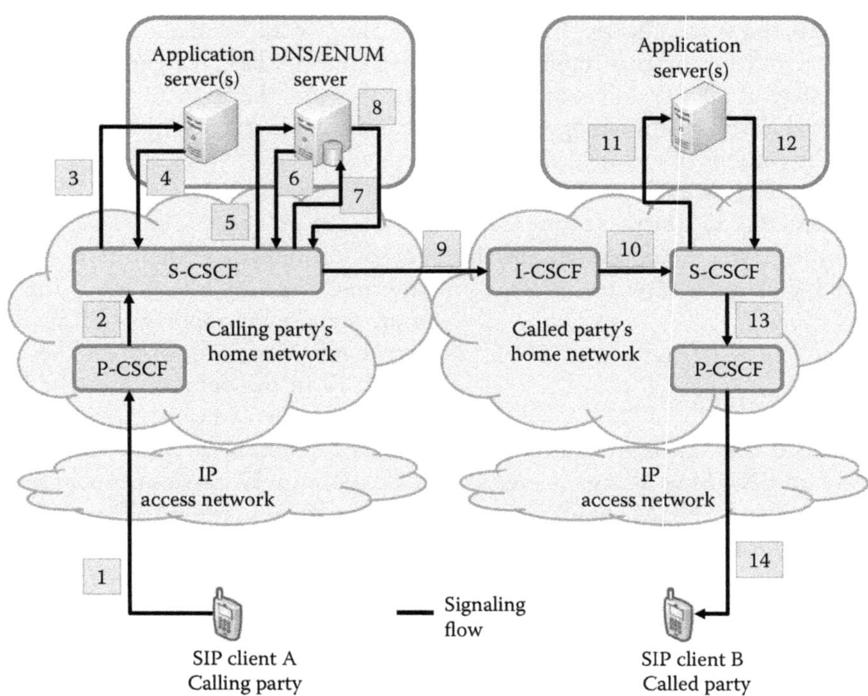

Figure 8.9 Point-to-point call flows between IP subscribers when both subscribers have separate home networks. (Copyright IETF. Reproduced with permission.)

in Figure 8.8, we have shown the media gateway controller (MGC), signaling gateway (SG), and media gateway that are used to provide interfaces between the IP and TDM network. The MGC and SG enable interworking between SIP and ISUP/SS-7 signaling schemes using technical standards as described in Section 14.4. Similarly, the protocol between the MGC and MG can use signaling protocols like H.248-family of technical standards including SIP. For showing the use of ENUM in SIP, we are not showing these interworking protocols in the call flow example for the sake of simplicity. Figure 8.8 shows the following steps that are carried out to set up and route the call through the IP network to the PSTN network:

1. The SIP client A of the calling party calls the E.164 number (e.g., 1-732-490-2533) in order to reach SIP client B of the called party.
2. The P-CSCF proxy in the calling party's network that is the contact point for the SIP client A intercepts the call and sends the S-CSCF proxy of this domain.
3. The S-CSCF proxy communicates with the application server to provide subscriber services.
4. The application server checks the service features of the SIP client A for providing services and returns the call to the S-CSCF proxy.
5. The S-CSCF queries the DNS/ENUM server with the E.164 number (e.g., 1-732-490-2533).
6. The DNS/ENUM server does not return a SIP URI, since the server does not contain a NAPTR record for this PSTN number.
7. The S-CSCF proxy sends the call to the BGCF proxy to route the call to the PSTN network.
8. The BGCF proxy finds the appropriate PSTN gateway (i.e., MGC/SG/MG) that will route the call over the PSTN network to the called party cost-effectively meeting performances. (Note: In parallel, MGC sends the call signaling messages to the MG as shown in step 11 for transferring media between the called and calling party as soon as the call setup is successfully completed.)
9. The PSTN gateway (i.e., MGC/SG) routes the call to the PSTN network.
10. The PSTN network then routes the call to the PSTN client B (e.g., 1-732-490-2533) of the called party. A session is established between the two end points, and bearer traffic between them is routed through the IP access, IP backbone, IP/PSTN GW (i.e., MG), and PSTN networks.

If both subscribers remain in the IP network, the main steps to set up and route the call are depicted in Figure 8.9.

1. The SIP client A of the calling party calls the E.164 number (e.g., 1-732-490-2533) in order to reach SIP client B of the called party.
2. The P-CSCF proxy in the calling party's network that is the contact point for the SIP client A intercepts the call and sends the S-CSCF proxy of this domain.
3. The S-CSCF proxy communicates with the application server to provide subscriber services.
4. The application server checks the service features of the SIP client A for providing services and returns the call to the S-CSCF proxy.
5. The S-CSCF queries the DNS/ENUM server with the E.164 number (e.g., 1-732-490-2533).
6. The DNS/ENUM server returns the SIP URI of sip:ClientB@ims.rrr.com.
7. The S-CSCF proxy queries the DNS/ENUM server again to get the host IP address for ims.rrr.com.
8. The DNS/ENUM server returns the IP address for ims.rrr.com to the S-CSCF proxy. This IP address is the address of the I-CSCF proxy of the called party's home network.
9. The S-CSCF proxy of the calling party's home network then sends the call to the I-CSCF proxy of the called party's home network.
10. The I-CSCF proxy sends the call to the S-CSCF of the called party's home network. (Although not shown, the I-CSCF proxy queries the home subscriber server in the called party home network to determine which S-CSCF proxy is currently serving client B.)
11. The S-CSCF proxy then communicates with the application server of the called party's home network to provide subscriber services.
12. The application server of the called party's home network replies back to the S-CSCF proxy invoking services of the called party.
13. The S-CSCF proxy of the called party's network then routes the to the P-CSCF proxy through which the SIP client B of the called party is being connected.
14. The P-CSCF proxy then sends the call to the SIP client B of the called party. A session is established between the two end points, and bearer traffic between them is routed through the IP access and backbone networks.

8.3.9 ENUM Implementation Issues

ENUM implementations have some issues related to Character Sets (Non-ASCII Character, Case Sensitivity, Regexp Field Delimiter, and Regexp Meta-Character), Unsupported NAPTRs, ENUM NAPTR Processing, and Nonterminal NAPTR Processing. Some highlights of those issues are provided below, although more detail can be found in RFC 5483.

8.3.9.1 Character Sets

- **Non-ASCII Character:** If the Regexp filed contain non-ASCII characters and there are multibyte characters within an ENUM NAPTR, incorrect processing may well result from the UTF-8-unaware systems.
- **Case Sensitivity:** The case-sensitivity flag that can reside in any static text in the Repl subfield of the Regexp field is inappropriate for ENUM, and should not be provisioned into E2U NAPTRs.
- **Regexp Field Delimiter:** It is not possible to select a delimiter character of the Regexp field that cannot appear in one of the subfields. A client may attempt to process this as a standard delimiter and interpret the Regexp field contents differently from the system that provisioned it.
- **Regexp Meta-Character:** In ENUM, the ERE subfield Regexp may include the application-specific meta-character that needs to be escaped. Not escaping the meta-character produces an invalid ERE.

8.3.9.2 Unsupported NAPTRs

An ENUM client may discard a NAPTR received in response to an ENUM query because of the following: NAPTR is syntactically or semantically incorrect, the NAPTR has a different (nonempty) DDDS Application identifier from the E2U used in ENUM, the NAPTR's ERE does not match the AUS for this ENUM query, the ENUM client does not recognize any ENUM service held in this NAPTR, or this NAPTR (only) contains an ENUM service that is unsupported. These conditions should not cause the whole ENUM query to terminate, and processing should continue with the next NAPTR in the returned RR Set (RRSet).

8.3.9.3 ENUM NAPTR Processing

ENUM is a DDDS application, and the way in which NAPTRs in an RRSet are processed reflects this. The sequence of processing needs to be done seeing the combination of ORDER and PREFERENCE/PRIORITY field values. Once the NAPTRs are sorted into sequence, further processing is done to determine if each of the NAPTRs is appropriate for this ENUM evaluation. These steps must be followed strictly to avoid any processing errors.

8.3.9.4 Nonterminal NAPTR Processing

An ENUM RRSet that contains a nonterminal NAPTR record may hold as its target another domain that has a set of NAPTRs. In effect, this is similar to the nonterminal

NAPTR being replaced by the NAPTRs contained in the domain to which it points. It may create a set of problems:

- Nonterminal NAPTER domains may not be under the control of the ENUM management system.
- Cascaded domains may create loops.
- The nonterminal NAPTR may have a different ORDER value from that in the referring nonterminal NAPTR.
- The set of specifications defining complex and multi-layered DDDS and its applications may contain a set of fields with Nonterminal NAPTRs such as Flags, Services, Regular Expression, and Replacement. The systematic interpretations and appropriate use of these fields and their contents may be prone to errors.

8.3.9.5 Backwards Compatibility

The change in syntax of the Services field of the NAPTR that reflects a refinement of the concept of ENUM processing may create backward compatibility problems unless implemented very carefully.

8.3.9.6 Collected Implications for ENUM Provisioning

ENUM NAPTRs should be provisioned complying with all the recommendations described earlier, such as Character Sets (Non-ASCII Character, Case Sensitivity, Regexp Field Delimiter, and Regexp Meta-Character), Unsupported NAPTRs, ENUM NAPTR Processing, and Nonterminal NAPTR Processing.

8.3.9.7 Collected Implications for ENUM Clients

ENUM clients should not discard NAPTRs in which they detect characters outside the US-ASCII printable range.

8.4 DSN and ENUM Security

The security of ENUM services depends on the DNS that provides mapping between E.164 and the IP addresses storing the appropriate data. DNS uses the hierarchy of distributed databases of the name parent of e164.arpa international domain name. The public data stored in DNS registries of Tiers 1, 2, and 3 (Figure 8.4) undergoes changes by the appropriate authorities. The popularity of DNS has made it almost a general-purpose server for access control to resources, traffic management, load balancing, active planning of topology of communications, and many others. As a result, DNS servers have become attractive places for attackers. Like all DNS services, the data of ENUM services becomes the focus of security threats such as cache poisoning for denial of service (DoS) and Masquerading, client flooding, vulnerabilities in dynamic updates, information leakage, and compromising authoritative data, to name a few.

8.4.1 Cache Poisoning

In cache poisoning, an attacker takes advantage by forging the query forwarding capability of a DNS server to another server. If the server passes the query onto another DNS server that has incorrect information, whether placed there intentionally or unintentionally, then cache poisoning can occur. This cache poisoning is also known as DNS spoofing. For example, earlier BIND software that implements a DNS protocol, a DNS server responding to a query, but not necessarily with an answer, filled in the additional records section of the DNS response message with information that did not necessarily relate to the answer. This partial hint response has been highly susceptible to cache poisoning by a malicious user. A DNS server accepting this response did not perform any necessary checks to assure that the additional information was correct or even related in some way to the answer indicating that the responding server had appropriate authority over those records. The native DNS server accepts this information and adds to the cache corruption problem. Another problem has been that there was not a mechanism in place to assure that the answer received was related to the original question. The DNS server receiving the response caches the answer, again contributing to the cache corruption problem.

Rogue DNS servers pose a threat because they facilitate attack techniques such as host name spoofing and DNS spoofing. DNS pointer records are used in host name spoofing. It differs slightly from most DNS spoofing techniques in that all the transactions that transpire are legitimate according to the DNS protocol, while this is not necessarily the case for other types of DNS spoofing. With host name spoofing, the DNS server legitimately attempts to resolve a PTR query using a legitimate DNS server for the zone belonging to that PTR. It is the PTR record in the zone's data file on the primary server that is purposely configured to point somewhere else, typically a trusted host for another site. Host name spoofing can have a TTL of 0 resulting in no caching of the misleading information, even though the host name is being spoofed.

The DoS attack is one of the objectives of the DNS cache poisoning objectives by the attacker. This objective is achieved by sending back the negative response for a DNS name that could otherwise be resolved. This can result in DoS for the client wishing to communicate in some manner with the DNS name in the query. DoS can be accomplished in several ways by taking advantage of negative responses that indicate that the DNS name in the query cannot be resolved. By sending back the negative response for a DNS name that could otherwise be resolved, it results in a DoS for the client wishing to communicate in some manner with the DNS name in the query. The other way DoS is accomplished is for the rogue server to send a response that redirects the client to a different system that does not contain the service the client desires. Another DoS associated with cache poisoning involves inserting a CNAME record into a cache that refers to itself as the canonical name.

A more potential objective of DNS cache poisoning is masquerading, where DNS caches redirect communications to masquerade as a trusted entity. If this is accomplished, an attacker can intercept, analyze, or intentionally corrupt the communications. An attacker can give the injected cache a short time-to-live, making it appear and disappear quickly enough to avoid detection. Masquerading attacks are possible simply because a number of IP-based applications use host names or IP addresses as a mechanism of providing host-based authentication. This burdens the DNS with the responsibility of maintaining up-to-date and accurate information, neither of which the DNS alone can assure. An attacker can make use of these shortcomings within the DNS to masquerade as a trusted host. Host-based authentication is vulnerable to host name spoofing.

8.4.2 Client Flooding

The lack of strong authentication of DNS responses for a given query by a client can cause flooding. The attacker makes it appear that the responses are coming from the expected name server, and the DNS client fails to detect the origin of the response due to the lack of capability of strong authentication. This attack can be used instead of DNS spoofing when attempting to host-name spoof an application.

8.4.3 Dynamic Updates Vulnerability

The DNS Dynamic Update protocol has provisions to control what systems are allowed to dynamically update a primary server. However, it has very weak form of access control and is vulnerable to threats such as IP spoofing of the system performing the updates, or compromise of the system. For example, protocols such as DHCP can then make use of the DNS Dynamic Update protocol to add and delete RR on demand. These updates take place on the primary server for the zone. The updates take the form of additions and deletions. An attacker who is able to successfully accomplish either can perform a variety of dynamic updating attacks against the primary server. They can range from DoS attacks, such as the deletion of records, to malicious redirection, for instance, by changing IP address information for an RR being sent in an update.

8.4.4 Information Leakage

DNS zone transfers can leak information concerning internal networks to a potential attacker. Blocking zone transfers proves to be a futile effort in preventing such leaks of information. An intruder can make use of DNS tools to automatically query IP addresses in a domain space in an attempt to learn the DNS host name or to find IP addresses that are not assigned. Knowing the unused IP addresses may allow an intruder to use IP spoofing to masquerade as a host of a trusted network. The system may be vulnerable to an attack using an unassigned IP address if the system does not specify every host that it trusts but trusts an entire IP network.

8.4.5 Compromising Authoritative Data

The gains of administrative privileges by an attacker, although this attack is not DND specific, may allow modifying zone information for which the server is authoritative. Careful configuration of the DNS server can provide some protection to these threats. The appropriate security measures needed to provide adequate protection within the DNS could only be accomplished through DSN security extensions (DNSSEC) published IETF RFCs such as RFCs 4033–4035, 5155, and 5910. They provide a set of extensions to DNS, which provide origin authentication of DNS data, data integrity, and authenticated denial of existence. DNSSEC services protect against most of the threats to the DNS. There are several distinct classes of threats to the DNS, most of which are DNS-related instances of more general problems, but a few of which are specific to peculiarities of the DNS protocol. However, DNSSEC does not provide confidentiality of data and does not protect against distributed DDoS attacks.

8.5 Summary

We have discussed that ENUM has been developed for extending the DNS that enables translation between not only host names and IP addresses for translation between E.164 numbers and associated services. In this context, we have explained the DNS architecture along with discovering of SIP entities using DNS. ENUM's DNS-based tiered architecture and ENUM functional architecture for implementation in North America are also described. It is noted that ENUM relies on the DDDS that converts string inputs into URI in its absolute form for its operation as it is an application of DDDS. Examples are provided on how ENUM can be used for SIP services. ENU/DNS security and implementation issues and their possible remedies are also explained. We have also explained elaborately how the DNS can be used for locating/discovering SIP entities.

With the advent of new contact methods like home number, office number, mobile number, fax number, office e-mail address, home e-mail address, instant messaging address, and others, ENUM can enable using a single registered contact number to map to other methods of contact. For example, an ENUM-compliant e-mail application can query the DNS using an E.164 number and what is returned is an associated e-mail address. Once the e-mail address is returned, the e-mail application can then send an e-mail message to the end user. Similarly, this same E.164 number can be entered in a web browser to retrieve an associated web page. All this can be accomplished through the use of only the end-user phone number, an E.164 number. A variety service possibilities can be created using ENUM. Intelligent applications can be created to allowing potentially multiple methods of contacting someone in the event the primary method is unavailable. Even ENUM can be used to place a call to an office based on the time of day using the E.164 number. During out-of-office hours, if users can be reached using the primary number, an application like e-mail or video mail can be invoked instead automatically. Order and preference values that are assigned in ENUM record can be used to reach the user at different times of a day and at different days of a week. In short, many possible intelligent multimedia services can be offered using ENUM.

PROBLEMS

1. What are the DNS namespace, RRs, and name servers? Explain each of these DNS functionalities using examples.
2. How are the SIP entities located/discovered using DNS in the context of the following: client usage, selecting transport protocol, determining port and IP address, detail of RFC 2782, stateful and stateless proxy, server usage, constructing SIP URIs, and selecting transport protocol?
3. What is DDDS algorithm? What is ENUM? How is the DDDS applied to ENUM, and what is the expected output?
4. Explain the use of ENUM with compound NAPTRs. Explain ENUM operations with examples.
5. How is ENUM used for providing SIP services? Explain in detail using examples.
6. What are the implementation issues in ENUM in the context of the following: character sets, unsupported NAPTRs, ENUM NAPTR processing, backwards compatibility, ENUM provisioning, and ENUM clients?
7. Discuss in detail the DNS and ENUM security related to the following: cache poisoning, client flooding, and compromising authoritative data.

Chapter 9

Routing in SIP

Abstract

Session Initiation Protocol (SIP) messages have defined many inherent mechanisms for routing of signaling messages between its entities over the SIP network. We describe all of those routing capabilities in SIP. The SIP registrar is a routing database, while a SIP proxy routes the SIP messages to other proxies and user agents (UAs) along with source–destination paths. However, the routing over a specific path may depend on many criteria, such as administrative policies, load balancing, user preferences, static versus dynamic routing, and others. An incoming SIP message may have multiple addresses of record (AORs) and Contact Uniform Resource Identifiers (URIs), and the routing of the message to a unique location at a given device and time where and when the UA can be reached successfully is a huge challenge in real-time communications. SIP has defined the Record-Route header with Globally Routable UA URI (GRUU) to reach a user. We also describe the SIP routing schemes based on the following, in addition to static and dynamic routing: GRUU, Caller Preferences, and Location. In addition, we also explain the loop-detection algorithm in routing over the SIP network.

9.1 Introduction

Session Initiation Protocol (SIP) request and response messages need to be routed to the destination SIP entities, and routing in SIP is used for sending SIP messages to the final designations locating the SIP entities. Many factors such as technical criteria (e.g., load balancing, service features), administrative policies (e.g., routing through peering partners), economic issues (e.g., least-cost path), routing methodologies (e.g., static destination versus dynamically varying destination, strict versus loose), user preferences (e.g., call forwarding to certain destinations), and other criteria may influence routing decisions for taking a given path and physical destination. The contact address of the destination user must be known or resolved appropriately for routing the call. A SIP user registers its contact address with the SIP registrar server. Note that the routing operation using SIPS Uniform Resource Identifier (URI) is described in Section 4.2.3.

9.2 SIP Registrar

SIP register is a database where a SIP user registers their contact information where they can be reached knowing or discovering the registrar server address (see Section 3.3). Internet Protocol (IP) addresses are temporary because they change frequently. To solve this problem, SIP has developed a concept of permanent SIP address for the user known as the address of record (AOR) that is permanently associated with a user described in Chapter 4. An AOR is temporarily bound to the current contact of the SIP entity (user or service). The bindings are stored in the register database by the SIP UA using REGISTER request (Figure 9.1).

For example, Bob (U1) sends a SIP REGISTER request (M1) to the SIP Registrar server (R1). It is assumed that Bob has not previously registered with this server. In Figure 9.1, we have assumed that there are three separate domains: example.com, network.com, and office.com. The request includes the user's contact list. This flow shows the use of HTTP Digest for authentication using Transport Layer Security (TLS) transport (Request for Comment [RFC] 3665). TLS transport is used due to the lack of integrity protection in HTTP Digest and the danger of

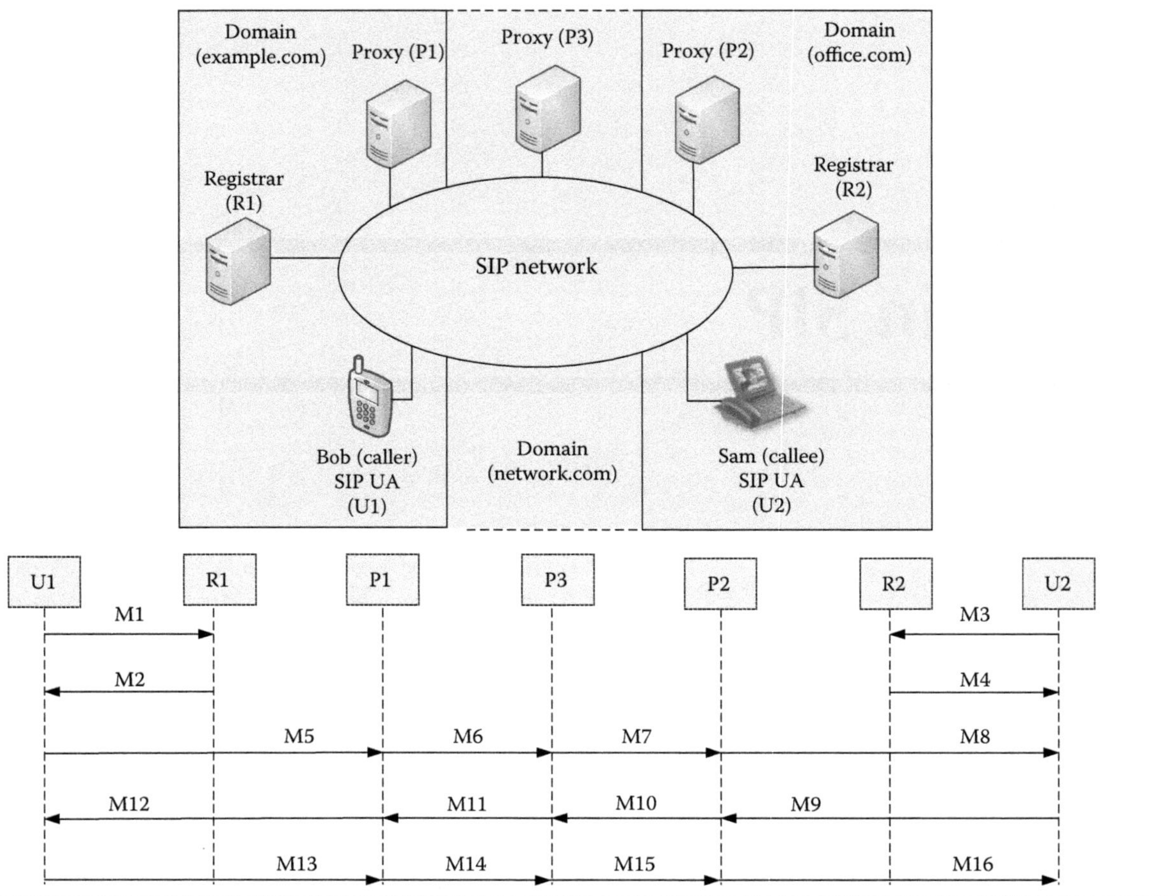

Figure 9.1 SIP network, functional entities, and message flows. (Copyright IETF. Reproduced with permission.)

registration hijacking without it, as described in RFC 3261 (see Section 9.11.1.1). Bob enters his valid user ID and password. Bob's SIP client encrypts the user information according to the challenge (not shown here) issued by the SIP Registrar server and sends the response to the SIP Registrar server. The SIP Registrar server validates the user's credentials. It registers the user in its contact database and returns a response (200 OK) to Bob's SIP client. The response includes the user's current contact list in Contact headers. The format of the authentication shown is HTTP digest.

M1 REGISTER Bob -> SIP Server

```
REGISTER sips:ss2.biloxi.example.com SIP/2.0
Via: SIP/2.0/TLS client.biloxi.example.
com:5061;branch=z9hG4bKnashd92
Max-Forwards: 70
From: Bob <sips:bob@biloxi.example.
com>;tag=ja743ks76zlflH
To: Bob <sips:bob@biloxi.example.com>
Call-ID: 1j9FpLxk3uxtm8tn@biloxi.example.com
CSeq: 2 REGISTER
Contact: <sips:bob@client.biloxi.example.com>
Authorization: Digest username="bob",
realm="atlanta.example.com"
nonce="ea9c8e88df84f1cec4341ae6cbe5a359",
opaque="",
uri="sips:ss2.biloxi.example.com",
response="dfe56131d1958046689d83306477ecc"
Content-Length: 0
```

M2 200 OK SIP Server -> Bob

```
SIP/2.0 200 OK
Via: SIP/2.0/TLS client.biloxi.example.
com:5061;branch=z9hG4bKnashd92
      ;received=192.0.2.201
From: Bob <sips:bob@biloxi.example.
com>;tag=ja743ks76zlflH
To: Bob <sips:bob@biloxi.example.
com>;tag=37GkEhwl6
Call-ID: 1j9FpLxk3uxtm8tn@biloxi.example.com
CSeq: 2 REGISTER
Contact: <sips:bob@client.biloxi.example.
com>;expires=3600
Content-Length: 0
```

Similar is the case with another user, Sam, for registration (contents of messages M3 and M4 not shown) with its

SIP Registrar server (R2) located in its domain (office.com). The user's contact information is updated by the user as one changes one's location. A user can have multiple contact information registered at the same time, indicating that one needs to be tried in multiple locations forking the request, as one can be available in one of these registered addresses. It should be noted that the SIP proxy server or location server may collect the contact information of SIP users from SIP registrars and create location databases for routing purposes. However, the protocols that are used for communications between registrars, proxies, or location servers are beyond the scope of SIP.

9.3 SIP Proxy

The SIP proxy server is usually the functional entity that is responsible for routing between intradomain and interdomain for SIP messages (see Section 3.11). The proxy must inspect the SIP Request-URI of the request because this may contain the headers like Route/Route-Record. The Route header field is used to force routing for a request through the listed set of proxies, for example, Route: <sip:bigbox3.site3.atlanta.com;lr>, <sip:server10.biloxi.com;lr>. The Record-Route header field is inserted by proxies in a request to force future requests in the dialog to be routed through the proxy, for example, Record-Route: <sip:server10.biloxi.com;lr>, sip:bigbox3.site3.atlanta.com;lr. In the absence of local policy to the contrary, the processing a proxy performs on a request containing a Route header field can be summarized in the following steps (RFC 3261).

1. The proxy will inspect the Request-URI. If it indicates a resource owned by this proxy, the proxy will replace it with the results of running a location service. Otherwise, the proxy will not change the Request-URI.
2. The proxy will inspect the URI in the topmost Route header field value. If it indicates this proxy, the proxy removes it from the Route header field (this route node has been reached).
3. The proxy will forward the request to the resource indicated by the URI in the topmost Route header field value or in the Request-URI if no Route header field is present. The proxy determines the address, port, and transport to use when forwarding the request by applying the procedures in step 4 to that URI. If no strict-routing elements are encountered on the path of the request, the Request-URI will always indicate the target of the request.
4. If the Request-URI contains a maddr parameter, the proxy must check to see if its value is in the set of addresses or domains the proxy is configured to be responsible for. If the Request-URI has a maddr parameter with a value the proxy is responsible for, and the request was received using the port and transport indicated (explicitly or by default) in the Request-URI, the proxy MUST strip the maddr and any nondefault port or transport parameter, and continue processing as if those values had not been present in the request.
5. A request may arrive with a maddr matching the proxy, but on a port or transport different from that indicated in the URI. Such a request needs to be forwarded to the proxy using the indicated port and transport. If the first value in the Route header field indicates this proxy, the proxy must remove that value from the request.

This scenario is the basic SIP trapezoid, U1 -> P1 -> P3-> P2 -> U2, with both proxies record-routing (Figure 9.1). Here is the flow. U1 sends (M5):

```
INVITE sip:callee@office.com SIP/2.0
Contact: sip:caller@u1.example.com
```

to P1. P1 is an outbound proxy. P1 is not responsible for office.com and does not have any direct relationship with this domain, so it looks it up in the Domain Name System (DNS) and sends it to the proxy (P3) of the network domain. It also adds a Record-Route header field value (M6):

```
INVITE sip:callee@office.com SIP/2.0
Contact: sip:caller@u1.example.com
Record-Route: <sip:p1.example.com;lr>
```

P2 gets this and queries the DNS and sends this to the proxy (P2) that is responsible for the domain (office.com) adding the Route-Record header keeping it in the routing path (M7):

```
INVITE sip:callee@office.com SIP/2.0
Contact: sip:caller@u1.example.com
Record-Route: <sip:p3.network.com;lr>
Record-Route: <sip:p1.example.com;lr>
```

P2 gets this. It is responsible for domain.com, so it runs a location service and rewrites the Request-URI. It also adds a Record-Route header field value. There is no Route header field, so it resolves the new Request-URI to determine where to send the request (M8):

```
INVITE sip:callee@u2.office.com SIP/2.0
Contact: sip:caller@u1.example.com
Record-Route: <sip:p2.office.com;lr>
Record-Route: <sip:p3.network.com;lr>
Record-Route: <sip:p1.example.com;lr>
```

The callee at u2.office.com gets this and responds with a 200 OK (M9):

```
SIP/2.0 200 OK
Contact: sip:callee@u2.office.com
Record-Route: <sip:p2.office.com;lr>
Record-Route: <sip:p3.network.com;lr>
Record-Route: <sip:p1.example.com;lr>
```

The callee at u2 also sets its dialog state's remote target URI to sip:caller@u1.example.com and its route set to

```
(<sip:p2.office.com;lr>,<sip:p3.network.
com;lr>,<sip:p1.example.com;lr>)
```

This is forwarded by P2 to P3 to P1 to U1 as normal. Now, U1 sets its dialog state's remote target URI to sip:callee@u2.office.com and its route set to

```
(<sip:p1.example.com;lr>,<sip:p3.network.
com;lr>,<sip:p2.office.com;lr>)
```

The messages M10, M11, and M12 are not shown here and are left for exercises.

Since all the route set elements contain the lr parameter, U1 constructs the following BYE request (M13):

```
BYE sip:callee@u2.office.com SIP/2.0
Route: <sip:p1.example.com;lr>,<sip:p3.
network.com;lr>,<sip:p2.office.com;lr>
```

As any other element (including proxies) would do, it resolves the URI in the topmost Route header field value using DNS to determine where to send the request. This goes to P1. P1 notices that it is not responsible for the resource indicated in the Request-URI so it does not change it. It does see that it is the first value in the Route header field, so it removes that value, and forwards the request to P3 (M14):

```
BYE sip:callee@u2.office.com SIP/2.0
Route: <sip:p3.network.com;lr>,<sip:p2.
domain.com;lr>
```

Similarly, P3 examines that it is not responsible for the resource indicated by the Request-URI and does not change it and removes its first value in the Route header field value, and forwards the request to P2 (M15):

```
BYE sip:callee@u2.office.com SIP/2.0
Route: <sip:p2.office.com;lr>
```

P2 also notices it is not responsible for the resource indicated by the Request-URI (it is responsible for office.com, not u2.office.com), so it does not change it. It does see itself in the first Route header field value, so it removes it and forwards the following to u2.office.com based on a DNS lookup against the Request-URI (M16):

```
BYE sip:callee@u2.office.com SIP/2.0
```

9.4 Traversing a Strict-Routing Proxy

In this scenario, a dialog is established across four proxies, each of which adds Record-Route header field values. The third proxy implements the strict-routing procedures specified in RFC 2543 and many works in progress (not relevant to Figure 9.1):

```
U1 -> P1 -> P2 -> P3 -> P4 -> U2
```

The INVITE arriving at U2 contains:

```
INVITE sip:callee@u2.domain.com SIP/2.0
Contact: sip:caller@u1.example.com
Record-Route: <sip:p4.domain.com;lr>
Record-Route: <sip:p3.middle.com>
Record-Route: <sip:p2.example.com;lr>
Record-Route: <sip:p1.example.com;lr>
```

which U2 responds to with a 200 OK. Later, U2 sends the following BYE request to P4 based on the first Route header field value:

```
BYE sip:caller@u1.example.com SIP/2.0
Route: <sip:p4.domain.com;lr>
Route: <sip:p3.middle.com>
Route: <sip:p2.example.com;lr>
Route: <sip:p1.example.com;lr>
```

P4 is not responsible for the resource indicated in the Request-URI, so it will leave it alone. It notices that it is the element in the first Route header field value so it removes it. It then prepares to send the request based on the now first Route header field value of sip:p3.middle.com; however, it notices that this URI does not contain the lr parameter, so before sending, it reformats the request to be

```
BYE sip:p3.middle.com SIP/2.0
Route: <sip:p2.example.com;lr>
Route: <sip:p1.example.com;lr>
Route: <sip:caller@u1.example.com>
```

P3 is a strict router, so it forwards the following to P2:

```
BYE sip:p2.example.com;lr SIP/2.0
Route: <sip:p1.example.com;lr>
Route: <sip:caller@u1.example.com>
```

P2 sees the request-URI is a value it placed into a Record-Route header field, so before further processing, it rewrites the request to be

```
BYE sip:caller@u1.example.com SIP/2.0
Route: <sip:p1.example.com;lr>
```

P2 is not responsible for u1.example.com, so it sends the request to P1 based on the resolution of the Route header field value. P1 notices itself in the topmost Route header field value, so it removes it, resulting in

```
BYE sip:caller@u1.example.com SIP/2.0
```

Since P1 is not responsible for u1.example.com and there is no Route header field, P1 will forward the request to u1.example.com based on the Request-URI.

9.5 Rewriting Record-Route Header Field Values

In this scenario, U1 and U2 are in different private namespaces and they enter a dialog through a proxy P1, which acts as a gateway between the namespaces (not relevant to Figure 9.1).

```
U1 -> P1 -> U2
```

U1 sends

```
INVITE sip:callee@gateway.leftprivatespace.
com SIP/2.0
Contact: <sip:caller@u1.leftprivatespace.com>
```

P1 uses its location service and sends the following to U2:

```
INVITE sip:callee@rightprivatespace.com
SIP/2.0
Contact: <sip:caller@u1.leftprivatespace.com>
Record-Route: <sip:gateway.rightprivatespace.
com;lr>
```

U2 sends this 200 (OK) back to P1:

```
SIP/2.0 200 OK
Contact: <sip:callee@u2.rightprivatespace.com>
Record-Route: <sip:gateway.rightprivatespace.
com;lr>
```

P1 rewrites its Record-Route header parameter to provide a value that U1 will find useful, and sends the following to U1:

```
SIP/2.0 200 OK
Contact: <sip:callee@u2.rightprivatespace.
com>
Record-Route: <sip:gateway.leftprivatespace.
com;lr>
Later, U1 sends the following BYE request to
P1:
BYE sip:callee@u2.rightprivatespace.com
SIP/2.0
Route: <sip:gateway.leftprivatespace.com;lr>
```

which P1 forwards to U2 as

```
BYE sip:callee@u2.rightprivatespace.com
SIP/2.0
```

9.5.1 Problems and Recommendation

Record-Route rewriting in responses described earlier is not the optimal way of handling multihomed and transport protocol-switching situations. Furthermore, the consequence of doing rewriting is that the route set seen by the caller is different from the route set seen by the callee, and this has at least two negative implications (RFC 5658):

- The route set gets edited by the proxy in the response and, as a result, the callee cannot sign the route set. It implies that end-to-end protection of the route set cannot be supported by the protocol violating the Internet's principles of openness and breaking the end-to-end connectivity.
- A proxy must implement special multihoming logic in view of multiple interfaces. When a proxy forwards a request, it usually performs an output interface calculation and writes information resolving to the output interface into the URI of the Record-Route header. When handling responses, the proxy must inspect the Record-Route header(s) and will look for an input interface, and selectively edit them to reference the correct output interface although it implies more processing as it will be done for all responses forwarded by the proxy.

The double Record-Route approach described next is recommended to avoid rewriting the Record-Route (RFC 5658). This recommendation applies to all uses of Record-Route rewriting by proxies, including transport protocol-switching and multihomed proxies.

9.6 Record-Routing with Globally Routable UA URI

The Globally Routable UA URI (GRUU) defined in RFC 5627 has been described earlier. The GRUU is a URI that routes to a specific UA instance. However, there are two distinct requirements for record-routing (R-R) for the GRUU:

- R-R in the originating domain
- R-R in the terminating domain

These requirements avoid unnecessary, and possibly problematic, spirals of requests.

If (i) an originating authoritative proxy receives a dialog-forming request, (ii) and the Contact header field contains a GRUU in the domain of the proxy, (iii) and that GRUU is a valid one in the domain of the proxy, (iv) and that GRUU is associated with the AOR matching the authenticated identity of the requestor (assuming such authentication has been performed), (v) and the request contains Record-Route header fields, then the authoritative proxy must record-route. If all of these conditions are true, except that the GRUU is associated with an AOR that did not match the authenticated identity of the requestor, it is recommended that the proxy reject the request with a 403 (Forbidden) response.

If (i) a terminating authoritative proxy receives a dialog-forming request, (ii) and the Request-URI contains a URI in the location service (either a GRUU or an AOR), (iii) and the contact selected for sending the request has an instance ID and is bound to a GRUU, (iv) and the registration contains Path URI, then the authoritative proxy must record-route.

If a proxy is in either the originating or terminating domain, but is not an authoritative proxy, the proxy may record-route. If a proxy in the terminating domain requires mid-dialog requests to pass through it for whatever reason (firewall traversal, accounting, etc.), the proxy must still record-route and must not assume that a UA will utilize its GRUU in the Contact header field of its response (which would cause mid-dialog requests to pass through the proxy without record-routing).

Implementers should note that, if a UA uses a GRUU in its contact, and a proxy inserted itself into the Path header field of a registration, that proxy will be receiving mid-dialog requests regardless of whether it record-routes or not. The only distinction is what URI the proxy will see in the top-most Route header field of mid-dialog requests. If the proxy record-routes, it will see that URI. If it does not, it will see the Path URI it inserted.

9.7 Double Route-Record

The Record-Route rewriting that we have described earlier creates some problems when a proxy has to change some of those parameters between its incoming and outgoing interfaces (multihomed proxies, transport protocol switching, or IPv4 to IPv6 scenarios, and others), the question arises on what should be put in Record-Route header(s). It is not possible to make one header have the characteristics of both interfaces at the same time. Record-Route rewriting in responses is not the optimal way of handling multihomed and transport protocol-switching situations. Additionally, the consequence of doing rewriting is that the route set seen by the caller is different from the route set seen by the callee, and this has at least two negative implications:

1. The callee cannot sign the route set because it gets edited by the proxy in the response. Consequently, end-to-end protection of the route set cannot be supported by the protocol. This means the Internet's principles of openness and end-to-end connectivity are broken.
2. A proxy must implement special *multihomed* logic. During the request-forwarding phase, it performs an output interface calculation and writes information resolving to the output interface into the URI of the Record-Route header. When handling responses, the proxy must inspect the Record-Route header(s), look for an input interface, and selectively edit them to reference the correct output interface. Since this lookup has to be done for all responses forwarded by the proxy, this technique implies a CPU drag.

The serious drawbacks of the rewriting technique have been removed with the help of the double Route-Routing scheme (RFC 5658). This technique is also backward compatible with the rewriting of the Record-Route as described above, and can also solve the spiraling request problem. When double Record-Routing scheme is used, the proxy will have to handle the subsequent in-dialog request(s) as a spiral, and consequently devote resources to maintain transactions required to handle the spiral.

To avoid a spiral, the proxy can be smart and scan an extra Route header ahead to determine whether the request will spiral through it. If it does, it can optimize the second spiral through itself. Even though this is an implementation decision, it is much more efficient to avoid spiraling. Therefore, implementers can choose that a proxy may remove two Route headers instead of one when using the double Record-Routing. We have taken an example that shows a basic call flow (Figure 9.2) using double Record-Routing in a multihomed IPv4 to IPv6 proxy (RFC 5658), and annotates the dialog state on each SIP UA.

SIP Proxy P1 is dual-homed in IP4 and IPv6 network acting the proxy serving UAs U1 (howell.domain.com) and U2 (atlanta.domain.com), respectively. The address configurations of dual-stack proxy P1 are 192.0.2.254:5060 on the IPv4 interface and 2001:db8::1 on the IPv6 interface. The call flow messages with double Route-Record are explained in Figure 9.2, omitting some mandatory SIP headers for simplicity.

The caller (U1) sends INVITE to the callee (U2) via its outgoing proxy (P1):

F1 INVITE U1 -> P1 (192.0.2.254:5060)

```
INVITE sip:joe@howell.network.com SIP/2.0
Route: <sip:192.0.2.254:5060;lr>
From: Joe <joe@howell.network.com>;tag=1234
To: Ken <sip:ken@atlanta.network.com>
Contact: <sip:joe@192.0.2.1>
```

The proxy (P1) receives the message (F1) from Joe (U1) and adds Route-Record header field for both of its interfaces of IPv4 and IPv6, and then it sends the INVITE message (F2) to Ken (U1):

F2 INVITE P1 (2001:db8::1) -> U2

```
INVITE sip: joe@howell.network.com SIP/2.0
Record-Route: <sip:[2001:db8::1];lr>
```

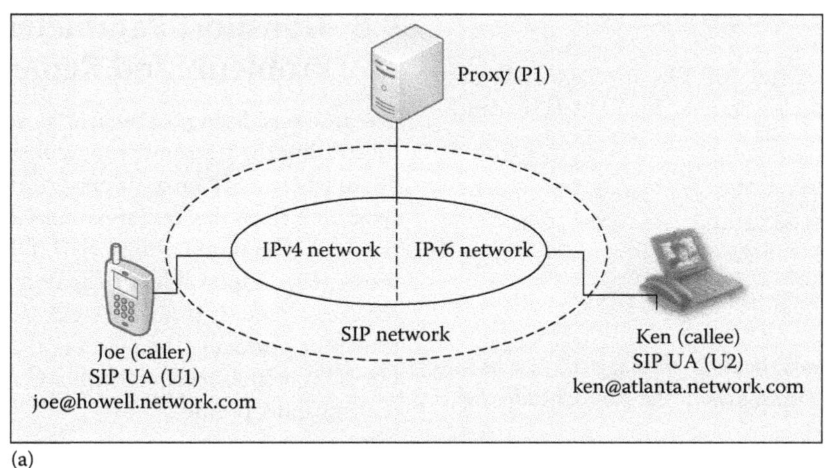

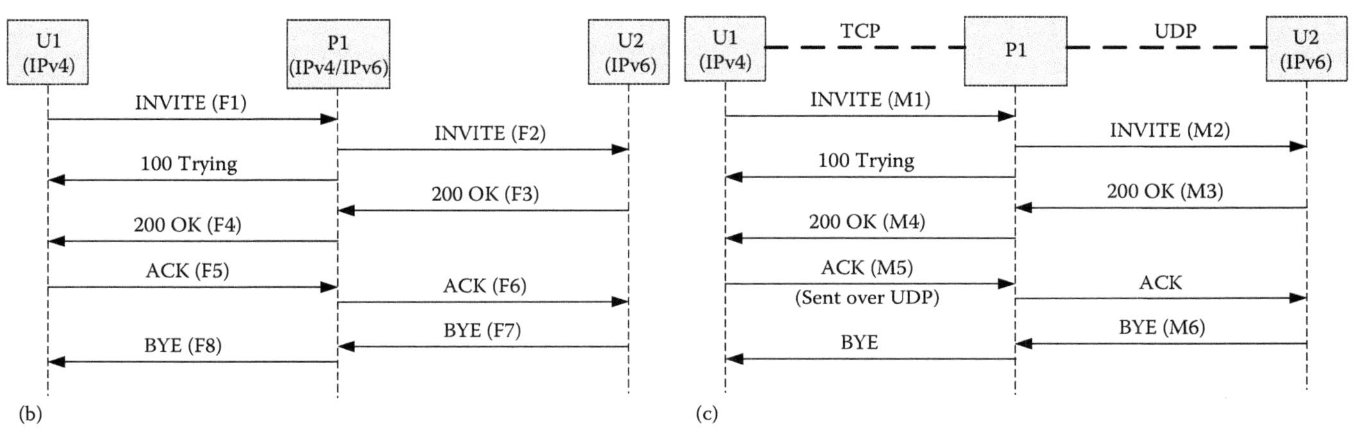

Figure 9.2 Example of double Route-Record: (a) SIP and IP network configuration, (b) call flows with IPv4–IPv6 multi-homed proxy, and (c) call flows with TCP/UDP transport protocol switching. (Copyright IETF. Reproduced with permission.)

```
Record-Route: <sip:192.0.2.254:5060;lr>
From: Joe <sip:joe@howell.network.
com>;tag=1234
To: Ken <sip:ken@atlanta.network.com>
Contact: <sip:joe@192.0.2.1>
```

Ken's UA (U2) receives INVITE message (F2) from proxy (P1). However, the dialog state at Ken's UA (U2) can be described as follows:

```
Local URI      = sip:ken@atlanta.network.com
Remote URI     = sip:joe@howell.network.com
Remote target= sip:joe@192.0.2.1
Route Set      = sip:[2001:db8::1];lr
                 sip:192.0.2.254:5060:lr
```

Ken's UA (U2) processes the message (F2) and sends the 200 OK message (F3) to the proxy (P1) adding the route set in the double Route-Record header field:

F3 200 OK U2 -> P1 (2001:db8::1)

```
SIP/2.0 200 OK
Record-Route: <sip:[2001:db8::1];lr>
Record-Route: <sip:192.0.2.254:5060;lr>
From: Joe <sip: joe@howell.network.
com>;tag=1234
To: Ken <sip:ken@atlanta.network.
com>;tag=4567
Contact:<sip:ken@[2001:db8::33]>
```

The proxy (P1) receives the 200 OK messages (F3) from Ken's UA (U2) and forwards the message (F4) to Joes UA (U1):

F4 200 OK P1 -> U1

```
SIP/2.0 200 OK
Record-Route: <sip:[2001:db8::1];lr>
Record-Route: <sip:192.0.2.254:5060;lr>
From: Joe <sip:joe@howell.network.
com>;tag=1234
To: Ken <sip:ken@atlanta.network.
com>;tag=4567
```

```
Contact: <sip:ken@[2001:db8::33]>
```

Joe's UA (U1) receives the 200 OK message (F4) from the proxy (P1), and the dialog state at Joe's UA (U1) can be described as follows:

```
Local URI    = sip:joe@howell.network.com
Remote URI = sip:ken@atlanta.network.com
Remote target = sip:bob@[2001:db8::33]
Route Set = sip:192.0.2.254:5060:lr
              sip:[2001:db8::1];lr
```

Now Joe's UA (U1) sends the ACK message (F5) via its outgoing proxy (P1) adding both routes in the Route header field:

F5 ACK U1 -> P1 (192.0.2.254:5060)

```
ACK sip:ken@[2001:db8::33] SIP/2.0
Route: <sip:192.0.2.254:5060:lr>
Route: <sip:[2001:db8::1];lr>
From: Joe <sip:joe@howell.network.
com>;tag=1234
To: Ken <sip:ken@atlanta.network.
com>;tag=4567
```

The proxy (P1) receives the ACK message (F5) from Joe's UA (U1) and forwards the ACK message (F6) to Ken's UA (U2) after removing both Route header fields:

F6 ACK P1 (2001:db8::1) -> U2

```
ACK sip:ken@[2001:db8::33] SIP/2.0
From: Alice <sip:alice@atlanta.example.
com>;tag=1234
To: Bob <sip:bob@biloxi.example.com>;tag=4567
```

The session is now established between Joe and Ken. At the end of the session, Ken's UA (U2) sends the BYE Messages (F7) via the proxy (P2) adding both routes in Route header fields:

F7 BYE U2 -> P1 (2001:db8::1)

```
BYE sip:alice@192.0.2.1 SIP/2.0
Route: <sip:[2001:db8::1];lr>
Route: <sip:192.0.2.254:5060:lr>
From: Ken <sip:ken@atlanta.network.
com>;tag=4567
To: Joe <sip:joe@howell.network.com>;tag=1234
```

The proxy (P1) receives the BYE message (F7) from Ken's UA (U2) and forwards the BYE message (F8) to Joe's UA (U1) after removing both Route header fields:

F8 BYE P1 (192.0.2.254:5060) -> U1

```
BYE sip:alice@192.0.2.1 SIP/2.0
From: Ken <sip:ken@atlanta.network.
com>;tag=4567
To: Joe <sip:joe@howell.network.com>;tag=1234
```

9.8 Transport Parameter Usage Problems and Remedies

We are considering a scenario as shown in Figure 9.2c for illustrating the transport protocol-switching problems (RFC 5658) where a SIP proxy is performing the transport protocol switching from the Transmission Control Protocol (TCP) to the User Datagram Protocol (UDP). In this example, the proxy (P1), responsible for the domain howell.domain.com, receives a request from Joe's UA (U1), which uses the TCP transport protocol. The proxy (P1) sends this request to Ken UA (U2), which registers with a Contact specifying UDP as the transport protocol.

9.8.1 UA Implementation

We assume that the proxy (P1) receives an initial request from Joe over the TCP and forwards it to Ken over the UDP (Figure 9.2c). For subsequent requests, it is expected that the TCP could continue to be used between Joe and P1, and the UDP between P1 and Ken. However, this cannot happen if a numeric IP address is used and no transport parameter is set on Record-Route URI. This happens because of procedures described in RFC 3263. We have provided the call flows with messages M1–M6 omitting some mandatory parameters of SIP for simplicity as stated below:

M1 INVITE Joe's UA (U1) -> Proxy (P1) (192.0.2.1/tcp)

```
INVITE sip:ken@atlanta.network.com SIP/2.0
Route: <sip:192.0.2.1;lr;transport=tcp>
From: Joe<sip:joe@howell.network.
com>;tag=1234
To: Ken <sip:ken@atlanta.network.com>
Contact: <sip:joe@u1.howell.network.
com;transport=tcp>
```

M2 INVITE Proxy (P1) -> Ken's UA (U2) (u2.atlanta.network.com/udp)

```
INVITE sip: ken@atlanta.network.
com;transport=udp SIP/2.0
Record-Route: <sip:192.0.2.1;lr> (Note: No
transport parameter is used.)
From: Joe<sip:joe@howell.network.
com>;tag=1234
To: Ken <sip:ken@atlanta.network.com>
Contact: < sip:joe@u1.howell.network.
com;transport=tcp>
```

Dialog State at Ken's UA (U2):

```
Local URI     = sip:ken@atlanta.network.com
Remote URI    = sip:joe@howell.network.com
Remote target = sip:joe@u1.howell.network.
com;transport = tcp
Route Set     = sip:192.0.2.1;lr
```

M3 200 OK Ken's UA (U2) -> Proxy (P1) (192.0.2.1/udp)

```
SIP/2.0 200 OK
Record-Route: <sip:192.0.2.1;lr>
From: Joe <sip:joe@howell.network.
com>;tag=1234
To: Ken <sip:ken@atlanta.network.
com>;tag=4567
Contact: <sip:ken@u2.atlanta.network.com>
```

M4 200 OK Proxy (P1) -> Joe's UA (U1) (u1.howell.network.com/tcp)

```
SIP/2.0 200 OK
Record-Route: <sip:192.0.2.1;lr>
From: Joe <sip:joe@howell.network.
com>;tag=1234
To: Ken <sip:ken@atlanta.network.
com>;tag=4567
Contact: <sip:ken@u2.atlanta.network.com>
```

Dialog State at Joe's UA (U1):

```
Local URI     = sip:joe@howell.network.com
Remote URI    = sip: ken@atlanta.network.com
Remote target = sip:ken@u2.atlanta.network.com
Route Set     = sip:192.0.2.1;lr
```

M5 ACK Joe's UA (U1) -> Proxy (P1) (192.0.2.1/udp)

```
ACK sip:ken@u2.atlanta.network.com SIP/2.0
Route: <sip:192.0.2.1;lr>
From: Ken <sip:ken@atlanta.network.
com>;tag=1234
To: Ken <sip:ken@atlanta.network.
com>;tag=4567
```

M6 BYE Ken's UA (U2) -> Proxy (P1) (192.0.2.1/udp)

```
BYE sip:joe@u1.howell.network.
com;transport=tcp SIP/2.0
Route: <sip:192.0.2.1;lr>
From: Ken <sip:ken@atlanta.network.
com>;tag=4567
To: Joe <sip:joe@howell.network.com>;tag=1234
```

9.8.1.1 Transport Switching Issues

In message M2 of the call flow example shown earlier in Figure 9.2c, the proxy (P1) does not insert any transport parameter in the Record-Route URI, and in subsequent in-dialog requests of U1, like the ACK sent in M5. This is sent according to the behavior specified in RFC 3261 (Section 3.6.2). It implies that the route set is used without any transport parameter, and if the procedures described in RFC 3263 (see Section 8.2.4) are applied, the Route sip:192.0.2.1 will resolve to a UDP transport by default (since no transport parameter is present here), and no Naming Authority Pointer (NAPTR) request will be performed since this is a numeric IP address. In general, the interoperability problems arise when a UA (e.g., U1) is trying to send the ACK: it is not ready to change its transport protocol for a mid-dialog request and just fails to do so, requiring the proxy implementer to insert the transport protocol in the Record-Route URI.

A more important generic question is this: What happens if the proxy had Record-Routed its logical name (howell.network.com)? The protocol-switching problem can only be avoided only if the resulting transport protocol per procedures described in RFC 3263 (see Section 8.2.4) is UDP since Ken is to be contacted over UDP per this example. For any other resulting transport protocol, the transport protocol-switching problems will occur as described above (RFC 5658). Also, if one of the UAs sends an initial request using a different transport than the one retrieved from the DNS, this scenario would be problematic.

In practice, there are multiple situations where UA implementations do not use logical names and NAPTR records when sending an initial request to a proxy. This happens, for instance, when (RFC 5658)

1. UAs offer the ability to choose the transport to be used for initial requests, even if they support RFC 3263 (see Section 8.2.4). This is a frequent UA functionality that is justified by the following use cases:
   - When it is not possible to change the DNS server configuration and the implementation does not support all the transport protocols that could be configured by default in DNS (e.g., TLS)
   - When the end user wants to choose his transport protocol for whatever reason, for example, needing to force TCP, avoiding UDP/congestion, retransmitting, fragmenting, or other problems

   This ability to force the transport protocol in UAs for initial requests should be avoided.

   - Selecting the transport protocol in the configuration of an outbound proxy means that the procedure described in RFC 3263 is bypassed for initial requests. As a consequence, if the proxy Record-Routed with no transport parameter as is recommended in RFC 3261 (see Section 2.8.2), the UA will be forced to use the procedure of RFC 3263 as preferred transport for subsequent requests anyway, which leads to the problematic scenario described in Figure 9.2c.
2. UAs decide to always keep the same transport for a given dialog. This choice is erratic, since if the proxy is not Record-Routing, the callee may receive the subsequent request through a transport that is not the one put in its Contact. If a UA really wants to avoid transport protocol switching between the initial and

subsequent request, it should rely on DNS records for that; thus, it should avoid configuring statically the outbound proxy with a numeric IP address. A logical name, with no transport parameter, should be used instead.

3. UAs do not support RFC 3263 (see Section 8.2.4) at all, or do not have any DNS server available. In that case, as illustrated previously, forcing Joe's UA (U1) to switch from TCP to UDP between the initial request and subsequent request(s) is clearly not the desired default behavior, and it typically leads to interoperability problems. UA implementations should then be ready to change the transport protocol between initial and subsequent requests. In theory, any UA or proxy using UDP must also be prepared to use TCP for requests that exceed the size limit of path maximum transmission unit (MTU), as described in RFC 3261 (see Section 3.13.1.1).

9.8.2 Proxy Implementation

To prevent UA implementation problems, and to maintain a reasonable level of interoperability, the situation can be improved on the proxy side. Thus, if the transport protocol changed between its incoming and outgoing sides, the proxy should use the double Record-Route technique and should add a transport parameter to each of the Record-Route URIs it inserts. When TLS is used on the transport on either side of the proxy, the URI placed in the Record-Route header field must encode a next hop that will be reached using TLS. There are two ways for this to work. The first way is for the URI placed in the Record-Route to be a SIPS URI. The second is for the URI placed in the Record-Route to be constructed such that application of resolution procedures of RFC 3262 to that URI results in TLS being selected. Proxies compliant with this specification must not use a transport=tls parameter on the URI placed in the Record-Route because the transport=tls usage was deprecated in RFC 3261.

Record-Route rewriting may also be used. However, the recommendation to put a transport protocol parameter on Record-Route URI does not apply when the proxy has changed the transport protocol due to the size of UDP requests as per RFC 3261 (see Section 3.13.1.1). As an illustration of the previous example, it means one of the following processing (RFC 5658) will be performed:

- **Double Record-Routing:** The proxy inserts two Record-Route headers into the SIP request. The first one is set, in this example, to Record-Route: <sip:192.0.2.1;lr;transport=tcp>; the second one is set to Record-Route: <sip:192.0.2.1;lr> with no transport, or with transport=udp, which basically means the same thing.
- **Record-Route rewriting on responses:** In the INVITE request sent in M2, the proxy puts the outgoing transport protocol in the transport parameter of Record-Route URI. By doing so, Ken's UA (U2) will correctly send its BYE request in M6 using the same transport protocol as previous messages of the same dialog. The proxy rewrites the Record-Route when processing the 200 OK response, changing the transport parameter *on the fly* to transport=tcp, so that the Route set will appear to be <sip:192.0.2.1;lr;transport=tcp> for UA1 and <sip:192.0.2.1;lr;transport=udp> for U2.

It is a common practice in proxy implementations to support double Record-Route and to insert the transport parameter in the Record-Route URI. This practice is acceptable as long as all SIP elements that may be in the path of subsequent requests support that transport. This restriction needs an explanation. Let us imagine we have two proxies, P1 at p1.howell.network.com and P2 on the path of an initial request. P1 is Record-Routing and changes the transport from UDP to Stream Control Transmission Protocol (SCTP) because the P2 URI resolves to SCTP applying RFC 3263 (see Section 8.2.4). Consequently, the proxy P1 inserts two Record-Route headers:

```
Record-Route: <sip:p1.howell.network.
com;transport=udp> and
Record-Route: <sip:p1.howell.network.
com;transport=sctp>.
```

The problem arises if P2 is not Record-Routing because the SIP element downstream of P2 will be asked to reach P1 using SCTP for any subsequent, in-dialog request from the callee, and this downstream SIP element may not support that transport. To handle this situation, RFC 5658 recommends that a proxy should apply the double Record-Routing technique as soon as it changes the transport protocol between its incoming and outgoing sides. If proxy P2 in the example above would follow this recommendation, it would perform double Record-Routing and the downstream element would not be forced to send requests over a transport it does not support. By extension, a proxy should also insert a Record-Route header for any multihomed situation (as the ones described here: scheme changes, sigcomp, IPv4/IPv6, transport changes) that may affect the processing of proxies being on the path of subsequent requests.

9.8.3 Symmetric Response Routing

The SIP (RFC 3261) operates over UDP and TCP. When used with UDP, responses to requests are returned to the source address the request came from, and to the port written into the topmost Via header field value of the request.

This results in a *hybrid* way of computing the destination of the response. Half of the information (specifically, the IP address) is taken from the IP packet headers, and the other half (specifically, the port) from the SIP message headers. SIP operates in this manner so that a server can listen for all messages, both requests and responses, on a single IP address and port. This helps improve scalability. However, this behavior is not desirable in many cases, most notably when the client is behind a network address translation (NAT). In that case, the response will not properly traverse the NAT, since it will not match the binding established with the request.

Furthermore, there is currently no way for a client to examine a response and determine the source port that the server saw in the corresponding request. In RFC 3261, SIP provides the client with the source IP address that the server saw in the request, but not the port. The source IP address is conveyed in the *received* parameter in the topmost Via header field value of the response. This information has proved useful for basic NAT traversal, debugging purposes, and support of multihomed hosts. However, it is incomplete without the port information. RFC 3581 defines a new parameter for the Via header field, called *rport*, that allows a client to request that the server send the response back to the source IP address and port where the request came from. The rport parameter is analogous to the *received* parameter, except that rport contains a port number, not the IP address.

9.8.3.1 Client Behavior

The client behavior specified here affects the transport processing defined in SIP (RFC 3261, see Section 3.1). A client, compliant to this specification (clients include UACs and proxies), may include an rport parameter in the top Via header field value of requests it generates. This parameter must have no value; it serves as a flag to indicate to the server that this extension is supported and requested for the transaction. When the client sends the request, if the request is sent using UDP, the client must be prepared to receive the response on the same IP address and port it used to populate the source IP address and source port of the request. For backwards compatibility, the client MUST still be prepared to receive a response on the port indicated in the sent-by field of the topmost Via header field value, as specified in SIP (RFC 3261, see Section 3.1.2.1).

When there is a NAT between the client and server, the request will create (or refresh) a binding in the NAT. This binding must remain in existence for the duration of the transaction in order for the client to receive the response. Most UDP NAT bindings appear to have a timeout of about 1 minute. This exceeds the duration of non-INVITE transactions. Therefore, responses to a non-INVITE request will be received while the binding is still in existence. INVITE transactions can take an arbitrarily long amount of time to complete. As a result, the binding may expire before a final response is received. To keep the binding fresh, the client should retransmit its INVITE every 20 seconds or so. These retransmissions will need to take place even after receiving a provisional response. A UA may execute the binding lifetime discovery algorithm defined in RFC 5389 (see Section 14.3) to determine the actual binding lifetime in the NAT. If it is longer than 1 minute, the client should increase the interval for request retransmissions up to half of the discovered lifetime. If it is shorter than 1 minute, it should decrease the interval for request retransmissions to half of the discovered lifetime. Note that discovery of binding lifetimes can be unreliable (RFC 5389, see Section 14.3).

9.8.3.2 Server Behavior

The server behavior specified here affects the transport processing defined in SIP (RFC 3261, see Section 3.13.2). When a server compliant to this specification (which can be a proxy or UA server [UAS]) receives a request, it examines the topmost Via header field value. If this Via header field value contains an rport parameter with no value, it must set the value of the parameter to the source port of the request. This is analogous to the way in which a server will insert the received parameter into the topmost Via header field value. In fact, the server must insert a received parameter containing the source IP address that the request came from, even if it is identical to the value of the *sent-by* component. Note that this processing takes place independent of the transport protocol. When a server attempts to send a response, it examines the topmost Via header field value of that response. If the sent-protocol component indicates an unreliable unicast transport protocol, such as UDP, and there is no maddr parameter, but there is both a received parameter and an rport parameter, the response must be sent to the IP address listed in the received parameter, and the port in the rport parameter. The response must be sent from the same address and port that the corresponding request was received on.

This effectively adds a new processing step between bullets two and three in SIP (RFC 3261, see Section 3.13.2.2). The response must be sent from the same address and port that the request was received on in order to traverse symmetric NATs. When a server is listening for requests on multiple ports or interfaces, it will need to remember the one on which the request was received. For a stateful proxy, storing this information for the duration of the transaction is not an issue. However, a stateless proxy does not store state between a request and its response, and therefore cannot remember the address and port on which a request was received. To properly implement this specification, a stateless proxy can encode the destination address and port of a request into the Via header field value that it inserts. When the response arrives, it can extract this information and use it to forward the response.

9.8.3.3 Example

A client sends an INVITE to a proxy server that looks like, in part

```
INVITE sip:user@example.com SIP/2.0
Via: SIP/2.0/UDP 10.1.1.1:4540;rport;branch
=z9hG4bKkjshdyff
```

This INVITE is sent with a source port of 4540 and a source IP address of 10.1.1.1. The proxy is at 192.0.2.2 (proxy.example.com), listening on both port 5060 and 5070. The client sends the request to port 5060. The request passes through a NAT on the way to the proxy, so that the source IP address appears as 192.0.2.1 and the source port as 9988. The proxy forwards the request, but not before appending a value to the rport parameter in the proxied request:

```
INVITE sip:user@example.com SIP/2.0
Via: SIP/2.0/UDP proxy.example.
com;branch=z9hG4bKkjsh77
Via: SIP/2.0/UDP 10.1.1.1:4540;received=192.0
.2.1;rport=9988
;branch=z9hG4bKkjshdyff
```

This request generates a response that arrives at the proxy:

```
SIP/2.0 200 OK
Via: SIP/2.0/UDP proxy.example.
com;branch=z9hG4bKkjsh77
Via: SIP/2.0/UDP 10.1.1.1:4540;received=192.0.
2.1;rport=9988
;branch=z9hG4bKkjshdyff
```

The proxy strips its top Via header field value, and then examines the next one. It contains both a received parameter and an rport parameter. The server follows the rules specified in Section 1.4 and sends the response to IP address 192.0.2.1, port 9988, and sends it from port 5060 on 192.0.2.2:

```
SIP/2.0 200 OK
Via: SIP/2.0/UDP 10.1.1.1:4540;received=192.0.
2.1;rport=9988
;branch=z9hG4bKkjshdyff
```

This packet matches the binding created by the initial request. Therefore, the NAT rewrites the destination address of this packet back to 10.1.1.1, and the destination port back to 4540. It forwards this response to the client, which is listening for the response on that address and port. The client properly receives the response.

9.9 Caller Preferences-Based Routing

9.9.1 Overview

When a SIP server defined in RFC 3261 (see Section 2.4.4.3) receives a request, there are a number of decisions it can make regarding the processing of the request. These include

- Whether to proxy or redirect the request
- Which URIs to proxy or redirect to
- Whether to fork or not
- Whether to search recursively or not
- Whether to search in parallel or sequentially

The server can base these decisions on any local policy. This policy can be statically configured, or can be based on execution of a program or database access. However, the administrator of the server is the not the only entity with an interest in request processing. There are at least three parties that have an interest:

- The administrator of the server
- The user who sent the request
- The user to whom the request is directed

The directives of the administrator are embedded in the policy of the server. The preferences of the user to whom the request is directed (referred to as the callee, even though the request method may not be INVITE) can be expressed most easily through a script written in some type of scripting language, such as the Call Processing Language (CPL) specified in RFC 2824. However, no mechanism exists to incorporate the preferences of the user that sent the request (also referred to as the caller, even though the request method may not be INVITE). For example, the caller might want to speak to a specific user, but wants to reach them only at work, because the call is a business call. As another example, the caller might want to reach a user, but not their voice mail, since it is important that the caller talk to the called party. In both of these examples, the caller's preference amounts to having a proxy make a particular routing choice on the basis of the preferences of the caller. This extension allows the caller to have these preferences met. It does so by specifying mechanisms by which a caller can provide preferences on processing of a request. There are two types of preferences. One of them, called request handling preferences, are encapsulated in the Request-Disposition header field. They provide specific request handling directives for a server. The other, called feature preferences, is present in the Accept-Contact and Reject-Contact header fields. They allow the caller to provide a feature set defined in RFC 2533 (see Section 3.4.3) that expresses its preferences on the characteristics of the UA that is to be reached.

These are matched with a feature set provided by a UA to its registrar specified in RFC 3840 (see Section 3.4). The extension is of a very general purpose, and not tied to a particular service. Rather, it is a tool that can be used in the development of many services. One example of a service enabled by caller preferences is a *one number* service. A user can have a single identity (their SIP URI) for all of their devices—their cell phone, personal digital assistance (PDA), work phone, home phone, and so on. If the caller wants to reach the user at their business phone, they simply select *business phone* from a pull-down menu of options when calling that URI. Users would no longer need to maintain and distribute separate identities for each device. RFC 3841 that is described in this section specifies a set of extensions to the SIP that allow a caller to express preferences about request handling in servers. These preferences include the ability to select which URI a request gets routed to, and to specify certain request handling directives in proxies and redirect servers. It does so by defining three new request header fields (Accept-Contact, Reject-Contact, and Request-Disposition) that specify the caller's preferences. Note that we have defined the following items in Section 2.2: caller, feature preferences, request handling preferences, and explicit preference.

9.9.2 Operation

When a caller sends a request, it can optionally include new header fields that request certain handling at a server. These preferences fall into two categories. The first category, called request handling preferences, is carried in the Request-Disposition header field. It describes specific behavior that is desired at a server. Request handling preferences include whether the caller wishes the server to proxy or redirect, and whether sequential or parallel search is desired. These preferences can be applied at every proxy or redirect server on the call signaling path. The second category of preferences, called feature preferences, is carried in the Accept-Contact and Reject-Contact header fields. These header fields contain feature sets, represented by the same feature parameters that are used to indicate capabilities defined in RFC 3840 (see Section 3.4). Here, the feature parameters represent the caller's preferences. The Accept-Contact header field contains feature sets that describe UAs that the caller would like to reach. The Reject-Contact header field contains feature sets that, if matched by a UA, imply that the request should not be routed to that UA.

Proxies use the information in the Accept-Contact and Reject-Contact header fields to select among contacts in their target set. When neither of those header fields is present, the proxy computes implicit preferences from the request. These are caller preferences that are not explicitly placed into the request but can be inferred from the presence of other message components. As an example, if the request method is INVITE, this is an implicit preference to route the call to a UA that supports the INVITE method. Both request handling and feature preferences can appear in any request, not just INVITE. However, they are only useful in requests where proxies need to determine a request target. If the domain in the request URI is not owned by any proxies along the request path, those proxies will never access a location service, and therefore, never have the opportunity to apply the caller preferences. This makes sense because typically, the request URI will identify a UAS for mid-dialog requests. In those cases, the routing decisions were already made on the initial request, and it makes no sense to redo them for subsequent requests in the dialog.

9.9.3 UAC Behavior

A caller wishing to express preferences for a request includes Accept-Contact, Reject-Contact, or Request-Disposition header fields in the request, depending on their particular preferences. No additional behavior is required after the request is sent. The Accept-Contact, Reject-Contact, and Request-Disposition header fields in an ACK for a non-2xx final response, or in a CANCEL request, must be equal to the values in the original request being acknowledged or cancelled. This is to ensure proper operation through stateless proxies. If the UAC wants to determine whether servers along the path understand the header fields described in this specification, it includes a Proxy-Require header field with a value of *pref* specified in RFC 3840 (see Section 3.4) in its request. If the request should fail with a 420 response code, the UAC knows that the extension is not supported. In that case, it should retry, and may decide whether or not to use caller preferences. A UA should only use Proxy-Require if knowledge about support is essential for handling of the request. Note that, in any case, caller preferences can only be considered preferences—there is no guarantee that the requested service will be executed. As such, inclusion of a Proxy-Require header field does not mean that the preferences will be executed, just that the caller preferences extension is understood by the proxies.

9.9.3.1 Request Handling Preferences

The Request-Disposition header field specifies caller preferences for how a server should process a request. Its value is a list of tokens, each of which specifies a particular processing directive. The syntax of the header field can be found in Section 2.4.1.2.

9.9.3.2 Feature Set Preferences

A UAC can indicate caller preferences for the capabilities of a UA that should be reached or not reached as a result of sending a SIP request. To do that, it adds one or more

Accept-Contact and Reject-Contact header field values. Each header field value contains a set of feature parameters that define a feature set. The syntax of the header field can be found in Section 2.4.1.2. Each feature set is constructed as described in RFC 3840 (see Section 3.4). The feature sets placed into these header fields may overlap; that is, a UA may indicate preferences for feature sets that match according to the matching algorithm of RFC 2533 (see Section 3.4.3). A UAC can express explicit preferences for the methods and event packages supported by a UA. It is recommended that a UA include a term in an Accept-Contact feature set with the sip.methods feature tag (note, however, that even though the name of this feature tag is sip.methods, it would be encoded into the Accept-Contact header field as just *methods*), whose value includes the method of the request. When a UA sends a SUBSCRIBE request, it is recommended that a UA include a term in an Accept-Contact feature set with the sip.events feature tag, whose value includes the event package of the request. Whether these terms are placed into a new feature set, or whether they are included in each feature set, is at the discretion of the implementer. In most cases, the right effect is achieved by including a term in each feature set. As an example, the following Accept-Contact header field expresses a desire to route a call to a mobile device, using feature parameters taken from RFC 3840 (see Section 3.4):

```
Accept-Contact: *;mobility="mobile";methods
="INVITE"
```

The Reject-Contact header field allows the UAC to specify that a UA should not be contacted if it matches any of the values of the header field. Each value of the Reject-Contact header field contains a "*," purely to align the syntax with guidelines for SIP extensions, and is parameterized by a set of feature parameters. Any UA whose capabilities match the feature set described by the feature parameters matches the value. The Accept-Contact header field allows the UAC to specify that a UA should be contacted if it matches some or all of the values of the header field. Each value of the Accept-Contact header field contains a "*," and is parameterized by a set of feature parameters. Any UA whose capabilities match the feature set described by the feature parameters matches the value. The precise behavior depends heavily on whether the *require* and *explicit* parameters are present. When both of them are present, a proxy will only forward the request to contacts that have explicitly indicated that they support the desired feature set. Any others are discarded. As such, a UAC should only use *require* and *explicit* together when it wishes the call to fail unless a contact definitively matches. It is possible that a UA supports a desired feature but did not indicate it in its registration. When a UAC uses both *explicit* and *require*, such a contact would not be reached. As a result, this combination is often not the one a UAC will want.

When only *require* is present, it means that a contact will not be used if it does not match. If it does match, or if it is not known whether it is a complete match, the contact is still used. A UAC would use *require* alone when a nonmatching contact is useless. This is common for services where the request simply cannot be serviced without the necessary features. An example is support for specific methods or event packages. When only *require* is present, the proxy will also preferentially route the request to the UA that represents the best match. Here, *best* means that the UA has explicitly indicated that it supports more of the desired features than any other. Note, however, that this preferential routing will never override an ordering provided by the called party. The preferential routing will only choose among contacts of equal *q*-value. When only *explicit* is present, it means that all contacts provided by the callee will be used. However, if the contact is not an explicit match, it is tried last among all other contacts with the same *q*-value. The principal difference, therefore, between this configuration and the usage of both *require* and *explicit* is the fallback behavior for contacts that do not match explicitly. Here, they are tried as a last resort. If *require* is also present, they are never tried. Finally, if neither *require* nor *explicit* is present, it means that all contacts provided by the callee will be used. However, if the contact does not match, it is tried last among all other contacts with the same *q*-value. If it does match, the request is routed preferentially to the best match. This is a common configuration for preferences that, if not honored, will still allow for a successful call, and the greater the match, the better.

9.9.4 UAS Behavior

When a UAS compliant to this specification receives a request whose request-URI corresponds to one of its registered contacts, it should apply the behavior described later as if it were a proxy for the domain in the request-URI. The UAS acts as if its location database contains a single request target for the request-URI. That target is associated with a feature set. The feature set is the same as the one placed in the registration of the URI in the request-URI. If a UA had registered against multiple separate AORs, and the contacts registered for each had different capabilities, it will have used a different URI in each registration, so it can determine which feature set to use.

This processing occurs after the client authenticates and authorizes the request, but before the remainder of the general UAS processing described in RFC 3261 (see Section 3.1.3.1). If, after performing this processing, there are no URI left in the target set, the UA should reject the request with a 480 response. If there is a URI remaining (there was only one to begin with), the UA proceeds with request processing as per RFC 3261 (see Section 3.1). Having a UAS perform the matching operations as if it were a proxy allows certain caller preferences to be honored, even if the proxy does not support the extension. A UAS should process any queue directive present in a Request-Disposition header field in the request. All other directives must be ignored.

9.9.5 Proxy Behavior

Proxy behavior consists of two orthogonal sets of rules—one for processing the Request-Disposition header field and one for processing the URI and feature set preferences in the Accept-Contact and Reject-Contact header fields. In addition to processing these headers, a proxy may add one if not present, or add a value to an existing header field, as if it were a UAC. This is useful for a proxy to request processing in downstream proxies in the implementation of a feature. However, a proxy must not modify or remove an existing header field value. This is particularly important when S/MIME is used. The message signature could include the caller preferences header fields, allowing the UAS to verify that, even though proxies may have added header fields, the original caller preferences were still present.

9.9.5.1 Request-Disposition Processing

If the request contains a Request-Disposition header field and it is the owner of the domain in the Request URI, the server should execute the directives described later, unless it has local policy configured to direct it otherwise.

9.9.5.2 Preference and Capability Matching

A proxy compliant to this specification must not apply the preferences matching operation described here to a request unless it is the owner of the domain in the request URI, and accessing a location service that has capabilities associated with request targets. However, if it is the owner of the domain, and accessing a location service that has capabilities associated with request targets, it should apply the processing described in this section. Typically, this is a proxy that is using a registration database to determine the request targets. However, if a proxy knows about capabilities through some other means, it should apply the processing defined here as well. If it does perform the processing, it must do so as described below. The processing is described through a conversion from the syntax described in this specification to RFC 2533 (see Section 3.4.3) syntax, followed by a matching operation and a sorting of resulting contact values. The usage of RFC 2533 syntax as an intermediate step is not required; it only serves as a useful tool to describe the behavior required of the proxy. A proxy can use any steps it likes, so long as the results are identical to the ones that would be achieved with the processing described here.

9.9.5.2.1 Extracting Explicit Preferences

The first step in proxy processing is to extract explicit preferences. To do that, it looks for the Accept-Contact and Reject-Contact header fields. For each value of those header fields, it extracts the feature parameters. These are the header field parameters whose name is audio, automata, class, duplex, data, control, mobility, description, events, priority, methods, extensions, schemes, application, video, language, type, isfocus, actor, or text, or whose name begins with a plus (+) (RFC 3840, see Section 3.4). The proxy converts all of those parameters to the syntax based on the rules in RFC 2533 (see Section 3.4.3).

The result will be a set of feature set predicates in conjunctive normal form, each of which is associated with one of the two preference header fields. If there was a req-parameter associated with a header field value in the Accept-Contact header field, the feature set predicate derived from that header field value is said to have its require flag set. Similarly, if there was an explicit-param associated with a header field value in the Accept-Contact header field, the feature set predicate derived from that header field value is said to have its explicit flag set.

9.9.5.2.2 Extracting Implicit Preferences

If, and only if, the proxy did not find any explicit preferences in the request (because there was no Accept-Contact or Reject-Contact header field), the proxy extracts implicit preferences. These preferences are ones implied by the presence of other information in the request. First, the proxy creates a conjunction with no terms. This conjunction represents a feature set that will be associated with the Accept-Contact header field, as if it were included there. Note that there is no modification of the message implied—only an association for the purposes of processing. Furthermore, this feature set has its require flag set, but not its explicit flag. The proxy then adds terms to the conjunction for the two implicit preference types below.

- **Methods**

  One implicit preference is the method. When a UAC sends a request with a specific method, it is an implicit preference to have the request routed only to UAs that support that method. To support this implicit preference, the proxy adds a term to the conjunction of the following form:

  ```
  (sip.methods=[method of request])
  ```

- **Event packages**

  For requests that establish a subscription per RFC 6665 (see Section 5.2), the Event header field is another expression of an implicit preference. It expresses a desire for the request to be routed only to a server that supports the given event package. To support this implicit preference, the proxy adds a term to the conjunction of the following form:

```
(sip.events=[value of the Event header
field])
```

9.9.5.2.3 Constructing Contact Predicates

The proxy then takes each URI in the target set (the set of URI it is going to proxy or redirect to), and obtains its capabilities as an RFC 2533-formatted feature set predicate. This is called a contact predicate. If the target URI was obtained through a registration, the proxy computes the contact predicate by extracting the feature parameters from the Contact header field (see Section 2.8) and then converting them to a feature predicate. To extract the feature parameters, the proxy follows these steps:

- Create an initial, empty list of feature parameters.
- If the Contact URI parameters included the audio, automata, class, duplex, data, control, mobility, description, events, priority, methods, schemes, application, video, actor, language, isfocus, type, extensions, or text parameters, those are copied into the list.
- If any Contact URI parameter name begins with a "+," it is copied into the list if the list does not already contain that name with the plus removed. In other words, if the video feature parameter is in the list, the +video parameter would not be placed into the list. This conflict should never arise if the client were compliant to RFC 3840 (see Section 3.4), since it is illegal to use the + form for encoding of a feature tag in the base set. If the URI in the target set had no feature parameters, it is said to be immune to caller preference processing. This means that the URI is removed from the target set temporarily, the caller preferences processing described below is executed, and then the URI is added back in.

Assuming the URI has feature parameters, they are converted to syntax using the rules of RFC 2533 (see Section 3.4.3). The resulting predicate is associated with a *q*-value. If the contact predicate was learned through a REGISTER request, the *q*-value is equal to the *q*-value in the Contact header field parameter, else 1.0 if not specified. As an example, consider the following registered Contact header field:

```
Contact: <sip:user@example.com>;audio;video;
mobility="fixed";
+sip.message="TRUE";other-param=66372;
methods="INVITE,OPTIONS,BYE,CANCEL,ACK";
schemes="sip,http"
```

This would be converted into the following predicate:

```
(& (sip.audio=TRUE)
(sip.video=TRUE)
(sip.mobility=fixed)
(sip.message=TRUE)
(| (sip.methods=INVITE) (sip.methods=OPTIONS)
(sip.methods=BYE)
(sip.methods=CANCEL) (sip.methods=ACK))
(| (sip.schemes=sip) (sip.schemes=http)))
```

Note that *other-param* was not considered a feature parameter, since it is neither a base tag nor did it begin with a leading +.

9.9.5.2.4 Matching

It is important to note that the proxy does not have to know anything about the meaning of the feature tags that it is comparing in order to perform the matching operation. The rules for performing the comparison depend on syntactic hints present in the values of each feature tag. For example, a predicate such as (foo>=4) implies that the feature tag *foo* is a numeric value. The matching rules in RFC 2533 (see Section 3.4.3) only require an implementation to know whether the feature tag is a numeric, token, or quoted string (Booleans can be treated as tokens). Quoted strings are always matched using a case-sensitive matching operation. Tokens are matched using case-insensitive matching. These two cases are differentiated by the presence of angle brackets around the feature tag value. When these brackets are present (i.e., ;+sip.foo="<value>"), it implies case sensitive string comparison. When they are not present, (i.e., (;+sip.bar="val"), it implies case insensitivity. Numerics are matched using normal mathematical comparisons.

First, the proxy applies the predicates associated with the Reject-Contact header field. For each contact predicate, each Reject-Contact predicate (i.e., each predicate associated with the Reject-Contact header field) is examined. If that Reject-Contact predicate contains a filter for a feature tag, and that feature tag is not present anywhere in the contact predicate, that Reject-Contact predicate is discarded for the processing of that contact predicate. If the Reject-Contact predicate is not discarded, it is matched with the contact predicate using the matching operation of RFC 2533 (see Section 3.4.3). If the result is a match, the URI corresponding to that contact predicate is discarded from the target set. The result is that Reject-Contact will only discard URIs where the UA has explicitly indicated support for the features that are not wanted.

Next, the proxy applies the predicates associated with the Accept-Contact header field. For each contact that remains in the target set, the proxy constructs a matching set, Ms. Initially; this set contains all of the Accept-Contact predicates. Each of those predicates is examined. It is matched with the contact predicate using the matching operation of RFC 2533 (see Section 3.4.3). If the result is not a match, and the Accept-Contact predicate had its require flag set, the URI corresponding to that contact predicate is discarded from the target set. If the result is not a match but the Accept-Contact predicate did not have its require flag set, that Contact URI is not discarded from the target set; however, the Accept-Contact predicate is removed from the matching set for that contact.

For each contact that remains in the target set, the proxy computes a score for that contact against each predicate in the contact's matching set. Let the number of terms in the Accept-Contact predicate conjunction be equal to *N*. Each term in that predicate contains a single feature tag. If the contact predicate has a term containing that same feature tag, the score is incremented by 1/*N*. If the feature tag was not present in the contact predicate, the score remains unchanged. On the basis of these rules, the score can range between 0 and 1.

The required and explicit tags are then applied, resulting in potential modification of the score and the target set. This process is summarized in Figure 9.3. If the score for the contact predicate against that Accept-Contact predicate was <1, the Accept-Contact predicate had an explicit tag, and if the predicate also had a require tag, the Contact URI corresponding to that contact predicate is dropped. If, however, the predicate did not have a require tag, the score is set to 0. If there was no explicit tag, the score is unchanged. The next step is to combine the scores and the *q*-values associated with the predicates in the matching set, to arrive at an overall caller preference, Qa. For those URIs in the target set that remain, there will be a score that indicates its match against each Accept-Contact predicate in the matching set. If there are M Accept-Contact predicates in the matching set, there will be M scores S1 through SM, for each contact. The overall caller preference, Qa, is the arithmetic average of S1 through SM.

At this point, any URIs that were removed from the target set because they were immune from caller preferences are added back in, and the Qa for that URI is set to 1.0. The purpose of the caller preference Qa is to provide an ordering for any contacts remaining in the target set, if the callee has not provided an ordering. To do this, the contacts remaining in the target set are sorted by the *q*-value provided by the callee. Once sorted, they are grouped into equivalence classes, such that all contacts with the same *q*-value are in the same equivalence class. Within each equivalence class, the contacts are then ordered on the basis of their Qa values. The result is an ordered list of contacts that is used by the proxy. If there were no URIs in the target set after the application of the processing in this section, and the caller preferences were based on implicit preferences, the processing in this section is discarded, and the original target set, ordered by their original *q*-values, is used. This handles the case where implicit preferences for the method or event packages resulted in the elimination of all potential targets. By going back to the original target set, those URIs will be tried, and result in the generation of a 405 or 489 response. The UAC can then use this information to try again, or report the error to the user. Without reverting to the original target set, the UAC would see a 480 response, and have no knowledge of why their request failed. Of course, the target set can also be empty after the application of explicit preferences.

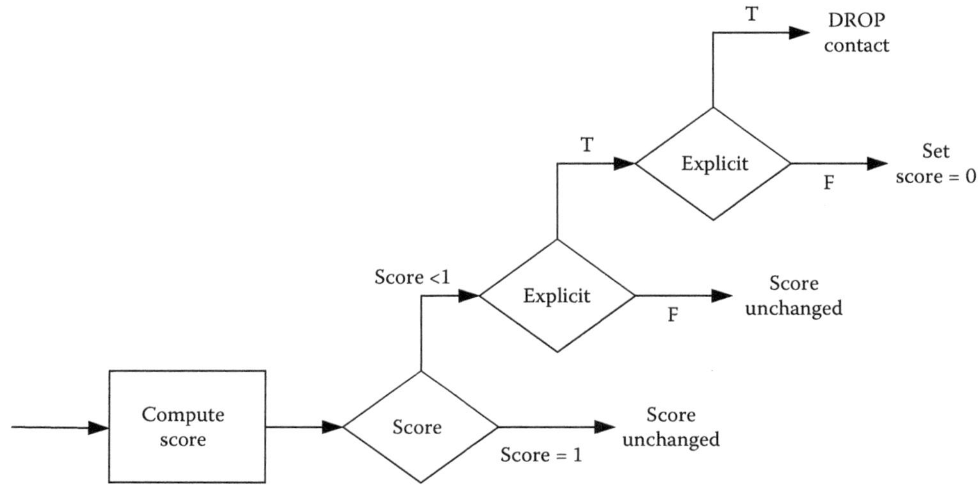

Figure 9.3 Applying the score. (Copyright IETF. Reproduced with permission.)

This will result in the generation of a 480 by the proxy. This behavior is acceptable, and indeed, desirable in the case of explicit preferences. When the caller makes an explicit preference, it is agreeing that its request might fail because of a preference mismatch. One might try to return an error indicating the capabilities of the callee, so that the caller could perhaps try again. However, doing so results in the leaking of potentially sensitive information to the caller without authorization from the callee, and therefore this specification does not provide a means for it. If a proxy server is recursing, it adds the Contact header fields returned in the redirect responses to the target set, and reapplies the caller preferences algorithm. If the server is redirecting, it returns all entries in the target set. It assigns *q*-values to those entries so that the ordering is identical to the ordering determined by the processing above. However, it must not include the feature parameters for the entries in the target set. If it did, the upstream proxy server would apply the same caller preferences once more, resulting in a double application of those preferences. If the redirect server does wish to include the feature parameters in the Contact header field, it must redirect using the original target set and original *q*-values before the application of caller preferences.

9.9.5.2.5 Example

Consider the following example, which is contrived but illustrative of the various components of the matching process. There are five registered Contacts for sip:user@example.com. They are

```
Contact: sip:u1@h.example.com;audio;video;
methods="INVITE,BYE";q=0.2
Contact: sip:u2@h.example.com;audio="FALSE";
methods="INVITE";actor="msg-taker";q=0.2
Contact: sip:u3@h.example.
com;audio;actor="msg-taker";
methods="INVITE";video;q=0.3
Contact: sip:u4@h.example.com;audio;methods
="INVITE,OPTIONS";q=0.2
Contact: sip:u5@h.example.com;q=0.5
```

An INVITE sent to sip:user@example.com contained the following caller preferences header fields:

```
Reject-Contact:  *;actor="msg-taker";video
Accept-Contact:  *;audio;require
Accept-Contact:  *;video;explicit
Accept-Contact:  *;methods="BYE";class
                 ="business";q=1.0
```

There are no implicit preferences in this example because explicit preferences are provided. The proxy first removes u5 from the target set, since it is immune from caller preferences processing. Next, the proxy processes the Reject-Contact header field. It is a match for all four remaining contacts, but only an explicit match for u3. That is because u3 is the only one that explicitly indicated support for video, and explicitly indicated it is a message taker. Thus, u3 gets discarded and the others remain.

Next, each of the remaining three contacts is compared against each of the three Accept-Contact predicates. u1 is a match to all three, earning a score of 1.0 for the first two predicates, and 0.5 for the third (the methods feature tag was present in the contact predicate, but the class tag was not). u2 does not match the first predicate. Because that predicate has a require tag, u2 is discarded. u4 matches the first predicate, earning a score of 1.0. u4 matches the second predicate; however, since the match is not explicit (the score is 0.0, in fact), the score is set to zero (it was already zero, so nothing changes). u4 does not match the third predicate. At this point, u1 and u4 remain. u1 matched all three Accept-Contact predicates, so its matching set contains all three, with scores of 1, 1, and 0.5. u4 matches the first two predicates, with scores of 1.0 and 0.0. Qa for u1 is 0.83 and Qa for u4 is 0.5. u5 is added back in with a Qa of 1.0.

Next, the remaining contacts in the target set are sorted by *q*-value. u5 has a value of 0.5, u1 has a *q*-value of 0.2 and so does u4. There are two equivalence classes. The first has a *q*-value of 0.5, and consists of just u5. Since there is only one member of the class, sorting within the class has no impact. The second equivalence class has a *q*-value of 0.2. Within that class, the two contacts, u1 and u4, are ordered on the basis of their values of Qa. u1 has a Qa of 0.83, and u4, a Qa of 0.5. Thus, u1 comes first, followed by u4. The resulting overall ordered set of contacts in the target set is u5, u1, and then u4.

9.9.6 *Mapping Feature Parameters to a Predicate*

Mapping between feature parameters and a feature set predicate, formatted according to the syntax of RFC 2533 (see Section 3.4.3), is trivial. It is just the opposite of the process described in RFC 3840 (see Section 3.4). Starting from a set of feature-param, the procedure is as follows. Construct a conjunction. Each term in the conjunction derives from one feature-param. If the feature-param has no value, it is equivalent, in terms of the processing which follows, as if it had a value of TRUE. If the feature-param value is a tag-value-list, the element of the conjunction is a disjunction. There is one term in the disjunction for each tag-value in the tag-value-list. Consider now the construction of a filter from a tag-value. If the tag-value starts with an exclamation mark (!), the filter is of the form

```
(! <filter from remainder>)
```

where <filter from remainder> refers to the filter that would be constructed from the tag-value if the exclamation mark had not been present.

If the tag-value starts with an octothorpe (#), the filter is a numeric comparison. The comparator is either =, > =, < =, or a range based on the next characters in the phrase. If the next characters are =, > =, or < =, the filter is of the form

```
(name comparator compare-value)
```

where *name* is the name of the feature parameter after it has been decoded (see below in the next paragraph), and the comparator is either =, > =, or < = depending on the initial characters in the phrase. If the remainder of the text in the tag-value after the equal contains a decimal point (implying a rational number), the decimal point is shifted right *N* times until it is an integer, *I*. The compare-value above is then set to *I*/10***N*, where 10***N* is the result of computing the number 10 to the *N*th power.

If the value after the octothorpe is a number, the filter is a range. The format of the filter is

```
(name=<remainder>)
```

where *name* is the feature tag after it has been decoded (see below this paragraph), and <remainder> is the remainder of the text in the tagvalue after the #, with any decimal numbers converted to a rational form, and the colon replaced by a double dot (..). If the tag-value does not begin with an octothorpe (it is a tokennobang or boolean), the filter is of the form

```
(name=tag-value)
```

where *name* is the feature tag after it has been decoded (see below this paragraph). If the feature-param contains a string-value (based on the fact that it begins with a left angle bracket [<] and ends with a right angle bracket [>]), the filter is of the form

```
(name="qdtext")
```

Note the explicit usage of quotes around the qdtext, which indicate that the value is a string. In RFC 2533 (see Section 3.4.3), strings are compared using case-sensitive rules and tokens are compared using case-insensitive rules. Feature tags, as specified in RFC 2506 (see Section 2.11), cannot be directly represented as header field parameters in the Contact, Accept-Contact, and Reject-Contact header fields. This is due to an inconsistency in the grammars and in the need to differentiate feature parameters from parameters used by other extensions. As such, feature tag values are encoded from RFC 2506 format to yield an enc-feature-tag, and then are decoded into RFC 2506 format. The decoding process is simple. If there is a leading plus (+) sign, it is removed. Any exclamation point (!) is converted to a colon (:) and any single quote (') is converted to a forward slash (/). If there was no leading plus sign, and the remainder of the encoded name was audio, automata, class, duplex, data, control, mobility, description, events, priority, methods, schemes, application, video, actor, isfocus, extensions, or text, the prefix *sip.* is added to the remainder of the encoded name to compute the feature tag name. As an example, the Accept-Contact header field

```
Accept-Contact:*;mobility="fixed"
;events="!presence,message-summary"
;language="en,de";description="<PC>";+sip
.newparam
;+rangeparam="#-4:+5.125"
```

would be converted to the following feature predicate:

```
(& (sip.mobility=fixed)
(| (! (sip.events=presence)) (sip.
events=message-summary))
(| (language=en) (language=de))
(sip.description="PC")
(sip.newparam=TRUE)
(rangeparam=-4..5125/1000))
```

9.9.7 Header Field Definitions

RFC 3841 defines three new header fields—Accept-Contact, Reject-Contact, and Request-Disposition; the descriptions of these fields are provided in Section 2.8.2.

9.9.7.1 Request Disposition

The Request-Disposition header field specifies caller preferences for how a server should process a request. Its value is a list of tokens, each of which specifies a particular directive. Note that a compact form, using the letter d, has been defined. The directives are grouped into types. There can be only one directive of each type per request (e.g., you cannot have both *proxy* and *redirect* in the same Request-Disposition header field). When the caller specifies a directive, the server should honor that directive. The following types of directives are defined:

- **Proxy-directive:** This type of directive indicates whether the caller would like each server to proxy (*proxy*) or redirect (*redirect*).
- **Cancel-directive:** This type of directive indicates whether the caller would like each proxy server to send a CANCEL request downstream (*cancel*) in response to a 200 OK from the downstream server (which is the normal mode of operation, making it redundant), or whether this function should be left to the caller (*no-cancel*). If a proxy receives a request with this parameter set to nocancel, it should not CANCEL any outstanding branches upon receipt of a 2xx. However, it would still send CANCEL on any outstanding branches upon receipt of a 6xx.
- **Fork-directive:** This type of directive indicates whether a proxy should fork a request (*fork*), or

proxy to only a single address (*no-fork*). If the server is requested not to fork, the server should proxy the request to the *best* address (generally the one with the highest *q*-value). If there are multiple addresses with the highest *q*-value, the server chooses one based on its local policy. The directive is ignored if redirect has been requested.

- **Recurse-directive:** This type of directive indicates whether a proxy server receiving a 3xx response should send requests to the addresses listed in the response (*recurse*), or forward the list of addresses upstream toward the caller (*no-recurse*). The directive is ignored if redirect has been requested.
- **Parallel-directive:** For a forking proxy server, this type of directive indicates whether the caller would like the proxy server to proxy the request to all known addresses at once (*parallel*), or go through them sequentially, contacting the next address only after it has received a non-2xx or non-6xx final response for the previous one (*sequential*). The directive is ignored if redirect has been requested.
- **Queue-directive**: If the called party is temporarily unreachable, for example, because it is in another call, the caller can indicate that it wants to have its call queued (*queue*) or rejected immediately (*no-queue*). If the call is queued, the server returns 182 Queued.

Example:

```
Request-Disposition: proxy, recurse, parallel
```

The set of request disposition directives is not extensible on purpose. This is to avoid a proliferation of new extensions to SIP that are *tunneled* through this header field.

9.9.7.2 Accept-Contact and Reject-Contact Header Fields

Section 2.8.2 describes in detail these header fields. Note that a compact form, with the letter a, has been defined for the Accept-Contact header field, and with the letter j for the Reject-Contact header field.

9.9.8 Augmented BNF

The ABNF for the Request-Disposition header field is repeated as follows for convenience, although all SIP syntaxes are provided in Section 2.4.1.2:

```
Request-Disposition  =     ("Request-
                           Disposition"/"d")
                           HCOLON
                           directive *(COMMA
                           directive)
directive            =     proxy-directive/
                           cancel-directive/
                           fork-directive/
                           recurse-directive/
                           parallel-directive/
                           queue-directive
proxy-directive     = "proxy"/"redirect"
cancel-directive    = "cancel"/"no-cancel"
fork-directive      = "fork"/"no-fork"
recurse-directive   = "recurse"/"no-recurse"
parallel-directive = "parallel"/"sequential"
queue-directive     = "queue"/"no-queue"
```

The ABNF for the Accept-Contact and Reject-Contact header fields is

```
Accept-Contact =  ("Accept-Contact"/"a")
                  HCOLON ac-value
                  *(COMMA ac-value)
Reject-Contact =  ("Reject-Contact"/"j")
                  HCOLON rc-value
                  *(COMMA rc-value)
ac-value       =  "*" *(SEMI ac-params)
rc-value       =  "*" *(SEMI rc-params)
ac-params      =  feature-param/req-param
                  /explicit-param/
                  generic-param
                  ;;feature param from RFC
                  3840 (see Section 2.4.2.1)
                  ;;generic-param from RFC
                  3261 (see Section;; 2.4.1.2)
rc-params      =  feature-param/generic-param
req-param      =  "require"
explicit-param =  "explicit"
```

Despite the ABNF, there must not be more than one req-param or explicit-param in an ac-params. Furthermore, there can only be one instance of any feature tag in feature-param.

9.10 Location-Based Routing

9.10.1 Overview

The location-based routing in SIP provides mechanisms for routing of SIP messages based on geographic location information among the SIP entities over the SIP network. SIP conveys geographic location information of a Target to a Location Recipient (LR). SIP acts as a Using Protocol of location information, as defined in RFC 3693. Three SIP header fields defined in RFC 6442, Geolocation, Geolocation-Routing, and Geolocation-Error, which carry a reference to a Location Object (LO), grant permission to route a SIP request based on the location-value, and provide error notifications specific to location errors, respectively. The Geolocation header field conveys the location information of the SIP functional entities. The Geolocation-Routing header field indicates whether SIP functional entities can route the messages within the SIP network based on the information provided in the location object. The Geolocation-Error header field is used to convey location-specific errors within a response.

The Geolocation and Geolocation-Routing header fields can be included in the following SIP requests (see Section 15.3): INVITE, REGISTER, OPTIONS, BYE, UPDATE, INFO, MESSAGE, REFER, SUBSCRIBE, NOTIFY, and PUBLISH. In addition, the 424 Bad Location Information response code is a rejection of the request due to its location contents, indicating location information that was malformed or not satisfactory for the recipient's purpose or could not be dereferenced. A more detailed description of these header field and response codes is provided in the SIP message header section. The Location Object may appear in a MIME body attached to the SIP request, or it may be a remote resource in the network. The location information embedded in SIP message header fields can be conveyed on end-to-end using SIP request messages, and the SIP functional entities can make routing decisions based on the location of the Location Target.

A Target is an entity whose location is being conveyed per RFC 3693. Thus, a Target could be a SIP UA, some other IP device (a router or a personal computer) that does not have a SIP stack, a non-IP device (a person or a black phone), or even a noncommunications device (a building or store front). In no way does this document assume that the SIP UA client that sends a request containing a location object is necessarily the Target. The location of a Target conveyed within SIP typically corresponds to that of a device controlled by the Target, for example, a mobile phone; however, such devices can be separated from their owners, and moreover, in some cases, the UA may not know its own location. In the SIP context, a location recipient will most likely be a SIP UA, but owing to the mediated nature of SIP architectures, location information conveyed by a single SIP request may have multiple recipients, as any SIP proxy server in the signaling path that inspects the location of the Target must also be considered a Location Recipient. In presence-like architectures, an intermediary that receives publications of location information and distributes them to watchers acts as a Location Server per RFC 3693. This location conveyance mechanism can also be used to deliver URIs pointing to such Location Servers where prospective Location Recipients can request Location Objects.

9.10.2 Basic SIP Location Conveyance Operations

We will provide some examples that will provide the basic idea about the operation of SIP location conveyance. Figure 9.4a shows a SIP network consisting of a caller with SIP UA (U2), a callee with SIP UA (U2), SIP intermediary, and a location server (LS).

Each entity is aware of the SIP location capabilities as described earlier. Alice (U1) is the Target, and Bob (U2) is a location recipient (LR). A SIP intermediary may be a SIP proxy or even an entity with SIP B2BUA capability that may need to inspect and modify the SIP message body for location information. Any SIP entity that receives and inspects location information is an LR; therefore, this SIP intermediary that receives a SIP request is potentially an LR. It should be noted that it does not mean that such an intermediary necessarily has to route the SIP request based on the location information. If a SIP UA performs the location function, we identify it as capability with LS. However, in some use cases, location information passes through the LS, a dedicated server, that keeps the location information for the entire SIP network. LS may even be managed by a third party.

9.10.2.1 Location Conveyed by Value

First, we take the example of location conveyance where Alice calls Bob directly and no other functional entities are involved. In Figure 9.4b, the call flows show that Alice is both the Target and the LS that is conveying her location directly to Bob, who acts as an LR. This conveyance is point-to-point: it does not pass through any SIP-layer intermediary. A Location Object appears by-value in the initial SIP request as a MIME body, and Bob responds to that SIP request as appropriate. There is a Bad Location Information response code introduced within this document to specifically inform Alice if she conveys bad location to Bob, for example, Bob "cannot parse the location provided," or "there is not enough location information to determine where Alice is."

9.10.2.2 Location Conveyed as a Location URI

Now we consider the call flows shown in Figure 9.4c that shows a little more complication by showing a diagram of indirect location conveyance from Alice to Bob, where Bob's entity has to retrieve the location object from a third party server. Here, the location information is conveyed indirectly, via a location URI carried in the SIP request (more of those details in the following sections). If Alice sends Bob this location URI, Bob will need to dereference the URI—analogous to Content Indirection (RFC 4483, see Section 16.6)—in order to request the location information. In general, the LS provides the location value to Bob instead of Alice directly for conveyance to Bob. From a user interface perspective, Bob the user would not know that this information was gathered from LS indirectly rather than culled from the SIP request; practically, this does not affect the operation of location-based applications.

The example given in this section is only illustrative, not normative. In particular, applications can choose to dereference a location URI at any time, possibly several times, or

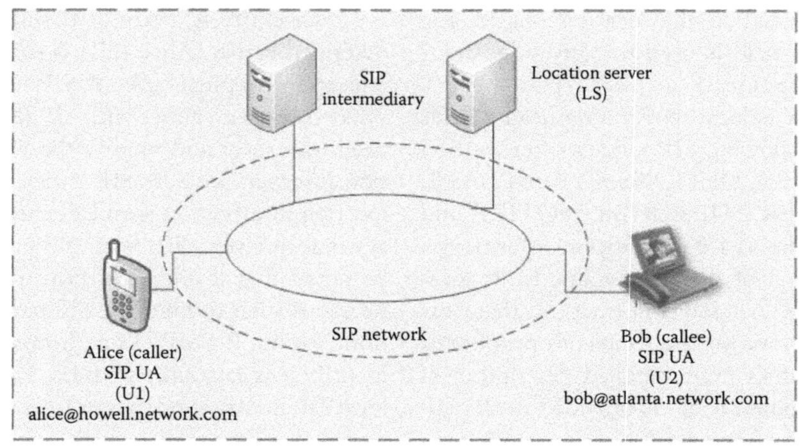

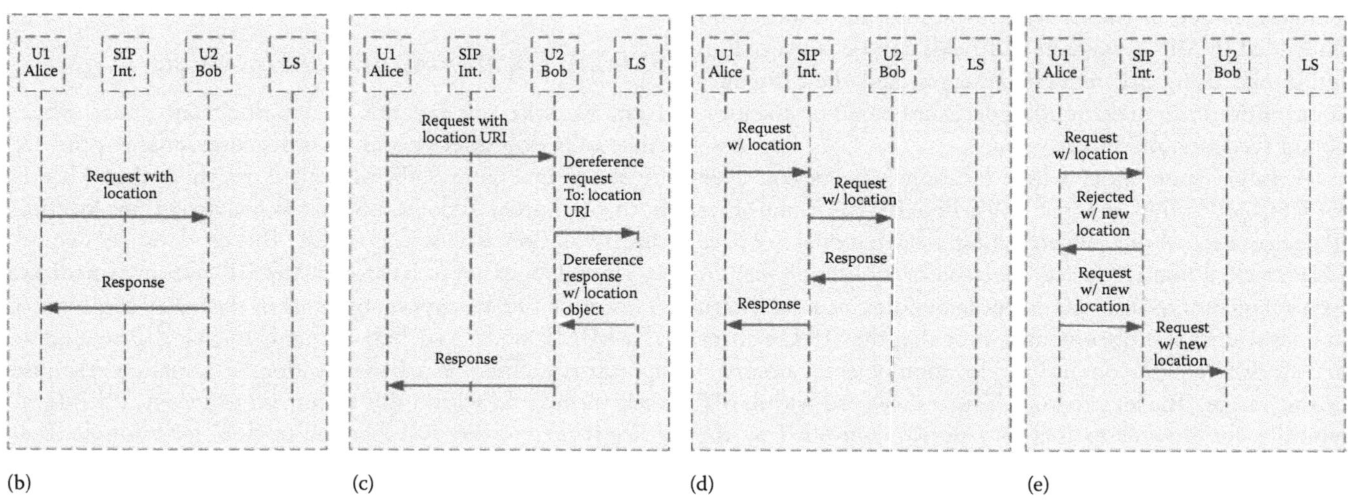

Figure 9.4 Location conveyance in SIP: (a) SIP network and functional entities, (b) location conveyed by value, (c) location conveyed by URI, (d) location conveyed through a SIP intermediary, and (e) SIP intermediary replacing bad location. (Copyright IETF. Reproduced with permission.)

potentially not at all. Applications receiving a location URI in a SIP transaction need to be mindful of timers used by different transactions. In particular, the means of dereferencing the location URI take longer than the SIP transaction timeout (Timer C; see Section 3.12) as INVITE and rely on mechanisms other than the transaction's response code to convey location errors, when returning such errors are necessary.

9.10.2.3 Location Conveyed through a SIP Intermediary

In Figure 9.4d, we introduce the idea of a SIP intermediary into the example to illustrate the role of proxying in the location architecture. This intermediary can be a SIP proxy or it can be a B2BUA. In this message flow, the SIP intermediary could act as an LR, in addition to Bob. The primary use for intermediaries consuming location information is location-based routing. In this case, the intermediary chooses a next hop for the SIP request by consulting a specialized location service that selects forwarding destinations based on the geographical location information contained in the SIP request. However, the most common case will be one in which the SIP intermediary receives a request with location information (conveyed either by-value or by-reference) and does not know or care about Alice's location, or support this extension, and merely passes it on to Bob. In this case, the intermediary does not act as a Location Recipient. When the intermediary is not an LR, this use case is the same as the one described earlier in that case of location conveyed by value.

Note that an intermediary does not have to perform location-based routing in order to be a location recipient. It could be the case that a SIP intermediary that does not perform location-based routing does care when Alice includes her location; for example, it could care that the location information is complete or that it correctly identifies where Alice is. The best example of this is intermediaries that verify location information for emergency calling, but it could also be for any location-based routing, for example, contacting your favorite local pizza delivery service, making sure that organization has Alice's proper location in the initial SIP request. There is another scenario in which the SIP intermediary cares about location and is not an LR, one in which the intermediary inserts another location of the Target, Alice in this case, into the request, and forwards it. This secondary insertion is generally not advisable because downstream SIP entities will not be given any guidance about which location to believe is better, more reliable, less prone to error, more granular, worse than the other location, or just plain wrong. This example takes a "you break it, you buy it" approach to dealing with second locations placed into a SIP request by an intermediary entity. That entity becomes completely responsible for all location within that SIP request.

9.10.2.4 SIP Intermediary Replacing Bad Location

If the SIP intermediary rejects the message due to unsuitable location information, the SIP response will indicate there was Bad Location Information in the SIP request and provide a location-specific error code indicating what Alice needs to do to send an acceptable request as shown in Figure 9.4e. In this last use case, the SIP intermediary wishes to include a LO indicating where it understands Alice to be. Thus, it needs to inform her UA of what location it will include in any subsequent SIP request that contains her location. In this case, the intermediary can reject Alice's request and, through the SIP response, convey to her the best way to repair the request in order for the intermediary to accept it. Overriding location information provided by the user requires a deployment where an intermediary necessarily knows better than an end user—after all, it could be that Alice has an on-board GPS, and the SIP intermediary only knows her nearest cell tower. Which is more accurate location information? Currently, there is no way to tell which entity is more accurate or which is wrong, for that matter. This shows the limitation of the location service that does not specify how to indicate which location is more accurate than another.

As an aside, it is not envisioned that any SIP-based emergency services request (i.e., IP-911 or 112 type of call attempt) will receive a corrective Bad Location Information response from an intermediary. Most likely, in that scenario, the SIP intermediary would act as a B2BUA and insert into the request by-value any appropriate location information for the benefit of Public Safety Answering Point (PSAP) call centers to expedite call reception by the emergency services personnel, thereby minimizing any delay in call establishment time. The implementation of these specialized deployments is, however, outside the scope of this document.

9.10.2.5 Location URIs in Message Bodies

In the case where an LR sends a 424 Bad Location Information response and wishes to communicate suitable location-by-reference rather than location-by-value, the 424 response must include a content-indirection body per RFC 4483.

9.10.2.6 Location Profile Negotiation

Figure 9.4c introduces the concept of sending location indirectly. If a location URI is included in a SIP request, the sending UA must also include a Supported header field indicating which location profiles it supports. Two option tags for location profiles are defined by this document: geolocation-sip and geolocation-http. Future specifications may define further location profiles per the IANA policy. The geolocation-sip option tag signals support for acquiring location information via the presence event package of SIP defined in RFC 3856. A location recipient who supports this option can send a SUBSCRIBE request and parse a resulting NOTIFY containing a PIDF-LO object. The URI schemes supported by this option include sip, sips, and pres.

The geolocation-http option tag signals support for acquiring location information via HTTP defined in RFCs 7230–7235. A location recipient who supports this option can request location with an HTTP GET and parse a resulting 200 response containing a Presence Information Data Format-Location Object (PIDF-LO) defined in RFC 4119 (see Section 2.8). The URI schemes supported by this option include http and https. A failure to parse the 200 response, for whatever reason, will return a Dereference Failure indication to the original location sending UA to inform it that location was not delivered as intended. If the location URI receiver does not understand the URI scheme sent to it, it will return an Unsupported header value of the option tag from the SIP request, and include the option tag of the preferred URI scheme in the response's Supported header field.

9.10.3 Geolocation Examples

9.10.3.1 Location-by-Value (in Coordinate Format)

This example shows an INVITE message with a coordinate location. In this example, the SIP request uses a sips-URI defined in RFC 3261 (see Section 4.2), meaning that this message is protected using TLS on a hop-by-hop basis.

```
INVITE sips:bob@biloxi.example.com SIP/2.0
Via: SIPS/2.0/TLS pc33.atlanta.example.
com;branch=z9hG4bK74bf9
Max-Forwards: 70
To: Bob <sips:bob@biloxi.example.com>
From: Alice <sips:alice@atlanta.example.
com>;tag=9fxced76sl
Call-ID: 3848276298220188511@atlanta.example.
com
Geolocation: <cid:target123@atlanta.example.
com>
Geolocation-Routing: no
Accept: application/SDP, application/pidf
CSeq: 31862 INVITE
Contact: <sips:alice@atlanta.example.com>
Content-Type: multipart/mixed;
boundary=boundary1
Content-Length:...

--boundary1

Content-Type: application/SDP

...Session Description Protocol (SDP) goes
here

--boundary1

Content-Type: application/pidf
Content-ID: <target123@atlanta.example.com>

<?xml version="1.0" encoding="UTF-8"?>

<presence
       xmlns="urn:ietf:params:xml:ns:pidf"
       xmlns:gp="urn:ietf:params:xml:ns:pidf:
       geopriv10"
       xmlns:gbp="urn:ietf:params:xml:ns:pidf
       :geopriv10:basicPolicy"
       xmlns:cl="urn:ietf:params:xml:ns:pidf:
       geopriv10:civicAddr"
       xmlns:gml="http://www.opengis.net/gml"
       xmlns:dm="urn:ietf:params:xml:ns:pidf:
       data-model"
       entity="pres:alice@atlanta.example.
       com">
       <dm:device id="target123-1">
              <gp:geopriv>
                     <gp:location-info>
                            <gml:location>
                                   <gml:Point

srsName="urn:ogc:def:crs:EPSG::4326">
                            <gml:pos>32.86726 -

                            97.16054</gml:pos>
                                   </gml:Point>
                            </gml:location>
                     </gp:location-info>
                     <gp:usage-rules>
              <gbp:retransmission-allowed>
                                   false
</gbp:retransmission-allowed>

<gbp:retention-expiry>

2010-11-14T20:00:00Z
</gbp:retention-expiry>
                     </gp:usage-rules>
                     <gp:method>802.11</
                     gp:method>
              </gp:geopriv>
              <dm:deviceID>mac:1234567890ab</
              dm:deviceID>
              <dm:timestamp>2010-11-
              04T20:57:29Z</dm:timestamp>
       </dm:device>
</presence>

--boundary1--
```

The Geolocation header field from the above INVITE:

```
Geolocation: <cid:target123@atlanta.example.
com>
```

"..." indicates the content-ID location (RFC 2392, see Section 2.8.2) within the multipart message body of where location information is. The other message body part is SDP. The *cid:* eases message body parsing and disambiguates multiple parts of the same type. If the Geolocation header field did not contain a cid: scheme, for example, it could look like this location URI:

```
Geolocation: <sips:target123@server5.atlanta.
example.com>
```

... the existence of a non-cid: scheme indicates this is a location URI, to be dereferenced to learn the Target's location. Any node wanting to know where the target is located would subscribe to the SIP presence event package (RFC 3856) at

```
sips:target123@server5.atlanta.example.com
```

9.10.3.2 Two Locations Composed in Same Location Object Example

This example shows the INVITE message after a SIP intermediary rejected the original INVITE. This INVITE contains the composed LO sent by the SIP intermediary that includes where the intermediary understands Alice to be. The rules of RFC 5491 are followed in this construction. This example is here, but ought not to be taken as occurring very often. In fact, this example is believed to be a corner case of location conveyance applicability.

```
INVITE sips:bob@biloxi.example.com SIP/2.0
Via: SIPS/2.0/TLS pc33.atlanta.example.
com;branch=z9hG4bK74bf0
Max-Forwards: 70
To: Bob <sips:bob@biloxi.example.com>
From: Alice <sips:alice@atlanta.example.
com>;tag=9fxced76sl
Call-ID: 3848276298220188512@atlanta.example.
com
Geolocation: <cid:target123@atlanta.example.
com>
Geolocation-Routing: no
Accept: application/SDP, application/pidf
CSeq: 31863 INVITE
Contact: <sips:alice@atlanta.example.com>
Content-Type: multipart/mixed;
boundary=boundary1
Content-Length:...

--boundary1

Content-Type: application/SDP

...SDP goes here

--boundary1

Content-Type: application/pidf
Content-ID: <target123@atlanta.example.com>

<?xml version="1.0" encoding="UTF-8"?>

<presence
       xmlns="urn:ietf:params:xml:ns:pidf"
       xmlns:gp="urn:ietf:params:xml:ns:pidf:
       geopriv10"
       xmlns:gbp="urn:ietf:params:xml:ns:pidf
       :geopriv10:basicPolicy"
       xmlns:dm="urn:ietf:params:xml:ns:pidf:
       data-model"
       xmlns:cl="urn:ietf:params:xml:ns:pidf:
       geopriv10:civicAddr"
       xmlns:gml="http://www.opengis.net/gml"
       entity="pres:alice@atlanta.example.
       com">
       <dm:device id="target123-1">
              <gp:geopriv>
                     <gp:location-info>
                            <gml:location>
                                   <gml:Point
srsName="urn:ogc:def:crs:EPSG::4326">

<gml:pos>32.86726 -97.16054</gml:pos>
                                   </gml:Point>
                            </gml:location>
                     </gp:location-info>
                     <gp:usage-rules>

<gbp:retransmission-allowed>false
</gbp:retransmission-allowed>

<gbp:retention-expiry>2010-11-14T20:00:00Z
</gbp:retention-expiry>
                     </gp:usage-rules>
                     <gp:method>802.11</
                     gp:method>
              </gp:geopriv>
              <dm:deviceID>mac:1234567890ab</
dm:deviceID>
              <dm:timestamp>2010-11-
              04T20:57:29Z</dm:timestamp>
       </dm:device>
       <dm:person id="target123">
              <gp:geopriv>
                     <gp:location-info>
                            <cl:civicAddress>
                            <cl:country>US</
                            cl:country>
                            <cl:A1>Texas</
                            cl:A1>
                     <cl:A3>Colleyville</
                     cl:A3>
                            <cl:RD>Treemont</
                            cl:RD>
                            <cl:STS>Circle</
                            cl:STS>
                            <cl:HNO>3913</
                            cl:HNO>
                            <cl:FLR>1</cl:FLR>
                            <cl:NAM>Haley's
                            Place</cl:NAM>
                            <cl:PC>76034</
                            cl:PC>
                           </cl:civicAddress>
                    </gp:location-info>
                     <gp:usage-rules>
              <gbp:retransmission-allowed>
                     false
       </gbp:retransmission-allowed>
<gbp:retention-expiry>2010-11-14T20:00:00Z
                     </gbp:retention-expiry>
              </gp:usage-rules>
              <gp:method>triangulation</
              gp:method>
              </gp:geopriv>
              <dm:timestamp>2010-11-
              04T12:28:04Z</dm:timestamp>
       </dm:person>
</presence>

--boundary1--
```

9.11 Loop Detection

Loop detection is the fundamental property of the SIP entities when they route through forwarding of SIP messages. RFC 3261 (see Section 3.11.3) describes that a SIP entity may check for forwarding loops before forwarding a request examining the Via header field. If the request contains a Via header field with a sent-by value that equals a value placed into previous requests by the proxy, the request has been forwarded by this element before. The request has either looped or is legitimately spiraling through the element. To determine if the request has looped, the element may perform the branch parameter calculation described in RFC 3261 (see Section 3.11.6) on this message and compare it to the parameter received in that Via header field. If the parameters match, the request has looped. If they differ, the request is spiraling, and processing continues. If a loop is detected, the element may return a 482 Loop Detected response. However, this loop-detection procedure is highly insufficient to detect loops of SIP messages. RFC 5393 shows how this vulnerability enables an attack against SIP networks where a small number of legitimate, even authorized, SIP requests can stimulate massive amounts of proxy-to-proxy traffic.

RFC 5393 that is described here in the context of loop detection shows that, taking advantage of the forking capability, requests will continue to propagate down this tree until Max-Forwards reaches zero, creating a storm (see Section 19.9) of 408 Request Timeout responses and/or a storm of CANCEL requests will also be propagating through the tree along with the INVITE requests. RFC 5393 strengthens loop-detection requirements on SIP proxies when they fork requests (i.e., forward a request to more than one destination), and corrects and clarifies the description of the loop-detection algorithm such proxies are required to implement. Additionally, it defines a Max-Breadth header field for limiting the number of concurrent branches pursued for any given request. If there is insufficient value set in the Max-Breadth header field to carry out a desired parallel forking, a proxy sends the 440 Max-Breadth Exceeded response code. The Max-Breadth mechanism only limits concurrency. It does not limit the total number of branches a request can traverse over its lifetime. However, an attacker with access to a sufficient number of distinct resources will still be able to stimulate a very large number of messages. The number of concurrent messages will be limited by the Max-Breadth mechanism, so the entire set will be spread out over a long period of time, giving operators better opportunity to detect the attack and take corrective measures outside the scope of RFC 5393 recommendations. More work is needed to prevent this form of attack.

9.11.1 Enhancements in Loop-Detection Algorithm

9.11.1.1 Treatment of Via Header Field

The proxy must insert a Via header field value into the copy before the existing Via header field values using the procedure described in RFC 3261 (see Section 2.8). The Via header field indicates the transport used for the transaction and identifies the location where the response is to be sent. A Via header field value is added only after the transport that will be used to reach the next hop has been selected, which may involve the usage of the procedures in RFC 3263 (see Section 8.2.4). When the UAC creates a request, it must insert a Via into that request. The protocol name and protocol version in the header field must be SIP and 2.0, respectively. The Via header field value must contain a branch parameter. This parameter is used to identify the transaction created by that request. This parameter is used by both the client and the server. The branch parameter value must be unique across space and time for all requests sent by the UA. The exceptions to this rule are CANCEL and ACK for non-2xx responses. As discussed below, a CANCEL request will have the same value of the branch parameter as the request it cancels. As discussed in RFC 3261 (see Section 3.12.1.1.3), an ACK for a non-2xx response will also have the same branch ID as the INVITE whose response it acknowledges.

The uniqueness property of the branch ID parameter, to facilitate its use as a transaction ID, was not part of RFC 2543 obsoleted by RFC 3261. The branch ID inserted by an element compliant with this specification must always begin with the characters z9hG4bK. These seven characters are used as a magic cookie (seven is deemed sufficient to ensure that an older RFC 2543 implementation would not pick such a value), so that servers receiving the request can determine that the branch ID was constructed in the fashion described by this specification (i.e., globally unique). Beyond this requirement, the precise format of the branch token is implementation defined. The Via header maddr, ttl, and sent-by components will be set when the request is processed by the transport layer (RFC 3261, see Section 3.13). Via processing for proxies are described in RFC 3261 (see Sections 3.11.6 and 3.11.7). This implies that the proxy will compute its own branch parameter, which will be globally unique for that branch, and will contain the requisite magic cookie. Note that following only the guidelines in RFC 3261 (see Section 3.1.2.1.7) will result in a branch parameter that will be different for different instances of a spiraled or looped request through a proxy.

However, proxies required to perform loop detection by RFC 5393 have an additional constraint on the value they place in the Via header field. Such proxies should create a branch value separable into two parts in any implementation-dependent way. The existence of these two parts is a requirement of the loop-detection procedure. If a proxy chooses to employ some other mechanism, it is the implementer's responsibility to verify that the detection properties defined by the requirements placed on these two parts are achieved. The first part of the branch value must satisfy the constraints of RFC 3261 (see Section 3.1.2.1.7). The second part is used to perform loop detection and distinguish loops from spirals. This second part must vary with any field used by the location service logic in determining where to retarget or forward this request. This is necessary to distinguish looped requests from spirals by allowing the proxy to recognize if none of the values affecting the processing of the request have changed. Hence, the second part must depend at least on the received Request-URI and any Route header field values used when processing the received request. Implementers need to take care to include all fields used by the location service logic in that particular implementation. This second part must not vary with the request method. CANCEL and non-200 ACK requests must have the same branch parameter value as the corresponding request they cancel or acknowledge. This branch parameter value is used in correlating those requests at the server handling them as described in RFC 3261 (see Sections 3.12.2.3 and 3.2).

9.11.1.2 Updates in Loop-Detection Algorithm

RFC 5393 replaces all of item 4 in Section 16.3 of RFC 3261 (see Section 3.11.3.4) and mandates that proxies required to perform loop detection must perform the following loop-detection test before forwarding a request. Each Via header field value in the request whose sent-by value matches a value placed into previous requests by this proxy must be inspected for the *second part* as defined earlier (Section 4.2.1 of RFC 5393). This second part will not be present if the message was not forked when that Via header field value was added. If the second field is present, the proxy must perform the second-part calculation described earlier (Section 4.2.1 of RFC 5393) on this request and compare the result to the value from the Via header field. If these values are equal, the request has looped and the proxy must reject the request with a 482 Loop Detected response. If the values differ, the request is spiraling and processing continues to the next step.

9.11.1.2.1 Impact of Loop Detection on Overall Network Performance

These requirements and the recommendation to use the loop-detection mechanisms in this document make the favorable trade of exponential message growth for work that is, at worst, order n^2 as a message crosses n proxies. Specifically, this work is order m*n, where m is the number of proxies in the path that fork the request to more than one location. In practice, m is expected to be small. The loop-detection algorithm expressed here per RFC 5393 requires a proxy to inspect each Via element in a received request. In the worst case, where a message crosses N proxies, each of which loop detect, proxy k does k inspections, and the overall number of inspections spread across the proxies handling this request is the sum of k from $k = 1$ to $k = N$, which is $N(N + 1)/2$.

9.11.1.3 Note to Implementers

A common way to create the second part of the branch parameter value when forking a request is to compute a hash over the concatenation of the Request-URI, any Route header field values used during processing the request, and any other values used by the location service logic while processing this request. The hash should be chosen so that there is a low probability that two distinct sets of these parameters will collide. Because the maximum number of inputs that need to be compared is 70, the chance of a collision is low even with a relatively small hash value, such as 32 bits. CRC-32c as specified in RFC 4960 is a specific acceptable function, as is MD5 of RFC 1321. Note that MD5 is being chosen purely for noncryptographic properties. An attacker who can control the inputs in order to produce a hash collision can attack the connection in a variety of other ways. When forming the second part using a hash, implementations should include at least one field in the input to the hash that varies between different transactions attempting to reach the same destination to avoid repeated failure should the hash collide.

The Call-ID and CSeq fields would be good inputs for this purpose. A common point of failure to interoperate has been due to parsers objecting to the contents of another element's Via header field values when inspecting the Via stack for loops. Implementers need to take care to avoid making assumptions about the format of another element's Via header field value beyond the basic constraints placed on that format by RFC 3261 (see Section 2.8). In particular, parsing a header field value with unknown parameter names, parameters with no values, or parameter values with or without quoted strings must not cause an implementation to fail. Removing, obfuscating, or in any other way modifying the branch parameter values in Via header fields in a received request before forwarding it removes the ability for the node that placed that branch parameter into the message to perform loop detection. If two elements in a loop modify branch parameters this way, a loop can never be detected.

9.11.2 Max-Breadth Header Field

The Max-Breadth mechanism defined here limits the total number of concurrent branches caused by a forked SIP request. With this mechanism, all proxyable requests are assigned a positive integral Max-Breadth value, which denotes the maximum number of concurrent branches this request may spawn through parallel forking as it is forwarded from its current point. When a proxy forwards a request, its Max-Breadth value is divided among the outgoing requests. In turn, each of the forwarded requests has a limit on how many concurrent branches it may spawn. As branches complete, their portion of the Max-Breadth value becomes available for subsequent branches, if needed. If there is insufficient

Max-Breadth to carry out a desired parallel fork, a proxy can return the 440 Max-Breadth Exceeded response defined in this document. This mechanism operates independently from Max-Forwards. Max-Forwards limits the depth of the tree a request may traverse as it is forwarded from its origination point to each destination it is forked to. As discussed earlier, the number of branches in a tree of even limited depth can be made large (exponential with depth) by leveraging forking.

Each such branch has a pair of SIP transaction state machines associated with it. The Max-Breadth mechanism limits the number of branches that are active (those that have running transaction state machines) at any given point in time. Max-Breadth does not prevent forking. It only limits the number of concurrent parallel forked branches. In particular, a Max-Breadth of 1 restricts a request to pure serial forking rather than restricting it from being forked at all. A client receiving a 440 Max-Breadth Exceeded response can infer that its request did not reach all possible destinations. Recovery options are similar to those when receiving a 483 Too Many Hops response, and include affecting the routing decisions through whatever mechanisms are appropriate to result in a less broad search, or refining the request itself before submission to make the search space smaller. Figure 9.5 adopted from RFC 5393 depicts an example of how the combination of Max-Breadth and Max-Forwards is working in view of different scenarios of forking: Parallel, Sequential, and None.

9.11.2.1 Max-Breadth Header Field

The Max-Breadth header field takes a single positive integer as its value. The Max-Breadth header field value takes no parameters. For each response context defined in RFC 3261 (see Section 3.12) in a proxy, RFC 5393 defines two positive integral values: Incoming Max-Breadth and Outgoing Max-Breadth. Incoming Max-Breadth is the value in the Max-Breadth header field in the request that formed the response context. Outgoing Max-Breadth is the sum of the Max-Breadth header field values in all forwarded requests in the response context that have not received a final response.

9.11.2.2 Proxy Behavior

If a SIP proxy receives a request with no Max-Breadth header field value, it must add one, with a value that is recommended to be 60. Proxies must have a maximum allowable Incoming Max-Breadth value, which is recommended to be 60. If this maximum is exceeded in a received request, the proxy must overwrite it with a value that should be no greater than its allowable maximum. All proxied requests must contain a single Max-Breadth header field value. SIP proxies must not allow the Outgoing Max-Breadth to exceed the Incoming Max-Breadth in a given response context. If a SIP proxy determines a response context has insufficient Incoming Max-Breadth to carry out a desired parallel fork, and the proxy is unwilling/unable to compensate by forking serially or sending a redirect, that proxy must return a 440 Max-Breadth Exceeded response.

Notice that these requirements mean a proxy receiving a request with a Max-Breadth of 1 can only fork serially, but it is not required to fork at all—it can return a 440 instead. Thus, this mechanism is not a tool a UA can use to force all proxies in the path of a request to fork serially. A SIP proxy may distribute Max-Breadth in an arbitrary fashion between active branches. A proxy should not use a smaller amount of Max-Breadth than was present in the original request unless the Incoming Max-Breadth exceeded the proxy's maximum acceptable value. A proxy must not decrement Max-Breadth for each hop or otherwise use it to restrict the *depth* of a request's propagation.

9.11.2.3 Reusing Max-Breadth

Because forwarded requests that have received a final response do not count toward the Outgoing Max-Breadth, whenever a final response arrives, the Max-Breadth that was used on that branch becomes available for reuse. Proxies should be prepared to reuse this Max-Breadth in cases where there may be elements left in the target set.

9.11.2.4 UA Behavior

A UA client may place a Max-Breadth header field value in outgoing requests. If so, this value is recommended to be 60. This mechanism does not affect UAS behavior. A UAS receiving a request with a Max-Breadth header field will ignore that field while processing the request.

9.11.2.5 Implementation Note

9.11.2.5.1 Treatment of CANCEL

Since CANCEL requests are never proxied, a Max-Breadth header field value is meaningless in a CANCEL request. Sending a CANCEL in no way affects the Outgoing Max-Breadth in the associated INVITE response context. Receiving a CANCEL in no way affects the Incoming Max-Breadth of the associated INVITE response context.

9.11.2.5.2 Reclamation of Max-Breadth on 2xx Responses

Whether 2xx responses free up Max-Breadth is mostly a moot issue, since proxies are forbidden to start new branches in this case. However, there is one caveat. A proxy

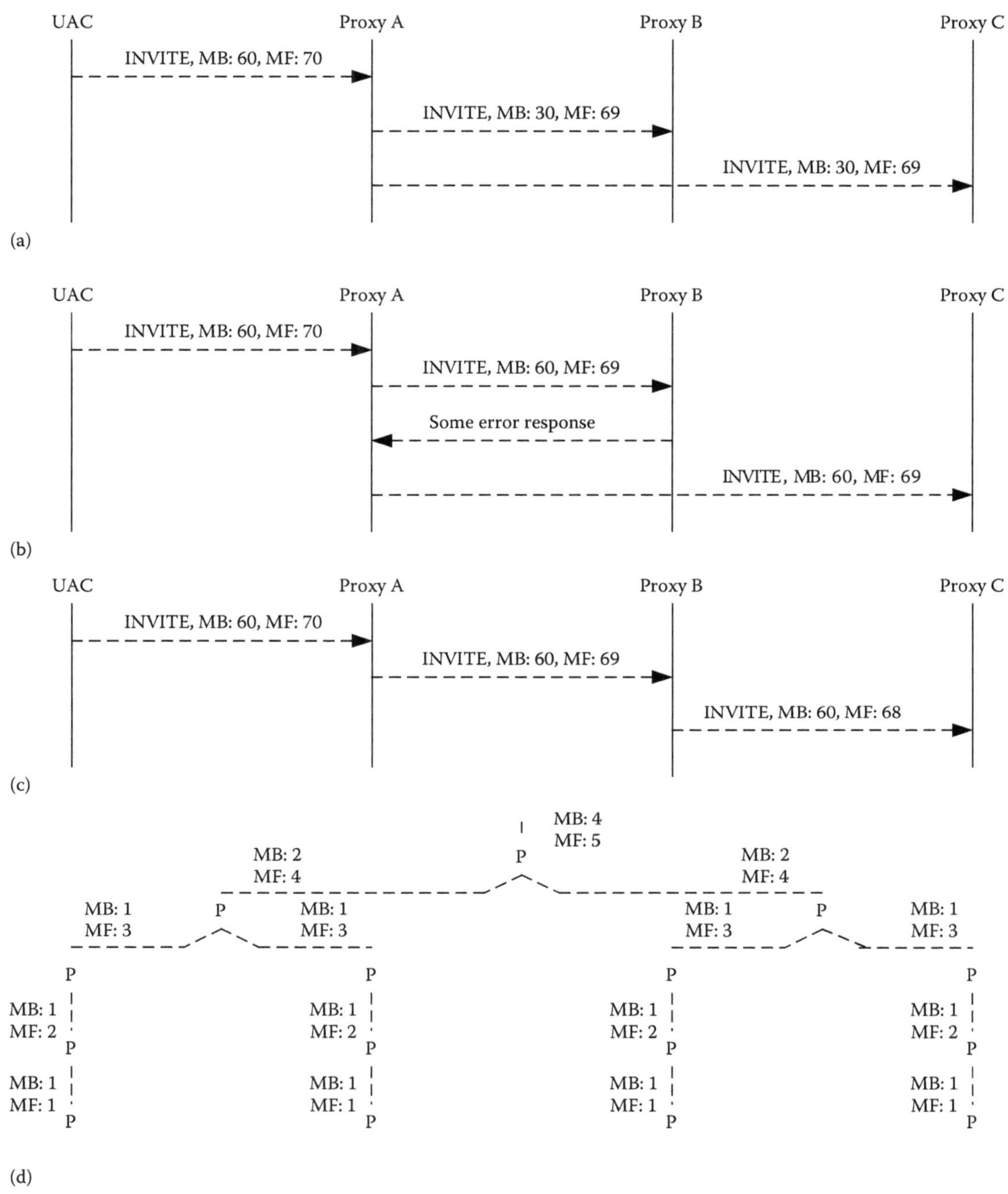

Figure 9.5 Max-Breadth and Max-Forwards example: (a) parallel forking, (b) sequential forking, (c) no forking, and (d) combined working of Max-Breadth and Max-Forwards. (Copyright IETF. Reproduced with permission.)

may receive multiple 2xx responses for a single forwarded INVITE request. Also, implementations following RFC 2543 obsoleted by RFC 3261 may send back a 6xx followed by a 2xx on the same branch. Implementations that subtract from the Outgoing Max-Breadth when they receive a 2xx response to an INVITE request must be careful to avoid bugs caused by subtracting multiple times for a single branch.

9.11.2.5.3 Max-Breadth and Automaton UAs

Designers of automaton UAs including B2BUAs, gateways, exploders, and any other element that programmatically sends requests as a result of incoming SIP traffic should consider whether Max-Breadth limitations should be placed on outgoing requests. For example, it is reasonable to design B2BUAs to carry the Max-Breadth value from incoming requests into requests that are sent as a result. Also, it is reasonable to place Max-Breadth constraints on sets of requests sent by exploders when they may be leveraged in an amplification attack.

9.11.2.6 Parallel and Sequential Forking

Inherent in the definition of this mechanism is the ability of a proxy to reclaim apportioned Max-Breadth while forking sequentially. The limitation on Outgoing Max-Breadth is applied to concurrent branches only. For example, if a proxy receives a request with a Max-Breadth of 4 and has eight targets to forward it to, that proxy may parallel fork to four of these targets initially (each with a Max-Breadth of 1, totaling an Outgoing Max-Breadth of 4). If one of these transactions completes with a failure response, the outgoing Max-Breadth drops to 3, allowing the proxy to forward to one of the four remaining targets (again, with a Max-Breadth of 1).

9.11.2.7 Max-Breadth Split Weight Selection

There are a variety of mechanisms for controlling the weight of each fork branch. Fork branches that are given more Max-Breadth are more likely to complete quickly (because it is less likely that a proxy down the line will be forced to fork sequentially). By the same token, if it is known that a given branch will not fork later on, a Max-Breadth of 1 may be assigned with no ill effect. This would be appropriate, for example, if a proxy knows the branch is using the UA-initiated connection management over the SIP network defined in RFC 5626 (see Section 15.2).

9.12 Summary

We have describe how routing is done in the SIP network, including the use of Route, Route-Record, and double Router-Record header. The registration and routing schemes used by different SIP functional entities over the SIP network are explained. However, there are some interoperability issues that are faced when rewriting of Record-Route and transport switching are performed. We are summarizing the recommendations for avoiding these interoperability issues as discussed earlier:

- Record-Route rewriting is presented as a technique that may be used; however, its drawbacks need to be noted as explained.
- The double Record-Routing technique described earlier should be used.
- The Record-Route header interoperability problems on transport protocol switching outlined here should be avoided using the recommended UA and proxy implementations described here. Proxies should use double Record-Routing for any multihomed situation that may affect the further processing, and they should put transport protocol parameters on Record-Route URIs in some circumstances. UAs should not offer options to overwrite the transport for initial requests. UAs should rely on DNS to express their desired transport and should avoid IP addresses with transport parameters in this case. Lastly, UAs should be ready to switch transports between the initial request and further in-dialog messages.

PROBLEMS

1. How does a SIP registrar act as the routing database? Explain in detail with examples.
2. How does a SIP proxy route incoming SIP messages? Explain in detail with examples.
3. How does a strict-routing SIP proxy handle incoming SIP messages? Explain in detail with examples.
4. What are the procedures for rewriting SIP Record-Route header field values? What are the problems in doing so for routing? What are the recommended solutions for these problems?
5. Explain the Record-Routing with GRUU using detailed examples. Explain the double Route-Record with examples.
6. What are the problems for switching the transport protocol, for example, switching from TCP to UDP? How are these problems solved by the SIP entities: UA and proxy?
7. What is caller preference-based routing in SIP? Explain with examples. How does a UAC handle this routing scheme for the following preferences: request handling and feature set? Explain the behavior of UAS with examples.
8. How does a SIP proxy behave for the caller preference-based routing scheme in processing the Request-Disposition? Explain with examples.
9. How does a SIP proxy behave for the caller preference-based routing scheme in matching preference and capability of the following: extracting explicit and implicit preferences and constructing contact predicates? How are the feature parameters mapped to a predicate? Explain all of these items with examples.
10. What is the location-based routing in SIP? How are the basic SIP location conveyance operations performed for the following: location conveyed by value, location URI, through a SIP intermediary, and location URIs in message bodies? How does a SIP intermediary replace a bad location?
11. How is a SIP location profile negotiated? Explain the SIP location-based routing using geolocation examples

as follows: location-by-value (in coordinate format) and two locations composed in same location object.

12. How is the geopriv privacy maintained in SIP location-based routing? Describe the overall security issues and their solutions in the SIP location-based routing.
13. How does the looping occur in routing SIP messages? Explain the loop-detection algorithm that is used in SIP. What is the impact in overall performance of the loop-detection over the SIP network?
14. How is the SIP Max-Breadth header field used in avoiding the routing loop over the SIP network? How is the Max-Breadth header field reused? Explain the proxy and UA behavior in using the Max-Breadth header field in avoiding the routing loop over the SIP network.
15. Explain the parallel and sequential forking for avoiding the route loop in using the Max-Breadth header field over the SIP network. Explain the same in using the Max-Breadth header field with split weight selection.
16. Explain in detail the Max-Breadth header field's effect on the forking-based amplification attacks. Recommend remedies against these attacks.

Chapter 10

User and Network-Asserted Identity in SIP

Abstract

We describe the user identity and the Network-Asserted Identity (NAI) that can be used over the Session Initiation Protocol (SIP) network. A SIP user may have multiple identities to be used for many purposes, and some of the user identities may be public while others can be private identities. All of these user identities can be shared with other SIP users for communications as appropriate. Although user identities can be both public and private, a NAI is considered always applicable over the private SIP network. The details of both user identity and NAI are provided here.

10.1 Introduction

The user identity in Session Initiation Protocol (SIP) usually describes a unique public identity of a user that is shared with others so that they can contact the user. The user can be a single user, a group of users, a service, or a device. In some cases, the user identity in SIP can be a private identity that is only shared within a certain closed group without making it public, such as the user's identity for access control, billing, and charging by a service provider. As explained earlier in the context of the user's address registration, the user identity in SIP is sometimes called address of record (AOR), which usually looks like `sip:username@domain` (e.g., sip:joe@network.com). The SIP user agent (UA) registers the user's SIP identity with the SIP registrar server. The SIP server binds the user's SIP identity to the network address of user SIP UA (its contact address). This lets others who know the user's AOR call without knowing the SIP UA's user network address.

Unless a user is integrated with an existing SIP network, the SIP identity a user chooses can be anything. However, the domain part of user's identity (`sip:`sip:joe@network.com) should be one of the domains known by the SIP proxy that is responsible for the service in this domain because the proxy forwards requests to the user SIP UA's contact address. In SIP networks, the Network-Asserted Identity (NAI) is defined as an identity initially derived by a SIP network intermediary as a result of an authentication process. However, NAI is used in a private SIP network and NAIs are exchanged within networks of securely interconnected trusted nodes and UAs. A trusted domain is created as per Spec(T) security specification among the trusted nodes, and the network nodes are connected securely in accordance to Spec(T).

10.2 Multiple User Identities

A user may have multiple devices, especially if the user is mobile, where the user can be reached. For example, a service provider, as Third Generation Partnership Project's (3GPP's) Internet Protocol (IP) multimedia subsystem (IMS) specification allows, may permit a user to have several SIP user identities (SUIs). Different SUIs may serve as aliases for a particular user. These SUIs are totally interchangeable because they are associated to the same set of services and are transparently associated to the same devices. The user may use them to differentiate between different groups of contacts for different purposes, such as relatives versus friends versus strangers. A user may typically have a telephone Uniform Resource Identifier (tel URI) as an alias to a SIP URI. Different indoor units (IDUs) may also permit the user to endorse several personas (e.g., member of an association, owner of a private business). In this case, the IDUs may be associated to different service profiles and possibly to different devices (but they can also be associated to the same).

It has also opened a very powerful feature that is the possibility to associate a single SUI to virtually all the services of a user, although this feature may seem to conflict with the previous one. All services, like audio, video, data sharing, instant messaging, presence, and related communications services, can be accessed through a single SUI, making it independent from the devices and access technologies being used. If the user's e-mail address, the most popular means of contacting a user, happens to correspond to this SUI, this may finally be the unique address that can be used in one's business card or otherwise, and all services can be provided to the user using this single address. The possibility of accessing a host of services through a single SUI can also be extremely beneficial to the services themselves. Only one of these addresses may be used as the key to discover all others dynamically, although a user may have multiple identities and addresses. It implies that a user can discover a whole lot of information about another user and use it for the delivery of sophisticated services.

10.3 Public User Identity

The public user identity in SIP is the unique identity of a user that is shared with other users publicly for contacting the user, and can be expressed in SIP URI, SIPS URI, or tel URI. However, a user can subscribe one or multiple public identities for contacting the user by others using one of those addresses. The multiple identities may be used by a user for different purposes, as described earlier. A service provider to which a user subscribes to may use the different identities of the user using a certain set of rules. For example, per 3GPP IMS specifications, the subscriber needs to register at least one of the addresses with the provider's IMS network.

For the subscriber who has multiple public identities, IMS defines implicit registration sets. That is, once any one of these public identities in the set is registered or deregistered, all other identities of the set are also registered or deregistered. The use of the same SIP URI as an identity by a user for both fixed and mobile networking environments will have the possibility to prevail for universal communications of all media. In another context, for IMS network, 3GPP has also defined the public service identity (PSI) that enables users to directly access public services such as conferencing services, including media bridging using SIP or SIPS URI indicating a certain service at an application server that is not related to a certain user.

10.4 Private User Identity

The private user identity in SIP is used for security reasons and, unlike the public user identity, the private identity is not used for routing over the SIP network. With respect to privacy and anonymity, users, groups, or institution may determine when, how, and to what extent the information related to them is to be revealed to other parties. SIP has mechanisms that can allow distinguishing between different information (Personal, Location, and Call) that a user might keep private:

- SIP header fields like To, From, Call-Id, Contact, Organization, Sever, and User-Agent may carry personal information related to the user's identity, device, and place.
- SIP message-body containing a Session Description Protocol (SDP) part as well as headers like Via, Contact, Router, and Route-Record may carry location information that indicates IP address, host, network, and service provider of the user.
- The overall call information containing all the headers and message-body indicates that a user is making a call and with whom the user is communicating.

Some headers cannot be concealed by a UA itself because they are used in routing. However, those headers could be concealed by an intermediary that subsequently takes responsibility for directing messages to and from the anonymous user. The UA must have some way to request such privacy services from the network. For that purpose, SIP header, Privacy, is defined in Requests for Comment (RFCs) 3323 (see Section 20.2) and 3325 (see Sections 2.8, 10.4, and 20.3) and can be used to specify privacy handling for requests and responses:

```
Privacy-hdr = "Privacy" HCOLON priv-value
*(";" priv-value)
priv-value = "header"/"session"/"user"/"none"
/"critical"/"id"/token
```

UAs should include a Privacy header when network-provided privacy is required. Note that some intermediaries may also add the Privacy header to messages, including privacy services. However, such intermediaries should only do so if they are operating at a user's behest, for example, if a user has an administrative arrangement with the operator of the intermediary that it will add such a Privacy header. An intermediary must not modify the Privacy header in any way if the *none* priv-value is already specified. The priv-value field that is used to control the level of needed privacy setting value is described as follows:

- **Header:** The user requests that a privacy service obscure those headers that cannot be completely expunged of identifying information without the assistance of intermediaries such as Via and Contact that cannot be anonymized by the SIP UA. Also, no unnecessary headers should be added by the service that might reveal personal information about the originator of the request.

- **Session:** The user requests that a privacy service provide anonymization for the session described in SIP message-body by the SDP initiated by this message. This will mask the IP address from which the session traffic would ordinarily appear to originate. When session privacy is requested, UAs must not encrypt SDP bodies in messages. Note that requesting session privacy in the absence of any end-to-end session encryption raises some serious security concerns.
- **User:** This privacy level is usually set only by intermediaries, to communicate that user-level privacy functions must be provided by the network, presumably because the UA is unable to provide them. UAs may, however, set this privacy level for REGISTER requests, but should not set *user*-level privacy for other requests.
- **None:** The user requests that a privacy service apply no privacy functions to this message, regardless of any preprovisioned profile for the user or default behavior of the service. UAs can specify this option when they are forced to route a message through a privacy service that will, if no Privacy header is present, apply some privacy functions that the user does not desire for this message. Intermediaries must not remove or alter a Privacy header whose priv-value is *none*. UAs must not populate any other values of the priv-value field, including *critical*, in a Privacy header that contains a value of *none*.
- **Critical:** The user asserts that the privacy services requested for this message are critical, and that, therefore, if these privacy services cannot be provided by the network, this request should be rejected. Criticality cannot be managed appropriately for responses.
- **Id:** The presence of this privacy type in a Privacy header field indicates that the user would like the NAI (RFC 3324, see Section 10.5) to be kept private with respect to SIP entities outside the Trust Domain with which the user authenticated. Note that a user requesting multiple types of privacy must include all of the requested privacy types in its Privacy header field value.

SIP needs to enable a network of trusted SIP servers to assert the identity of authenticated users in a trusted manner and still respect the privacy references of the users. P-Asserted-Identity and P-Preferred-Identity header (RFC 3325, see Sections 2.8, 10.4, and 20.3) of SIP described in earlier sections accommodate these needs of both service providers and users. Note that we have described more appropriate use of asserted identities (P-Asserted- and P-Preferred-Identity) updating RFC 3235 (see the next section).

10.4.1 P-Asserted-Identity

The P-Asserted-Identity header field described earlier must use SIP, SIPS, or tel URI if there is only one value. If there are two values, one value must be a SIP or SIPS URI and the other must be a tel URI. It is used among trusted SIP entities to carry the identity of a user sending a SIP message as it was verified by authentication. A proxy server that handles a message can, after authenticating the originating user, insert such a P-Asserted-Identity header field into the message and forward it to other trusted proxies. A proxy that is about to forward a message to a proxy server or UA that it does not trust must remove all the P-Asserted-Identity header field values if the user requested that this information be kept private. The use of this header is only applicable inside a trusted administrative domain with previously agreed-upon policies for generation, transport, and usage of such information.

10.4.2 P-Preferred-Identity

The P-Preferred-Identity header field described earlier is used from a UA to a trusted proxy to carry the identity the user sending the SIP message wishes to be used for the P-Asserted-Header field value that the trusted element will insert. Like P-Asserted-Identity, this header also must use a SIP, SIPS, or tel URI if there is only one value. If there are two values, one value must be a SIP or SIPS URI and the other must be a tel URI.

10.4.3 Identity

The Identity header field described earlier defines a mechanism for securely identifying originators of SIP messages that can be used for both intradomain and interdomain through conveying a signature used for validating the identity. Either SIP UA or the SIP proxy acting as the authentication service signs the hash calculated over the identity string and adds the Identity header to the SIP request. The same procedure can be used in the SIP response message if the call is not retargeted to reach the callee.

10.4.3.1 Connected Identity

The Identity header field described earlier cannot be signed in the SIP response message by the authentication service located in the callee's domain if the call is retargeted to reach the callee because the AOR URI provided in the To header by the caller SIP request message will be different. RFC 4916 (see Section 20.4) deprecates this requirement of the To and From headers for being the same in a given dialog of RFC 3261 introducing a new option tag from-change for providing a positive indication of support in the Supported header field. In this case, the retargeted callee with whom the call has finally been established can be signed by the authentication service of the retargeted caller's domain, although the URI of the To header field of the SIP request message is different because the callee is located in the retargeted domain. This type of call establishment with signed Identity header for the retargeted callee is defined as the connected identity.

10.4.4 Recommended Use of Asserted Identity with SIP Messages

SIP has a mechanism for conveying the identity of the originator of a request by means of the P-Asserted-Identity and P-Preferred-Identity header fields. These header fields are specified for use in requests using a number of SIP methods, in particular the INVITE method. However, RFC 3325 (see Sections 10.4.1 and 10.4.2) does not specify the insertion of the P-Asserted-Identity header field by a trusted UA client (UAC); does not specify the use of P-Asserted-Identity and P-Preferred-Identity header fields with certain SIP methods such as UPDATE, REGISTER, MESSAGE, and PUBLISH; and does not specify how to handle an unexpected number of URIs or unexpected URI schemes in these header fields. This document extends RFC 3325 to cover these situations. RFC 5876 that is described here extends RFC 3325 (see Section 10.4) by allowing inclusion of the P-Asserted-Identity header field by a UAC in the same Trust Domain as the first proxy, and allowing use of P-Asserted-Identity and P-Preferred-Identity header fields in any request except ACK and CANCEL. The reason for these two exceptions is that ACK and CANCEL requests cannot be challenged for digest authentication. RFC 3325 (see Sections 10.4.1 and 10.4.2) allows the P-Asserted-Identity and P-Preferred-Identity header fields each to contain at most two URIs, where one is a SIP or SIPS URI (RFC 3261, see Section 4.2.1) and the other is a tel URI (RFC 3966, see Section 4.2.2).

This may be unduly restrictive in the future, for example, if there is a need to allow other URI schemes, if there is a need to allow both a SIP and a SIPS URI, or if there is a need to allow more than one URI with the same scheme (e.g., a SIP URI based on a telephone number and a SIP URI that is not based on a telephone number). This specification (RFC 5876) therefore provides forwards compatibility by mandating tolerance to the receipt of unexpected URIs. RFC 3325 (see Sections 10.4.1 and 10.4.2) is unclear on the use of P-Asserted-Identity in responses. In contrast to requests, there is no means in SIP to challenge a UA to provide SIP digest authentication in a response. As a result, there is currently no standardized mechanism whereby a proxy can authenticate a UA server (UAS). Since authenticating the source of a message is a prerequisite for asserting an identity, this specification (RFC 5876) does not specify the use of the P-Asserted-Identity header field in responses. This may be the subject of a future update to RFC 3325 (see Sections 10.4.1 and 10.4.2). Also, RFC 5876 does not specify the use of the P-Preferred-Identity header field in responses, as this would serve no purpose in the absence of the ability for a proxy to insert the P-Asserted-Identity header field. The security issues are described in Section 19.2.2.

10.4.4.1 Inclusion of P-Asserted-Identity by a UAC

RFC 3325 (see Sections 10.4.1 and 10.4.2) does not include procedures for a UAC to include the P-Asserted-Identity header field in a request. This can be meaningful if the UAC is in the same Trust Domain as the first downstream SIP entity. Examples of types of UACs that are often suitable for inclusion in a Trust Domain are as follows: public switched telephone network (PSTN) gateways, Media servers, Application servers (or B2BUAs) that act as URI list servers (RFC 5363, see Section 19.6), and Application servers (or B2BUAs) that perform third-party call control. In the particular case of a PSTN gateway, the PSTN gateway might be able to assert an identity received from the PSTN, the proxy itself having no means to authenticate such an identity. Likewise, in the case of certain application server or B2BUA arrangements, the application server or B2BUA may be in a position to assert an identity of a user on the other side of that application server or B2BUA. In accordance with RFC 3325 (see Sections 10.4.1 and 10.4.2), nodes within a Trust Domain (see Section 10.5) must behave in accordance with a Spec(T), and this principle needs to be applied between a UAC and its proxy as part of the condition to consider the UAC to be within the same Trust Domain. The normal proxy procedures of RFC 3325 ensure that the header field is removed or replaced if the first proxy considers the UAC to be outside the Trust Domain. This update to RFC 3325 clarifies that a UAC may include a P-Asserted-Identity header field in a request in certain circumstances.

10.4.4.2 Inclusion of P-Asserted-Identity in Any Request

There are several use cases that would benefit from the use of the P-Asserted-Identity header field in an UPDATE request. These use cases apply within a Trust Domain where the use of asserted identity is appropriate (see RFC 3325). In one example, an established call passes through a gateway to the PSTN. The gateway becomes aware that the remote party in the PSTN has changed, for example, due to call transfer. By including the P-Asserted-Identity header field in an UPDATE request, the gateway can convey the identity of the new remote party to the peer SIP UA. Note that the (re-) INVITE method could be used in this situation. However, this forces an offer–answer exchange, which typically is not required in this situation. Also, it involves three messages rather than two. In another example, a B2BUA that is a 3PCC (RFC 3725, see Section 18.3) wishes to join two calls together, one of which is still waiting to be answered and potentially is forked to different UAs. At this point in time, it is not possible to trigger the normal offer–answer exchange between the two joined parties, because of the mismatch between a single dialog on the one side and potentially multiple early dialogs on the other side, so this action must wait until one of the called UAs answers.

However, it would be useful to give an early indication to each user concerned of the identity of the user to which they will become connected when the call is answered. In other words, it would provide the new calling UA with the identity of the new called user and provide the new called UA(s) with the identity of the new calling user. This can be achieved by the B2BUA sending an UPDATE request with a P-Asserted-Identity header field on the dialogs concerned. Within a Trust Domain, a P-Asserted-Identity header field could advantageously be used in a REGISTER request between an edge proxy that has authenticated the source of the request and the registrar. Within a Trust Domain, a P-Asserted-Identity header field could advantageously be used in a MESSAGE request to assert the source of a page-mode instant message. This would complement its use in an INVITE request to assert the source of an instant-message session or any other form of session. Similarly, between a UAC and first proxy that are not within the same Trust Domain, a P-Preferred-Identity header field could be used in a MESSAGE request to express a preference when the user has several identities. Within a Trust Domain, a P-Asserted-Identity header field could advantageously be used in a PUBLISH request to assert the source of published state information.

This would complement its use in SUBSCRIBE and NOTIFY requests. Similarly, between a UAC and first proxy that are not within the same Trust Domain, a P-Preferred-Identity header field could be used in a PUBLISH request to express a preference when the user has several identities. Thus, there are several examples where P-Asserted-Identity could be used in requests with methods for which there is no provision in RFC 3325 (see Sections 10.4.1 and 10.4.2). This leaves a few methods for which use cases are less obvious, but the inclusion of P-Asserted-Identity would not cause any harm. In any requests, the header field would simply assert the source of that request, whether or not this is of any use to the UAS. Inclusion of P-Asserted-Identity in a request requires that the original asserter of an identity be able to authenticate the source of the request. This implies the ability to challenge a request for SIP digest authentication, which is not possible with ACK and CANCEL requests. Therefore, ACK and CANCEL requests need to be excluded. Similarly, there are examples where P-Preferred-Identity could be used in requests with methods for which there is no provision in RFC 3325 or any other RFC (with the exception of ACK and CANCEL). This update to RFC 3325 allows a P-Asserted-Identity or P-Preferred-Identity header field to be included in any request except ACK and CANCEL.

10.4.4.3 Dialog Implications

A P-Asserted-Identity header field in a received request asserts the identity of the source of that request and says nothing about the source of subsequent received requests claiming to relate to the same dialog. The recipient can make its own deductions about the source of subsequent requests not containing a P-Asserted-Identity header field. This document does not change RFC 3325 in this respect.

10.4.4.4 SIP Entity Behavior

This document updates RFC 3325 (see Sections 10.4.1 and 10.4.2) by allowing a P-Asserted-Identity header field to be included by a UAC within the same Trust Domain and by allowing a P-Asserted-Identity or P-Preferred-Identity header field to appear in any request except ACK or CANCEL.

10.4.4.4.1 UAC Behavior

A UAC may include a P-Asserted-Identity header field in any request except ACK and CANCEL to report the identity of the user on behalf of which the UAC is acting and whose identity the UAC is in a position to assert. A UAC should do so only in cases where it believes it is in the same Trust Domain as the SIP entity to which it sends the request and where it is connected to that SIP entity in accordance with the security requirements of RFC 3325. A UAC should not do so in other circumstances and might instead use the P-Preferred-Identity header field. A UAC must not include both header fields. A UAC may include a P-Preferred-Identity header field in any request except ACK or CANCEL. Inclusion of a P-Asserted-Identity or P-Preferred-Identity header field in a request is not limited to the methods allowed in RFC 3325.

10.4.4.4.2 Proxy Behavior

If a proxy receives a request containing a P-Asserted-Identity header field from a UAC within the Trust Domain, it must behave as it would for a request from any other node within the Trust Domain, in accordance with the rules of RFC 3325 for a proxy. Note that this implies that the proxy must have authenticated the sender of the request in accordance with the Spec(T) (see Section 10.5) in force for the Trust Domain, and determined that the sender is indeed part of the Trust Domain. If a proxy receives a request (other than ACK or CANCEL) containing a P-Asserted-Identity or P-Preferred-Identity header field, it must behave in accordance with the rules of RFC 3325 for a proxy, even if the method is not one for which RFC 3325 specifies the use of that header field.

10.4.4.4.3 Registrar Behavior

If a registrar receives a REGISTER request containing a P-Asserted-Identity header field, it must disregard the asserted identity unless it is received from a node within the Trust Domain. If the node is within the Trust Domain (the node having been authenticated by some means), the registrar MAY use this as evidence that the registering UA has been authenticated and is represented by the identity asserted in the header field.

10.4.4.4.4 UAS Behavior

If a UAS receives any request (other than ACK or CANCEL) containing a P-Asserted-Identity header field, it must behave in accordance with the rules of RFC 3325 for a UAS, even if the method is not one for which RFC 3325 specifies the use of that header field.

10.4.4.4.5 General Handling

An entity receiving a P-Asserted-Identity or P-Preferred-Identity header field can expect the number of URIs and the combination of URI schemes in the header field to be in accordance with RFC 3325, any updates to RFC 3325, or any Spec(T) (see Section 10.5) that states otherwise. If an entity receives a request containing a P-Asserted-Identity or P-Preferred-Identity header field containing an unexpected number of URIs or unexpected URI schemes, it must act as follows: ignore any URI with an unexpected URI scheme; ignore any URI for which the expected maximum number of URIs with the same scheme occurred earlier in the header field; and ignore any URI whose scheme is not expected to occur in combination with a scheme that occurred earlier in the header field. In the absence of a Spec(T) determining otherwise, this document does not change the RFC 3325 requirement that allows each of these header fields to contain at most two URIs, where one is a SIP or SIPS URI and the other is a tel URI; however, future updates to this document may relax that requirement. In the absence of such a relaxation or a Spec(T) determining otherwise, the RFC 3325 requirement means that an entity receiving a request containing a P-Asserted-Identity or P-Preferred-Identity header field must act as follows:

- Ignore any URI with a scheme other than SIP, SIPS, or tel.
- Ignore a second or subsequent SIP URI, a second or subsequent SIPS URI, or a second or subsequent tel URI.
- Ignore a SIP URI if a SIPS URI occurred earlier in the header field and vice versa.

A proxy must not forward a URI when forwarding a request, if that URI is to be ignored in accordance with the requirement above. When a UAC or a proxy sends a request containing a P-Asserted-Identity header field to another node in the Trust Domain, if that other node complies with RFC 3325 but not with this specification, and if the method is not one for which RFC 3325 specifies the use of the P-Asserted-Identity header field, and if the request also contains a Privacy header field with value *id*, as specified in RFC 3325, the other node might not handle the Privacy header field correctly. To prevent incorrect handling of the Privacy header field with value *id*, the Spec(T) in force for the Trust Domain should require all nodes to comply with this specification. If this is not the case, a UAC or a proxy should not include a P-Asserted-Identity header field in a request if the method is not one for which RFC 3325 specifies use of the P-Asserted-Identity header field and if the request also contains a Privacy header field with value *id*.

10.5 Network-Asserted Identity

10.5.1 Overview

A NAI defined in RFC 3324 is an identity initially derived by a SIP network intermediary as a result of an authentication process. We will describe here that there is a need for exchange of the NAI within networks of securely interconnected trusted nodes and to UAs securely connected to such networks. SIP allows users to assert their identity in a number of ways, for example, using the From header. However, there is no requirement for these identities to be anything other than the user's desired alias. An authenticated identity of a user can be obtained using SIP Digest Authentication (or by other means). However, UAs do not always have the necessary key information to authenticate another UA.

A NAI is an identity initially derived by a SIP network intermediary as a result of an authentication process. This may or may not be based on SIP Digest Authentication. This document describes short-term requirements for the exchange of NAIs within networks of securely interconnected trusted nodes and also to UAs with secure connections to such networks. Such a network is described in this document as a Trust Domain, and we present a strict definition of trust and Trust Domain for the purposes of this document. These short-term requirements provide only for the exchange of NAI within a Trust Domain and to an entity directly connected to the Trust Domain. General requirements for transport of NAIs on the Internet are out of scope of this document. Note that we have described more appropriate use of asserted identities updating RFC 3235 including NAI and maintaining privacy in Section 20.2.8.4.

10.5.2 Trust Domain Identities, NAI, and Trust Domain Specification

10.5.2.1 Trust Domain Identities

An identity, for the purposes of the Trust Domain as specified here per RFC 3324, can be a SIP, SIPS or tel URI, and optionally a Display Name. The URI must be meaningful to the domain identified in the URI (in the case of SIP or SIPS URIs) or the owner of the E.164 number (in the case of tel URIs), in the sense that when used as a SIP Request-URI in a request sent to that domain/number range owner, it would cause the request to be routed to the user/line that is associated with the identity, or to be processed by service logic running on that user's behalf. If the URI is a SIP or SIPS URI, then depending on the local policy of the domain identified in the URI, the URI may identify some specific entity, such as a person. If the URI is a tel URI, then depending on the local policy of the owner of the number range within which the telephone number lies, the number may identify some specific entity, such as a telephone line. However, it should be noted that identifying the owner of the number range is a less straightforward process than identifying the domain that owns a SIP or SIPS URI.

10.5.2.2 Network-Asserted Identity

A NAI is an identity derived by a SIP network entity as a result of an authentication process, which identifies the authenticated entity in the sense above. In the case of a SIP or SIPS URI, the domain included in the URI must be within the Trust Domain. In the case of a tel URI, the owner of the E.164 number in the URI must be within the Trust Domain. The authentication process used, or at least its reliability/strength, is a known feature of the Trust Domain using the NAI mechanism, that is, in the language of described below, it is defined in Spec(T).

10.5.2.3 Trust Domains

A Trust Domain for the purposes of NAI is a set of SIP nodes (UAC, UAS, proxies, or other network intermediaries) that are trusted to exchange NAI information in the sense described here. A node can be a member of a Trust Domain, T, only if the node is known to be compliant to a certain set of specifications, Spec(T), which characterize the handling of NAI within the Trust Domain, T. Trust Domains are constructed by human beings who know the properties of the equipment they are using/deploying. In the simplest case, a Trust Domain is a set of devices with a single owner/operator who can accurately know the behavior of those devices. Such simple Trust Domains may be joined into larger Trust Domains by bilateral agreements between the owners/operators of the devices. We say a node is *trusted* (with respect to a given Trust Domain) if and only if it is a member of that domain. We say that a node, A, in the domain is *trusted by* a node, B (or "B trusts A"), if and only if

- There is a secure connection between the nodes.
- B has configuration information indicating that A is a member of the Trust Domain.

Note that B may or may not be a member of the Trust Domain. For example, B may be a UA that trusts a given network intermediary, A (e.g., its home proxy). A *secure connection* in this context means that messages cannot be read by third parties, cannot be modified by third parties without detection, and that B can be sure that the message really did come from A. The level of security required is a feature of the Trust Domain, that is, it is defined in Spec(T). Within this context, SIP signaling information received by one node from a node that it trusts is known to have been generated and passed through the network according to the procedures of the particular specification set Spec(T), and therefore can be known to be valid, or at least as valid as specified in the specifications Spec(T). Equally, a node can be sure that signaling information passed to a node that it trusts will be handled according to the procedures of Spec(T). For these capabilities to be useful, Spec(T) must contain requirements as to how the NAI is generated, how its privacy is protected, and how its integrity is maintained as it is passed around the network. A reader of Spec(T) can then make an informed judgment about the authenticity and reliability of network asserted information received from the Trust Domain T.

The term *trusted* (with respect to a given Trust Domain) can be applied to a given node in an absolute sense—it is just equivalent to saying the node is a member of the Trust Domain. However, the node itself does not know whether another arbitrary node is trusted, even within the Trust Domain. It does know about certain nodes with which it has secure connections as described above. With the definition above, statements such as "A trusted node shall..." are just shorthand for "A node compliant to this specification shall...." Statements such as "When a node receives information from a trusted node..." are not valid, because one node does not have complete knowledge about all the other nodes in the Trust Domain. Statements such as "When a node receives information from another node that it trusts..." are valid, and should be interpreted according to two criteria described above. The above relationships are illustrated in Figure 10.1.

- A, B, and C are part of the same Trust Domain.
- A trusts C, but A does not trust B.
- Since E knows that B is inside of the Trust Domain, E trusts B, but B does not trust E.
- B does not trust F, and F does not trust B.

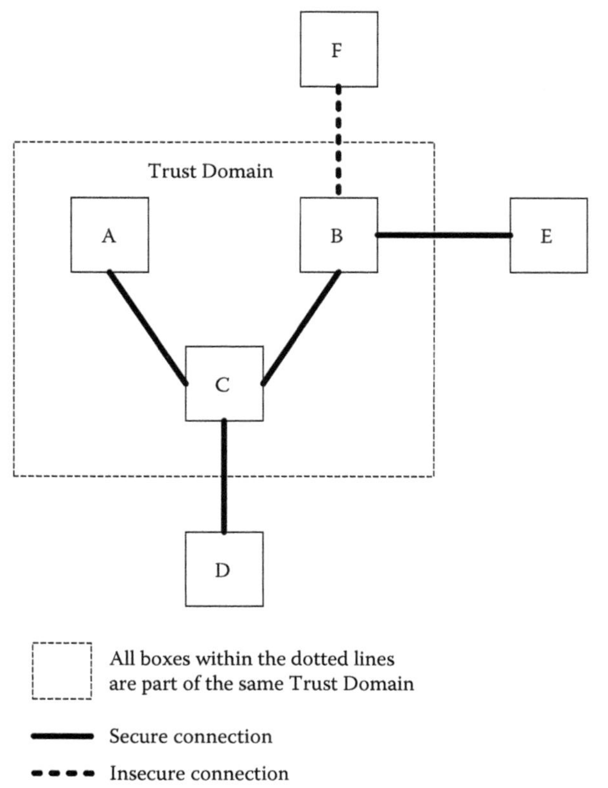

Figure 10.1 Trust Domain. (Copyright IETF. Reproduced with permission.)

10.5.2.4 Spec(T)

An aspect of the definition of a Trust Domain is that all the elements in that domain are compliant to a set of configurations and specifications generally referred to as Spec(T). Spec(T) is not a specification in the sense of a written document; rather, it is an agreed-upon set of information that all elements are aware of. Proper processing of the asserted identities requires that the elements know what is actually being asserted, how it was determined, and what the privacy policies are. All of that information is characterized by Spec(T).

10.5.3 Generation of NAI

A NAI is generated by a network intermediary following an Authentication process that authenticates the entity (say, UA) to be identified. The Authentication processes used are a characteristic feature of the Trust Domain, and must be specified in Spec(T). It shall be possible for a UA to provide a preferred identity to the network intermediary, which may be used to inform the generation of the NAI according to the policies of the Trust Domain.

10.5.4 Transport of NAI

10.5.4.1 Sending of NAI within a Trust Domain

It shall be possible for one node within a Trust Domain to securely send a NAI to another node that it trusts.

10.5.4.2 Receiving of NAI within a Trust Domain

It shall be possible for one node within a Trust Domain to receive a NAI from another node that it trusts.

10.5.4.3 Sending of NAI to Entities outside the Trust Domain

If a node, A, within the Trust Domain, is trusted by a node, B, outside the Trust Domain, then it shall be possible for A to securely send a NAI to B, if allowed by the privacy policies of the user that has been identified, and the Trust Domain. This is most often used to pass a NAI directly to a UA.

10.5.4.4 Receiving of NAI by a Node outside the Trust Domain

It shall be possible for a node outside the Trust Domain to receive a NAI from a node that it trusts. NAI received in this way may be considered valid, and used for display to the user, input data for services, etc. NAI information received by one node from a node that it does not trust carries no guarantee of authenticity or integrity because it is not known that the procedures of Spec(T) were followed to generate and transport the information. Such information must not be used, that is, it shall not be displayed to the user, passed to other nodes, used as input data for services, and others.

10.5.5 Parties with NAIs

A NAI identifies the originator of the message in which it was received. For example, a NAI received in an initial INVITE (outside the context of any existing dialog) identifies the calling party.

- A NAI received in a 180 Ringing response to such an INVITE identifies the party who is ringing.
- A NAI received in a 200 response to such an INVITE identifies the party who has answered.

10.5.6 Types of NAI

It shall be possible to assert multiple identities associated with a given party (in a given message), provided that these are of distinct types. The types of identity supported shall be SIP, SIPS, and tel URIs, all of which identify the user as described earlier. It is not required to transport both a SIP and SIPS URI. It shall be possible for the capability to transport additional types of identity associated with a single party to be introduced in the future.

10.6 Summary

We have described the SIP user identity used over SIP networks that can be both public and private. In addition, we have described the NAI that is used over the private SIP network and is exchanged among the secure trusted SIP network intermediaries created by a trusted domain in accordance with the Spec(T). The three categories of private user identities defined are as follows: P-Asserted-Identity, P-Preferred-Identity, and Connected Identity. For NAI, we have defined the trusted domain, Spec(T), NAI generation, and different types of NAIs. Finally, we have explained the security implications for using both user identity and NAI over the SIP networks.

PROBLEMS

1. Why does a SIP user like to use multiple identities? Explain in detail using examples.
2. What is public user identity and how is it being used by a SIP user over the public Internet? Explain the public user identity using examples.
3. What are the definitions of the three categories of private user identities: P-Asserted-Identity, P-Preferred-Identity, and Connected Identity? How are these private user identities used by a SIP user over the private IP network? Explain these private user identities using examples.
4. What is the NAI? What is a Trust Domain? What is Spec(T)? How can the NAI be useful in creating a private Trust Domain over the private SIP network? Explain the NAI, Trust Domain, and Spect(T) using detailed examples.
5. How is a NAI generated? How is the NAI transported over the private SIP network considering the following: sending and receiving of NAI over a trusted domain, sending of NAI to entities outside a Trust Domain, and receiving of NAI by a node outside the Trust Domain? Explain using detailed examples.
6. How do parties with NAIs operate within the private SIP network? What are the different types of NAIs? What are the security implications for using NAIs?

Chapter 11

Early Media in SIP

Abstract

We describe early media in detail because it is an important feature for the Session Initiation Protocol (SIP) network for the generation of ringtone and others, for altering the SIP user before the establishment of the session. We explain the problems, including media clipping, that have been created by early media because of its peculiar behavior over the SIP network. A number of early-media solution models are discussed in dealing with its complicated characteristics based on the fact that it cannot be declined, modified, or identified by the receiving parties, or media and the codec of early media may not match at the receiving side as no negotiations are allowed. We also address the security implications of dealing with early media briefly, although more details about its security features are provided in Section 19.2.2.5.

11.1 Introduction

Early media refers to media, such as audio and video, that is exchanged between the callee and the caller before a particular session is accepted by the called party. Within a dialog, early media occurs from the moment the initial INVITE is sent until the user agent (UA) server (UAS) generates a final response. It may be unidirectional or bidirectional, and can be generated by the caller, the callee, or both. Typical examples of early media generated by the callee are ringing tone and announcements, for example, queuing status. Early media generated by the caller typically consists of voice commands or dual-tone multifrequency (Request for Comment [RFC] 4733, see Section 16.10) tones to drive interactive voice response (IVR) systems. The basic SIP specification of RFC 3261 only supports very simple early-media mechanisms. These simple mechanisms have a number of problems that relate to media clipping, forking, bandwidth availability, and security, and do not satisfy the requirements of most applications. Media clipping occurs when the user (or the machine generating media) believes that the media session is already established but the establishment process has not finished yet.

The user starts speaking (i.e., generating media), and the first few syllables or even the first few words are lost. Another form of media clipping (not related to early media either) occurs in the caller-to-callee direction. When the callee picks up and starts speaking, the UAS sends a 200 OK response with an answer, in parallel with the first media packets. If the first media packets arrive at the UA client (UAC) before the answer and the caller starts speaking, the UAC cannot send media until the 200 OK response from the UAS arrives. In the case of forking, the INVITE message of the caller is forked; it may also introduce media clipping. This happens when the UAC receives different answers to its offer in several provisional responses from different UASs, and the UAC needs to present it to the user. If the early media consists of audio, playing several audio streams to the user at the same time may be confusing. On the other hand, other media types (e.g., video) can be presented to the user at the same time. For example, the UAC can build a mosaic with the different inputs.

11.2 Early Media and Session Establishment in SIP

We need to understand the issues related to early media in the context of the session establishment in brief before presenting two early-media solutions. This will let us keep separate features that are intrinsic to SIP, for example, media being played before the 200 OK to avoid media clipping, from early-media operations. SIP uses the offer–answer model (RFC 3264, see Section 3.8.4) to negotiate session parameters. One of the UAs—the offerer—prepares a session description that is called the offer. The other UA—the answerer—responds with another session description called the answer. This two-way handshake allows both UAs to agree on the session parameters to be used to exchange media. The offer–answer model decouples the offer–answer exchange from the messages used to transport the session descriptions. For example, the offer can be sent in an INVITE request and the answer can arrive in the 200 OK response for that INVITE, or, alternatively, the offer can be sent in the 200 OK for an empty INVITE and the answer can be sent in the ACK. When reliable provisional responses (RFC 3262; see Sections 2.5, 2.8.2, and 2.10) and UPDATE requests (RFC 3311, see Section 3.8.3) are used, there are many more possible ways to exchange offers and answers.

Media clipping occurs when the user (or the machine generating media) believes that the media session is already established but the establishment process has not finished yet. The user starts speaking (i.e., generating media), and the first few syllables or even the first few words are lost. When the offer–answer exchange takes place in the 200 OK response and in the ACK, media clipping is unavoidable. The called user starts speaking at the same time the 200 OK is sent, but the UAS cannot send any media until the answer from the UAC arrives in the ACK. On the other hand, media clipping does not appear in the most common offer–answer exchange, for example, an INVITE with an offer and a 200 OK with an answer. UACs are ready to play incoming media packets as soon as they send an offer because they cannot count on the reception of the 200 OK to start playing out media for the caller; SIP signaling and media packets typically traverse different paths, and thus, media packets may arrive before the 200 OK response.

Another form of media clipping (not related to early media either) occurs in the caller-to-callee direction. When the callee picks up and starts speaking, the UAS sends a 200 OK response with an answer, in parallel with the first media packets. If the first media packets arrive at the UAC before the answer and the caller starts speaking, the UAC cannot send media until the 200 OK response from the UAS arrives. If the media starts flowing before the call establishment and the bandwidth is not reserved for supporting the media, there may not be enough bandwidth between the source and destination path to support the early media especially in the case of multiple early media flowing due to forking. An early-media-specific risk may be the attempts by attackers to exploit the different charging policies some operators apply to early and regular media. When UAs are allowed to exchange early media for free but are required to pay for regular media sessions, rogue UAs may try to establish a bidirectional early-media session and never send a 200 OK response for the INVITE.

11.3 Early-Media Solution Models

The peculiarity of early media is that it cannot be declined, modified, or identified by the receiving parties, or media and the codec of early media may not match at the receiving side as no negotiations are allowed. Over the years, a good number of solutions for these problems of early media have been proposed. However, two solutions, namely early media with early-session disposition type and early media with P-Early-Media header field described in RFC 3960 (see Section 11.4.7) and RFC 5009 (see Section 11.5), respectively, have emerged as good ones for solving the early-media problems in some closed networking environments, although these are not applicable in the Internet in general. We describe these two solution models in the subsequent sections:

- Early-Media Solution Model with Disposition-Type: Early-Session
- Early-Media Solution Model with P-Early-Media Header

11.4 Early-Media Solution Model with Disposition-Type: Early-Session

11.4.1 Overview

Early media refers to media (e.g., audio and video) that is exchanged before a particular session is accepted by the called user. Within a dialog, early media occurs from the moment the initial INVITE is sent until the UAS generates a final response. It may be unidirectional or bidirectional, and can be generated by the caller, the callee, or both. Typical examples of early media generated by the callee are ringing tone and announcements (e.g., queuing status). Early media generated by the caller typically consists of voice commands or dual-tone multifrequency (DTMF) tones to drive IVR systems. RFC 3959 that is described here defines a new disposition type (early-session) for the Content-Disposition header field in SIP for addressing the early-media solution. The treatment of *early-session* bodies is similar to the treatment of *session* bodies. That is, they follow the offer–answer model.

Their only difference is that session descriptions whose disposition type is *early-session* are used to establish early-media sessions within early dialogs, as opposed to regular sessions within regular dialogs. Although we are explaining the Disposition-Type: Early-Session extension here, we will be cross-referencing RFC 3960 (see Section 11.4.7) that provides the early-media solution models using this extension. The basic SIP specification described in RFC 3261 only supports very simple early-media mechanisms. These simple mechanisms have a number of problems related to forking and security, and do not satisfy the requirements of most applications. RFC 3960 (see Section 11.4.7), which uses this SIP extension, Disposition-Type: Early-Session by RFC 3959, goes beyond the mechanisms defined in RFC 3261 and describes two models of early media using SIP:

- Gateway model
- Application server model

Although both early-media models described in RFC 3960 are superior to the one specified in RFC 3261, the gateway model still presents a set of issues. In particular, the gateway model does not work well with forking. Nevertheless, the gateway model is needed because some SIP entities (in particular, some gateways) cannot implement the application server model. The application server model addresses some of the issues present in the gateway model. This model uses the early-session disposition type specified in this document.

11.4.2 Issues Related to Early-Media Session Establishment

Traditionally, early-media sessions have been established in the same way as regular sessions. That is, using an offer–answer exchange where the disposition type of the session descriptions is *session*. Application servers perform an offer–answer exchange with the UAC to exchange early media exclusively, while UASs use the same offer–answer exchange, first to exchange early media, and once the regular dialog is established, to exchange regular media. This way of establishing early-media sessions is known as the gateway model specified in RFC 3960 (see Section 11.4.7), which presents some issues related to forking and security. These issues exist when this model is used by either an application server or by a UAS. Application servers may not be able to generate an answer for an offer received in the INVITE. The UAC created the offer for the UAS, and thus, it may have applied end-to-end encryption or have included information (e.g., related to key management) that the application server is not supposed to use. Therefore, application servers need a means to perform an offer–answer exchange with the UAC that is independent from the offer–answer exchange between both UAs.

UASs using the offer–answer exchange that will carry regular media for sending and receiving early media can cause media clipping described in RFC 3960 (see Section 11.4.7). Some UACs cannot receive early media from different UASs at the same time. Thus, when an INVITE forks and several UASs start sending early media, the UAC mutes all the UASs but one (which is usually chosen at random). If the UAS that accepts the INVITE (i.e., sends a 200 OK) was muted, a new offer–answer exchange is needed to unmute it. This usually causes media clipping. Therefore, UASs need a means of performing an offer–answer exchange with the UAC to exchange early media that is independent from the offer–answer exchanged used to exchange regular media. A potential solution to this need would be to establish a different dialog using a globally routable Uniform Resource Identifier (URI) to perform an independent offer–answer exchange. This dialog would be labeled as a dialog for early media and would be somehow related to the original dialog at the UAC. However, performing all the offer–answer exchanges within the original dialog has many advantages:

- It is simpler.
- It does not have synchronization problems because all the early dialogs are terminated when the session is accepted.
- It does not require globally routable URIs.
- It does not introduce service interaction issues related to services that may be wrongly applied to the new dialog.
- It makes firewall management easier.

This way of performing offer–answer exchanges for early media is referred to as the application server model specified in RFC 3960 (see Section 11.4.7). This model uses the early-session disposition type defined in the following section.

11.4.3 Early-Session Disposition Type

We define a new disposition type for the Content-Disposition header field: early-session. UAs must use early-session bodies to establish early-media sessions in the same way as they use session bodies to establish regular sessions, as described in RFCs 3261 and 3264 (see Section 3.8.4). Particularly, early-session bodies must follow the offer–answer model and may appear in the same messages as session bodies do with the exceptions of 2xx responses for an INVITE and ACKs. Nevertheless, it is not recommended that early offers in INVITEs be included because they can fork, and the UAC could receive multiple early answers establishing early-media streams at roughly the same time. Also, the use of the same transport address (Internet Protocol [IP] address plus port) in a session body and in an early-session body is not recommended. Using different transport addresses (e.g., different ports) to receive early and regular media makes it easy to detect the start of the regular media.

If a UA needs to refuse an early-session offer, it must do so by refusing all the media streams in it. When Session Description Protocol (SDP) (see Section 7.7) is used, this is done by setting the port number of all the media streams to zero. This is the same mechanism that UACs use to refuse regular offers that arrive in a response to an empty INVITE. An early-media session established using early-session bodies must be terminated when its corresponding early dialog is terminated or it transitions to a regular dialog. It is recommended that UAs generating regular and early-session descriptions use, as long as it is possible, the same codecs in both. This way, the remote UA does not need to change codecs when the early-session transitions to a regular session.

11.4.4 Preconditions

RFC 3312 (see Section 15.4) defines a framework for preconditions for SDP. Early sessions may contain preconditions, which are treated in the same way as preconditions in regular sessions. That is, the UAs do not exchange media, and the called user is not alerted until the preconditions are met.

11.4.5 Option Tag

We define an option tag to be used in the Require and Supported header fields: early-session. A UA adding the early-session option tag to a message indicates that it understands the early-session disposition type.

11.4.6 Example

Figure 11.1 shows the message flow between two UAs. INVITE (F1) has an early-session option tag in its Supported header field and the body shown in Figure 11.2. The UAS sends back a response with two body parts, as shown in Figure 11.3: one of disposition-type session and the other early-session. The session body part is the answer to the offer

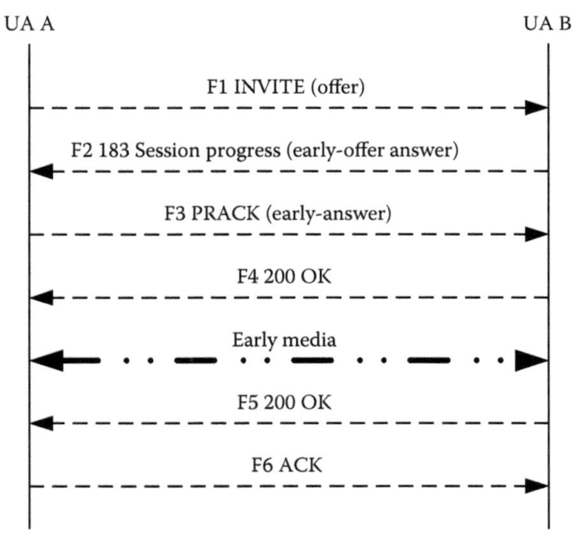

Figure 11.1 Message flow. (Copyright IETF. Reproduced with permission.)

```
Content-Type: application/sdp
Content-Disposition: session
v=0
o=alice 2890844730 2890844731 IN IP4 host.example.com
s=
c=IN IP4 192.0.2.1
t=0 0
m=audio 20000 RTP/AVP 0
```

Figure 11.2 Offer.

```
Content-Type: multipart/mixed; boundary="boundary1"
Content-Length: 401
--boundary1
Content-Type: application/sdp
Content-Disposition: session
v=0
o=Bob 2890844725 2890844725 IN IP4 host.example.org
s=
c=IN IP4 192.0.2.2
t=0 0
m=audio 30000 RTP/AVP 0
--boundary1
Content-Type: application/sdp
Content-Disposition: early-session
v=0
o=Bob 2890844714 2890844714 IN IP4 host.example.org
s=
c=IN IP4 192.0.2.2
t=0 0
m=audio 30002 RTP/AVP 0
--boundary1--
```

Figure 11.3 Early offer and answer.

```
Content-Type: application/sdp
Content-Disposition: early-session
v=0
o=alice 2890844717 2890844717 IN IP4 host.example.com
s=
c=IN IP4 192.0.2.1
t=0 0
m=audio 20002 RTP/AVP 0
```

Figure 11.4 Early answer.

in the INVITE. The early-session body part is an offer to establish an early-media session. When the UAC receives the 183 Session Progress response, it sends the answer to the early-session offer in a PRACK, as shown in Figure 11.4. This early-media session is terminated when the early dialog transitions to a regular dialog.

11.4.7 Early-Media Solution with Application Server and Gateway Model

The early-media model that uses the SIP extension of Content-Disposition: Early-Session solves most of the issues related to the early media. RFC 3960 that is described here provides much superior mechanisms for early media to those defined in RFC 3261, and describes two models of early-media implementations using SIP:

- **Application server model:** The UAC indicates support for the early-session disposition type defined in RFC 3959 using the early-session option tag. The application server model consists of having the UAS behave as an application server to establish early-media sessions with the UAC. The application server model addresses solves most of the early-media-related problems.
- **Gateway model:** The gateway model does not need any extension in SIP. Unlike the application server model, it does not even need to use the early-session disposition type. As a result, unlike the application server model, the gateway model cannot solve many of the issues related to forking and ringtone generation of early media. The gateway model is primarily applicable in situations where the UA cannot distinguish between early media and regular media, as in the case of devices like IP–public switched telephone network (IP–PSTN) gateway that supports SIP over the IP side and ISUP (Integrated Services Digital Network User Part) over the PSTN side. The IP–PSTN gateway receives media from the PSTN over a circuit, and sends it to the IP network. The gateway is not aware of the contents of the media, and it does not exactly know when the transition from early to regular media takes place. From the PSTN perspective, the circuit is a continuous source of media.

11.4.7.1 Application Server Model

The application server model consists of having the UAS behave as an application server to establish early-media sessions with the UAC. As described earlier, the UAC indicates support for the early-session disposition type using the early-session option tag. This way, UASs know that they can keep offer–answer exchanges for early media, Content-Disposition: Early-Session, separate from regular media using a different session disposition type for the early media. It requires an option tag to be used in the Require and Supported header fields: early-session. A UA adding the early-session option tag to a message indicates that it understands the early-session disposition type. Sending early media using a different offer–answer exchange than the one used for sending regular media helps avoid media clipping in cases of forking. The UAC can reject or mute new offers for early media without muting the sessions that will carry media when the original INVITE is accepted. The UAC can give priority to media received over the latter sessions. This way, the application server model transitions from early to regular media at the right moment.

Having a separate offer–answer exchange for early media also helps UACs decide whether or not local ringing should be generated. If a new early session is established and that early session contains at least an audio stream, the UAC can assume that there will be incoming early media and it can then avoid generating local ringing. An alternative model would include the addition of a new stream, with an *early media* label, to the original session between the UAC and the UAS using an UPDATE instead of establishing a new early session. We have chosen to establish a new early session to be coherent with the mechanism used by application servers that are not colocated with the UAS. This way, the UAS uses the same mechanism as any application server in the network to interact with the UAC.

11.4.7.1.1 In-Band versus Out-of-Band Session Progress Information

It should be noted that, even when the application server model is used, a UA will have to choose which early-media sessions are muted and which ones are rendered to the user. To make this choice easier for UAs, it is strongly recommended that information that is not essential for the session not be transmitted using early media. For instance, UAs should not use early media to send special ringing tones. The status code and the reason phrase in SIP can already inform the remote user about the progress of session establishment, without incurring the problems associated with early media.

11.4.7.1.2 Alert-Info Header Field

The Alert-Info header field allows specifying an alternative ringing content, such as ringing tone, to the UAC. This header field tells the UAC which tone should be played in case local ringing is generated; however, it does not tell the UAC when to generate local ringing. A UAC should follow the rules described above for ringing tone generation in both models. If, after following those rules, the UAC decides to play local ringing, it can then use the Alert-Info header field to generate it.

11.4.7.1.3 Security Considerations

All media-related security features defined in SIP are also applicable for the early media. An early-media-specific risk roughly equivalent to forms of *toll fraud* as described earlier may be attempted by attackers due to the different charging policies by the service providers differentiating between early media and regular media. For example, if the charging policy states that the early media is free while the regular media is chargeable during the session, rogue UAs may try to establish a bidirectional early-media session and never send a 200 OK response for the INVITE. On the other hand, some application servers (e.g., IVR systems) use bidirectional early media to obtain information from the callers (e.g., the PIN code of a calling card). Thus, it is not recommended that operators disallow bidirectional early media. Instead, operators should consider a remedy of charging early-media exchanges that last too long, or stopping them at the media level (according to the operator's policy).

11.4.7.1.4 Limitations in Application Server Model

If the unknown, untrusted network or network with different early-media policies is connected to a private SIP network of a managed administrative domain (e.g., Third Generation Partnership Project's Internet Multimedia System [3GPP's IMS] network) via a gateway and the gateway becomes the primary requestor of early media over this managed SIP network, the application server model cannot be used for early media. In this situation, the P-Early-Media header-based early model described later can be used within a transitive Trust Domain.

11.4.7.2 Gateway Model

The gateway model does not use any SIP signaling indication for early media as described earlier because unintelligent gateways like IP–PSTN cannot differentiate between the early media and the regular media. Although both early-media models described in this document are superior to the one specified in RFC 3261, the gateway model still presents a set of issues. In particular, the gateway model does not work well with forking. Nevertheless, the gateway model is needed because some SIP entities (in particular, some gateways) cannot implement the application server model. SIP uses the offer–answer model to negotiate session parameters as described earlier. An offer–answer exchange that takes place before a final response for the INVITE is sent establishes an *early* media session.

Early-media sessions terminate when a final response for the INVITE is sent. If the final response is a 200 OK, the early-media session transitions to a regular media session. If the final response is a non-200 class final response, the early-media session is simply terminated. Not surprisingly, media exchanged within an early-media session is referred to as early media. The gateway model consists of managing early-media sessions using offer–answer exchanges in reliable provisional responses, PRACKs, and UPDATEs. The gateway model is seriously limited in the presence of forking, as described in the following section. Therefore, its use is only acceptable when the UA cannot distinguish between early and regular media, as described later. In any other situation (the majority of UAs), use of the application server model described earlier is strongly recommended instead.

11.4.7.2.1 Forking

In the absence of forking, assuming that the initial INVITE contains an offer, the gateway model does not introduce media clipping. Following normal SIP procedures, the UAC is ready to play any incoming media as soon as it sends the initial offer in the INVITE. The UAS sends the answer in a reliable provisional response and can send media as soon as there is media to send. Even if the first media packets arrive at the UAC before the 1xx response, the UAC will play them. It should be noted that, in some situations, the UAC needs to receive the answer before being able to play any media. UAs in such a situation (e.g., quality of service, media authorization, or media encryption is required) use preconditions (RFC 4032, see Section 15.4.12) to avoid media clipping. On the other hand, if the INVITE forks, the gateway model may introduce media clipping. This happens when the UAC receives different answers to its offer in several provisional responses from different UASs. The UAC has to deal with bandwidth limitations and early-media session selection.

If the UAC receives early media from different UASs, it needs to present it to the user. If the early media consists of audio, playing several audio streams to the user at the same time may be confusing. On the other hand, other media types (e.g., video) can be presented to the user at the same time. For example, the UAC can build a mosaic with the different inputs. However, even with media types that can be played at the same time to the user, if the UAC has limited bandwidth, it will not be able to receive early media from all the different UASs at the same time. Therefore, many times, the UAC needs to choose a single early-media session and *mute* those sending UPDATE requests. It is difficult to decide which early-media sessions carry more important information from the caller's perspective. In fact, in some scenarios, the UA cannot even correlate media packets with their particular SIP early dialog. Therefore, UACs typically pick one early dialog randomly and mute the rest.

If one of the early-media sessions that was muted transitions to a regular media session (i.e., the UAS sends a 2xx response), media clipping is likely. The UAC typically sends an UPDATE with a new offer (upon reception of the 200 OK for the INVITE) to unmute the media session. The UAS cannot send any media until it receives the offer from the UAC. Therefore, if the caller starts speaking before the offer from the UAC is received, his words will get lost. Having the UAS send the UPDATE to unmute the media session (instead of the UAC) does not avoid media clipping in the backward direction, and it causes possible race conditions.

11.4.7.2.2 Ringing-Tone Generation

In the PSTN, telephone switches typically play ringing tones for the caller, indicating that the callee is being alerted.

When, where, and how these ringing tones are generated has been standardized (i.e., the local exchange of the callee generates a standardized ringing tone while the callee is being alerted). It makes sense for a standardized approach to provide this type of feedback for the user in a homogeneous environment such as the PSTN, where all the terminals have a similar user interface. This homogeneity is not found among SIP UAs. SIP UAs have different capabilities, different user interfaces, and may be used to establish sessions that do not involve audio at all. Because of this, the way a SIP UA provides the user with information about the progress of session establishment is a matter of local policy. For example, a UA with a Graphical User Interface (GUI) may choose to display a message on the screen when the callee is being alerted, while another UA may choose to show a picture of a phone ringing instead. Many SIP UAs choose to imitate the user interface of PSTN phones.

They provide a ringing tone to the caller when the callee is being alerted. Such a UAC is supposed to generate ringing tones locally for its user as long as no early media is received from the UAS. If the UAS generates early media (e.g., an announcement or a special ringing tone), the UAC is supposed to play it rather than generate the ringing tone locally. The problem is that, sometimes, it is not an easy task for a UAC to know whether it will be receiving early media or it should generate local ringing. A UAS can send early media without using reliable provisional responses (very simple UASs do that), or it can send an answer in a reliable provisional response without any intention of sending early media (this is the case when preconditions are used). Therefore, by only looking at the SIP signaling, a UAC cannot be sure whether there will be early media for a particular session. The UAC needs to check if media packets are arriving at a given moment. An implementation could even choose to look at the contents of the media packets, since they could carry only silence or comfort noise. With this in mind, a UAC should develop its local policy regarding local ringing generation. For example, a POTS (Plain Old Telephone Service)-like SIP UA could implement the following local policy:

- Unless a 180 Ringing response is received, never generate local ringing.
- If a 180 Ringing has been received but there are no incoming media packets, generate local ringing.
- If a 180 Ringing has been received and there are incoming media packets, play them and do not generate local ringing.

Note that a 180 Ringing response means that the callee is being alerted, and a UAS should send such a response if the callee is being alerted, regardless of the status of the early-media session. At first sight, such a policy may look difficult to implement in decomposed UAs (i.e., media gateway controller and media gateway); however, this policy is the same as the one described earlier, which must be implemented by any UA. That is, any UA should play incoming media packets (and stop local ringing tone generation if it was being performed) to avoid media clipping, even if the 200 OK response has not arrived. Thus, the tools to implement this early-media policy are already available to any UA that uses SIP.

Furthermore, while it is not desirable to standardize a common local policy to be followed by every SIP UA, a particular subset of more or less homogeneous SIP UAs could use the same local policy by convention. Examples of such subsets of SIP UAs may be "all the PSTN/SIP gateways" or "every 3GPP IMS terminal." However, defining the particular common policy that such groups of SIP devices may use is outside the scope of this document.

11.4.7.2.3 Absence of an Early-Media Indicator

The SIP, as opposed to other signaling protocols, does not provide an early-media indicator. That is, there is no information about the presence or absence of early media in SIP. Such an indicator could be potentially used to avoid the generation of local ringing tone by the UAC when UAS intends to provide an in-band ringing tone or some type of announcement. However, in the majority of the cases, such an indicator would be of little use due to the way SIP works.

One important reason limiting the benefit of a potential early-media indicator is the loose coupling between SIP signaling and the media path. SIP signaling traverses a different path than the media. The media path is typically optimized to reduce the end-to-end delay (e.g., minimum number of intermediaries), while the SIP signaling path typically traverses a number of proxies providing different services for the session. Hence, it is very likely that the media packets with early media reach the UAC before any SIP message that could contain an early-media indicator.

Nevertheless, sometimes SIP responses arrive at the UAC before any media packet. There are situations in which the UAS intends to send early media but cannot do it straight away. For example, UAs using Interactive Connectivity Establishment (RFC 5245, see Section 14.3) may need to exchange several Session Traversal of UDP through NAT (Network Address Translation) (STUN) (RFC 5389, see Section 14.3) messages before being able to exchange media. In this situation, an early-media indicator would keep the UAC from generating a local ringing tone during this time. However, while the early media is not arriving at the UAC, the user would not be aware that the remote user is being alerted, even though a 180 Ringing had been received. Therefore, a better solution would be to apply a local ringing tone until the early-media packets could be sent from the UAS to the UAC. This solution does not require any early-media indicator. Moreover, it should be noted that migrations from local ringing tone to early media at the UAC happen in the presence of forking as well; one UAS sends a 180 Ringing response, and later, another UAS starts sending early media.

11.4.7.2.4 Limitations of the Gateway Model

Most of the limitations of the gateway model are described earlier. It produces media clipping in forking scenarios and requires media detection to generate local ringing properly. These issues are addressed by the application server model, described earlier, which is the recommended way of generating early media that is not continuous with the regular media generated during the session. The gateway model allows for individual networks to create local policy with respect to the handling of early media, but does not address the case where a network is interconnected with other networks with unknown, untrusted, or different early-media policies. In this situation, the P-Early-Media header-based model described in RFC 5009 (Section 11.5) becomes a natural extension of this gateway model that is applicable within a transitive Trust Domain.

11.5 Early-Media Solution Model with P-Early-Media Header

Like the earlier model, early media with the P-Early-Media header model also provides the solution for early media in a closed SIP network (e.g., 3GPP's IMS network) under the same administrative domain, and does not need to use the Disposition-Type: Early-Media option tag, as explained earlier. This header field is also useful in any SIP network that is interconnected with other SIP networks and needs to control the flow of media in the early dialog state. This document defines the use of the P-Early-Media header field for use within SIP (RFC 3261) messages in certain SIP networks to authorize the cut-through of backward or forward early media when permitted by the early-media policies of the networks involved.

11.5.1 Early-Media Policy

The private P-Early-Media header field is intended for use in a SIP network that has the following characteristics:

- Its early-media policy prohibits the exchange of early media between end users.
- It is interconnected with other SIP networks that have unknown, untrusted, or different policies regarding early media.
- It has the capability to *gate* (enable/disable) the flow of early media to/from user equipment.

Within an isolated SIP network, it is possible to gate early media associated with all end points within the network to enforce a desired early-media policy among network end points. However, when a SIP network is interconnected with other SIP networks, only the boundary node connected to the external network can determine which early-media policy to apply to a session established between end points on different sides of the boundary. The P-Early-Media header field provides a means for this boundary node to communicate this early-media policy decision to other nodes within the network.

11.5.2 Early-Media Application Environments

The P-Early-Media header of SIP can only be applied in closed networking environments. For example, a private SIP network that emulates a traditional circuit switched telephone network will benefit from using this header field. Despite the limitations, there are sufficiently useful specialized deployments for the use of P-Early-Media in SIP networks under the following networking conditions:

1. The use of this private P-Early-Media header field is only applicable inside a Trust Domain as defined in RFC 3324 (see Section 10.5). Nodes in such a Trust Domain are explicitly trusted by its users and end systems to authorize early-media requests only when allowed by the early-media policy within the Trust Domain.
2. The private P-Early-Media header field cannot be applied for a general early-media authorization communications model suitable for interdomain use or use in the Internet at large. Furthermore, since the early-media requests are not cryptographically certified, they are subject to forgery, replay, and falsification in any architecture that does not meet the requirements of the Trust Domain.
3. An early-media request also lacks an indication of who specifically is making or modifying the request, and so it must be assumed that the Trust Domain is making the request. Therefore, the information is only meaningful when securely received from a node known to be a member of the Trust Domain.
4. Although this extension can be used with parallel forking, it does not improve on the known problems with early-media and parallel forking, as described in RFC 3960, unless one can assume the use of symmetric RTP.

11.5.3 Early-Media Authorization

PSTN networks typically provide call progress information as backward early media from the terminating switch toward the calling party. PSTN networks also use forward early media from the calling party toward the terminating switch under some circumstances for applications, such as digit collection for secondary dialing. PSTN networks typically allow backward or forward early media since they are used for the purpose of progressing the call to the answer state and do not involve the exchange of data between end points.

In a SIP network, backward early media flows from the UAS toward the UAC. Forward early media flows from the UAC toward the UAS. SIP networks by default allow both forms of early media, which may carry user data, once the media path is established. Early media is typically desirable with a PSTN gateway as UAS, but not with SIP user equipment as UAS.

To prevent the exchange of user data within early media while allowing early media via PSTN gateways, a SIP network may have a policy to prohibit backward early media from SIP user equipment and to prohibit forward media toward SIP user equipment, either of which may contain user data. A SIP network containing both PSTN gateways and SIP end devices, for example, can maintain such an early-media policy by gating *off* any early media with a SIP end device acting as UAS, gating *on* early media with a SIP end device acting as UAC, and gating *on* early media at each PSTN gateway.

Unfortunately, a SIP network interconnected with another SIP network may have no means of assuring that the interconnected network is implementing a compatible early-media policy, thus allowing the exchange of user data within early media under some circumstances. For example, if a network A allows all early media with user equipment as UAC and an interconnected network B allows all early media with user equipment as UAS, any session established between user equipment as UAC in A and user equipment as UAS in B will allow bidirectional user data exchange as early media. Other combinations of early-media policies may also produce similar undesirable results. The purpose of the P-Early-Media header is to allow a SIP network interconnected to other SIP networks with different early-media policies to correctly identify and enable authorized early media according to its policies.

11.5.3.1 Backward Early Media

Backward early media in the PSTN typically comprises call progress information, such as ringing feedback (*ringback*), or announcements regarding special handling such as forwarding. It may also include requests for further information, such as a credit card number to be entered as forward early media in the form of DTMF tones or speech. Backward early media of this type provides information to the calling party strictly for the purpose of indicating that the call is progressing and involves no exchange of data between end users. The usual PSTN charging policy assumes that no data is exchanged between users until the call has been answered.

A terminating SIP UA outside of the SIP network, on the other hand, may provide any user data in a backward early-media stream. Thus, if the network implements the usual early-media policy, the network equipment gating the backward early-media flow for the originating UA must distinguish between authorized early media from a terminating SIP end point and unauthorized early media from another SIP device outside of the network. Given the assumption of a transitive trust relationship between SIP servers in the network, this can be accomplished by including some information in a backward SIP message that identifies the presence of authorized backward early media.

Since it is necessary to verify that this indication comes from a trusted source, it is necessary for each server on the path back to the originating UA to be able to verify the trust relationship with the previous server and to remove such an indication when it cannot do so. A server on the boundary to an untrusted SIP network can assure that no indication of authorized backward early media passes from an external UAS to a UAC within the network. Thus, the use of a private header field that can be modified by SIP proxies is to be preferred over the use of a Multipurpose Internet Mail Extensions attachment that cannot be modified in this way.

11.5.3.2 Forward Early Media

Forward early media is less common than backward early media in the PSTN. It is typically used to collect secondary dialed digits, to collect credit card numbers, or to collect other DTMF or speech responses for the purpose of further directing the call. Forward early media in the PSTN is always directed toward a network server for the purpose of indicating that a call is progressing and involves no exchange of data between end users.

A terminating SIP UA outside of the SIP network, on the other hand, may receive any user data in a forward early-media stream. Thus, if the network implements the usual early-media policy, the network equipment gating the forward early-media flow for the originating UA must distinguish between a terminating end point that is authorized to receive forward early media, and another SIP device outside of the network that is not authorized to receive forward early media containing user data. This authorization can be accomplished in the same manner as for backward early media by including some information in a backward SIP message that identifies that the terminating side is authorized to receive forward early media.

11.5.4 Applicability of Content-Disposition and Application/Gateway Model

The private P-Early-Media header can be applicable to the gateway model defined in RFC 3960 (see Section 11.4.7), since the PSTN gateway is the primary requestor of early media in a private SIP network of a given administrative domain (e.g., 3GPP's IMS network). For the same reason, neither the application server model of RFC 3960, nor the early-session disposition type defined in RFC 3959 (see Section 11.4) is applicable in this situation. The gateway model of RFC 3960 allows for individual networks to create local policy with respect to the handling of early media, but does not address the case where a network is interconnected with other networks with unknown, untrusted, or different early-media policies. In this communications environment, the P-Early-Media header like this is essential. Because without the kind of information in the P-Early-Media header field, it is not possible for the network to determine whether cut-through of early media could lead to the transfer of data between end users during session establishment. Thus, the P-Early-Media header is a natural extension of the gateway model of RFC 3960 that is applicable within a transitive Trust Domain.

11.5.5 Operation

The P-Early-Media header field is used for the purpose of requesting and authorizing requests for backward or forward early media. A UAC capable of recognizing the P-Early-Media header field may include the header field in an INVITE request. The P-Early-Media header field in an INVITE request contains the *supported* parameter. As members of the Trust Domain, each proxy receiving an INVITE request must decide whether to insert or delete the P-Early-Media header field before forwarding. A UAS receiving an INVITE request can use the presence of the P-Early-Media header field in the request to decide whether to request early-media authorization in subsequent messages toward the UAC.

After receiving an incoming INVITE request, the UAS requesting backward or forward early media will include the P-Early-Media header field in a message toward the UAC within the dialog, including direction parameter(s) that identify for each media line in the session whether the early-media request is for backward media, forward media, both, or neither. The UAS can change its request for early media by including a modified P-Early-Media header field in a subsequent message toward the UAC within the dialog. Each proxy in the network receiving the P-Early-Media header field in a message toward the UAC has the responsibility of assuring that the early-media request comes from an authorized source. If a P-Early-Media header field arrives from either an untrusted source, a source not allowed to send backward early media, or a source not allowed to receive forward early media, then the proxy may remove the P-Early-Media header field or alter the direction parameter(s) of the P-Early-Media header field before forwarding the message, based on local policy.

A proxy in the network not receiving the P-Early-Media header field in a message toward the UAC may insert one based on local policy. If the proxy also performs gating of early media, then it uses the parameter(s) of the P-Early-Media header field to decide whether to open or close the gates for backward and forward early-media flow(s) between the UAs. The proxy performing gating of early media may also add a *gated* parameter to the P-Early-Media header field before forwarding the message so that other gating proxies in the path can choose to leave open their gates.

If the UAC is a trusted server within the network (e.g., a PSTN gateway), then the UAC may use the parameter(s) of the P-Early-Media header field in messages received from the UAS to decide whether to perform early-media gating or cut-through, and to decide whether to render backward early media in preference to generating ringback based on the receipt of a 180 Ringing response. If the UAC is associated with user equipment, then the network will have assigned a proxy the task of performing early-media gating, so that the parameter(s) of the P-Early-Media header field received at such a UAC do not require that the UAC police the early-media flow(s); however, they do provide additional information that the UAC may use to render media. The UAC and proxies in the network may also insert, delete, or modify the P-Early-Media header field in messages toward the UAS within the dialog according to local policy; however, the interpretation of the header field when used in this way is a matter of local policy and not defined herein. The use of direction parameter(s) in this header field could be used to inform the UAS of the final early-media authorization status.

11.5.6 Limitations of the P-Early-Media Header Field

The P-Early-Media header field does not apply to any SDP with Content-Disposition: Early-Session defined in RFC 3959 (see Section 11.4). When parallel forking occurs, there is no reliable way to correlate early-media authorization in a dialog with the media from the corresponding end point unless one can assume the use of symmetric RTP, since the SDP messages do not identify the RTP source address of any media stream. When a UAC or proxy receives multiple early dialogs and cannot accurately identify the source of each media stream, it should use the most restrictive early-media authorization it receives on any of the dialogs to decide the policy to apply toward all received media.

When early-media usage is desired for any reason and one cannot assume the use of symmetric RTP, it is advisable to disable parallel forking using caller preferences defined in RFC 3841. Although the implementation of media gating is not defined in this specification (RFC 5009), note that media gating must be implemented carefully in the presence of NATs and protocols that aid in network address translation traversal. Media gating may also introduce a potential for media clipping that is similar to that created during parallel forking or any other feature that may disable early media, such as custom ringback.

11.5.7 P-Early-Media Header Field

The private P-Early-Media header field with the supported parameter may be included in an INVITE request to indicate that the UAC or a proxy on the path recognizes the header field. This header is not used in the Internet. A network entity may request the authorization of early media or change a request for authorization of early media by including the P-Early-Media header field in any message allowed by Table 2.5, Section 2.8, within the dialog toward the sender of the INVITE request. The P-Early-Media header field includes one or more direction parameters where each has one of the values sendrecv, sendonly, recvonly, or inactive, following the convention used for the SDP stream directionality of RFCs 3264 (see Section 3.8.4) and 4566 (see Section 7.7).

Each parameter applies, in order, to the media lines in the corresponding SDP messages establishing session media. Unrecognized parameters shall be silently discarded. Nondirection parameters are ignored for purposes of early-media authorization. If there are more direction parameters than media lines, the excess shall be silently discarded. If there are fewer direction parameters than media lines, the value of the last direction parameter shall apply to all remaining media lines. A message directed toward the UAC containing a P-Early-Media header field with no recognized direction parameters shall not be interpreted as an early-media authorization request.

The parameter value sendrecv indicates a request for authorization of early media associated with the corresponding media line, both from the UAS toward the UAC and from the UAC toward the UAS (both backward and forward early media). The value sendonly indicates a request for authorization of early media from the UAS toward the UAC (backward early media), and not in the other direction. The value recvonly indicates a request for authorization of early media from the UAC toward the UAS (forward early media), and not in the other direction. The value inactive indicates either a request that no early media associated with the corresponding media line be authorized, or a request for revocation of authorization of previously authorized early media. The P-Early-Media header field in any message within a dialog toward the sender of the INVITE request may also include the nondirection parameter gated to indicate that a network entity on the path toward the UAS is already gating the early media, according to the direction parameter(s). When included in the P-Early-Media header field, the gated parameter shall come after all direction parameters in the parameter list.

When receiving a message directed toward the UAC without the P-Early-Media header field and no previous early-media authorization request has been received within the dialog, the default early-media authorization depends on local policy and may depend on whether the header field was included in the INVITE request. After an early-media authorization request has been received within a dialog, and a subsequent message is received without the P-Early-Media header field, the previous early-media authorization remains unchanged. The P-Early-Media header field in any message within a dialog toward the UAS may be ignored or interpreted according to local policy.

The P-Early-Media header field does not interact with SDP offer–answer procedures in any way. Early-media authorization is not influenced by the state of the SDP offer–answer procedures (including preconditions and directionality) and does not influence the state of the SDP offer–answer procedures. The P-Early-Media header field may or may not be present in messages containing SDP. The most recently received early-media authorization applies to the corresponding media line in the session established for the dialog until receipt of the 200 OK response to the INVITE request, at which point all media lines in the session are implicitly authorized. Early-media flow in a particular direction requires that early media in that direction is authorized, that media flow in that direction is enabled by the SDP direction attribute for the stream, and that any applicable preconditions RFC 3312 (see Section 15.4) are met. Early-media authorization does not override the SDP direction attribute or preconditions state, and the SDP direction attribute does not override early-media authorization.

11.5.7.1 Procedures at the UAC

A UAC may include the P-Early-Media header field with the supported parameter in an INVITE request to indicate that it recognizes the header field. A UAC receiving a P-Early-Media header field may use the parameter(s) of the header field to gate or cut-through early media, and to decide whether to render early media from the UAS to the UAC in preference to any locally generated ringback triggered by a 180 Ringing response. If a proxy is providing the early-media gating function for the UAC, then the gateway model of RFC 3960 for rendering of early media is applicable. A UAC without a proxy in the network performing early-media gating that receives a P-Early-Media header field should perform gating or cut-through of early media according to the parameter(s) of the header field.

11.5.7.2 Procedures at the UAS

A UAS that is requesting authorization to send or receive early media may insert a P-Early-Media header field with appropriate parameters(s) in any message allowed in Tables 2.5 and 2.10 (see Section 2.8) toward the UAC within the dialog.

A UAS may request changes in early-media authorization by inserting a P-Early-Media header field with appropriate parameter(s) in any subsequent message allowed in Tables 2.5 and 2.10 (see Section 2.8) toward the UAC within the dialog. If the P-Early-Media header field is not present in the INVITE request, the UAS may choose to suppress early-media authorization requests and may choose to execute alternate early-media procedures.

11.5.7.3 Procedures at the Proxy

When forwarding an INVITE request, a proxy may add, retain, or delete the P-Early-Media header field, depending on local policy and the trust relationship with the sender or receiver of the request. When forwarding a message allowed in Tables 2.5 and 2.10 (see Section 2.8) toward the UAC, a proxy may add, modify, or delete a P-Early-Media header field, depending on local policy and the trust relationship with the sender or receiver of the message. In addition, if the proxy controls the gating of early media for the UAC, it should use the contents of the P-Early-Media header field to gate the early media, according to the definitions of the header field parameters defined earlier.

11.6 Summary

We have explained in detail the characteristics of early media that can be offered over the SIP network. A variety of early-media services can be provided over the SIP network such as ringtone, announcement, video messages, and others. It is described how the peculiar behavior of early media has created a number of problems, including media clipping. Moreover, early media can be forked by SIP proxies, which aggravates the problems further. A number of solutions have been articulated for early media, and the pros and cons of each model are described. In addition, the security aspects of early media are briefly addressed here, although more details can be found in Section 19.2.2.5.

PROBLEMS

1. What is early media? Why is it needed? What can be the forms of early-media services over the SIP network? Which characteristics of early media are considered peculiar?
2. What are the problems created by early-media services over the SIP network, including forking of early media? Explain in detail with examples using SIP call flows that also include media clipping caused by early media.
3. What is the early-media solution model with Disposition-Type: Early-Session? How does this model solve the early-media session establishment problems? What are the limitations of this model? How are the security issues resolved with the solution model? Explain with detailed examples using SIP call flows.
4. What is the early-media application server solution? Explain in detail using SIP call flows. What are the security implications of this solution model? What are the limitations of this model? Explain with detailed examples using SIP call flows.
5. What is the early-media gateway solution model? Explain in detail using SIP call flows. What are the security implications of this solution model, if any? What are the limitations of this model? Explain with detailed examples using SIP call flows.
6. How do the early-media policy and application environments affect the P-Early-Media SIP header solution model? How does this model provide early-media authorization?
7. What is the early media P-Early-Media SIP header solution model? Explain in detail using SIP call flows.
8. How is the early-media disposition type and application/gateway solution model applicable to the P-Early-Media solution model? Explain with detailed examples using SIP call flows.
9. What are the security implications of this solution model? What are the limitations of this model? Explain with detailed examples using SIP call flows.

Chapter 12

Service and Served-User Identity in SIP

Abstract

We describe the service identification (ID) that represents services that cannot be standardized directly for the public Internet at large. We explain the creation of service IDs using some canonical forms based on some hints of services that can be obtained indirectly knowing the user-level service-agnostic Session Initiation Protocol (SIP) signaling messages. In this connection, we explain the service Uniform Resource Names, asserted-services, and preferred-service IDs that can privately be used for identification of services over the SIP network. In addition, the served-user IDs that are used for handling of services are articulated.

12.1 Introduction

Any service identification (ID) is a user-level representation of services, and the Session Initiation Protocol (SIP) signaling messages are used for invoking those services. However, the SIP signaling itself is user-level service agnostic. The interpretations of services knowing the hints of the SIP signaling messages either from the header or from the message body are not standardized and are subject to controversies. New real-time and near-real-time services are emerging at a very high rate, and a new horizon of future services that are yet to be imagined will be coming in full force. It is a perilous situation to deal with service IDs and the processing of those user-level services through interpretations of some service IDs. Some guidelines are provided in Request for Comment (RFC) 5897 (Sections 12.1 through 12.3) in this direction for the creation of service IDs and processing of services so that interoperability failures, perils with frauds, misinterpretation of services, and other fatal mistakes can be minimized, if not fully avoided.

In some closed SIP networking environments creating Trust Domain under a single administrative domain, some private SIP headers have been created that provide asserted IDs of services, such as RFC 6050 (see Section 12.3), although processing of unique services from those service identities are only applicable for that particular administrative domain only and cannot be used in the Internet at large. Similarly, although implicitly related to services, some rather different kind of private IDs have been created, known as Served-User IDs, such as those defined in RFC 5502 (see Section 12.4), which indicate whether a given user is being served for providing services by the functional entities in the SIP network based on the services profile of that particular user. Earlier, we have described that a few private service Uniform Resource Identifiers (URIs) have been created for invoking some specific services over the SIP network in a very limited way. This approach cannot be used indefinitely for several reasons:

- No URI can be standardized for any specific service in accordance to the definition of the URI standard.
- A huge number of services distinguishing from some minor ones to highly complex features that already exist cannot be designated using all nonstandard service URIs, and only the future can tell how great will be the number of services to be created.

In view of this, it appears that the approach that has been taken through the creation of service IDs using some canonical forms are more reasonable as well as manageable without breaking any standards. In the subsequent sections, we describe the communications service IDs, asserted service IDs, and served-user IDs for providing service-based user profiles.

12.2 Communications Service ID

The SIP carries signaling messages for session establishments for invoking services. A given SIP signaling message that represents a unique service must also be unique. For example, if the Session Description Protocol (SDP) message body contains a specific audio codec with its definitive functional and performances characteristics, it will represent a specific audio service and the same unique signaling scheme will always represent the same service, and all users are expected to have the same experiences for this service. There are a number of points that we can make, as follows:

- Expressions used in the signaling message for representation of the service in the SIP signaling layer.
- Processing of the signaling message for representation of the service in the service (or application) layer.
- Experiences of users for the same service at the user level. If the end users have been in control of the services, and the network or networks that interconnect the end users are not involved in providing services in the service (or application) layer, then things would be simpler.

However, the session establishment and reestablishment within a given call in SIP even for a single media can be highly complex, and the intermediate functional entities within the network may have to play a role such as for media bridging, transfer/diversion of the call-leg, mid-call charging, digit collection, emergency call, and many other services that a caller may have to get. In many cases, the processing of a service from a given SIP signaling message knowing the SDP message body and hints from the headers, as well as user experiences of the same service, may not always be the same especially if the service provided within the network or networks are different. If we add multimedia on the top of a single media, for each of those call features, things will get more complicated. In this respect, RFC 5897 (Sections 12.1 through 12.3) provides some guidelines for using the service ID that is the process of determining or signaling the user-level use case that is driving the signaling being utilized by the user agent (UA). The recommendations for service ID are summarized in the following sections.

12.2.1 Derived Service ID

Derived service ID—where an identifier for a service is obtained by inspection of the signaling and of other contextual data (such as subscriber profile)—is reasonable, and when done properly, does not lead to the perils described above. However, declarative service ID—where UAs indicate what the service is, separate from the rest of the signaling—leads to the perils described above. If it appears that the signaling currently defined in standards is not sufficient to identify the service, it may be due to a lack of sufficient signaling to convey what is needed, or may be because request URIs should be used for differentiation and they are not being so used. By applying the litmus tests described later, network designers can determine whether the system is attempting to perform a declarative service ID.

12.2.2 SIP's Expressiveness for Negotiation

One of SIP's key strengths is its ability to negotiate a common view of a session between participants. This means that the service that is ultimately received can vary wildly, depending on the types of end points in the call and their capabilities. Indeed, this fact becomes even more evident when calls are set up between domains. As such, when performing derived service ID, domains should be aware that sessions may arrive from different networks and different end points. Consequently, the service ID algorithm must be complete—meaning that it computes the best answer for any possible signaling message that might be received and any session that might be set up.

In a homogeneous environment, the process of service ID is easy. The service provider will know the set of services they are providing, and, based on the specific call flows for each specific service, can construct rules to differentiate one service from another. However, when different providers interconnect, or when different end points are introduced, assumptions about what services are used, and how they are signaled, no longer apply. To provide the best user experience possible, a provider doing service ID needs to perform a *best-match* operation, such that any legal SIP signaling—not just the specific call flows running within their own network among a limited set of endpoints—is mapped to the appropriate service.

12.2.3 Presence

Presence can help a great deal with providing unique URIs for different services. If a user wishes to contact another user and knows only the AOR for the target, as is usually the case, the user can fetch the presence document for the target. That document, in turn, can contain numerous services URIs for contacting the target with different services. Those URIs can then be used in the Request-URI for differentiation. When possible, this is the best solution to the problem. It should be noted that, unlike service URIs described earlier, the URI itself will provide the address of a given service, but the service itself must be uniquely understood from the description of the services provided somewhere else.

12.2.4 Intradomain

Service identifiers themselves are not bad; derived service ID allows each domain to cache the results of the service ID process for usage by another network element within the same domain. However, service identifiers are fundamentally useful within a particular domain, and any such header must be stripped at a network boundary. Consequently, the process of service ID and their associated service identifiers are always an intradomain operation.

12.2.5 Device Dispatch

Device dispatch should be done following the principles of RFC 3841 (see Section 9.9), using implicit preferences based on the signaling. For example, RFC 5688 (Sections 12.2.5 and 12.3.2) defines a new UA capability that can be used to dispatch requests based on different types of application media streams. However, it is a mistake to try and use a service identifier as a UA capability. Consider a service called *multimedia telephony*, which adds video to the existing public switched telephone network (PSTN) experience. A user has two devices, one of which is used for multimedia telephony and the other strictly for a voice-assisted game. It is tempting to have the telephony device include a UA capability (RFC 3840, see Section 3.4) called multimedia telephony in its registration. A calling multimedia telephony device can then include the Accept-Contact header field (RFC 3841, see Section 9.9) containing this feature tag. The proxy serving the called party, applying the basic algorithms of RFC 3841, will correctly route the call to the terminating device.

However, if the calling party is not within the same domain, and the calling domain does not know about or use this feature tag, there will be no Accept-Contact header field, even if the calling party was using a service that is a good match for multimedia telephony. In such a case, the call may be delivered to both devices, but it will yield a poorer user experience. That is because device dispatch was done using a declarative service ID. The best way to avoid this problem is to use feature tags that can be matched to well-defined signaling features—media types, required SIP extensions, and so on. In particular, the golden rule is that the granularity of feature tags must be equivalent to the granularity of individual features that can be signaled in SIP.

12.3 Asserted- and Preferred-Service ID

12.3.1 Overview

The concept of *service* within SIP has no hard and fast rules. As described earlier, RFC 5897 provides general guidance on what constitutes a service within SIP and what does not. This document also makes use of the terms *derived service ID* and *declarative service ID* as defined in Sections 12.1 through 12.3 (RFC 5897). It clearly states that the declarative service ID of the process by which a UA inserts a moniker into a message that defines the desired service, separate from explicit and well-defined protocol mechanisms is harmful. During a session setup, proxies may need to understand what service the request is related to in order to know what application server (AS) to contact or other service logic to invoke. The SIP INVITE request contains all of the information necessary to determine the service. However, the calculation of the service may be computational and database intensive. For example, a given Trust Domain's definition of a service might include request authorization. Moreover, the analysis may require examination of the SDP.

For example, an INVITE request with video SDP directed to a video-on-demand Request-URI could be marked as an Internet Protocol (IP) television session. An INVITE request with push-to-talk over cellular (PoC) routes could be marked as a PoC session. An INVITE request with a Require header field containing an option tag of *foogame* could be marked as a foogame session. If the information contained within the SIP INVITE request is not sufficient to uniquely identify a service, the remedy is to extend the SIP signaling to capture the missing element.

By providing a mechanism to compute and store the results of the domain-specific service calculation, that is, the derived service ID, this optimization allows a single trusted proxy to perform an analysis of the request and authorize the requestor's permission to request such a service. The proxy may then include a service identifier that relieves other trusted proxies and trusted UAs from performing further duplicate analysis of the request for their service ID purposes. In addition, this extension allows UA clients (UACs) outside the Trust Domain to provide a hint of the requested service. The private P-Asserted-Service and private P-Preferred-Service header defined in RFC 6050 (see Section 12.3) enable a network of trusted SIP servers to assert the service of authenticated users. The use of these extensions is only applicable inside an administrative domain with previously agreed-upon policies for generation, transport, and usage of such information, and does not offer a general service ID model suitable for use between different Trust Domains or for use in the Internet at large.

These headers do not provide for the dialog or transaction to be rejected if the service is not supported end-to-end. SIP provides other mechanisms, such as the option-tag and use of the Require and Proxy-Require header fields, where such functionality is required. No explicitly signaled service ID exists, and the session proceeds for each node's definition of the service in use, on the basis of information contained in the SDP and in other SIP header fields.

This mechanism is specifically for managing the information needs of intermediate routing devices between the calling user and the user represented by the Request-URI. In support of this mechanism, a Uniform Resource Name (URN) is defined to identify the services. This URN has wider applicability to additionally identify services and terminal applications. Between end users, caller preferences and callee capabilities as specified in RFC 3840 and RFC 3841 provide an appropriate mechanism for indicating such service and application ID. These mechanisms have been extended by RFC 5688 (see Sections 9.5 through 9.8) to provide further capabilities in this area. The P-Asserted-Service header field contains a URN. This is supported by the P-Preferred-Service header field that also contains a URN and that allows the UA to express preferences regarding the decisions made on service within the Trust Domain. An example of the P-Asserted-Service header field is

```
P-Asserted-Service: urn:urn-7:3gpp-service.
exampletelephony.version1
```

A proxy server that handles a request can, after authenticating the originating user in some way (e.g., digest authentication) to ensure that the user is entitled to that service, insert such a P-Asserted-Service header field into the request and forward it to not sufficient to uniquely identify a service, the remedy is to extend the SIP signaling to capture the missing element. We provide further explanation here per RFC 5897. A proxy server or UA that it does not trust removes all the P-Asserted-Service header field values. Thus, the services are labeled by means of an informal URN that provides a hierarchical structure for defining services and subservices, and provides an address that can be resolvable for various purposes outside the scope of this document, for example, to obtain information about the service so described.

12.3.2 Applicability Statement

The use of the P-Asserted-Service and P-Preferred-Service header fields defined in RFC 6050 is only applicable inside a Trust Domain. All functional entities of the network create a Trust Domain, T, authenticating each other's Network-Asserted Identity using valid identities expressed in SIP URI, SIPS URI, tel URI, or optional display name complying with a certain set of specification, spec (T), as defined in RFC 3324 (see Section 12.3). Nodes in such a Trust Domain are explicitly trusted by its users and end systems to publicly assert the service of each party, and they have common and agreed-upon definitions of services and homogeneous service offerings. The means by which the network determines the service to assert is not defined in RFC 6050 (see Section 12.3).

As explained earlier, this service model is not suitable for interdomain use or use in the Internet at large. Its assumptions about the trust relationship between the user and the network may not be suitable in many applications. For example, these extensions do not accommodate a model whereby end users can independently assert their service by use of the extensions defined here. End users assert their service by including the SIP and SDP parameters that correspond to the service they require. Furthermore, since the asserted services are not cryptographically certified, they are subject to forgery, replay, and falsification in any architecture that does not meet the requirements of RFC 3324 (see Section 10.5). The asserted services also lack an indication of who specifically is asserting the service, and so it must be assumed that a member of the Trust Domain is asserting the service. Therefore, the information is only meaningful when securely received from a node known to be a member of the Trust Domain. Despite these limitations, there are sufficiently useful specialized deployments that meet the assumptions described above and can accept the limitations that result, to warrant the informational publication of this mechanism.

12.3.3 Header Fields

We have provided augmented Backus–Naur Form (ABNF) syntaxes of all SIP header field in Section 2.4.1. However, we are repeating syntaxes for these two header fields for convenience: P-Asserted-Service and P-Preferred Service.

12.3.3.1 P-Asserted-Service Header

The P-Asserted-Service header field is used among trusted SIP entities (typically intermediaries) to carry the service information of the user sending a SIP message. The P-Asserted-Service header field carries the information of the derived service ID. While the declarative service ID can assist in deriving the value transferred in this header field, this should be in the form of streamlining the correct derived service ID.

```
PAssertedService = "P-Asserted-Service"
                   HCOLON
                   PAssertedService-value
PAssertedService-value = Service-ID *(COMMA
                         Service-ID)
```

Note the following:

- The definition of Service-ID has been provided in ABNF in the subsequent section.
- Proxies can (and will) add and remove this header field.
- Tables 2.5 and 2.10 (Section 2.8) show the relationship between P-Asserted-Service header field, Proxy, and Request Messages.

Syntactically, there may be multiple P-Asserted-Service header fields in a request. The semantics of multiple P-Asserted-Service header fields appearing in the same request is not defined at this time in RFC 6050. Implementations of this specification must provide only one P-Asserted-Service header field value.

12.3.3.2 P-Preferred-Service Header

The P-Preferred-Service header field is used by a UA sending the SIP request to provide a hint to a trusted proxy of the preferred service that the user wishes to be used for the P-Asserted-Service field value that the trusted element will insert. The P-Preferred-Service header field carries the information of the declarative service ID. Such information should only be used to assist in deriving the derived service ID at the recipient entity.

```
PPreferredService = "P-Preferred-Service"
                    HCOLON
                    PPreferredService-value
PPreferredService-value = Service-ID *(COMMA
Service-ID)
```

Note the following:

- The definition of Service-ID has been provided in ABNF in the subsequent section.
- Tables 2.5 and 2.10 (Section 2.8) show the relationship between P-Preferred-Service header field, Proxy, and Request Messages.

Syntactically, there may be multiple P-Preferred-Service header fields in a request. The semantics of multiple P-Preferred-Service header fields appearing in the same request is not defined at this time in RFC 6050 (see Section 12.3). Implementations of this specification must only provide one P-Preferred-Service header field value.

12.3.3.3 Service and Application Definition

Service definitions and characteristics are beyond the scope of this document. Other standards organizations, vendors, and operators may define their own services and register them. A hierarchical structure is defined consisting of service identifiers or application identifiers, and subservice identifiers. The service and subservice identifiers are as described earlier. The URN may also be used to identify a service or an application between end users for use within the context of RFC 3840 (see Section 3.4) and RFC 3841 (see Section 9.9). The Internet Assigned Number Authority (IANA) maintains a registry of service identifier values that have been assigned. However, subservice identifiers are not managed by IANA. It is the responsibility of the organization that registered the service to manage the subservices.

12.3.3.4 Service URN

The service URN scheme is defined in according to RFC 3406 and needs to be registered with IANA. The URN scheme is defined as an informal namespace ID (NID). The declaration of syntactic structure of URN consists of a hierarchical service identifier or application identifier, with a sequence of labels separated by periods. The leftmost label is the most significant one and is called *top-level service identifier*, while names to the right are called *subservices* or *subapplications*. The set of allowable characters is the same as that for domain names provided in RFC 1123 and a subset of the labels allowed in RFC 3958. Labels are case insensitive and must be specified in all lowercase. For any given service identifier, labels can be removed right-to-left and the resulting URN is still valid, referring a more generic service, with the exception of the top-level service identifier and possibly the first subservice or subapplication identifier.

Labels cannot be removed beyond a defined basic service; for example, the label w.x may define a service, but the label w may only define an assignment authority for assigning subsequent values and not define a service in its own right. In other words, if a service identifier w.x.y.z exists, the URNs w.x and w.x.y are also valid service identifiers; however, w may not be a valid service identifier if it merely defines who is responsible for defining x.

```
Service-ID = "urn:urn-7:" urn-service-id
urn-service-id = top-level *("."
sub-service-id)
top-level = let-dig [*26let-dig]
sub-service-id = let-dig [*let-dig]
let-dig = ALPHA/DIGIT/"-"
```

While the naming convention above uses the term *service*, all the constructs are equally applicable to identifying applications within the UA.

1. Relevant ancillary documentation: None.
2. Identifier uniqueness considerations: A service identifier identifies a service, and an application identifier an application indicated in the service or application registration. Uniqueness is guaranteed by the IANA registration.
3. Identifier persistence considerations: The service or application identifier for the same service or application is expected to be persistent, although there naturally cannot be a guarantee that a particular service will continue to be available globally or at all times.
4. Process of identifier assignment: The process of identifier assignment is described in the IANA considerations.
5. Process for identifier resolution: There is no single global resolution service for service identifiers or application identifiers.
6. Rules for lexical equivalence: Service identifiers are compared according to case-insensitive string equality.
7. Conformance with URN syntax: The ABNF in the “Declaration of syntactic structure” above constrains the syntax for this URN scheme.

8. Validation mechanism: Validation determines whether a given string is currently a validly assigned URN provided in RFC 3406. Owing to the distributed nature of usage and since not all services are available everywhere, validation in this sense is not possible.
9. Scope: The scope for this URN can be local to a single domain, or may be more widely used.

12.3.4 Usage of Header Fields in Requests

12.3.4.1 Procedures at UACs

The UAC may insert a P-Preferred-Service in a request that creates a dialog, or a request outside of a dialog. This information can assist the proxies in identifying appropriate service capabilities to apply to the call. This information must not conflict with other SIP or SDP information included in the request. Furthermore, the SIP or SDP information needed to signal the functionality of this service must be present. Thus, if a service requires a video component, then the SDP has to include the media line associated with that video component; it cannot be assumed from the P-Preferred-Service header field value. Similarly, if the service requires particular SIP functionality for which a SIP extension and a Require header field value is defined, then the request has to include that SIP signaling as well as the P-Preferred-Service header field value. A UAC that is within the same Trust Domain as the proxy to which it sends a request (e.g., a media gateway or AS) may insert a P-Asserted-Service header field in a request that creates a dialog, or a request outside of a dialog. This information must not conflict with other SIP or SDP information included in the request. Furthermore, the SIP or SDP information needed to signal the functionality of this service must be present.

12.3.4.2 Procedures at Intermediate Proxies

A proxy in a Trust Domain can receive a request from a node that it trusts or a node that it does not trust. When a proxy receives a request from a node it does not trust and it wishes to add a P-Asserted-Service header field, the proxy must identify the service appropriate to the capabilities (e.g., SDP) in the request, and may authenticate the originator of the request (to determine whether the user is subscribed for that service). Where the originator of the request is authenticated, the proxy must use the identity that results from this checking and authentication to insert a P-Asserted-Service header field into the request.

When a proxy receives a request containing a P-Preferred-Service header field, the proxy may use the contents of that header field to assist in determining the service to be included in a P-Asserted-Service header field (for instance, to prioritize the order of comparison of filter criteria for potential services that the request could match). The proxy must not use the contents of the P-Preferred-Service header field to identify the service without first checking against the capabilities (e.g., SDP) contained in the request. If the proxy inserts a P-Asserted-Service header field in the request, the proxy must remove the P-Preferred-Service header field before forwarding the request; otherwise, the proxy should include the P-Preferred-Service header field when forwarding the request.

If the proxy receives a request from a node that it trusts, it can use the information in the P-Asserted-Service header field, if any, as if it had authenticated the user itself. If there is no P-Asserted-Service header field present, or it is not possible to match the request to a specific service as identified by the service identifier, a proxy may add one containing it using its own analysis of the information contained in the SIP request. If the proxy received the request from an element it does not trust and there is a P-Asserted-Service header present, the proxy must replace that header field's contents with a new analysis or remove that header field. The analysis performed to identify such service identifiers is outside the scope of this document. However, it is perfectly valid as a result of the analysis not to include any service identifier in the forwarded request, and thus not include a P-Asserted-Service header field. If a proxy forwards a request to a node outside the proxy's Trust Domain, there must not be a P-Asserted-Service header field in the forwarded request.

12.3.4.3 Procedures at UA Servers

For a UA server (UAS) outside the Trust Domain, the P-Asserted-Service header is removed before it reaches this entity; therefore, there are no procedures for such a device. However, if a UAS receives a request from a previous element that it does not trust, it must not use the P-Asserted-Service header field in any way. If a UA is part of the Trust Domain from which it received a request containing a P-Asserted-Service header field, then it can use the value freely; however, it must ensure that it does not forward the information to any element that is not part of the Trust Domain.

12.3.5 Usage of Header Fields in Responses

There is no usage of these header fields in responses.

12.3.6 Examples of Usage

In this example, proxy.example.com creates a P-Asserted-Service header field from the user identity it discovered from SIP digest authentication, the list of services appropriate to that user, and the services that correspond to the SDP information included in the request. Note that F1 and F2 are about identifying the user and do not directly form part of the capability described here. It forwards this information to a trusted proxy that forwards it to a trusted gateway. Note that these examples consist of partial SIP messages that illustrate only those header fields relevant to the authenticated identity problem.

* F1 useragent.example.com -> proxy.example.com

```
INVITE sip:+14085551212@example.com SIP/2.0
Via: SIP/2.0/TCP useragent.example.
com;branch=z9hG4bK-123
To: <sip:+14085551212@example.com>
From: "Anonymous" <sip:anonymous@anonymous.
invalid>;tag=9802748
Call-ID: 245780247857024504
CSeq: 1 INVITE
Max-Forwards: 70

v=0
o=- 2987933615 2987933615 IN IP6
5555::aaa:bbb:ccc:ddd
s=-
c=IN IP6 5555::aaa:bbb:ccc:ddd
t=0 0
m=audio 3456 RTP/AVPF 97 96
b=AS:25.4
a=curr:qos local sendrecv
a=curr:qos remote none
a=des:qos mandatory local sendrecv
a=des:qos mandatory remote sendrecv
a=sendrecv
a=rtpmap:97 AMR
a=fmtp:97 mode-set=0,2,5,7; maxframes
```

* F2 proxy.example.com -> useragent.example.com

```
SIP/2.0 407 Proxy Authorization
Via: SIP/2.0/TCP useragent.example.
com;branch=z9hG4bK-123
To: <sip:+14085551212@example.com>;tag=123456
From: "Anonymous" <sip:anonymous@anonymous.
invalid>;tag=9802748
Call-ID: 245780247857024504
CSeq: 1 INVITE
Proxy-Authenticate:.... realm="sip.example.
com"
```

* F3 useragent.example.com -> proxy.example.com

```
INVITE sip:+14085551212@example.com SIP/2.0
Via: SIP/2.0/TCP useragent.example.
com;branch=z9hG4bK-124
To: <sip:+14085551212@example.com>
From: "Anonymous" <sip:anonymous@anonymous.
invalid>;tag=9802748
Call-ID: 245780247857024504
CSeq: 2 INVITE
Max-Forwards: 70
Proxy-Authorization: realm="sip.example.com"
user="bjohnson"

v=0
o=- 2987933615 2987933615 IN IP6
5555::aaa:bbb:ccc:ddd
s=-
c=IN IP6 5555::aaa:bbb:ccc:ddd
t=0 0
m=audio 3456 RTP/AVPF 97 96
b=AS:25.4
a=curr:qos local sendrecv
a=curr:qos remote none
a=des:qos mandatory local sendrecv
a=des:qos mandatory remote sendrecv
a=sendrecv
a=rtpmap:97 AMR
a=fmtp:97 mode-set=0,2,5,7; maxframes
```

* F4 proxy.example.com -> proxy.pstn.example (trusted)

```
INVITE sip:+14085551212@proxy. pstn.example
SIP/2.0
Via: SIP/2.0/TCP useragent.example.
com;branch=z9hG4bK-124
Via: SIP/2.0/TCP proxy.example.
com;branch=z9hG4bK-abc
To: <sip:+14085551212@example.com>
From: "Anonymous" <sip:anonymous@anonymous.
invalid>;tag=9802748
Call-ID: 245780247857024504
CSeq: 2 INVITE
Max-Forwards: 69
P-Asserted-Service: urn:urn-7:3gpp-service.
exampletelephony.version1

v=0
o=- 2987933615 2987933615 IN IP6
5555::aaa:bbb:ccc:ddd
s=-
c=IN IP6 5555::aaa:bbb:ccc:ddd
t=0 0
m=audio 3456 RTP/AVPF 97 96
b=AS:25.4
a=curr:qos local sendrecv
a=curr:qos remote none
a=des:qos mandatory local sendrecv
a=des:qos mandatory remote sendrecv
a=sendrecv
a=rtpmap:97 AMR
a=fmtp:97 mode-set=0,2,5,7; maxframes
```

* F5 proxy.pstn.example -> gw.pstn.example (trusted)

```
INVITE sip:+14085551212@gw.pstn.example
SIP/2.0
Via: SIP/2.0/TCP useragent.example.
com;branch=z9hG4bK-124
Via: SIP/2.0/TCP proxy.example.
com;branch=z9hG4bK-abc
Via: SIP/2.0/TCP proxy.pstn.
example;branch=z9hG4bK-a1b2
To: <sip:+14085551212@example.com>
From: "Anonymous" <sip:anonymous@anonymous.
invalid>;tag=9802748
```

```
Call-ID: 245780247857024504
CSeq: 2 INVITE
Max-Forwards: 68
P-Asserted-Service: urn:urn-7:3gpp-service.
exampletelephony.version1

v=0
o=- 2987933615 2987933615 IN IP6
5555::aaa:bbb:ccc:ddd
s=-
c=IN IP6 5555::aaa:bbb:ccc:ddd
t=0 0
m=audio 3456 RTP/AVPF 97 96
b=AS:25.4
a=curr:qos local sendrecv
a=curr:qos remote none
a=des:qos mandatory local sendrecv
a=des:qos mandatory remote sendrecv
a=sendrecv
a=rtpmap:97 AMR
a=fmtp:97 mode-set=0,2,5,7; maxframes
```

12.4 Served-User ID for Handling Services

We are dealing with served-user ID in particular that is expressed explicitly for a given service; however, the type of service or the service ID is known implicitly. For example, the SIP INVITE message itself expresses the kinds of services that are being requested directly in the SDP message body, and may express services or provide hints for services implicitly in the message headers. If the served-user identity is known, the kind of services that the user obtained from the SIP network can also be known directly or implicitly. However, the most important use of the P-Served-User header field (RFC 5502) lies somewhere else: routing within the SIP-aware AS farm, where a host of ASs may be used for serving a SIP call with distributed service architecture. A high-level description is provided; now, this header can be used for providing SIP services by multiple ASs in inter-AS communication environments.

12.4.1 P-Served-User Header

The private P-Served-User header field defined in RFC 5502 conveys the identity of the served user and the session case parameter that applies to this particular communication session and application invocation. The header is not used in the Internet in general. The session case parameter is used to indicate the category of the served user: originating served user or terminating served user, and registered user or unregistered user. Note that there can be many kinds of ASs in the farm for providing a variety of services to the SIP users based on different subscription types.

The served user to a proxy or AS is the user whose service profile is accessed by that SIP proxy that may be known as the serving SIP proxy, for example, Serving–Call Session Control Function (S-CSCF) of Third Generation Partnership Project's (3GPP's) IP Multimedia System (IMS) network or AS when an initial request is received that is originated by, originated on behalf of, or terminated to that user. There may also be the distributed servers/databases, for example, home subscriber server (HSS) of 3GPP's IMS network, that store the user profiles. This profile, in turn, provides some useful information (preferences or permissions) for processing at a proxy and, potentially, at an AS. For providing specific services to the respective users, some service-specific filter criteria (SSFC) are stored in the server/database (e.g., HSS of 3GPP's IMS network) as part of the user profile and are downloaded to the serving SIP proxy upon user registration. For example, 3GPP's IMS network also uses the service-specific filter criteria.

The P-Served-User header field is very useful for the large-scale distributed SIP network especially where a variety of SIP-aware ASs are employed for providing services in a more scalable way. A large distributed fixed or mobile SIP network (e.g., 3GPP's IMS network) of a given administrative domain may have multiple SIP proxies playing different roles, and the AS farm is distributed over a large geographical area and provides services to SIP users. All functional entities of the network create a Trust Domain, T, authenticating each other's Network-Asserted Identity using valid identities expressed in SIP URI, SIPS URI, tel URI, or optionally display name complying with a certain set of specification, spec (T), as defined in RFC 3324 (see Section 10.5). SIP proxies may have the service control interface (SCI), for example, IP multimedia Service Control (ISC) interface of 3GPP's IMS network, with many ASs and servers/databases. A proxy may have multiple SCIs of different ASs to fulfill the service requirements of the users that are served by this particular proxy. In addition, SIP proxies may have SIP interfaces with ASs/servers.

Some implementations of the SIP network may use the original dialog identifier (ODI) to the request that will allow the serving SIP proxy to identify the message on the incoming side, even if its dialog ID has been changed by the AS (e.g., AS performing third-party call control). In addition, the originating ID presentation (OIP) service may also be implemented to provide the terminating user with the possibility of receiving trusted (i.e., network-provided) identity information in order to identify the originating user. For example, 3GPP's IMS network has specified both ODI and OPI services. It should be noted that the SIP Identity and Identity-Info header field specified in RFC 4474 (see Sections 2.8 and 19.4.8) and connected identity specified with the from-change tag may be the standard way of doing the identity presentation instead of using OIP that is non-SIP standard. We use both ODI and OIP later as an example for the purpose of showing the usefulness of the P-Served-User header field.

12.4.2 Application Service Invocation

We describe the following scenarios in the context of the large-scale distributed SIP network where the capability gaps of the SIP signaling messages that can be fulfilled by the P-Served-User header field are identified:

- General Scenario
- Diversion
  - Continue on terminating leg, but finish subsequent terminating SSFC first
  - Create new originating leg and provide originating SSFC processing
- Call out of the blue
  - On behalf of user B, but service profile of service identity C

In summary, all those scenarios describe the following SIP capability gaps:

- The identity of the served user can be conveyed on the SCI interface in order to be able to offer real-world application services.
- It is required that, in addition to the served-user identity, the session case needs to be conveyed in order to be able to offer appropriate services to the served user.

12.4.2.1 General Scenarios

A SIP proxy that serves as a registrar may handle originating and terminating session states for users allocated to it. This means that any call that is originated by a specific user or any call that is terminated to that specific user will pass through that particular proxy that is allocated to that user. At the time of servicing the call, it may also imply that this particular serving SIP proxy that is allocated for a specific user will download the profile of this particular user from the server/database (e.g., HSS of 3GPP's IMS network). This user profile tells this serving SIP proxy whether the user is allowed to originate or terminate calls or whether an AS needs to be linked in over the particular SCI interface. The user profile information that determines whether a particular initial request needs to be sent to a particular AS is decided using the SSFC criteria. For the serving SIP proxy to be able to meet its responsibilities, it needs to determine on which user's behalf it is performing its tasks and which session case is applicable for the particular request. As explained earlier, the session case distinguishes the originating and terminating call cases, and determines whether or not the particular user is registered.

When the serving SIP proxy determines that for an incoming initial request the originating call case applies, it determines the served user by looking at the P-Asserted-Identity header field defined in RFC 3325 (see Sections 2.8, 10.4, and 20.3), which carries the Network-Asserted Identity of the originating user. When, after filtering through the SCI for this initial request, the serving proxy may decide to forward the request to an AS, the AS has to go through a similar process of determining the session case and the served user. Since it should come to the same conclusion that this is an originating session case, it also has to look at the P-Asserted-Identity header field to determine the served user.

When the serving proxy determines that for an incoming initial request, the terminating call case applies, it determines the served user by looking at the Request-URI defined in RFC 3261, which carries the identity of the intended terminating user. When, after processing through the SSFC for this initial request, the serving proxy may decide to forward the request to an AS, the AS has to go through a similar process of determining the session case and the served user. Since it should come to the same conclusion that this is a terminating session case, it also has to look at the Request-URI to determine the served user.

In the originating case, it can be observed that while the P-Asserted-Identity header field just represents the originating user when it enters the serving proxy, it is overloaded with another meaning when it is sent to an AS over the SSFC interface. This other meaning is that it serves as a representation of the served user. In the terminating case, a similar overloading happens to the Request-URI; while it first only represented the identity of the intended terminating user, it is overloaded with another meaning when it is sent to an AS over the ISC interface. This other meaning is that it serves as a representation of the served user. In basic call scenarios, this does not show up as a problem; however, once more complicated service scenarios (notably forwarding services) need to be realized, it poses severe limitations. Such scenarios are brought forward in the following subsections. In those situations, the P-Served-User header field overcomes those limitations and is very useful in providing real-world application services using a distributed SIP network and a distributed AS farm, making the large-scale network scalable.

12.4.2.2 Call Diversion Continuing on Terminating Leg

This scenario deals with the diversion of the same call continuing on the terminating leg but finishing on the subsequent terminating SSFC first. Imagine a service scenario where a user B has a terminating service that diverts the call to a different destination but is required to still execute subsequent terminating services for the same user. This means that this particular user has multiple SSFCs configured that are applicable for an incoming initial request. When the serving SIP proxy receives an initial INVITE request, it analyzes the request and determines that the session case is for a terminating registered user, and then it determines the served user to be user B by looking at the Request-URI. Now the serving proxy starts the SSFC processing. The first SSFC that matches the INVITE request causes the INVITE to be forwarded over the SCI interface to an AS that hosts user B's diversion service by adding the AS and serving proxy's own host names to the Route header. The serving proxy may add an ODI to the serving proxy's own host name (e.g., ODI is used in 3GPP's IMS network) on the Route header. This ODI, even if its dialog ID may have been changed by an AS for some reason, allows the serving proxy to correlate an INVITE coming from an AS over the SCI interface to the existing session that forwarded the INVITE to the AS in the first place.

When the AS receives the initial INVITE request, it analyzes the request and determines that the session case is for a terminating registered user, and then it determines the served user to be user B by looking at the Request-URI. On the basis of some criteria depending on implementation, the diversion service may conclude that the request needs to be diverted to another user or application C. It does this by changing the Request-URI to C. It may record the Request-URI history by using the History-Info header field defined in RFC 4244. Then, the AS removes itself from the Route header and routes the INVITE request back to the serving SIP proxy by using the topmost Route header field. When the serving SIP proxy receives the INVITE over the ISC interface, it can see that the Route header contains its own host name and an ODI that correlates to an existing terminating session for user B. This can be used by the serving SIP proxy to analyze whether there are still unexecuted SSFCs. (Note that the implementation behavior of the serving SIP proxy on receiving an INVITE with a changed Request-URI is to terminate the SCI processing and to route the request based on the new Request-URI value.)

The process repeats itself. The INVITE is forwarded to the AS that is associated with this particular SSFC. When the AS receives the initial INVITE request, it analyzes the request and determines that the session case is for a terminating registered user, and then it determines the served user to be user C by looking at the Request-URI. This is clearly wrong, as the user being served is still user B. This scenario clearly shows the problem that occurs when the Request-URI is overloaded with the meanings *intended target identity* and *served user* with the operation as described earlier. Moreover, it shows that this use case cannot be realized without introducing a mechanism that conveys information about the served user from the serving SIP proxy to the AS. Use of the History-Info element does not solve this problem as it does not tell the AS which user is being served; it just presents a history of diversions that might not be even caused by the systems serving this particular user.

12.4.2.3 Call Diversion Creating New Originating Leg

We are now considering a scenario where the call is diverted, creating a new originating leg and providing originating SSFC processing. Imagine a service scenario where a user B has a terminating service that diverts the call to a different destination. It is required that a forwarded call leg is handled as an originating call leg and that originating services for user B are executed. This means that this particular user has one or more SSFCs configured that are applicable for an outgoing initial request. When the serving SIP proxy receives an initial INVITE request, it analyzes the request and determines that the session case is for a terminating registered user, and then it determines the served user to be user B by looking at the Request-URI. Now, the serving SIP proxy starts the SSFC processing. The first SSFC that matches the INVITE request causes the INVITE to be forwarded over the ISC interface to an AS that hosts user B's diversion service by adding the AS and serving SIP proxy's own host names to the Route header. The serving SIP proxy adds an ODI to the serving SIP proxy's own host name on the Route header. This allows the serving SIP proxy to correlate an INVITE coming from an AS over the ISC interface to the existing session that forwarded the INVITE to the AS in the first place.

When the AS receives the initial INVITE request, it analyzes the request and determines that the session case is for a terminating registered user, and then it determines the served user to be user B by looking at the Request-URI. On the basis of some criteria, the diversion service concludes that the request needs to be diverted to another user or application C. It does this by changing the Request-URI to C. It may record the Request-URI history by using the History-Info header field defined in RFC 4244. Then, the AS removes itself from the Route header. To make sure that the request is handled as a new originating call on behalf of user B, the AS adds the *orig* parameter to the topmost route header. Then, it routes the INVITE request back to the serving SIP proxy by using this topmost Route header field. When the serving SIP proxy receives the INVITE over the ISC interface, it can see that the topmost Route header contains its own host name and an orig parameter. Because the topmost Route header contains the orig parameter, the serving SIP proxy concludes that the INVITE should be handled as if a call is originated by the served user. The served user is determined from the P-Asserted-Identity header to be user A. This is clearly wrong, as the user being served is and should be user B. For the sake of discussion, let us assume that the serving SIP proxy can determine that the served user is user B.

Then, the procedure would continue as follows: The serving SIP proxy starts the originating SSFC processing; the first SSFC that matches the INVITE request causes the INVITE to be forwarded over the ISC interface to an AS that hosts an originating service of user B by adding the AS and serving SIP proxy's own host names to the Route header. The serving SIP proxy adds an ODI to the serving SIP proxy's own host name on the Route header. The INVITE is forwarded to the AS that is associated with this particular SSFC. When the AS receives the initial INVITE request, it analyzes the request and determines that the session case is for an originating registered user, and then it determines the served user to be user A by looking at the P-Asserted-Identity. This is clearly wrong, as the user being served is and should be user B. This scenario clearly shows the problem that occurs when the P-Asserted-Identity is overloaded with the meanings *call originator* and *served user* with the operation as described earlier. It shows that this use case cannot be realized without introducing a mechanism that conveys information about the served user from the serving SIP proxy to the AS, and from the AS to the serving SIP proxy. Use of the History-Info element does not solve this problem as it does not tell the AS which user is being served, but just presents a history of diversions that might not be even caused by the systems serving this particular user.

12.4.2.4 Call Out of the Blue

This scenario is dealing with the call that is coming out of the blue on behalf of user B, but the service profile happens to be of service identity C. There are services that need to be able to initiate a call, whereby the call appears to be coming from a user B but the service profile on behalf of service identity C needs to be executed in the serving SIP proxy. When a call needs to appear as coming from user B, it means that the P-Asserted-Identity needs to contain B's identity. For example, 3GPP's IMS network uses OIP service that uses the P-Asserted-Identity to present the call originator. This makes sense because that is the main meaning expressed by the P-Asserted-Identity header field. It is clear that no INVITE request can be constructed currently that would achieve both requirements expressed in the first paragraph, because the P-Asserted-Identity is overloaded with two meanings on the ISC interface. When the serving SIP proxy receives this request, it will determine that the served user is user B, which is not what we want to achieve.

12.4.3 P-Served-User Header Field Usage, Definition, and Syntax

We explain this header field here again for detailed explanations, although all header fields can be seen in Section 2.8. This header field can be added to initial requests for a dialog or stand-alone requests, which are routed between nodes in a Trust Domain for P-Served-User. The P-Served-User header field contains an identity of the user that represents the served user. The *sescase* parameter may be used to convey whether the initial request is originated by the served user or destined for the served user. The *regstate* parameter may be used to indicate whether the initial request is for a registered or unregistered user. The ABNF, defined in RFC 5234, syntax of the P-Served-User header field is as follows:

```
P-Served-User =  "P-Served-User" HCOLON
PServedUser- value *(SEMI served-user-param)
served-user-param =  sessioncase-param/
                     registration-state-param
                     /generic-param
PServedUser-value =  name-addr/addr-spec
sessioncase-param =  "sescase" EQUAL
                     "orig"/"term"
registration-state-param = "regstate" EQUAL
                           "unreg"/"reg"
                           EQUAL, HCOLON,
                           SEMI, name-addr,
                           addr-spec, and
                           generic-param are
                           defined in RFC
                           3261.
```

The following is an example of a P-Served-User header field:

```
P-Served-User: <sip:user@example.com>;
sescase=orig; regstate=reg
```

12.4.4 Proxy Behavior: Generating the P-Served-User Header

Proxies that support the header must only insert the header in initial requests for a dialog or in stand-alone requests when the following conditions hold:

- The proxy has the capability to determine the served user for the current request.
- The next hop is part of the same Trust Domain for P-Served-User.

When the above conditions do not hold, the proxy must not insert the header.

12.4.5 Proxy Behavior: Consuming the P-Served-User Header

A proxy that supports the header must, upon receiving from a trusted node the P-Served-User header in initial requests for a dialog or in stand-alone requests, take the value of the P-Served-User header to represent the served user in operations that require such information. A proxy that supports the header must remove the header from requests or responses when the header was received from a node outside the Trust Domain for P-Served-User before further forwarding the message. A proxy that supports the header must remove the header from requests or responses when the next hop is a node outside the Trust Domain for P-Served-User before further forwarding the message.

12.4.6 Applicability and Limitations

The use of the P-Served-User header field extensions is only applicable inside a Trust Domain for served user and cannot be used in the Internet in general, as described earlier. Nodes in such a Trust Domain explicitly trust each other to convey the served user and to be responsible for withholding that information outside of the Trust Domain. The means by which the network determines the served user and the policies that are executed for a specific served user is not considered in RFC 5502. The served-user information lacks an indication of whom or what specifically determined the served user, and so it must be assumed that the Trust Domain determined the served user. Therefore, the information is only meaningful when securely received from a node known to be a member of the Trust Domain. Because the served user typically only has validity in one administrative domain, it is in general not suitable for interdomain use or use in the Internet at large. Despite these limitations, there are sufficiently useful specialized deployments that meet the assumptions described above, and that can accept the limitations that result, to warrant the informational publication of this mechanism, for example, a closed network like 3GPP's IMS.

12.5 Summary

We have explained why service IDs cannot be standardized for services over the public Internet in general. However, we have described how service IDs can be created using some canonical forms based on some hints of services that are provided by the user-level service-agnostic SIP signaling. The P-Preferred service ID, service URNs, and usage of these header fields are described. In addition, the P-Served-User ID that is used for handling of services are presented. The behaviors of all SIP entities in processing the services and P-Preferred service IDs are explained in detail. All of these service-related IDs can be used in private intradomain communications, but are not suitable for interdomain or public Internet communications. Finally, the security concerns in using these identities are addressed.

PROBLEMS

1. What are IDs used in SIP service-agnostic? Why are service IDs not officially standardized for use over the public Internet?
2. How do you suggest to identify communication services from signaling messages of SIP including presence and device dispatch? Describe in detail using examples in intradomain communication environments.
3. Do the IDs in SIP signaling messages provide sufficient hints for services over the SIP network that will provide interoperability? If not, what are the mechanisms that can be used for creation of service IDs over the private SIP network? Justify your recommendation with examples.
4. What are the P-Asserted-Service and P-Preferred-Service SIP header fields? Explain the usage of these header fields in request messages in SIP for the following: UAC, UAS, and proxy. Why are these header fields not required to be used in SIP response messages? Explain in detail the usage of these headers by using examples.
5. What are the security concerns in handling of services using the P-Asserted-Service and P-Preferred-Service SIP headers? How are these security concerns mitigated?
6. What is the P-Served-User SIP header? How does it help in handling of services over the SIP network in general? Explain using general scenarios for invocation of services.
7. Explain the use of the P-Served-User field for invocation of services for the following cases: diversion—continue on terminating leg, but finish subsequent terminating SSFC first; diversion—create new originating leg and provide originating SSFC processing; and call out of the blue—on behalf of user B, but service profile of service identity C.
8. What are the security concerns in handling of services using the P-Served-User and P-Preferred-Service SIP headers? How are these security concerns mitigated?

Chapter 13

Connections Management and Overload Control in SIP

Abstract

The Session Initiation Protocol (SIP), being an application layer protocol, forms the notion of end-to-end logical connections known as network flows, in the form of registrations or dialog-forming requests/responses between the SIP communicating functional entities, including user agents (UAs) and proxies. The management of these end-to-end connections in the form of network flows of SIP messages for reusing by proxies in the routing of SIP messages is very important, especially in the face of failures of SIP and network entities. The flow-based connection setup, keep-alive mechanisms, connection management by SIP entities, and illustrations of connection management are described in detail. In addition, the overload control of SIP entities, which is a prime requirement for the next-generation large-scale SIP networks, is articulated in great detail. Two types of overload control, known as loss-based and rate-based control algorithms, that complement each other are explained. The general behaviors of SIP entities for both overload control mechanisms are described in detail. The SIP extensions that are required for both connection management and overload control are also provided.

13.1 Introduction

The Session Initiation Protocol (SIP) enables end-to-end communications between user agents (UAs) after establishing a session that may last from a few seconds to hours. SIP proxies may route the SIP request/response messages sent by UAs. These SIP messages that may be sent over Transmission Control Protocol (TCP) or User Datagram Protocol (UDP) create a logical notion of connections in the SIP application layer, in the form of dialog-forming requests/responses including registration messages. We articulate how the SIP layer can manage those logical connections that can be reused by SIP logical entities for routing messages, especially in view of failures of SIP and network entities. It requires some new parameters in SIP that are used to characterize the logical connection. RFC 5626 that specifies the SIP connection management is described. On the other hand, it is critical that overload control of SIP entities are essential for the next-generation SIP networks. Recently, two kinds of overload control mechanisms, known as loss-based and rate-based overload controls, have been proposed in Request for Comment (RFC) 7339 and the International Engineering Task Force (IETF) draft [RATE-CONTROL], respectively. The loss-based control mechanism described in RFC 7339 requires some extensions in SIP parameters for the Via header. The rate-based overload control mechanism complements the loss-based control, taking care of more granularity of the overload control, including limiting the upper bound of the load of the client. Both of these overload control mechanisms, including their algorithms, are described.

13.2 Connections Management in SIP Network

13.2.1 Overview

The key idea of connections management in SIP specified in RFC 5626 that is described here is that when a UA sends a

REGISTER request or a dialog-forming request, the proxy can later use this same network flow that appears to be end-to-end connections between the communicating entities, whether this is a bidirectional stream of UDP datagrams, a TCP connection, or an analogous concept in another transport protocol, to forward any incoming requests that need to go to this UA in the context of the registration or dialog. In this context, the term flow used in SIP apparently may constitute a connection using the parameters defined in RFC 5626, such as flow token, instant-id, and reg-id that are specified by a UA at the time of registration as well as ob parameter used in the Path header. The flow token is an identifier that uniquely identifies a flow that can be included in a SIP Uniform Resource Identifier (URI). The reg-id refers to the value of a new header field parameter for the Contact header field. When a UA registers multiple times, each for a different flow, each concurrent registration gets a unique reg-id value. The instance-id refers to the value of the sip.instance media feature tag, which appears as a +sip.instance Contact header field parameter and is a Uniform Resource Name (URN) that uniquely identifies this specific UA instance. Note that the registration with multiple telephone addresses of record (AORs) for client-initiated outbound connection is described in Section 3.3.5.

The ob parameter is a SIP URI parameter that has a different meaning depending on context. In a Path header field value, it is used by the first edge proxy to indicate that a flow token was added to the URI. In a Contact or Route header field value, it indicates that the UA would like other requests in the same dialog to be routed over the same flow. In addition, RFC 5626 defines the *outbound* option tag, 430 Flow Failed, and 439 First Hop Lacks Outbound response code. A registrar places the outbound option tag in a Require header to indicate to the registering UA that the registrar used registrations using the binding rules defined in RFC 5626. The response 430 Flow Failed code is used by an edge proxy to indicate to the Authoritative Proxy that a specific flow to a UA instance has failed. The 439 First Hop Lacks Outbound Support response code is used by a registrar to indicate that it supports the outbound feature described in this specification, but that the first outbound proxy that the user is attempting to register through does not. In addition, keep-alive mechanisms are also used and a UA may register over multiple flows at the same time for improving reliability, and the keep-alive schemes will make sure that flows are active. If any flow goes down and the connection is not available because of server failures within the network path, the UA will able to get connected using any one of the remaining alternate flows.

The keep-alive mechanism is also used to keep network address translator (NAT) bindings open and to allow the UA to detect when a flow has failed. As a result, connections management using flow mechanisms allows keeping end-to-end persistence connections with UAs despite the existence of firewalls and NATs, or the use of Transport Layer Security (TLS) with server-provided certificates over TCP and failures and rebooting of servers in the network path. To illustrate different kinds of proxies in a large SIP network, RFC 5626 has defined some terms like authoritative proxy and edge proxy (EP). An authoritative proxy that handles non-REGISTER requests for a specific AOR, performs the logical Location Server lookup described in RFC 3263 (see Section 8.2), and forwards those requests to specific Contact URIs. An edge proxy is any proxy that is located topologically between the registering UA and the authoritative proxy. A UA can have multiple connections bindings with any number of proxies over the SIP network.

13.2.2 Flow-Based Connections Setup

In connections mechanisms, each UA has a unique instance-id that stays the same for this UA even if the UA reboots or is power cycled. Each UA can register multiple times over different flows for the same SIP AOR to achieve high reliability. Each registration includes the instance-id for the UA and a reg-id label that is different for each flow. The registrar can use the instance-id to recognize that two different registrations both correspond to the same UA. The registrar can use the reg-id label to recognize whether a UA is creating a new flow or refreshing or replacing an old one, possibly after a reboot or a network failure. For achieving reliability, a UA can set up connection bindings with multiple logical outbound proxies/registrars running on different hosts or multiple edge proxies of a given administrative domain. When a proxy goes to route a message to a UA for which it has a binding, it can use any one of the flows on which a successful registration has been completed.

A failure to deliver a request on a particular flow can be tried again on an alternate flow. Proxies can determine which flows go to the same UA by comparing the instance-id. Proxies can tell that a flow replaces a previously abandoned flow by looking at the reg-id. When sending a dialog-forming request, a UA can also ask its first edge proxy to route subsequent requests in that dialog over the same flow. This is necessary whether the UA has registered or not. UAs use a simple periodic message as a keep-alive mechanism to keep their flow to the proxy or registrar alive. For connection-oriented transports such as TCP, this is based on carriage-return and line-feed sequences (CRLF), while for transports that are not connection oriented, this is accomplished by using a SIP-specific usage profile of Session Traversal of UDP through NAT (STUN) specified in RFC 5389 (see Section 14.3).

13.2.3 Keep-Alive Mechanisms

Two keep-alive mechanisms are specified in RFC 5626: CRLF keep-alive and STUN keep-alive. Each of these mechanisms uses a client-to-server *ping* keep-alive and a corresponding server-to-client *pong* message. This ping–pong sequence allows the client, and optionally the server, to tell if its flow is still active and useful for SIP traffic. The server responds to pings by sending pongs. If the client does not receive a pong in response to its ping (allowing for retransmission for STUN as described in RFC 5389; see Section 8.2.4), it declares the flow dead and opens a new flow in its place. However, RFC 5626 (see Section 13.2) has suggested timer values for these client keep-alive mechanisms. These timer values were chosen to keep most NAT and firewall bindings open, to detect unresponsive servers within 2 minutes, and mitigate against the avalanche restart problem.

However, the client may choose different timer values to suit its needs, for example, to optimize battery life. In some environments, the server can also keep track of the time since a ping was received over a flow to guess the likelihood that the flow is still useful for delivering SIP messages. When the UA detects that a flow has failed or that the flow definition has changed, the UA needs to reregister and will use the backoff mechanism described later to provide congestion relief when a large number of agents simultaneously reboot. A keep-alive mechanism needs to keep NAT bindings refreshed; for connections, it also needs to detect failure of a connection; and for connectionless transports, it needs to detect flow failures including changes to the NAT public mapping. For connection-oriented transports such as TCP (RFC 0793) and Stream Control Transmission Protocol (SCTP; RFC 4960), this specification describes a keep-alive approach based on sending CRLFs. For connectionless transport, such as UDP (RFC 0768), this specification describes using STUN (RFC 5389, see Section 8.2.4) over the same flow as the SIP traffic to perform the keep-alive. UAs and proxies are also free to use native transport keep-alives; however, the application may not be able to set these timers on a per-connection basis, and the server certainly cannot make any assumption about what values are used. Use of native transport keep-alives is beyond the scope of this document.

13.2.3.1 CRLF Keep-Alive Technique

This approach can only be used with connection-oriented transports such as TCP or SCTP. The client periodically sends a double-CRLF (the ping), then waits to receive a single CRLF (the pong). If the client does not receive a pong within an appropriate amount of time, it considers the flow failed. It should be noted that sending a CRLF over a connection-oriented transport is backwards compatible because of requirements in Section 2.4.2 (RFC 3261), but only implementations that support this specification will respond to a ping with a pong.

13.2.3.2 STUN Keep-Alive Technique

This approach can only be used for connection-less transports, such as UDP. For connection-less transports, a flow definition could change because a NAT device in the network path reboots and the resulting public Internet Protocol (IP) address or port mapping for the UA changes. To detect this, STUN requests are sent over the same flow that is being used for the SIP traffic. The proxy or registrar acts as a limited STUN server on the SIP signaling port. Again, the STUN mechanism is very robust and allows the detection of a changed IP address and port.

13.2.4 Grammar

RFC 5626 defines a new header field Flow-Timer, and new Contact header field parameters, reg-id and +sip.instance. The grammar includes the definitions from RFC 3261. Flow-Timer is an extension-header from the message-header in the RFC 3261 augmented Backus–Naur Form (ABNF). The ABNF is repeated here for convenience, although all SIP syntaxes are provided in Section 2.4.1:

```
Flow-Timer      = "Flow-Timer" HCOLON 1*DIGIT
contact-params = /c-p-reg/c-p-instance
c-p-reg         = "reg-id" EQUAL 1*DIGIT; 1 to
                  (2^31 - 1)
c-p-instance    = "+sip.instance" EQUAL DQUOTE
                  "<" instance-val ">" DQUOTE
instance-val    = 1*uric; defined in RFC 3261
```

The value of the reg-id must not be 0 and must be less than 2^31.

13.2.5 Connections Management Procedures for SIP Entities

13.2.5.1 User Agent

13.2.5.1.1 Instance ID Creation

Each UA must have an Instance Identifier URN defined in RFC 2141 that uniquely identifies the device. Usage of a URN provides a persistent and unique name for the UA instance. It also provides an easy way to guarantee uniqueness within the AOR. This URN must be persistent across power cycles of the device. The instance ID must not change as the device moves from one network to another.

A UA should create a Universally Unique Identifier (UUID) URN specified in RFC 4122 as its instance-id. The UUID URN allows for noncentralized computation of a URN based on time, unique names such as a medium access control (MAC) address, or a random number generator. If a URN scheme other than UUID is used, the UA must only use URNs for which an RFC (from the IETF stream) defines how the specific URN needs to be constructed and used in the +sip.instance Contact header field parameter for outbound behavior. To convey its instance-id in both requests and responses, the UA includes a sip.instance media feature tag as a UA characteristic defined in RFC 3840 (see Sections 2.11 and 3.4). This media feature tag is encoded in the Contact header field as the +sip.instance Contact header field parameter. One case where a UA could prefer to omit the sip.instance media feature tag is when it is making an anonymous request or when some other privacy concern requires that the UA not reveal its identity.

When the instance ID is used in this specification, it is *extracted* from the value in the sip.instance media feature tag. Thus, equality comparisons are performed using the rules for URN equality that are specific to the scheme in the URN. If the element performing the comparisons does not understand the URN scheme, it performs the comparisons using the lexical equality rules defined in RFC 2141. Lexical equality could result in two URNs being considered unequal when they are actually equal. In this specific usage of URNs, the only element that provides the URN is the SIP UA instance identified by that URN. As a result, the UA instance has to provide lexically equivalent URNs in each registration it generates. This is likely to be normal behavior in any case; clients are not likely to modify the value of the instance ID so that it remains functionally equivalent to (yet lexicographically different from) previous registrations.

13.2.5.1.2 Connection-Oriented Registrations

To provide reliability for connections management per RFC 5626, a UA must support sets with at least two outbound proxy URIs and should support sets with up to four URIs. For each outbound proxy URI in the set, the UA client (UAC) should send a REGISTER request using this URI as the default outbound proxy. Alternatively, the UA could limit the number of flows formed to conserve battery power, for example. If the set has more than one URI, the UAC must send a REGISTER request to at least two of the default outbound proxies from the set. UAs that support RFC 5626 must include the outbound option tag in a Supported header field in a REGISTER request in addition to other and headers and parameters used for the normal registration. REGISTER requests must include an instance-id media feature tag as specified earlier. A UAC conforming to this specification must include in the Contact header field, a reg-id parameter that is distinct from other reg-id parameters used in other registrations that use the same +sip.instance Contact header field parameter and AOR. Each one of these registrations will form a new flow from the UA to the proxy. The sequence of reg-id values does not have to be sequential but must be exactly the same sequence of reg-id values each time the UA instance power cycles or reboots, so that the reg-id values will collide with the previously used reg-id values. This is so that the registrar can replace the older registrations.

For refreshing a binding and for removing a binding, subsequent REGISTER requests use the same instance-id and reg-id values as the corresponding initial registration where the binding was added. Registrations that merely refresh an existing binding are sent over the same flow as the original registration where the binding was added. If a reregistration is rejected with a recoverable error response, for example, by a 503 Service Unavailable containing a Retry-After header, the UAC should not tear down the corresponding flow if the flow uses a connection-oriented transport such as TCP. As long as pongs are received in response to pings, the flow should be kept active until a nonrecoverable error response is received. This prevents unnecessary closing and opening of connections. In an initial registration or reregistration in the case of the third-party registrations, a UA must not include a reg-id header field parameter in the Contact header field if the registering UA is not the same instance as the UA referred to by the target Contact header field. This practice is occasionally used to install forwarding policy into registrars. A UAC also must not include an instance-id feature tag or reg-id Contact header field parameter in a request to unregister all Contacts (a single Contact header field value with the value of "*").

13.2.5.1.3 Sending Connection-Oriented Non-REGISTER Requests

UAs that support this specification should include the outbound option tag in a Supported header field in a request that is not a REGISTER request and finds a protocol, IP address, and port for the next-hop URI using the Domain Name System (DNS). For protocols that do not use TLS, if the UAC has an existing flow to this IP address, and port with the correct protocol, then the UAC must use the existing connection. For TLS protocols, there must also be a match between the host production in the next hop and one of the URIs contained in the subjectAltName in the peer certificate. If the UAC cannot use one of the existing flows, then it should form a new flow by sending a datagram or opening a new connection to the next hop, as appropriate for the transport protocol.

Typically, a UAC using the procedures of this document and sending a dialog-forming request will want all subsequent requests in the dialog to arrive over the same flow. If the UAC is using a Globally Routable UA URI (GRUU) specified in RFC 5627 that was instantiated using a Contact header field value that included an *ob* parameter, the UAC sends the request over the flow used for registration, and subsequent requests will arrive over that same flow. If the UAC is not using such a GRUU, then the UAC adds an ob parameter to its Contact header field value. This will cause all subsequent requests in the dialog to arrive over the flow instantiated by the dialog-forming request. This case is typical when the request is sent before registration, such as in the initial subscription dialog for the configuration framework.

13.2.5.2 Edge Proxy

13.2.5.2.1 Processing Register Requests

When an edge proxy receives a registration request with a reg-id header field parameter in the Contact header field, it needs to determine if it (the edge proxy) will have to be visited for any subsequent requests sent to the UA identified in the Contact header field, or not. If the edge proxy is the first hop, as indicated by the Via header field, it must insert its URI in a Path header field value as described in RFC 3327 (see Section 2.8.2). If it is not the first hop, it might still decide to add itself to the Path header based on local policy. In addition, if the edge proxy is the first SIP node after the UAC, the edge proxy either must store a *flow token* (containing information about the flow from the previous hop) in its Path URI or reject the request. The flow token must be an identifier that is unique to this network flow. The flow token may be placed in the user part of the URI. In addition, the first node must include an ob URI parameter in its Path header field value. If the edge proxy is not the first SIP node after the UAC, it must not place an ob URI parameter in a Path header field value. The edge proxy can determine if it is the first hop by examining the Via header field.

13.2.5.2.2 Generating Flow Tokens

It is impractical to keep all of the states of the flow tokens as described earlier especially in the case when the proxy reboots after the crash. A proxy can use any algorithm it wants as long as the flow token is unique to a flow, the flow can be recovered from the token, and the token cannot be modified by attackers. RFC 5626 provides an example for generation of the flow token for the stateless proxy.

13.2.5.2.3 Forwarding Non-REGISTER Requests

When an edge proxy receives a request, it applies normal routing procedures with the following additions. If the edge proxy receives a request where the edge proxy is the host in the topmost Route header field value, and the Route header field value contains a flow token, the proxy follows the procedures of this section. Otherwise, the edge proxy skips the procedures in this section, removes itself from the Route header field, and continues processing the request. The proxy decodes the flow token and compares the flow in the flow token with the source of the request to determine if this is an incoming or an outgoing request. If the flow in the flow token identified by the topmost Route header field value matches the source IP address and port of the request, the request is an outgoing request; otherwise, it is an incoming request.

13.2.5.2.4 Processing Incoming Non-REGISTER Requests

If the Route header value contains an ob URI parameter, the Route header was probably copied from the Path header in a registration. If the Route header value contains an ob URI parameter, and the request is a new dialog-forming request, the proxy needs to adjust the route set to ensure that subsequent requests in the dialog can be delivered over a valid flow to the UA instance identified by the flow token. A simple approach to satisfy this requirement is for the proxy to add a Record-Route header field value that contains the flow token, by copying the URI in the Route header minus the ob parameter. Next, regardless of whether the Route header field contains an ob URI parameter or not, the proxy removes the Route header field value and forwards the request over the *logical flow* identified by the flow token, which is known to deliver data to the specific target UA instance. If the flow token has been tampered with, the proxy should send a 403 Forbidden response. If the flow no longer exists, the proxy should send a 430 Flow Failed response to the request.

13.2.5.2.5 Processing Outgoing Non-REGISTER Requests

For mid-dialog requests to work with outbound UAs, the requests need to be forwarded over some valid flow to the appropriate UA instance. If the edge proxy receives an outgoing dialog-forming request, the edge proxy can use the presence of the ob URI parameter in the UAC's Contact URI (or the topmost Route header field) to determine if the edge proxy needs to assist in mid-dialog request routing. Implementation note: specific procedures at the edge proxy to ensure that mid-dialog requests are routed over an existing flow are not part of this specification. However, an approach such as having the edge proxy add a Record-Route header with a flow token is one way to ensure that mid-dialog requests are routed over the correct flow.

13.2.5.2.6 Keep-Alive Handling

All edge proxies compliant with this specification must implement support for STUN NAT keep-alives on their SIP UDP ports as described earlier. When a server receives a double CRLF sequence between SIP messages on a connection-oriented transport such as TCP or SCTP, it must immediately respond with a single CRLF over the same connection. The last proxy to forward a successful registration response to a UA may include a Flow-Timer header field if the response contains the outbound option tag in a Require header field value in the response. The reason a proxy would send a Flow-Timer is if it wishes to detect flow failures proactively and take appropriate action (e.g., log alarms provide alternative treatment if incoming requests for the UA are received, etc.). The server must wait for an amount of time larger than the Flow-Timer in order to have a grace period to account for transport delay.

13.2.5.3 Registrar

RFC 5626 updates the definition of a binding in RFC 3261 (see Section 3.3) and RFC 3327 (see Section 2.8.2). Registrars that implement this specification must support the Path header mechanism defined in RFC 3327 (see Section 2.8.2). When receiving a REGISTER request, the registrar must check from its Via header field if the registrar is the first hop or not. If the registrar is not the first hop, it must examine the Path header of the request. If the Path header field is missing or it exists but the first URI does not have an ob URI parameter, then outbound processing must not be applied to the registration. In this case, the following processing applies: if the REGISTER request contains the reg-id and the outbound option tag in a Supported header field, then the registrar must respond to the REGISTER request with a 439 First Hop Lacks Outbound Support defined in RFC 5626 response; otherwise, the registrar must ignore the reg-id parameter of the Contact header. See Section 2.6, Table 2.4 for more information on the 439 response code. A Contact header field value with an instance-id media feature tag but no reg-id header field parameter is valid (this combination will result in the creation of a GRUU, as described in the GRUU specification in RFC 5627), but one with a reg-id but no instance-id is not valid. If the registrar processes a Contact header field value with a reg-id but no instance-id, it simply ignores the reg-id parameter.

A registration containing a reg-id header field parameter and a nonzero expiration is used to register a single UA instance over a single flow, and can also deregister any Contact header field with zero expiration. Therefore, if the Contact header field contains more than one header field value with nonzero expiration and any of these header field values contain a reg-id Contact header field parameter, the entire registration should be rejected with a 400 Bad Request response. The justification for recommending rejection versus making it mandatory is that the receiver is allowed by RFC 3261 to squelch (not respond to) excessively malformed or malicious messages. If the Contact header did not contain a reg-id Contact header field parameter or if that parameter was ignored as described above, the registrar must not include the outbound option tag in the Require header field of its response. The registrar must be prepared to receive, simultaneously for the same AOR, some registrations that use instance-id and reg-id, and some registrations that do not. The registrar may be configured with local policy to reject any registrations that do not include the instance-id and reg-id, or with Path header field values that do not contain the ob URI parameter.

If the Contact header field does not contain a +sip.instance Contact header field parameter, the registrar processes the request using the Contact binding rules defined in RFC 3261. When a +sip.instance Contact header field parameter and a reg-id Contact header field parameter are present in a Contact header field of a REGISTER request (after the Contact header validation as described above), the corresponding binding is between an AOR and the combination of the instance-id (from the +sip.instance Contact header parameter) and the value of reg-id Contact header field parameter. The registrar must store in the binding the Contact URI, all the Contact header field parameters, and any Path header field values. (Even though the Contact URI is not used for binding comparisons, it is still needed by the authoritative proxy to form the target set.) Provided that the UAC had included an outbound option tag (defined in Section 2.10) in a Supported header field value in the REGISTER request, the registrar must include the outbound option tag in a Require header field value in its response to that REGISTER request.

If the UAC has a direct flow with the registrar, the registrar must store enough information to uniquely identify the network flow over which the request arrived. For common operating systems with TCP, this would typically be just the handle to the file descriptor where the handle would become invalid if the TCP session was closed. For common operating systems with UDP, this would typically be the file descriptor for the local socket that received the request, the local interface, and the IP address and port number of the remote side that sent the request. The registrar may store this information by adding itself to the Path header field with an appropriate flow token. If the registrar receives a reregistration for a specific combination of AOR, and instance-id and reg-id values, the registrar MUST update any information that uniquely identifies the network flow over which the request arrived if that information has changed, and should update the time the binding was last updated. To be compliant with this specification, registrars that can receive SIP requests directly from a UAC without intervening edge proxies must implement the same keep-alive mechanisms as edge proxies described earlier. Registrars with a direct flow with a UA may include a Flow-Timer header in a 2xx class registration response that includes the outbound option tag in the Require header.

13.2.5.4 Authoritative Proxy Procedures: Forwarding Requests

When a proxy uses the location service to look up a registration binding and then proxies a request to a particular contact, it selects a contact to use normally, with a few additional rules:

- The proxy must not populate the target set with more than one contact with the same AOR and instance-id at a time.
- If a request for a particular AOR and instance-id fails with a 430 Flow Failed defined in RFC 5626 response, the proxy should replace the failed branch with another target if one is available with the same AOR and instance-id, but a different reg-id.
- If the proxy receives a final response from a branch other than a 408 Request Timeout or a 430 Flow Failed response, the proxy must not forward the same request to another target representing the same AOR and instance-id. The targeted instance has already provided its response.

The proxy uses the next-hop target of the message and the value of any stored Path header field vector in the registration binding to decide how to forward and populate the Route header in the request. If the proxy is colocated with the registrar and stored information about the flow to the UA that created the binding, then the proxy must send the request over the same logical flow saved with the binding, since that flow is known to deliver data to the specific target UA instance's network flow that was saved with the binding. Implementation note: typically, this means that for TCP, the request is sent on the same TCP socket that received the REGISTER request.

For UDP, the request is sent from the same local IP address and port over which the registration was received, to the same IP address and port from which the REGISTER was received. If a proxy or registrar receives information from the network that indicates that no future messages will be delivered on a specific flow, then the proxy must invalidate all the bindings in the target set that use that flow (regardless of AOR). Examples of this are a TCP socket closing or receiving a destination unreachable ICMP (Internet Control Message Protocol) error on a UDP flow. Similarly, if a proxy closes a file descriptor, it MUST invalidate all the bindings in the target set with flows that use that file descriptor.

13.2.5.5 Registration Call Flows Managing Client-Initiated Connection

We have provided an example message flow from RFC 5626 that extends the registration scheme defined in RFC 3261 (see Section 3.3) as explained earlier. These call flows illustrate most of the concepts related to the client-initiated outbound connection management by the registration server. In many cases, Via, Content-Length, and Max-Forwards headers are omitted for brevity and readability. In these examples, edge proxy 1 (EP1) and edge proxy 2 (EP2) are outbound proxies, and Proxy is the authoritative proxy. The section is subdivided into independent calls flows; however, they are structured in sequential order of a hypothetical sequence of call flows. We have considered that the outbound-proxy-set is already configured on Bob's UA for the sake of simplicity.

13.2.5.5.1 Registration

Now that Bob's UA is configured with the outbound proxy set, whether through configuration or using the configuration framework procedures of the previous section, Bob's UA sends REGISTER requests through each edge proxy (Figure 13.1) in the set. Once the registrations succeed, Bob's UA begins sending CRLF keep-alive messages about every 2 minutes.

In message F1 (Figure 13.1), Bob's UA sends its first registration through the first edge proxy in the outbound-proxy-set by including a loose route. The UA includes an instance-id and reg-id in its Contact header field value. Note the option tags in the Supported header.

Message F1:

```
REGISTER sip:example.com SIP/2.0
Via: SIP/2.0/TCP
192.0.2.2;branch=z9hG4bKnashds7
Max-Forwards: 70
From: Bob <sip:bob@example.
com>;tag=7F94778B653B
To: Bob <sip:bob@example.com>
Call-ID: 16CB75F21C70
CSeq: 1 REGISTER
Supported: path, outbound
Route: <sip:ep1.example.com;lr>
Contact:
<sip:bob@192.0.2.2;transport=tcp>;reg-id=1
       ;+sip.
instance="<urn:uuid:00000000-0000-1000-8000-
AABBCCDDEEFF>"
Content-Length: 0
```

Message F2 is similar to F1, but EP1 removes the Route header field value, decrements Max-Forwards, and adds its Via header field value. Since EP1 is the first edge proxy, it adds a Path header with a flow token and includes the ob parameter.

```
Path: <sip:VskztcQ/S8p4WPbOnHbuyh5iJvJIW3ib@
ep1.example.com;lr;ob>
```

Since the response to the REGISTER (message F3) contains the outbound option tag in the Require header field, Bob's UA will know that the registrar used outbound

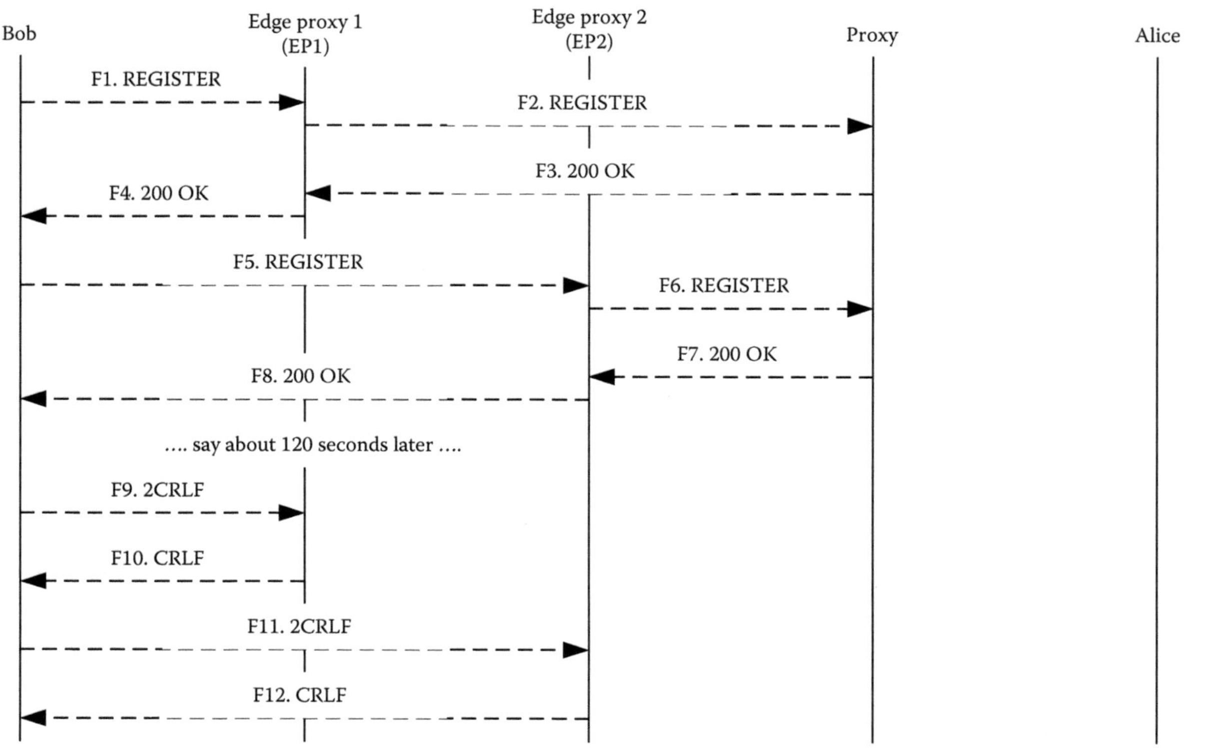

Figure 13.1 Registration call flows managing outbound connections. (Copyright IETF. Reproduced with permission.)

binding rules. The response also contains the currently active Contacts and the Path for the current registration.

Message F3:

```
SIP/2.0 200 OK
Via: SIP/2.0/TCP 192.0.2.15;branch=z9hG4bKnui
qisi
Via: SIP/2.0/TCP
192.0.2.2;branch=z9hG4bKnashds7
From: Bob <sip:bob@example.
com>;tag=7F94778B653B
To: Bob <sip:bob@example.
com>;tag=6AF99445E44A
Call-ID: 16CB75F21C70
CSeq: 1 REGISTER
Supported: path, outbound
Require: outbound
Contact: <sip:bob@192.0.2.2;transport=tcp>;
reg-id=1;expires=3600
      ;+sip.
instance="<urn:uuid:00000000-0000-1000-8000-
AABBCCDDEEFF>"
Path: <sip:VskztcQ/S8p4WPbOnHbuyh5iJvJIW3ib@
ep1.example.com;lr;ob>
Content-Length: 0
```

The second registration through EP2 (message F5) is similar except that the Call-ID has changed, the reg-id is 2, and the Route header goes through EP2.

Message F5:

```
REGISTER sip:example.com SIP/2.0
Via: SIP/2.0/TCP
192.0.2.2;branch=z9hG4bKnqr9bym
Max-Forwards: 70
From: Bob <sip:bob@example.
com>;tag=755285EABDE2
To: Bob <sip:bob@example.com>
Call-ID: E05133BD26DD
CSeq: 1 REGISTER
Supported: path, outbound
Route: <sip:ep2.example.com;lr>
Contact:
<sip:bob@192.0.2.2;transport=tcp>;reg-id=2
      ;+sip.
instance="<urn:uuid:00000000-0000-1000-8000-
AABBCCDDEEFF>"
Content-Length: 0
```

Likewise in message F6, EP2 adds a Path header with flow token and ob parameter.

```
Path: <sip:wazHDLdIMtUg6r0I/oRZ15zx3zHE1w1Z@
ep2.example.com;lr;ob>
```

Message F8 tells Bob's UA that outbound registration was successful, and shows both Contacts. Note that only the Path corresponding to the current registration is returned.

Message F8:

```
SIP/2.0 200 OK
Via: SIP/2.0/TCP
192.0.2.2;branch=z9hG4bKnqr9bym
From: Bob <sip:bob@example.
com>;tag=755285EABDE2
To: Bob <sip:bob@example.
com>;tag=49A9AD0B3F6A
Call-ID: E05133BD26DD
Supported: path, outbound
Require: outbound
CSeq: 1 REGISTER
Contact: <sip:bob@192.0.2.2;transport=tcp>;
reg-id=1;expires=3600
;+sip.instance="<urn:uuid:
00000000-0000-1000-8000-AABBCCDDEEFF>"
Contact: <sip:bob@192.0.2.2;transport=tcp>;
reg-id=2;expires=3600
;+sip.instance="<urn:uuid:
00000000-0000-1000-8000-AABBCCDDEEFF>"
Path: <sip:wazHDLdIMtUg6r0I/oRZ15zx3zHE1w1Z@
ep2.example.com;lr;ob>
Content-Length: 0
```

13.2.5.5.2 Incoming Call and Proxy Crash

Let us suppose that, after registration, EP1 crashes and reboots (Figure 13.2); before Bob's UA notices that its flow to EP1 is no longer responding, Alice calls Bob. Bob's authoritative proxy first tries the flow to EP1, but EP1 no longer has a flow to Bob, so it responds with a 430 Flow Failed response. The proxy removes the stale registration and tries the next binding for the same instance.

Message F13:

```
INVITE sip:bob@example.com SIP/2.0
To: Bob <sip:bob@example.com>
From: Alice <sip:alice@a.example>;tag=02935
Call-ID: klmvCxVWGp6MxJp2T2mb
CSeq: 1 INVITE
```

Bob's proxy rewrites the Request-URI to the Contact URI used in Bob's registration, and places the path for one of the registrations toward Bob's UA instance into a Route header field. This Route goes through EP1.

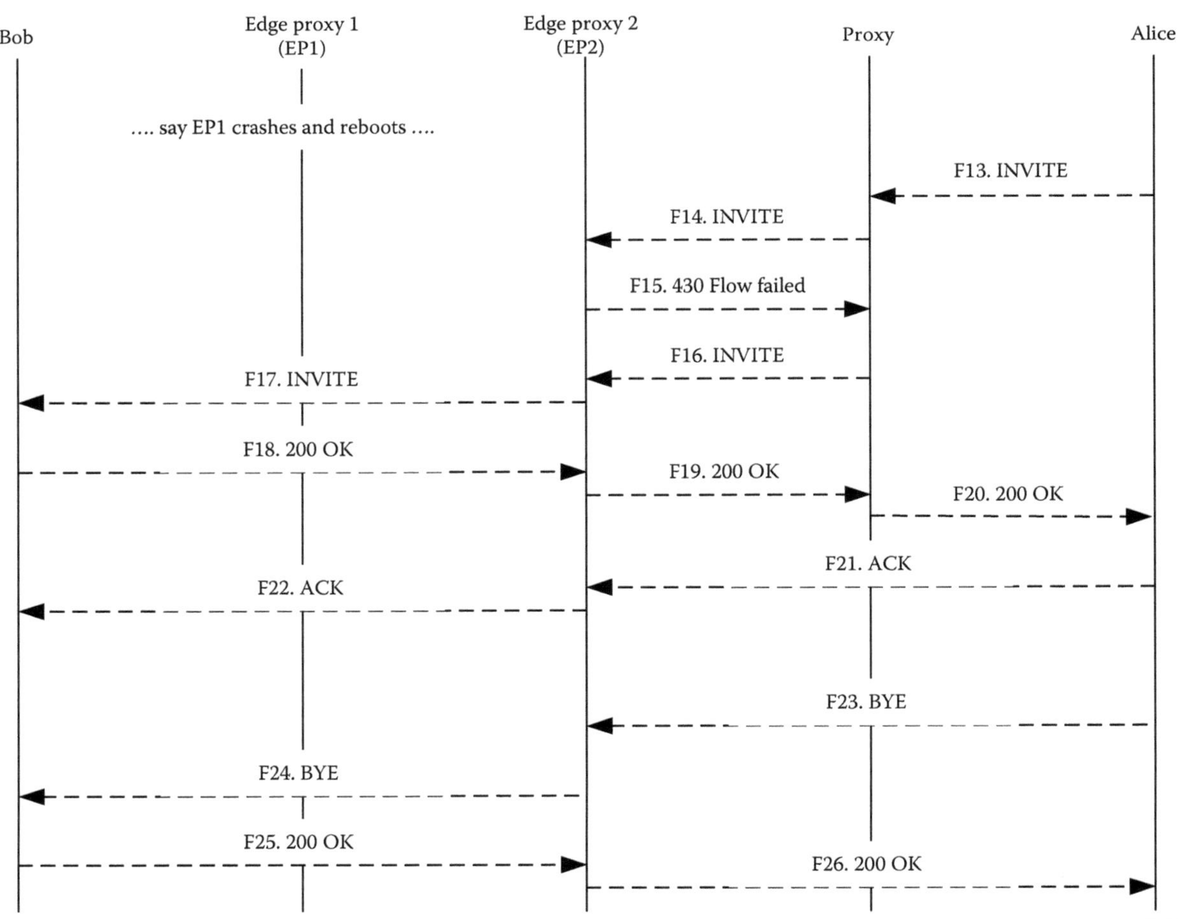

Figure 13.2 Incoming call and proxy crash. (Copyright IETF. Reproduced with permission.)

Message F14:

```
INVITE sip:bob@192.0.2.2;transport=tcp
SIP/2.0
To: Bob <sip:bob@example.com>
From: Alice <sip:alice@a.example>;tag=02935
Call-ID: klmvCxVWGp6MxJp2T2mb
CSeq: 1 INVITE
Route: <sip:VskztcQ/S8p4WPbOnHbuyh5iJvJIW3ib@
ep1.example.com;lr;ob>
```

Since EP1 just rebooted, it does not have the flow described in the flow token. It returns a 430 Flow Failed response.

Message F15:

```
SIP/2.0 430 Flow Failed
To: Bob <sip:bob@example.com>
From: Alice <sip:alice@a.example>;tag=02935
Call-ID: klmvCxVWGp6MxJp2T2mb
CSeq: 1 INVITE
```

The proxy deletes the binding for this path and tries to forward the INVITE again, this time with the path through EP2.

Message F16:

```
INVITE sip:bob@192.0.2.2;transport=tcp
SIP/2.0
To: Bob <sip:bob@example.com>
From: Alice <sip:alice@a.example>;tag=02935
Call-ID: klmvCxVWGp6MxJp2T2mb
CSeq: 1 INVITE
Route: <sip:wazHDLdIMtUg6r0I/oRZ15zx3zHE1w1Z@
ep2.example.com;lr;ob>
```

In message F17, EP2 needs to add a Record-Route header field value, so that any subsequent in-dialog messages from Alice's UA arrive at Bob's UA. EP2 can determine it needs to Record-Route since the request is a dialog-forming request and the Route header contained a flow token and an ob parameter. This Record-Route information is passed back to Alice's UA in the responses (messages F18, F19, and F20).

Message F17:

```
INVITE sip:bob@192.0.2.2;transport=tcp
SIP/2.0
To: Bob <sip:bob@example.com>
From: Alice <sip:alice@a.example>;tag=02935
Call-ID: klmvCxVWGp6MxJp2T2mb
CSeq: 1 INVITE
Record-Route:
<sip:wazHDLdIMtUg6r0I/oRZ15zx3zHE1w1Z@ep2.
example.com;lr>
```

Message F18:

```
SIP/2.0 200 OK
To: Bob <sip:bob@example.com>;tag=skduk2
From: Alice <sip:alice@a.example>;tag=02935
Call-ID: klmvCxVWGp6MxJp2T2mb
CSeq: 1 INVITE
Record-Route:
      <sip:wazHDLdIMtUg6r0I/oRZ15zx3zHE1w1Z@
ep2.example.com;lr>
```

At this point, both UAs have the correct route set for the dialog. Any subsequent requests in this dialog will route correctly. For example, the ACK request in message F21 is sent from Alice's UA directly to EP2. The BYE request in message F23 uses the same route set.

Message F21:

```
ACK sip:bob@192.0.2.2;transport=tcp SIP/2.0
To: Bob <sip:bob@example.com>;tag=skduk2
From: Alice <sip:alice@a.example>;tag=02935
Call-ID: klmvCxVWGp6MxJp2T2mb
CSeq: 1 ACK
Route: <sip:wazHDLdIMtUg6r0I/oRZ15zx3zHE1w1Z@
ep2.example.com;lr>
```

Message F23:

```
BYE sip:bob@192.0.2.2;transport=tcp SIP/2.0
To: Bob <sip:bob@example.com>;tag=skduk2
From: Alice <sip:alice@a.example>;tag=02935
Call-ID: klmvCxVWGp6MxJp2T2mb
CSeq: 2 BYE
Route: <sip:wazHDLdIMtUg6r0I/oRZ15zx3zHE1w1Z@
ep2.example.com;lr>
```

13.2.5.5.3 Reregistration

Somewhat later, Bob's UA sends keep-alive messages to both its edge proxies (Figure 13.3), but it discovers that the flow with EP1 failed. Bob's UA reregisters through EP1 using the same reg-id and Call-ID it previously used.

Message F30:

```
REGISTER sip:example.com SIP/2.0
From: Bob <sip:bob@example.
com>;tag=7F94778B653B
To: Bob <sip:bob@example.com>
Call-ID: 16CB75F21C70
CSeq: 2 REGISTER
Supported: path, outbound
Route: <sip:ep1.example.com;lr>
Contact:
<sip:bob@192.0.2.2;transport=tcp>;reg-id=1
```

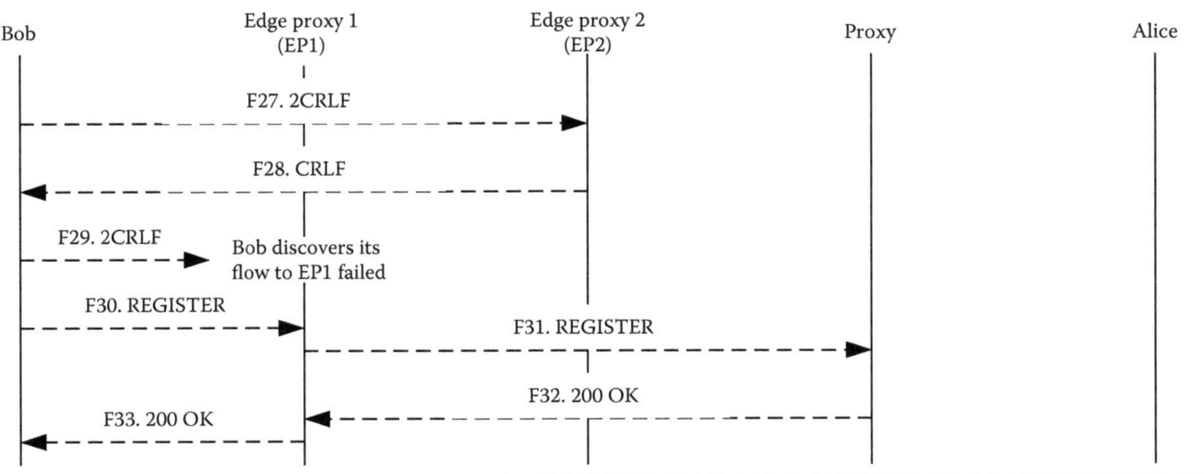

Figure 13.3 Call flows with reregistration. (Copyright IETF. Reproduced with permission.)

```
;+sip.instance="<urn:uuid:
00000000-0000-1000-8000-AABBCCDDEEFF>"
```

In message F31, EP1 inserts a Path header with a new flow token:

```
Path: <sip:3yJEbr1GYZK9cPYk5Snocez6DzO7w+AX@
ep1.example.com;lr;ob>
```

13.2.5.5.4 Outgoing Call

Finally, Bob makes an outgoing call (Figure 13.4) to Alice. Bob's UA includes an ob parameter in its Contact URI in message F34. EP1 adds a Record-Route with a flow token in message F38. The route set is returned to Bob in the response (messages F37, F38, and F39), and either Bob or Alice can send in-dialog requests.

Message F34:

```
INVITE sip:alice@a.example SIP/2.0
From: Bob <sip:bob@example.com>;tag=ldw22z
To: Alice <sip:alice@a.example>
Call-ID: 95KGsk2V/Eis9LcpBYy3
CSeq: 1 INVITE
Route: <sip:ep1.example.com;lr>
Contact: <sip:bob@192.0.2.2;transport=tcp;ob>
```

In message F35, EP1 adds the following Record-Route header.

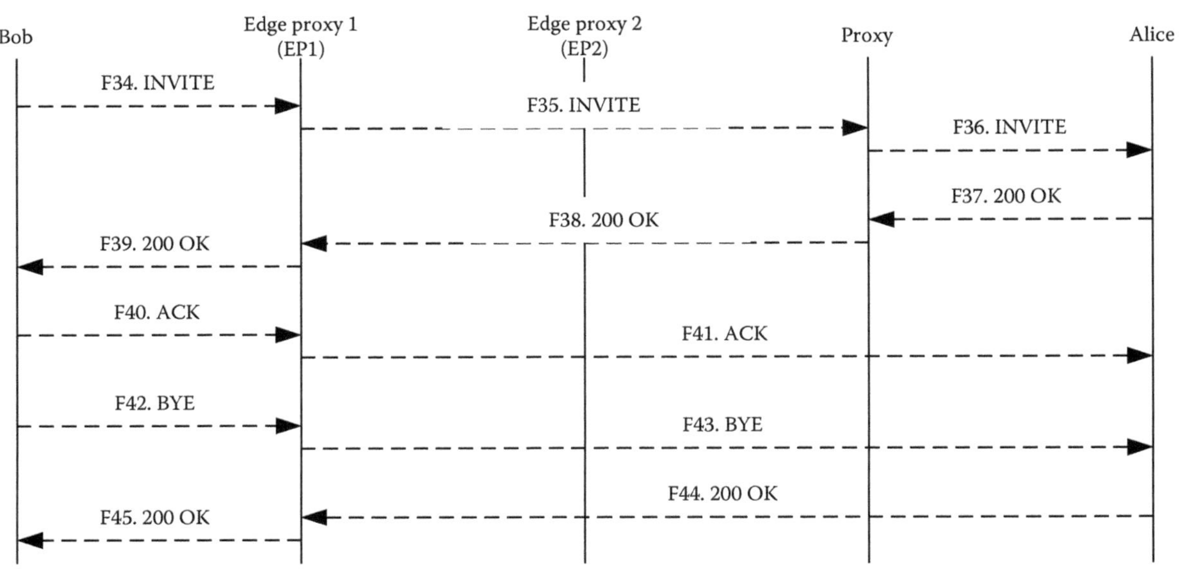

Figure 13.4 Outgoing call flows after reregistration. (Copyright IETF. Reproduced with permission.)

```
Record-Route:
      <sip:3yJEbr1GYZK9cPYk5Snocez6DzO7w+AX@
ep1.example.com;lr>
```

When EP1 receives the BYE (message F42) from Bob's UA, it can tell that the request is an outgoing request (since the source of the request matches the flow in the flow token) and simply deletes its Route header field value and forwards the request on to Alice's UA.

Message F42:

```
BYE sip:alice@a.example SIP/2.0
From: Bob <sip:bob@example.com>;tag=ldw22z
To: Alice <sip:alice@a.example>;tag=plqus8
Call-ID: 95KGsk2V/Eis9LcpBYy3
CSeq: 2 BYE
Route: <sip:3yJEbr1GYZK9cPYk5Snocez6DzO7w+AX@
ep1.example.com;lr>
Contact: <sip:bob@192.0.2.2;transport=tcp;ob>
```

13.2.6 Keep-Alive Mechanisms in SIP Network

Keep-alives are used for refreshing NAT/firewall bindings and detecting flow failure. Flows can fail for many reasons, including the rebooting of NATs and the crashing of edge proxies. As described earlier, a UA that registers will begin sending keep-alives after an appropriate registration response. A UA that does not register (e.g., a public switched telephone network [PSTN] gateway behind a firewall) can also send keep-alives under certain circumstances. Under specific circumstances, a UAC might be allowed to send STUN keep-alives even if the procedures in registration described earlier were not completed, provided that there is an explicit indication that the target first-hop SIP node supports STUN keep-alives. For example, this applies to a nonregistering UA, or to a case where the UA registration succeeded but the response did not include the outbound option tag in the Require header field. It should be noted that a UA can always send a double CRLF (a ping) over connection-oriented transports as this is already allowed by RFC 3261 (see Section 2.4.2.5). However a UA that did not register using outbound registration cannot expect a CRLF in response (a pong) unless the UA has an explicit indication that CRLF keep-alives are supported as described in this section.

Likewise, a UA that did not successfully register with outbound procedures needs explicit indication that the target first-hop SIP node supports STUN keep-alives before it can send any STUN messages. A configuration option indicating keep-alive support for a specific target is considered an explicit indication. If these conditions are satisfied, the UA sends its keep-alives according to the same guidelines as those used when UAs register; these guidelines are described below. The UA needs to detect when a specific flow fails. The UA actively tries to detect failure by periodically sending keep-alive messages using one of the techniques described in the following sections. If a flow with a registration has failed, the UA follows the procedures earlier to form a new flow to replace the failed one. When a successful registration response contains the Flow-Timer header field, the value of this header field is the number of seconds the server is prepared to wait without seeing keep-alives before it could consider the corresponding flow dead.

Note that the server would wait for an amount of time larger than the Flow-Timer in order to have a grace period to account for transport delay. The UA must send keep-alives at least as often as this number of seconds. If the UA uses the server-recommended keep-alive frequency, it should send its keep-alives so that the interval between each keep-alive is randomly distributed between 80% and 100% of the server-provided time. For example, if the server suggests 120 seconds, the UA would send each keep-alive with a different frequency between 95 and 120 seconds. If no Flow-Timer header field was present in a register response for this flow, the UA can send keep-alives at its discretion. The sections below provide recommended default values for these keep-alives. The client needs to perform normal SIP DNS resolution described in RFC 3263 (see Section 8.2.4) on the URI from the outbound-proxy-set to pick a transport. Once a transport is selected, the UA selects the keep-alive approach that is recommended for that transport.

13.2.6.1 Keep-Alive with CRLF

This approach must only be used with connection-oriented transports such as TCP or SCTP; it must not be used with connection-less transports such as UDP. A UA that forms flows checks if the configured URI to which the UA is connecting resolves to a connection-oriented transport (e.g., TCP and TLS over TCP). For this mechanism, the client ping is a double-CRLF sequence, and the server pong is a single CRLF, as defined in the ABNF below:

```
CRLF          =    CR LF
double-CRLF   =    CR LF CR LF
CR            =    %x0D
LF            =    %x0A
```

The ping and pong need to be sent between SIP messages and cannot be sent in the middle of a SIP message. If sending over TLS, the CRLFs are sent inside the TLS-protected channel. If sending over a SigComp compressed data stream described in RFC 3320, the CRLF keep-alives are sent inside the compressed stream. The double CRLF is considered a single SigComp message. The specific mechanism for representing these characters is an implementation-specific matter to be handled by the SigComp compressor at the sending end. If a pong is not received within 10 seconds after sending a ping (or immediately after processing any incoming message being received when that 10 seconds expires), then the client MUST treat the flow as failed. Clients MUST support this CRLF keep-alive. However, this value of 10-second timeout was selected to be long enough that it allows plenty of time for a server to send a response even if the server is temporarily busy with an administrative activity. At the same time, it was selected to be small enough that a UA registered to two redundant servers with unremarkable hardware uptime could still easily provide very high levels of overall reliability. Although some Internet protocols are designed for round-trip times over 10 seconds, SIP for real-time communications is not really usable in these types of environments, as users often abandon calls before waiting much more than a few seconds.

When a Flow-Timer header field is not provided in the most recent success registration response, the proper selection of keep-alive frequency is primarily a trade-off between battery usage and availability. The UA must select a random number between a fixed or configurable upper bound and a lower bound, where the lower bound is 20% less than the upper bound. The fixed upper bound or the default configurable upper bound should be 120 seconds (95 seconds for the lower bound) where battery power is not a concern, and 840 seconds (672 seconds for the lower bound) where battery power is a concern. The random number will be different for each keep-alive ping. The rationale for the selection of time values is as follows: the 120-second upper bound was chosen on the basis of the idea that for a good user experience, failures normally will be detected in this amount of time and a new connection will be set up. The 14-minute upper bound for battery-powered devices was selected on the basis of NATs with TCP timeouts as low as 15 minutes. Operators that wish to change the relationship between load on servers and the expected time that a user might not receive inbound communications will probably adjust this time. The 95-second lower bound was chosen so that the jitter introduced will result in a relatively even load on the servers after 30 minutes.

13.2.6.2 Keep-Alive with STUN

The STUN-based keep-alive approach must only be used with connection-less transports, such as UDP; it must not be used for connection-oriented transports such as TCP and SCTP. A UA that forms flows checks if the configured URI to which the UA is connecting resolves to use the UDP transport. The UA can periodically perform keep-alive checks by sending STUN specified in RFC 5389 (see Section 8.2.4) Binding Requests over the flow as described in the subsequent section. Clients must support STUN-based keep-alives. When a Flow-Timer header field is not included in a successful registration response, the time between each keep-alive request should be a random number between 24 and 29 seconds.

Note on selection of time values: the upper bound of 29 seconds was selected, as many NATs have UDP timeouts as low as 30 seconds. The 24-second lower bound was selected so that after 10 minutes, the jitter introduced by different timers will make the keep-alive requests unsynchronized to evenly spread the load on the servers. Note that the short NAT timeouts with UDP have a negative impact on battery life. If a STUN Binding Error Response is received, or if no Binding Response is received after seven retransmissions (16 times the STUN RTO timer—where RTO is an estimate of round-trip time), the UA considers the flow failed. If the XOR-MAPPED-ADDRESS in the STUN Binding Response changes, the UA MUST treat this event as a failure on the flow.

13.2.6.2.1 STUN Keep-Alive Processing

The STUN keep-alive processing is only applicable to the SIP transport layer that allows SIP and STUN Binding Requests to be mixed over the same flow, and constitutes a new STUN usage. The STUN messages are used to verify that connectivity is still available over a UDP flow, and to provide periodic keep-alives. These STUN keep-alives are always sent to the next SIP hop. STUN messages are not delivered end-to-end. The only STUN messages required by this usage are Binding Requests, Binding Responses, and Binding Error Responses. The UAC sends Binding Requests over the same UDP flow that is used for sending SIP messages. These Binding Requests do not require any STUN attributes. The corresponding Binding Responses do not require any STUN attributes except the XOR-MAPPED-ADDRESS. The UA server (UAS), proxy, or registrar responds to a valid Binding Request with a Binding Response that must include the XOR-MAPPED-ADDRESS attribute. If a server compliant to this section receives SIP requests on a given interface and UDP port, it must also provide a limited version of a STUN server on the same interface and UDP port. Note that it is easy to distinguish STUN and SIP packets sent over UDP because the first octet of a STUN Binding method has a value of 0 or 1, while the first octet of a SIP message is never a 0 or 1. Because sending and receiving binary STUN data on the same ports used for SIP is a significant and nonbackwards compatible change to RFC 3261, this section requires a number of checks before sending STUN messages to a SIP node.

If a SIP node sends STUN requests (e.g., due to incorrect configuration) despite these warnings, the node could be blacklisted for UDP traffic. A SIP node must not send STUN requests over a flow unless it has an explicit indication that the target next-hop SIP server claims to support this specification. UACs must not use an ambiguous configuration option such as "Work through NATs?" or "Do keep-alives?" to imply next-hop STUN support. A UAC may use the presence of an ob URI parameter in the Path header in a registration response as an indication that its first edge proxy supports the keep-alives defined in this document. Typically, a SIP node first sends a SIP request and waits to receive a 2xx class response over a flow to a new target destination, before sending any STUN messages. When scheduled for the next NAT refresh, the SIP node sends a STUN request to the target. Once a flow is established, failure of a STUN request (including its retransmissions) is considered a failure of the underlying flow. For SIP over UDP flows, if the XOR-MAPPED-ADDRESS returned over the flow changes, this indicates that the underlying connectivity has changed, and is considered a flow failure. The SIP keep-alive STUN usage requires no backwards compatibility with RFC 5389 (see Section 8.2.4).

13.2.6.2.2 Use with SigComp

When STUN is used together with SigComp specified in RFC 3320 compressed SIP messages over the same flow, the STUN messages are simply sent uncompressed, outside of SigComp. This is supported by multiplexing STUN messages with SigComp messages by checking the two topmost bits of the message. These bits are always 1 for SigComp, or 0 for STUN. All SigComp messages contain a prefix (the five most significant bits of the first byte are set to 1) that does not occur in UTF-8 of RFC 3629 encoded text messages; thus, for applications that use this encoding (or ASCII encoding), it is possible to multiplex uncompressed application messages and SigComp messages on the same UDP port. The most significant two bits of every STUN Binding method are both zeroes. This, combined with the magic cookie, aids in differentiating STUN packets from other protocols when STUN is multiplexed with other protocols on the same port.

13.2.6.3 Flow-Recovery Mechanisms

The flow-recovery mechanisms are described in RFC 5626 when a flow used in registration fails. When a flow used for registration (through a particular URI in the outbound-proxy-set) fails, the UA needs to form a new flow to replace the old flow and replace any registrations that were previously sent over this flow. Each new registration must have the same reg-id value as the registration it replaces. This is done in much the same way as forming a brand new flow. However, if there is a failure in forming this flow, the UA needs to wait a certain amount of time before retrying to form a flow to this particular next hop.

The amount of time to wait depends if the previous attempt at establishing a flow was successful. For the purposes of this section, a flow is considered successful if outbound registration succeeded and, if keep-alives are in use on this flow, at least one subsequent keep-alive response was received. The number of seconds to wait is computed in the following way. If all of the flows to every URI in the outbound-proxy-set have failed, the base time is set to a lower value (with a default of 30 seconds); otherwise, in the case where at least one of the flows has not failed, the base time is set to a higher value (with a default of 90 seconds). The upper-bound wait time (W) is computed by taking 2 raised to the power of the number of consecutive registration failures for that URI, and multiplying this by the base time, up to a configurable maximum time (with a default of 1800 seconds).

$$W = \min[T_m, \{T_b(2^f)\}]$$

where

T_m = max time (maximum time), T_b = base time (baseline time), and f = consecutive failures.

These times may be configurable in the UA. The three times are

- T_m with a default of 1800 seconds
- T_b (if all failed) with a default of 30 seconds
- T_b (if all have not failed) with a default of 90 seconds

For example, if the base time is 30 seconds, and there were three failures, then the upper-bound wait time is min[1800, $\{30(2^3)\}$] or 240 seconds. The actual amount of time the UA waits before retrying registration (the retry delay time) is computed by selecting a uniform random time between 50% and 100% of the upper-bound wait time.

The UA MUST wait for at least the value of the retry delay time before trying another registration to form a new flow for that URI (a 503 Service Unavailable response code to an earlier failed registration attempt with a Retry-After header field value may cause the UA to wait longer). To be explicitly clear on the boundary conditions: when the UA boots, it immediately tries to register. If this fails and no registration on other flows succeed, the first retry happens somewhere between 30 and 60 seconds after the failure of the first registration request. If the number of consecutive failures is large enough that the maximum of 1800 seconds is reached, the UA will keep trying indefinitely with a random time of 15 to 30 minutes between each attempt. The default flow registration backoff times are defined in Table 13.1 (Appendix A of RFC 5626). The base time used for the flow reregistration backoff times are configurable. If the base-time-all-fail value is set to the default of 30 seconds and the base-time-not-failed value is set to the default of 90 seconds, Table 13.1 shows the resulting amount of time the UA will wait to retry registration.

Table 13.1 Default Flow Registration Backoff Times

No. of Reg Failures	*All Flows Unusable*	*>1 Nonfailed Flow*
0	0 s	0 s
1	30–60 s	90–180 s
2	1–2 min	3–6 min
3	2–4 min	6–12 min
4	4–8 min	12–24 min
5	8–16 min	15–30 min
6	15–30 min	15–30 min

Source: Copyright IETF. Reproduced with permission.

13.2.7 Connection Management Example

We have taken the connections management call flow example in a SIP network as shown in Figure 13.5 adopted from RFC 5626. Two outbound edge proxy (EP) servers denoted by EP1 and EP2, proxy servers, one authoritative proxy server simply termed as proxy, and one configuration server (CS) are in the SIP network of the example.com administrative domain. An authoritative proxy handles non-REGISTER requests for a specific AOR and performs the location server lookup as described in RFC 3261 (see Section 3.3). An EP is the one that can be located between the registering UA and the authoritative proxy topologically. Some header fields like Via, Content-Length, and Max-Forwards are omitted for brevity and readability.

13.2.7.1 Configuration Subscription

Figure 13.5b shows the call flows of how Bob's UA obtains the configuration package of the outbound-proxy-set assuming that Bob's UA has not been configured yet. Bob's UA sends a SUBSCRIBE request for the UA profile configuration package through polling (Expires is zero). After receiving the NOTIFY request, Bob's UA fetches the external configuration and obtains a configuration file that contains the outbound-proxy-set sip:ep1.example.com;lr and sip:ep2.example.com;lr. Note that the configuration package is obtained using a different protocol other than SIP, such as HTTPS, which is not shown. In this example, the DNS server happens to be configured so that sip: example.com resolves to EP1 and EP2.

In this example (Figure 13.5b), the first message is as follows:

Message F1:

```
SUBSCRIBE sip:00000000-0000-1000-8000-
AABBCCDDEEFF@example.com
SIP/2.0
Via: SIP/2.0/TCP 192.0.2.2;branch=z9hG4bKnlsd
kdj2
Max-Forwards: 70
From: <anonymous@example.com>;tag=23324
To: <sip:00000000-0000-1000-8000-
AABBCCDDEEFF@example.com>
Call-ID: nSz1TWN54x7My0GvpEBj
CSeq: 1 SUBSCRIBE
Event: ua-profile;profile-type=device
;vendor="example.com";model="uPhone";
version="1.1"
Expires: 0
Supported: path, outbound
Accept: message/external-body,
application/x-uPhone-config
Contact: <sip:192.0.2.2;transport=tcp;ob>
;+sip.instance="<urn:uuid:
00000000-0000-1000-8000-AABBCCDDEEFF>"
Content-Length: 0
```

In message F2, EP1 adds the following Record-Route header:

```
Record-Route:
<sip:GopIKSsn0oGLPXRdV9BAXpT3coNuiGKV@ep1.
example.com;lr>
```

In message F5, the configuration server sends a NOTIFY with an external URL for Bob to fetch his configuration. The NOTIFY has a Subscription-State header that ends the subscription.

Message F5:

```
NOTIFY sip:192.0.2.2;transport=tcp;ob SIP/2.0
Via: SIP/2.0/TCP
192.0.2.5;branch=z9hG4bKn81dd2
Max-Forwards: 70
To: <anonymous@example.com>;tag=23324
From: <sip:00000000-0000-1000-8000-
AABBCCDDEEFF@example.com>;tag=0983
Call-ID: nSz1TWN54x7My0GvpEBj
CSeq: 1 NOTIFY
Route: <sip:GopIKSsn0oGLPXRdV9BAXpT3coNuiGKV@
ep1.example.com;lr>
Subscription-State: terminated;
reason=timeout
Event: ua-profile
Content-Type: message/external-body;
access-type="URL"
;expiration="Thu, 01 Jan 2009 09:00:00 UTC"
;URL="http://example.com/uPhone.cfg"
;size=9999;hash=10AB568E91245681AC1B
Content-Length: 0
```

EP1 receives this NOTIFY request, strips off the Route header, extracts the flow token, calculates the correct flow, and forwards the request message F6 over that flow to Bob. Bob's UA fetches the configuration file and learns the outbound-proxy-set.

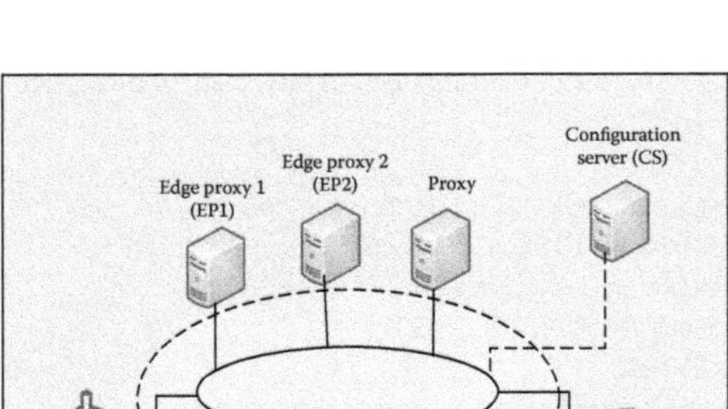

(a)

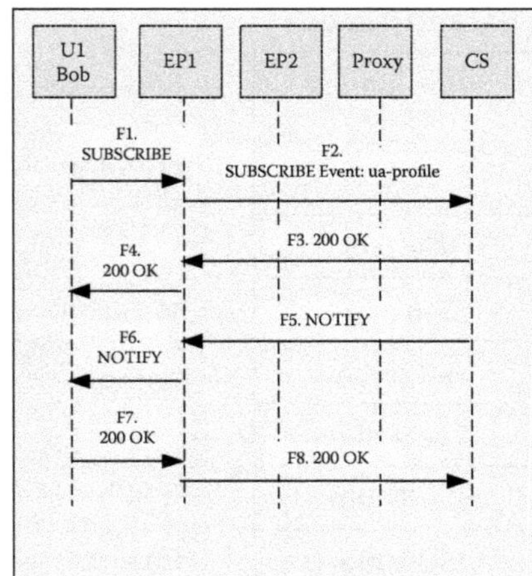

(b)

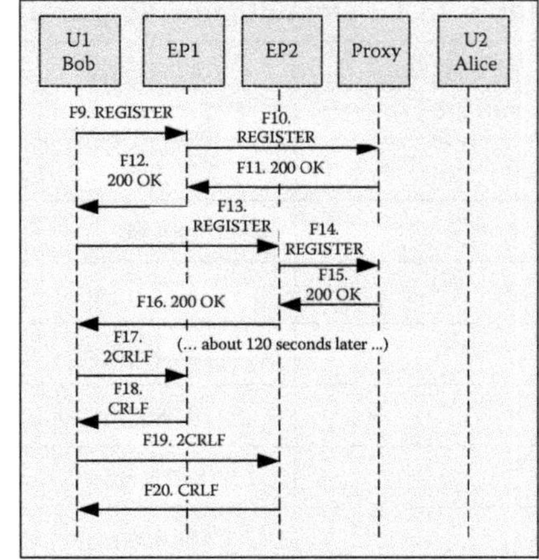

(c)

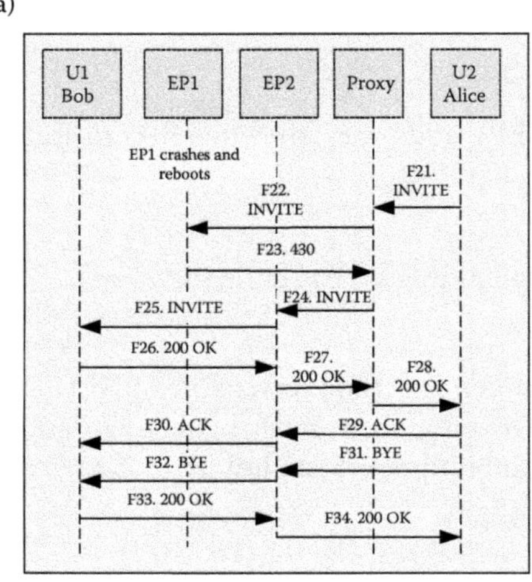

(d)

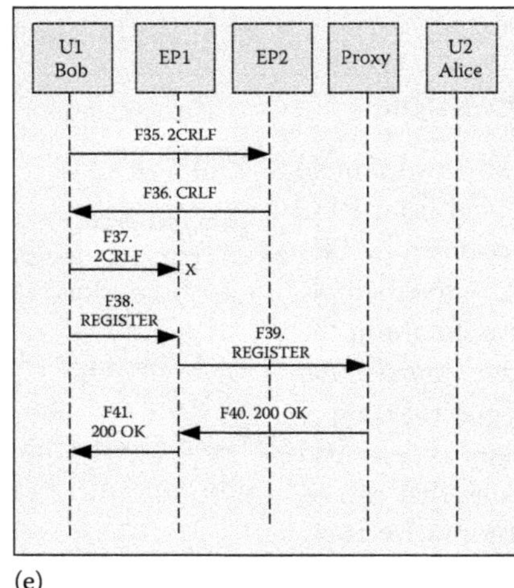

(e)

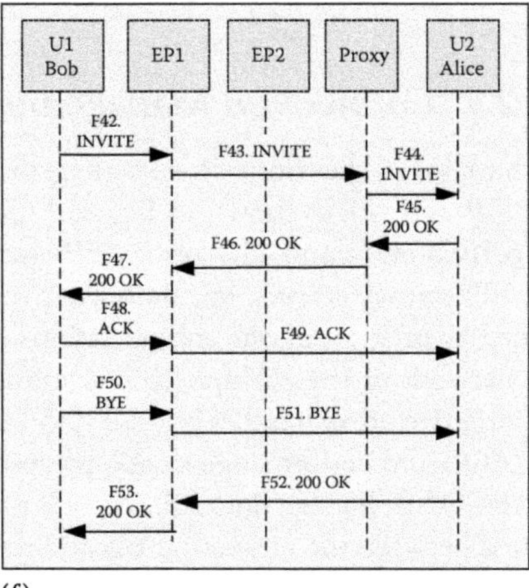

(f)

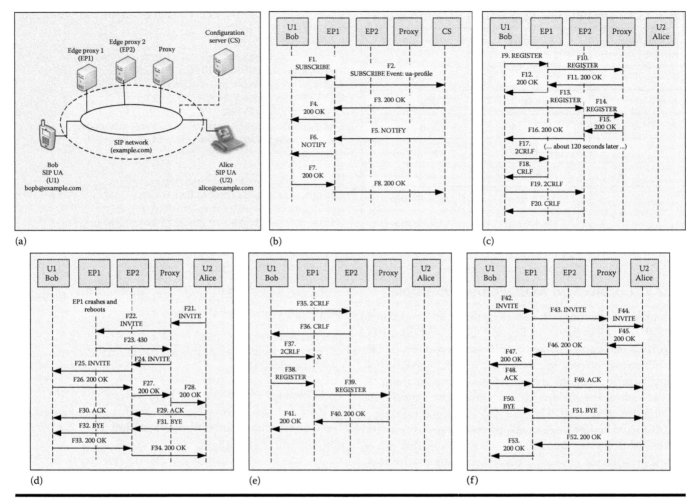

Figure 13.5 Connections management in SIP example: (a) SIP network and (b, c, d, e, and f) connections management call flows. (Copyright IETF. Reproduced with permission.)

13.2.7.2 Registration

The next step is the registration (Figure 13.5c) now that Bob's UA is configured with the outbound-proxy-set; whether through configuration or using other mechanisms, Bob's UA sends REGISTER requests through each edge proxy in the set. Once the registrations succeed, Bob's UA begins sending CRLF keep-alives about every 2 minutes. In message F9, Bob's UA sends its first registration through the first edge proxy in the outbound-proxy-set by including a loose route. The UA includes an instance-id and reg-id in its Contact header field value. Note the option tags in the Supported header.

Message F9:

```
REGISTER sip:example.com SIP/2.0
Via: SIP/2.0/TCP
192.0.2.2;branch=z9hG4bKnashds7
Max-Forwards: 70
From: Bob <sip:bob@example.com>
;tag=7F94778B653B
To: Bob <sip:bob@example.com>
Call-ID: 16CB75F21C70
CSeq: 1 REGISTER
Supported: path, outbound
Route: <sip:ep1.example.com;lr>
Contact:
<sip:bob@192.0.2.2;transport=tcp>;reg-id=1
;+sip.instance="<urn:uuid:
00000000-0000-1000-8000-AABBCCDDEEFF>"
Content-Length: 0
```

The registrar will challenge this registration to authenticate Bob (not shown here). When the registrar adds an entry for this contact under the AOR for Bob, the registrar also keeps track of the connection over which it received this registration. The registrar saves the instance-id (<urn:uuid:00000000-0000-1000-8000-AABBCCDDEEFF>) and reg-id (1) along with the rest of the Contact header field. If the instance-id and reg-id are the same as a previous registration for the same

AOR, the registrar replaces the old Contact URI and flow information. This allows a UA that has rebooted to replace its previous registration for each flow with minimal impact on overall system load.

When Alice sends a request to Bob, although not shown here, Bob's authoritative proxy selects the target set. The proxy forwards the request to elements in the target set based on the proxy's policy. The proxy looks at the target set and uses the instance-id to understand if two targets both end up routing to the same UA. When the proxy goes to forward a request to a given target, it looks and finds the flows over which it received the registration. The proxy then forwards the request over an existing flow, instead of resolving the Contact URI using the procedures in RFC 3263 (see Section 8.2.4) and trying to form a new flow to that contact. Message F10 is similar. EP1 removes the Route header field value, decrements Max-Forwards, and adds its Via header field value. Since EP1 is the first edge proxy, it adds a Path header with a flow token and includes the ob parameter.

```
Path: <sip:VskztcQ/S8p4WPbOnHbuyh5iJvJIW3ib@
ep1.example.com;lr;ob>
```

Since the 200 OK response message F11 to the REGISTER contains the outbound option tag in the Require header field, Bob's UA will know that the registrar used outbound binding rules. The response also contains the currently active Contacts and the Path for the current registration.

Message F11:

```
SIP/2.0 200 OK
Via: SIP/2.0/TCP 192.0.2.15;branch=z9hG4bKnui
qisi
Via: SIP/2.0/TCP
192.0.2.2;branch=z9hG4bKnashds7
From: Bob <sip:bob@example.com>
;tag=7F94778B653B
To: Bob <sip:bob@example.com>
;tag=6AF99445E44A
Call-ID: 16CB75F21C70
CSeq: 1 REGISTER
Supported: path, outbound
Require: outbound
Contact: <sip:bob@192.0.2.2;transport=tcp>;
reg-id=1;expires=3600
;+sip.instance="<urn:uuid:
00000000-0000-1000-8000-AABBCCDDEEFF>"
Path: <sip:VskztcQ/S8p4WPbOnHbuyh5iJvJIW3ib@
ep1.example.com;lr;ob>
Content-Length: 0
```

The second registration message F13 through EP2 is similar except that the Call-ID has changed, the reg-id is 2, and the Route header goes through EP2.

Message F13:

```
REGISTER sip:example.com SIP/2.0
Via: SIP/2.0/TCP
192.0.2.2;branch=z9hG4bKnqr9bym
Max-Forwards: 70
From: Bob <sip:bob@example.com>
;tag=755285EABDE2
To: Bob <sip:bob@example.com>
Call-ID: E05133BD26DD
CSeq: 1 REGISTER
Supported: path, outbound
Route: <sip:ep2.example.com;lr>
Contact:
<sip:bob@192.0.2.2;transport=tcp>;reg-id=2
;+sip.instance="<urn:uuid:
00000000-0000-1000-8000-AABBCCDDEEFF>"
Content-Length: 0
```

Likewise in message F14, EP2 adds a Path header with flow token and ob parameter.

```
Path: <sip:wazHDLdIMtUg6r0I/oRZ15zx3zHE1w1Z@
ep2.example.com;lr;ob>
```

Message F16 tells Bob's UA that outbound registration was successful, and shows both Contacts. Note that only the Path corresponding to the current registration is returned.

Message F16:

```
SIP/2.0 200 OK
Via: SIP/2.0/TCP
192.0.2.2;branch=z9hG4bKnqr9bym
From: Bob <sip:bob@example.com>
;tag=755285EABDE2
To: Bob <sip:bob@example.com>
;tag=49A9AD0B3F6A
Call-ID: E05133BD26DD
Supported: path, outbound
Require: outbound
CSeq: 1 REGISTER
Contact: <sip:bob@192.0.2.2;transport=tcp>;
reg-id=1;expires=3600
;+sip.instance="<urn:uuid:
00000000-0000-1000-8000-AABBCCDDEEFF>"
Contact: <sip:bob@192.0.2.2;transport=tcp>;
reg-id=2;expires=3600
;+sip.
instance="<urn:uuid:00000000-0000-1000-8000-
AABBCCDDEEFF>"
Path: <sip:wazHDLdIMtUg6r0I/oRZ15zx3zHE1w1Z@
ep2.example.com;lr;ob>
Content-Length: 0
```

13.2.7.3 Incoming Call in View of Proxy Crash

In another example (Figure 13.5d), we are considering that EP1 crashes and reboots after the registration of Bob with the authoritative proxy. Before Bob's UA notices that its flow to EP1 is no longer responding, Alice calls Bob sending an INVITE message F21. Bob's authoritative proxy first tries the flow to EP1, but EP1 no longer has a flow to Bob, so it responds with a 430 Flow Failed response message F23. The proxy removes the stale registration and tries the next binding for the same instance.

Message F21:

```
INVITE sip:bob@example.com SIP/2.0
To: Bob <sip:bob@example.com>
From: Alice <sip:alice@a.example>;tag=02935
Call-ID: klmvCxVWGp6MxJp2T2mb
CSeq: 1 INVITE
```

Bob's proxy rewrites the Request-URI to the Contact URI used in Bob's registration, and places the path for one of the registrations toward Bob's UA instance into a Route header field. This Route goes through EP1.

Message F22:

```
INVITE sip:bob@192.0.2.2;transport=tcp
SIP/2.0
To: Bob <sip:bob@example.com>
From: Alice <sip:alice@a.example>;tag=02935
Call-ID: klmvCxVWGp6MxJp2T2mb
CSeq: 1 INVITE
Route: <sip:VskztcQ/S8p4WPbOnHbuyh5iJvJIW3ib@
ep1.example.com;lr;ob>
```

Since EP1 just rebooted, it does not have the flow described in the flow token. It returns a 430 Flow Failed response message F23.

Message F23:

```
SIP/2.0 430 Flow Failed
To: Bob <sip:bob@example.com>
From: Alice <sip:alice@a.example>;tag=02935
Call-ID: klmvCxVWGp6MxJp2T2mb
CSeq: 1 INVITE
```

The proxy deletes the binding for this path and tries to forward the INVITE again, this time with the path through EP2:

Message F24:

```
INVITE sip:bob@192.0.2.2;transport=tcp
SIP/2.0
To: Bob <sip:bob@example.com>
From: Alice <sip:alice@a.example>;tag=02935
Call-ID: klmvCxVWGp6MxJp2T2mb
CSeq: 1 INVITE
Route: <sip:wazHDLdIMtUg6r0I/oRZ15zx3zHE1w1Z@
ep2.example.com;lr;ob>
```

In message F25, EP2 needs to add a Record-Route header field value, so that any subsequent in-dialog messages from Alice's UA arrive at Bob's UA. EP2 can determine it needs to Record-Route since the request is a dialog-forming request and the Route header contained a flow token and an ob parameter. This Record-Route information is passed back to Alice's UA in the responses (messages F26, F27, and F28).

Message F25:

```
INVITE sip:bob@192.0.2.2;transport=tcp
SIP/2.0
To: Bob <sip:bob@example.com>
From: Alice <sip:alice@a.example>;tag=02935
Call-ID: klmvCxVWGp6MxJp2T2mb
CSeq: 1 INVITE
Record-Route:
<sip:wazHDLdIMtUg6r0I/oRZ15zx3zHE1w1Z@ep2.
example.com;lr>
```

Message F26:

```
SIP/2.0 200 OK
To: Bob <sip:bob@example.com>;tag=skduk2
From: Alice <sip:alice@a.example>;tag=02935
Call-ID: klmvCxVWGp6MxJp2T2mb
CSeq: 1 INVITE
Record-Route:
<sip:wazHDLdIMtUg6r0I/oRZ15zx3zHE1w1Z@ep2.
example.com;lr>
```

At this point, both UAs have the correct route set for the dialog. Any subsequent requests in this dialog will route correctly. For example, the ACK request in message F29 is sent from Alice's UA directly to EP2. The BYE request in message #31 uses the same route set.

Message F29:

```
ACK sip:bob@192.0.2.2;transport=tcp SIP/2.0
To: Bob <sip:bob@example.com>;tag=skduk2
From: Alice <sip:alice@a.example>;tag=02935
Call-ID: klmvCxVWGp6MxJp2T2mb
CSeq: 1 ACK
Route: <sip:wazHDLdIMtUg6r0I/oRZ15zx3zHE1w1Z@
ep2.example.com;lr>
```

Message F31:

```
BYE sip:bob@192.0.2.2;transport=tcp SIP/2.0
To: Bob <sip:bob@example.com>;tag=skduk2
From: Alice <sip:alice@a.example>;tag=02935
Call-ID: klmvCxVWGp6MxJp2T2mb
CSeq: 2 BYE
Route: <sip:wazHDLdIMtUg6r0I/oRZ15zx3zHE1w1Z@
ep2.example.com;lr>
```

13.2.7.4 Reregistration

Next, we are considering a reregistration scenario (Figure 13.5e). Somewhat later, Bob's UA sends keep-alives to both its edge proxies, but it discovers that the flow with EP1 failed. Bob's UA reregisters through EP1 using the same reg-id and Call-ID it previously used.

Message F38:

```
REGISTER sip:example.com SIP/2.0
From: Bob <sip:bob@example.com>
;tag=7F94778B653B
To: Bob <sip:bob@example.com>
Call-ID: 16CB75F21C70
CSeq: 2 REGISTER
Supported: path, outbound
Route: <sip:ep1.example.com;lr>
Contact:
<sip:bob@192.0.2.2;transport=tcp>;reg-id=1
;+sip.instance="<urn:uuid:
00000000-0000-1000-8000-AABBCCDDEEFF>"
In message #39, EP1 inserts a Path header
with a new flow token:
Path: <sip:3yJEbr1GYZK9cPYk5Snocez6DzO7w+AX@
ep1.example.com;lr;ob>
```

13.2.7.5 Outgoing Call

Finally, the call flows for the outgoing call is taken. Bob makes an outgoing call to Alice. Bob's UA includes an ob parameter in its Contact URI in message F42. EP1 adds a Record-Route with a flow token in message F43. The route set is returned to Bob in the response (messages F45, F46, and F47), and either Bob or Alice can send in-dialog requests.

Message F42:

```
INVITE sip:alice@a.example SIP/2.0
From: Bob <sip:bob@example.com>;tag=ldw22z
To: Alice <sip:alice@a.example>
Call-ID: 95KGsk2V/Eis9LcpBYy3
CSeq: 1 INVITE
Route: <sip:ep1.example.com;lr>
Contact: <sip:bob@192.0.2.2;transport=tcp;ob>
```

In message F43, EP1 adds the following Record-Route header.

```
Record-Route:
<sip:3yJEbr1GYZK9cPYk5Snocez6DzO7w+AX@ep1.
example.com;lr>
```

When EP1 receives the BYE message F50 from Bob's UA, it can tell that the request is an outgoing request (since the source of the request matches the flow in the flow token) and simply deletes its Route header field value and forwards the request on to Alice's UA.

Message F50:

```
BYE sip:alice@a.example SIP/2.0
From: Bob <sip:bob@example.com>;tag=ldw22z
To: Alice <sip:alice@a.example>;tag=plqus8
Call-ID: 95KGsk2V/Eis9LcpBYy3
CSeq: 2 BYE
Route: <sip:3yJEbr1GYZK9cPYk5Snocez6DzO7w+AX@
ep1.example.com;lr>
Contact: sip:bob@192.0.2.2;transport=tcp;ob
```

13.2.8 Connection Reuse in SIP

RFC 5923 that is described here enables a pair of communicating proxies to reuse a congestion-controlled connection between themselves for sending requests in the forwards and backwards direction. Because the connection is essentially aliased for requests going in the backwards direction, reuse is predicated upon both the communicating endpoints authenticating themselves using X.509 certificates through TLS. For this reason, we only consider connection reuse for TLS over TCP and TLS over SCTP. RFC 5923 also provides guidelines on connection reuse and virtual SIP servers, and the interaction of connection reuse and DNS service (SRV) lookups in SIP. SIP entities can communicate using either unreliable/connectionless (e.g., UDP) or reliable/connection-oriented (e.g., TCP, SCTP) transport protocols. When SIP entities use a connection-oriented protocol (such as TCP or SCTP) to send a request, they typically originate their connections from an ephemeral port. In the following example, A listens for SIP requests over TLS on TCP port 5061 (the default port for SIP over TLS over TCP), but uses an ephemeral port (port 49160) for a new connection to B. These entities could be SIP UAs or SIP proxy servers. The SIP includes the notion of a persistent connection, which is a mechanisms to ensure that responses to a request reuse the existing connection that is typically still available, as well as reusing the existing connections for other requests sent by the originator of the connection. However, new requests sent in the backwards direction, in the example shown in Figure 13.6a, requests from B destined to A, are unlikely to reuse the existing connection. This frequently causes a pair of SIP entities to use one connection for requests sent in each direction, as shown in Figure 13.6b.

Unlike TCP, TLS connections can be reused to send requests in the backwards direction since each end can be authenticated when the connection is initially set up. Once the authentication step has been performed, the situation can be thought to resemble the picture in Figure 13.6a, except that A and B both use a single shared connection, for example, between port 49160 on A and port 5061 on B. When A wants to send a request to B, it will reuse this connection, and when B wants to send a request to A, it will reuse the same connection.

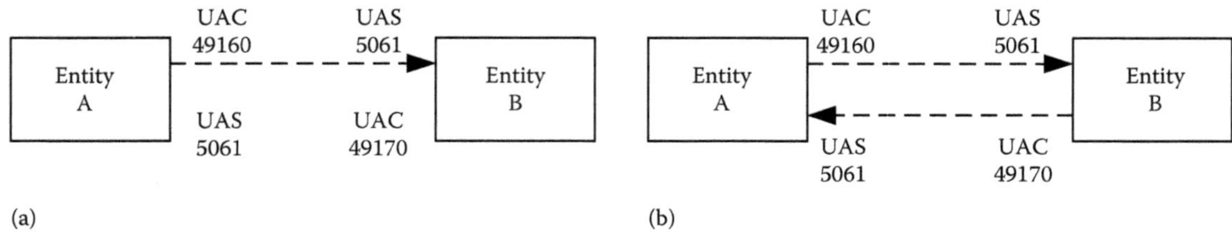

Figure 13.6 Connection requests between A and B: (a) unidirectional connection for requests from A to B, and (b) two connections for requests between A and B. (Copyright IETF. Reproduced with permission.)

13.2.8.1 Applicability

The applicability of the mechanism described in this document is for two adjacent SIP entities to reuse connections when they are agnostic about the direction of the connection; that is, either end can initiate the connection. SIP entities that can only open a connection in a specific direction—perhaps because of network address translation and firewalls—reuse their connections using the mechanism described in the outbound document RFC 5626 (see Section 13.2). RFC 5923 concerns connection reuse, not persistent connections (see definitions of these in Section 2.2). Behavior for persistent connections is specified in RFC 3261 (see Section 3.13) and is not altered by this memo. RFC 5923 documents that it is good practice to only reuse those connections where the identity of the sender can be verified by the receiver. Thus, TLS (RFC 5246) connections (over any connection-oriented transport) formed by exchanging X.509 certificates can be reused because they authoritatively establish the identities of the communicating parties.

13.2.8.2 Benefits of TLS Connection Reuse

Opening an extra connection where an existing one is sufficient can result in potential scaling and performance problems. Each new connection using TLS requires a TCP three-way handshake, a handful of round trips to establish TLS, typically expensive asymmetric authentication and key generation algorithms, and certificate verification. This can lead to a buildup of considerable queues as the server CPU becomes saturated by the TLS handshakes it is already performing. Consider the call flow shown in Figure 13.7 where proxy A and proxy B use the Record-Route mechanism to stay involved in a dialog. Proxy B will establish a new TLS connection just to send a BYE request.

Setting up a second connection (from B to A above) for subsequent requests, even requests in the context of an existing dialog (e.g., re-INVITE request or BYE request after an initial INVITE request, or a NOTIFY request after a SUBSCRIBE request or a REFER request), can also cause excessive delay (especially in networks with long round-trip times). Thus, it is advantageous to reuse connections whenever possible. From the user expectation point of view, it is advantageous if the re-INVITE requests or UPDATE requests are handled automatically and rapidly in order to avoid media and session state from being out of step. If a re-INVITE request requires a new TLS connection, the re-INVITE request could be delayed by several extra round-trip times. Depending on the round-trip time, this combined delay could be perceptible or even annoying to a human user. This is especially problematic for some common SIP call flows (e.g., the recommended example flow in RFC 3725 [see Section 18.3, Figure 18.1e] uses many re-INVITE requests). However, the mechanism described in RFC 5923 can mitigate the delays associated with subsequent requests as explained next.

13.2.8.3 Overview of Operation

We now explain this working in more detail in the context of communication between two adjacent proxies. Without any loss of generality, the same technique can be used for connection reuse between a UAC and an edge proxy, or between an edge proxy and a UAS, or between a UAC and a UAS. P1 and P2 are proxies responsible for routing SIP requests to UAs that use them as edge proxies (see Figure 13.8).

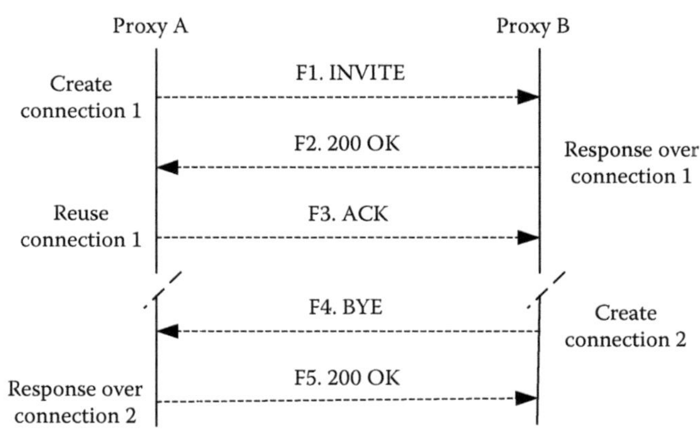

Figure 13.7 Multiple connections for requests. (Copyright IETF. Reproduced with permission.)

For illustration purposes, the discussion below uses TCP as a transport for TLS operations. Another streaming transport, such as SCTP, can be used as well. The act of reusing a connection is initiated by P1 when it adds an *alias* header field parameter (see Section 2.4.1) to the Via header field. When P2 receives the request, it examines the topmost Via header field. If the Via header contained an alias header field parameter, P2 establishes a binding such that subsequent requests going to P1 will reuse the connection; that is, requests are sent over the established connection. With reference to Figure 13.8, in order for P2 to reuse a connection for requests in the backwards direction, it is important that the validation model for requests sent in this direction (i.e., P2 to P1) is equivalent to the normal *connection in each direction* model, wherein P2 acting as client would open up a new connection in the backwards direction and validate the connection by examining the X.509 certificate presented. The act of reusing a connection needs the desired property that requests get delivered in the backwards direction only if they would have been delivered to the same destination had connection reuse not been employed. To guarantee this property, the X.509 certificate presented by P1 to P2 when a TLS connection is first authenticated is cached for later use.

To aid the discussion of connection reuse, this document defines a data structure called the connection alias table (or simply, alias table), which is used to store aliased addresses and is used by UAs to search for an existing connection before a new one is opened up to a destination. It is not the intent of this memo to standardize the implementation of an alias table; rather, we use it as a convenience to aid subsequent discussions. P1 gets a request from one of its upstream UAs, and after performing RFC 3263 (see Section 8.2.4) server selection, arrives at a resolved address of P2. P1 maintains an alias table, and it populates the alias table with the IP address, port number, and transport of P2 as determined through RFC 3263 server selection. P1 adds an alias header field parameter to the topmost Via header field (inserted by it) before sending the request to P2. The value in the sent-by production rule of the Via header field (including the port number) and the transport over which the request was sent become the advertised address of P1:

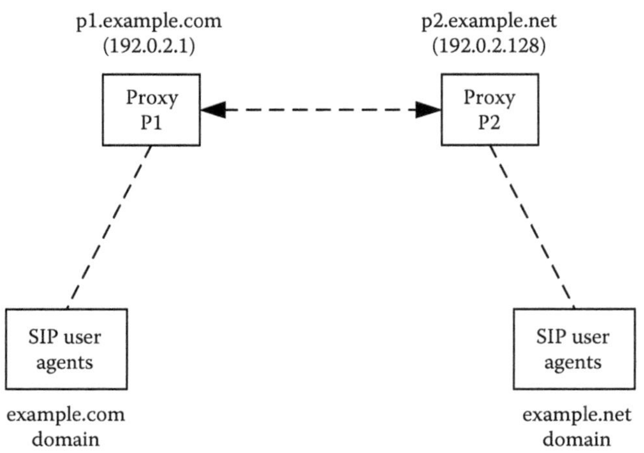

Figure 13.8 Proxy setup. (Copyright IETF. Reproduced with permission.)

```
Via: SIP/2.0/TLS p1.example.com
;branch=z9hG4bKa7c8dze;alias
```

Assuming that P1 does not already have an existing aliased connection with P2, P1 now opens a connection with P2. P2 presents its X.509 certificate to P1 for validation (see Section 19.2.2). Upon connection authentication and acceptance, P1 adds P2 to its alias table. P1's alias table now looks like

Destination IP Address	*Destination Port*	*Destination Transport*	*Destination Identity*	*Alias Descriptor*
...				
192.0.2.128	5061	TLS	sip:example.net, sip:p2.example.net	25

Subsequent requests that traverse from P1 to P2 will reuse this connection; that is, the requests will be sent over the descriptor 25. The following columns in the alias table created at the client warrant an explanation:

- The IP address, port, and transport are a result of executing the RFC3263 server resolution process on a next-hop URI.
- The entries in the fourth column consists of the identities of the server as asserted in the X.509 certificate presented by the server. These identities are cached by the client after the server has been duly authenticated (see Section 19.2.2).
- The entry in the last column is the socket descriptor over which P1, acting as a client, actively opened a TLS connection. At some later time, when P1 gets a request from one of the UAs in its domain, it will reuse the aliased connection accessible through socket descriptor 25, if and only if all of the following conditions hold:
  - P1 determines through the RFC 3263 (see Section 8.2.4) server resolution process that the {transport, IP-address, port} tuple of P2 is {TLS, 192.0.2.128, 5061}.
  - The URI used for the RFC 3263 server resolution matches one of the identities stored in the cached certificate (fourth column).

When P2 receives the request, it examines the topmost Via header field to determine whether P1 is willing to use this connection as an aliased connection (i.e., accept requests from P2 toward P1). The Via header field at P2 now looks like the following (the received header field parameter is added by P2):

```
Via: SIP/2.0/TLS p1.example.com;branch=z9hG4b
Ka7c8dze;alias;
                              received=192.0.2.1
```

The presence of the alias Via header field parameter indicates that P1 supports aliasing on this connection. P2 now authenticates the connection (see Section 19.2.2), and if the authentication was successful, P2 creates an alias to P1 using the advertised address in the topmost Via header field. P2's alias table looks like the following:

Destination IP Address	*Destination Port*	*Destination Transport*	*Destination Identity*	*Alias Descriptor*
...				
192.0.2.1	5061	TLS	sip:example.com, sip:p2.example.com	18

There are a few items of interest here:

- The IP address field is populated with the source address of the client.
- The port field is populated from the advertised address (topmost Via header field), if a port is present in it, or 5061 if not.
- The transport field is populated from the advertised address (topmost Via header field).
- The entries in the fourth column consist of the identities of the client as asserted in the X.509 certificate presented by the client. These identities are cached by the server after the client has been duly authenticated (see Section 19.2.2).
- The entry in the last column is the socket descriptor over which the connection was passively accepted. At some later time, when P2 gets a request from one of the UAs in its domain, it will reuse the aliased connection accessible through socket descriptor 18 if and only if all of the following conditions hold:
  - P2 determines through RFC3263 server resolution process that the {transport, IP-address, port} tuple of P1 is {TLS, 192.0.2.1, 5061}.
  - The URI used for RFC3263 server resolution matches one of the identities stored in the cached certificate (fourth column).
  - The network address inserted in the Destination IP Address column is the source address as seen by P2 (i.e., the received header field parameter). It could be the case that the host name of P1 resolves to different IP addresses due to round-robin DNS. However, the aliased connection is to be established with the original sender of the request.

13.2.8.4 Requirements

The following are the requirements that motivated this specification:

- A connection-sharing mechanism should allow SIP entities to reuse existing connections for requests and responses that originated from either peer in the connection.
- A connection-sharing mechanism must not require clients to send all traffic from well-known SIP ports.
- A connection-sharing mechanism must not require configuring ephemeral port numbers in DNS.
- A connection-sharing mechanism must prevent unauthorized hijacking of other connections.
- Connection sharing should persist across SIP transactions and dialogs.
- Connection sharing must work across name-based virtual SIP servers.
- There is no requirement to share a complete path for ordinary connection reuse. Hop-by-hop connection sharing is more appropriate.

13.2.8.5 Normative Behavior

13.2.8.5.1 Client Behavior

Clients should keep connections up as long as they are needed. Connection reuse works best when the client and the server maintain their connections for long periods of time. Clients, therefore, should not automatically drop connections on completion of a transaction or termination of a dialog. The mechanism for connection reuse uses a new Via header field parameter. The alias header field parameter is included in a Via header field value to indicate that the client wants to create a transport layer alias. The client places its advertised address in the Via header field value (in the sent-by production). If the client places an alias header field parameter in the topmost Via header of the request, the client should keep the connection open for as long as the resources on the host operating system allow it to, and that the client must accept requests over this connection, in addition to the default listening port, from its downstream peer. Furthermore, the client should reuse the connection when subsequent requests in the same or different transactions are destined to the same resolved address. Note that RFC 3261 (see Section 3.13) states that a response arrives over the same connection that was opened for a request.

Whether or not to allow an aliased connection ultimately depends on the recipient of the request; that is, the client does not get any confirmation that its downstream peer created the alias, or indeed that it even supports this specification. Thus, clients must not assume that the acceptance of a request by a server automatically enables connection aliasing. Clients must continue receiving requests on their default port. Clients must authenticate the connection before forming an alias (see Section 19.2.2). Once the server has been authenticated, the client must cache, in the alias table, the identity (or identities) of the server as determined in RFC 5922 (see Section 19.4.6). The client must also populate the destination IP address, port, and transport of the server in the alias table; these fields are retrieved from executing RFC3263 (see Section 8.2.4) server resolution process on the next-hop URI. Finally, the client must populate the alias descriptor field with the connection handle (or identifier) used to connect to the server. Once the alias table has been updated with a resolved address, and the client wants to send a new request in the direction of the server, the client reuses the connection only if all of the following conditions hold:

- The client uses the RFC3263 resolution on a URI and arrives at a resolved address contained in the alias table.
- The URI used for RFC3263 server resolution matches one of the identities stored in the alias table row corresponding to that resolved address.

Clients must be prepared for the case that the connection no longer exists when they are ready to send a subsequent request over it. In such a case, a new connection must be opened to the resolved address, and the alias table updated accordingly. This behavior has an adverse side effect when a CANCEL request or an ACK request for a non-2xx response is sent downstream. Normally, these would be sent over the same connection over which the INVITE request was sent. However, if between the sending of the INVITE request and subsequent sending of the CANCEL request or ACK request to a non-2xx response, the connection was closed, then the client should open a new connection to the resolved address and send the CANCEL request or ACK request there instead. The client may insert the newly opened connection into the alias table.

13.2.8.5.2 Server Behavior

Servers should keep connections up unless they need to reclaim resources. Connection reuse works best when the client and the server maintain their connections for long periods of time. Servers, therefore, should not automatically drop connections on completion of a transaction or termination of a dialog. When a server receives a request over TLS whose topmost Via header field contains an alias header field parameter, it signifies that the upstream client will leave the connection open beyond the transaction and dialog lifetime, and that subsequent transactions and dialogs that are destined to a resolved address that matches the identifiers in the advertised address in the topmost Via header field can reuse this connection. Whether or not to use, in the reverse direction, a connection marked with the alias Via header field parameter ultimately depends on the policies of the server. It can choose to honor it, and thereby send subsequent requests over the aliased connection. If the server chooses not to honor an aliased connection, the server must allow the request to proceed as though the alias header field parameter was not present in the topmost Via header. This assures interoperability with RFC3261 server behavior. Clients can include the alias header field parameter without fear that the server will reject the SIP request because of its presence.

Servers must be prepared to deal with the case that the aliased connection no longer exists when they are ready to send a subsequent request over it. This can occur if the peer ran out of operating system resources and had to close the connection. In such a case, the server must open a new connection to the resolved address, and the alias table updated accordingly. If the sent-by production of the Via header field contains a port, the server must use it as a destination port. Otherwise, the default port is the destination port. Servers must authenticate (see Section 19.2.2) the connection before forming an alias. The server, if it decides to reuse the connection, must cache in the alias table the identity (or identities) of the client as they appear in the X.509 certificate subjectAlternativeName extension field. The server also populates the destination IP address, port, and transport in the alias table from the topmost Via header field (using the *;received* parameter for the destination IP address). If the port number is omitted, a default port number of 5061 is to be used. Finally, the server populates the alias descriptor field with the connection handle (or identifier) used to accept the connection from the client (see Section 2.1 for the contents of the alias table). Once the alias table has been updated, and the server wants to send a request in the direction of the client, it reuses the connection only if all of the following conditions hold:

- The server, which acts as a client for this transaction, uses the RFC3263 resolution process on a URI and arrives at a resolved address contained in the alias table.
- The URI used for RFC3263 server resolution matches one of the identities stored in the alias table row corresponding to that resolved address.

13.2.8.5.3 Closing a TLS connection

Either the client or the server may terminate a TLS session by sending a TLS closure alert. Before closing a TLS connection, the initiator of the closure must either wait for any outstanding SIP transactions to complete, or explicitly abandon them. After the initiator of the close has sent a closure alert, it must discard any TLS message until it has received a similar alert from its peer. The receiver of the closure alert must not start any new SIP transactions after the receipt of the closure alert.

13.2.8.6 Connection Reuse and SRV Interaction

Connection reuse has an interaction with the DNS SRV load balancing mechanism. To understand the interaction, consider Figure 13.9.

Here, the proxy uses the DNS SRV to load balance across the three servers, S1, S2, and S3. Using the connect reuse mechanism specified in this document, over time the proxy will maintain a distinct aliased connection to each of the servers. However, once this is done, subsequent traffic is load balanced across the three downstream servers in the normal manner.

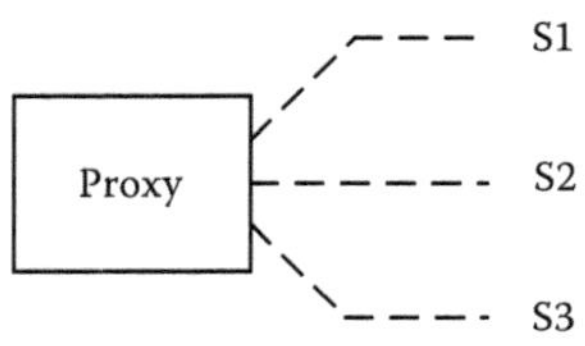

Figure 13.9 Load balancing.

13.3 Loss-Based Overload Control in SIP Network

13.3.1 Overview

Like any network element, a SIP server (RFC 3261, see Section 2.4.4) can suffer from overload when the number of SIP messages it receives exceeds the number of messages it can process. Overload can pose a serious problem for a network of SIP servers. During periods of overload, the throughput of a network of SIP servers can be significantly degraded. In fact, overload may lead to a situation where the retransmissions of dropped SIP messages may overwhelm the capacity of the network. This is often called *congestion collapse*. Overload is said to occur if a SIP server does not have sufficient resources to process all incoming SIP messages. These resources may include CPU processing capacity, memory, input/output, or disk resources. For overload control, this document only addresses failure cases where SIP servers are unable to process all SIP requests because of resource constraints. There are other cases where a SIP server can successfully process incoming requests but has to reject them due to failure conditions unrelated to the SIP server being overloaded. For example, a PSTN gateway that runs out of trunks but still has plenty of capacity to process SIP messages should reject incoming INVITEs using a 488 Not Acceptable Here response (RFC 4412, see Section 2.8).

Similarly, a SIP registrar that has lost connectivity to its registration database but is still capable of processing SIP requests should reject REGISTER requests with a 500 Server Error response (RFC 3261, see Section 2.6). Overload control does not apply to these cases, and SIP provides appropriate response codes for them. The SIP provides a limited mechanism for overload control through its 503 Service Unavailable response code. However, this mechanism cannot prevent overload of a SIP server, and it cannot prevent congestion collapse. In fact, the use of the 503 Service Unavailable response code may cause traffic to oscillate and shift between SIP servers, thereby worsening an overload condition. A detailed discussion of the SIP overload problem, the problems with the 503 Service Unavailable response code, and the requirements for a SIP overload control mechanism can be found in RFC 5390 (see Section 13.3.9).

RFC 7339 that is described here defines the protocol for communicating overload information between SIP servers and clients so that clients can reduce the volume of traffic sent to overloaded servers, avoiding congestion collapse and increasing useful throughput. It describes the Via header parameters used for overload control communication. In addition, the general behavior of SIP servers and clients involved in overload control is specified. RFC 7339 specifies the loss-based overload control scheme that is mandatory to implement for this specification. However, it allows other overload control schemes to be supported as well. To do so effectively, the expectations and primitive protocol parameters common to all classes of overload control schemes are described here.

13.3.2 Operations

We provide an overview of how the overload control mechanism operates by introducing the overload control parameters. The next section provides more details and normative behavior on the parameters listed below. Because overload control is performed hop-by-hop, the Via header parameter is attractive since it allows two adjacent SIP entities to indicate support for, and exchange information associated with, overload control specified in RFC 6357 that describes the design for management of overload in SIP handling overload conditions. Additional advantages of this choice are discussed here later. An alternative mechanism using SIP event packages was also considered, and the characteristics of that choice are further outlined here.

RFC 7339 defines four new parameters for the SIP Via header for overload control. These parameters provide a mechanism for conveying overload control information between adjacent SIP entities. The *oc* parameter is used by a SIP server to indicate a reduction in the number of requests arriving at the server. The *oc-algo* parameter contains a token or a list of tokens corresponding to the class of overload control algorithms supported by the client. The server chooses one algorithm from this list. The *oc-validity* parameter establishes a time limit for which overload control is in effect, and the *oc-seq* parameter aids in sequencing the responses at the client. These parameters are discussed in detail in the next section.

13.3.3 Via Header Parameters for Overload Control

The four Via header parameters that are introduced by RFC 7339 are described here. Further context about how to interpret these under various conditions is provided in the next section.

13.3.3.1 Parameter: oc

This parameter is inserted by the SIP client and updated by the SIP server. A SIP client must add an oc parameter to the topmost Via header it inserts into every SIP request. This provides an indication to downstream neighbors that the client supports overload control. There must not be a value associated with the parameter (the value will be added by the server). The downstream server must add a value to the oc parameter in the response going upstream to a client that included the oc parameter in the request. Inclusion of a value to the parameter represents two things. First, upon the first contact (see the next section), addition of a value by the server to this parameter indicates (to the client) that the downstream server supports overload control as defined in this document. Second, if overload control is active, then it indicates the level of control to be applied. When a SIP client receives a response with the value in the oc parameter filled in, it must reduce, as indicated by the oc and oc-algo parameters, the number of requests going downstream to the SIP server from which it received the response.

13.3.3.2 Parameter: oc-algo

This parameter is inserted by the SIP client and updated by the SIP server. A SIP client MUST add an oc-algo parameter to the topmost Via header it inserts into every SIP request, with a default value of *loss*. This parameter contains names of one or more classes of overload control algorithms. A SIP client must support the loss-based overload control scheme and must insert at least the token *loss* as one of the oc-algo parameter values. In addition, the SIP client may insert other tokens, separated by a comma, in the oc-algo parameter if it supports other overload control schemes such as a rate-based scheme (see Section 13.4). Each element in the comma-separated list corresponds to the class of overload control algorithms supported by the SIP client. When more than one class of overload control algorithms is present in the oc-algo parameter, the client may indicate algorithm preference by ordering the list in a decreasing order of preference. However, the client cannot assume that the server will pick the most preferred algorithm. When a downstream SIP server receives a request with multiple overload control algorithms specified in the oc-algo parameter (optionally sorted by decreasing order of preference), it chooses one algorithm from the list and must return the single selected algorithm to the client.

Once the SIP server has chosen a mutually agreeable class of overload control algorithms and communicated it to the client, the selection stays in effect until the algorithm is changed by the server. Furthermore, the client must continue to include all the supported algorithms in subsequent requests; the server must respond with the agreed-to algorithm until the algorithm is changed by the server. The selection should stay the same for a nontrivial duration of time to allow the overload control algorithm to stabilize its behavior described later. The oc-algo parameter does not define the exact algorithm to be used for traffic reduction; rather, the intent is to use any algorithm from a specific class of algorithms that affect traffic reduction similarly. For example, the reference default overload rate control algorithm described later can be used as a loss-based algorithm, or it can be substituted by any other loss-based algorithm that results in equivalent traffic reduction.

13.3.3.3 Parameter: oc-validity

This parameter may be inserted by the SIP server in a response; it must not be inserted by the SIP client in a request. This parameter contains a value that indicates an interval of time (measured in milliseconds) that the load reduction specified in the value of the oc parameter should be in effect. The default value of the oc-validity parameter is 500 (milliseconds). If the client receives a response with the oc and oc-algo parameters suitably filled in, but no oc-validity parameter, the SIP client should behave as if it had received oc-validity=500.

A value of 0 in the oc-validity parameter is reserved to denote the event that the server wishes to stop overload control, or to indicate that it supports overload control but is not currently requesting any reduction in traffic specified later. A nonzero value for the oc-validity parameter must only be present in conjunction with an oc parameter. A SIP client must discard a nonzero value of the oc-validity parameter if the client receives it in a response without the corresponding oc parameter being present as well. After the value specified in the oc-validity parameter expires and until the SIP client receives an updated set of overload control parameters from the SIP server, overload control is not in effect between the client and the downstream SIP server.

13.3.3.4 Parameter: oc-seq

This parameter must be inserted by the SIP server in a response; it must not be inserted by the SIP client in a request. This parameter contains an unsigned integer value that indicates the sequence number associated with the oc parameter. This sequence number is used to differentiate two oc parameter values generated by an overload control algorithm at two different instants in time. The oc parameter values generated by an overload control algorithm at time t and $t + 1$ must have an increasing value in the oc-seq parameter. This allows the upstream SIP client to properly collate out-of-order responses. Note that a timestamp can be used as a value of the oc-seq parameter.

If the value contained in the oc-seq parameter overflows during the period in which the load reduction is in effect, then the oc-seq parameter must be reset to the current timestamp or an appropriate base value. Also note that a client implementation can recognize that an overflow has occurred when it receives an oc-seq parameter whose value is significantly less than several previous values. Note that an oc-seq parameter whose value does not deviate significantly from the last several previous values is symptomatic of a tardy packet. However, overflow will cause the oc-seq parameter value to be significantly less than the last several values. If an overflow is detected, then the client should use the overload parameters in the new message, even though the sequence number is lower. The client should also reset any internal state to reflect the overflow so that future messages following the overflow will be accepted.

13.3.4 General Behavior

When forwarding a SIP request, a SIP client uses the SIP procedures of RFC 3263 (see Section 8.2.4) to determine the next-hop SIP server. The procedures of RFC 3263 take a SIP URI as input, extract the domain portion of that URI for use as a lookup key, query the DNS to obtain an ordered set of one or more IP addresses with a port number, and transport corresponding to each IP address in this set—the Expected Output.

After selecting a specific SIP server from the Expected Output, a SIP client determines whether overload controls are currently active with that server. If overload controls are currently active (and the oc-validity period has not yet expired), the client applies the relevant algorithm to determine whether or not to send the SIP request to the server. If overload controls are not currently active with this server (which will be the case if this is the initial contact with the server, the last response from this server had oc-validity=0, or the time period indicated by the oc-validity parameter has expired), the SIP client sends the SIP message to the server without invoking any overload control algorithm.

13.3.4.1 Determining Support for Overload Control

If a client determines that this is the first contact with a server, the client must insert the oc parameter without any value and must insert the oc-algo parameter with a list of algorithms it supports. This list must include *loss* and may include other algorithm names approved by the Internet Assigned Numbers Authority and described in corresponding documents. The client transmits the request to the chosen server. If a server receives a SIP request containing the oc and oc-algo parameters, the server must determine if it has already selected the overload control algorithm class with this client. If it has, the server should use the previously selected algorithm class in its response to the message.

If the server determines that the message is from a new client or a client the server has not heard from in a long time, the server must choose one algorithm from the list of algorithms in the oc-algo parameter. It must put the chosen algorithm as the sole parameter value in the oc-algo parameter of the response it sends to the client. In addition, if the server is currently not in an overload condition, it must set the value of the oc parameter to be 0 and may insert an oc-validity=0 parameter in the response to further qualify the value in the oc parameter. If the server is currently overloaded, it must follow the procedures described below. A client that supports the rate-based overload control scheme (see Section 13.4) will consider oc=0 as an indication not to send any requests downstream at all. Thus, when the server inserts oc-validity=0 as well, it is indicating that it does support overload control, but it is not under overload mode right now.

13.3.4.2 Creating and Updating the Overload Control Parameters

A SIP server provides overload control feedback to its upstream clients by providing a value for the oc parameter to the topmost Via header field of a SIP response, that is, the Via header added by the client before it sent the request to the server. Since the topmost Via header of a response will be removed by an upstream client after processing it, overload control feedback contained in the oc parameter will not travel beyond the upstream SIP client. A Via header parameter therefore provides hop-by-hop semantics for overload control feedback (RFC 6357) even if the next-hop neighbor does not support this specification. The oc parameter can be used in all response types, including provisional, success, and failure responses. We also explained later the special consideration on transporting overload control parameters in a 100 Trying response. A SIP server can update the oc parameter in a response, asking the client to increase or decrease the number of requests destined to the server or to stop performing overload control altogether.

A SIP server that has updated the oc parameter should also add an oc-validity parameter. The oc-validity parameter defines the time in milliseconds during which the overload control feedback specified in the oc parameter is valid. The default value of the oc-validity parameter is 500 (milliseconds). When a SIP server retransmits a response, it should use the oc and oc-validity parameter values consistent with the overload state at the time the retransmitted response was sent. This implies that the values in the oc and oc-validity parameters may be different than the ones used in previous retransmissions of the response. Because responses sent over UDP may be subject to delays in the network and arrive out of order, the oc-seq parameter aids in detecting a stale oc parameter value.

Implementations that are capable of updating the oc and oc-validity parameter values during retransmissions must insert the oc-seq parameter. The value of this parameter must be a set of numbers drawn from an increasing sequence. Implementations that are not capable of updating the oc and oc-validity parameter values during retransmissions—or implementations that do not want to do so because they will have to regenerate the message to be retransmitted—must still insert an oc-seq parameter in the first response associated with a transaction; however, they do not have to update the value in subsequent retransmissions.

The oc-validity and oc-seq Via header parameters are only defined in SIP responses and must not be used in SIP requests. These parameters are only useful to the upstream neighbor of a SIP server (i.e., the entity that is sending requests to the SIP server) since the client is the entity that can offload traffic by redirecting or rejecting new requests. If requests are forwarded in both directions between two SIP servers (i.e., the roles of upstream/downstream neighbors change), there are also responses flowing in both directions. Thus, both SIP servers can exchange overload information.

This specification provides a good overload control mechanism that can protect a SIP server from overload. However, if a SIP server wants to limit advertisements of overload control capability for privacy reasons, it might decide to perform overload control only for requests that are received on a secure transport, such as TLS. Indicating support for overload control on a request received on an untrusted link can leak privacy in the form of capabilities supported by the server. To limit the knowledge that the server supports overload control, a server can adopt a policy of inserting overload control parameters in only those requests received over trusted links such that these parameters are only visible to trusted neighbors.

13.3.4.3 Determining the oc Parameter Value

The value of the oc parameter is determined by the overloaded server using any pertinent information at its disposal. The only constraint imposed by this document is that the server control algorithm must produce a value for the oc parameter that it expects the receiving SIP clients to apply to all downstream SIP requests (dialog forming as well as in-dialog) to this SIP server. Beyond this stipulation, the process by which an overloaded server determines the value of the oc parameter is considered out of the scope of this document. Note that this stipulation is required so that both the client and server have a common view of which messages the overload control applies to. With this stipulation in place, the client can prioritize messages as discussed in Section 13.3.4.10.1. As an example, a value of oc=10 when the loss-based algorithm is used implies that 10% of the total number of SIP requests (dialog forming as well as in-dialog) are subject to reduction at the client. Analogously, a value of oc=10 when the rate-based algorithm (see Section 13.4) is used indicates that the client should send SIP requests at a rate of 10 SIP requests or fewer per second.

13.3.4.4 Processing the Overload Control Parameters

A SIP client should remove the oc, oc-validity, and oc-seq parameters from all Via headers of a response received, except for the topmost Via header. This prevents overload control parameters that were accidentally or maliciously inserted into Via headers by a downstream SIP server from traveling upstream. The scope of overload control applies to unique combinations of IP and port values. A SIP client maintains the overload control values received (along with the address and port number of the SIP servers from which they were received) for the duration specified in the oc-validity parameter or the default duration. Each time a SIP client receives a response with an overload control parameter from a downstream SIP server, it compares the oc-seq value extracted from the Via header with the oc-seq value stored for this server.

If these values match, the response does not update the overload control parameters related to this server, and the client continues to provide overload control as previously negotiated. If the oc-seq value extracted from the Via header is larger than the stored value, the client updates the stored values by copying the new values of the oc, oc-algo, and oc-seq parameters from the Via header to the stored values. Upon such an update of the overload control parameters, the client restarts the validity period of the new overload control parameters. The overload control parameters now remain in effect until the validity period expires or the parameters are updated in a new response. Stored overload control parameters must be reset to default values once the validity period has expired.

13.3.4.5 Using the Overload Control Parameter Values

A SIP client must honor the overload control values it receives from downstream neighbors. The SIP client must not forward more requests to a SIP server than allowed by the current oc and oc-algo parameter values from that particular downstream server. When forwarding a SIP request, a SIP client uses the SIP procedures of RFC 3263 to determine the next-hop SIP server. The procedures of RFC 3263 (see Section 8.2.4) take a SIP URI as input, extract the domain portion of that URI for use as a lookup key, query the DNS to obtain an ordered set of one or more IP addresses with a port number, and transport corresponding to each IP address in this set—the Expected Output.

After selecting a specific SIP server from the Expected Output, the SIP client determines if it already has overload control parameter values for the server chosen from the Expected Output. If the SIP client has a nonexpired oc parameter value for the server chosen from the Expected Output, then this chosen server is operating in overload control mode. Thus, the SIP client determines if it can or cannot forward the current request to the SIP server based on the oc and oc-algo parameters and any relevant local policy. The particular algorithm used to determine whether or not to forward a particular SIP request is a matter of local policy and may take into account a variety of prioritization factors. However, this local policy should transmit the same number of SIP requests as the sample algorithm defined by the overload control scheme being used.

13.3.4.6 Forwarding the Overload Control Parameters

Overload control is defined in a hop-by-hop manner. Therefore, forwarding the contents of the overload control parameters is generally not recommended and should only be performed if permitted by the configuration of SIP servers. This means that a SIP proxy should strip the overload control parameters inserted by the client before proxying the request further downstream. Of course, when the proxy acts as a client and proxies the request downstream, it is free to add overload control parameters pertinent to itself in the Via header it inserted in the request.

13.3.4.7 Terminating Overload Control

A SIP client removes overload control if one of the following events occur:

- The oc-validity period previously received by the client from this server (or the default value of 500 milliseconds if the server did not previously specify an oc-validity parameter) expires.
- The client is explicitly told by the server to stop performing overload control using the oc-validity=0 parameter. A SIP server can decide to terminate overload control by explicitly signaling the client. To do so, the SIP server must set the value of the oc-validity parameter to 0. The SIP server must increment the value of oc-seq and should set the value of the oc parameter to 0.

Note that the loss-based overload control scheme described later can effectively stop overload control by setting the value of the oc parameter to 0. However, the rate-based scheme (see Section 13.4) needs an additional piece of information in the form of oc-validity=0. When the client receives a response with a higher oc-seq number than the one it most recently processed, it checks the oc-validity parameter. If the value of the oc-validity parameter is 0, this indicates to the client that overload control of messages destined to the server is no longer necessary, and the traffic can flow without any reduction. Furthermore, when the value of the oc-validity parameter is 0, the client should disregard the value in the oc parameter.

13.3.4.8 Stabilizing Overload Algorithm Selection

Realities of deployments of SIP necessitate that the overload control algorithm may be changed upon a system reboot or a software upgrade. However, frequent changes of the overload control algorithm must be avoided. Frequent changes of the overload control algorithm will not benefit the client or the server as such flapping does not allow the chosen algorithm to stabilize. An algorithm change, when desired, is simply accomplished by the SIP server choosing a new algorithm from the list in the client's oc-algo parameter and sending it back to the client in a response.

The client associates a specific algorithm with each server it sends traffic to, and when the server changes the algorithm, the client must change its behavior accordingly. Once the server selects a specific overload control algorithm for a given client, the algorithm should not change the algorithm associated with that client for at least 3600 seconds (1 hour). This period may involve one or more cycles of overload control being in effect, and then being stopped depending on the traffic and resources at the server. Note that one way to accomplish this involves the server saving the time of the last algorithm change in a lookup table, indexed by the client's network identifiers. The server only changes the oc-algo parameter when the time since the last change has surpassed 3600 seconds.

13.3.4.9 Self-Limiting

In some cases, a SIP client may not receive a response from a server after sending a request. RFC 3261 states that when a timeout error is received from the transaction layer, it must be treated as if a 408 Request Timeout status code has been received. If a fatal transport error is reported by the transport layer, the condition MUST be treated as a 503 Service Unavailable status code. In the event of repeated timeouts or fatal transport errors, the SIP client must stop sending requests to this server. The SIP client should periodically probe if the downstream server is alive using any mechanism at its disposal. Clients should be conservative in their probing (e.g., using an exponential backoff) so that their aliveness probes do not exacerbate an overload situation. Once a SIP client has successfully received a normal response for a request sent to the downstream server, the SIP client can resume sending SIP requests. It should, of course, honor any overload control parameters it may receive in the initial, or later, responses.

13.3.4.10 Responding to an Overload Indication

A SIP client can receive overload control feedback indicating that it needs to reduce the traffic it sends to its downstream server. The client can accomplish this task by sending some of the requests that would have gone to the overloaded element to a different destination. It needs to ensure, however, that this destination is not in overload and is capable of processing the extra load. A client can also buffer requests in the hope that the overload condition will resolve quickly and the requests can still be forwarded in time. In many cases, however, it will need to reject these requests with a 503 Service Unavailable response without the Retry-After header.

13.3.4.10.1 Message Prioritization at Hop before an Overloaded Server

During an overload condition, a SIP client needs to prioritize requests and select those requests that need to be rejected or redirected. This selection is largely a matter of local policy. It is expected that a SIP client will follow local policy as long as the result in reduction of traffic is consistent with the overload algorithm in effect at that node. Accordingly, the normative behavior in the next three paragraphs should be interpreted with the understanding that the SIP client will aim to preserve local policy to the fullest extent possible. A SIP client should honor the local policy for prioritizing SIP requests such as policies based on message type, for example, INVITEs versus requests associated with existing sessions. A SIP client should honor the local policy for prioritizing SIP requests based on the content of the Resource-Priority header (RPH) (RFC 4412, see Section 2.8). Specific (namespace. value) RPH contents may indicate high-priority requests that should be preserved as much as possible during overload. The RPH contents can also indicate a low-priority request that is eligible to be dropped during times of overload.

A SIP client should honor the local policy for prioritizing SIP requests relating to emergency calls as identified by the SOS URN (RFC 5031, see Section 16.11.2) indicating an emergency request. This policy ensures that when a server is overloaded and nonemergency calls outnumber emergency calls in the traffic arriving at the client, the few emergency calls will be given preference. If, on the other hand, the server is overloaded and the majority of calls arriving at the client are emergency in nature, then no amount of message prioritization will ensure the delivery of all emergency calls if the client is to reduce the amount of traffic as requested by the server. A local policy can be expected to combine both the SIP request type and the prioritization markings, and it should be honored when overload conditions prevail.

13.3.4.10.2 Rejecting Requests at an Overloaded Server

If the upstream SIP client to the overloaded server does not support overload control, it will continue to direct requests to the overloaded server. Thus, for the nonparticipating client, the overloaded server must bear the cost of rejecting some requests from the client as well as the cost of processing the nonrejected requests to completion. It would be fair to devote the same amount of processing at the overloaded server to the combination of rejection and processing from a nonparticipating client as the overloaded server would devote to processing requests from a participating client. This is to ensure that SIP clients that do not support this specification do not receive an unfair advantage over those that do. A SIP server that is in overload and has started to throttle incoming traffic must reject some requests from nonparticipating clients with a 503 Service Unavailable response without the Retry-After header.

13.3.4.11 Provisional Response and Overload Control

The overload control information sent from a SIP server to a client is transported in the responses. While implementations can insert overload control information in any response, special attention should be accorded to overload control information transported in a 100 Trying response. Traditionally, the 100 Trying response has been used in SIP to quench retransmissions. In some implementations, the 100 Trying message may not be generated by the transaction user (TU) nor consumed by the TU. In these implementations, the 100 Trying response is generated at the transaction layer and sent to the upstream SIP client. At the receiving SIP client, the 100 Trying is consumed at the transaction layer by inhibiting the retransmission of the corresponding request. Consequently, implementations that insert overload control information in the 100 Trying cannot assume that the upstream SIP client passed the overload control information in the 100 Trying to their corresponding TU. For this reason, implementations that insert overload control information in the 100 Trying must reinsert the same (or updated) overload control information in the first non-100 Trying response being sent to the upstream SIP client.

13.3.4.12 Example

Consider a SIP client, P1, which is sending requests to another downstream SIP server, P2. The following snippets of SIP messages demonstrate how the overload control parameters work.

```
INVITE sips:user@example.com SIP/2.0
Via: SIP/2.0/TLS p1.example.net;
branch=z9hG4bK2d4790.1;oc;oc-algo="loss,A"
...
SIP/2.0 100 Trying
Via: SIP/2.0/TLS p1.example.net;
branch=z9hG4bK2d4790.1;received=192.0.2.111;
oc=0;oc-algo="loss";oc-validity=0
...
```

In the messages above, the first line is sent by P1 to P2. This line is a SIP request; because P1 supports overload control, it inserts the oc parameter in the topmost Via header that it created. P1 supports two overload control algorithms: loss and an algorithm called A. The second line, a SIP response, shows the topmost Via header amended by P2 according to this specification and sent to P1. Because P2 also supports overload control and chooses the loss-based scheme, it sends *loss* back to P1 in the oc-algo parameter. It also sets the value of the oc and oc-validity parameters to 0 because it is not currently requesting overload control activation. Had P2 not supported overload control, it would have left the oc and oc-algo parameters unchanged, thus allowing the client to know that it did not support overload control. At some later time, P2 starts to experience overload. It sends the following SIP message indicating that P1 should decrease the messages arriving to P2 by 20% for 0.5 seconds.

```
SIP/2.0 180 Ringing
Via: SIP/2.0/TLS p1.example.net;
branch=z9hG4bK2d4790.3;received=192.0.2.111;
oc=20;oc-algo="loss";oc-validity=500;
oc-seq=1282321615.782
...
```

After some time, the overload condition at P2 subsides. It then changes the parameter values in the response it sends to P1 to allow P1 to send all messages destined to P2.

```
SIP/2.0 183 Queued
Via: SIP/2.0/TLS p1.example.net;
branch=z9hG4bK2d4790.4;received=192.0.2.111;
oc=0;oc-algo="loss";oc-validity=0;oc-
seq=1282321892.439
...
```

13.3.5 Loss-Based Overload Control Scheme

Under a loss-based approach, a SIP server asks an upstream neighbor to reduce the number of requests it would normally forward to this server by a certain percentage. For example, a SIP server can ask an upstream neighbor to reduce the number of requests this neighbor would normally send by 10%. The upstream neighbor then redirects or rejects 10% of the traffic originally destined for that server. This section specifies the semantics of the overload control parameters associated with the loss-based overload control scheme. The general behavior of SIP clients and servers is specified in Section 2.1, and is applicable to SIP clients and servers that implement loss-based overload control.

13.3.5.1 Special Parameter Values

The loss-based overload control scheme is identified using the token *loss*. This token appears in the oc-algo parameter list sent by the SIP client. Upon entering the overload state, a SIP server that has selected the loss-based algorithm will assign a value to the oc parameter. This value must be in the range of [0, 100], inclusive. This value indicates to the client the percentage by which the client is to reduce the number of requests being forwarded to the overloaded server. The SIP client may use any algorithm that reduces the traffic it sends to the overloaded server by the amount indicated. Such an algorithm should honor the message prioritization discussed earlier. While a particular algorithm is not subject to standardization, for completeness, a default algorithm for loss-based overload control is provided in the next section.

13.3.5.2 Default Algorithm

We describe a default algorithm that a SIP client can use to throttle SIP traffic going downstream by the percentage loss value specified in the oc parameter. The client maintains two categories of requests. The first category will include requests that are candidates for reduction, and the second category will include requests that are not subject to reduction except when all messages in the first category have been rejected and further reduction is still needed. Earlier directives are provided on identifying messages for inclusion in the second category. The remaining messages are allocated to the first category. Under overload condition, the client converts the value of the oc parameter to a value that it applies to requests in the first category. As a simple example, if oc=10 and 40% of the requests should be included in the first category, then

```
10 / 40 * 100 = 25
```

Or, 25% of the requests in the first category can be reduced to obtain an overall reduction of 10%. The client uses random discard to achieve the 25% reduction of messages in the first category. Messages in the second category proceed downstream unscathed. To affect the 25% reduction rate from the first category, the client draws a random number between 1 and 100 for the request picked from the first category. If the random number is less than or equal to the converted value of the oc parameter, the request is not forwarded; otherwise, the request is forwarded. A reference algorithm is shown below.

```
       cat1: = 80.0 // Category 1 -- Subject
//to reduction
       cat2: = 100.0 - cat1 // Category 2
//-- Under normal operations,
//only subject to reduction after category 1
//is exhausted.
//Note that the above ratio is simply a
//reasonable default.
//The actual values will change through
//periodic sampling as the traffic mix
//changes over time.

       while (true) {

//We're modeling message processing as a
//single work queue that contains both
//incoming and outgoing messages.

       sip_msg := get_next_message_from_work_
       //queue()
       update_mix(cat1, cat2) // See Note
//below
       switch (sip_msg.type) {
       case outbound request:
       destination := get_next_hop(sip_msg)
       oc_context :=
       get_oc_context(destination)
       if (oc_context == null) {
       send_to_network(sip_msg) // Process it
//normally by sending the request to the next
//hop since this particular destination is
//not subject to overload.

       }
       else {

//Determine if server wants to enter in
//overload or is in
//overload.

       in_oc := extract_in_oc(oc_context)
       oc_value := extract_oc(oc_context)
       oc_validity :=
       extract_oc_validity(oc_context)
       if (in_oc == false or oc_validity is
not in effect) {
       send_to_network(sip_msg) // Process it
//normally by sending the request to the next
//hop since this particular destination is
//not subject to overload. Optionally, clear
//the oc context for this server (not shown).

       }
       else { // Begin performing overload
//control.
       r := random()
       drop_msg := false
       category :=
       assign_msg_to_category(sip_msg)
       pct_to_reduce_cat1 = oc_value / cat1 *
       100
       if (oc_value <= cat1) { // Reduce all
//msgs from category 1
       if (r <= pct_to_reduce_cat1 &&
       category == cat1) {
       drop_msg := true
       }
       }
       else { // oc_value > category 1.
       //Reduce 100% of msgs from

//category 1 and remaining from category 2.

       pct_to_reduce_cat2 = (oc_value - cat1) /
        cat2 * 100
       if (category == cat1) {
       drop_msg := true
       }
       else {
       if (r <= pct_to_reduce_cat2) {
       drop_msg := true;
       }
       }
       }
       if (drop_msg == false) {
       send_to_network(sip_msg) // Process it
       //normally by sending the request to
       //the next hop.
       }
       else {

//Do not send request downstream; handle it
//locally by generating response (if a proxy)
//or treating it as an error (if a user
//agent).

       }
       } // End perform overload control.
       }
       end case // outbound request
       case outbound response:
       if (we are in overload) {
```

```
add_overload_parameters(sip_msg)
}
send_to_network(sip_msg)
end case // outbound response
case inbound response:
if (sip_msg has oc parameter values) {
create_or_update_oc_context() // For
//the specific server that sent the
//response, create or update the oc
//context, i.e., extract the values of
//the oc-related parameters and store
//them for later use.

}
process_msg(sip_msg)
end case // inbound response
case inbound request:
if (we are not in overload) {
process_msg(sip_msg)
}
else { // We are in overload.
if (sip_msg has oc parameters) {
//Upstream client supports
process_msg(sip_msg) // oc; only sends
//important requests.
}
else { // Upstream client does not
//support oc
if (local_policy(sip_msg) says process
message) {
process_msg(sip_msg)
}
else {
send_response(sip_msg, 503)
}
}
}
end case // inbound request
}
}
```

Note that a simple way to sample the traffic mix for category 1 and category 2 is to associate a counter with each category of message. Periodically (every 5–10 seconds), get the value of the counters, and calculate the ratio of category 1 messages to category 2 messages since the last calculation. Example: In the last 5 seconds, a total of 500 requests arrived at the queue. Of the 500 messages, 450 were subject to reduction, and 50 out of 500 were classified as requests not subject to reduction. On the basis of this ratio, cat1 := 90 and cat2 := 10, so a 90/10 mix will be used in overload calculations.

13.3.6 Relationship with Other SIP Load Control Schemes

The overload control mechanism described here is reactive in nature, and apart from the message prioritization directives earlier, the mechanisms described here per RFC 7339 will not discriminate requests based on user identity, filtering action, and arrival time. SIP networks that require proactive overload control mechanisms can upload user-level load control filters as described in RFC 7200 in the context of the SIP load-control event package. Local policy will also dictate the precedence of different overload control mechanisms applied to the traffic. Specifically, in a scenario where load control filters are installed by signaling neighbors (RFC 7200) and the same traffic can also be throttled using the overload control mechanism, local policy will dictate which of these schemes shall be given precedence. Interactions between the two schemes are out of the scope of this document.

13.3.7 Syntax

RFC 7339 specification extends the existing definition of the Via header field parameters of RFC 3261. The ABNF (RFC 5234) syntax for this is provided as follows for convenience although all SIP syntaxes are shown in Section 2.4.1:

```
via-params =/ oc/oc-validity/oc-seq/oc-algo
oc = "oc" [EQUAL oc-num]
oc-num = 1*DIGIT
oc-validity = "oc-validity" [EQUAL delta-ms]
oc-seq = "oc-seq" EQUAL 1*12DIGIT "."
1*5DIGIT
oc-algo = "oc-algo" EQUAL DQUOTE algo-list
*(COMMA algo-list)
DQUOTE
algo-list = "loss"/*(other-algo)
other-algo = %x41-5A/%x61-7A/%x30-39
delta-ms = 1*DIGIT
```

13.3.8 Design Considerations for Overload Control

The specific design considerations are explained here for the overload control mechanism described above. However, general design considerations for SIP overload control can be found in RFC 6357, which was not described here for brevity.

13.3.8.1 SIP Mechanism

A SIP mechanism is needed to convey overload feedback from the receiving to the sending SIP entity. A number of different alternatives exist to implement such a mechanism.

13.3.8.1.1 SIP Response Header

Overload control information can be transmitted using a new Via header field parameter for overload control. A SIP server can add this header parameter to the responses it is sending upstream to provide overload control feedback to its upstream neighbors. This approach has the following characteristics:

- A Via header parameter is lightweight and creates very little overhead. It does not require the transmission of additional messages for overload control and does not increase traffic or processing burdens in an overload situation.
- Overload control status can frequently be reported to upstream neighbors since it is a part of a SIP response. This enables the use of this mechanism in scenarios where the overload status needs to be adjusted frequently. It also enables the use of overload control mechanisms that use regular feedback, such as window-based overload control.
- With a Via header parameter, overload control status is inherent in SIP signaling and is automatically conveyed to all relevant upstream neighbors, that is, neighbors that are currently contributing traffic. There is no need for a SIP server to specifically track and manage the set of current upstream or downstream neighbors with which it should exchange overload feedback.
- Overload status is not conveyed to inactive senders. This avoids the transmission of overload feedback to inactive senders, which do not contribute traffic. If an inactive sender starts to transmit while the receiver is in overload, it will receive overload feedback in the first response and can adjust the amount of traffic forwarded accordingly.
- A SIP server can limit the distribution of overload control information by only inserting it into responses to known upstream neighbors. A SIP server can use transport-level authentication (e.g., via TLS) with its upstream neighbors.

13.3.8.1.2 SIP Event Package

Overload control information can also be conveyed from a receiver to a sender using a new event package. Such an event package enables a sending entity to subscribe to the overload status of its downstream neighbors and receive notifications of overload control status changes in NOTIFY requests. This approach has the following characteristics:

- Overload control information is conveyed decoupled from SIP signaling. It enables an overload control manager, which is a separate entity, to monitor the load on other servers and provide overload control feedback to all SIP servers that have set up subscriptions with the controller.
- With an event package, a receiver can send updates to senders that are currently inactive. Inactive senders will receive a notification about the overload and can refrain from sending traffic to this neighbor until the overload condition is resolved. The receiver can also notify all potential senders once they are permitted to send traffic again. However, these notifications do generate additional traffic, which adds to the overall load.
- A SIP entity needs to set up and maintain overload control subscriptions with all upstream and downstream neighbors. A new subscription needs to be set up before/while a request is transmitted to a new downstream neighbor. Servers can be configured to subscribe at boot time. However, this would require additional protection to avoid the avalanche restart problem for overload control. Subscriptions need to be terminated when they are not needed any more, which can be done, for example, using a timeout mechanism.
- A receiver needs to send NOTIFY messages to all subscribed upstream neighbors in a timely manner when the control algorithm requires a change in the control variable (e.g., when a SIP server is in an overload condition). This includes active as well as inactive neighbors. These NOTIFYs add to the amount of traffic that needs to be processed. To ensure that these requests will not be dropped due to overload, a priority mechanism needs to be implemented in all servers these requests will pass through.
- As overload feedback is sent to all senders in separate messages, this mechanism is not suitable when frequent overload control feedback is needed.
- A SIP server can limit the set of senders that can receive overload control information by authenticating subscriptions to this event package.
- This approach requires each proxy to implement UA functionality (UAS and UAC) to manage the subscriptions.

13.3.8.2 Backwards Compatibility

A new overload control mechanism needs to be backwards compatible so that it can be gradually introduced into a network and function properly if only a fraction of the servers support it. Hop-by-hop overload control design (RFC 6357) has the advantage that it does not require that all SIP entities in a network support it. It can be used effectively between two adjacent SIP servers if both servers support overload control and does not depend on the support from any other server or UA. The more SIP servers in a network support hop-by-hop overload control, the better protected the network is against occurrences of overload.

A SIP server may have multiple upstream neighbors from which only some may support overload control. If a server would simply use this overload control mechanism, only those that support it would reduce traffic. Others would keep sending at the full rate and benefit from the throttling by the servers that support overload control. In other words, upstream neighbors that do not support overload control would be better off than those that do. A SIP server should therefore follow the behavior outlined earlier to handle clients that do not support overload control.

13.3.9 Salient Features of Overload Control

RFC 7339 specified here provide the following benefits meeting the overload control for the SIP network requirements specified in RFC 5390:

- The overload control mechanism allows an overloaded SIP server to maintain a reasonable level of throughput as it enters into congestion mode by requesting the upstream clients to reduce traffic destined downstream.
- When a SIP server enters overload mode, it requests the upstream clients to throttle the traffic destined to it. As a consequence of this, the overloaded SIP server itself generates proportionally less downstream traffic, thereby limiting the impact on other elements in the network.
- On the server side, the overload condition is determined monitoring *S* and reporting a load feedback *F* as a value to the oc parameter. On the client side, a throttle *T* is applied to requests going downstream based on *F*. This specification does not prescribe any value for *S* nor a particular value for *F*. The oc-algo parameter allows for automatic convergence to a particular class of overload control algorithm. There are suggested default values for the oc-validity parameter.
- The mechanism is designed to reduce congestion when a pair of communicating entities support it. If a downstream overloaded SIP server does not respond to a request in time, a SIP client will attempt to reduce traffic destined toward the nonresponsive server.
- The mechanism does not assume that it will only be deployed in environments with completely trusted elements. The overload control information is shared between a pair of communicating entities. Consequently, a confidential and authenticated channel can be used for this communication. However, if such a channel is not available, then the needed security ramifications are specified.
- The mechanism provides a way for an element to throttle the amount of traffic it receives from an upstream element. This throttling is graded to a great extent with the current 503 Service Unavailable mechanism.
- A SIP client that has overload information from multiple downstream servers will not retry the request on another element. However, if a SIP client does not know the overload status of a downstream server, it may send the request to that server.
- The mechanism supports servers that receive requests from a large number of different upstream elements, where the set of upstream elements is not enumerable. There are no constraints on the number of upstream clients.
- The mechanism supports servers that receive requests from a finite set of upstream elements, where the set of upstream elements is enumerable. There are no constraints on the number of upstream clients.
- The mechanism works between servers in different domains. There are no inherent limitations on using overload control between domains. However, interconnection points that engage in overload control between domains will have to populate and maintain the overload control parameters as requests cross domains.
- The mechanism does not dictate a specific algorithm for prioritizing the processing of work within a proxy during times of overload. It must permit a proxy to prioritize requests based on any local policy so that certain ones, such as a call for emergency services or a call with a specific value of the RPH field (RFC 4412, see Section 2.8), are given preferential treatment, such as not being dropped, being given additional retransmission, or being processed ahead of others.
- The mechanism provides unambiguous directions to clients on when they should retry a request and when they should not. This especially applies to TCP connection establishment and SIP registrations in order to mitigate against an avalanche restart. The scheme provides normative behavior on when to retry a request after repeated timeouts, and fatal transport errors resulting from communications with a nonresponsive downstream SIP server.
- The mechanism has capabilities to function properly in cases where a network element fails, is so overloaded that it cannot process messages, or cannot communicate owing to a network failure or network partition. It is not able to provide explicit indications of the nature of the failure or its levels of congestion, because it provides normative behavior on when to retry a request after repeated timeouts and fatal transport errors resulting from communications with a nonresponsive downstream SIP server.
- The mechanism attempts to minimize the overhead of the overload control messaging. Overload control messages are sent in the topmost Via header, which is always processed by the SIP elements.
- The overload mechanism tries to prevent malicious attacks, including denial-of-service and distributed denial-of-service attacks.
- Overload control information is shared between a pair of communicating entities, and a confidential and authenticated channel can be used for this communication. However, if such a channel is not available, then the security ramifications specified by the mechanism should be used.

- The overload mechanism is unambiguous about whether a load indication applies to a specific IP address, host, or URI so that an upstream element can determine the load of the entity to which a request is to be sent.
- The specification for the overload mechanism gives guidance on which message types might be desirable to process over others during times of overload, based on SIP-specific considerations. For example, it may be more beneficial to process a SUBSCRIBE refresh with Expires of zero than a SUBSCRIBE refresh with a nonzero expiration (since the former reduces the overall amount of load on the element) or to process re-INVITEs over new INVITEs.
- In a mixed environment of elements that do and do not implement the overload mechanism, no disproportionate benefit accrues to the users or operators of the elements that do not implement the mechanism. An element that does not implement overload control does not receive any measure of extra benefit.
- The overload mechanism ensures that the system remains stable. When the offered load drops from above the overall capacity of the network to below the overall capacity, the throughput should stabilize and become equal to the offered load. The specified overload control mechanism ensures the stability of the system.
- It is possible to disable the reporting of load information toward upstream targets based on the identity of those targets. An operator of a SIP server can configure the SIP server to only report overload control information for requests received over a confidential channel, for example. However, note that this introduces a modicum of extra configuration.
- The overload mechanism can also work in cases where there is a load balancer in front of a farm of proxies. Depending on the type of load balancer, this requirement is met. A load balancer fronting a farm of SIP proxies could be a SIP-aware load balancer or one that is not SIP-aware. If the load balancer is SIP-aware, it can make conscious decisions on throttling outgoing traffic toward the individual server in the farm based on the overload control parameters returned by the server. On the other hand, if the load balancer is not SIP-aware, then there are other strategies to perform overload control.

13.4 Rate-Based Overload Control in SIP Network

13.4.1 Overview

We have described a promising SIP-based overload control solution in the earlier section specified in RFC 7339 (see Section 13.3). That solution provides a communication scheme for overload control algorithms. It also includes a default loss-based overload control algorithm that makes it possible for a set of clients to limit offered load toward an overloaded server. However, such a loss control algorithm is sensitive to variations in load so that any increase in load would be directly reflected by the clients in the offered load presented to the overloaded servers. More important, a loss-based control scheme cannot guarantee an upper bound on the offered load from the clients toward an overloaded server, and requires frequent updates that may have implications for stability. The use of SIP in large-scale next-generation networks requires that SIP-based networks provide adequate control mechanisms for handling traffic growth. In particular, SIP networks must be able to handle traffic overloads gracefully, maintaining transaction throughput by preventing congestion collapse.

The IETF draft [1] that is described here proposes an overload control and the rate-based overload control algorithm that complements the loss-based control scheme, using the same signaling within the framework defined in RFC 7339 (see Section 13.3). The rate-based control guarantees an upper bound on the rate, constant between server updates, of requests sent by clients toward an overloaded server. The trade-off is in terms of algorithmic complexity since the overloaded server is more likely to use a different target (maximum rate) for each client than the loss-based approach. The proposed rate-based overload control algorithm mitigates congestion in SIP networks while adhering to the overload signaling scheme in RFC 7339 and presenting a rate-based control as an optional alternative to the default loss-based control scheme in RFC 7339.

13.4.2 Rate-Based Algorithm Scheme

13.4.2.1 Objective

The server is the one protected by the overload control algorithm defined here, and the client is the one that throttles traffic toward the server. Following the procedures defined in RFC 7339 (see Section 13.3), the server and clients signal one another's support for rate-based overload control. Then, periodically, the server relies on internal measurements (e.g., CPU utilization or queuing delay) to evaluate its overload state and estimate a target maximum SIP request rate in number of requests per second (as opposed to target percent loss in the case of loss-based control). When in overload, the server uses the Via header field oc parameter of RFC 7339 of SIP responses in order to inform the clients of its overload state and of the target maximum SIP request rate for that client. Upon receiving the oc parameter with a target maximum SIP request rate, each client throttles new SIP requests toward the overloaded server.

13.4.2.2 Via Header Field Parameters for Overload Control

The use of the Via header field oc parameter informs clients of the desired maximum rate. They are defined in RFC 7339 (see Section 13.3) and summarized below:

- **oc:** Used by clients in SIP requests to indicate (RFC 7339, see Section 13.3) support and by servers to indicate the load reduction amount in the loss algorithm, and the maximum rate, in messages per second, for the rate-based algorithm described here.
- **oc-algo:** Used by clients in SIP requests to advertise supported overload control algorithms and by servers to notify clients of the algorithm in effect.
- **values:** loss (default), rate (optional).
- **oc-validity:** Used by servers in SIP responses to indicate an interval of time (milliseconds) that the load reduction should be in effect. A value of 0 is reserved for the server to stop overload control. A nonzero value is required in all other cases.
- **oc-seq:** A sequence number associated with the oc parameter. Consult Section Section 13.3.3 for an illustration of the Via header field oc parameter usage.

13.4.2.3 Client and Server Rate-Control Algorithm Selection

Per RFC 7339 (see Section 13.3), new clients indicate supported overload control algorithms to servers by inserting oc and oc-algo, with the names of the supported algorithms, in the Via header field of SIP requests destined to servers. The inclusion by the client of the token *rate* indicates that the client supports a rate-based algorithm. Conversely, servers notify clients of the selected overload control algorithm through the oc-algo parameter in the Via header field of SIP responses to clients. The inclusion by the server of the token *rate* in the oc-algo parameter indicates that the rate-based algorithm has been selected by the server. Support of rate-based control must be indicated by clients including the token *rate* in the oc-algo list. Selection of rate-based control must be indicated by servers by setting oc-algo to the token *rate*.

13.4.2.4 Server Operation

The actual algorithm used by the server to determine its overload state and estimate a target maximum SIP request rate is beyond the scope of this document. However, the server MUST periodically evaluate its overload state and estimate a target SIP request rate beyond which it would become overloaded. The server must determine how it will allocate the target SIP request rate among its clients. The server may set the same rate for every client, or may set different rates for different clients. The maximum rate determined by the server for a client applies to the entire stream of SIP requests, even though throttling may only affect a particular subset of the requests, since as per RFC 7339 (see Section 13.3), request prioritization is a client's responsibility. When setting the maximum rate for a particular client, the server may need take into account the workload (e.g., CPU load per request) of the distribution of message types from that client. Furthermore, because the client may prioritize the specific types of messages it sends while under overload restriction, this distribution of message types may be different from (e.g., either higher or lower CPU load) the message distribution for that client under nonoverload conditions.

Note that the oc parameter for the rate algorithm is an upper bound (in messages per second) on the traffic sent by the client to the server. The client may send traffic at a rate significantly lower than the upper bound for a variety of reasons. In other words, when multiple clients are being controlled by an overloaded server, at any given time some clients may receive requests at a rate below their target (maximum) SIP request rate, while others above that target rate. However, the resulting request rate presented to the overloaded server will converge toward the target SIP request rate. Upon detection of overload and the determination to invoke overload controls, the server must follow the specifications in RFC 7339 (see Section 13.3) to notify its clients of the allocated target SIP request rate, and that rate-based control is in effect. The server must use the oc parameter (RFC 7339) to send a target SIP request rate to each of its clients. When a client supports the default loss algorithm and not the rate algorithm, the client would be handled in the same way as described here [1].

13.4.2.5 Client Operation

13.4.2.5.1 Default Algorithm

In determining whether or not to transmit a specific message, the client may use any algorithm that limits the message rate to the oc parameter in units of messages per second. For ease of discussion, we define T = 1/[oc parameter] as the target inter-SIP request interval. The algorithm may be strictly deterministic, or it may be probabilistic. It may, or may not, have a tolerance factor, to allow for short bursts, as long as the long-term rate remains below $1/T$. The algorithm may have provisions for prioritizing traffic. If the algorithm requires other parameters (in addition to T, which is 1/[oc parameter]), they may be set autonomously by the client, or they may be negotiated between client and server independently of the SIP-based overload control solution. In either case, the coordination is out of scope for this document. The default algorithms presented here (one without provisions for prioritizing traffic, one with provisions) are only examples. To throttle new SIP requests at the rate specified by the oc parameter sent by the server to its clients, the client may use the proposed default algorithm for rate-based control or any other equivalent algorithm that forward messages in conformance with the upper bound of $1/T$ messages per second. The default leaky bucket algorithm is presented here [2]. The algorithm makes it possible for clients to deliver SIP requests at a rate specified by the oc parameter with tolerance parameter *TAU* (preferably configurable).

Conceptually, the leaky bucket algorithm can be viewed as a finite capacity bucket whose real-valued content drains out at a continuous rate of 1 unit of content per time unit and whose content increases by the increment T for each forwarded SIP request. T is computed as the inverse of the rate specified by the oc parameter, namely $T = 1/$[oc parameter]. Note that when the oc parameter is 0 with a nonzero oc-validity, then the client should reject 100% of SIP requests destined to the overload server. However, when the oc-validity value is 0, the client should immediately stop throttling. If, at a new SIP request arrival, the content of the bucket is less than or equal to the limit value *TAU*, then the SIP request is forwarded to the server; otherwise, the SIP request is rejected. Note that the capacity of the bucket (the upper bound of the counter) is $(T + TAU)$. The tolerance parameter *TAU* determines how close the long-term admitted rate is to an ideal control that would admit all SIP requests for arrival rates less than $1/T$, and then admit SIP requests precisely at the rate of $1/T$ for arrival rates above $1/T$. In particular, at mean arrival rates close to $1/T$, it determines the tolerance to deviation of the interarrival time from T (the larger the *TAU*, the more tolerance to deviations from the interdeparture interval T).

This deviation from the interdeparture interval influences the admitted rate burstiness, or the number of consecutive SIP requests forwarded to the server (burst size proportional to *TAU* over the difference between $1/T$ and the arrival rate). In situations where clients are configured with some knowledge about the server (e.g., operator preprovisioning), it can be beneficial to choose a value of *TAU* based on how many clients will be sending requests to the server. Servers with a very large number of clients, each with a relatively small arrival rate, will generally benefit from a smaller value for *TAU* in order to limit queuing (and hence response times) at the server when subjected to a sudden surge of traffic from all clients. Conversely, a server with a relatively small number of clients, each with a proportionally larger arrival rate, will benefit from a larger value of *TAU*. Once the control has been activated, at the arrival time of the kth new SIP request, $t_a(k)$, the content of the bucket is provisionally updated to the value

$$X' = X - (t_a(k) - LCT)$$

where X is the value of the leaky bucket counter after arrival of the last forwarded SIP request, and *LCT* is the time at which the last SIP request was forwarded.

If X' is less than or equal to the limit value *TAU*, then the new SIP request is forwarded and the leaky bucket counter X is set to X' (or to 0 if X' is negative) plus the increment T, and *LCT* is set to the current time $t_a(k)$. If X' is greater than the limit value *TAU*, then the new SIP request is rejected, and the values of X and *LCT* are unchanged. When the first response from the server has been received, indicating control activation (oc-validity > 0), *LCT* is set to the time of activation, and the leaky bucket counter is initialized to the parameter TAU_0 (preferably configurable), which is 0 or larger but less than or equal to *TAU*. *TAU* can assume any positive real number value and is not necessarily bounded by T. $TAU = 4 * T$ is a reasonable compromise between burst size and throttled rate adaptation at low offered rates. Note that specification of a value for *TAU* and any communication or coordination between servers are beyond the scope of this document. A reference algorithm is shown below.

No priority case:

```
//T: inter-transmission interval, set to 1 /
//[oc parameter]
//TAU: tolerance parameter
//ta: arrival time of the most recent arrival
//received by the client
//LCT: arrival time of last SIP request that
//was sent to the server
//(initialized to the first arrival time)
//X: current value of the leaky bucket
//counter (initialized to TAU0)
//After most recent arrival, calculate
//auxiliary variable Xp

        Xp = X - (ta - LCT);
        if (Xp ≤ TAU) {

//Transmit SIP request
//Update X and LCT

        X = max(0, Xp) + T;
        LCT = ta;
        }else {
//Reject SIP request
//Do not update X and LCT
        }
```

13.4.2.5.2 Priority Treatment

As with the loss-based algorithm of RFC 7339 (see Section 13.3), a client implementing the rate-based algorithm also prioritizes messages into two or more categories of requests: requests that are candidates for reduction and requests not subject to reduction (except under extenuating circumstances when there are no messages in the first category that can be reduced). Accordingly, the proposed leaky bucket implementation is modified to support priority using two thresholds for SIP requests in the set of request candidates for reduction. With two priorities, the proposed leaky bucket requires two thresholds $TAU_1 < TAU_2$:

- All new requests would be admitted when the leaky bucket counter is at or below TAU_1.
- Only higher-priority requests would be admitted when the leaky bucket counter is between TAU_1 and TAU_2.
- All requests would be rejected when the bucket counter is at or above TAU_2.

This can be generalized to n priorities using n thresholds for $n > 2$ in the obvious way. With a priority scheme that relies on two tolerance parameters (TAU_2 influences the priority traffic, TAU_1 influences the nonpriority traffic), always set $TAU_1 < TAU_2$ (TAU is replaced by TAU_1 and TAU_2). Setting both tolerance parameters to the same value is equivalent to having no priority. TAU_1 influences the admitted rate the same way as TAU does when no priority is set. Moreover, the larger the difference between TAU_1 and TAU_2, the closer the control is to strict priority queuing. TAU_1 and TAU_2 can assume any positive real number value and are not necessarily bounded by T. Reasonable values for TAU_0, TAU_1, and TAU_2 are

$$TAU_0 = 0, TAU_1 = \frac{1}{2} * TAU_2 \text{ and } TAU_2 = 10 * T$$

Note that specification of a value for TAU_1 and TAU_2, and any communication or coordination between servers are beyond the scope of this document. A reference algorithm is shown below.

Priority case:

```
//T: inter-transmission interval, set to 1 /
//[oc parameter]
//TAU1: tolerance parameter of no-priority
//SIP requests
//TAU2: tolerance parameter of priority SIP
//requests
//ta: arrival time of the most recent arrival
//received by the client
//LCT: arrival time of last SIP request that
//was sent to the server
//(initialized to the first arrival time)
//X: current value of the leaky bucket
//counter (initialized to TAU0)
//After most recent arrival, calculate
//auxiliary variable Xp
      Xp = X -(ta - LCT);
      if (AnyRequestReceived && Xp ≤ TAU1)
|| (PriorityRequestReceived &&
      Xp ≤ TAU2 & & Xp > TAU1 {
//Transmit SIP request
//Update X and LCT
      X = max(0, Xp) + T;
      LTC = Ta;
      }else {
//Reject SIP request
//Do not update X and LCT
}
```

13.4.2.5.3 Optional Enhancement: Avoidance of Resonance

As the number of client sources of traffic increases or the throughput of the server decreases, the maximum rate admitted by each client needs to decrease, and therefore the value of T becomes larger. Under some circumstances, for example, if the traffic arises very quickly simultaneously at many sources, the occupancies of each bucket can become synchronized, resulting in the admissions from each source being close in time, and batched or very *peaky* arrivals at the server, which not only gives rise to control instability but also to very poor delays and even lost messages. An appropriate term for this is *resonance* [3]. If the network topology is such that resonance can occur, then a simple way to avoid resonance is to randomize the bucket occupancy at two appropriate points: At the activation of control and whenever the bucket empties, as follows. After updating the value of the leaky bucket to X', generate a value u as follows:

```
      if X' > 0, then u = 0
      else if X' ≤ 0, then let u be set to a
uniformly distributed random value
      between -1/2 and +1/2
if X' > 0, then u = 0
else if X' ≤ 0, then let u be set to a random
value uniformly distributed between -1/2 and
+1/2.
```

Then, (only) if the arrival is admitted, increase the bucket by an amount $T + uT$, which will therefore be just T if the bucket has not emptied, or lie between $T/2$ and $3T/2$ if it has. This randomization should also be done when control is activated; that is, instead of simply initializing the leaky bucket counter to TAU_0, initialize it to $TAU_0 + uT$, where u is uniformly distributed as stated above. Since activation would have been a result of response to a request sent by the client, the second term in this expression can be interpreted as being the bucket increment following that admission. This method has the following characteristics:

- If TAU_0 is chosen to be equal to u and all sources were to activate control at the same time owing to an extremely high request rate, then the time until the first request admitted by each client would be uniformly distributed over [0,*T*].

- The maximum occupancy is $TAU + \left(\frac{3}{2}\right)T$ rather than $TAU + T$ without randomization.
- For the special case of *classic gapping*, where $TAU = 0$, then the minimum time between admissions is uniformly distributed over $\left[\frac{T}{2}, \frac{3T}{2}\right]$, and the mean time between admissions is the same, that is, $T + \frac{R}{2}$ where R is the request arrival rate.
- As high load randomization rarely occurs, there is no loss of precision of the admitted rate, even though the randomized *phasing* of the buckets remains.

13.4.3 Example

Adapting the example in RFC 7339 (see Section 13.3), where client P1 sends requests to a downstream server P2:

```
INVITE sips:user@example.com SIP/2.0
Via: SIP/2.0/TLS p1.example.net;
branch=z9hG4bK2d4790.1;received=192.0.2.111;
oc;oc-algo="loss,rate"
...
SIP/2.0 100 Trying
Via: SIP/2.0/TLS p1.example.net;
branch=z9hG4bK2d4790.1;received=192.0.2.111;
oc=0;oc-algo="rate";oc-validity=0;
oc-seq=1282321615.781
...
```

In the messages above, the first line is sent by P1 to P2. This line is a SIP request; because P1 supports overload control, it inserts the oc parameter in the topmost Via header field that it created. P1 supports two overload control algorithms: loss and rate. The second line, a SIP response, shows the top most Via header field amended by P2 according to this specification and sent to P1. Because P2 also supports overload control, it chooses the rate-based scheme and sends that back to P1 in the oc-algo parameter. It uses oc-validity=0 to indicate no overload control. In this example, oc=0; however, oc could be any value as oc is ignored when oc-validity=0. At some later time, P2 starts to experience overload. It sends the following SIP message indicating P1 should send SIP requests at a rate no greater than or equal to 150 SIP requests per second and for a duration of 1000 milliseconds.

```
SIP/2.0 180 Ringing
Via: SIP/2.0/TLS p1.example.net;
branch=z9hG4bK2d4790.1;received=192.0.2.111;
oc=150;oc-algo="rate";oc-validity=1000;
oc-seq=1282321615.782
...
```

13.4.4 Syntax

This specification extends the existing definition of the Via header field parameters of RFC 3261 (see Section 2.8) as follows:

```
algo-list/="rate"
```

13.5 Summary

We have defined the notion of logical connection, known as network flows of SIP messages, in the form of dialog forming and registration between the SIP entities for end-to-end communications in the SIP application layer. These flow-based logical connections can be reused for routing of messages by SIP entities especially for proxies. The flow-based connection setup, keep-alive mechanisms connection management procedures, registration of client-initiated procedures by SIP entities, flow-recovery mechanisms, and connection management examples are explained in great detail. Like connection management, the growing needs of overload control for the next-generation large-scale SIP networks have resulted in extensions in SIP. The loss-based and rate-based overload control mechanisms that complement each other are explained along with their load control algorithms. The general behavior of SIP entities related to determining support for overload control, creating and updating the control parameters, processing and using, terminating, stabilizing, self-limiting, responding with overload indication, and dealing with provisional response by the overload control is described. It is explained that the rate-based overload mechanism uses a different load control algorithm, but uses the same SIP signaling messages that are used by the loss-based control. The examples for both control mechanisms are discussed.

PROBLEMS

1. What is the logical connection known as the network flows of SIP messages? Why is it useful? Articulate with examples. How does it differ with that of TCP or UDP?
2. How are the flow-based connections set up over the SIP network? Describe in detail the roles that are played by SIP entities in setting up the connection.
3. What is the keep-alive mechanism? Describe the CRLF and STUN keep-alive techniques. How do they help in managing the logical connection of network flows?
4. Describe in detail the procedures for connection management by UA, edge proxy, and registrar for both RGISTER and non-REGISTER messages as applicable.

5. Describe the connection management procedures by the authoritative proxy.
6. Describe the registration call flows managing client-initiated connection for registration, incoming call and proxy crash, reregistration, and outgoing call.
7. Describe the keep-alive mechanism in the SIP network with CRLF and STUN.
8. Describe the flow-recovery mechanisms in the SIP network with call flow example: configuration subscription, registration, and incoming proxy in view of proxy crash, reregistration, and outgoing call.
9. Why is overload control needed in the SIP network? How does the overload control mechanism operate? What are the requirements that the overload control mechanism in the SIP network need to satisfy?
10. Explain the functions of the parameters that are being extended for the SIP Via header: oc, oc-algo, oc-validity, and oc-seq.
11. Explain the general behavior in determining support for overload control, creating and updating the control parameters, processing and using, terminating, stabilizing, self-limiting, responding with overload indication, and dealing with provisional response by the overload control along with examples.
12. Describe the loss-based overload control scheme. What are its special parameter values? What is its default algorithm?
13. Develop a detailed design architecture for implementation of the loss-based overload control mechanism along with SIP mechanism and backward compatibility.
14. Describe in detail the security features that the overload control mechanism need to take care of.
15. What is the rate-based overload control mechanism? How does it complement the load-based overload control mechanism?
16. Describe the rate-based control algorithm scheme along with Via header filed, client and server rate control algorithm selection, server, and client operation with examples.

References

1. Noel, E. and Williams, P.M., "Session Initiation Protocol (SIP) rate control," draft-ietf-soc-overload-rate-control-10.txt, IETF Draft, Work in Progress, April 10, 2015.
2. "Traffic control and congestion control in B-ISDN," ITU-T Recommendation I.371, 2000.
3. Erramilli, A. and Forys, L.J., "Traffic synchronization effects in teletraffic systems," ITC-13, 1991.

Chapter 14

Interworking Services in SIP

Abstract

We describe how Session Initiation Protocol (SIP) signaling messages and media streams can cross intermediaries like session border controllers (SBCs) and network address translators (NATs), providing end-to-end seamless interworking services among the SIP end points. SBCs are being deployed between the two network boundaries by network operators. We address how interoperability can be offered, avoiding proprietary implementations. A whole new set of protocols have been created for NAT crossing, making NATs a kind of SIP application-aware back-to-back user agent devices, which can be used by SIP user agents for NAT crossing. The NAT crossing by SIP itself is a rather big area and requires a stand-alone separate discussion. We only briefly summarize this topic for the sake of brevity. In addition, we address the SIP public switched telephone network/Integrated Services Digital Network (PSTN/ISDN) protocol interworking that enables real-time communications between Internet Protocol (IP) and PSTN/ISDN end points. Again, the interworking between the IP packet switching-based IP telephony and circuit-switched-based telephony is also a huge area, and we only briefly address this topic here by providing some basic ideas of interworking.

14.1 Introduction

Intermediary devices like session border controllers (SBCs) and network address translators (NATs) have created serious technical hurdles for real-time multimedia communications. SBCs usually handle both signaling and media traffic between two network boundaries for topology hiding, quality of service (QOS), facilitating NAT crossing, and other purposes. SBCs are being implemented in a proprietary manner and have caused interoperability issues among multivendor environments. Similarly, NAT crossing is also a problem. However, in NATs, this is primarily because their operation characteristics are only tuned to the Transmission Control Protocol (TCP) and User Datagram Protocol (UDP) transport protocols, but not to real-time transport protocols like Real-Time Transport Protocol (RTP) and others that run over TCP/UDP. Moreover, the operational characteristics of real-time and non-real-time application protocols are also fundamentally different. The non-real-time application protocols over only the TCP/UDP can easily cross NATs, while real-time application protocols, which use, for example, RTP/UDP or RTP/TCP, cannot cross NATs. In this section, we describe some of the NAT-crossing protocols that enable real-time application protocols like SIP to cross NATs, and enable end-to-end communications over the Internet Protocol (IP) network between the SIP end points. However, these NAT-crossing protocols make a NAT application-aware device, like a SIP-aware device acting as the back-to-back user agent (B2BUA). Moreover, the key interworking aspects between SIP and public switched telephone network/Integrated Services Digital Network (PSTN/ISDN) protocols are addressed here briefly. We describe only the SIP-T interworking that provides the basic framework for interworking between two disparate sets of call control protocols of a packet-switching and circuit-switching network.

14.2 SIP Session Border Controller

14.2.1 Objective

The deployment of SIP in enterprise or residential customer environments has given rise to the use of another intermediary functional entity known as the SBC that often carries both SIP signaling and media to meet some requirements, as follows:

- Perimeter defense, for example, access control, topology hiding, and denial-of-service (DoS) prevention and detection
- Functionality not available in the end points, for example, NAT traversal and protocol interworking or repair
- Traffic management, for example, media monitoring and QOS

Even though many SBCs currently behave in ways that can break end-to-end security and influence feature negotiations, there is clearly a market for them. Network operators need many of the features current SBCs provide, and often there are no standard mechanisms available to provide them. SBCs are typically deployed at the border between two networks. The reason for this is that network policies are typically enforced at the edge of the network.

On the basis of this marketing trend of SIP deployment, Request for Comment (RFC) 5853 has been created to provide some implementation guidance for SBCs so that SBC products from different vendors may interoperate abiding by this framework, preventing the proliferation of non-interoperable proprietary SBC products. This specification describes functions implemented in SBCs. A special focus is given to those practices that conflict with SIP architectural principles in some way. This RFC also explores the underlying requirements of network operators that have led to the use of these functions and practices in order to identify protocol requirements and determine whether those requirements are satisfied by existing specifications, or if additional work on standards is required.

14.2.2 Background on SBCs

The term SBC is relatively nonspecific since it is not standardized or defined anywhere. Nodes that may be referred to as SBCs but do not implement SIP are outside the scope of this document. SBCs usually sit between two service provider networks in a peering environment, or between an access network and a backbone network to provide service to residential or enterprise customers. They provide a variety of functions to enable or enhance session-based multimedia services (e.g., SIP-based voice over IP) as described above. Some of these functions may also get integrated into other SIP elements, such as prepaid platforms, Third Generation Partnership Project (3GPP) Proxy-Call Session Control Function (P-CSCF), Interrogating-CSPF (I-CSPF) [1], and others.

SIP-based SBCs can implement behavior that is equivalent to a *privacy service* (RFC 3323, see Section 20.2) performing both Header Privacy and Session Privacy because, as stated earlier, they usually handle both signaling and media acting as the B2BUAs. SBCs often modify certain SIP headers and message bodies that proxies are not allowed to modify. The transparency of these B2BUAs varies depending on the functions they perform. For example, some SBCs modify the session description carried in the message and insert a Record-Route entry. Other SBCs replace the value of the Contact header field with the SBCs' address, and generate a new Call-ID and new To and From tags. Figure 14.1 shows the logical architecture of an SBC, which includes a signaling and a media component. In this chapter, the terms outer network and inner network are used to describe these two networks.

An SBC is logically associated with the inner network, and it typically provides functions such as controlling and protecting access to the inner network from the outer network. The SBC itself is configured and managed by the organization operating the inner network. In some scenarios, SBCs operate with users' (implicit or explicit) consent; however, in others, they operate without users' consent (this latter case can potentially cause problems). For example, if an SBC in the same administrative domain as a set of enterprise users performs topology hiding, the enterprise users can choose to

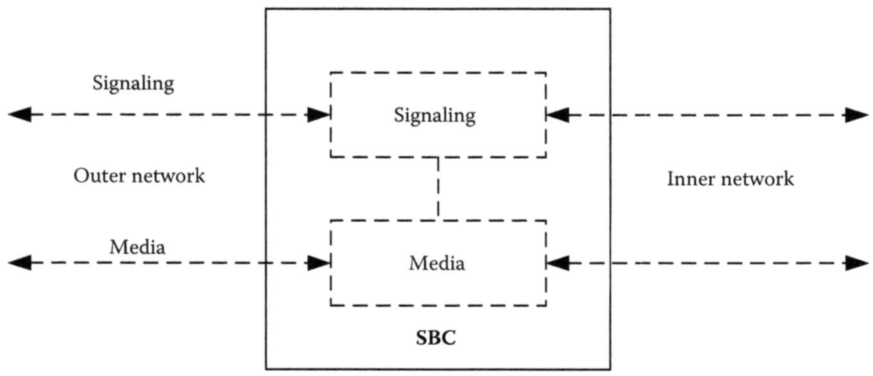

Figure 14.1 SBC architecture. (Copyright IETF. Reproduced with permission.)

route their SIP messages through it. If they choose to route through the SBC, then the SBC can be seen as having the users' implicit consent. Another example is a scenario where a service provider has broken gateways and it deploys an SBC in front of them for protocol repair reasons. Users can choose to configure the SBC as their gateway and, thus, the SBC can be seen as having the users' implicit consent.

14.2.2.1 Peering Scenario

A typical peering scenario involves two network operators who exchange traffic with each other. An example peering scenario is illustrated in Figure 14.2. An originating gateway (GW-A1) in operator A's network sends an INVITE that is routed to the SBC in operator B's network. Then, the SBC forward it to the SoftSwitch (SS-B). The SoftSwitch responds with a redirect (3xx) message back to the SBC that points to the appropriate terminating gateway (GW-B1) in operator B's network. If operator B does not have an SBC, the redirect message would go to operator A's originating gateway. After receiving the redirect message, the SBC sends the INVITE to the terminating gateway.

From the SBC's perspective, operator A is the outer network and operator B is the inner network. Operator B can use the SBC, for example, to control access to its network, protect its gateways and SoftSwitches from unauthorized use and DoS attacks, and monitor the signaling and media traffic. It also simplifies network management by minimizing the number of Access Control List (ACL) entries in the gateways. The gateways do not need to be exposed to the peer network, and they can restrict access (both media and signaling) to the SBCs. The SBC helps ensure that only media from sessions the SBC authorizes will reach the gateway.

14.2.2.2 Access Scenario

In an access scenario, presented in Figure 14.3, the SBC is placed at the border between the access network (outer network) and the operator's network (inner network) to control access to the operator's network, protect its components

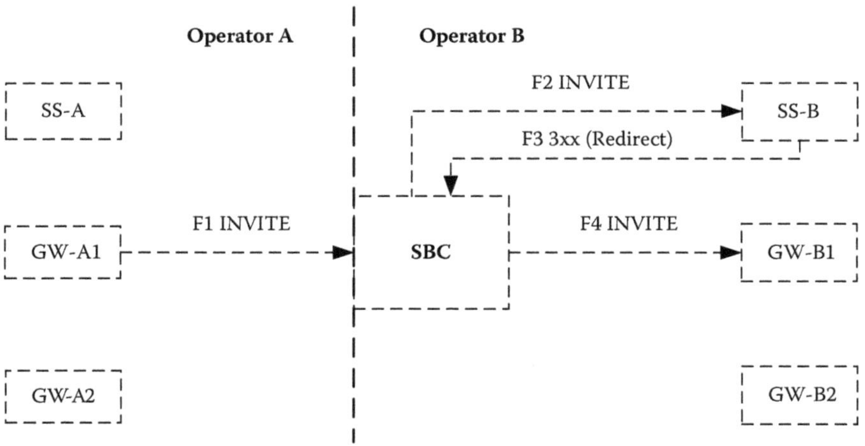

Figure 14.2 Peering with SBC. (Copyright IETF. Reproduced with permission.)

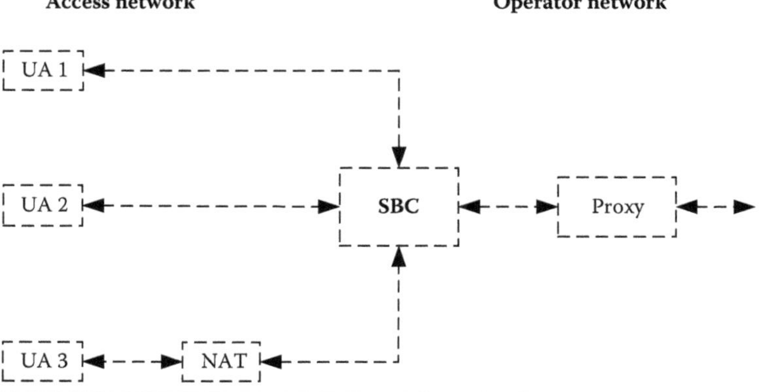

Figure 14.3 Access scenario with SBC. (Copyright IETF. Reproduced with permission.)

(media servers, application servers, gateways, etc.) from unauthorized use and DoS attacks, and monitor the signaling and media traffic. Also, since the SBC is call stateful, it may provide access control functions to prevent oversubscription of the access links. End points are configured with the SBC as their outbound proxy address. The SBC routes requests to one or more proxies in the operator network.

The SBC may be hosted in the access network (e.g., this is common when the access network is an enterprise network), or in the operator network (e.g., this is common when the access network is a residential or small business network). Despite where the SBC is hosted, it is managed by the organization maintaining the operator network. Some end points may be behind enterprise or residential NATs. In cases where the access network is a private network, the SBC is a NAT for all traffic. It is noteworthy that SIP traffic may have to traverse more than one NAT. The proxy usually does authentication or authorization for registrations and outbound calls. The SBC modifies the REGISTER request so that subsequent requests to the registered address of record are routed to the SBC. This is done either with a Path header or by modifying the Contact to point at the SBC. The scenario presented in this section is a general one, and it applies also to other similar settings. One example from a similar setting is the one where an access network is the open Internet, and the operator network is the network of a SIP service provider.

14.2.3 Functions of SBCs

This section lists those functions that are used in SBC deployments in current communication networks. Each subsection describes a particular function or feature, the operators' requirements for having it, explanation of any impact to the end-to-end SIP architecture, and a concrete implementation example. Each section also discusses potential concerns specific to that particular implementation technique. Suggestions for alternative implementation techniques that may be more architecturally compatible with SIP are outside the scope of this document. All the examples given in this section are simplified; only the relevant header lines from SIP and Session Description Protocol (SDP) messages are displayed.

14.2.3.1 Topology Hiding

14.2.3.1.1 General Information and Requirements

Topology hiding consists of limiting the amount of topology information given to external parties. Operators have a requirement for this functionality because they do not want the IP addresses of their equipment (proxies, gateways, application servers, and others) to be exposed to outside parties. This may be because they do not want to expose their equipment to DoS attacks, they may use other carriers for certain traffic and do not want their customers to be aware of it, or they may want to hide their internal network architecture from competitors or partners. In some environments, the operator's customers may wish to hide the addresses of their equipment, or the SIP messages may contain private, nonroutable addresses. The most common form of topology hiding is the application of header privacy (RFC 3323, see Section 20.2), which involves stripping Via and Record-Route headers, replacing the Contact header, and even changing Call-IDs. However, in deployments that use IP addresses instead of domain names in headers that cannot be removed (e.g., From and To headers), the SBC may replace these IP addresses with its own IP address or domain name. For reference, there are also other ways of hiding topology information than inserting an intermediary, like an SBC, to the signaling path. One of the ways is the user agent (UA)-driven privacy mechanism (RFC 5767, see Section 20.6.2), where the UA can facilitate the concealment of topology information.

14.2.3.1.2 Architectural Issues

Performing topology hiding, as described above, by SBCs that do not have the users' consent presents some issues. This functionality is based on a hop-by-hop trust model as opposed to an end-to-end trust model. The messages are modified without the subscriber's consent and could potentially modify or remove information about the user's privacy, security requirements, and higher-layer applications that are communicated end-to-end using SIP. Neither UA in an end-to-end call has any way to distinguish the SBC actions from a man-in-the-middle (MITM) attack. The topology hiding function does not work well with Authenticated Identity Management (RFC 4474, see Sections 2.8 and 19.4.8) in scenarios where the SBC does not have any kind of consent from the users. The Authenticated Identity Management mechanism is based on a hash value that is calculated from parts of From, To, Call-ID, CSeq, Date, and Contact header fields plus from the whole message body. If the authentication service is not provided by the SBC itself, the modification of the aforementioned header fields and the message body is in violation of RFC 4474. Some forms of topology hiding are in violation, because they are, for example, replacing the Contact header of a SIP message.

14.2.3.1.3 Example

The current way of implementing topology hiding consists of having an SBC act as a B2BUA and removing all traces of topology information (e.g., Via and Record-Route entries) from outgoing messages. Imagine the following example

```
INVITE sip:callee@u2.domain.example.com SIP/2.0
Via: SIP/2.0/UDP p3.middle.example.com;branch=z9hG4bK48jq9w174131.1
Via: SIP/2.0/UDP p2.example.com;branch=z9hG4bK18an6i9234172.1
Via: SIP/2.0/UDP p1.example.com;branch=z9hG4bK39bn2e5239289.1
Via: SIP/2.0/UDP u1.example.com;branch=z9hG4bK92fj4u7283927.1
Contact: sip:caller@u1.example.com
Record-Route: <sip:p3.middle.example.com;lr>
Record-Route: <sip:p2.example.com;lr>
Record-Route: <sip:p1.example.com;lr>
```

Figure 14.4 INVITE request before topology hiding.

```
INVITE sip:callee@u2.domain.example.com SIP/2.0
Via: SIP/2.0/UDP p4.domain.example.com;branch=z9hG4bK92es3w230129.1
Contact: sip:caller@u1.example.com
Record-Route: <sip:p4.domain.example.com;lr>
```

Figure 14.5 INVITE request after topology hiding.

scenario: the SBC (p4.domain.example.com) receives an INVITE request from the inner network, which in this case is an operator network. The received SIP message is shown in Figure 14.4.

Then, the SBC performs a topology hiding function. In this scenario, the SBC removes and stores all existing Via and Record-Route headers, and then inserts Via and Record-Route header fields with its own SIP Uniform Resource Identifier (URI). After the topology hiding function, the message could appear as shown in Figure 14.5.

Like a regular proxy server that inserts a Record-Route entry, the SBC handles every single message of a given SIP dialog. If the SBC loses state (e.g., the SBC restarts for some reason), it may not be able to route messages properly (note: some SBCs preserve the state information also on restart). For example, if the SBC removes Via entries from a request and then restarts, thus losing state, the SBC may not be able to route responses to that request, depending on the information that was lost when the SBC restarted. This is only one example of topology hiding. Besides topology hiding (i.e., information related to the network elements is being hidden), SBCs may also do identity hiding (i.e., information related to identity of subscribers is being hidden). While performing identity hiding, SBCs may modify Contact header field values and other header fields containing identity information. The header fields containing identity information is listed in RFC 3323 (see Section 20.2). Since the publication of RFC 3323, the following header fields containing identity information have been defined: P-Asserted-Identity, Referred-By, Identity, and Identity-Info.

14.2.3.2 Media Traffic Management

14.2.3.2.1 General Information and Requirements

Media traffic management is the function of controlling media traffic. Network operators may require this functionality in order to control the traffic being carried on their network on behalf of their subscribers. Traffic management helps the creation of different kinds of billing models (e.g., video telephony can be priced differently than voice-only calls), and it also makes it possible for operators to enforce the usage of selected codecs. One of the use cases for media traffic management is the implementation of intercept capabilities that are required to support audit or legal obligations. It is noteworthy that the legal obligations mainly apply to operators providing voice services, and those operators typically have infrastructure (e.g., SIP proxies acting as B2BUAs) for providing intercept capabilities even without SBCs. Since the media path is independent of the signaling path, the media may not traverse through the operator's network unless the SBC modifies the session description. By modifying the session description, the SBC can force the media to be sent through a media relay that may be colocated with the SBC.

This kind of traffic management can be done, for example, to ensure a certain QOS level, or to ensure that subscribers are using only allowed codecs. It is noteworthy that the SBCs do not have direct ties to routing topology and they do not, for example, change bandwidth reservations on Traffic Engineering tunnels, nor do they have direct interaction with the routing protocol. Some operators do not want to manage the traffic, but only to monitor it to collect statistics and make sure that they are able to meet any business-service-level agreements with their subscribers or partners. The protocol techniques, from the SBC's viewpoint, needed for monitoring media traffic are the same as for managing media traffic. SBCs on the media path are also capable of dealing with the *lost BYE* issue if either end point dies in the middle of the session. The SBC can detect that the media has stopped flowing, and issue a BYE to both sides to clean up any state in other intermediate elements and the end points. One possible form of media traffic management is that SBCs terminate media streams and SIP dialogs by generating BYE requests. This kind of procedure can take place, for example, in a situation where the subscriber runs out of credits. Media management is needed to ensure that the subscriber cannot just ignore the BYE request generated by the SBC and continue its media sessions.

14.2.3.2.2 Architectural Issues

Implementing traffic management in this manner requires the SBC to access and modify the session descriptions (i.e., offers and answers) exchanged between the UAs. Consequently, this approach does not work if UAs encrypt or integrity-protect their message bodies end-to-end. Again, messages are modified without subscriber consent, and UAs do not have any way to distinguish the SBC actions from an attack by an MITM. Furthermore, this is in violation of Authenticated Identity Management specified in RFC 4474 (see Sections 2.8 and 19.4.8). The insertion of a media relay can prevent nonmedia uses of the media path, for example, the media path key agreement. Sometimes this type of prevention is intentional, but it is not always necessary, for example, if an SBC is used just for enabling media monitoring but not for interception. There are some possible issues related to media relaying. If media relaying is not done in the correct manner, it may break functions like Explicit Congestion Notification (ECN) and Path Maximum Transmission Unit Discovery (PMTUD).

Media relays easily break such IP and transport-layer functionalities that rely on the correct handling of the protocol fields. Some especially sensitive fields are, for example, ECN and Type of Service (TOS) fields and the Do Not Fragment (DF) bit. The way in which media traffic management functions impedes innovation. The reason for the impediment is that, in many cases, SBCs need to be able to support new forms of communication (e.g., extensions to the SDP protocol) before new services can be put into use, which slows the adoption of new innovations. If an SBC directs many media streams through a central point in the network, it is likely to cause a significant amount of additional traffic to a path to that central point. This might create possible bottleneck in the path. In this application, the SBC may originate messages that the user may not be able to authenticate as coming from the dialog peer or the SIP registrar/proxy.

14.2.3.2.3 Example

Traffic management may be performed in the following way: the SBC behaves as a B2BUA and inserts itself, or some other entity under the operator's control, in the media path. In practice, the SBC modifies the session descriptions carried in the SIP messages. As a result, the SBC receives media from one UA and relays it to the other UA, and performs the identical operation with media traveling in the reverse direction. As mentioned earlier, codec restriction is a form of traffic management. The SBC restricts the codec set negotiated in the offer–answer exchange (RFC 3264, see Section 3.8.4) between the UAs. After modifying the session descriptions, the SBC can check whether or not the media stream corresponds to what was negotiated in the offer–answer exchange. If it differs, the SBC has the ability to terminate the media stream or take other appropriate (configured) actions (e.g., raise an alarm). Consider the following example scenario: the SBC receives an INVITE request from the outer network, which in this case is an access network. The received SIP message contains the SDP session descriptor shown in Figure 14.6.

```
v=0
o=owner 2890844526 2890842807 IN IP4 192.0.2.4
c=IN IP4 192.0.2.4
m=audio 49230 RTP/AVP 96 98
a=rtpmap:96 L8/8000
a=rtpmap:98 L16/16000/2
```

Figure 14.6 Request before media management.

```
v=0
o=owner 2890844526 2890842807 IN IP4 192.0.2.4
c=IN IP4 192.0.2.4
m=audio 49230 RTP/AVP 96
a=rtpmap:96 L8/8000
```

Figure 14.7 Request body after media management.

In this example, the SBC performs the media traffic management function by rewriting the m= line, and removing one a= line according to some (external) policy. Figure 14.7 shows the session description after the traffic management function.

Media traffic management has a problem where the SBC needs to understand the SDP and all extensions used by the UAs. This means that in order to use a new extension (e.g., an extension to implement a new service) or a new SDP, SBCs in the network may need to be upgraded in conjunction with the end points. It is noteworthy that a similar problem, but with header fields, applies to, for example, the topology hiding function described earlier. Certain extensions that do not require active manipulation of the session descriptors to facilitate traffic management will be able to be deployed without upgrading existing SBCs, depending on the degree of transparency the SBC implementation affords. In cases requiring an SBC modification to support the new protocol features, the rate of service deployment may be affected.

14.2.3.3 Fixing Capability Mismatches

14.2.3.3.1 General Information and Requirements

SBCs fixing capability mismatches enable communications between UAs with different capabilities or extensions. For example, an SBC can enable a plain SIP (RFC 3261) UA to connect to a 3GPP network, or enable a connection between UAs that support different IP versions, different codecs, or that are in different address realms. Operators have a requirement and a strong motivation for performing capability mismatch fixing, so that they can provide transparent communication across different domains. In some cases, different SIP extensions or methods to implement the same SIP application (like monitoring session liveness, call history/diversion, etc.) may also be interworked through the SBC.

14.2.3.3.2 Architectural Issues

SBCs that are fixing capability mismatches do it by inserting a media element into the media path using the procedures described earlier. Therefore, these SBCs have the same concerns as SBCs performing traffic management: the SBC may modify SIP messages without consent from any of the UAs. This may break end-to-end security and application extensions negotiation. The capability mismatch fixing is a fragile function in the long term. The number of incompatibilities built into various network elements is increasing the fragility and complexity over time. This might lead to a situation where SBCs need to be able to handle a large number of capability mismatches in parallel.

14.2.3.3.3 Example

Consider the following example scenario (Figure 14.8) where the inner network is an access network using IPv4 and the outer network is using IPv6. The SBC receives an INVITE request with a session description from the access network (Figure 14.8).

```
INVITE sip:callee@ipv6.domain.example.com SIP/2.0
Via: SIP/2.0/UDP 192.0.2.4
Contact: sip:caller@u1.example.com
v=0
o=owner 2890844526 2890842807 IN IP4 192.0.2.4
c=IN IP4 192.0.2.4
m=audio 49230 RTP/AVP 96
a=rtpmap:96 L8/8000
```

Figure 14.8 Request before capability match.

Then, the SBC performs a capability mismatch fixing function. In this scenario, the SBC inserts Record-Route and Via headers and rewrites the c= line from the sessions descriptor. Figure 14.9 shows the request after the capability mismatch adjustment.

This message is then sent by the SBC to the onward IPv6 network.

```
INVITE sip:callee@ipv6.domain.com SIP/2.0
Record-Route: <sip:[2001:DB8::801:201:2ff:fe94:8e10];lr>
Via: SIP/2.0/UDP sip:[2001:DB8::801:201:2ff:fe94:8e10]
Via: SIP/2.0/UDP 192.0.2.4
Contact: sip:caller@u1.example.com
v=0
o=owner 2890844526 2890842807 IN IP4 192.0.2.4
c=IN IP6 2001:DB8::801:201:2ff:fe94:8e10
m=audio 49230 RTP/AVP 96
a=rtpmap:96 L8/8000
```

Figure 14.9 Request after capability match.

14.2.3.4 Maintaining SIP-Related NAT Bindings

14.2.3.4.1 General Information and Requirements

NAT traversal in this instance refers to the specific message modifications required to assist a UA in maintaining SIP and media connectivity when there is a NAT device located between a UA and a proxy/registrar and, possibly, any other UA. The primary purpose of the NAT traversal function is to keep up a control connection to UAs behind NATs. This can, for example, be achieved by generating periodic network traffic that keeps bindings in NATs alive. SBCs' NAT traversal function is required in scenarios where the NAT is outside the SBC (i.e., not in cases where the SBC itself acts as a NAT).

An SBC performing a NAT traversal function for a UA behind a NAT sits between the UA and the registrar of the domain. NATs are widely deployed in various access networks today, so operators have a requirement to support it. When the registrar receives a REGISTER request from the UA and responds with a 200 OK response, the SBC modifies such a response, decreasing the validity of the registration (i.e., the registration expires sooner). This forces the UA to send a new REGISTER to refresh the registration sooner than it would have done on receiving the original response from the registrar. The REGISTER requests sent by the UA refresh the binding of the NAT before the binding expires.

Note that the SBC does not need to relay all the REGISTER requests received from the UA to the registrar. The SBC can generate responses to REGISTER requests received before the registration is about to expire at the registrar. Moreover, the SBC needs to deregister the UA if this fails to refresh its registration in time, even if the registration at the registrar would still be valid. SBCs can also force traffic to go through a media relay for NAT traversal purposes. A typical call has media streams in two directions. Even though SBCs can force media streams from both directions to go through a media relay, in some cases, it is enough to relay only the media from one direction (e.g., in a scenario where only the other end point is behind a NAT).

14.2.3.4.2 Architectural Issues

This approach to NAT traversal does not work if end-to-end confidentiality or integrity-protection mechanisms are used (e.g., S/MIME, see Section 19.6). The SBC would be seen as an MITM modifying the messages between the UA and the registrar. There is also a problem related to the method of how SBCs choose the value for the validity of a registration period. This value should be as high as possible, but it still needs to be low enough to maintain the NAT binding. Some SBCs do not have any deterministic method for choosing a suitable value. However, SBCs can just use a suboptimal, relatively small value that usually works. An example from such value is 15 seconds (RFC 5405).

NAT traversal for media using SBCs poses a few issues as well. For example, an SBC normally guesses the recipient's public IP address on one of the media streams relayed by the SBC by snooping on the source IP address of another media stream relayed by the same SBC. This causes security and interoperability issues since the SBC can end up associating wrong destination IP addresses on media streams it is relaying. For example, an attacker may snoop on the local IP address and ports used by the SBC for media relaying the streams and send a few packets from a malicious IP address to these destinations. In most cases, this can cause media streams in the opposite directions to divert traffic to the attacker, resulting in a successful MITM or DoS attack. A similar example of an interoperability issue is caused when an end point behind a NAT attempts to switch the IP address of the media streams by using a re-INVITE. If any media packets are reordered or delayed in the network, they can cause the SBC to block the switch from happening even if the re-INVITE successfully goes through.

14.2.3.4.3 Example

Consider the following example scenario: the SBC resides between the UA and Registrar. Previously, the UA has sent a REGISTER request to the Registrar, and the SBC receives the registration response shown in Figure 14.10.

```
SIP/2.0 200 OK
From: Bob <sip:bob@biloxi.example.com>;tag=a73kszlfl
To: Bob <sip:bob@biloxi.example.com>;tag=34095828jh
CSeq: 1 REGISTER
Contact: <sips:bob@client.biloxi.example.com>;expires=3600
```

Figure 14.10 Response before NAT maintenance function.

```
SIP/2.0 200 OK
From: Bob <sip:bob@biloxi.example.com>;tag=a73kszlfl
To: Bob <sip:bob@biloxi.example.com>;tag=34095828jh
CSeq: 1 REGISTER
Contact: <sips:bob@client.biloxi.example.com>;expires=60
```

Figure 14.11 Manipulated response for NAT traversal.

When performing the NAT traversal function, the SBC may rewrite the expiry time to coax the UA to reregister before the intermediating NAT decides to close the pinhole. Figure 14.11 shows a possible modification of the response from Figure 14.10.

Naturally, other measures could be taken in order to enable the NAT traversal (e.g., non-SIP keep-alive messages); however, this example illustrates only one mechanism for preserving the SIP-related NAT bindings.

14.2.3.5 Access Control

14.2.3.5.1 General Information and Requirements

Network operators may wish to control what kind of signaling and media traffic their network carries. There is strong motivation and a requirement to do access control on the edge of an operator's network. Access control can be based on, for example, link-layer identifiers, IP addresses, or SIP identities. This function can be implemented by protecting the inner network with firewalls and configuring them so that they only accept SIP traffic from the SBC. This way, all the SIP traffic entering the inner network needs to be routed though the SBC, which only routes messages from authorized parties or traffic that meets a specific policy that is expressed in the SBC administratively. Access control can be applied to either only the signaling or both the signaling and media. If it is applied only to the signaling, then the SBC might behave as a proxy server. If access control is applied to both the signaling and media, then the SBC behaves in a similar manner as explained earlier. A key part of media-layer access control is that only media for authorized sessions is allowed to pass through the SBC or associated media relay devices. Operators implement some functionalities, like NAT traversal for example, in an SBC instead of other elements in the inner network for several reasons:

- Preventing packets from unregistered users to mitigate chances of DoS attack
- Prioritization or rerouting of traffic based on user or service, like E911 as it enters the network
- Performing a load-balancing function or reducing the load on other network equipment

In environments where there is limited bandwidth on the access links, the SBC can compute the potential bandwidth use by examining the codecs present in SDP offers and answers. With this information, the SBC can reject sessions before the available bandwidth is exhausted to allow existing sessions to maintain acceptable QOS. Otherwise, the link could become oversubscribed and all sessions would experience a deterioration in QOS. SBCs may contact a policy server to determine whether sufficient bandwidth is available on a per-session basis.

14.2.3.5.2 Architectural Issues

Since the SBC needs to handle all SIP messages, this function has scalability implications. In addition, the SBC is a single point of failure from an architectural point of view. However, in practice, many current SBCs have the capability of supporting redundant configuration, which prevents the loss of calls or sessions in the event of a failure on a single node. If access control is performed only on behalf of signaling, then the SBC is compatible with general SIP architectural principles; however, if it is performed for signaling and for media, then there are similar problems as described earlier.

14.2.3.5.3 Example

Figure 14.12 shows a call flow where the SBC is providing both signaling and media access control (ACKs omitted for brevity).

In this scenario, the SBC first identifies the caller, so it can determine whether or not to give signaling access to the caller. This might be achieved using information gathered during registration, or by other means. Some SBCs may rely on the proxy to authenticate the UA placing the call. After identification, the SBC modifies the session descriptors in INVITE and 200 OK messages in a way so that the media is going to flow through the SBC itself. When the media starts flowing, the SBC can inspect whether the callee and caller use the codec(s) upon which they had previously agreed.

14.2.3.6 Protocol Repair

14.2.3.6.1 General Information and Requirements

SBCs are also used to repair protocol messages generated by clients that are not fully standard compliant, or are badly implemented. Operators may wish to support protocol repair if they want to support as many clients as possible. It is noteworthy that this function affects only the signaling component of an SBC, and that the protocol repair function is not the same as protocol conversion (i.e., making translation between two completely different protocols).

14.2.3.6.2 Architectural Issues

In many cases, doing protocol repair for SIP header fields can be seen as being compatible with SIP architectural principles, and it does not violate the end-to-end model of SIP. The SBC repairing protocol message behaves as a proxy server that is liberal in what it accepts and strict in what it sends. However, protocol repair may break security mechanisms that do cryptographical computations on SIP header values. Attempting protocol repair for SIP message bodies that contain, for example, SDP is incompatible with Authenticated Identity Management (RFC 4474, see Sections 2.8 and 19.4.8) and end-to-end security mechanisms such as S/MIME. A similar problem related to increasing complexity, as explained earlier, also affects protocol repair function.

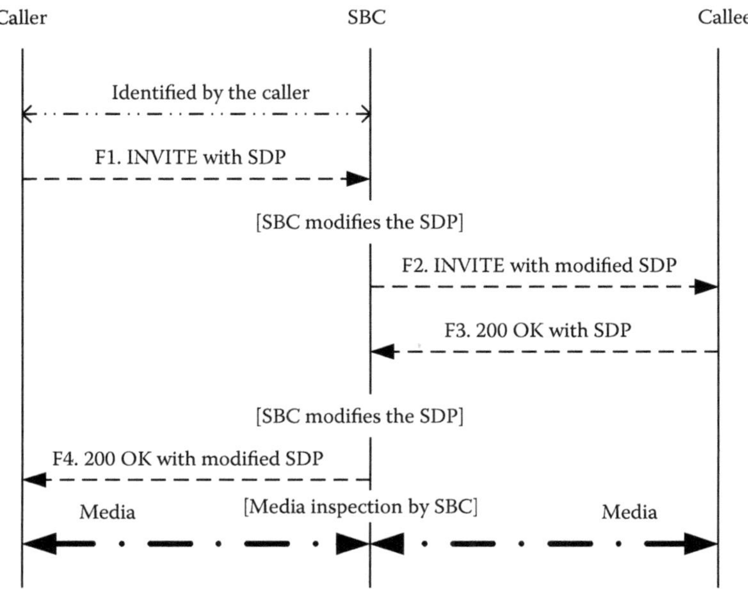

Figure 14.12 Example access call flow. (Copyright IETF. Reproduced with permission.)

```
INVITE sip:callee@sbchost.example.com
Via: SIP/2.0/UDP u1.example.com:5060;lr
From: Caller <sip:caller@one.example.com>
To: Callee <sip:callee@two.example.com>
Call-ID: 18293281@u1.example.com
CSeq: 1 INVITE
Contact: sip:caller@u1.example.com
```

Figure 14.13 Request from a relatively new client.

14.2.3.6.3 Example

The SBC can, for example, receive an INVITE message from a relatively new SIP UA as illustrated in Figure 14.13.

If the SBC does protocol repair, it can rewrite the *lr* parameter on the Via header field into the form lr=true in order to support some older, badly implemented SIP stacks. It could also remove excess white spaces to make the SIP message more human readable.

14.2.3.7 Media Encryption

14.2.3.7.1 General Information and Requirements

SBCs are used to perform media encryption/decryption at the edge of the network. This is the case when media encryption (e.g., SRTP, see Section 7.3) is used only on the access network (outer network) side and the media is carried unencrypted in the inner network. Some operators provide the ability to do legal interception while still giving their customers the ability to encrypt media in the access network. One possible way to do this is to perform a media encryption function.

14.2.3.7.2 Architectural Issues

While performing a media encryption function, SBCs need to be able to inject either themselves, or some other entity, to the media path. It must be noted that this kind of behavior is the same as a classical MITM attack. Owing to this, the SBCs have the same architectural issues as explained earlier.

14.2.3.7.3 Example

Figure 14.14 shows an example where the SBC is performing media-encryption-related functions (ACKs omitted for brevity).

First, the UA client (UAC) sends an INVITE request, and the first SBC modifies the session descriptor in a way that it injects itself to the media path. The same happens in the second SBC. Then, the UA server replies with a 200 OK response and the SBCs inject themselves in the returning media path. After signaling, the media starts flowing, and both SBCs perform media encryption and decryption.

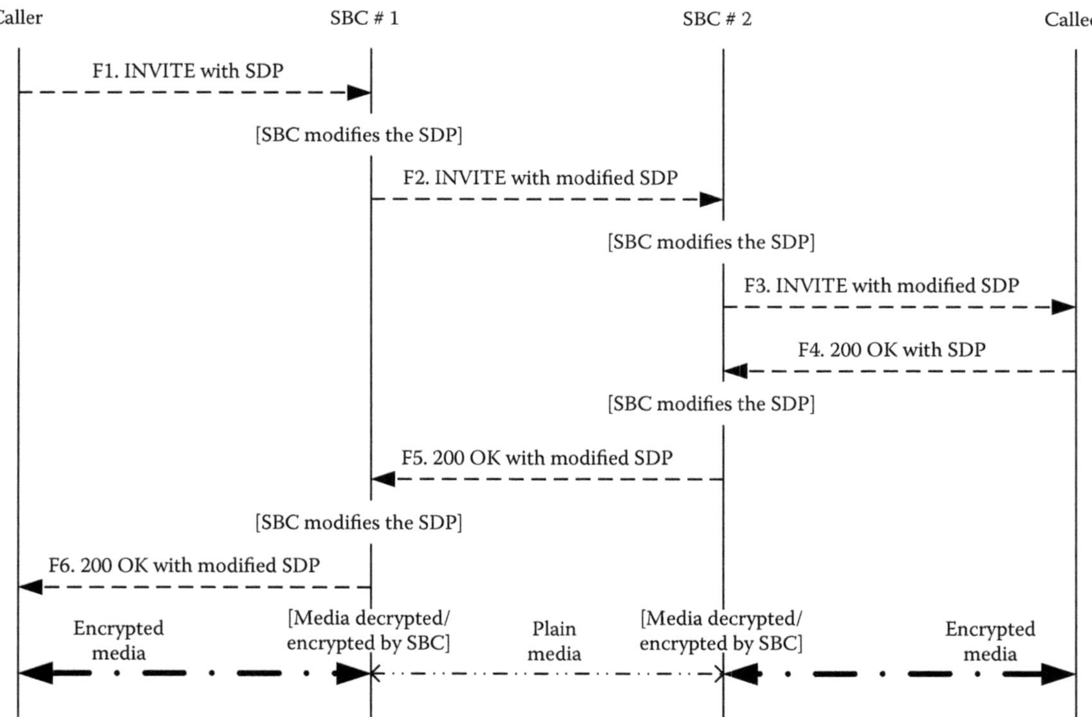

Figure 14.14 Media encryption example. (Copyright IETF. Reproduced with permission.)

14.2.4 Derived Requirements for Future SIP Standardization Work

Some of the functions listed in this chapter are more SIP-unfriendly than others. This list of requirements is derived from the functions that break the principles of SIP in one way or another when performed by SBCs that do not have the users' consent. The derived requirements are as follows:

- There should be a SIP-friendly way to hide network topology information. Currently, this is done by stripping and replacing header fields, which is against the principles of SIP on behalf of some header fields.
- There should be a SIP-friendly way to direct media traffic through intermediaries. Currently, this is done by modifying session descriptors, which is against the principles of SIP.
- There should be a SIP-friendly way to fix capability mismatches in SIP messages. This requirement is harder to fulfill on complex mismatch cases, like the 3GPP/SIP (RFC 3261) network mismatch. Currently, this is done by modifying SIP messages, which may violate end-to-end security, on behalf of some header fields.

The first two requirements do not have an existing standardized solution today. There is ongoing work in the Internet Engineering Task Force (IETF) for addressing the second requirement, such as SIP session policies, TURN (see Section 14.3), and ICE (see Section 14.3). Nonetheless, future work is needed in order to develop solutions to these requirements.

14.3 NAT Crossing by SIP

14.3.1 Overview

Being an application-layer signaling protocol, SIP's messages usually consist of two parts: header and message body. The header part, which contains the *public* addresses of the SIP functional entities for routing of SIP signaling messages, consists of SIP, SIP Security, or telephone URIs. These URIs can then be translated into public IP addresses along with the port numbers of the corresponding transport protocols such as UDP, TCP, or others. Similarly, the SIP message body may contain the public addresses of media such as audio, video, and data applications, in terms of public IP addresses as well as ports of UDP, TCP, or other transport protocols expressed in SDP or other protocols for communications between the parties once the session is established. It should be noted that the IP addresses and port numbers that are dynamically allocated during the call/session in SIP are also communicated between the calling and called parties.

However, the network address translation is used by the network administrator for their private internal networks using *private* IP addresses and port numbers hiding the internal network topologies for security reasons or nonavailability of the public IP addresses. The NAT that is considered a network-layer (or even layer 4 in some cases) device usually maps the internal private IP addresses and port numbers into public IP and port numbers. The key is when a calling, called, or both parties reside behind NATs, their private IP and port numbers will not be known a priori first for routing of the SIP signaling messages before the session is set up and then for routing of the media between the communicating parties once the session is established. Moreover, there are different kinds of NATs, and the behavior of one kind of NAT significantly differs from that of another.

The NAT crossing by SIP has drained huge resources, including extensions in SDP in the IETF breaking the basic tenet of the Open Standard International (OSI) protocol stack where each layer is supposed to work independently of all other layers for scalability. A key issue has been that a NAT opens and closes its pinholes for communications based on policies that depend on the layer 3/4 properties and parameters of the order of a few seconds to minutes, while a SIP session and the media flows of the session may continue for hours if not days. The pinhole opening and closing policies are again handled by the upper-layer firewall (FW). In fact, the NAT and FW close hand-by-hand. If NAT and FW are not collocated, an application protocol needs to be used between the two, and, often, these protocols are proprietary.

It turns out that SIP, being an upper application-layer protocol, needs to be NAT-aware, that is, a lower-layer (layer 3 or 4) device, in order to cross NATs. That is, enhancements in NAT functionalities need to be made like a gateway that is aware of the network layer to the SIP application layer as if acting as a SIP B2BUA. Session Traversal of UDP through NAT (STUN) (RFC 5389), Traversal Using Relays around NAT (TURN) (RFC 5766), and Interactive Connectivity Establishment (ICE) (RFC 5245) protocols have been developed to cross the NATs by SIP so that, first, the session is established and then the media is transferred between the conferencing end points. Each of these NAT-crossing protocols has its own pros, cons, and particular usages depending on different network settings. We will only discuss some basic features of NAT crossing.

14.3.2 NAT-Crossing Protocols

14.3.2.1 STUN

The primary purpose of the STUN protocol is to discover the presence and types of NATs and firewalls between them, and the public IP network including Internet for the applications like SIP. In addition, applications such as SIP can determine the public IP addresses allocated to them by the NAT. However, STUN, as its name implies, only works with NATs such as full-cone NATs that use UDP transport protocols, and also cannot work with symmetric NATs thereby raising security concerns. The STUN functional entity, for example, implemented in a stand-alone server, must have the public IP address. Figure 14.15 shows an example of STUN server configuration that can be used in the SIP network by the SIP functional entities (e.g., UAs and proxies) to be aware of the STUN protocol acting as the STUN client/server.

Figure 14.15a depicts a STUN client on the SIP phone or other end-point device sending packets via the NAT/FW on the STUN server that has the public IP address. The STUN server answers back with information about the IP address and ports from which the packets were received (Figure 14.15a). In this way, the STUN server detects the type of NAT device through which the packets were sent. The STUN client in the SIP end point uses this information in constructing its headers so that external contacts can reach them without the need for any other device or technique. Figure 14.15b shows the communications between hosts that are residing behind NATs once the public addresses are discovered using the STUN protocol. It should be noted that the media goes to the hosts directly via the respective NATs without any involvement of the STUN server.

14.3.2.2 TURN

We have seen that STUN does not work for NATs that are symmetric or use connection-oriented transport protocol such as TCP where the duration of the transport connection, unlike connectionless UDP protocol, is dependent on the application type. In these situations, if a host like the SIP end point is located behind a NAT, then in certain situations it can be impossible for that host to communicate directly with other SIP hosts (peers). The TURN protocol is an extension of STUN and allows the SIP host to control the operation of the relay and to exchange packets with its peers using the relay. Working for both connection-oriented (e.g., TCP) and connectionless (e.g., UDP) transport protocols along with full-cone and symmetric NATs, TURN provides the same protection as that created by symmetric NATs/firewalls because it connects clients behind a NAT to a single peer. Note that TURN differs from some other relay control protocols in that it allows a client to communicate with multiple peers using a single relay address.

Any data received by the TURN server is forwarded as it acts as the relay. However, it can be seen that the TURN client on the inside NAT/FW can then be on the receiving end (but not the sending end, thereby limiting applicability) of a connection that is requested by the client on the inside. That is, it only allows the inbound traffic through a NAT/FW where the TURN client is in control. In addition, the media must go through the TURN server because it relays both incoming and outgoing media stream, consuming significant bandwidth. Extra media delays are introduced because of relaying and extra hops that the media needs to go over the network. Consequently, the use of the TURN server limits the scalability for NAT-crossing implementations of multimedia applications like SIP over the IP network.

14.3.2.3 ICE

ICE allows application end points like SIP to discover other peers residing behind NATs/FWs and then establish a connection. ICE itself is a complex protocol that encompasses all the functionalities of STUN, TURN, and other protocols

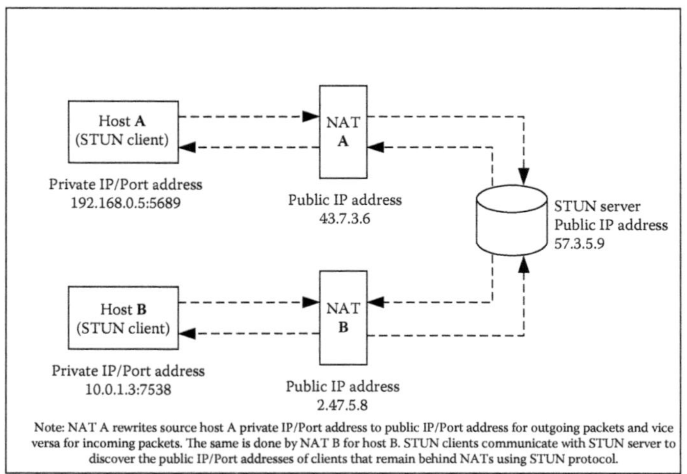

(a)

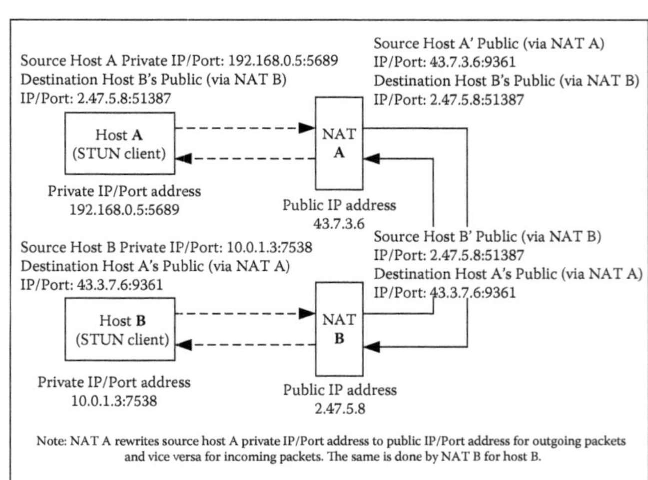

(b)

Figure 14.15 STUN protocol: (a) address discovery by STUN clients residing behind NATs and (b) communications between hosts residing behind NATs.

for solving NAT/FW-crossing problems that are faced by applications like SIP. It encompasses multiple solutions and is regarded as one that will always enable the connection, regardless of the number of NATs involved. ICE essentially incorporates all the functionalities that are needed by applications like SIP for NAT/FW crossing. It requires that the SIP entities (e.g., UAs) need to be ICE-aware. However, ICE can be used by any protocol utilizing the offer–answer model, such as the SIP. ICE takes over the control for opening and closing of pinholes to let the communication through from the NAT/FW. Figure 14.15 depicts the NAT/FW crossing by SIP end points using ICE. In some complicated scenarios, ICE may not work where the NAT/FW deviates from the behaviors that are expected by STUN, TURN, and ICE. In those cases, extensions are needed in ICE.

14.4 SIP–PSTN/ISDN Protocols Interworking

14.4.1 Overview

SIP is a new generation of a networked multimedia protocol that separates between the signaling/call/session control and the media flows for both point-to-point and multipoint communications. A SIP call/session can have many lags/subsessions, and each of these lags/subsessions can be controlled, established, and tear down independently without affecting others. A family of PSTN/ISDN protocols have emerged over many years, such as Channel Associated Signaling (CAS), ISDN, ISDN User Part (ISUP), QSIG (ITU-T Q-Series Signaling Standard), and others. In addition, many variations of each of these protocols have been created in each region/country worldwide. However, in PSTN/ISDN protocols, the signaling/call/session and media flows are tightly coupled together including the physical circuits of the PSTN/ISDN.

As a result, PSTN/ISDN protocols are extremely inflexible to deal with multiple media of a given multimedia application where each media needs to be controlled and manipulated independently with a given call/session, not to mention about the individual call-leg/subsession. In view of this, the interworking between SIP and PSTN/ISDN protocols has become very difficult for mapping on a one-to-one basis. The PSTN/ISDN protocol information that cannot be translated or mapped to SIP messages will be lost if the call routes back to the PSTN. In many cases, the part of the PSTN/ISDN protocols that cannot be translated/mapped into SIP, encapsulation is made putting into the SIP message body carrying in MIME bodies. Many IETF interworking standards such as SIP for Telephony (SIP-T) (RFC 3372), SIP–ISUP (RFC 3398), SIP-QSIG (RFC 4497), and others have been created. We are only providing a brief framework of SIP interworking with PSTN/ISDN protocols following SIP-T here.

14.4.2 SIP-PSTN/ISDN Protocols Interworking Framework

RFC 3372 provides a framework for the integration of legacy PSTN/ISDN protocols into SIP messages taking a couple of basic SIP–ISUP interworking call flow examples. SIP-T provides the two characteristics through techniques known as encapsulation and translation/mapping, respectively. At a SIP–ISUP gateway, ISUP messages are encapsulated within SIP so that information necessary for services is not discarded in the SIP request. However, intermediaries like proxy servers that make routing decisions for SIP requests cannot be expected to understand ISUP; thus, simultaneously, some critical information is translated from an ISUP message into the corresponding SIP headers in order to determine how the SIP request will be routed. Table 14.1 shows the summary of the interworking framework.

Let us take a simple interworking example, as shown in Figure 14.16, that shows that an IP network is connecting the two different PSTN/ISDN networks. The call is originating in the PSTN/ISDN and is terminating in another PSTN/ISDN network via the IP network, while the ISUP and SIP call signaling protocol is used for the PSTN/ISDN and the IP network, respectively. We have shown two media gateway controllers (MGC) that act as the gateway between the IP and PSTN/ISDN networks. It should be noted that the MGC will have both signaling and media interfaces. The SIP proxy servers are usually responsible for routing SIP requests (based on the Request-URI) to the eventual end points. At this, the originating MGC will not know at which a SIP call will terminate toward the destination end point.

Table 14.1 SIP–PSTN/ISUP Protocols Interworking Framework Summary

SIP-PSTN/ISDN Protocols Interworking Requirements	*SIP-T Functions (RFC 3372)*
Transparency of ISUP signaling	Encapsulation of ISUP in the SIP body
Routability of SIP messages with dependencies on ISUP	Translation of ISUP information into the SIP header
Transfer of mid-call ISUP signaling messages	Use of the SIP INFO method (RFC 6086) for mid-message call signaling

Source: Copyright IETF. Reproduced with permission.

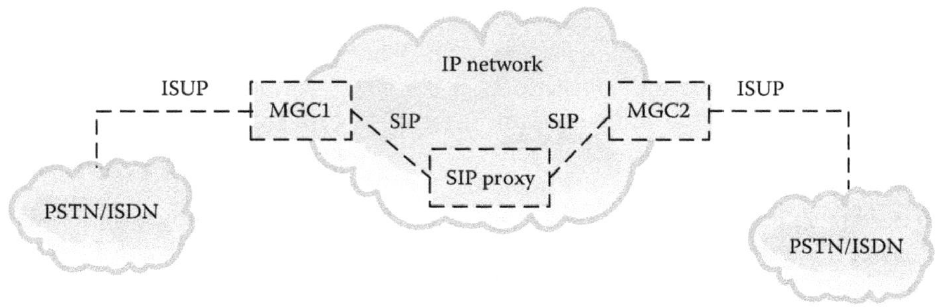

Figure 14.16 PSTN origination–PSTN termination (SIP bridging). (Copyright IETF. Reproduced with permission.)

Therefore, the originator does not select from the flows described in this section, as a matter of static configuration or on a per-call basis; rather, each call is routed by the SIP network independently, and it may instantiate any of the flows below as the routing logic the network dictates. When a call destined for the SIP network originates in the PSTN, an ISUP message will eventually be received by the gateway that is the point of interconnection with the PSTN network. This gateway is from the perspective of the SIP UAC for this call setup request.

Traditional SIP routing is used in the IP network to determine the appropriate point of termination (in this instance, a gateway) and to establish a SIP dialog and begin negotiation of a media session between the origination and termination end points. The egress gateway then signals ISUP to the PSTN/ISDN, reusing any encapsulated ISUP present in the SIP request it receives as appropriate. A very elementary call flow for SIP bridging is shown in Figure 14.17.

This scenario (Figures 14.16 and 14.17), which shows calls originating and terminating in PSTN/ISDN networks interconnected by the IP backbone network, is also known as the SIP trunking configuration. SIP trunking has been very successful in early deployment of SIP because the large traffic volume passing over the IP backbone network interconnecting PSTN/ISDN networks requires only a small portion of network bandwidth because of packet switching as opposed to circuit switching. In addition, it is easy to integrate the equipment of different vendors for interoperability by using a single SIP standard, while there are different variations of PSTN/ISDN standards worldwide. Many other scenarios of

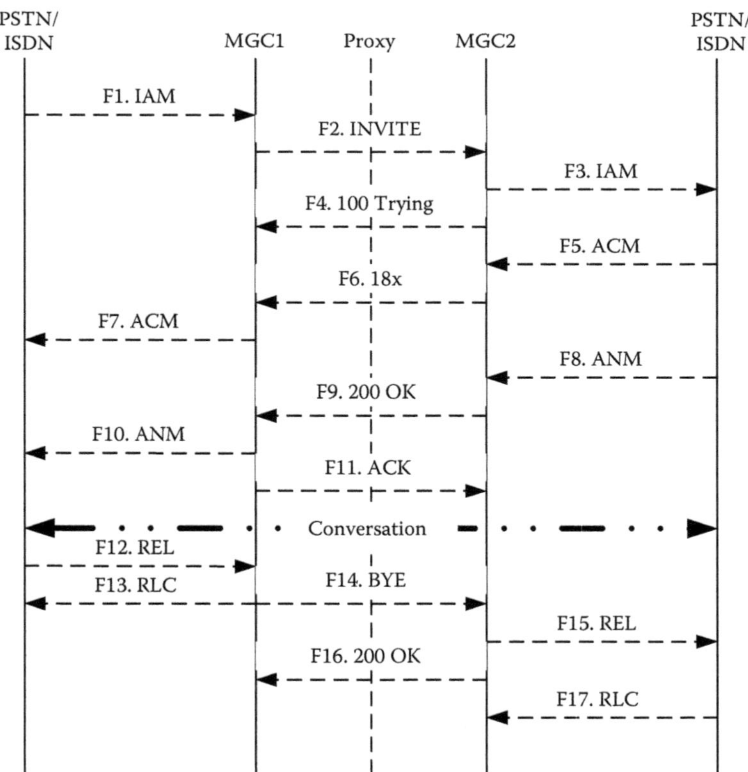

Figure 14.17 Elementary call flows. (Copyright IETF. Reproduced with permission.)

call flows can occur as follows: PSTN/ISDN origination—IP termination and IP origination, PSTN/ISDN termination. We summarize them below.

If the gateway (say, MGC) is the originator that receives an ISUP request, it must always perform both encapsulation and translation of ISUP, regardless of where the originator might guess the request will terminate. If the terminator does not understand ISUP, it ignores it while performing standard SIP processing. If the terminator does understand ISUP, and needs to signal to the PSTN/ISDN, it should reuse the encapsulated ISUP if it understands the variant. The terminator should perform the following steps:

1. Extract the ISUP from the message body, and use this ISUP as a message template. Note that if there is no encapsulated ISUP in the message, the gateway should use a canonical template for the message type in question (a prepopulated ISUP message configured in the gateway) instead.
2. Translate the headers of the SIP request into ISUP parameters, overwriting any values in the message template.
3. Apply any local policies in populating parameters. An intermediary must be able to route a call based on the choice of routable elements in the SIP headers.
4. The SIP INFO method should be used for carrying any mid-call control information over the SIP network that is generated during a session while the PSTN/ISDN network has its own method of carrying the mid-call information.

14.5 Summary

It is explained how NATs have created serious communications problems for multimedia communications over the public IP networks breaking the basic tenet of logically independent OSI protocol stacks that provide interoperability and scalability. STUN, TURN, and ICE, which have been developed for discovering the addresses of hosts residing behind different kinds of NATs using private IP and port addresses, are described briefly. The pros and cons of each kind of NAT-crossing protocols are articulated. The key interworking aspects between the SIP and PSTN/ISDN protocols are discussed briefly. The SIP-T interworking framework that has been developed in the IETF is described. The details of many other SIP-PSTN/ISDN protocols interworking standards that have been developed based on this framework are not addressed for the sake of brevity.

PROBLEMS

1. Describe different ways of opening and closing pinholes for communications between private and public IP networks.
2. Describe the pinhole opening and closing functionalities of different kinds of NATs that use the TCP and UDP transport protocols.
3. How do the pinholes opening and closing operations of NATs differ in dealing with non-multimedia applications like simple text-based file transfer versus multimedia applications like SIP?
4. Describe in detail how STUN clients discover the IP/port addresses for the hosts that reside behind NATs as shown in Figure 14.16a. Describe the call flows for communications between hosts A and B that reside in a private IP network behind NATs as shown in Figure 14.16b.
5. What are the specific kinds of NATs that will work for each kind of NAT-crossing protocol: STUN, TURN, and ICE? Describe the operational properties of the STUN, TURN, and ICE protocols for NAT crossing by SIP. Compare the pros and cons of each kind of NAT-crossing protocol.
6. Describe the detailed call flows for each kind of NATs that are appropriate for STUN, TURN, and ICE, respectively, for communications between SIP end points that reside behind NATs using audio and video.
7. What are the main problems for interworking among the PSTN/ISDN protocol standards among different regions and countries worldwide? Why is SIP so successful in providing interoperability among all of its standards worldwide?
8. Describe the key functional characteristics of the CAS, ISDN, ISUP, and QSIG protocols.
9. Describe the key functional characteristics of the SIP-T framework. Describe the call flows for SIP trunking as shown in Figure 14.17. Write all functional fields of each signaling message: IAM, ACM, ANM, REL, RLC, INVITE, 100 Trying, 18x, 200 OK, ACK, and BYE.
10. Describe the call flows when a call originates from the SIP network and terminates in the PSTN/ISDN network, and vice versa.

Reference

1. 3GPP, "IP Multimedia Subsystem (IMS); Stage 2," 3GPP TS 23.228 10.0.0, March 2010.

Chapter 15

Resource Priority and Quality of Service in SIP

Abstract

We describe resource prioritization over the Session Initiation Protocol (SIP) network that differentiates in providing services of different types of calls. Emergency calls need to be processed with higher priority than ordinary calls, and SIP network resources that need to be allocated accordingly are explained here. The priority levels of calls that are designated with different registered Internet Assigned Numbers Authority namespaces by different authorities based on policies are described. The preemption of calls that may be needed for serving the higher-priority calls in view of limited resources is described along with behavior of SIP entities. In addition, preemption events with access and network, preemption cause codes, and semantics are articulated. The SIP quality-of-service (QOS) requirements described in the application layer by multimedia applications need to be met at the time of the session setup before completion of the session establishment. It imposes a kind of precondition for setting up the successful session should QOS requirements need to be met. The preconditions for meeting the SIP application QOS needs through using the network layer QOS signaling protocol for reservation of resources are explained with detailed examples. The SIP QOS requirements that are expressed by the Session Description Protocol (SDP) attached as the message body of SIP signaling messages are negotiated between the end points. The QOS negotiations using the SDP offer–answer model are described in addition to mapping of QOS flows on SDP media streams. We have also described SDP and SIP signaling messages compression that save bandwidth. The SIP message body in some cases may be very large. In this connection, we describe the SDP and SIP signaling compression that save bandwidth for the signaling traffic. Finally, the security aspects of SIP QOS, such as authentication and authorization, confidentiality and integrity, anonymity, and denial-of-service attacks, which are very critical for users, are elaborated.

15.1 Introduction

The Session Initiation Protocol (SIP) network requires performances to be provided while supporting real-time multimedia applications in setting up sessions. Multimedia applications consisting of audio, video, or data-sharing applications will have different performance requirements for different kinds of media that they consist of. SIP signaling messages need to carry those performance requirements at the time of initiating the session establishment. Consequently, there needs to be differentiating capability for prioritizing resources while sharing the same network by all applications, including real-time, near-real-time, and non-real-time, both at the call/session signaling level and at the media-transfer level. For example, an emergency call will have higher priority than the nonemergency call. Request for Comment (RFC) 4412 (see Section 15.2) that is described here provides this capability in SIP through its extensions. The Resource-Priority header enables SIP to differentiate in handling calls of different priority levels. With the introduction of the SIP Resource-Priority header, it also allows the preemption of calls for (scarce) resource reasons if the resources are insufficient for a particular session to continue.

However, the resources that are required to support the needs of the multimedia applications in terms of bandwidth, and others, reside primarily in the network layer. It implies that session establishment should not take place until there are enough resources in the network for meeting the upper-layer performance requirements. This situation imposes a kind of precondition for setting up the session. RFC 3312 (see Section 15.4) that is described here provides mechanisms to define those preconditions in meeting the quality-of-service (QOS) requirements before setting up SIP sessions. The network layer QOS signaling protocols, like the Resource ReSerVation Protocol (RSVP), that reserves the network resources mapping the SIP application layer QOS requirements are described in detail. The multimedia application QOS parameters are being carried over the Session Description Protocol (SDP) used in the message body of SIP signaling messages. Different media streams may have different QOS requirements, and the QOS flows need to be mapped to the appropriate media streams appropriately. In addition, SDP offer–answer model allows negotiating appropriate QOS for each of the media streams between the SIP end points. RFCs 3524 (see Section 15.5) and 5432 (see Section 15.6) that are described here specify QOS mapping to media streams and QOS negotiations between the end points, respectively.

15.2 Communications Resource Priority in SIP

15.2.1 Overview

During emergencies, communications resources (including telephone circuits, Internet Protocol [IP] bandwidth, and gateways between the circuit-switched and IP networks) may become congested. Congestion can occur due to heavy usage, loss of resources caused by the natural or man-made disaster, and attacks on the network during man-made emergencies. This congestion may make it difficult for persons charged with emergency assistance, recovery, or law enforcement to coordinate their efforts. As IP networks become part of converged or hybrid networks, along with public and private circuit-switched (telephone) networks, it becomes necessary to ensure that these networks can assist during such emergencies. Also, users may want to interrupt their lower-priority communications activities and dedicate their end-system resources to the high-priority communications attempt if a high-priority communications request arrives at their end system.

There are many IP-based services that can assist during emergencies. RFC 4412 covers real-time communications applications involving SIP (RFC 3261), including Voice over IP, multimedia conferencing, instant messaging, and presence. SIP applications may involve at least five different resources that may become scarce and congested during emergencies. These resources include gateway resources, circuit-switched network resources, IP network resources, receiving end-system resources, and SIP proxy resources. IP network resources are beyond the scope of SIP signaling and are therefore not considered here.

Even if the resources at the SIP element itself are not scarce, a SIP gateway may mark outgoing calls with an indication of priority, for example, on an ISUP (Integrated Services Digital Network User Part) Initial Address Message (IAM) originated by a SIP gateway with the public switched telephone network (PSTN). To improve emergency response, it may become necessary to prioritize access to SIP-signaled resources during periods of emergency-induced resource scarcity. We call this *resource prioritization*. The mechanism itself may well be in place at all times, but may only materially affect call handling during times of resource scarcity. Currently, SIP does not include a mechanism that allows a request originator to indicate to a SIP element that it wishes the request to invoke such resource prioritization. To address this need, this document adds a SIP element that labels certain SIP requests.

RFC 4412 defines two new SIP header fields for communications resource priority, called Resource-Priority and Accept-Resource-Priority. The Resource-Priority header field may be used by SIP user agents (UAs), including PSTN gateways and terminals, and SIP proxy servers to influence their treatment of SIP requests, including the priority afforded to PSTN calls. For PSTN gateways, the behavior translates into analogous schemes in the PSTN, for example, the ITU Recommendation Q.735.3 [1] prioritization mechanism, in both the PSTN-to-IP and IP-to-PSTN directions. ITU Recommendation I.255.3 [2] is another example. A SIP request with a Resource-Priority indication can be treated differently in these situations:

- The request can be given elevated priority for access to PSTN gateway resources, such as trunk circuits.
- The request can interrupt lower-priority requests at a user terminal, such as an IP phone.
- The request can carry information from one multilevel priority domain in the telephone network (e.g., using the facilities of Q.735.3 [1]) to another, without the SIP proxies themselves inspecting or modifying the header field.
- In SIP proxies and back-to-back UAs, requests of higher priorities may displace existing signaling requests or bypass PSTN gateway capacity limits in effect for lower priorities.

This header field is related to, but differs in semantics from, the Priority header field of RFC 3261 (see Section 2.8). The Priority header field describes the importance that the SIP request should have for the receiving human or its agent. For example, that header may be factored into decisions about call routing to mobile devices and assistants, and about call acceptance when the call destination is busy. The Priority header field does not affect the usage of PSTN gateway or proxy resources, for example. In addition, SIP user agent client (UAC) can assert any Priority value, and usage of Resource-Priority header field values is subject to authorization. While the Resource-Priority header field does not directly influence the forwarding behavior of IP routers or the use of communications resources such as packet forwarding priority, procedures for using this header field to cause such influence may be defined in other documents.

Existing implementations of RFC 3261 that do not participate in the resource-priority mechanism follow the normal rules of RFC 3261 (repeating from Section 3.1.3.2): "If a UAS does not understand a header field in a request (that is, the header field is not defined in this specification or in any supported extension), the server must ignore that header field and continue processing the message." Thus, the use of this mechanism is wholly invisible to existing implementations unless the request includes the Require header field with the resource-priority option tag. The mechanism described here can be used for emergency preparedness in emergency telecommunications systems, but is only a small part of an emergency preparedness network and is not restricted to such use. The mechanism aims to satisfy the requirements in RFC 3487. RFC 3487 is structured so that it works in all SIP and Real-Time Transport Protocol (RTP) specified in RFC 3550 (see Section 7.2) and transparent networks.

In such networks, all network elements and SIP proxies let valid SIP requests pass through unchanged. This is important since it is likely that this mechanism will often be deployed in networks where the edge networks are unaware of the resource-priority mechanism and provide no special privileges to such requests. The request then reaches a PSTN gateway or set of SIP elements that are aware of the mechanism. For conciseness, we refer to SIP proxies and UAs that act on the Resource-Priority header field as resource-priority actors (RP actors). It is likely to be common that the same SIP element will handle requests that bear the Resource-Priority header fields and those that do not. Government entities and standardization bodies have developed several different priority schemes for their networks. Users would like to be able to obtain authorized priority handling in several of these networks, without changing SIP clients. Also, a single call may traverse SIP elements that are run by different administrations and subject to different priority mechanisms. Since there is no global ordering among those priorities, we allow each request to contain more than one priority value drawn from these different priority lists, called a namespace in this document.

Typically, each SIP element only supports one such namespace, but we discuss what happens if an element needs to support multiple namespaces. Since gaining prioritized access to resources offers opportunities to deny service to others, it is expected that all such prioritized calls are subject to authentication and authorization, using standard SIP security or other appropriate mechanisms. Since calls may traverse multiple administrative domains with different namespaces or multiple elements with the same namespace, it is strongly suggested that all such domains and elements apply the same algorithms for the same namespace, as otherwise the end-to-end experience of privileged users may be compromised.

15.2.2 Resource-Priority SIP Header Field

We are describing the Resource-Priority and Accept-Resource-Priority SIP header field syntax in more detail for convenience, although all SIP syntaxes are described in Section 2.4.1. The behaviors of SIP entities for processing these headers are described in the next section.

15.2.2.1 Resource-Priority Header Field

The Resource-Priority request header field marks a SIP request as desiring prioritized access to resources, as described in Section 15.1. There is no protocol requirement that all requests within a SIP dialog or session use the Resource-Priority header field. Local administrative policy may mandate the inclusion of the Resource-Priority header field in all requests. Implementations of this specification must allow inclusion to be either by explicit user request or automatic for all requests. The syntax of the Resource-Priority header field is described below. The token-nodot production is used from SIP Event Notification RFC 6665 (see Section 5.2).

```
Resource-Priority = "Resource-Priority"
                    HCOLON r-value *(COMMA
                    r-value)
r-value           = namespace "." r-priority
namespace         = token-nodot
r-priority        = token-nodot
token-nodot       = 1*(alphanum/"-"/"!"/"%"/
                    "*" /"_"/"+"/"‘"/"’"/"~")
```

An example Resource-Priority header field is shown below:

```
Resource-Priority: dsn.flash
```

The *r*-value parameter in the Resource-Priority header field indicates the resource priority desired by the request originator. Each resource value (*r*-value) is formatted as namespace "." priority value. The value is drawn from the namespace identified by the *namespace* token. Namespaces and priorities are case-insensitive ASCII tokens that do not contain periods. Thus, dsn.flash and DSN.Flash, for example, are equivalent. Each namespace has at least one priority value. Namespaces and priority values within each namespace must be registered with the Internet Assigned Numbers Authority (IANA). Initial namespace registrations are described here. Since a request may traverse multiple administrative domains with multiple different namespaces, it is necessary to be able to enumerate several different namespaces within the same message.

However, a particular namespace must not appear more than once in the same SIP message. These may be expressed equivalently as either comma-separated lists within a single header field, as multiple header fields, or as some combination. The ordering of *r*-values within the header field has no significance. Thus, for example, the following header snippets are equivalent:

```
Resource-Priority: dsn.flash, wps.3
Resource-Priority: wps.3, dsn.flash
Resource-Priority: wps.3
Resource-Priority: dsn.flash
```

15.2.2.2 Accept-Resource-Priority Header Field

The Accept-Resource-Priority response header field enumerates the resource values (*r*-values) a SIP user agent server (UAS) is willing to process. (This does not imply that a call with such values will find sufficient resources and succeed.) The syntax of the Accept-Resource-Priority header field is as follows:

```
Accept-Resource-Priority = "Accept-Resource-
                           Priority" HCOLON
                           [r-value *(COMMA
                           r-value)]
```

An example is given below:

```
Accept-Resource-Priority:  dsn.flash-
                           override, dsn.
                           flash, dsn.
                           immediate, dsn.
                           priority, dsn.
                           routine
```

Some administrative domains may choose to disable the use of the Accept-Resource-Priority header for revealing too much information about that domain in responses. However, this behavior is not recommended, as this header field aids in troubleshooting.

15.2.2.3 Resource-Priority Header Field Usage

The usage of the Resource-Priority and Accept-Resource-Priority header fields by all SIP methods and functional entities is shown in Table 2.5, Section 2.8.

15.2.2.4 Resource-Priority Option Tag

RFC 4412 also defines the resource-priority option tag. The behavior is described in Section 15.2.

15.2.3 Behavior of SIP Elements That Receive Prioritized Requests

15.2.3.1 General Rules

The Resource-Priority header field is potentially applicable to all SIP request messages. At a minimum, implementations of the following request types MUST support the Resource-Priority header to be in compliance with this specification: INVITE, ACK, PRACK, UPDATE, and REFER. Implementations should support the Resource-Priority header field in the following request types: MESSAGE, SUBSCRIBE, and NOTIFY.

Note that this does not imply that all implementations have to support all request methods listed. If a SIP element receives the Resource-Priority header field in a request other than those listed above, the header may be ignored, according to the rules of RFC 3261. In short, an RP actor performs the following steps when receiving a prioritized request:

- If the RP actor recognizes none of the namespaces, it treats the request as if it had no Resource-Priority header field.
- It ascertains that the request is authorized according to local policy to use the priority levels indicated. If the request is not authorized, it rejects it. Examples of authorization policies are discussed in Security Considerations.
- If the request is authorized and resources are available (no congestion), it serves the request as usual. If the request is authorized but resources are not available (congestion), it either preempts other current sessions or inserts the request into a priority queue.

15.2.3.2 Usage of Require Header with Resource-Priority

Following standard SIP behavior, if a SIP request contains the Require header field with the resource-priority option tag, a SIP UA MUST respond with a 420 Bad Extension if it does not support the SIP extensions described in this document. It then lists resource-priority in the Unsupported header field included in the response. The use of the resource-priority option tag in Proxy-Require header field is not recommended.

15.2.3.3 OPTIONS Request with Resource-Priority

An OPTIONS request can be used to determine if an element supports the mechanism. A compliant implementation should return an Accept-Resource-Priority header field in OPTIONS responses enumerating all valid resource values, but an RP actor may be configured not to return such values or only to return them to authorized requestors. Following standard SIP behavior, OPTIONS responses must include the Supported header field that includes the resource-priority option tag. According to RFCs 3261 and 3840 (see Sections 3.4 and 3.5), proxies that receive a request with a Max-Forwards header field value of zero may answer the OPTIONS request, allowing a UAC to discover the capabilities of both proxy and UASs.

15.2.3.4 Approaches for Preferential Treatment of Requests

SIP elements may use the resource-priority mechanism to modify a variety of behaviors, such as routing requests, authentication requirements, override of network capacity controls, or logging. The resource-priority mechanism may influence the treatment of the request itself, the marking of outbound PSTN calls at a gateway, or of the session created by the request. (Here, we use the terms session and call interchangeably, both implying a continuous data stream between two or more parties. Sessions are established by SIP dialogs.) Below, we define two common algorithms, namely, preemption and priority queuing. Preemption applies only to sessions created by SIP requests, while both sessions and request handling can be subject to priority queuing. Both algorithms can sometimes be combined in the same element, although none of the namespaces described in this document do this. Algorithms can be defined for each namespace or, in some cases, can be specific to an administrative domain. Other behavior, such as request routing or network management controls, is not defined by this specification. Naturally, only SIP elements that understand this mechanism and the namespace and resource value perform these algorithms. We also discuss what happens if an RP actor does not understand priority values contained in a request.

15.2.3.4.1 Preemption

An RP actor following a preemption policy may disrupt an existing session to make room for a higher-priority incoming session. Since sessions may require different amounts of bandwidth or a different number of circuits, a single higher-priority session may displace more than one lower-priority session. Unless otherwise noted, requests do not preempt other requests of equal priority. As noted above, the processing of SIP requests itself is not preempted. Thus, since proxies do not manage sessions, they do not perform preemption. RFC 4411 (see Section 15.3) contains more details and examples of this behavior. UAS behavior for preemption is discussed here.

15.2.3.4.2 Priority Queuing

In a priority queuing policy, requests that find no available resources are queued to the queue assigned to the priority value. Unless otherwise specified, requests are queued in a first-come, first-served order. Each priority value may have its own queue, or several priority values may share a single queue. If a resource becomes available, the RP actor selects the request from the highest-priority nonempty queue according to the queue service policy. For first-come, first-served policies, the request from that queue that has been waiting the longest is served. Each queue can hold a finite number of pending requests. If the per-priority-value queue for a newly arriving request is full, the request is rejected immediately, with the status codes specified here. In addition, a priority queuing policy may impose a waiting time limit for each priority class, whereby requests that exceed a specified waiting time are ejected from the queue and a 408 Request Timeout failure response is returned to the requestor. Finally, an RP actor may impose a global queue size limit summed across all queues and drop waiting lower-priority requests with a 408 Request Timeout failure response. This does not imply preemption, since the session has not been established yet. UAS behavior for queuing is discussed later.

15.2.3.5 Error Conditions

We describe the error behavior that is shared among multiple types of RP actors (including various instances of UAS such as trunk gateways, line gateways, and IP phones) and proxies. A request containing a resource-priority indication can fail for four reasons:

- The RP actor does not understand the priority value.
- The requestor is not authenticated.
- An authenticated requestor is not authorized to make such a request.
- There are insufficient resources for an authorized request.

We treat these error cases in the order that they typically arise in the processing of requests with Resource-Priority headers. However, this order is not mandated. For example, an RP actor that knows that a particular resource value cannot be served or queued may, as a matter of local policy, forgo authorization, since it would only add processing load without changing the outcome.

15.2.3.5.1 No Known Namespace or Priority Value

If an RP actor does not understand any of the resource values in the request, the treatment depends on the presence of the Require resource-priority option tag:

1. Without the option tag, the RP actor treats the request as if it contained no Resource-Priority header field and processes it with default priority. Resource values that are not understood must not be modified or deleted.
2. With the option tag, it must reject the request with a 417 Unknown Resource-Priority response code.

Making the first case the default is necessary since otherwise there would be no way to successfully complete any calls in the case where a proxy on the way to the UAS shares no common namespaces with the UAC; however, the UAC and UAS do have such a namespace in common. In general, as noted, a SIP request can contain more than one Resource-Priority header field. This is necessary if a request needs to traverse different administrative domains, each with its own set of valid resource values. For example, the ETS namespace might be enabled for US government networks that also support the Defense Switched Network (DSN) or Defense Red Switched Network (DRSN) namespaces for most individuals in those domains. A 417 Unknown Resource-Priority response may, according to local policy, include an Accept-Resource-Priority header field enumerating the acceptable resource values.

15.2.3.5.2 Authentication Failure

If the request is not authenticated, a 401 Unauthorized or 407 Proxy Authentication Required response is returned to allow the requestor to insert appropriate credentials.

15.2.3.5.3 Authorization Failure

If the RP actor receives an authenticated request with a namespace and priority value it recognizes but the originator is not authorized for that level of service, the element must return a 403 Forbidden response.

15.2.3.5.4 Insufficient Resources

Insufficient resource conditions can occur on proxy servers and UASs, typically trunk gateways, if an RP actor receives an authorized request, has insufficient resources, and the request neither preempts another session nor is queued. A request can fail because the RP actor has either insufficient processing capacity to handle the SIP request, or insufficient bandwidth or trunk capacity to establish the requested session for session-creating SIP requests. If the request fails because the RP actor cannot handle the signaling load, the RP actor responds with 503 Service Unavailable. If there is not enough bandwidth, or if there is an insufficient number of trunks, a 488 Not Acceptable Here response indicates that the RP actor is rejecting the request due to media path availability, such as insufficient gateway resources. In that case, RFC 3261 advises that a 488 response (see Section 2.6) should include a Warning header field with a reason for the rejection; warning code 370 Insufficient Bandwidth is typical. For systems implementing queuing, if the request is queued, the UAS will return 408 Request Timeout if the request exceeds the maximum configured waiting time in the queue.

15.2.3.5.5 Busy

Resource contention also occurs when a call request arrives at a UAS that is unable to accept another call, because the UAS either has just one line appearance or has active calls on all line appearances. If the call request indicates an equal- or lower-priority value when compared with all active calls present on the UAS, the UAS returns a 486 Busy Here response. If the request is queued instead, the UAS will return a 408 Request Timeout if the request exceeds the maximum configured waiting time in the device queue. If a proxy gets 486 Busy Here responses on all branches, it can then return a 600 Busy Everywhere response to the caller.

15.2.4 UAC Behavior

SIP UACs supporting this specification must be able to generate the Resource-Priority header field for requests that require elevated resource access priority. As stated previously, the UAC should be able to generate more than one resource value in a single SIP request. Upon receiving a 417 Unknown Resource-Priority response, the UAC may attempt a subsequent request with the same or different resource value. If available, it should choose authorized resource values from the set of values returned in the Accept-Resource-Priority header field.

15.2.4.1 Preemption Algorithm

A UAC that requests a priority value that may cause preemption must understand a Reason header field in the BYE request explaining why the session was terminated, as discussed in RFC 4411 (see Section 15.3).

15.2.4.2 Queuing Policy

By standard SIP rules, a UAC must be prepared to receive a 182 Queued response from an RP actor that is currently at capacity, but that has put the original request into a queue. A UAC may indicate this queued status to the user by some audio or visual indication to prevent the user from interpreting the call as having failed.

15.2.5 UAS Behavior

The precise effect of the Resource-Priority indication depends on the type of UAS, the namespace, and local policy.

15.2.5.1 Preemption Algorithm

A UAS compliant with this specification MUST terminate a session established with a valid namespace and lower-priority value in favor of a new session setup with a valid namespace and higher relative priority value, unless local policy has some form of call-waiting capability enabled. If a session is terminated, the BYE method is used with a Reason header field indicating why and where the preemption took place. Implementers have a number of choices in how to implement preemption at IP phones with multiple line presences, that is, with devices that can handle multiple simultaneous sessions. Naturally, if that device has exhausted the number of simultaneous sessions, one of the sessions needs to be replaced. If the device has spare sessions, an implementation may choose to alert the callee to the arrival of a higher-priority call. Details may also be set by local or namespace policy. RFC 4411 (see Section 15.3) provides additional information in the case of purposeful or administrative termination of a session by including the Reason header in the BYE message that states why the BYE was sent (in this case, a preemption event). The mechanisms in that document allow indication of where the termination occurred (at the UA, within a reservation, at a IP/PSTN gateway) and include call flow examples of each reason.

15.2.5.2 Queue Policy

A UAS compliant with this specification should generate a 182 Queued response if that element's resources are busy, until it is able to handle the request and provide a final response. The frequency of such provisional messages is governed by RFC 3261 (see Section 2.6).

15.2.6 Proxy Behavior

SIP proxies MAY ignore the Resource-Priority header field. SIP proxies may reject any unauthenticated request bearing that header field. When the Require header field is included in a message, it ensures that in parallel forking, only branches that support the resource-priority mechanism succeed. If Secure/Multipurpose Internet Mail Extensions (S/MIME) encapsulation is used according to RFC 3261 (see Section 19.6), special considerations apply. As shown in Table 2.5, Section 2.8, the Resource-Priority header field can be modified by proxies and thus is exempted from the integrity checking described in RFC 3261 (see Section 19.6). Since it may need to be inspected or modified by proxies, the header field must also be placed in the *outer* message if the UAC would like proxy servers to be able to act on the header information. Similar considerations apply if parts of the message are integrity protected or encrypted as described in RFC 3420 (see Section 2.8.2).

If S/MIME is not used, or if the Resource-Priority header field is in the outer header, SIP proxies may downgrade or upgrade the Resource-Priority of a request or insert a new Resource-Priority header if allowed by local policy. If a stateful proxy has authorized a particular resource-priority level, and if it offers differentiated treatment to responses containing resource-priority levels, the proxy should ignore any higher value contained in responses, to prevent colluding UAs from artificially raising the priority level. A SIP proxy may use the Resource-Priority indication in its routing decisions, for example, to retarget to a SIP node or SIP Uniform Resource Identifier (URI) that is reserved for a particular resource priority. There are no special considerations for proxies when forking requests containing a resource-priority indication. Otherwise, the proxy behavior is the same as for UASs described above.

15.2.7 Third-Party Authentication

In some cases, the RP actor may not be able to authenticate the requestor or determine whether an authenticated user is authorized to make such a request. In these circumstances, the SIP entity may avail itself of general SIP mechanisms that are not specific to this application. The authenticated identity management mechanism RFC 3893 (see Section 19.4.7) allows a third party to verify the identity of the requestor and to certify this toward an RP actor. In networks with mutual trust, the SIP-asserted identity mechanism specified in RFC 3325 (see Sections 2.8, 10.4, and 20.3) can help the RP actor determine the identity of the requestor.

15.2.8 Backwards Compatibility

The resource-priority mechanism described in this document is fully backwards compatible with SIP systems following RFC 3261. Systems that do not understand the mechanism can only deliver standard, not elevated, service priority. UASs and proxies can ignore any Resource-Priority header field just like any other unknown header field, and then treat the request like any other request. Naturally, the request may still succeed.

15.2.9 Examples

The SDP message body and the BYE and ACK exchanges/call flows are the same as in RFC 3665 and are omitted for brevity.

15.2.9.1 Simple Call

In this scenario (Figure 15.1), user A completes a call to user B directly. The call from A to B is marked with a resource-priority indication.

F1 INVITE User A -> User B

```
INVITE sip:UserB@biloxi.example.com SIP/2.0
Via: SIP/2.0/TCP client.atlanta.example.
com:5060;branch=z9hG4bK74bf9
Max-Forwards: 70
From: BigGuy <sip:UserA@atlanta.example.com>
;tag=9fxced76sl
To: LittleGuy <sip:UserB@biloxi.example.com>
Call-ID: 3848276298220188511@atlanta.example.
com
CSeq: 1 INVITE
Resource-Priority: dsn.flash
Contact: <sip:UserA@client.atlanta.example.
com;transport=tcp>
Content-Type: application/SDP
Content-Length:...
...
```

F2 180 Ringing User B -> User A

```
SIP/2.0 180 Ringing
Via: SIP/2.0/TCP client.atlanta.example.
com:5060;branch=z9hG4bK74bf9
      ;received=192.0.2.101
From: BigGuy <sip:UserA@atlanta.example.com>
;tag=9fxced76sl
To: LittleGuy <sip:UserB@biloxi.example.com>
;tag=8321234356
Call-ID: 3848276298220188511@atlanta.example.
com
CSeq: 1 INVITE
Contact: <sip:UserB@client.biloxi.example.
com;transport=tcp>
Content-Length: 0
```

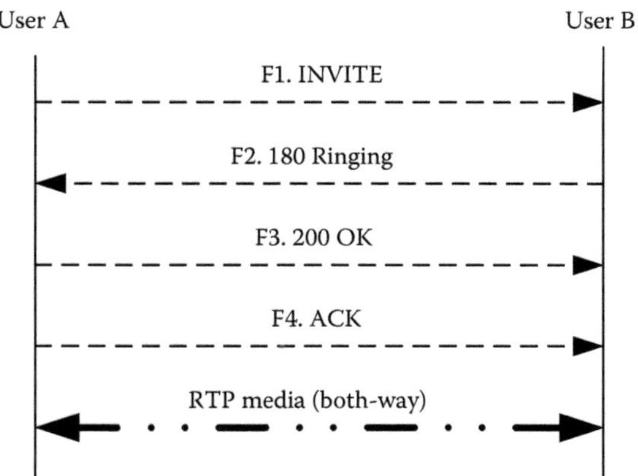

Figure 15.1 Simple call flows. (Copyright IETF. Reproduced with permission.)

F3 200 OK User B -> User A

```
SIP/2.0 200 OK
Via: SIP/2.0/TCP client.atlanta.example.
com:5060;branch=z9hG4bK74bf9
      ;received=192.0.2.101
From: BigGuy <sip:UserA@atlanta.example.com>
;tag=9fxced76sl
To: LittleGuy <sip:UserB@biloxi.example.com>
;tag=8321234356
Call-ID: 3848276298220188511@atlanta.example.
com
CSeq: 1 INVITE
Contact: <sip:UserB@client.biloxi.example.
com;transport=tcp>
Content-Type: application/SDP
Content-Length:...
...
```

15.2.9.2 Receiver Does Not Understand Namespace

In this example (Figure 15.2), the receiving UA does not understand the dsn namespace and thus returns a 417 Unknown Resource-Priority status code. We omit the message details for messages F5 through F7, since they are essentially the same as in the first example.

F1 INVITE User A -> User B

```
INVITE sip:UserB@biloxi.example.com SIP/2.0
Via: SIP/2.0/TCP client.atlanta.example.com
:5060;branch=z9hG4bK74bf9
Max-Forwards: 70
From: BigGuy <sip:UserA@atlanta.example.com>
;tag=9fxced76sl
To: LittleGuy <sip:UserB@biloxi.example.com>
Call-ID: 3848276298220188511@atlanta.example.
com
CSeq: 1 INVITE
Require: resource-priority
Resource-Priority: dsn.flash
Contact: <sip:UserA@client.atlanta.example.
com;transport=tcp>
Content-Type: application/SDP
Content-Length:...
...
```

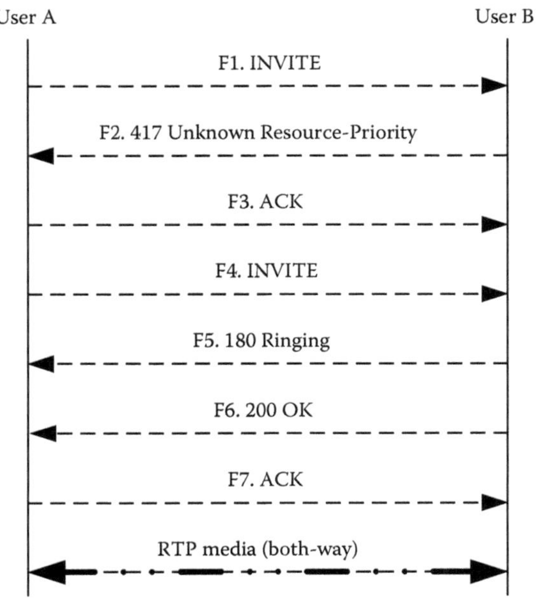

Figure 15.2 Call flows where receiver does not understand namespace. (Copyright IETF. Reproduced with permission.)

F2 417 Resource-Priority failed User B -> User A

```
SIP/2.0 417 Unknown Resource-Priority
Via: SIP/2.0/TCP client.atlanta.example.com
:5060;branch=z9hG4bK74bf9
      ;received=192.0.2.101
From: BigGuy <sip:UserA@atlanta.example.com>
;tag=9fxced76sl
To: LittleGuy <sip:UserB@biloxi.example.com>
;tag=8321234356
Call-ID: 3848276298220188511@atlanta.example.
com
CSeq: 1 INVITE
Accept-Resource-Priority: q735.0, q735.1,
q735.2, q735.3, q735.4
Contact: <sip:UserB@client.biloxi.example.
com;transport=tcp>
Content-Type: application/SDP
Content-Length: 0
```

F3 ACK User A -> User B

```
ACK sip:UserB@biloxi.example.com SIP/2.0
Via: SIP/2.0/TCP client.atlanta.example.com
:5060;branch=z9hG4bK74bd5
Max-Forwards: 70
From: BigGuy <sip:UserA@atlanta.example.com>
;tag=9fxced76sl
To: LittleGuy <sip:UserB@biloxi.example.com
>;tag=8321234356
Call-ID: 3848276298220188511@atlanta.example.
com
CSeq: 1 ACK
Content-Length: 0
```

F4 INVITE User A -> User B

```
INVITE sip:UserB@biloxi.example.com SIP/2.0
Via: SIP/2.0/TCP client.atlanta.example.com
:5060;branch=z9hG4bK74bf9
Max-Forwards: 70
From: BigGuy <sip:UserA@atlanta.example.com>
;tag=9fxced76sl
To: LittleGuy <sip:UserB@biloxi.example.com>
Call-ID: 3848276298220188511@atlanta.example.
com
CSeq: 2 INVITE
Require: resource-priority
Resource-Priority: q735.3
Contact: <sip:UserA@client.atlanta.example.
com;transport=tcp>
Content-Type: application/SDP
Content-Length:...
...
```

15.2.10 Handling Multiple Concurrent Namespaces

15.2.10.1 General Rules

A single SIP request may contain resource values from multiple namespaces. As noted earlier, an RP actor disregards all namespaces it does not recognize. This specification only addresses the case where an RP actor then selects one of the remaining resource values for processing, usually choosing the one with the highest relative priority. If an RP actor understands multiple namespaces, it must create a local total ordering across all resource values from these namespaces, maintaining the relative ordering within each namespace. It is recommended that the same ordering be used across an administrative domain. However, there is no requirement that such ordering be the same across all administrative domains.

15.2.10.2 Examples of Valid Orderings

Table 15.1 shows a set of examples of an RP actor that supports two namespaces, foo and bar. Foo's priority-values are 3 (highest), then 2, and then 1 (lowest), and bar's priority-values are C (highest), then B, and then A (lowest). Five lists of acceptable priority orders the SIP element may use are shown in Table 15.1.

15.2.10.3 Examples of Invalid Orderings

On the basis of the priority order of the namespaces in Table 15.1, the combinations in Table 15.2 are examples of orderings that are not acceptable and must not be configurable. These examples are invalid since the global orderings are not consistent with the namespace-internal order.

Table 15.1 Valid Examples of Resource-Priority Actor Supporting Two Namespaces

Example 1		*Example 2*		*Example 3*	*Priority Level*
Foo.3		Foo.3		Bar.C	Highest priority
Foo.2		Bar.C		Foo.3	
Foo.1	or	Foo.2	or	Foo.2	
Bar.C		Bar.B		Foo.1	
Bar.B		Foo.1		Bar.B	
Bar.A		Bar.A		Bar.A	Lowest priority
	Example 4				*Priority Level*
	Bar.C				Highest priority
or	Foo.3		Bar.B		
	Foo.2		Bar.A		
	Foo.1				Lowest priority

Source: Copyright IETF. Reproduced with permission.

Note: In the last example, Bar.A and Bar.B are ignored.

Table 15.2 Invalid Examples of Resource-Priority Actor Supporting Two Namespaces

Example 1		*Example 2*	*or*	*Example 3*	*Priority Level*
Foo.3		Foo.3		Bar.C	Highest priority
Foo.2		Bar.A		Foo.1	
Foo.1	or	Foo.2	or	Foo.3	
Bar.C		Bar.B		Foo.2	
Bar.A		Foo.1		Bar.A	
Bar.B		Bar.A		Bar.B	Lowest priority
	Example 4				*Priority Level*
	Bar.C				Highest priority
or	Foo.1		Bar.B		
	Foo.3		Bar.A		
	Foo.2				Lowest priority

Source: Copyright IETF. Reproduced with permission.

Note: In Example 1, Bar.A is ordered higher than Bar.B; in Example 2, Bar.A is ordered higher than Bar.B and Bar.C; in Example 3, Foo.1 is ordered higher than Foo.2 and Foo.3; in Example 4, Foo.1 is ordered higher than Foo.3 and Foo.2.

15.2.11 Registering Namespaces

Organizations considering the use of the Resource-Priority header field should investigate whether an existing combination of namespace and priority-values meets their needs. For example, emergency first responders worldwide are discussing utilizing this mechanism for preferential treatment in future networks. Jurisdictions should attempt to reuse existing IANA-registered namespaces where possible, as a goal of this document is not to have unique namespaces per jurisdiction serving the same purpose, with the same usage of priority levels. This will greatly increase interoperability and reduce development time, and probably reduce future confusion if there is ever a need to map one namespace to another in an interworking function. Below, we describe the steps necessary to register a new namespace. A new namespace must be defined in a Standards Track RFC, following the IANA Standards Action policy specified in RFC in RFC 5226, and must include the following facets:

- It must define the namespace label, a unique namespace label within the IANA registry for the SIP Resource-Priority header field.
- It must enumerate the priority levels (i.e., *r*-priority values) the namespace is using. Note that only finite lists are permissible, not unconstrained integers or tokens, for example.
- The priority algorithm, as described earlier, identifies whether the namespace is to be used with priority queuing (*queue*) or preemption (*preemption*). If queuing is used, the namespace may indicate whether normal-priority requests are queued. If there is a new *intended algorithm* other than preemption or priority queuing, the algorithm must be described, taking into account all RP actors (UAC, UAS, proxies).
- A namespace may either reference an existing list of priority values or define a new finite list of priority values in relative priority order for IANA registration within the sip-parameters Resource-Priority priority-values registry. New priority-values should not be added to a previously IANA-registered list associated with a particular namespace, as this may cause interoperability

Table 15.3 Features for IANA Resource-Priority Namespace Registration

Namespace	*Levels*	*Intended Algorithm*	*New Warning Code*	*New Representation of Code*	*Reference*
<label>	<# of levels>	<preemption or queue>	<new warn code>	<new resp. code>	<RFC>

Source: Copyright IETF. Reproduced with permission.

problems. Unless otherwise specified, it is assumed that all priority values confer higher priority than requests without a priority value.

- Any new SIP response codes unique to this new namespace need to be explained and registered.
- The reference document must specify and describe any new Warning header field (see Section 2.8) warn-codes.
- The document needs to specify a new row for Table 15.3 that summarizes the features of the namespace and is included into IANA resource-priority namespace registration.

If information on new response codes, rejection codes, or error behaviors is omitted, it is to be assumed that the namespace defines no new parameters or behaviors. However, the following namespace (Table 15.4) has already been defined with IANA registration and the following sections describe all these registered namespaces.

15.2.12 Namespace Definitions

15.2.12.1 Overview

This specification defines five unique namespaces below: DSN, DRSN, Q735, ETS, and WPS, constituting their registration with IANA. Each IANA registration contains the facets defined earlier. For recognizability, we label the namespaces in capital letters, but note that namespace names are case insensitive and are customarily rendered as lowercase in protocol requests.

15.2.12.2 DSN Namespace

The DSN namespace comes from the name of a US government network called Defense Switched Network. The DSN namespace has a finite list of relative priority-values, listed as follows from lowest priority to highest priority:

```
(lowest)      dsn.routine
              dsn.priority
              dsn.immediate
              dsn.flash
(highest)     dsn.flash-override
```

The DSN namespace uses the preemption algorithm described earlier

15.2.12.3 DRSN Namespace

The DRSN namespace comes from the name of a US government network, called Defense Red Switched Network. The DRSN namespace defines the following resource values, listed from lowest priority to highest priority:

```
(lowest)      drsn.routine
              drsn.priority
              drsn.immediate
              drsn.flash
              drsn.flash-override
(highest)     drsn.flash-override-override
```

The DRSN namespace uses the preemption algorithm described earlier. The DRSN namespace differs in one

Table 15.4 Registered IANA Resource-Priority Namespace

Namespace <label>	*Levels <# of levels>*	*Intended Algorithm <preemption or queue>*	*New Warning Code <new warn code>*	*New Representation of Code <new resp. code>*	*Reference <RFC>*
dsn	5	Preemption	No	No	RFC4412
drsn 6	6	Preemption	No	No	RFC4412
q735	5	Preemption	No	No	RFC4412
ets	5	Queue	No	No	RFC4412
wps	5	Queue	No	No	RFC4412

algorithmic aspect from the DSN and Q735 namespaces. The behavior for the flash-override-override priority value differs from the other values. Normally, requests do not preempt those of equal priority, but a newly arriving flash-override-override request will displace another one of equal priority if there are insufficient resources. This can also be expressed as saying that flash-override-override requests defend themselves as flash-override only.

15.2.12.4 Q735 Namespace

Q.735.3 [1] was created to be a commercial version of the operationally equivalent DSN specification for Multilevel Precedence and Preemption (MLPP). The Q735 namespace is defined here in the same manner. The Q735 namespace defines the following resource values, listed from lowest priority to highest priority:

```
(lowest)      q735.4
              q735.3
              q735.2
              q735.1
(highest)     q735.0
```

The Q735 namespace operates according to the preemption algorithm described earlier.

15.2.12.5 ETS Namespace

The ETS namespace derives its name indirectly from the name of the US government telecommunications service, called Government Emergency Telecommunications Service (or GETS), though the organization responsible for the GETS service chose the acronym ETS for its GETS over IP service, which stands for Emergency Telecommunications Service. The ETS namespace defines the following resource values, listed from lowest priority to highest priority:

```
(lowest)      ets.4
              ets.3
              ets.2
              ets.1
(highest)     ets.0
```

The ETS namespace operates according to the priority queuing algorithm described earlier.

15.2.12.6 WPS Namespace

The WPS namespace derives its name from the Wireless Priority Service, defined in GSM and other wireless technologies. The WPS namespace defines the following resource values, listed from lowest priority to highest priority:

```
(lowest)      wps.4
              wps.3
              wps.2
              wps.1
(highest)     wps.0
```

The WPS namespace operates according to the priority queuing algorithm described earlier.

15.3 Preemption Events in SIP

15.3.1 Overview

With the introduction of the SIP Resource-Priority header in RFC 4412 (see Section 15.2), there became the possibility of sessions being torn down for (scarce) resource reasons, meaning there were not enough resources for a particular session to continue. Certain domains will implement this mechanism where resources may become constrained either at the SIP UA or at congested router interfaces where more important sessions are to be completed at the expense of less important sessions. Which sessions are more or less important than others will not be discussed here. What is proposed in RFC 4411 that is described here is a SIP (RFC 3261) extension to synchronize SIP elements as to why a preemption event occurred and which type of preemption event occurred, as viewed by the element that performed the preemption of a session.

RFC 4411 proposes an IANA registration extension to the SIP Reason header to be included in a BYE Method Request as a result of a session preemption event, either at a UA, or somewhere in the network involving a reservation-based protocol such as the RSVP or Next Steps in Signaling (NSIS). However, this specification does not attempt to address routers failing in the packet path; instead, it addresses a deliberate tear down of a flow between UAs, and informs the terminated UA(s) with an indication of what occurred.

The SIP Reason header is an application layer feedback mechanism to synchronize SIP elements of events; the particular event explained here deals with preemption of a session. Q.850 [3] provides an indication for preemption (cause=8) and for preemption *circuit reserved for reuse* (cause=9). Q.850 cause=9 does not apply to IP, as IP has no concept of circuits. Some domains wish to differentiate appropriate IP reasons for preemption of sessions and to indicate topologically where the preemption event occurred. No other means exists today to give feedback as to why a session was torn down on preemption grounds.

In the event that a session is terminated for a specific reason that can (or should) be shared with SIP servers and UAs sharing dialog, the Reason header (RFC 3326, see Section 2.8) was created to be included in the BYE Request. This was not the only Method for this new header; RFC 3326 also discusses the CANCEL Method usage.

RFC 4411 defines two use cases in which new preemption Reason values are necessary:

- **Access Preemption Event (APE):** This is when a UA receives a new SIP session request message with a valid RP (Resource-Priority) value that is higher than the one associated with the currently active session at that UA. The UA must discontinue the existing session in order to accept the new one (according to local policy of some domains).
- **Network Preemption Event (NPE):** This is when a network element, such as a router, reaches capacity on a particular interface and has the ability to statefully choose which session(s) will remain active when a new session/reservation is signaled for under the parameters outlined in SIP preconditions per RFC 3312 (see Section 15.4) that would otherwise overload that interface (perhaps adversely affecting all sessions). In this case, the router must terminate one or more reservations of lower priority in order to allow this higher-priority reservation access to the requested amount of bandwidth (according to local policy of some domains).

The semantics for these two cases have been registered with IANA for the new protocol value Preemption for the Reason Header field, with four cause values for the above preemption conditions. Additionally, this document will create a new IANA registry for reason-text strings that are not currently defined through existing SIP Response codes or Q.850 [3] cause codes. This new registry will be useful for future protocols used by the SIP Reason header.

We are using an existing SIP RFC 3312 (see Section 15.4) as the starting point for NPEs. RFC 3312 set rules surrounding SIP interaction using a reservation protocol for QOS preconditions, using RSVP as the example protocol. That effort did not preclude other preconditions or future protocol work from becoming a means of preconditions. NSIS is a new reservation protocol effort that specifies a preemption operation similar to RSVP's ResvErr message involving the NSIS NOTIFY message in RFC 5974 with a Transient error code 0x04000005 (Resources Preempted). Note that SIP itself does not cause RSVP or NSIS reservation signaling to start or end. That operation is part of a separate API within each UA.

15.3.2 Access Preemption Events

As mentioned previously, APEs occur at the UA. It does not matter which UA in a unicast or multicast session this happens to (the UAC or UAS of a session). If local policy dictates in a particular domain rules regarding the functionality of a UA, there must be a means by which that UA (not the user) informs the other UA(s) why a session was just torn down prematurely. The appropriate mechanism is the BYE method. The user of the other far side UA will not understand why that session "just went away" without there being a means of informing the UA of what occurred (if this event was purposeful). Through this type of indication to the preempted UA, it can indicate to the user of that device appropriately.

The rules within a domain surrounding the UA to be informed can be different from the rules for informing the user. Local policy should determine if the user should be informed of the specific reason. This indication in SIP will provide a means for the UA to react in a locally determined way, if appropriate (play a certain tone or tone sequence, point toward a special announcement uri, cause the UA's visual display to do something, etc.). Figure 15.3 illustrates the scenario. UA1 invites UA2 to a session with the resource-priority level of 3 (levels 1 and 2 are higher in this domain, and the namespace element is not necessary for this discussion).

After the session between UA1 and UA2 is established, UA3 invites UA2 to a new session with an RP of 2 (a higher priority than the current session between UA1 and UA2). Local policy within this domain dictates that UA2 must preempt all existing calls of lower priority in order to accept a higher-priority call. What Reason value could be inserted above to mean *preemption* at a UA? There are several choices: 410 Gone, 480 Temporarily Unavailable, 486 Busy Here, and 503 Service Unavailable. The use of any of these here is questionable because the session is already established. It is further complicated if there needs to be a difference in the Reason value for an APE versus an NPE (which is a requirement here). The limits of Q.850 [3] have been stated previously. It should be possible to configure UAs receiving a preemption indication to indicate to the user that no particular type of preemption occurred. There are some domains that might prefer their users to remain unaware of the specifics of network behavior. This should not ever prevent a known preemption indication from being sent in a BYE from a UA.

15.3.2.1 Effects of Preemption at the UA

If two UAs are in a session and one UA must preempt that session to accept another session, a BYE method message is the appropriate mechanism to perform this task. However, taking this a step further, if a UA is the common point of a three-way (or more) ad hoc conference and must preempt all sessions in that conference due to receipt of a higher-priority session request (that this UA must accept), then a BYE message must be sent to all UAs in that ad hoc conference.

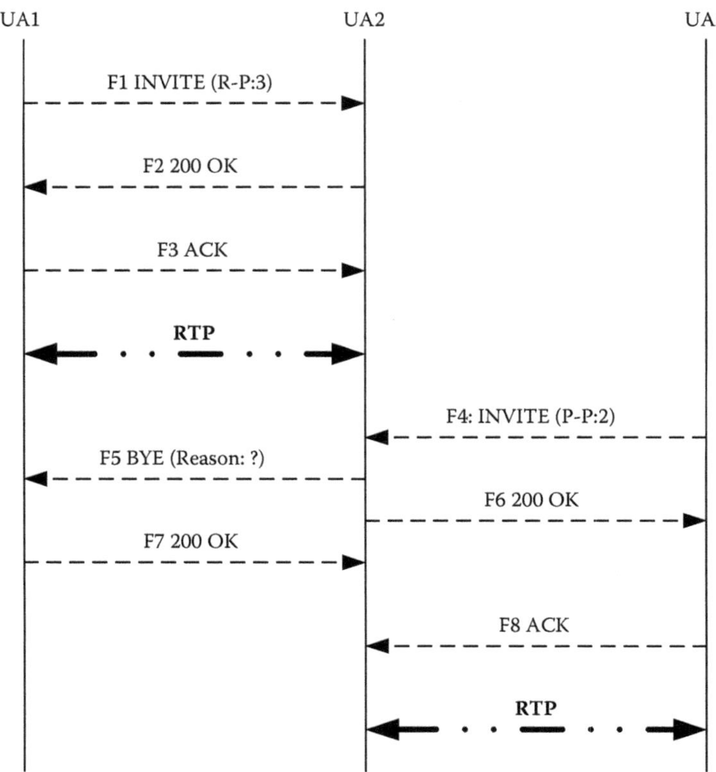

Figure 15.3 Access preemption with obscure reason. (Copyright IETF. Reproduced with permission.)

15.3.2.2 Reason Header Requirements for APEs

The addition of an appropriate Reason value for an APE as described above and shown in Figure 15.3 meets the following requirements:

- Create a means by which one UA can inform another UA (within the same active session) that the active session between the two devices is being purposely preempted at one UA for a higher-priority session request from another UA.
- Create a means by which all relevant SIP elements can be informed of this APE to a specific session. For example: perhaps SIP servers that have incorporated a Record-Route header into that session setup need to be informed of this occurrence.
- Create a means of informing all participants in an ad hoc conference that the primary UA (the mixer) has preempted the conference by accepting a higher-priority session request.
- Create a separate indication for the APE than the one used for an NPE (described in Section 15.3.3) in the session BYE message.
- Create a means to generate a specific indication of a preemption event at the UA to inform all relevant SIP entities, yet have the ability to generalize this indication (based on local policy) to the receiving UA such that this UA cannot display more information than the domain wants the user to see.

15.3.3 Network Preemption Events

NPEs are instances in which an intermediate router between SIP UAs preempts one or more sessions at one of its interfaces to place a higher-priority session through that interface. Within RSVP, there exists a means to execute this functionality per RFC 2205: ResvErr messages (RSVP), which travel downstream toward appropriate receivers. The ResvErr message (RSVP) has the ability to carry within it a code indicating why a reservation is being torn down. The ResvErr does not travel upstream to the other UA. This document proposes that a SIP message be generated to synchronize all relevant SIP elements to this preemption event, including the upstream UA. Creating another Reason value describing that a network element preempted the session is necessary in certain domains.

Figures 15.4 and 15.5 illustrate a network preemption scenario with RSVP. NSIS, not shown in examples here, can be imagined from RFC 5974 with a NOTIFY error message indicating that a reservation has been preempted with the Transient ERROR_SPEC 0x04000005. SIP behavior will be identical using either reservation protocol.

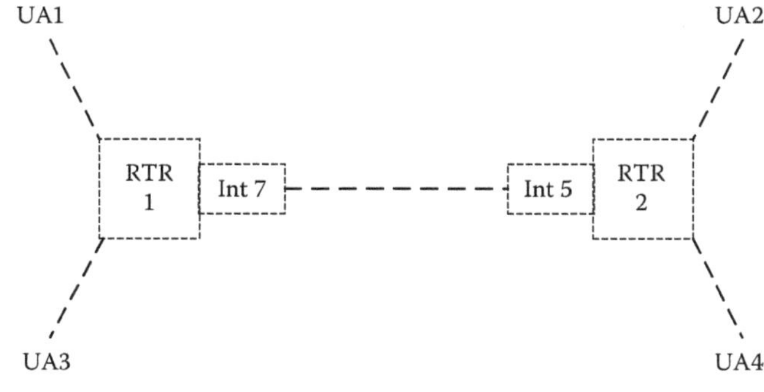

Figure 15.4 Network diagram scenario A. (Copyright IETF. Reproduced with permission.)

UA1 invites UA2 to a session with the resource-priority level of 3 (levels 1 and 2 are higher in this domain) and is accepted. This SIP signaling translated the resource-priority value to an appropriate RSVP priority level for that flow. The link between router 1 and router 2 became saturated with this session reservation between UA1 and UA2 (in this example).

After the session between UA1 and UA2 is established, UA3 invites UA4 to a new session with a resource-priority level of 2 (a higher priority than the current reservation between UA1 and UA2). Again, the priority value within the Resource-Priority header of this INVITE is translated into an appropriate RSVP priority (that is also higher in relative priority to the UA1_UA2 session/RSVP flow). When this second, higher-priority session is signaled, one Path message goes from UA3 to UA4, resulting in the RESV message going from UA4 back to UA3. Because this link between the two routers is at capacity (at Int 7 in Figure 15.4), router 1 will (in this example) make the decision or will communicate with another network entity that will make the decision to preempt lower-priority BW to ensure that this higher-priority session reservation is completed. A ResvErr message (RSVP) is sent to UA2. The result is that UA2 will know that there has been a preemption event in a router (because the ResvErr message has an error code within it, stating *preemption*). At this point, UA1 will not know anything of this preemption. If there are any SIP proxies between UAs 1 and 2 (perhaps that inserted a Record-Route header), each will also need to be informed as to why this reservation was torn down.

Figure 15.5 shows the call flow with router 2 from Figure 15.4 included at the RSVP layer sending the

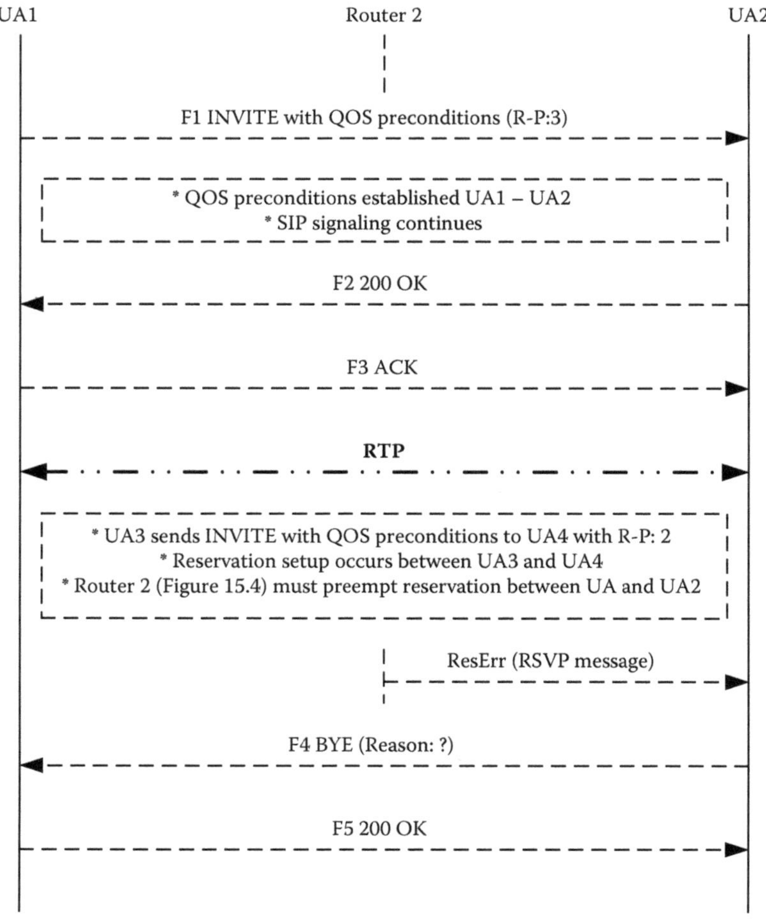

Figure 15.5 Network preemption with obscure reason. (Copyright IETF. Reproduced with permission.)

ResvErr message. A complete call flow including all UAs and routers is not shown here for diagram complexity reasons. The complete signaling between UA3 and UA4 is also not included.

What Reason value could be inserted above to mean "preemption at a router interface"? There are several choices: 410 Gone, 480 Temporarily Unavailable, 486 Busy Here, and 503 Service Unavailable. The use of any of these here is questionable because the session is already established. It is further complicated if there needs to be a difference between the Reason value for an APE versus an NPE. The limits of Q.850 [3] have already been stated previously, showing there is nothing in that spec to indicate a problem in an IP network. To state that all preemptions are equal is possible, but will not provide adequate information. Therefore, another Reason Header value is necessary to differentiate the APE from the NPE.

15.3.3.1 Reason Header Requirements for NPEs

The Reason header enhances the following capabilities for the appropriate SIP signaling in reaction to an NPE:

- Create a means of informing the far-end UA that an NPE has occurred in an intermediate router.
- Create a means by which all relevant SIP elements can be informed of an NPE to a specific session, for example, perhaps SIP servers have incorporated a Record-Route header into that session setup.
- Create a means of informing all participants in an ad hoc conference that the primary UA (the mixer) has been preempted by an NPE.
- Create a separate description of the NPE relative to an APE in SIP.

15.3.4 Hybrid Infrastructure Preemption Events

If user 1 is in a non-IP portion of infrastructure (using a Time Division Multiplexing [TDM] phone) in a session with a UA through a SIP gateway, and if the TDM portion had the ability to preempt the session and indicate to the SIP gateway when it did such a preemption, the SIP gateway would need to be able to convey this preemption event into the SIP portion of this session just as if user 1 were a UA in the session. Figure 15.6 shows a diagram of this.

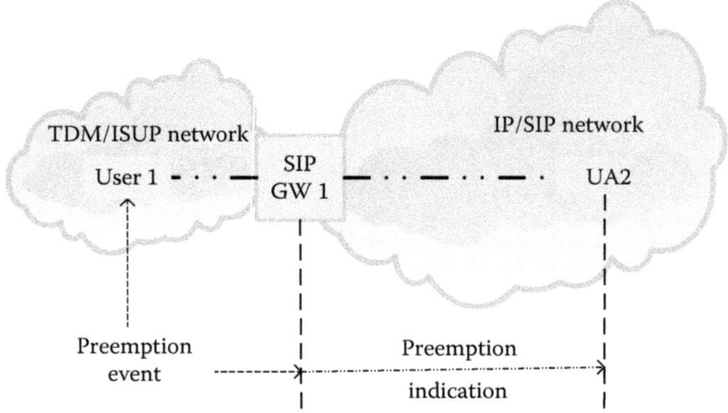

Figure 15.6 TDM/IP preemption event. (Copyright IETF. Reproduced with permission.)

15.3.4.1 Hybrid Infrastructure Requirements

The Reason header enhances the following capabilities for the appropriate SIP signaling unique to the topology involving both IP infrastructure and TDM (or non-IP) infrastructure.

- Create a means of informing the far-end UA in a dialog through a SIP gateway with a non-IP phone that the TDM portion of the session indicated to the SIP gateway that a preemption event terminated the session.
- Create a means of identifying this preemption event uniquely with respect to an access preemption and NPE.

15.3.5 Preemption Reason Header Cause Codes and Semantics

RFC 4411 defines the following new protocol value for the protocol field of the Reason header field in RFC 3326 (see Section 2.8):

Preemption: The cause parameter contains a preemption cause code.

The preemption cause codes are shown in Table 15.5.

Example syntax for the preemption types in Table 15.5 are as follows:

```
Reason: preemption ;cause=1 ;text="UA
Preemption"
Reason: preemption ;cause=2 ;text="Reserved
Resources Preempted"
Reason: preemption ;cause=3 ;text="Generic
Preemption"
Reason: preemption ;cause=4 ;text="Non-IP
Preemption"
```

We provide use cases and extended definitions for the above four cause codes with message flow diagrams in the sections below.

Table 15.5 Preemption Cause Code

Value	*Default Text*	*Description*
1	UA Preemption	The session has been preempted by a UA.
2	Reserved Resources	The session preemption has been preempted, initiated within the network via a purposeful RSVP preemption occurrence, and not a link error.
3	Generic Preemption	This is a limited-use preemption indication to be used on the final leg to the preempted UA to generalize the event.
4	Non-IP Preemption	Session preemption has occurred in a non-IP portion of the infrastructure, and this is the Reason cause code given by the SIP gateway.

15.3.5.1 APE Reason Code

A more elaborate description of the APE cause=1 is as follows:

> A UA in a session has purposely preempted a session and is informing the far-end UA, or UAs (if part of a conference), and SIP proxies (if stateful of the session's transactions).

An example usage of this header value would be

```
Reason: preemption; cause=1; text="UA
Preemption"
```

15.3.5.1.1 APE Call Flow

Figure 15.7 replicates the call flow from Figure 15.3, but with an appropriate Reason value indication that was proposed earlier above.

UA1 invites UA2 to a session with the resource-priority level of 3 (levels 1 and 2 are higher in this domain). After the session between UA1 and UA2 is established, UA3 invites UA2 to a new session with an RP of 2 (a higher priority than the current session to UA1). Local policy within this domain dictates that UA2 must preempt all existing calls of lower

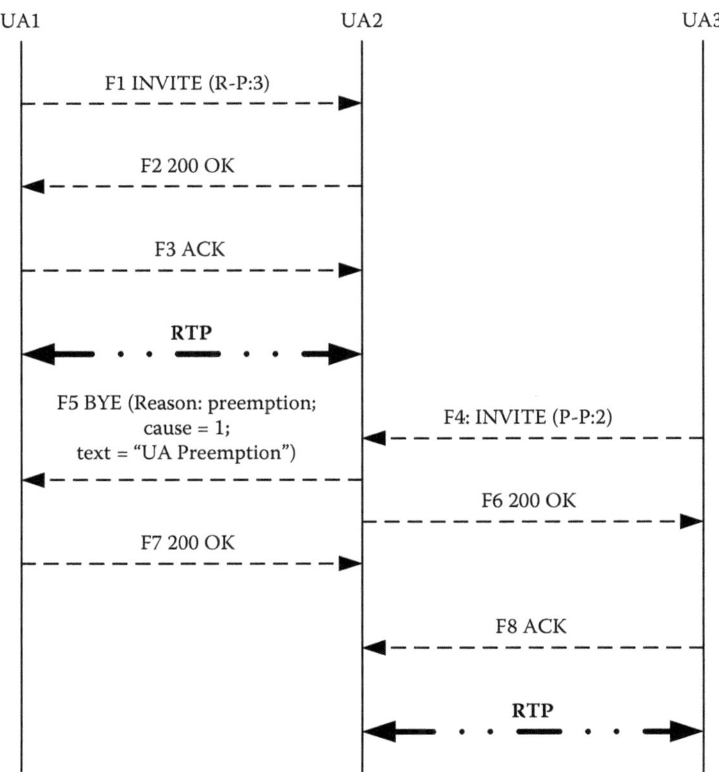

Figure 15.7 Access preemption with reason: UA preemption. (Copyright IETF. Reproduced with permission.)

priority in order to accept a higher-priority call. UA2 sends a BYE Request message with a Reason header with a value of UA Preemption. This will inform the far-end UA (UA1) and all relevant SIP elements (e.g., SIP Proxies). The cause code is unique to what is proposed in the RSVP Preemption Event for differentiation purposes.

15.3.5.2 NPE Reason Code

A more elaborate description of the Reserved Resources Preempted Event cause=2 is as follows:

> A router has preempted a reservation flow and generated a reservation error message: a ResvErr traveling downstream in RSVP, and a NOTIFY in NSIS. The UA receiving the preemption error message generates a BYE request toward the far-side UA with a Reason Header with this value, indicating that somewhere between two or more UAs, a router has administratively preempted this session.

An example usage of this header value would be

```
Reason: Preemption :cause=2 ;text="Reserved
Resources Preempted"
```

15.3.5.2.1 NPE Call Flow

Figure 15.8 replicates the call flow from Figure 15.7, but with an appropriate Reason value indication that was proposed earlier. Above is the call flow with router 2 from Figure 15.4 included at the RSVP layer sending the Resv messages (RSVP).

A complete call flow including all UAs and routers is not included for diagram complexity reasons. The signaling between UA3 and UA4 is also not included. Upon receipt of the ResvErr message (RSVP) with the preemption error code, UA2 can now appropriately inform UA1 why this event occurred. This BYE message will also inform all relevant SIP elements, synchronizing them. The cause value is unique to that proposed earlier for APEs for differentiation purposes.

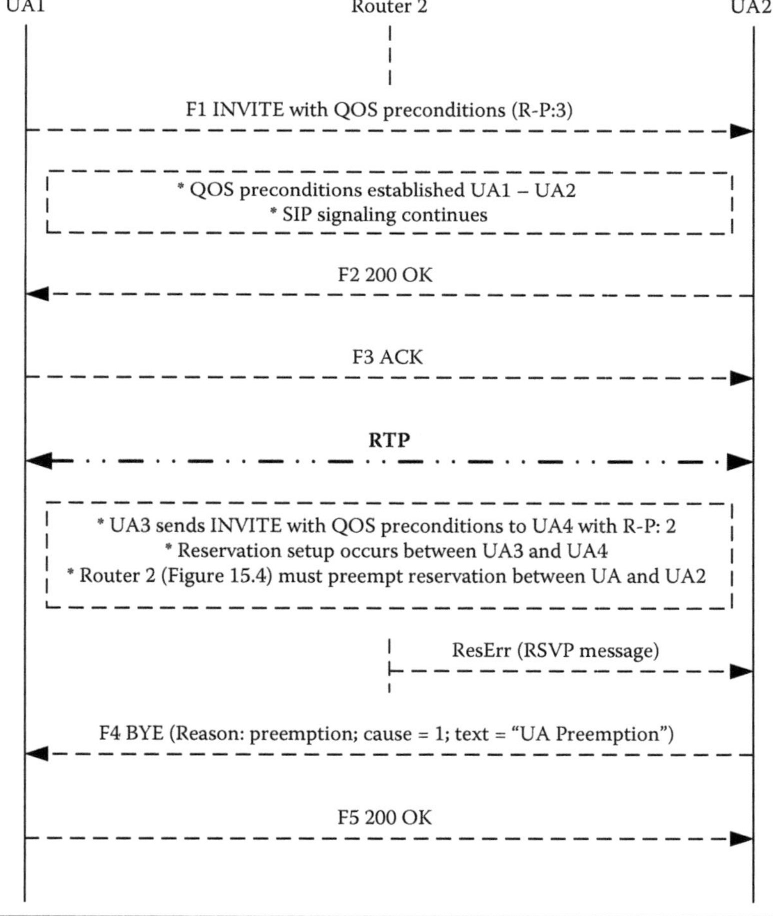

Figure 15.8 Network preemption with Reserved Resources Preempted. (Copyright IETF. Reproduced with permission.)

15.3.5.3 Generic Preemption Event Reason Code

A more elaborate description of the Generic Preemption Event cause=3 is as follows:

> This cause code is for infrastructures that do not wish to provide the preempted UA with a more precise reason than just preemption. It is possible that UAs will have code that will indicate the type of preemption event that is contained in the Reason header, and certain domains have expressed this as not being optimal, and wanted to generalize the indication. This must not be the initial indication within these domains, as valuable traffic analysis and other NM applications will be generalized as well. If this cause value is to be implemented, it should only be done at the final SIP Proxy in such a way that the cause value indicating which type of preemption event actually occurred is changed to this generalized preemption indication to be received by the preempted UA.

An example usage of this header value would be

```
Reason: preemption ;cause=3 ;text="Generic
Preemption"
```

15.3.5.4 Non-IP Preemption Event Reason Code

A more elaborate description of the Non-IP Preemption Event cause=4 is as follows:

> A session exists in a hybrid IP/non-IP infrastructure and the preemption event occurs in the non-IP portion, and was indicated by that portion that this call termination was due to preemption. This is the indication that would be generated by a SIP gateway toward the SIP UA that is being preempted, traversing whichever SIP proxies are involved in session signaling (a question of server state).

An example usage of this header value would be

```
Reason: preemption ;cause=4 ;text="Non-IP
Preemption"
```

15.3.5.4.1 Non-IP Preemption Event Call Flow

Figure 15.9 is a simple call flow diagram of the Non-IP Preemption Event. In this case, UA1 signals user 3 to a session. Once established, there is a preemption event in the non-IP portion of the session/call, and the TDM portion has the ability to inform the SIP gateway of this type of event.

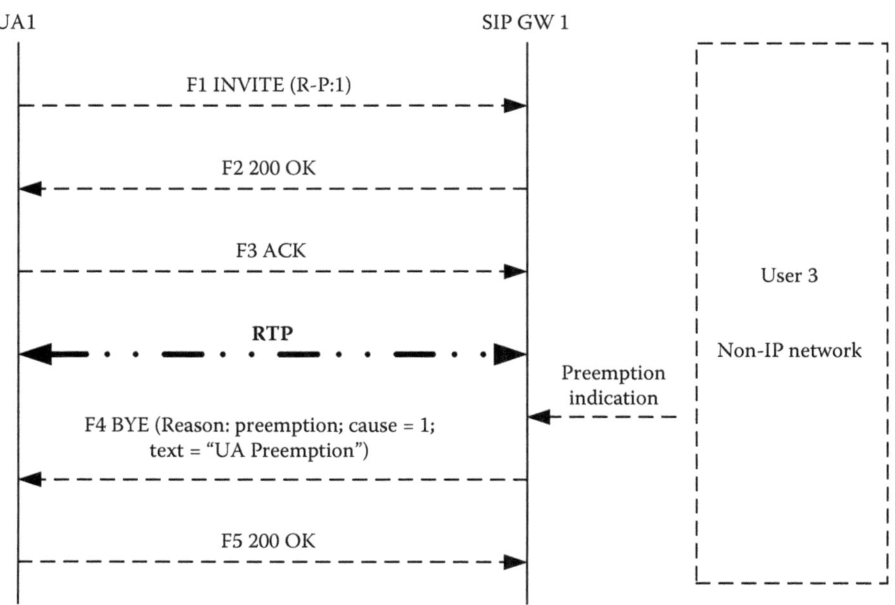

Figure 15.9 Non-IP preemption flow. (Copyright IETF. Reproduced with permission.)

This non-IP signal can be translated into SIP signaling (into the BYE session termination message). Within this BYE, there should be a Reason header indicating such an event to synchronize all SIP elements.

15.4 QOS in SIP

15.4.1 Overview

RFC 3312 that is described here defines a generic framework for preconditions, which are extensible through IANA registration. We describe how network QOS can be made a precondition for the establishment of sessions initiated by the SIP. These preconditions require that the participant reserve network resources before continuing with the session. We do not define new QOS reservation mechanisms; these preconditions simply require a participant to use existing resource reservation mechanisms before beginning the session. Some architectures require that at session establishment time, once the callee has been alerted, the chances of a session establishment failure are minimum. One source of failure is the inability to reserve network resources for a session. To minimize *ghost rings*, it is necessary to reserve network resources for the session before the callee is alerted. However, the reservation of network resources frequently requires learning the IP address, port, and session parameters from the callee. This information is obtained as a result of the initial offer–answer exchange carried in SIP.

This exchange normally causes the phone to ring, thus introducing a chicken-and-egg problem: resources cannot be reserved without performing an initial offer–answer exchange, and the initial offer–answer exchange cannot be done without performing resource reservation. The solution is to introduce the concept of a precondition. A precondition is a set of constraints about the session, which are introduced in the offer. The recipient of the offer generates an answer, but does not alert the user or otherwise proceed with session establishment. That only occurs when the preconditions are met. This can be known through a local event (such as a confirmation of a resource reservation), or through a new offer sent by the caller. This document deals with sessions that use SIP as a signaling protocol and SDP to describe the parameters of the session. We have chosen to include the QOS preconditions in the SDP description rather than in the SIP header because preconditions are stream specific. To ensure that session establishment does not take place until certain preconditions are met, we distinguish between two different state variables that affect a particular media stream: current status and desired status. This document defines the QOS status. The desired status consists of a threshold for the current status. Session establishment stops until the current status reaches or surpasses this threshold. Once this threshold is reached or surpassed, session establishment resumes. For example, the following values for current and desired status would not allow session establishment to resume:

- Current status = resources reserved in the send direction
- Desired status = resources reserved in both (sendrecv) directions

On the other hand, the values of the example below would make session establishment resume:

- Current status = resources reserved in both (sendrecv) directions
- Desired status = resources reserved in the send direction

These two state variables define a certain piece of state of a media stream the same way the direction attribute or the codecs in use define other pieces of state. Consequently, we treat these two new variables in the same way as other SDP media attributes are treated in the offer–answer model used by SIP (see Section 3.8.4): they are exchanged between two UAs using an offer and an answer in order to have a shared view of the status of the session. Figure 15.10 shows

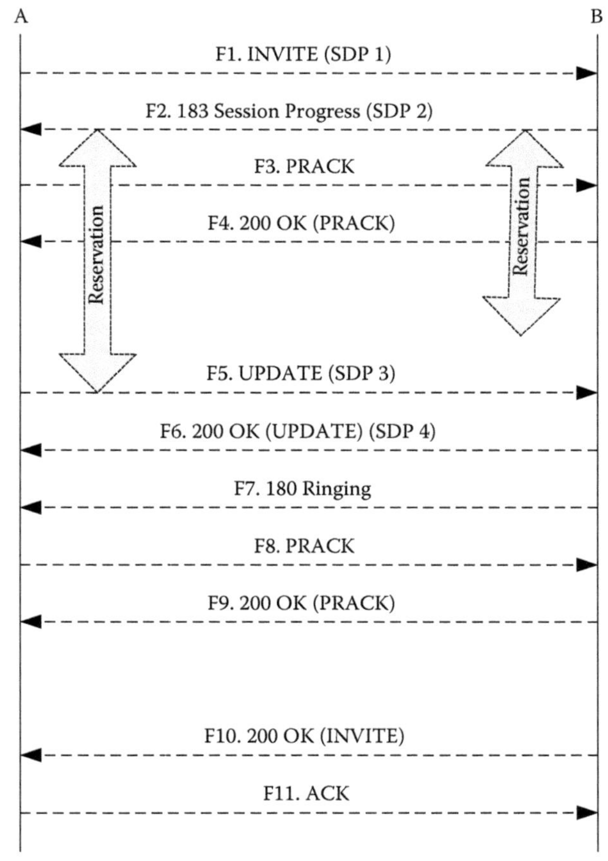

Figure 15.10 Basic session establishment using preconditions. (Copyright IETF. Reproduced with permission.)

a typical message exchange between two SIP UAs using preconditions.

A includes QOS preconditions in the SDP of the initial INVITE. A does not want B to be alerted until there are network resources reserved in both directions (sendrecv) end-to-end. B agrees to reserve network resources for this session before alerting the callee. B will handle resource reservation in the B->A direction, but needs A to handle the A->B direction. To indicate so, B returns a 183 (Session Progress) response to A asking A to start resource reservation and to confirm to B as soon as the A->B direction is ready for the session. A and B both start resource reservation. B finishes reserving resources in the B->A direction, but does not alert the user yet, because network resources in both directions are needed. When A finishes reserving resources in the A->B direction, it sends an UPDATE to B. B returns a 200 OK response for the UPDATE, indicating that all the preconditions for the session have been met. At this point in time, B starts alerting the user, and session establishment completes normally.

15.4.2 SDP Parameters

We define the following media-level SDP attributes:

```
current-status     = "a=curr:" precondition-
                     type SP status-type SP
                     direction-tag
desired-status     = "a=des:" precondition-
                     type SP strength-tag SP
                     status-type SP
                     direction-tag
confirm-status     = "a=conf:" precondition-
                     type SP status-type SP
                     direction-tag
precondition-type  = "qos"/token
strength-tag       = ("mandatory" | "optional"
                     | "none"
                   = | "failure" |"unknown")
status-type        = ("e2e" | "local" |
                     "remote")
direction-tag      = ("none" | "send" | "recv"
                     | "sendrecv")
```

- **Current status:** The current status attribute carries the current status of network resources for a particular media stream.
- **Desired status:** The desired status attribute carries the preconditions for a particular media stream. When the direction tag of the current status attribute with a given precondition type/status type for a particular stream is equal to (or better than) the direction tag of the desired status attribute with the same precondition type/status type for that stream, then the preconditions are considered to be met for that stream.
- **Confirmation status:** The confirmation status attribute carries threshold conditions for a media stream. When the status of network resources reach these conditions, the peer UA will send an update of the session description containing an updated current status attribute for this particular media stream.
- **Precondition type:** This document defines QOS preconditions. Extensions may define other types of preconditions.
- **Strength tag:** The strength tag indicates whether or not the callee can be alerted in case the network fails to meet the preconditions.
- **Status type:** We define two types of status: end-to-end and segmented. The end-to-end status reflects the status of the end-to-end reservation of resources. The segmented status reflects the status of the access network reservations of both UAs. The end-to-end status corresponds to the tag e2e defined above and the segmented status to the tags *local* and *remote*. End-to-end status is useful when end-to-end resource reservation mechanisms are available. The segmented status is useful when one or both UAs perform resource reservations on their respective access networks.
- **Direction tag:** The direction tag indicates the direction in which a particular attribute (current, desired or confirmation status) is applicable to.

The values of the tags send, recv, local, and remote represent the point of view of the entity generating the SDP description. In an offer, send is the direction offerer->answerer and local is the offerer's access network. In an answer, send is the direction answerer->offerer and local is the answerer's access network. The following example shows these new SDP attributes in two media lines of a session description:

```
m=audio 20000 RTP/AVP 0
a=curr:qos e2e send
a=des:qos optional e2e send
a=des:qos mandatory e2e recv
m=audio 20002 RTP/AVP 0
a=curr:qos local sendrecv
a=curr:qos remote none
a=des:qos optional local sendrecv
a=des:qos mandatory remote sendrecv
```

15.4.3 Usage of Preconditions with Offer–Answer

Parameter negotiation in SIP is carried out using the offer–answer model described in RFC 3264 (see Section 3.8.2). The idea behind this model is to provide a shared view of the session parameters for both UAs once the answer has been received by the offerer. This section describes which values our new SDP attributes can take in an answer, depending on their value in the offer. To achieve a shared view of the status of a media stream, we define a model that consists of three tables: both UAs implement a local status table, and each offer–answer exchange has a transaction status table associated to it. The offerer generates a transaction status table identical to its local status table and sends it to the answerer in the offer. The answerer uses the information of this transaction status table to update its local status table. The answerer also updates the transaction status table fields that were out of date and returns this table to the offerer in the answer. The offerer can then update its local status table with the information received in the answer. After this offer–answer exchange, the local status tables of both UAs are synchronized. They now have a common view of the status of the media stream. Sessions that involve several media streams implement these tables per media stream. Note, however, that this is a model of UA behavior, not of software. An implementation is free to take any approach that replicates the external behavior this model defines.

15.4.3.1 Generating an Offer

Both UAs must maintain a local precondition status, which is referred to as a *local status table*. Tables 15.6 and 15.7 show the format of these tables for both the end-to-end and the segmented status types. For the end-to-end status type, the table contains two rows; one for each direction (i.e., send and recv). A value of *yes* in the Current field indicates the successful reservation of that resource in the corresponding direction. *No* indicates that resources have not been reserved yet. The Desired Strength field indicates the strength of the preconditions in the corresponding direction. The table for the segmented status type contains four rows: both directions in the local access network and in the peer's access network.

Table 15.6 Table for the End-to-End Status Type

Direction	*Current*	*Desired Strength*
Send	No	Mandatory
Recv	No	Mandatory

Table 15.7 Table for the Segmented Status Type

Direction	*Current*	*Desired Strength*
Local send	No	None
Local recv	No	None
Remote send	No	Optional
Remote recv	No	None

The meaning of the fields is the same as in the end-to-end case.

Before generating an offer, the offerer must build a transaction status table with the current and the desired status for each media stream. The different values of the strength tag for the desired status attribute have the following semantics:

- None: no resource reservation is needed. Optional: the UAs should try to provide resource reservation, but the session can continue regardless of whether or not this provision is possible.
- Mandatory: the UAs must provide resource reservation. Otherwise, session establishment must not continue.

The offerer then decides whether it is going to use the end-to-end status type or the segmented status type. If the status type of the media line will be end-to-end, the UA generates records with the desired status and the current status for each direction (send and recv) independently, as shown in Table 15.6.

If the status type of the media line will be segmented, the UA generates records with the desired status, and the current status for each direction (send and recv) and each segment (local and remote) independently, as shown in Table 15.7.

At the time of sending the offer, the offerer's local status table and the transaction status table contain the same values. With the transaction status table, the UA must generate the current-status and the desired-status lines following the syntax of Section 15.4.2 and the rules described below.

15.4.3.1.1 SDP Encoding

For the end-to-end status type, the UA must generate one current status line with the tag e2e for the media stream. If the strength tags for both directions are equal (e.g., both *mandatory*) in the transaction status table, the UA must add one desired status line with the tag *sendrecv*. If both tags are different, the UA must include two desired status lines, one with the tag send and the other with the tag recv. The semantics of two lines with the same strength tag, one with a send tag and the other with a recv tag, is the same as one sendrecv line. However, to achieve a more compact encoding, we have chosen to make the latter format mandatory. For the segmented status type, the UA must generate two current status lines: one with the tag local and the other with the tag remote. The UA must add one or two desired status lines per segment (i.e., local and remote). If, for a particular segment (local or remote), the tags for both directions in the transaction status table are equal (e.g., both mandatory), the UA must add one desired status line with the tag sendrecv. If both tags are different, the UA must include two desired status lines, one with the tag send and the other with the tag recv. Note that the rules above apply to the desired strength tag *none* as well. This way, a UA that supports QOS but does not intend to use them adds desired-status lines with the strength tag none. Since this tag can be upgraded in the answer, as described later, the answerer can request QOS reservation without a need of another offer–answer exchange. The example below shows the SDP corresponding to Tables 15.6 and 15.7.

```
m=audio 20000 RTP/AVP 0
a=curr:qos e2e none
a=des:qos mandatory e2e sendrecv
m=audio 20002 RTP/AVP 0
a=curr:qos local none
a=curr:qos remote none
a=des:qos optional remote send
a=des:qos none remote recv
a=des:qos none local sendrecv
```

15.4.3.2 Generating an Answer

When the answerer receives the offer, it recreates the transaction status table using the SDP attributes contained in the offer. The answerer updates both its local status and the transaction status table following the rules below:

Desired Strength: We define an absolute ordering for the strength tags: *none*, *optional*, and *mandatory*. Mandatory is the tag with the highest grade, and none the tag with the lowest grade. An answerer may upgrade the desired strength in any entry of the transaction status table, but it must not downgrade it. Therefore, it is OK to upgrade a row from none to optional, from none to mandatory, or from optional to mandatory, but not the other way around.

Current Status: For every row, the value of the Current field in the transaction status table, and in the local status table of the answerer, have to be compared. Table 15.8 shows the four possible combinations. If both fields have the same value (two first rows of Table 15.8), nothing needs to be updated. If the Current field of the transaction status table is *yes* and the field of the local status table is *no* (third row of Table 15.8), the latter must be set to *yes*. If the Current field of the transaction status table is *no* and the field of the local status table is *yes* (fourth row of Table 15.8), the answerer needs to check if it has local information (e.g., a confirmation of a resource reservation has been received) about that particular current status. If it does, the Current field of the transaction status table is set to *yes*. If the answerer does not have local information about that current status, the Current field of the local status table must be set to *no*.

Table 15.8 Possible Values for the Current Fields

Transaction Status Table	*Local Status Table*	*New Values Transaction/Local*
No	No	No/no
Yes	Yes	Yes/yes
Yes	No	Yes/yes
No	Yes	Depends on location information

Table 15.9 Values of Tags in Offers and Answers

Offer	*Answer*
Send	Recv
Recv	Send
Local	Remote
Remote	Local

Table 15.9 shows the values of tags that need to be used in offers and answers. Note that RFC 4032 (see Section 15.4.12) has updated RFC 3312, and, accordingly, Table 15.8 needs to be updated as shown in Table 15.10 in Section 15.4.12. Once both tables have been updated, an answer must be generated following the rules described earlier, taking into account that send, recv, local, and remote tags have to be inverted in the answer, as shown in Table 15.9.

At the time the answer is sent, the transaction status table and the answerer's local status table contain the same values. Therefore, this answer contains the shared view of the status of the media line in the current-status attribute and the negotiated strength and direction tags in the desired-status attribute. If the resource reservation mechanism used requires participation of both UAs, the answerer should start resource reservation after having sent the answer and the offerer should start resource reservation as soon as the answer is received. If participation of the peer UA is not needed (e.g., segmented status type), the offerer may start resource reservation before sending the offer and the answerer may start it before sending the answer. The status of the resource reservation of a media line can change between two consecutive offer–answer exchanges. Therefore, both UAs must keep their local status tables up to date, using local information throughout the duration of the session.

15.4.4 Suspending and Resuming Session Establishment

A UAS that receives an offer with preconditions should not alert the user until all the mandatory preconditions are met; session establishment is suspended until that moment (e.g., a PSTN gateway reserves resources without sending signaling to the PSTN.) A UAS may receive an INVITE request with no offer in it. In this case, the UAS will provide an offer in a reliable 1xx response. The UAC will send the answer in another SIP request (i.e., the PRACK for the 1xx). If the offer and the answer contain preconditions, the UAS should not alert the user until all the mandatory preconditions in the answer are met. Note that in this case, a UAS providing an initial offer with preconditions, a 180 Ringing response with preconditions, will never be sent, since the UAS cannot alert the user until all the preconditions are met.

A UAS that is not capable of unilaterally meeting all of the mandatory preconditions must include a confirm-status attribute in the SDP (offer or answer) that it sends. Furthermore, the SDP (offer or answer) that contains this confirm-status attribute must be sent as soon as allowed by the SIP offer–answer rules. While session establishment is suspended, UAs should not send any data over any media stream. In the case of RTP (see Section 7.7), neither RTP nor Real-Time Transport Control Protocol (RTCP) packets are sent. A UAS knows that all the preconditions are met for a media line when its local status table has a value of *yes* in all the rows whose strength tag is mandatory. When the preconditions of all the media lines of the session are met, session establishment should resume. For an initial INVITE suspending and resuming session establishment is very intuitive. The callee will not be alerted until all the mandatory preconditions are met. However, offers containing preconditions sent in the middle of an ongoing session need further explanation. Both UAs should continue using the old session parameters until all the mandatory preconditions are met. At that moment, the UAs can begin using the new session parameters.

15.4.5 Status Confirmation

The confirm-status attribute may be used in both offers and answers. This attribute represents a threshold for the resource reservation. When this threshold is reached or surpassed, the UA must send an offer to the peer UA, reflecting the new current status of the media line as soon as allowed by the SIP offer–answer rules. If this threshold is crossed again (e.g., the network stops providing resources for the media stream), the UA must send a new offer as well, as soon as allowed by the SIP offer–answer rules. If a peer has requested confirmation on a particular stream, an agent must mark that stream with a flag in its local status table. When all the rows with this flag have a Current value of *yes*, the UA must send a new offer to the peer. This offer will contain the current status of resource reservation in the current-status attributes. Later, if any of the rows with this flag transition to *no*, a new offer must be sent as well. Confirmation attributes are not negotiated. The answerer uses the value of the confirm-status attribute in the offer and the offerer uses the value of this attribute in the answer. For example, if a UA receives an SDP description with the following attributes:

```
m=audio 20002 RTP/AVP 0
a=curr:qos local none
a=curr:qos remote none
a=des:qos mandatory local sendrecv
a=des:qos mandatory remote sendrecv
a=conf:qos remote sendrecv
```

It will send an offer as soon as it reserves resources in its access network (remote tag in the received message) for both directions (sendrecv).

15.4.6 Refusing an Offer

We define a new SIP status code:

```
Server-Error = "580"; Precondition Failure
```

When a UAS acting as an answerer cannot or is not willing to meet the preconditions in the offer, it should reject the offer by returning a 580 Precondition-Failure response. Using the 580 Precondition Failure status code to refuse an offer is useful when the offer comes in an INVITE or in an UPDATE request. However, SIP does not provide a means to refuse offers that arrive in a response (1xx or 2xx) to an INVITE. If a UAC generates an initial INVITE without an offer and receives an offer in a 1xx or 2xx response that is not acceptable, it should respond to this offer with a correctly formed answer, and immediately send a CANCEL or a BYE. If the offer comes in a 1xx or 2xx response to a re-INVITE, A would not have a way to reject it without terminating the session at the same time. The same recommendation given in RFC 3261 (see Section 3.8) applies here:

> The UAS must ensure that the session description overlaps with its previous session description in media formats, transports, other parameters that require support from the peer. This is to avoid the need for the peer to reject the session description. If, however, it is unacceptable to A, A should generate an answer with a valid session description, and then send a BYE to terminate the session.

580 Precondition Failure responses and BYE and CANCEL requests indicating failure to meet certain preconditions should contain an SDP description indicating which desired status triggered the failure. Note that this SDP description is not an offer or an answer, since it does not lead to the establishment of a session. The format of such a description is based on the last SDP (an offer or an answer) received from the remote UA.

For each m= line in the last SDP description received, there must be a corresponding m= line in the SDP description indicating failure. This SDP description must contain exactly the same number of m= lines as the last SDP description received. The port number of every m= line must be set to zero, but the connection address is arbitrary. The desired status line corresponding to the precondition that triggered the failure must use the *failure* strength tag, as shown in the example below:

```
m=audio 20000 RTP/AVP 0
a=des:qos failure e2e send
```

15.4.6.1 Rejecting a Media Stream

In the offer–answer model, when an answerer wishes to reject a media stream, it sets its port to zero. The presence of preconditions does not change this behavior; streams are still rejected by setting their port to zero. Both the offerer and the answerer must ignore all the preconditions that affect a stream with its port set to zero. They are not taken into consideration to decide whether or not session establishment can resume.

15.4.7 Unknown Precondition Type

This document defines the *qos* tag for QOS preconditions. New precondition types defined in the future will have new associated tags. A UA that receives an unknown precondition type, with a mandatory strength tag in an offer, must refuse the offer unless the only unknown mandatory preconditions have the local tag. In this case, the UA does not need to be involved in order to meet the preconditions. The UA will ask for confirmation of the preconditions and, when the confirmation arrives, it will resume session establishment. A UA refusing an offer follows the rules described in Section 15.4.6.1, but instead of the tag failure, it uses the tag *unknown*, as shown in the example below:

```
m=audio 20000 RTP/AVP 0
a=des:foo unknown e2e send
```

15.4.8 Multiple Preconditions per Media Stream

A media stream may contain multiple preconditions. Different preconditions MAY have the same precondition type and different status types (e.g., end-to-end and segmented QOS preconditions) or different precondition types (this document only defines the qos precondition type, but extensions may define more precondition types in the future). All the preconditions for a media stream must be met in order to resume session establishment. The following example shows a session description that uses both end-to-end and segmented status types for a media stream.

```
m=audio 20000 RTP/AVP 0
a=curr:qos local none
a=curr:qos remote none
a=des:qos mandatory local sendrecv
a=des:qos mandatory remote sendrecv
a=curr:qos e2e none
a=des:qos optional e2e sendrecv
```

15.4.9 Option Tag for Preconditions

We define the option tag *precondition* for use in the Require and Supported header fields. An offerer must include this tag in the Require header field if the offer contains one or more mandatory strength tags. If all the strength tags in the description are optional or none, the offerer must include this tag in either a Supported header field or in a Require header field. It is, however, recommended that the Supported header field be used in this case. The lack of preconditions in the answer would indicate that the answerer did not support this extension. The mapping of offers and answers to SIP requests and responses is performed following the rules given in RFC 3311 (see Section 3.8.3). Therefore, a UA including preconditions in the SDP must support the PRACK and UPDATE methods. Consequently, it must include the 100rel (see Section 2.10) option tag in the Supported header field and should include an Allow header field with the UPDATE tag (RFC 3311, see Section 3.8.3).

15.4.10 Indicating Capabilities

The offer–answer model (RFC 3264, see Section 3.8.4) describes the format of a session description to indicate capabilities. This format is used in responses to OPTIONS requests. A UA that supports preconditions should add desired status lines indicating the precondition types supported for each media stream. These lines must have the none strength tag, as shown in the example below:

```
m=audio 0 RTP/AVP 0
a=rtpmap:0 PCMU/8000
a=des:foo none e2e sendrecv
a=des:qos none local sendrecv
```

Note that when this document was published, the precondition type foo had not been registered. It is used here in the session description above to provide an example with multiple precondition types. A UA that supports this framework should add a precondition tag to the Supported header field of its responses to OPTIONS requests.

15.4.11 Examples

The following examples cover both status types: end-to-end and segmented.

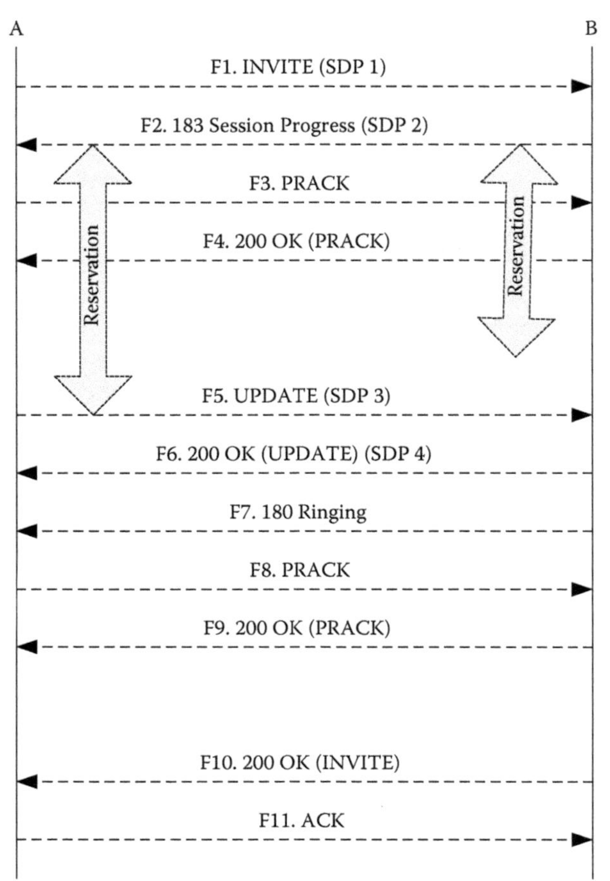

Figure 15.11 Example using the end-to-end status type. (Copyright IETF. Reproduced with permission.)

15.4.11.1 End-to-End Status Type

The call flow of Figure 15.11 shows a basic session establishment using the end-to-end status type. The SDP descriptions of this example are shown below:

SDP 1: A includes end-to-end QOS preconditions in the initial offer.

```
m=audio 20000 RTP/AVP 0
c=IN IP4 192.0.2.1
a=curr:qos e2e none
a=des:qos mandatory e2e sendrecv
```

SDP 2: Since B uses RSVP, it can know when resources in its send direction are available, because it will receive RESV messages from the network. However, it does not know the status of the reservations in the other direction. B requests confirmation for resource reservations in its recv direction to the peer UA A in its answer.

```
m=audio 30000 RTP/AVP 0
c=IN IP4 192.0.2.4
a=curr:qos e2e none
a=des:qos mandatory e2e sendrecv
a=conf:qos e2e recv
```

After having sent the answer, B starts reserving network resources for the media stream. When A receives this answer (F2), it starts performing resource reservation as well. Both UAs use RSVP, so A sends PATH messages toward B and B sends PATH messages toward A. As time passes, B receives RESV messages confirming the reservation. However, B waits until resources in the other direction are reserved as well since it did not receive any confirmation and the preconditions still have not been met.

SDP 3: When A receives RESV messages it sends an updated offer (F5) to B:

```
m=audio 20000 RTP/AVP 0
c=IN IP4 192.0.2.1
a=curr:qos e2e send
a=des:qos mandatory e2e sendrecv
```

SDP 4: B responds with an answer (F6) that contains the current status of the resource reservation (i.e., sendrecv):

```
m=audio 30000 RTP/AVP 0
c=IN IP4 192.0.2.4
a=curr:qos e2e sendrecv
a=des:qos mandatory e2e sendrecv
```

At this point in time, session establishment resumes and B returns a 180 Ringing response (F7). Let us assume that in the middle of the session, A wishes to change the IP address where it is receiving media. Figure 15.12 shows this scenario.

SDP 1: A includes an offer in a re-INVITE (F1). A continues to receive media on the old IP address (192.0.2.1), but is ready to receive media on the new one as well (192.0.2.2):

```
m=audio 20000 RTP/AVP 0
c=IN IP4 192.0.2.2
a=curr:qos e2e none
a=des:qos mandatory e2e sendrecv
```

SDP 2: B includes a conf attribute in its answer. B continues sending media to the old remote IP address (192.0.2.1)

```
m=audio 30000 RTP/AVP 0
c=IN IP4 192.0.2.4
a=curr:qos e2e none
a=des:qos mandatory e2e sendrecv
a=conf:qos e2e recv
```

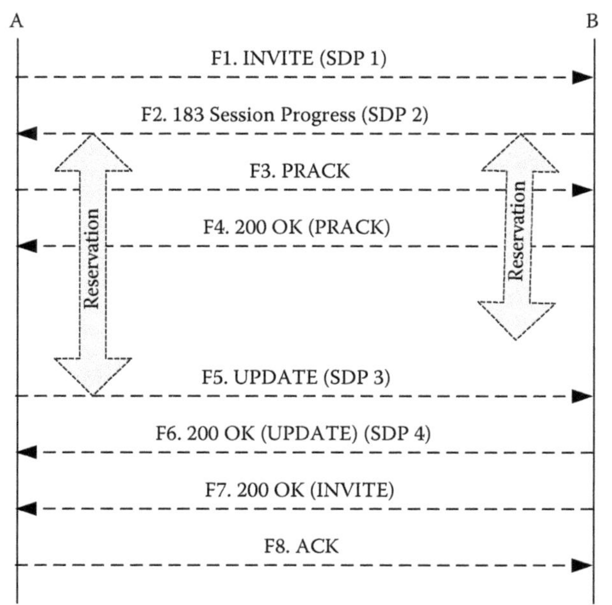

Figure 15.12 Session modification with preconditions. (Copyright IETF. Reproduced with permission.)

SDP 3: When A receives RESV messages it sends an updated offer (F5) to B:

```
m=audio 20000 RTP/AVP 0
c=IN IP4 192.0.2.2
a=curr:qos e2e send
a=des:qos mandatory e2e sendrecv
```

SDP 4: B responds with an answer (F6), indicating that the preconditions have been met (current status sendrecv). It is now that B begins sending media to the new remote IP address (192.0.2.2).

```
m=audio 30000 RTP/AVP 0
c=IN IP4 192.0.2.4
a=curr:qos e2e sendrecv
a=des:qos mandatory e2e sendrecv
```

15.4.11.2 Segmented Status Type

The call flow of Figure 15.13 shows a basic session establishment using the segmented status type. The SDP descriptions of this example are shown below:

SDP 1: A includes local and remote QOS preconditions in the initial offer. Before sending the initial offer, A reserves resources in the access network. This is indicated in the local current status of the SDP below:

```
m=audio 20000 RTP/AVP 0 8
c=IN IP4 192.0.2.1
```

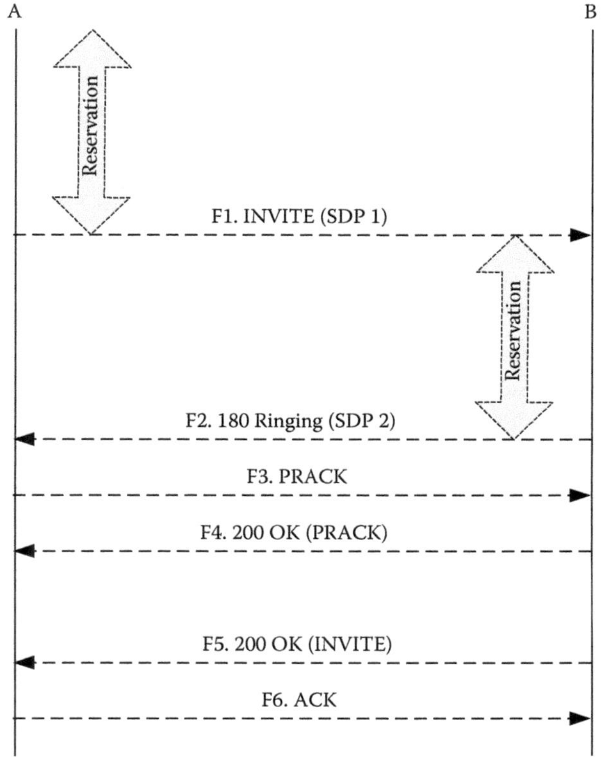

Figure 15.13 Example using the segmented status type. (Copyright IETF. Reproduced with permission.)

```
a=curr:qos local sendrecv
a=curr:qos remote none
a=des:qos mandatory local sendrecv
a=des:qos mandatory remote sendrecv
```

SDP 2: B reserves resources in its access network and, since all the preconditions are met, returns an answer in a 180 Ringing response (F3).

```
m=audio 30000 RTP/AVP 0 8
c=IN IP4 192.0.2.4
a=curr:qos local sendrecv
a=curr:qos remote sendrecv
a=des:qos mandatory local sendrecv
a=des:qos mandatory remote sendrecv
```

Let us assume that after receiving this response, A decides that it wants to use only PCM u-law (payload 0), as opposed to both PCM u-law and A-law (payload 8). It would send an UPDATE to B, possibly before receiving the 200 OK for the INVITE (F5). The SDP would look like

```
m=audio 20000 RTP/AVP 0
c=IN IP4 192.0.2.1
a=curr:qos local sendrecv
a=curr:qos remote sendrecv
a=des:qos mandatory local sendrecv
a=des:qos mandatory remote sendrecv
```

B would generate an answer for this offer and place it in the 200 OK for the UPDATE. Note that this last offer–answer to reduce the number of supported codecs may arrive to the UAS after the 200 OK response has been generated. This would mean that the session is established before A has reduced the number of supported codecs. To avoid this situation, the UAC could wait for the first answer from the UA before setting its local current status to sendrecv.

15.4.11.3 Offer in a SIP Response

The call flow of Figure 15.14 shows a basic session establishment where the initial offer appears in a reliable 1xx response. This example uses the end-to-end status type. The SDP descriptions of this example are shown below.

The first INVITE (F1) does not contain a session description. Therefore, the initial offer is sent by B in a reliable 183 Session Progress response.

SDP 1: B includes end-to-end QOS preconditions in the initial offer. Since B uses RSVP, it can know when resources in its send direction are available, because it will receive RESV messages from the network. However, it does not know the status of the reservations in the other direction. B requests confirmation for resource reservations in its recv direction, to the peer UA A, in its answer.

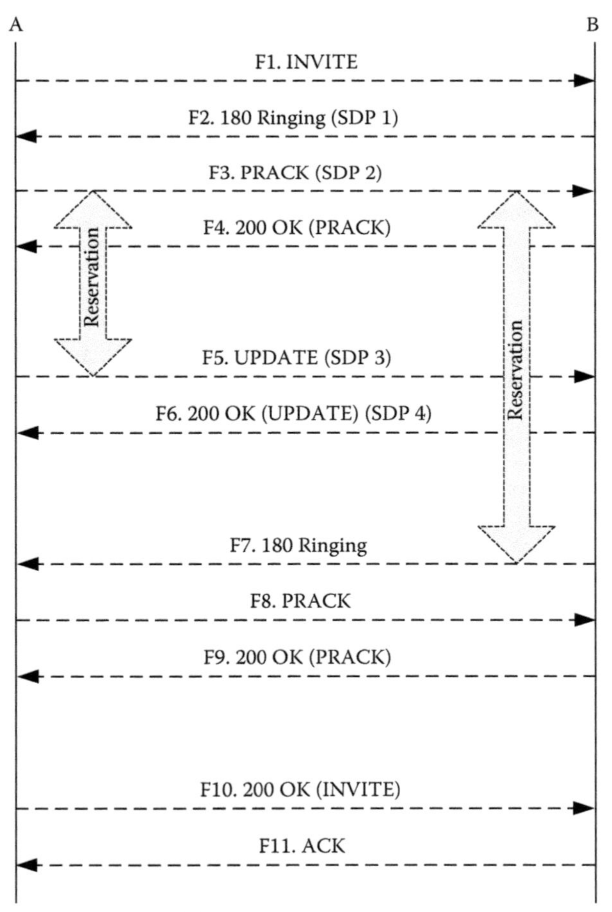

Figure 15.14 Example of an initial offer in a 1xx response. (Copyright IETF. Reproduced with permission.)

```
m=audio 30000 RTP/AVP 0
c=IN IP4 192.0.2.4
a=curr:qos e2e none
a=des:qos mandatory e2e sendrecv
a=conf:qos e2e recv
```

SDP 2: A includes its answer in the PRACK for the 183 Session Progress response.

```
m=audio 20000 RTP/AVP 0
c=IN IP4 192.0.2.1
a=curr:qos e2e none
a=des:qos mandatory e2e sendrecv
```

After having sent the answer, A starts reserving network resources for the media stream. When B receives this answer (F3), it starts performing resource reservation as well. Both UAs use RSVP, so A sends PATH messages toward B and B sends PATH messages toward A.

SDP 3: When A receives RESV messages it sends an updated offer (F5) to B:

```
m=audio 20000 RTP/AVP 0
c=IN IP4 192.0.2.1
a=curr:qos e2e send
a=des:qos mandatory e2e sendrecv
```

SDP 4: B responds with an answer (F6) that contains the current status of the resource reservation (i.e., recv):

```
m=audio 30000 RTP/AVP 0
c=IN IP4 192.0.2.4
a=curr:qos e2e recv
a=des:qos mandatory e2e sendrecv
```

As time passes, B receives RESV messages confirming the reservation. At this point in time, session establishment resumes and B returns a 180 Ringing response (F7).

15.4.12 Enhancements in Precondition Procedures and Use in Session Mobility

RFC 3312 (see Sections 15.4.1 through 15.4.11) defines the framework for SIP preconditions, which is a generic framework that allows SIP UAs to suspend the establishment of a session until a set of preconditions are met. Although only QOS preconditions have been defined thus far, this framework supports different types of preconditions. RFC 4032 that is described here updates some of the procedures in RFC 3312 (see Sections 15.4.1 through 15.4.11) for using SIP preconditions in situations that involve session mobility. RFC 3312 focuses on media sessions that do not move around. That is, media is sent between the same end points throughout the duration of the session. Nevertheless, media sessions established by SIP are not always static. SIP offers mechanisms to provide session mobility, namely re-INVITEs and UPDATEs (see Section 3.8.3). While existing implementations of RFC 3312 can probably handle session mobility, there is a need to explicitly point out the issues involved and make a slight update on some of the procedures defined there in. With the updated procedures defined in this specification (RFC 4032), messages carrying precondition information become more explicit about the current status of the preconditions. Specifically, we now allow answers to downgrade current status values (this was disallowed by RFC 3312). We consider moving an existing stream to a new location as equivalent to establishing a new stream. Therefore, answers moving streams to new locations set all the current status values in their answers to *no* and start a new precondition negotiation from scratch.

15.4.12.1 Defining New Precondition Types

Specifications defining new precondition types need to discuss the topics described in this section. Having clear definitions of new precondition types is essential to ensure interoperability among different implementations.

15.4.12.1.1 Precondition Type Tag

New precondition types must have an associated precondition type tag (e.g., qos is the tag for QOS preconditions). Any new preconditions must be registered with IANA per RFC 3312 guideline.

15.4.12.1.2 Status Type

RFC 3312 defines two status types: end-to-end and segmented. Specifications defining new precondition types must indicate which status applies to the new precondition. New preconditions can use only one status type or both. For example, the QOS preconditions defined in RFC 3312 (see Sections 15.4.1 through 15.4.11) can use both.

15.4.12.1.3 Precondition Strength

RFC 3312 (see Sections 15.4.1 through 15.4.11) defines optional and mandatory preconditions. Specifications defining new precondition types must describe whether or not optional preconditions are applicable, and in case they are, what is the expected behavior of a UA on reception of optional preconditions.

15.4.12.1.4 Suspending and Resuming Session Establishment

RFC 3312 (see Section 15.4.4) describes the behavior of UAs from the moment session establishment is suspended, due to a set of preconditions, until it is resumed when these preconditions are met. In general, the called user is not alerted until the preconditions are met. In addition to not alerting the user, each precondition type must define any extra actions UAs should perform or refrain from performing when session establishment is suspended. The behavior of media streams during session suspension is therefore part of the definition of a particular precondition type. Some precondition types may allow media streams to send and receive packets during session suspension; others may not. Consequently, the following paragraph from RFC 3312 only applies to QOS preconditions:

> While session establishment is suspended, UAs should not send any data over any media stream. In the case of RTP, neither RTP nor RTCP packets are sent.

To clarify the previous paragraph, the control messages used to establish connections in connection-oriented transport protocols (e.g., Transmission Control Protocol [TCP] SYNs) are not affected by the previous rule. Thus, UAs follow standard rules, for example, the SDP *setup* attribute (RFC 4145), to decide when to establish the connection, regardless of QOS preconditions. New precondition types must also describe the behavior of UAs on reception of a re-INVITE or an UPDATE with preconditions for an ongoing session.

15.4.12.2 Issues Related to Session Mobility

RFC 3312 (se Section 15.4.3) describes how to use SIP preconditions with the offer–answer model (RFC 3264, see Section 3.8.4). RFC 3312 gives a set of rules that allow a UA to communicate changes in the current status of the preconditions to the remote UA. The idea is that a given UA knows about the current status of some part of the preconditions (e.g., send direction of the QOS precondition) through local information (e.g., an RSVP RESV is received indicating that resource reservation was successful). The UAC informs the UAS about changes in the current status by sending an offer to the UAS. The UAS, in turn, could (if needed) send an offer to the UAC informing it about the status of the part of the preconditions the UAS has local information about.

Note that UASs do not usually send updates about the current status to the UAC because UASs are the ones resuming session establishment when all the preconditions are met. Therefore, rather than performing an offer–answer exchange to inform the UAC that all the preconditions are met, they

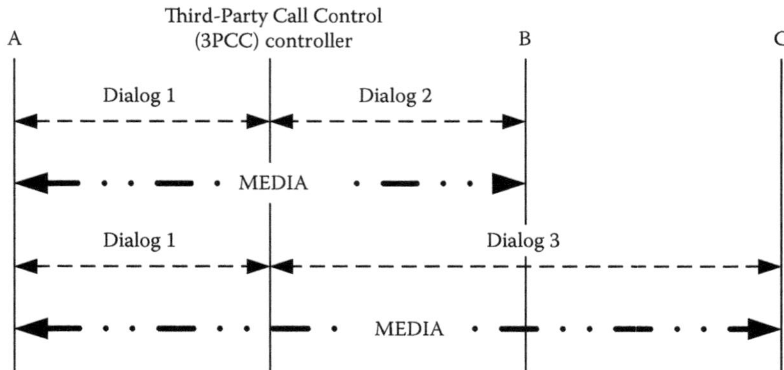

Figure 15.15 Session mobility using 3PCC. (Copyright IETF. Reproduced with permission.)

simply send a 180 Ringing response indicating that session establishment has been resumed. While RFC 3312 (see Sections 15.4.1 through 15.4.11) allows updating current status information using the methods described above, it does not allow downgrading current status values in answers, as shown in the third row of Table 13.8 (Table 3 of RFC 3312). Figure 15.10 shows how performing such a downgrade in an answer would sometimes be needed.

The Third-Party Call Control (3PCC) (RFC 3725, see Section 18.3) controller in Figure 15.15 has established a session between A and B using dialog 1 toward A and dialog 2 toward B. At that point, the controller wants A to have a session with C instead of B. To transfer A to C (configuration shown at the bottom of Figure 15.15), the controller sends an empty (no offer) re-INVITE to A. Since A does not know that the session will be moved, its offer in the 200 OK states that the current status of the media stream in the send direction is *yes*. After contacting C establishing dialog 3, the controller sends back an answer to A. This answer contains a new destination for the media (C) and should have downgraded the current status of the media stream to *no*, since there is no reservation of resources between A and C.

15.4.12.2.1 Update to RFC 3312

Below is a set of new rules that update RFC 3312 to address the issues above. The rule below applies to offerers moving a media stream to a new address:

> When a stream is being moved to a new transport address, the offerer must set all current status values about which it does not have local information about to *no*.

Note that for streams using segmented status (as opposed to end-to-end status), the fact that the address for the media stream at the local segment changes may or may not affect the status of preconditions at the remote segment. However, moving an existing stream to a new location, from the preconditions point of view, is like establishing a new stream. Therefore, it is appropriate to set all the current status values to *no* and start a new precondition negotiation from scratch. The updated Table 15.10 and rules below apply to an answerer that is moving a media stream. It implies that Table 15.8 (Table 3 of RFC 3312) needs to be updated to allow answerers to downgrade current status values (as shown in Table 15.10 per RFC 4032). Note that the offerer was not aware of the move when it generated the offer.

An answerer must downgrade the current status values received in the offer if it has local information about them or if the media stream is being moved to a new transport address. Note that for streams using segmented status, the address change at the answerer may or may not affect the status of the preconditions at the offerer's segment. However, as stated above, moving an existing stream to a new location, from the preconditions point of view, is like establishing a new stream. Therefore, it is appropriate to set all the current status values to *no* and start a new precondition negotiation from scratch. Table 15.10 applies to an offerer that receives an answer that updates or downgrades its local status tables.

Table 15.10 Possible Values for the Current Fields (Updated Version of Table 15.8, Section 15.4.3.2 per RFC 4032)

Transaction Status Table	*Local Status Table*	*New Values Transaction/ Local*
No	No	No/No
Yes	Yes	Yes/Yes
Yes	No	Depends on local information
No	Yes	Depends on local information

Table 15.11 Offerer Updated Local Status

Transaction Status Table	*Local Status Table*	*New Values Local Status*
No	No	No
Yes	Yes	Yes
Yes	No	Yes
No	Yes	No

Offerers should update their local status tables when they receive an answer, as shown in Table 15.11.

15.4.12.2.2 Desired Status

The desired status that a UA wants for a media stream after the stream is moved to a new transport address may be different than the desired status negotiated for the stream originally. A UA, for instance, may require mandatory QOS over a low-bandwidth link but be satisfied with optional QOS when the stream is moved to a high-bandwidth link. If the new desired status is higher than the previous one (e.g., optional to mandatory), the UA, following RFC 3312 (see Sections 15.4.1 through 15.4.11) procedures, may upgrade its desired status in an offer or in an answer. If the new desired status is lower than the previous one (i.e., mandatory to optional), the UA, following RFC 3312 procedures as well, may downgrade its desired status only in an offer (i.e., not in an answer.)

15.4.13 SIP Performance Metrics

RFC 6076 defines a set of common metrics and their usage to evaluate the performance of SIP. The metrics provide a kind of common basis for understanding and quantifying performance expectations between service providers, vendors, and the users of services based on SIP, although the application of each performance metric will differ significantly based on the features and capabilities used by SIP end users under different circumstances. Different multimedia-rich complex scenarios for SIP signaling messages in using these performance metrics are not addressed in RFC 6076. We leave this to readers as an exercise to develop their own multimedia-rich complex scenarios and analyze these SIP performance metrics. The metrics defined in this document do not take into consideration the impairment or failure of actual application processing of a request or response. The metrics do not distinguish application processing time from other sources of delay, such as packet transfer delay. Metrics designed to quantify single device application processing performance are beyond the scope of this document. This specification does not provide any numerical objectives or acceptance threshold values for the SIP performance metrics.

15.4.13.1 Registration Request Delay

The Registration Request Delay (RRD) metric is calculated using the following formula only for the successful registration:

RRD = Time of final response – time of REGISTER request

In a successful registration attempt, RRD is defined as the time interval from when the first bit of the initial REGISTER message containing the necessary information is passed by the originating UA to the intended registrar, until the last bit of the 200 OK is received indicating the registration attempt has completed successfully. This dialog includes an expected authentication challenge before receiving the 200 OK. Note that the registration using Globally Routable UA URI (GRUU) (see Section 4.3), client-initiated connection management (see Section 13.2), and the variations of different authentications schemes (see Section 19.4) in SIP may differ significantly than that of the usual registration described in RFC 3261 (see Section 3.3), and RFC 6076 has not discussed the implications of RRD in those contexts.

15.4.13.2 Ineffective Registration Attempts

Ineffective registration attempts (IRAs) are utilized to detect failures or impairments causing the inability of a registrar to receive a UA REGISTER request. This metric is measured at the originating UA. The output value of this metric is numerical and should be reported as a percentage of registration attempts. This metric is calculated as a percentage of total REGISTER requests. The IRA percentage is calculated using the following formula:

$$\text{IRA \%} = \frac{\text{Number of IRAs}}{\text{Total number of REGISTER requests}} \times 100$$

A failed registration attempt is defined as a final failure response to the initial REGISTER request. It usually indicates a failure received from the destination registrar or interim proxies, or failure due to a timeout of the REGISTER request at the originating UA. A failure response is described as a 4xx (excluding 401, 402, and 407 nonfailure challenge response codes), 5xx, or possible 6xx message. A timeout failure is identified by timer F expiring. IRAs may be used to detect problems in downstream signaling functions, which may be impairing the REGISTER message from reaching the intended registrar, or it may indicate a registrar has become overloaded and is unable to respond to the request. Note that, like RRD, the IRA using GRUU (see Section 4.3), client-initiated connection management (see Section 13.2), and the variations of different authentications schemes (see Section 19.4) in SIP may differ significantly from that of the usual registration described in RFC 3261 (see Section 3.3), and RFC 6076 has not discussed the implications of IRAs in those contexts.

15.4.13.3 Session Request Delay

The Session Request Delay (SRD) metric is utilized to detect failures or impairments causing delays in responding to a UA session request. SRD is measured for both successful and failed session setup requests independently as this metric usually relates to a user experience. The duration associated with success and failure responses will likely vary substantially, and the desired output time associated with each will be significantly different in many cases. It is measured at the originating UA only. The output value of this metric must indicate whether the output is for successful or failed session requests and should be stated in units of seconds. The SRD is calculated using the following formula:

SRD = Time of status indicative response − time of INVITE request

15.4.13.3.1 Successful Session Setup SRD

In a successful request attempt, SRD is defined as the time interval from when the first bit of the initial INVITE message containing the necessary information is sent by the originating UA to the intended mediation or destination agent, until the last bit of the first provisional response is received indicating an audible or visual status of the initial session setup request. (Note: In some cases, the initial INVITE may be forked. In this case, all dialogs along with 200 OK answers need to be considered. In many forking cases, the situations might be more complicated. Each case, need to be taken into account accordingly.) In SIP, the message indicating status would be a non-100 Trying provisional message received in response to an INVITE request. In some cases, a non-100 Trying provisional message is not received, but rather a 200 message is received as the first status message instead. In these situations, the 200 message would be used to calculate the interval. In most circumstances, this metric relies on receiving a non-100 Trying message. The use of the PRACK method (RFC 3262, see Section 2.5) may improve the quality and consistency of the results.

15.4.13.3.2 Failed Session Setup SRD

In a failed request attempt, SRD is defined as the time interval from when the first bit of the initial INVITE message containing the necessary information is sent by the originating agent or user to the intended mediation or destination agent, until the last bit of the first provisional response or a failure indication response. A failure response is described as a 4xx (excluding 401, 402, and 407 nonfailure challenge response codes), 5xx, or possible 6xx message. A change in the metric output might indicate problems in downstream signaling functions, which may be impairing the INVITE message from reaching the intended UA or may indicate changes in end-point behavior. While this metric calculates the delay associated with a failed session request, the metric Ineffective Session Attempts (ISAs) described later is used for calculating a ratio of session attempt failures

15.4.13.4 Session Disconnect Delay

The Session Disconnect Delay (SDD) metric is utilized to detect failures or impairments delaying the time necessary to end a session. SDD is measured independently for both successful and failed session disconnects. The SDD is calculated using the following formula:

SDD = Time of 2xx or timeout − time of completion message (BYE)

SDD is defined as the interval between the first bit of the sent session completion message, such as a BYE, and the last bit of the subsequently received 2xx response. In some cases, a recoverable error response, such as a 503 Retry-After, may be received. In such situations, these responses should not be used as the end time for this metric calculation. Instead, the successful (2xx) response related to the recovery message is used.

15.4.13.5 Session Duration Time

The Session Duration Time (SDT) metric is used to detect problems (e.g., poor audio quality) causing short session durations. SDT is measured for both successful and failed session completions independently. It can be measured from either end-point UA involved in the SIP dialog. The SDT is calculated using the following formula:

SDT = Time of BYE or timeout − time of 200 OK response to INVITE request

This metric does not calculate the duration of sessions leveraging early media. For example, some automated response systems only use early media by responding with a SIP 183 Session Progress message with the SDP connecting the originating UA with the automated message. Usually, in these sessions, the originating UA never receives a 200 OK, and the message exchange ends with the originating UA sending a CANCEL.

15.4.13.5.1 Successful Session Duration SDT

In a successful session completion, SDT is calculated as an average and is defined as the duration of a dialog defined by the interval between receipt of the first bit of a 200 OK response to an INVITE, and receipt of the last bit of an associated BYE message indicating dialog completion. Retransmissions of the 200 OK and ACK messages due to network impairments do not reset the metric timers.

15.4.13.5.2 Failed Session Completion SDT

In some cases, no response is received after a session completion message is sent and potentially retried. In this case, SDT is defined as the interval between receiving the first bit of a 200 OK response to an INVITE, and the resulting timer F expiration.

15.4.13.6 Session Establishment Ratio

The Session Establishment Ratio (SER) metric is used to detect the ability of a terminating UA or downstream proxy to successfully establish sessions per new session INVITE requests. SER is defined as the ratio of the number of new session INVITE requests resulting in a 200 OK response, to the total number of attempted INVITE requests less INVITE requests resulting in a 3xx response. It is measured at the originating UA only. The output value of this metric is numerical and should be adjusted to indicate a percentage of successfully established sessions. The SER is calculated using the following formula:

$$\text{SER}\,\% = \frac{\begin{array}{c}\text{Number of INVITE requests}\\ \text{with associated 200 OK}\end{array}}{\begin{array}{c}\text{Total number of INVITE requests} -\\ \text{Number of invite requests with 3xx response}\end{array}} \times 100$$

15.4.13.7 Session Establishment Effectiveness Ratio

The Session Establishment Effectiveness Ratio (SEER) metric is complementary to SER, but is intended to exclude the potential effects of an individual user of the target UA from the metric. SEER is defined as the ratio of the number of INVITE requests resulting in a 200 OK response and INVITE requests resulting in a 480, 486, 600, or 603, to the total number of attempted INVITE requests less INVITE requests resulting in a 3xx response. The response codes 480, 486, 600, and 603 were chosen because they clearly indicate the effect of an individual user of the UA. It is possible an individual user could cause a negative effect on the UA. The SEER is calculated using the following formula:

$$\text{SEER} = \frac{\begin{array}{c}\text{Number of INVITE requests}\\ \text{with associated 200, 480, 600, or 603}\end{array}}{\begin{array}{c}\text{Total number of INVITE requests} -\\ \text{Number of invite requests with 3xx response}\end{array}} \times 100$$

15.4.13.8 Ineffective Session Attempts

ISAs occur when a proxy or agent internally releases a setup request with a failed or overloaded condition. This metric is similar to Ineffective Machine Attempts (IMAs) in telephony applications of SIP. The output value of this metric is numerical and should be adjusted to indicate a percentage of ISAs. The following failure responses provide a guideline for this criterion:

- 408 Request Timeout
- 500 Server Internal Error
- 503 Service Unavailable
- 504 Server Time-out

This set was derived in a similar manner as described for SEER. In addition, 408 failure responses may indicate an overloaded state with a downstream element; however, there are situations other than overload that may cause an increase in 408 responses. This metric is calculated as a percentage of total session setup requests. The ISA percentage is calculated using the following formula:

$$\text{ISA}\,\% = \frac{\text{Number of ISAs}}{\text{Total number of session requests}} \times 100$$

15.4.13.9 Session Completion Ratio

A Session Completion Ratio (SCR) is defined as a SIP dialog that completes without failing due to a lack of response from an intended proxy or UA. The output value of this metric is numerical and should be adjusted to indicate a percentage of successfully completed sessions. This metric is calculated as a percentage of total sessions completed successfully. The SCR percentage is calculated using the following formula:

$$\text{SCR}\% = \frac{\text{Number of successfully completed sessions}}{\text{Total number of session requests}} \times 100$$

15.5 SDP Media Streams Mapping to QOS Flows

15.5.1 Overview

Resource reservation protocols assign network resources to particular flows of IP packets. When a router receives an IP packet, it applies a filter in order to map the packet to the flow it belongs. The router provides the IP packet with the QOS corresponding to its flow. Routers typically use the source and the destination IP addresses and port numbers to filter packets. Multimedia sessions typically contain multiple media streams (e.g., an audio stream and a video stream). To provide QOS for a multimedia session, it is necessary to map all the media streams to resource reservation flows. This mapping can be performed in different ways. Two possible ways are to map all the media streams to a single resource reservation flow or to map every single media stream to a different resource reservation flow. Some applications require that the former type of mapping is performed, while other applications require the latter. It is even possible that a mixture of both mappings is required for a particular media session. For instance, a multimedia session with three media streams might require that two of them are mapped into a single reservation flow while the third media stream uses a second reservation flow. RFC 3524 that is described here defines the SDP syntax needed to express how media streams need to be mapped into reservation flows. It allows requesting a group of media streams to be mapped into a single resource reservation flow. It also specifies a new *semantics* attribute called Single Reservation Flow (SRF).

15.5.2 SRF Semantics

We define a new semantics attribute within the SDP grouping framework: SRF. Media lines grouped using SRF semantics should be mapped into the same resource reservation flow. Media lines that do not belong to a particular SRF group should not be mapped into the reservation flow used for that SRF group. Note that an SRF group may consist of a single media line. In that case, following the definition above, that media line will be mapped into one reservation flow. That reservation flow will carry traffic from that media line, and from no other media lines.

15.5.3 Applicability Statement

The way resource reservation works in some scenarios makes it unnecessary to use the mechanism described in this document. Some resource reservation protocols allow the entity generating the SDP session description to allocate resources in both directions (i.e., sendrecv) for the session. In this case, the generator of the session description can chose any particular mapping of media flows and reservation flows. The mechanism described in this document is useful when the remote party needs to be involved in the resource reservation.

15.5.4 Examples

For this example, we have chosen to use SIP to transport SDP sessions and RSVP (RFC 2205) to establish reservation flows. However, other protocols or mechanisms could be used instead without affecting the SDP syntax. A UA receives a SIP INVITE with the SDP below:

```
v=0
o=Laura 289083124 289083124 IN IP4 one.
example.com
t=0 0
c=IN IP4 192.0.0.1
a=group:SRF 1 2
m=audio 30000 RTP/AVP 0
a=mid:1
m=video 30002 RTP/AVP 31
a=mid:2
```

This UA uses RSVP to perform resource reservation. Since both media streams are part of an SRF group, the UA will establish a single RSVP session. An RSVP session is defined by the triple: (DestAddress, ProtocolId[, DstPort]). Table 15.12 shows the parameters used to establish the RSVP session. If the same UA received an SDP session description with the same media streams but without the group line, it would be free to map the two media streams into two different RSVP sessions.

15.5.5 IANA Registration: SDP Attribute for Group

This specification has registered the following new semantics attribute for the SDP grouping framework with IANA. It has been registered in the SDP parameters registry under Semantics for the *group* SDP attribute:

Semantics	*Token*	*Reference*
Single Reservation Flow	SRF	RFC 3524

Table 15.12 Parameters Needed to Establish the RSVP Session

Session Number	*DestAddress*	*ProtocolId*	*DstPort*
1	192.0.0.1	UDP	Any

15.6 QOS Mechanism Selection in SDP

15.6.1 Overview

The offer–answer model (RFC 3264, see Section 3.8.4) for SDP (RFC 4566, see Section 7.7) does not provide any mechanism for end points to negotiate the QOS mechanism to be used for a particular media stream. Even when QOS preconditions (RFC 3312, see Section 15.4) are used, the choice of the QOS mechanism is left unspecified and is up to the end points. End points that support more than one QOS mechanism need a way to negotiate which one to use for a particular media stream. Examples of QOS mechanisms are RSVP (RFC 2205) and NSIS (RFC 5974). RFC 5432 that is described herein defines a mechanism that allows end points to negotiate the QOS mechanism to be used for a particular media stream. However, the fact that end points agree on a particular QOS mechanism does not imply that that particular mechanism is supported by the network. In any case, the information the end points exchange to negotiate QOS mechanisms, as defined in RFC 5432, can be useful for a network operator to resolve a subset of the QOS interoperability problem—namely, to ensure that a mechanism commonly acceptable to the end points is chosen and make it possible to debug potential misconfiguration situations. Note that discovering which QOS mechanisms are supported at the network layer is out of the scope of this RFC 5432.

15.6.2 SDP Attribute Definitions

This document defines the qos-mech-send and qos-mech-recv session and media-level SDP (RFC 4566, see Section 7.7) attributes. The following is their Augmented Backus-Naur Form (RFC 5234) syntax, which is based on the SDP (RFC 4566) grammar:

```
attribute          =  /qos-mech-send-attr
attribute          =  /qos-mech-recv-attr
qos-mech-send-attr =  "qos-mech-send" ":"
                      [[SP] qos-mech *(SP
                      qos-mech)]
qos-mech-recv-attr =  "qos-mech-recv" ":"
                      [[SP] qos-mech *(SP
                      qos-mech)]
qos-mech           =  "rsvp"/"nsis"/
                      extension-mech
extension-mech     =  token
```

The qos-mech token identifies a QOS mechanism that is supported by the entity generating the session description. A token that appears in a qos-mech-send attribute identifies a QOS mechanism that can be used to reserve resources for traffic sent by the entity generating the session description. A token that appears in a qos-mech-recv attribute identifies a QOS mechanism that can be used to reserve resources for traffic received by the entity generating the session description. The qos-mech-send and qos-mech-recv attributes are not interdependent; one can be used without the other. The following is an example of an m= line with qos-mech-send and qos-mech-recv attributes:

```
m=audio 50000 RTP/AVP 0
a=qos-mech-send: rsvp nsis
a=qos-mech-recv: rsvp nsis
```

15.6.3 Offer–Answer Behavior

Through the use of the qos-mech-send and qos-mech-recv attributes, an offer–answer exchange allows end points to come up with a list of common QOS mechanisms sorted by preference. However, note that end points negotiate in which direction QOS is needed using other mechanisms, such as preconditions (RFC 3312, see Section 15.4). End points may also use other mechanisms to negotiate, if needed, the parameters to use with a given QOS mechanism (e.g., bandwidth to be reserved).

15.6.3.1 Offerer Behavior

Offerers include a qos-mech-send attribute with the tokens corresponding to the QOS mechanisms (in order of preference) that are supported in the send direction. Similarly, offerers include a qos-mech-recv attribute with the tokens corresponding to the QOS mechanisms (in order of preference) that are supported in the receive direction.

15.6.3.2 Answerer Behavior

On receiving an offer with a set of tokens in a qos-mech-send attribute, the answerer takes those tokens corresponding to QOS mechanisms that it supports in the receive direction and includes them, in order of preference, in a qos-mech-recv attribute in the answer. On receiving an offer with a set of tokens in a qos-mechrecv attribute, the answerer takes those tokens corresponding to QOS mechanisms that it supports in the send direction and includes them, in order of preference, in a qos-mech-send attribute in the answer. When ordering the tokens in a qos-mech-send or a qos-mech-recv attribute by preference, the answerer may take into account its own preferences and those expressed in the offer. However, the exact algorithm to be used to order such token lists is outside the scope of this specification. Note that if the answerer does not have any QOS mechanism in common with the offerer, it will return empty qos-mech-send and qos-mechrecv attributes.

15.6.3.3 Resource Reservation

Once the offer–answer exchange completes, both offerer and answerer use the token lists in the qos-mech-send and qos-mech-recv attributes of the answer to perform resource reservations. Offerers and answerers should attempt to use the QOS mechanism with highest priority in each direction first. If an end point (the offerer or the answerer) does not succeed in using the mechanism with highest priority in a given direction, it should attempt to use the next QOS mechanism in order of priority in that direction, and so on. If an end point unsuccessfully tries all the common QOS mechanisms for a given direction, the end point may attempt to use additional QOS mechanisms not supported by the remote end point. This is because there may be network entities out of the end point's control (e.g., an RSVP proxy) that make those mechanisms work.

15.6.3.4 Subsequent Offer–Answer Exchanges

If, during an established session for which the QOS mechanism to be used for a given direction was agreed upon using the mechanism defined in this specification, an end point receives a subsequent offer that does not contain the QOS selection attribute corresponding to that direction (i.e., the qos-mech-send or qos-mech-recv attribute is missing), the end points should continue using the same QOS mechanism used up to that moment.

15.6.4 Example

The following is an offer–answer exchange between two end points using the qos-mech-send and qos-mech-recv attributes. Parts of the session descriptions are omitted for clarity purposes. The offerer generates the following session description, listing both RSVP and NSIS for both directions. The offerer would prefer to use RSVP and, thus, includes it before NSIS.

```
m=audio 50000 RTP/AVP 0
a=qos-mech-send: rsvp nsis
a=qos-mech-recv: rsvp nsis
```

The answerer supports NSIS in both directions, but not RSVP. Consequently, it returns the following session description:

```
m=audio 55000 RTP/AVP 0
a=qos-mech-send: nsis
a=qos-mech-recv: nsis
```

15.6.5 IANA Registration: SDP Attribute and Token for QOS

This specification registers two new SDP attributes and creates a new registry for QOS mechanisms.

15.6.5.1 SDP Attribute: qos-mech-send

This specification has registered the following att-field under the SDP parameters registry:

- Attribute name: qos-mech-send
- Long-form attribute name: QOS Mechanism for the Send Direction
- Type of attribute: Session and Media levels
- Subject to charset: No
- Purpose of attribute: To list QOS mechanisms supported in the send direction
- Allowed attribute values: IANA Registered Tokens

15.6.5.2 SDP Attribute: qos-mech-recv

The IANA has registered the following SDP att-field under the SDP parameters registry:

- Attribute name: qos-mech-recv
- Long-form attribute name: QOS Mechanism for the Receive Direction
- Type of attribute: Session and Media levels
- Subject to charset: No
- Purpose of attribute: To list QOS mechanisms supported in the receive direction
- Allowed attribute values: IANA Registered Tokens

15.6.5.3 QOS Mechanism Tokens

The IANA has created a subregistry for QOS mechanism token values to be used in the qos-mech-send and qos-mech-recv attributes under the SDP parameters registry. The initial values for the subregistry are as follows:

QOS Mechanism	*Reference*
rsvp	RFC 5432
nsis	RFC 5432

As per the terminology in RFC 5226, the registration policy for new QOS mechanism token values shall be Specification Required.

15.7 SIP Signaling Compression

The SIP and SDP signaling messages compression standards use the signaling compression (SigComp) framework specified in RFC 3320. RFC 3320 provides a multiple compression/decompression algorithm framework to compress and decompress text-based protocols, such as SIP and

SDP. When compression is used in SIP, the compression achieves its maximum rate once a few message exchanges have taken place. This is because the first message the compressor sends to the decompressor is only partially compressed, as there is not a previously stored state to compress against. As the goal is to compress as much as possible, it seems sensible to investigate a mechanism to boost the compression rate from the first message. RFC 3485 defines a static dictionary standard for the text-based SIP and SDP protocol. The dictionary is to be used in conjunction with SIP, SDP, and SigComp (RFC 3320). The static SIP/SDP dictionary constitutes a SigComp state that can be referenced in the first SIP message that the compressor sends out. The dictionary is compression algorithm independent and provides higher efficiency for compression of SIP/SDP messages.

Note that a SIP client sending a request to a SIP server typically may perform a DNS lookup for the domain name of the server. When Naming Authority Pointer or Service records are available for the server, the client can specify the type of service it wants. The service in this context is the transport protocol to be used by SIP (e.g., User Datagram Protocol [UDP], TCP, or Stream Control Transmission Protocol). A SIP server that supports different transport protocols will have different DNS entries. Since it is foreseen that the number of transport protocols supported by a particular application layer protocol is not going to grow dramatically, having a DNS entry per transport seems like a scalable enough solution. However, sometimes it is necessary to include new layers between the transport protocol and the application layer protocol. Examples of these layers are transport layer security and compression. If DNS was used to discover the availability of these layers for a particular server, the number of DNS entries needed for that server would grow dramatically. It can be seen that, in supporting all different transport protocols, it will not be scalable with a growing list of DNS entries because each entry for each transport protocol needs to show, for example, whether or not the transport layer security protocol and signaling compression (SigComp) algorithms along with their port numbers are used for each transport protocol or a combination of different transport protocols.

RFC 3486 describes a mechanism to signal that compression is desired for one or more SIP messages. It also states when it is appropriate to send compressed SIP messages to a SIP entity. The SIP/SDP statically defined dictionary standard for compression uses the SigComp (RFC 3320) framework for compressing messages generated by application protocols. The SigComp framework is intentionally designed to be application agnostic so that it can be applied to any application protocol. Consequently, many application-dependent specifics are left out of the base standard. It is intended that a separate specification be used to describe those specifics when SigComp is applied to a particular application protocol. As a result, the SIP/SDP compression standard needs to be more specific to the SIP/SDP signaling messages for optimizing the compression further. RFC 5049 describes some specifics that apply when Signaling Compression is applied to the SIP, such as default minimum values of SigComp parameters, compartment and state management, and a few issues on SigComp over TCP. Any implementation of SigComp for use with SIP must conform to this specification (RFC 5049) and SigComp, and in addition, support the SIP and SDP static dictionary.

Note that the static SIP/SDP dictionary constitutes a SigComp state that can be referenced in the first SIP message that the compressor sends out boosting the compression of SIP and SDP, but, unfortunately, does not have any effect in XML-based presence documents. SIP is extended by the SIP events notification framework to provide subscriptions and notifications of SIP events. One example of such event notification mechanism is presence, which is expressed in XML documents called presence documents. Typically, presence documents can contain large amounts of data. The size of this data is dependent on the number of presentities that a watcher is subscribed to and the amount of information supplied by the presentity. As a result, this can impose a problem in environments where resources are scarce (e.g., low-bandwidth links with high latency), and the presence service is offered at low or no cost. This is the case, for example, of some wireless networks and devices. It is reasonable to try to minimize the impact of bringing the presence service to wireless networks under these circumstances. Work has been done to mitigate the impact of transferring large amounts of presence documents between end points. For example, the partial PIDF (Presence Information Data Format) reduces the amount of data transferred between the end points. RFC 5112 defines the presence-specific static dictionary that SigComp can use in order to compress presence documents to achieve higher efficiency. The dictionary is compression algorithm independent. The detailed description of SIP, SDP, SIP event packages, and Presence is beyond the scope of this section.

15.8 Summary

We have described both resource-priority and QOS of the SIP network that are related to the application layer. The different SIP calls that will have different priority levels are expressed in the SIP Resource-Priority header. However, these priority levels are defined by different authorities based on their policies. We have described the IANA-registered namespaces, namely DSN, DRSN, Q735, ETS, and WPS, that can be designated in the Resource-Priority header. The implication of allocations of network resources is that SIP calls may even need to be preempted for providing services based on priority levels if there are insufficient resources to support all the calls concurrently. We have described the behavior of SIP entities in handling the priority-based calls, including dealing with preemption. In addition, preemption events that represent instances where network routers between SIP UAs preempt calls/sessions for the interfaces that handle SIP traffic are explained in two areas: NPEs and APEs.

The SIP session cannot be successfully established if there are insufficient resources over the network should QOS requirements in the SIP application layer need to be met. We have described the preconditions in SIP in detail for supporting QOS over SIP networks. We have explained how SIP application QOS requirements need to be met using preconditions invoking the network layer QOS signaling protocols such as RSVP for appropriate resources reservation at the time of the session setup. However, SIP QOS requirements for different media streams are negotiated between the SIP end points. SDP that is carried over the SIP message body of the signaling messages express the QOS parameters for different media used by multimedia applications. We have described how SDP offer–answer model is used for negotiating QOS between SIP UAs in addition to mapping of QOS flows to the SDP media streams appropriately. The SIP and SDP compression that saves the bandwidth for the signaling traffic is described. Finally, authentication and authorization, confidentiality and integrity, anonymity, and denial-of-service attacks that are very critical for users for offering QOS over SIP networks are explained elaborately.

PROBLEMS

1. Why is priority of the call/session needed over the SIP network? Describe the detailed features of the SIP Resource-Priority and Accept-Resource-Priority headers, including the option tags.
2. Describe the behavior of all SIP elements that receive prioritized requests, including preemption and priority queuing. What can be the possible error conditions in handling the priority over the SIP network? Explain in detail.
3. Explain the SIP UAC and UAS behavior in detail with preemption algorithm and queuing priority. What is the proxy behavior in handling the SIP Resource-Priority header?
4. How does the third-party authentication work in requesting the resource priority? Are the Resource-Priority and Accept-Resource-Priority headers backwards compatible in SIP? Explain with call flows.
5. How are the multiple concurrent namespaces handled in SIP? Explain the general rules, valid and invalid orderings.
6. What is the QOS namespace? What are there multiple namespaces? Explain with detail examples the following namespaces: DSN, DRSN, Q735, ETS, and WPS.
7. Explain the security aspects in offering resource-priority over the SIP networks: authentication and authorization, confidentiality and integrity, anonymity, and denial-of-service attacks.
8. What is preemption event in SIP? What are the access, network, and hybrid-infrastructure preemption events? Explain in detail including their appropriate reason codes.
9. Why is the precondition needed in SIP in offering QOS over the SIP network? How is the precondition in QOS related to the preemption? How is preemption related to the priority levels in SIP networks?
10. How is the SDP offer–answer model used in QOS negotiations with preconditions between the SIP end points? Explain with call flows.
11. Explain with call flows how the suspension, resumption, and rejection of session establishment is done in offering QOS with preconditions over the SIP network.
12. How is the unknown the precondition type used over the SIP network in offering QOS? How are the multiple preconditions per media handled? How is the option tag for precondition used? How are the capabilities of the SIP end points indicated? Explain with examples the following: end-to-end status type, segmented status type, and offer in a SIP response.
13. Explain in detail with examples how SDP media streams are mapped to QOS flows.
14. Explain how QOS mechanisms are selected in SDP, including the definition of SDP attributes. Describe the SDP offer–answer behavior of offerer and answerer with examples. How is resource reservation done? How are the subsequent offer–answer exchanges done?
15. Explain in brief all aspects of SDP and SIP compression.

References

1. International Telecommunications Union, "Stage 3 description for community of interest supplementary services using Signaling System No. 7: Multi-level Precedence and Preemption," Recommendation Q.735.3, March 1993.
2. International Telecommunications Union, "Integrated Services Digital Network (ISDN)—General structure and service capabilities—Multi-level Precedence and Preemption," Recommendation I.255.3, July 1990.
3. Usage of cause and location in the Digital. Subscriber Signalling System No. 1 and the. Signalling System No. 7 ISDN User Part. ITU-T Recommendation Q.850, 1998.

Chapter 16

Call Services in SIP

Abstract

The use of SIP signaling messages can create a huge number of real-time networked multimedia services. The call services show some preliminary examples of how multimedia-rich intelligence services can be created. The creation of RT multimedia service is a limitless opportunity whose true potential needs to be explored with deep inventive insights. We only describe a few SIP call services, including call transfer, call diversion, referring calls to multiple resources, call services with content indirection, third-party transcoding call services, INFO method with mid-call information transfer and INFO Packages, call control user-to-user information services, call services using dual-tone multifrequency, and emergency call services. Each of these basic call services can offer/create a host of many other rich multimedia call services extending the basic call service. The detail of each basic call service and its extensions are explained along with call flow examples.

16.1 Introduction

The details of the Session Initiation Protocol (SIP) along with different capabilities, features, quality of service (QOS), and others are discussed throughout many chapters. In this chapter, we are describing an entirely new thing: how SIP signaling mechanisms can be used to create multimedia-rich call services. We have taken some examples of basic call services: call transfer, call diversion, referring calls to multiple resources, call services with content indirection, third-party transcoding services, INFO method with mid-call information transfer, call control user-to-user information (UUI) services, dual-tone multifrequency (DTMF) call service, and emergency call services. The basic call transfer is really the use of the SIP REFER method for transferring to another party. It is explained that the transfer cannot be easy for RT communications because the other party can be busy, or even if the party is not busy, it may not answer the call, or many other situations for which the transfer may not be successful. For each of those unsuccessful transfer conditions, the transferor needs to know what has been the cause for the call not being transferred. In addition, the security/privacy aspect of the transferring of call needs to be handled appropriately. Knowing each of these failure conditions, the next course of action can be decided. The same basic call transfer can be extended with many other features such as transfer with consultation hold, transfer with Referred-By, transfer as an ad hoc conference, transfer with multiparties, referring the call to multiple resources, and other call transfer services. For each of these call transfer services, the behaviors of SIP entities will be different.

Call services with content indirection facilitate to specify the content of the SIP message body indirectly as SIP, unlike Hypertext Transfer Protocol (HTTP), is not a general-purpose data transport protocol because there can be numerous reasons for this, including that SIP can be used for setting up the sessions in wireless environments where bandwidth is very scarce. The SIP message body may contain a huge amount of data that can be referred via URL or other means, and the user can retrieve those data later while leaving the base SIP to serve its main objectives: create, modify, or terminate sessions with one or more participants. Third-party transcoding call services facilitate media transcoding such as speech-to-text, text-to-speech, and others. In addition, they also deal with media transcoding architecture: transcoding services in parallel and multiple transcoding in series. The mid-call information service using SIP INFO method allows transferring user information, such as DTMF and others, after the session is established. It has opened a way to create more multimedia-rich call services using SIP. Some examples of SIP INFO Packages are provided to show the creation of more multimedia-rich intelligent services. Interestingly, UUI call services, which transfer user information at the time of the call setup as opposed to after the establishment of the session as in the case of INFO, are also described. A new SIP header has been created specifically to indicate this UUI that usually restricts the transfer of user information to a few hundred bytes for providing interoperability with public switched telephone network/Integrated Services Digital Network (PSTN/ISDN) protocols. Call services using DTMF are also briefly explained. Finally, emergency call services using SIP and IP networks are also described.

16.2 Call Transfer and Related Call Services

16.2.1 Overview

Some examples of relatively simple SIP call services are provided in Request for Comment (RFC) 5359: Call Hold, 3-Way Conference, Find-Me, Music on Hold, Incoming Call Screening, Unattended Transfer Outgoing, Call Screening, Attended Transfer, Call Park, Instant Messaging Transfer, Call Pickup, Unconditional Call Forwarding, Automatic Redial, Call Forwarding on Busy, Click to Dial, and Call Forwarding on No Answer. However, more complicated call services described in RFC 5589 are described here. We describe the Call Transfer capabilities in SIP using the REFER method and Replaces header to provide a number of transfer services, including blind transfer, consultative transfer, and attended transfer. This work is part of the SIP multiparty call control framework. The mechanisms discussed here are most closely related to traditional, basic, and consultation hold transfers. This chapter details the use of the REFER method and Replaces header field to achieve call transfer. A user agent (UA) that fully supports the transfer mechanisms described in this chapter supports REFER and Replaces in addition to other capabilities of SIP. A UA should use a Contact Uniform Resource Identifier (URI) and supports the Target-Dialog header field (see Section 2.8).

16.2.2 Actors and Roles

There are three actors in a given transfer event, each playing one of the following roles:

- Transferee: the party being transferred to the Transfer Target
- Transferor: the party initiating the transfer
- Transfer Target: the new party being introduced into a call with the Transferee

The following roles are used to describe transfer requirements and scenarios:

- Originator: wishes to place a call to the Recipient. This actor is the source of the first INVITE in a session, to either a Facilitator or a Screener.
- Facilitator: receives a call or out-of-band request from the Originator, establishes a call to the Recipient through the Screener, and connects the Originator to the Recipient. Typically, a Facilitator acts on behalf of the Originator.
- Screener: receives a call ultimately intended for the Recipient and transfers the calling party to the Recipient, if appropriate. Typically, a Screener acts on behalf of the Recipient.

16.2.3 Requirements

1. Any party in a SIP session must be able to transfer any other party in that session at any point in that session.
2. The Transferor and the Transferee must not be removed from a session as part of a transfer transaction. At first glance, this requirement may seem to indicate that the user experience in a transfer must be significantly different from what a current Private Branch Exchange (PBX) or Centrex user expects. As the call flows in this document show, this is not the case. A client may preserve the current experience. In fact, without this requirement, some forms of the current experience (ringback on transfer failure, for instance) will be lost.
3. The Transferor must know whether or not the transfer was successful.
4. The Transferee must be able to replace an existing dialog with a new dialog.
5. The Transferor and Transferee should indicate their support for the primitives required to achieve transfer.
6. The Transferor should provide the Transfer Target and Transferee with information about the nature and progress of the transfer operation being attempted.

To meet these requirements, the transfer operation can be modeled as an ad hoc conference between three parties, as discussed later.

16.2.4 Using REFER to Achieve Call Transfer

A REFER can be issued by the Transferor to cause the Transferee to issue an INVITE to the Transfer Target. Note that a successful REFER transaction does not terminate the session between the Transferor and the Transferee. If those parties wish to terminate their session, they must do so with a subsequent BYE request. The media negotiated between the Transferee and the Transfer Target is not affected by the media that had been negotiated between the Transferor and the Transferee. In particular, the INVITE issued by the Transferee will have the same SDP body it would have if the Transferee had initiated that INVITE on its own. Furthermore, the disposition of the media streams between the Transferor and the Transferee is not altered by the REFER method. Agents may alter a session's media through additional signaling. For example, they may make use of the SIP hold re-INVITE or conferencing extensions described in the conferencing framework (RFC 4353).

To perform the transfer, the Transferor and Transferee could reuse an existing dialog established by an INVITE to send the REFER. This would result in a single dialog shared by two uses—an invite usage and a subscription usage. The call flows for this are shown in detail later. However, the approach described in this document is to avoid dialog reuse. The issues and difficulties associated with dialog reuse are described in RFC 5057 (see Section 3.6.5). Motivations for reusing the existing dialog include the following:

1. There was no way to ensure that a REFER on a new dialog would reach the particular end point involved in a transfer. Many factors, including details of implementations and changes in proxy routing between an INVITE and a REFER, could cause the REFER to be sent to the wrong place. Sending the REFER down the existing dialog ensured it got to the end point to which we were already talking.
2. It was unclear how to associate an existing invite usage with a REFER arriving on a new dialog, where it was completely obvious what the association was when the REFER came on the INVITE usage's dialog.
3. There were concerns with authorizing out-of-dialog REFERs. The authorization policy for REFER in most implementations piggybacks on the authorization policy for INVITE (which is, in most cases, based simply on "I placed or answered this call").

Globally Routable UA URIs (GRUUs) (see Section 4.2) can be used to address problem 1. Problem 2 can be addressed using the Target-Dialog header field (see Section 2.8). In the immediate term, this solution to problem 2 allows the existing REFER authorization policy to be reused. As a result, if the Transferee supports the target-dialog extension and the Transferor knows the Contact URI is routable outside the dialog, the REFER should be sent in a new dialog. If the nature of the Contact URI is not known or if support for the target-dialog extension is not known, the REFER should be sent inside the existing dialog. A Transferee must be prepared to receive a REFER either inside or outside a dialog. One way that a Transferor could know that a Contact URI is routable outside a dialog is by validation (e.g., sending an OPTIONS and receiving a response), or if it satisfies the properties described in the GRUU specification (see Section 4.3).

This document does not prescribe the flows and examples precisely as they are shown, but rather the flows illustrate the principles for best practice for the transfer feature. The call flows represent well-reviewed examples of SIP usage to implement transfer with REFER, which are the Best Common Practice according to International Engineering Task Force (IETF) consensus. In most of the following examples, the Transferor is in the atlanta.example.com domain, the Transferee is in the biloxi.example.com, and the Transfer Target is in the chicago.example.com domain.

16.2.5 Basic Transfer

Basic Transfer consists of the Transferor providing the Transfer Target's contact to the Transferee. The Transferee attempts to establish a session using that contact and reports the results of that attempt to the Transferor. The signaling relationship between the Transferor and Transferee is not terminated, so the call is recoverable if the Transfer Target cannot be reached. Note that the Transfer Target's contact information has been exposed to the Transferee. The provided contact can be used to make new calls in the future. The participants in a basic transfer should indicate support for the REFER and NOTIFY methods in Allow header fields in INVITE, 200 OK to INVITE, and OPTIONS messages. Participants should also indicate support for Target-Dialog in the Supported header field. The diagrams below show the first line of each message. The first column of the figure shows the dialog used in that particular message. In these diagrams, media is managed through re-INVITE holds; however, other mechanisms (e.g., mixing multiple media streams at the UA or using the conferencing extensions) are valid.

Selected message details are shown, labeled as message F1, F2, etc. Each of the flows below shows the dialog between the Transferor and the Transferee remaining connected (on hold) during the REFER process. While this provides the greatest flexibility for recovery from failure, it is not necessary. If the Transferor's agent does not wish to participate in the remainder of the REFER process and has no intention of assisting with recovery from transfer failure, it could emit a BYE to the Transferee as soon as the REFER transaction completes. This flow is sometimes known as *unattended transfer* or *blind transfer*. Figure 16.1 shows transfer when the Transferee utilizes a GRUU and supports the target-dialog extension and indicates this to the Transferor. As a result, the Transferor sends the REFER outside the INVITE dialog. The Transferee is able to match this REFER to the existing dialog using the Target-Dialog header field in the REFER, which references the existing dialog.

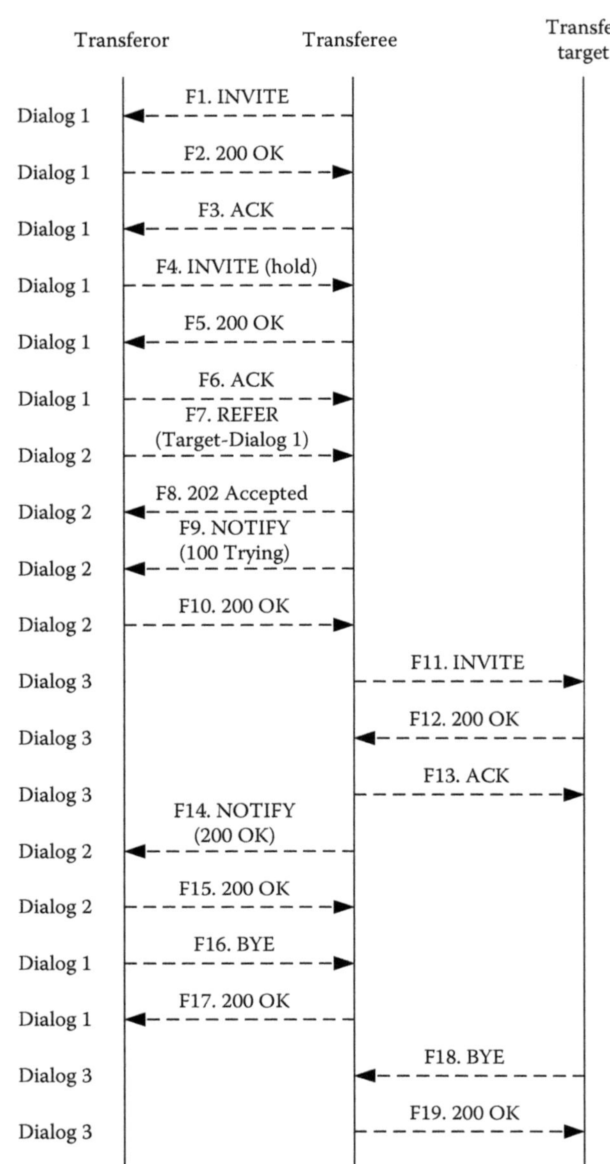

Figure 16.1 Basic transfer call flow. (Copyright IETF. Reproduced with permission.)

16.2.5.1 Successful Transfer

Figure 16.1 shows the call flows of a successful call transfer utilizing GRUU when both parties support the dialog extension using GRUU. All SIP messages for the successful call transfer are shown in detail.

F1 INVITE Transferee -> Transferor

```
INVITE sips:transferor@atlanta.example.com
SIP/2.0
Via: SIP/2.0/TLS
192.0.2.4;branch=z9hG4bKnas432
Max-Forwards: 70
To: <sips:transferor@atlanta.example.com>
From: <sips:transferee@biloxi.example.com>
;tag=7553452
Call-ID: 090459243588173445
CSeq: 29887 INVITE
Allow: INVITE, ACK, CANCEL, OPTIONS, BYE,
REFER, NOTIFY
Supported: replaces, gruu, tdialog
Contact: <sips:3ld812adkjw@biloxi.example.
com;gr=3413kj2ha>
Content-Type: application/sdp
Content-Length: ...
```

F2 200 OK Transferor -> Transferee

```
SIP/2.0 200 OK
Via: SIP/2.0/TLS
192.0.2.4;branch=z9hG4bKnas432
To: <sips:transferor@atlanta.example.com>
;tag=31kdl4i3k
From: <sips:transferee@biloxi.example.com>
;tag=7553452
Call-ID: 090459243588173445
CSeq: 29887 INVITE
Allow: INVITE, ACK, CANCEL, OPTIONS, BYE,
REFER, NOTIFY
Supported: replaces, gruu, tdialog
Contact: <sips:4889445d8kjtk3@atlanta.
example.com;gr=723jd2d>
Content-Type: application/sdp
Content-Length: ...
```

F3 REFER Transferor -> Transferee

```
REFER sips:3ld812adkjw@biloxi.example.
com;gr=3413kj2ha SIP/2.0
Via: SIP/2.0/TLS pc33.atlanta.example.
com;branch=z9hG4bKna9
Max-Forwards: 70
To: <sips:3ld812adkjw@biloxi.example.
com;gr=3413kj2ha>
From: <sips:transferor@atlanta.example.com>
;tag=1928301774
Call-ID: a84b4c76e66710
CSeq: 314159 REFER
Allow: INVITE, ACK, CANCEL, OPTIONS, BYE,
REFER, NOTIFY
Supported: gruu, replaces, tdialog
Require: tdialog
Refer-To: <sips:transfertarget@chicago.
example.com>
Target-Dialog:
090459243588173445;local-tag=7553452
;remote-tag=31kdl4i3k
Contact: <sips:4889445d8kjtk3@atlanta.
example.com;gr=723jd2d>
Content-Length: 0
```

F4 NOTIFY Transferee -> Transferor

```
NOTIFY sips:4889445d8kjtk3@atlanta.example.
com;gr=723jd2d SIP/2.0
Via: SIP/2.0/TLS
192.0.2.4;branch=z9hG4bKnas432
Max-Forwards: 70
To: <sips:transferor@atlanta.example.com>
;tag=1928301774
From: <sips:3ld812adkjw@biloxi.example.
com;gr=3413kj2ha>
      ;tag=a6c85cf
Call-ID: a84b4c76e66710
CSeq: 73 NOTIFY
Contact: <sips:3ld812adkjw@biloxi.example.
com;gr=3413kj2ha>
Allow: INVITE, ACK, CANCEL, OPTIONS, BYE,
REFER, NOTIFY
Supported: replaces, tdialog
Event: refer
Subscription-State: active;expires=60
Content-Type: message/sipfrag
Content-Length: ...
SIP/2.0 100 Trying
```

F5 INVITE Transferee -> Transfer Target

```
INVITE sips:transfertarget@chicago.example.
com SIP/2.0
Via: SIP/2.0/TLS 192.0.2.4;branch=z9hG4bK
nas41234
Max-Forwards: 70
To: <sips:transfertarget@chicago.example.com>
From: <sips:transferee@biloxi.example.com>
;tag=j3kso3iqhq
Call-ID: 90422f3sd23m4g56832034
CSeq: 521 REFER
Allow: INVITE, ACK, CANCEL, OPTIONS, BYE,
REFER, NOTIFY
Supported: replaces, gruu, tdialog
Contact: <sips:3ld812adkjw@biloxi.example.
com;gr=3413kj2ha>
Content-Type: application/sdp
Content-Length: ...
```

F6 NOTIFY Transferee -> Transferor

```
NOTIFY sips:4889445d8kjtk3@atlanta.example.
com;gr=723jd2d SIP/2.0
Via: SIP/2.0/TLS
192.0.2.4;branch=z9hG4bKnas432
Max-Forwards: 70
To: <sips:transferor@atlanta.example.com>
;tag=1928301774
From: <sips:3ld812adkjw@biloxi.example.
com;gr=3413kj2ha>
      ;tag=a6c85cf
Call-ID: a84b4c76e66710
CSeq: 74 NOTIFY
Contact: <sips:3ld812adkjw@biloxi.example.
com;gr=3413kj2ha>
Allow: INVITE, ACK, CANCEL, OPTIONS, BYE,
REFER, NOTIFY
Supported: replaces, tdialog
Event: refer
Subscription-State:
terminated;reason=noresource
Content-Type: message/sipfrag
Content-Length: ...
SIP/2.0 200 OK
```

16.2.5.2 Transfer with Dialog Reuse

In this scenario, depicted in Figure 16.2, the Transferor does not know the properties of the Transferee's Contact URI or does not know that the Transferee supports the Target-Dialog header field. As a result, the REFER is sent inside the INVITE dialog.

F1 INVITE Transferee -> Transferor

```
INVITE sips:transferor@atlanta.example.com
SIP/2.0
Via: SIP/2.0/TLS
192.0.2.4;branch=z9hG4bKnas432
Max-Forwards: 70
To: <sips:transferor@atlanta.example.com>
From: <sips:transferee@biloxi.example.com>
;tag=7553452
Call-ID: 090459243588173445
CSeq: 29887 INVITE
Allow: INVITE, ACK, CANCEL, OPTIONS, BYE,
REFER, NOTIFY
Supported: replaces
Contact: <sips:transferee@192.0.2.4>
Content-Type: application/sdp
Content-Length: ...
```

F2 200 OK Transferor -> Transferee

```
SIP/2.0 200 OK
Via: SIP/2.0/TLS
192.0.2.4;branch=z9hG4bKnas432
To: <sips:transferor@atlanta.example.com>
;tag=31kdl4i3k
From: <sips:transferee@biloxi.example.com>
;tag=7553452
Call-ID: 090459243588173445
CSeq: 29887 INVITE
Allow: INVITE, ACK, CANCEL, OPTIONS, BYE,
REFER, NOTIFY
Supported: gruu, replaces
Contact: <sips:4889445d8kjtk3@atlanta.
example.com;gr=723jd2d>
Content-Type: application/sdp
Content-Length: ...
```

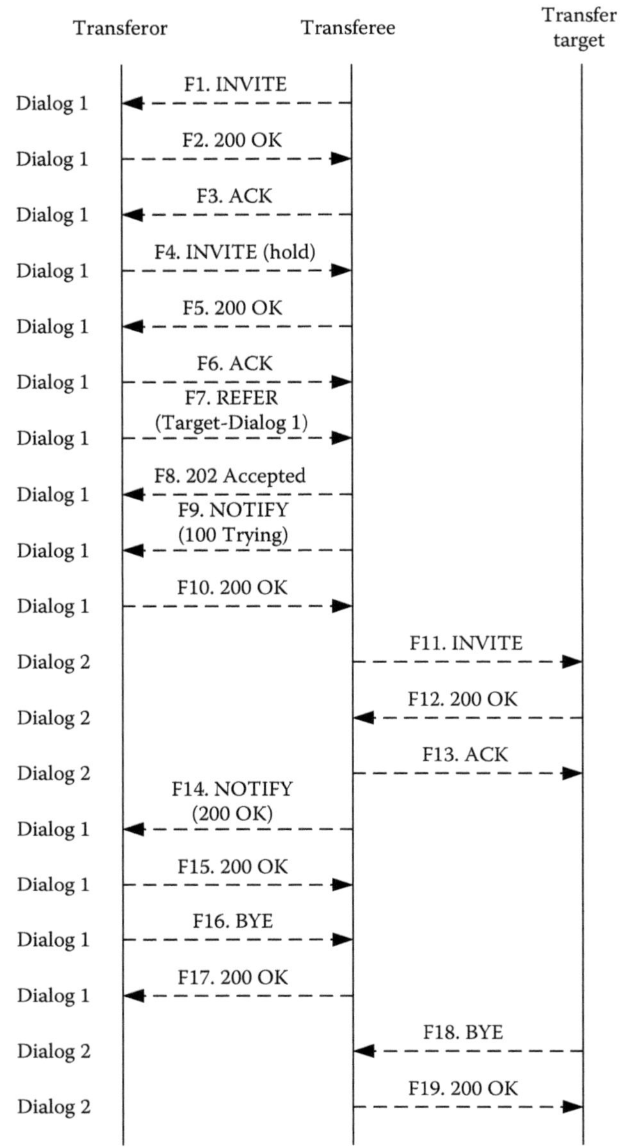

Figure 16.2 Transfer with dialog reuse. (Copyright IETF. Reproduced with permission.)

F3 REFER Transferor -> Transferee

```
REFER sips:transferee@192.0.2.4 SIP/2.0
Via: SIP/2.0/TLS pc33.atlanta.example.
com;branch=z9hG4bKna9
Max-Forwards: 70
To: <sips:transferee@biloxi.example.com>
;tag=7553452
From: <sips:transferor@atlanta.example.com>
;tag=31kdl4i3k
Call-ID: 090459243588173445
CSeq: 314159 REFER
Allow: INVITE, ACK, CANCEL, OPTIONS, BYE,
REFER, NOTIFY
Supported: replaces
Refer-To: <sips:transfertarget@chicago.
example.com>
Contact: <sips:4889445d8kjtk3@atlanta.
example.com;gr=723jd2d>
Content-Length: 0
```

F4 NOTIFY Transferee -> Transferor

```
NOTIFY sips:4889445d8kjtk3@atlanta.example.
com;gr=723jd2d SIP/2.0
Via: SIP/2.0/TLS
192.0.2.4;branch=z9hG4bKnas432
Max-Forwards: 70
To: <sips:transferor@atlanta.example.com>
;tag=31kdl4i3k
From: <sips:transferee@biloxi.example.com>
;tag=7553452
Call-ID: 090459243588173445
CSeq: 29888 INVITE
Contact: <sips:3ld812adkjw@biloxi.example.
com;gr=3413kj2ha>
Allow: INVITE, ACK, CANCEL, OPTIONS, BYE,
REFER, NOTIFY
Supported: replaces
Event: refer
Subscription-State: active;expires=60
Content-Type: message/sipfrag
Content-Length: ...
SIP/2.0 100 Trying
```

F5 INVITE Transferee -> Transfer Target

```
INVITE sips:transfertarget@chicago.example.
com SIP/2.0
Via: SIP/2.0/TLS 192.0.2.4;branch=z9hG4bK
nas41234
Max-Forwards: 70
To: <sips:transfertarget@chicago.example.com>
From: <sips:transferee@biloxi.example.com>
;tag=j3kso3iqhq
Call-ID: 90422f3sd23m4g56832034
CSeq: 521 REFER
Allow: INVITE, ACK, CANCEL, OPTIONS, BYE,
REFER, NOTIFY
Supported: replaces
Contact: <sips:transferee@192.0.2.4>
Content-Type: application/sdp
Content-Length: ...
```

F6 NOTIFY Transferee -> Transferor

```
NOTIFY sips:4889445d8kjtk3@atlanta.example.
com;gr=723jd2d SIP/2.0
Via: SIP/2.0/TLS
192.0.2.4;branch=z9hG4bKnas432
Max-Forwards: 70
To: <sips:transferor@atlanta.example.com>
;tag=31kdl4i3k
From: <sips:transferee@biloxi.example.com>
;tag=7553452
Call-ID: 090459243588173445
```

```
CSeq: 29889 INVITE
Contact: <sips:3ld812adkjw@biloxi.example.
com;gr=3413kj2ha>
Allow: INVITE, ACK, CANCEL, OPTIONS, BYE,
REFER, NOTIFY
Supported: replaces
Event: refer
Subscription-State:
terminated;reason=noresource
Content-Type: message/sipfrag
Content-Length: ...
SIP/2.0 200 OK
```

16.2.5.2.1 Failed Transfer

This section shows examples of failed transfer attempts. After the transfer failure occurs, the Transferor takes the Transferee off hold and resumes the session.

16.2.5.2.2 Target Busy

Figure 16.3 shows the call flows where the call transferred has failed when the transfer target is busy.

16.2.5.2.3 Transfer Target Does Not Answer

Figure 16.4 describes the call flows where the transferred has not been successful because the transfer target did not answer the call.

16.2.6 Transfer with Consultation Hold

Transfer with consultation hold involves a session between the Transferor and the Transfer Target before the transfer actually takes place. This is implemented with SIP Hold and Transfer as described above. A good feature is for the Transferor to let the target know that the session relates to an intended transfer. Since many UAs render the display name in the From header field to the user, a consultation INVITE could contain a string such as "Incoming consultation from Transferor with intent to transfer Transferee," where the display names of the transferor and transferee are included in the string.

16.2.6.1 Exposing Transfer Target

The Transferor places the Transferee on hold, establishes a call with the Transfer Target (Figure 16.5) to alert them to the impending transfer, terminates the connection with the Transfer Target, and then proceeds with transfer as above. This variation can be used to provide an experience similar to that expected by current PBX and Centrex users. To (hopefully) improve clarity, non-REFER transactions have been collapsed into one indicator with the arrow showing the direction of the request.

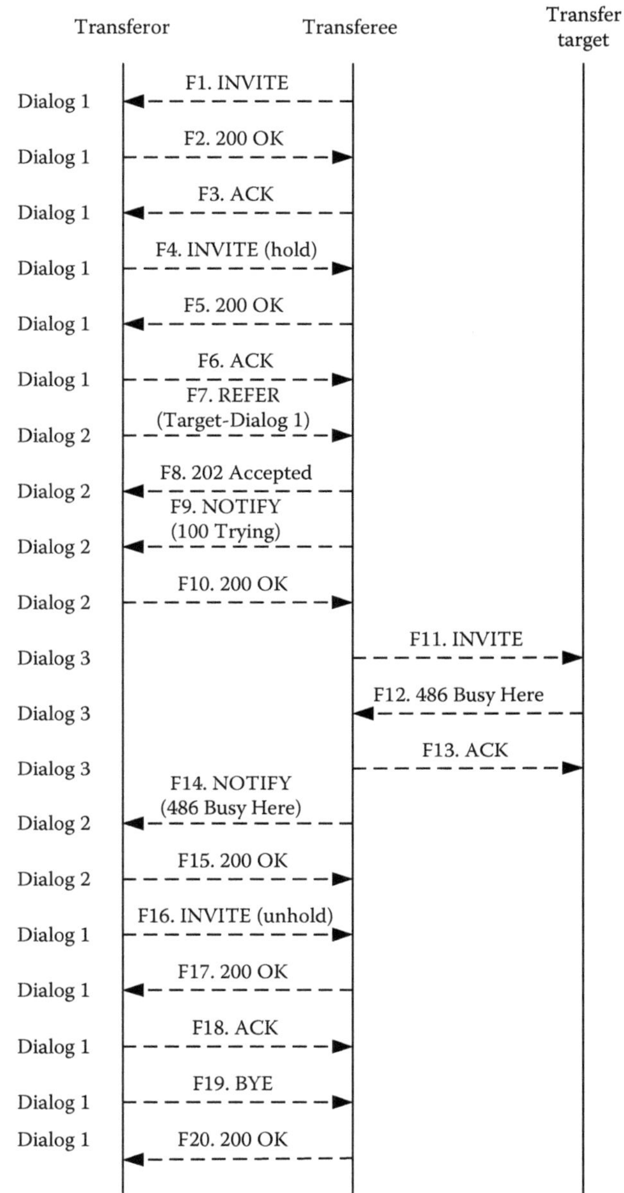

Figure 16.3 Failed transfer—target busy. (Copyright IETF. Reproduced with permission.)

16.2.6.2 Protecting Transfer Target

The Transferor places the Transferee on hold, establishes a call with the Transfer Target, and then reverses their roles, transferring the original Transfer Target to the original Transferee. This has the advantage of hiding information about the original Transfer Target from the original Transferee. On the other hand, the Transferee's experience is different than in current systems. The Transferee is effectively called back by the Transfer Target. One of the problems with this simplest implementation of a target protecting transfer is that the Transferee is receiving a new call from

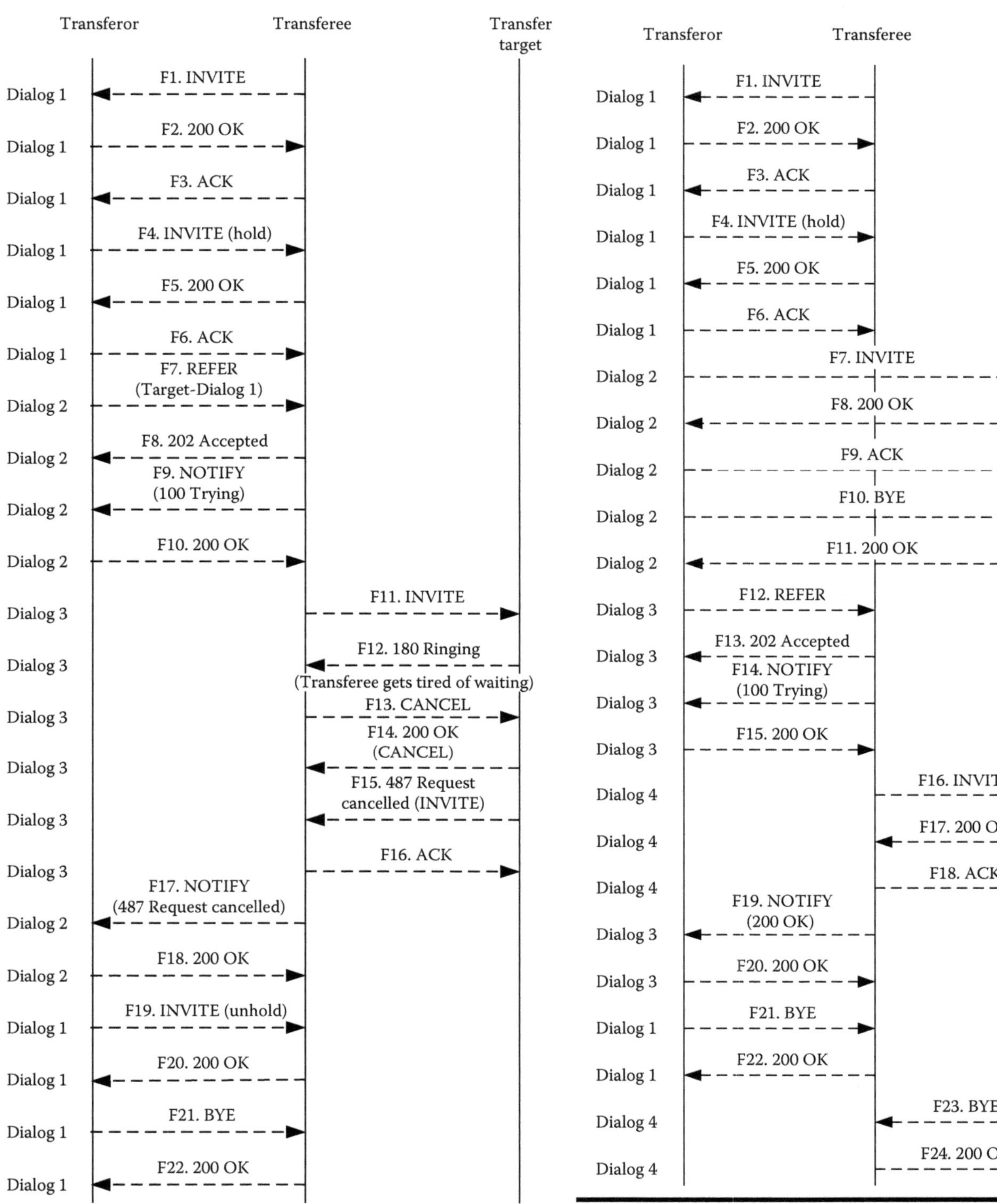

Figure 16.4 Failed transfer—target does not answer. (Copyright IETF. Reproduced with permission.)

Figure 16.5 Transfer with consultation hold—exposing Transfer Target. (Copyright IETF. Reproduced with permission.)

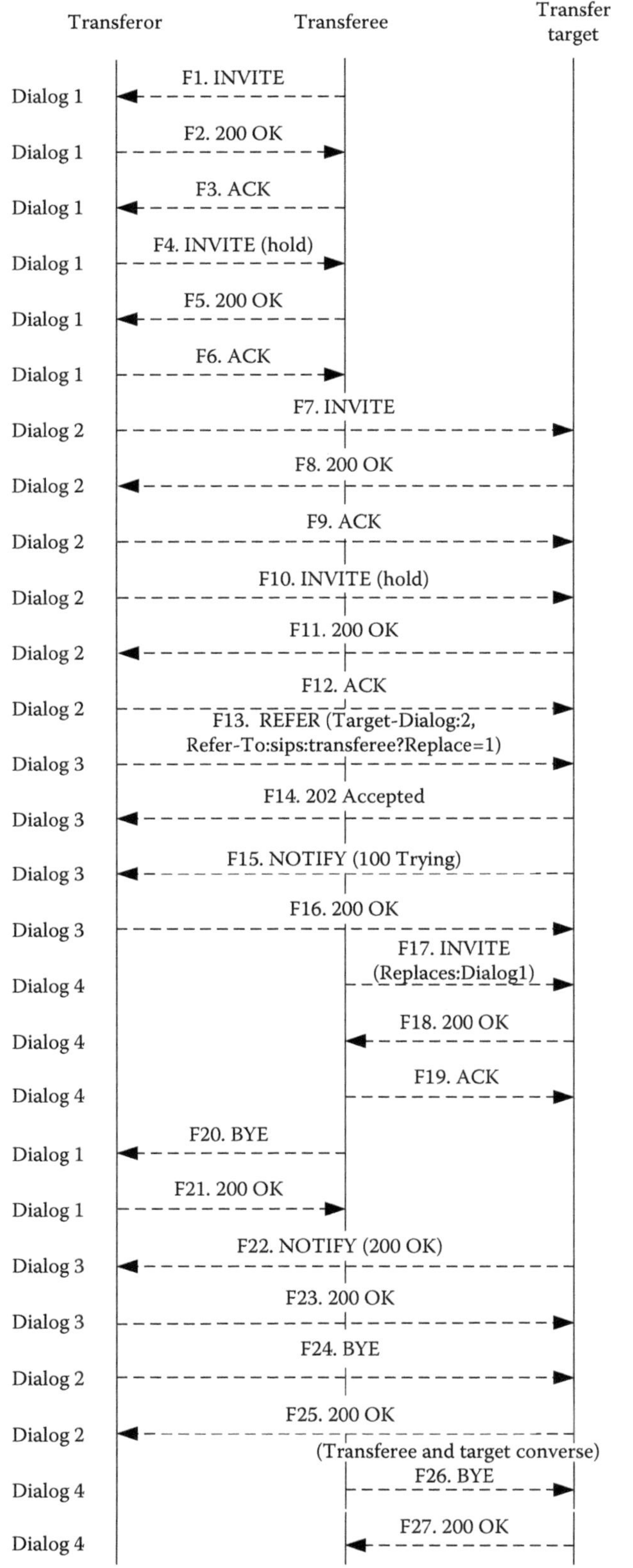

Figure 16.6 Transfer protecting Transfer Target. (Copyright IETF. Reproduced with permission.)

the Transfer Target. Unless the Transferee's agent has a reliable way to associate this new call with the call it already has with the Transferor, it will have to alert the new call on another appearance. If this, or some other call-waiting-like user interface were not available, the Transferee might be stuck returning a Busy-Here to the Transfer Target, effectively preventing the transfer.

There are many ways that correlation could be provided. The dialog parameters could be provided directly as header parameters in the Refer-To URI, for example. The Replaces mechanism (RFC 3891, see Section 2.8.2) uses this approach and solves this problem nicely. For the call flows below (Figure 16.6), dialog1 means dialog identifier 1, and consists of the parameters of the Replaces header for dialog 1. In RFC 3891, this is the Call-ID, To-tag, and From-tag. Note that the Transferee's agent emits a BYE to the Transferor's agent as an immediate consequence of processing the Replaces header. The Transferor knows that both the Transferee and the Transfer Target support the Replaces header from the Supported: replaces header contained in the 200 OK responses from both. In this scenario, the Transferee utilizes a GRUU as a Contact URI for reasons discussed earlier. Note that the conventions used in the SIP Torture Test Messages (RFC 4475) document are reused, specifically the <allOneLine> tag.

F1 INVITE Transferee -> Transferor

```
INVITE sips:transferor@atlanta.example.com
SIP/2.0
Via: SIP/2.0/TLS
192.0.2.4;branch=z9hG4bKnas432
Max-Forwards: 70
To: <sips:transferor@atlanta.example.com>
From: <sips:transferee@biloxi.example.com>
;tag=7553452
Call-ID: 090459243588173445
CSeq: 29887 INVITE
Allow: INVITE, ACK, CANCEL, OPTIONS, BYE,
REFER, NOTIFY
Supported: replaces, gruu
Contact: <sips:3ld812adkjw@biloxi.example.
com;gr=3413kj2ha>
Content-Type: application/sdp
Content-Length: ...
```

F2 200 OK Transferor -> Transferee

```
SIP/2.0 200 OK
Via: SIP/2.0/TLS
192.0.2.4;branch=z9hG4bKnas432
To: <sips:transferor@atlanta.example.com>
;tag=31431
From: <sips:transferee@biloxi.example.com>
;tag=7553452
Call-ID: 090459243588173445
CSeq: 29887 INVITE
```

```
Allow: INVITE, ACK, CANCEL, OPTIONS, BYE,
REFER, NOTIFY
Supported: replaces, gruu, tdialog
Contact: <sips:4889445d8kjtk3@atlanta.
example.com;gr=723jd2d>
Content-Type: application/sdp
Content-Length: ...
```

F3 INVITE Transferor -> Transfer Target

```
INVITE sips:transfertarget@chicago.example.
com SIP/2.0
Via: SIP/2.0/TLS pc33.atlanta.example.
com;branch=z9hG4bKnas432
Max-Forwards: 70
To: <sips:transfertarget@chicago.example.com>
From: <sips:transferor@atlanta.example.com>
;tag=763231
Call-ID: 592435881734450904
CSeq: 29887 INVITE
Allow: INVITE, ACK, CANCEL, OPTIONS, BYE,
REFER, NOTIFY
Supported: gruu, replaces, tdialog
Require: replaces
Contact: <sips:4889445d8kjtk3@atlanta.
example.com;gr=384i32lw3>
Content-Type: application/sdp
Content-Length: ...
```

F4 200 OK Transfer Target -> Transferor

```
SIP/2.0 200 OK
Via: SIP/2.0/TLS pc33.atlanta.example.
com;branch=z9hG4bKnas432
      ;received=192.0.2.1
To: <sips:transfertarget@chicago.example.com>
;tag=9m2n3wq
From: <sips:transferor@atlanta.example.com>
;tag=763231
Call-ID: 592435881734450904
CSeq: 29887 INVITE
Allow: INVITE, ACK, CANCEL, OPTIONS, BYE,
REFER, NOTIFY
Supported: replaces, gruu, tdialog
Contact: <sips:482n4z24kdg@chicago.example.
com;gr=8594958>
Content-Type: application/sdp
Content-Length: ...
```

F5 REFER Transferor -> Transfer Target

```
REFER sips:482n4z24kdg@chicago.example.
com;gr=8594958 SIP/2.0
Via: SIP/2.0/TLS pc33.atlanta.example.
com;branch=z9hG4bKnashds9
Max-Forwards: 70
To: <sips:482n4z24kdg@chicago.example.
com;gr=8594958>
From: <sips:transferor@atlanta.example.com>
;tag=1928301774
Call-ID: a84b4c76e66710
CSeq: 314159 REFER
Allow: INVITE, ACK, CANCEL, OPTIONS, BYE,
REFER, NOTIFY
Supported: gruu, replaces, tdialog
Require: tdialog
<allOneLine>
      Refer-To: <sips:3ld812adkjw@biloxi.
      example.com;gr=3413kj2ha
      ?Replaces=090459243588173445%
      3Bto-tag%3D7553452%3Bfrom-tag%3D31431>
</allOneLine>
Target-Dialog:
592435881734450904;local-tag=9m2n3wq
      ;remote-tag=763231
Contact: <sips:4889445d8kjtk3@atlanta.
example.com;gr=723jd2d>
Content-Length: 0
```

F6 INVITE Transfer Target -> Transferee

```
INVITE sips:3ld812adkjw@biloxi.example.
com;gr=3413kj2ha SIP/2.0
Via: SIP/2.0/TLS client.chicago.example.
com;branch=z9hG4bKnaslu84
Max-Forwards: 70
To: <sips:3ld812adkjw@biloxi.example.
com;gr=3413kj2ha>
From: <sips:transfertarget@chicago.example.com>
;tag=341234
Call-ID: kmzwdle3dl3d08
CSeq: 41 INVITE
Allow: INVITE, ACK, CANCEL, OPTIONS, BYE,
REFER, NOTIFY
Supported: gruu, replaces, tdialog
Contact: <sips:482n4z24kdg@chicago.example.
com;gr=8594958>
Replaces:
090459243588173445;to-tag=7553452;from-
tag=31431
Content-Type: application/sdp
Content-Length: ...
```

16.2.6.3 Attended Transfer

The Transferor places the Transferee on hold, establishes a call with the Transfer Target to alert them to the impending transfer, places the target on hold, then proceeds with transfer (Figure 16.7) using an escaped Replaces header field in the Refer-To header. This is another common service expected by current PBX and Centrex users. The Contact URI of the Transfer Target should be used by the Transferor as the Refer-To URI, unless the URI is suspected or known to not be routable outside the dialog. Otherwise, the address of record (AOR) of the Transfer Target should be used. That is, the same URI that the Transferor used to establish the session with the Transfer Target should be used. In case the triggered INVITE is routed to a different UA than the Transfer

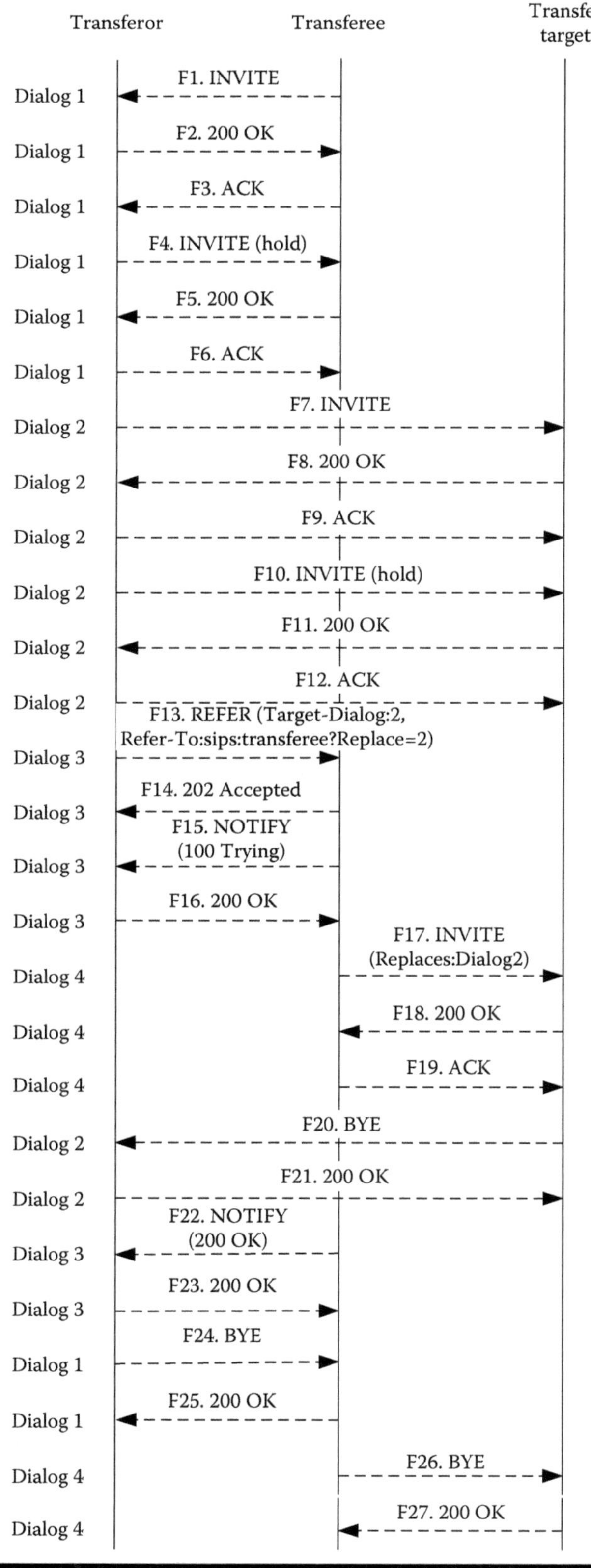

Figure 16.7 Attended transfer call flow. (Copyright IETF. Reproduced with permission.)

Target, the Require: replaces header field should be used in the triggered INVITE. (This is to prevent an incorrect UA that does not support Replaces from ignoring the Replaces and answering the INVITE without a dialog match.) It is possible that proxy/service routing may prevent the triggered INVITE from reaching the same UA. If this occurs, the triggered invite will fail with a timeout, 403, 404, and other error messages (see Section 2.6). The Transferee may then retry the transfer with the Refer-To URI set to the Contact URI.

F1 INVITE Transferee -> Transferor

```
INVITE sips:transferor@atlanta.example.com
SIP/2.0
Via: SIP/2.0/TLS
192.0.2.4;branch=z9hG4bKnas432
Max-Forwards: 70
To: <sips:transferor@atlanta.example.com>
From: <sips:transferee@biloxi.example.com>
;tag=7553452
Call-ID: 090459243588173445
CSeq: 29887 INVITE
Allow: INVITE, ACK, CANCEL, OPTIONS, BYE,
REFER, NOTIFY
Supported: replaces, gruu, tdialog
Contact: <sips:3ld812adkjw@biloxi.example.
com;gr=3413kj2ha>
Content-Type: application/sdp
Content-Length: ...
```

F2 200 OK Transferor -> Transferee

```
SIP/2.0 200 OK
Via: SIP/2.0/TLS
192.0.2.4;branch=z9hG4bKnas432
To: <sips:transferor@atlanta.example.com>
;tag=31431
From: <sips:transferee@biloxi.example.com>
;tag=7553452
Call-ID: 090459243588173445
CSeq: 29887 INVITE
Allow: INVITE, ACK, CANCEL, OPTIONS, BYE,
REFER, NOTIFY
Supported: replaces, gruu, tdialog
Contact: <sips:4889445d8kjtk3@atlanta.
example.com;gr=723jd2d>
Content-Type: application/sdp
Content-Length: ...
```

F3 INVITE Transferor -> Transfer Target

```
INVITE sips:transfertarget@chicago.example.
com SIP/2.0
Via: SIP/2.0/TLS pc33.atlanta.example.
com;branch=z9hG4bKnas432
Max-Forwards: 70
To: <sips:transfertarget@chicago.example.com>
```

```
From: <sips:transferor@atlanta.example.com>
;tag=763231
Call-ID: 592435881734450904
CSeq: 29887 INVITE
Allow: INVITE, ACK, CANCEL, OPTIONS, BYE,
REFER, NOTIFY
Supported: gruu, replaces, tdialog
Require: replaces
Contact: <sips:4889445d8kjtk3@atlanta.
example.com;gr=384i32lw3>
Content-Type: application/sdp
Content-Length: ...
```

F4 200 OK Transfer Target -> Transferor

```
SIP/2.0 200 OK
Via: SIP/2.0/TLS pc33.atlanta.example.
com;branch=z9hG4bKnas432
       ;received=192.0.2.1
To: <sips:transfertarget@chicago.example.com>
;tag=9m2n3wq
From: <sips:transferor@atlanta.example.com>
;tag=763231
Call-ID: 592435881734450904
CSeq: 29887 INVITE
Allow: INVITE, ACK, CANCEL, OPTIONS, BYE,
REFER, NOTIFY
Supported: replaces, gruu
Contact: <sips:482n4z24kdg@chicago.example.
com;gr=8594958>
Content-Type: application/sdp
Content-Length: ...
```

F5 REFER Transferor -> Transferee

```
REFER sips:3ld812adkjw@biloxi.example.
com;gr=3413kj2ha SIP/2.0
Via: SIP/2.0/TLS pc33.atlanta.example.
com;branch=z9hG4bKnashds9
Max-Forwards: 70
To: <sips:3ld812adkjw@biloxi.example.
com;gr=3413kj2ha>
From: <sips:transferor@atlanta.example.com>
;tag=1928301774
Call-ID: a84b4c76e66710
CSeq: 314159 REFER
Require: tdialog
<allOneLine>
       Refer-To: <sips:482n4z24kdg@chicago.
       example.com;gr=8594958?
       Replaces=592435881734450904%
       3Bto-tag%3D9m2n3wq%3Bfrom-tag3D763231>
</allOneLine>
Target-Dialog:
592435881734450904;local-tag=9m2n3wq
;remote-tag=763231
Contact: <sips:4889445d8kjtk3@atlanta.
example.com;gr=723jd2d>
Content-Length: 0
```

F6 INVITE Transferee -> Transfer Target

```
INVITE sips:482n4z24kdg@chicago.example.
com;gr=8594958 SIP/2.0
Via: SIP/2.0/TLS
192.0.2.4;branch=z9hG4bKnaslu82
Max-Forwards: 70
To: <sips:482n4z24kdg@chicago.example.
com;gr=8594958>
From: <sips:transferee@biloxi.example.com>
;tag=954
Call-ID: kmzwdle3dl3d08
CSeq: 41 INVITE
Allow: INVITE, ACK, CANCEL, OPTIONS, BYE,
REFER, NOTIFY
Supported: gruu, replaces, tdialog
Contact: <sips:3ld812adkjw@biloxi.example.
com;gr=3413kj2ha>
Replaces:
592435881734450904;to-tag=9m2n3wq;from-
tag=763231
Content-Type: application/sdp
Content-Length: ...
```

16.2.6.4 Recovery When One Party Does Not Support REFER

If protecting or exposing the Transfer Target is not a concern, it is possible to complete a transfer (Figure 16.8) with consultation hold when only the transferor and one other party support REFER. Note that a 405 Method Not Allowed might be returned instead of the 501 Not Implemented response.

16.2.6.5 Attended Transfer without Knowing GRUU

It is a requirement of RFC 3261 that a Contact URI be globally routable even outside the dialog. It implies that the Contact URI should be a globally routable UA URI. However, due to RFC 2543 (obsoleted by RFC 3261) UAs and some architectures such as network address translator (NAT)/Firewall traversal, screening proxies, application layer gateways, and others, this will not always be the case. As a result, the method of attended transfer shown in Figures 16.6 through 16.8 should only be used if the Contact URI is known to be routable outside the dialog. Figure 16.9 shows such a scenario where the Transfer Target Contact URI is not routable outside the dialog, so the triggered INVITE is sent to the AOR of the Transfer Target.

Attended Transfer: Contact URI Not Known to Route to a Unique UA

F1 INVITE Transferor -> Transfer Target

```
INVITE sips:transfertarget@chicago.example.
com SIP/2.0
```

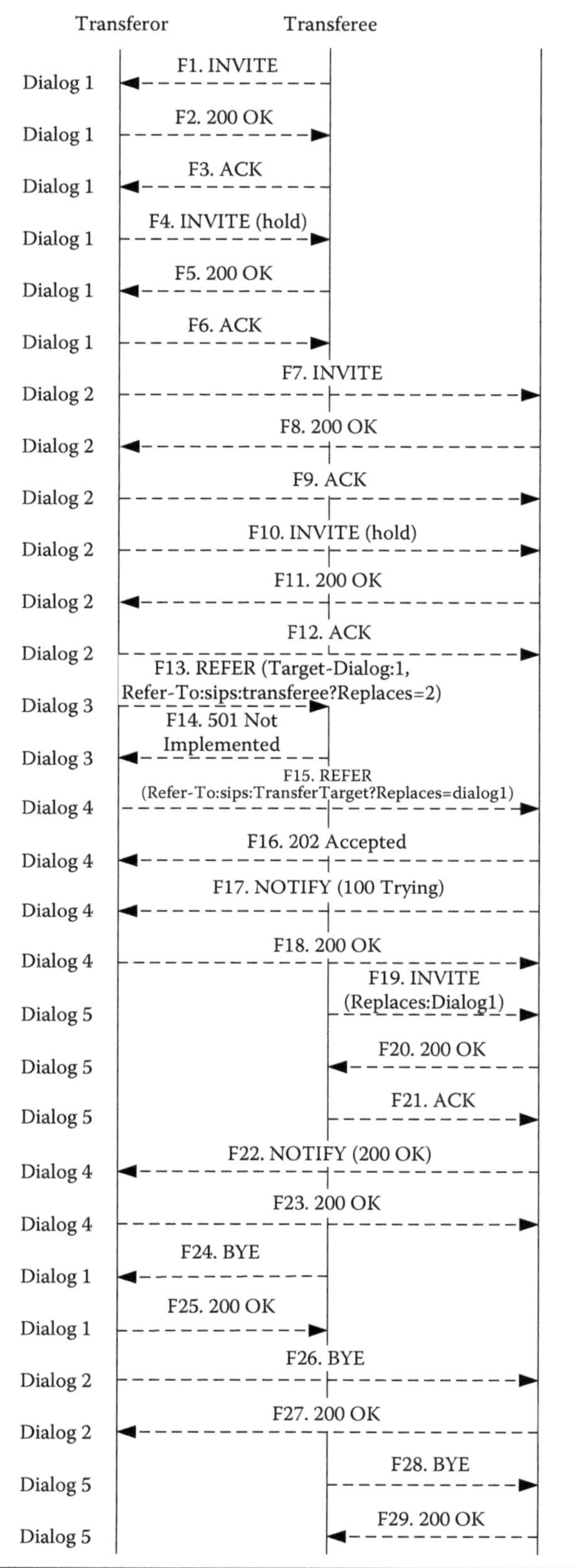

Figure 16.8 Recovery when one party does not support REFER. (Copyright IETF. Reproduced with permission.)

```
Via: SIP/2.0/TLS pc33.atlanta.example.
com;branch=z9hG4bK76
Max-Forwards: 70
To: <sips:transfertarget@chicago.example.com>
From: <sips:transferor@atlanta.example.com>
;tag=763231
Call-ID: 090459243588173445
CSeq: 29887 INVITE
Allow: INVITE, ACK, CANCEL, OPTIONS, BYE,
REFER, NOTIFY
Supported: replaces
Contact: <sips:transferor@pc33.atlanta.
example.com>
Content-Type: application/sdp
Content-Length: ...
```

F2 200 OK Transfer Target -> Transferee

```
SIP/2.0 200 OK
Via: SIP/2.0/TLS pc33.atlanta.example.
com;branch=z9hG4bKnas432
;received=192.0.2.1
To: <sips:transfertarget@chicago.example.com>
;tag=9m2n3wq
From: <sips:transferor@atlanta.example.com>
;tag=763231
Call-ID: 090459243588173445
CSeq: 29887 INVITE
Allow: INVITE, ACK, CANCEL, OPTIONS, BYE,
REFER, NOTIFY
Supported: replaces
Contact: <sips:transfertarget@client.chicago.
example.com>
Content-Type: application/sdp
Content-Length: ...
```

F3 REFER Transferor -> Transferee

```
REFER sips:transferee@192.0.2.4 SIP/2.0
Via: SIP/2.0/TLS pc33.atlanta.example.
com;branch=z9hG4bKnashds9
Max-Forwards: 70
To: <sips:transferee@biloxi.example.com>
;tag=a6c85cf
From: <sips:transferor@atlanta.example.com>
;tag=1928301774
Call-ID: a84b4c76e66710
CSeq: 314160 REFER
<allOneLine>
       Refer-To: <sips:transfertarget@
       chicago.example.com?Replaces=
       090459243588173445%3Bto-tag%3D9m2n3wq%
       3Bfrom-tag%3D763231
       &Require=replaces>
<allOneLine>
Contact: <sips:transferor@pc33.atlanta.
example.com>
Content-Length: 0
```

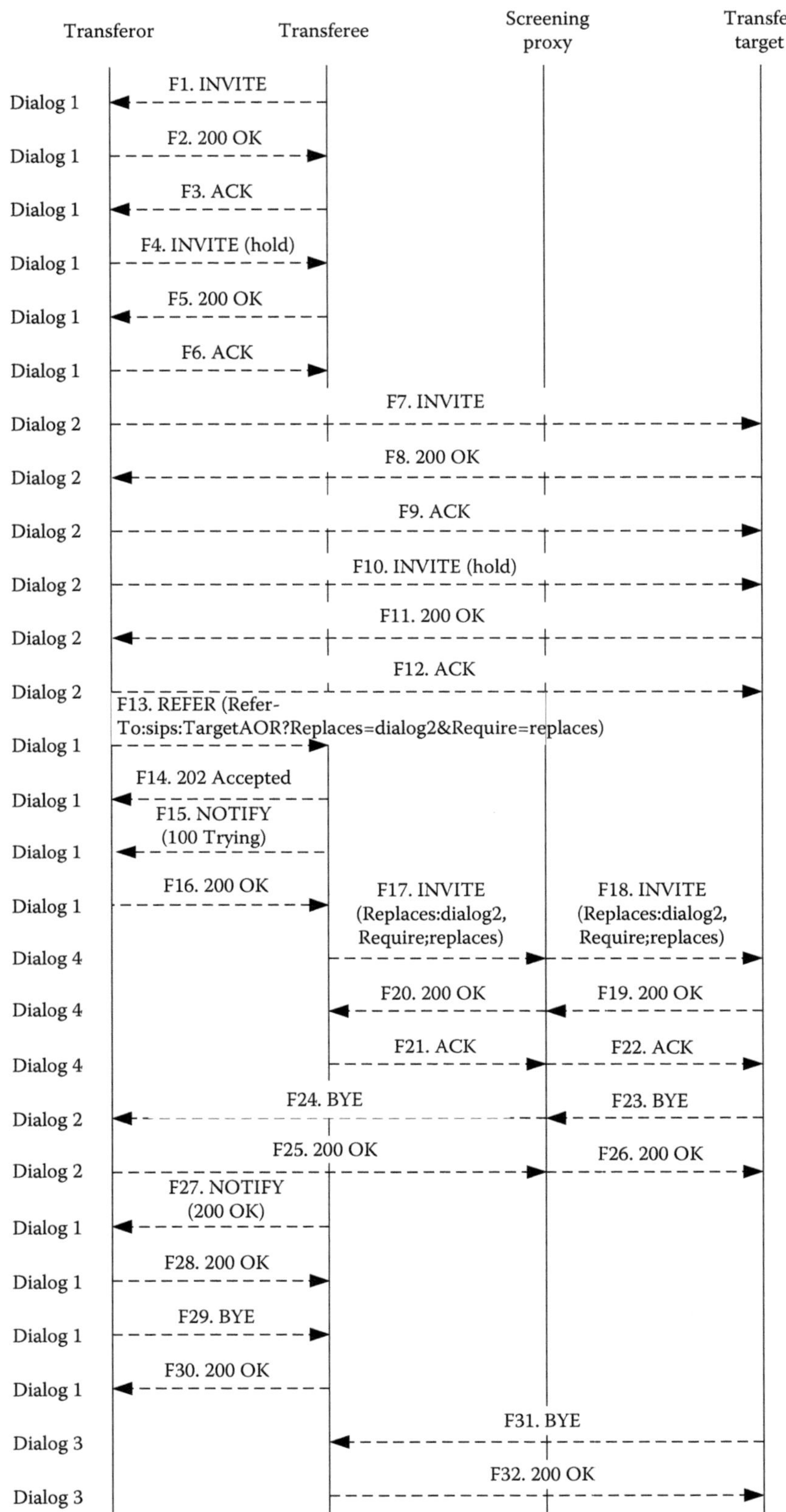

Figure 16.9 Attended transfer call flow with a contact URI not known to be globally routable. (Copyright IETF. Reproduced with permission.)

F4 INVITE Transferee -> Transfer Target

```
INVITE sips:transfertarget@chicago.example.
com SIP/2.0
Via: SIP/2.0/TLS
192.0.2.4;branch=z9hG4bKnaslu82
Max-Forwards: 70
To: <sips:transfertarget@chicago.example.com>
From: <sips:transferee@biloxi.example.com>
;tag=954
Call-ID: 20482817324945934422930
CSeq: 42 INVITE
Allow: INVITE, ACK, CANCEL, OPTIONS, BYE,
REFER, NOTIFY
Supported: replaces
Contact: <sips:transferee@192.0.2.4>
Replaces:
090459243588173445;to-tag=9m2n3wq;from-
tag=763231
Require: replaces
Content-Type: application/sdp
Content-Length: ...
```

F5 NOTIFY Transferee -> Transferor

```
NOTIFY sips:transferor@pc33.atlanta.com
SIP/2.0
Via: SIP/2.0/TLS
192.0.2.4;branch=z9hG4bKnas432
Max-Forwards: 70
To: <sips:transferor@atlanta.example.com>
;tag=1928301774
From: <sips:transferee@biloxi.example.com>
;tag=a6c85cf
Call-ID: a84b4c76e66710
CSeq: 76 NOTIFY
Contact: <sips:31d812adkjw@biloxi.example.
com;gr=3413kj2ha>
Allow: INVITE, ACK, CANCEL, OPTIONS, BYE,
REFER, NOTIFY
Supported: replaces
Event: refer;id=98873867
Subscription-State:
terminated;reason=noresource
Content-Type: message/sipfrag
Content-Length: ...
SIP/2.0 200 OK
```

Figure 16.10 shows a failure case in which the AOR URI fails to reach the Transfer Target. As a result, the transfer is retried with the Contact URI, at which point it succeeds. Note that there is still no guarantee that the correct end point will be reached, and the result of this second REFER may also be a failure. In that case, the Transferor could fall back to unattended transfer or give up on the transfer entirely. Since two REFERs are sent within the dialog creating two distinct subscriptions, the Transferee uses the *id* parameter in the Event header field to distinguish notifications for the two subscriptions.

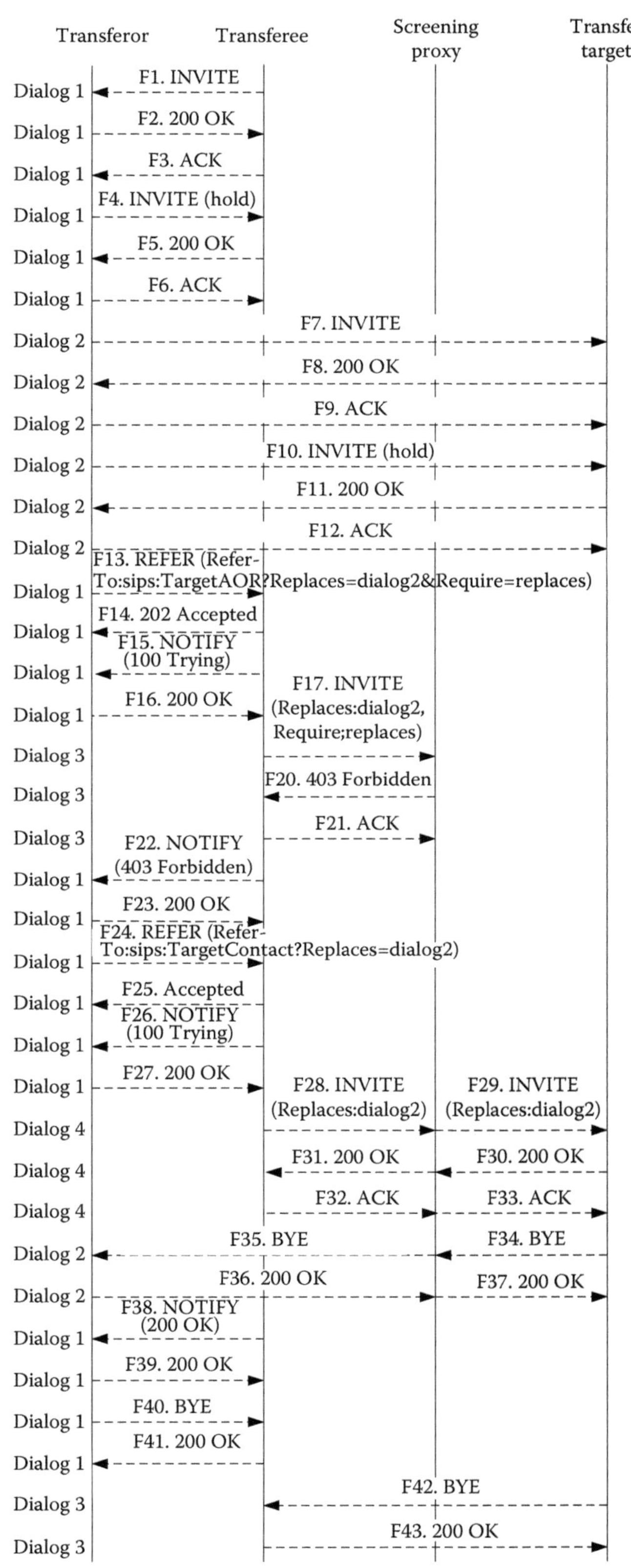

Figure 16.10 Attended transfer call flow with nonroutable contact URI and AOR failure. (Copyright IETF. Reproduced with permission.)

F1 INVITE Transferor -> Transfer Target

```
INVITE sips:transfertarget@chicago.example.
com SIP/2.0
Via: SIP/2.0/TLS pc33.atlanta.example.
com;branch=z9hG4bK76
Max-Forwards: 70
To: <sips:transfertarget@chicago.example.com>
From: <sips:transferor@atlanta.example.com>
;tag=763231
Call-ID: 090459243588173445
CSeq: 29887 INVITE
Allow: INVITE, ACK, CANCEL, OPTIONS, BYE,
REFER, NOTIFY
Supported: replaces
Contact: <sips:transferor@pc33.atlanta.
example.com>
Content-Type: application/sdp
Content-Length: ...
```

F2 200 OK Transfer Target -> Transferee

```
SIP/2.0 200 OK
Via: SIP/2.0/TLS pc33.atlanta.example.
com;branch=z9hG4bKnas432
;received=192.0.2.1
To: <sips:transfertarget@chicago.example.com>
;tag=9m2n3wq
From: <sips:transferor@atlanta.example.com>
;tag=763231
Call-ID: 090459243588173445
CSeq: 29887 INVITE
Allow: INVITE, ACK, CANCEL, OPTIONS, BYE,
REFER, NOTIFY
Supported: replaces
Contact: <sips:transfertarget@client.chicago.
example.com>
Content-Type: application/sdp
Content-Length: ...
```

F3 REFER Transferor -> Transferee

```
REFER sips:transferee@192.0.2.4 SIP/2.0
Via: SIP/2.0/TLS pc33.atlanta.example.
com;branch=z9hG4bKnashds9
Max-Forwards: 70
To: <sips:transferee@biloxi.example.com>
;tag=a6c85cf
From: <sips:transferor@atlanta.example.com>
;tag=1928301774
Call-ID: a84b4c76e66710
CSeq: 314159 REFER
<allOneLine>
       Refer-To: <sips:transfertarget@
       chicago.example.com?Replaces=
       090459243588173445%3Bto-tag%3D9m2n
       3wq%3Bfrom-tag%3D763231
       &Require=replaces>
</allOneLine>
Contact: <sips:transferor@pc33.atlanta.
example.com>
Content-Length: 0
```

F4 NOTIFY Transferee -> Transferor

```
NOTIFY sips:transferor@pc33.atlanta.com
SIP/2.0
Via: SIP/2.0/TLS
192.0.2.4;branch=z9hG4bKnas432
Max-Forwards: 70
To: <sips:transferor@atlanta.example.com>
;tag=1928301774
From: <sips:transferee@biloxi.example.com>
;tag=a6c85cf
Call-ID: a84b4c76e66710
CSeq: 74 NOTIFY
Contact: <sips:3ld812adkjw@biloxi.example.
com;gr=3413kj2ha>
Allow: INVITE, ACK, CANCEL, OPTIONS, BYE,
REFER, NOTIFY
Supported: replaces
Event: refer;id=314159
Subscription-State:
terminated;reason=noresource
Content-Type: message/sipfrag
Content-Length: ...
SIP/2.0 403 Forbidden
```

F5 REFER Transferor -> Transferee

```
REFER sips:transferee@192.0.2.4 SIP/2.0
Via: SIP/2.0/TLS pc33.atlanta.example.
com;branch=z9hG4bKnashds9
Max-Forwards: 70
To: <sips:transferee@biloxi.example.com>
;tag=a6c85cf
From: <sips:transferor@atlanta.example.com>
;tag=1928301774
Call-ID: a84b4c76e66710
CSeq: 314160 REFER
<allOneLine>
       Refer-To: <sips:transfertarget@client.
       chicago.example.com
       ?Replaces=090459243588173445%
       3Bto-tag%3D9m2n3wq
       %3Bfrom-tag%3D763231>
</allOneLine>
Contact: <sips:transferor@pc33.atlanta.
example.com>
Content-Length: 0
```

F6 INVITE Transferee -> Transfer Target

```
INVITE sips:transfertarget@client.chicago.
example.com SIP/2.0
Via: SIP/2.0/TLS
192.0.2.4;branch=z9hG4bKnaslu82
Max-Forwards: 70
To: <sips:transfertarget@chicago.example.com>
```

```
From: <sips:transferee@biloxi.example.com>
;tag=954
Call-ID: 20482817324945934422930
CSeq: 42 INVITE
Allow: INVITE, ACK, CANCEL, OPTIONS, BYE,
REFER, NOTIFY
Supported: replaces
Contact: <sips:transferee@192.0.2.4>
Replaces:
090459243588173445;to-tag=9m2n3wq;from-
tag=763231
Content-Type: application/sdp
Content-Length: ...
```

F7 NOTIFY Transferee -> Transferor

```
NOTIFY sips:transferor@pc33.atlanta.com
SIP/2.0
Via: SIP/2.0/TLS
192.0.2.4;branch=z9hG4bKnas432
Max-Forwards: 70
To: <sips:transferor@atlanta.example.com>
;tag=1928301774
From: <sips:transferee@biloxi.example.com>
;tag=a6c85cf
Call-ID: a84b4c76e66710
CSeq: 76 NOTIFY
Contact: <sips:3ld812adkjw@biloxi.example.
com;gr=3413kj2ha>
Allow: INVITE, ACK, CANCEL, OPTIONS, BYE,
REFER, NOTIFY
Supported: replaces
Event: refer;id=314160
Subscription-State:
terminated;reason=noresource
Content-Type: message/sipfrag
Content-Length: ...
SIP/2.0 200 OK
```

To prevent this scenario from happening, the Transfer Target should use a Contact URI that is routable outside the dialog, which will result in the call flow of Figure 16.7.

16.2.6.6 Semi-Attended Transfer

In any of the consultation hold flows above, the Transferor may decide to terminate its attempt to contact the Transfer Target before that session is established. Most frequently, that will be the end of the scenario; however, in some circumstances, the Transferor may wish to proceed with the transfer action. For example, the Transferor may wish to complete the transfer knowing that the Transferee will end up eventually talking to the Transfer Target's voice-mail service. Some PBX systems support this feature, sometimes called *semi-attended transfer*, which is effectively a hybrid between a fully attended transfer and an unattended transfer. A call flow is shown in Figure 16.11. In this flow, the Transferor's UA continues the transfer as an attended transfer even after

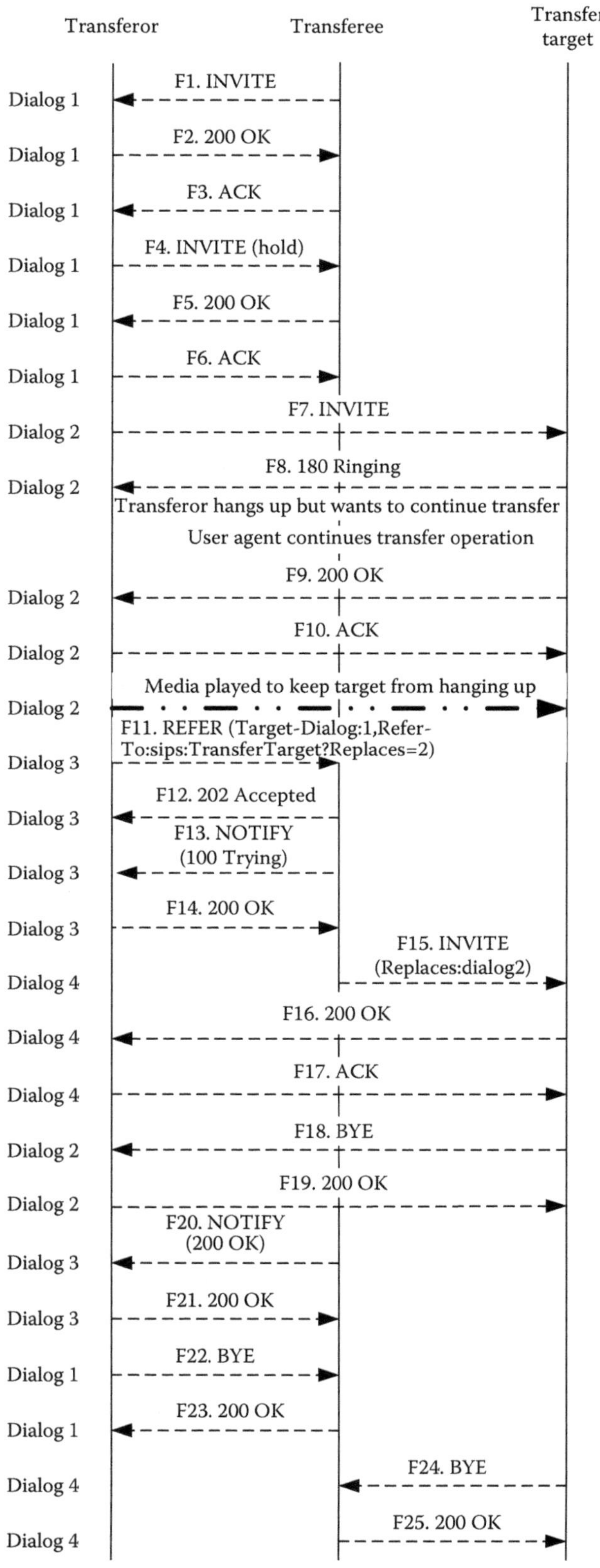

Figure 16.11 Recommended semi-attended transfer call flow. (Copyright IETF. Reproduced with permission.)

the Transferor hangs up. Note that media must be played to the Transfer Target upon answer—otherwise, the Target may hang up and the resulting transfer operation will fail.

Two other possible semi-attended transfer call flows are shown in Figures 16.12 and 16.13. However, these call flows are not recommended because of race conditions. In both of these flows, when the Transferor hangs up, the Transferor attempts to revert to unattended transfer by sending a CANCEL to the target. This can result in two race conditions. One is that the target answers despite the CANCEL and the resulting unattended transfer fails. This race condition can be eliminated by the Transferor waiting to send the REFER until the 487 response from the target is returned. Instead of a 487, a 200 OK may be returned, indicating that the target has answered the consultation call.

In this case, the call flow in Figure 16.13 must be followed. In this flow, the Transferor must play some kind of media to the Target to prevent the Target from hanging up, or the transfer will fail. That is, the human at the Transfer Target will hear silence from when they answer (message F1) until the transfer completes (message F3 and they are talking to the Transferee unless some media is played, message F2). The second race condition occurs in Figure 16.12 if the Transfer Target goes off hook after the CANCEL is received and the 487 returned. This may result in a 486 Busy Here response to the unattended transfer. The recommended call flow of Figure 16.11 does not utilize a CANCEL and does not suffer from these race conditions.

16.2.6.7 Attended Transfer Fallback to Basic Transfer

In this flow, an attempted attended transfer fails so the Transferor falls back to basic transfer. The call flow in Figure 16.14 shows the use of Require: replaces in the INVITE sent by the Transferor to the Transfer Target in which the Transferor's intention at the time of sending the INVITE to the Transfer Target was known to be to complete an attended transfer. Since the Target does not support Replaces, the INVITE is rejected with a 420 Bad Extension response, and the Transferor switches from attended transfer to basic transfer immediately.

Figure 16.15 shows the use of OPTIONS when the Transferee and Transfer Target do not explicitly indicate support for the REFER method and Replaces header fields in Allow and Supported header fields, and the Transferor did not have the intention of performing an attended transfer when the INVITE to the Target was sent. In dialog 1, the Transferor determines, using OPTIONS, that the Transferee does support REFER and Replaces. As a result, the Transferor begins the attended transfer by placing the Transferee on hold and calling the Transfer Target. Using an OPTIONS in dialog 2, the Transferor determines that the target does not

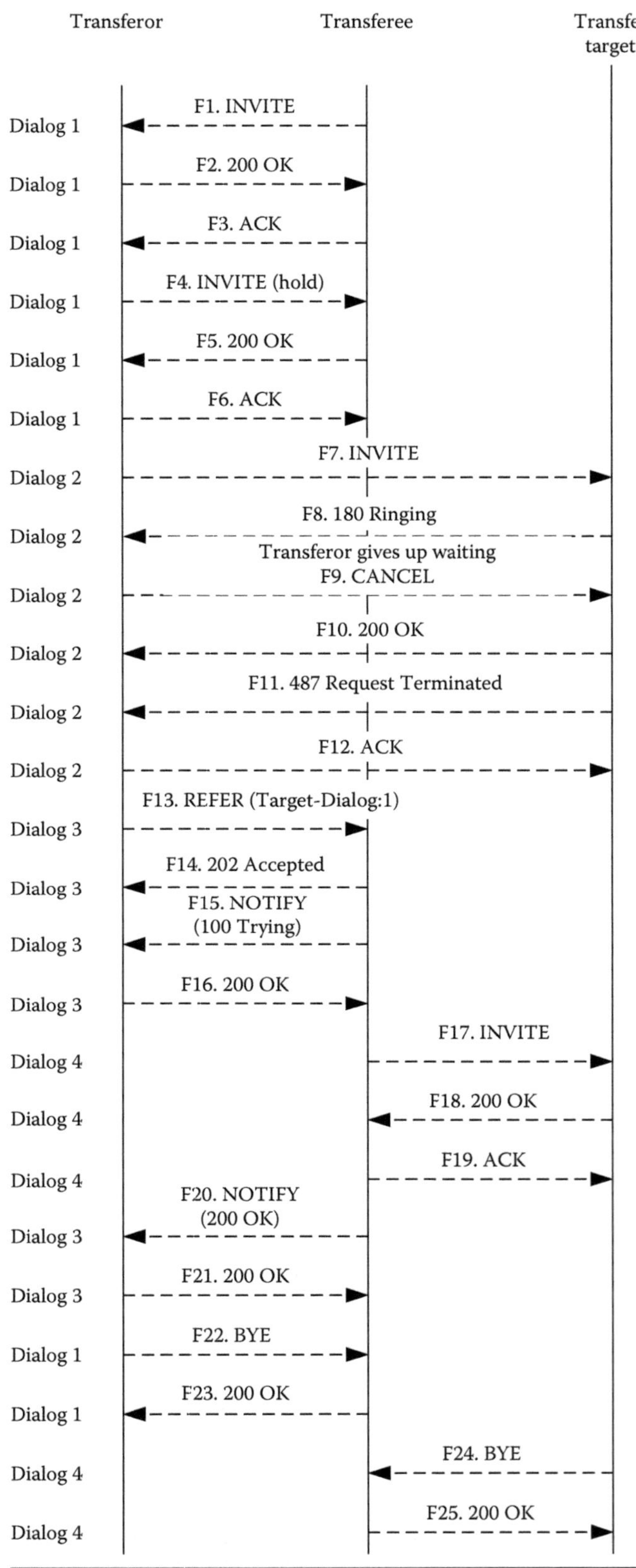

Figure 16.12 Semi-attended transfer as blind transfer call flow (not recommended). (Copyright IETF. Reproduced with permission.)

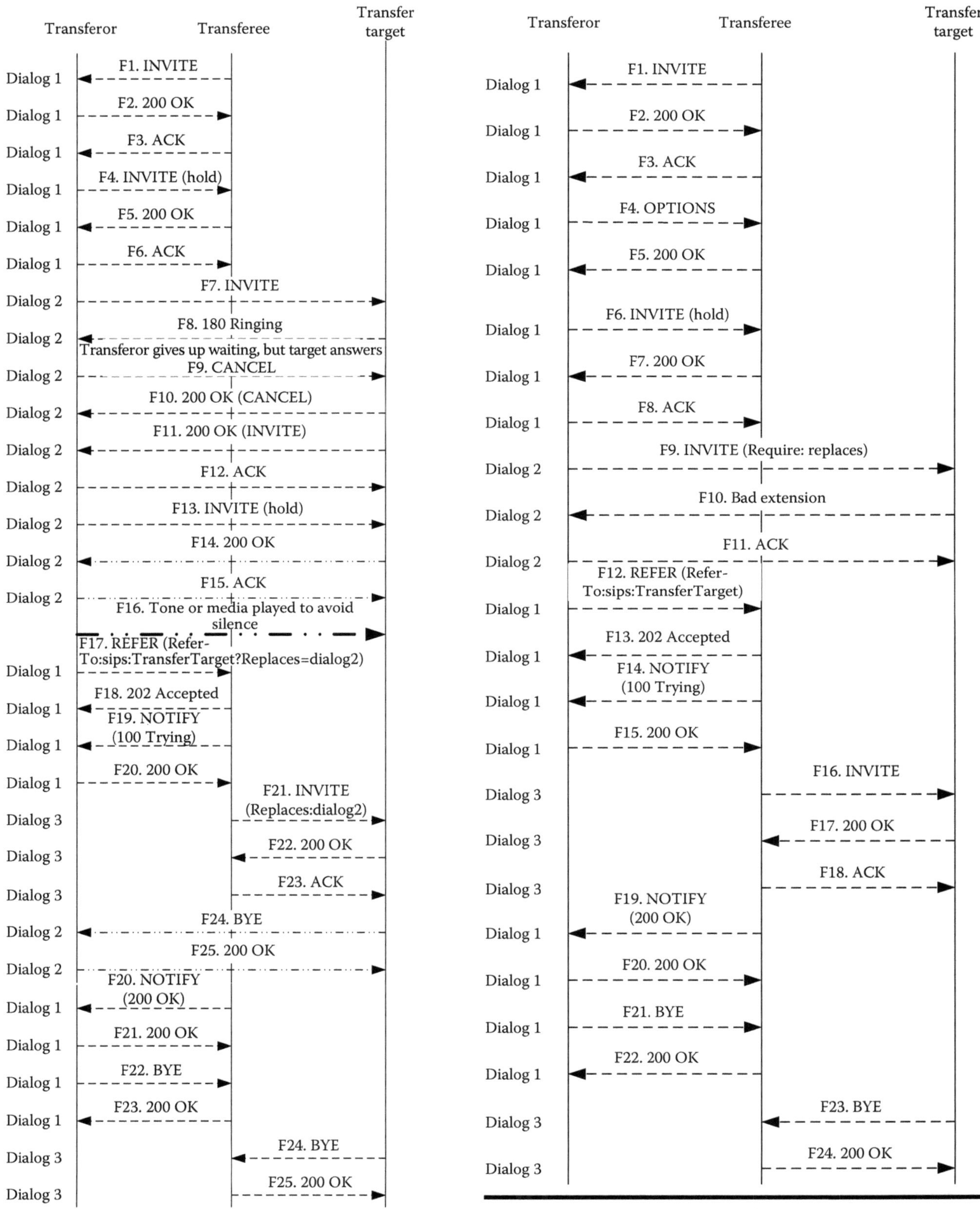

Figure 16.13 Semi-attended transfer as attended transfer call flow (not recommended). (Copyright IETF. Reproduced with permission.)

Figure 16.14 Attended transfer fallback to basic transfer using Require: replaces. (Copyright IETF. Reproduced with permission.)

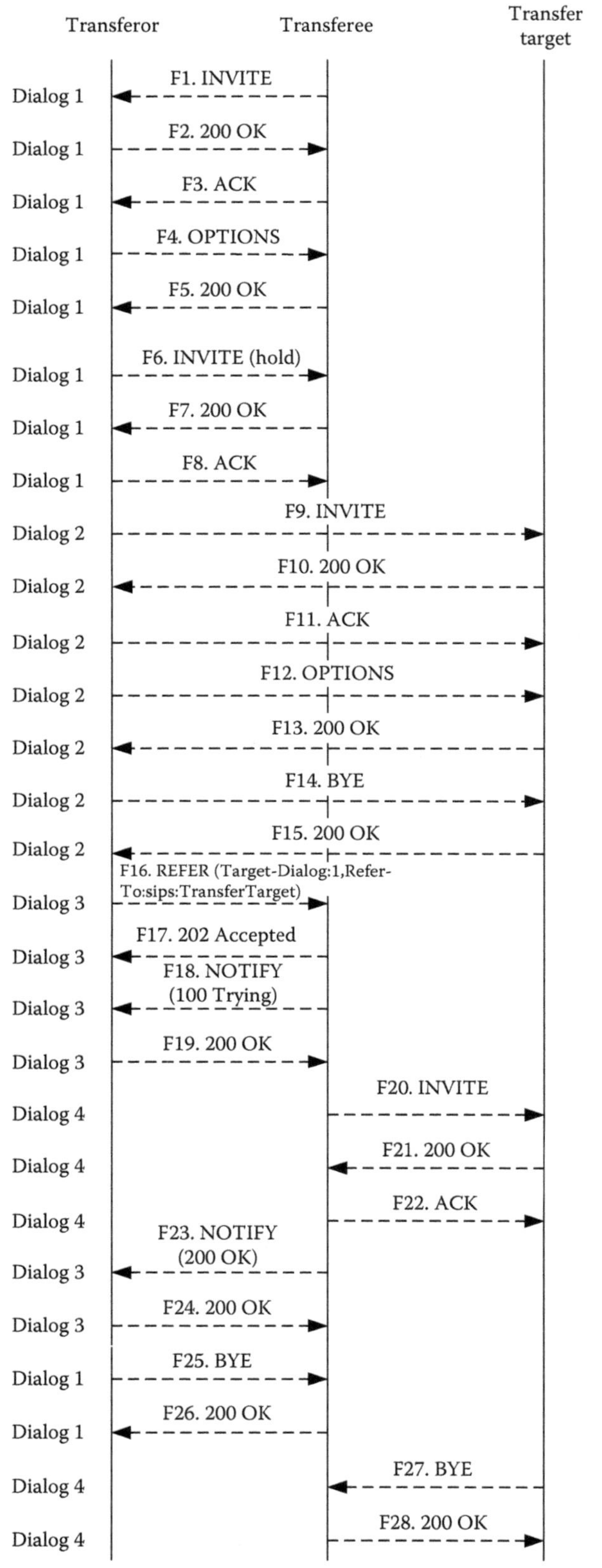

Figure 16.15 Attended transfer fallback to basic transfer. (Copyright IETF. Reproduced with permission.)

support either REFER or Replaces, making attended transfer impossible. The Transferor then ends dialog 2 by sending a BYE, then sends a REFER to the Transferee using the AOR URI of the Transfer Target.

16.2.7 Transfer with Referred-By

In the previous examples, the Transfer Target does not have definitive information about what party initiated the transfer, or, in some cases, even that transfer is taking place. The Referred-By mechanism (RFC 3892, see Section 2.8) provides a way for the Transferor to provide the Transferee with a way to let the Transfer Target know what party initiated the transfer. The simplest and least secure approach just involves the inclusion of the Referred-By header field in the REFER, which is then copied into the triggered INVITE. However, a more secure mechanism involves the Referred-By security token, which is generated and signed by the Transferor and passed in a message body to the Transferee then to the Transfer Target. The call flow in Figure 16.16 shows the Referred-By header field and body in the REFER F5 and triggered INVITE F6. Note that the Secure/Multipurpose Internet Mail Extensions (S/MIME) (see Section 2.8) signature is not shown in the example below. The conventions used in the SIP Torture Test Messages (RFC 4475) document are reused, specifically the <hex> and <allOneLine> tags.

F5 REFER Transferor -> Transferee

```
REFER sips:3ld812adkjw@biloxi.example.
com;gr=3413kj2ha SIP/2.0
Via: SIP/2.0/TLS pc33.atlanta.example.
com;branch=z9hG4bK392039842
Max-Forwards: 70
To: <sips:3ld812adkjw@biloxi.example.
com;gr=3413kj2ha>
From: <sips:transferor@atlanta.example.com>
;tag=1928301774
Call-ID: a84b4c76e66710
CSeq: 314160 REFER
<allOneLine>
       Refer-To: <sips:482n4z24kdg@chicago.
       example.com;gr=8594958
       ?Replaces=090459243588173445%
       3Bto-tag%3D9m2n3wq%3Bfrom-tag
       %3D763231&Require=replaces>
</allOneLine>
Supported: gruu, replaces, tdialog
Require: tdialog
Referred-By: <sips:transferor@atlanta.
example.com>
       ;cid="20398823.2UWQFN309shb3@atlanta.
example.com"
```

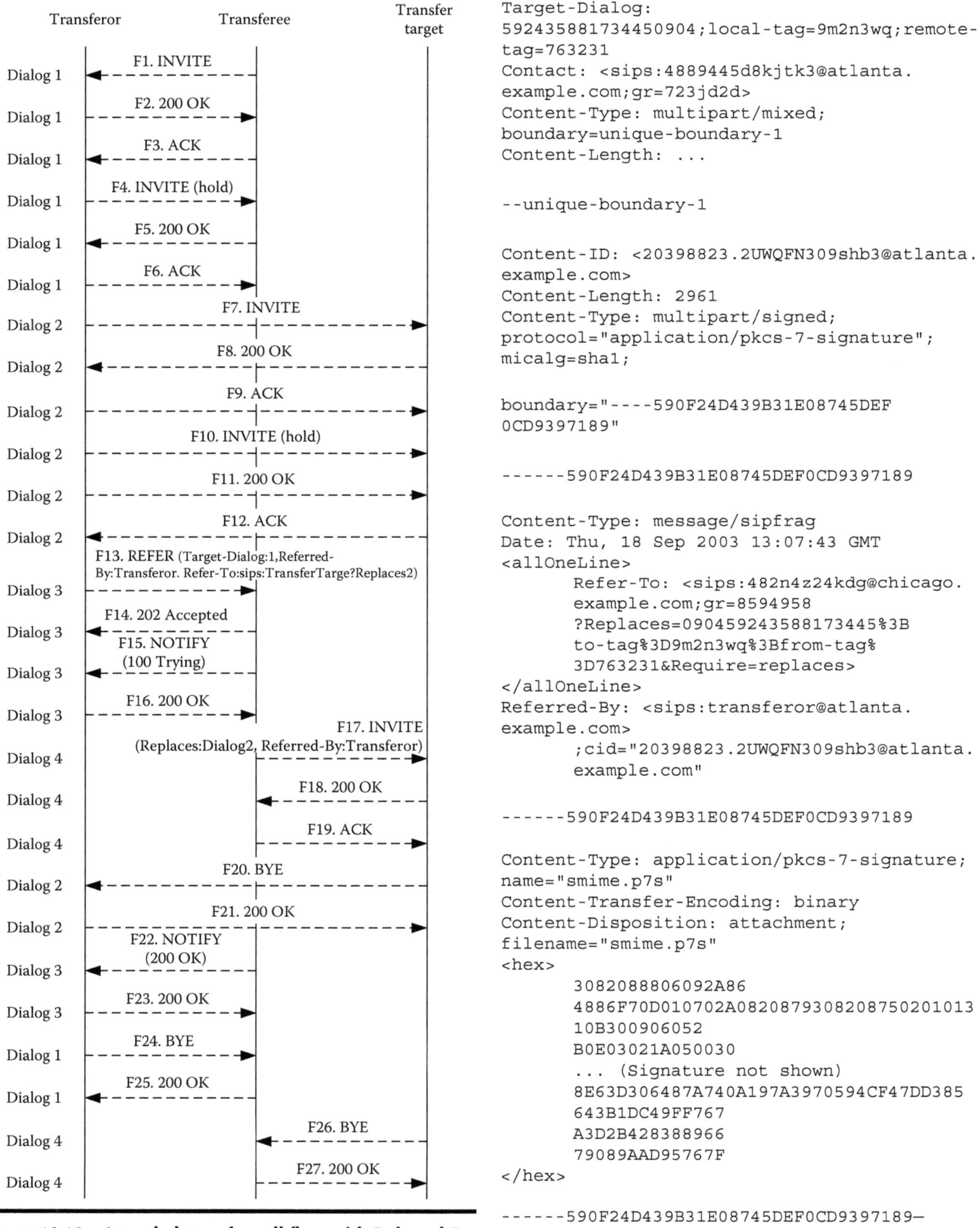

Figure 16.16 Attended transfer call flow with Referred-By. (Copyright IETF. Reproduced with permission.)

```
Target-Dialog:
592435881734450904;local-tag=9m2n3wq;remote-
tag=763231
Contact: <sips:4889445d8kjtk3@atlanta.
example.com;gr=723jd2d>
Content-Type: multipart/mixed;
boundary=unique-boundary-1
Content-Length: ...

--unique-boundary-1

Content-ID: <20398823.2UWQFN309shb3@atlanta.
example.com>
Content-Length: 2961
Content-Type: multipart/signed;
protocol="application/pkcs-7-signature";
micalg=sha1;

boundary="----590F24D439B31E08745DEF
0CD9397189"

------590F24D439B31E08745DEF0CD9397189

Content-Type: message/sipfrag
Date: Thu, 18 Sep 2003 13:07:43 GMT
<allOneLine>
       Refer-To: <sips:482n4z24kdg@chicago.
       example.com;gr=8594958
       ?Replaces=090459243588173445%3B
       to-tag%3D9m2n3wq%3Bfrom-tag%
       3D763231&Require=replaces>
</allOneLine>
Referred-By: <sips:transferor@atlanta.
example.com>
       ;cid="20398823.2UWQFN309shb3@atlanta.
       example.com"

------590F24D439B31E08745DEF0CD9397189

Content-Type: application/pkcs-7-signature;
name="smime.p7s"
Content-Transfer-Encoding: binary
Content-Disposition: attachment;
filename="smime.p7s"
<hex>
       3082088806092A86
       4886F70D010702A0820879308208750201013
       10B300906052
       B0E03021A050030
       ... (Signature not shown)
       8E63D306487A740A197A3970594CF47DD385
       643B1DC49FF767
       A3D2B428388966
       79089AAD95767F
</hex>

------590F24D439B31E08745DEF0CD9397189–

--unique_boundary-1
```

F6 INVITE Transferee -> Transfer Target

```
INVITE sips:482n4z24kdg@chicago.example.
com;gr=8594958 SIP/2.0
Via: SIP/2.0/TLS referee.example;branch=z9hG4
bKffe209934aac
To: <sips:482n4z24kdg@chicago.example.
com;gr=8594958>
From: <sips:transferee@biloxi.example.com>
;tag=2909034023
Call-ID: fe9023940-a3465@referee.example
CSeq: 889823409 INVITE
Max-Forwards: 70
Contact: <sips:3ld812adkjw@biloxi.example.
com;gr=3413kj2ha>
Referred-By: <sips:transferor@atlanta.
example.com>
       ;cid="20398823.2UWQFN309shb3@atlanta.
       example.com"
Replaces:090459243588173445;to-
tag=9m2n3wq;fromtag=76323
Require: replaces
Supported: gruu, replaces, tdialog
Content-Type: multipart/mixed;
boundary=my-boundary-9
Content-Length: ...

--my-boundary-9

Content-Type: application/sdp
Content-Length: 156

v=0
o=referee 2890844526 2890844526 IN IP4
referee.example
s=Session SDP
c=IN IP4 referee.example
t=0 0
m=audio 49172 RTP/AVP 0
a=rtpmap:0 PCMU/8000

--my-boundary-9

Content-Length: 2961
Content-Type: multipart/signed;
protocol="application/pkcs-7-signature";
micalg=sha1;

boundary="----590F24D439B31E08745DEF
0CD9397189"

------590F24D439B31E08745DEF0CD9397189

Content-Type: message/sipfrag
Date: Thu, 18 Sep 2003 13:07:43 GMT
<allOneLine>
       Refer-To: <sips:transfertarget@
       chicago.example.com;
       Replaces=090459243588173445%3B
       to-tag%3D9m2n3wq%3Bfrom-tag%
       3D763231&Require=replaces>
</allOneLine>
Referred-By: <sips:transferor@atlanta.
example.com>
       ;cid="20398823.2UWQFN309shb3@atlanta.
       example.com"

------590F24D439B31E08745DEF0CD9397189

Content-Type: application/pkcs-7-signature;
name="smime.p7s"
Content-Transfer-Encoding: binary
Content-Disposition: attachment;
filename="smime.p7s"
<hex>
       3082088806092A86
       4886F70D010702A082087930820875020101310
       B300906052
       B0E03021A050030
       ... (Signature not shown)
       8E63D306487A740A197A3970594CF47DD38564
       3B1DC49
       FF767A3D2B428388966
       79089AAD95767F
</hex>

------590F24D439B31E08745DEF0CD9397189–

--my-boundary-9--
```

16.2.8 Transfer as an Ad Hoc Conference

In this flow, shown in Figure 16.17, Bob does an attended transfer of Alice to Carol. To keep both Alice and Carol fully informed of the nature and state of the transfer operation, Bob acts as a focus (RFC 4579, see Sections 2.2 and 2.4.4.1) and hosts an ad hoc conference involving Alice, Bob, and Carol. Alice and Carol subscribe to the conference package (RFC 4575) of Bob's focus, which allows them to know the exact status of the operation. After the transfer operation is complete, Bob deletes the conference. This call flow meets requirement 6 as described earlier. NOTIFY messages related to the refer package are indicated as NOTIFY (refer), while NOTIFYs related to the Conference INFO Package are indicated as NOTIFY (Conf-Info). Note that any type of semi-attended transfer in which media mixing or relaying could be implemented using this model. In addition to simply mixing, the focus could introduce additional media signals such as simulated ringtone or on-hold announcements to improve the user experience.

16.2.9 Transfer with Multiple Parties

In this example, shown in Figure 16.18, the Originator places a call to the Facilitator who reaches the Recipient through the Screener. The Recipient's contact information is exposed to the Facilitator and the Originator. This example

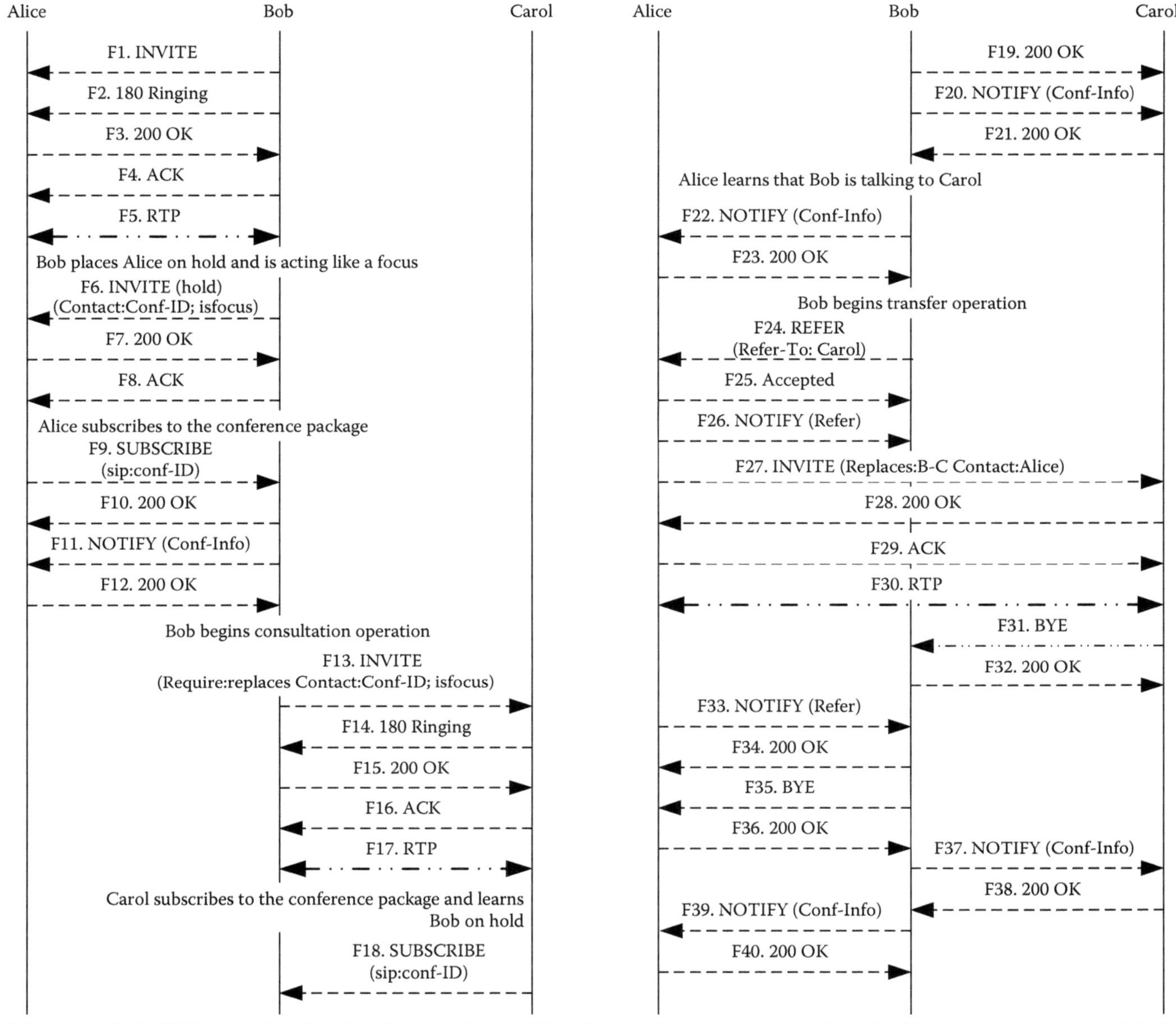

Figure 16.17 Attended transfer as an ad hoc conference. (Copyright IETF. Reproduced with permission.)

is provided for clarification of the semantics of the REFER method only, and it should not be used as the design of an implementation.

16.2.10 Gateway Transfer Issues

A gateway in SIP acts as a UA. As a result, the entire preceding discussion and call flows apply equally well to gateways as native SIP end points. However, there are some gateway-specific issues that are documented in this section. While this discussion focuses on the common cases involving PSTN gateways, similar situations exist for other gateways, such as H.323/SIP gateways.

16.2.10.1 Coerce Gateway Hairpins to the Same Gateway

To illustrate how a hairpin situation can occur in transfer, consider this example. The original call dialog is setup with the Transferee residing on the PSTN side of a SIP gateway. The Transferor is a SIP phone purely in the IP space. The Transfer Target is on the PSTN side of a SIP gateway as well. After completing the transfer (regardless of consultative or blind), the Transferee is in a call with the Transfer Target (both on the PSTN side of a gateway). It is often desirable to remove the gateway(s) out of the loop. This is likely to only be possible if both legs of the target call are on the same

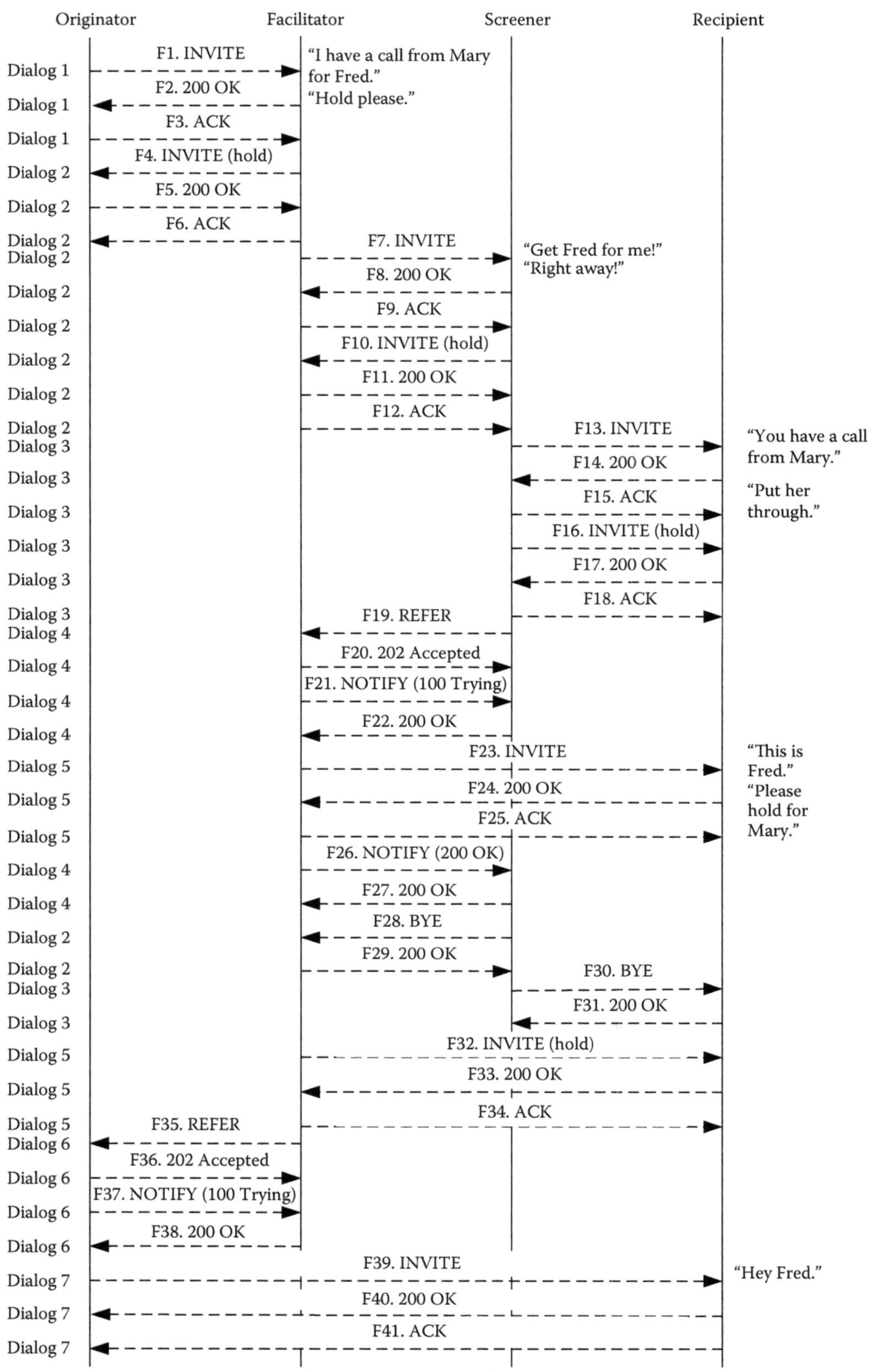

Figure 16.18 Transfer with multiple parties: example. (Copyright IETF. Reproduced with permission.)

gateway. With both legs on the same gateway, it may be able to invoke the analogous transfer on the PSTN side. Then, the target call would not involve the gateway.

Thus, the problem is how to give the proxy enough information so that it knows to route the call to the same gateway. With a simple single call that hairpins, the incoming and outgoing leg have the same dialog. The proxy should have enough information to optimize the routing. In the consultative transfer scenario, it is desirable to coerce the consultative INVITE out the same gateway as the original call to be transferred. However, there is no way to relate the consultation with the original call. In the consultative case, the target call INVITE includes the Replaces header, which contains dialog information that can be used to relate it to the consultation. However, there is no information that relates the target call to the original. In the blind transfer scenario, it is desirable to coerce the target call onto the same gateway as the original call. However, the same problem exists in that the target dialog cannot be related to the original dialog.

In either transfer scenario, it may be desirable to push the transfer operation onto the non-SIP side of the gateway. Presumably, this is not possible unless all of the legs go out the same gateway. If the gateway supports more than one trunk group, it might also be necessary to get all of the legs on the same trunk group in order to perform the transfer on the non-SIP side of the gateway. Solutions to these gateway-specific issues may involve new extensions to SIP in the future.

16.2.10.2 Consultative-Turned-Blind Gateway Glare

In the consultative transfer case turned blind, there is a glare-like problem. The Transferor initiates the consultation INVITE; the Transferor gets impatient and hangs up, transitioning this to a blind transfer. The Transfer Target on the gateway (connected through a PSTN switch to a single line or dumb analog phone) rings. The user answers the phone just after the CANCEL is received by the Transfer Target. The REFER and INVITE for the target call are sent. The Transferee attempts to set up the call on the PSTN side, but gets either a busy response or lands in the user's voice mail as the user has the handset in hand and off hook. This is another example of a race condition that this call flow can cause. The recommended behavior is to use the approach described earlier.

16.2.11 Call Services with Shared Appearances of a SIP AOR

RFC 7463 that is described here specifies the requirements and implementation of a group telephony feature commonly known as Bridged Line Appearance (BLA) or Multiple Line Appearance (MLA), or Shared Call/Line Appearance (SCA). When implemented using the SIP, it is referred to as shared appearances of an AOR since SIP does not have the concept of lines. This feature is commonly offered in IP Centrex services and IP Private Branch Exchange (IPBX) offerings, and is likely to be implemented on SIP IP telephones and SIP feature servers used in a business environment. This feature allows several UAs to share a common AOR, learn about calls placed and received by other UAs in the group, and pick up or join calls within the group. A variant of this feature is known as Single Line Extension. This specification discusses use cases, lists requirements, and defines extensions to implement this feature. This specification updates RFCs 3261 and 4235.

In traditional telephony, the line is physical. A common scenario in telephony is for a number of business telephones to share a single or a small number of lines. The sharing or appearance of these lines between a number of phones is what gives this feature its name. A common scenario in SIP is for a number of business telephones to share a single or a small number of AOR URIs. In addition, an AOR can have multiple appearances on a single UA in terms of the user interface. The appearance number relates to the user interface for the telephone; typically, each appearance of an AOR has a visual display (lamp that can change color or blink or a screen icon) and a button (used to select the appearance) where each appearance number is associated with a different dialog to/from the AOR. The telephony concept of line appearance is still relevant to SIP due to the user interface considerations. It is important to keep the appearance number construct because

1. Human users are used to the concept and will expect it in replacement systems (e.g., an overhead page announcement says, "Joe, pick up line 3").
2. It is a useful structure for user interface representation.

The purpose of the appearance number is to identify active calls to facilitate sharing between users (e.g., passing a call from one user to another). If a telephone has enough buttons/lamps, the appearance number could be the positional sequence number of the button. If not, it may still be desirable to present the call state, but the appearance number should be displayed so that users know which call, for example, is on hold on which key. In this specification (RFC 7463), except for the usage scenarios in the next section, we will use the term *appearance* rather than *line appearance* since SIP does not have the concept of lines. Note that this does not mean that a conventional telephony user interface (lamps and buttons) must be used: implementations may use another metaphor as long as the appearance number is readily apparent to the user. Each AOR has a separate appearance numbering space. As a result, a given UA user interface may have multiple occurrences of the same appearance number, but they will be for different AORs.

16.2.11.1 Usage Scenarios

The following examples are common applications of the shared appearances feature and are mentioned here as informative use cases. All these example usages can be supported by the shared appearances feature described in this document. The main differences relate to the user interface considerations of the device.

Executive/Assistant Arrangement. The appearances on the executive's UA also appear on the assistant's UA. The assistant may answer incoming calls to the executive and then place the call on hold for the executive to pick up. The assistant can always see the state of all calls on the executive's UA.

16.2.11.1.1 Call Group

Users with similar business needs or tasks can be assigned to specific groups and share an AOR. For example, an IT department staff of five might answer a help line that has three appearances on each phone in the IT work area. A call answered on one phone can be put on hold and picked up on another phone. A shout or an instant message (IM) to another staff member can result in them taking over a call on a particular appearance. Another phone can request to be added/joined/bridged to an existing appearance resulting in a conference call.

Single Line Extension. In this scenario, incoming calls are offered to a group of UAs. When one answers, the other UAs are informed. If another UA in the group seizes the line (i.e., goes off hook), it is immediately bridged or joined in with the call. This mimics the way residential telephone extensions usually operate.

16.2.11.1.2 Changing UAs

A user is on a call on one UA and wishes to change devices and continue the call on another UA. They place the call on hold, note the appearance number of the call, then walk to another UA. They are able to identify the same appearance number on the other UA, pick up the call, and continue the conversation.

16.2.11.2 Shared Appearance Implementation

The following list describes the operation of the shared appearances feature.

1. A UA is configured with the AOR of a shared appearance group. It registers against the AOR, then attempts a dialog state subscription to the AOR. If the subscription fails, loops back to itself, or returns an error, it knows there is no State Agent and hence no Appearance Agent, and this feature is not implemented.
2. If the subscription receives a 200 OK, the UA knows there is a State Agent and that the feature is implemented. The UA then follows the steps in this list.
3. Information learned about the dialog state of other UAs in the group is rendered to the user.
4. Incoming calls are forked to all UAs in the group, and any may answer. UAs receive the appearance number to use in rendering the incoming call in a NOTIFY from the Appearance Agent and in the INVITE itself. The UA will also receive a notification if the call is answered by another UA in the group so this information can be rendered to the user.
5. For outgoing calls, the operation depends on the implementation. If the user seizes a particular appearance number for the call, the UA publishes the trying state dialog information with the desired appearance number and waits for a 2xx response before sending the INVITE.
6. For outgoing calls, if the user does not seize a particular appearance or does not care, the INVITE can be sent immediately, and the appearance number learned as the call progresses from a notification from the Appearance Agent.
7. For outgoing calls, if the user does not want an appearance number assigned, such as during a consultation call or if a UA is fetching *service media* such as music on hold (RFC 7088), the UA also publishes before sending the INVITE but does not include an appearance number in the publication.
8. Established calls within the group may be joined (bridged) or taken (picked) by another UA. Information in the dialog package notifications can be used to construct Join or Replaces header fields. Since the same appearance number is used for these types of operations, this information is published before sending the INVITE Join or INVITE Replaces.
9. The Appearance Agent may not have direct access to the complete dialog state of some or all of the UAs in the group. If this is the case, the Appearance Agent will subscribe to the dialog state of individual UAs in the group to obtain this information. In any case, the Appearance Agent will send normal notifications (via the subscriptions established by the UAs in step 1) every time the aggregate dialog state of the AOR changes, including when calls are placed, answered, placed on and off hold, and hung up.

16.2.11.3 Definitions

RFC 7463 normatively defines three new terminologies as follows: Appearance Number, Seizing, and Selecting (or Not-Seizing). The detail of these definitions is provided in

Section 2.2. In addition, the functional elements that are required for implementation of the system to implement services specific to the Shared Appearances of a SIP AOR consists of

1. UAs that support publications, subscriptions, and notifications for the SIP dialog event package, and the shared appearance dialog package extensions and behavior.
2. An Appearance Agent consisting of a State Agent for the dialog event package that implements an Event State Compositor (see Section 5.2) and the shared appearance dialog package extensions and behavior. The Appearance Agent also has logic for assigning and releasing appearance numbers and resolving appearance number contention.
3. A forking proxy server that can communicate with the State Agent.
4. A registrar that supports the registration event package. The behavior of these elements is described normatively in the following sections after the definitions of the dialog package extensions.

16.2.11.4 Shared Appearance Dialog Package Extensions

RFC 7463 normatively defines four new elements described below in the subsections as extensions to the SIP Dialog Event package (RFC 4235), and the schema is defined in the next section. The elements are <appearance>, <exclusive>, <joined-dialog>, and <replaced-dialog>, which are subelements of the <dialog> element. The detailed description of the extended event package is provided in this specification (RFC 7463). RFC 7463 also describes user interfaces for the Shared Appearance/AOR, Interoperability with Non-Shared Appearance UA server (UAS), and call flows. We have not included these here for the sake of brevity.

16.2.11.5 Alert-Info Appearance Parameter Definition

This specification (RFC 7463) extends RFC 3261 to add an appearance parameter to the Alert-Info header field and also to allow proxies to modify or delete the Alert-Info header field. The changes to the augmented Backus–Naur Form (ABNF) in RFC 3261 (also see Section 2.4.1) are

```
alert-param       = LAQUOT absoluteURI RAQUOT
                    *(SEMI(generic-param/
                    appearance-param))
appearance-param  = "appearance" EQUAL 1*DIGIT
```

A proxy inserting an appearance Alert-Info parameter follows normal Alert-Info policies. To indicate the appearance number for this dialog, the proxy adds the Alert-Info header field with the appearance parameter to the INVITE. If an Alert-Info is already present, the proxy adds the appearance parameter to the Alert-Info header field. If an appearance number parameter is already present (associated with another AOR or by mistake), the value is rewritten adding the new appearance number. There must not be more than one appearance parameter in an Alert-Info header field.

If no special ringtone is desired, a normal ringtone should be indicated using the urn:alert:service:normal in the Alert-Info, as per RFC 7462. The appearance number present in an Alert-Info header field should be rendered by the UA to the user, following the guidelines of RFC 7463. If the INVITE is forwarded to another AOR, the appearance parameter in the Alert-Info should be removed before forwarding outside the group. The determination as to what value to use in the appearance parameter can be done at the proxy that forks the incoming request to all the registered UAs.

There is a variety of ways the proxy can determine what value it should use to populate this parameter. For example, the proxy could fetch this information by initiating a SUBSCRIBE (see Section 5.2) request with Expires: 0 to the Appearance Agent for the AOR to fetch the list of lines that are in use. Alternatively, it could act like a UA that is a part of the shared appearance group and SUBSCRIBE to the State Agent like any other UA. This would ensure that the active dialog information is available without having to poll on a need basis. It could keep track of the list of active calls for the appearance AOR based on how many unique INVITE requests it has forked to or received from the appearance AOR. Another approach would be for the Proxy to first send the incoming INVITE to the Appearance Agent, which would redirect to the shared appearance group URI and escape the proper Alert-Info header field for the Proxy to recurse and distribute to the other UAs in the group. The Appearance Agent needs to know about all incoming requests to the AOR in order to seize the appearance number. One way in which this could be done is for the Appearance Agent to register against the AOR with a higher *q*-value. This will result in the INVITE being sent to the Appearance Agent first, then being offered to the UAs in the group.

RFC 7463 registers the two SIP header fields defining new parameters as shown below through Internet Assigned Numbers Authority (IANA) registration:

Header Field	*Parameter Name*	*Predefined Values*	*Reference*
Event	shared	No	RFC 7463
Alert-Info	appearance	No	RFC 7463

16.2.12 Completion of Call Services in SIP

The *completion of calls* feature defined in RFC 6910 that is described here allows the caller of a failed call to be notified when the callee becomes available to receive a call. For the realization of a basic solution without queuing, this document references the usage of the dialog event package (RFC 4235) that is described as Automatic Redial in "Session Initiation Protocol Service Examples" (RFC 5359). For the realization of a more comprehensive solution with queuing, this specification (RFC 6910) introduces an architecture for implementing these features in the SIP where completion-of-calls implementations associated with the caller's and callee's end points cooperate to place the caller's request for completion of calls into a queue at the callee's end point; when a caller's request is ready to be serviced, reattempt of the original, failed call is then made. The architecture is designed to interoperate well with existing completion of call solutions in other networks. Note that RFC 6910 describes in detail the caller's agent and callee's monitor behavior along with the call completion event package in great detail. However, we have not addressed those for the sake of brevity. Instead, we have described some examples for basic call flows in explaining the call completion services.

For the purpose of this service, RFC 6910 has defined the following terminology: callee, caller, callee's monitor, caller's agent, completion of calls (CC), CC activation, CC to busy subscriber (CCBS), CC on no reply (CCNR), CC call, CC indicator, CC recall, CC recall events, CC recall timer, CC request, CC service duration timer, CC queue, CC entity (CCE), failed call, original call, retain option, Signaling System 7 (SS7), CC on not logged-in (CCNL), and subscriber (see Section 2.2).

16.2.12.1 Solution

16.2.12.1.1 Completion of Call Architecture

The CC architecture augments each caller's UA (or UA client [UAC]) wishing to use the CC features with a CC agent (also written as *caller's agent*). It augments each callee's UA (or UAS) wishing to be the target of the CC features with a CC monitor (also written as *callee's monitor*). The caller's agent and callee's monitor functions can be integrated into the respective UAs, be independent end systems, or be provided by centralized application servers. The two functions, though associated with the two UAs (caller and callee), also may be provided as services by the end points' home proxies or by other network elements. Though it is expected that a UA that implements CC will have both functions so that it can participate in CC as both caller and callee, the two functions are independent of each other. A caller's agent may service more than one UA as a collective group if a caller or population of users will be shared between the UAs, and especially if the UAs share an AOR. The caller's agent monitors calls made from the caller's UA(s) in order to determine their destinations and (potentially) their final response statuses, and the Call-Info header fields of provisional and final responses to invoke the CC feature. A callee's monitor may service more than one UA as a collective group if a callee or population of users will be shared between the UAs, and especially if the UAs share an AOR. The callee's monitor may supply the callee's UAS(s) with Call-Info header field values for provisional and final responses. The callee's monitor also instantiates a presence server used to monitor the caller's availability for CC recall.

The callees using the UA(s) may be able to indicate to the callee's monitor when they wish to receive CC calls. To allow flexibility and innovation, most of the interaction between the caller's agent, the caller(s) (user(s)), and the caller's UA(s) is out of the scope of this document. Similarly, most of the interaction between the callee's monitor, the callee(s), and the callee's UA(s) is out of the scope of this document, as is the policy by which the callee's monitor arbitrates between multiple CC requests. The caller's agent must be capable of performing a number of functions relative to the UA(s). The method by which it does so is outside the scope of this document. The callee's monitor must be capable of performing a number of functions relative to the UA(s). The method by which it does so is outside the scope of RFC 6910. As a proof of concept, simple caller's agents and callee's monitors can be devised that interact with users and UAs entirely through standard SIP mechanisms such as event framework (RFC 6665, see Section 5.2), secure shell (RFC 4235), and REFER (RFC 3515, see Section 2.5). The callers using the UA(s) can indicate to the caller's agent when they wish to avail themselves of CC for a recently made call that the callers determined to be unsuccessful.

The caller's agent monitors the status of the caller's UA(s) to determine when they are available to be used for a CC recall. The caller's agent can communicate to the caller's UA(s) that a CC recall is in progress, and inquire if the relevant caller is available for the CC recall. The callee's monitor may utilize several methods to monitor the status of the callee's UA(s) or their users for availability to receive a CC call. This can be achieved through monitoring calls made to the callee's UA(s) to determine the callee's status, the identity of callers, and the final responses for incoming calls. In a system with rich presence information, the presence information may directly provide this status. In a more restricted system, this determination can depend on the mode of the CC call in question, which is provided by the URI "m" parameter. For example, a UA is considered available for CCBS (m=BS) when it is not busy, but a UA is considered available for CCNR (m=NR) when it becomes not busy after being busy with an established call. The callee's monitor maintains information about the set of INVITEs received by the callee's UA(s) considered unsuccessful by the caller. In practice, the callee's monitor may remove knowledge about an incoming dialog from its set if local policy at the callee's monitor establishes that the dialog is no longer eligible for CC activations.

16.2.12.1.2 Completion of Call Procedures

The caller's UA sends an INVITE to a request-URI. One or more forks of this request reach one or more of the callee's UAs. If the CC feature is available, the callee's monitor (note there can be a monitor for each of the callee's UAs) inserts a Call-Info header field with its URI and with purpose=call-completion in appropriate non-100 provisional or final responses to the initial INVITE and forwards them to the caller. The provisional response should be sent reliably if the INVITE contained a Supported header field with the option tag 100rel. On receipt of a non-100 provisional or a final response with the indication that the CC feature is available, the calling user can invoke the CC feature.

The caller indicates to the caller's agent that he wishes to invoke CC services on the recent call. Note that from the SIP point of view, the INVITE may have been successful, but from the user's point of view, the call may have been unsuccessful. For example, the call may have connected to the callee's voice mail, which would return a 200 status to the INVITE but from the caller's point of view is *no reply*. To receive information necessary for the caller to complete the call at the callee, the caller's agent subscribes to the call-completion event package at the callee's monitor.

The possibility of the caller completing the call at the callee is also known as the CC state (cc-state) of the caller. The cc-states comprehend the values *queued* and *ready* (for CC). To receive information from all destinations where the callee will be reachable, the caller's agent sends a SUBSCRIBE request for the call-completion event package to the original destination URI of the call, and to all known URIs of the callees' monitors (which are provided by Call-Info header fields in provisional and final responses to the INVITE). Each callee's monitor uses the subscription as an indication that the caller is interested in using the CC feature with regard to the particular callee.

Each callee's monitor keeps a list or queue of subscriptions from callers' agents, representing the requests from the callers' agents to the callee's monitor for CC services. These subscriptions are created, refreshed, and terminated according to the procedures of RFC 6665. Upon receiving a SUBSCRIBE request from the caller's agent, the callee's monitor instantiates a presence state for the caller's UA that can be modified by the caller's UA to indicate its availability for the CC call. Upon instantiation, the caller's presence status at the callee's monitor is *open*. When the callee's monitor determines that the callee or callee's UA is available for a CC call, it selects a caller to execute the CC call and sends a CC event update (cc-state: ready) via a NOTIFY request to the selected subscription of the caller's agent, telling it to begin the CC call to the callee's UA. When the caller's agent receives this update, it initiates a CC recall by calling the caller's UA and then starts the CC call to the callee's UA, using third-party call control (3PCC) procedures in accordance with RFC 3725 (see Section 18.3). The caller's agent can also check by other means whether the caller is available to initiate the CC call to the callee's UA. If the caller is available, the caller's agent directs the caller's UA to initiate the CC call to the callee's UA.

The caller's agent marks the CC call as such by adding a specific SIP URI parameter to the Request-URI, so it can be given precedence by the callee's monitor in reaching the callee's UA. If the caller is not available on receipt of the *ready for recall* notification, the caller's agent suspends the CC request at the callee's monitor by sending a PUBLISH request containing presence information to the presence server of the callee's monitor, informing the server that the presence status is *closed*. Once the caller becomes available for a CC call again, the caller's agent resumes the CC request by sending another PUBLISH request to the callee's monitor, informing the monitor that the presence status is open. On receipt of the suspension request, the callee's monitor performs the monitoring for the next nonsuspended CC request in the queue. On receipt of the resume from the previously suspended caller's agent that was at the top of the queue, the callee's monitor performs callee monitoring for this caller's agent.

When the CC call fails, there are two possible options: the CC feature has to be activated again by the caller's agent subscribing to the callee's monitor, or CC remains activated and the original CC request retains its position in the queue if the retain option is supported. The retain option (see Section 1.3) determines the behavior of the callee's monitor when a CC call fails. If the retain option is supported, CC remains activated, and the original CC request retains its position in the queue. Otherwise, the CC feature is deactivated, and the caller's agent would have to subscribe again to reactivate it. A monitor that supports the retain option provides the cc-service-retention header in its CC events. A caller's agent that also supports the retain option uses the presence of this header to know not to generate a new CC request after a failed CC call.

Monitors not supporting the retain option do not provide the cc-service-retention header. A failed CC call causes the CC request to be deleted from the queue, and these monitors will terminate the corresponding subscription of the caller's agent to inform that agent that its CC request is no longer in the queue. A caller's agent that does not support the retain option can also terminate its subscription when a CC call fails, so it is possible that both the caller's agent and the callee's monitor may be signaling the termination of the subscription concurrently. This is a normal SIP events (RFC 6665, see Section 5.2) scenario. After the subscription is terminated, the caller's agent may create a new subscription to reactivate the CC feature for the original call.

16.2.12.1.3 Automatic Redial as a Fallback

Automatic Redial is a simple end-to-end design. An Automatic Redial scenario is described in RFC 5359. This solution is based on the usage of the dialog event package. If the callee is busy when the call arrives, then the caller subscribes to the callee's call state. The callee's UA sends a notification when the callee's call state changes. This means the caller is also notified when the callee's call state changes to *terminated*. The caller is alerted, then the caller's UA starts a call establishment to the callee again. If several callers have subscribed to a busy callee's call state, they will be notified at the same time that the call state has changed to terminated. The problem with this solution is that it might happen that several recalls are started at the same time. This means it is a heuristic approach with no guarantee of success. There is no interaction between CC and Automatic Redial, as there is a difference in the behavior of the callee's monitor and the caller when using the dialog event package for receiving dialog information or for aggregating a CC state.

16.2.12.1.4 Differences from SS7

SIP CC differs in some ways from the CCBS and CCNR features of SS7, which is used in the PSTN. For ease of understanding, we enumerate some of the differences here. As there is no equivalent to the forking mechanism in SS7, in the PSTN, calls can be clearly differentiated as successful or unsuccessful. Owing to the complex forking situations that are possible in SIP, a call may fail from the point of view of the user and yet have a success response from SIP's point of view. (This can occur even in simple situations, e.g., a call to a busy user that falls over to his voice mail receives a SIP success response, even though the caller may consider it *busy subscriber*.) Thus, the caller must be able to invoke CC even when the original call appeared to succeed. To support this, the caller's agent must record successful calls as well as unsuccessful calls.

In SIP, only the caller's UA or service system on the originating side and the callee's UA or service system on the terminating side need to support CC for CC to work successfully between the UAs. Intermediate SIP systems (proxies or back-to-back user agents [B2BUAs]) do not need to implement CC; they only need to be transparent to the usual range of SIP messages. In the PSTN, additionally, intermediate nodes like media gateway controllers have to implement the CC service.

16.2.12.2 Completion of Call Queue Model

The callee's monitor manages CC for a single URI. This URI is likely to be a published AOR, or more likely non-voicemail AOR, but it may be as narrowly scoped as a single UA's contact URI. The callee's monitor manages a dynamic set of CC entities (called CCEs), which represent CC requests, or equivalently, the existing incoming CC subscriptions. This set is also called a queue, because a queue data structure often aids in implementing the policies of the callee's monitor for selecting CCEs for CC recall. Each CCE has an availability state, determined through the caller's presence status at the callee's monitor. A presence status of open represents a CCE's availability state of *available*, and a presence status of closed represents a CCE's availability state of *unavailable*. Each CCE has a recall state that is visible via subscriptions. The recall state is either *queued* or *ready*.

Each CCE carries the From URI of the SUBSCRIBE request that caused its creation. CC subscriptions arrive at the callee's monitor by addressing the URIs the callee's monitor returns in Call-Info header fields. The request-URI of the SUBSCRIBE request determines the queue to which the resulting CCE is added. The resulting subscription reports the status of the queue. The base event data is the status of all the CCEs in the queue, but the data returned by each subscription is filtered to report only the status of that subscription's CCE. (Further standardization may define means for obtaining more comprehensive information about a queue.) When a CCE is created, it is given the availability state available and recall state queued. When the callee's monitor receives Presence Information Data Format (PIDF) bodies (RFC 3863) via PUBLISH requests (RFC 3903, see Section 5.2), these PUBLISH requests are expected to be sent by subscribers to indirectly suspend and resume their CC requests by modifying its CCE availability state.

A CCE is identified by the request-URI (if it was taken from a CC event notification that identifies the CCE) or the From URI of the request (matching the From URI recorded in the CCE). Receipt of a PUBLISH with status open sets the availability state of the CCE to available (resume); status closed sets the availability state of the CCE to unavailable (suspend). A CC request is eligible for recall only when its CCE's availability state is available and the m value of the CCE also indicates an available state. The callee's monitor must not select for recall any CC requests that fail to meet those criteria. Within that constraint, the selections made by the callee's monitor are determined by its local policy. Often, a callee's monitor will choose the acceptable CCE that has been in the queue the longest.

When the callee's monitor has selected a CCE for recall, it changes the CCE's recall state from queued to ready, which triggers a notification on the CCE's subscription. If a selected subscriber then suspends its request by sending a PUBLISH with the presence status closed, the CCE becomes unavailable, and the callee's monitor changes the CCE's recall state to queued. This may cause another CCE (e.g., a CCE that has been in the queue for less time) to be selected for recall. The caller's presence status at the callee's monitor is terminated when the caller completes its CC call or when the subscription of the caller's agent at the callee's monitor is terminated.

16.2.12.3 Examples

A basic call flow, with only the most significant messages of a CC activation and invocation is shown in Figure 16.19 (please note that this is an example, and there may be variations in the failure responses).

The original call is an ordinary INVITE. It fails due to no-response (ring-no-answer). In this case, the callee's governing proxy generates a 487 response because the proxy canceled the INVITE to the UA when it rang too long without an answer. The 487 Request Terminated response carries a Call-Info header field with purpose=call-completion. The Call-Info header field positively indicates that CC is available for this failed fork of the call. The m=NR parameter indicates that it failed due to no-response, which is useful for PSTN interworking and assessing presence information in the callee's monitor. The URI in the Call-Info header field (<sip:456@z.b.com>) is where the caller's agent should subscribe for CC processing. Ideally, it is a globally routable URI for the callee's monitor. In practice, it may be the callee's AOR, and the SUBSCRIBE will be routed to the callee's monitor only because it specifies Event: call-completion. CC is activated by sending a SUBSCRIBE to all known callee's monitor URIs. These can be provided by the Call-Info header field in the response to the INVITE.

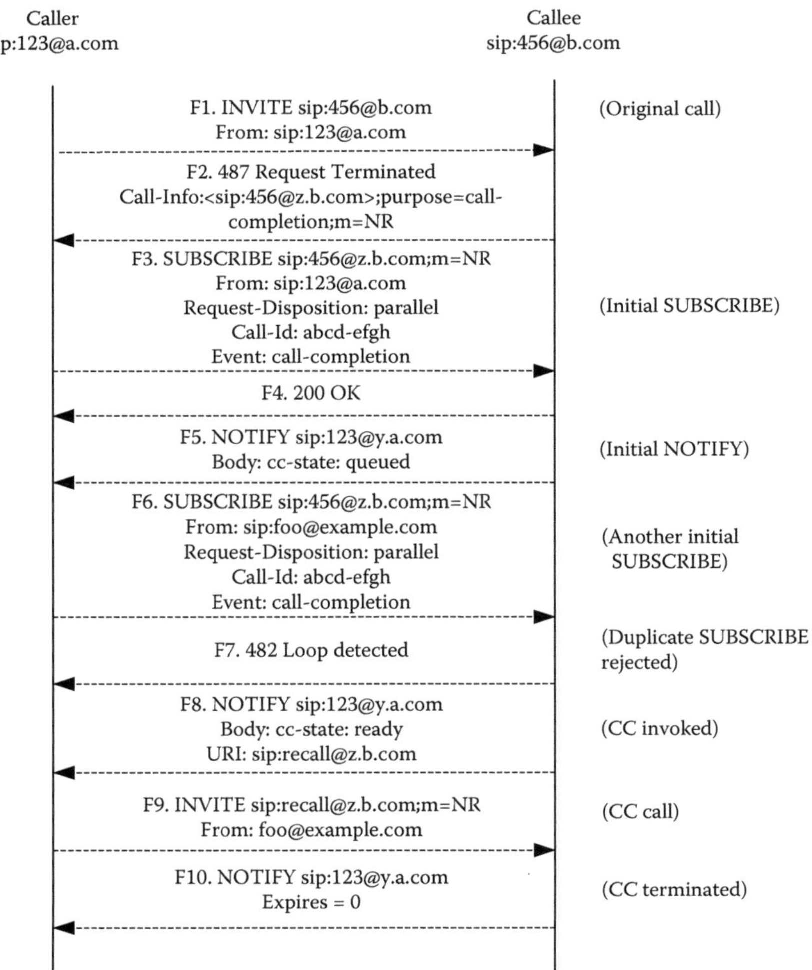

Figure 16.19 Basic call flow of CC activation and invocation (only the most significant messages). (Copyright IETF. Reproduced with permission.)

Additionally, the caller's agent needs to include the original request-URI in its set of callee's monitor URIs, because the call may have forked to additional callees whose responses the caller has not seen. (A SUBSCRIBE to the request-URI alone is used in cases where the caller's agent has not received or cannot remember any callee's monitor URI.) The caller's agent adds to these URIs an m parameter (if possible). In this case, the caller's agent forks the SUBSCRIBE to two destinations as defined by RFC 3261 (see Section 3.1.3.2.2), with appropriate Request-Disposition. The first SUBSCRIBE is to the URI from Call-Info. The second SUBSCRIBE is to the original request-URI and reaches the same callee's monitor. Because it has the same Call-Id as the SUBSCRIBE that has already reached the callee's monitor, the callee's monitor rejects it with a 482, thus avoiding redundant subscriptions.

The initial NOTIFY for the successful SUBSCRIBE has cc-state: queued in its body. Eventually, this caller is selected for CC and is informed of this via a NOTIFY containing cc-state: ready. This NOTIFY carries a URI to which the INVITE for the CC call should be sent. In practice, this may be the AOR of the callee. The caller generates a new INVITE to the URI specified in the NOTIFY, or if there was no such URI or if the caller's agent cannot remember it, it may use the original request-URI. The caller adds the m parameters (if possible), to specify CC processing. Finally, the subscription for the CC request is terminated by the callee's monitor.

Another flow, with only the most significant messages of CC suspension and resumption shown, is demonstrated in Figure 16.20.

The caller is selected for CC and is informed of this via a NOTIFY request containing cc-state: ready. At this time, the caller is not available for the CC recall. For updating its presence event state at the callee's presence server, the caller sends a PUBLISH request informing the presence server that the PIDF state is closed. The PUBLISH request is sent (in order of preference) as follows: (F1) out-of-dialog to the CC URI as received in the NOTIFY, (F2) within the corresponding SUBSCRIBE dialog, (F3) out-of-dialog to the corresponding callee's monitor URI received in the Call-Info header field of the NOTIFY, or (F4) out-of-dialog to the remote Contact address of the corresponding SUBSCRIBE dialog. When the caller is again available for the CC recall, the caller updates his presence event state at the callee's presence server by generating a PUBLISH request informing the

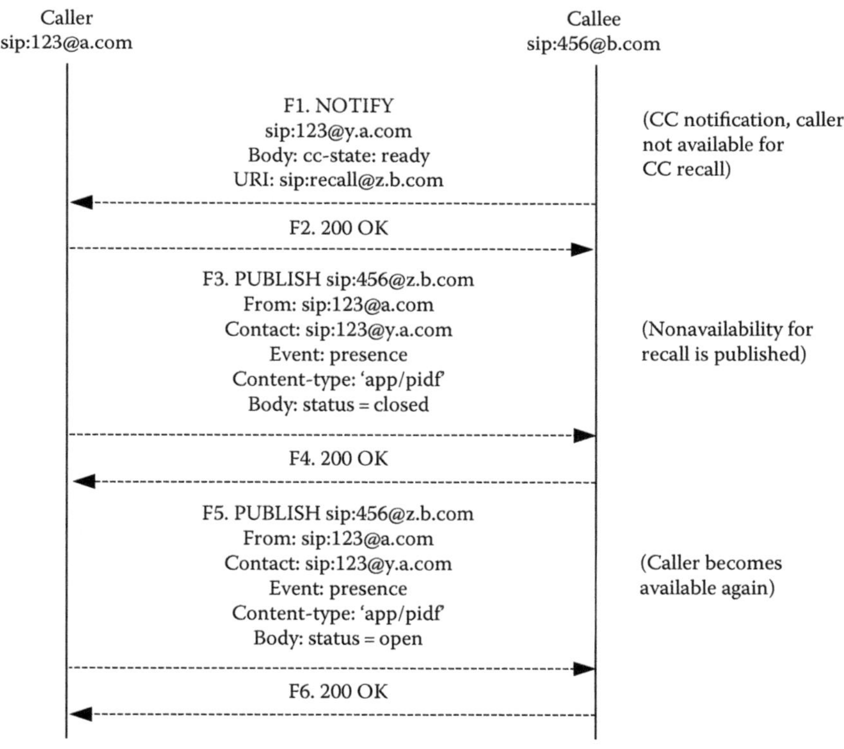

Figure 16.20 Basic call flow of CC suspension and resumption (only the most significant messages). (Copyright IETF. Reproduced with permission.)

server that the PIDF state is open; this request will otherwise be constructed in the same way as the suspended PUBLISH request.

16.2.12.4 IANA Considerations

16.2.12.4.1 SIP Event Package Registration for CC

This specification registers an event package, based on the registration procedures defined in RFC 6665 (see Section 5.2). The following information is required for such a registration:

Package name: call-completion
Is this registration for a Template-Package: No
Published specification: RFC 6910

16.2.12.4.2 MIME Registration for application/call-completion

MIME media type name: application.
MIME subtype name: call-completion.
Required parameters: None.
Optional parameters: None.
Encoding considerations: Consists of lines of UTF-8-encoded characters, ending with carriage return line feed (CRLF).
Security considerations: There are no security considerations internal to the media type. Its typical usage involves the security considerations described in RFC 6910.
Interoperability considerations: See RFC 6910.
Published specification: RFC 6910.
Applications that use this media type: Implementations of the CC features of the SIP.
Additional information:
Magic number(s): None.
File extension(s): Not expected to be stored in files.
Macintosh file type code(s): Not expected to be stored in files.
Person and e-mail address to contact for further information: Martin Huelsemann, martin.huelsemann@telekom.de.
Intended usage: LIMITED USE.
Restrictions on usage: None.
Author/Change controller: IETF.

16.2.12.4.3 SIP/SIPS URI Parameter m

This specification defines one new SIP/SIPS URI parameter m as per the registry created by RFC 3969. It is used to identify that an INVITE request is a CC call, or to further identify that a SUBSCRIBE request is for the call-completion event package. The parameter may have a value that describes the type of the CC operation, as described in this specification.

Name of the parameter: m
Predefined values: yes
Reference: RFC 6910

16.2.12.4.4 purpose Parameter Value call-completion

This specification adds a new predefined value *call-completion* for the *purpose* header field parameter of the Call-Info header field. This modifies the registry header field parameters and parameter values by adding this RFC as a reference to the line for header field Call-Info and parameter name purpose:

Header field: Call-Info
Parameter name: purpose
Predefined values: yes
Reference: RFC 3261, RFC 5367, and RFC 6910

16.2.12.4.5 m Header Parameter for Call-Info

This specification extends RFC 3261 to add a new header field parameter m to the Call-Info header field. This adds a row to the registry header field parameters and parameter values:

Header field: Call-Info
Parameter name: m
Predefined values: yes
Reference: RFC 6910
The predefined values are BS, NR.

16.3 Call Diversion Indication

16.3.1 Overview

We are describing an informational RFC 5806 that is an historical record, one proposed for call diversion indication capability in SIP. This capability was met in SIP by other proposed extensions in SIP, but we are discussing what could have been done using this alternative method should researchers find any interesting technical insights in the future. RFC 5806 proposed an extension to SIP. This extension would provide the ability for the called SIP UA to identify from whom the call was diverted and why the call was diverted. The extension defined a general header, Diversion, which conveys the diversion information from other SIP UAs and proxies to the called UA. This extension would allow enhanced support for various features, including

Unified Messaging, Third-Party Voice Mail, and Automatic Call Distribution (ACD). SIP UAs and SIP proxies that receive diversion information may use this as supplemental information for feature invocation decisions. RFC 5589 (see Section 16.2) provides similar services to call diversion indication using REFER, Refer-To, Referred-By, NOTIFY/SUBSCRIBE, and other methods and headers. Examples provided in this RFC may be compared with those of the call diversion indication described here.

16.3.2 Diversion and History-Info Header Interworking in SIP

Although the SIP History-Info header is the solution adopted in IETF, the nonstandard Diversion header is nevertheless widely implemented and used for conveying call-diversion-related information in SIP signaling. This document describes a recommended interworking guideline between the Diversion header and the History-Info header to handle call diversion information. In addition, an interworking policy is proposed to manage the headers' coexistence. The History-Info header is described in RFC 4244 (see Section 2.8) and the nonstandard Diversion header is described, as Historic, in RFC 5806 (see above, Section 16.3.1). Since the Diversion header is used in many existing network implementations for the transport of call diversion information, its interworking with the SIP History-Info standardized solution is needed. This work is intended to enable the migration from nonstandard implementations and deployment toward IETF specification-based implementations and deployment.

For some Voice over IP (VoIP)-based services (e.g., voice mail, Interactive Voice Recognition, or ACD), it is helpful for the called SIP UA to identify from whom and why the session was diverted. For this information to be used by various service providers or by applications, it needs to pass through the network. This is possible with two different SIP headers: the History-Info header defined in RFC 4244 (see Sections 2.4.1 and 2.8) and the historic Diversion header defined in RFC 5806 (see above, Section 16.3.1), which are both able to transport diversion information in SIP signaling. Although the Diversion header is not standardized, it is widely used. Therefore, it is useful to have guidelines make this header interwork with the standard History-Info header. Note that the new implementation and deployment of the Diversion header is strongly discouraged. RFC 6044 provides a mechanism for header-content translation between the Diversion header and the History-Info header.

16.3.2.1 Background

The History-Info header (RFC 4244, see Section 2.8) and its extension for forming SIP service URIs (including Voice-Mail URI) (RFC 4458, see Section 4.4) are recommended by the IETF to convey redirection information. They are also recommended in the Communication Diversion (CDIV) service Third Generation Partnership Project (3GPP) specification [10]. Originally, the Diversion header was described in a document that was submitted to the SIP Working Group. It has been published now as RFC 5806 (see above, Section 16.3.1) for the historical record and to provide a reference for this RFC 6044. This header contains a list of diverting URIs and associated information providing specific information as the reason for the call diversion. Most existing SIP-based implementations have implemented the Diversion header when no standard solution was ready to deploy.

The IETF has finally standardized the History-Info header, partly because it can transport general history information. This allows the receiving part to determine how and why the session is received. As the History-Info header may contain further information than call diversion information, it is critical to avoid losing information and be able to extract the relevant data using the retargeting cause URI parameter described in RFC 4458 (see Section 4.4) for the transport of the diversion reason. The Diversion header and the History-Info header have different syntaxes, described below. Note that the main difference is that the History-Info header is a chronological writing header, whereas the Diversion header applies a reverse chronology (i.e., the first diversion entry read corresponds to the last diverting user).

16.3.2.2 Problem Statement

16.3.2.2.1 Interworking Requirements and Scope

This section provides the baseline terminology used in the rest of the document and defines the scope of interworking between the Diversion header and the History-Info header. There are many ways in which SIP signaling can be used to modify a session destination before it is established, and there are many reasons for doing so. The behavior of the SIP entities that will have to further process the session downstream will sometimes vary depending on the reasons that lead to changing the destination, for example, whether it is for a simple proxy to route the session or for an application server to provide a supplementary service. The Diversion header and the History-Info header differ in the approach and scope of addressing this problem. For clarity, the following vocabulary is used in this document:

- Retargeting/redirecting: refers to the process of a proxy server/UAC changing a URI in a request and thus changing the target of the request. These terms are defined in RFC 4244. The History-Info header is used to capture retargeting information.
- Call forwarding/call diversion/communication diversion: these terms are equivalent and refer to the

CDIV supplementary services, based on the ISDN Communication diversion supplementary services and defined in 3GPP [10]. They are applicable to entities that are intended to modify the original destination of an IP multimedia session during or before the session establishment.

This document does not intend to describe when or how History-Info or Diversion headers should be used. Hereafter, we provide a clarification on the context in which interworking is required. The Diversion header has exactly the same scope as the call diversion service, and each header entry reflects a call diversion invocation. The Diversion header is used for recording call-forwarding information, which could be useful to network entities downstream. Today, this SIP header is implemented by several manufacturers and is deployed in networks.

The History-Info header is used to store all retargeting information, including call diversion information. In practice, the History-Info header (RFC 4244, see Section 2.8) is used to convey call-diversion-related information by using a cause URI parameter (RFC 4458, see Section 4.4) in the relevant entry. Note, however, that the use of cause URI parameter (RFC 4458) in a History-Info entry for a call diversion is specific to the 3GPP specification [10]. RFC 4458 focuses on retargeting toward a voice-mail server and does not specify whether the cause URI parameter should be added in a URI for other cases. As a consequence, implementations that do not use the cause URI parameter for call-forwarding information are not considered for the mapping described in this document. Nevertheless, some recommendations are given in the next sections on how to avoid the loss of nonmapped information at the boundary between a network region using the History-Info header and one using the Diversion header.

Since both headers address call-forwarding needs, diverting information could be mixed up or be inconsistent if both are present in an uncoordinated fashion in the INVITE request. Thus, the Diversion and History-Info headers must not independently coexist in the same session signaling. This document addresses how to convert information between the Diversion header and the History-Info header, and when and how to preserve both headers to cover additional cases. For the transportation of consistent diversion information downstream, it is necessary to make the two headers interwork. Interworking between the Diversion header and the History-Info header is introduced in Sections 2.1 and 2.2. Since the coexistence scenario may vary from one use case to another, guidelines regarding headers interaction are proposed.

16.3.2.2.2 Interworking Recommendations

Interworking function:

In a normal case, the network topology assumption is that the interworking described in this document should be performed by a specific SIP border device that is aware, by configuration, that it is at the border between two regions, one using History-Info header and one using Diversion header. As History-Info header is a standard solution, a network using the Diversion header must be able to provide information to a network using the History-Info header. In this case, to avoid header coexistence, it is required to replace, as often as possible, the Diversion header with the History-Info header in the INVITE request during the interworking. Since the History-Info header has a wider scope than the Diversion header, it may be used for other needs and services than call diversion.

In addition to trace call diversion information, the History-Info header also acts as a session history and can store all successive R-URI values. Consequently, even if it should be better to remove the History-Info header after the creation of the Diversion header to avoid confusion, the History-Info header must remain unmodified in the SIP signaling if it contains supplementary (nondiversion) information. It is possible to have History-Info headers that do not have values that can be mapped into the Diversion header. In this case, no interworking with the Diversion header should be performed, and it must be defined per implementation what to do in this case. This point is left out of the scope of this document. As a conclusion, it is recommended to have local policies minimizing the loss of information and find the best way to keep it up to the terminating UA. The following paragraphs describe the basic common use case.

SIP Network/Terminal Using Diversion to SIP Network/Terminal Using History-Info Header:

When the Diversion header is used to create a History-Info header, the Diversion header must be removed in the outgoing INVITE. It is considered that all of the information present in the Diversion header is transferred in the History-Info header. If a History-Info header is present in the incoming INVITE (in addition to Diversion header), the Diversion header and History-Info header present must be mixed, and only the diversion information not yet present in the History-Info header must be inserted as a last entry (more recent) in the existing History-Info header, as recommended in RFC 4244 (see Section 2.8).

SIP Network/Terminal Using History-Info Header to SIP Network/Terminal Using Diversion Header:

When the History-Info header is interpreted to create a Diversion header, some precautions must be taken. If the History-Info header contains only call-forwarding information, then it must be deleted after the interworking. If the History-Info header contains other information, then only the information of concern to the diverting user must be used to create entries in the Diversion header, and the History-Info header must be kept as received in the INVITE and forwarded downstream. Note that the History-Info header could be used for other reasons than call diversion services, for example, by a service that needs to know if a specific application server had been invoked in the signaling path.

If the call is later forwarded to a network using the History-Info header, it would be better not to lose history information due to passing though the network that only supports Diversion headers. A recommended solution must not disrupt the standard behavior, and networks that do not implement the History-Info header must be transparent to a received History-Info header. If a Diversion header is present in the incoming INVITE (in addition to the History-Info header), only diversion information present in the History-Info header but not in the Diversion header must be inserted from the last entry (more recent) into the existing Diversion header, as recommended in RFC 5806 (see above, Section 16.3.1). Note that the chronological order could not be certified. If previous policy recommendations are respected, this case should not happen.

Forking case:

The History-Info header enables the recording of sequential forking for the same served user. During an interworking, from the History-Info header to the Diversion header, the History-Info entries containing a forking situation (with an incremented *index* parameter) could possibly be mapped if it contains a call-forwarding *cause* parameter. The interworking entity could choose to create only a Diversion entry or not apply the interworking. The choice could be done according to a local policy. The same logic is applied for an interworking with Voice-Mail URI.

16.3.2.3 Header Syntax Reminders

16.3.2.3.1 History-Info Header Syntax

(Also see Section 2.4.1; reproduced here for convenience.)

```
History-Info        = "History-Info" HCOLON
                      hi-entry *(COMMA
                      hi-entry)
hi-entry            = hi-targeted-to-uri *(SEMI
                      hi-param)
hi-targeted-to-uri = name-addr
hi-param            = hi-index/hi-extension
hi-index            = "index" EQUAL 1*DIGIT
                      *(DOT 1*DIGIT)
hi-extension        = generic-param
```

The History-Info header is specified in RFC 4244 (see Sections 2.4.1 and 2.8). The topmost History-Info entry (first in the list) corresponds to the oldest history information. A hi-entry may contain a cause URI parameter expressing the diversion reason. This optional cause URI parameter is defined in RFC 4458 (see Section 4.4) with the following syntax:

```
cause-param="cause" EQUAL Status-Code
```

This parameter is also named cause-param and should be inserted in the History-Info entry (URI) of the diverted-to user in case of call diversion as recommended in the 3GPP CDIV specification [10]. The cause values used in the cause-param for the diverting reason are listed in the RFC 4458 (see Section 4.4), and because it is a parameter dedicated to call-forwarding service, its presence is used to determine that a hi-entry is a diverting user. More precisely, each diverting user is located in the hi-entry before the one containing a cause-param with a cause value as listed in RFC 4458. Moreover, the Reason header defined in RFC 3326 (see Section 2.8) should be escaped in the hi-entry of the diverting user when the call diversion is due to a received SIP response. The Reason header contains a cause parameter set to the true SIP response code received (Status-Code). Therefore, in case of call diversion due to a SIP response, both cause parameters should be used. The complexity is that these parameters could be used at the same time in the History-Info header but not in the same hi-entry and not with the same meaning. Only the cause-param is dedicated to call diversion service. The cause Reason header parameter is not taken into account in the mapping with a Diversion header.

RFC 4458 (see Section 4.4) also defines the *target* URI parameter, which could be inserted in a R-URI and consequently in the hi-targeted-to-uri. This parameter is used to keep the diverting user address in the downstream INVITE request in Voice-Mail URI implementation. As this information is already present in the hi-entries, the target URI parameter is not taken into account regarding the interworking with the Diversion header. From the Diversion header, it could be possible to create the target URI parameter in the hi-entries or in the R-URI; however, this possibility is based on local policies not described in this document. A Privacy header, as defined in RFC 3323 (see Section 20.2), could also be included in hi-entries with the *history* value defined in the RFC 4244 (see Sections 2.4.1 and 2.8). The index parameter is a string of digits, separated by dots, to indicate the number of forward hops and retargets. Note that a history entry could contain the gr parameter. Regardless of the rules concerning the gr parameter defined in Ref. [10], which must be applied, this parameter has no impact on the mapping and must only be copied with the served user address.

Example:

History-Info:

```
<sip: diverting_user1_addr?Privacy=none?Reaso
n=SIP%3Bcause%3D302>;index=1,
<sip: diverting_user2_addr;cause=480?Privacy=
history>;index=1.1,
<sip:last_diversion_target;cause=486>;
index=1.1.1
```

Policy concerning histinfo option tag in Supported header: according to RFC 4244 (see Section 2.8), a proxy that receives a Request with the histinfo option tag in the Supported header should return captured History-Info in subsequent, provisional, and final responses to the Request. The behavior depends on whether or not the local policy supports the capture of History-Info.

16.3.2.3.2 Diversion Header Syntax

The following text is restating the exact syntax that the production rules in RFC 5806 define, but using RFC 5234 ABNF:

```
Diversion           = "Diversion" HCOLON
                      diversion-params
                      *(COMMA
                      diversion-params)
diversion-params    = name-addr *(SEMI
                      (diversion-reason/
                      diversion-counter/
                      diversion-limit/
                      diversion-privacy/
                      diversion-screen/
                      diversion-extension))
diversion-reason    = "reason" EQUAL
                      ("unknown"/"user-busy"/
                      "no-answer"
                      /"unavailable"
                      /"unconditional"/"time-
                      of-day"/"do-not-
                      disturb"/"deflection"
                      /"follow-me"/"out-of-
                      service"/"away"/token/
                      quoted-string)
diversion-counter   = "counter" EQUAL
                      1*2DIGIT
diversion-limit     = "limit" EQUAL 1*2DIGIT
diversion-privacy   = "privacy" EQUAL
                      ("full"/"name"/"uri"/
                      "off"/token/
                      quoted-string)
diversion-screen    = "screen" EQUAL
                      ("yes"/"no"/token/
                      quoted-string)
diversion-extension = token [EQUAL (token/
                      quoted-string)]
```

Note that the Diversion header could be used in the comma-separated format, as described below, and in a header-separated format. Both formats could be combined a received INVITE as recommended in RFC 3261.

Example:

Diversion:

```
diverting_user2_addr; reason="user-busy";
counter=1; privacy=full,
diverting_user1_addr; reason="unconditional";
counter=1; privacy=off
```

16.3.2.4 Headers in SIP Method

The recommended interworking presented in this document should apply only for INVITE requests. In 3xx responses, both headers could be present. When a proxy wants to interwork with a network supporting the other header field, it should apply the interworking between the Diversion header and the History-Info header in the 3xx response. When a recursing proxy redirects an initial INVITE after receiving a 3xx response, it should add as a last entry either a Diversion header or a History-Info header (according to its capabilities) in the forwarded INVITE. Local policies could apply to send the received header in the next INVITE. Other messages where History-Info could be present are not used for the call-forwarding service and should not be changed into a Diversion header. The destination network must be transparent to the received History-Info header. Note that the following mapping is inspired from the ISDN User Part (ISUP) to the SIP interworking described in Ref. [11].

16.3.2.5 Diversion Header to History-Info Header

The following text is valid only if no History-Info is present in the INVITE request. If at least one History-Info header is present, the interworking function must adapt its behavior to respect the chronological order. For N Diversion entries, $N + 1$ History-Info entries must be created. To create the History-Info entries in the same order than during a session establishment, the Diversion entries must be mapped from the bottommost until the topmost. Each Diversion entry shall be mapped into a History-Info entry. An additional History-Info entry (the last one) must be created with the diverted-to party address present in the R-URI of the received INVITE. The mapping is described below.

The first entry created in the History-Info header contains

- A hi-targeted-to-uri with the name-addr parameter of the bottommost Diversion header.
- If a privacy parameter is present in the bottommost Diversion entry, then a Privacy header could be escaped in the History-Info header as described below.
- An index set to 1.

For each following Diversion entry (from bottom to top), the History-Info entries are created as follows (from top to bottom):

Source		*Destination*	
Diversion header component:		History-Info header component:	
name-addr		hi-targeted-to-uri	
Reason of the previous Diversion entry		cause-param (not present in the first created hi-entry)	
	unknown	404 (default *cause* value)	
	unconditional	302	
	user-busy	486	
	no-answer	408	
	deflection	480 or 487	
	unavailable	404	
	time-of-day	404 (default)	
	do-not-disturb	404 (default)	
	follow-me	404 (default)	
	out-of-service	404 (default)	
	away	404 (default)	
Counter		hi-index	
	1 or parameter not present	The previous created index is incremented with .1.	
	Superior to 1 (i.e., N)	Create $N-1$ placeholder History entry with the previous index incremented with .1. Then, the History-Info header created with the Diversion entry with the previous index incremented with .1	
Privacy		Privacy header escaped in the hi-targeted-to-uri	
	full	history	
	Off	Privacy header field absent or none	
	name	history	
	uri	history	

A last History-Info entry is created and contains

- A hi-targeted-to-uri with the Request-URI of the INVITE request.
- A cause-param from the topmost Diversion entry, mapped from the diversion-reason as described above.
- If a privacy parameter is present in the topmost Diversion entry, then a Privacy header could be escaped in the History-Info header as described above.
- An index set to the previous created index and incremented with .1.

Notes:

1. For other optional Diversion parameters, there is no recommendation as History-Info header does not provide equivalent parameters.
2. For values of the diversion-reason values that are mapped with a recommended default value, it could also be possible to choose another value. The cause-param URI parameter offers less possible values than the diversion-reason parameter. However, it has been considered that cause-param values list was sufficient to implement CDIV service as defined in 3GPP [10] as it covers a large portion of cases.
3. The Diversion header could contain a Tel: URI in the name-addr parameter, but it seems not possible to have a Tel: URI in the History-Info header. RFC 3261 gives

an indication as to the mapping between sip: and Tel: URIs; however, in this particular case, it is difficult to assign a valid hostport as the diversion has occurred in a previous network and a valid hostport is difficult to determine. Thus, it is suggested that in case of Tel: URI in the Diversion header, the History-Info header should be created with a SIP URI with user=phone.

4. The Diversion header allows carrying a counter that retains information about the number of successive redirections. The History-Info header does not have an equivalent because to trace and count the number of diversion, it is necessary to count the cause parameters containing a value associated to a call diversion. Reading the index value is not enough. With the use of the *placeholder* entry, the History-Info header entries could reflect the real number of diversions that occurred. Example of placeholder entry in the History-Info header:

```
<sip:unknown@unknown.
invalid;cause=xxx>;index=1.1
<sip:bob_addr;cause=404>;index=1.1.1
```

cause=xxx reflects the diverting reason of a previous diverting user. For a placeholder hi-entry, the value 404 must be taken for the cause-param and, thus, located in the next hi-entry. Concerning local policies recommendations about headers coexistence in the INVITE request, see Section 16.3.2.2.2.

16.3.2.6 *History-Info Header to Diversion Header*

To create the Diversion entries in the same order than during a session establishment, the History-Info entries must be mapped from the topmost to the bottommost. The first History-Info header entry selected will be mapped into the last Diversion header entry and so on. One Diversion header entry must be created for each History-Info entry, with a cause-param reflecting a diverting reason as listed in RFC 4458 (see Sections 2.4.1 and 2.8). In this case, the History-Info header must be mapped into the Diversion header as follows:

	Source	*Destination*	
History-Info header component:		Diversion header component:	
hi-targeted-to-uri of the History-Info that precedes the one containing a diverting cause-param		name-addr	
cause-param		Reason	
	404	unknown (default value)	
	302	unconditional	
	486	user-busy	
	408	no-answer	
	480 or 487	deflection	
	503	unavailable	
hi-index		Counter	
	Mandatory parameter for History-Info reflecting the chronological order of the information.	The counter is set to 1.	
Privacy header RFC 3323 (see Section 20.2) escaped in the hi-targeted-to-uri of the History-Info, which precedes the one containing a diverting cause-param. Optional parameter for History-Info, this Privacy indicates that this specific History-Info header should not be forwarded.		Privacy	
	history	full	
	Privacy header field absent or none	Off	

Note that for other optional History-Info parameters, there is no recommendation as Diversion header does not provide equivalent parameters. Concerning local policies recommendations about headers coexistence in the INVITE request, see Section 16.3.2.2.2.

16.3.2.7 *Examples*

16.3.2.7.1 Example with Diversion Header Changed into History-Info Header

INVITE last_diverting_target

Diversion:

```
diverting_user3_address;reason=unconditional;
counter=1;privacy=off,
```

```
diverting_user2_address;reason=user-
busy;counter=1;privacy=full,
diverting_user1_address;reason=no-
answer;counter=1;privacy=off
```

Mapped into:

History-Info:

```
<sip: diverting_user1_address; privacy=none>;
index=1,
<sip: diverting_user2_address; cause=408?priv
acy=history>;index=1.1,
<sip: diverting_user3_address; cause=486?priv
acy=none>;index=1.1.1,
<sip: last_diverting_target;
cause=302>;index=1.1.1.1
```

16.3.2.7.2 Example with History-Info Header Changed into Diversion Header

History-Info:

```
<sip: diverting_user1_address?privacy=
history>; index=1,
<sip: diverting_user2_address; cause=302?
privacy=none>;index=1.1,
<sip: last_diverting_target;
cause=486>;index=1.1.1
```

Mapped into:

Diversion:

```
diverting_user2_address; reason=user-busy;
counter=1; privacy=off,
diverting_user1_address;
reason=unconditional; counter=1;
privacy=full
```

Note that RFC 6044 also provides call flow examples for the following scenario: two SIP networks using a History-Info header that interworks with a SIP network using a Diversion header. We leave these to readers as an exercise.

16.4 Call Services Using Session Border Controller

16.4.1 Overview

We have modeled the outlines of the book to bind all SIP RFCs within the framework of RFC 3261 as if the book itself were a super-RFC 3261. We have deferred to provide how the SIP-based scalable networking architecture can be built using all SIP functional capabilities that are described in all SIP RFCs. The scope of building scalable SIP networking architecture especially for the global carrier network is a huge one. A single book or several books may not be good enough to address all the details of implementation issues of SIP-based networking. One example can be provided to see the enormous efforts that 3GPP is offering for decades in building the SIP-based implementation architectural specifications. However, we have taken an exception to provide a brief description in building the scalable architecture of a single SIP-based functional entity such as the session border controller (SBC). We have described the SIP SBC in Section 14.2 that is used by customers in various networking environments, including enterprise networks, for the following reasons: topology hiding, media traffic management, fixing capability mismatches, maintaining SIP-related NAT bindings, access control, protocol repair, and media encryption.

We have also explained that the SBC has two separate distinct functions: signaling control and media control. We have described the overall end-to-end networking architecture considering a single monolithic functional entity along with their advantages and disadvantages. Despite the emergence of the IP/Internet telephony over two decades, only a small percentage of the total telephony traffic is passed over the pure IP/Internet. More than 90% of the total IP/Internet telephony traffic may be passed over the time division multiplexing (TDM)/circuit-switched based access lines that are not considered high-speed. In recent years, with the advent of everything-over-IP networking environments, all RT and near-RT multimedia applications with new customer experiences that were unimaginable and unheard of in plain old telephone service (POTS) are becoming SIP based. With respect to signaling traffic, the SIP-based presence information and forking of SIP calls due to use of multiple devices by a given user are expected to cause an increase of the SIP signaling traffic enormously in the future because the seamless use of SIP for all kinds of real-time (RT) and near-RT multimedia applications for simplicity and scalable operations is removing the bottleneck of multiprotocol applications.

On the other hand, with the demise of page-mode short message service (SMS), the session-mode Message Session Relay Protocol (MSRP) that may include audio and video in addition to text/graphics will increase the media traffic even for mobile environments, as high-capacity long-term evolution (LTE) wireless networks are becoming a reality. As a result, the mix of SIP signaling traffic and the media traffic generated by the SIP-based sessions that will be carried over the SBC are becoming highly disproportionate. The media traffic that may be flowing over the SBC in the future may become a couple of times higher than that of the signaling traffic depending on networking configurations and mix of SIP users. It implies that a monolithic single physical entity of an SBC carrying both signaling and media traffic will not be scalable under all networking environments. A distributed SBC architecture meeting all the customer requirements as described earlier will be the logical choice for providing scalability. In this section, we describe the different scenarios of the distributed architectures of the SBC.

16.4.2 Distributed SBC Architecture

The distributed SBC architecture separates the signaling and media plane function into two physical entities known as signaling controller and media controller, respectively, as depicted in Figure 16.21. Note that the SBC signaling plane acts as the SIP B2BUA. We have shown that the communication between these two functional entities is done using a separate protocol like H.248 [8]. The H.248 protocol was standardized in ITU-T at the time when H.323 [9] had been developed primarily for interfacing the TDM-based PSTN/ISDN telephony network to the IP-based IP/Internet H.323- and SIP-based VoIP telephony network providing scalability and interoperability. This SBC architecture is also popularly known as the SoftSwitch architecture.

Some also opine that SIP can also be used instead of H.248 as SIP has much more powerful functional capabilities than those of H.248. However, no standard has been published yet for using SIP for communications between the signaling and media controllers. The separation between the signaling and media plane has solved the most important problem—the scaling of the signaling and media plane independently because there is an enormous mismatch between the signaling and media traffic as explained earlier. Moreover, the routing of signaling and media traffic can be optimized independently as required without forcing one to follow the other. The NAT crossing function that handles the media traffic can also be integrated in the media plane operating under the control of the signaling plane of SBC. For example, when the SIP session is progressed to a point where a media path needs to be established, the signaling plane sends an H.248 command for opening the gate with hole punching for NAT crossing. However, the same operation is also true for media plane whether there is NAT or not. The logical call flows still remain the same for all operations as shown in Section 14.2, except that we have not included the operations of H.248 protocol as shown here.

More important, the implication of separation between the signaling and media plane goes much deeper in the distributed IP/Internet telephony networking architecture should customers want to deploy SBCs for the large-scale global network meeting those requirements as described in the beginning, despite their limitations in being a closed network. For instance, the traffic and geographical distribution can be such that a single SBC signaling controller may need to control multiple media controllers for scalable operations and traffic route optimization creating a one-to-many or many-to-one communications topology. In other examples, there can be many signaling controllers as well as many media controllers communicating in many-to-many fashion for scalable operations of the network. In the next section, we provide some examples of those distributed SBC architectures resulting the following benefits: cost-reduction with high availability configurations and scalability of both signaling and media capacity.

16.4.2.1 Single Signaling Controller with Multiple Media Controllers

The regional and local geographical topology and traffic concentration of a SIP network for any enterprise is such that a single signaling controller is good enough to meet the optimum network design criteria; the distributed SBC-based SIP network architecture may look like as shown in Figure 16.22.

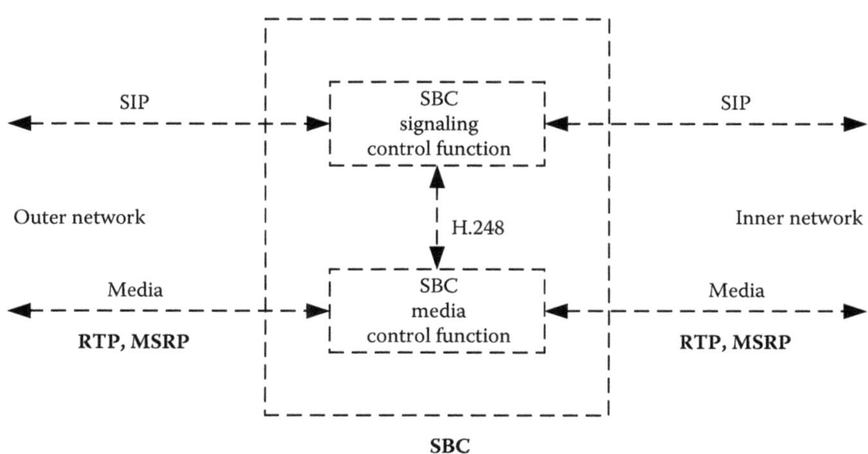

Figure 16.21 Distributed SBC architecture with separation of signaling and media control function.

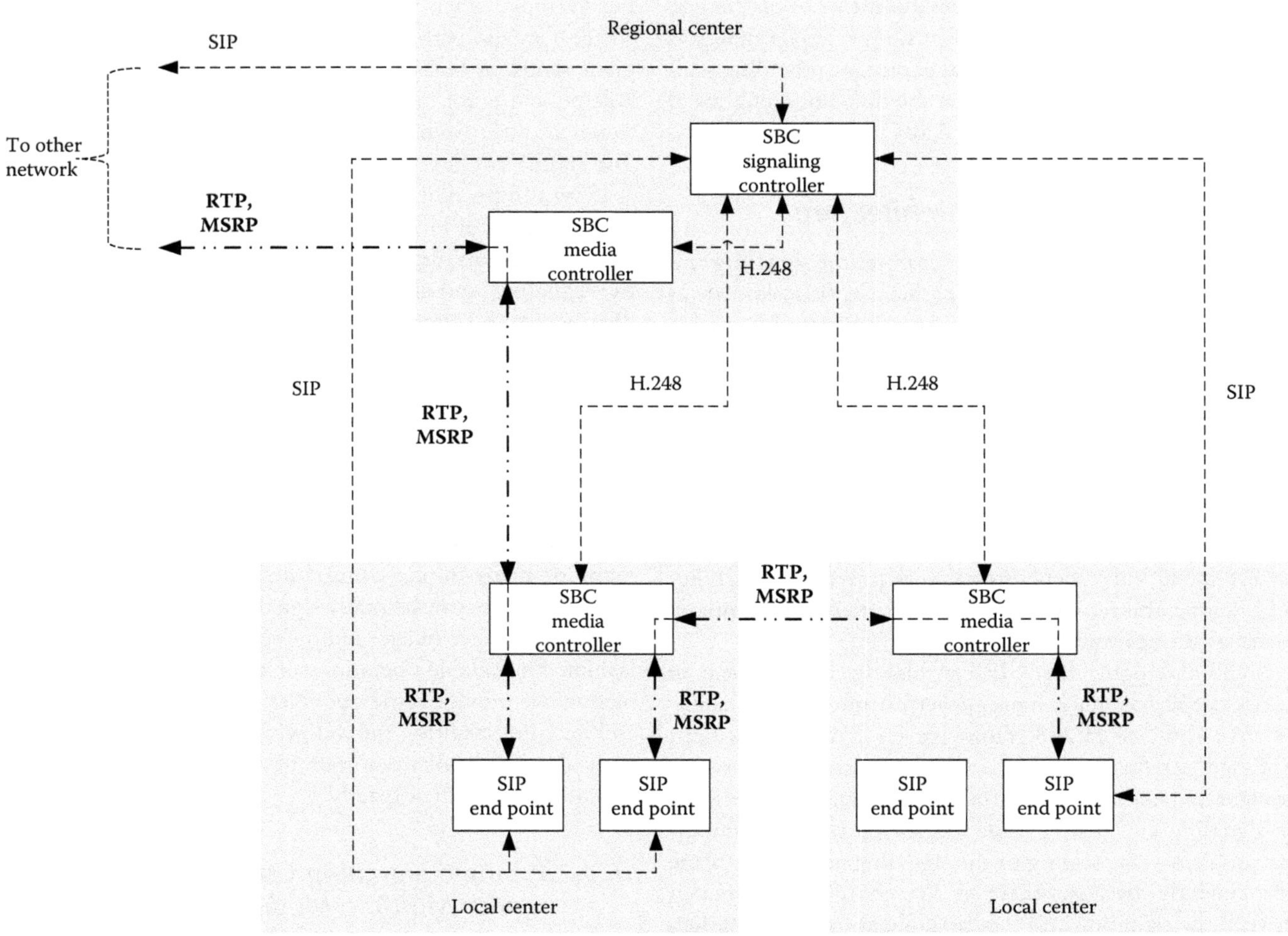

Figure 16.22 Distributed SBC-based SIP network architecture consisting of a single signaling controller with multiple media controllers.

Note that this network can be thought as being geographically distributed with logically centralized control from the SIP signaling point of view. Sometimes, this kind of network configuration is known as on-net and off-net call distribution services. This architecture shows how the media path can be optimized for communications, thereby reducing costs between the SIP end points independently when the signaling controller is physically decoupled from the media controller. Although there are multiple media controllers that can take care of one another in case of any media controller failures increasing the reliability and availability of media communications, the same is not true for the SIP signaling traffic.

16.4.2.2 Multiple Signaling and Media Controllers

We now provide an example of the distributed SBC architecture that uses multiple signaling and media controllers as depicted in Figure 16.23. This architecture shows that, unlike Figure 16.21, there are multiple signaling controllers that increase the reliability and availability of the signaling traffic in case of signaling controller failures.

Note that the communications protocol between the signaling controllers is also SIP. In this way, many kinds of SBC-based distributed SIP network architectures can be designed meeting all the requirements that SBCs need to meet from enterprise and home networking environments. Next, we will explain the SIP trunking architecture briefly using an example.

16.4.2.3 SBC-Based SIP Trunking Network Architecture

We now explain one of the most popular SIP network architectures, popularly known as the SIP trunking network architectures. The initial most successful deployment of SIP has been based on this SBC-based distributed network architecture as depicted in Figure 16.24.

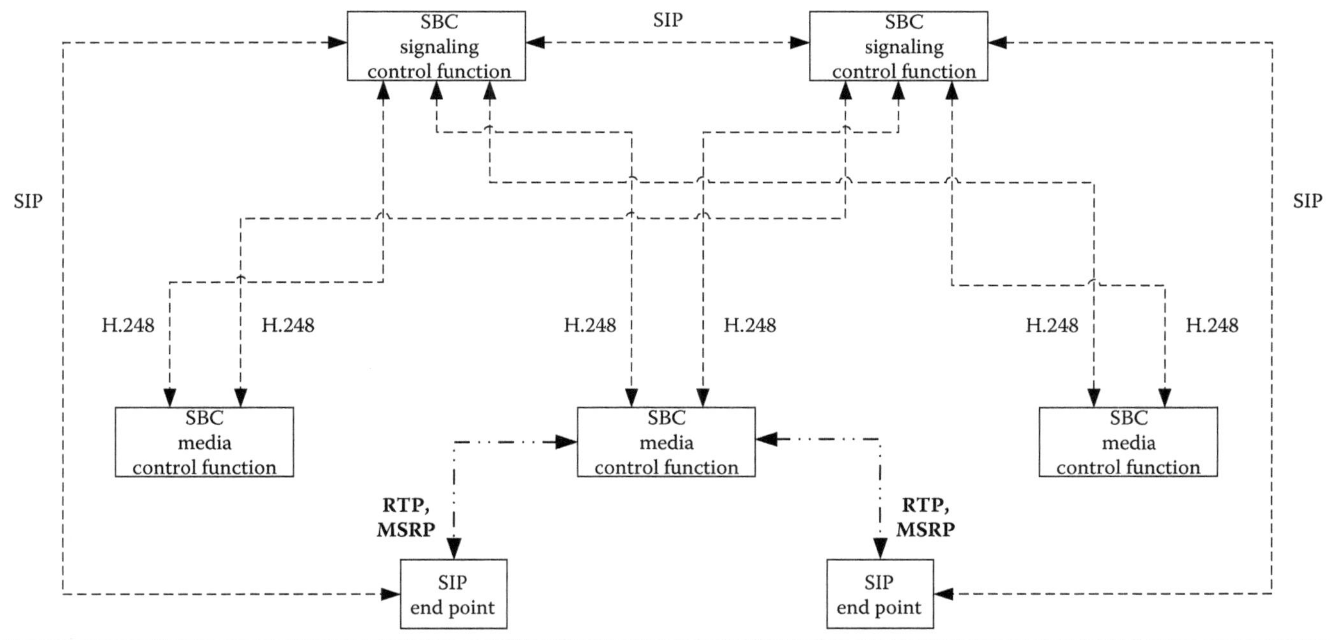

Figure 16.23 Distributed SBC-based SIP network architecture with multiple signaling and media controllers.

Note that we have shown a high-level SoftSwitch architecture that uses decoupling SBC-based signaling and media function along with SIP-ISUP/CAS signaling interworking function (IWF) for interfacing both TDM and IP network. Again, there can be one or more media controllers that may be located near the signaling controller or may be distributed geographically depending on the network configurations. However, a SoftSwitch usually interfaces both the TDM and IP networks and is acting like a gateway. The SIP trunking architecture has historically been a successful implementation architecture from the volume point of view, interconnecting multiple geographically disparate PSTN/ISDN networks over the large-scale IP backbone network improving economies of scale. In Figure 16.24b, SIP trunking network configuration, isolated PSTN/ISDN circuit-switched networks are interconnected via packet-switched IP backbone network offering multiplexing gain with audio silence suppression and busty data traffic of multimedia applications. Moreover, the centralized least-cost routing of the multimedia traffic over the IP backbone network will offer economic benefits. The bandwidth-saving codecs, audio transcoding, and audio/video media bridging that require specialized hardware will benefit from the geographically distributed SBC-based media controllers under the control of the logically centralized signaling controller loosely termed as the distributed *logical* SoftSwitch architecture. All PSTN/ISDN telephony users may not be aware about the use of the SIP trunking over the long-haul IP backbone network. There can be many variations of this *star*-based SIP trunking architecture in implementations, although the basic objectives may remain the same.

As more and more users start using SIP-based IP telephony, this architecture also offers a graceful migration as time goes by. For example, Figure 16.25 provides a distributed architecture where newer SIP-based IP telephony end points are coexisting with the SBC-based trunking networking. In this distributed SIP-based IP telephony architecture, the IP network itself offers the valuable, much richer RT and near-RT multimedia services directly to its native SIP-based end points.

Both SIP-based IP and PSTN/ISDN telephony users can also communicate, simultaneously interworking with each other. We have not explained each of these RT and near-RT multimedia services for both kinds of IP and PSTN/ISDN end points for the sake of brevity. Note that, like the distributed SBC architecture, each kind of SIP-based application server also needs to be geographically distributed while acting as a single logically centralized application server for scalability and reliability of the large-scale global SIP-based IP/Internet telephony network. It is needless to explain how much urgent it is to do so, especially for the audio and video bridging media servers. All of this special attention is provided to the next generation of SIP-based distributed RT and near-RT multimedia application service architecture for each kind of application for building scalable networks for offering SIP-based services. The recent completion of IETF standard activities related to the initial sets of multimedia conferencing services is pointing development in this direction. The experiences of implementations of these few

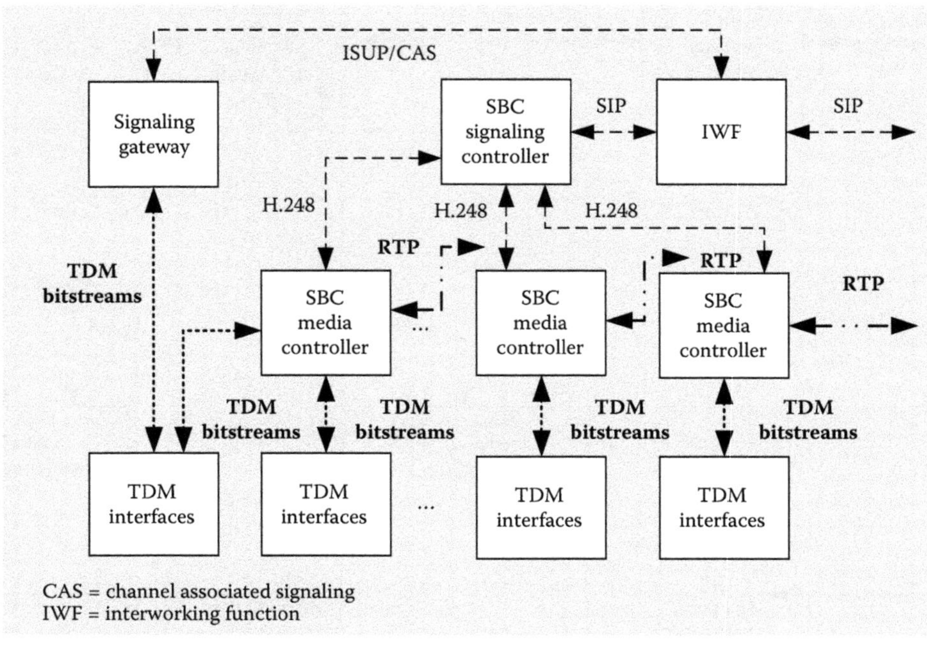

(a)

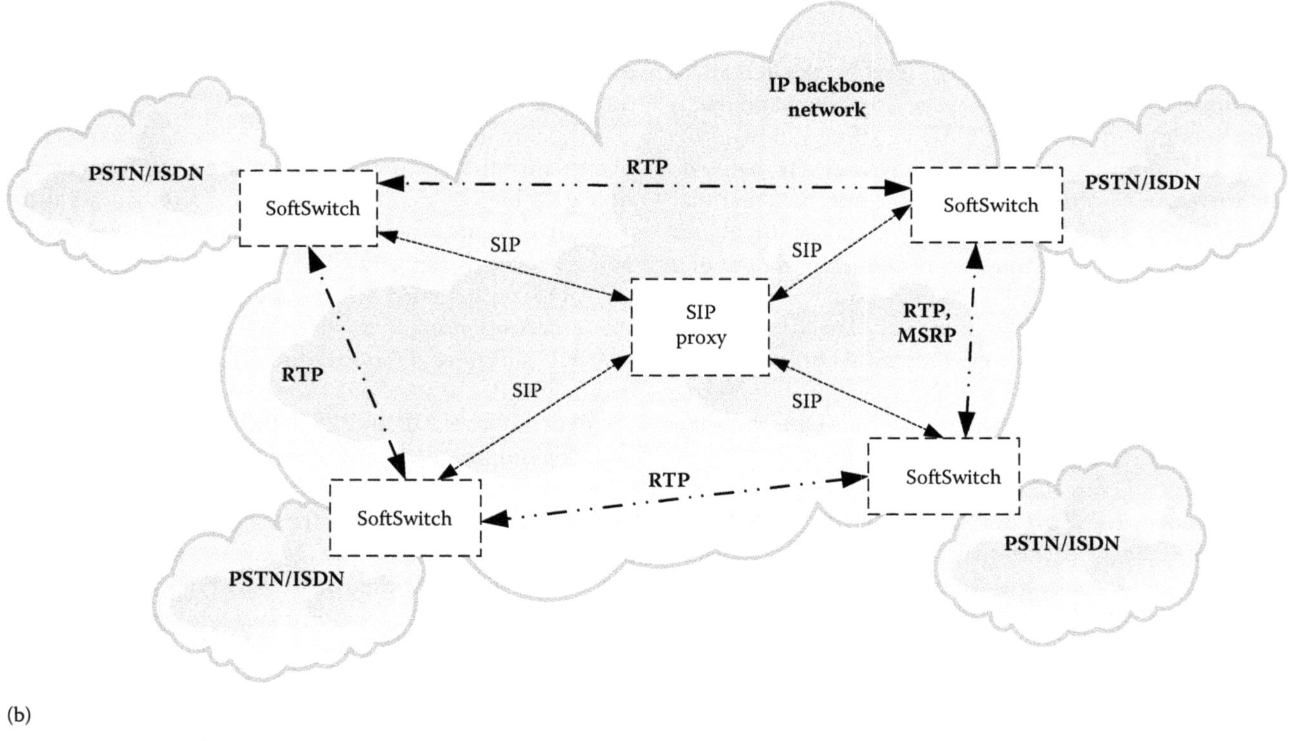

(b)

Figure 16.24 SBC-based SIP trunking architecture: (a) high-level SoftSwitch architecture and (b) trunking architecture.

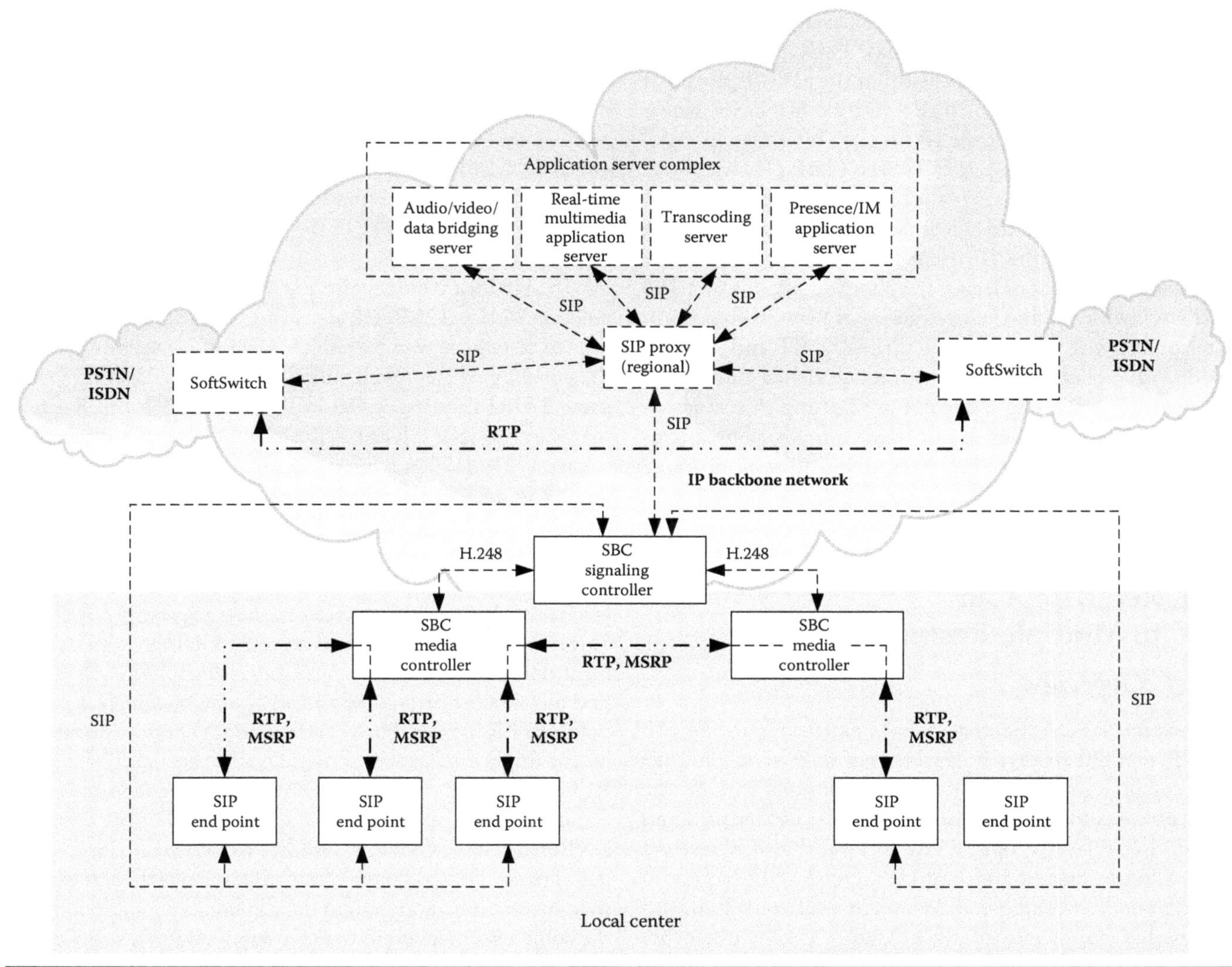

Figure 16.25 Graceful migration of the distributed SBC-based SIP trunking architecture to SIP-based IP telephony network.

sets of multimedia conferencing architectures will usher much greater multimedia-rich experiences for new commercial and residential users. In turn, it will create a new demand for building much better multimedia applications and corresponding service architectures in the future.

16.4.3 Conclusion

We have explained how the separation between the signaling and media plane of the SBC architecture provides scalability, enhanced reliability, and economy of scale for the RT and near-RT multimedia services. The primary reason has been that the distribution of signaling and media traffic for SIP-based multimedia applications differ significantly, especially media traffic becomes much higher in proportion to that of the signaling traffic. It demands that the signaling and media entities require scaling independently. Only the physical separation between the signaling and the media entities of SBC makes it possible to do so where the signaling entity needs to control each of those geographically distributed media entities acting as a single logically centralized signaling controller. However, it brings another issue in that we need to use a protocol for communications between the signaling and media controllers. We have taken H.248 [8] as the protocol standardized in the ITU-T. Although SIP could be another alternative to H.248 with much richer capabilities, no SIP standard has been published thus far. We have left all the call flows using the distributed SBC architecture as an exercise for the following (as discussed in Section 14.2): topology hiding, media traffic management, fixing capability mismatches, maintaining SIP-related NAT bindings, access control, protocol repair, and media encryption.

In the context of the distributed SBC-architecture, we have explained how the so-called SoftSwitch architecture has evolved a long time ago while ITU-T developed the H.248 protocol. Later on, the SoftSwitch-based SIP trunking architecture has been the most successful in the early deployment that allows the evolution of the large-scale SIP-based native IP telephony services over the IP network offering a graceful migration path for the legacy POTS/PSTN/ISDN telephony services. Even after almost two decades of IP telephony services, the low-speed circuit-switched lines are still carrying more than 90% of the IP telephony traffic because of the existing huge amount of legacy telephony lines built over 100 years worldwide. With the emergence of new SIP-based all-IP telephony with much richer multimedia RT and near-RT broadband applications, users with much richer multimedia experiences throughout the world are causing this situation to change. We have pointed out how more distributed scalable and reliable SIP-based services architecture needs to be developed in the future.

16.5 Referring Call to Multiple Resources

16.5.1 Overview

We describe RFC 5368 that defines extensions to the SIP REFER method so that it can be used to refer to multiple resources in a single request. These extensions include the use of pointers to URI lists in the Refer-To header field and the multiple-refer SIP option tag. The SIP REFER method allows a UA to request a second UA to send a SIP request to a third party. For example, if Alice is in a call with Bob, and decides that Bob needs to talk to Carol, Alice can instruct her SIP UA to send a REFER request to Bob's UA providing Carol's SIP Contact information. Assuming Bob has given it permission, Bob's UA will attempt to call Carol using that contact. That is, it will send an INVITE request to that contact. A number of applications need to request this second UA to initiate transactions toward a set of destinations. In one example, the moderator of a conference may want the conference server to send BYE requests to a group of participants. In another example, the same moderator may want the conference server to INVITE a set of new participants. We define an extension to the REFER method so that REFER requests can be used to refer other UAs (such as conference servers) to multiple destinations. In addition, this mechanism uses the suppression of the REFER method implicit subscription specified in RFC 4488 (see Section 2.8.2).

16.5.2 Operation

We describe an application of URI-list services (RFC 5363, see Section 19.7) that allows a URI-list service to receive a SIP REFER request containing a list of targets. The URI-list service invokes the requested SIP method to each of the targets contained in the list. This type of URI-list service is referred to as a REFER-Recipient throughout this document. This document defines an extension to the SIP REFER method that allows a SIP UAC to include a URI list (RFC 4826) of REFER-Targets in a REFER request and send it to a REFER-Recipient. The REFER-Recipient creates a new SIP request for each entry in the URI list and sends it to each REFER-Recipient.

The URI list that contains the list of targets is used in conjunction with RFC 5364 to allow the sender to indicate the role (e.g., *to*, *cc*, or *anonymous*) in which REFER-Target is involved in the signaling. We represent multiple targets of a REFER request using a URI list as specified in RFC 4826. A REFER-Issuer that wants to refer a REFER-Recipient to a set of destinations creates a SIP REFER request. The Refer-To header contains a pointer to a URI list, which is included in a body part, and an option tag in the Require header field: multiple-refer. This option tag indicates the requirement to support the functionality described in this specification. When the REFER-Recipient receives such a request, it creates a new request per REFER-Target and sends them, one to each REFER-Target. This document does not provide any mechanism for REFER-Issuers to find out about the results of a REFER request containing multiple REFER-Targets. Furthermore, it does not provide support for the implicit subscription mechanism that is part of the SIP REFER method. The way REFER-Issuers are kept informed about the results of a REFER is service specific. For example, a REFER-Issuer sending a REFER request to invite a set of participants to a conference can discover which participants were successfully brought into the conference by subscribing to the conference state event package specified in RFC 4575 (see Sections 2.2 and 2.4.4.1).

16.5.3 Multiple-Refer SIP Option Tag

A new SIP option tag is defined for the Require and Supported header fields: multiple-refer. A UA including the multiple-refer option tag in a Supported header field indicates compliance with this specification. A UA generating a REFER with a pointer to a URI list in its Refer-To header field must include the multiple-refer option tag in the Require header field of the REFER.

16.5.4 Suppressing REFER's Implicit Subscription

REFER requests with a single REFER-Target establish implicitly a subscription to the refer event. The REFER-Issuer is informed about the result of the transaction toward the REFER-Target through this implicit subscription. As described in RFC 3515 (see Section 2.5), NOTIFY requests sent as a result of an implicit subscription created by a REFER request contain a body of type message/sipfrag (RFC 3420, see Section 2.8.2) that describes the status of the transaction initiated by the REFER-Recipient. In the case of a REFER-Issuer that generates a REFER with multiple REFER-targets, the REFER-Issuer is typically already subscribed to other event packages that can provide the information about the result of the transactions toward the REFER-Targets. For example, a moderator instructing a conference server to send a BYE request to a set of participants is usually subscribed to the conference state event package for the conference. Notifications to this event package will keep the moderator and the rest of the subscribers informed of the current list of conference participants. Most of the applications using the multiple REFER technology described in this memo do not need its implicit subscription.

Consequently, a SIP REFER-Issuer generating a REFER request with multiple REFER-Targets should include the norefersub option tag in a Require header field and should include a Refer-Sub header field set to *false* to indicate that no notifications about the requests should be sent to the REFER-Issuer. The REFER-Recipient should honor the suggestion and also include a Refer-Sub header field set to false in the 200 (OK) response. The norefersub SIP option tag and the Refer-Sub header field (see Section 2.8) are specified in RFC 4488. Note that a condition for the REFER-Issuer to include a Refer-Sub header is that the REFER-Issuer is sure that the REFER request will not fork. At the time of writing, there is no extension that allows to report the status of several transactions over the implicit subscription associated with a REFER dialog. That is the motivation for this document to recommend the usage of the norefersub option tag. If in the future such an extension is defined, REFER-Issuers using it could refrain from using the norefersub option tag and use the new extension instead.

16.5.5 URI-List Format

As described in RFC 5363 (see Section 19.7), specifications of individual URI-list services need to specify a default format for recipient-list bodies used within the particular service. The default format for recipient-list (RFCs 4826 and 5364) bodies for REFER-Issuers and REFER-Recipients is used. REFER-Recipients handling recipient-list bodies must support both of these formats. Both REFER-Issuers and REFER-Recipients may support other formats. As described in RFC 5364, each URI can be tagged with a copyControl attribute set to either *to*, *cc*, or *bcc*, indicating the role in which the target will get the referred SIP request. However, depending on the target SIP method, a copyControl attribute lacks sense. For example, while a copyControl attribute can be applied to INVITE requests, it does not make sense with mid-dialog requests such as BYE requests.

In addition to the copyControl attribute, URIs can be tagged with the anonymize attribute (also specified in RFC 5364) to prevent that the REFER-Recipient discloses the target URI in a URI list. Additionally, RFC 5364 defines a recipient-list-history body that contains the list of targets. The default format for recipient-list-history bodies for conference services is also extended (RFCs 4826 and 5364). REFER-Recipients supporting this specification MUST support both of these formats; REFER-Targets may support these formats. Both REFER-Recipients and REFER-Targets may support other formats. Nevertheless, RFC 4826 provides features such as hierarchical lists and the ability to include entries by reference relative to the XML Configuration Access Protocol (XCAP) root URI that are not needed by the multiple REFER service defined in this document. Figure 16.26 shows an example of a flat list that follows the resource-list document.

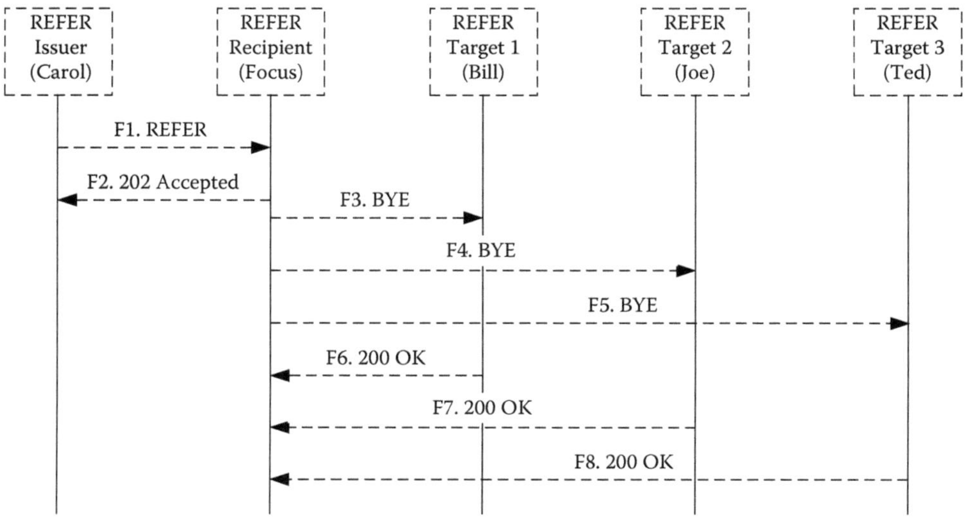

Figure 16.26 URI list.

16.5.6 Behavior of SIP REFER-Issuers

As indicated in Sections 1.4 and 2.1, a SIP REFER-Issuer that creates a REFER request with multiple REFER-Targets includes a multiple-refer and norefersub option tags in the Require header field and, if appropriate, a Refer-Sub header field set to false. The REFER-Issuer includes the set of REFER-Targets in a recipient-list body whose disposition type is recipient-list (RFC 5363, see Section 19.7). The URI-list body is further described earlier. The Refer-To header field of a REFER request with multiple REFER-Targets must contain a pointer (i.e., a Content-ID URL as per RFC 2392, see Section 2.8.2) that points to the body part that carries the URI list. The REFER-Issuer should not include any particular URI more than once in the URI list. RFC 4826 provides features such as hierarchical lists and the ability to include entries by reference relative to the XCAP root URI. However, these features are not needed by the multiple REFER service defined in this document. Therefore, when using the default resource list document, SIP REFER-Issuers generating REFER requests with multiple REFER-Targets should use flat lists (i.e., no hierarchical lists) and should not use <entry-ref> elements.

16.5.7 Behavior of REFER-Recipients

The REFER-Recipient follows the rules of RFC 3515 (see Section 2.5) to determine the status code of the response to the REFER. The REFER-Recipient should not create an implicit subscription, and should add a Refer-Sub header field set to false in the 200 OK response. The incoming REFER request typically contains a URI-list document or reference with the actual list of targets. If this URI list includes resources tagged with the copyControl attribute set to a value of *to* or *cc*, and if the request is appropriate for the service, for example, it is not received mid-dialog, the REFER-Recipient should include a URI list in each of the outgoing requests. This list should be formatted according to RFCs 4826 and 5364. The REFER-Recipient must follow the procedures specified in RFC 4826 with respect to handling of the anonymize, count, and copyControl attributes.

RFC 5363 (see Section 19.7) discusses cases when duplicated URIs are found in a URI list. To avoid duplicated requests, REFER-Recipients must take those actions specified in RFC 5363 into account to avoid sending a duplicated request to the same target. If the REFER-Recipient includes a URI list in an outgoing request, it must include a Content-Disposition header field, specified in RFC 2183 (see Section 2.8.2), with the value set to recipient-list-history and a handling parameter, specified in RFC 3204, set to optional. Since the multiple REFER service does not use hierarchical lists nor may lists that include entries by reference to the XCAP root URI, a REFER-Recipient receiving a URI list with more information than what has been described in Section 2.2 discard all the extra information. The REFER-Recipient follows the rules in RFC 3515 (see Section 2.5) to generate the necessary requests toward the REFER-Targets, acting as if it had received a regular (no URI list) REFER per each URI in the URI list.

16.5.8 Example

Figure 16.27 shows an example flow where a REFER-Issuer sends a multiple-REFER request to the focus of a conference, which acts as the REFER-Recipient. The REFER-Recipient generates a BYE request per REFER-Target. Details for using

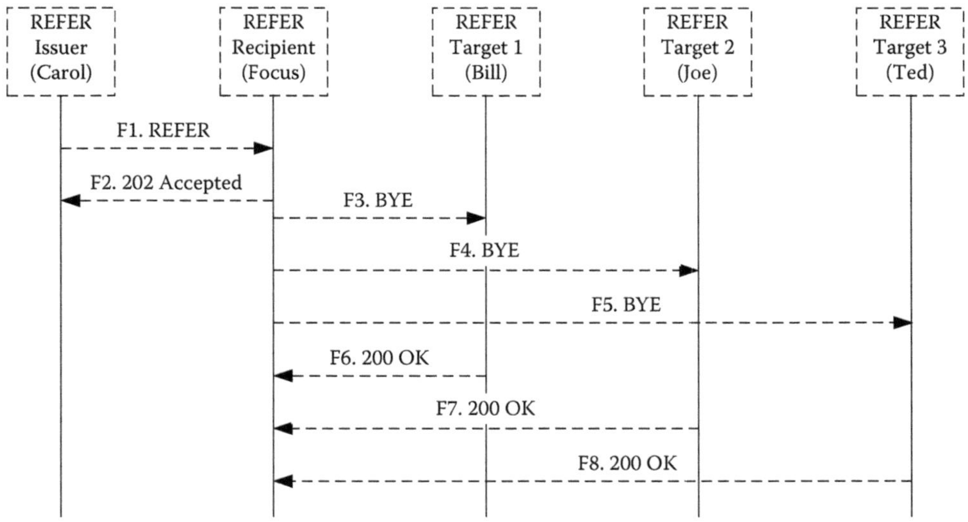

Figure 16.27 Example flow of a REFER request containing multiple REFER-Targets. (Copyright IETF. Reproduced with permission.)

```
REFER sip:conf-123@example.com;gruu;opaque=hha9s8d-999a SIP/2.0
Via: SIP/2.0/TCP client.chicago.example.com
        ;branch=z9hG4bKhjhs8ass83
Max-Forwards: 70
To: "Conference 123" <sip:conf-123@example.com>
From: Carol <sip:carol@chicago.example.com>;tag=32331
Call-ID: d432fa84b4c76e66710
CSeq: 2 REFER
Contact: <sip:carol@client.chicago.example.com>
Refer-To: <cid:cn35t8jf02@example.com>
Refer-Sub: false
Require: multiple-refer, norefersub
Allow: INVITE, ACK, CANCEL, OPTIONS, BYE, REFER, SUBSCRIBE, NOTIFY
Allow-Events: dialog
Accept: application/sdp, message/sipfrag
Content-Type: application/resource-lists+xml
Content-Disposition: recipient-list

Content-Length: 362

Content-ID: <cn35t8jf02@example.com>

<?xml version="1.0" encoding="UTF-8"?>

<resource-lists xmlns="urn:ietf:params:xml:ns:resource-lists"
                xmlns:xsi="http://www.w3.org/2001/XMLSchema-instance">
        <list>
                <entry uri="sip:bill@example.com?method=BYE" />
                <entry uri="sip:joe@example.org?method=BYE" />
                <entry uri="sip:ted@example.net?method=BYE" />
        </list>
</resource-lists>
```

Figure 16.28 REFER request with multiple REFER-Targets.

REFER request to remove participants from a conference are specified in RFC 4579 (see Sections 2.2 and 2.4.4.1).

The REFER request (F1) contains a Refer-To header field that includes a pointer to the message body, which carries a list with the URIs of the REFER-Targets. In this example, the URI list does not contain the copyControl attribute extension. The REFER's Require header field carries the multiple-refer and norefersub option tags. The Request-URI is set to a GRUU (as a guarantee that the REFER request will not fork). The Refer-Sub header field is set to false to request the suppression of the implicit subscription. Figure 16.28 shows an example of this REFER request. The resource list document contains the list of REFER-Target URIs along with the method of the SIP request that the REFER-Recipient generates.

Figure 16.29 shows an example of the BYE request (F3) that the REFER Recipient sends to the first REFER-Target.

```
BYE sip:bill@example.com SIP/2.0
Via: SIP/2.0/TCP conference.example.com
        ;branch=z9hG4bKhjhs8assmm
Max-Forwards: 70
From: "Conference 123" <sip:conf-123@example.com>;tag=88734
To: <sip:bill@example.com>;tag=29872
Call-ID: d432fa84b4c34098s812
CSeq: 34 BYE
Content-Length: 0
```

Figure 16.29 BYE request.

16.6 Call Services with Content Indirection

16.6.1 Overview

SIP is a signaling protocol that is used to create, modify, or terminate sessions with one or more participants. SIP messages, like HTTP, are syntactically composed of a start line, one or more headers, and an optional body. Unlike HTTP, SIP is not designed as a general-purpose data transport protocol. There are numerous reasons why it might be desirable to specify the content of the SIP message body indirectly. For bandwidth-limited applications such as cellular wireless, indirection provides a means to annotate the (indirect) content with meta-data, which may be used by the recipient to determine whether or not to retrieve the content over a resource-limited link. It is also possible that the content size to be transferred might overwhelm intermediate signaling proxies, thereby unnecessarily increasing network latency. For time-sensitive

SIP applications, this may be unacceptable. Indirect content can remedy this by moving the transfer of this content out of the SIP signaling network and into a potentially separate data transfer channel. There may also be scenarios where the session-related data (body) that needs to be conveyed does not directly reside on the end point or UA. In such scenarios, it is desirable to have a mechanism whereby the SIP message can contain an indirect reference to the desired content. The receiving party would then use this indirect reference to retrieve the content via a non-SIP transfer channel such as HTTP, File Transfer Protocol (FTP), or Lightweight Directory Access Protocol.

The purpose of content indirection is purely to provide an alternative transport mechanism for SIP MIME body parts. With the exception of the transport mechanism, indirect body parts are equivalent to, and should have the same treatment as, in-line body parts. Previous attempts in RFC 3261 at solving the content indirection problem made use of the text/uri-list MIME type. While attractive for its simplicity (a list of URIs delimited by end-of-line markers), it failed to satisfy a number of the requirements for a more general-purpose content indirection mechanism in SIP. Most notably lacking is the ability to specify various attributes on a per-URI basis. These attributes might include version information, the MIME type of the referenced content, and others. RFC 2017 defines a strong candidate for a replacement for the text/uri-list MIME type. RFC 2017 defines an extension to the message/external-body MIME type originally defined in RFC 2046. The extension that RFC 2017 makes allows a generic URI to specify the location of the content rather than protocol-specific parameters for FTP, and others as originally defined in RFC 2046. Although it provides most of the functionality needed for a SIP content indirection mechanism, RFC 2017 by itself is not a complete solution.

RFC 4488 that is described here defines an extension to the URL MIME External-Body Access-Type to satisfy the content indirection requirements for the SIP. These extensions are aimed at allowing any MIME part in a SIP message to be referred to indirectly via a URI. The requirements can be classified as applying either to the URI, which indirectly references the desired content, or to the content itself. Where possible, existing MIME parameters and entity headers are used to satisfy those requirements. MIME (Content-Type) parameters are the preferred manner of describing the URI, while entity headers are the preferred manner of describing the (indirect) content. Note that RFC 2045 can be seen for a description of most of these entity headers and MIME parameters.

16.6.2 Use-Case Examples

There are several examples of using the content indirection mechanism. These are examples only and are not intended to limit the scope or applicability of the mechanism.

16.6.2.1 Presence Notification

The information carried in a presence document could exceed the recommended size for a SIP NOTIFY request, particularly if the document carries aggregated information from multiple end points. In such a situation, it would be desirable to send the NOTIFY request with an indirect pointer (Figure 16.30) to the presence document, which could then be retrieved by, for example, HTTP.

In this example, the presence server returns an HTTP URI pointing to a presence document on the presence server, which the watcher can then fetch by using an HTTP GET.

16.6.2.2 Document Sharing

During an instant messaging conversation, a useful service is document sharing, wherein one party sends an instant messaging MESSAGE request with an indirect pointer (Figure 16.31) to a document that is meant to be rendered by the

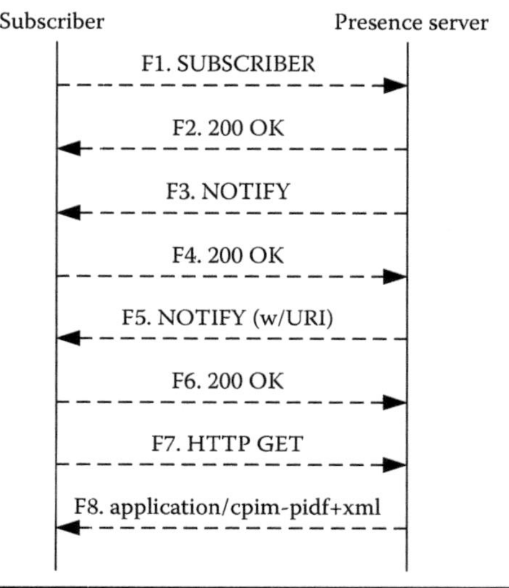

Figure 16.30 Presence notification with content indirection. (Copyright IETF. Reproduced with permission.)

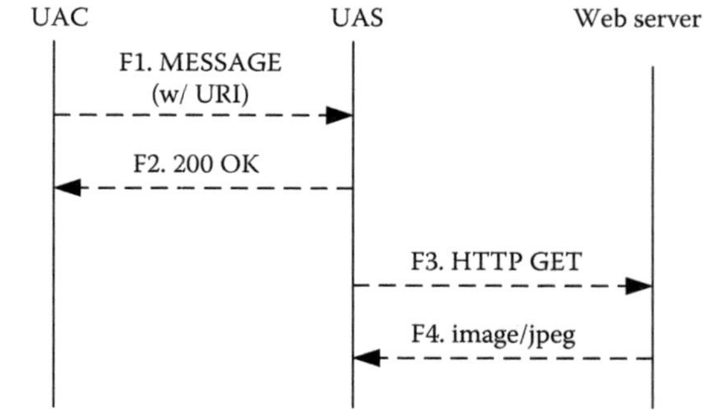

Figure 16.31 MESSAGE method with content indirection. (Copyright IETF. Reproduced with permission.)

remote party. Carrying such a document directly in the MESSAGE request is not an appropriate use of the signaling channel. Furthermore, the document to be shared may reside on a completely independent server from that of the originating party.

In this example, a user UAC wishes to exchange a JPEG image that she has stored on her web server with user UAS with whom she has an IM conversation. She intends to render the JPEG inline in the IM conversation. The recipient of the MESSAGE request launches an HTTP GET request to the web server to retrieve the JPEG image.

16.6.3 Requirements

- It must be possible to specify the location of content via a URI. Such URIs must conform to RFC 3986.
- It must be possible to specify the length of the indirect content.
- It must be possible to specify the type of the indirect content.
- It must be possible to specify the disposition of each URI independently.
- It must be possible to label each URI to identify if and when the content referred to by that URI has changed. Applications of this mechanism may send the same URI more than once. The intention of this requirement is to allow the receiving party to determine whether the content referenced by the URI has changed, without having to retrieve that content. Examples of ways the URI could be labeled include a sequence number, time stamp, and version number. When used with HTTP, the entity-tag (ETAG) mechanism, as defined in RFCs 7230–7235, may be appropriate. Note that we are labeling not the URI itself but the content to which the URI refers, and that the label is therefore effectively *metadata* of the content itself.
- It must be possible to specify the time span for which a given URI is valid. This may or may not be the same as the lifetime for the content itself.
- It must be possible for the UAC and the UAS to indicate support of this content indirection mechanism. A fallback mechanism should be specified in the event that one of the parties is unable to support content indirection.
- It must be possible for the UAC and UAS to negotiate the type of the indirect content when using the content indirection mechanism.
- It must be possible for the UAC and UAS to negotiate support for any URI scheme to be used in the content indirection mechanism. This is in addition to the ability to negotiate the content type.
- It should be possible to ensure the integrity and confidentiality of the URI when it is received by the remote party.
- It must be possible to process the content indirection without human intervention.
- It must allow for indirect transference of content in any SIP message that would otherwise carry that content as a body.

16.6.4 Application of MIME-URI Standard to Content Indirection

We have explained earlier that RFC 2017 provides most of the functionality needed for a SIP content indirection mechanism; however, RFC 2017 by itself is not a complete solution. We describe the following text of RFC 2017 that meets the requirements for content indirection in SIP.

16.6.4.1 Specifying Support for Content Indirection

A UAC/UAS indicates support for content indirection by including the message/external-body MIME type in the Accept header. The UAC/UAS may supply additional values in the Accept header to indicate the content types that it is willing to accept, either directly or through content indirection. UAs supporting content indirection must support content indirection of the application/sdp MIME type. For example:

```
Accept: message/external-body, image/*,
application/sdp
```

16.6.4.2 Mandatory Support for HTTP URI

Applications that use this content indirection mechanism must support the HTTP URI scheme. Additional URI schemes may be used, but a UAC/UAS must support receiving a HTTP URI for indirect content if it advertises support for content indirection. The UAS may advertise alternate access schemes in the schemes parameter of the Contact header in the UAS response to the UAC's session establishment request (e.g., INVITE, SUBSCRIBE), as described in RFC 3840 (see Section 3.4).

16.6.4.3 Rejecting Content Indirection

If a UAS receives a SIP request that contains a content indirection payload and the UAS cannot or does not wish to support such a content type, it must reject the request with a 415 Unsupported Media Type response as defined in SIP

RFC 3261 (see Section 2.6). In particular, the UAC should note the absence of the message/external-body MIME type in the Accept header of this response to indicate that the UAS does not support content indirection, or the absence of the particular MIME type of the requested comment to indicate that the UAS does not support the particular media type.

16.6.4.4 Specifying the Location of the Content via a URI

The URI for the indirect content is specified in a URI parameter of the message/external-body MIME type (RFC 2046). An access-type parameter indicates that the external content is referenced by a URI. HTTP URI specifications must conform to RFC 3986. For example:

```
Content-Type: message/external-body;
access-type="URL";
              URL="http://www.example.com/
              the-indirect-content"
```

16.6.4.5 Marking Indirect Content Optional

Some content is not critical to the context of the communication if there is a fetch or conversion failure. The content indirection mechanism uses the Critical-Content mechanism described in RFC 3459. In particular, if the UAS is unable to fetch or render an optional body part, then the server must not return an error to the UAC.

16.6.4.6 Specifying Versioning Information for the URI

To determine whether the content indirectly referenced by the URI has changed, a Content-ID entity header is used. The syntax of this header is defined in RFC 2045. Changes in the underlying content referred to by a URI must result in a change in the Content-ID associated with that URI. Multiple SIP messages carrying URIs that refer to the same content should reuse the same Content-ID, to allow the receiver to cache this content and to avoid unnecessary retrievals. The Content-ID is intended to be globally unique and should be temporally unique across SIP dialogs. For example:

```
Content-ID: <4232423424@www.example.com>
```

16.6.4.7 Specifying the URI Lifetime

The URI supplied by the Content-Type header is not required to be accessible or valid for an indefinite period of time. Rather, the supplier of the URI must specify the time period for which this URI is valid and accessible. This is done through an EXPIRATION parameter of the Content-Type. The format of this expiration parameter is an RFC 1123 date–time value. This is further restricted in this application to use only GMT time, consistent with the Date: header in SIP. This is a mandatory parameter. Note that the date–time value can range from minutes to days or even years. For example:

```
Content-Type: message/external-body;
              expiration="Mon, 24 June 2002
              09:00:00 GMT"
```

16.6.4.8 Specifying the Type of the Indirect Content

To support existing SIP mechanisms for the negotiation of content types, a Content-Type entity header should be present in the entity (payload) itself. If the protocol (scheme) of the URI supports its own content negotiation mechanisms (e.g., HTTP), this header may be omitted. The sender must, however, be prepared for the receiving party to reject content indirection if the receiver is unable to negotiate an appropriate MIME type by using the underlying protocol for the URI scheme. For example:

```
Content-Type: message/external-body;
              access-type="URL";
              expiration="Mon, 24 June 2002
              09:00:00 GMT";
              URL="http://www.example.com/
              the-indirect-content"
              <CRLF>
              Content-Type: application/sdp
              Content-Disposition: session
              <CRLF>
```

16.6.4.9 Specifying the Size of the Indirect Content

When known in advance, the size of the indirect content in bytes should be supplied via a size parameter on the Content-Type header. This is an extension of RFC 2017 but is in line with other access types defined for the message/external-body MIME type in RFC 2046. The content size is useful for the receiving party to make a determination about whether to retrieve the content. As with directly supplied content, a UAS may return a 513 Message Too Long error response in the event that the content size is too large. Size is an optional parameter. For example:

```
Content-Type: message/external-body;
              access-type="URL";
```

```
          expiration="Mon, 24 June 2002
          09:00:00 GMT";
          URL="http://www.example.com/
          the-indirect-content";
          size=4123
```

16.6.4.10 Specifying the Purpose of the Indirect Content

A Content-Disposition entity header must be present for all indirect content. For example:

```
Content-Type: message/external-body;
          access-type="URL";
      expiration="Mon, 24 June 2002 09:00:00
      GMT";
      URL="http://www.example.com/
      the-indirect-content"
<CRLF>
Content-Type: image/jpeg
Content-Disposition: render
```

16.6.4.11 Specifying Multiple URIs for Content Indirection

If there is a need to send multiple URIs for content indirection, an appropriate multipart MIME type should be used. Each URI must be contained in a single entity. Indirect content may be mixed with directly supplied content. This is particularly useful with the multipart/alternative MIME type. Note that RFC 4483 does not change the meanings of the various multipart flavors, particularly multipart/related, as described in RFC 2387.

For example:

```
MIME-Version: 1.0
Content-Type: multipart/mixed;
boundary=boundary42

--boundary42

Content-Type: text/plain; charset=us-ascii
The company announcement for June, 2002
follows:

--boundary42

Content-Type: message/external-body;
      access-type="URL";
      expiration="Mon, 24 June 2002 09:00:00
      GMT";
      URL="http://www.example.com/
      announcements/07242002";
      size=4123
Content-Type: text/html
Content-Disposition: render

--boundary42--
```

16.6.4.12 Specifying a Hash Value for the Indirect Content

If the sender knows the specific content being referenced by the indirection, and if the sender wishes the recipient to be able to validate that this content has not been altered from that intended by the sender, the sender includes a SHA-1 (RFC 3174) hash of the content. If it is included, the hash is encoded by extending the MIME syntax (RFC 2046) to include a *hash* parameter for the content type message/external-body, whose value is a hexadecimal encoding of the hash. For example:

```
Content-Type: message/external-body;
             access-type="URL";
             expiration="Mon, 24 June 2002
             09:00:00 GMT";
             URL="http://www.example.com/
             the-indirect-content.au";
             size=52723;
             hash=10AB568E91245681AC1B
<CRLF>
Content-Disposition: render
```

16.6.4.13 Freeform Text to Comments about the Indirect Content

One may use the Content-Description entity header to provide optional, freeform text to comment on the indirect content. This text may be displayed to the end user but must not used by other elements to determine the disposition of the body. For example:

```
Content-Type: message/external-body;
             access-type="URL";
             expiration="Mon, 24 June 2002
             09:00:00 GMT";
             URL="http://www.example.com/
             the-indirect-content";
             size=52723
<CRLF>
Content-Description: Multicast gaming session
Content-Disposition: render
```

16.6.4.14 Relationship to Call-Info, Error-Info, and Alert-Info Headers

SIP defines three headers (see Section 2.8) that supply additional information with regard to a session, a particular error response, or alerting. All three of these headers allow the UAC or UAS to indicate additional information through a URI. They may be considered a form of content indirection. The content indirection mechanism defined in this document is not intended as a replacement for these headers. Rather, the headers defined in SIP must be used in preference to this mechanism, where applicable, because of the well-defined semantics of those headers.

16.6.5 Examples

16.6.5.1 Single Content Indirection

```
INVITE sip:boromir@example.com SIP/2.0
From: <sip:gandalf@example.net>;tag=347242
To: <sip:boromir@example.com>
Call-ID: 3573853342923422@example.net
CSeq: 2131 INVITE
Accept: message/external-body application/sdp
Content-Type: message/external-body;
             ACCESS-TYPE=URL;
             URL="http://www.example.net/
             party/06/2002/announcement";
             EXPIRATION="Sat, 20 Jun 2002
             12:00:00 GMT";
             size=231
Content-Length: 105
Content-Type: application/sdp
Content-Disposition: session
Content-ID: <4e5562cd1214427d@example.net>
```

16.6.5.2 Multipart MIME with Content Indirection

```
MESSAGE sip:boromir@example.com SIP/2.0
From: <sip:gandalf@example.net>;tag=34589882
To: <sip:boromir@example.com>
Call-ID: 9242892442211117@example.net
CSeq: 388 MESSAGE
Accept: message/external-body, text/html,
text/plain,
             image/*, text/x-emoticon
MIME-Version: 1.0
Content-Type: multipart/mixed;
boundary=zz993453

--zz993453

Content-Type: message/external-body;
access-type="URL";
             expiration="Mon, 24 June 2002
             09:00:00 GMT";
             URL="http://www.example.net/
             company_picnic/image1.png";
             size=234422
Content-Type: image/png
Content-ID: <9535035333@example.net>
Content-Disposition: render
Content-Description: Kevin getting dunked in
the wading pool

--zz993453
Content-Type: message/external-body;
             access-type="URL";
             expiration="Mon, 24 June 2002
             09:00:00 GMT";
             URL="http://www.example.net/
             company_picnic/image2.png";
             size=233811
Content-Type: image/png
Content-ID: <1134299224244@example.net>
Content-Disposition: render
Content-Description: Peter on his tricycle

--zz993453--
```

16.7 Transcoding Call Services

16.7.1 Transcoding Services Framework

16.7.1.1 Overview

RFC 5369 that is described here provides a framework for transcoding with SIP how two SIP UAs can discover incompatibilities that prevent them from establishing a session (e.g., lack of support for a common codec or common media type). RFC 4117 that is described in Section 16.7.2 specifies how to invoke transcoding services using SIP and 3PCC. This way of invocation meets the requirements for SIP regarding transcoding services invocation to support deaf, hard-of-hearing, and speech-impaired individuals, and for other purposes. When such incompatibilities are found, the UAs need to invoke transcoding services to successfully establish the session. The two methods that allow for invocation of transcoding services are as follows:

- The 3PCC specified in RFC 4117 (see Section 16.7.2).
- The conference bridge transcoding service described in RFC 5370 (see Section 16.7.3).

Two UAs involved in a SIP dialog may find it impossible to establish a media session due to a variety of incompatibilities. Assuming that both UAs understand the same session description format, for example, SDP (RFC 4566, see Section 7.7), incompatibilities can be found at the UA level and at the user level. At the UA level, both terminals may not support any common codec or may not support common media types (e.g., a text-only terminal and an audio-only terminal). At the user level, a deaf person will not understand anything said over an audio stream. Note that both models meet the requirements regarding transcoding services invocation in RFC 3351, which support deaf, hard-of-hearing, and speech-impaired individuals.

To make communications possible in the presence of incompatibilities, UAs need to introduce intermediaries that provide transcoding services to a session. From the SIP point of view, the introduction of a transcoder is done in the same way to resolve both user level and UA level incompatibilities. Thus, the invocation mechanisms described in this document are generally applicable to any type of incompatibility related to how the information that needs to be communicated is encoded. Furthermore, although this framework focuses on transcoding, the mechanisms described are applicable to media manipulation in general. It would be possible to use them, for example, to invoke a server that simply increases the volume of an audio stream. This document does not describe media server discovery. That is an orthogonal problem that one can address using UA provisioning or other methods.

16.7.1.2 Discovery of the Need for Transcoding Services

According to the one-party consent model defined in RFC 3238, services that involve media manipulation invocation are best invoked by one of the end points involved in the communication, as opposed to being invoked by an intermediary in the network. Following this principle, one of the end points should be the one detecting that transcoding is needed for a particular session. To decide whether or not transcoding is needed, a UA needs to know the capabilities of the remote UA. In accordance to offer–answer model, a UA acting as an offerer (RFC 3264, see Section 3.8.4) typically obtains this knowledge by downloading a presence document that includes media capabilities (e.g., Bob is available on a terminal that only supports audio) or by getting an SDP description of media capabilities as defined in RFC 3264.

Presence documents are typically received in a NOTIFY request (RFC 6665, see Section 5.2) as a result of a subscription. SDP media capability descriptions are typically received in a 200 OK response to an OPTIONS request or in a 488 Not Acceptable Here response to an INVITE. In the absence of presence information, routing logic that involves parallel forking to several UAs may make it difficult (or impossible) for the caller to know which UA will answer the next call attempt. For example, a call attempt may reach the user's voice mail while the next one may reach a SIP phone where the user is available. If both terminating UAs have different capabilities, the caller cannot know, even after the first call attempt, whether or not transcoding will be necessary for the session. This is a well-known SIP problem that is referred to as Heterogeneous Error Response Forking Problem (HEREP). Resolving HERFP is outside the scope of this book.

It is recommended that an offerer does not invoke transcoding services before making sure that the answerer does not support the capabilities needed for the session. Making wrong assumptions about the answerer's capabilities can lead to situations where two transcoders are introduced (one by the offerer and one by the answerer) in a session that would not need any transcoding services at all. An example of the situation above is a call between two Global System for Mobile Communications (GSM) phones (without using transcoding-free operation). Both phones use a GSM codec, but the speech is converted from GSM to Pulse Code Modulation (PCM) by the originating Mobile Switching Center (MSC), and from PCM back to GSM by the terminating MSC. Note that transcoding services can be symmetric (e.g., speech-to-text plus text-to-speech) or asymmetric (e.g., a one-way speech-to-text transcoding for a hearing-impaired user that can talk).

16.7.1.3 Transcoding Service Invocation

Once the need for transcoding for a particular session has been identified as described earlier, one of the UAs needs to invoke transcoding services. As stated earlier, transcoder location is outside the scope of this document. Thus, we assume that the UA invoking transcoding services knows the URI of a server that provides them. Invoking transcoding services from a media transcoding server (T) for a session between two user parties/agents (A and B) involves establishing two media sessions; one between A and T and another between T and B. How to invoke T's services (i.e., how to establish both A–T and T–B sessions) depends on how we model the transcoding service. We have considered two models for invoking a transcoding service. The first is to use 3PCC (RFC 3725, see Section 18.3). The second is to use a (dial-in and dial-out) conference bridge that negotiates the appropriate media parameters on each individual leg (i.e., A–T and T–B). In the following sections, we describe the 3PCC model and the conference bridge transcoding invocation model.

16.7.2 Third-Party Transcoding Services

16.7.2.1 Overview

The 3PCC for the conferencing in SIP is defined in RFC 3725 (see Section 18.3). RFC 4117 is using the same 3PCC model for transcoding invocation with SIP where a transcoding server provides a particular transcoding service (e.g., speech-to-text) is identified by a URI. A UA that wishes to invoke that service sends an INVITE request to that URI establishing a number of media streams. The way the transcoder manipulates and manages the contents of those media streams (e.g., the text received over the text stream is transformed into speech and sent over the audio stream) is service specific. All the call flows in this document use SDP. The same call flows could be used with another SDP that provides similar session description capabilities.

In the 3PCC transcoding model defined here, the UA invoking the transcoding service has a signaling relationship with the transcoder and another signaling relationship with the remote UA. There is no signaling relationship between the transcoder and the remote UA, as shown in Figure 16.32.

This model is suitable for advanced end points that are able to perform 3PCC. It allows end points to invoke transcoding services on a stream basis. That is, the media streams that need transcoding are routed through the transcoder, while the streams that do not need it are sent directly between the end points. This model also allows invoking one transcoder for the sending direction and a different one for the receiving direction of the same stream. Invoking a transcoder in the middle of an ongoing session is also quite simple. This is useful when session changes occur (e.g., an audio session is upgraded to an audio/video session) and the end points cannot cope with the changes (e.g., they had common audio codecs but no common video codecs). The privacy level that is achieved using 3PCC is high, since the transcoder does not see the signaling between both end points. In this model, the transcoder only has access to the information that is strictly needed to perform its function.

16.7.2.2 Transcoding Call Control Flows

Given two UAs (A and B) and a transcoding server (T), the invocation of a transcoding service consists of establishing two sessions: A–T and T–B. How these sessions are established depends on which party, caller (A) or the callee (B), invokes the transcoding services. Next, we describe the callee and caller invocation of the transcoding service. In all

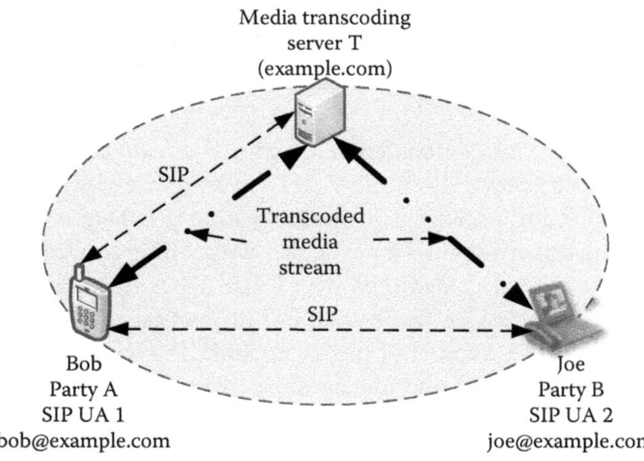

Figure 16.32 3PCC model. (Copyright IETF. Reproduced with permission.)

our 3PCC flows, we have followed the general principle that a 200 OK response from the transcoding service has to be received before contacting the callee. This tries to ensure that the transcoding service will be available when the callee accepts the session.

Still, the transcoding service does not know the exact type of transcoding it will be performing until the callee accepts the session. Thus, there is always the chance of failing to provide transcoding services after the callee has accepted the session. A system with more stringent requirements could use preconditions to avoid this situation. When preconditions are used, the callee is not alerted until everything is ready for the session. We define some terms here just only for explaining some example call flows of the third-party transcoding services as follows:

- SDP A: A session description generated by A. It contains, among other things, the transport address (IP address and port number) where A wants to receive media for each particular stream.
- SDP B: A session description generated by B. It contains, among other things, the transport address where B wants to receive media for each particular stream.
- SDP A+B: A session description that contains, among other things, the transport address where A wants to receive media and the transport address where B wants to receive media.
- SDP TA: A session description generated by T and intended for A. It contains, among other things, the transport address where T wants to receive media from A.
- SDP TB: A session description generated by T and intended for B. It contains, among other things, the transport address where T wants to receive media from B.
- SDP TA+TB: A session description generated by T that contains, among other things, the transport address where T wants to receive media from A and the transport address where T wants to receive media from B.

16.7.2.3 Callee's Invocation

In this scenario, B receives an INVITE from A, and B decides to introduce T in the session. Figure 16.32 shows the call flow for this scenario. In Figure 16.33, A can both hear and speak, and B is a deaf user with a speech impairment. A proposes to establish a session that consists of an audio stream (F1). B wants to send and receive only text, so it invokes a transcoding service T that will perform both speech-to-text and text-to-speech conversions (F2). The session descriptions of Figure 16.33 are partially shown below.

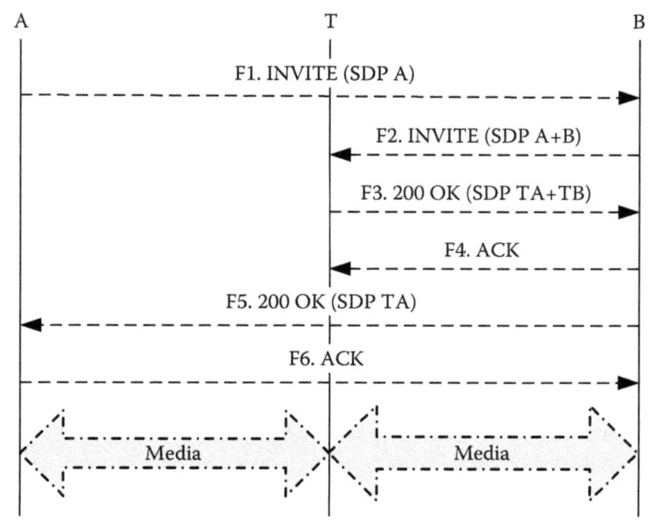

Figure 16.33 Callee's invocation of a transcoding service. (Copyright IETF. Reproduced with permission.)

(F1) INVITE SDP A

```
m=audio 20000 RTP/AVP 0
c=IN IP4 A.example.com
```

(F2) INVITE SDP A+B

```
m=audio 20000 RTP/AVP 0
c=IN IP4 A.example.com
m=text 40000 RTP/AVP 96
c=IN IP4 B.example.com
a=rtpmap:96 t140/1000
```

(F3) 200 OK SDP TA+TB

```
m=audio 30000 RTP/AVP 0
c=IN IP4 T.example.com
m=text 30002 RTP/AVP 96
c=IN IP4 T.example.com
a=rtpmap:96 t140/1000
```

(F5) 200 OK SDP TA

```
m=audio 30000 RTP/AVP 0
c=IN IP4 T.example.com
```

Four media streams (i.e., two bidirectional streams) have been established at this point:

1. Audio from A to T.example.com:30000
2. Text from T to B.example.com:40000
3. Text from B to T.example.com:30002
4. Audio from T to A.example.com:20000

When either A or B decides to terminate the session, it sends a BYE indicating that the session is over. If the first INVITE (F1) received by B is empty (no session description), the call flow is slightly different. Figure 16.34 shows the messages involved. B may have different reasons for invoking T before knowing A's session description. B may want to hide its lack of native capabilities, and therefore wants to return a session description with all the codecs that B supports, plus all the codecs that T supports. Or T may provide recording services (besides transcoding), and B wants T to record the conversation, regardless of whether transcoding is needed.

This scenario (Figure 16.34) is a bit more complex than the previous one. In INVITE (F2), B still does not have SDP A, so it cannot provide T with that information. When B finally receives SDP A in (F6), it has to send it to T. B sends an empty INVITE to T (F7) and gets a 200 OK with SDP TA+TB (F8). In general, this SDP TA+TB can be different than the one sent in (F3). That is why B needs to send the updated SDP TA to A in (F9). A then sends a possibly updated SDP A (10) and B sends it to T in (12). On the other hand, if T happens to return the same SDP TA+TB in (F8) as in (F3), B can skip messages (F9), (F10), and (F11). Thus, implementers

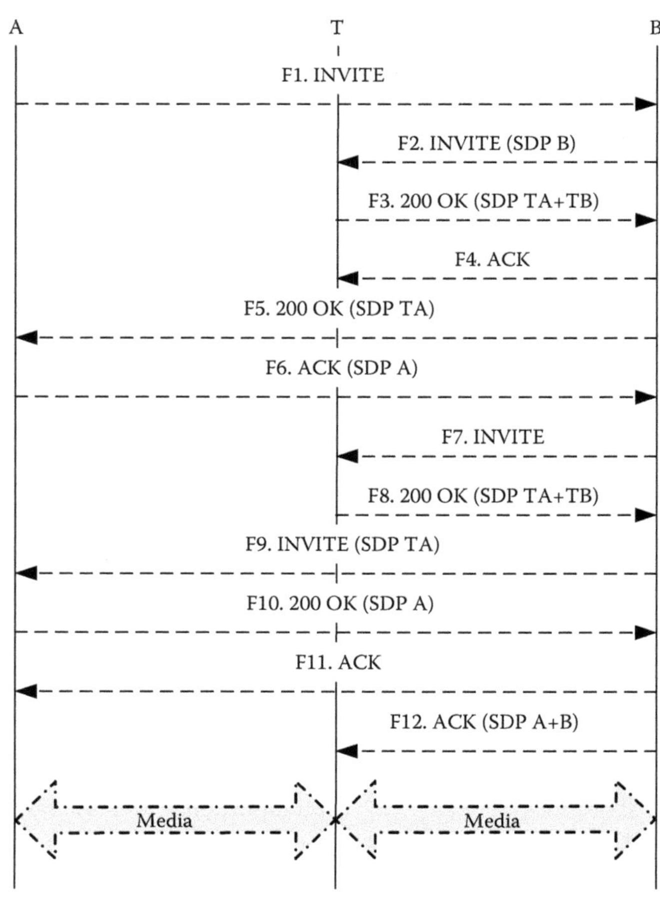

Figure 16.34 Callee's invocation after initial INVITE without SDP. (Copyright IETF. Reproduced with permission.)

of transcoding services are encouraged to return the same session description in (F8) as in (F3) in this type of scenario. The session descriptions of this flow are shown below:

(F2) INVITE SDP A+B

```
m=audio 20000 RTP/AVP 0
c=IN IP4 0.0.0.0
m=text 40000 RTP/AVP 96
c=IN IP4 B.example.com
a=rtpmap:96 t140/1000
```

(F3) 200 OK SDP TA+TB

```
m=audio 30000 RTP/AVP 0
c=IN IP4 T.example.com
m=text 30002 RTP/AVP 96
c=IN IP4 T.example.com
a=rtpmap:96 t140/1000
```

(F5) 200 OK SDP TA

```
m=audio 30000 RTP/AVP 0
c=IN IP4 T.example.com
```

(F6) ACK SDP A

```
m=audio 20000 RTP/AVP 0
c=IN IP4 A.example.com
```

(F8) 200 OK SDP TA+TB

```
m=audio 30004 RTP/AVP 0
c=IN IP4 T.example.com
m=text 30006 RTP/AVP 96
c=IN IP4 T.example.com
a=rtpmap:96 t140/1000
```

(F9) INVITE SDP TA

```
m=audio 30004 RTP/AVP 0
c=IN IP4 T.example.com
(10) 200 OK SDP A
m=audio 20002 RTP/AVP 0
c=IN IP4 A.example.com
```

(F12) ACK SDP A+B

```
m=audio 20002 RTP/AVP 0
c=IN IP4 A.example.com
m=text 40000 RTP/AVP 96
c=IN IP4 B.example.com
a=rtpmap:96 t140/1000
```

Four media streams (i.e., two bidirectional streams) have been established at this point:

1. Audio from A to T.example.com:30004
2. Text from T to B.example.com:40000
3. Text from B to T.example.com:30006
4. Audio from T to A.example.com:20002

16.7.2.4 Caller's Invocation

In this scenario, A wishes to establish a session with B using a transcoding service. A uses 3PCC to set up the session between T and B. The call flow we provide here is slightly different from the ones in RFC 3725 (see Section 18.3). In 3PCC, the controller establishes a session between two UAs, which are the ones deciding the characteristics of the streams. Here, A wants to establish a session between T and B, but A wants to decide how many and which types of streams are established. That is why A sends its session description in the first INVITE (F1) to T, as opposed to the media-less initial INVITE recommended by the 3PCC model. Figure 16.35 shows the call flow for this scenario. We do not include the session descriptions of this flow since they are very similar to those in Figure 16.34. In this flow, if T returns the same SDP TA+TB in (F8) as in (F2), messages (F9), (F10), and (F11) can be skipped.

16.7.2.5 Receiving the Original Stream

Sometimes, as pointed out in the requirements for SIP in support of deaf, hard-of-hearing, and speech-impaired individuals specified in RFC 3351, a user wants to receive both the original stream (e.g., audio) and the transcoded stream (e.g., the output

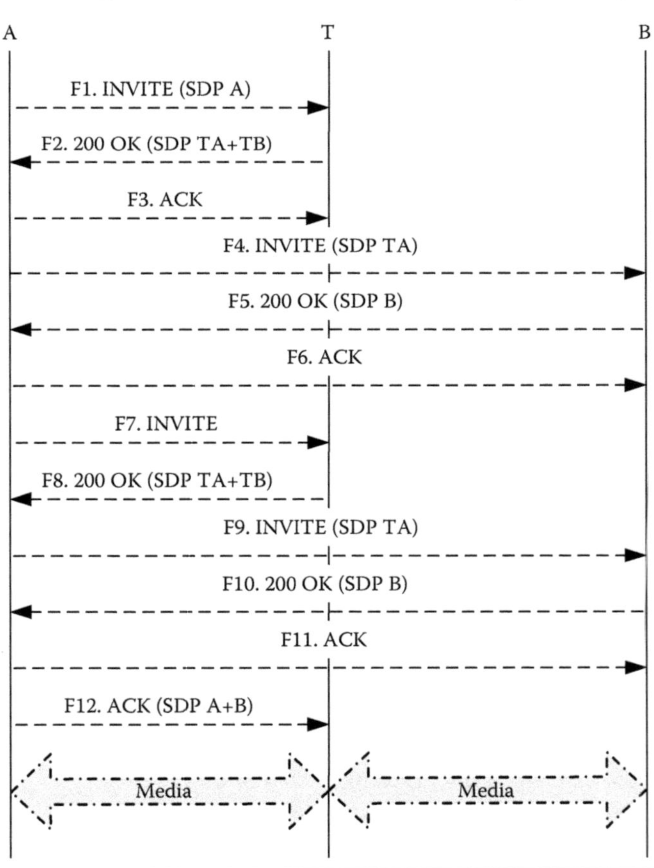

Figure 16.35 Caller's invocation of a transcoding service. (Copyright IETF. Reproduced with permission.)

of the speech-to-text conversion). There are various possible solutions for this problem. One solution consists of using the SDP group attribute with Flow Identification (FID) semantics (RFC 3351). FID allows requesting that a stream is sent to two different transport addresses in parallel, as shown below:

```
a=group:FID 1 2
m=audio 20000 RTP/AVP 0
c=IN IP4 A.example.com
a=mid:1
m=audio 30000 RTP/AVP 0
c=IN IP4 T.example.com
a=mid:2
```

The problem with this solution is that the majority of the SIP UAs do not support FID. Moreover, only a small fraction of the few UAs that support FID also support sending simultaneous copies of the same media stream at the same time. In addition, FID forces both copies of the stream to use the same codec. Therefore, we recommend that T (instead of a UA) replicates the media stream. The transcoder T receiving the following session description performs speech-to-text and text-to-speech conversions between the first audio stream and the text stream. In addition, T copies the first audio stream to the second audio stream and sends it to A.

```
m=audio 40000 RTP/AVP 0
c=IN IP4 B.example.com
m=audio 20000 RTP/AVP 0
c=IN IP4 A.example.com
a=recvonly
m=text 20002 RTP/AVP 96
c=IN IP4 A.example.com
a=rtpmap:96 t140/1000
```

16.7.2.6 *Transcoding Services in Parallel*

Transcoding services sometimes consist of human relays (e.g., a person performing speech-to-text and text-to-speech conversions for a session). If the same person is involved in both conversions (i.e., from A to B and from B to A), he/she has access to all of the conversation. To provide some degree of privacy, sometimes two different persons are allocated to do the job (i.e., one person handles A→B and the other B→A). This type of disposition is also useful for automated transcoding services, where one machine converts text to synthetic speech (text-to-speech) and another performs voice recognition (speech-to-text). The scenario described above involves four different sessions: A-T1, T1-B, B-T2, and T2-A. Figure 16.36 shows the call flow where A invokes T1 and T2. Note this example uses unidirectional media streams (i.e., sendonly or recvonly) to clearly identify which transcoder handles media in which direction. Nevertheless, nothing precludes the use of bidirectional streams in this scenario. They could be used, for example, by a human relay to ask for clarifications (e.g., I did not get that, could you repeat, please?) to the party he or she is receiving media from.

(F1) INVITE SDP AT1

```
m=text 20000 RTP/AVP 96
c=IN IP4 A.example.com
a=rtpmap:96 t140/1000
a=sendonly
m=audio 20000 RTP/AVP 0
c=IN IP4 0.0.0.0
a=recvonly
```

(F2) INVITE SDP AT2

```
m=text 20002 RTP/AVP 96
c=IN IP4 A.example.com
a=rtpmap:96 t140/1000
a=recvonly
m=audio 20000 RTP/AVP 0
c=IN IP4 0.0.0.0
a=sendonly
```

(F3) 200 OK SDP T1A+T1B

```
m=text 30000 RTP/AVP 96
c=IN IP4 T1.example.com
a=rtpmap:96 t140/1000
a=recvonly
m=audio 30002 RTP/AVP 0
c=IN IP4 T1.example.com
a=sendonly
```

(F5) 200 OK SDP T2A+T2B

```
m=text 40000 RTP/AVP 96
c=IN IP4 T2.example.com
a=rtpmap:96 t140/1000
a=sendonly
m=audio 40002 RTP/AVP 0
c=IN IP4 T2.example.com
a=recvonly
```

(F7) INVITE SDP T1B+T2B

```
m=audio 30002 RTP/AVP 0
c=IN IP4 T1.example.com
a=sendonly
m=audio 40002 RTP/AVP 0
c=IN IP4 T2.example.com
a=recvonly
```

(F8) 200 OK SDP BT1+BT2

```
m=audio 50000 RTP/AVP 0
c=IN IP4 B.example.com
a=recvonly
m=audio 50002 RTP/AVP 0
c=IN IP4 B.example.com
a=sendonly
```

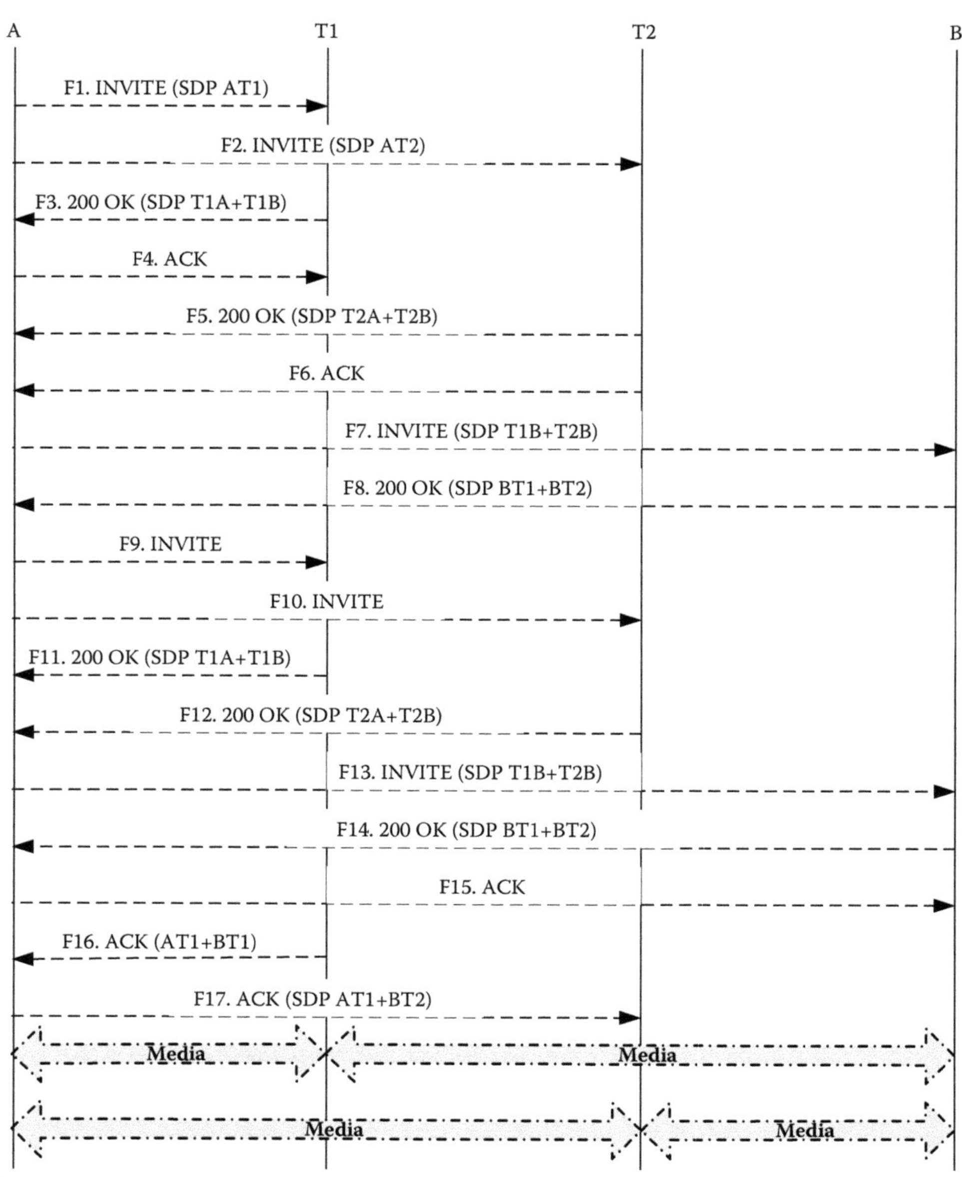

Figure 16.36 Transcoding services in parallel. (Copyright IETF. Reproduced with permission.)

(F11) 200 OK SDP T1A+T1B

```
m=text 30000 RTP/AVP 96
c=IN IP4 T1.example.com
a=rtpmap:96 t140/1000
a=recvonly
m=audio 30002 RTP/AVP 0
c=IN IP4 T1.example.com
a=sendonly
```

(F12) 200 OK SDP T2A+T2B

```
m=text 40000 RTP/AVP 96
c=IN IP4 T2.example.com
a=rtpmap:96 t140/1000
a=sendonly
m=audio 40002 RTP/AVP 0
c=IN IP4 T2.example.com
a=recvonly
```

Since T1 has returned the same SDP in (F11) as in (F3), and T2 has returned the same SDP in (F12) as in (F5), messages (F13), (F14), and (F15) can be skipped.

(F16) ACK SDP AT1+BT1

```
m=text 20000 RTP/AVP 96
c=IN IP4 A.example.com
a=rtpmap:96 t140/1000
a=sendonly
```

```
m=audio 50000 RTP/AVP 0
c=IN IP4 B.example.com
a=recvonly
```

(F17) ACK SDP AT2+BT2

```
m=text 20002 RTP/AVP 96
c=IN IP4 A.example.com
a=rtpmap:96 t140/1000
a=recvonly
m=audio 50002 RTP/AVP 0
c=IN IP4 B.example.com
a=sendonly
```

Four media streams have been established at this point:

1. Text from A to T1.example.com:30000
2. Audio from T1 to B.example.com:50000
3. Audio from B to T2.example.com:40002
4. Text from T2 to A.example.com:20002

Note that B, the UA server, needs to support two media streams: sendonly and recvonly. At present, some UAs, although they support a single sendrecv media stream, do not support a different media line per direction. Implementers are encouraged to build support for this feature.

16.7.2.7 Multiple Transcoding Services in Series

In a distributed environment, a complex transcoding service (e.g., English text to Spanish speech) is often provided by several servers. For example, one server performs English text to Spanish text translation, and its output is fed into a server that performs text-to-speech (TTS) conversion. The flow in Figure 16.37 shows how A invokes T1 and T2.

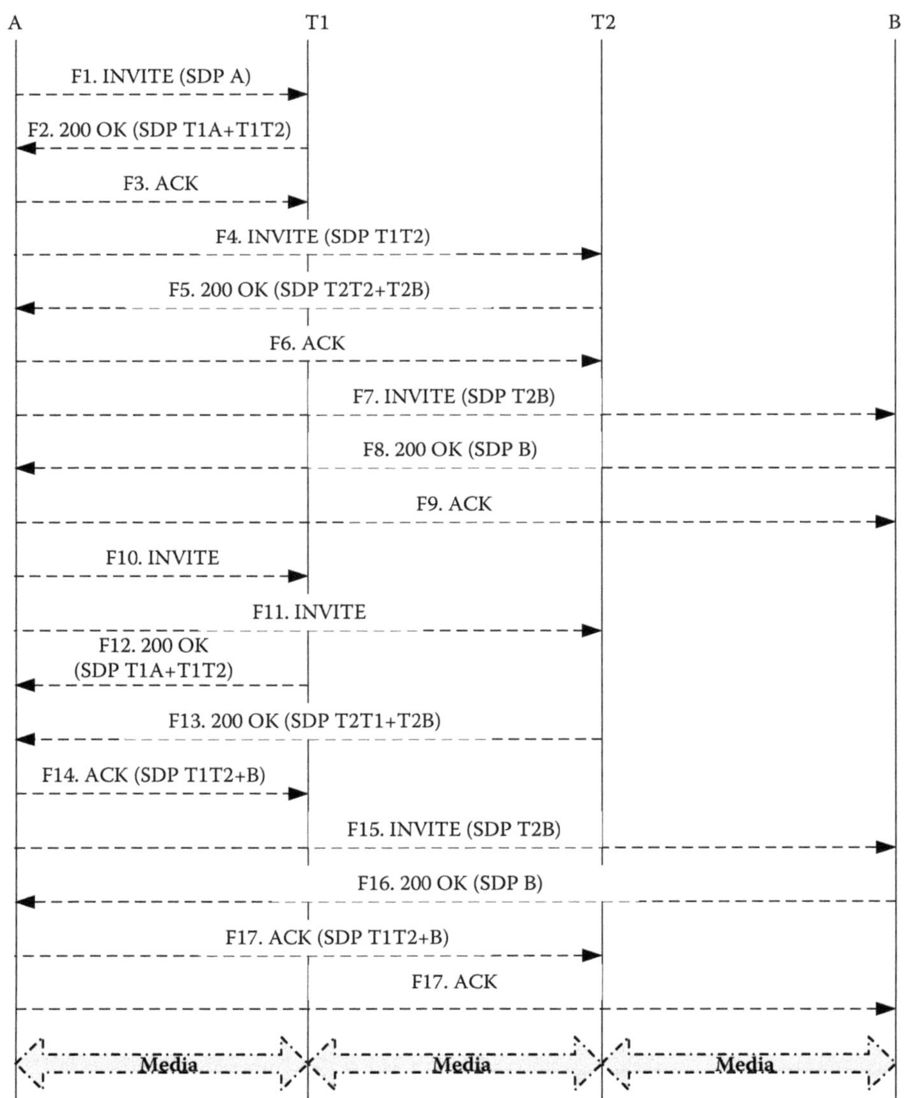

Figure 16.37 Transcoding services in serial. (Copyright IETF. Reproduced with permission.)

16.7.3 Conference Bridging Transcoding Call Control Flows

16.7.3.1 Overview

We have described earlier (RFC 5369, see Section 16.7.1) how two SIP UAs can discover incompatibilities that prevent them from establishing a session (e.g., lack of support for a common codec or for a common media type). When such incompatibilities are found, the UAs need to invoke transcoding services to successfully establish the session. We now describe (RFC 5370) how to invoke transcoding services using the conference bridge model. This way of invocation meets the requirements for SIP regarding transcoding services invocation to support deaf, hard-of-hearing, and speech-impaired individuals.

In the conference bridge model for transcoding invocation, a transcoding server that provides a particular transcoding service (e.g., speech-to-text) behaves as a B2BUA between both UAs and is identified by a URI. As shown in Figure 16.38, both UAs, A and B, exchange signaling and media with the transcoder T. The UAs do not exchange any traffic (signaling or media) directly between them.

Next, we describe how the caller A or the callee B, respectively, can use the conference bridge model to invoke transcoding services from T.

16.7.3.2 Caller's Invocation

UA A needs to perform two operations to invoke transcoding services from T for a session between UA A and UA B. UA A needs to establish a session with T and provide T with UA B's URI so that T can generate an INVITE toward UA B.

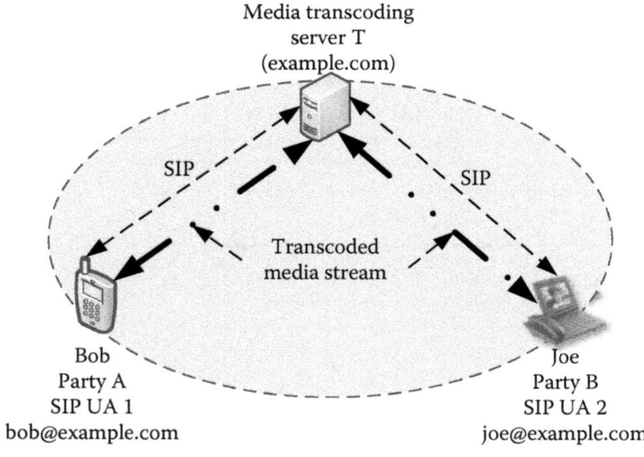

Figure 16.38 Conference bridge model. (Copyright IETF. Reproduced with permission.)

16.7.3.2.1 Procedures at the UA

UA A uses the procedures for RFC 5366, which describes the conference establishment, to provide T with B's URI using the same INVITE that establishes the session between A and T. That is, UA A adds to the INVITE a body part whose disposition type is recipient secured URI-list services (RFC 5363, see Section 19.7). This body part consists of a URI-list that contains a single URI: UA B's URI. Note that the transcoding model described here is modeled as a two-party conference server. Consequently, this document focuses on two-party sessions that need transcoding. Multiparty sessions can be established using INVITE requests with multiple URIs in their bodies, as specified in RFC 5366.

16.7.3.2.2 Procedures at the Transcoder

On receiving an INVITE with a URI-list body, the transcoder follows the procedures in RFC 5366 to generate an INVITE request toward the URI contained in the URI-list body. Note that the transcoder acts as a B2BUA, not as a proxy. Additionally, the transcoder must generate the From header field of the outgoing INVITE request using the same value as the From header field included in the incoming INVITE request, subject to the privacy requirements specified in RFC 3323 (see Section 20.2) and RFC 3325 (see Sections 2.8, 10.4, and 20.3) expressed in the incoming INVITE request. Note that this does not apply to the tag parameter.

The session description the transcoder includes in the outgoing INVITE request depends on the type of transcoding service that particular transcoder provides. For example, a transcoder resolving audio codec incompatibilities would generate a session description listing the audio codecs the transcoder supports. When the transcoder receives a final response for the outgoing INVITE requests, it generates a new final response for the incoming INVITE request. This new final response should have the same status code as the one received in the response for the outgoing INVITE request. If a transcoder receives an INVITE request with a URI-list with more than one URI, it should return a 488 Not Acceptable (Max 1 URI allowed in URI-list) response.

16.7.3.2.3 Example

Figure 16.39 shows the message flow for the caller's invocation of a transcoder T. The caller A sends an INVITE (F1) to the transcoder (T) to establish the session A–T. Following the procedures in RFC 5366, the caller A adds a body part whose disposition type is recipient-secured URI-list (RFC 5363, see Section 19.7).

The following example shows an INVITE with two body parts: an SDP (RFC 4566, see Section 7.7) session description and a URI-list.

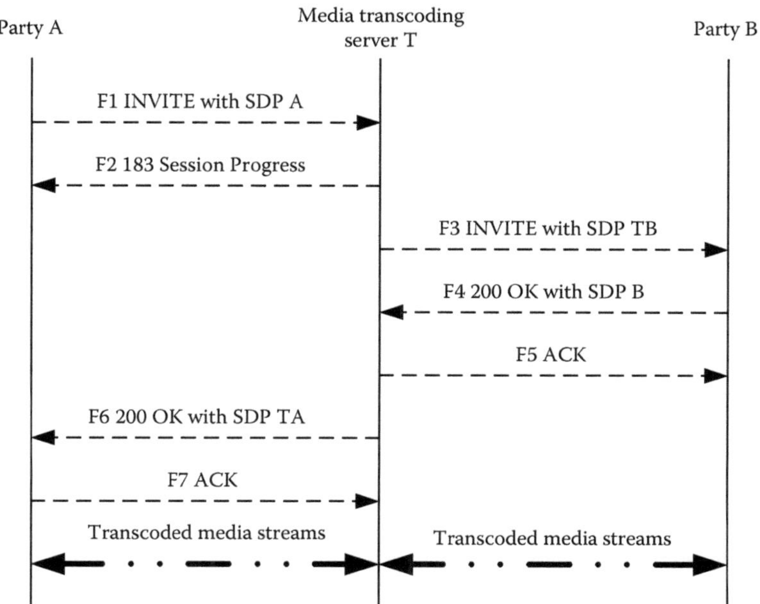

Figure 16.39 Successful invocation of a transcoder by the caller. (Copyright IETF. Reproduced with permission.)

```
INVITE sip:transcoder@example.com SIP/2.0
Via: SIP/2.0/TCP client.chicago.example.com
;branch=z9hG4bKhjhs8ass83
Max-Forwards: 70
To: Transcoder <sip:transcoder@example.org>
From: A <sip:A@chicago.example.com>;tag=32331
Call-ID: d432fa84b4c76e66710
CSeq: 1 INVITE
Contact: <sip:A@client.chicago.example.com>
Allow: INVITE, ACK, CANCEL, OPTIONS, BYE,
REFER,
SUBSCRIBE, NOTIFY
Allow-Events: dialog
Accept: application/sdp, message/sipfrag
Require: recipient-list-invite
Content-Type: multipart/
mixed;boundary="boundary1"
Content-Length: 556

--boundary1

Content-Type: application/sdp
v=0
o=example 2890844526 2890842807 IN IP4
chicago.example.com
s=-
c=IN IP4 192.0.2.1
t=0 0
m=audio 50000 RTP/AVP 0
a=rtpmap:0 PCMU/8000

--boundary1

Content-Type: application/resource-lists+xml
Content-Disposition: recipient-list
<?xml version="1.0" encoding="UTF-8"?>
<resource-lists xmlns="urn:ietf:params:xml:ns
:resource-lists"
       xmlns:xsi="http://www.w3.org/2001/
       XMLSchema-instance">
       <list>
              <entry uri="sip:B@example.org"/>
       </list>
</resource-lists>

--boundary1--
```

On receiving the INVITE, the transcoder generates a new INVITE toward the callee. The transcoder acts as a B2BUA, not as a proxy. Therefore, this new INVITE (F3) belongs to a different transaction than the INVITE (F1) received by the transcoder. When the transcoder receives a final response (F4) from the callee, it generates a new final response (F6) for INVITE (F1). This new final response (F6) has the same status code as the one received in the response from the callee (F4).

16.7.3.2.4 Unsuccessful Session Establishment

Figure 16.40 shows a similar message flow as the one in Figure 16.39. Nevertheless, this time, the callee generates a non-2xx final response (F4). Consequently, the transcoder generates a non-2xx final response (F6) toward the caller as well.

The ambiguity in this flow is that, if the provisional response (F2) gets lost, the caller does not know whether the 603 Decline response means that the initial INVITE (F1) was rejected by the transcoder or that the INVITE generated by the transcoder (F4) was rejected by the callee. The use of

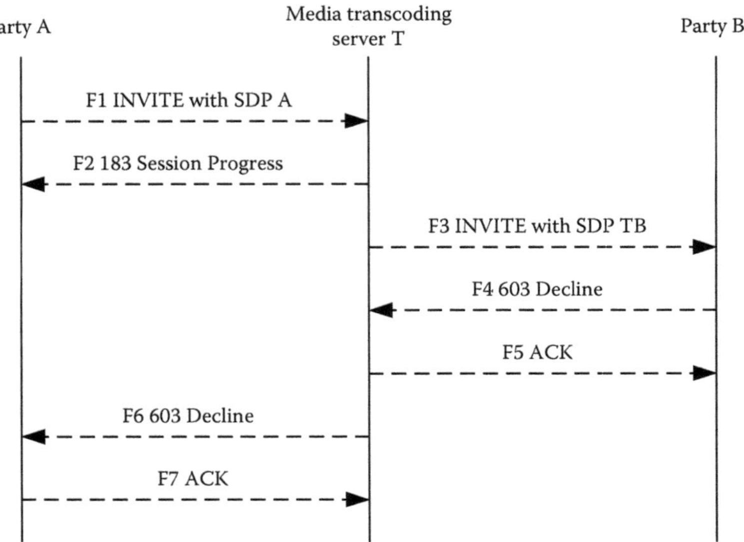

Figure 16.40 Unsuccessful session establishment. (Copyright IETF. Reproduced with permission.)

the History-Info header field (RFC 4244, see Section 2.8) between the transcoder and the caller resolves the previous ambiguity. Note that this ambiguity problem could also have been resolved by having transcoders act as a pure conference bridge. The transcoder would respond with a 200 OK to the INVITE request from the caller, and it would generate an outgoing INVITE request toward the callee. The caller would get information about the result of the latter INVITE request by subscribing to the conference event package (RFC 4575) at the transcoder. Although this flow would have

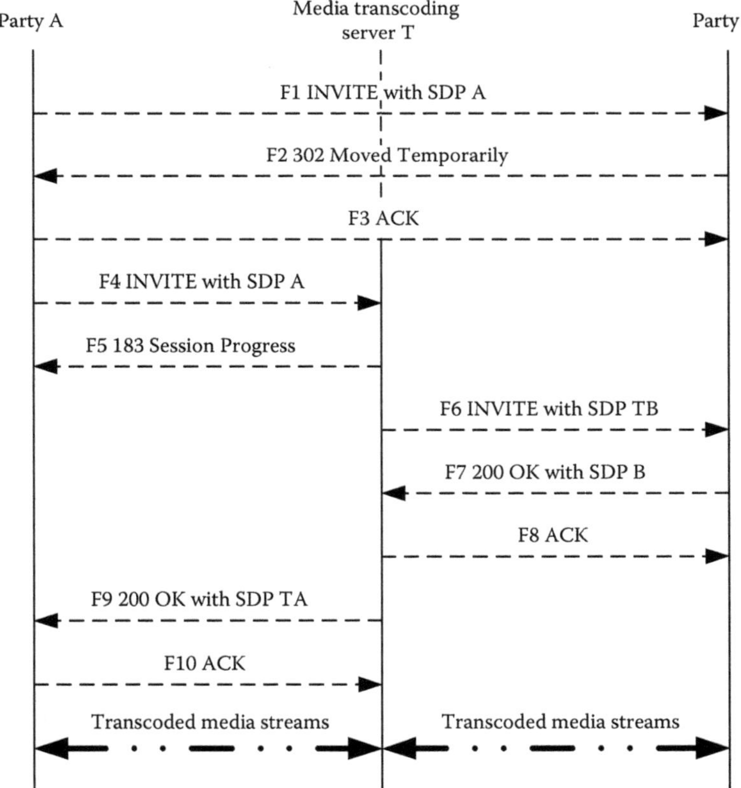

Figure 16.41 Callee's invocation of a transcoder. (Copyright IETF. Reproduced with permission.)

resolved the ambiguity problem without requiring support for the History-Info header field, it is more complex, requires a higher number of messages, and introduces higher session setup delays. That is why it was not chosen to implement transcoding services.

16.7.3.3 Callee's Invocation

If a UA receives an INVITE with a session description that is not acceptable, it can redirect it to the transcoder by using a 302 Moved Temporarily response. The Contact header field of the 302 Moved Temporarily response contains the URI of the transcoder plus a ?body= parameter. This parameter contains a recipient-list body with B's URI. Note that some escaping (e.g., for CRLFs) is needed to encode a recipient-list body in such a parameter. Figure 16.41 shows the message flow for this scenario.

Note that the syntax resulting from encoding a body into a URI as described earlier is quite complex. It is actually simpler for callees to invoke transcoding services using the 3PCC transcoding model as described earlier instead.

16.8 INFO Method—Mid-Call Information Transfer

16.8.1 Overview

RFC 6086 that is described here defines a method, INFO, for the SIP. The purpose of the INFO message is to carry application-level information between end points, using the SIP dialog signaling path. Note that the INFO method is not used to update the characteristics of a SIP dialog or session, but to allow the applications that use the SIP session to exchange information (which might update the state of those applications). Use of the INFO method does not constitute a separate dialog usage. INFO messages are always part of, and share the fate of, an invite dialog usage (RFC 5057, see Sections 3.6.5 and 16.2). INFO messages cannot be sent as part of other dialog usages, or outside an existing dialog. This document also defines an INFO Package mechanism. An INFO Package specification defines the content and semantics of the information carried in an INFO message associated with the INFO Package. The INFO Package mechanism also provides a way for UAs to indicate for which INFO Packages they are willing to receive INFO requests, and which INFO Package a specific INFO request is associated with. A UA uses the Recv-Info header field, on a per-dialog basis, to indicate for which INFO Packages it is willing to receive INFO requests. A UA can indicate an initial set of INFO Packages during dialog establishment and can indicate a new set during the lifetime of the invite dialog usage.

Note that a UA can use an empty Recv-Info header field (a header field without a value) to indicate that it is not willing to receive INFO requests for any INFO Package, while still informing other UAs that it supports the INFO Package mechanism. When a UA sends an INFO request, it uses the Info-Package header field to indicate which INFO Package is associated with the request. One particular INFO request can only be associated with a single INFO Package.

16.8.2 Motivation

A number of applications, standardized and proprietary, make use of the INFO method as it was previously defined in RFC 2976 (obsoleted by RFC 6087), here referred to as *legacy INFO usage*. These include but are not limited to the following:

- RFC 3372 (see Section 14.4.2) specifies the encapsulation of ISDN User Part in SIP message bodies. ITU-T and the 3GPP have specified similar procedures.
- ECMA-355 [12] specifies the encapsulation of QSIG in SIP message bodies.
- RFC 5022 specifies how INFO is used as a transport mechanism by the Media Server Control Markup Language (MSCML) protocol. MSCML uses an option tag in the Require header field to ensure that the receiver understands the INFO content.
- RFC 5707 specifies how INFO is used as a transport mechanism by the Media Server Markup Language (MSML) protocol.
- Companies have been using INFO messages in order to request fast video update. Currently, a standardized mechanism, based on the RTCP, has been specified in RFC 5168.
- Companies have been using INFO messages in order to transport DTMF tones. All mechanisms are proprietary and have not been standardized.

Some legacy INFO usages are also recognized as being shortcuts to more appropriate and flexible mechanisms. Furthermore, RFC 2976 did not define mechanisms that would enable a SIP UA to indicate (a) the types of applications and contexts in which the UA supports the INFO method or (b) the types of applications and contexts with which a specific INFO message is associated. Because legacy INFO usages do not have associated INFO Packages, it is not possible to use the Recv-Info and Info-Package header fields with legacy INFO usages. That is, a UA cannot use the Recv-Info header field to indicate for which legacy INFO usages it is willing to receive INFO requests, and a UA cannot use the Info-Package header field to indicate with which legacy INFO usage an INFO request is associated.

Owing to the problems described above, legacy INFO usages often require static configuration to indicate the types of applications and contexts for which the UAs support the INFO method, and the way they handle application information transported in INFO messages. This has caused interoperability problems in the industry. To overcome these problems, the SIP Working Group has spent significant discussion time over many years, coming to an agreement on whether it was more appropriate to fix INFO (by defining a registration mechanism for the ways in which it was used) or to deprecate it altogether (with the usage described in RFC 3398 being grandfathered as the sole legitimate usage). Although it required substantial consensus building and concessions by those more inclined to completely deprecate INFO, the eventual direction of the working group was to publish a framework for registration of INFO Packages as defined in this specification.

16.8.2.1 Applicability and Backwards Compatibility

We describe here an RFC 6086-specified method, INFO, for the SIP (RFC 3261), and an INFO Package mechanism. As RFC 6086 obsoletes RFC 2976, for backwards compatibility, we also specify a *legacy* mode of usage of the INFO method that is compatible with the usage previously defined in RFC 2976, here referred to as *legacy INFO Usage*. For backwards compatibility purposes, this document does not deprecate legacy INFO usages, and does not mandate users to define INFO Packages for such usages. However,

- A UA must not insert an Info-Package header field in a legacy INFO request (as described later, an INFO request associated with an INFO Package always contains an Info-Package header field).
- Any new usage must use the INFO Package mechanism defined in this specification, since it does not share the issues associated with legacy INFO usage, and since INFO Packages can be registered with IANA.

16.8.3 UAs Are Allowed to Enable Both Legacy INFO Usages and Info

INFO Package usages are a part of the same invite dialog usage, but UAs shall not mix legacy INFO usages and INFO Package usages in order to transport the same application-level information. If possible, UAs shall prefer the usage of an INFO Package.

16.8.4 INFO Method

16.8.4.1 General

The INFO method (RFC 6086) provides a mechanism for transporting application-level information that can further enhance a SIP application. Later, we provide more details on the types of applications for which the use of INFO is appropriate. This section describes how a UA handles INFO requests and responses, as well as the message bodies included in INFO messages.

16.8.4.2 INFO Request

16.8.4.2.1 INFO Request Sender

An INFO request can be associated with an INFO Package described later, or associated with a legacy INFO usage. The construction of the INFO request is the same as any other nontarget refresh request within an existing invite dialog usage as described in RFC 3261 (see Section 2.8.2). When a UA sends an INFO request associated with an INFO Package, it must include an INFO-Package header field that indicates which INFO Package is associated with the request. A specific INFO request can be used only for a single INFO Package. When a UA sends an INFO request associated with a legacy INFO usage, there is no INFO Package associated with the request, and the UA must not include an Info-Package header field in the request. The INFO request must not contain a Recv-Info header field. A UA can only indicate a set of INFO Packages for which it is willing to receive INFO requests by using the SIP methods (and their responses) listed in Section 16.8.5. A UA must not send an INFO request outside an invite dialog usage and must not send an INFO request for an INFO Package inside an invite dialog usage if the remote UA has not indicated willingness to receive that INFO Package within that dialog.

If a UA receives a 469 Bad INFO Package response to an INFO request, based on RFC 5057 (see Sections 3.6.5 and 16.2), the response represents a Transaction Only failure, and the UA must not terminate the invite dialog usage. Owing to the possibility of forking, the UA that sends the initial INVITE request must be prepared to receive INFO requests from multiple remote UAs during the early dialog phase. In addition, the UA must be prepared to receive different Recv-Info header field values from different remote UAs. Note that if the UAS (receiver of the initial INVITE request) sends an INFO request just after it has sent the response that creates the dialog, the UAS needs to be prepared for the possibility that the INFO request will reach the UAC before the dialog-creating response, and might therefore be rejected by the UAC. In addition, an INFO request might be rejected due to a race condition, if a UA sends the INFO request at the same time that the remote UA sends a new set of INFO Packages for which it is willing to receive INFO requests.

16.8.4.2.2 INFO Request Receiver

If a UA receives an INFO request associated with an INFO Package that the UA has not indicated willingness to receive, the UA must send a 469 Bad INFO Package response described later, which contains a Recv-Info header field with INFO Packages for which the UA is willing to receive INFO requests. The UA must not use the response to update the set of INFO Packages, but simply to indicate the current set. In the terminology of multiple dialog usages (RFC 5057, see Sections 3.6.5 and 16.2), this represents a Transaction Only failure, and does not terminate the invite dialog usage. If a UA receives an INFO request associated with an INFO Package, and the message-body part with Content-Disposition Info-Package described below has a MIME type that the UA supports but not in the context of that INFO Package, it is recommended that the UA send a 415 Unsupported Media Type response. The UA may send other error responses, such as Request Failure (4xx), Server Failure (5xx), and Global Failure (6xx), in accordance with the error-handling procedures (see Section 2.6). Otherwise, if the INFO request is syntactically correct and well structured, the UA must send a 200 OK response. Note that if the application needs to reject the information that it received in an INFO request, that needs to be done on the application level. That is, the application needs to trigger a new INFO request that contains information that the previously received application data was not accepted. Individual INFO Package specifications need to describe the details for such procedures.

16.8.4.2.3 SIP Proxies

Proxies need no additional behavior beyond that described in RFC 3261 to support INFO.

16.8.4.3 INFO Message Body

16.8.4.3.1 INFO Request Message Body

The purpose of the INFO request is to carry application-level information between SIP UAs. The application information data is carried in the payload of the message body of the INFO request. Note that an INFO request associated with an INFO Package can also include information associated with the INFO Package using Info-Package header field parameters. If an INFO request associated with an INFO Package contains a message-body part, the body part is identified by a Content-Disposition header field Info-Package value. The body part can contain a single MIME type, or it can be a multipart (RFC 5621) that contains other body parts associated with the INFO Package. UAs MUST support multipart body parts in accordance with RFC 5621. Note that an INFO request can also contain other body parts that are meaningful within the context of an invite dialog usage but are not specifically associated with the INFO method and the application concerned. When a UA supports a specific INFO Package, the UA must also support message-body MIME types in accordance with that INFO Package. However, in accordance with RFC 3261, the UA still indicates the supported MIME types using the Accept header.

16.8.4.3.2 INFO Response Message Body

A UA must not include a message body associated with an INFO Package in an INFO response. Message bodies associated with INFO Packages must only be sent in INFO requests. A UA may include a message body that is not associated with an INFO Package in an INFO response.

16.8.4.4 Order of Delivery

The INFO Package mechanism does not define a delivery order mechanism. INFO Packages can rely on the CSeq header field to detect if an INFO request is received out of order. If specific applications need additional mechanisms for order of delivery, those mechanisms, and related procedures, are specified as part of the associated INFO Package (e.g., the use of sequence numbers within the application data).

16.8.5 INFO Packages

16.8.5.1 General

An INFO Package specification defines the content and semantics of the information carried in an INFO message associated with an INFO Package. The INFO Package mechanism provides a way for UAs to indicate for which INFO Packages they are willing to receive INFO requests, and with which INFO Package a specific INFO request is associated.

16.8.5.2 UA Behavior

16.8.5.2.1 General

This section describes how a UA handles INFO Packages, how a UA uses the Recv-Info header field, and how the UA acts in re-INVITE rollback situations.

16.8.5.2.2 UA Procedures

A UA that supports the INFO Package mechanism must indicate, using the Recv-Info header field, the set of INFO Packages for which it is willing to receive INFO requests for a specific session. A UA can list multiple INFO Packages in a single Recv-Info header field, and the UA can use multiple Recv-Info header fields. A UA can use an empty Recv-Info header field, that is, a header field without any header field values. A UA provides its set of INFO Packages for which it is willing to receive INFO requests during the dialog establishment. A UA can update the set of INFO Packages during the invite dialog usage. If a UA is not willing to receive INFO requests for any INFO Packages, during dialog establishment or later during the invite dialog usage, the UA must indicate this by including an empty Recv-Info header field. This informs other UAs that the UA still supports the INFO Package mechanism. Example: If a UA has previously indicated INFO Packages *foo* and *bar* in a Recv-INFO header field, and the UA during the lifetime of the invite dialog usage wants to indicate that it does not want to receive INFO requests for any INFO Packages anymore, the UA sends a message with an empty Recv-Info header field. Once a UA has sent a message with a Recv-Info header field containing a set of INFO Packages, the set is valid until the UA sends a new Recv-Info header field containing a new, or empty, set of INFO Packages.

Once a UA has indicated that it is willing to receive INFO requests for a specific INFO Package, and a dialog has been established, the UA must be prepared to receive INFO requests associated with that INFO Package until the UA indicates that it is no longer willing to receive INFO requests associated with that INFO Package. For a specific dialog usage, a UA must NOT send an INFO request associated with an INFO Package until it has received an indication that the remote UA is willing to receive INFO requests for that INFO Package, or after the UA has received an indication that the remote UA is no longer willing to receive INFO requests associated with that INFO Package. Note that when a UA sends a message that contains a Recv-Info header field with a new set of INFO Packages for which the UA is willing to receive INFO requests, the remote UA might, before it receives the message, send an INFO request based on the old set of INFO Packages. In this case, the receiver of the INFO requests rejects, and sends a 469 Bad INFO Package response to, the INFO request.

If a UA indicates multiple INFO Packages that provide similar functionality, it is not possible to indicate a priority order of the INFO Packages, or to indicate that the UA wishes to only receive INFO requests for one of the INFO Packages. It is up to the application logic associated with the INFO Packages, and particular INFO Package specifications, to describe application behavior in such cases. For backwards compatibility purposes, even if a UA indicates support of the INFO Package mechanism, it is still allowed to enable legacy INFO usages. In addition, if a UA indicates support of the INFO method using the Allow header field (RFC 3261), it does not implicitly indicate support of the INFO Package mechanism. Per RFC 3261, a UA must use the Recv-Info header field to indicate that it supports the INFO Package mechanism. Likewise, even if a UA uses the Recv-Info header field to indicate that it supports the INFO Package mechanism, in addition the UA still indicates support of the INFO method using the Allow header. This document does not define a SIP option tag (see Section 2.10) for the INFO Package mechanism. However, an INFO Package specification can define an option tag associated with the specific INFO Package, as described later.

16.8.5.2.3 Recv-Info Header Field Rules

The text below defines rules on when a UA is required to include a Recv-Info header field in SIP messages. Later, we list the SIP methods for which a UA can insert a Recv-Info header field in requests and responses.

- The sender of an initial INVITE request must include a Recv-Info header field in the initial INVITE request, even if the sender is not willing to receive INFO requests associated with any INFO Package.
- The receiver of a request that contains a Recv-Info header field must include a Recv-Info header field in a reliable 18x/2xx response to the request, even if the request contains an empty Recv-Info header field, and even if the header field value of the receiver has not changed since the previous time it sent a Recv-Info header field.
- A UA must not include a Recv-Info header field in a response if the associated request did not contain a Recv-Info header field.

Note that in contrast to the rules for generating SDP answers, the receiver of a request is not restricted to generating its own set of INFO Packages as a subset of the INFO Package set received in the Info-Package header field of the request. As with SDP answers, the receiver can include the same Recv-Info header field value in multiple responses (18x/2xx) for the same INVITE/re-INVITE transaction, but the receiver MUST use the same Recv-Info header field value (if included) in all responses for the same transaction.

16.8.5.2.4 INFO Package Fallback Rules

If the receiver of a request that contains a Recv-Info header field rejects the request, both the sender and receiver of the request must roll back to the set of INFO Packages that was used before the request was sent. This also applies to the case where the receiver of an INVITE/re-INVITE request has included a Recv-Info header field in a provisional response, but later rejects the request. Note that the dialog state rollback rules for INFO Packages might differ from the rules for other types of dialog state information (SDP, target, and others).

16.8.5.3 REGISTER Processing

The INFO method (RFC 6086) allows a UA to insert a Recv-INFO header field in a REGISTER request. However, a UA shall not include a header value for a specific INFO Package unless the particular INFO Package specification describes how the header field value shall be interpreted and used by the registrar, for example, to determine request targets. Rather than using the Recv-Info header field to determine request targets, it is recommended to use more appropriate mechanisms, for example, based on RFC 3840 (see Section 3.4). However, this document does not define a feature tag for the INFO Package mechanism, or a mechanism to define feature tags for specific INFO Packages.

16.8.6 Formal INFO Method Definition and Header Fields

16.8.6.1 INFO Method

We have defined all SIP methods including the new INFO method per RFC 6086 in Section 2.5, replacing the definition and registrations found in RFC 2976 (obsoleted by RFC 6086). We have described all SIP header fields including this new the INFO header fields per RFC 6086 in Section 2.8.

16.8.6.2 Info-Package Header Field

We add Info-Package per RFC 6086 to the definition of the element message-header in the SIP message grammar. We have described the Info-Package header field usage earlier. For the purposes of matching Info-Package types indicated in Recv-Info with those in the Info-Package header field value, one compares the Info-package-name portion of the Info-package-type portion of the Info-Package header field octet by octet with that of the Recv-Info header field value. That is, the INFO Package name is case sensitive. Info-package-param is not part of the comparison checking algorithm. This document does not define values for Info-Package types. Individual INFO Package specifications define these values.

16.8.7 INFO Package Considerations

16.8.7.1 General

This section covers considerations to take into account when deciding whether the usage of an INFO Package is appropriate for transporting application information for a specific use case.

16.8.7.2 Appropriateness of INFO Package Usage

When designing an INFO Package, for application-level information exchange, it is important to consider: is signaling, using INFO requests, within a SIP dialog, an appropriate mechanism for the use case? Is it because it is the most reasonable and appropriate choice, or merely because "it is easy"? Choosing an inappropriate mechanism for a specific use case can cause negative effects in SIP networks where the mechanism is used.

16.8.7.3 INFO Request Rate and Volume

INFO messages differ from many other sorts of SIP messages in that they carry application information, and the size and rate of INFO messages are directly determined by the application. This can cause application information traffic to interfere with other traffic on that infrastructure, or to self-interfere when data rates become too high. There is no default throttling mechanism for INFO requests. Apart from the SIP session establishment, the number of SIP messages exchanged during the lifetime of a normal SIP session is rather small. Some applications, like those sending DTMF tones, can generate a burst of up to 20 messages per second. Other applications, like constant GPS location updates, could generate a high rate of INFO requests during the lifetime of the invite dialog usage.

A designer of an INFO Package, and the application that uses it, need to consider the impact that the size and the rate of the INFO messages have on the network and on other traffic, since it normally cannot be ensured that INFO messages will be carried over a congestion-controlled transport protocol end-to-end. Even if an INFO message is sent over such a transport protocol, a downstream SIP entity might forward the message over a transport protocol that does not provide congestion control. Furthermore, SIP messages tend to be relatively small, on the order of 500 bytes to 32,000 bytes. SIP is a poor mechanism for direct exchange of bulk data beyond these limits, especially if the headers plus body exceed the UDP maximum transmission unit (RFC 0768). Appropriate mechanisms for such traffic include the HTTP (RFCs 7230-7235), the MSRP (RFC 4975, see Section 6.3.3), or other media plane data transport mechanisms. RFC 5405 provides additional guidelines for applications using UDP that may be useful background reading.

16.8.8 Alternative Mechanisms

16.8.8.1 Alternative SIP Signaling Plane Mechanisms

16.8.8.1.1 General

This subsection describes some alternative mechanisms for transporting application information on the SIP signaling plane, using SIP messages.

16.8.8.1.2 SUBSCRIBE/NOTIFY

An alternative for application-level interaction is to use subscription-based events (RFC 6665, see Section 20.2) that use the SIP SUBSCRIBE and NOTIFY methods. Using that mechanism, a UA requests state information, such as keypad presses from a device to an application server, or key-map images from an application server to a device. Event Packages (RFC 6665) perform the role of disambiguating the context of a message for subscription-based events. The INFO Package mechanism provides similar functionality for application information exchange using invite dialog usages (RFC 5057, see Section 3.6.5 and 16.2). While an INFO request is always part of, and shares the fate of, an existing invite dialog usage, a SUBSCRIBE request creates a separate dialog usage (RFC 5057) and is normally sent outside an existing dialog usage.

The subscription-based mechanism can be used by SIP entities to receive state information about SIP dialogs and sessions, without requiring the entities to be part of the route set of those dialogs and sessions. As SUBSCRIBE/NOTIFY messages traverse through stateful SIP proxies and B2BUAs, the resource impact caused by the subscription dialogs needs to be considered. The number of subscription dialogs per user also needs to be considered. As for any other SIP signaling plane-based mechanism for transporting application information, the SUBSCRIBE/NOTIFY messages can put a significant burden on intermediate SIP entities that are part of the dialog route set, but do not have any interest in the application information transported between the end users.

16.8.8.1.3 MESSAGE

The MESSAGE method (RFC 3428, see Sections 2.5 and 6.3.1) defines one-time instant message exchange, typically for sending MIME contents for rendering to the user.

16.8.8.2 Alternative SIP Media Plane Mechanisms

16.8.8.2.1 General

In SIP, media plane channels associated with SIP dialogs are established using SIP signaling, but the data exchanged on the media plane channel does not traverse SIP signaling intermediates; thus, if there will be a lot of information exchanged, and there is no need for the SIP signaling intermediaries to examine the information, it is recommended to use a media plane mechanism rather than a SIP signaling-based mechanism. A low-latency requirement for the exchange of information is one strong indicator for using a media channel. Exchanging information through the SIP routing network can introduce hundreds of milliseconds of latency.

16.8.8.2.2 Media Resource Control Protocol

One mechanism for media plane exchange of application data is the Media Resource Control Protocol (MRCP) (see Section 7.6), where a media plane connection-oriented channel, such as a Transmission Control Protocol (TCP) (RFC 0793) or Stream Control Transmission Protocol (SCTP) (RFC 4960), stream is established.

16.8.8.2.3 Message Session Relay Protocol

MSRP (RFC 4975, see Section 6.3.3) defines session-based instant messaging as well as bulk file transfer and other such large-volume uses.

16.8.8.3 Alternative Non-SIP-Related Mechanisms

Another alternative is to use a SIP-independent mechanism, such as HTTP (RFCs 7230—7035). In this model, the UA knows about a rendezvous point to which it can direct HTTP requests for the transfer of information. Examples include encoding of a prompt to retrieve in the SIP Request URI (RFC 4240, see Section 4.4.2) or the encoding of a SUBMIT target in a VoiceXML (see Section 17.2.3) script.

16.8.9 INFO Package Requirements

16.8.9.1 General

This section provides guidance on how to define an INFO Package, and what information needs to exist in an INFO Package specification. If, for an INFO Package, there is a need to extend or modify the behavior described in this document, that behavior must be described in the INFO Package specification. It is bad practice for INFO Package specifications to repeat procedures defined in this document, unless needed for purposes of clarification or emphasis. INFO Package specifications must not weaken any behavior designated with *should* or *must* in this specification. However, INFO Package specifications may strengthen *should*, *may*, or *recommended* requirements to *must* if applications associated with the INFO Package require it. INFO Package specifications must address the issues defined in the following subsections, or document why an issue is not applicable to the specific INFO Package. Earlier, we have described alternative mechanisms that should be considered as part of the process for solving a specific use case, when there is a need for transporting application information.

16.8.9.2 Overall Description

The INFO Package specification must contain an overall description of the INFO Package: what type of information is carried in INFO requests associated with the INFO Package, and for what types of applications and functionalities UAs can use the INFO Package. If the INFO Package is defined for a specific application, the INFO Package specification must state which application UAs can use the INFO Package with.

16.8.9.3 Applicability

The INFO Package specification must describe why the INFO Package mechanism, rather than some other mechanism, has been chosen for the specific use case to transfer application information between SIP end points. Common reasons can be a requirement for SIP proxies or B2BUAs to see the transported application information (which would not be the case if the information was transported on a media path), or that it is not seen as feasible to establish separate dialogs (subscription) in order to transport the information. Section 2.4 provides more information and describes alternative mechanisms that one should consider for solving a specific use case.

16.8.9.4 INFO Package Name

The INFO Package specification MUST define an INFO Package name that UAs use as a header field value (e.g., infoX) to identify the INFO Package in the Recv-INFO and Info-Package header fields. The header field value must conform to the ABNF defined earlier. The INFO Package mechanism does not support package versioning. Specific INFO Package message-body payloads can contain version information, which is handled by the applications associated with the INFO Package. However, such a feature is outside the scope of the generic INFO Package mechanism. Note that even if an INFO Package name contains version numbering (e.g., foo_v2), the INFO Package mechanism does not distinguish a version number from the rest of the INFO Package name.

16.8.9.5 INFO Package Parameters

The INFO Package specification may define INFO Package parameters that can be used in the Recv-Info or Info-Package header fields, together with the header field value that indicates the INFO Package name. The INFO Package specification must define the syntax and semantics of the defined parameters. In addition, the specification must define whether a specific parameter is applicable to only the Recv-Info header field, only the Info-Package header field, or to both. By default, an INFO Package parameter is only applicable to the INFO Package for which the parameter has been explicitly defined. INFO Package parameters defined for specific INFO Packages can share the name with parameters defined for other INFO Packages, but the parameter semantics are specific to the INFO Package for which they are defined. However, when choosing the name of a parameter, it is recommended to not use the same name as an existing parameter for another INFO Package if the semantics of the parameters are different.

16.8.9.6 SIP Option Tags

The INFO Package specification may define SIP option tags, which can be used as described in RFC 3261 (see Section 2.10). The registration requirements for option tags are defined in RFC 5727.

16.8.9.7 INFO Message-Body Parts

The INFO Package specification must define which message-body part MIME types are associated with the INFO Package. The specification must either define those body parts, including the syntax, semantics, and MIME type of each body part, or refer to other documents that define the body parts. If multiple message-body part MIME types are associated with an INFO Package, the INFO Package specification must define whether UAs need to use multipart body parts, in order to include multiple body parts in a single INFO request.

16.8.9.8 INFO Package Usage Restrictions

If there are restrictions on how UAs can use an INFO Package, the INFO Package specification must document such restrictions. There can be restrictions related to whether UAs are allowed to send overlapping (outstanding) INFO requests associated with the INFO Package, or whether the UA has to wait for the response for a previous INFO request associated with the same INFO Package. There can also be restrictions related to whether UAs need to support and use other SIP extensions and capabilities when they use the INFO Package, and if there are restrictions related to how UAs can use the INFO Package together with other INFO Packages. As the SIP stack might not be aware of INFO Package-specific restrictions, it cannot be assumed that overlapping requests would be rejected. As explained earlier, UAs will normally send a 200 OK response to an INFO request. The application logic associated with the INFO Package needs to handle situations where UAs do not follow restrictions associated with the INFO Package.

16.8.9.9 Rate of INFO Requests

If there is a maximum or minimum rate at which UAs can send INFO requests associated with the INFO Package within a dialog, the INFO Package specification must document the rate values. If the rates can vary, the INFO Package specification may define INFO Package parameters that UAs can use to indicate or negotiate the rates. Alternatively, the rate information can be part of the application data information associated with the INFO Package.

16.8.9.10 INFO Package Security Considerations

If the application information carried in INFO requests associated with the INFO Package requires a certain level of security, the INFO Package specification must describe the mechanisms that UAs need to use to provide the required security. If the INFO Package specification does not require any additional security, other than what the underlying SIP provides, this must be stated in the INFO Package specification.

Note that in some cases, it may not be sufficient to mandate TLS (RFC 5246) in order to secure the INFO Package payload, since intermediaries will have access to the payload, and because beyond the first hop, there is no way to assure subsequent hops will not forward the payload in clear text. The best way to ensure secure transport at the application level is to have the security at the application level. One way of achieving this is to use end-to-end security techniques such as S/MIME (see Section 19.6).

16.8.9.11 Implementation Details

It is strongly recommended that the INFO Package specification define the procedure regarding how implementers shall implement and use the INFO Package, or refer to other locations where implementers can find that information. Note that sometimes an INFO Package designer might choose to not reveal the details of an INFO Package. However, in order to allow multiple implementations to support the INFO Package, INFO Package designers are strongly encouraged to provide the implementation details.

16.8.10 Examples

It is recommended that the INFO Package specification provide demonstrative message flow diagrams, paired with complete messages and message descriptions. Note that example flows are by definition informative, and do not replace normative text.

16.8.10.1 Indication of Willingness to Receive INFO Packages

16.8.10.1.1 Initial INVITE Request

The UAC sends an initial INVITE request, where the UAC indicates that it is willing to receive INFO requests for INFO Packages P and R.

```
INVITE sip:bob@example.com SIP/2.0
Via: SIP/2.0/TCP pc33.example.
com;branch=z9hG4bK776
Max-Forwards: 70
To: Bob <sip:bob@example.com>
From: Alice <sip:alice@example.com>
;tag=1928301774
Call-ID: a84b4c76e66710@pc33.example.com
CSeq: 314159 INVITE
Recv-Info: P, R
Contact: <sip:alice@pc33.example.com>
Content-Type: application/sdp
Content-Length: ...
...
```

The UAS sends a 200 OK response back to the UAC, where the UAS indicates that it is willing to receive INFO requests for INFO Packages R and T.

```
SIP/2.0 200 OK
Via: SIP/2.0/TCP pc33.example.
com;branch=z9hG4bK776;
received=192.0.2.1
To: Bob <sip:bob@example.com>;tag=a6c85cf
From: Alice <sip:alice@example.com>
;tag=1928301774
Call-ID: a84b4c76e66710@pc33.example.com
CSeq: 314159 INVITE
Contact: <sip:bob@pc33.example.com>
Recv-Info: R, T
Content-Type: application/sdp
Content-Length: ...
...
```

The UAC sends an ACK request.

```
ACK sip:bob@pc33.example.com SIP/2.0
Via: SIP/2.0/TCP pc33.example.
com;branch=z9hG4bK754
Max-Forwards: 70
To: Bob <sip:bob@example.com>;tag=a6c85cf
From: Alice <sip:alice@example.com>
;tag=1928301774
Call-ID: a84b4c76e66710@pc33.example.com
CSeq: 314159 ACK
Content-Length: 0
```

16.8.10.1.2 Target Refresh

The UAC sends an UPDATE request within the invite dialog usage, where the UAC indicates (using an empty Recv-Info header field) that it is not willing to receive INFO requests for any INFO Packages.

```
UPDATE sip:bob@pc33.example.com SIP/2.0
Via: SIP/2.0/TCP pc33.example.
com;branch=z9hG4bK776
Max-Forwards: 70
To: Bob <sip:bob@example.com>;tag=a6c85cf
From: Alice <sip:alice@example.com>
;tag=1928301774
Call-ID: a84b4c76e66710@pc33.example.com
CSeq: 314163 UPDATE
Recv-Info:
Contact: <sip:alice@pc33.example.com>
Content-Type: application/sdp
Content-Length: ...
...
```

The UAS sends a 200 OK response back to the UAC, where the UAS indicates that it is willing to receive INFO requests for INFO Packages R and T.

```
SIP/2.0 200 OK
Via: SIP/2.0/TCP pc33.example.
com;branch=z9hG4bK893;
received=192.0.2.1
To: Bob <sip:bob@example.com>;tag=a6c85cf
From: Alice <sip:alice@example.com>
;tag=1928301774
Call-ID: a84b4c76e66710@pc33.example.com
CSeq: 314163 INVITE
Contact: <sip:alice@pc33.example.com>
Recv-Info: R, T
Content-Type: application/sdp
Content-Length: ...
...
```

16.8.10.2 INFO Request Associated with INFO Package

16.8.10.2.1 Single Payload with INFO Package

The UA sends an INFO request associated with INFO Package foo.

```
INFO sip:alice@pc33.example.com SIP/2.0
Via: SIP/2.0/UDP 192.0.2.2:5060;branch=z9hG4b
Knabcdef
To: Bob <sip:bob@example.com>;tag=a6c85cf
From: Alice <sip:alice@example.com>
;tag=1928301774
Call-Id: a84b4c76e66710@pc33.example.com
CSeq: 314333 INFO
Info-Package: foo
Content-type: application/foo
Content-Disposition: Info-Package
Content-length: 24
I am a foo message type
```

16.8.10.3 Multipart INFO with INFO Package

16.8.10.3.1 Non-Info Package Body Part

SIP extensions can sometimes add body part payloads into an INFO request, independent of the INFO Package. In this case, the INFO Package payload gets put into a multipart MIME body, with a Content-Disposition header field that indicates which body part is associated with the INFO Package.

```
INFO sip:alice@pc33.example.com SIP/2.0
Via: SIP/2.0/UDP 192.0.2.2:5060;branch=z9hG4b
Knabcdef
To: Alice <sip:alice@example.net>;tag=1234567
From: Bob <sip:bob@example.com>;tag=abcdefg
Call-Id: a84b4c76e66710@pc33.example.com
CSeq: 314400 INFO
Info-Package: foo
Content-Type: multipart/
mixed;boundary="theboundary"
Content-Length: ...

--theboundary

Content-Type: application/mumble
...
<mumble stuff>
--theboundary
Content-Type: application/foo-x
Content-Disposition: Info-Package
Content-length: 59

I am a foo-x message type, and I belong to
Info Package foo

--theboundary--
```

16.8.10.3.2 Multiple Body Parts inside Multipart Body Part

Multiple body part payloads can be associated with a single INFO Package. In this case, the body parts are put into a multipart MIME body, with a Content-Disposition header field that indicates which body part is associated with the INFO Package.

```
INFO sip:alice@pc33.example.com SIP/2.0
Via: SIP/2.0/UDP 192.0.2.2:5060;branch=z9hG4b
Knabcdef
To: Alice <sip:alice@example.net>;tag=1234567
From: Bob <sip:bob@example.com>;tag=abcdefg
Call-Id: a84b4c76e66710@pc33.example.com
CSeq: 314423 INFO
Info-Package: foo
Content-Type: multipart/
mixed;boundary="theboundary"
Content-Disposition: Info-Package
Content-Length: ...

--theboundary

Content-Type: application/foo-x

Content-length: 59

I am a foo-x message type, and I belong to
Info Package foo
<mumble stuff>

--theboundary

Content-Type: application/foo-y
Content-length: 59

I am a foo-y message type, and I belong to
Info Package foo

--theboundary--
```

16.8.10.3.3 Single Body Part inside Multipart Body Part

The body part payload associated with the INFO Package can have a Content-Disposition header field value other than Info-Package. In this case, the body part is put into a multipart MIME body, with a Content-Disposition header field that indicates which body part is associated with the INFO Package.

```
INFO sip:alice@pc33.example.com SIP/2.0
Via: SIP/2.0/UDP 192.0.2.2:5060;branch=z9hG4b
Knabcdef
To: Alice <sip:alice@example.net>;tag=1234567
From: Bob <sip:bob@example.com>;tag=abcdefg
Call-Id: a84b4c76e66710@pc33.example.com
CSeq: 314423 INFO
Info-Package: foo
Content-Type: multipart/
mixed;boundary="theboundary"
Content-Disposition: Info-Package
Content-Length: ...

--theboundary

Content-Type: application/foo-x
Content-Disposition: icon
Content-length: 59
I am a foo-x message type, and I belong to
Info Package foo
--theboundary--
```

16.9 SIP Call Control UUI Transfer Services

16.9.1 Overview

RFC 6567 that is described here defines SIP UUI data as application-specific information that is related to a session being established using SIP. It is assumed that the application is running in both end points in a two-party session. That is, the application interacts with both the UAs in a SIP session. To function properly, the application needs a small piece of information, the UUI, to be transported at the time of session establishment. This information is essentially opaque data to SIP—it is unrelated to SIP routing, authentication, or any other SIP function. This application can be considered to be operating at a higher layer on the protocol stack. As a result, SIP should not interpret, understand, or perform any operations on the UUI. Should this not be the case, then the information being transported is not considered UUI, and another SIP-specific mechanism will be needed to transport the information (such as a new header field). In particular, this mechanism creates no requirements on intermediaries such as proxies, B2BUAs, and SBCs.

UUI is defined this way for two reasons. First, this definition supports a strict layering of protocols and data. Providing information and understanding of the UUI to the transport layer (SIP in this case) would not provide any benefits and instead could create cross-layer coupling. Second, it is neither feasible nor desirable for a SIP UA to understand the information; instead, the goal is for the UA to simply pass the information as efficiently as possible to the application that does understand the information. An important application is the interworking with UUI in ISDN, specifically the transport of the call control-related ITU-T Q.931 UUI Element (UUIE) [3] and ITU-T Q.763 UUI Parameter [2] data in SIP. ISDN UUI is widely used in the PSTN today in contact centers and call centers. These applications are currently transitioning away from using ISDN for session establishment to using SIP. Native SIP end points will need to implement a similar service and be able to interwork with this ISDN service.

Note that the distinction between call control UUI and non-call control UUI is very important. SIP already has a mechanism for sending arbitrary UUI data between UAs during a session or dialog—the SIP INFO (RFC 6086, see Section 16.8) method. Call control UUI, in contrast, must be exchanged at the time of setup and needs to be carried in the INVITE and a few other methods and responses. Applications that exchange UUI but do not have a requirement that it be transported and processed during call setup can simply use SIP INFO and do not need a new SIP extension. In this document, four different use-case call flows are discussed. Next, the requirements for call control UUI transport are discussed.

16.9.2 Requirements for UUI Transport

RFC 6567 states the requirements for the transport of call control UUI solution that needs to be met as follows:

- REQ-1: The mechanism will allow UAs to insert and receive UUI data in SIP call setup requests and responses. SIP messages covered by this include INVITE requests and end-to-end responses to the INVITE, that is, 18x and 200 responses. UUI data may also be inserted in 3xx responses to an INVITE. However, if a 3xx response is recursed on by an intermediary proxy, the resulting INVITE will not contain the UUI data from only one 3xx response. In a scenario where a proxy forks an INVITE to multiple UASs that include UUI data in 3xx responses, if a 3xx response is the best response sent upstream by the proxy, it will contain the UUI data from only one 3xx response.
- REQ-2: The mechanism will allow UAs to insert and receive UUI data in SIP dialog terminating requests and responses.

- Q.931 UUI supports inclusion in release and release completion messages. SIP messages covered by this include BYE and 200 OK responses to a BYE.
- REQ-3: The mechanism will allow UUI to be inserted and retrieved in SIP redirects and referrals. SIP messages covered by this include REFER requests and 3xx responses to INVITE requests.
- REQ-4: The mechanism will allow UUI to be able to survive proxy retargeting or redirection of the request. Retargeting is a common method of call routing in SIP and must not result in the loss of UUI.
- REQ-5: The mechanism should not require processing entities to dereference a URL in order to retrieve the UUI data. Passing a pointer or link to the UUI data will not meet the RT processing considerations and would complicate interworking with the PSTN.
- REQ-6: The mechanism will support interworking with call-control related DSS1 information elements or QSIG information elements and ISUP parameters.
- REQ-7: The mechanism will allow a UAC to learn that a UAS understands the UUI mechanism.
- REQ-8: The mechanism will allow a UAC to require that a UAS understands the call control UUI mechanism and have a request routed on the basis of this information. If the request cannot be routed to a UAS that understands the UUI mechanism, the request will fail. This could be useful in ensuring that a request destined for the PSTN is routed to a gateway that supports the UUI mechanism rather than an otherwise equivalent PSTN gateway that does not support the ISDN mechanism. Note that support of the UUI mechanism does not, by itself, imply that a particular application is supported (see REQ-10).
- REQ-9: The mechanism will allow proxies to remove a particular application usage of UUI data from a request or response. This is a common security function provided by border elements to header fields such as Alert-Info or Call-Info URIs. There is no requirement for UAs to be able to determine if a particular usage of UUI data has been removed from a request or response.
- REQ-10: The mechanism will provide the ability for a UA to discover which application usages of UUI another UA understands or supports. The creation of a registry of application usages for the UUI mechanism is implied by this requirement. The ISDN service utilizes a field known as the protocol discriminator, which is the first octet of the ISDN UUI data, for this purpose.
- REQ-11: The UUI is a sequence of octets. The solution will provide a mechanism of transporting at least 128 octets of user data and a one-octet protocol discriminator, that is, 129 octets in total. There is the potential for non-ISDN services to allow UUI to be larger than 128 octets. However, users of the mechanism will need be cognizant of the size of SIP messages and the ability of parsers to handle extremely large values.
- REQ-12: The recipient of UUI will be able to determine the entity that inserted the UUI. It is acceptable that this is performed implicitly where it is known that there is only one other end UA involved in the dialog. Where that does not exist, some other mechanism will need to be provided. The UUI mechanism does not introduce stronger authorization requirements for SIP; instead, the mechanism needs to be able to utilize existing SIP approaches for request and response identity. This requirement comes into play during redirection, retargeting, and referral scenarios.
- REQ-13: The mechanism will allow integrity protection of the UUI. This allows the UAS to be able to know that the UUI has not been modified or tampered with by intermediaries. Note that there are trade-offs between this requirement and requirement REQ-9 for proxies and border elements to remove UUI. One possible way to satisfy both of these requirements is to utilize hop-by-hop protection. This property is not guaranteed by the protocol in the ISDN application.
- REQ-14: The mechanism will allow end-to-end privacy of the UUI. Some UUI may contain private or sensitive information and may require different security handling from the rest of the SIP message. Note that this property is not available in the ISDN application.
- REQ-15: The mechanism will allow both end-to-end and hop-by-hop security models. The hop-by-hop model is required by the ISDN UUI service.

16.9.3 Possible Approaches for UUI Transport in SIP

Two other possible mechanisms for transporting UUI data will be described: MIME body and URI parameter transport.

16.9.3.1 Why INFO Is Not Used

Since the INFO method (RFC 6086, see Section 16.8) was developed for ISUP interworking of UUI, it might seem to be the logical choice here. For non-call control UUI, INFO can be utilized for end-to-end transport. However, for transport of call control UUI, INFO cannot be used. As the call flows in RFC 6567 show, the information is related to an attempt to establish a session and needs to be passed with the session setup request (INVITE), responses to that INVITE, or session termination requests. As a result, it is not possible to use INFO in these cases.

16.9.3.2 Why Other Protocol Encapsulations Are Not Used

Other protocols have the ability to transport UUI data. For example, consider the ITU-T Recommendation Q.931 User–user information element [3] and the ITU-T Recommendation Q.763 UUI parameter [2]. In addition, the Narrowband Signaling System (NSS) [1] is also able to transport UUI data. Should one of these protocols be in use, and present in both UAs, then utilizing these other protocols to transport UUI data might be a logical solution. Essentially, this is just adding an additional layer in the protocol stack. In these cases, SIP is not transporting the UUI data; it is encapsulating another protocol, and that protocol is transporting the UUI data. Once a mechanism to transport that other protocol using SIP exists, the UUI data transport function is essentially obtained without any additional effort or work.

16.9.3.3 Why MIME Is Not Used

One method of transport is to use a MIME body. This is in keeping with the SIP-T architecture (RFC 3372, see Section 2.8.2) in which MIME bodies are used to transport ISUP information. Since the INVITE will normally have a SDP message body, the resulting INVITE with SDP and UUI data will be multipart MIME. This is not ideal as many SIP UAs do not support multipart MIME INVITEs. A bigger problem is the insertion of a UUI message body by a redirect server or in a REFER. The body would need to be encoded in the Contact URI of the 3xx response or the Refer-To URI of a REFER. Currently, the authors are not aware of any UAs that support this capability today for any body type. As such, the complete set of semantics for this operation would need to be determined and defined. Some issues will need to be resolved, such as, do all the Content-* header fields have to be included as well? What if the included Content-Length does not agree with the included body? Since proxies cannot remove a body from a request or response, it is not clear how this mechanism could meet REQ-9.

The requirement for integrity protection could be met by the use of an S/MIME signature over the body, as defined in Securing MIME bodies, Section 23.3 of RFC 3261 (see Section 2.8.2). Alternatively, this could be achieved using RFC 4474 (see Sections 2.8 and 19.4.8). The requirement for end-to-end privacy could be met using S/MIME encryption or using encryption at the application layer. However, note that neither S/MIME nor RFC 4474 enjoys deployment in SIP today. An example:

```
<allOneLine>
       Contact: <sip:+12125551212@gateway.
       example.com?Content-Type =
       application/uui&body=ZeGl9i2icVqaNVail
       T6F5iJ90m6mvuTS4OK05M0vDk0Q4Xs>
</allOneLine>
```

As such, the MIME body approach meets REQ-1, REQ-2, REQ-4, REQ-5, REQ-7, REQ-11, REQ-13, and REQ-14. Meeting REQ-12 seems possible, although the authors do not have a specific mechanism to propose. Meeting REQ-3 is problematic but not impossible for this mechanism. However, this mechanism does not seem to be able to meet REQ-9.

16.9.3.4 Why URI Parameter Is Not Used

Another proposed approach is to encode the UUI data as a URI parameter. This UUI parameter could be included in a Request-URI or in the Contact URI or Refer-To URI. It is not clear how it could be transported in a response that does not have a Request-URI, or in BYE requests or responses.

```
<allOneLine>
       Contact: <sip:+12125551212@gateway.
       example.com;uui=ZeGl9i2icVqaNVailT
       6F5iJ90m6mvuTS4OK05M0vDk0Q4Xs>
</allOneLine>
```

An INVITE sent to this Contact URI would contain UUI data in the Request-URI of the INVITE. The URI parameter has a drawback in that a URI parameter carried in a Request-URI will not survive retargeting by a proxy as shown in RFC 6567 described later. That is, if the URI is included with an AOR instead of a Contact URI, the URI parameter in the Request-URI will not be copied over to the Contact URI, resulting in the loss of the information. Note that if this same URI were present in a Refer-To header field, the same loss of information would occur. The URI parameter approach would meet REQ-3, REQ-5, REQ-7, REQ-9, and REQ-11. It is possible the approach could meet REQ-12 and REQ-13. The mechanism does not appear to meet REQ-1, REQ-2, REQ-4, and REQ-14.

16.9.3.5 Why SIP Extensions for UUI Transport Are Used

This section describes how the User-to-User header field meets the requirements in RFC 6567 described earlier. The header field can be included in INVITE requests and responses and BYE requests and responses, meeting REQ-1 and REQ-2. For redirection and referral use cases and REQ-3, the header field is included (escaped) within the Contact or Refer-To URI. Since SIP proxy forwarding and retargeting does not affect header fields, the header field meets REQ-4. The UUI header field will carry the UUI data and not a pointer to the data, so REQ-5 is met. Since the basic design of the UUI header field is similar to the ISDN UUI service, interworking with PSTN protocols is straightforward and is documented in a separate specification in RFC 7434 described in the next section, meeting REQ-6. Requirements REQ-7,

REQ-8, and REQ-10 relate to discovery of the mechanism and supported packages, and hence applications. REQ-7 relates to support of the UUI header field, while REQ-8 relates to routing based on support of the UUI header field.

REQ-7 is met by defining a new SIP option tag uui. The use of a Require:uui in a request or Supported:uui in a SIP OPTIONS response could be used to require or discover support of the mechanism. The presence of a Supported:uui or Require:uui header field can be used by proxies to route to an appropriate UA, meeting REQ-8. However, note that only UAs are expected to understand the UUI data—proxies and other intermediaries do not. REQ-10 is met by utilizing SIP feature tags (RFC 3840, see Section 2.11). For example, the feature tag sip.uui-isdn could be used to indicate support of the ISDN UUI package, or sip.uui-pk1 could be used to indicate support for a particular package, pk1. Proxies commonly apply policy to the presence of certain SIP header fields in requests by either passing them or removing them from requests. REQ-9 is met by allowing proxies and other intermediaries to remove UUI header fields in a request or response based on policy. Carrying UUI data elements of at least 129 octets is trivial in the UUI header field, meeting REQ-11. Note that avoiding having very large UUI data elements is a good idea, as SIP header fields have traditionally not been large.

To meet REQ-12 for the redirection and referral use cases, the History-Info header field (RFC 7044, see Section 2.8) can be used. In these retargeting cases, the changed Request-URI will be recorded in the History-Info header field along with the identity of the element that performed the retargeting. The requirement for integrity protection in REQ-13 could be met by the use of an S/MIME signature over a subset of header fields, as defined in "SIP Header Privacy and Integrity using S/MIME: Tunneling SIP" of RFC 3261 (see Section 19.6). Note that the lack of deployment of S/MIME with SIP means that, in general, REQ-13 is not met. The requirement of REQ-14 for end-to-end privacy could be met using S/MIME or using encryption at the application layer. Note that the use of S/MIME to secure the UUI data will result in an additional body being added to the request. Hop-wise TLS (RFC 5246) allows the header field to meet REQ-15 for hop-by-hop security.

16.9.4 SIP Extensions for UUI Transport

RFC 7433 that is described next specifies the transport of UUI data using SIP. It defines a mechanism for the transport of general-application UUI data and for the transport of the call control-related ITU-T Recommendation Q.931 user–user information element [3] and ITU-T Recommendation Q.763 UUI parameter [2] data in SIP. UUI data is widely used in the PSTN today for contact centers and call centers. There is also a trend for the related applications to transition from ISDN to SIP. The UUI extension for SIP may also be used for native SIP UAs implementing similar services and to interwork with ISDN services. Note that, in most cases, there is an a priori understanding between the UAs in regard to what to do with received UUI data. This document enables the definition of packages and related attributes that can make such understandings more explicit. The UUI mechanism is designed to meet the use cases, requirements, and call flows for SIP call control UUI detailed in RFC 6567 described later.

The mechanism is a new SIP header field, along with a new SIP option tag. The header field carries the UUI data, along with parameters indicating the encoding of the UUI data, the UUI package, and optionally the content of the UUI data. The package definition contains details about how a particular application can utilize the UUI mechanism. The header field can be included (sometimes called *escaped*) into URIs supporting referral and redirection scenarios. In these scenarios, the History-Info header field is used to indicate the inserter of the UUI data. The SIP option tag can be used to indicate support for the header field. Support for the UUI header field indicates that a UA is able to extract the information in the UUI data and pass it up the protocol stack. Individual packages using the UUI mechanism can utilize SIP media feature tags to indicate that a UA supports a particular UUI package. Guidelines for defining UUI packages are provided.

16.9.5 Normative Definition

RFC 7433 defines a new SIP header field User-to-User to transport call control UUI data to meet the requirements in RFC 6567 described earlier. To help tag and identify the UUI data used with this header field, *purpose*, *content*, and *encoding* header field parameters are defined. The purpose header field parameter identifies the package that defines the generation and usage of the UUI data for a particular application. The value of the purpose parameter is the package name, as registered in the UUI Packages subregistry with IANA. For the case of interworking with the ISDN UUI service, the ISDN UUI service interworking package is used. The default value for the purpose header field is isdn-uui, as defined here per RFC 7434. If the purpose header field parameter is not present, the ISDN UUI must be used. The content header field parameter identifies the actual content of the UUI data. If not present, the default content defined for the package must be used.

Newly defined UUI packages must define or reference at least a default content value. The encoding header field parameter indicates the method of encoding the information in the UUI data associated with a particular content value. This specification only defines encoding=hex. If the encoding header field parameter is not present, the default encoding defined for the package must be used. UUI data is considered an opaque series of octets. This mechanism must not be used to convey a URL or URI, since the Call-Info header field in RFC 3261 (see Section 2.8) already supports this use case.

16.9.5.1 Syntax for UUI Header Field

The UUI header field can be present in INVITE requests and responses and in BYE requests and responses. Note that when the UUI header is used in responses, it can only be utilized in end-to-end responses, for example, 1xx (excluding 100 Trying), 2xx, and 3xx responses. The following syntax specification uses the ABNF as described in RFC 5234 and extends RFC 3261 (where token, quoted-string, and generic-param are defined) here again for convenience although all SIP header syntaxes are provided in Section 2.4.1:

```
UUI="User-to-User" HCOLON uui-value *(COMMA
uui-value)
uui-value=uui-data *(SEMI uui-param)
uui-data=token/quoted-string
uui-param=pkg-param/cont-param/enc-param/
generic-param
pkg-param="purpose" EQUAL pkg-param-value
pkg-param-value=token
cont-param="content" EQUAL cont-param-value
cont-param-value=token
enc-param="encoding" EQUAL enc-param-value
enc-param-value=token/"hex"
```

Each package defines how many User-to-User header fields of each package may be present in a request or a response. A sender may include multiple User-to-User header fields, and a receiver must be prepared to receive multiple User-to-User header fields. Consistent with the rules of SIP syntax, the syntax defined in this document allows any combination of individual User-to-User header fields or User-to-User header fields with multiple comma separated UUI data elements. Any size limitations on the UUI data for a particular purpose are to be defined by the related UUI package. UAs shall ignore UUI data from packages or encoding that they do not understand. For redirection use cases, the header field is included (escaped) within the Contact URI. For referral use cases, the header field is included (escaped) within the Refer-To URI. For example, if a UA supports this specification, it should include any UUI data included in a redirection URI (if the UUI data and encoding is understood).

Note that redirection can occur multiple times to a request. Currently, UAs that support attended transfer support the ability to include a Replaces header field (RFC 3891, see Section 2.8.2) into a Refer-To URI, and when acting upon this URI, UAs add the Replaces header field to the triggered INVITE. This sort of logic and behavior is utilized for the UUI header field (i.e., the UUI header field is included in the triggered INVITE). The UA processing the REFER or the 3xx response to the INVITE should support the UUI mechanism. If the REFER or redirect target does not support UUI, the UUI header will be discarded as per RFC 3261. However, this may limit the utility of use cases that depend on the UUI being supported by all elements. Here is an example of an included User-to-User header field from the redirection response F2 of Figure 16.43 in RFC 6567:

```
<allOneLine>
       Contact: <sip:+12125551212@gateway.
       example.com?User-to-User =
       56a390f3d2b7310023a2%3Bencoding%3Dhex%
       3Bpurpose%3Dfoo%3B
       content%3Dbar>
</allOneLine>
```

The resulting INVITE (F4) would contain

```
User-to-User: 56a390f3d2b7310023a2;encoding=
hex;purpose=foo;content=bar
```

16.9.5.2 Hex Encoding Definition

This specification defines hex encoding of UUI data. When the value of hex is used in the encoding parameter of a header field, the data is encoded using base16 encoding according to Section 8 of RFC 4648. The hex-encoded value is normally represented using the token construction from RFC 3261, although the quoted-string construction is permitted, in which case the quotes must be ignored. If a canonicalized version of a normally case-insensitive hex encoded UUI data object is needed for a digital signature or integrity checking, then the base16 encoding with all upper case must be used.

16.9.5.3 Source Identity of UUI Data

It is important for the recipient of UUI data to know the identity of the UA that inserted the UUI data. In a request without a History-Info header field, the identity of the entity that inserted the UUI data will be assumed to be the source of the SIP message. For a SIP request, typically this is the UA identified by the URI in the From header field or a P-Asserted-Identity (RFC 3325, see Sections 2.8, 10.4, and 20.3) header field. In a request with a History-Info header field, the recipient needs to parse the Targeted-to-URIs present (hi-targeted-to-uri defined in RFC 7044, see Section 2.8) to see if any included User-to-User header fields are present. If an included User-to-User header field is present and matches the UUI data in the request, this indicates that redirection has taken place, resulting in the inclusion of UUI data in the request.

The inserter of the UUI data will be the UA identified by the Targeted-to-URI of the History-Info element before the element with the included UUI data. In a response, the inserter of the UUI data will be the identity of the UA that generated the response. Typically, this is the UA identified in the To header field of the response. Note that any updates to this identity by use of the SIP connected identity extension (RFC 4916, see Section 20.4) or other identity modifiers will update this information. For an example of History-Info and redirection, consider Figure 16.43 from RFC 6567 where the Originating UA is Carol, the Redirector Bob, and the Terminating UA Alice. The INVITE F4 containing UUI data could be

```
INVITE sips:alice@example.com SIP/2.0
Via: SIP/2.0/TLS lab.example.com:5061
;branch=z9hG4bKnashds9
To: Bob <sips:bob@example.com>
From: Carol <sips:carol@example.com>
;tag=323sf33k2
Call-ID: dfaosidfoiwe83ifkdf
Max-Forwards: 70
Contact: <sips:carol@lab.example.com>
Supported: histinfo
User-to-User: 342342ef34;encoding=hex
History-Info: <sips:bob@example.com>;index=1

<allOneLine>
       History-Info: <sips:alice@example.
       com?Reason=SIP%3Bcause%3D302
       &User-to-User=342342ef34%3Bencoding%3D
       hex>;index=1.1;rc=1
</allOneLine>
```

Without the redirection captured in the History-Info header field, Alice would conclude that the UUI data was inserted by Carol. However, the History-Info containing UUI data (index = 1.1) indicates that the inserter was Bob (index = 1). To enable maintaining a record of the inserter identity of UUI data, UAs supporting this mechanism should support History-Info (RFC 7044, see Section 2.8) and include Supported: hist-info in all requests and responses. If a border element such as a proxy or a B2BUA removes a History-Info header field containing a User-to-User parameter, the UA consuming the UUI data may not be able at the SIP level to identify the source of the UUI data.

16.9.6 Guidelines for UUI Packages

UUI packages defined using this SIP UUI mechanism must follow the Standards Action guideline as defined in RFC 5226 and publish a Standards Track RFC that describes the usage. Note that this mechanism is not suitable for the transport of arbitrary data between UAs. The following guidelines are provided to help determine if this mechanism is appropriate or not. The SIP UUI mechanism is applicable when all of the following conditions are met:

- The information is generated and consumed by an application during session setup using SIP, but the application is not necessarily SIP aware.
- The behavior of SIP entities that support it is not significantly changed (as discussed in Section 4 of RFC 5727).
- UAs are the generators and consumers of the UUI data. Proxies and other intermediaries may route on the basis of the presence of a User-to-User header field or a particular package tag but do not otherwise consume or generate the UUI data.
- There are no privacy issues associated with the information being transported (e.g., geolocation or emergency-related information are examples of inappropriate UUI data).
- The UUI data is not being utilized for User-to-User Remote Procedure Calls (RPCs).

UUI packages define the semantics for a particular application usage of UUI data. The content defines the syntax of the UUI data, while the encoding defines the encoding of the UUI data for the content. Each content is defined as a stream of octets, which allows multiple encodings of that content. For example, packages may define

- The SIP methods and responses in which the UUI data may be present.
- The maximum number of UUI data elements that may be inserted into a request or response. The default is one per encoding. Note that a UA may still receive a request with more than this maximum number due to redirection. The package needs to define how to handle this situation.
- The default values for content and encoding if they are not present. If the same UUI data may be inserted multiple times with different encodings, the package needs to state this. A package may support and define multiple contents and their associated encodings and reuse contents defined by other packages.
- Any size limitations on the UUI data. Size needs to be specified in terms of the octet stream output of the content, since the size of the resulting uui-data element will vary depending on the encoding scheme.

A package must define a purpose header field value to identify the package in the coding. A package must describe the new application that is utilizing the UUI data and provide some use-case examples. The default content value must be defined or referenced in another document for the package. Additional allowed contents may also be defined or referenced. Any restrictions on the size of the UUI data must be described. In addition, a package may define a media feature tag per RFC 3840 (see Section 2.11) to indicate support for this UUI package. For example, the media feature tag sip.

uui-pk1 could be defined to indicate support for a UUI package named pk1. The definition of a new SIP option tag solely to identify support for a UUI package is not recommended unless there are additional SIP behaviors needed to implement this feature. RFC 7434 also provides the example UUI package definition.

16.9.6.1 Extensibility

New content values must describe the semantics of the UUI data and valid encodings, and give some example use cases. A previously defined UUI content value can be used in a new package. In this case, the semantics and usage of the content by the new package is defined within the new package. New UUI content types cannot be added to existing packages—instead, a new package would need to be defined. New content values that are defined are added to the IANA registry with a Standards Track RFC, which needs to discuss the issues in this section. If no new encoding value is defined for a content, the encoding defaults to hex as defined in this document. In this case, the hex value will be explicitly stated via the encoding parameter as the encoding for the content.

New encoding values associated with a new content must reference a specific encoding scheme (such as hex, which is defined in this specification) or define the new encoding scheme. A previously defined UUI encoding value can be used with a newly defined content. In this case, the usage of the encoding is defined by the content definition. New UUI encodings cannot be added to existing contents—instead, a new content would need to be defined. Newly defined encoding values are added to the IANA registry with a Standards Track RFC, which needs to discuss the issues in this section.

16.9.7 Use Cases

We now discuss four use cases (UA-to-UA, Retargeting, Redirection, and Referral) for the transport of call control UUI specified in RFC 6567 (see Section 16.9.1). These use cases will help motivate the requirements for SIP call control UUI.

16.9.7.1 User Agent to User Agent

In this scenario, the originating UA includes UUI in the INVITE sent through a proxy to the terminating UA. The terminating UA can use the UUI in any way. If it is an ISDN gateway, it could map the UUI into the appropriate DSS1 [4] information element, QSIG [5] information element, or ISUP parameter. Alternatively, the using application might render the information to the user, or use it during alerting

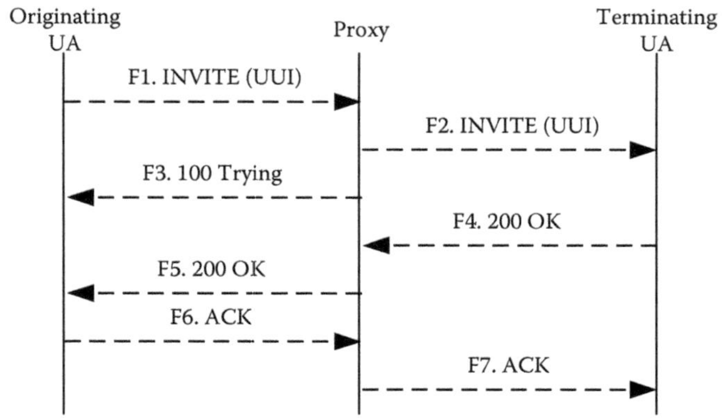

Figure 16.42 Call flow with UUI exchanged between originating and terminating UAs. (Copyright IETF. Reproduced with permission.)

or as a lookup for a screen pop. In this case, the proxy does not need to understand the UUI mechanism; however, normal proxy rules should result in the UUI being forwarded without modification. This call flow is shown in Figure 16.42 (RFC 6567).

16.9.7.2 Proxy Retargeting

In this scenario, the originating UA includes UUI in the INVITE request sent through a proxy to the terminating UA. The proxy retargets the INVITE request, changing its Request-URI to a URI that addresses the terminating UA. The UUI data is then received and processed by the terminating UA. This call flow is identical to Figure 16.32 except that the proxy retargets the request, that is, changes the Request-URI as directed by some unspecified process. The UUI in the INVITE request needs to be passed unchanged through this proxy retargeting operation. Note that the contents of the UUI are not used by the proxy for routing, as the UUI has only end-to-end significance between UAs.

16.9.7.3 Redirection

In this scenario, UUI is inserted by an application that utilizes a SIP Redirect Server. The UUI is then included in the INVITE request sent by the originating UA to the terminating UA. In this case, the originating UA does not necessarily need to support the UUI mechanism but does need to support the SIP redirection mechanism used to include the UUI data. Two examples of UUI with redirection (transfer and diversion) are defined in Refs. [6] and [7]. Note that this case may not precisely map to an equivalent ISDN service use case. This is because there is no one-to-one mapping between elements in a SIP network and elements in an ISDN network. Also, there is no exact one-to-one mapping between SIP call control and ISDN call control. However,

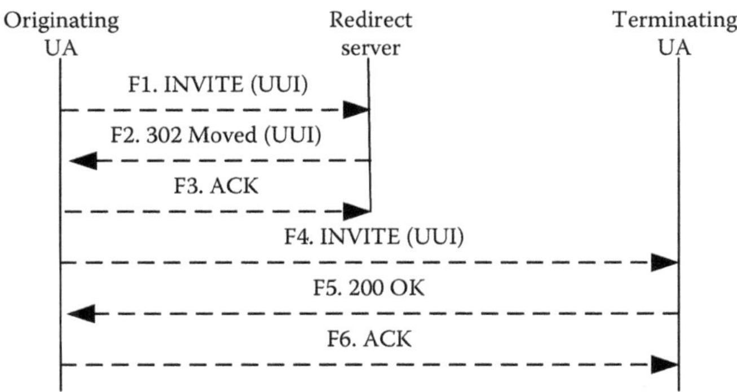

Figure 16.43 Call flow with UUI exchanged between redirect server and terminating UA. (Copyright IETF. Reproduced with permission.)

this should not prevent the usage of SIP call control UUI in these cases. Instead, these slight differences between the SIP UUI mechanism and the ISDN service need to be carefully noted and discussed in an interworking specification. Figure 16.43 (RFC 6567) shows this scenario, with the Redirect Server inserting UUI that is then included in the INVITE request F4 sent to the terminating UA.

A common example application of this call flow is an Automatic Call Distributer in a PSTN contact center. The originator would be a PSTN gateway. The ACD would act as a Redirect Server, inserting UUI based on called number, calling number, time of day, and other information. The resulting UUI would be passed to the agent's handset, which acts as the terminating UA. The UUI could be used to look up information for rendering to the agent at the time of call answering. This redirection scenario and the referral scenario in the next section are the most important scenarios for contact center applications. Incoming calls to a contact center almost always are redirected or referred to a final destination, sometimes multiple times, based on collected information and business logic. The ability to pass along UUI in these call redirection scenarios is critical.

16.9.7.4 Referral

In this scenario, the application uses a UA to initiate a referral, which causes an INVITE request to be generated between the originating UA and terminating UA with UUI data inserted by the referrer UA. Note that this REFER method could be part of a transfer operation, or it might be unrelated to an existing call, such as out-of-dialog REFER request. In some cases, this call flow is used in place of the redirection call flow: the referrer immediately answers the call and then sends the REFER request. This scenario is shown in Figure 16.44 (RFC 6567).

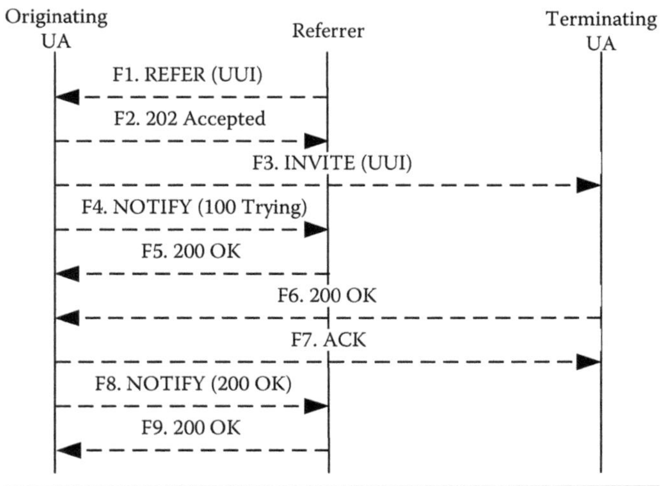

Figure 16.44 Call flow with referral and UUI. (Copyright IETF. Reproduced with permission.)

16.10 Call Services Using DTMF

The DTMF is a signaling system that identifies the dialed number on a DTMF key pad or pushbutton. The legacy PSTN/ISDN telephone system uses the multifrequency dialing that is used by DTMF eliminating the need of the telecom operator used between the caller and the callee, and has ushered the automated dialing in the telephone switching centers. DTMF, as the name suggests, uses a combination of two sine-wave tones to represent a key, which are called row and column frequencies as they correspond to the layout of a telephone keypad as depicted in Figure 16.45.

The combination of different sine waves with high and low frequencies prevents misinterpretation of the harmonics.

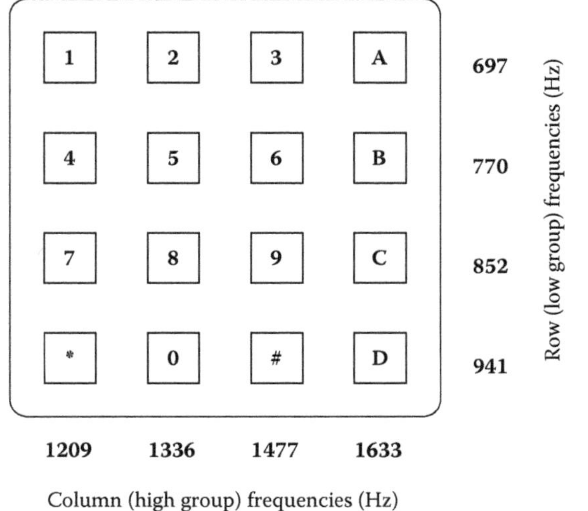

Figure 16.45 DTMF keypad system.

Also, the frequencies for DTMF are so chosen that none have a harmonic relationship with the others and that mixing the frequencies would not produce sum or product frequencies that could mimic another valid tone. The high-group frequencies (the column tones) are slightly louder than the low group to compensate for the high-frequency roll-off of voice audio systems. DTMF tones are able to represent 1 of the 16 different states or symbols on the keypad. This is equivalent to 4 bits of data, also known as nibble. DTMF has clearly been extended to purposes beyond simply dialing a telephone number. Interactive Voice Systems prompt us for all sorts of things that we answer with button presses. We log into our voice-mail systems and retrieve our messages with DTMF. If so inclined, even music can be played using DTMF.

Depending on the origin of the DTMF signals, they can start out in a separate stream, or that separate stream might be created by stripping the tones out of an audio conversation. An example of the latter would be a gateway that converts analog to SIP. Problems can arise from this stripping that need to be considered. The converter must hear the tone before stripping it out, and sometimes there is leakage where the very beginning of the tone makes its way through. This might cause a voice-mail system to hear two tones for a single tone. One would come from the RFC 2833 stream and the other in the voice stream. Fortunately, conversion hardware is getting better and better, and these problems have become less common (albeit a bear to debug when they occur). Thus, in terms of SIP, how is this RFC 2833 stream created and managed? Through SDP, of course. SDP is used to describe the voice stream (e.g., G.729) and it is also used to inform the recipient that RFC 2833 is available. Specifically, it uses something called telephone event. Here is an example of an SDP media description that you might see in the body of an Invite message. Note the format of 0–15. This represents the 10 digits plus *, #, A, B, D, E, and Flash.

```
m=audio 12346 RTP/AVP 101
a=rtpmap:101 telephone-event/8000
a=fmtp:101 0-15
```

The purpose of RFC 2833 has been to create a separate stream for DTMF to allow voice codecs to strictly deal with creating the best possible voice stream using the fewest number of bytes. Note that we do not need to send those DTMF signals on the same connection that we send our audio conversation with use of RFC 2833. Instead, we send them out-of-band on their own stream allowing even to compress the voice signal without altering the DTMF signals. The newly developed RFC 4733 obsoletes RFC 2833 using much richer functionalities. RFC 4733 captures and expands upon the basic framework defined in RFC 2833, but retains only the most basic event codes. It sets up an IANA registry to which other event code assignments may be added. Companion documents add event codes to this registry relating to modem, fax, text telephony, and channel-associated signaling events. The remainder of the event codes defined in RFC 2833 are conditionally reserved in case other documents revive their use.

RFC 4733 provides a number of clarifications to RFC 2833. However, it specifically differs from RFC 2833 by removing the requirement that all compliant implementations support the DTMF events. Instead, compliant implementations taking part in out-of-band negotiations of media stream content indicate what events they support. This memo adds three new procedures to the RFC 2833 framework: subdivision of long events into segments, reporting of multiple events in a single packet, and the concept and reporting of state events. RFC 4734 updates RFC 4733 to add event codes for modem, fax, and text telephony signals when carried in the telephony event RTP payload. It supersedes the assignment of event codes for this purpose in RFC 2833, and therefore obsoletes that part of RFC 2833.

Furthermore, RFC 5244 updates RFC 4733 to add event codes for telephony signals used for channel-associated signaling when carried in the telephony event RTP payload. It supersedes and adds to the original assignment of event codes for this purpose in RFC 2833. Some of the RFC 2833 events have been deprecated because their specification was ambiguous, erroneous, or redundant. In fact, the degree of change of RFC 2833 is such that implementations of the present document are fully backwards compatible with RFC 2833 implementations only in the case of full ABCD-bit signaling. RFC 5244 further expands and improves the coverage of signaling systems compared with RFC 2833. The details of RFCs 4733, 4734, and 5244 have not been addressed here for the sake of brevity.

16.11 Emergency Call Services in SIP

16.11.1 Overview

Emergency calls are being supported worldwide by every government for helping citizens by using law enforcement authorities. Emergency calls need to support at least the exact location of the caller so that assistance can be provided. SIP, being the call control signaling protocol used over the IP network and public Internet, supports the emergency calls. The traditional emergency calls are usually provided using only a single media like audio over the circuit switched PSTN networks where calls are routed through public safety access points (PSAPs). However, SIP can support emergency calls with audio, video, or data applications over both fixed and mobile wireless network infrastructures. It has opened a new era of supporting emergency calls with multimedia, providing emergency support for users with more vividness and accuracy. Unlike PSTN, the support of emergency calls over packet switched networks like IP using new call control protocols like SIP has not yet emerged due to the lack of international standards that require time for their development.

Of late, the IETF has created a host of standards primarily defining the Emergency Telecommunications Service (ETS) requirements and frameworks in RFCs 3523, 3689, 3690, 4190, 4375, 4542, 4958, 5012, 5031, 5069, 6061, 6443, 6881, and others for IP network infrastructures like IP-based PSAPs, policies for supporting single and multiple administrative domains, URNs for emergency services, dealing with security and threats faced by emergency calls, best current practice (BCP) for supporting ETS, extensions in SIP/SDP, call preemption, and many other functional capabilities needed for support. Going forward, many more standards need to be created to achieve the full potential for supporting media-rich, functionality-rich multimedia emergency calls over IP networks. The detailed description of all functionalities for supporting emergency calls using SIP over IP/Internet infrastructures is beyond the scope of this section. A brief outline is provided in the next section, limiting the description to the context of the IP/Internet.

16.11.2 Emergency Services Uniform Resource Name

The exact location of the emergency call is the most essential criterion in order to provide assistance to the user. Moreover, the type of location can be civic, postal, geospatial, and others. RFC 5031 has standardized the initial emergency Uniform Resource Name (URN), as shown in Figure 16.46. This figure also includes the URN for the emergency counseling services. In addition, RFC 6061 specifies the URN namespace for the National Emergency Number Association (NENA).

Figure 16.46 shows only two root domains: SOS and Counseling. Some of the subdomains of these root domains that have been registered with the IANA are also depicted. Note that many more subdomains of these root and subroot domains can be created as required. RFCs 6116 and 6117 have specified the DNS mechanisms for the dynamic discovery and delegation system that can be used for the emergency call information of the SOS and the Counseling DNS tree for the location information. The delegation tree branch may even include the street address, street number, and cube and floor number. The support for the PASPs over the IP/Internet is described in RFC 6443. Section 16.11 describes in detail how the DNS NAPTR records for SOS or Counseling can support automatic routing.

We have described that a SIP call is routed using the Request-URI. Chapter 9 described in detail the routing in SIP. The SOS URI shall be used for routing the emergency calls. The feature tag will indicate the type of service that has been requested by the caller. RFC 6443 describes how SIP UAs, proxy servers, and PSAPs support processing and routing for emergency calls, including intermediate devices that exist between end devices or applications and the access network.

16.11.3 Multilevel Precedence and Preemption

One of the most important requirements in supporting emergency calls is to provide priority. That is, emergency calls ought to be handled, processed, and routed on the basis of their respective priority types, even preempting ongoing existing calls at the call/session level. In addition, the resources of both application and network level must be prioritized in serving the emergency calls based on its priority levels. To meet this requirement, RFC 4542 defines the Multilevel Precedence and Preemption (MLPP). MLPP is an architecture for a

Service	Reference	Description
sos	RFC 5031	Emergency services
sos.ambulance		Ambulance service
sos.animal-control		Animal control
sos.fire		Fire service
sos.gas		Gas leaks and gas emergencies
sos.marine		Maritime search and rescue
sos.mountain		Mountain rescue
sos.physician		Physician referral service
sos.poison		Poison control center
sos.police		Police, law enforcement
counseling		Counseling services
counseling.children		Counseling for children
counseling.mental-health		Mental health counseling
counseling.suicide		Suicide prevention hotline

Figure 16.46 Initial IANA registration for emergency and counseling services.

prioritized call handling service such that in times of emergency. The precedence types, in descending order of priority level, are Flash Override Override, Flash Override, Flash, Immediate, Priority, and Routine.

The resource priority that needs to be provided by SIP functional entities like UAs and proxies are defined in RFC 3487 (see Section 15.2.1). Consequently, the SIP will route the emergency calls via the IP-based PSAPs handling, processing, and routing the calls serving with appropriate priorities, even preempting lower-priority calls if needed between the source and the destination. QOS signaling protocols, such as Resource Reservation Protocol, can be used for network resource reservation-based priority precedence. The security features for emergency calls are described in RFC 5069. The description of interworking between the IP/Internet and PSTN emergency calls is beyond the scope of this chapter.

16.12 Summary

We have described some basic call services that are being created using SIP signaling messages. Service creation using SIP signaling messages is a huge area, and more intelligent multimedia-rich applications can be created in the future by new innovators. We have shown how a variety of different call services can be created using only the REFER method. Unlike non-RT services, the creation of RT multimedia services demands a different kind of solutions. For example, to transfer a call to another party, we need to consider whether the other party is available, busy, or willing to accept a call at that particular moment in real time, including security/privacy. Even if the transfer is not successful, the next course of action needs to be decided on the basis of the kind of unsuccessful call transfer. In addition, if the call is transferred to multiple parities, it creates more complexities in view of dealing with each of these parties separately, knowing the status of each one.

We have explained why call services for content indirection is needed as SIP is not a general-purpose data transfer protocol. Third-party transcoding call services provide STT, TTS, and other media transcoding. The SIP INFO method and User-to-User header are used in call services for transferring user information during the mid-call after the session establishment and at the time of session setup time, respectively. DTMF call services have also been discussed briefly. Finally, we have described the emerging standards for supporting emergency calls over the IP/Internet. The emergency and counseling root URN and their subdomains are explained. The emergency SOS URI address resolution and the automatic routing of the call using the DNS are discussed. Emergency call priority using MLPP and resource-priority, which are essential for the successful completion of emergency calls, are also articulated. In the future, more innovative intelligent RT networked multimedia services can be created using SIP signaling mechanisms.

PROBLEMS

1. What is the basic call transfer in SIP? Explain with call flow examples using REFER to achieve call transfer under following conditions: successful transfer and transfer with dialog reuse (failed transfer: target busy and transfer target does not answer).
2. What is call transfer with consultation hold? Explain using SIP call flows for the following scenarios: exposing and protecting transfer target, attended transfer, recovery when one party does not support REFER, attended transfer using GRUU known for routing the call to a unique UA, semi-attended transfer, and attended transfer fallback to basic transfer.
3. Explain the use of SIP call flows for the following circumstances: call transfer with Referred-By, transfer as an ad hoc conference and transfer with multiple parties.
4. What are the issues in call transfer with a gateway? Explain with SIP call flows the call transfer issues related to the gateway: coerce gateway hairpins to the same gateway and consultative-turned-blind glare.
5. What is the call diversion indication specified in RFC 5806? Explain with detailed call flows. Why is RFC 5806 an informational RFC published although not used in SIP? How is this capability offered in SIP by other means that are standardized by Standards Track RFCs?
6. Why is the distributed SBC architecture needed in SIP? Explain the logical operation of distributed SBC architecture if there are only two physical entities: signaling controller (SC) and media controller (MC). Which protocol would you choose between the SC and MC, and why? Describe the logical functional capabilities of H.248 protocol briefly. Will H.248 protocol satisfy the needs of SBC?
7. Develop call flows for the distributed SIP-based SBC assuming that there is only a single physical entity of SC and MC for the following, choosing your own networking topology along the line of Section 14.2: topology hiding, media traffic management, fixing capability mismatches, maintaining SIP-related NAT bindings, access control, protocol repair, and media encryption.
8. What is a so-called SoftSwitch architecture that uses the distributed SIP-based SBC? Explain the SIP trunking architecture, developing your own topology along with call flows.

9. Explain the evolution of the so-called SoftSwitch-based SIP trunking architecture evolution to the all SIP-based IP telephony architectures along with RT and near-RT SIP application server architecture from the legacy POTS/PSTN/ISDN telephony architecture along with call flows choosing your own network architecture.
10. Develop a distributed SIP-based RT and near-RT service architecture for the large-scale global network architecture. Extend this SIP-based server architecture for providing end-to-end SIP-based telephony services along with distributed SBC architecture in the local centers along with call flows.
11. Define an operation scenario for referring call to multiple parties. Why is the multiple-refer SIP option tag useful for this purpose? Explain with SIP call flows the following for referring calls to multiple resources: suppressing REFER's implicit subscription, behavior of SIP REFER-Issuers, and behavior of REFER recipients.
12. Why is content indirection needed in SIP? Explain using use cases: presence notification, and document sharing. How is RFC 2017 used in solving the content indirection problems in SIP? Explain in detail.
13. What is the media transcoding service? Why is it needed in SIP? Explain with SIP call flows the third-party transcoding call services for the following: callee's and caller's invocation, receiving the original stream, and transcoding services in parallel, and multiple transcoding services in series. Explain the conferencing mode transcoding call services with detailed SIP call flows.
14. Why is the INFO method needed in SIP? What are the special characteristics of the INFO method that make it fundamentally different from other SIP methods? Explain the behavior of all SIP entities in processing the INFO method. Describe in detail the INFO request and response message body and order of delivery.
15. How are the INFO Packages created? Explain the SIP UA behavior related to INFO Packages: general, procedures, Recv-Info header field rules, and INFO Package fallback rules.
16. Explain in detail the things that need to be considered for the INFO Package: appropriateness of usage, request rate and volume, alternative SIP signaling mechanisms (SUBSCRIBE/NOTIFY and MESSAGE), and alternative SIP media plane mechanisms (MRCP and MSRP).
17. What are the requirements of the INFO Package? Explain with SIP call flows for the INFO method for the following scenarios: willingness to receive INFO Packages (INVITE and Target Refresh), INFO request associated with INFO Package (Single INFO Payload and Multipart INFO [non-Info Package body part, multiple body parts inside multiple body part, and single body part inside multipart body part]).
18. What are the differences between the INFO method and User-to-User header in SIP? What are the requirements that UUI needs to meet in SIP? Why are INFO, MIME, and URI not used in transferring the call control UUI? Explain the guidelines for UUI packages. Explain with call flows UUI use cases for the following: UA-to-UA, proxy retargeting, redirection, and referral.
19. Explain with detailed SIP call flows the call services using DTMF.
20. Explain with detailed SIP call flows how emergency services are offered using SIP over the IP network including the use of emergency URNs and MLPP.
21. How does the emergency call over the IP/Internet differ from that over the PSTN network?
22. What are the IETF standards that are being standardized for supporting emergency calls over the IP/Internet? Explain each one of these standards briefly.
23. Explain the emergency root SOS URN. How can the subdomains of the root SOS domain be created? How is the emergency URI resolved using the DNS? How does the DNS NAPTAR record help in routing emergency calls?
24. Describe how the SIP Request-URI helps in routing emergency calls over the SIP network.
25. What is MLLP? Describe each kind of priority level as described in RFC 4542.
26. Describe how emergency calls are routed over the IP/Internet with SIP using MLLP and resource priority.
27. Describe the security aspects of emergency calls over the IP/Internet.
28. Develop an architecture that interworks between the IP/Internet and the PSTN.

References

1. ITU-T, "The Narrowband Signaling Syntax (NSS)—Syntax definition," ITU-T Recommendation Q.1980.1, Available at http://www.itu.int/itudoc/itu-t/aap/sg11aap/history/q1980.1/q1980.1.html.
2. ITU-T, "Signaling System No. 7—ISDN User Part formats and codes," ITU-T Recommendation Q.763, Available at http://www.itu.int/rec/T-REC-Q.763-199912-I/en.
3. ITU-T, "ISDN user-network interface layer 3 specification for basic call control," ITU-T Recommendation Q.931, Available at http://www.itu.int/rec/T-REC-Q.931-199805-I/en.
4. ITU-T, "ISDN Digital Subscriber Signaling System No. 1 (DSS1)—Signaling specifications for frame mode switched

and permanent virtual connection control and status monitoring," ITU-T Recommendation Q.933, Available at http://www.itu.int/rec/T-REC-Q.933/en.

5. ECMA, "Private Integrated Services Network (PISN)—Circuit Mode Bearer Services—Inter-exchange Signaling Procedures and Protocol (QSIG-BC)," Standard ECMA-143, December 2001.
6. ANSI, "Telecommunications–Integrated Services Digital Network (ISDN)–Explicit Call Transfer Supplementary Service," ANSI T1.643-1995.
7. ETSI, "Integrated Services Digital Network (ISDN); Diversion supplementary services," ETSI ETS 300 207-1, Ed. 1, 1994.
8. Recommendation ITU-T H.248.1 (03/2013): Gateway control protocol: Version 3.
9. Recommendation ITU-T H.323 (2009): Packet-based multimedia communications.
10. Third Generation Partnership Project, "Technical Specification Group Core Network and Terminals; Communication Diversion (CDIV) using IP Multimedia (IM)Core Network (CN) subsystem; Protocol specification (Release 8), 3GPP TS 24.604," December 2008.
11. Third Generation Partnership Project, "Technical Specification Group Core Network and Terminals; Interworking between the IP Multimedia (IM) Core Network (CN) Subsystem and Circuit Switched (CS) networks (Release 8)," December 2008.
12. Standard ECMA-355 (www.ecma-international.org): Corporate Telecommunication Networks-Tunnelling of QSIG over SIP 3rd edition, June 2008.

Chapter 17

Media Server Interfaces in SIP

Abstract

Media server interfaces use a lot of stimulus signaling that encompasses a wide range of mechanisms, ranging from clicking on hyperlinks, to pressing buttons, to traditional dual-tone multifrequency input. Request for Comment (RFC) 5629 describes a framework for the interaction between users and Session Initiation Protocol (SIP)-based applications. The stimulus signaling allows a user agent to interact with an application without knowledge of the semantics of that application. Application interaction can be either functional or stimulus. Functional interaction requires the user device to understand the semantics of the application, whereas stimulus interaction does not. Stimulus signaling allows for applications to be built without requiring modifications to the user device. The services invoked from media server are examples of SIP-based applications creation using a kind of stimulus signaling. The details of session establishment and termination, media negotiation using Session Description Protocol offer–answer model, returning data (e.g., collected utterance or digit information) from the media server to the application server, and other services using SIP interfaces are discussed. We have taken the SIP interface to VoiceXML media server specified in RFC 5552 as an example in this chapter. Similarly, the audio, video, or data media bridging/mixing server for multimedia conferencing in SIP also demands that the media server needs to be distributed for scalability, especially for the large-scale SIP network. It should be noted that the media services are a huge area that need to be looked into for the creation of more scalable multimedia services, making them distributed for the generation large-scale next SIP network.

17.1 Introduction

Session Initiation Protocol (SIP) interfaces to the VoiceXML media server specified in Request for Comment (RFC) 5552 (see Section 17.2) are used to initiate, establish, and tear down the sessions between the media server and the user while the application servers control the media server. The VoiceXML sessions are characterized by synthesized speech, digitized audio, recognition of spoken and dual-tone multifrequency (DTMF) key input, recording of audio and video, telephony, and mixed-initiative conversations. However, the VoiceXML media server standards along with MEDIACTRL protocol and packages mechanism have been created by the World Wide Web Consortium (W3C). In addition to the execution of the session, SIP triggers the execution of a specified VoiceXML application simultaneously. First, we describe the VoiceXML use cases: public switched telephone network (PSTN) interactive voice response (IVR) services with application servers, PSTN IVR service node, media resource function (MRF) defined in Third Generation Partnership Project (3GPP), Call Control eXtensible Markup Language (CCXML) and VoiceXML interaction, and other cases. The VoiceXML session establishment and termination, media support including early media, audio and video codecs and DTMF, data transfer to the application server, outbound calling, and call transfer (Blind, Bridge, and Consultation) are described here. In all of those media services, the key is the stimulus signaling specified in RFC 5629 which allows a user agent (UA) to interact with an application without knowledge of the semantics of that application as indicated earlier.

17.2 SIP Interface to VoiceXML Media Server

17.2.1 Overview

VoiceXML [1,2] is a W3C standard for creating audio and video dialogs that feature synthesized speech, digitized audio, recognition of spoken and DTMF key input, recording of audio and video, telephony, and mixed-initiative conversations. VoiceXML allows web-based development and content delivery paradigms to be used with interactive video and voice response applications. RFC 5552 describes a SIP (RFC 3261) interface to VoiceXML media services. Commonly, application servers controlling media servers use this protocol for pure VoiceXML processing capabilities. SIP is responsible for initiating a media session to the VoiceXML media server and simultaneously triggering the execution of a specified VoiceXML application. This protocol is an adjunct to the full MEDIACTRL protocol and packages mechanism. The interface described here leverages a mechanism for identifying dialog media services first described in RFC 4240 (see Section 4.4.2). The interface has been updated and extended to support the W3C Recommendation for VoiceXML 2.0 [1] and VoiceXML 2.1 [2]. A set of commonly implemented functions and extensions has been specified, including VoiceXML dialog preparation, outbound calling, video media support, and transfers. VoiceXML session variable mappings have been defined for SIP with an extensible mechanism for passing application-specific values into the VoiceXML application. Mechanisms for returning data to the application server have also been added.

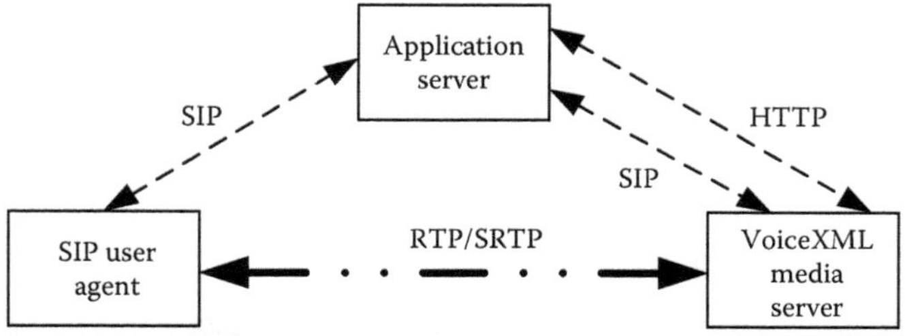

Figure 17.1 IVR services by SIP application server using VoiceXML media server. (Copyright IETF. Reproduced with permission.)

17.2.2 Use Cases

The VoiceXML media service user in this document is generically referred to as an application server. In practice, it is intended that the interface defined by this document be applicable across a wide range of use cases. Several intended use cases are described below.

17.2.2.1 IVR Services with Application Servers

SIP application servers provide services to users of the network. Typically, there may be several application servers in the same network, each specialized in providing a particular service. Throughout this specification and without loss of generality, we posit the presence of an application server specialized in providing IVR services. A typical configuration for this use case is illustrated in Figure 17.1.

Assuming the application server also supports HTTP, the VoiceXML application may be hosted on it and served up via HTTP (RFCs 7230-7235). Note, however, that the web model allows the VoiceXML application to be hosted on a separate (HTTP) application server from the (SIP) application server that interacts with the VoiceXML media server via this specification. It is also possible for a static VoiceXML application to be stored locally on the VoiceXML media server, leveraging the VoiceXML 2.1 [2] <data> mechanism to interact with a web/application server when dynamic behavior is required. The viability of static VoiceXML applications is further enhanced by the mechanisms through which the application server can make session-specific information available within the VoiceXML session context. The approach described in this document is sometimes termed the *delegation model*—the application server is essentially delegating programmatic control of the human–machine interactions to one or more VoiceXML documents running on the VoiceXML media server. During the human–machine interactions, the application server remains in the signaling path and can respond to results returned from the VoiceXML media server or other external network events.

17.2.2.2 PSTN IVR Service Node

While this section is intended to enable enhanced use of VoiceXML as a component of larger systems and services, it is intended that devices that are completely unaware of this specification remain capable of invoking VoiceXML services offered by a VoiceXML media server compliant with this document. A typical configuration for this use case is shown in Figure 17.2.

Note also that beyond the invocation and termination of a VoiceXML dialog, the semantics defined for call transfers using REFER are intended to be compatible with standard, existing Internet Protocol (IP)/PSTN gateways.

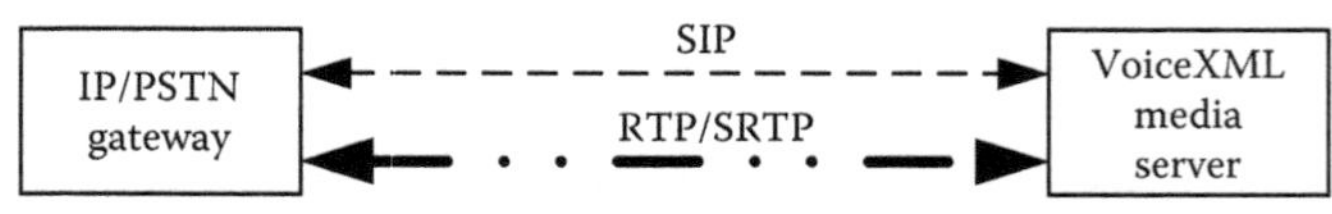

Figure 17.2 IVR services to IP/PSTN gateway from SIP network. (Copyright IETF. Reproduced with permission.)

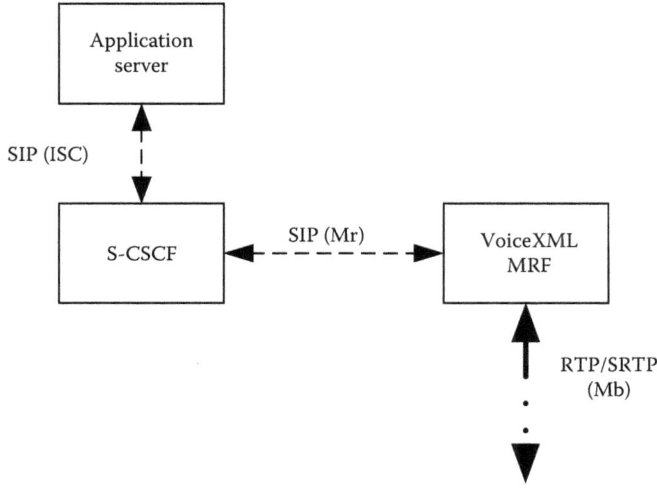

Figure 17.3 IVR services in 3GPP IMS network. (Copyright IETF. Reproduced with permission.)

17.2.2.3 3GPP IP Multimedia Subsystem MRF

The 3GPP IP Multimedia Subsystem (IMS) [3] defines an MRF used to offer media-processing services such as conferencing, transcoding, and prompt/collect. The capabilities offered by VoiceXML are ideal for offering richer media-processing services in the context of the MRF. In this architecture, the interface defined here corresponds to the *Mr* interface to the MRFC (MRF controller); the implementation of this interface might use separated MRFC and MRFP (MRF processor) elements (as per the IMS architecture), or might be an integrated MRF (as is a common practice). The diagram in Figure 17.3 is highly simplified and shows a subset of nodes typically involved in MRF interactions.

It should be noted that while the MRF will primarily be used by the application server via the Serving Call Session Control Function (S-CSCF) that is a SIP proxy in 3GPP architecture [3], it is also possible for calls to be routed directly to the MRF without the involvement of an application server. Although the above is described in terms of the 3GPP IMS architecture, it is intended that it is also applicable to 3GPP2, Next-Generation Network (NGN), and PacketCable architectures that are converging with 3GPP IMS standards.

17.2.2.4 CCXML and VoiceXML Interaction

CCXML 1.0 [4] applications provide services mainly through controlling the interaction between connections, conferences, and dialogs. Although CCXML is capable of supporting arbitrary dialog environments, VoiceXML is commonly used as a dialog environment in conjunction with CCXML applications; CCXML is specifically designed to effectively support the use of VoiceXML. CCXML 1.0 defines language elements that allow for dialogs to be prepared, started, and terminated; it further allows for data to be returned by the dialog environment, for call transfers to be requested (by the dialog) and responded to by the CCXML application, and for arbitrary eventing between the CCXML application and running dialog application. The interface described in this document can be used by CCXML 1.0 implementations to control VoiceXML media servers. Note, however, that some CCXML language features require eventing facilities between CCXML and VoiceXML sessions that go beyond what is defined in this specification. For example, VoiceXML-controlled call transfers and mid-dialog, application-defined events cannot be fully realized using this specification alone. A SIP event package (RFC 6665, see Section 5.2) may be used in addition to this specification to provide extended eventing.

17.2.2.5 Other Use Cases

In addition to the use cases described in some detail above, there are a number of other intended use cases that are not described in detail, such as

- Use of a VoiceXML media server as an adjunct to an IP-based Private Branch Exchange/Automatic Call Distributor (PBX/ACD), possibly to provide voice mail/messaging, automated attendant, or other capabilities.
- Invocation and control of a VoiceXML session that provides the voice modality component in a multimodal system.

17.2.2.6 Functional Features

- **Application server:** A SIP application server hosts and executes services, in particular by terminating SIP sessions on a media server. The application server MAY also act as an HTTP server in interactions with media servers.
- **VoiceXML media server:** A VoiceXML interpreter including a SIP-based interpreter context and the requisite media-processing capabilities to support VoiceXML functionality.
- **VoiceXML session:** A VoiceXML session is a multimedia session comprising at least a SIP UA, a VoiceXML media server, the data streams between them, and an executing VoiceXML application.
- **VoiceXML Dialog:** Equivalent to a VoiceXML session.

17.2.3 VoiceXML Session Establishment and Termination

This section describes how to establish a VoiceXML session, with or without preparation, and how to terminate a session. This section also addresses how session information is made available to VoiceXML applications.

17.2.3.1 Service Identification

The SIP Request-URI is used to identify the VoiceXML media service. The user part of the SIP Request-URI is fixed to *dialog*. This is done to ensure compatibility with RFC 4240, since this document extends the dialog interface defined in that specification and because this convention from RFC 4240 (see Section 4.4.2) is widely adopted by existing media servers. Standardizing the SIP Request-URI including the user part also improves interoperability between application servers and media servers, and reduces the provisioning overhead that would be required if use of a media server by an application server required an individually provisioned Uniform Resource Identifier (URI). In this respect, this document (and RFC 4240) do not add semantics to the user part, but rather standardize the way that targets on media servers are provisioned. Furthermore, since application servers—and not human beings—are generally the clients of media servers, issues such as interpretation and internationalization do not apply. Exposing a VoiceXML media service with a well-known address may enhance the possibility of exploitation: the VoiceXML media server is RECOMMENDED to use standard SIP mechanisms to authenticate end points as discussed in Section 2.5. The initial VoiceXML document is specified with the voicexml parameter. In addition, parameters are defined that control how the VoiceXML media server fetches the specified VoiceXML document. The list of parameters defined by this specification is as follows (note that the parameter names are case insensitive):

- **voicexml:** URI of the initial VoiceXML document to fetch. This will typically contain an HTTP URI, but may use other URI schemes, for example, to refer to local, static VoiceXML documents. If the voicexml parameter is omitted, the VoiceXML media server may select the initial VoiceXML document by other means, such as by applying a default, or may reject the request.
- **maxage:** Used to set the max-age value of the Cache-Control header in conjunction with VoiceXML documents fetched using HTTP, as per RFCs 7230–7235. If omitted, the VoiceXML media server will use a default value.
- **maxstale:** Used to set the max-stale value of the Cache-Control header in conjunction with VoiceXML documents fetched using HTTP, as per RFCs 7230–7235. If omitted, the VoiceXML media server will use a default value.
- **method:** Used to set the HTTP method applied in the fetch of the initial VoiceXML document. Allowed values are *get* or *post* (case insensitive). The default is get.
- **postbody:** Used to set the application/x-www-form-urlencoded encoded [5] HTTP body for post requests (or is otherwise ignored).
- **ccxml:** Used to specify a JSON value (RFC 4627) that is mapped to the session.connection.ccxml VoiceXML session variable.
- **aai:** Used to specify a JSON value (RFC 4627) that is mapped to the session.connection.aai VoiceXML session variable.

Other application-specific parameters may be added to the Request-URI and are exposed in VoiceXML session variables. Formally, the Request-URI for the VoiceXML media service has a fixed user part dialog. Seven URI parameters are defined (see the definition of uri-parameter in augmented Backus–Naur Form in Section 2.4.1).

```
dialog-param    = "voicexml=" vxml-url;
                  vxml-url follows the URI
                  ; syntax defined in RFC 3986
maxage-param    = "maxage=" 1*DIGIT
maxstale-param  = "maxstale=" 1*DIGIT
method-param    = "method=" ("get"/"post")
postbody-param  = "postbody=" token
ccxml-param     = "ccxml=" json-value
aai-param       = "aai=" json-value
json-value      = false/
                  null/
                  true/
                  object/
                  array/
                  number/
                  string ; defined in RFC 7158
                  (obsoletes RFC 4627)
```

In addition, RFC 5552 has registered the following parameters in the SIP/SIPS URI parameters registry of the Internet Assigned Numbers Authority, in accordance to policy of RFC 3969:

Parameter Name	*Predefined Values*	*Reference*
maxage	No	RFC 5552
maxstale	No	RFC 5552
method	get/post	RFC 5552
postbody	No	RFC 5552
ccml	No	RFC 5552
aai	No	RFC 5552

Parameters of the Request-URI in subsequent re-INVITEs are ignored. One consequence of this is that the VoiceXML media server cannot be instructed by the application server to change the executing VoiceXML application after a VoiceXML session has been started. Special characters contained in the dialog-param, postbody-param, ccxml-param, and aai-param values must be URL-encoded (*escaped*) as required by the SIP URI syntax, for example, "?" (%3f), "=" (%3d), and ";" (%3b). The VoiceXML media server MUST therefore unescape these parameter values before making use of them or exposing them to running VoiceXML applications. It is important that the VoiceXML media server only unescape the parameter values once since the desired VoiceXML URI value could itself be URL encoded, for example.

Since some applications may choose to transfer confidential information, the VoiceXML media server must support the sips: scheme. Informative note: With respect to the postbody-param value, since the application/x-www-form-urlencoded content itself escapes non-alphanumeric characters by inserting %HH replacements, the escaping rules above will result in the % characters being further escaped in addition to the & and = name/value separators. As an example, the following SIP Request-URI identifies the use of VoiceXML media services, with http://appserver.example.com/promptcollect.vxml as the initial VoiceXML document, to be fetched with max-age/max-stale values of 3600s/0s, respectively:

```
sip:dialog@mediaserver.example.com; \
      voicexml=http://appserver.example.com
      /promptcollect.vxml; \
      maxage=3600;maxstale=0
```

17.2.3.2 Initiating a VoiceXML Session

A VoiceXML session is initiated via the application server using a SIP INVITE. Typically, the application server will be specialized in providing VoiceXML services. At a minimum, the application server may behave as a simple proxy by rewriting the Request-URI received from the UA to a Request-URI suitable for consumption by the VoiceXML media server specified earlier. For example, a UA might present a dialed number:

```
tel:+1-201-555-0123
```

that the application server maps to a directory assistance application on the VoiceXML media server with a Request-URI of

```
sip:dialog@ms1.example.com; \
      voicexml=http://as1.example.com
      /da.vxml
```

Certain header values in the INVITE message to the VoiceXML media server are mapped into VoiceXML session variables and are specified in Section 17.2.3.4. On receipt of the INVITE, the VoiceXML media server issues a provisional response, 100 Trying, and commences the fetch of the initial VoiceXML document. The 200 OK response indicates that the VoiceXML document has been fetched and parsed correctly and is ready for execution. Application execution commences on receipt of the ACK (except if the dialog is being prepared as specified later). Note that the 100 Trying response will usually be sent on receipt of the INVITE in accordance with RFC 3261, since the VoiceXML media server cannot, in general, guarantee that the initial fetch will complete in less than 200 milliseconds. However, certain implementations may be able to guarantee response times to the initial INVITE, and thus may not need to send a 100 Trying response. As an optimization, before sending the 200 OK response, the VoiceXML media server may execute the application up to the point of the first VoiceXML waiting state or prompt flush.

A VoiceXML media server, like any SIP UA, may be unable to accept the INVITE request for a variety of reasons. For instance, a Session Description Protocol (SDP) offer contained in the INVITE might require the use of codecs that are not supported by the media server. In such cases, the media server should respond as defined by RFC 3261. However, there are error conditions specific to VoiceXML, as follows:

1. If the Request-URI does not conform to this specification, a 400 Bad Request must be returned (unless it is used to select other services not defined by this RFC 5552 specification).
2. If a URI parameter in the Request-URI is repeated, then the request MUST be rejected with a 400 Bad Request response.
3. If the Request-URI does not include a voicexml parameter, and the VoiceXML media server does not elect to use a default page, the VoiceXML media server must return a final response of 400 Bad Request, and it should include a Warning header with a three-digit code of 399 and a human-readable error message.
4. If the VoiceXML document cannot be fetched or parsed, the VoiceXML media server must return a final response of 500 Server Internal Error and should include a Warning header with a three-digit code of 399 and a human-readable error message.

Informative note: Certain applications may pass a significant amount of data to the VoiceXML dialog in the form of Request-URI parameters. This may cause the total size of the INVITE request to exceed the maximum transmission unit of the underlying network. In such cases, applications/

implementations must take care either to use a transport appropriate to these larger messages (such as Transmission Control Protocol) or to use alternative means of passing the required information to the VoiceXML dialog (such as supplying a unique session identifier in the initial VoiceXML URI and later using that identifier as a key to retrieve data from the HTTP server).

17.2.3.3 Preparing a VoiceXML Session

In certain scenarios, it is beneficial to prepare a VoiceXML session for execution before running it. A previously prepared VoiceXML session is expected to execute with minimal delay when instructed to do so. If a media-less SIP dialog is established with the initial INVITE to the VoiceXML media server, the VoiceXML application will not execute after receipt of the ACK. To run the VoiceXML application, the application server must issue a re-INVITE to establish a media session. A media-less SIP dialog can be established by sending an SDP containing no media lines in the initial INVITE. Alternatively, if no SDP is sent in the initial INVITE, the VoiceXML media server will include an offer in the 200 OK message, which can be responded to with an answer in the ACK with the media port(s) set to 0. Once a VoiceXML application is running, a re-INVITE that disables the media streams (i.e., sets the ports to 0) will not otherwise affect the executing application (except that recognition actions initiated while the media streams are disabled will result in noinput timeouts).

17.2.3.4 Session Variable Mappings

The standard VoiceXML session variables are assigned values according to

- **session.connection.local.uri:** Evaluates to the SIP URI specified in the To header of the initial INVITE.
- **session.connection.remote.uri:** Evaluates to the SIP URI specified in the From header of the initial INVITE.
- **session.connection.redirect:** This array is populated by information contained in the History-Info (RFC 4244) header in the initial INVITE or is otherwise undefined. Each entry (hi-entry) in the History-Info header is mapped, in reverse order, into an element of the session.connection.redirect array. Properties of each element of the array are determined as follows:
  - uri—Set to the hi-targeted-to-uri value of the History-Info entry
  - pi—Set to *true* if hi-targeted-to-uri contains a Privacy=history parameter, or if the INVITE Privacy header includes *history*; *false* otherwise
  - si—Set to the value of the *si* parameter if it exists, undefined otherwise
  - reason—Set verbatim to the value of the Reason parameter of hi-targeted-to-uri session.connection. protocol.name: evaluates to *sip*. Note that this is intended to reflect the use of SIP in general, and does not distinguish between whether the media server was accessed via SIP or SIPS procedures
- **session.connection.protocol.version:** Evaluates to 2.0.
- **session.connection.protocol.sip.headers:** This is an associative array where each key in the array is the noncompact name of a SIP header in the initial INVITE converted to lowercase (note the case conversion does not apply to the header value). If multiple header fields of the same field name are present, the values are combined into a single comma-separated value. Implementations must at a minimum include the Call-ID header and may include other headers. For example, session.connection.protocol.sip.headers evaluates to the Call-ID of the SIP dialog.
- **session.connection.protocol.sip.requesturi:** This is an associative array where the array keys and values are formed from the URI parameters on the SIP Request-URI of the initial INVITE. The array key is the URI parameter name converted to lowercase (note the case conversion does not apply to the parameter value). The corresponding array value is obtained by evaluating the URI parameter value as a JSON value (RFC 4627) in the case of the ccxml-param and aai-param values and otherwise as a string. In addition, the array's toString() function returns the full SIP Request-URI. For example, assuming a Request-URI of sip:dialog@example.com;voicexml=http://example.com;aai=%7b"x":1%2c"y":true%7d, then session.connection.protocol.sip.requesturi["voicexml"] evaluates to http://example.com, session.connection.protocol.sip.requesturi["aai"].x evaluates to 1 (type Number), session.connection.protocol.sip.requesturi["aai"].y evaluates to true (type Boolean), and session.connection.protocol.sip.requesturi evaluates to the complete Request-URI (type String) sip:dialog@example.com;voicexml=http://example.com;aai={"x":1,"y":true}.
- **session.connection.aai:** Evaluates to session.connection.protocol.sip.requesturi["aai"].
- **session.connection.ccxml:** Evaluates to session.connection.protocol.sip.requesturi["ccxml"].
- **session.connection.protocol.sip.media:** This is an array where each array element is an object with the following properties:
  - type—This required property indicates the type of the media associated with the stream. The value is a string. It is strongly recommended that the following values are used for common types of media: *audio* for audio media and *video* for video media.

- direction—This required property indicates the directionality of the media relative to session connection originator. Defined values are sendrecv, sendonly, recvonly, and inactive.
- session.connection.originator—Defined values are sendrecv, sendonly, recvonly, and inactive.
- format—This property is optional. If defined, the value of the property is an array. Each array element is an object that specifies information about one format of the media (there is an array element for each payload type on the m-line). The object contains at least one property called *name* whose value is the Multipurpose Internet Mail Extension (MIME) subtype of the media format (MIME subtypes are registered in RFC 4855). Other properties may be defined with string values; these correspond to required and, if defined, optional parameters of the format.

As a consequence of this definition, there is an array entry in session.connection.protocol.sip.media for each nondisabled m-line for the negotiated media session. Note that this session variable is updated if the media session characteristics for the VoiceXML session change (i.e., due to a re-INVITE). For example, consider a connection with bidirectional G.711 mu-law audio sampled at 8 kHz. In this case, session.connection.protocol.sip.media[0].type evaluates to audio, session.connection.protocol.sip.media[0].direction to sendrecv, session.connection.protocol.sip.media[0].format[0].name evaluates to audio/PCMU, and session.connection.protocol.sip.media[0].format[0].rate evaluates to 8000. Note that when accessing SIP headers and Request-URI parameters via the session.connection.protocol.sip.headers and session.connection.protocol.sip.requesturi associative arrays defined above, applications can choose between two semantically equivalent ways of referring to the array. For example, either of the following can be used to access a Request-URI parameter named *foo*:

```
session.connection.protocol.sip
.requesturi["foo"]
session.connection.protocol.sip.requesturi.foo
```

However, it is important to note that not all SIP header names or Request-URI parameter names are valid ECMAScript identifiers, and as such, can only be accessed using the first form (array notation). For example, the Call-ID header can only be accessed as session.connection.protocol.sip.headers; attempting to access the same value as session.connection.protocol.sip.headers.call-id would result in an error.

17.2.3.5 Terminating a VoiceXML Session

The application server can terminate a VoiceXML session by issuing a BYE to the VoiceXML media server. Upon receipt of a BYE in the context of an existing VoiceXML session, the VoiceXML media server MUST send a 200 OK response and must throw a connection.disconnect.hangup event to the VoiceXML application. If the Reason header (RFC 3326, see Section 2.8) is present on the BYE request, then the value of the Reason header is provided verbatim via the _message variable within the catch element's anonymous variable scope. The VoiceXML media server may also initiate termination of the session by issuing a BYE request. This will typically occur as a result of encountering a <disconnect> or <exit> in the VoiceXML application, due to the VoiceXML application running to completion, or due to unhandled errors within the VoiceXML application.

17.2.3.6 Examples

17.2.3.6.1 Basic Session Establishment

Figure 17.4 illustrates an application server setting up a VoiceXML session on behalf of a UA.

17.2.3.6.2 VoiceXML Session Preparation

Figure 17.5 demonstrates the preparation of a VoiceXML session. In this example, the VoiceXML session is prepared before placing an outbound call to a UA, and is started as soon as the UA answers. The [answer1:0] notation is used to indicate an SDP answer with the media ports set to 0.

Implementation detail: offer2' is derived from offer2—it duplicates the m-lines and a-lines from offer2. However, offer2' differs from offer2 since it must contain the same o-line as used in answer1:0 but with the version number incremented. Also, if offer1 has more m-lines than offer2, then offer2' must be padded with extra (rejected) m-lines.

17.2.3.6.3 Media Resource Control Protocol Establishment

Media Resource Control Protocol (MRCP) (RFC 6787, see Section 7.6) is a protocol that enables clients such as a VoiceXML media server to control media service resources such as speech synthesizers, recognizers, verifiers, and identifiers residing in servers on the network. Figure 17.6 illustrates how a VoiceXML media server may establish an MRCP session in response to an initial INVITE. In Figure 17.6, the VoiceXML media server is responsible for establishing a session with the MRCP (RFC 6787, see Section 7.6) media resource server before sending the 200 OK response to the initial INVITE.

The VoiceXML media server will perform the appropriate offer–answer with the MRCP media resource server based on the SDP capabilities of the application server and the MRCP media resource server. The VoiceXML media server will change the offer received from step F1 to establish an MRCP session in step (F5) and will re-write the SDP to

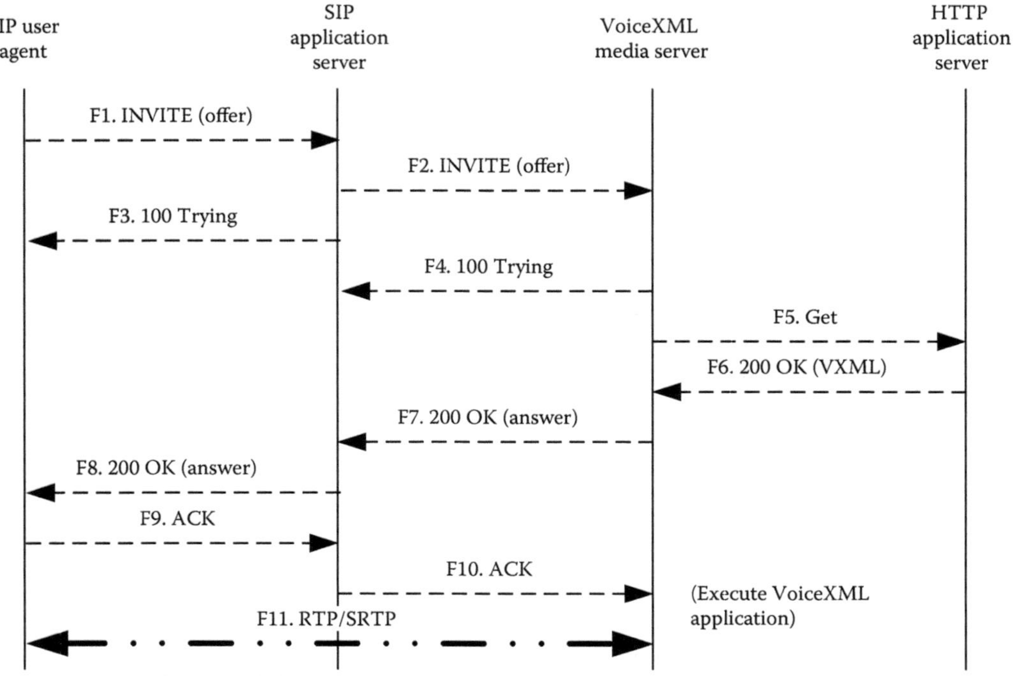

Figure 17.4 Basic session establishment for VoiceXML session. (Copyright IETF. Reproduced with permission.)

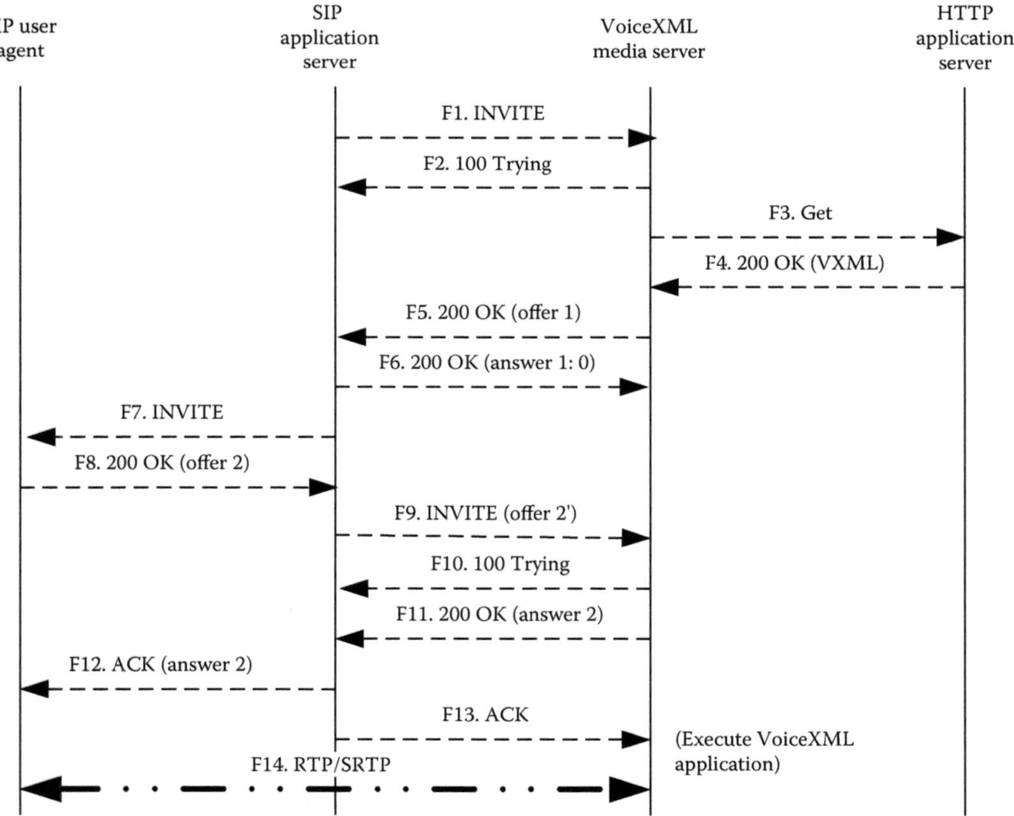

Figure 17.5 Preparation for VoiceXML session. (Copyright IETF. Reproduced with permission.)

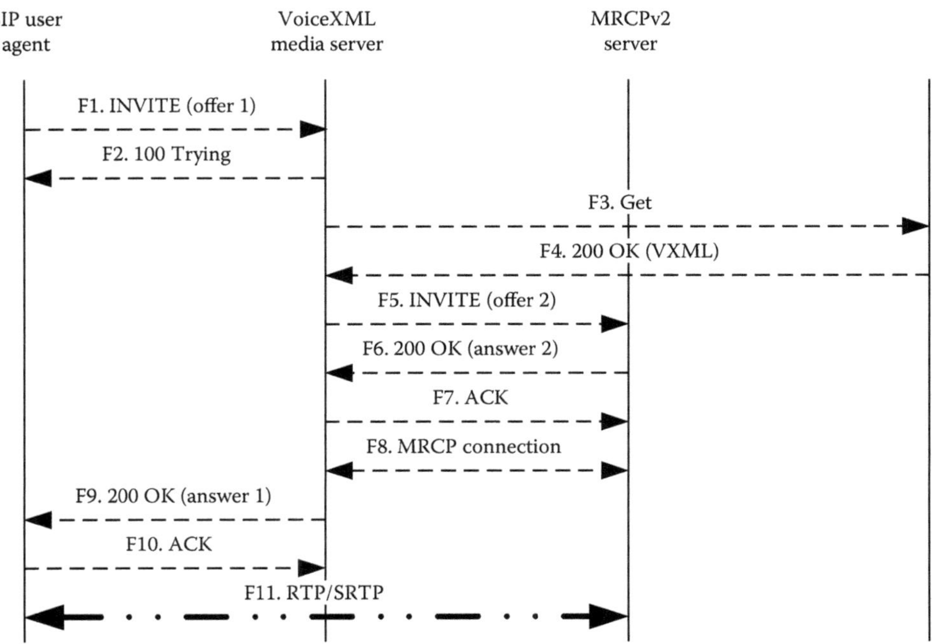

Figure 17.6 VoiceXML session using MRCP server. (Copyright IETF. Reproduced with permission.)

include an m-line for each MRCP resource to be used and other required SDP modifications as specified by MRCP. Once the VoiceXML media server performs the offer–answer with the MRCP media resource server, it will establish an MRCP control channel in step (F8). The MRCP resource is deallocated when the VoiceXML media server receives or sends a BYE (not shown).

17.2.4 Media Support

This section describes the mandatory and optional media support required by this interface.

17.2.4.1 Offer–Answer

The VoiceXML media server MUST support the standard offer–answer mechanism of (RFC 3264, see Section 3.8.4). In particular, if an SDP offer is not present in the INVITE, the VoiceXML media server will make an offer in the 200 OK response listing its supported codecs.

17.2.4.2 Early Media

The VoiceXML media server may support establishment of early media streams as described in RFC 3960 (see Section 11.4.7.2). This allows the application server to establish media streams between a UA and the VoiceXML media server in parallel with the initial VoiceXML document being processed (which may involve dynamic VoiceXML page generation and interaction with databases or other systems). This is useful primarily for minimizing the delay in starting a VoiceXML session, particularly in cases where a session with the UA already exists but the media stream associated with that session needs to be redirected to a VoiceXML media server. Figure 17.7 demonstrates the use of early media (using the gateway model defined in RFC 3960, see Section 11.4.7.2).

Although RFC 3960 prefers the use of the application server model for early media over the gateway model, the primary issue with the gateway model—forking—is significantly less common when issuing requests to VoiceXML media servers. This is because VoiceXML media servers respond to all requests with 200 OK responses in the absence of unusual errors, and they typically do so within several hundred milliseconds. This makes them unlikely targets in forking scenarios, since alternative targets of the forking process would virtually never be able to respond more quickly than an automated system, unless they are themselves automated systems, in which case, there is little point in setting up a response time race between two automated systems.

Issues with ringing tone generation in the gateway model are also mitigated, both by the typically quick 200 OK response time and because this specification mandates that no media packets are generated until the receipt of an ACK (thus eliminating the need for the UA to perform media packet analysis). Note that the offer of early media by a VoiceXML media server does not imply that the referenced VoiceXML application can always be fetched and executed successfully. For instance, if the HTTP application server were to return a 4xx response in step F10 above, or if the provided VoiceXML content was not valid, the VoiceXML

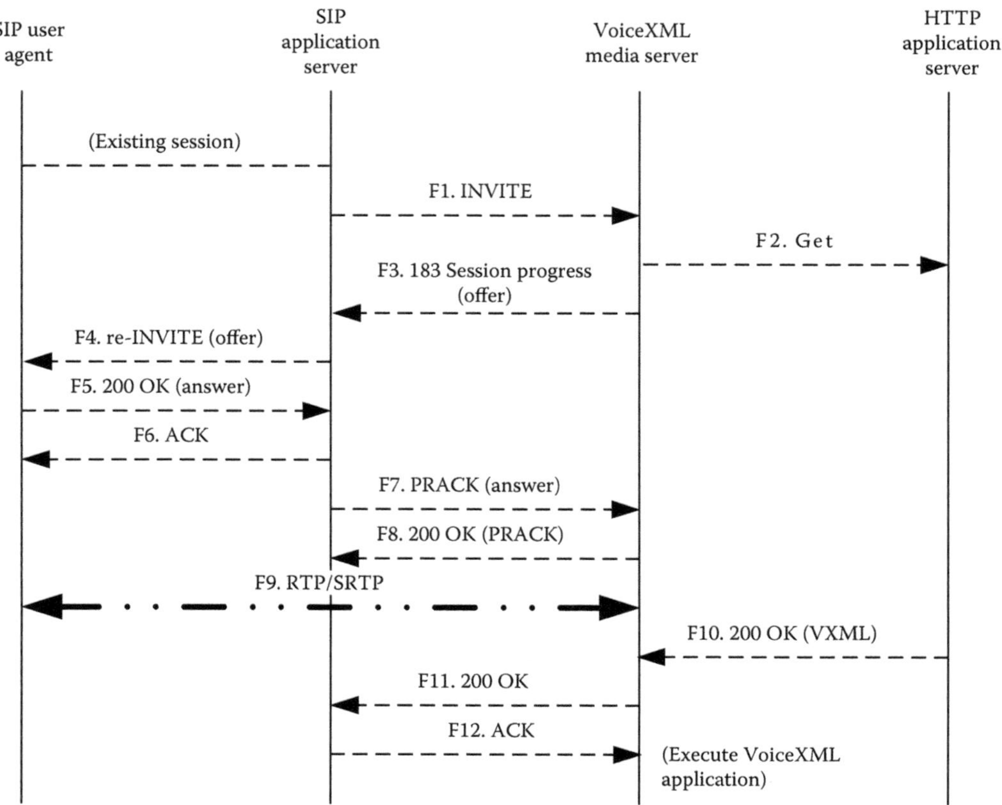

Figure 17.7 VoiceXML session for early media services. (Copyright IETF. Reproduced with permission.)

media server would still return a 500 response. At this point, it would be the responsibility of the application server to tear down any media streams established with the media server.

17.2.4.3 Modifying the Media Session

The VoiceXML media server must allow the media session to be modified via a re-INVITE and should support the UPDATE method (RFC 3311, see Section 3.8.3) for the same purpose. In particular, it must be possible to change streams between sendrecv, sendonly, and recvonly as specified in RFC 3264 (see Section 3.8.4). Unidirectional streams are useful for announcement- or listening-only (hotword). The preferred mechanism for putting the media session on hold is specified in RFC 3264, that is, the UA modifies the stream to be sendonly and mutes its own stream. Modification of the media session does not affect VoiceXML application execution (except that recognition actions initiated while on hold will result in noinput timeouts).

17.2.4.4 Audio and Video Codecs

For the purposes of achieving a basic level of interoperability, this section specifies a minimal subset of codecs and Real-Time Transport Protocol (RTP) (RFC 3550, see Section 7.2) payload formats that MUST be supported by the VoiceXML media server. For audio-only applications, G.711 mu-law and A-law MUST be supported using the RTP payload type 0 and 8 (RFC 3551, see Section 7.2). Other codecs and payload formats may be supported. Video telephony applications, which employ a video stream in addition to the audio stream, are possible in VoiceXML 2.0/2.1 through the use of multimedia file container formats such as the .3gp [6] and .mp4 formats [7]. Video support is optional for this specification. If video is supported, then

1. H.263 Baseline (RFC 4629) must be supported. For legacy reasons, the 1996 version of H.263 may be supported using the RTP payload format defined in RFC 2190/4628 (payload type 34 specified in RFC 3551, see Section 7.2).
2. Adaptive Multirate (AMR) narrow-band audio (RFC 4867) should be supported.
3. MPEG-4 video (RFC 6416) should be supported.
4. MPEG-4 Advanced Audio Coding (AAC) audio (RFC 6416) should be supported.
5. Other codecs and payload formats may be supported.

Video record operations carried out by the VoiceXML media server typically require receipt of an intraframe before the recording can commence. The VoiceXML media server should use the mechanism described in RFC 4585 to request that a new intraframe be sent. Since some applications may choose to transfer confidential information, the VoiceXML media server must support SRTP (RFC 3711, see Section 7.3).

17.2.4.5 DTMF

DTMF events (RFC 4733, see Section 16.10) must be supported. When the UA does not indicate support for RFC 4733, the VoiceXML media server may perform DTMF detection using other means, such as detecting DTMF tones in the audio stream. Implementation note: the reason only telephone-events (RFC 4733) must be used when the UA indicates support of it is to avoid the risk of double detection of DTMF if detection on the audio stream was simultaneously applied.

17.2.5 Returning Data to the Application Server

This section discusses the mechanisms for returning data (e.g., collected utterance or digit information) from the VoiceXML media server to the application server.

17.2.5.1 HTTP Mechanism

At any time during the execution of the VoiceXML application, data can be returned to the application server via HTTP using standard VoiceXML elements such as <submit> or <subdialog>. Notably, the <data> element in VoiceXML 2.1 [2] allows data to be sent to the application server efficiently without requiring a VoiceXML page transition and is ideal for short VoiceXML applications such as *prompt and collect*. For most applications, it is necessary to correlate the information being passed over HTTP with a particular VoiceXML session. One way this can be achieved is to include the SIP Call-ID (accessible in VoiceXML via the session.connection.protocol.sip.headers array) within the HTTP POST fields. Alternatively, a unique POST-back URI can be specified as an application-specific URI parameter in the Request-URI of the initial INVITE (accessible in VoiceXML via the session.connection.protocol.sip .requesturi array). Since some applications may choose to transfer confidential information, the VoiceXML media server must support the https: scheme.

17.2.5.2 SIP Mechanism

Data can be returned to the application server via the expr or namelist attribute on <exit> or the namelist attribute on <disconnect>. A VoiceXML media server must support encoding of the expr/namelist data in the message body of a BYE request sent from the VoiceXML media server as a result of encountering the <exit> or <disconnect> element. A VoiceXML media server may support inclusion of the expr/namelist data in the message body of the 200 OK message in response to a received BYE request (i.e., when the VoiceXML application responds to the connection.disconnect .hangup event and subsequently executes an <exit> element with the expr or namelist attribute specified). Note that sending expr/namelist data in the 200 OK response requires that the VoiceXML media server delay the final response to the received BYE request until the VoiceXML application's post-disconnect final processing state terminates. This mechanism is subject to the constraint that the VoiceXML media server must respond before the UAC's timer F expires (defaults to 32 seconds).

Moreover, for unreliable transports, the UAC will retransmit the BYE request according to the rules of RFC 3261 (see Section 3.10). The VoiceXML media server should implement the recommendations of RFC 4320 (see Section 3.12.2.5) regarding when to send the 100 Trying provisional response to the BYE request. If a VoiceXML application executes a <disconnect> [2] and then subsequently executes an <exit> with namelist information, the namelist information from the <exit> element is discarded. Namelist variables are first converted to their JSON value equivalent (RFC 4627) and encoded in the message body using the application/x-www-form-urlencoded format content type [5]. The behavior resulting from specifying a recording variable in the namelist or an ECMAScript object with circular references is not defined. If the expr attribute is specified on the <exit> element instead of the namelist attribute, the reserved name __exit is used. To allow the application server to differentiate between a BYE resulting from a <disconnect> from one resulting from an <exit>, the reserved name __reason is used, with a value of *disconnect* (without brackets) to reflect the use of VoiceXML's <disconnect> element, and a value of *exit* (without brackets) to an explicit <exit> in the VoiceXML document. If the session terminates for other reasons (such as the media server encountering an error), this parameter may be omitted, or may take on platform-specific values prefixed with an underscore.

This specification extends the application/x-www-form-urlencoded by replacing non-ASCII characters with one or more octets of the UTF-8 representation of the character, with each octet in turn replaced by %HH, where HH represents the uppercase hexadecimal notation for the octet value and % is a literal character. As a consequence, the Content-Type header field in a BYE message containing expr/namelist data MUST be set to application/x-www-form-urlencoded;charset=utf-8. The following table provides some examples of <exit> usage and the corresponding result content.

<exit> Usage	*Result Content*
<exit/>	__reason=exit
<exit expr="5"/>	__exit=5&__reason=exit
<exit expr="'done'"/	__exit="done"& __reason=exit
<exit expr="userAuthorized"/>	__exit=true&__reason=exit
<exit namelist="pin errors"/>	pin=1234&errors=0& __reason=exit

Assuming the following VoiceXML variables and values:

```
userAuthorized=true
pin=1234
errors=0
```

For example, consider the VoiceXML snippet:

```
...
<exit namelist="id pin"/>
...
```

If id equals 1234 and pin equals 9999, say, the BYE message would look similar to

```
BYE sip:user@pc33.example.com SIP/2.0
Via: SIP/2.0/UDP 192.0.2.4;branch=z9hG4bKnas
hds10
Max-Forwards: 70
From: sip:dialog@example.com;tag=a6c85cf
To: sip:user@example.com;tag=1928301774
Call-ID: a84b4c76e66710
CSeq: 231 BYE
Content-Type:
application/x-www-form-
urlencoded;charset=utf-8
Content-Length: 30

id=1234&pin=9999&__reason=exit
```

Since some applications may choose to transfer confidential information, the VoiceXML media server must support the S/MIME encoding of SIP message bodies.

17.2.6 Outbound Calling

Outbound calls can be triggered via the application server using third-party call control (RFC 3725, see Section 18.3). Flow IV from RFC 3725 (see Figure 18.1b, Section 18.3) is recommended in conjunction with the VoiceXML session preparation mechanism. This flow has several advantages over others, as follows:

1. Selection of a VoiceXML media server and preparation of the VoiceXML application can occur before the call is placed to avoid the callee experiencing delays.
2. Avoidance of timing difficulties that could occur with other flows due to the time taken to fetch and parse the initial VoiceXML document.
3. The flow is IPv6 compatible.

An example flow for an application server-initiated outbound call has been provided earlier.

17.2.7 Call Transfer

While VoiceXML is at its core a dialog language, it also provides optional call transfer capability. VoiceXML's transfer capability is particularly suited to the PSTN IVR Service Node use case described earlier. It is not recommended to use VoiceXML's call transfer capability in networks involving application servers. Rather, the application server itself can provide call routing functionality by taking signaling actions based on the data returned to it from the VoiceXML media server via HTTP or in the SIP BYE message.

If VoiceXML transfer is supported, the mechanism described in this section must be employed. The transfer flows specified here are selected on the basis that they provide the best interworking across a wide range of SIP devices. CCXML<->VoiceXML implementations, which require tight coupling in the form of bidirectional eventing to support all transfer types defined in VoiceXML, may benefit from other approaches, such as the use of SIP event packages (RFC 6665, see Section 5.2). In what follows, the provisional responses have been omitted for clarity.

17.2.7.1 Blind

The blind-transfer sequence is initiated by the VoiceXML media server via a REFER message on the original SIP dialog. The Refer-To header contains the URI for the called party, as specified via the dest or destexpr attributes on the VoiceXML <transfer> tag. If the REFER request is accepted, in which case the VoiceXML media server will receive a 2xx response, the VoiceXML media server throws the connection.disconnect.transfer event and will terminate the VoiceXML session with a BYE message. For blind transfers, implementations may use RFC 4488 (see Section 2.8) to suppress the implicit subscription associated with the REFER message. If the REFER request results in a non-2xx response, the <transfer>'s form item variable (or event raised) depends on the SIP response and is specified in the following table. Note that this indicates that the transfer request was rejected.

SIP Response	*<transfer> variable/event*
404 Not Found	error.connection. baddestination
405 Method Not Allowed	error.unsupported. transfer.blind
503 Service Unavailable	error.connection. noresource
(No response)	network_busy
(Other 3xx/4xx/5xx/6xx)	unknown

An example is illustrated in Figure 17.8 (provisional responses and NOTIFY messages corresponding to provisional responses have been omitted for clarity).

If the aai or aaiexpr attribute is present on <transfer>, it is appended to the Refer-To URI as a parameter named *aai* in the REFER method. Reserved characters are URL encoded as required for SIP/SIPS URIs (RFC 3261, see Section 4.2). The mapping of values outside of the ASCII range is platform specific.

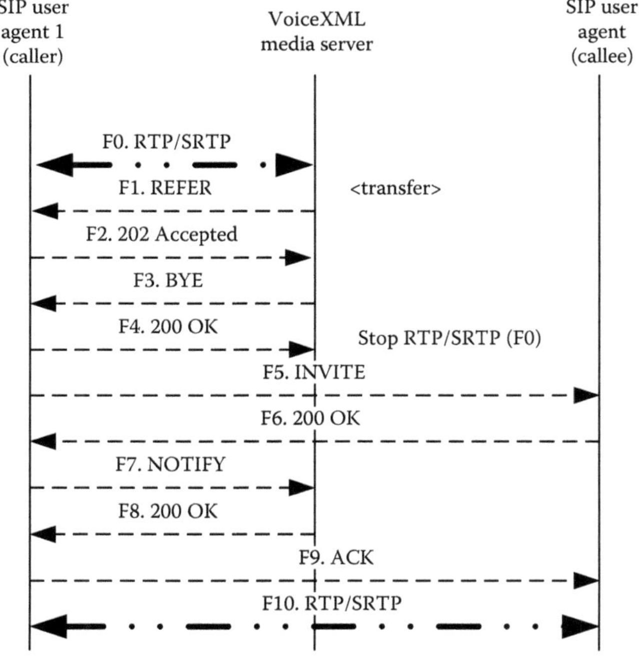

Figure 17.8 Blind transfer using REFER for VoiceXML session. (Copyright IETF. Reproduced with permission.)

17.2.7.2 Bridge

The bridge transfer function results in the creation of a small multiparty session involving the caller, the VoiceXML media server, and the callee. The VoiceXML media server invites the callee to the session and will eject the callee if the transfer is terminated. If the aai or aaiexpr attribute is present on <transfer>, it is appended to the Request-URI in the INVITE as a URI parameter named aai. Reserved characters are URL encoded as required for SIP/SIPS URIs (RFC 3261, see Section 4.2). The mapping of values outside of the ASCII range is platform specific. During the transfer attempt, audio specified in the transferaudio attribute of <transfer> is streamed to UA 1. A VoiceXML media server may play early media received from the callee to the caller if the transferaudio attribute is omitted. The bridge transfer sequence is illustrated in Figure 17.9. The VoiceXML media server (acting as a UAC) makes a call to UA 2 with the same codecs used by UA 1. When the call setup is complete, RTP flows between UA 2 and the VoiceXML media server. This stream is mixed with that of UA 1.

If a final response is not received from UA 2 from the INVITE and the connecttimeout expires (specified as an attribute of <transfer>), the VoiceXML media server will issue a CANCEL to terminate the transaction and the <transfer>'s form item variable is set to noanswer. If INVITE results in a non-2xx response, the <transfer>'s form item variable (or event raised) depends on the SIP response and is specified in Table 17.1.

Once the transfer is established, the VoiceXML media server can *listen* to the media stream from UA 1 to perform speech or DTMF hotword, which when matched results in a near-end disconnect, that is, the VoiceXML media server issues a BYE to UA 2 and the VoiceXML application continues with UA 1. A BYE will also be issued to UA 2 if the call duration exceeds the maximum duration specified in the maxtime attribute on <transfer>. If UA 2 issues

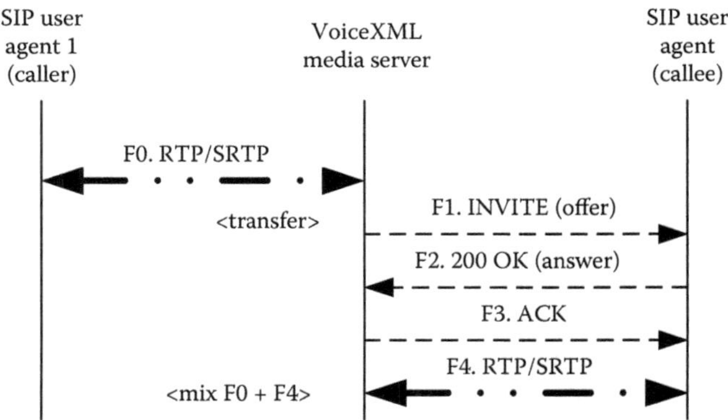

Figure 17.9 Bridge transfer for VoiceXML session. (Copyright IETF. Reproduced with permission.)

Table 17.1 SIP Responses for Error Conditions

SIP Response	*<transfer> variable/event*
404 Not Found	error.connection. baddestination
405 Method Not Allowed	error.unsupported. transfer.blind
408 Request Timeout	noanswer
486 Busy Here	busy
503 Service Unavailable	error.connection. noresource
(No response)	network_busy
(Other 3xx/4xx/5xx/6xx)	unknown

a BYE during the transfer, the transfer terminates and the VoiceXML <transfer>'s form item variable receives the value far_end_disconnect. If UA 1 issues a BYE during the transfer, the transfer terminates and the VoiceXML event connection.disconnect.transfer is thrown.

17.2.7.3 Consultation

The consultation transfer (also called attended transfer specified in RFC 5359) is similar to a blind transfer except that the outcome of the transfer call setup is known and the caller is not dropped as a result of an unsuccessful transfer attempt. Consultation transfer commences with the same flow as for bridge transfer except that the RTP streams are not mixed at step (F4) and error.unsupported.transfer. consultation supplants error.unsupported.transfer.bridge. Assuming a new SIP dialog with UA 2 is created, the remainder of the sequence follows as illustrated in Figure 17.10 (provisional responses and NOTIFY messages corresponding to provisional responses have been omitted for clarity). Consultation transfer (Figure 17.10) makes use of the Replaces header (RFC 3891, see Section 2.8.2) such that UA 1 calls UA 2 and replaces the latter's SIP dialog with the VoiceXML media server with a new SIP dialog between the caller and callee.

If a response other than 202 Accepted is received in response to the REFER request sent to UA 1, the transfer terminates and an error.unsupported.transfer.consultation event is raised. In addition, a BYE is sent to UA 2 to terminate the established outbound leg. The VoiceXML media server uses receipt of a NOTIFY message with a sipfrag message of 200 OK to determine that the consultation transfer has succeeded. When this occurs, the connection.disconnect.transfer event will be thrown to the VoiceXML application, and a BYE is sent to UA 1 to terminate the session.

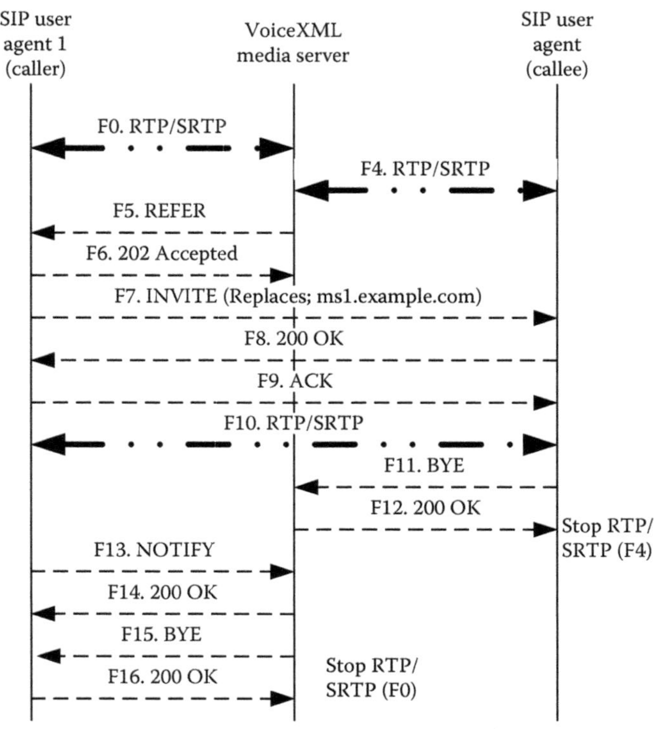

Figure 17.10 Consultation transfer for VoiceXML session. (Copyright IETF. Reproduced with permission.)

A NOTIFY message with a non-2xx final response sipfrag message body will result in the transfer terminating and the associated VoiceXML input item variable being set to *unknown*. Note that as a consequence of this mechanism, implementations must not use RFC 4488 (see Sections 2.8.2 and 16.6.1) to suppress the implicit subscription associated with the REFER message for consultation transfers.

17.3 Summary

We have described media server interfaces in SIP taking VoiceXML media server standardized in W3C as an example. The important principle for the creation of these kinds of media application services is the interaction between users and SIP-based applications, which is termed as the stimulus signaling specified in RFC 5629. In stimulus signaling, users can interact with an application without knowledge of the semantics of that application. We have explained how SIP establishes and terminates the VoiceXML session between the users and the application server in addition to the execution of a specified VoiceXML application simultaneously for the following: media support including early media, audio and video codecs, and DTMF; media negotiation using SDP offer–answer model; data transfer to the application server; outbound calling; and call transfer (blind, bridge, and consultation). Similarly, the media (audio, video, and data application) bridging/mixing application servers also need to create many multimedia services for the multiparty multimedia conferencing distributive for offering multimedia services with scalability over the large-scale next-generation SIP networks. This is a hugely growing area for multimedia services creation, and some of the works in this area have been progressing in the International Engineering Task Force; however, we have not addressed these for the sake of brevity.

PROBLEMS

1. What is stimulus signaling? Explain the stimulus signaling framework in detail as specified in RFC 5629.
2. How does stimulus signaling help in the context of services creation using SIP interfaces to the VoiceXML media application server within the framework specified in RFC 5629?
3. Explain the use cases in detail for the SIP interfaces to the VoiceXML media server for the following scenarios: IVR services, PSTN IVR server node, IMS MRF, CCXML, and VoiceXML.
4. Describe in detail the VoiceXML session establishment and termination using SIP explaining the following steps: service identification, initiating and preparing the VoiceXML session, session variable mappings, and terminating the VoiceXML session.
5. Explain in detail using SIP call flows for media services to the SIP users for the following cases: basic session establishments, VoiceXML session preparation, and MRCP establishment.
6. Explain the VoiceXML media services to the SIP users using detailed call flows, step by step as follows: media negotiations using SDP offer–answer model, support of early media, modifying the media session, support of audio and video codecs, and DTMF.
7. Explain how the data collected utterance or digit information during the session between the SIP user and the VoiceXML media server is transferred to the application server using the following mechanisms: HTTP and SIP.
8. Explain using SIP call flows creating a scenario of the outbound calling while the session is established between the SIP user and the VoiceXML server in addition to between two SIP users.
9. Explain with detailed SIP call flows creating a call transfer service scenario of the session between the two SIP users making VoiceXML server a part of the session for the following call services: blind, bridge, and consultation.

References

1. McGlashan, S., Burnett, D., Carter, J., Danielsen, P., Ferrans, J., Hunt, A., Lucas, B., Porter, B., Rehor, K., and Tryphonas, S., "Voice Extensible Markup Language (VoiceXML) version 2.0," W3C Recommendation, March 2004.
2. Oshry, M., Auburn, R.J., Baggia, P., Bodell, M., Burke, D., Burnett, D., Candell, E., Kilic, H., McGlashan, S., Lee, A., Porter, B., and Rehor, K., "Voice Extensible Markup Language (VoiceXML) version 2.1," W3C Candidate Recommendation, June 2005.
3. 3GPP, "3rd Generation Partnership Project: Network architecture (Release 6)," 3GPP TS 23.002 v6.6.0, December 2004.
4. Auburn, R.J., "Voice Browser Call Control: CCXML version 1.0," W3C Working Draft, June 2005.
5. Raggett, D., Le Hors, A., and Jacobs, I., "HTML 4.01 specification," W3C Recommendation, December 1999.
6. 3GPP, "Transparent end-to-end packet switched streaming service (PSS); 3GPP file format (3GP)," 3GPP TS 26.244 v6.4.0, December 2004.
7. "Information technology. Coding of audio-visual objects. MP4 file format," ISO/IEC 14496-14:2003, October 2003.

Chapter 18

Multiparty Conferencing in SIP

Abstract

We describe multipoint multimedia conferencing among the multiple parties using Session Initiation Protocol (SIP). We explain that multiparty multimedia conferencing is a hugely complicated application. The requirements of multipoint multimedia conferencing go far beyond the capabilities of SIP signaling messages, and SIP is being used in conjunction with newly developed application protocols like Binary Floor Control Protocol. Media bridging/mixing is another complicated application that is needed for making conferencing architecture scalable. However, we address only the basic third-party centralized multiparty conferencing that use the basic SIP capabilities described in Request for Comment 3261. All other complicated multipoint multimedia conferencing rich in more intelligent multimedia functionalities, including application sharing, have not been addressed for the sake of brevity.

18.1 Introduction

Multiparty multimedia conferencing is itself a hugely complex application because it needs media negotiations, media bridging/mixing, application sharing, floor control, conference scheduling, and many other capabilities dealing with multiple conferencing end points. Moreover, multiparty multimedia conferencing can be provided using both centralized and distributive architecture. The distributive multiparty multimedia conferencing architecture is yet to be addressed in Session Initiation Protocol (SIP) because it is a much more complex architecture that needs deeper research for solving all the problems. The International Engineering Task Force (IETF) standards have recently completed a good amount of work related to centralized multiparty multimedia conferencing in SIP, which needs a completely separate stand-alone discussion. However, we have only provided the third-party call control (3PCC) centralized conferencing that is based only on the basic capabilities of SIP defined in Request for Comment (RFC) 3261. Many 2PCC scenarios are described here on how the same sets of conferencing requirements can be met using different conferencing architectures using SIP. The pros and cons of each of these 2PCC conference architectures are also described in detail.

18.2 Multiparty Multimedia Conferencing

Multiparty conferencing requires both SIP for call control signaling protocol and Session Description Protocol (SDP) for media negotiations among multiple parties (i.e., consisting of more than two parties). SDP is carried in the messages body of the SIP signaling protocol, and the simplicity of SDP media session description architecture has made it rather successful for many of the less complex multimedia point-to-point calls. If there are more than two parties in conferencing, the key is that media bridging (also termed as mixing) needs to be done. Media bridging is the key functionality that makes multipoint conferencing fundamentally different from that of two-party conferencing. Moreover, each kind of media stream, such as audio, video, or application, will again have different ways of doing bridging. Each of these bridged media will then be required to be sent to each participating party.

Media negotiations and media bridging of multiparty conferencing are the fundamental challenges of call signaling protocols like SIP and media negotiation schemes like SDP. Another problem is that media bridging of all parties need to be done centrally because distributed media bridging dynamically is very difficult, if not impossible. In addition, the creation of a multiparty call evolving from a two-party call dynamically where media bridging is needed to a centralized place is not possible with the present SIP/SDP protocol. This is especially because of the way the protocol architecture of SDP that is used for media negotiations has been developed.

Consequently, there has been a basic assumption that a centralized functional entity such as conference controller is a priori known to all multiparty conferences. The conference controller is dialed-in by the conferencing parties or dialed-out to the conferencing parties. In this way, one of the problems is knowing the central point of contact where every multiparty participant will be communicating to have the star-like topology for conferencing. This centralized controller may also take the responsibility of media bridging and other functionalities for conferencing, if not controlling. RFC 3725, known as the 3PCC, is being developed as if a centralized controller is setting up the multiparty conference. This has been a simple SIP multiparty conference architecture, although it is riddled with many problems where the conference setup may fail in many circumstances. Later on, RFC 5239 (see Sections 2.2, 2.4.4.1, and 4.2.1.6) describes the framework of the multiparty conferencing system and its mechanisms, along with the conference controller known as *focus* user agent (UA). Conference-aware UA, and Conference-unaware UA, along with well-defined Conference Factory Uniform Resource Identifier (URI), have been standardized. Although we have included some definitions and addressing schemes of RFC 5239 in those sections, the detail description of RFC 5239 is out of scope of this book.

Multiparty conferencing with multimedia requires a host with very rich and complex functionalities, namely conference control including floor control, conference objects that are manipulated during the conference, audio and video bridging, sharing/bridging of a variety of data applications, media channel control, and many others. These functions do not belong to SIP call control functions, and non-SIP protocols are needed. In this respect, the Centralized Conference Manipulation Protocol (CCMP) (RFC 6503), Binary Floor Control Protocol (BFCP) (RFC 4582), Conference Object Model (RFC 6501), Mixer for Media Control Channel (RFC 6505), and other functionalities for multiparty multimedia conferencing have been standardized. It is beyond the scope of this chapter to deal with all those aspects of conferencing here. However, we briefly outline some of the 3PCCs here.

18.3 Third-Party Multiparty Conferencing

3PCC provides mechanisms for the creation of multiparty conference calls in a star-like point-to-point fashion from a centralized controller. In fact, 3PCC refers to the general ability to manipulate calls between two or multiple parties. It is assumed that the controller knows the addresses of all parties and when to dial-out the participants or the address of the controller is a priori known to all conference participants for dial-in. Call control, including modifications of signaling messages, is done by the controller acting as the back-to-back UA (B2BUA). It is also possible that the media bridge can be used to dial-out or dial-in as another party by the controller. A controller is a SIP UA that wishes to create a session between two other UAs. 3PCC is often used for operator services (where an operator creates a call that connects two or more participants together) and multimedia conferencing.

Many SIP services are possible through 3PCC. These include the traditional ones on the public switched telephone network (PSTN), but also new ones such as click-to-dial, mid-call announcements, media transcoding, call transfer, and others. For example, click-to-dial allows a user to click on a web page when they wish to speak to a customer service representative. The web server then creates a call between the user and a customer service representative. The call can be between two phones, a phone and an Internet Protocol (IP) host, or two IP hosts. 3PCC is possible using only the mechanisms specified within RFC 3261. In addition, many other services are possible using other methods and mechanisms defined in other SIP-related RFCs. Indeed, many possible approaches can be used for the 3PCC; however, we describe here some examples of the call setup following RFC 3725, each with different benefits and drawbacks. The use of 3PCC also becomes more complex when aspects of the call utilize SIP extensions or optional features of SIP.

18.3.1 3PCC Call Establishment

The controller that establishes the call between two or multiple parties is termed as the third party (RFC 3725) because the establishment of the session is orchestrated by the controller that is not a party among the conference participants. It is implied that the controller somehow has the prior intelligence to set up the multiparty conference. The mechanisms by which a controller will be fed this intelligence may itself be another application that RFC 3725 does not describe. The controller can play a significant role in setting up the sessions among the participants, which may be very simple to very complex. Figure 18.1 shows different primitives of operations that a controller can play in establishing the calls in the SIP network that consists of three parties and a controller. Subsequent call flows described here are similar to RFC 3725.

Note that we have used the connection address of 0.0.0.0, which, although recommended by RFC 3264 (see Section 3.8.4), has numerous drawbacks. It is anticipated that a future specification will recommend use of a domain within the invalid Domain Name System top-level domain

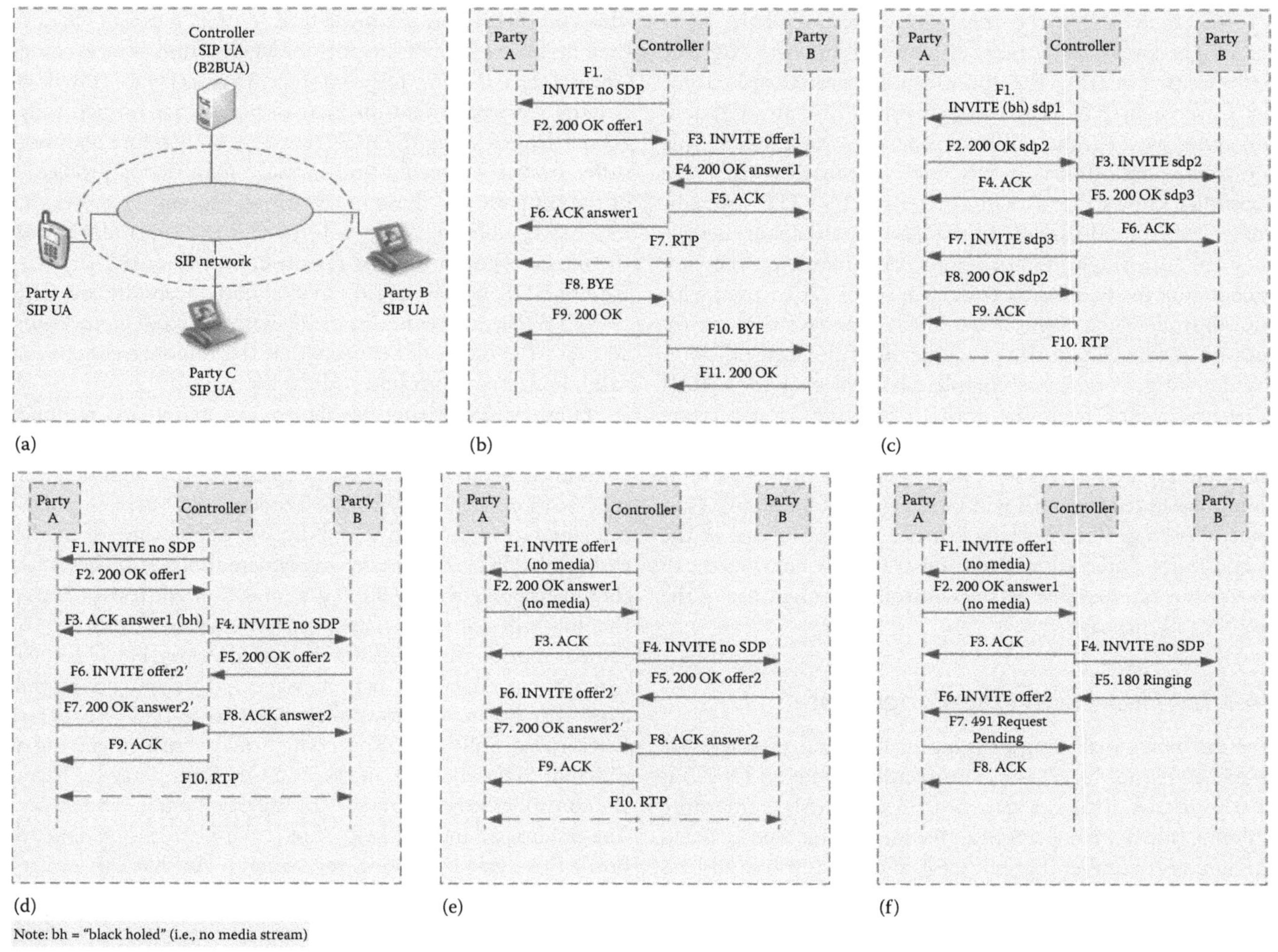

Figure 18.1 3PCC call flows in SIP network: (a) SIP network, (b) simplest flows, (c) flows with ping-ponging of INVITEs, (d) flows with unknown entities, (e) efficient flows with unknown entities, and (f) flows with error handling. (Copyright IETF. Reproduced with permission.)

instead of the 0.0.0.0 IP address. As a result, implementers are encouraged to track such developments once they arise. In addition, RFC 6157 describes how the IPv4 SIP UAs can communicate with IPv6 SIP UAs (and vice versa) at the signaling layer as well as exchange media once the session has been successfully set up. Both single- and dual-stack (i.e., IPv4-only and IPv4/IPv6) UAs are also considered. We have not discussed these scenarios in the 3PCC call flows here.

18.3.1.1 Simplest Multiparty Call Flows

The simplest 3PCC is depicted in Figure 18.1b. The controller first sends a SIP message INVITE (F1) with no SDP to party A. That is, this INVITE message has no session description. Party A's phone rings, and party A answers. This results in a 200 OK (F2) message that contains an offer as defined in RFC 3264 (see Section 3.8.4). The controller needs to send its answer in the ACK message, as mandated by RFC 3261. To obtain the answer, it sends the offer it received from party A (offer1) in an INVITE message (F3) to party B. Party B's phone rings. When party B answers, the 200 OK message (F4) contains the answer to this offer, answer1. The controller sends an ACK message (F5) to party B, and then passes answer1 to A in an ACK message (F6) sent to it. Because the offer was generated by A and the answer generated by B, the actual media session is between A and B. Therefore, Real-time Transport Protocol (RTP) (F7) media flows between parties A and B. This flow is simple, requires no manipulation of the SDP by the controller, and works for any media types supported by both end points. However, it has a serious timeout problem. User B may not answer the call immediately.

The result is that the controller cannot send the ACK to A right away. This causes A to retransmit the 200 OK response periodically. The 200 OK will be retransmitted for 64*T1 seconds (RFC 3261, see Section 3.12). If an ACK does not arrive by then, the call is considered to have failed. This limits the applicability of this flow to scenarios where the controller knows that B will answer the INVITE immediately. Once the calls are established, both participants believe they are in a single point-to-point call. However, they are exchanging media directly with each other, rather than with the controller. The controller is involved in two dialogs, yet sees no media. Since the controller is still a central point for signaling, it now has complete control over the call. If it receives a BYE from one of the participants, it can create a new BYE and hang up with the other participant. This is shown in Figure 17.1b as well, in messages F8 through F11. It should be noted that this will be the general behavior of the controller in dealing with BYE messages sent by one of the participants. Later, we will also describe how continued call processing can be done by the controller through use of the re-INVITE message.

18.3.1.2 Flows with Ping-Ponging of INVITEs

The call flows with ping-ponging of INVITE messages are shown in Figure 18.1c. The controller first sends an INVITE (F1) to user A. This is a standard INVITE (F1), containing an offer (sdp1) with a single audio media line, one codec, a random port number (but not zero), and a connection address of 0.0.0.0. This creates an initial media stream that is *black holed* (bh), since no media (or Real-time Transport Control Protocol packets defined in RFC 3550, see Section 7.2) will flow from A. The INVITE causes A's phone to ring. When party A answers, the 200 OK (F2) contains an answer, sdp2, with a valid address in the connection line. It then generates a second INVITE (F3). This INVITE is addressed to user B, and it contains sdp2 as the offer to B. Note that the role of sdp2 has changed. In the 200 OK (F2), it was an answer, but in the INVITE (F3), it is an offer. Fortunately, all valid answers are valid initial offers. At the same time, the controller also sends an ACK (F4) to party A as it has been due immediately in response to A's 200 OK (F2) for stopping retransmissions or timeout. The INVITE (F3) causes B's phone to ring. When it answers, it generates a 200 OK (F5) with an answer, sdp3. As usual, the controller then generates an ACK (F6). Next, it sends a re-INVITE (F7) to A containing sdp3 as the offer. Once again, there has been a reversal of roles. sdp3 of message F5 has been an answer, and now it is an offer to party A in INVITE (F7).

Fortunately, an answer to an answer recast as an offer is, in turn, a valid offer. This re-INVITE generates a 200 OK (F8) with sdp2, assuming that A does not decide to change any aspects of the session as a result of this re-INVITE (F7). This 200 OK (F8) is acknowledged in ACK message F9, and then media can flow from A to B. Media from B to A could already start flowing once message F5 was sent. This flow has the advantage that all final responses are immediately acknowledged using the ACK message. It therefore does not suffer from the timeout and message-inefficiency problems of the simplest call flows in the earlier section. However, it, too, has troubles. First, it requires that the controller know the media types to be used for the call (since it must generate a bh SDP, which requires media lines). Secondly, the first INVITE (F1) to A contains media with a 0.0.0.0 connection address. The controller expects that the response contains a valid, nonzero connection address for A.

However, experience has shown that many UAs respond to an offer of a 0.0.0.0 connection address with an answer containing a 0.0.0.0 connection address. The offer–answer specification of RFC 3264 (see Section 3.8.4) explicitly tells implementers not to do this; however, at the time of publication of RFC 3725, many implementations still did. If A should respond with a 0.0.0.0 connection address in sdp2, the flow will not work. The most serious flaw in this flow is the assumption that the 200 OK (F8) to the re-INVITE (F7) contains the same SDP as in message 2. This may not be the case. If it is not, the controller needs to re-INVITE party B with that SDP (say, sdp4), which may result in getting a different SDP, say sdp5, in the 200 OK from party B. Then, the controller needs to re-INVITE party A again, and so on. The result is an infinite loop of re-INVITEs. It is possible to break this cycle by having very smart UAs that can return the same SDP whenever possible, or really smart controllers that can analyze the SDP to determine if a re-INVITE is really needed. However, RFC 3725 recommends keeping this mechanism simple, and avoids SDP awareness in the controller. As a result, this flow is not really workable. This 3PCC call flow is therefore not recommended by RFC 3725.

18.3.1.3 Flows with Unknown Entities

The call flows with the parties whose media compositions for the sessions are not known to the controller are shown in Figure 18.1d. First, the controller sends an INVITE (F1) to user A without any SDP because the controller does not need to assume anything about the media composition of the session. Party A's phone rings. When party A answers, a 200 OK (F2) is generated containing its offer, offer1. The controller generates an immediate ACK (F3) containing an answer (F3). This answer (F3) is a bh SDP, with its connection address equal to 0.0.0.0. The controller then sends an INVITE (F4) to B without SDP. This causes party B's phone to ring. When party B answers, a 200 OK (F5) is sent, containing their offer, offer2. This SDP is used to create a re-INVITE (F6) back to party A. That re-INVITE (F6) is based on offer2, but may need to be reorganized to match up media lines, or to trim media lines. For example, if offer1 contained an audio and a video line, in that order, but offer2 contained just an audio line, the controller would need to add a video line to the offer (setting its port to zero) to create offer2′.

Since this is a re-INVITE (F6), it should complete quickly in the general case. That is good since user B is retransmitting their 200 OK (F5), waiting for an ACK. The SDP in the 200 OK (F7) from A, answer2', may also need to be reorganized or trimmed before sending it an ACK (F8) to B as answer2. Finally, an ACK (F9) is sent to A, and then media can flow. This flow has many benefits. First, it will usually operate without any spurious retransmissions or timeouts (although this may still happen if a re-INVITE is not responded to quickly). Secondly, it does not require the controller to guess the media that will be used by the participants. There are some drawbacks. The controller does need to perform SDP manipulations. Specifically, it must take some SDP, and generate another SDP that has the same media composition but has connection addresses equal to 0.0.0.0. This is needed for message F3. Secondly, it may need to reorder and trim SDP Y so that its media lines match up with those in some other SDP, Z. Thirdly, the offer from B (offer2, message F5) may have no codecs or media streams in common with the offer from A (offer 1, message F2). The controller will need to detect this condition and terminate the call. Finally, the flow is far more complicated than the simplest and elegant call flows shown in Figure 17.1b.

18.3.1.4 Efficient Flows with Unknown Entities

The call flows with reduced complexities shown in Figure 18.1e are a variation of the call flows shown in Figure 18.1d with the parties whose media compositions for the sessions are not known to the controller. The actual message flow is identical, but the SDP placement and construction differ. The initial INVITE (F1) contains SDP with no media at all, meaning that there are no m-lines. This is valid, and implies that the media makeup of the session will be established later through a re-INVITE described in RFC 3264 (see Section 3.8.4). Once the INVITE is received, user A is alerted. When the party A answers the call, the 200 OK (F2) has an answer with no media either. This is acknowledged by the controller sending an ACK message (F3). The flow from this point onwards is identical to flows shown in Figure 18.1d. However, the manipulations required to convert offer2 to offer2′, and answer2′ to answer2, are much simpler. Indeed, no media manipulations are needed at all.

The only change that is needed is to modify the origin lines, so that the origin line in offer2′ is valid based on the value in offer1 (validity requires that the version increments by one, and that the other parameters remain unchanged). There are some limitations associated with this flow. First, user A will be alerted without any media having been established yet. This means that user A will not be able to reject or accept the call based on its media composition. Secondly, both A and B will end up answering the call (i.e., generating a 200 OK) before it is known whether there is compatible media. If there is no media in common, the call can be terminated later with a BYE. However, the users will have already been alerted, resulting in user annoyance and possibly resulting in billing events.

18.3.2 Recommendations for 3PCC Call Setups

The call flows shown Figure 18.1b represent the simplest and the most efficient flows. This flow should be used by a controller if it knows with certainty that user B is actually an automaton that will answer the call immediately. This is the case for devices such as media servers, conferencing servers, and messaging servers, for example. Since we expect a great deal of 3PCCs to be to automata, special casing in this scenario is reasonable. For calls to unknown entities, or to entities known to represent people, it is recommended that flows shown in Figure 18.1e be used for 3PCC. Call flows shown in Figure 18.1d may be used instead, but they provide no additional benefits over flows of Figure 18.1e. However, flows shown in Figure 18.1c should not be used because of the potential for infinite ping-ponging of re-INVITEs.

Several of these flows use a bh connection address of 0.0.0.0. This is an IPv4 address with the property that packets sent to it will never leave the host that sent them; they are just discarded. Those flows are therefore specific to IPv4. For other network or address types, an address with an equivalent property should be used. In most cases, including the recommended flows, user A will hear silence while the call to B completes. This may not always be ideal. It can be remedied by connecting the caller to a music-on-hold source while the call to B occurs. In addition, RFC 6157 can be used for IPv4 and IPv6 network scenarios that are not shown here.

18.3.3 Multiparty Call Establishment Error Handling

Numerous error cases may occur in establishing the multiparty calls, which merit discussion. With all of the call flows described earlier, one call is established to party A, and then the controller attempts to establish a call to party B. However, this call attempt may fail, for any number of reasons. User B might be busy (resulting in a 486 Busy Here response to the INVITE), there may not be any media in common, the requests may time out, and so on. If the call attempt to B should fail, it is recommended that the controller send a BYE to A. This BYE should include a Reason header defined in RFC 3326 (see Section 2.8), which carries the status code from the error response. This will inform user A of the precise reason for the failure. The information is important from a user interface perspective. For example, if A was calling from a black phone, and B generated a 486 Busy Here, the BYE will contain a Reason code of 486 Busy Here, and this could be used to generate a local busy signal so that A knows that B is busy.

Another error condition worthy of discussion is shown in Figure 18.1f. After the controller establishes the dialog with party A (messages F1–F3), it attempts to contact B (message F4). Contacting party B may take some time. During that interval, party A could possibly attempt a re-INVITE, providing an updated offer. However, the controller cannot pass this offer on to B, since it has an INVITE transaction pending with it. As a result, the controller needs to reject the request. It is recommended that a 491 Request Pending response be used. The situation here is similar to the glare condition described in RFC 3261, and thus the same error handling is sensible. However, user A is likely to retry its request (as a result of the 491 Request Pending), and this may occur before the exchange with B is completed. In that case, the controller would respond with another 491 Request Pending.

18.3.4 Continued Call Processing in 3PCC

In continuation of the call flows of Figure 18.1e after setting the RTP (F10), if the controller receives a re-INVITE from one of the participants, it can forward it to the other participant. Depending on which flow was used, this may require some manipulation on the SDP before passing it on. However, the controller need not *proxy* the SIP messages received from one of the parties. Since it is a B2BUA, it can invoke any signaling mechanism on each dialog, as it sees fit. For example, if the controller receives a BYE from A, it can generate a new INVITE to a third party, C, and connect B to that participant instead. A call flow for this is shown in Figure 18.2a, assuming the case where C represents an end user, not an automaton.

From here, new parties can be added, removed, transferred, and so on, as the controller sees fit. In many cases, the controller will be required to modify the SDP exchanged between the participants in order to affect these changes. In particular, the version number in the SDP will need to be changed by the controller in certain cases. Should the controller issue an SDP offer on its own (e.g., to place a call on hold), it would need to increment the version number in the SDP offer. The other participant in the call will not know that the controller has done this, and any subsequent offer it generates will have the wrong version number as far as its peer is concerned. As a result, the controller will be required to modify the version number in SDP messages to match what the recipient is expecting. It is important to point out that the call need not have been established by the controller in order for the processing of this section to be used. Rather, the controller could have acted as a B2BUA during a call established by A toward B (or vice versa).

18.3.5 3PCC and Early Media

Early media represents the condition where the session is established (as a result of the completion of an offer–answer exchange), yet the call itself has not been accepted. This is usually used to convey tones or announcements regarding progress of the call. Handling of early media in a third-party call is straightforward. Figure 18.2b shows the case where user B generates early media before answering the call. The flow is almost identical to flows of Figure 18.1e. The only difference is that user B generates a reliable provisional response (F5) defined in RFC 3262 instead of a final response, and answer2 is carried in a PRACK (F9) instead of an ACK. When party B finally does accept the call (F12), there is no change in the session state, and therefore, no signaling needs to be done with user A. The controller simply acknowledges the 200 OK (F13) to confirm the dialog. The case where user A generates early media is more complicated, and is shown in Figure 18.2c. The flow is based on call flows of Figure 18.1e. The controller sends an INVITE (F1) to user A, with an offer containing no media streams. User A generates a reliable provisional response (F2) containing an answer with no media streams.

The controller acknowledges this provisional response (F2) sending PRACK (F3). Now, the controller sends an INVITE (F5) without SDP to user B. User B's phone rings, and the user answers resulting in a 200 OK (F6) with an offer, offer2. The controller now needs to update the session parameters with user A. However, since the call has not been answered, it cannot use a re-INVITE. Rather, it uses a SIP UPDATE request (F7) defined RFC 3311, passing the offer (after modifying it to get the origin field correct). User A generates its answer in the 200 OK (F8) to the UPDATE. This answer is passed to user B in the ACK (F9) message. When user A finally answers (F11), there is no change in session state, so the controller simply acknowledges the 200 OK sending the ACK (F12) message. Note that it is likely that there will be clipping of media in this call flow. User A is likely a PSTN gateway, and has generated a provisional response because of early media from the PSTN side. The PSTN will deliver this media even though the gateway does not have anywhere to send it, since the initial offer from the controller had no media streams. When user B answers, media can begin to flow. However, any media sent to the gateway from the PSTN up to that point will be lost.

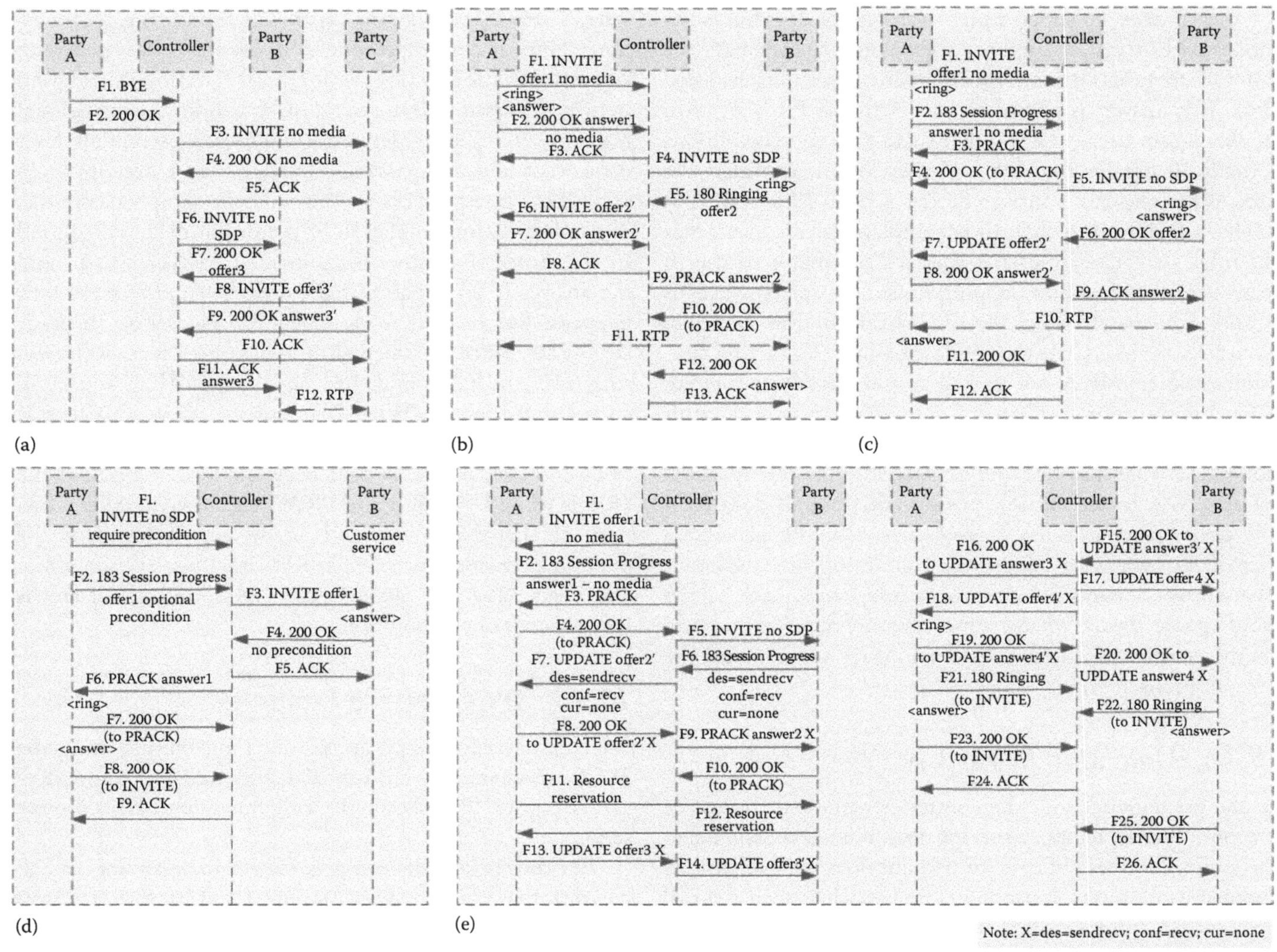

Figure 18.2 3PCC: (a) continued call processing, (b) simple early media, (c) complex early media, (d) controller initiated SDP preconditions, and (e) party-initiated SDP preconditions. (Copyright IETF. Reproduced with permission.)

18.3.6 3PCC and SDP Preconditions

A SIP extension has been specified that allows for the coupling of signaling and resource reservation described in RFC 3312 (see Section 15.4). This specification relies on exchanges of session descriptions before completion of the call setup. These flows are initiated when certain SDP parameters are passed in the initial INVITE. As a result, the interaction of this mechanism with 3PCC is not obvious, and worth detailing.

18.3.6.1 Initiation by Controller

In one usage scenario, the controller wishes to make use of preconditions in order to avoid the call failure scenarios documented in the earlier section. Specifically, the controller can use preconditions in order to guarantee that neither party is alerted unless there is a common set of media and codecs. It can also provide both parties with information on the media composition of the call before they decide to accept it. The flow for this scenario is shown in Figure 18.2d. In this example, we assume that user B is an automaton or agent of some sort that will answer the call immediately. Therefore, the flow is based on call flows of Figure 18.1b. The controller sends an INVITE to user A containing no SDP, but with a Require header indicating that preconditions are required. This specific scenario (an INVITE without an offer, but with a Require header indicating preconditions) is not described in RFC 3312 (see Section 15.4). It is recommended that the UA server respond with an offer in a 1xx including the media streams it wishes to use for the call, and, for each, list all preconditions it supports as optional. Of course, the user is not alerted at this time. The controller takes this offer and passes it to user B (F3).

User B does not support preconditions, or does but is not interested in them. Therefore, when it answers the call, the 200 OK contains an answer without any preconditions listed (F4). This answer is passed to user A in the PRACK (F6). At this point, user A knows that there are no preconditions actually in use for the call, and therefore, it can alert the user. When the call is answered, user A sends a 200 OK (F8) to the controller and the call is complete. In the event that the offer generated by user A was not acceptable to user B (e.g., because of nonoverlapping codecs or media), user B would immediately reject the INVITE (F3). The controller would then CANCEL the request to user A. In this situation, neither user A nor user B would have been alerted, achieving the desired effect. It is interesting to note that this property is achieved using preconditions even though it does not matter what specific types of preconditions are supported by user A. It is also entirely possible that user B does actually desire preconditions. In that case, it might generate a 1xx of its own with an answer containing preconditions. That answer would still be passed to user A, and both parties would proceed with whatever measures are necessary to meet the preconditions. Neither user would be alerted until the preconditions are met.

18.3.6.2 Initiation by Party A

In the previous section, the controller requested the use of preconditions to achieve a specific goal. It is also possible that the controller does not care (or perhaps does not even know) about preconditions, but one of the participants in the call does care. A call flow for this case is shown in Figure 18.2e. The controller follows the call flows of Figure 18.1e; it has no specific requirements for support of the preconditions specification of RFC 3312 (see Section 15.4). Therefore, it sends an INVITE (F1) with SDP that contains no media lines. User A is interested in supporting preconditions, and does not want to ring its phone until resources are reserved. Since there are no media streams in the INVITE, it cannot reserve resources for media streams, and therefore it cannot ring the phone until they are conveyed in a subsequent offer and then reserved. Therefore, it generates a 183 Session Progress (F2) message with the answer, and does not alert the user. The controller acknowledges this 183 Session Progress provisional response sending the PRACK message (F3), and A responds to the PRACK (F3) message with 200 OK (F4). At this point, the controller attempts to bring B into the call. It sends B an INVITE without SDP (F5). B is interested in having preconditions for this call. Therefore, it generates its offer in a 183 Session Progress (F6) message that contains the appropriate SDP attributes. The controller passes this offer to A in an UPDATE request (F7).

The controller uses UPDATE because the call has not been answered yet, and therefore, it cannot use a re-INVITE. User A sees that its peer is capable of supporting preconditions. Since it desires preconditions for the call, it generates an answer in the 200 OK (F8) to the UPDATE. This answer, in turn, is passed to B in the PRACK (F9) for the provisional response. Now, both sides perform resource reservation. User A succeeds first, and passes an updated session description in an UPDATE request (F13). The controller simply passes this to A, after the manipulation of the origin field, as required in call flows of Figure 18.1e, in an UPDATE (F14), and the answer (F15) is passed back to A (F16). The same flow happens, but from B to A, when B's reservation succeeds (F17–F20). Since the preconditions have been met, both sides ring (F21 and F22), and then both answer (F23 and F25), completing the call. What is important about this flow is that the controller does not know anything about preconditions. It merely passes the SDP back and forth as needed. The trick is using UPDATE and PRACK to pass the SDP when needed. That determination is made entirely based on the offer–answer rules described in RFC 3311 (see Section 3.8.3) and RFC 3262 (see Sections 2.5, 2.8.2, and 2.10), and is independent of preconditions.

18.3.7 3PCC Service Examples

We have considered two applications for offering using the 3PCC mechanisms: click-to-dial and mid-call announcement. Figure 18.3 shows the call flows for both of these services.

For the click-to-dial service, Figure 18.3a shows the SIP network that contains user A's phone and browser, controller, and customer service, while Figure 18.3b shows the call flows. Note that both phone and browser capability can also be implemented in a single device. Figure 18.3c depicts the SIP network with user A's phone, called party B's phone, controller, and media server, while Figure 18.3d describes the call flows for the mid-call announcement services.

18.3.7.1 Click-to-Dial

In the click-to-dial service, a user is browsing the web page of an e-commerce site and would like to speak to a customer service representative. The user clicks on a link, and a call is placed to a customer service representative. When the representative picks up, the phone on the user's desk rings. When the user picks up, the customer service representative is there, ready to talk to the user. The call flow for this service is given in Figure 18.3b. It is identical to that of Figure 18.1e, with the exception that the service is triggered through an HTTP POST request when the user clicks on the link. Normally, this POST request would contain neither the number of the user nor that of the customer service representative. The user's number would typically be obtained by the web application from backend databases, since the user would have

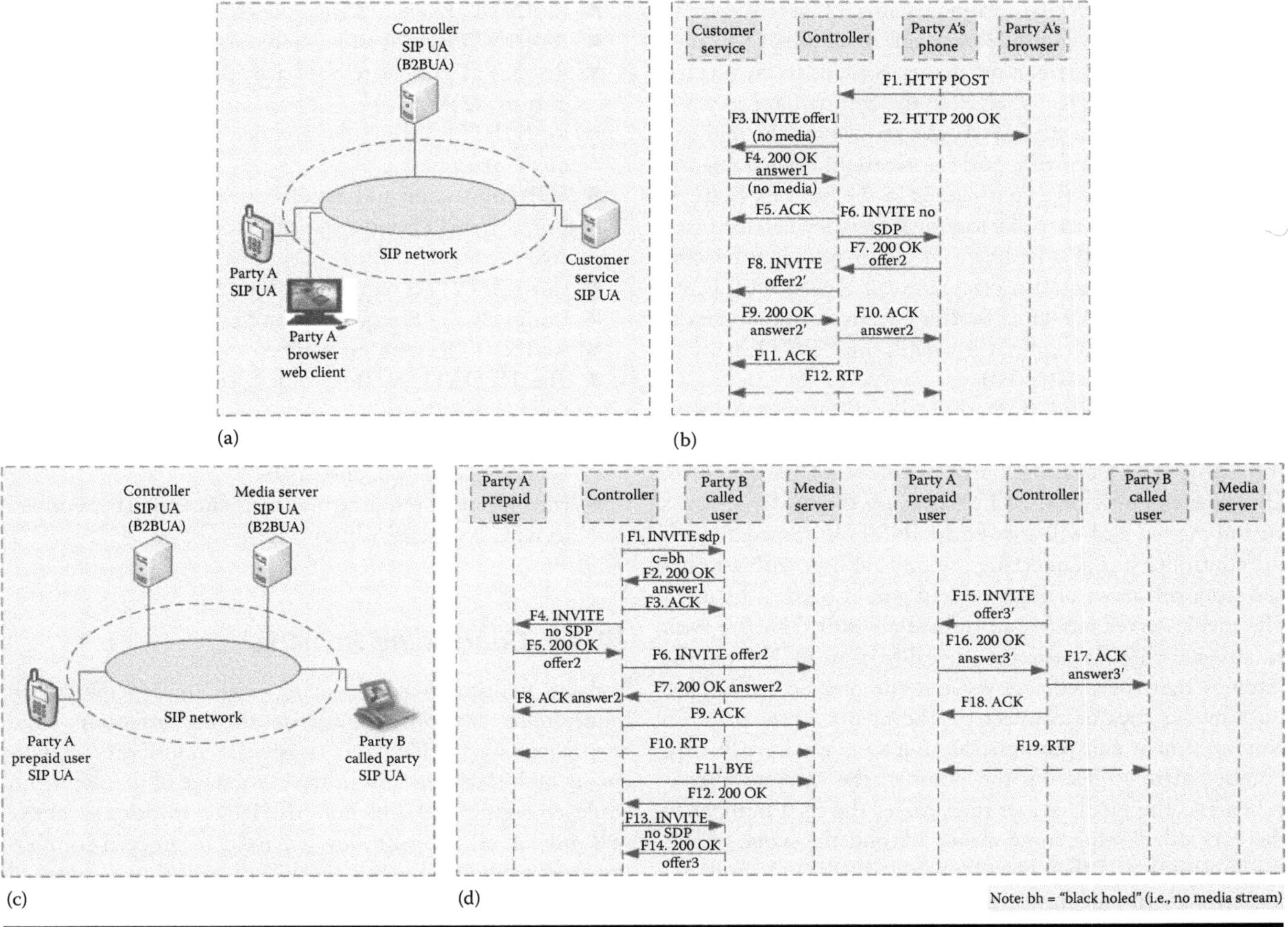

Figure 18.3 3PCC service examples: (a) click-to-dial SIP network, (b) click-to-dial call flows, (c) mid-call announcement SIP network, and (d) mid-call announcement call flows. (Copyright IETF. Reproduced with permission.)

presumably logged into the site, giving the server the needed context. The customer service number would typically be obtained through provisioning. Thus, the HTTP POST is actually providing the server nothing more than an indication that a call is desired.

We note that this service can be provided through other mechanisms, namely PSTN/Internet Interworking (PINT) described in RFC 2848. However, there are numerous differences between the way in which the service is provided by PINT and the way in which it is provided here as described in RFC 3725:

- The PINT solution enables calls only between two PSTN end points. The solution described here allows calls between PSTN phones (through SIP enabled gateways) and native IP phones.
- When used for calls between two PSTN phones, the solution here may result in a portion of the call being routed over the Internet. In PINT, the call is always routed only over the PSTN. This may result in better-quality calls with the PINT solution, depending on the codec in use and quality-of-service capabilities of the network routing the Internet portion of the call.
- The PINT solution requires extensions to SIP (PINT is an extension to SIP), whereas the solution described here is done with baseline SIP.
- The PINT solution allows the controller (acting as a PINT client) to *step out* once the call is established. The solution described here requires the controller to maintain call state for the entire duration of the call.

18.3.7.2 Mid-Call Announcement

The 3PCC mechanism described here can also be used to enable mid-call announcements. Consider a service for prepaid calling cards. Once the prepaid call is established, the system needs to set a timer to fire when they run out of minutes. We would like the user to hear an announcement that tells them to enter a credit card to continue when this timer fires. Once they enter the credit card info, more money is added to the prepaid card, and the user is reconnected to the destination party. We consider here the usage of 3PCC just for playing the mid-call dialog to collect the credit card information. We assume the call is set up so that the controller is in the call as a B2BUA. We wish to connect the caller to a media server when the timer fires. The flow for this is shown in Figure 18.3d. When the timer expires, the controller places the called party with a connection address of 0.0.0.0 (F1). This effectively *disconnects* the called party. The controller then sends an INVITE without SDP to the prepaid caller (F4).

The offer returned from the caller (F5) is used in an INVITE to the media server that will be collecting digits (F6). This is an instantiation of call flows of Figure 18.1b. This flow can only be used here because the media server is an automaton, and will answer the INVITE immediately. If the controller was connecting the prepaid user with another end user, call flows of Figure 18.1d would need to be used. The media server returns an immediate 200 OK (F7) with an answer, which is passed to the caller in an ACK (F8). The result is that the media server and the prepaid caller have their media streams connected. The media server plays an announcement and prompts the user to enter a credit card number. After collecting the number, the card number is validated. The media server then passes the card number to the controller (using some means beyond the scope of this specification), and then hangs up the call (F11). After hanging up with the media server, the controller reconnects the user to the original called party. To do this, the controller sends an INVITE without SDP to the called party (F13). The 200 OK (F14) contains an offer, offer3. The controller modifies the SDP as shown in Figure 18.1d, and passes the offer in an INVITE to the prepaid user (F15). The prepaid user generates an answer in a 200 OK (F16), which the controller passes to user B in the ACK (F17). At this point, the caller and called party are reconnected.

18.3.8 3PCC Implementation Recommendations

Most of the work involved in supporting 3PCC is within the controller. A standard SIP UA should be controllable using the mechanisms described here. However, 3PCC relies on a few features that might not be implemented. As such, we recommend that implementers of UA servers support the following as described in RFC 3725:

- Offers and answers that contain a connection line with an address of 0.0.0.0
- Re-INVITE requests that change the port to which media should be sent
- Re-INVITEs that change the connection address
- Re-INVITEs that add a media stream
- Re-INVITEs that remove a media stream (setting its port to zero)
- Re-INVITEs that add a codec among the set in a media stream
- SDP connection address of zero
- Initial INVITE requests with a connection address of zero
- Initial INVITE requests with no SDP
- Initial INVITE requests with SDP but no media lines
- Re-INVITEs with no SDP
- The UPDATE method described in RFC 3311 (see Section 3.8.3)
- Reliability of provisional responses in RFC 3262 (see Sections 2.5, 2.8.2, and 2.10)
- Integration of resource management and SIP described in RFC 3312 (see Section 15.4)

18.3.9 Concluding Remarks

Scalable multiparty conferencing with interoperability in multivendor environments needs further attention from researchers worldwide. The large-scale multiparty conferencing architecture is still in the early stage of development, while emerging SIP and non-SIP RFCs mentioned above will provide glimpses on how we need to proceed in offering most of the media-rich, intelligent, real-time networked multimedia services. The ease of use, like clicking on a URL, and scalable multiparty conferencing services with utmost reliability and a variety application sharing among businesses, universities, governments, academic institutions, and domestic users worldwide are of paramount need. Should these technical challenges be met in the future, multiparty conferencing with audio, video, and data applications would create a new thrilling era of real-time presence, providing a feeling of intimacy as if all parties are close together and geographical distance is merely an illusion.

18.4 Summary

We have described the key problems of offering multiparty conferencing using SIP/SDP. The simple SDP media description architecture that has been very attractive for the initial less media-rich point-to-point call has posed a huge challenge for multiparty multimedia conferencing. The multiparty 3PCC conference architecture has been described using SIP/SDP per RFC 3725, where the controller sets up the multipart call in a star-like, point-to-point, centralized conferencing topology under many assumptions. Even then, multiparty conferencing call establishment may fail under many circumstances. We have explained each of those error cases that need to be taken care of. We have also clarified that a huge amount of research work still needs to be done, although there are many other multiparty conferencing-related SIP and non-SIP application protocols like CCMP, BFCP, media channel mixer, and others that are being standardized to fill many of the gaps for centralized conferencing only, but the detail descriptions of those beyond the scope of this chapter.

PROBLEMS

1. What are the fundamental functional differences between two-party point-to-point and multiparty conference calls?
2. What are the limitations of single or multiple media negotiations with the media description architecture of multiparty conferencing?
3. Describe the problems of developing a multiparty call control architecture that needs media bridging evolving from the initial two-party point-to-point call using SIP/SDP.
4. What are the assumptions made with the third-party centralized controller to set up the multiparty conference call using SIP/SDP, which is described in RFC 3725?
5. Describe the 3PCC call flows using SIP/SDP for the following: (a) simplest flows, (b) flows with ping-ponging of INVITEs, (c) flows with unknown entities, and (d) efficient flows with unknown entities. Provide detailed descriptions of every header and message body field of each SIP/SDP message of each call establishment flows of (a) through (d).
6. Describe all limitations of each call establishment flows of (a) through (d) of item 5.
7. What are the recommendations of 3PCC call setups per RFC 3725?
8. How can 3PCC call establishment errors be handled in general?
9. Describe the 3PCC call flows using SIP/SDP for continued call processing along with each header and message-body field of each message.
10. Describe the 3PCC call flows with early media using SIP/SDP for continued call processing along with each header and message-body field of each message.
11. Describe the 3PCC call flows with SDP preconditions using SIP/SDP for the following along with their limitations, if any: (a) initiation by the controller and (b) initiation by the first party (say, A). Provide detailed descriptions for every header and message-body field of each SIP/SDP message of each call establishment flows of (a) and (b).
12. Describe the 3PCC call flows using SIP/SDP for the following services along with their limitations, if any: (a) click-to-dial and (b) mid-call announcement. Provide detailed descriptions of every header and message-body field of each SIP/SDP message of each call establishment flows of (a) and (b).
13. What are the implementation recommendations of 3PCC call setups per RFC 3725?
14. Describe the security recommendations using some examples for the 3PCC call setups and services per RFC 3725: authentication, authorization, end-to-end encryption, and integrity.
15. Describe the limitations, and suggest probable solutions for the worldwide large-scale 3PCC multiparty audio, video, and application sharing (including media bridging) conferencing services architecture recommended in RFC 3725 for providing scalability and interoperability in multivendor environments.

Chapter 19

Security Mechanisms in SIP

Abstract

The inherent security capabilities that are available in Session Initiation Protocol (SIP) are discussed in this section. SIP security is required in two levels: session level and media level. Session-level security deals with SIP signaling messages, while SIP media-level security is handled by secure media transport protocols like SRTP and ZRTP, which are extensions of the Real-Time Transmission Protocol. We do not deal with media-level security because it in itself needs more detailed treatment that is beyond the scope of this book. However, we explain the Session Description Protocol (SDP) media-level cryptographic features that are used for media streams once the session is set up, and that are negotiated using SIP/SDP messages. First, we explain the session-and media-level security of SIP. Second, the functionality for negotiating the security mechanisms used between a SIP UA and its next-hop SIP entity at the session level is provided. Third, all security mechanisms of SIP are described in detail. Fourth, we explain the SIP session setup that includes security features using an example of a call flow. Fifth, we explain the possible security threats that are being faced in the context of SIP that is an application-layer protocol. Finally, means to mitigate security threats using existing security mechanisms in SIP are provided. In this context, how the lower-transport-layer security capabilities complement SIP application-layer security features is discussed. However, a separate chapter is devoted to describing privacy and anonymity in SIP.

19.1 Introduction

Security services in Session Initiation Protocol (SIP) are important because SIP services primarily deal with human communications in real time over the fixed or mobile wireline or wireless networks. Moreover, networked multimedia RT and near-RT communications not only use SIP/SDP signaling messages for session setups and teardowns, but also use audio, video, and/or data application media protocols and payloads once sessions are setup. SIP communications may include all aspects of human life, including commercial and financial industries, governments, and private households including individuals. Countering sophisticated cyberattacks has made SIP security services more important. In general, five categories of security services are offered in SIP described in this section as follows:

Authentication: This is the identification of a certain entity and verification of that identity using credentials (e.g., digital signature) that can assure the identification and can be trusted for the communication/transmission. The entity can be a human user, an end device, a consumer/provider of a service, or others. In case of two parties, termed as mutual authentication, the authentication can be made during communicating through security key exchanges authenticating the identity of the peer. It can also be termed as identity or entity authentication. Sometimes, a message may also need to be authenticated. In this case, the authentication usually deals with the origin of the message as opposed to the message itself, and is termed as data origin authentication. For example, Hypertext Transfer Protocol (HTTP) authentication is used in SIP.

Authorization: This deals with the access rights to various resources, application subsystems, functionality, and data. Various policies, access control models, and security levels are used as means of supporting authorization. They are used to support confidentiality and integrity. For example, SIP call-level priority, the kind of media to be used, resource-level priority, and many other functions in SIP may be subject to authorization. Indirectly, it also implies that the authorized entity will be authenticated before providing authorization.

Integrity: In information security, integrity ensures that the data used maintains consistency over its entire life cycle and is free from deliberate or accidental modification. Integrity protection ensures the recipient that a received data/message has not been tampered along the end-to-end transmission path. Integrity protects information against malicious attacks and communication errors and failures. Data/message integrity service is provided in addition to confidentiality in information security.

Confidentiality: This deals only with the secrecy of the information or data that passes through from one party to another through the network. That is, data/information can only be kept confidential between the trusted entities. For example, confidentiality enables a message to be encrypted using a key so that only the recipients who possess the appropriate key can retrieve the original message by decrypting the message. It does not deal with the privacy of a person, although it offers a kind of privacy service to the information/data. SIP has mechanisms for encrypting messages for providing confidentiality.

Nonrepudiation: This deals with the need to prove that a certain action has been taken by an identity without plausible deniability. It implies that one party of a transaction cannot deny having received a transaction nor can the other party deny having sent a transaction. Nonrepudiation enables holding people accountable for their actions. It provides a verifiable proof that the transaction has taken place between the entities. Nonrepudiation security services can be provided using SIP.

19.2 Multilevel Security Characteristics in SIP

19.2.1 Overview

SIP is a complex signaling protocol that is used by networked multimedia applications where call/session signaling messages and the media streams that are transferred between the communications after establishment of the SIP call/session follow entirely different paths. There are two stages of communications: in the first stage, the session is set up and the second stage is followed by the media streams that have been negotiated using the Session Description Protocol (SDP) carried in the SIP message body during the call establishment. Signaling messages use SIP protocol, whereas multimedia streams use entirely different sets of real-time media transport (e.g., Real-Time Transport Protocol [RTP], Secure RTP [SRTP], and ZRTP) and data application sharing application (e.g., ITU-T T-series, instant messaging [IM], e-mails, web applications) protocols.

In addition, both SIP signaling messages and media streams may move via different SIP and network functional entities between the source–destination paths. For multiparty conferring, audio, video, or data application mixing/bridging is needed. Again, these application-layer signaling and media protocols also need the support of the lower-transport-layer protocols (e.g., User Datagram Protocol [UDP], Transmission Control Protocol [TCP], Stream Control Transmission Protocol [SCTP], Transport Layer Security [TLS], and Datagram Transport Layer Security [DTLS]). SIP security involves of all of those application and transport layers together in addition to the two-stage approach explained earlier.

19.2.2 Session-Level Security

The security of the SIP session establishment is the most important part of SIP security because all the security features that are negotiated for the media level to be used in the second stage are decided during the session setup. We will see in the subsequent sections that if there is no adequate security for the session establishment, then media-level security cannot be provided. All security mechanisms that are addressed here are primarily focused on the SIP session-level security that includes both SIP signaling message headers and SIP message body that includes SDP. We start first on how SIP security mechanisms can be agreed upon between the communicating entities using SIP security-related headers that were later added to SIP specifications. Furthermore, authentication, authorization, integrity, confidentiality, and nonrepudiation at the SIP session level are discussed in detail in the subsequent sections.

19.2.2.1 SIP REFER Method Security

The REFER request message described in Section 2.5 extends the basic SIP Request for Comment (RFC) 3261. However, the security considerations described in the base SIP RFC (RFC 3261) are also applicable to the REFER transaction. In particular, the implementation requirements and considerations related to the threat model described in Section 19.9 for securing a generic SIP transaction are specifically applicable to the RFER request. Special consideration is warranted for the authorization policies applied to REFER requests and for the use of message/sipfrag (RFC 3420, see Section 2.8.2) to convey the results of the referenced request.

19.2.2.1.1 Constructing a Refer-To Uniform Resource Identifier

This mechanism relies on providing contact information for the referred-to resource to the party being referred. Care should be taken to provide a suitably restricted Uniform Resource Identifier (URI) if the referred-to resource should be protected.

19.2.2.1.2 Authorization Considerations for REFER

We are clarifying some authorization issues specific to the SIP REFER method here, although SIP authorization in general that is specified in Section 19.5 is also applicable for this request message. As described for the REFER method in Section 2.5, an implementation can receive a REFER request with a Refer-To URI containing an arbitrary scheme. For instance, a user could be referred to an online service by using a telnet URI. Customer service could refer a customer to an order-tracking web page using an HTTP URI. The SIP REFER method allows a user agent (UA) to reject a REFER request when it cannot process the referenced scheme. It also requires the UA to obtain authorization from its user before attempting to use the URI. Generally, this could be achieved by prompting the user with the full URI and with a question such as "Do you wish to access this resource (yes/no)?" Of course, URIs can be arbitrarily long and are occasionally constructed with malicious intent, so care should be taken to avoid surprises even in the display of the URI itself (such as partial display or crashing). Furthermore, care should be taken to expose as much information about the reference as possible to the user to mitigate the risk of being misled into a dangerous decision. For instance, the Refer-To header may contain a display name along with the URI. Nothing ensures that any property implied by that display name is shared by the URI. For instance, the display name may contain *secure* or *president* and when the URI indicates sip:agent59@telemarketing.example.com. Thus, prompting the user with the display name alone is insufficient.

In some cases, the user can provide authorization for some REFER requests ahead of time by providing policy to the UA. This is appropriate, for instance, for call transfer as described in RFC 5589 (see Section 16.2). Here, a properly authenticated REFER request within an existing SIP dialog to a sip:, sips:, or tel: URI may be accepted through policy without interactively obtaining the user's authorization. Similarly, it may be appropriate to accept a properly authenticated REFER to an HTTP URI if the referror is on an explicit list of approved referrors. In the absence of such preprovided authorization, the user must interactively provide authorization to reference the indicated resource. To see the danger of a policy that blindly accepts and acts on an HTTP URI, for example, consider a web server configured to accept requests only from clients behind a small organization's firewall. As it sits in this soft-creamy-middle environment where the small organization trusts all its members and has little internal security, the web server is frequently behind on maintenance, leaving it vulnerable to attack through maliciously constructed URIs (resulting perhaps in running arbitrary code provided in the URI).

If a SIP UA inside this firewall blindly accepted a reference to an arbitrary HTTP URI, an attacker outside the firewall could compromise the web server. On the other hand, if the UA's user has to take positive action (such as responding to a prompt) before acting on this URI, the risk is reduced to the same level as the user clicking on the URI in a web browser or e-mail message. The conclusion in the above paragraph generalizes to URIs with an arbitrary scheme. An agent that takes automated action to access a URI with a given scheme risks being used to indirectly attack another host that is vulnerable to some security flaw related to that scheme. This risk and the potential for harm to that other host is heightened when the host and agent reside behind a common policy-enforcement point such as a firewall. Furthermore, this agent increases its exposure to denial-of-service (DoS) attacks through resource exhaustion, especially if each automated action involves opening a new connection. UAs should take care when handing an arbitrary URI to a third-party service such as that provided by some modern operating systems, particularly if the UA is not aware of the scheme and the possible ramifications using the protocols it indicates. The opportunity for violating the principal of least surprise is very high.

19.2.2.1.3 Considerations for the Use of message/sipfrag

Using message/sipfrag bodies to return the progress and results of a REFER request is extremely powerful. Careless use of that capability can compromise confidentiality and privacy. Here are a couple of simple, somewhat contrived, examples to demonstrate the potential for harm:

- Circumventing privacy

  Suppose Alice has a UA that accepts REFER requests to SIP INVITE URIs, and NOTIFYs the referrer of the progress of the INVITE by copying each response to the INVITE into the body of a NOTIFY. Suppose further that Carol (see Section 2.5 for REFER method) has a reason to avoid Mallory and has configured her system at her proxy to only accept calls from a certain set of people she trusts (including Alice), so that Mallory does not learn when she is around, or what UA she is actually using. Mallory can send a REFER to Alice, with a Refer-To URI indicating Carol. If Alice can reach Carol, the 200 OK Carol sends gets returned to Mallory in a NOTIFY, letting him know not only that Carol is around, but also the IP address of the agent she is using.

- Circumventing confidentiality

  Suppose Alice, with the same UA as above, is working at a company that is working on the greatest SIP device ever invented—the SIP FOO. The company has been working for months building the device and the marketing materials, carefully keeping the idea, even the name of the idea secret (since a FOO is one of those things that anybody could do if they just had the idea first). FOO is up and running, and anyone at the company can use it, but it is not available outside the company firewall. Mallory has heard rumor that Alice's company is onto something big, and has even managed to get his hands on a URI that he suspects might have something to do with it. He sends a REFER to ALICE with the mysterious URI and as Alice connects to the FOO, Mallory gets NOTIFYs with bodies containing server: FOO/v0.9.7.

- Limiting the breach

  For each of these cases, and in general, returning a carefully selected subset of the information available about the progress of the reference through the NOTIFYs mitigates risk. The minimal implementation for the REFER method described in Section 2.5 exposes the least information about what the agent operating on the REFER request has done, and is least likely to be a useful tool for malicious users.

- Cut, paste, and replay considerations

  The mechanism defined in this specification is not directly susceptible to abuse through copying the message/sipfrag (RFC 5589, see Section 16.2) bodies from NOTIFY requests and inserting them, in whole or in part, in future NOTIFY requests associated with the same or a different REFER. Under this specification the agent replying to the REFER request is in complete control of the content of the bodies of the NOTIFY it sends. There is no mechanism defined here requiring this agent to faithfully forward any information from the referenced party. Thus, saving a body for later replay gives the agent no more ability to affect the mechanism defined in this document at its peer than it has without that body. Similarly, capture of a message/sipfrag body by eavesdroppers will give them no more ability to affect this mechanism than they would have without it.

  Future extensions may place additional constraints on the agent responding to REFER to allow using the message/sipfrag body part in a NOTIFY to make statements like "I contacted the party you referred me to, and here is cryptographic proof." These statements might be used to affect the behavior of the receiving UA. This kind of extension will need to define additional mechanism to protect itself from copy-based attacks.

19.2.2.2 P-Asserted- and Preferred-Services Identification Security

We have discussed the P-Asserted-Services and P-Preferred-Services Identification header field in Section 12.3 (RFC 6050). The mechanism provides a partial consideration of the problem of service identification in SIP. For example, these mechanisms provide no means by which end users can securely share service information end-to-end without a trusted service provider. This information is secured by transitive trust, which is only as reliable as the weakest link in the chain of trust. The Trust Domain provides a set of servers where the characteristics of the service are agreed for that service identifier value, and where the calling user is entitled to use that service. RFC 5897 (see Sections 12.1 through 12.3) identifies the impact of allowing such service identifier values to *leak* outside of the Trust Domain, including implications on interoperability, and stifling of service innovation.

In addition to interoperability and stifle in services innovative issues, the declarative service identification can lead to fraud. If a provider uses the service identifier for billing and accounting purposes, or for authorization purposes, it opens an avenue for attack. The user can construct the signaling message so that its actual effect (which is the service the user will receive) is what the user desires, but the user places a service identifier into the request (which is what is used for billing and authorization) that identifies a cheaper service, or one that the user is not authorized to receive. In such a case, the user will receive service, and not be billed properly for it. If, however, the domain administrator derived the service identifier from the signaling itself (derived service identification), the user cannot lie. If they did lie, they would not get the desired service. Consider the example of Internet Protocol television (IPTV) versus multimedia conferencing. If multimedia conferencing is cheaper, the user could send an INVITE for an IPTV session, but include a service identifier that indicates multimedia conferencing.

The user gets the service associated with IPTV, but at the cost of multimedia conferencing. This same principle shows up in other places—for example, in the identification of an emergency services call (see Section 16.11). It is desirable to give emergency services calls special treatment, such as being free and authorized even when the user cannot otherwise make calls, and to give them priority. If emergency calls were indicated through something other than the target of the call being an emergency services Uniform Resource Name (URN) (RFC 5031, see Section 16.11.2), it would open an avenue for fraud. The user could place any desired URI in the request-URI, and indicate separately, through a declarative identifier, that the call is an emergency services call. This would then get special treatment but of course would get routed to the target URI. The only way to prevent this fraud is to consider an emergency call as any call whose target is an emergency services URN. Thus, the service identification here is based on the target of the request. When the target is an emergency services URN, the request can get special treatment. The user cannot lie, since there is no way to separately indicate that this is an emergency call, besides targeting it to an emergency URN.

RFC 5876 (see Section 10.4.4) raises the following additional security considerations. When adding a P-Asserted-Identity header field to a message, an entity must have authenticated the source of the message by some means. One means is to challenge the sender of a message to provide SIP Digest authentication. Responses cannot be challenged, and also ACK and CANCEL requests cannot be challenged. Therefore, this document limits the use of P-Asserted-Identity to requests other than ACK and CANCEL. When sending a request containing the P-Asserted-Identity header field and also the Privacy header field with value *id* to a node within the Trust Domain, special considerations apply if that node does not support this specification. Section 10.5.2 makes a special provision for this case.

When receiving a request containing a P-Asserted-Identity header field, a proxy will trust the assertion only if the source is known to be within the Trust Domain and behaves in accordance with a Spec(T), which defines the security requirements. This applies regardless of the nature of the resource (UA or proxy). One example where a trusted source might be a UA is a public switched telephone network (PSTN) gateway. In this case, the UA can assert an identity received from the PSTN, with the proxy itself having no means to authenticate such an identity. A SIP entity must not trust an identity asserted by a source outside the Trust Domain. Typically, a UA under the control of an individual user (such as a desk phone or mobile phone) should not be considered part of a Trust Domain. When receiving a response from a node outside the Trust Domain, a proxy has no standardized SIP means to authenticate the source of the response. For this reason, this document does not specify the use of P-Asserted-Identity or P-Preferred-Identity in responses.

19.2.2.3 Feature Tags Security

Feature tags described in Section 2.11 can provide sensitive information about a user or a UA. As such, RFC 3840 cautions against providing sensitive information to another party. Once this information is given out, any use may be made of it, including relaying to a third party as in this specification. A REFER-Issuer must not create or guess feature tags. Instead, a feature tag included in a REFER should be discovered in an authenticated and secure method (such as an OPTIONS response or from a remote target URI in a dialog) directly from the REFER-Target. It is recommended that the REFER-Issuer includes in the Refer-To header field all feature tags that were listed in the most recent Contact header field of the REFER-Target.

A feature tag provided by a REFER-Issuer cannot be authenticated or certified directly from the REFER request. As such, the REFER-Recipient must treat the information as a hint. If the REFER-Recipient application logic or user's action depends on the presence of the expressed feature, the feature tag can be verified. For example, in order to do so, the REFER-Recipient can directly send an OPTIONS query to the REFER-Target over a secure (e.g., mutually authenticated and integrity-protected) connection. This protects the REFER-Recipient against the sending of incorrect or malicious feature tags.

19.2.2.4 Offer–Answer Security

There are numerous attacks possible if an attacker can modify offers or answers described in Section 3.8.4 in transit. Generally, these include diversion of media streams (enabling eavesdropping), disabling of calls, and injection of unwanted media streams. If a passive listener can construct fake offers, and inject those into an exchange, similar attacks are possible. Even if an attacker can simply observe offers and answers, they can inject media streams into an existing conversation. Offer–answer relies on transport within an application signaling protocol, such as SIP. It also relies on that protocol for security capabilities. Because of the attacks described above, that protocol MUST provide a means for end-to-end authentication and integrity protection of offers and answers.

It should offer encryption of bodies to prevent eavesdropping. However, media injection attacks can alternatively be resolved through authenticated media exchange, and therefore the encryption requirement is a *should* instead of a *must*. Replay attacks are also problematic. An attacker can replay an old offer, perhaps one that had put media on hold, and thus disable media streams in a conversation. Therefore, the application protocol must provide a secure way to sequence offers and answers, and to detect and reject old offers or answers, and SIP meets all of these requirements.

19.2.2.5 Network-Asserted Identity Security

The Network-Asserted Identity (NAI) requirements described in Section 10.5 are not intended to result in a mechanism with general applicability between arbitrary hosts on the

Internet. Rather, the intention is to state requirements for a mechanism to be used within a community of devices that are known to obey the specification of the mechanism (Spec(T)) and between which there are secure connections. Such a community is known here as a Trust Domain. The requirements on the mechanisms used for security and to initially derive the NAI must be part of the specification Spec(T). The requirements also support the transfer of information from a node within the Trust Domain, via a secure connection to a node outside the Trust Domain. Use of this mechanism in any other context has serious security shortcomings, namely that there is absolutely no guarantee that the information has not been modified, or was even correct in the first place.

19.2.2.6 Location Information Security

RFC 6442 (see Section 9.10), which specifies the target's location information creation and distribution, describes the security of the target. Conveyance of the physical location of a UA raises privacy concerns (see Section 20.2), and depending on use, there probably will be authentication and integrity concerns. RFC 6442 (see Section 9.10) calls for conveyance to be accomplished through secure mechanisms, like Secure/Multipurpose Internet Mail Extension (S/MIME) (see Section 19.6) encrypting message bodies (although this is not widely deployed), or TLS protecting the overall signaling or conveyance location-by-reference and requiring all entities that dereference location to authenticate themselves. In location-based routing cases, encrypting the location payload with an end-to-end mechanism such as S/MIME is problematic because one or more proxies on the path need the ability to read the location information to retarget the message to the appropriate new destination UA server (UAS). Data can only be encrypted to a particular, anticipated target, and thus if multiple recipients need to inspect a piece of data, and those recipients cannot be predicted by the sender of data, encryption is not a very feasible choice. Securing the location hop-by-hop, using TLS, protects the message from eavesdropping and modification in transit, but exposes the information to all proxies on the path as well as the end point.

In most cases, the UA has no trust relationship with the proxy or proxies providing location-based routing services, so such end-to-middle solutions might not be appropriate either. When location information is conveyed by reference, however, one can properly authenticate and authorize each entity that wishes to inspect location information. This does not require that the sender of data anticipate who will receive data, and it does permit multiple entities to receive it securely; however, it does not obviate the need for preassociation between the sender of data and any prospective recipients. Obviously, in some contexts, this preassociation cannot be presumed; when it is not, effectively unauthenticated access to location information must be permitted. In this case, choosing pseudo-random URIs for location-by-reference, coupled with path encryption like SIP Secure (SIPS), can help ensure that only entities on the SIP signaling path learn the URI. Thus, it can restore rough parity with sending location-by-value. Location information is especially sensitive when the identity of its target is obvious. Note that there is the ability, according to RFC 3693 (see Sections 2.8 and 9.10.1), to have an anonymous identity for the target's location. This is accomplished by the use of an unlinkable pseudonym in the entity= attribute of the <presence> element defined in RFC 4479. However, this can be problematic for routing messages based on location covered in RFC 4479.

Moreover, anyone fishing for information would correlate the identity at the SIP layer with that of the location information referenced by SIP signaling. When a UA inserts location, the UA sets the policy on whether to reveal its location along the signaling path—as discussed earlier, as well as flags in the PIDF-LO defined in RFC 4119 (see Section 2.8). UA client (UAC) implementations must make such capabilities conditional on explicit user permission, and must alert the user that location is being conveyed. This SIP extension offers the default ability to require permission to process location while the SIP request is in transit. The default for this is set to *no*. There is an error explicitly describing how an intermediary asks for permission to view the target's location, plus a rule stating the user has to be made aware of this permission request. There is no end-to-end integrity on any locationValue or locationErrorValue header field parameter (or middle-to-end if the value was inserted by an intermediary), so recipients of either header field need to implicitly trust the header field contents, and take whatever precautions each entity deems appropriate given this situation.

19.2.2.7 Early-Session Option Tags Security

We have discussed the Early-Session option tags in Section 11.4 in the context of the early-media solution model with Disposition-Type SIP message header. The security implications of using early-session bodies in SIP are the same as when using session bodies; they are part of the offer–answer model. SIP uses the offer–answer model to establish early sessions in both the gateway and the application server models. UAs generate a session description, which contains the transport address (i.e., IP address plus port) where they want to receive media, and send it to their peer in a SIP message. When media packets arrive at this transport address, the UA assumes that they come from the receiver of the SIP message carrying the session description. Nevertheless, attackers may attempt to gain access to the contents of the SIP message and send packets to the transport address contained in the session description.

To prevent this situation, UAs should encrypt their session descriptions (e.g., using S/MIME). Still, even if a UA encrypts its session descriptions, an attacker may try to guess the transport address used by the UA and send media packets to that address. Guessing such a transport address is sometimes easier than it may seem because many UAs always pick up the same initial media port. To prevent this situation, UAs should use media-level authentication mechanisms (e.g., SRTP; see Section 7.3). In addition, UAs that wish to keep their communications confidential should use media-level encryption mechanisms (e.g., SRTP).

Attackers may attempt to make a UA send media to a victim as part of a DoS attack. This can be done by sending a session description with the victim's transport address to the UA. To prevent this attack, the UA should engage in a handshake with the owner of the transport address received in a session description (just verifying willingness to receive media) before sending a large amount of data to the transport address. This check can be performed by using a connection-oriented transport protocol, by using STUN (see Section 14.3.2.1) in an end-to-end fashion, or by the key exchange in SRTP (see Section 7.3). In any event, note that the previous security considerations are not early-media specific, but apply to the usage of the offer–answer model in SIP to establish sessions in general.

Additionally, an early-media-specific risk (roughly speaking, an equivalent to forms of *toll fraud* in the PSTN) attempts to exploit the different charging policies some operators apply to early and to regular media. When UAs are allowed to exchange early media for free, but are required to pay for regular media sessions, rogue UAs may try to establish a bidirectional early-media session and never send a 2xx response for the INVITE. On the other hand, some application servers (e.g., interactive voice response systems) use bidirectional early media to obtain information from the callers (e.g., the personal identification number [PIN] code of a calling card). Thus, we do not recommend that operators disallow bidirectional early media. Instead, operators should consider a remedy of charging early-media exchanges that last too long, or stopping them at the media level (according to the operator's policy).

19.2.2.8 Early-Media Security

We have described early media in SIP in Chapter 11. The use of this P-Early-Media header field is only applicable inside a Trust Domain, as defined in RFC 3324 (see Section 10.5). As stated earlier, this header does not offer a general early-media authorization model suitable for interdomain use or use in the Internet at large. No confidentiality concerns are associated with the P-Early-Media header field. It is desirable to maintain the integrity of the direction parameters in the header field across each hop between servers to avoid the potential for unauthorized use of early media. It is assumed that the P-Early-Media header field is used within the context of a given administrative Trust Domain (e.g., Third Generation Partnership Project IP multimedia subsystem [3GPP IMS] network) or a similar Trust Domain, consisting of a collection of SIP servers maintaining pairwise security associations.

Within the Trust Domain of a network, it is only necessary to police the use of the P-Early-Media header field at the boundary to user equipment served by the network and at the boundary to peer networks. It is assumed that boundary servers in the Trust Domain of a network will have local policy for the treatment of the P-Early-Media header field as it is sent to or received from any possible server external to the network. Since boundary servers are free to modify or remove any P-Early-Media header field in SIP messages forwarded across the boundary, the integrity of the P-Early-Media header field can be verified to the extent that the connections to external servers are secured. The authenticity of the P-Early-Media header field can only be assured to the extent that the external servers are trusted to police the authenticity of the header field.

19.2.2.9 Served-User Identification Security

We have described the Served-User Identification in SIP in Section 12.4. The P-Served-User header field defined in this document is to be used in an environment where elements are trusted and where attackers are not supposed to have access to the protocol messages between those elements. Traffic protection between network elements is sometimes achieved by using IPsec, and sometimes by physically protecting the network. In any case, the environment where the P-Served-User header field will be used ensures the integrity and the confidentiality of the contents of this header field. The Spec(T) that defines the Trust Domain for P-Served-User must require that member nodes understand the P-Served-User header extension.

There is a security risk if a P-Served-User header field is allowed to propagate out of the Trust Domain where it was generated. In that case, user-sensitive information would be revealed. To prevent such a breach from occurring, proxies must not insert the header when forwarding requests to a hop that is located outside the Trust Domain. When forwarding the request to a node in the Trust Domain, proxies must not insert the header unless they have sufficient knowledge that the route set includes another proxy in the Trust Domain that understands the header, such as the home proxy. There is no automatic mechanism to learn the support for this specification. Proxies must remove the header when forwarding requests to nodes that are not in the Trust Domain or when the proxy does not have knowledge of any other proxy included in the route set that will remove it before it is routed to any node that is not in the Trust Domain.

19.2.2.10 Connection Reuse Security

RFC 5923 (see Section 13.2.8) presents requirements and a mechanism for reusing existing connections easily. Unauthenticated connection reuse would present many opportunities for rampant abuse and hijacking. Authenticating connection aliases is essential to prevent connection hijacking. For example, a program run by a malicious user of a multiuser system could attempt to hijack SIP requests destined for the well-known SIP port from a large relay proxy.

19.2.2.10.1 Authenticating TLS Connections: Client View

When a TLS client establishes a connection with a server, it is presented with the server's X.509 certificate. Authentication proceeds as described in RFC 5922 (see Section 19.4.6).

19.2.2.10.2 Authenticating TLS Connections: Server View

A TLS server conformant to this specification must ask for a client certificate; if the client possesses a certificate, it will be presented to the server for mutual authentication, and authentication proceeds as described in RFC 5922 (see Section 19.4.6). If the client does not present a certificate, the server must proceed as if the *alias* header field parameter was not present in the topmost Via header. In this case, the server must not update the alias table.

19.2.2.10.3 Connection Reuse and Virtual Servers

Virtual servers present special considerations for connection reuse. Under the name-based virtual server scheme, one SIP proxy can host many virtual domains using one IP address and port number. If adequate defenses are not put in place, a connection opened to a downstream server on behalf of one domain can be reused to send requests in the backwards direction to a different domain. The Destination Identity column in the alias table has been added to aid in such defenses. Virtual servers must only perform connection reuse for TLS connections; virtual servers must not perform connection reuse for other connection-oriented transports. To understand why this is the case, note that the alias table caches not only which connections go to which destination addresses, but also which connections have authenticated themselves as responsible for which domains. If a message is to be sent in the backwards direction to a new SIP domain that resolves to an address with a cached connection, the cached connection cannot be used because it is not authenticated for the new domain.

As an example, consider a proxy P1 that hosts two virtual domains—example.com and example.net—on the same IP address and port. RFC 3263 (see Section 8.2.4) server resolution is set up such that a Domain Name System (DNS) lookup of example.com and example.net both resolve to an {IP-address, port, transport} tuple of {192.0.2.1, 5061, TLS}. A UA in the example.com domain sends a request to P1 causing it to make a downstream connection to its peering proxy, P2, and authenticating itself as a proxy in the example.com domain by sending it a X.509 certificate asserting such an identity. P2's alias table now looks like the following:

Destination IP Address	*Destination Port*	*Destination Transport*	*Destination Identity*	*Alias Descriptor*
...				
192.0.2.1	5061	TLS	sip:example.com	18

At some later point in time, a UA in P2's domain wants to send a request to a UA in the example.net domain. P2 performs an RFC 3263 (see Section 8.2.4) server resolution process on sips:example.net to derive a resolved address tuple {192.0.2.1, 5061, TLS}. It appears that a connection to this network address is already cached in the alias table; however, P2 cannot reuse this connection because the destination identity (sip:example.com) does not match the server identity used for RFC 3261 resolution (sips:example.net). Hence, P2 will open up a new connection to the example.net virtual domain hosted on P1. P2's alias table will now look like

Destination IP Address	*Destination Port*	*Destination Transport*	*Destination Identity*	*Alias Descriptor*
...				
192.0.2.1	5061	TLS	sip:example.com	18
192.0.2.1	5061	TLS	sip:example.net	54

The identities conveyed in an X.509 certificate are associated with a specific TLS connection. With the absence of such a guarantee of an identity tied to a specific connection, a normal TCP or SCTP connection cannot be used to send requests in the backwards direction without a significant risk of inadvertent (or otherwise) connection hijacking. The above discussion details the impact on P2 when connection reuse is desired for virtual servers. There is a subtle but important impact on P1 as well. P1 should keep separate alias tables for the requests served from the UAs in the example.com domain from those served by the UAs in the example.net domain. This is so that the boundary between the two domains is preserved; P1 must not open a connection on behalf of one domain and reuse it to send a new request on behalf of another domain.

19.2.2.11 Loss-Based Overload Control Security

We have described the overload control in SIP networks in Section 13.3. Overload control mechanisms can be used by an attacker to conduct a DoS attack on a SIP entity if the attacker can pretend that the SIP entity is overloaded. When such a forged overload indication is received by an upstream SIP client, it will stop sending traffic to the victim. Thus, the victim is subject to a DoS attack. To better understand the threat model, consider the diagram in Figure 19.1.

Here, requests travel downstream from the left-hand side, through proxy P1, toward the right-hand side; responses travel upstream from the right-hand side, through P1, toward the left-hand side. Proxies Pa, Pb, and P1 support overload control. L1 and L2 are labels for the links connecting P1 to the upstream clients and downstream servers. If an attacker is able to modify traffic between Pa and P1 on link L1, it can cause a DoS attack on P1 by having Pa not send any traffic to P1. Such an attack can proceed by the attacker modifying the response from P1 to Pa such that Pa's Via header is changed to indicate that all requests destined toward P1 should be dropped. Conversely, the attacker can simply remove any oc, oc-validity, and oc-seq markings added by P1 in a response to Pa. In such a case, the attacker will force P1 into overload by denying request quenching at Pa even though Pa is capable of performing overload control.

Similarly, if an attacker is able to modify traffic between P1 and Pb on link L2, it can change the Via header associated with P1 in a response from Pb to P1 such that all subsequent requests destined toward Pb from P1 are dropped. In essence, the attacker mounts a DoS attack on Pb by indicating false overload control. Note that it is immaterial whether Pb supports overload control or not; the attack will succeed as long as the attacker is able to control L2. Conversely, an attacker can suppress a genuine overload condition at Pb by simply removing any oc, oc-validity, and ocseq markings added by Pb in a response to P1. In such a case, the attacker will force P1 into sending requests to Pb even under overload conditions because P1 would not be aware that Pb supports overload control. Attacks that indicate false overload control are best mitigated by using TLS in conjunction with applying BCP 38 (RFC 2827). Attacks that are mounted to suppress genuine overload conditions can be similarly avoided by using TLS on the connection. Generally, TCP or WebSockets (RFC 6455) in conjunction with BCP 38 makes it more difficult for an attacker to insert or modify messages, but may still prove inadequate against an adversary that controls links L1 and L2. TLS provides the best protection from an attacker with access to the network links.

Another way to conduct an attack is to send a message containing a high overload feedback value through a proxy that does not support this extension. If this feedback is added to the second Via header (or all Via headers), it will reach the next upstream proxy. If the attacker can make the recipient believe that the overload status was created by its direct downstream neighbor (and not by the attacker further downstream), the recipient stops sending traffic to the victim. A precondition for this attack is that the victim proxy does not support this extension since it would not pass through overload control feedback otherwise. A malicious SIP entity could gain an advantage by pretending to support this specification but never reducing the amount of traffic it forwards to the downstream neighbor. If its downstream neighbor receives traffic from multiple sources that correctly implement overload control, the malicious SIP entity would benefit since all other sources to its downstream neighbor would reduce load. Note that the solution to this problem depends on the overload control method. With rate-based, window-based, and other similar overload control algorithms that promise to produce no more than a specified number of requests per unit time, the overloaded server can regulate the traffic arriving to it.

However, when using loss-based overload control, such policing is not always obvious since the load forwarded depends on the load received by the client. To prevent such attacks, servers should monitor client behavior to determine whether they are complying with overload control policies. If a client is not conforming to such policies, then the server should treat it as a nonsupporting client described earlier. Finally, a distributed DoS (DDoS) attack could cause an honest server to start signaling an overload condition. Such a DDoS attack could be mounted without controlling the communications links since the attack simply depends on

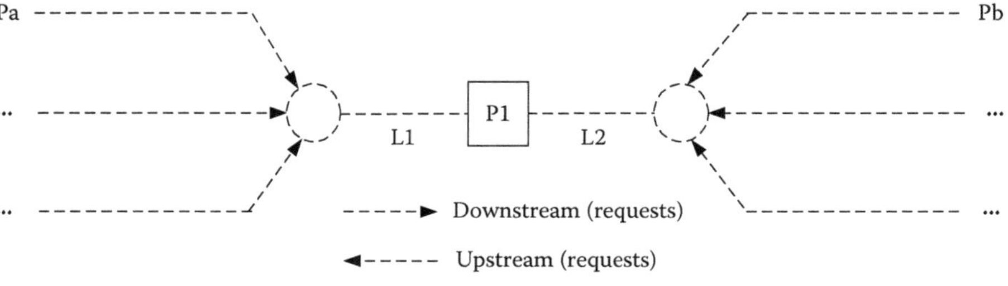

Figure 19.1 Downstream and upstream requests through SIP proxy.

the attacker injecting a large volume of packets on the communication links. If the honest server attacked by a DDoS attack has a long oc-validity interval and the attacker can guess this interval, the attacker can keep the server overloaded by synchronizing the DDoS traffic with the validity period. While such an attack may be relatively easy to spot, mechanisms for combating it are outside the scope of this document and, of course, since attackers can invent new variations, the appropriate mechanisms are likely to change over time.

19.2.2.12 Session Border Controller Security

We have described the session border controller (SBC) in SIP networks in Section 14.2. Many of the functions of the SBC have important security and privacy implications. One major security problem is that many functions implemented by SBCs (e.g., topology hiding and media traffic management) modify SIP messages and their bodies without the UAs' consent. The result is that the UAs may interpret the actions taken by an SBC as a man-in-the-middle (MITM) attack. SBCs modify SIP messages because it allows them to, for example, protect elements in the inner network from direct attacks. SBCs that place themselves (or another entity) on the media path can be used to eavesdrop on conversations. Since, often, UAs cannot distinguish between the actions of an attacker and those of an SBC, users cannot know whether they are being eavesdropped on or if an SBC on the path is performing some other function. SBCs place themselves on the media path because it allows them to, for example, perform legal interception.

On a general level, SBCs prevent the use of end-to-end authentication. This is because SBCs need to be able to perform actions that look like MITM attacks, and in order for UAs to communicate, they must allow those type of attacks. It other words, UAs cannot use end-to-end security. This is especially harmful because other network elements, besides SBCs, are then able to do similar attacks. However, in some cases, UAs can establish encrypted media connections between one another. One example is a scenario where SBC is used for enabling media monitoring but not for interception.

An SBC is a single point of failure from the architectural point of view. This makes it an attractive target for DoS attacks. The fact that some functions of SBCs require those SBCs to maintain session-specific information makes the situation even worse. If the SBC crashes (or is brought down by an attacker), ongoing sessions experience undetermined behavior. If the International Engineering Task Force (IETF) decides to develop standard mechanisms to address the requirements presented in Section 14.2.4, the security- and privacy-related aspects of those mechanisms will, of course, need to be taken into consideration.

19.2.2.13 Resource-Priority Security

19.2.2.13.1 Background

We have described resource priority in SIP in Section 15.2. Any resource-priority mechanism can be abused to obtain resources and thus deny service to other users. An adversary may be able to take over a particular PSTN gateway, cause additional congestion during emergencies affecting the PSTN, or deny service to legitimate users. In SIP end systems, such as IP phones, this mechanism could inappropriately terminate existing sessions and calls. Thus, while the indication itself does not have to provide separate authentication, SIP requests containing this header are very likely to have higher authentication requirements than those without. These authentication and authorization requirements extend to users within the administrative domain, as later interconnection with other administrative domains may invalidate earlier assumptions on the trustworthiness of users. Below, we describe authentication and authorization aspects, confidentiality and privacy requirements, protection against DoS attacks, and anonymity requirements. Naturally, the general discussion in RFC 3261 (see Section 19.9) applies. All UAs and proxy servers that support this extension must implement SIP over TLS specified in RFC 3546, the sips URI scheme as described in RFC 3261 (see Section 19.12.2), and Digest Authentication (see Section 19.4.5) as described in RFC 3261. In addition, UAs that support this extension should also implement S/MIME (see Section 19.6) as described in RFC 3261 to allow for signing and verification of signatures over requests that use this extension.

19.2.2.13.2 Authentication and Authorization

Prioritized access to network and end-system resources imposes particularly stringent requirements on authentication and authorization mechanisms, since access to prioritized resources may influence overall system stability and performance and not just result in theft of, say, a single phone call. Under certain emergency conditions, the network infrastructure, including its authentication and authorization mechanism, may be under attack. Given the urgency during emergency events, normal statistical fraud detection may be less effective, thus placing a premium on reliable authentication. Common requirements for authentication mechanisms apply, such as resistance to replay, cut-and-paste, and bid-down attacks.

Authentication may be SIP based or use other mechanisms. Use of Digest authentication or S/MIME is recommended for UAS authentication. Digest authentication requires that the parties share a common secret, thus limiting its use across administrative domains. SIP systems employing resource priority should implement S/MIME at least for integrity, as described in RFC 3261 (see Section 19.6).

However, in some environments, receipt of asserted identity specified in RFC 3325 (see Sections 2.8, 10.4, and 20.3) from a trusted entity may be sufficient authorization. Trait-based authorization specified in RFC 4484 (see Section 19.5.1) "entails an assertion by an authorization service of attributes associated with an identity" and may be appropriate for this application. With trait-based authorization, a network element can directly determine, by inspecting the certificate, that a request is authorized to obtain a particular type of service, without having to consult a mapping mechanism that converts user identities to authorizations. Authorization may be based on factors besides the identity of the caller, such as the requested destination. Namespaces may also impose particular authentication or authorization considerations that are stricter than the baseline described here.

19.2.2.13.3 Confidentiality and Integrity

Calls that use elevated resource-priority levels provided by the Resource-Priority header field are likely to be sensitive and often need to be protected from intercept and alteration. In particular, requirements for protecting the confidentiality of communications relationships may be higher than those for normal commercial service. For SIP, the To, From, Organization, and Subject header fields are examples of particularly sensitive information. Systems must implement encryption at the transport level using TLS and may implement other transport-layer or network-layer security mechanisms. UACs should use the sips URI to request a secure transport association to the destination. The Resource-Priority header field can be carried in the SIP message header or can be encapsulated in a message fragment carried in the SIP message body specified in RFC 3420 (see Section 2.8.2). To be considered valid authentication for the purposes of this specification, S/MIME-signed SIP messages or fragments must contain, at a minimum, the Date, To, From, Call-ID, and Resource-Priority header fields. Encapsulation in S/MIME body parts allows the user to protect this header field against inspection or modification by proxies.

However, in many cases, proxies will need to authenticate and authorize the request, so encapsulation would be undesirable. Removal of a Resource-Priority header field or downgrading its priority value affords no additional opportunities to an adversary, since that man in the middle could simply drop or otherwise invalidate the SIP request and thus prevent call completion. Only SIP elements within the same administrative Trust Domain employing a secure channel between their SIP elements will trust a Resource-Priority header field that is not appropriately signed. Others will need to authenticate the request independently. Thus, insertion of a Resource-Priority header field or upgrading the priority value has no further security implications except causing a request to fail (see discussion in the previous paragraph).

19.2.2.13.4 Anonymity

Some users may wish to remain anonymous to the request destination. Anonymity for requests with resource priority is no different from that for any other authenticated SIP request. For the reasons noted earlier, users have to authenticate themselves toward the SIP elements carrying the request where they desire resource-priority treatment. The authentication may be based on capabilities and norms, not necessarily their civil name. Clearly, they may remain anonymous toward the request destination, using the NAI and general privacy mechanism described in RFC 3323 (see Section 20.2).

19.2.2.13.5 DoS Attacks

As noted, systems described here are likely to be subject to deliberate DoS attacks during certain types of emergencies. DoS attacks may be launched on the network itself as well as on its authentication and authorization mechanism. As noted, systems should minimize the amount of state, computation, and network resources that an unauthorized user can command. The system must not amplify attacks by causing the transmission of more than one packet to a network address whose reachability has not been verified.

19.2.2.14 Preemption Events Security

We have described the preemption events in SIP in Section 15.3. Eavesdropping on this header field should not prevent proper operation of the SIP protocol, although some domains utilizing this mechanism for notifying and synchronizing SIP elements will likely want the integrity to be assured. It is therefore recommended that integrity protection be applied when using this header to prevent unwanted changes to the field and snooping of the messages. The accepted choices for providing integrity protection in SIP are TLS (see Section 3.13) and S/MIME (see Section 19.6).

19.2.2.15 Quality-of-Service Security

We have discussed quality-of-service (QOS) signaling mechanisms in SIP using SDP in the message body in Sections 15.4 and 15.5. An attacker may attempt to add, modify, or remove qos-mech-send and qos-mech-recv attributes from a session description. This could result in an application behaving in an undesirable way. For example, the end points under attack may not be able to find a common QOS mechanism to use. Consequently, it is strongly recommended that integrity and authenticity protection be applied to SDP session descriptions carrying these attributes. For session descriptions carried in SIP, S/MIME (see Section 19.6) is the natural choice to provide such end-to-end integrity protection.

19.2.2.16 Call Transfer Security

The call transfer that is explained in detail in Section 16.2 is implemented using the REFER and Replaces call control primitives in SIP. As such, the security considerations detailed in the REFER and Replaces must be followed. The security addresses the issue of protecting the address of record (AOR) URI of a Transfer Target in Sections 16.2.6.2 through 16.2.7. Any REFER request must be appropriately authenticated and authorized using standard SIP mechanisms or else calls may be hijacked. A UA may use local policy or human intervention in deciding whether or not to accept a REFER. In generating NOTIFY responses based on the outcome of the triggered request, care should be taken in constructing the message/sipfrag body to ensure that no private information is leaked. An INVITE containing a Replaces header field should only be accepted if it has been properly authenticated and authorized using standard SIP mechanisms, and the requestor is authorized to perform dialog replacement. Special care is needed if the replaced dialog utilizes additional media streams compared with the original dialog. In this case, the user must authorize the addition of new media streams in a dialog replacement. For example, the same mechanism used to authorize the addition of a media stream in a re-INVITE could be used.

19.2.2.17 Call Referring to Multiple Resources Security

We have described referring calls to multiple resources in Section 16.5. Given that a REFER-Recipient accepting REFER requests with multiple REFER-targets acts as a URI-list service, implementations of this type of server MUST follow the security-related rules that include opt-in lists and mandatory authentication and authorization of clients. Additionally, REFER-Recipients should only accept REFER requests within the context of an application that the REFER-Recipient understands (e.g., a conferencing application). This implies that REFER-Recipients must not accept REFER requests for methods they do not understand. The idea behind these two rules is that REFER-Recipients are not used as dumb servers whose only function is to fan-out random messages they do not understand.

19.2.2.18 Content-Indirection Security

We have articulated the call services with content indirection in SIP in Section 16.6. Any content-indirection mechanism introduces additional security concerns. By its nature, content indirection requires an extra processing step and information transfer. There are a number of potential abuses of a content indirection mechanism:

- Content indirection allows the initiator to choose an alternative protocol with weaker security or known vulnerabilities for the content transfer (e.g., asking the recipient to issue an HTTP request that results in a basic authentication challenge).
- Content indirection allows the initiator to ask the recipient to consume additional resources in the information transfer and content processing, potentially creating an avenue for DoS attacks (e.g., an active File Transfer Protocol Universal Resource Locator [URL] consuming two connections for every indirect-content message).
- Content indirection could be used as a form of port-scanning attack where the indirect-content URL is actually a bogus URL pointing to an internal resource of the recipient. The response to the content indirection request could reveal information about open (and vulnerable) ports on these internal resources.
- A content-indirection URL can disclose sensitive information about the initiator such as an internal user name (as part of an HTTP URL) or possibly geolocation information.

Fortunately, all of these potential threats can be mitigated through careful screening of both the indirect-content URIs that are received and those that are sent. Integrity and confidentiality protection of the indirect-content URI can prevent additional attacks as well. For confidentiality, integrity, and authentication, this content-indirection mechanism relies on the security mechanisms outlined in RFC 3261 (see Section 19.6). In particular, the usage of S/MIME (see Section 19.6) provides the necessary mechanism to ensure integrity, protection, and confidentiality of the indirect-content URI and associated parameters. Securing the transfer of the indirect content is the responsibility of the underlying protocol used for this transfer. If HTTP is used, applications implementing this content-indirection method should support the HTTPS URI scheme for secure transfer of content and must support the upgrading of connections to TLS (see Section 3.13), by using starttls.

Note that a failure to complete HTTPS or starttls (e.g., due to certificate or encryption mismatch) after having accepted the indirect content in the SIP request is not the same as rejecting the SIP request, and it may require additional user–user communication for correction. Note that this document does not advocate the use of transitive trust. That is, just because the UAS receives a URI from a UAC that the UAS trusts, the UAS should not implicitly trust the object referred to by the URI without establishing its own trust relationship with the URI provider. Access control to the content referenced by the URI is not defined by this specification. Access control mechanisms may be defined by the protocol for the scheme of the indirect-content URI. If the UAC knows the content in advance, the UAC should include a hash parameter in the content indirection.

The hash parameter is a hexadecimal-encoded SHA-1 (RFC 3174) hash of the indirect content. If a hash value is included, the recipient MUST check the indirect content against that hash and indicate any mismatch to the user. In addition, if the hash parameter is included and the target URI involves setting up a security context using certificates, the UAS must ignore the results of the certificate validation procedure, and instead verify that the hash of the (canonicalized) content received matches the hash presented in the content-indirection hash parameter. If the hash parameter is not included, the sender should use only schemes that offer message integrity (such as https:). When the hash parameter is not included and security using certificates is used, the UAS must verify any server certificates, by using the UAS's list of trusted top-level certificate authorities. If hashing of indirect content is not used, the content returned to the recipient by exercise of the indirection might have been altered from that intended by the sender.

19.2.2.19 Third-Party Call Control Multiparty Conferencing Security

The multiparty conferencing in SIP using third-party call control (3PCC) mechanisms are provided in Section 18.3. We are describing the security schemes for this in the following sections.

19.2.2.19.1 Authorization and Authentication

In most uses of SIP INVITE, whether or not a call is accepted is based on a decision made by a human when presented information about the call, such as the identity of the caller. In other cases, automata answer the calls, and whether or not they do so may depend on the particular application to which SIP is applied. For example, if a caller makes a SIP call to a voice portal service, the call may be rejected unless the caller has previously signed up (perhaps via a website). In other cases, call handling policies are made based on automated scripts, such as those described by the Call Processing Language (CPL) in RFC 3880. Frequently, those decisions are also made on the basis of the identity of the caller. These authorization mechanisms would be applied to normal first-party calls and third-party calls, as these two are indistinguishable. As a result, it is important for these authorization policies to continue to operate correctly for third-party calls. Of course, third-party calls introduce a new party—the one initiating the third-party call. Do the authorizations policies apply based on the identity of that third party, or do they apply based on the participants in the call? Ideally, the participants would be able to know the identities of both other parties, and have authorization policies be based on those, as appropriate. However, this is not possible using existing mechanisms.

As a result, the next best thing is for the INVITE requests to contain the identity of the third party. Ultimately, this is the user who is requesting communication, and it makes sense for call authorization policies to be based on that identity. This requires, in turn, that the controller authenticate itself as that third party. This can be challenging, and the appropriate mechanism depends on the specific application scenario. In one common scenario, the controller is acting on behalf of one of the participants in the call. A typical example is click-to-dial, where the controller and the customer service representative are run by the same administrative domain. Indeed, for the purposes of identification, the controller can legitimately claim to be the customer service representative. In this scenario, it would be appropriate for the INVITE to the end user to contain a From field identifying the customer service representative, and authenticate the request using S/MIME (see Section 19.6) signed by the key of the customer service representative (which is held by the controller). This requires the controller to actually have credentials with which it can authenticate itself as the customer support representative.

In many other cases, the controller is representing one of the participants, but does not possess their credentials. Unfortunately, there are currently no standardized mechanisms that allow a user to delegate credentials to the controller in a way that limits their usage to specific 3PCC operations. In the absence of such a mechanism, the best that can be done is to use the display name in the From field to indicate the identity of the user on whose behalf the call is being made. It is recommended that the display name be set to "[controller] on behalf of [user]," where user and controller are textual identities of the user and controller, respectively. In this case, the URI in the From field would identify the controller. In other situations, there is no real relationship between the controller and the participants in the call. In these situations, ideally the controller would have a means to assert that the call is from a particular identity (which could be one of the participants, or even a third party, depending on the application), and to validate that assertion with a signature using the key of the controller. The security features described in RFCs 4474 (see Section 19.4.8) and 4916 (see Section 20.4) can be used for authenticated identity management and connected identity in 3PCC scenarios, respectively.

19.2.2.19.2 End-to-End Encryption and Integrity

With 3PCC, the controller is actually one of the participants as far as the SIP dialog is concerned. Therefore, encryption and integrity of the SIP messages, as provided by S/MIME, will occur between participants and the controller, rather than directly between participants. However, integrity, authenticity, and confidentiality of the media sessions can be provided through a controller. End-to-end media security is based on the exchange of keying material within SDP described in RFC 4568 (see Sections 7.7.3 and 7.7.4).

The proper operation of these mechanisms with 3PCC depends on the controller behaving properly. So long as it is not attempting to explicitly disable these mechanisms, the protocols will properly operate between the participants, resulting in a secure media session that even the controller cannot eavesdrop or modify. Since 3PCC is based on a model of trust between the users and the controller, it is reasonable to assume it is operating in a well-behaved manner. However, there is no cryptographic means that can prevent the controller from interfering with the initial exchanges of keying materials. As a result, it is trivially possible for the controller to insert itself as an intermediary on the media exchange, if it should so desire.

19.2.2.20 Third-Party Encoding Services Security

RFC 3725 (see Sections 18.3 and 19.2.2.15) discusses security considerations that relate to the use of 3PCC in SIP. These considerations apply to this document, since it describes how to use 3PCC to invoke transcoding services. In particular, RFC 3725 states that end-to-end media security is based on the exchange of keying material within SDP and depends on the controller behaving properly. That is, the controller should not try to disable the security mechanisms offered by the other parties. As a result, it is trivially possible for the controller to insert itself as an intermediary on the media exchange, if it should so desire. In third-party encoding services described in Section 18.3, the controller is the UA invoking the transcoder, and there is a media session established using 3PCC between the remote UA and the transcoder.

Consequently, the attack described in RFC 3725 (see Section 19.2.2.1) does not constitute a threat because the controller is the UA invoking the transcoding service and it has access to the media anyway by definition. Thus, it seems unlikely that a UA would attempt to launch an attack against its own session by disabling security between the transcoder and the remote UA. Regarding end-to-end media security from the UAs' point of view, the transcoder needs access to the media in order to perform its function. Therefore, by definition, the transcoder behaves as a man in the middle. UAs that do not want a particular transcoder to have access to all the media exchanged between them can use a different transcoder for each direction. In addition, UAs can use different transcoders for different media types.

19.2.2.21 Conferencing Bridging Transcoding Services Security

Transcoders implementing conferencing bridging mode call services described in Sections 16.7 and 16.7.3 behave as a URI-list service. Therefore, the security considerations for URI-list services discussed in RFC 5363 (see Section 19.7) apply here as well. In particular, the requirements related to list integrity and unsolicited requests are important for transcoding services. UAs should integrity-protect URI-lists using mechanisms such as S/MIME (RFC 3850, see Section 19.6) or TLS (RFC 5246, see Section 3.13), which can also provide URI-list confidentiality if needed. Additionally, transcoders must authenticate and authorize users and may provide information about the identity of the original sender of the request in their outgoing requests by using the SIP Identity mechanism (RFC 4474, see Sections 2.8 and 19.4.8).

The requirement in RFC 5363 (see Section 19.7) to use opt-in lists deserves special discussion. The type of URI-list service implemented by transcoders following this specification does not produce amplification (only one INVITE request is generated by the transcoder on receiving an INVITE request from a UA) and does not involve a translation to a URI that may be otherwise unknown to the caller (the caller places the callee's URI in the body of its initial INVITE request). Additionally, the identity of the caller is present in the INVITE request generated by the transcoder. Therefore, there is no requirement for transcoders implementing this specification to use opt-in lists.

19.2.2.22 INFO Method Security

We have described the INFO method of SIP in Section 16.8. By eliminating multiple usages of INFO messages without adequate community review, and by eliminating the possibility of rogue SIP UAs confusing another UA by purposely sending unrelated INFO requests, we expect this document's clarification of the use of INFO to improve the security of the Internet. While rogue UAs can still send unrelated INFO requests, this mechanism enables the UAS and other security devices to associate INFO requests with Info Packages that have been negotiated for a session. If the content of the Info Package payload is private, UAs will need to use end-to-end encryption, such as S/MIME (see Section 19.6), to prevent access to the content. This is particularly important, as transport of INFO is likely not to be end-to-end, but through SIP proxies and back-to-back UAs (B2BUAs), which the user may not trust.

The INFO request transports application-level information. One implication of this is that INFO messages may require a higher level of protection than the underlying SIP dialog signaling. In particular, if one does not protect the SIP signaling from eavesdropping or authentication and repudiation attacks, for example, by using TLS (see Section 3.13) transport, then the INFO request and its contents will be vulnerable as well. Even with SIP/TLS, any SIP hop along the path from UAC to UAS can view, modify, or intercept INFO requests, as they can with any SIP request. This means some applications may require end-to-end encryption of the INFO payload, beyond, for example, hop-by-hop protection of the SIP signaling itself. Since the application dictates the level of security required, individual Info Packages have to enumerate these requirements. In any event, the Info Package mechanism described by this document provides the tools for such secure, end-to-end transport of application data. One interesting property of Info Package usage is that one can reuse the same digest-challenge mechanism used for INVITE-based authentication for the INFO request. For example, one could use a quality-of-protection (qop) value of authentication with integrity (auth-int), to challenge the request and its body, and prevent intermediate devices from modifying the body. However, this assumes the device that knows the credentials in order to perform the INVITE challenge is still in the path for the INFO request, or that the far-end UAS knows such credentials.

19.2.2.23 User-to-User Information Security

The user-to-user information (UUI) transfer service is discussed in Section 16.9. UUI data can potentially carry sensitive information that might require confidentiality protection for privacy or integrity protection from third parties that may wish to read or modify the UUI data. The three security models described in RFC 6567 (see Section 16.9) may be applicable for the UUI mechanism. One model treats the SIP layer as untrusted and requires end-to-end integrity protection or encryption. This model can be achieved by providing these security services at a layer above SIP. In this case, applications are encouraged to use their own integrity or encryption mechanisms before passing it to the SIP layer.

The second approach is for the application to pass the UUI without any protection to the SIP layer and require the SIP layer to provide this security. This approach is possible in theory, although its practical use would be extremely limited. To preserve multihop or end-to-end confidentiality and integrity of UUI data, approaches using S/MIME (see Section 19.6) or IPsec can be used. However, the lack of deployment of these mechanisms means that applications cannot in general rely on them being present. The third model utilizes a Trust Domain and relies on perimeter security at the SIP layer. This is the security model of the PSTN and ISDN where UUI is commonly used today. This approach uses hop-by-hop security mechanisms and relies on border elements for filtering and application of policy. Standard deployed SIP security mechanisms such as TLS transport offer privacy and integrity protection properties on a hop-by-hop basis at the SIP layer.

If the UUI data was included by the UA originator of the SIP request or response, normal SIP mechanisms can be used to determine the identity of the inserter of the UUI data. If the UUI data was included by a UA that was not the originator of the request, a History-Info header field can be used to determine the identity of the inserter of the UUI data. UAs can apply policy based on the origin of the UUI data using this information. In short, the UUI data included in an INVITE can be trusted as much as the INVITE itself. Note that it is possible that this mechanism could be used as a covert communication channel between UAs, conveying information unknown to the SIP network.

19.2.2.24 VoiceXML Media Server Security

We have described SIP interfaces to VoiceXML media server in Section 17.2. Exposing a VoiceXML media service with a well-known address may enhance the possibility of exploitation (e.g., an invoked network service may trigger a billing event). The VoiceXML media server is recommended to use standard SIP mechanisms of RFC 3261 to authenticate (see Section 19.4) requesting end points and authorize per local policy. Some applications may choose to transfer confidential information to or from the VoiceXML media server. To provide data confidentiality, the VoiceXML media server must implement the sips: and https: schemes in addition to S/MIME message-body encoding as described in RFC 3261 (see Section 19.6). The VoiceXML media server must support SRTP (see Section 7.3) to provide confidentiality, authentication, and replay protection for RTP media streams (including RTCP control traffic). To mitigate the possibility of DoS attacks, the VoiceXML media server is recommended (in addition to authenticating and authorizing end points described in Section 17.2) to provide mechanisms for implementing local policies such as the time limiting of VoiceXML application execution.

19.2.2.25 Security for Multiple Telephone AOR Registration

RFC 6140 (see Section 3.3.5), which describes the multiple telephone AOR registration, takes the unprecedented step of extending the previously defined REGISTER method to apply to more than one AOR. In general, this kind of change has the potential to cause problems at intermediaries, such as proxies, that are party to the REGISTER transaction. In particular, such intermediaries may attempt to apply policy to the user indicated in the To header field (i.e., the SIP–PBX's identity), without any knowledge of the multiple AORs that are being implicitly registered. The mechanism defined by this document solves this issue by adding an option tag to a Proxy-Require header field in such REGISTER requests. Proxies that are unaware of this mechanism will not process the requests, preventing them from misapplying policy. Proxies that process requests with this option tag are clearly aware of the nature of the REGISTER request and can make reasonable policy decisions. As noted in RFC 6140 (see Section 3.3.5), intermediaries need to take care if they use a policy token in the path and service route mechanisms, as doing so will cause them to apply the same policy to all users serviced by the same SIP Private Branch Exchange (SIP–PBX). This may frequently be the correct behavior, but circumstances can arise in which differentiation of user policy is required.

RFC 6140 (see Section 3.3.5) also notes that these techniques use a token or cookie in the Path or Service-Route header values, and that this value will be shared among all AORs associated with a single registration. Because this information will be visible to UAs under certain conditions, proxy designers using this mechanism in conjunction with the techniques described in this document need to take care that doing so does not leak sensitive information. One of the key properties of the outbound client connection mechanism discussed in RFC 6140 (see Section 3.3.5) is the assurance that a single connection is associated with a single user and cannot be hijacked by other users. With the mechanism defined in this document, such connections necessarily become shared between users. However, the only entity in a position to hijack calls as a consequence is the SIP–PBX itself. Because the SIP–PBX acts as a registrar for all the potentially affected users, it already has the ability to redirect any such communications as it sees fit. In other words, the SIP–PBX must be trusted to handle calls in an appropriate fashion, and the use of the outbound connection mechanism introduces no additional vulnerabilities.

The ability to learn the identity and registration state of every user on the PBX (RFC 6140, see Section 3.3.5) is invaluable for diagnostic and administrative purposes. For example, this allows the SIP–PBX to determine whether all its extensions are properly registered with the SSP. However, this information can also be highly sensitive, as many organizations may not wish to make their entire list of phone numbers available to external entities. Consequently, SSP servers are advised to use explicit (i.e., whitelist) and configurable policies regarding who can access this information, with very conservative defaults (e.g., an empty access list or an access list consisting only of the PBX itself). The procedure for the generation of temporary Globally Routable UA URIs (GRUUs) requires the use of a Hashed Message Authentication Code (HMAC) to detect any tampering that external entities may attempt to perform on the contents of a temporary GRUU. The mention of HMACSHA256-80 in RFC 6140 (see Section 3.3.5) is intended solely as an example of a suitable HMAC algorithm. Since all HMACs used in this document are generated and consumed by the same entity, the choice of an actual HMAC algorithm is entirely up to an implementation, provided that the cryptographic properties are sufficient to prevent third parties from spoofing GRUU-related information. The procedure for the generation of temporary GRUUs also requires the use of RSA keys. The selection of the proper key length for such keys requires careful analysis, taking into consideration the current and foreseeable speed of processing for the period of time during which GRUUs must remain anonymous, as well as emerging cryptographic analysis methods.

The most recent guidance from RSA Laboratories [1] suggests a key length of 2048 bits for data that needs protection through the year 2030, and a length of 3072 bits thereafter. Similarly, implementers are warned to take precautionary measures to prevent unauthorized disclosure of the private key used in GRUU generation. Any such disclosure would result in the ability to correlate temporary GRUUs to each other and, potentially, to their associated PBXs. Furthermore, the use of RSA decryption when processing GRUUs received from arbitrary parties can be exploited by DoS attackers to amplify the impact of an attack: because of the presence of a cryptographic operation in the processing of such messages, the CPU load may be marginally higher when the attacker uses (valid or invalid) temporary GRUUs in the messages employed by such an attack. Normal DoS mitigation techniques, such as rate-limiting processing of received messages, should help reduce the impact of this issue as well. Finally, good security practices should be followed regarding the duration an RSA key is used. For implementers, this means that systems must include an easy way to update the public key provided to the SIP–PBX. To avoid immediately invalidating all currently issued temporary GRUUs, the SSP servers should keep the retired RSA key around for a grace period before discarding it. If decryption fails based on the new RSA key, then the SSP server can attempt to use the retired key instead. By contrast, the SIP–PBXs must discard the retired public key immediately and exclusively use the new public key.

19.2.3 Media-Level Security

The SIP media-level security is a huge area that needs a complete separate discussion all by itself. We have also briefly discussed SRTP and ZRTP that deals with the real-time audio-video media streams in Sections 7.3 and 7.4, respectively. We have also described the TLS and DTLS that provides security at the transport layer (see Sections 3.1.2.1, 4.2.3, 19.1, 19.4.6, 19.4.11, 19.10, and 19.12.4.3). It is believed that non-real-time data applications that, unlike real-time audio-video media, do not need synchronization will be protected by TLS and DTLS appropriately. However, we are providing the SDP security features that allow negotiating the cryptographic mechanisms to be used for media security during the SIP session establishment time.

19.2.3.1 SDP Media Security Description

The SDP security attribute descriptions defined in RFCs 4568, 5029, and 5939 enable the conferencing parties in two-party unicast communication to exchange security parameters and keys that can be used to set up SRTP (RFC 3171, see Section 7.3) and ZRTP (RFC 6191, Section 7.4) cryptographic contexts. A new media-level SDP attribute called *crypto* describes the cryptographic suite, key parameters, and session parameters for the preceding unicast media line. The crypto attribute must only appear at the SDP media level (not at the session level). The crypto attributes, known as the SDP security description (SDES) specified in RFC 4568 (see Sections 7.7.3 and 7.7.4), that are used for media encryption are expressed with the following structure:

```
a=crypto:<tag> <crypto-suite> <key-params>
[<session-params>]
```

The fields tag, crypto-suite, key-params, and session-params are described as follows:

- **Tag:** The `<tag>` is unique among all crypto attributes for a given media line in SDP. It is used with the SDP offer–answer model specified in RFC 3264 (see Section 3.8.4) and determine which of several offered crypto attributes were chosen by the answerer. In the offer–answer model, the tag is a negotiated parameter.
- **Crypto-Suite:** The `<crypto-suite>` field is an identifier that describes the encryption and authentication algorithms (e.g., AES_CM_128_HMAC_SHA1_80) for the transport in question. The possible values for the crypto-suite parameter are defined within the context of the transport, that is, each transport defines a separate namespace for the set of crypto-suites. For example, the crypto-suite AES_CM_128_HMAC_SHA1_80 defined within the context RTP/SAVP transport applies to secure RTP only; the string may be reused for another transport (e.g., RTP/SAVPF, but a separate definition would be needed. In the SDP offer–answer model, the crypto-suite is a negotiated parameter.
- **Key parameters:** The `<key-params>` field provides one or more sets of keying material for the crypto-suite in question. The field consists of a method indicator followed by a colon, and the actual keying information as shown below:

  ```
  key-params=<key-method> ":" <key-info>
  ```

  Keying material might be provided by different means from that for key-params; however, the detail discussion of SDP keying parameters is beyond the scope of this Book. Only one method is defined in this document, namely, *inline*, which indicates that the actual keying material is provided in the key-info field itself.

  There is a single namespace for the key method, that is, the key method is transport independent. New key methods (e.g., use of a URL) may be defined in a Standards Track RFC in the future. Although the key method itself may be generic, the accompanying key-info definition is specific not only to the key method but also to the transport in question. Key-info encodes keying material for a crypto-suite, which defines that keying material. New key methods must be registered with the IANA.

  `<Key-info>` is defined as a general octet string; further transport and key method-specific syntax and semantics must be provided in a Standards Track RFC for each combination of transport and key method that uses it. Note that such definitions are provided within the context of both a particular transport (e.g., RTP/SAVP) and a specific key method (e.g., inline). The Internet Assigned Numbers Authority (IANA) will register the list of supported key methods for each transport.

  When multiple keys are included in the key parameters, it must be possible to determine which of the keys is being used in a given media packet by a simple inspection of the media packet received; a trial-and-error approach between the possible keys must not be performed. For SRTP, this could be achieved by use of Master Key Identifiers (RFC 3711, see Section 7.3). Use of `<From, To>` values are not supported in SRTP security descriptions. In the SDP offer–answer model, the key parameter is a declarative parameter.
- **Session parameters:** Session parameters are specific to a given transport and their use is optional in the security descriptions framework, where they are just defined as general character strings. If session parameters are to be used for a given transport, then transport-specific syntax and semantics must be provided in a Standards Track RFC.

  In the SDP offer–answer model, session parameters may be either negotiated or declarative; the definition of specific session parameters must indicate whether they are negotiated or declarative. Negotiated parameters apply to data sent in both directions, whereas declarative parameters apply only to media sent by the entity that generated the SDP. Thus, a declarative parameter in an offer applies to media sent by the offerer, whereas a declarative parameter in an answer applies to media sent by the answerer.

Multimedia streams such as audio and video are carried via RTP that does not offer media security. However, SRTP (see Section 7.3) and ZRTP (see Section 7.4) are designed extending RTP for offering media security. However, media security needs cryptographic suite and parameters that are required to be agreed upon between the conferencing parties through negotiations. The SIP session is established and the media that need to be sent is negotiated using INVITE and SDP offer–answer model. The cryptographic algorithms and parameters that will be used for encryption of each medium are negotiated during the session using the SDES parameters of SDP described above for using SRTP or ZRTP.

Once the security parameters are agreed upon during negotiations using the SDP offer–answer model, then the SRTP or ZRTP cryptographic algorithms are used for media encryption. The encrypted media payloads are then sent on an end-to-end basis between the end points. The huge descriptions are provided in SRTP and ZRTP protocol specifications for providing media security for audio, video, and data applications. The detailed description of media security provided by these two protocols is beyond the scope of this chapter and needs to be addressed separately.

19.2.3.2 SDP Media Streams Security Preconditions

19.2.3.2.1 Overview

The concept of an SDP specified in RFC 4566 (see Section 7.7) precondition is defined in RFC 3312 (see Section 15.4) as updated by RFC 4032. A precondition is a condition that has to be satisfied for a given media stream in order for session establishment or modification to proceed. When a (mandatory) precondition is not met, session progress is delayed until the precondition is satisfied or the session establishment fails. For example, RFC 3312 defines the QOS precondition, which is used to ensure availability of network resources before establishing (i.e., alerting) a call. Media streams can either be provided in clear text and with no integrity protection, or some kind of media security can be applied, for example, confidentiality or message integrity. For example, the audio/video profile of RTP (see Section 7.2) is normally used without any security services, whereas SRTP (see Section 7.3) is always used with security services.

When media stream security is being negotiated, for example, using the mechanism defined in SDP security descriptions, both the offerer and the answerer (RFC 3264, see Section 3.8.4) need to know the cryptographic parameters being used for the media stream; the offerer may provide multiple choices for the cryptographic parameters, or the cryptographic parameters selected by the answerer may differ from those of the offerer (e.g., the key used in one direction versus the other). In such cases, to avoid media clipping, the offerer needs to receive the answer before receiving any media packets from the answerer. This can be achieved by using a security precondition that ensures the successful negotiation of media stream security parameters for a secure media stream before session establishment or modification. A security precondition defined in RFC 5027 that is described here can be used to delay session establishment or modification until media stream security for a secure media stream has been negotiated successfully.

19.2.3.2.2 Security Precondition Definition

The semantics for a security precondition defined in RFC 5027 are that the relevant cryptographic parameters (cipher, key, etc.) for a secure media stream are known to have been negotiated in the direction(s) required. If the security precondition is used with a nonsecure media stream, the security precondition is, by definition, satisfied. A secure media stream is here defined as a media stream that uses some kind of security service (e.g., message integrity, confidentiality, or both), regardless of the cryptographic strength of the mechanisms being used.

- As an extreme example of this, secure RTP using the NULL encryption algorithm and no message integrity would be considered a secure media stream, whereas use of plain RTP would not. Note, however, that SRTP (RFC 3711) discourages the use of SRTP without message integrity.
- Security preconditions do not guarantee that an established media stream will be secure. They merely guarantee that the recipient of the media stream packets will be able to perform any relevant decryption and integrity checking on those media stream packets. Please refer to Sections 19.2.3.2.3 through 19.2.3.2.5 for further security considerations.

The security precondition type is defined by the string *sec*, and hence we modify the grammar found in RFC 3312 (see Section 15.4) as follows:

```
precondition-type   =     "sec"/"qos"/token
```

RFC 3312 (see Section 15.4) defines support for two kinds of status types, namely segmented and end-to-end. The security precondition type defined here must be used with the end-to-end status type; use of the segmented status type is undefined. A security precondition can use the strength tag *mandatory*, *optional*, or *none*. When a security precondition with a strength tag of mandatory is received in an offer, session establishment or modification must be delayed until the security precondition has been met, that is, the relevant cryptographic parameters (cipher, key, etc.) for a secure media stream are known to have been negotiated in the direction(s) required. When a mandatory security precondition is offered, and the answerer cannot satisfy the security precondition (e.g., because the offer was for a secure media stream, but it did not include the necessary parameters to establish the secure media stream keying material for example), the offered media stream must be rejected as described in RFC 3312. The delay of session establishment defined here implies that alerting of the called party must not occur and media for which security is being negotiated MUST NOT be exchanged until the precondition has been satisfied. In cases where secure media and other nonmedia data is multiplexed on a media stream, for example, when Interactive Connectivity Establishment (ICE) (RFC 5245, see Section 14.3) is being used, the nonmedia data is allowed to be exchanged before the security precondition is satisfied.

When a security precondition with a strength tag of optional is received in an offer, the answerer must generate its answer SDP as soon as possible. Since session progress is not delayed in this case, the answerer does not know when the offerer is able to process secure media stream packets, and hence clipping may occur. If the answerer wants to avoid clipping and delay session progress until he knows the offerer has received the answer, the answerer must increase the strength of the security precondition by using a strength tag of mandatory in the answer. Note that use of a mandatory precondition in an offer requires the presence of a SIP Require header field containing the option tag *precondition*: any SIP UA that does not support a mandatory precondition will consequently reject such requests that also has unintended ramifications for SIP forking described in RFC 5393 (see Section 19.9). To get around this, an optional security precondition and the SIP Supported header field containing the option tag precondition can be used instead.

When a security precondition with a strength tag of none is received, processing continues as usual. The none strength tag merely indicates that the offerer supports the following security precondition—the answerer may upgrade the strength tag in the answer as described in RFC 3312. The direction tags defined in RFC 3312 (see Section 15.4) are interpreted as follows:

- **send:** Media stream security negotiation is at a stage where it is possible to send media packets to the other party, and the other party will be able to process them correctly from a security point of view, that is, decrypt or integrity check them as necessary. The definition of *media packets* includes all packets that make up the media stream. In the case of secure RTP for example, it includes SRTP as well as SRTCP. When media and nonmedia packets are multiplexed on a given media stream (e.g., when ICE is being used), the requirement applies to the media packets only.
- **recv:** Media stream security negotiation is at a stage where it is possible to receive and correctly process media stream packets sent by the other party from a security point of view.

The precise criteria for determining when the other party is able to correctly process media stream packets from a security point of view depend on the secure media stream protocol being used as well as the mechanism by which the required cryptographic parameters are negotiated.

We here provide details for SRTP negotiated through SDP security descriptions as defined in RFC 4568:

- When the offerer requests the *send* security precondition, it needs to receive the answer before the security precondition is satisfied. The reason for this is twofold. First, the offerer needs to know where to send the media. Secondly, in the case where alternative cryptographic parameters are offered, the offerer needs to know which set was selected. The answerer does not know when the answer is actually received by the offerer (which, in turn, will satisfy the precondition), and hence the answerer needs to use the confirm-status attribute (RFC 3312, see Section 15.4). This will make the offerer generate a new offer showing the updated status of the precondition.
- When the offerer requests the *recv* security precondition, it also needs to receive the answer before the security precondition is satisfied. The reason for this is straightforward: the answer contains the cryptographic parameters that will be used by the answerer for sending media to the offerer; before receipt of these cryptographic parameters, the offerer is unable to authenticate or decrypt such media.

When security preconditions are used with the Key Management Extensions for the SDP (RFC 4567), the details depend on the actual key management protocol being used. After an initial offer–answer exchange in which the security precondition is requested, any subsequent offer–answer sequence for the purpose of updating the status of the precondition for a secure media stream should use the same key material as the initial offer–answer exchange. This means that the key-mgmt attribute lines (RFC 4567), or crypto attribute lines (RFC 4568) in SDP offers, that are sent in response to SDP answers containing a confirm-status field (RFC 3312, see Section 15.4) should repeat the same data as that sent in the previous SDP offer. If applicable to the key management protocol or SDP security description, the SDP answers to these SDP offers should repeat the same data in the key-mgmt attribute lines (RFC 4568) or crypto attribute lines (RFC 4567) as that sent in the previous SDP answer.

Of course, this duplication of key exchange during precondition establishment is not to be interpreted as a replay attack. This issue may be solved if, for example, the SDP implementation recognizes that the key management protocol data is identical in the second offer–answer exchange and avoids forwarding the information to the security layer for further processing. Offers with security preconditions in re-INVITEs or UPDATEs follow the rules given in RFC 3312 (see Section 15.4), that is, "Both UAs should continue using the old session parameters until all the mandatory preconditions are met. At that moment, the UAs can begin using the new session parameters." At that moment, we furthermore require that UAs must start using the new session parameters for media packets being sent. The UAs should be prepared to process media packets received with either the old or the new session parameters for a short period of time to accommodate media packets in transit. Note that this may involve iterative security processing of the received media packets during that period of time. RFC 3264 (see Section 3.8.4) lists several techniques to help alleviate the problem of determining when a received media packet was generated according to the old or new offer–answer exchange.

19.2.3.2.3 SDP Security Description Examples

The call flow of Figure 19.2 shows a basic session establishment using the SIP and SDP security descriptions (RFC 4568) with security descriptions for the secure media stream (SRTP in this case).

The SDP descriptions of this example are shown below—we have omitted the details of the SDP security descriptions as well as any SIP details for clarity of the security precondition described here:

SDP 1: A includes a mandatory end-to-end security precondition for both the send and receive direction in the initial offer as well as a *crypto* attribute RFC 4568 (see Sections 7.7.3 and 7.7.4), which includes keying material that can be used by A to generate media packets. Since B does not know any of the security parameters yet, the current status (see RFC 3312, see Section 15.4) is set to none. A's local status table (see RFC 3312) for the security precondition is as follows:

Direction	*Current*	*Desired Strength*	*Confirm*
send	no	mandatory	no
recv	no	mandatory	no

and the resulting offer SDP is
m=audio 20000 RTP/SAVP 0
c=IN IP4 192.0.2.1
a=curr:sec e2e none
a=des:sec mandatory e2e sendrecv
a=crypto:foo...

SDP 2: When B receives the offer and generates an answer, B knows the (send and recv) security parameters of both A and B. From a security perspective, B is now able to receive media from A, so B's recv security precondition is *yes*. However, A does not know any of B's SDP information, so B's send security precondition is *no*. B's local status table therefore looks as follows:

Direction	*Current*	*Desired Strength*	*Confirm*
send	no	mandatory	no
recv	yes	mandatory	no

B requests A to confirm when A knows the security parameters used in the send and receive direction (it

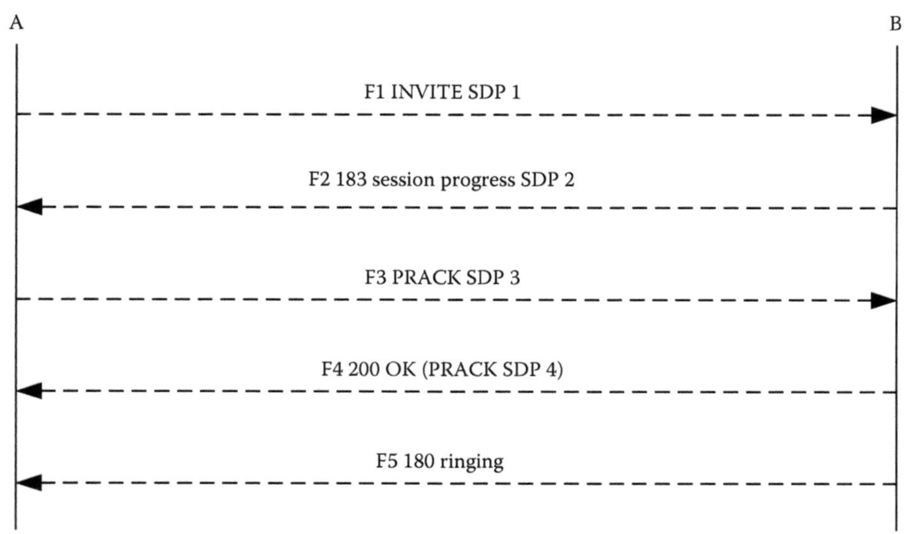

Figure 19.2 Security preconditions with SDP security description example. (Copyright IETF. Reproduced with permission.)

would suffice for B to ask for confirmation of A's send direction only) and hence the resulting answer SDP becomes

m=audio 30000 RTP/SAVP 0
c=IN IP4 192.0.2.4
a=curr:sec e2e recv
a=des:sec mandatory e2e sendrecv
a=conf:sec e2e sendrecv
a=crypto:bar...

SDP 3: When A receives the answer, A updates its local status table based on the rules in RFC 3312 (see Section 15.4). A knows the security parameters of both the send and receive direction and hence A's local status table is updated as follows:

Direction	*Current*	*Desired Strength*	*Confirm*
send	yes	mandatory	yes
recv	yes	mandatory	yes

Since B requested confirmation of the send and recv security preconditions, and both are now satisfied, A immediately sends an updated offer (F3) to B showing that the security preconditions are satisfied:

m=audio 20000 RTP/SAVP 0
c=IN IP4 192.0.2.1
a=curr:sec e2e sendrecv
a=des:sec mandatory e2e sendrecv
a=crypto:foo...

Note that we here use PRACK (RFC 3262, see Sections 2.5, 2.8.2, and 2.10) instead of UPDATE (RFC 3311, see Section 3.8.3) since the precondition is satisfied immediately, and the original offer–answer exchange is complete.

SDP 4: Upon receiving the updated offer, B updates its local status table based on the rules in RFC 3312 (see Section 15.4), which yields the following:

Direction	*Current*	*Desired Strength*	*Confirm*
send	yes	mandatory	no
recv	yes	mandatory	no

B responds with an answer (F4) that contains the current status of the security precondition (i.e., sendrecv) from B's point of view:

m=audio 30000 RTP/SAVP 0
c=IN IP4 192.0.2.4
a=curr:sec e2e sendrecv
a=des:sec mandatory e2e sendrecv
a=crypto:bar...

B's local status table indicates that all mandatory preconditions have been satisfied, and hence session establishment resumes; B returns a 180 Ringing response (F5) to indicate alerting.

19.2.3.2.4 Key Management Extension for SDP Example

The call flow of Figure 19.3 shows a basic session establishment using the SIP and Key Management Extensions for SDP (RFC 4567) with security descriptions for the secure media stream (SRTP in this case).

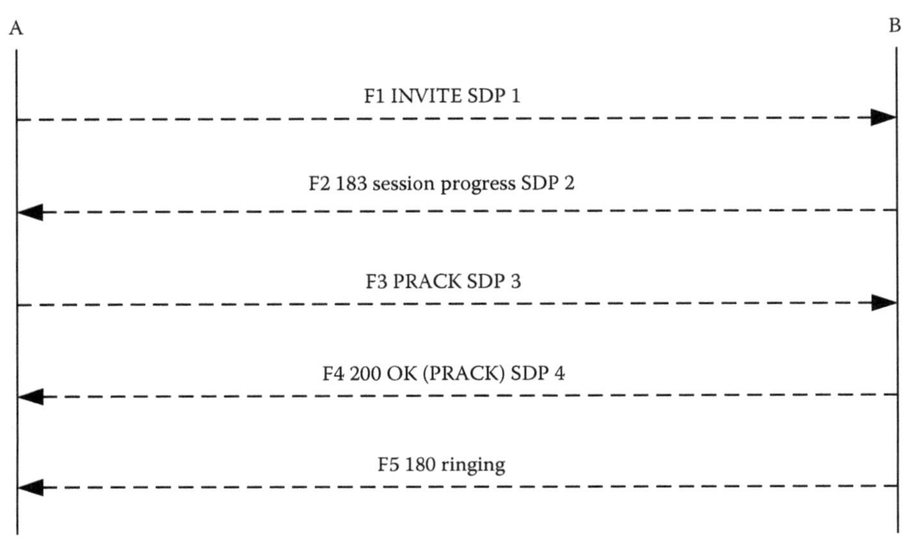

Figure 19.3 Security preconditions with key management extensions for SDP example. (Copyright IETF. Reproduced with permission.)

The SDP descriptions of this example are shown below—we show an example use of Multimedia Internet KEYing (MIKEY) (RFC 3830) with the Key Management Extensions; however, we have omitted the details of the MIKEY parameters as well as any SIP details for clarity of the security precondition described here:

SDP1: A includes a mandatory end-to-end security precondition for both the send and receive direction in the initial offer as well as a key-mgmt attribute (RFC 4567), which includes keying material that can be used by A to generate media packets. Since B does not know any of the security parameters yet, the current status (see RFC 3312, see Section 15.4) is set to none. A's local status table (see RFC 3312) for the security precondition is as follows:

Direction	*Current*	*Desired Strength*	*Confirm*
send	no	mandatory	no
recv	no	mandatory	no

and the resulting offer SDP is
m=audio 20000 RTP/SAVP 0
c=IN IP4 192.0.2.1
a=curr:sec e2e none
a=des:sec mandatory e2e sendrecv
a=key-mgmt:mikey AQAFgM0X...

SDP 2: When B receives the offer and generates an answer, B knows the (send and recv) security parameters of both A and B. B generates keying material for sending media to A; however, A does not know B's keying material, so the current status of B's send security precondition is *no*. B does know A's SDP information, so B's recv security precondition is *yes*. B's local status table therefore looks as follows:

Direction	*Current*	*Desired Strength*	*Confirm*
send	no	mandatory	no
recv	yes	mandatory	no

B requests A to confirm when A knows the security parameters used in the send and receive direction and hence the resulting answer SDP becomes
m=audio 30000 RTP/SAVP 0
c=IN IP4 192.0.2.4
a=curr:sec e2e recv
a=des:sec mandatory e2e sendrecv
a=conf:sec e2e sendrecv
a=key-mgmt:mikey AQAFgM0X...

Note that the actual MIKEY data in the answer differs from that in the offer; however, we have only shown the initial and common part of the MIKEY value above.

SDP 3: When A receives the answer, A updates its local status table based on the rules in RFC 3312 (see Section 15.4). A now knows all the security parameters of both the send and receive direction and hence A's local status table is updated as follows:

Direction	*Current*	*Desired Strength*	*Confirm*
send	yes	mandatory	yes
recv	yes	mandatory	yes

Since B requested confirmation of the send and recv security preconditions, and both are now satisfied, A immediately sends an updated offer (F3) to B showing that the security preconditions are satisfied:
m=audio 20000 RTP/SAVP 0
c=IN IP4 192.0.2.1
a=curr:sec e2e sendrecv
a=des:sec mandatory e2e sendrecv
a=key-mgmt:mikey AQAFgM0X...

SDP 4: Upon receiving the updated offer, B updates its local status table based on the rules in RFC 3312, which yields the following:

Direction	*Current*	*Desired Strength*	*Confirm*
send	yes	mandatory	no
recv	yes	mandatory	no

B responds with an answer (F4) that contains the current status of the security precondition (i.e., sendrecv) from B's point of view:
m=audio 30000 RTP/SAVP 0
c=IN IP4 192.0.2.4
a=curr:sec e2e sendrecv
a=des:sec mandatory e2e sendrecv
a=key-mgmt:mikey AQAFgM0X...

B's local status table indicates that all mandatory preconditions have been satisfied, and hence session establishment resumes; B returns a 180 Ringing response (F5) to indicate alerting.

19.2.3.2.5 Security Considerations

In addition to the general security considerations for preconditions provided in RFC 3312 (see Section 15.4), the following security issues should be considered. Security preconditions delay session establishment until cryptographic parameters required to send or receive media for a media stream have been negotiated. Negotiation of such parameters can fail for a variety of reasons, including policy preventing use of certain cryptographic algorithms, keys, and other security parameters. If an attacker can remove security preconditions or downgrade the strength tag from an offer–answer exchange, the attacker can thereby cause user alerting for a session that may have no functioning media. This is likely to cause inconvenience to both the offerer and the answerer.

Similarly, security preconditions can be used to prevent clipping due to race conditions between offer–answer exchanges and secure media stream packets based on that offer–answer exchange. If an attacker can remove or downgrade the strength tag of security preconditions from an offer–answer exchange, the attacker can cause clipping to occur in the associated secure media stream. Conversely, an attacker might add security preconditions to offers that do not contain them or increase their strength tag. This, in turn, may lead to session failure (e.g., if the answerer does not support it), heterogeneous error response forking problems, or a delay in session establishment that was not desired. Use of signaling integrity mechanisms can prevent all of the above problems. Where intermediaries on the signaling path (e.g., SIP proxies) are trusted, it is sufficient to use only hop-by-hop integrity protection of signaling, for example, IPSec or TLS. In all other cases, end-to-end integrity protection of signaling (e.g., S/MIME, see Section 19.6) must be used. Note that the end-to-end integrity protection must cover not only the message body, which contains the security preconditions, but also the SIP Supported and Require headers, which may contain the precondition option tag. If only the message body were integrity protected, removal of the precondition option tag could lead to clipping (when a security precondition was otherwise to be used), whereas addition of the option tag could lead to session failure (if the other side does not support preconditions).

However, security preconditions do not guarantee that an established media stream will be secure. They merely guarantee that the recipient of the media stream packets will be able to perform any relevant decryption and integrity checking on those media stream packets. Current SDP (RFC 4566, see Section 7.7) and associated offer–answer procedures (RFC 3264, see Section 3.8.4) allows only a single type of transport protocol to be negotiated for a given media stream in an offer–answer exchange.

Negotiation of alternative transport protocols (e.g., plain and secure RTP) is currently not defined. Thus, if the transport protocol offered (e.g., secure RTP) is not supported, the offered media stream will simply be rejected. There is, however, work in progress to address that. For example, the SDP Capability Negotiation framework (RFC 5939) defines a method for negotiating the use of a secure or a nonsecure transport protocol by use of SDP and the offer–answer model with various extensions. Such a mechanism introduces a number of security considerations in general; however, use of SDP Security Preconditions with such a mechanism introduces the following security precondition specific security considerations.

A basic premise of negotiating secure and nonsecure media streams as alternatives is that the offerer's security policy allows for nonsecure media. If the offer were to include secure and nonsecure media streams as alternative offers, and media for either alternative may be received before the answer, then the offerer may not know if the answerer accepted the secure alternative. An active attacker thus may be able to inject malicious media stream packets until the answer (indicating the chosen secure alternative) is received. From a security point of view, it is important to note that use of security preconditions (even with a mandatory strength tag) would not address this vulnerability since security preconditions would effectively apply only to the secure media stream alternatives. If the nonsecure media stream alternative was selected by the answerer, the security precondition would be satisfied by definition, the session could progress, and (nonsecure) media could be received before the answer is received.

19.3 Security Mechanisms Negotiation

SIP uses HTTP authentication and other security mechanisms where multiple alternative methods and algorithms are available to choose from. All security mechanisms may not be suitable under all circumstances of different security threats. For example, RFC 2617 (see Section 19.4.5) describes that some of those security features are vulnerable to MITM attacks. It is also difficult, or sometimes even impossible, to know whether a specific security mechanism is truly unavailable to a SIP peer entity, or if in fact an MITM attack is in action. In certain small networks, these issues are not very relevant, as the administrators of such networks can deploy appropriate software versions and set up policies for using exactly the right type of security. However, SIP is also expected to be deployed to hundreds of millions of small devices with little or no possibilities for coordinated security policies, let alone software upgrades, which necessitates the need for the negotiation functionality to be available from the very beginning of deployment. RFC 3329 described here provides negotiation capabilities for the security mechanisms between a SIP UA and its first-hop SIP entity. The security negotiations need to abide by the following objectives:

- The entities involved in the security agreement process need to find out exactly which security mechanisms to apply, preferably without excessive additional roundtrips.

- The selection of security mechanisms itself needs to be secure. Traditionally, all security protocols use a secure form of negotiation. For instance, after establishing mutual keys through Diffie–Hellman (DH), the Internet Key Exchange (IKE) protocol sends hashes of the previously sent data including the offered crypto mechanisms (RFC 4306). This allows the peers to detect if the initial, unprotected offers were tampered with.
- The entities involved in the security agreement process need to be able to indicate success or failure of the security agreement process.

19.3.1 Security Mechanisms Negotiation

19.3.1.1 Operation

We are considering a hypothetical security mechanisms negotiation message flow as described in RFC 3329 in Figure 19.4. The message flow illustrates how the mechanism defined in this document works:

- Step 1: Clients wishing to use this specification can send a list of their supported security mechanisms along the first request to the server.
- Step 2: Servers wishing to use this specification can challenge the client to perform the security agreement procedure. The security mechanisms and parameters supported by the server are sent along in this challenge.
- Step 3: The client then proceeds to select the highest-preference security mechanism they have in common and to turn on the selected security.
- Step 4: The client contacts the server again, now using the selected security mechanism. The server's list of supported security mechanisms is returned as a response to the challenge.

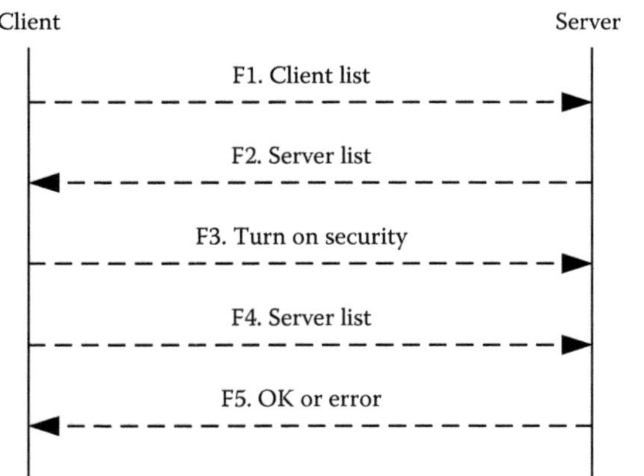

Figure 19.4 Security mechanisms negotiation message flow. (Copyright IETF. Reproduced with permission.)

- Step 5: The server verifies its own list of security mechanisms in order to ensure that the original list had not been modified.

This procedure is stateless for servers (unless the used security mechanisms require the server to keep some state). The client and the server lists are both static (i.e., they do not and cannot change based on the input from the other side). Nodes may, however, maintain several static lists, one for each interface, for example. Between steps 1 and 2, the server may set up a non-self-describing security mechanism if necessary. Note that with this type of security mechanisms, the server is necessarily stateful. The client would set up the non-self-describing security mechanism between steps 2 and 4.

19.3.1.2 Syntax for SIP Security Headers

We define three new SIP header fields, namely Security-Client, Security-Server, and Security-Verify. The notation used in the augmented Backus–Naur Form (ABNF) definitions for the syntax elements in this section is repeated here as used in SIP (see Section 2.4.1) for convenience, and any elements not defined in this section are as defined in SIP and the documents to which it refers:

```
security-client  = "Security-Client" HCOLON
                   sec-mechanism *(COMMA
                   sec-mechanism)
security-server  = "Security-Server" HCOLON
                   sec-mechanism *(COMMA
                   sec-mechanism)
security-verify  = "Security-Verify" HCOLON
                   sec-mechanism *(COMMA
                   sec-mechanism)
sec-mechanism    = mechanism-name *(SEMI
                   mech-parameters)
mechanism-name   = ("digest"/"tls"/
                   "ipsec-ike"/
                   "ipsec-man"/token)
mech-parameters  = (preference/
                   digest-algorithm/
                   digest-qop/digest-verify/
                   extension)
preference       = "q" EQUAL qvalue
                   qvalue=("0" ["." 0*3DIGIT])
                   /("1" ["." 0*3("0")])
digest-algorithm  = "d-alg" EQUAL token
digest-qop        = "d-qop" EQUAL token
digest-verify     = "d-ver" EQUAL LDQUOT 32LHEX
                   RDQUOT
extension        = generic-param
```

Note that qvalue is already defined in the SIP ABNF (RFC 3261, see Section 2.4.1). We have copied its definitions here for completeness. The parameters described by the ABNF above have the following semantics:

- **Mechanism-name:** This token identifies the security mechanism supported by the client, when it appears in a Security-Client header field, or by the server, when it appears in a Security-Server or in a Security-Verify header field. The mechanism-name tokens are registered with the IANA. This specification defines four values:
  - *tls* for TLS (RFC 4346)
  - *digest* for HTTP Digest (RFC 4306)
  - *ipsec-ike* for IPsec with IKE (RFC 4301)
  - *ipsec-man* for manually keyed IPsec without IKE
- **Preference:** The *q*-value indicates a relative preference for the particular mechanism. The higher the value the more preferred the mechanism is. All the security mechanisms MUST have different *q*-values. It is an error to provide two mechanisms with the same *q*-value.
- **Digest-algorithm:** This optional parameter is defined here only for HTTP Digest in order to prevent the bidding-down attack for the HTTP Digest algorithm parameter. The content of the field may have same values as defined in RFC 4306 for the *algorithm* field.
- **Digest-qop:** This optional parameter is defined here only for HTTP Digest (RFC 4306) in order to prevent the bidding-down attack for the HTTP Digest qop parameter. The content of the field may have same values as defined in RFC 4306 for the *qop* field.
- **Digest-verify:** This optional parameter is defined here only for HTTP Digest (RFC 4306) in order to prevent the bidding-down attack for the SIP security mechanism agreement (this document). The content of the field is counted exactly the same way as request-digest in RFC 4306 except that the Security-Server header field is included in the A2 parameter. If the qop directive's value is *auth* or is unspecified, then A2 is
  - A2 = Method ":" digest-uri-value ":" security-server
  - If the qop value is auth-int, then A2 is
  - A2 = Method ":" digest-uri-value ":" H(entity-body) ":"
  - security-server

  All linear white spaces in the Security-Server header field MUST be replaced by a single space (SP) before calculating or interpreting the digest-verify parameter. Method, digest-uri-value, entity-body, and any other HTTP Digest parameter are as specified in RFC 4306.

Note that this specification does not introduce any extension or change to HTTP Digest (RFC 4306). This specification only reuses the existing HTTP Digest mechanisms to protect the negotiation of security mechanisms between SIP entities.

19.3.1.3 SIP Protocol Operation

This section deals with the protocol details involved in the negotiation between a SIP UA and its next-hop SIP entity. Throughout the text, the next-hop SIP entity is referred to as the first-hop proxy or outbound proxy. However, the reader should bear in mind that a UAS can also be the next hop for a UAC.

19.3.1.3.1 Client Initiated

If a client ends up using TLS to contact the server because it has followed the rules specified in RFC 3263 (see Section 8.2.4), the client must not use the security agreement procedure of this specification. If a client ends up using non-TLS connections because of the rules in RFC 3263, the client may use the security agreement of this specification to detect DNS spoofing, or to negotiate some other security than TLS. A client wishing to use the security agreement of this specification must add a Security-Client header field to a request addressed to its first-hop proxy (i.e., the destination of the request is the first-hop proxy). This header field contains a list of all the security mechanisms that the client supports. The client should not add preference parameters to this list. The client MUST add both a Require and Proxy-Require header field with the value sec-agree to its request.

The contents of the Security-Client header field may be used by the server to include any necessary information in its response. A server receiving an unprotected request that contains a Require or Proxy-Require header field with the value sec-agree must respond to the client with a 494 (Security Agreement Required) response. The server must add a Security-Server header field to this response listing the security mechanisms that the server supports. The server must add its list to the response even if there are no common security mechanisms in the client's and server's lists. The server's list must not depend on the contents of the client's list. The server MUST compare the list received in the Security-Client header field with the list to be sent in the Security-Server header field. When the client receives this response, it will choose the common security mechanism with the highest *q*-value. Therefore, the server MUST add the necessary information so that the client can initiate that mechanism (e.g., a Proxy-Authenticate header field for HTTP Digest).

When the client receives a response with a Security-Server header field, it must choose the security mechanism in the server's list with the highest *q*-value among all the mechanisms that are known to the client. Then, it must initiate that particular security mechanism. This initiation may be carried out without involving any SIP message exchange (e.g., establishing a TLS connection). If an attacker modified the Security-Client header field in the request, the server may not include in its response the information needed to establish the common security mechanism with the highest preference value (e.g., the Proxy-Authenticate header field is missing). A client detecting such a lack of information in the response must consider the current security agreement process aborted, and may try to start it again by sending a new request with a Security-Client header field as described above.

All the subsequent SIP requests sent by the client to that server should make use of the security mechanism initiated in the previous step. These requests must contain a Security-Verify header field that mirrors the server's list received previously in the Security-Server header field. These requests MUST also have both a Require and Proxy-Require header fields with the value sec-agree. The server must check that the security mechanisms listed in the Security-Verify header field of incoming requests correspond to its static list of supported security mechanisms. Note that, following the standard SIP header field comparison rules, both lists have to contain the same security mechanisms in the same order to be considered equivalent. In addition, for each particular security mechanism, its parameters in both lists need to have the same values. The server can proceed processing a particular request if, and only if, the list was not modified. If modification of the list is detected, the server must respond to the client with a 494 Security Agreement Required response. This response must include the server's unmodified list of supported security mechanisms.

If the list was not modified, and the server is a proxy, it must remove the sec-agree value from both the Require and Proxy-Require header fields, and then remove the header fields if no values remain. Once the security has been negotiated between two SIP entities, the same SIP entities may use the same security when communicating with each other in different SIP roles. For example, if a UAC and its outbound proxy negotiate some security, they may try to use the same security for incoming requests (i.e., the UA will be acting as a UAS). The user of a UA should be informed about the results of the security mechanism agreement. The user may decline to accept a particular security mechanism, and abort further SIP communications with the peer.

19.3.1.3.2 Server Initiated

A server decides to use the security agreement described in this document based on local policy. If a server receives a request from the network interface that is configured to use this mechanism, it must check that the request has only one Via entry. If there are several Via entries, the server is not the first-hop SIP entity, and it must not use this mechanism. For such a request, the server must return a 502 Bad Gateway response. A server that decides to use this agreement mechanism must challenge unprotected requests with one Via entry regardless of the presence or the absence of any Require, Proxy-Require, or Supported header fields in incoming requests.

A server that by policy requires the use of this specification and receives a request that does not have the sec-agree option tag in a Require, Proxy-Require, or Supported header field must return a 421 Extension Required response. If the request had the sec-agree option tag in a Supported header field, it must return a 494 Security Agreement Required response. In both situations, the server must also include in the response a Security-Server header field listing its capabilities and a Require header field with an option tag sec-agree in it. The server must also add necessary information so that the client can initiate the preferred security mechanism (e.g., a Proxy-Authenticate header field for HTTP Digest). Clients that support the extension defined in this document should add a Supported header field with a value of sec-agree.

19.3.1.4 Security Mechanism Initiation

Once the client chooses a security mechanism from the list received in the Security-Server header field from the server, it initiates that mechanism. Different mechanisms require different initiation procedures. If tls is chosen, the client uses the procedures to determine the URI to be used as an input to the DNS procedures of RFC 3263 (see Section 8.2.4). However, if the URI is a SIP URI, it must treat the scheme as if it were sips, not sip. If the URI scheme is not sip, the request must be sent using TLS. If digest is chosen, the 494 Security Agreement Required response will contain an HTTP Digest authentication challenge. The client must use the algorithm and qop parameters in the Security-Server header field to replace the same parameters in the HTTP Digest challenge. The client MUST also use the digest-verify parameter in the Security-Verify header field to protect the Security-Server header field as specified above.

To use ipsec-ike, the client attempts to establish an IKE connection to the host part of the Request-URI in the first request to the server. If the IKE connection attempt fails, the agreement procedure must be considered to have failed, and must be terminated. Note that ipsec-man will only work if the communicating SIP entities know which keys and other parameters to use. It is outside the scope of this specification to describe how this information can be made known to the peers. All rules for minimum implementations, such as mandatory-to-implement algorithms, apply as defined in RFCs 4301–4303. In both IPsec-based mechanisms, it is expected that appropriate policy entries for protecting SIP have been configured or will be created before attempting to use the security agreement procedure, and that SIP communications use port numbers and addresses according to these policy entries. It is outside the scope of this specification to describe how this information can be made known to the peers, but it would typically be configured at the same time as the IKE credentials or manual security associations have been entered.

19.3.1.5 Duration of Security Associations

Once a security mechanism has been negotiated, both the server and the client need to know until when it can be used. All the mechanisms described in this document have a different way of signaling the end of a security association. When TLS is used, the termination of the connection indicates that a new negotiation is needed. IKE negotiates the duration of a security association. If the credentials provided by a client using digest are no longer valid, the server will rechallenge the client. It is assumed that when IPsec-man is used, the same out-of-band mechanism used to distribute keys is used to define the duration of the security association.

19.3.1.6 Header-Field Use

The three header fields (Security-Client, Security-Server, and Security-Verify) may be used to negotiate the security mechanisms between a UAC and other SIP entities, including UAS, proxy, and registrar. Information about the use of headers in relation to SIP methods and proxy processing is summarized in Section 2.8.

19.3.2 Backwards Compatibility

The use of this extension in a network interface is a matter of local policy. Different network interfaces may follow different policies, and consequently the use of this extension may be situational by nature. UA and server implementations must be configurable to operate with or without this extension. A server that is configured to use this mechanism may also accept requests from clients that use TLS based on the rules defined in RFC 3263 (see Section 8.2.4). Requests from clients that do not support this extension, and do not support TLS, cannot be accepted. This obviously breaks interoperability with some SIP clients. Therefore, this extension should be used in environments where it is somehow ensured that every client implements this extension or is able to use TLS. This extension may also be used in environments where insecure communication is not acceptable if the option of not being able to communicate is also accepted.

19.3.3 Security Algorithms Negotiation Example

19.3.3.1 Client Initiated

A UA negotiates (Figure 19.5) the security mechanism to be used with its outbound proxy without knowing beforehand which mechanisms the proxy supports. The OPTIONS method can be used here to request the security capabilities of the proxy. In this way, the security can be initiated even before the first INVITE is sent via the proxy.

The UAC sends an OPTIONS request to its outbound proxy, indicating at the same time that it is able to negotiate security mechanisms and that it supports TLS and HTTP Digest (F1). The outbound proxy responds to the UAC with its own list of security mechanisms—IPsec and TLS (F2). The only common security mechanism is TLS, so they establish a TLS connection between them. When the connection is

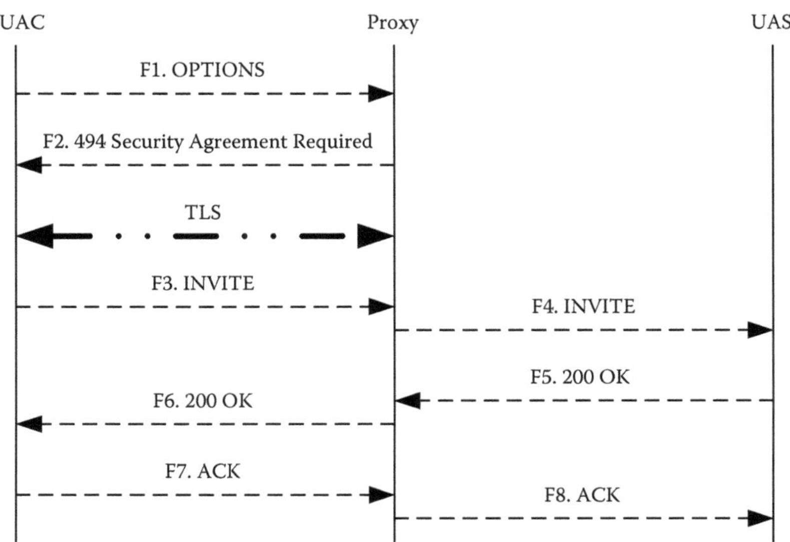

Figure 19.5 Negotiation initiated by the client. (Copyright IETF. Reproduced with permission.)

successfully established, the UAC sends an INVITE request over the TLS connection just established (F3). This INVITE contains the server's security list. The server verifies it, and since it matches its static list, it processes the INVITE and forwards it to the next hop. If this example was run without Security-Server header in step 2, the UAC would not know what kind of security the other one supports, and would be forced to error-prone trials. More seriously, if the Security-Verify was omitted in step 3, the whole process would be prone to MITM attacks. An attacker could spoof ICMP Port Unreachable message on the trials, or remove the stronger security option from the header in step 1, therefore substantially reducing the security.

```
F1: OPTIONS sip:proxy.example.com SIP/2.0
   Security-Client: tls
   Security-Client: digest
   Require: sec-agree
   Proxy-Require: sec-agree
F2. SIP/2.0 494 Security Agreement Required
   Security-Server: ipsec-ike;q=0.1
   Security-Server: tls;q=0.2
F3. INVITE sip:proxy.example.com SIP/2.0
   Security-Verify: ipsec-ike;q=0.1
   Security-Verify: tls;q=0.2
   Route: sip:callee@domain.com
   Require: sec-agree
   Proxy-Require: sec-agree
```

The 200 OK response (F6) for the INVITE and the ACK (F7) are also sent over the TLS connection. The ACK will contain the same Security-Verify header field as the INVITE (F3).

19.3.3.2 Server Initiated

In the example of Figure 19.6, the client sends an INVITE toward the callee using an outbound proxy. This INVITE does not contain any Require header field.

The proxy, following its local policy, does not accept the INVITE. It returns a 421 Extension Required (F2) with a Security-Server header field that lists IPsec-IKE and TLS. Since the UAC supports IPsec-IKE, it performs the key exchange and establishes a security association with the proxy. The second INVITE (F4) and the ACK (F8) contain a Security-Verify header field that mirrors the Security-Server header field received in the 421. The INVITE (F4), the 200 OK (F7), and the ACK (F8) are sent using the security association that has been established.

```
F1: INVITE sip:uas.example.com SIP/2.0
F2: SIP/2.0 421 Extension Required
   Security-Server: ipsec-ike;q=0.1
   Security-Server: tls;q=0.2
F4: INVITE sip:uas.example.com SIP/2.0
   Security-Verify: ipsec-ike;q=0.1
   Security-Verify: tls;q=0.2
```

19.3.4 Security Considerations

This specification is about making it possible to select between various SIP security mechanisms in a secure manner. In particular, the method presented herein allows current networks using, for instance, HTTP Digest, to be securely upgraded to, for instance, IPsec without requiring a simultaneous

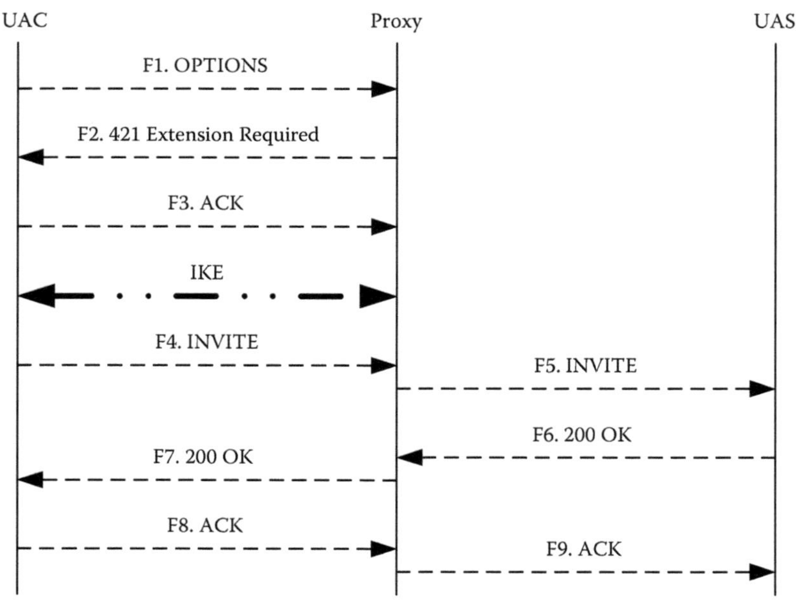

Figure 19.6 Server-initiated security negotiation. (Copyright IETF. Reproduced with permission.)

modification in all equipment. The method presented in this specification is secure only if the weakest proposed mechanism offers at least integrity and replay protection for the Security-Verify header field. The security implications of this are subtle, but do have a fundamental importance in building large networks that change over time. Given that the hashes are produced also using algorithms agreed upon in the first unprotected messages, one could ask what the difference in security really is. Assuming integrity protection is mandatory and only secure algorithms are used, we still need to prevent MITM attackers from modifying other parameters, such as whether encryption is provided or not. Let us first assume two peers capable of using both strong and weak security.

If the initial offers are not protected in any way, any attacker can easily *downgrade* the offers by removing the strong options. This would force the two peers to use weak security between them. However, if the offers are protected in some way—such as by hashing or repeating them later when the selected security is really on—the situation is different. It would not be sufficient for the attacker to modify a single message. Instead, the attacker would have to modify both the offer message as well as the message that contains the hash/repetition. More important, the attacker would have to forge the weak security that is present in the second message, and would have to do so in real time between the sent offers and the later messages. Otherwise, the peers would notice that the hash is incorrect. If the attacker is able to break the weak security, the security method or the algorithm should not be used.

In conclusion, the security difference is making a trivial attack possible versus demanding the attacker to break algorithms. An example of where this has a serious consequence is when a network is first deployed with integrity protection (such as HTTP Digest), and then later new devices are added that support also encryption (such as TLS). In this situation, an insecure negotiation procedure allows attackers to trivially force even new devices to use only integrity protection. Possible attacks against the security agreement include the following:

- Attackers could try to modify the server's list of security mechanisms in the first response. This would be revealed to the server when the client returns the received list using the security.
- Attackers could also try to modify the repeated list in the second request from the client. However, if the selected security mechanism uses encryption, this may not be possible; if it uses integrity protection, any modifications will be detected by the server.
- Attackers could try to modify the client's list of security mechanisms in the first message. The client selects the security mechanism based on its own knowledge of its own capabilities and the server's list; hence, the client's choice would be unaffected by any such modification. However, the server's choice could still be affected as described below:
  - If the modification affected the server's choice, the server and client would end up choosing different security mechanisms in step 3 or 4 of Figure 19.6. Since they would be unable to communicate to each other, this would be detected as a potential attack. The client would either retry or give up in this situation.
  - If the modification did not affect the server's choice, there is no effect.
- Finally, attackers may also try to reply old security agreement messages. Each security mechanism must provide replay protection. In particular, HTTP Digest implementations should carefully utilize existing reply protection options such as including a time stamp to the nonce parameter, and using nonce counters (RFC 4306).

All clients that implement this specification must select HTTP Digest, TLS, IPsec, or any stronger method for the protection of the second request.

19.3.5 Syntax of IPsec–3GPP Security Headers

The 3gpp document [3] extends the security agreement framework described in this document with a new security mechanism: ipsec-3gpp. This security mechanism and its associated parameters are used in the 3GPP IMS. The ABNF definitions below follow the syntax of SIP (RFC 3261, see Section 2.4.1):

```
mechanism-name=("ipsec-3gpp")
mech-parameters=(algorithm/protocol/mode/
encrypt-algorithm/spi/
port1/port2)
algorithm="alg" EQUAL ("hmac-md5-96"/
"hmac-sha-1-96")
protocol="prot" EQUAL ("ah"/"esp")
mode="mod" EQUAL ("trans"/"tun")
encrypt-algorithm="ealg" EQUAL
("des-ede3-cbc"/"null")
spi="spi" EQUAL spivalue
spivalue=10DIGIT; 0 to 4294967295
port1="port1" EQUAL port
port2="port2" EQUAL port
port=1*DIGIT
```

The parameters described by the ABNF above have the following semantics:

- **Algorithm:** This parameter defines the used authentication algorithm. It may have a value of hmac-md5-96 for HMAC-MD5-96 (RFC 2403), or hmac-sha-1-96 for HMAC-SHA-1-96 (RFC 2404). The algorithm parameter is mandatory.

- **Protocol:** This parameter defines the IPsec protocol. It may have a value of *ah* for AH (RFC 4302), or *esp* for ESP (RFCs 4303 & 4305). If no Protocol parameter is present, the protocol will be ESP by default.
- **Mode:** This parameter defines the mode in which the IPsec protocol is used. It may have a value of *trans* for transport mode, or a value of *tun* for tunneling mode. If no Mode parameter is present, the IPsec protocol is used in transport mode.
- **Encrypt-algorithm:** This parameter defines the used encryption algorithm. It may have a value of des-ede3-cbc for 3DES (Triple Data Encryption System) (RFC 2451), or *null* for no encryption. If no Encrypt-algorithm parameter is present, encryption is not used.
- **Spi:** This parameter defines the SPI number used for inbound messages.
- **Port1:** This parameter defines the destination port number for inbound messages that are protected.
- **Port2:** This parameter defines the source port number for outbound messages that are protected. Port 2 is optional.

The communicating SIP entities need to know beforehand which keys to use. It is also assumed that the underlying IPsec implementation supports selectors that allow all transport protocols supported by SIP to be protected with a single security association. The duration of security association is the same as in the expiration interval of the corresponding registration binding.

19.4 Authentication in SIP

19.4.1 Background

The development SIP security solution that requires end-to-end authentication for the communicating parties is primarily because of the intermediaries over the SIP network that route the SIP calls to the SIP end users. The lack of a global public key infrastructure and limited usage of the client certificates have created serious problems for the authentication service in an end-to-end fashion. Figure 19.7a depicts the classic SIP trapezoid signaling communications between two end points located in two different administrative domains via two SIP proxy servers.

The communication includes end SIP UA A to middle outbound proxy A (end-to-middle), middle proxy A to middle proxy B (middle-to-middle), middle inbound proxy B to end SIP UA B (middle-to-end). However, RTP/SRTP/RCTP/SRTCP media flows directly between the end SIP UA A and end SIP UA B (end-to-end). It clearly implies that a lot of hop-by-hop, end-to-end, end-to-middle, middle-to-middle, and middle-to-end security issues are required to be taken care of in SIP. Consequently, unlike traditional text-based non-real-time data applications, the authentication of SIP UA A (Alice) to SIP UA B (Bob), and the security of the real-time multimedia traffic transferred between Alice and Bob after establishment of the SIP session securely are really complicated. A typical security solution is provided considering a SIP authentication server that plays a logical role for security being a part of a SIP outbound proxy due to lack of the end-to-end security solution in SIP. Figure 19.7b shows a modified version of Figure 19.7a where outbound proxy A is

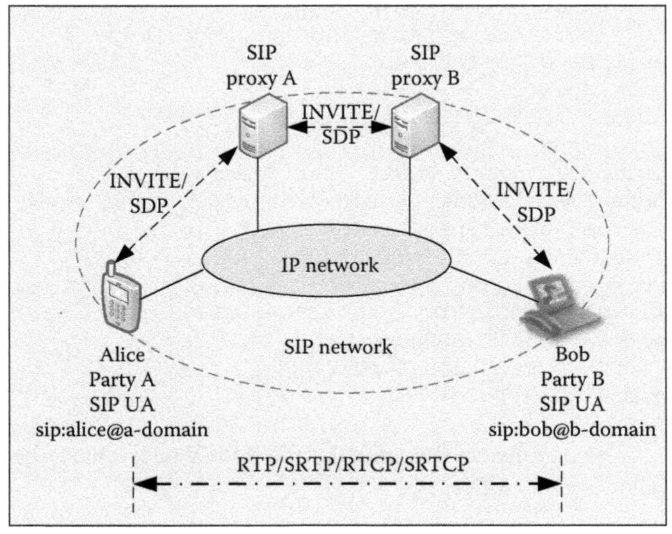

(a)

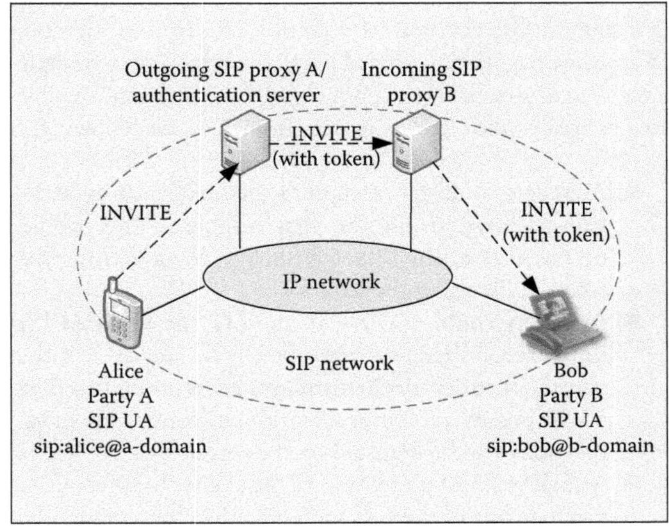

(b)

Figure 19.7 SIP call flows: (a) SIP trapezoid and (b) SIP authenticated identities.

playing the role of the authentication server. The core idea of the authentication service can be described as follows:

- Alice sends a SIP INVITE message through outbound proxy A that is playing the role of the SIP authentication server. The outgoing proxy authenticates the user using a set of security policies that are used in this administrative domain.
- Alice is authenticated and authorized by proxy A creating and cryptographically signing an authentication token for the user. In this way, proxy A will assert the SIP UA's identity, known as the asserted identity (see Chapter 10) and that UA A (Alice) was authenticated by adding a digitally signed token (see Figure 19.7b shown as token) to the SIP message. The digital signature is computed over a number of additional fields of the SIP message discussed later in order to protect their integrity and that of the overall message.
- Proxy A then shares this identity of SIP UA A with others, including proxy B, as necessary. The SIP message along with the asserted identity is sent to proxy B. Proxy B/SIP UA B (Bob) inspects the content of the token as necessary. Of course, the processing steps will involve verification of the digital signature along with other functions.

The key advantage for the incoming proxy and the called party is that they only require knowing, or having to discover, the certificates of the authentication services they interact with. It does not require for interaction with the certificates of each individual by the incoming proxy (e.g., proxy B) and the called party (e.g., SIP UA B, Bob), thereby scaling the authentication and authorization services especially for the large-scale SIP network. In turn, although this security service provides scalability, this approach exposes another important security problem known as the user privacy. Proxy B that remains in another administrative domain as well as the called party (e.g., SIP UA B, Bob) will be able to know the identity of the calling party (e.g., SIP UA A, Alice). This security issue in SIP invites to offer privacy and anonymity services for SIP users. We have devoted a separate chapter (see Chapter 20) to deal with SIP privacy and anonymity services. It reveals the fact that we need to address security in SIP in an integrated manner that includes all functions: authentication, authorization, integrity, confidentiality, privacy/anonymity, and nonrepudiation.

Note that SIP providing a stateless, challenge-based mechanism for authentication (RFC 3261) is based on authentication in HTTP (RFC 2617) that is described here. Any time that a proxy server or UA receives a request (with the exceptions given in Section 19.4.2), it may challenge the initiator of the request to provide assurance of its identity. Once the originator has been identified, the recipient of the request should ascertain whether or not this user is authorized to make the request in question. No authorization systems are recommended or discussed in this document. The Digest authentication mechanism described in this section provides message authentication and replay protection only, without message integrity or confidentiality. Protective measures above and beyond those provided by Digest need to be taken to prevent active attackers from modifying SIP requests and responses. Note that due to its weak security, the usage of Basic authentication has been deprecated. Servers must not accept credentials using the Basic authorization scheme, and servers also must not challenge with Basic. This is a change from RFC 2543 (obsoleted by RFC 3261).

19.4.2 Framework

The framework for SIP authentication closely parallels that of HTTP defined in RFC 2617. In particular, the ABNF for auth-scheme, auth-param, challenge, realm, realm-value, and credentials is identical (although the usage of Basic as a scheme is not permitted). In SIP, a UAS uses the 401 Unauthorized response to challenge the identity of a UAC. Additionally, registrars and redirect servers may make use of 401 Unauthorized responses for authentication, but proxies must not, and instead may use the 407 Proxy Authentication Required response. The requirements for inclusion of the Proxy-Authenticate, Proxy-Authorization, WWW-Authenticate, and Authorization in the various messages are identical to those described in RFC 2617.

Since SIP does not have the concept of a canonical root URL, the notion of protection spaces is interpreted differently in SIP. The realm string alone defines the protection domain. This is a change from RFC 2543 (obsoleted by RFC 3261), in which the Request-URI and the realm together defined the protection domain. This previous definition of protection domain caused some amount of confusion since the Request-URI sent by the UAC and the Request-URI received by the challenging server might be different, and indeed the final form of the Request-URI might not be known to the UAC. Also, the previous definition depended on the presence of a SIP URI in the Request-URI and seemed to rule out alternative URI schemes (e.g., the tel URL). Operators of UAs or proxy servers that will authenticate received requests must adhere to the following guidelines for creation of a realm string for their server:

- Realm strings must be globally unique. It is recommended that a realm string contain a host name or domain name, following the recommendation in Section 3.2.1 of RFC 2617.
- Realm strings should present a human-readable identifier that can be rendered to a user.

For example:

```
INVITE sip:bob@biloxi.com SIP/2.0
Authorization: Digest realm="biloxi.com",
<...>
```

Generally, SIP authentication is meaningful for a specific realm, a protection domain. Thus, for Digest authentication, each such protection domain has its own set of user names and passwords. If a server does not require authentication for a particular request, it may accept a default user name, *anonymous*, which has no password (password of ""). Similarly, UACs representing many users, such as PSTN gateways, may have their own device-specific user name and password, rather than accounts for particular users, for their realm.

While a server can legitimately challenge most SIP requests, there are two requests defined by this document that require special handling for authentication: ACK and CANCEL. Under an authentication scheme that uses responses to carry values used to compute nonces (such as Digest), some problems come up for any requests that take no response, including ACK. For this reason, any credentials in the INVITE that were accepted by a server MUST be accepted by that server for the ACK. UACs creating an ACK message will duplicate all of the Authorization and Proxy-Authorization header field values that appeared in the INVITE to which the ACK corresponds. Servers MUST NOT attempt to challenge an ACK.

Although the CANCEL method does take a response (a 2xx), servers must not attempt to challenge CANCEL requests since these requests cannot be resubmitted. Generally, a CANCEL request should be accepted by a server if it comes from the same hop that sent the request being canceled (provided that some sort of transport or network layer security association, as described in Section 19.12.2.1, is in place).

When a UAC receives a challenge, it should render to the user the contents of the *realm* parameter in the challenge (which appears in either a WWW-Authenticate header field or Proxy-Authenticate header field) if the UAC device does not already know of a credential for the realm in question. A service provider that preconfigures UAs with credentials for its realm should be aware that users will not have the opportunity to present their own credentials for this realm when challenged at a preconfigured device.

Finally, note that even if a UAC can locate credentials that are associated with the proper realm, the potential exists that these credentials may no longer be valid or that the challenging server will not accept these credentials for whatever reason (especially when anonymous with no password is submitted). In this instance, a server may repeat its challenge, or it may respond with a 403 Forbidden. A UAC must not re-attempt requests with the credentials that have just been rejected (though the request may be retried if the nonce was stale).

19.4.3 User-to-User Authentication

When a UAS receives a request from a UAC, the UAS may authenticate the originator before the request is processed. If no credentials (in the Authorization header field) are provided in the request, the UAS can challenge the originator to provide credentials by rejecting the request with a 401 Unauthorized status code. The WWW-Authenticate response-header field must be included in 401 Unauthorized response messages. The field value consists of at least one challenge that indicates the authentication scheme(s) and parameters applicable to the realm. An example of the WWW-Authenticate header field in a 401 challenge is as follows:

```
WWW-Authenticate: Digest
realm="biloxi.com",
qop="auth,auth-int",
nonce="dcd98b7102dd2f0e8b11d0f600bfb0c093",
opaque="5ccc069c403ebaf9f0171e9517f40e41"
```

When the originating UAC receives the 401 Unauthorized, it should, if it is able, reoriginate the request with the proper credentials. The UAC may require input from the originating user before proceeding. Once authentication credentials have been supplied (either directly by the user, or discovered in an internal keyring), UAs should cache the credentials for a given value of the To header field and realm, and attempt to reuse these values on the next request for that destination. UAs may cache credentials in any way they would like.

If no credentials for a realm can be located, UACs may attempt to retry the request with a user name of anonymous and no password (a password of ""). Once credentials have been located, any UA that wishes to authenticate itself with a UAS or registrar—usually, but not necessarily, after receiving a 401 Unauthorized response—may do so by including an Authorization header field with the request. The Authorization field value consists of credentials containing the authentication information of the UA for the realm of the resource being requested, as well as parameters required in support of authentication and replay protection. An example of the Authorization header field is

```
Authorization: Digest username="bob",
realm="biloxi.com",
nonce="dcd98b7102dd2f0e8b11d0f600bfb0c093",
uri="sip:bob@biloxi.com",
qop=auth,
nc=00000001,
cnonce="0a4f113b",
response="6629fae49393a05397450978507c4ef1",
opaque="5ccc069c403ebaf9f0171e9517f40e41"
```

When a UAC resubmits a request with its credentials after receiving a 401 Unauthorized or 407 Proxy Authentication Required response, it MUST increment the CSeq header field value as it would normally when sending an updated request.

19.4.4 Proxy-to-User Authentication

Similarly, when a UAC sends a request to a proxy server, the proxy server may authenticate the originator before the request is processed. If no credentials (in the Proxy-Authorization header field) are provided in the request, the proxy can challenge the originator to provide credentials by rejecting the request with a 407 Proxy Authentication Required status code. The proxy must populate the 407 Proxy Authentication Required message with a Proxy-Authenticate header field value applicable to the proxy for the requested resource.

The use of Proxy-Authenticate and Proxy-Authorization parallel are described in RFC 2543 (obsoleted by RFC 3261), with one difference. Proxies must not add values to the Proxy-Authorization header field. All 407 Proxy Authentication Required responses must be forwarded upstream toward the UAC following the procedures for any other response. It is the UAC's responsibility to add the Proxy-Authorization header field value containing credentials for the realm of the proxy that has asked for authentication.

If a proxy were to resubmit a request adding a Proxy-Authorization header field value, it would need to increment the CSeq in the new request. However, this would cause the UAC that submitted the original request to discard a response from the UAS, as the CSeq value would be different. When the originating UAC receives the 407 Proxy Authentication Required, it should, if it is able, reoriginate the request with the proper credentials. It should follow the same procedures for the display of the realm parameter that are given above for responding to 401. If no credentials for a realm can be located, UACs may attempt to retry the request with a user name of anonymous and no password (a password of ""). The UAC should also cache the credentials used in the reoriginated request. The following rule is recommended for proxy credential caching.

If a UA receives a Proxy-Authenticate header field value in a 401/407 response to a request with a particular Call-ID, it should incorporate credentials for that realm in all subsequent requests that contain the same Call-ID. These credentials must not be cached across dialogs; however, if a UA is configured with the realm of its local outbound proxy, when one exists, then the UA may cache credentials for that realm across dialogs. Note that this does mean a future request in a dialog could contain credentials that are not needed by any proxy along the Route header path. Any UA that wishes to authenticate itself to a proxy server—usually, but not necessarily, after receiving a 407 Proxy Authentication Required response—may do so by including a Proxy-Authorization header field value with the request. The Proxy-Authorization request-header field allows the client to identify itself (or its user) to a proxy that requires authentication. The Proxy-Authorization header field value consists of credentials containing the authentication information of the UA for the proxy or realm of the resource being requested.

A Proxy-Authorization header field value applies only to the proxy whose realm is identified in the realm parameter (this proxy may previously have demanded authentication using the Proxy-Authenticate field). When multiple proxies are used in a chain, a Proxy-Authorization header field value must not be consumed by any proxy whose realm does not match the realm parameter specified in that value. Note that if an authentication scheme that does not support realms is used in the Proxy-Authorization header field, a proxy server must attempt to parse all Proxy-Authorization header field values to determine whether one of them has what the proxy server considers to be valid credentials. Because this is potentially very time consuming in large networks, proxy servers should use an authentication scheme that supports realms in the Proxy-Authorization header field.

If a request is forked, as described in RFC 3261 (see Section 3.11.7), various proxy servers or UAs may wish to challenge the UAC. In this case, the forking proxy server is responsible for aggregating these challenges into a single response. Each WWW-Authenticate and Proxy-Authenticate value received in responses to the forked request must be placed into the single response that is sent by the forking proxy to the UA; the ordering of these header field values is not significant. When a proxy server issues a challenge in response to a request, it will not proxy the request until the UAC has retried the request with valid credentials. A forking proxy may forward a request simultaneously to multiple proxy servers that require authentication, each of which, in turn, will not forward the request until the originating UAC has authenticated itself in their respective realm. If the UAC does not provide credentials for each challenge, the proxy servers that issued the challenges will not forward requests to the UA where the destination user might be located, and therefore, the virtues of forking are largely lost. When resubmitting its request in response to a 401 Unauthorized or 407 Proxy Authentication Required that contains multiple challenges, a UAC may include an Authorization value for each WWW-Authenticate value and a Proxy-Authorization value for each Proxy-Authenticate value for which the UAC wishes to supply a credential.

As noted above, multiple credentials in a request should be differentiated by the realm parameter. It is possible for multiple challenges associated with the same realm to appear in the same 401 Unauthorized or 407 Proxy Authentication Required. This can occur, for example, when multiple proxies within the same administrative domain, which use a common realm, are reached by a forking request. When it retries a request, a UAC may therefore supply multiple credentials in Authorization or Proxy-Authorization header fields with the same realm parameter value. The same credentials should be used for the same realm.

19.4.5 Digest Authentication Scheme

This section describes the modifications and clarifications required to apply the HTTP Digest authentication scheme to SIP. The SIP scheme usage is almost completely identical to that for HTTP (RFC 2617). Since RFC 2543 (obsoleted by RFC 3261) is based on HTTP Digest as defined in RFC 2069, SIP servers supporting RFC 2617 must ensure they are backwards compatible with RFC 2069. Procedures for this backwards compatibility are specified in RFC 2617. Note, however, that SIP servers must not accept or request Basic authentication. The rules for Digest authentication follow those defined in RFC 2617, with HTTP/1.1 replaced by SIP/2.0 in addition to the following differences:

- The URI included in the challenge has the following ABNF: URI=SIP-URI/SIPS-URI.
- The ABNF in RFC 2617 has an error in that the uri parameter of the Authorization header field for HTTP Digest authentication is not enclosed in quotation marks. (The example in Section 3.5 of RFC 2617 is correct.) For SIP, the uri must be enclosed in quotation marks.
- The ABNF for digest-uri-value is `digest-uri-value=Request-URI`; as defined in Section 2.4.1.
- The example procedure for choosing a nonce based on Etag does not work for SIP.
- The text in RFC 2617 regarding cache operation does not apply to SIP.
- RFC 2617 requires a server check that the URI in the request line and the URI included in the Authorization header field point to the same resource. In a SIP context, these two URIs may refer to different users, due to forwarding at some proxy. Therefore, in SIP, a server may check that the Request-URI in the Authorization header field value corresponds to a user for whom the server is willing to accept forwarded or direct requests, but it is not necessarily a failure if the two fields are not equivalent.
- As a clarification to the calculation of the A2 value for message integrity assurance in the Digest authentication scheme, implementers should assume, when the entity-body is empty (i.e., when SIP messages have no body), that the hash of the entity-body resolves to the MD5 hash of an empty string, or: `H(entity-body) =MD5("")="d41d8cd98f00b204e9800998ecf8 427e"`.
- RFC 2617 notes that a cnonce value must not be sent in an Authorization (and by extension Proxy-Authorization) header field if no qop directive has been sent. Therefore, any algorithms that have a dependency on the cnonce (including MD5-Sess) require that the qop directive be sent. Use of the qop parameter is optional in RFC 2617 for the purposes of backwards compatibility with RFC 2069 (note: RFC 2069 was obsoleted by RFC 2617); since RFC 2543 (obsoleted by RFC 3261) was based on RFC 2069, the qop parameter must unfortunately remain optional for clients and servers to receive. However, servers must always send a qop parameter in WWW-Authenticate and Proxy-Authenticate header field values. If a client receives a qop parameter in a challenge header field, it must send the qop parameter in any resulting authorization header field.

RFC 2543 did not allow usage of the Authentication-Info header field (it effectively used RFC 2069). However, we now allow usage of this header field, since it provides integrity checks over the bodies and provides mutual authentication. RFC 2617 defines mechanisms for backwards compatibility using the qop attribute in the request. These mechanisms must be used by a server to determine if the client supports the new mechanisms in RFC 2617 that were not specified in RFC 2069 (obsoleted by 2617).

19.4.6 Domain Certificates over TLS for Authentication in SIP

19.4.6.1 Background

The TLS (RFC 5246) protocol is available in an increasing number of SIP implementations. To use the authentication capabilities of TLS, certificates as defined by the Internet X.509 Public Key Infrastructure specified in RFC 5280 are required. Existing SIP specifications do not sufficiently specify how to use certificates for domain (as opposed to host) authentication.

RFC 5922 that is described here provides guidance to ensure interoperability and uniform conventions for the construction and interpretation of certificates used to identify their holders as being authoritative for the domain. The description in RFC 5922 is pertinent to an X.509 PKIX-compliant certificate used for a TLS connection. More specifically, this specification describes how to encode and extract the identity of a SIP domain in a certificate and how to use that identity for SIP domain authentication. As such, this specification is relevant both to implementers of SIP and to issuers of certificates.

19.4.6.2 Problem Statement

TLS uses X.509 Public Key Infrastructure (RFC 5280) to bind an identity or a set of identities, to the subject of an X.509 certificate. While RFC 3261 provides adequate guidance on the use of X.509 certificates for S/MIME (see Section 19.6), it is relatively silent on the use of such certificates for TLS. With respect to certificates for TLS, Section 26.3.1 of RFC 3261 says,

> Proxy servers, redirect servers, and registrars should possess a site certificate whose subject corresponds to their canonical host name. The security properties of TLS and S/MIME as used in SIP are different: X.509 certificates for S/MIME are generally used for end-to-end authentication and encryption; thus, they serve to bind the identity of a user to the certificate and RFC 3261 is sufficiently clear that in certificates used for S/MIME, the subjectAltName field will contain the appropriate identity.

On the other hand, X.509 certificates used for TLS serve to bind the identities of the per-hop domain sending or receiving the SIP messages. However, the lack of guidelines in RFC 3261 on exactly where to put identities—in the subjectAltName field or carried as a Common Name (CN) in the Subject field—of an X.509 certificate created ambiguities. Following the accepted practice of the time, legacy X.509 certificates were allowed to store the identity in the CN field of the certificate instead of the currently specified subjectAltName extension. Lack of further guidelines on how to interpret the identities, which identity to choose if more than one identity is present in the certificate, the behavior when multiple identities with different schemes were present in the certificate, etc., lead to ambiguities when attempting to interpret the certificate in a uniform manner for TLS use.

We now describe how the certificates are to be used for mutual authentication when both the client and server possess appropriate certificates, and normative behavior for matching the DNS query string with an identity stored in the X.509 certificate. Furthermore, a certificate can contain multiple identities for the subject in the subjectAltName extension (the *subject* of a certificate identifies the entity associated with the public key stored in the public key field). As such, this document specifies appropriate matching rules to encompass various subject identity representation options. Finally, we also provide guidelines to service providers for assigning certificates to SIP servers.

19.4.6.3 SIP Domain to Host Resolution

Routing in SIP is performed by having the client execute RFC 3263 (see Section 8.2.4) procedures on a URI, called the Application Unique String (AUS). These procedures take as input a SIP AUS (the SIP URI), extract the domain portion of that URI for use as a lookup key, and query the DNS (see Section 8.2) to obtain an ordered set of one or more IP addresses with a port number and transport corresponding to each IP address in the set (the Expected Output). If the transport indicates the use of TLS, then a TLS connection is opened to the server on a specific IP address and port. The server presents an X.509 certificate to the client for verification as part of the initial TLS handshake. The client extracts identifiers from the Subject, and any subjectAltName extension in the certificate and compares these values to the domain part extracted from the original SIP URI (the AUS). If any identifier match is found, the server is considered to be authenticated and subsequent signaling can now proceed over the TLS connection. Matching rules for X.509 certificates and the normative behavior for clients is specified here.

As an example, consider a request that is to be routed to the SIP address sips:alice@example.com. This address requires a secure connection to the SIP domain example.com (the sips scheme mandates a secure connection). Through a series of DNS manipulations, the domain name is mapped to a set of host addresses and transports. The entity attempting to create the connection selects an address appropriate for use with TLS from this set. When the connection is established to that server, the server presents a certificate asserting the identity sip:example.com. Since the domain part of the SIP AUS matches the subject of the certificate, the server is authenticated. SIPS (see Section 4.2.1) borrows this pattern of server certificate matching from HTTPS. However, RFC 2818 prefers that the identity be conveyed as a subjectAltName extension of type dNSName rather than the common practice of conveying the identity in the CN field of the Subject field.

Similarly, this document recommends that the SIP domain identity be conveyed as a subjectAltName extension of type uniformResourceIdentifier (see Section 19.4.11). A domain name in an X.509 certificate is properly interpreted only as a sequence of octets that is to be compared with hierarchy. For example, a valid certificate for example.com does not imply that the owner of that certificate has any relationship at all to subname.example.com.

19.4.6.4 Need for Mutual Interdomain Authentication

Let us consider the SIP interdomain communications as depicted in Figure 19.8. A user, alice@example.com, invites bob@example.net for a multimedia communication session. Alice's outbound proxy, proxy-A.example.com, uses normal RFC 3263 (see Section 8.2.4) resolution rules to find a proxy proxy-B.example.net in the example.net domain that uses TLS.

Proxy A actively establishes an interdomain TLS connection with proxy B, and each presents a certificate to authenticate that connection. In accordance with RFC 3261 (see Section 3.13), when a TLS connection is created between two proxies, each side of the connection should verify and inspect the certificate of the other, noting the domain name

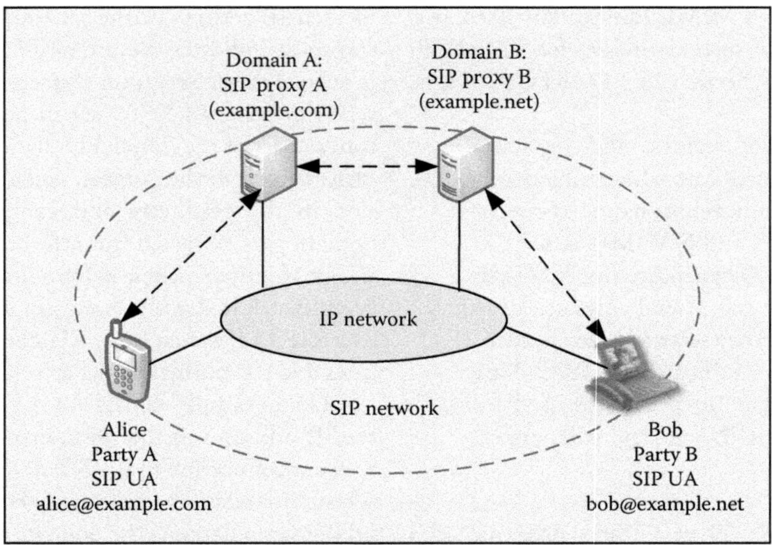

Figure 19.8 SIP trapezoid with interdomain communications. (Copyright IETF. Reproduced with permission.)

that appears in the certificate for comparison with the header fields of SIP messages. However, RFC 3261 is silent on whether to use the subjectAltName or CN of the certificate to obtain the domain name, and which takes precedence when there are multiple names identifying the holder of the certificate. The authentication problem for proxy A is straightforward: in the certificate, proxy A receives from proxy B; proxy A looks for an identity that is a SIP URI (sip:example.net) or a DNS name (example.net) that asserts proxy B's authority over the example.net domain. The normative behavior for a TLS client like proxy A is specified here.

The problem for proxy B is slightly more complex since it accepts the TLS request passively. Thus, proxy B does not possess an equivalent AUS that it can use as an anchor in matching identities from proxy A's certificate. RFC 3261 (see Section 19.12.3.2.2), only tells proxy B to "compare the domain asserted by the certificate with the 'domainname' portion of the From header field in the INVITE request." The difficulty with that instruction is that the *domainname* in the From header field is not always that of the domain from which the request is received. The normative behavior for a TLS server like proxy B that passively accepts a TLS connection and requires authentication of the sending peer domain is provided here.

19.4.6.5 Certificate Usage by SIP Service Provider

It is possible for service providers to continue the practice of using existing certificates for SIP usage with the identity conveyed only in the Subject field; however, they should carefully consider the following advantages of conveying identity in the subjectAltName extension field:

- The subjectAltName extension can hold multiple values, so the same certificate can identify multiple servers or sip domains.
- There is no fixed syntax specified for the Subject field, so issuers vary in how the field content is set. This forces a recipient to use heuristics to extract the identity, again increasing opportunities for misinterpretation.

Because of these advantages, service providers are strongly encouraged to obtain certificates that contain the identity or identities in the subjectAltName extension field. When assigning certificates to authoritative servers, a SIP service provider must ensure that the SIP domain used to reach the server appears as an identity in the subjectAltName field, or for compatibility with existing certificates, the Subject field of the certificate. In practice, this means that a service provider distributes to its users SIP URIs whose domain portion corresponds to an identity for which the service provider has been issued a certificate.

19.4.6.6 Behavior of SIP Entities

This section normatively specifies the behavior of SIP entities when using X.509 certificates to determine an authenticated SIP domain identity. The first two subsections apply to all SIP implementations that use TLS to authenticate the peer; the next section describes how to extract a set of SIP identities from the certificate obtained from a TLS peer, and Sections 4.2.3

and 19.4.6 specifies how to compare SIP identities. The remaining subsections provide context for how and when these rules are to be applied by entities in different SIP roles.

19.4.6.6.1 Finding SIP Identities in a Certificate

Implementations (both clients and server) must determine the validity of a certificate by following the procedures described in RFC 5280. As specified by Section 4.2.1.12 of RFC 5280, implementations must check for restrictions on certificate usage declared by any extendedKeyUsage extensions in the certificate. The SIP Extended Key Usage (EKU) document (RFC 5924, see Section 19.4.6.8) defines an extendedKeyUsage for SIP. Given an X.509 certificate that the above checks have found to be acceptable, the following describes how to determine what SIP domain identity or identities the certificate contains. A single certificate can serve more than one purpose—that is, the certificate might contain identities not acceptable as SIP domain identities, or might contain one or more identities that are acceptable for use as SIP domain identities.

- Examine each value in the subjectAltName field. The subjectAltName field and the constraints on its values are defined in Section 4.2.1.6 of RFC 5280. The subjectAltName field can be absent or can contain one or more values. Each value in the subjectAltName has a type; the only types acceptable for encoding a SIP domain identity shall be as follows: if the scheme of the URI is not sip, then the implementation must not accept the value as a SIP domain identity.

  If the scheme of the URI value is sip, and the URI value that contains a userpart (there is an "@"), the implementation must not accept the value as a SIP domain identity (a value with a userpart identifies an individual user, not a domain). If the scheme of the URI value is sip, and there is no userinfo component in the URI (there is no @), then the implementation must accept the hostpart as a SIP domain identity. Note that URI scheme tokens are always case insensitive. An implementation must accept a DNS identifier as a SIP domain identity if and only if no other identity is found that matches the sip URI type described above.
- If and only if the subjectAltName does not appear in the certificate, the implementation may examine the CN field of the certificate. If a valid DNS name is found there, the implementation may accept this value as a SIP domain identity. Accepting a DNS name in the CN value is allowed for backwards compatibility; however, when constructing new certificates, consider the advantages of using the subjectAltName extension field described earlier.

The above procedure yields a set containing zero or more identities from the certificate. A client uses these identities to authenticate a server, and a server uses them to authenticate a client.

19.4.6.6.2 Comparing SIP Identities

When an implementation (either client or server) compares two values as SIP domain identities: Implementations must compare only the DNS name component of each SIP domain identifier; an implementation must not use any scheme or parameters in the comparison. Implementations must compare the values as DNS names, which means that the comparison is case insensitive as specified by RFC 4343. Implementations MUST handle Internationalized Domain Names (IDNs) in accordance with Section 7.2 of RFC 5280. Implementations MUST match the values in their entirety: Implementations must not match suffixes. For example, foo .example.com does not match example.com.

Implementations must not match any form of wildcard, such as a leading "." or "*." with any other DNS label or sequence of labels. For example, *.example.com matches only *.example.com but not foo.example.com. Similarly, .example.com matches only .example.com, and does not match foo.example. com. RFC 2818 (HTTP over TLS) allows the dNSName component to contain a wildcard; for example, DNS:*.example. com. RFC 5280, while not disallowing this explicitly, leaves the interpretation of wildcards to the individual specification. RFC 3261 does not provide any guidelines on the presence of wildcards in certificates. Through the rule above, this document prohibits such wildcards in certificates for SIP domains.

19.4.6.6.3 Client Behavior

A client uses the domain portion of the SIP AUS to query a (possibly untrusted) DNS to obtain a result set, which is one or more Service (SRV) and A records identifying the server for the domain. The SIP server, when establishing a TLS connection, presents its certificate to the client for authentication. The client must determine the SIP domain identities in the server certificate using the procedure described earlier. Then, the client must compare the original domain portion of the SIP AUS used as input to the RFC 3263 (see Section 8.2.4) server location procedures to the SIP domain identities obtained from the certificate.

- If there were no identities found in the server certificate, the server is not authenticated.
- If the domain extracted from the AUS matches any SIP domain identity obtained from the certificate when compared as described above, the server is authenticated for the domain. If the server is not authenticated, the client MUST close the connection immediately.

19.4.6.6.4 Server Behavior

When a server accepts a TLS connection, the server presents its own X.509 certificate to the client. Servers that wish to authenticate the client will ask the client for a certificate. If the client possesses a certificate, that certificate is presented to the server. If the client does not present a certificate, the client must not be considered authenticated. Whether or not to close a connection if the client does not present a certificate is a matter of local policy, and depends on the authentication needs of the server for the connection. Some currently deployed servers use Digest authentication to authenticate individual requests on the connection, and choose to treat the connection as authenticated by those requests for some purposes.

If the local server policy requires client authentication for some local purpose, then one element of such a local policy might be to allow the connection only if the client is authenticated. For example, if the server is an inbound proxy that has peering relationships with the outbound proxies of other specific domains, the server might allow only connections authenticated as coming from those domains. When authenticating the client, the server must obtain the set of SIP domain identities from the client certificate as described earlier.

Because the server accepted the TLS connection passively, unlike a client, the server does not possess an AUS for comparison. Nonetheless, server policies can use the set of SIP domain identities gathered from the certificate described above to make authorization decisions. For example, a very open policy could be to accept an X.509 certificate and validate the certificate using the procedures in RFC 5280. If the certificate is valid, the identity set is logged. Alternatively, the server could have a list of all SIP domains the server is allowed to accept connections from; when a client presents its certificate, for each identity in the client certificate, the server searches for the identity in the list of acceptable domains to decide whether or not to accept the connection. Other policies that make finer distinctions are possible. The decision of whether or not the authenticated connection to the client is appropriate for use to route new requests to the client domain is independent of whether or not the connection is authenticated; the connect-reuse RFC 4474 (see Sections 2.8 and 19.4.8) discusses this aspect in more detail.

19.4.6.6.5 Proxy Behavior

A proxy must use the procedures defined earlier for a UAS when authenticating a connection from a client. A proxy must use the procedures defined for a UAC earlier when requesting an authenticated connection to a UAS. If a proxy adds a Record-Route when forwarding a request with the expectation that the route is to use secure connections, the proxy must insert into the Record-Route header a URI that corresponds to an identity for which the proxy has a certificate; if the proxy does not insert such a URI, then creation of a secure connection using the value from the Record-Route as the AUS will be impossible.

19.4.6.6.6 Registrar Behavior

A SIP registrar, acting as a server, follows the normative behavior described above. When the SIP registrar accepts a TLS connection from the client, the SIP registrar presents its certificate. Depending on the registrar policies, the SIP registrar can challenge the client with HTTP Digest.

19.4.6.6.7 Redirect Server Behavior

A SIP redirect server follows the normative behavior of a UAS as specified above.

19.4.6.6.8 Virtual SIP Servers and Certificate Content

In the *virtual hosting* cases where multiple domains are managed by a single application, a certificate can contain multiple subjects by having distinct identities in the subjectAltName field as specified in RFC 4474 (see Sections 2.8). Clients seeking to authenticate a server on such a virtual host can still follow the directions described earlier to find the identity matching the SIP AUS used to query DNS. Alternatively, if the TLS client hello server_name extension as defined in RFC 6066 is supported, the client should use that extension to request a certificate corresponding to the specific domain (from the SIP AUS) with which the client is seeking to establish a connection.

19.4.6.6.9 Security Considerations

The goals of TLS (when used with X.509 certificates) include the following security guarantees at the transport layer: confidentiality—packets tunneled through TLS can be read only by the sender and receiver; integrity—packets tunneled through TLS cannot be undetectably modified on the connection between the sender and receiver; authentication—each principal is authenticated to the other as possessing a private key for which a certificate has been issued. Moreover, this certificate has not been revoked, and is verifiable by a certificate chain leading to a (locally configured) trust anchor. We expect appropriate processing of domain certificates to provide the following security guarantees at the application level:

- Confidentiality: SIPS messages from alice@example.com to bob@example.net can be read only by alice@example.com, bob@example.net, and SIP proxies issued with domain certificates for example.com or example.net.

- Integrity: SIPS messages from alice@example.com to bob@example.net cannot be undetectably modified on the links between alice@example.com, bob@example .net, and SIP proxies issued with domain certificates for example.com or example.net.
- Authentication: alice@example.com and proxy.example.com are mutually authenticated; moreover, proxy. example.com is authenticated to alice@example.com as an authoritative proxy for domain example.com. Similar mutual authentication guarantees are given between proxy.example.com and proxy.example.net, and between proxy.example.net and bob@example. net. As a result, alice@example.com is transitively mutually authenticated to bob@example.net (assuming trust in the authoritative proxies for example.com and example.net).

19.4.6.6.10 Connection Authentication Using Digest

Digest authentication in SIP provides for authentication of the message sender to the challenging UAS. As commonly deployed, digest authentication provides only very limited integrity protection of the authenticated message, and has no provision for binding the authentication to any attribute of the transport. Many existing SIP deployments have chosen to use the Digest authentication of one or more messages on a particular transport connection as a way to authenticate the connection itself—by implication, authenticating other (unauthenticated) messages on that connection. Some even choose to similarly authenticate a UDP source address and port based on the digest authentication of another message received from that address and port. This use of digest goes beyond the assurances that the Digest Authentication mechanism was designed to provide. A SIP implementation should not use the Digest Authentication of one message on a TCP connection or from a UDP peer to infer any authentication of any other messages on that connection or from that peer. Authentication of the domain at the other end of a connection should be accomplished using TLS and the certificate validation rules described by this specification instead.

19.4.6.7 Nonnormative Changes and Updates in RFC 3261

RFC 5922 (see Section 19.4.11) provides nonnormative changes and updates of RFC 3261 as follows:

- Additions

  The content of Sections 19.4.6.3 through 19.4.6.6 can be incorporated as subsections within a section that describes SIP domain authentication. The contents of Section 19.4.6.6.10 can be incorporated into the Security Considerations section of the new document. All normative references from this document can be carried forward to its successor.
- Changes

  The following paragraph describes changes in specific sections of RFC 3261 that need to be modified in the successor document to align them with the content of this document. In each of the following, the token <domain-authentication> is a reference to the section added as described above in "Additions."
- Changes to Section 26.3.1 of RFC 3261

  The current text says: "Proxy servers, redirect servers, and registrars should possess a site certificate whose subject corresponds to their canonical host name." The suggested replacement for the above is: "Proxy servers, redirect servers, registrars, and any other server that is authoritative for some SIP purpose in a given domain should possess a certificate whose subjects include the name of that SIP domain."

19.4.6.8 EKU for X.509 Certificates for Authentication

We have explained earlier that the certificates need to be restricted specific to a particular domain in SIP. In this regard, RFC 5924 that is explained here specifies an EKU X.509 certificate extension for restricting the applicability of a certificate to use with SIP services. The extension indicates one or more purposes for which the certified public key is valid. In addition to providing rules for SIP implementations, this also provides guidance to issuers of certificates for use with SIP.

Assume that alice@example.com creates an INVITE for bob@example.net; her UA routes the request to some proxy in her domain, example.com. Suppose also that example. com is a large organization that maintains several SIP proxies, and her INVITE arrived at an outbound proxy proxy-A. example.com. To route the request onward, proxy A uses RFC 3263 (see Section 8.2.4) resolution and finds that proxy-B.example.net is a valid proxy for example.net that uses TLS. Proxy-A.example.com requests a TLS connection to Proxy-B.example.net, and in the TLS handshake each one presents a certificate to authenticate that connection. The validation of these certificates by each proxy to determine whether or not their peer is authoritative for the appropriate SIP domain is defined earlier (RFC 5922, see Section 19.4.6).

A SIP domain name is frequently textually identical to the same DNS name used for other purposes. For example, the DNS name example.com can serve as a SIP domain name, an e-mail domain name, and a web service name. Since these different services within a single organization might be administered independently and hosted separately, it is desirable that a certificate be able to bind the DNS name to its usage as a SIP domain name without creating the implication that the entity presenting the certificate is also authoritative for some other purpose. A mechanism is needed to allow the certificate issued to a proxy to be restricted such that the subject name(s) that the certificate contains are valid only for use in SIP. In our example, proxy B possesses a certificate making proxy B authoritative as a SIP server for the domain example.net; furthermore, proxy B has a policy that requires the client's SIP domain to be authenticated through a similar certificate. Proxy A is authoritative as a SIP server for the domain example.com; when proxy A makes a TLS connection to proxy B, the latter accepts the connection based on its policy.

19.4.6.8.1 Restricting Usage to SIP

This memo defines a certificate profile for restricting the usage of a domain name binding to usage as a SIP domain name. Section 4.2.1.12 of RFC 5280 defines a mechanism for this purpose: an Extended Key Usage (EKU) attribute, where the purpose of the EKU extension is described as follows: if the extension is present, then the certificate must only be used for one of the purposes indicated. If multiple purposes are indicated, the application need not recognize all purposes indicated, as long as the intended purpose is present. Certificate using applications may require that the EKU extension be present and that a particular purpose be indicated in order for the certificate to be acceptable to that application. A Certificate Authority issuing a certificate whose purpose is to bind a SIP domain identity without binding other non-SIP identities MUST include an id-kp-sipDomain attribute in the EKU extension value shown in the next section.

19.4.6.8.2 EKU Values for SIP Domains

RFC 5280 specifies the EKU X.509 certificate extension for use in the Internet. The extension indicates one or more purposes for which the certified public key is valid. The EKU extension can be used in conjunction with the key usage extension, which indicates how the public key in the certificate is used, in a more basic cryptographic way.

The EKU extension syntax is repeated here for convenience:

```
ExtKeyUsageSyntax   ::  = SEQUENCE SIZE (1..
                          MAX) OF KeyPurposeId
KeyPurposeId        ::  = OBJECT IDENTIFIER
```

This specification defines the KeyPurposeId id-kp-sipDomain. Inclusion of this KeyPurposeId in a certificate indicates that the use of any Subject names in the certificate is restricted to use by a SIP service (along with any usages allowed by other EKU values).

```
id-kp OBJECT IDENTIFIER ::  ={iso(1)
                             identified-
                             organization(3)
                             dod(6) internet(1)
                             security(5)
                             mechanisms(5)
                             pkix(7) 3}
id-kp-sipDomain OBJECT IDENTIFIER:: = {id-kp
                                      20}
```

19.4.6.8.3 Using the SIP EKU in a Certificate

Domain certificates in the SIP (RFC 5922, see Section 19.4.6) contains the steps for finding an identity (or a set of identities) in an X.509 certificate for SIP. To determine whether the usage of a certificate is restricted to serve as a SIP certificate only, implementations must perform the steps given below as a part of the certificate validation.

The implementation must examine the EKU value(s):

- If the certificate does not contain any EKU values (the EKU extension does not exist), it is a matter of local policy whether or not to accept the certificate for use as a SIP certificate. Note that since certificates not following this specification will not have the id-kp-sip-Domain EKU value, and many do not have any EKU values, the more interoperable local policy would be to accept the certificate.
- If the certificate contains the id-kp-sipDomain EKU extension, then implementations of this specification must consider the certificate acceptable for use as a SIP certificate.
- If the certificate does not contain the id-kp-sipDomain EKU value, but does contain the id-kp-anyExtendedKeyUsage EKU value, it is a matter of local policy whether or not to consider the certificate acceptable for use as a SIP certificate.
- If the EKU extension exists, but does not contain any of the idkp-sipDomain or id-kp-anyExtendedKeyUsage EKU values, then the certificate must not be accepted as valid for use as a SIP certificate.

19.4.6.8.4 Implications for a Certification Authority

The procedures and practices employed by a certification authority MUST ensure that the correct values for the EKU extension and subjectAltName are inserted in each certificate that is issued. For certificates that indicate authority over a SIP domain, but not over services other than SIP, certificate authorities must include the idkp-sipDomain EKU extension.

19.4.6.8.5 Security Considerations

This memo defines an EKU X.509 certificate extension that restricts the usage of a certificate to a SIP service belonging to an autonomous domain. Relying parties can execute applicable policies (such as those related to billing) on receiving a certificate with the id-kp-sipDomain EKU value. An id-kp-sipDomain EKU value does not introduce any new security or privacy concerns.

19.4.6.9 Certificate and Credential Management Service for SIP

RFC 3261, as amended by RFC 3853, provides a mechanism for end-to-end encryption and integrity using S/MIME (RFC 5751, see Section 19.6). Several security properties of RFC 3261 depend on S/MIME, and yet it has not been widely deployed. One reason is the complexity of providing a reasonable certificate distribution infrastructure. RFC 6072 specifies a way to address discovery, retrieval, and management of certificates for SIP deployments. Combined with the SIP Identity (RFC 4474, see Section 19.4.8) specification, this specification allows users to have certificates that are not signed by any well-known certification authority while still strongly binding the user's identity to the certificate. In addition, this specification provides a mechanism that allows SIP UAs such as IP phones to enroll and get their credentials without any more configuration information than they commonly have today. The end user expends no extra effort. The definitions of certificate and credentials are provided in Section 2.2.

The general approach is to provide a new SIP service referred to as a *credential service* that allows SIP UAs to subscribe to other users' certificates using a new SIP event package (RFC 6665, see Section 5.2). The certificate is delivered to the subscribing UA in a corresponding SIP NOTIFY request. An authentication service as described in the SIP Identity (RFC 4474, see Section 19.4.8) specification can be used to vouch for the identity of the sender of the certificate by using the sender's proxy domain certificate to sign the NOTIFY request. The authentication service is vouching that the sender is allowed to populate the SIP From header field value. The sender of the message is vouching that this is an appropriate certificate for the user identified in the SIP From header field value. The credential service can manage public certificates as well as the user's private keys. Users can update their credentials, as stored on the credential service, using a SIP PUBLISH (RFC 3903, see Section 5.2) request. The UA authenticates to the credential service using a shared secret when a UA is updating a credential. Typically, the shared secret will be the same one that is used by the UA to authenticate a REGISTER request with the Registrar for the domain (usually with SIP Digest Authentication). The details of RFC 6072 for certificate and credential management of the SIP event package are not described here for the sake of brevity.

19.4.7 Authenticated Identity Body Format in SIP

19.4.7.1 Overview

RFC 3261 describes an integrity mechanism that relies on signing tunneled message/sip MIME bodies (see Section 19.6) within SIP requests. The purpose of this mechanism is to replicate the headers of a SIP request within a body carried in that request in order to provide a digital signature over these headers. The signature on this body also provides authentication. The core requirement that motivates the tunneled message/sip mechanism is the problem of providing a cryptographically verifiable identity within a SIP request. The baseline SIP protocol allows a UA to express the identity of its user in any of a number of headers. The primary place for identity information asserted by the sender of a request is the From header. The From header field contains a URI (like sip:alice@example.com) and an optional display-name (like Alice) that identifies the originator of the request. A user may have many identities that are used in different contexts.

Typically, this URI is an AOR that can be dereferenced in order to contact the originator of the request; specifically, it is usually the same AOR under which a user registers their devices in order to receive incoming requests. This AOR is assigned and maintained by the administrator of the SIP service in the domain identified by the host portion of the AOR. However, the From field of a request can usually be set arbitrarily by the user of a SIP UA; the From header of a message provides no internal assurance that the originating user can legitimately claim the given identity. Nevertheless, many SIP UAs will obligingly display the contents of the From field as the identity of the originator of a received request (as a sort of caller identification function), much as e-mail implementations display the From field as the sender's identity.

To provide the recipient of a SIP message with greater assurance of the identity of the sender, a cryptographic signature can be provided over the headers of the SIP request, which allows the signer to assert a verifiable identity. Unfortunately, a signature over the From header alone is insufficient because it could be cut-and-pasted into a replay or forwarding attack, and more headers are therefore needed to correlate a signature with a request. RFC 3261 therefore recommends copying all of the headers from the request into a signed MIME body; however, SIP messages can be large, and many of the headers in a SIP message would not be relevant in determining the identity of the sender or assuring reference integrity with the request; moreover, some headers may change in transit for perfectly valid reasons.

Thus, this large tunneled message/sip body will almost necessarily be at variance with the headers in a request when it is received by the UAS, and the burden on the UAS to determine which header changes were legitimate, and which were security violations. It is therefore desirable to find a happy medium—to provide a way of signing just enough headers that the identity of the sender can be ascertained and correlated with the request. message/sipfrag defined in RFC 3420 (see Section 2.8.2) provides a way for a subset of SIP headers to be included in a MIME body. RFC 3893 provides a more specific mechanism to derive integrity and authentication properties from an authenticated identity body, a digitally signed SIP message, or message fragment. A standard format for such bodies, known as Authenticated Identity Bodies (AIBs), is given in the next section. The AIB format described here is based on message/sipfrag.

For reasons of end-to-end privacy, it may also be desirable to encrypt AIBs. The procedures for this encryption are given here as well. This document proposes that the AIB format should be used instead of the existing tunneled message/sip mechanism described in RFC 3261 (see Section 19.6.4), in order to provide the identity of the caller; if integrity over other, unrelated headers is required, then the message/sip mechanism should be used.

19.4.7.2 AIB Format

As a way of sharing authenticated identity among parties in the network, a special type of MIME body format, the AIB format, is defined in this section. AIBs allow a party in a SIP transaction to cryptographically sign the headers that assert the identity of the originator of a message, and provide some other headers necessary for reference integrity. An AIB is a MIME body of type message/sipfrag. For more information on constructing sipfrags, including examples, see Section 2.8.2. This MIME body must have a Content-Disposition (see Section 2.8.2) disposition-type of aib, a new value defined in this document specifically for authenticated identity bodies. The Content-Disposition header should also contain a handling parameter indicating that this MIME body is optional; that is, if this mechanism is not supported by the UAS, it can still attempt to process the request.

AIBs using the message/sipfrag MIME type must contain the following headers when providing identity for an INVITE request: From, Date, Call-ID, and Contact; they should also contain the To and CSeq header. The security properties of these headers, and circumstances in which they should be used, are also described. AIBs may contain any other headers that help uniquely identify the transaction or provide related reference integrity. An example of the AIB format for an INVITE is

```
Content-Type: message/sipfrag
Content-Disposition: aib; handling=optional
From: Alice <sip:alice@example.com>
To: Bob <sip:bob@example.net>
Contact: <sip:alice@pc33.example.com>
Date: Thu, 21 Feb 2002 13:02:03 GMT
Call-ID: a84b4c76e66710
CSeq: 314159 INVITE
```

Unsigned AIBs MUST be treated by any recipients according to the rules set out in Section 2.3 for AIBs that do not validate. After the AIB has been signed, it should be added to existing MIME bodies in the request (such as SDP), if necessary by transitioning the outermost MIME body to a multipart/mixed format.

19.4.7.3 Example of a Request with AIB

The following shows a full SIP INVITE request with an AIB:

```
INVITE sip:bob@example.net SIP/2.0
Via: SIP/2.0/UDP pc33.example.com;
branch=z9hG4bKnashds8
To: Bob <sip:bob@example.net>
From: Alice <sip:alice@example.com>;
tag=1928301774
Call-ID: a84b4c76e66710
CSeq: 314159 INVITE
Max-Forwards: 70
Date: Thu, 21 Feb 2002 13:02:03 GMT
Contact: <sip:alice@pc33.example.com>
Content-Type: multipart/mixed;
boundary=unique-boundary-1

--unique-boundary-1

Content-Type: application/sdp
Content-Length: 147

v=0
o=UserA 2890844526 2890844526 IN IP4 example.
com
s=Session SDP
c=IN IP4 pc33.example.com
t=0 0
m=audio 49172 RTP/AVP 0
a=rtpmap:0 PCMU/8000
--unique-boundary-1
Content-Type: multipart/signed;
protocol="application/pkcs7-signature";
micalg=sha1; boundary=boundary42
Content-Length: 608

--boundary42

Content-Type: message/sipfrag
Content-Disposition: aib; handling=optional
From: Alice <sip:alice@example.com>
To: Bob <sip:bob@example.net>
Contact: <sip:alice@pc33.example.com>
Date: Thu, 21 Feb 2002 13:02:03 GMT
Call-ID: a84b4c76e66710
CSeq: 314159 INVITE

--boundary42
```

```
Content-Type: application/pkcs7-signature;
name=smime.p7s
Content-Transfer-Encoding: base64
Content-Disposition: attachment;
filename=smime.p7s;
handling=required
```


```
ghyHhHUujhJhjH77n8HHGTrfvbnj756tbB9HG4VQpfyF
467GhIGfHfYT6
4VQpfyF467GhIGfHfYT6jH77n8HHGghyHhHUujhJh756
tbB9HGTrfvbnj
n8HHGTrfvhJhjH776tbB9HG4VQbnj7567GhIGfHfYT6g
hyHhHUujpfyF4
7GhIGfHfYT64VQbnj756
```


```
--boundary42--

--unique-boundary-1--
```

19.4.7.4 AIBs for Identifying Third Parties

There are special-case uses of the INVITE method in which some SIP messages are exchanged with a third party before an INVITE is sent, and in which the identity of the third party needs to be carried in the subsequent INVITE. The details of addressing identity in such contexts are outside the scope of this document. At a high level, it is possible that identity information for a third party might be carried in a supplemental AIB. The presence of a supplemental AIB within a message would not preclude the appearance of a regular AIB as specified in this document. Example cases in which supplemental AIBs might appear include the following: The use of the REFER method, for example, has a requirement for the recipient of an INVITE to ascertain the identity of the referrer who caused the INVITE to be sent. Third-party call control specified in RFC 3725 (see Section 18.3) has an even more complicated identity problem. A central controller INVITEs one party, gathers identity information (and session context) from that party, and then uses this information to INVITE another party. Ideally, the controller would also have a way to share a cryptographic identity signature given by the first party invited by the controller to the second party invited by the controller. In both of these cases, the Call-ID and CSeq of the original request (3PCC INVITE or REFER) would not correspond with that of the request in by the subsequent INVITE, nor would the To or From.

In both the REFER case and the 3PCC case, the Call-ID and CSeq cannot be used to guarantee reference integrity, and it is therefore much harder to correlate an AIB to a subsequent INVITE request. Thus, in these cases, some other headers might be used to provide reference integrity between the headers in a supplemental AIB with the headers of a 3PCC or REFER-generated INVITE; however, this usage is outside of the scope of this document. In order for AIBs to be used in these third-party contexts, further specification work is required to determine which additional headers, if any, need to be included in an AIB in a specific third-party case, and how to differentiate the primary AIB in a message from a third-party AIB.

19.4.7.5 Identity in Non-INVITE Requests

The requirements for populating an AIB in requests within a dialog generally parallel those of the INVITE: From, Call-ID, Date, and Contact header fields are required. Some non-INVITE requests, however, may have different identity requirements. New SIP methods or extensions that leverage AIB security must identify any special identity requirements in the Security Considerations of their specification.

19.4.7.6 Identity in Responses

Many of the practices described in the preceding sections can be applied to responses as well as requests. Note that a new set of headers must be generated to populate the AIB in a response. The From header field of the AIB in the response to an INVITE must correspond to the AOR of the responder, not to the From header field received in the request. The To header field of the request must not be included. A new Date header field and Contact header field should be generated for the AIB in a response. The Call-ID and CSeq should, however, be copied from the request.

Generally, the To header field of the request will correspond to the AOR of the responder. In some architectures where retargeting is used, however, this need not be the case. Some recipients of response AIBs may consider it a cause for security concern if the To header field of the request is not the same as the AOR in the From header field of the AIB in a response.

19.4.7.7 Receiving an AIB

When a UA receives a request containing an AIB, it must verify the signature, including validating the certificate of the signer, and compare the identity of the signer (the subjectAltName) with, in the INVITE case, the domain portion of the URI in the From header field of the request (for non-INVITE requests, other headers may be subject to this comparison). The two should correspond exactly; if they do not, the UA must report this condition to its user before proceeding. UAs may distinguish between plausibly minor variations (the difference between example.com and sip.example.com) and major variations (example.com versus example.org) when reporting these discrepancies in order to give the user some idea of how to handle this situation.

Analysis and comparison of the Date, Call-ID, and Contact header fields, as explained later for providing security, must also be performed. Any discrepancies or violations must be reported to the user. When the originating UA of a request receives a response containing an AIB, it should compare the identity in the From header field of the AIB of the response with the original value of the To header field in the request. If these represent different identities, the UA should render the identity in the AIB of the response to its user. Note that a discrepancy in these identity fields is not necessarily an indication of a security breach; normal retargeting may simply have directed the request to a different final destination. Implementers therefore may consider it unnecessary to alert the user of a security violation in this case.

19.4.7.8 Encryption of Identity

Many SIP entities that support the use of S/MIME for signatures also support S/MIME encryption, as described in RFC 3261 (see Section 19.6.4.3). While encryption of AIBs entails that only the holder of a specific key can decrypt the body, that single key could be distributed throughout a network of hosts that exist under common policies. The security of the AIB is therefore predicated on the secure distribution of the key. However, for some networks (in which there are federations of trusted hosts under a common policy), the widespread distribution of a decryption key could be appropriate. Some telephone networks, for example, might require this model. When an AIB is encrypted, the AIB should be encrypted before it is signed. Implementations must still accept AIBs that have been signed and then encrypted.

19.4.7.9 Example of Encryption

The following is an example of an encrypted and signed AIB (without any of the preceding SIP headers). In a rendition of this body sent over the wire, the text wrapped in asterisks would be in ciphertext.

```
Content-Type: multipart/signed;
protocol="application/pkcs7-signature";
micalg=sha1; boundary=boundary42
Content-Length: 568
Content-Disposition: aib; handling=optional

--boundary42

Content-Type: application/pkcs7-mime;
smime-type=enveloped-data;
name=smime.p7m
Content-Transfer-Encoding: base64
Content-Disposition: attachment;
filename=smime.p7m
handling=required
Content-Length: 231

* Content-Type: message/sipfrag *
* Content-Disposition: aib; handling=optional *
* *
* From: sip:alice@example.com *
* Call-ID: a84b4c76e66710 *
* Contact: sip:alice@device21.example.com *
* Date: Thu, 21 Feb 2002 13:02:03 GMT *

--boundary42

Content-Type: application/pkcs7-signature;
name=smime.p7s
Content-Transfer-Encoding: base64
Content-Disposition: attachment;
filename=smime.p7s;
handling=required
ghyHhHUujhJhjH77n8HHGTrfvbnj756tbB9HG4VQpfyF
467GhIGfHfYT6
4VQpfyF467GhIGfHfYT6jH77n8HHGghyHhHUujhJh756
tbB9HGTrfvbnj
n8HHGTrfvhJhjH776tbB9HG4VQbnj7567GhIGfHfYT6g
hyHhHUujpfyF4
7GhIGfHfYT64VQbnj756

--boundary42--
```

19.4.7.10 Security Considerations

The purpose of an AIB is to provide an identity for the sender of a SIP message. This identity is held in the From header field of an AIB. While other headers are also included, they are provided solely to assist in detection of replays and cut-and-paste attacks leveraged to impersonate the caller. The contents of the From header field of a valid AIB are suitable for display as a Caller ID for the sender of the SIP message. RFC 3873 mandates the inclusion of the Contact, Date, Call-ID, and From header fields within an AIB, and recommends the inclusion of CSeq and To header fields, when message/sipfrag is used to represent the identity of a request's sender. If these headers are omitted, some important security properties of AIB are lost. In general, the considerations related to the inclusion of various headers in an AIB are the same as those given in RFC 3261 for including headers in tunneled message/sip MIME bodies (see Section 19.6.3).

The From header field indicates the identity of the sender of the message; were this header to be excluded, the creator of the AIB essentially would not be asserting an identity at all. The Date and Contact headers provide reference integrity and replay protection, as described in RFC 3261 (see Section 19.6.4.2). Implementations of this specification must follow the rules for acceptance of the Date header field in tunneled message/sip requests described in RFC 3261 (see Section 19.6.4.2); this ensures that outdated AIBs will not be replayed (the suggested interval is that the Date header must indicate a time within 3600 seconds of the receipt of a message). Implementations MUST also record Call-IDs received in AIBs, and must remember those Call-IDs for at least the duration of a single Date interval (i.e., 3600 seconds).

Accordingly, if an AIB is replayed within the Date interval, receivers will recognize that it is invalid because of a Call-ID duplication; if an AIB is replayed after the Date interval, receivers will recognize that it is invalid because the Date is stale. The Contact header field is included to tie the AIB to a particular device instance that generated the request. Were an active attacker to intercept a request containing an AIB, and cut-and-paste the AIB into their own request (reusing the From, Contact, Date, and Call-ID fields that appear in the AIB), they would not be eligible to receive SIP requests from the called UA, since those requests are routed to the URI identified in the Contact header field.

The To and CSeq header fields provide properties that are generally useful, but not for all possible applications of AIBs. If a new AIB is issued each time a new SIP transaction is initiated in a dialog, the CSeq header field provides a valuable property (replay protection for this particular transaction). If, however, one AIB is used for an entire dialog, subsequent transactions in the dialog would use the same AIB that appeared in the INVITE transaction. Using a single AIB for an entire dialog reduces the load on the generator of the AIB. The To header field usually designates the original URI that the caller intended to reach, and therefore it may vary from the Request-URI if retargeting occurs at some point in the network. Accordingly, including the To header field in the AIB helps identify cut-and-paste attacks in which an AIB sent to a particular destination is reused to impersonate the sender to a different destination. However, the inclusion of the To header field probably would not make sense for many third-party AIB cases, nor is its inclusion necessary for responses.

19.4.8 Cryptographic Authentication Scheme

In SIP, an identity is usually defined as a SIP URI, commonly a canonical AOR employed to reach a user (such as sip:alice@atlanta.example.com). RFC 3261 stipulates several places within a SIP request where a user can express an identity for themselves, notably the user-populated From header field. However, the recipient of a SIP request has no way to verify that the From header field has been populated appropriately, in the absence of some sort of cryptographic authentication mechanism. RFC 3261 also specifies a number of security mechanisms that can be employed by SIP UAs, including Digest, TLS, and S/MIME (implementations may support other security schemes as well). However, few SIP UAs today support the end-user certificates necessary to authenticate themselves (via S/MIME, e.g., see Section 19.6), and furthermore Digest authentication is limited by the fact that the originator and destination must share a prearranged secret.

It is desirable for SIP UAs to be able to send requests to destinations with which they have no previous association; one can receive a call from someone with whom one has no previous association, and still have a reasonable assurance that the person's displayed Caller-ID is accurate. A cryptographic approach can probably provide a much stronger and less-spoofable assurance of identity than the S/MIME (see Section 19.6) provides for SIP networks. Cryptographically assuring the identity of the end users that originate SIP requests is an essential need especially in an interdomain context. RFC 4474 enhances the authenticated identity management specifying a mechanism for securely identifying originators of SIP messages. It does so by defining two new SIP header fields—Identity, for conveying a signature used for validating the identity, and Identity-Info, for conveying a reference to the certificate of the signer satisfying the following critical requirements:

- The mechanism allows a UAC or a proxy server to provide a strong cryptographic identity assurance in a request that can be verified by a proxy server or UAS.
- UAs that receive identity assurances is able to validate these assurances without performing any network lookup.
- UAs that hold certificates on behalf of their user is capable of adding this identity assurance to requests.
- Proxy servers that hold certificates on behalf of their domain is capable of adding this identity assurance to requests. However, a UAC is not required to support this mechanism in order for an identity assurance to be added to a request in this fashion.
- The mechanism prevents replay of the identity assurance by an attacker.
- The mechanism is capable of protecting the integrity of SIP message bodies (to ensure that media offers and answers are linked to the signaling identity) and thereby provides full replay protection.
- It is also possible for a user to have multiple AORs (i.e., accounts or aliases) that it is authorized to use within a domain, and for the UAC to assert one identity while authenticating itself as another, related, identity, as permitted by the local policy of the domain.

19.4.8.1 Background

The usage of many SIP applications and services is governed by authorization policies as described earlier (see Section 19.1) and in Section 19.5. These policies may be automated, or they may be applied manually by humans. An example of the latter would be an Internet telephone application that displays the Caller-ID of a caller, which a human may review before answering a call. An example of the former would be a presence service that compares the identity of potential subscribers to a whitelist before determining whether it should accept or reject the subscription. In both of these cases, attackers might attempt to circumvent these authorization policies through impersonation. Since the primary identifier of the sender of a SIP request, the From header field, can be populated arbitrarily by the controller of a UA, impersonation is very simple today.

The mechanism (RFC 4474) that is described here aspires to provide a strong identity system for SIP in which authorization policies cannot be circumvented by impersonation. All UAs being RFC 3261-compliant support Digest authentication, which utilizes a shared secret, as a means for authenticating themselves to a SIP registrar. Registration allows a UA to express that it is an appropriate entity to which requests should be sent for a particular SIP AOR URI (e.g., sip:alice@atlanta.example.com). By the definition of identity used here, registration is a proof of the identity of the user to a registrar. However, the credentials with which a UA proves its identity to a registrar cannot be validated by just any UA or proxy server—these credentials are only shared between the UA and their domain administrator. Thus, this shared secret does not immediately help a user to authenticate to a wide range of recipients.

Recipients require a means of determining whether or not the *return address* identity of a non-REGISTER request (i.e., the From header field value) has legitimately been asserted. The AOR URI used for registration is also the URI with which a UA commonly populates the From header field of requests in order to provide a return address identity to recipients. From an authorization perspective, if you can prove you are eligible to register in a domain under a particular AOR, you can prove you can legitimately receive requests for that AOR, and accordingly, when you place that AOR in the From header field of a SIP request other than a registration (like an INVITE), you are providing a return address where you can legitimately be reached. In other words, if you are authorized to receive requests for that return address, logically, it follows that you are also authorized to assert that return address in your From header field. This is of course only one manner in which a domain might determine how a particular user is authorized to populate the From header field; as an aside, for other sorts of URIs in the From header field (like anonymous URIs), other authorization policies would apply.

Ideally, then, SIP UAs should have some way of proving to recipients of SIP requests that their local domain has authenticated them and authorized the population of the From header field. This document proposes a mediated authentication architecture for SIP in which requests are sent to a server in the user's local domain, which authenticates such requests (using the same practices by which the domain would authenticate REGISTER requests). Once a message has been authenticated, the local domain then needs some way to communicate to other SIP entities that the sending user has been authenticated and its use of the From header field has been authorized. This document addresses how that imprimatur of authentication can be shared.

RFC 3261 already describes an architecture very similar to this (see Sections 19.4.1 through 19.4.5), in which a UA authenticates itself to a local proxy server, which in turn authenticates itself to a remote proxy server via mutual TLS, creating a two-link chain of transitive authentication between the originator and the remote domain. While this works well in some architectures, there are a few respects in which this is impractical. For one, transitive trust is inherently weaker than an assertion that can be validated end-to-end. It is possible for SIP requests to cross multiple intermediaries in separate administrative domains, in which case transitive trust becomes even less compelling.

One solution to this problem is to use *trusted* SIP intermediaries that assert an identity for users in the form of a privileged SIP header. A mechanism for doing so (with the P-Asserted-Identity header) is given in RFC 3325 (see Sections 2.8 and 20.3). However, this solution allows only hop-by-hop trust between intermediaries, not end-to-end cryptographic authentication, and it assumes a managed network of nodes with strict mutual trust relationships, an assumption that is incompatible with widespread Internet deployment. Accordingly, this document specifies a means of sharing a cryptographic assurance of end-user SIP Identity in an interdomain or intradomain context that is based on the concept of an *authentication service* and a new SIP header, the Identity header. Note that the scope of this cryptographic authentication mechanism is limited to providing this identity assurance for SIP requests; solving this problem for SIP responses is more complicated and is a subject for future research.

This specification allows either a UA or a proxy server to provide identity services and to verify identities. To maximize end-to-end security, it is obviously preferable for end-users to acquire their own certificates and corresponding private keys; if they do, they can act as an authentication service. However, end-user certificates may be neither practical nor affordable, given the difficulties of establishing a Public Key Infrastructure (PKI) that extends to end users, and moreover, given the potentially large number of SIP UAs (phones, PCs, laptops, PDAs, gaming devices) that may be employed by a single user. In such environments, synchronizing keying material across multiple devices may be very complex and requires a good deal of additional end-point behavior. Managing several certificates for the various devices is also quite problematic and unpopular with users. Accordingly, in the initial use of this mechanism, it is likely that intermediaries will instantiate the authentication service role.

19.4.8.2 Cryptographic Operations

A high-level informative overview of the mechanisms is described here. Imagine the case where Alice, who has the home proxy of example.com and the AOR sip:alice@

example.com, wants to communicate with sip:bob@example.org. Alice generates an INVITE and places her identity in the From header field of the request. She then sends an INVITE over TLS to an authentication service proxy for her domain. The authentication service authenticates Alice (possibly by sending a Digest authentication challenge) and validates that she is authorized to assert the identity that is populated in the From header field. This value may be Alice's AOR, or it may be some other value that the policy of the proxy server permits her to use.

It then computes a hash over some particular headers, including the From header field and the bodies in the message. This hash is signed with the certificate for the domain (example.com, in Alice's case) and inserted in a new header field in the SIP message, the Identity header. The proxy, as the holder of the private key of its domain, is asserting that the originator of this request has been authenticated and that she is authorized to claim the identity (the SIP AOR) that appears in the From header field. The proxy also inserts a companion header field, Identity-Info, that tells Bob how to acquire its certificate, if he does not already have it. When Bob's domain receives the request, it verifies the signature provided in the Identity header, and thus can validate that the domain indicated by the host portion of the AOR in the From header field authenticated the user, and permitted the user to assert that From header field value. This same validation operation may be performed by Bob's UAS.

19.4.8.3 Authentication Service Behavior

RFC 4474 defines a new role for SIP entities called an authentication service. The authentication service role can be instantiated by a proxy server or a UA. Any entity that instantiates the authentication service role must possess the private key of a domain certificate. Intermediaries that instantiate this role must be capable of authenticating one or more SIP users that can register in that domain. Commonly, this role will be instantiated by a proxy server, since these entities are more likely to have a static host name, hold a corresponding certificate, and have access to SIP registrar capabilities that allow them to authenticate users in their domain. It is also possible that the authentication service role might be instantiated by an entity that acts as a redirect server; however, that is left as a topic for future work.

SIP entities that act as an authentication service must add a Date header field to SIP requests if one is not already present (see Syntax in Section 16.2.7, for information on how the Date header field assists verifiers). Similarly, authentication services must add a Content-Length header field to SIP requests if one is not already present; this can help verifiers to double-check that they are hashing exactly as many bytes of message body as the authentication service when they verify the message. Entities instantiating the authentication service role perform the following steps, in order, to generate an Identity header for a SIP request.

Step 1:

The authentication service must extract the identity of the sender from the request. The authentication service takes this value from the From header field; this AOR will be referred to here as the identity field. If the identity field contains a SIP or SIP Secure (SIPS) URI, the authentication service must extract the host name portion of the identity field and compare it to the domain(s) for which it is responsible (following the procedures in RFC 3261, Chapter 9, used by a proxy server to determine the domain(s) for which it is responsible). If the identity field uses the TEL URI scheme, the policy of the authentication service determines whether or not it is responsible for this identity. If the authentication service is not responsible for the identity in question, it should process and forward the request normally, but it must not add an Identity header; see below for more information on authentication service handling of an existing Identity header.

Step 2:

The authentication service must determine whether or not the sender of the request is authorized to claim the identity given in the identity field. In order to do so, the authentication service must authenticate the sender of the message. Some possible ways in which this authentication might be performed include the following:

If the authentication service is instantiated by a SIP intermediary (proxy server), it may challenge the request with a 407 response code using the Digest authentication scheme (or viewing a Proxy-Authentication header sent in the request, which was sent in anticipation of a challenge using cached credentials, as described in RFC 3261, Section 19.4.3). Note that if that proxy server is maintaining a TLS connection with the client over which the client had previously authenticated itself using Digest authentication, the identity value obtained from that previous authentication step can be reused without an additional Digest challenge.

If the authentication service is instantiated by a SIP UA, a UA can be said to authenticate its user on the grounds that the user can provision the UA with the private key of the domain, or preferably by providing a password that unlocks said private key. Authorization of the use of a particular user name in the From header field is a matter of local policy for the authentication service, one that depends greatly on the manner in which authentication is performed. For example, one policy might be as follows: the user name given in the *username* parameter of the Proxy-Authorization header must correspond exactly to the user name in the From header field of the SIP message. However, there are many cases in which this is too limiting or inappropriate; a realm might use *username* parameters in Proxy-Authorization that do not correspond to the user-portion of SIP From headers, or a user might manage multiple accounts in the same administrative domain.

In this latter case, a domain might maintain a mapping between the values in the *username* parameter of Proxy-Authorization, and a set of one or more SIP URIs that might legitimately be asserted for that user name. For example, the user name can correspond to the private identity as defined in 3GPP, in which case the From header field can contain any one of the public identities associated with this private identity. In this instance, another policy might be as follows: the URI in the From header field must correspond exactly to one of the mapped URIs associated with the *username* given in the Proxy-Authorization header. Various exceptions to such policies might arise for cases like anonymity; if the AOR asserted in the From header field uses a form like sip:anonymous@example.com, then the example.com proxy should authenticate that the user is a valid user in the domain and insert the signature over the From header field as usual.

Note that this check is performed on the addr-spec in the From header field (e.g., the URI of the sender, like sip:alice@atlanta.example.com); it does not convert the display-name portion of the From header field (e.g., Alice Atlanta). Authentication services may check and validate the display name as well, and compare it to a list of acceptable display-names that may be used by the sender; if the display name does not meet policy constraints, the authentication service must return a 403 response code. The reason phrase should indicate the nature of the problem; for example, Inappropriate Display Name. However, the display name is not always present, and in many environments the requisite operational procedures for display-name validation may not exist.

Step 3:

The authentication service should ensure that any preexisting Date header in the request is accurate. Local policy can dictate precisely how accurate the Date must be; a recommended maximum discrepancy of 10 minutes will ensure that the request is unlikely to upset any verifiers. If the Date header contains a time different by more than 10 minutes from the current time noted by the authentication service, the authentication service should reject the request. This behavior is not mandatory because a UAC could only exploit the Date header in order to cause a request to fail verification; the Identity header is not intended to provide a source of nonrepudiation or a perfect record of when messages are processed. Finally, the authentication service must verify that the Date header falls within the validity period of its certificate. For more information on the security properties associated with the Date header field value, see Section 19.4.8.7.

Step 4:

The authentication service must form the identity signature and add an Identity header to the request containing this signature. After the Identity header has been added to the request, the authentication service MUST also add an Identity-Info header. The Identity-Info header contains a URI from which its certificate can be acquired. Finally, the authentication service must forward the message normally.

19.4.8.3.1 Identity within a Dialog and Retargeting

Retargeting is broadly defined as the alteration of the Request-URI by intermediaries. More specifically, retargeting supplants the original target URI with one that corresponds to a different user, a user that is not authorized to register under the original target URI. By this definition, retargeting does not include translation of the Request-URI to a contact address of an end point that has registered under the original target URI, for example. When a dialog-forming request is retargeted, this can cause a few wrinkles for the Identity mechanism when it is applied to requests sent in the backwards direction within a dialog. This section provides some nonnormative considerations related to this case. When a request is retargeted, it may reach a SIP end point whose user is not identified by the URI designated in the To header field value.

The value in the To header field of a dialog-forming request is used as the From header field of requests sent in the backwards direction during the dialog, and is accordingly the header that would be signed by an authentication service for requests sent in the backwards direction. In retargeting cases, if the URI in the From header does not identify the sender of the request in the backwards direction, then clearly it would be inappropriate to provide an Identity signature over that From header. As specified above, if the authentication service is not responsible for the domain in the From header field of the request, it must not add an Identity header to the request, and it should process/forward the request normally.

Any means of anticipating retargeting, and so on, is outside the scope of this mechanism, and likely to have equal applicability to response identity as it does to requests in the backwards direction within a dialog. Consequently, no special guidance is given for implementers here regarding the *connected party* problem; authentication service behavior is unchanged if retargeting has occurred for a dialog-forming request. Ultimately, the authentication service provides an Identity header for requests in the backwards dialog when the user is authorized to assert the identity given in the From header field, and if they are not, an Identity header is not provided. Although retargeting has some benefits from a communications efficiency point of view, it may have many security problems, namely as follows: service hijacking, insecure responses, confidentiality problems, circumvention of blacklists, and rampant transitivity. However, these security problems of retargeted response identity can be solved meeting the following problems:

- In an ideal world, it would be possible for a UAC to have a strong assurance that intermediaries were behaving properly, and furthermore to have the capability to differentiate between properly behaving intermediaries and attackers.
- It must be possible for a UAC to detect when a request has been retargeted.
- A domain that changes the target of a request must be capable of informing the UAC of the new target(s).
- The mechanism must allow simple intradomain retargeting in cases where persistent TLS connections are used as a network address translation (NAT) traversal mechanism.
- It must be possible for a domain that changes the target of a request to inform the UAC of the new target(s) before contacting any of the new target(s). There must furthermore be a way for intermediaries to determine when UACs require prior information about new targets.
- It must be possible to preserve the privacy of targets and potential targets of requests.
- It must be possible to preserve the ordering of a target set desired by the domain that changes the target of a request.

19.4.8.4 Verifier Behavior

RFC 4474 introduces a new logical role for SIP entities called a server. When a verifier receives a SIP message containing an Identity header, it may inspect the signature to verify the identity of the sender of the message. Typically, the results of a verification are provided as input to an authorization process that is outside the scope of this document. If an Identity header is not present in a request, and one is required by local policy (e.g., based on a per-sending-domain policy, or a per-sending-user policy), then a 428 Use Identity Header response must be sent. To verify the identity of the sender of a message, an entity acting as a verifier must perform the following steps, in the order here specified.

Step 1:

The verifier must acquire the certificate for the signing domain. Implementations supporting this specification should have some means of retaining domain certificates (in accordance with normal practices for certificate lifetimes and revocation) in order to prevent themselves from needlessly downloading the same certificate every time a request from the same domain is received. Certificates cached in this manner should be indexed by the URI given in the Identity-Info header field value. Provided that the domain certificate used to sign this message is not previously known to the verifier, SIP entities should discover this certificate by dereferencing the Identity-Info header, unless they have some more efficient implementation-specific way of acquiring certificates for that domain. If the URI scheme in the Identity-Info header cannot be dereferenced, then a 436 Bad Identity-Info response must be returned. The verifier processes this certificate in the usual ways, including checking that it has not expired, that the chain is valid back to a trusted certification authority (CA), and that it does not appear on revocation lists. Once the certificate is acquired, it must be validated following the procedures in RFC 3280. If the certificate cannot be validated (it is self-signed and untrusted, or signed by an untrusted or unknown certificate authority, expired, or revoked), the verifier must send a 437 Unsupported Certificate response.

Step 2:

The verifier must follow the process described in Section 19.4.8.11.4 to determine if the signer is authoritative for the URI in the From header field.

Step 3:

The verifier must verify the signature in the Identity header field, following the procedures for generating the hashed digest-string described in Section 19.4.8.7. If a verifier determines that the signature on the message does not correspond to the reconstructed digest string, then a 438 Invalid Identity Header response must be returned.

Step 4:

The verifier must validate the Date, Contact, and Call-ID headers in the manner described in Section 19.4.8.11.1; recipients that wish to verify Identity signatures must support all of the operations described there. It must furthermore ensure that the value of the Date header falls within the validity period of the certificate whose corresponding private key was used to sign the Identity header.

19.4.8.5 Considerations for UA

This mechanism can be applied opportunistically to existing SIP deployments; accordingly, it requires no change to SIP UA behavior in order for it to be effective. However, because this mechanism does not provide integrity protection between the UAC and the authentication service, a UAC should implement some means of providing this integrity. TLS would be one such mechanism, which is attractive because it must be supported by SIP proxy servers, but is potentially problematic because it is a hop-by-hop mechanism. See Section 19.4.8.11.3 for more information about securing the channel between the UAC and the authentication service.

When a UAC sends a request, it must accurately populate the From header field with a value corresponding to an identity that it believes it is authorized to claim. In a request, it must set the URI portion of its From header to match a SIP, SIPS, or TEL URI AOR that it is authorized to use in the domain (including anonymous URIs, as described in RFC 3323; see Section 20.2). In general, UACs should not use the TEL URI form in the From header field (see Section 19.4.8.9). Note that this document defines a number of new 4xx response codes. If UAs support these response codes, they will be able to respond intelligently to Identity-based error conditions.

The UAC must also be capable of sending requests, including mid-call requests, through an *outbound* proxy (the authentication service). The best way to accomplish this is using preloaded Route headers and loose routing. For a given domain, if an entity that can instantiate the authentication service role is not in the path of dialog-forming requests, identity for mid-dialog requests in the backwards direction cannot be provided. As a recipient of a request, a UA that can verify signed identities should also support an appropriate user interface to render the validity of identity to a user. UA implementations should differentiate signed From header field values from unsigned From header field values when rendering to an end user the identity of the sender of a request.

19.4.8.6 Considerations for Proxy Servers

Domain policy may require proxy servers to inspect and verify the identity provided in SIP requests. A proxy server may wish to ascertain the identity of the sender of the message to provide spam prevention or call control services. Even if a proxy server does not act as an authentication service, it may validate the Identity header before it makes a forwarding decision for a request. Proxy servers must not remove or modify an existing Identity or Identity-Info header in a request.

19.4.8.7 Identity Header Syntax

RFC 4474 specifies two new SIP headers: Identity and Identity-Info. Each of these headers can appear only once in a SIP message. The grammar for these two headers is described following the ABNF in RFC 3261 (see Section 2.4.1) and is repeated here for convenience:

```
Identity="Identity" HCOLON
signed-identity-digest
signed-identity-digest=LDQUOT 32LHEX RDQUOT
Identity-Info="Identity-Info" HCOLON
ident-info
*(SEMI ident-info-params)
ident-info=LAQUOT absoluteURI RAQUOT
ident-info-params=ident-info-alg/
ident-info-extension
ident-info-alg="alg" EQUAL token
ident-info-extension=generic-param
```

The signed-identity-digest is a signed hash of a canonical string generated from certain components of a SIP request. To create the contents of the signed-identity-digest, the following elements of a SIP message must be placed in a bit-exact string in the order specified here, separated by a vertical line, "|" or %x7C, character:

- The AOR of the UA sending the message, or addr-spec of the From header field (referred to occasionally here as the *identity field*).
- The addr-spec component of the To header field, which is the AOR to which the request is being sent.
- The callid from Call-Id header field.
- The digit (1*DIGIT) and method (method) portions from CSeq header field, separated by a single space (ABNF SP, or %x20). Note that the CSeq header field allows linear white space (LWS) rather than SP to separate the digit and method portions, and thus the CSeq header field may need to be transformed in order to be canonicalized. The authentication service must strip leading zeros from the *digit* portion of the Cseq before generating the digest-string.
- The Date header field, with exactly one space each for each SP, and the weekday and month items case set as shown in BNF in RFC 3261. RFC 3261 specifies that the BNF for weekday and month is a choice among a set of tokens. The RFC 2234 rules for the BNF specify that tokens are case sensitive. However, when used to construct the canonical string defined here, the first letter of each week and month must be capitalized, and the remaining two letters must be lowercase. This matches the capitalization provided in the definition of each token. All requests that use the Identity mechanism must contain a Date header.

- The addr-spec component of the Contact header field value. If the request does not contain a Contact header, this field must be empty (i.e., there will be no white space between the fourth and fifth "|" characters in the canonical string).
- The body content of the message with the bits exactly as they are in the message (in the ABNF for SIP, the message body). This includes all components of multipart message bodies. Note that the message body does not include the CRLF separating the SIP headers from the message body, but does include everything that follows that CRLF. If the message has no body, then message body will be empty, and the final "|" will not be followed by any additional characters.

For more information on the security properties of these headers, and why their inclusion mitigates replay attacks, see Section 19.4.8.11 and RFC 3893 (see Sections 19.4.6.9 and 19.4.7). The precise formulation of this digest-string is, therefore (following the ABNF in RFC 3261)

```
digest-string=addr-spec "|" addr-spec "|"
callid "|"
1*DIGIT SP Method "|" SIP-date "|" [addr-
spec] "|"
message-body
```

Note again that the first addr-spec must be taken from the From header field value, the second addr-spec must be taken from the To header field value, and the third addr-spec must be taken from the Contact header field value, provided the Contact header is present in the request. After the digest-string is formed, it must be hashed and signed with the certificate for the domain. The hashing and signing algorithm is specified by the *alg* parameter of the Identity-Info header. This document defines only one value for the alg parameter: *rsa-sha1;*; further values must be defined in a Standards Track RFC. All implementations of this specification must support rsa-sha1. When the rsa-sha1 algorithm is specified in the alg parameter of Identity-Info, the hash and signature must be generated as follows: compute the results of signing this string with sha1WithRSAEncryption as described in RFC 3370 and base64 encode the results as specified in RFC 4648. A 1024-bit or longer RSA key must be used. The result is placed in the Identity header field. For detailed examples of the usage of this algorithm, see Section 19.4.8.8.

The absoluteURI portion of the Identity-Info header must contain a URI that dereferences to a resource containing the certificate of the authentication service. All implementations of this specification must support the use of HTTP and HTTPS URIs in the Identity-Info header. Such HTTP and HTTPS URIs must follow the conventions of RFC 2585, and for those URIs the indicated resource must be of the form application/pkix-cert described in that specification. Note that this introduces key life-cycle management concerns; were a domain to change the key available at the Identity-Info URI before a verifier evaluates a request signed by an authentication service, this would cause obvious verifier failures. When a rollover occurs, authentication services should thus provide new Identity-Info URIs for each new certificate, and should continue to make older key acquisition URIs available for a duration longer than the plausible lifetime of a SIP message (an hour would most likely suffice). The Identity-Info header field must contain an alg parameter. No other parameters are defined for the Identity-Info header in this document. Future Standards Track RFCs may define additional Identity-Info header parameters.

RFC 4474 adds the Identity and Identity-Info header field with new entries to Table 2 of RFC 3261 (see Table 2.5, Section 2.8). Note that this mechanism does not protect the CANCEL method as indicated in Table 2.5, Section 2.8. The CANCEL method cannot be challenged, because it is hop-by-hop, and accordingly the authentication service behavior for CANCEL would be significantly limited. Also, note that the REGISTER method uses Contact header fields in very unusual ways that complicate its applicability to this mechanism, and the use of Identity with REGISTER is consequently a subject for future study, although it is left as optional here for forward-compatibility reasons. The Identity and Identity-Info header must not appear in CANCEL.

19.4.8.8 Compliance Tests and Examples

The examples in this section illustrate the use of the Identity header in the context of a SIP transaction. Implementers are advised to verify their compliance with the specification against the following criteria:

- Implementations of the authentication service role must generate identical base64 identity strings to the ones shown in the Identity headers in these examples when presented with the source message and utilizing the appropriate supplied private key for the domain in question.
- Implementations of the verifier role must correctly validate the given messages containing the Identity header when utilizing the supplied certificates (with the caveat about self-signed certificates below).

Note that the following examples use self-signed certificates, rather than certificates issued by a recognized certificate authority. The use of self-signed certificates for this mechanism is not recommended, and it appears here only for illustrative purposes. Therefore, in compliance testing, implementations of verifiers should generate appropriate warnings about the use of self-signed certificates. Also, the example certificates in this section have placed their domain name subject in the subjectAltName field; in practice, certificate authorities may place domain names in other locations in the certificate (see Section 19.4.8.11.4 for more information). Note that all examples use the rsa-sha1 algorithm (RFCs 3110, 3370, 4359, and 4648). Bit-exact reference files for these messages and their various transformations are supplied here.

Bit-Exact Archive of Examples of Messages:

The following text block is an encoded, gzip-compressed TAR archive of files that represent the transformations performed on the examples of messages discussed in Section 2.6. It includes for each example:

- (foo).message: the original message
- (foo).canonical: the canonical string constructed from that message
- (foo).sha1: the SHA1 hash of the canonical string (hexadecimal)
- (foo).signed: the RSA-signed SHA1 hash of the canonical string (binary)
- (foo).signed.enc: the base64 encoding of the RSA-signed SHA1 hash of the canonical string as it would appear in the request
- (foo).identity: the original message with the Identity and Identity-Info headers added

Also included in the archive are two public key/certificate pairs, for atlanta.example.com and biloxi.example.org, respectively, including

- (foo).cer: the certificate of the domain
- (foo).privkey: the private key of the domain
- (foo).pubkey: the public key of the domain, extracted from the cert file for convenience

To recover the compressed archive file intact, the text of this document may be passed as input to the following Perl script (the output should be redirected to a file or piped to tar -xzvf -):

```
#!/usr/bin/perl
use strict;
my $bdata="";
use MIME::Base64;
while(<>) {
if (/-- BEGIN MESSAGE ARCHIVE --/../-- END
MESSAGE ARCHIVE --/) {
if (m/^\s*[^\s]+\s*$/) {
$bdata=$bdata. $_;
}
}
}
print decode_base64($bdata);
```

Alternatively, the base64 encoded block can be edited by hand to remove document structure lines and fed as input to any base64 decoding utility.

Encoded Reference Files:


```
-- BEGIN MESSAGE ARCHIVE --
H4sICFfaz0QCA25ld2lkZW50LnRhcgDsW0us5NhZ7gUS
wqiF2CAhFikiIQhFt992+U46it+u8qPK5Uc9WPlVfj/Kd
pXtomEDCxaAhFggISE2WSHCIoIFioQQC8gqAhRAQQTY8J
JAbMgGIYTv7b7T09PT0xNl+mqS3F8qVd3jY/uc85//+87
/nXOLoIv9oGjBB2/PIAiDSBwfv1GERInxG8EwAh6/37UH
MIQRKIljCI4+gGCUGKtP8Ad3YKemderJ5EFSBW1QN2Xxm
np5GtblqXqUPfIffBdZcet/p82conUee0H9sfsfhiACw17
nfwQa y+Dra+MkQGFkrI+TOPJgAt37/63bo2tjeHGuTVh
+bc6FOUub/E0poM7nLGqyLJ06Id3NGTocPxytMWF6jNJY
pDqIoXVLoDlmr+pNx+o7ztZ1ke8WtnXhFUClU5GGLZ6lO
3YN8T3P0Usm1GyG9lQGEiBXFE6+yPecSSvPykuV4TPB5n
e9xNEO8KxQVXnk3cqn/TaK3C3T7A08cRGokyJPUzmrV7k
5pHK7i5bQyOambNcDLxUmH9zMD2sl8FGa+WGtBG6bGe5n
HafvFnK5n0dnT6N1nmF0mgt3EK3OxQVdiuMzZrNOhPxNOF
37W7w4LmsLOA0Mpeqt7RTKTrDX1CztZgezbM7rLlvQeBn
hWzWOV5qDZEdMahLZTo8Wq0oZOL4XFgkgMhY4pNBdU53sH
VvlaIX5TjqH0+JkYXAXmmzgSI7H9N3RvHingrIOAUIzCp
h4GhsdHGDwET+WCO5SuDtwxXKNvneGYrWiQ5WhaTEJXb0
LXb6Trgd2DS0ZZscLWm6Bau3aO48HZK4GEWgzN2oRTuBaG/
vLXA+aZKh8kDBYyJj7bHWREXgjMWxIgFQrxPyxb3eUc3E
EH6iEptuYL1zFRCpr22rPXujFs9EPx0s+o67pbhzRa/eO
jvEZX+wjt1hHgKpDHdvdXJA5er1Y22tRXXed+KwyxzFad
FtZyW1st4E7V7ROO4Rqw5Cnx6ncXb/Z5ztdUOmx34dX3C
k8cydPc76+a5uO4XLTMI9Q3iIwDJBOloNbUahd5OK7FnQ
u637tL/cQdlSHel5tRVjh84Jfhl7pDfV2zZyPeEVs3D
3t8XoKAVzDo3YAad6sp4r8nCUbUmxUUWAL9lRiS848gHA
m+nZNcQF78RIY2lk6qq6DnFO30Q4B2JaLG2WTkcZ2uVx7
ezqGS4vqngA30c5r3KsI8ODevsvtFf6v6vicBsMd8j+ME
+Qt/0PjAnCsT5AQes//d8z/a4OerNZze4z+iczvXqwBtv
rI+7TMhDq3WqlMK9nlKt3a0z2RHGGlCQ8jMtubakAY2zoc
FupKgghFgbyFoS8BZx7Yl3mZXDZt5ZwYcj5kezmjEwY/YC
O4rk+lFQc+26mK7GYb+rhviUDaVKy2X5DZUvOAOd8VeYQ
UtOfJ6QxVKtCW0DakDRBDOb3cIk3hF7toGs5wBFldupDk
xU1TXS7dnKN1mgFumFWGNmhb8AJH0omt08VC23Jtj1O0A
9snZMFvA6KMp8s6FYZmkbj7RdcoudzWYdsCq+3SmrVIvq
9iqJOxaIu1+6ho406UU2vFohHFJNVUDOr4sEIxeK0O6nJ
KHFZhclxeLK4DpvUqSdSqG1+eerx35ELXrPfF5gzqBWs4
joD2qSUehFTp8aXsremUp0mrLxp+tnVMFALaFWhZHg6HW
orIohz2um5KZcV4QUcNh4BdC9HZV8ikckSn5WM83neiON
KavbQlS4MlANoplaQn67JbMLQ2XSPumQa1OD9iBLYPiyD
judXR4en9xuHQdHmIDGp6VsjyyBvTE85DwIJMty65T2PD
tkJqa4GzVa/KPcjRF8i38qUytVhdmrEUb1rqHDnx7lFyG
d+2RC1FCYwFOMErfKO3oymKyceFn8Q7oyfs1eqMEFsqJw
1oOfhmaoQNCmJluerLmeSox20+g1idmdZA7zKolVXLMvK
YTpCp3KwzlSHYhjpmBCGHXZEp1CnlI0nalZdxHPxtUDLs
EFlNGfqGBRCgY9CCd97wYpuQ4HlY8Kyus6wBZ3LIb0tNX
x2XmpOdd9EwqPv1VlB8Dgvdbr2S4dNWBnZVirLpQbgsh
0MSKJ646reXI3K8nKSLaHL9nlrRQdVtsbWRviDVDwyrTz
D+n9yPGf7fhP8j5kO3+I/AN/k/gZHYPf7fMf6vLEaZs++
FfvGg0pDIGkfRmLsj2PLX6R5NY6JGcywT6x9OCcDrOOGj
UgLwOk74qJQAvJYT3o3O93f6e3b958ZZ2cdvQ/55s/6D
vEf/QbBr/YeAifv4/yToP3DCsnQyfZP+s32j/mOO6Tp3ub
75uf6TLipXpDDH5DWVbp7VCzvesGxrnfDuWEEErgvprjN2
eda4aFS9PzVXGWzLmTSsmvSgcTQyfgYtK6/LkOsy4D2Fn
X15k4AAm6p+k9Y/FxD2LOBs+nMgph+o/YgXev+u9pM/74
6BZ4EotJ7YZ0qunQHXZJni8v5B4wWaXjKJTnfhLmWvRYM
zIXYbFjI5jFzInZwlZZR0gmoAGoi39e6ENYEk HsO0UyJ
7umXRkl/i+LGOLxE6zD3bkFOqoJYZrS3Mo5bYjjSc16cL
```

```
jwvABjZ3TbgwEIHu51MYjruBLihkPUwjBwTDKJjJ0MqZL
pQpjMVG40i2HhaHDtNTcH08ZDpASGdmVh2T7DzUC/SINb
E6epSnaWfJNGP36oT2b+QcHeOFULeg/XStYOQGpFdc6+EM
cDBKfXviBR7sukN3IxIljBR2fkm/UvlF3SHaEOu9Kng98
MJNO5PObPM9s20E9IU2zrbVNVXduLbrRP35fLmVfYCXdZ
9mrHGr+yzi5y5+n7CIsCNRdBx901oTYGirG/vMgJcPmP/
XeqHOxIMszduZuT2I2qEqFtsYT9j4suzz3WwHhFkxa4eV4
ATDkcJN0Tub7Obil4xiVww3PVTrTb0F53O84Qlbcl16TB
nsXHb33UWn26oCVojgnBJk1lLYPuAkDTkfL8mhkBJ2iWCp
iC5OB8ScQXFWUTvJ47o+sYS6nRFWkbHTIfaBwTGDU7PBx
RN5hsMn97rPvb3K/29B/nmz/kOit/wPI+NaYFz/49j9/s8
nR/8Jb/UfFixdZqes1VXSpDV93CxjcUVb/RwFc6SNybjHP
OfImvRJ2OKeEoQ6QBb58aQspcM86u350UQOEGHRULYsEc
0uDzIlkqqZ2q6txQOdKTuL4xNyu1G4OXtA95ICEEINTlm
B7GqdqrH0TG7jhdyXvs2yPshFrEmJ1dTmymAmDflxuQHl
pgjqeJi/pP8syEMjzOWtnCabMJmljbhsIwM1CpjqVwY78
D7TH/gcWSUkqF0uQRaDK2/pxB6UAouR+r3iqCEHiQ/mogx
SvcX05ukQ6jt7cTwPEr9uiHq7BWMT2xU51cIUhPOxTu0r
qannADguEKwdDeu1GNJz6bxXbOVynFKywvH7qaS7J1ZZb
IUp4WYQ7+LMtf5DoESp0loF6Q4K5LsNryOnNhebXZ9ujc
PAuPDMZJcd2w5Q4TNrBLsMy4WAaO7eoGbKZSo6CB4d5mIH
LiQZKDjKXfKzmXWj/zBro/IxNzemOTZbgzDarnmDbqXj4
GtxsYVSA1xHnVSTeSqZFpqCKiD0etuj2BwV5Yuz79UCog
lCNqgzaEh+IUyD1Y2YIgak3kTDfnaKW2XV7jkvYzcRL0v
Akdal3OL3Z0tAbEmp3VOqKMtQsmpJcxDMmytnzEcHh7Wto
B1yzTsNZhfJCYJ1Ap3SS+ACJj3MV5mGRp0y1Zos25ebOT
47nU8kSB8RD/UuR8cWGddFYbKR2F0op5BLi2jaLdE8Big
UVLYbE/b8eGdXOeNJ3M1I51WYCsm035/wcEMbO/yUnKcCq
66gTedIeGQW29O0lQNgtUB9ZL7Yy71YZETcymuNFIN1RK
0MGUr3Y5osBHZ9bhaYVlYvEewnVwN6Bf8/fvnnW9N/yBv9
B8Wge/z/jtB/Xk8JwOs44aNSAvA6TviolAC8lhPu9Z9X4n
8IHntOURax52R3G//jAvD5+S8MxbGb9R8K38f/nVgTV1du
6X7+OfwHvZNXWfC4rMOn15ecLPaCz9/uDdxe9cr8qTPDX
MwjiYAgRtx+iqDwhNnxT83o9DMTBJ4IgTtBRkdPYOwKpq
5weCKq5tOn9wnXJzn+b37F7cdM/2/M/2AUe3H+E7vZ/0
eg+/2fO7ExZicvAr3yUPTxB0T7xJivQOQx9BCwY+fq9i/QV
IwJTI2/HiOPsXfc2im86MmFikTMlQunifwGHm9Rnf6RUN
adU/vN1YQcS4S6zK8mTOlOPvt6/PncO60TPnEIb4Z7h4e
AWV5N6OtGPrvntcD07LaxVTMUgkkSewhwThtcTT4UmB4Cr
JNlj+bc1eRlXBsvGMHxavIc3h4C8+chcjX5dHPGWbOEcPl
YGXkrtajv8fEShNmNaezbQkRjewoX+alWtjYo5e2gGaTS
1iHlZ326uZQPgckLCyzSJ5f2TOoC0+RK10bj1szDVccKi
cPn6sDPUZ80Bg2BB40rEX4NLs9h20HKCfeaefXSw6rVcRn
Cp23hXyRXJPM1sc4oprAi6XSw126Fw2qBdlB4sJonn37Rp
0fz4jCO8mejtq2aKxB81Sfv2SX63DtOFj6pG+dREznwOE
5l0Y6PeaQERdhGV5Nx6O7R9TsM//OgaZwwuOP9Pwh7cf57
hH7i5vw3gd/j/z3+fyz4/1Gh/XsSwV6K/2skfwvveFP8Qy
Rxm/9hY43r+Efg+/Ofd2KGRMM/9VLu/5knkwM5IyjUP6A
4jPuI5wfUGEw4jsEocX2ghnQdGMbgA3bP8N9l8R+HReDf
efwj7/7/H0ZCOPHs/A95H/93YV/6P0b7Veqnf3f9W3/5n9/
42+/75f/65g/4f3X4+p/9w0/8wt8Mv/97f/jX/zt88Stf+/
Ljv/unb379+OvZvw3aN/7jn59+6vt/Q7n6sU3/RS36oT/
5cS+a/8pXGLL7gy+ReY1dET/8qa/+8Q9Wf/HlP6r/9DNf+
J9f+8Wf/c3f/vs/z4p/Eb8Q/PePfu2Xfu53rB/59381fv
IfH05+Xr6PwE9c/D8OCu9u4/+F/nt9BOBG/yXuz//djf77
bYoYwLcrXADfilhxv+B4a/EfF+e4fTtbQG+Kfxy6Pv+D4S
iMosTN+V9yzAnu4/9O4v9DN3k+ZHfoffs/6JgQ4NRkrtl
z84N2gdArCLmC0JtdoDfrDU/PT8bsu3xiNUFN/3875/PaN
BiH8Yt6CBS0Q2SDYcYEkSl9k75Nmkmn7ebWde2WLm3646
Jp2q7FtU2btq496EGcKMgu4sH5a4dN8NccCMLYP6AMwcv
+Bg/e1NMuZimTdlvXyWxx4/s5pQ0N5SXPk/d9nrclaSuHr
```



```
BhbaKb6cHiUHOYxWe8SBkK1CTFVTWbSpDDAGwjZ1vATeR
vaWPWnbFIhmsyQmKNYmhz38Sa7yG+ckGy5vJKSlF5E8v0
ev8mq3bwHPCTYqv9mVEAN9//p+Z+mf9qCMMvqv/+k4fnf
EiqCJbcJfVPnuyR/9XS0YxBorSR4jTK/zWywKUlfjUftl
EvWa4qqzKsSE0pyvrf629Ubir6awigcGnVEnP0IiZ5wjr4e
zjNiqr/IZ9IBl2eo6PU5BrITiUwg5p5yxcsOWqKUKXvOL
E7kHEhQBbtU0/Ek4+p4NDnGZ7zh0FiJvpETJxKFhKx6Is6
AXxicGmYUJmvxjXmDTk+qzBSuZMxq0aUKTszlE6WhdM3F
BkU5XZLCPT2l8UlHKOT1ubOBsqtnREzwI5G436TkSgkxz
YVkxr9bYbTDCFT/r0y9yshXUrRhlxRFG0sprxm2SY0q2/
NYCrMGwkDAo6GZ/t+MCqhh/4/MVf2Pvv7DDMz/wP8Pg/+
DyQEHyP+bUQE23P+JqD/zfxpZ9P5fewv8vwXo/d/W7Oec
jaRZhGWaZq04LtGUjCPIwkUQkrUXmI1xEstIUQmbOVD/
IdN/EyrAPfZ/Ff2z+v5P7RD03wpit+2TyoevQvtisv3jf
Jz48e1pxN3xs+1I74vpO89MxqurnY/XnlxeLFx702lcIj
vurZ8ods/MHQtevPD+bbBr+dR5amnN25XtflV+/fCLPbs
62/fO+OD7yqzx9EzqbtfLk4GznxZurp+JHZ0+7l5+tPr8
vtj2OfXr0sLKnHgrqM6DAv9H/f/bCnCP/Z+ufzOm9Pyfh
fVfS9hvJkXsN4ci/iZ7gtkGAAAAAAAAAAAAAAAAAAAAA
AAAABAPX4DY+BfEQB4AAA=-- END MESSAGE ARCHIVE --
```


19.4.8.8.1 Identity-Info with a Singlepart MIME body

Consider the following private key and certificate pair assigned to atlanta.example.com (rendered in OpenSSL format).

```
-----BEGIN RSA PRIVATE KEY-----
MIICXQIBAAKBgQDPPMBtHVoPkXV+Z6jq1LsgfTELVWpy2
BVUffJMPH06LL0cJSQOaIeVzIojzWtpauB7IylZKlAjB5
f429tRuoUiedCwMLKblWAqZt6eHWpCNZJ7lONcIEwnmh2n
AccKk83Lp/VH3tgAS/43DQoX2sndnYh+g8522Pzwg7EGWs
pzzwIDAQABAoGBAK0W3tnEFD7AjVQAnJNXDtx59Aa1Vu2
JEXe6oi+OrkFysJjbZJwsLmKtrgttPXOU8t2mZpi0wK4h
X4tZhntiwGKkUPC3h9Bjp+GerifP341RMyMO+6fPgjqOz
UDw+rPjjMpwD7AkcEcqDgbTrZnWv/QnCSaaF3xkUGfFkLx
5OKcRAkEA7UxnsE8XaT30tP/UUc51gNk2KGKgxQQTHopBc
ew9yfeCRFhvdL7jpaGatEi5iZwGGQQDVOVHUN1H0YLpHQ
jRowJBAN+R2bvA/Nimq464ZgnelEDPqaEAZWaD3kOfhS9+
vL7oqES+u5E0J7kXb7ZkiSVUg9XU/8PxMKx/DAz0dUm
OL+UCQH8C9ETUMI2uEbqHbBdVUGNk364CDFcndSxVh+34
KqJdjiYSx6VPPv26X9m7S0OydTkSgs3/4ooPxo8HaMqXm
80CQB+rxbB3UlpOohcBwFK9mTrlMB6Cs9ql66KgwnlL9u
kEhHHYozGatdXeoBCyhUsogdSU6/aSAFcvWEGtj7/vyJE
CQQCCS1lKgEXoNQPqONalvYhyyMZRXFLdD4gbwRPK1uXKY
pk3CkfFzOyfjeLcGPxXzq2qzuHzGTDxZ9PAepwX4RSk
-----END RSA PRIVATE KEY-----
```

```
-----BEGIN CERTIFICATE-----
MIIC3TCCAkagAwIBAgIBADANBgkqhkiG9w0BAQUFADBZ
MQswCQYDVQQGEwJVUzELMAkGA1UECAwCR0ExEDAOBgNVB
AcMB0F0bGFudGExDTALBgNVBAoMBElFVEYxHDAaBgNVBA
MME2F0bGFudGEuZXhhbXBsZS5jb20wHhcNMDUxMDI0MDY
zNjA2WhcNMDYxMDI0MDYzNjA2WjBZMQswCQYDVQQGEwJV
UzELMAkGA1UECAwCR0ExEDAOBgNVBAcMB0F0bGFudGExD
TALBgNVBAoMBElFVEYxHDAaBgNVBAMME2F0bGFudGEuZX
hhbXBsZS5jb20wgZ8wDQYJKoZIhvcNAQEBBQADgY0AMIGJ
AoGBAM88wG0dWg+RdX5nqOrUuyB9MQtVanLYFVR98kw8fT
osvRwlJA5oh5XMiiPNa2lq4HsjKVkqUCMHl/jb21G6hSJ
50LAwspuVYCpm3p4dakI1knuU41wgTCeaHacBxwqTzcu
n9Ufe2ABL/jcNChfayd2diH6DznbY/PCDsQZaynPPAgMB
AAGjgbQwgbEwHQYDVR0OBBYEFNmU/MrbVYcEKDr/20WIS
```

```
rG1j1rNMIGBBgNVHSMEejB4gBTZlPzK21WHBCg6/9tFiEq
xtY9azaFdpFswWTELMAkGA1UEBhMCVVMxCzAJBgNVBAgMA
kdBMRAwDgYDVQQHDAdBdGxhbnRhMQ0wCwYDVQQKDARJRV
RGMRwwGgYDVQQDDBNhdGxhbnRhLmV4YW1wbGUuY29tggE
AMAwGA1UdEwQFMAMBAf8wDQYJKoZIhvcNAQEFBQADgYEA
DdQYtswBDmTSTq0mt2117alm/XGFrb2zdbU0vorxRdOZ0
4qMyrIpXG1LEmnEOgcocyrXRBvq5p6WbZAcEQk0DsE3Ve
0Nc8x9nmvljW7GsMGFCnCuo4ODTf/1lGdVr9DeCzcj10Y
UQ3MRemDMXhY2CtDisLWl7SXOORcZAi1oU9w =
-----END CERTIFICATE-----
```


A user of atlanta.example.com, Alice, wants to send an INVITE to bob@biloxi.example.org. She therefore creates the following INVITE request, which she forwards to the atlanta.example.org proxy server that instantiates the authentication service role:

```
INVITE sip:bob@biloxi.example.org SIP/2.0
Via: SIP/2.0/TLS pc33.atlanta.example.com;
branch=z9hG4bKnashds8
To: Bob <sip:bob@biloxi.example.org>
From: Alice <sip:alice@atlanta.example.com>;
tag=1928301774
Call-ID: a84b4c76e66710
CSeq: 314159 INVITE
Max-Forwards: 70
Date: Thu, 21 Feb 2002 13:02:03 GMT
Contact: <sip:alice@pc33.atlanta.example.com>
Content-Type: application/sdp
Content-Length: 147
v=0
o=UserA 2890844526 2890844526 IN IP4 pc33.
atlanta.example.com
s=Session SDP
c=IN IP4 pc33.atlanta.example.com
t=0 0
m=audio 49172 RTP/AVP 0
a=rtpmap:0 PCMU/8000
```

When the authentication service receives the INVITE, it authenticates Alice by sending a 407 response. As a result, Alice adds an Authorization header to her request, and resends to the atlanta.example.com authentication service. Now that the service is sure of Alice's identity, it calculates an Identity header for the request. The canonical string over which the identity signature will be generated is the following (note that the first line wraps because of RFC editorial conventions):

```
sip:alice@atlanta.example.com|sip:bob@biloxi.
example.org|
a84b4c76e66710|314159 INVITE|Thu, 21 Feb 2002
13:02:03 GMT|
sip:alice@pc33.atlanta.example.com|v=0
o=UserA 2890844526 2890844526 IN IP4 pc33.
atlanta.example.com
s=Session SDP
c=IN IP4 pc33.atlanta.example.com
t=0 0
m=audio 49172 RTP/AVP 0
a=rtpmap:0 PCMU/8000
```

The resulting signature (sha1WithRsaEncryption) using the private RSA key given above, with base64 encoding, is the following:


```
ZYNBbHC00VMZr2kZt6VmCvPonWJMGvQTBDqghoWeLxJfz
B2a1pxAr3VgrB0SsSAaifsRdiOPoQZYOy2wrVghuhcsMb
HWUSFxI6p6q5TOQXHMmz6uEo3svJsSH49thyGnFVcnyaZ
++yRlBYYQTLqWzJ+KVhPKbfU/pryhVn9Yc6U=
```


Accordingly, the atlanta.example.com authentication service will create an Identity header containing that base64 signature string (175 bytes). It will also add an HTTPS URL where its certificate is made available. With those two headers added, the message looks like the following:

```
INVITE sip:bob@biloxi.example.org SIP/2.0
Via: SIP/2.0/TLS pc33.atlanta.example.com;
branch=z9hG4bKnashds8
To: Bob <sip:bob@biloxi.example.org>
From: Alice <sip:alice@atlanta.example.com>;
tag=1928301774
Call-ID: a84b4c76e66710
CSeq: 314159 INVITE
Max-Forwards: 70
Date: Thu, 21 Feb 2002 13:02:03 GMT
Contact: <sip:alice@pc33.atlanta.example.com>
```

Identity:

```
"ZYNBbHC00VMZr2kZt6VmCvPonWJMGvQTBDqghoWeLxJ
fzB2a1pxAr3VgrB0SsSAa
ifsRdiOPoQZYOy2wrVghuhcsMbHWUSFxI6p6q5TOQXHM
mz6uEo3svJsSH49thyGn
FVcnyaZ++yRlBYYQTLqWzJ+KVhPKbfU/pryhVn9Yc6U="
Identity-Info: <https://atlanta.example.com/
atlanta.cer>;alg=rsa-sha1
Content-Type: application/sdp
Content-Length: 147
v=0
o=UserA 2890844526 2890844526 IN IP4 pc33.
atlanta.example.com
s=Session SDP
c=IN IP4 pc33.atlanta.example.com
t=0 0
m=audio 49172 RTP/AVP 0
a=rtpmap:0 PCMU/8000
```

atlanta.example.com then forwards the request normally. When Bob receives the request, if he does not already know the certificate of atlanta.example.com, he dereferences the URL in the Identity-Info header to acquire the certificate. Bob then generates the same canonical string given above, from the same headers of the SIP request. Using this canonical string, the signed digest in the Identity header, and the certificate discovered by dereferencing the Identity-Info header, Bob can verify that the given set of headers and the message body have not been modified.

19.4.8.8.2 Identity for a Request with No MIME Body or Contact

Consider the following private key and certificate pair assigned to biloxi.example.org.


```
-----BEGIN RSA PRIVATE KEY-----
MIICXgIBAAKBgQC/obBYLRMPjskrAqWOiGPAUxI3/m2t
i7ix4caqCTAuFX5cLegQ7nmquLOHfIhxVIqT2f06UA0lO
o2NVofK9G7MTkVbVNiyAlLYUDEj7XWLDICf3ZHL6Fr/+C
F7wrQ9r4kv7XiJKxodVCCd/DhCT9Gp+VDoe8HymqOW/Ks
neriyIwIDAQABAoGBAJ7fsFIKXKkjWgj8ksGOthS3Sn19
xPSCyEdBxfEm2Pj7/Nzzeli/PcOaic0kJALBcnqN2fHEe
IGK/9xUBxTufgQYVJqvyHERs6rXX/iT4Ynm9t1905EiQ9
ZpHsrI/AMMUYA1QrGgAIHvZLVLzq+9KLDEZ+HQbuCLJXF
+6bl0Eb5BAkEA636oMANp0Qa3mYWEQ2utmGsYxkXSfyBb
18TCOwCty0ndBR24zyOJF2NbZS98Lz+Ga25hfIGw/JHKn
D9bOE88UwJBANBRSpd4bmS+m48R/13tRESAtHqydNinX0
kS/RhwHr7mkHTU3k/MFxQtx34I3GKzaZxMn0A66KS9v/S
HdnF+ePECQQCGe7QshyZ8uitLPtZDclCWhEKHqAQHmUEZ
vUF2VHLrbukLLOgHUrHNa24cILv4d3yaCVUetymNcuyTw
hKj24wFAkAOz/jx1EplN3hwL+NsllZoWI58uvu7/Aq2c3
czqaVGBbb317sHCYgKk0bAG3kwO3mi93/LXWT1cdiYVpm
BcHDBAkEAmpgkFj+xZu5gWASY5ujv+FCMP0WwaH5hTnXu
+tKePJ3d2IJZKxGnl6itKRN7GeRh9PSK0kZSqGFeVrvsJ
4Nopg==
-----END RSA PRIVATE KEY-----


-----BEGIN CERTIFICATE-----
MIIC1jCCAj+gAwIBAgIBADANBgkqhkiG9w0BAQUFADBXM
QswCQYDVQQGEwJVUzELMAkGA1UECAwCTVMxDzANBgNVBA
cMBkJpbG94aTENMAsGA1UECgwESUVURjEbMBkGA1UEAww
SYmlsb3hpLmV4YW1wbGUuY29tMB4XDTA1MTAyNDA2NDAy
NloXDTA2MTAyNDA2NDAyNlowVzELMAkGA1UEBhMCVVMxC
zAJBgNVBAgMAk1TMQ8wDQYDVQQHDAZCaWxveGkxDTALBg
NVBAoMBElFVEYxGzAZBgNVBAMMEmJpbG94aS5leGFtcGx
lLmNvbTCBnzANBgkqhkiG9w0BAQEFAAOBjQAwgYkCgYEA
v6GwWC0TD47JKwKljohjwFMSN/5trYu4seHGqgkwLhV+X
C3oEO55qrizh3yIcVSKk9n9OlANJTqNjVaHyvRuzE5FW1
TYsgJS2FAxI+11iwyAn92Ry+ha//ghe8K0Pa+JL+14iSs
aHVQgnfw4Qk/RqflQ6HvB8pqjlvyrJ3q4siMCAwEAAaOBs
TCBrjAdBgNVHQ4EFgQU0Z+RL47W/APDtc5BfSoQXuEFE/
wwfwYDVR0jBHgwdoAU0Z+RL47W/APDtc5BfSoQXuEFE/y
hW6RZMFcxCzAJBgNVBAYTAlVTMQswCQYDVQQIDAJNUzEPM
A0GA1UEBwwGQmlsb3hpMQ0wCwYDVQQKDARJRVRGMRswGQ
YDVQQDDBJiaWxveGkuZXhhbXBsZS5jb22CAQAwDAYDVR0
TBAUwAwEB/zANBgkqhkiG9w0BAQUFAAOBgQBiyKHIt8TXf
GNfpnJXi5jCizOxmY8Ygln8tyPFaeyq95TGcvTCWzdoBL
VpBD+fpRWrX/II5sE6VHbbAPjjVmKbZwzQAtppP2Fauj28
t94ZeDHN2vqzjfnHjCO24kG3Juf2T80ilp9YHcDwxjUFr
t86UnlC+yidyaTeusW5Gu7v1g==
-----END CERTIFICATE-----
```


Bob (bob@biloxi.example.org) now wants to send a BYE request to Alice at the end of the dialog initiated in the previous example. He therefore creates the following BYE request, which he forwards to the biloxi.example.org proxy server that instantiates the authentication service role:

```
BYE sip:alice@pc33.atlanta.example.com
SIP/2.0
Via: SIP/2.0/TLS 192.0.2.4;branch=z9hG4bKnas
hds10
Max-Forwards: 70
From: Bob <sip:bob@biloxi.example.org>;
tag=a6c85cf
To: Alice <sip:alice@atlanta.example.com>;
tag=1928301774
Call-ID: a84b4c76e66710
CSeq: 231 BYE
Content-Length: 0
```

When the authentication service receives the BYE, it authenticates Bob by sending a 407 response. As a result, Bob adds an Authorization header to his request, and resends to the biloxi.example.org authentication service. Now that the service is sure of Bob's identity, it prepares to calculate an Identity header for the request. Note that this request does not have a Date header field. Accordingly, the biloxi.example .org will add a Date header to the request before calculating the identity signature. If the Content-Length header were not present, the authentication service would add it as well. The baseline message is thus

```
BYE sip:alice@pc33.atlanta.example.com SIP/2.0
Via: SIP/2.0/TLS 192.0.2.4;branch=z9hG4bKnas
hds10
Max-Forwards: 70
From: Bob <sip:bob@biloxi.example.org>;
tag=a6c85cf
To: Alice <sip:alice@atlanta.example.com>;
tag=1928301774
Date: Thu, 21 Feb 2002 14:19:51 GMT
Call-ID: a84b4c76e66710
CSeq: 231 BYE
Content-Length: 0
```

Also note that this request contains no Contact header field. Accordingly, biloxi.example.org will place no value in the canonical string for the addr-spec of the Contact address. Also note that there is no message body, and accordingly, the signature string will terminate, in this case, with two vertical bars. The canonical string over which the identity signature will be generated is the following (note that the first line wraps because of RFC editorial conventions):

```
sip:bob@biloxi.example.org|sip:alice@atlanta.
example.com|
a84b4c76e66710|231 BYE|Thu, 21 Feb 2002
14:19:51 GMT||
```

The resulting signature (sha1WithRsaEncryption) using the private RSA key given above for biloxi.example.org, with base64 encoding, is the following:


```
sv5CTo05KqpSmtHt3dcEiO/1CWTSZtnG3iV+1nmurLXV/
HmtyNS7Ltrg9dlxkWzoeU7d7OV8HweTTDobV3itTmgPwC
FjaEmMyEI3d7SyN21yNDo2ER/Ovgtw0Lu5csIppPqOg1u
XndzHbG7mR6Rl9BnUhHufVRbp51Mn3w0gfUs=
```


Accordingly, the biloxi.example.org authentication service will create an Identity header containing that base64 signature string. It will also add an HTTPS URL where its certificate is made available. With those two headers added, the message looks like the following:

```
BYE sip:alice@pc33.atlanta.example.com
SIP/2.0
Via: SIP/2.0/TLS 192.0.2.4;branch=z9hG4bKnas
hds10
Max-Forwards: 70
From: Bob <sip:bob@biloxi.example.org>;
tag=a6c85cf
To: Alice <sip:alice@atlanta.example.com>;
tag=1928301774
Date: Thu, 21 Feb 2002 14:19:51 GMT
Call-ID: a84b4c76e66710
CSeq: 231 BYE
```

Identity:

```
"sv5CTo05KqpSmtHt3dcEiO/1CWTSZtnG3iV+1nmur
LXV/HmtyNS7Ltrg9dlxkWzo
eU7d7OV8HweTTDobV3itTmgPwCFjaEmMyEI3d7SyN21y
NDo2ER/Ovgtw0Lu5csIp
pPqOg1uXndzHbG7mR6Rl9BnUhHufVRbp51Mn3w0gfUs="
Identity-Info: <https://biloxi.example.org/
biloxi.cer>;alg=rsa-sha1
Content-Length: 0
```

biloxi.example.org then forwards the request normally.

19.4.8.9 Identity and the TEL URI Scheme

Since many SIP applications provide a Voice over IP (VoIP) service, telephone numbers are commonly used as identities in SIP deployments. In the majority of cases, this is not problematic for the identity mechanism described in this document. Telephone numbers commonly appear in the user-name portion of a SIP URI (e.g., sip:+17005551008@chicago.example.com;user=phone). That user name conforms to the syntax of the TEL URI scheme (RFC 3966, see Section 4.2.2). For this sort of SIP AOR, chicago.example.com is the appropriate signatory. It is also possible for a TEL URI to appear in the SIP To or From header field outside the context of a SIP or SIPS URI (e.g., tel:+17005551008). In this case, it is much less clear which signatory is appropriate for the identity. Fortunately for the identity mechanism, this form of the TEL URI is more common for the To header field and Request-URI in SIP than in the From header field, since the UAC has no option but to provide a TEL URI alone when the remote domain to which a request is sent is unknown.

The local domain, however, is usually known by the UAC, and accordingly it can form a proper From header field containing a SIP URI with a user name in TEL URI form. Implementations that intend to send their requests through an authentication service SHOULD put telephone numbers in the From header field into SIP or SIPS URIs whenever possible. If the local domain is unknown to a UAC formulating a request, it most likely will not be able to locate an authentication service for its request, and therefore the question of providing identity in these cases is somewhat moot. However, an authentication service MAY sign a request containing a TEL URI in the From header field. This is permitted in this specification strictly for forward compatibility purposes. In the longer-term, it is possible that ENUM (see Section 8.3) may provide a way to determine which administrative domain is responsible for a telephone number, and this may aid in the signing and verification of SIP identities that contain telephone numbers. This is a subject for future work.

19.4.8.10 Privacy Considerations

The identity mechanism presented in this document is compatible with the standard SIP practices for privacy described in RFC 3323 (see Section 20.2). A SIP proxy server can act both as a privacy service and as an authentication service. Since a UA can provide any From header field value that the authentication service is willing to authorize, there is no reason why private SIP URIs that contain legitimate domains (e.g., sip:anonymous@example.com) cannot be signed by an authentication service. The construction of the Identity header is the same for private URIs as it is for any other sort of URIs. Note, however, that an authentication service must possess a certificate corresponding to the host portion of the addr-spec of the From header field of any request that it signs; accordingly, using domains like anonymous.invalid will not be possible for privacy services that also act as authentication services. The assurance offered by the usage of anonymous URIs with a valid domain portion is "this is a known user in my domain that I have authenticated, but I am keeping its identity private." The use of the domain anonymous.invalid entails that no corresponding authority for the domain can exist, and as a consequence, authentication service functions are meaningless.

The header level of privacy described in RFC 3323 (see Section 20.2) requests that a privacy service alter the Contact header field value of a SIP message. Since the Contact header field is protected by the signature in an Identity header, privacy services cannot be applied after authentication services without a resulting integrity violation. RFC 3325 (see Sections 2.8, 10.4, and 20.3) defines the id priv-value token, which is specific to the P-Asserted-Identity header. The sort of assertion provided by the P-Asserted-Identity header is very different from the Identity header presented in this section.

It contains additional information about the sender of a message that may go beyond what appears in the From header field; P-Asserted-Identity holds a definitive identity for the sender that is somehow known to a closed network of intermediaries that presumably the network will use this identity for billing or security purposes. The danger of this network-specific information leaking outside of the closed network motivated the id priv-value token. The id priv-value token has no implications for the Identity header, and privacy services must not remove the Identity header when a priv-value of id appears in a Privacy header. Finally, note that unlike RFC 3325 (see Sections 2.8, 10.4, and 20.3), the mechanism described in this specification adds no information to SIP requests that have privacy implications.

19.4.8.11 Security Considerations

19.4.8.11.1 Handling of Digest-String Elements

RFC 4474 describes a mechanism that provides a signature over the Contact, Date, Call-ID, CSeq, To, and From header fields of SIP requests. While a signature over the From header field would be sufficient to secure a URI alone, the additional headers provide replay protection and reference integrity necessary to make sure that the Identity header will not be used in cut-and-paste attacks. In general, the considerations related to the security of these headers are the same as those given in RFC 3261 for including headers in tunneled message/sip MIME bodies (see Section 19.6.3 in particular). The following section details the individual security properties obtained by including each of these header fields within the signature; collectively, this set of header fields provides the necessary properties to prevent impersonation. The From header field indicates the identity of the sender of the message, and the SIP AOR URI in the From header field is the identity of a SIP user, for the purposes of this document.

The To header field provides the identity of the SIP user that this request targets. Providing the To header field in the Identity signature serves two purposes: first, it prevents cut-and-paste attacks in which an Identity header from legitimate request for one user is cut-and-pasted into a request for a different user; second, it preserves the starting URI scheme of the request, which helps prevent downgrade attacks against the use of SIPS. The Date and Contact headers provide reference integrity and replay protection, as described in RFC 3261 (see Section 19.6.4.2). Implementations of this specification must not deem valid a request with an outdated Date header field (the recommended interval is that the Date header must indicate a time within 3600 seconds of the receipt of a message). Implementations must also record Call-IDs received in valid requests containing an Identity header, and must remember those Call-IDs for at least the duration of a single Date interval (i.e., commonly 3600 seconds). Because a SIP-compliant UA never generates the same Call-ID twice, verifiers can use the Call-ID to recognize cut-and-paste attacks; the Call-ID serves as a nonce.

The result of this is that if an Identity header is replayed within the Date interval, verifiers will recognize that it is invalid because of a Call-ID duplication; if an Identity header is replayed after the Date interval, verifiers will recognize that it is invalid because the Date is stale. The CSeq header field contains a numbered identifier for the transaction, and the name of the method of the request; without this information, an INVITE request could be cut-and-pasted by an attacker and transformed into a BYE request without changing any fields covered by the Identity header, and, moreover, requests within a certain transaction could be replayed in potentially confusing or malicious ways. The Contact header field is included to tie the Identity header to a particular UA instance that generated the request. Were an active attacker to intercept a request containing an Identity header, and cut-and-paste the Identity header field into its own request (reusing the From, To, Contact, Date, and Call-ID fields that appear in the original message), the attacker would not be eligible to receive SIP requests from the called UA, since those requests are routed to the URI identified in the Contact header field.

However, the Contact header is only included in dialog-forming requests, so it does not provide this protection in all cases. It might seem attractive to provide a signature over some of the information present in the Via header field value(s). For example, without a signature over the sent-by field of the topmost Via header, an attacker could remove that Via header and insert its own in a cut-and-paste attack, which would cause all responses to the request to be routed to a host of the attacker's choosing. However, a signature over the topmost Via header does not prevent attacks of this nature, since the attacker could leave the topmost Via intact and merely insert a new Via header field directly after it, which would cause responses to be routed to the attacker's host *on their way* to the valid host, which has exactly the same end result.

Although it is possible that an intermediary-based authentication service could guarantee that no Via hops are inserted between the sending UA and the authentication service, it could not prevent an attacker from adding a Via hop after the authentication service, and thereby preempting responses. It is necessary for the proper operation of SIP for subsequent intermediaries to be capable of inserting such Via header fields, and thus it cannot be prevented.

As such, though it is desirable, securing Via is not possible through the sort of identity mechanism described in this document; the best known practice for securing Via is the use of SIPS.

This mechanism also provides a signature over the bodies of SIP requests. The most important reason for doing so is to protect SDP bodies carried in SIP requests. There is little purpose in establishing the identity of the user that originated a SIP request if this assurance is not coupled with a comparable assurance over the media descriptors. Note, however, that this is not perfect end-to-end security. The authentication service itself, when instantiated at an intermediary, could conceivably change the SDP (and SIP headers, for that matter) before providing a signature. Thus, while this mechanism reduces the chance that a replayer or MITM will modify SDP, it does not eliminate it entirely. Since it is a foundational assumption of this mechanism that the users trust their local domain to vouch for their security, they must also trust the service not to violate the integrity of their message without good reason. Note that RFC 3261 (see Section 3.11.6) states that SIP proxy servers must not add to, modify, or remove the message body.

In the end analysis, the Identity and Identity-Info headers cannot protect themselves. Any attacker could remove these headers from a SIP request, and modify the request arbitrarily afterwards. However, this mechanism is not intended to protect requests from MITMs who interfere with SIP messages; it is intended only to provide a way that SIP users can prove definitively that they are who they claim to be. At best, by stripping identity information from a request, an MITM could make it impossible to distinguish any illegitimate messages he would like to send from those messages sent by an authorized user. However, it requires a considerably greater amount of energy to mount such an attack than it does to mount trivial impersonations by just copying someone else's From header field. This mechanism provides a way that an authorized user can provide a definitive assurance of his identity that an unauthorized user, an impersonator, cannot.

One additional respect in which the Identity-Info header cannot protect itself is the alg parameter. The alg parameter is not included in the digest-string, and accordingly, an MITM might attempt to modify the alg parameter. However, it is important to note that preventing MITMs is not the primary impetus for this mechanism. Moreover, changing the alg would at worst result in some sort of bid-down attack, and at best cause a failure in the verifier. Note that only one valid alg parameter is defined in this document and that thus there is currently no weaker algorithm to which the mechanism can be bid down. alg has been incorporated into this mechanism for forward compatibility reasons in case the current algorithm exhibits weaknesses, and requires swift replacement, in the future.

19.4.8.11.2 Display Names and Identity

As a matter of interface design, SIP UAs might render the display-name portion of the From header field of a caller as the identity of the caller; there is a significant precedent in e-mail user interfaces for this practice. As such, it might seem that the lack of a signature over the display-name is a significant omission. However, there are several important senses in which a signature over the display-name does not prevent impersonation. In the first place, a particular display-name, like Jon Peterson, is not unique in the world; many users in different administrative domains might legitimately claim that name. Furthermore, enrollment practices for SIP-based services might have a difficult time discerning the legitimate display-name for a user; it is safe to assume that impersonators will be capable of creating SIP accounts with arbitrary display-names. The same situation prevails in e-mail today. Note that an impersonator who attempted to replay a message with an Identity header, changing only the display-name in the From header field, would be detected by the other replay protection mechanisms described in Section 19.4.8.11.1.

Of course, an authentication service can enforce policies about the display-name even if the display-name is not signed. The exact mechanics for creating and operationalizing such policies is outside the scope of this document. The effect of this policy would not be to prevent impersonation of a particular unique identifier like a SIP URI (since display-names are not unique identifiers), but to allow a domain to manage the claims made by its users. If such policies are enforced, users would not be free to claim any display-name of their choosing. In the absence of a signature, MITM attackers could conceivably alter the display-names in a request with impunity.

Note that the scope of this specification is impersonation attacks, however, and that an MITM might also strip the Identity and Identity-Info headers from a message. There are many environments in which policies regarding the display-name are not feasible. Distributing bit-exact and internationalizable display-names to end-users as part of the enrollment or registration process would require mechanisms that are not explored in this document. In the absence of policy enforcement regarding domain names, there are conceivably attacks that an adversary could mount against SIP systems that rely too heavily on the display-name in their user interface; however, this argues for intelligent interface design, not changes to the mechanisms. Relying on a nonunique identifier for identity would ultimately result in a weak mechanism.

19.4.8.11.3 Securing the Connection to the Authentication Service

The assurance provided by this mechanism is strongest when a UA forms a direct connection, preferably one secured by

TLS, to an intermediary-based authentication service. The reasons for this are twofold:

- If a user does not receive a certificate from the authentication service over this TLS connection that corresponds to the expected domain (especially when the user receives a challenge via a mechanism such as Digest), then it is possible that a rogue server is attempting to pose as an authentication service for a domain that it does not control, possibly in an attempt to collect shared secrets for that domain.
- Without TLS, the various header field values and the body of the request will not have integrity protection when the request arrives at an authentication service. Accordingly, a prior legitimate or illegitimate intermediary could modify the message arbitrarily.

Of these two concerns, the first is most material to the intended scope of this mechanism. This mechanism is intended to prevent impersonation attacks, not MITM attacks; integrity over the header and bodies is provided by this mechanism only to prevent replay attacks. However, it is possible that applications relying on the presence of the Identity header could leverage this integrity protection, especially body integrity, for services other than replay protection.

Accordingly, direct TLS connections should be used between the UAC and the authentication service whenever possible. The opportunistic nature of this mechanism, however, makes it very difficult to constrain UAC behavior, and, moreover, there will be some deployment architectures where a direct connection is simply infeasible and the UAC cannot act as an authentication service itself. Accordingly, when a direct connection and TLS are not possible, a UAC should use the SIPS mechanism, Digest auth-int for body integrity, or both when it can. The ultimate decision to add an Identity header to a request lies with the authentication service, of course; domain policy must identify those cases where the UAC's security association with the authentication service is too weak.

19.4.8.11.4 Domain Names and Subordination

When a verifier processes a request containing an Identity-Info header, it must compare the domain portion of the URI in the From header field of the request with the domain name that is the subject of the certificate acquired from the Identity-Info header. While it might seem that this should be a straightforward process, it is complicated by two deployment realities. In the first place, certificates have varying ways of describing their subjects, and may indeed have multiple subjects, especially in virtual hosting cases where multiple domains are managed by a single application. Secondly, some SIP services may delegate SIP functions to a subordinate domain and utilize the procedures in RFC 3263 (see Section 8.2.4) that allow requests for, say, example.com to be routed to sip.example.com. As a result, a user with the AOR sip:jon@example.com may process its requests through a host like sip.example.com, and it may be that latter host that acts as an authentication service. To meet the second of these problems, a domain that deploys an authentication service on a subordinate host MUST be willing to supply that host with the private keying material associated with a certificate whose subject is a domain name that corresponds to the domain portion of the AORs that the domain distributes to users.

Note that this corresponds to the comparable case of routing inbound SIP requests to a domain. When the Naming Authority Pointer (NAPTR) and SRV procedures of RFC 3263 (see Section 8.2.4) are used to direct requests to a domain name other than the domain in the original Request-URI (e.g., for sip:jon@example.com, the corresponding SRV records point to the service sip1.example.org), the client expects that the certificate passed back in any TLS exchange with that host will correspond exactly with the domain of the original Request-URI, not the domain name of the host. Consequently, to make inbound routing to such SIP services work, a domain administrator must similarly be willing to share the domain's private key with the service. This design decision was made to compensate for the insecurity of the DNS, and it makes certain potential approaches to DNS-based virtual hosting unsecurable for SIP in environments where domain administrators are unwilling to share keys with hosting services. A verifier MUST evaluate the correspondence between the user's identity and the signing certificate by following the procedures defined in RFC 2818, (Section 3.1 of RFC 2818). While RFC 2818 deals with the use of HTTP in TLS, the procedures described are applicable to verifying identity if one substitutes the host name of the server in HTTP for the domain portion of the user's identity in the From header field of a SIP request with an Identity header.

Because the domain certificates that can be used by authentication services need to assert only the host name of the authentication service, existing certificate authorities can provide adequate certificates for this mechanism. However, not all proxy servers and UAs will be able to support the root certificates of all certificate authorities, and, moreover, there are some significant differences in the policies by which certificate authorities issue their certificates. This document makes no recommendations for the usage of particular certificate authorities, nor does it describe any particular policies that certificate authorities should follow; however, it is anticipated that operational experience will create de facto standards for authentication services. Some federations of service providers, for example, might only trust certificates that have been provided by a certificate authority operated by the federation. It is strongly recommended that self-signed domain certificates should not be trusted by verifiers, unless some previous key exchange has justified such trust. For further information on certificate security and practices, see RFC 5280. The Security Considerations of RFC 5280 are applicable to this specification (RFC 4474).

19.4.8.11.5 Authorization and Transitional Strategies

Ultimately, the worth of an assurance provided by an Identity header is limited by the security practices of the domain that issues the assurance. Relying on an Identity header generated by a remote administrative domain assumes that the issuing domain used its administrative practices to authenticate its users. However, it is possible that some domains will implement policies that effectively make users unaccountable (e.g., ones that accept unauthenticated registrations from arbitrary users). The value of an Identity header from such domains is questionable. While there is no magic way for a verifier to distinguish *good* from *bad* domains by inspecting a SIP request, it is expected that further work in authorization practices could be built on top of this identity solution; without such an identity solution, many promising approaches to authorization policy are impossible. That much said, it is recommended that authentication services based on proxy servers employ strong authentication practices such as token-based identifiers.

One cannot expect the Identity and Identity-Info headers to be supported by every SIP entity overnight. This leaves the verifier in a compromising position; when it receives a request from a given SIP user, how can it know whether or not the sender's domain supports Identity? In the absence of ubiquitous support for identity, some transitional strategies are necessary. A verifier could remember when it receives a request from a domain that uses Identity, and in the future, view messages received from that domain without Identity headers with skepticism. A verifier could query the domain through some sort of callback system to determine whether or not it is running an authentication service. There are a number of potential ways in which this could be implemented; use of the SIP OPTIONS method is one possibility.

This is left as a subject for future work. In the long term, some sort of identity mechanism, either the one documented in this specification or a successor, must become mandatory-to-use for the SIP protocol; that is the only way to guarantee that this protection can always be expected by verifiers. Finally, it is worth noting that the presence or absence of the Identity headers cannot be the sole factor in making an authorization decision. Permissions might be granted to a message on the basis of the specific verified Identity or really on any other aspect of a SIP request. Authorization policies are outside the scope of this specification; however, this specification advises any future authorization work not to assume that messages with valid Identity headers are always good.

19.4.9 HTTP Digest Authentication Using AKA in SIP

19.4.9.1 Background

The HTTP Authentication Framework, described in RFC 2617 (see Sections 19.4.5 and 19.12.2.3), includes two authentication schemes: Basic and Digest. Both schemes employ a shared secret based mechanism for access authentication. The Basic scheme is inherently insecure in that it transmits user credentials in plain text. The Digest scheme improves security by hiding user credentials with cryptographic hashes, and additionally by providing limited message integrity. The Authentication and Key Agreement (AKA) [2] mechanism performs authentication and session key distribution in Universal Mobile Telecommunications System (UMTS) networks. AKA is a challenge–response-based mechanism that uses symmetric cryptography. AKA is typically run in a UMTS IM Services Identity Module (ISIM), which resides on a smart card-like device that also provides tamper-resistant storage of shared secrets.

RFC 3310 that is described here specifies a mapping of AKA parameters onto HTTP Digest authentication. In essence, this mapping enables the usage of AKA as a one-time password generation mechanism for Digest authentication. As the SIP Authentication Framework closely follows the HTTP Authentication Framework (see Sections 19.4.5 and 19.12.2.3), Digest AKA is directly applicable to SIP as well as any other embodiment of HTTP Digest. The following terminologies are defined in RFC 3310:

- AKA: authentication and key agreement.
- AuC: authentication center. The network element in mobile networks that can authorize users either in GSM or in UMTS networks.
- AUTN: authentication token. A 128-bit value generated by the AuC, which together with the RAND parameter authenticates the server to the client.
- AUTS: authentication token. A 112-bit value generated by the client upon experiencing an SQN synchronization failure.
- CK: cipher key. An AKA session key for encryption.
- IK: integrity key. An AKA session key for integrity check.
- ISIM: IP Multimedia Services Identity Module.
- PIN: personal identification number. Commonly assigned passcodes for use with automatic cash machines, smart cards, etc.
- RAND: random challenge. Generated by the AuC using the SQN.
- RES: authentication response. Generated by the ISIM.
- SIM: subscriber identity module. GSM counterpart for ISIM.

- SQN: sequence number. Both AuC and ISIM maintain the value of the SQN.
- UMTS: Universal Mobile Telecommunications System.
- XRES: expected authentication response. In a successful authentication, this is equal to RES.

19.4.9.2 AKA Mechanism Overview

This chapter describes the AKA operation in detail:

- A shared secret K is established beforehand between the ISIM and the Authentication Center (AuC). The secret is stored in the ISIM, which resides on a smart card-like, tamper-resistant device.
- The AuC of the home network produces an authentication vector AV, based on the shared secret K and a sequence number SQN. The authentication vector contains a random challenge RAND, network authentication token AUTN, expected authentication result XRES, a session key for integrity check IK, and a session key for encryption CK.
- The authentication vector is downloaded to a server. Optionally, the server can also download a batch of AVs, containing more than one authentication vector.
- The server creates an authentication request, which contains the random challenge RAND and the network authenticator token AUTN.
- The authentication request is delivered to the client.
- Using the shared secret K and the sequence number SQN, the client verifies the AUTN with the ISIM. If the verification is successful, the network has been authenticated. The client then produces an authentication response RES, using the shared secret K and the random challenge RAND.
- The authentication response, RES, is delivered to the server.
- The server compares the authentication response RES with the expected response, XRES. If the two match, the user has been successfully authenticated, and the session keys, IK and CK, can be used for protecting further communications between the client and the server.

When verifying the AUTN, the client may detect that the sequence numbers between the client and the server have fallen out of sync. In this case, the client produces a synchronization parameter AUTS, using the shared secret K and the client sequence number SQN. The AUTS parameter is delivered to the network in the authentication response, and the authentication can be tried again based on authentication vectors generated with the synchronized sequence number. The specification of the AKA mechanism and the generation of the cryptographic parameters AUTN, RES, IK, CK, and AUTS is developed by 3GPP [2].

19.4.9.3 Specification of Digest AKA

In general, the Digest AKA operation is identical to the Digest operation in RFC 2617 (see Sections 19.4.5 and 19.12.2.3). This chapter specifies the parts in which Digest AKA extends the Digest operation.

19.4.9.3.1 Algorithm Directive

To direct the client into using AKA for authentication instead of the standard password system, the RFC 2617-defined algorithm directive is overloaded in Digest AKA:

```
algorithm        = "algorithm" EQUAL (aka-
                   namespace/algorithm-value)
aka-namespace    = aka-version "-"
                   algorithm-value
aka-version      = "AKAv" 1*DIGIT
algorithm-value  = ("MD5"/"MD5-sess"/token)
```

Algorithm:
A string indicating the algorithm used in producing the digest and the checksum. If the directive is not understood, the nonce should be ignored, and another challenge (if one is present) should be used instead. The default aka-version is AKAv1. Further AKA versions can be specified, with version numbers assigned by IANA. When the algorithm directive is not present, it is assumed to be MD5. This indicates that AKA is not used to produce the Digest password.
Example:

```
Algorithm    =      AKAv1-MD5
```

If the entropy of the used RES value is limited (e.g., only 32 bits), reuse of the same RES value in authenticating subsequent requests and responses is not recommended. Such a RES value should only be used as a one-time password, and algorithms such as MD5-sess, which limit the amount of material hashed with a single key, by producing a session key for authentication, should not be used.

19.4.9.3.2 Creating a Challenge

To deliver the AKA authentication challenge to the client in Digest AKA, the nonce directive defined in RFC 2617 is extended:

```
nonce            = "nonce" EQUAL (aka-nonce/
                   nonce-value)
aka-nonce        = LDQUOT aka-nonce-value
RDQUOT
aka-nonce-value  = <base64 encoding of RAND,
                   AUTN, and server specific
                   data>
```

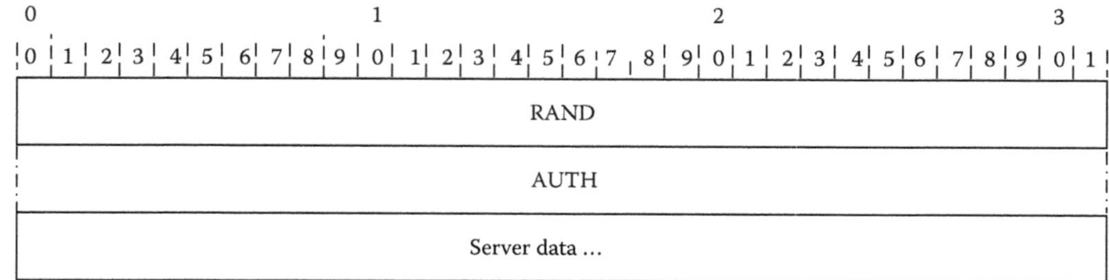

Figure 19.9 Generating the nonce value. (Copyright IETF. Reproduced with permission.)

nonce:
A parameter that is populated with the base64 (RFC 20454) encoding of the concatenation of the AKA authentication challenge RAND, the AKA AUTN token, and optionally some server specific data, as in Figure 19.9.
Example:

```
nonce  = "MzQ0a2xrbGtmbGtsZm9wb2tsc2tqaHJzZX
Ny9uQyMzMzMzQK="
```

If the server receives a client authentication containing the auts parameter defined in the next section that includes a valid AKA AUTS parameter, the server MUST use it to generate a new challenge to the client. Note that when the AUTS is present, the included response parameter is calculated using an empty password (password of ""), instead of a RES.

19.4.9.3.3 Client Authentication

When a client receives a Digest AKA authentication challenge, it extracts the RAND and AUTN from the nonce parameter, and assesses the AUTN token provided by the server. If the client successfully authenticates the server with the AUTN, and determines that the SQN used in generating the challenge is within expected range, the AKA algorithms are run with the RAND challenge and shared secret K. The resulting AKA RES parameter is treated as a password when calculating the response directive of RFC 2617 (see Sections 19.4.5 and 19.12.2.3).

19.4.9.3.4 Synchronization Failure

For indicating an AKA sequence number synchronization failure, and to resynchronize the SQN in the AuC using the AUTS token, a new directive is defined for the digest-response of the Authorization request header defined in RFC 2617:

```
Auts        =    "auts" EQUAL auts-param
auts-param  =    LDQUOT auts-value RDQUOT
auts-value  =    <base64 encoding of AUTS>
```

auts:
A string carrying a base64-encoded AKA AUTS parameter. This directive is used to resynchronize the server side SQN. If the directive is present, the client does not use any password when calculating its credentials. Instead, the client MUST calculate its credentials using an empty password (password of "".
Example:

```
auts   =      "CjkyMzRfOiwg5CfkJ2UK="
```

Upon receiving the auts parameter, the server will check the validity of the parameter value using the shared secret K. A valid AUTS parameter is used to resynchronize the SQN in the AuC. The synchronized SQN is then used to generate a fresh authentication vector AV, with which the client is then rechallenged.

19.4.9.3.5 Server Authentication

Even though AKA provides inherent mutual authentication with the AKA AUTN token, mutual authentication mechanisms provided by Digest may still be useful in order to provide message integrity. In Digest AKA, the server uses the AKA XRES parameter as password when calculating the response-auth of the Authentication-Info header defined in RFC 2617.

19.4.9.4 Example Digest AKA Operation

Figure 19.10 shows a message flow describing a Digest AKA process of authenticating a SIP request, namely the SIP REGISTER request.

F1: Initial request

```
REGISTER sip:home.mobile.biz SIP/2.0
```

F2: Response containing a challenge

```
SIP/2.0 401 Unauthorized
WWW-Authenticate: Digest
     realm="RoamingUsers@mobile.biz",
     nonce="CjPk9mRqNuT25eRkajM09uTl9nM09u
     Tl9nMz5OX25PZz== ",
```

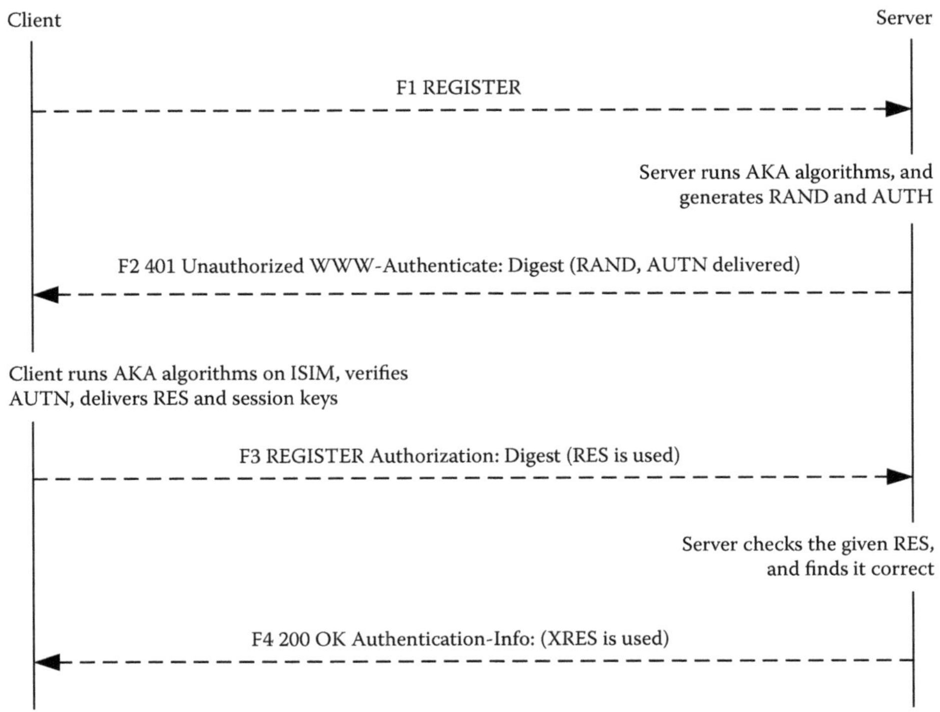

Figure 19.10 Message flow representing a successful authentication. (Copyright IETF. Reproduced with permission.)

```
       qop="auth,auth-int",
       opaque="5ccc069c403ebaf9f0171e9517f40
       e41",
       algorithm=AKAv1-MD5
```

F3: Request containing credentials

```
REGISTER sip:home.mobile.biz SIP/2.0
Authorization: Digest
       username="jon.dough@mobile.biz",
       realm="RoamingUsers@mobile.biz",
       nonce="CjPk9mRqNuT25eRkajM09uTl9nM09uT
       l9nMz5OX25PZz== ",
       uri="sip:home.mobile.biz",
       qop=auth-int,
       nc=00000001,
       cnonce="0a4f113b",
       response="6629fae49393a05397450978507c
       4ef1",
       opaque="5ccc069c403ebaf9f0171e9517f
       40e41"
```

F4: Successful response

```
SIP/2.0 200 OK
Authentication-Info:
       qop=auth-int,
       rspauth="6629fae49393a05397450978507c
       4ef1",
       cnonce="0a4f113b",
       nc=00000001
```

Figure 19.11 shows a message flow describing a Digest AKA authentication process, in which there is a synchronization failure.

F1: Initial request

```
REGISTER sip:home.mobile.biz SIP/2.0
```

F2: Response containing a challenge

```
SIP/2.0 401 Unauthorized
WWW-Authenticate: Digest
       realm="RoamingUsers@mobile.biz",
       qop="auth",
       nonce="CjPk9mRqNuT25eRkajM09uTl9nM09uT
l9nMz5OX25PZz== ",
       opaque="5ccc069c403ebaf9f0171e9517f
40e41",
       algorithm=AKAv1-MD5
```

F3: Request containing credentials

```
REGISTER sip:home.mobile.biz SIP/2.0
Authorization: Digest
       username="jon.dough@mobile.biz",
       realm="RoamingUsers@mobile.biz",
       nonce="CjPk9mRqNuT25eRkajM09uTl9nM09uT
       l9nMz5OX25PZz== ",
       uri="sip:home.mobile.biz",
       qop=auth,
       nc=00000001,
```

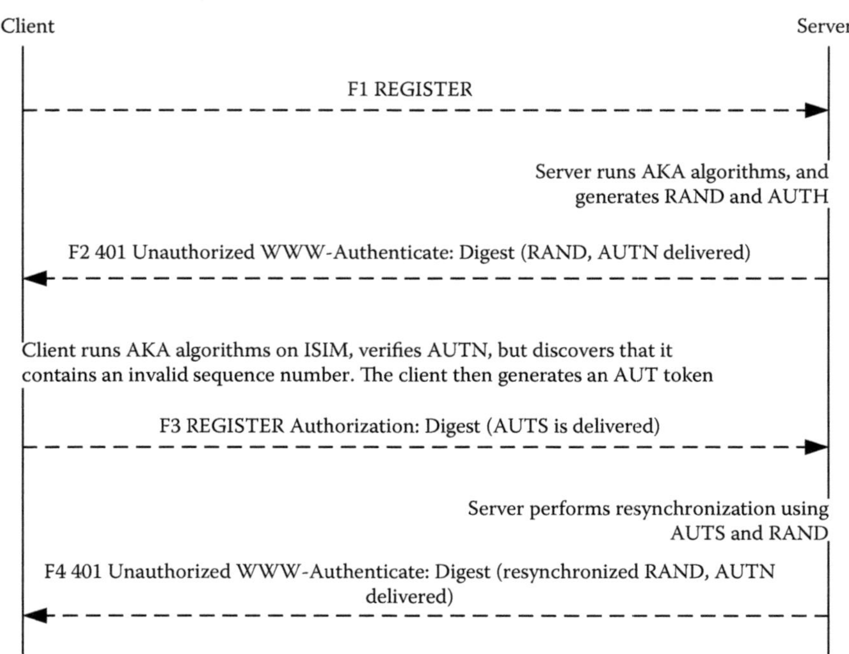

Figure 19.11 Message flow representing an authentication synchronization failure. (Copyright IETF. Reproduced with permission.)

```
        cnonce="0a4f113b",
        response="4429ffe49393c02397450934607c
        4ef1",
        opaque="5ccc069c403ebaf9f0171e9517f
        40e41",
        auts="5PYxMuX2NOT2NeQ="
```

F4: Response containing a new challenge

```
SIP/2.0 401 Unauthorized
WWW-Authenticate: Digest
        realm="RoamingUsers@mobile.biz",
        qop="auth,auth-int",
        nonce="9uQzNPbk9jM05Pbl5Pbl5DIz9uTl9uT
        l9jM0NTHk9uXk== ",
        opaque="dcd98b7102dd2f0e8b11d0f600bf
        b0c093",
        algorithm=AKAv1-MD5
```

19.4.9.5 Security Considerations

In general, Digest AKA is vulnerable to the same security threats as HTTP authentication (RFC 2617) that has been described in Sections 19.4.5 and 19.12.2.3. However, we are describing some relevant exceptions here in the context of Digest AKA.

19.4.9.5.1 Authentication of Clients Using Digest AKA

AKA is typically, though this is not a theoretical limitation, run on an ISIM application that usually resides in a tamper-resistant smart card. Interfaces to the ISIM exist, which enable the host device to request authentication to be performed on the card. However, these interfaces do not allow access to the long-term secret outside the ISIM, and the authentication can only be performed if the device accessing the ISIM has knowledge of a PIN code, shared between the user and the ISIM. Such PIN codes are typically obtained from user input, and are usually required when the device is powered on. The use of tamper-resistant cards with secure interfaces implies that Digest AKA is typically more secure than regular Digest implementations, as neither possession of the host device nor Trojan horses in the software give access to the long-term secret. Where a PIN scheme is used, the user is also authenticated when the device is powered on. However, there may be a difference in the resulting security of Digest AKA, compared with traditional Digest implementations, depending of course on whether those implementations cache/store passwords that are received from the user.

19.4.9.5.2 Limited Use of Nonce Values

The Digest scheme uses server-specified nonce values to seed the generation of the request-digest value. The server is free to construct the nonce in such a way that it may only be used from a particular client, for a particular resource, for a limited period of time or number of uses, or any other restrictions. Doing so strengthens the protection provided against, for example, replay attacks. Digest AKA limits the applicability of a nonce value to a particular ISIM. Typically, the ISIM is accessible only to one client device at a time. However, the nonce values are strong and secure even though limited to a particular ISIM. Additionally, this requires that the server is provided with the client identity before an authentication challenge can be generated. If a client identity is not available, an additional round trip is needed to acquire it. Such a case is analogous to an AKA synchronization failure. A server may allow each nonce value to be used only once by sending a next-nonce directive in the Authentication-Info header field of every response. However, this may cause a synchronization failure, and consequently some additional round trips in AKA, if the same SQN space is also used for other access schemes at the same time.

19.4.9.5.3 Multiple Authentication Schemes and Algorithms

In HTTP authentication, a UA MUST choose the strongest authentication scheme it understands and request credentials from the user, based on that challenge. In general, using passwords generated by Digest AKA with other HTTP authentication schemes is not recommended even though the realm values or protection domains would coincide. In these cases, a password should be requested from the end-user instead. Digest AKA passwords must not be reused with such HTTP authentication schemes, which send the password in clear. In particular, AKA passwords must not be reused with HTTP Basic. The same principle must be applied within a scheme if several algorithms are supported. A client receiving an HTTP Digest challenge with several available algorithms MUST choose the strongest algorithm it understands. For example, Digest with AKAv1-MD5 would be stronger than Digest with MD5.

19.4.9.5.4 Online Dictionary Attacks

Since user-selected passwords are typically quite simple, it has been proposed that servers should not accept passwords for HTTP Digest that are in the dictionary of RFC 2617. This potential threat does not exist in HTTP Digest AKA because the algorithm will use ISIM-originated passwords. However, the end user must still be careful with PIN codes. Even though HTTP Digest AKA password requests are never displayed to the end user, the end user will be authenticated to the ISIM via a PIN code. Commonly known initial PIN codes are typically installed to the ISIM during manufacturing and if the end users do not change them, there is a danger that an unauthorized user may be able to use the device. Naturally, this requires that the unauthorized user has access to the physical device, and that the end user has not changed the initial PIN code. For this reason, end users are strongly encouraged to change their PIN codes when they receive an ISIM.

19.4.9.5.5 Session Protection

Digest AKA is able to generate additional session keys for integrity (IK) and confidentiality (CK) protection. Even though this document does not specify the use of these additional keys, they may be used for creating additional security within HTTP authentication or some other security mechanism.

19.4.9.5.6 Replay Protection

AKA allows sequence numbers to be tracked for each authentication, with the SQN parameter. This allows authentications to be replay protected even if the RAND parameter happened to be the same for two authentication requests. More important, this offers additional protection for the case where an attacker replays an old authentication request sent by the network. The client will be able to detect that the request is old, and refuse authentication. This proves liveliness of the authentication request even in the case where an MITM attacker tries to trick the client into providing an authentication response, and then replaces parts of the message with something else. In other words, a client challenged by Digest AKA is not vulnerable for chosen plain text attacks. Finally, frequent sequence number errors would reveal an attack where the tamper-resistant card has been cloned and is being used in multiple devices. The downside of sequence number tracking is that servers must hold more information for each user than just their long-term secret, namely the current SQN value. However, this information is typically not stored in the SIP nodes, but in dedicated authentication servers instead.

19.4.9.5.7 Improvements to AKA Security

Even though AKA is perceived as a secure mechanism, Digest AKA is able to improve it. More specifically, the AKA parameters carried between the client and the server during authentication may be protected along with other parts of the message by using Digest AKA. This is not possible with plain AKA.

19.4.10 Key-Derivation Authentication Scheme in SIP

19.4.10.1 Background

SIP uses the Digest Authentication schemes (see Sections 19.4.5 and 19.12.2.3) with the general framework for access control and authentication, which is used by a server to challenge a client request and by a client to provide authentication information. The challenge–response framework relies on passwords chosen by users that usually have low entropy and weak randomness, and as a result cannot be used as cryptographic keys. While they cannot be used directly as cryptographic keys, the passwords can still be used to derive cryptographic keys, by using Key Derivation Function (KDF).

A Standards Track IETF draft [3] defines a key-derivation authentication scheme based on the KDF that could be used with the challenge–response authentication framework used by SIP to authenticate the user. The scheme allows two parties to establish a mutually authenticated communication channel based on a shared password, without ever sending the password on the wire. That is, the Key-Derivation scheme ensures that the password is never sent on the wire, and allows for a better secure storage of passwords, as it significantly increases the amount of computation needed to derive a key from a password in a dictionary attack. The Key-Derivation scheme creates a master-key that is derived from the password, which has a much better entropy than the password, to calculate a proof-of-possession (pop) for the shared password.

19.4.10.2 Operations

When an account is created, the server uses a KDF, a salt, a key length, and an iteration count to create a master-key based on the user's password, as defined in Ref. [4]. The server then stores the following information in the database: user name, iteration count, salt and master-key. Figure 19.12 describes the flow of messages at a high level based on the challenge–response framework.

With the challenge–response framework, the initial request from the client is sent without providing any credentials. When the server receives the initial request from the client, the server fetches the master-key associated with the user name provided in the request. The server then uses the master-key to create a pop using an HMAC-Hash function with the digest-string and nonce from the challenge. The digest-string, as defined in RFC 4474 (see Sections 2.8 and 19.4.8), is a list of SIP headers that must be hashed to create the pop defined in this document. The server then challenges the request and includes the Key-Derivation scheme with a kdf, a salt, a key size, an iteration count, a nonce, and pop. To be able to provide credentials to the server, the client must create the master-key as was done by the server when the account was initially created, as described above, using the parameters provided by the server in the challenge.

The client will then verify the pop sent by the server using its master-key, the digest-string of the incoming request, and the nonce provided in the challenge. The client then creates an initial request (F1) with a pop using an HMAC-Hash function and the master-key using the digest-string from the response concatenated with the nonce to be sent to the server. A valid response from the client will contain the Key-Derivation scheme, a nonce, and the pop parameter. When the server receives the response, it verifies the pop, and if that is valid, it sends a confirmation. At the end of the above process, the client and the server would have established a communication channel after completing a mutual authentication using the same

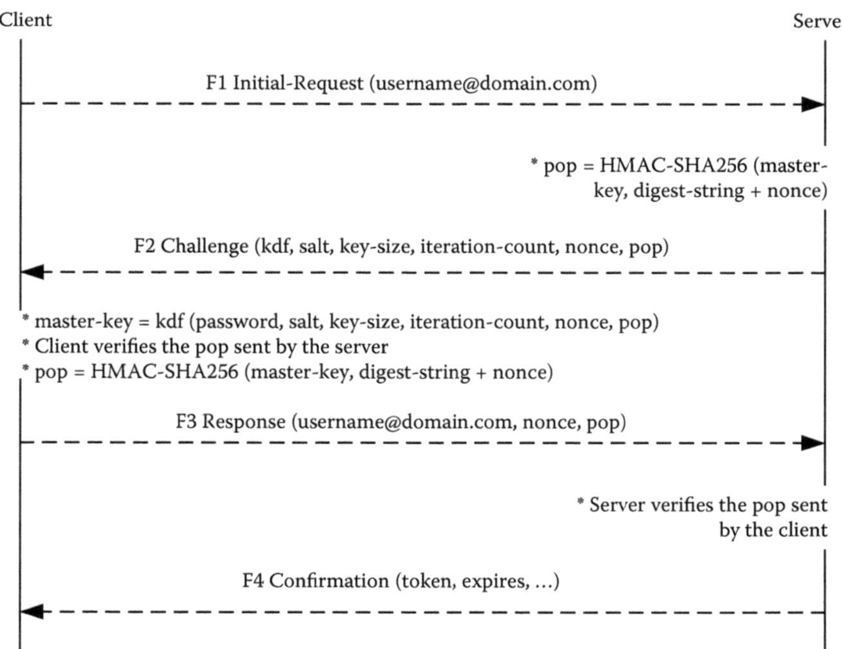

Figure 19.12 Message flows for key-derivation authentication scheme. (Copyright IETF. Reproduced with permission.)

master-key on both sides. Subsequent requests will be able to use the master-key to create pop to prove possession of the credentials.

19.4.10.3 Challenge

When a server receives a request from a client (F1), and an acceptable authorization is not sent, the server challenges the originator to provide credentials by rejecting the request and include the Key-Derivation scheme. The challenge (F2) should include the following parameters:

- **KDF** (REQUIRED): A deterministic algorithm used to derive cryptographic keys from a shared secret like a password. A good example of such a function is HMAC-SHA2-256.
- **Iterations** (OPTIONAL): The number of iterations that the KDF will be applied on the salt and password. The default value for this parameter is 1000.
- **Salt** (REQUIRED): A random value that is used to make sure that the same password will always be hashed differently. The salt MUST be generated using an approved random number generator.
- **Key-Size** (REQUIRED): The size of the derived key in bits.
- **nonce** (REQUIRED): A server-specified value that should be uniquely generated each time a challenge is made.
- **pop** (REQUIRED): The pop is derived from applying the HMAC-SHA256 on digest-string and a nonce using the master-key, as follows:

```
pop = HMAC-SHA256(master-key, digest-
string + nonce)
```

19.4.10.4 Response

The client first creates the master-key based on the parameters provided by the server in the challenge. The client then uses the master-key to verify the pop sent by the server; if that is successful, the client then uses the master-key to create a pop for the response (F3) to be sent to the server. The client is expected to retry the request, passing the nonce and pop with the Key-Derivation scheme.

- **nonce** (REQUIRED): A client-specified value that should be uniquely generated each time a response is made.
- **pop** (REQUIRED): The pop is derived from applying the HMAC-SHA256 on digest-string and a nonce using the master-key, as follows:

```
pop = HMAC-SHA256(master-key, digest-
string + nonce)
```

19.4.10.5 Confirmation

The server verifies the pop sent by the client. If the verification is successful, the server sends a confirmation (F4) to the client; otherwise, the server declines the request.

19.4.11 DNS-Based Authentication for TLS Sessions in SIP

19.4.11.1 Background

RFC 3261 defines how to use TLS in the SIP protocol (see Section 3.13), but does not describe the actual verification between a SIP request and a TLS server certificate in detail. RFC 5922 (see Section 19.4.5) updates RFC 3261 with a definition of how a SIP client matches a PKIX X.509 (RFC 5280) certificate provided by a TLS-enabled SIP server with the domain of a SIP request that caused the connection to be set up. Verification is done using the domain part of the SIP URI and the X.509 SubjectAltName extension of type dNSName or uniformResourceIdentifier. This is called *domain verification* as opposed to *host verification* in RFC 5922 (see Section 19.4.6). Including all domains hosted by a server in a server's certificate does not provide for a scalable and easily managed solution. Every time a service adds a domain, a new certificate will need to be provided, unless TLS Server Name Identification (SNI) is used, where each domain can have its own certificate. Having one certificate per domain and subdomain adds to the administration of a service. In addition, no known commercial CA offers certificate services with SIP URI's in the certificates.

Using DNSsec and DNS-based Authentication of Named Entities (DANE) (RFC 6698), the chain from a SIP uri to a TLS certificate changes, as outlined in this document. With DNSsec, the DNS lookups are authenticated and can be verified and trusted. A Standard Track IETF draft [5] describes a DANE-based chain of trust, matching the SRV host name with the contents of the certificate. The Standards Track IETF draft [6] that is described here explains how a SIP implementation can use DANE to set up a secure connection to a SIP server with TLS support. In addition, we describe how a server can provide support for RFC 5922 (see Section 19.4.6)-style clients with the same certificate, if needed. This draft adds an alternative to RFC 5922 so that SIP implementations supporting DANE can validate a SIP domain identity using secure DNS queries and the identity of the SIP host by verifying the certificate using the SRV host name found in a SubjectAltName extension of type DNSName in the certificate. The domain verification will now occur based on DNSsec and the TLS verification will be based on host names (host verification in RFC 5922). The specifications for DANE and the different ways a TLSA record can be constructed are described in RFC 6698.

19.4.11.2 Using DNS in the SIP Protocol

RFC 3263 (see Section 8.2.4) describes how a SIP implementation uses DNS to find the next-hop server. The first step is to look up a DNS NAPTR record for the domain part of the URI. NAPTR records are used by the target domain to indicate reachability using different transports. NAPTR may be used to indicate a preference for TLS/TCP connections. The result of the NAPTR lookup is a DNS name used to query for DNS SRV records. The list of DNS SRV records indicate host names that are queried to find A or AAAA records with IP addresses. SIP SRV records for TLS/TCP are using the prefix _sips._tcp, as in the DNS name _sips._tcp.example.com. A SIP implementation with no support for NAPTR may, based on configuration or URI scheme, choose to set up a TLS session to the target domain. In rare cases, no SRV lookup is done. This means that the implementation lacks capability to do load balancing and failover based on the information in the DNS. These types of clients are not considered in this document.

19.4.11.3 Importance of DNSsec for SIP

DNS relies on DNS lookups not only to find the next-hop server, but also for server administrators to provide failover and to load balance clients. The result of querying for one domain may need to SRV records or host names in another domain. Without DNSsec, an attacker can forge DNS replies and issue bogus DNS records, directing traffic to a bad server. This applies to calls as well as instant messaging, chat, and presence services.

19.4.11.4 DANE Applicability

It is important for implementers to understand the concept of secure DNSsec validation according to RFC 4033. For this specification to take effect, all DNS RRsets in the chain from SIP URI to IP address and TLSA record must be secure if DANE needs to be applicable. (This corresponds to the A.D. bit being set in the responses.) If any RRset is not secure, this specification does not apply and the implementation should fall back to RFC 5922 (see Section 19.4.6) behavior. If any of the responses are *bogus* according to DNSsec validation, the client must abort the connection.

19.4.11.5 TLSA Record Name

For the SIP protocol DANE usage, TLSA records are to be found in accordance with this IETF draft [5]. If the domain example.com's TLS SRV records point to sip01.example.com port 5042, then the corresponding TLSA record will be found using name_5042._tcp.sip01.example.com.

19.4.11.6 Procedures for DANE-Capable SIP Implementations

DANE-capable SIP implementations follow the procedures above to find an SRV host name and look for a TLSA record. If no TLSA record is found, the client should fall back to RFC 5922 (see Section 19.4.6). If a TLSA record is found, the client should never fall back to RFC 5922 behavior. If TLSA-based validation fails, the client MUST abort the connection attempt.

19.4.11.7 X.509 Certificate Validation

When using DANE-based validation, the client validates the SRV host name with the certificate using RFC 5922 (see Section 19.4.6) rules. A DANE-capable SIP implementation looks for the SRV host name in the list of SubjAltName DNSName extension fields. Only if there are no SubjAltName extension fields may the client look in the CN of the X.509 certificate according to RFC 5922. If the SRV host name is not found in the certificate, DANE validation fails and the client MUST abort the connection. Using the SRV host name for validation of a SIP domain identity is an update to RFC 5922.

19.4.11.8 Backwards Compatibility

RFC 5922 (see Section 19.4.6) implementations with no DANE support will be able to connect with the matching described in that document. SIP servers can use certificates that are compatible with both this specification and RFC 5922. This IETF draft [5] requires use of the TLS Server Name Indication (SNI) extension (RFC 6066). This is not a requirement in this document, since SIP certificates can support both RFC 5922 style validation and DANE-based validation with the same certificate.

19.4.11.9 Examples on Certificate Content

This section gives examples on certificate content and how they match a given URI. The X.509 PKIX Subject field CN value is abbreviated as CN, while the SubjAltName extension DNSName and uniformResourceIdentifier are abbreviated as SAN-DNS and SAN-URI, respectively. The certificates are tested with three different clients. A DANEaware client, an RFC 5922 (see Section 19.4.6) client with no DANE support, and a client that matches the SIP domain with the Common Name in the Subject of the certificate. The last example is not really covered by any SIP-related RFC and should be avoided.

Example 1: network.example.com

- Domain: network.example.com
- DNS SRV host for TLS: siphosting.example.net
- Certificate content
- CN: siphosting.example.net
- SAN-URI
- SAN-DNS
- Matching for DANE-aware SIP clients: Yes
- Matching for only RFC 5922 SIP clients: No
- Matching on CNAME only: No

Example 2: lundholm.example.com

- Domain: lundholm.example.com
- DNS SRV host for TLS: sipcrew.example.net
- Certificate content
- CN: randomname.example.net
- SAN-URI: sip:lundholm.example.com
- SAN-DNS: lundholm.example.com
- Matching for DANE-aware SIP clients: Yes
- Matching for only RFC 5922 (see Section 19.4.6) SIP clients: Yes

19.5 Authorization in SIP

19.5.1 Trait-Based Authorization in SIP

19.5.1.1 Overview

While some authentication mechanisms are described in the base SIP specification, trait-based authorization provides information used to make policy decisions based on the attributes of a participant in a session. This approach provides a richer framework for authorization, as well as allowing greater privacy for users of an identity system. RFC 4484 that is described here specifies requirements of the SIP (RFC 3261) for enabling trait-based authorization. This effort stems from the recognition that when SIP requests are received by a UAS, there are authorization requirements that are orthogonal to ascertaining of the identity of the UAC. Supplemental authorization information might allow the UAS to implement non-identity-based policies that depend on further attributes of the principal that originated a SIP request.

For example, in traditional SIP authorization architectures, the mere fact that a UAC has been authenticated by a UAS does not mean that the UAS will grant the UAC full access to its services or capabilities—in most instances, a UAS will compare the authenticated identity of the UAC to some set of users that are permitted to make particular requests (as a way of making an authorization decision). However, in large communities of users with few preexisting relationships (such as federations of discrete service providers), it is unlikely that the authenticated identity of a UAC alone will give a UAS sufficient information to decide how to handle a given request. Trait-based authorization entails an assertion by an authorization service of attributes associated with an identity. An assertion is a sort of document consisting of a set of these attributes that are wrapped within a digital signature provided by the party that generates the assertion (the operator of the authorization service). These attributes describe the trait or traits of the identity in question—facts about the principal corresponding to that identity.

For example, a given principal might be a faculty member at a university. An assertion for that principal's identity might state that they have the trait of "is a faculty member," and the assertion would be issued (and signed) by a university. When a UAS receives a request with this trait assertion, if it trusts the signing university, it can make an authorization decision based on whether or not faculty members are permitted to make the request in question, rather than just looking at the identity of the UAC and trying to discern whether or not they are a faculty member through some external means. Thus, these assertions allow a UAS to authorize a SIP request without having to store or access attributes associated with the identity of the UAC itself. Even complex authorization decisions based the presence of multiple disjointed attributes are feasible; for example, a faculty member could be part of the chemistry department, and both of these traits could be used to make authorization decisions in a given federation.

It is easy to see how traits can be used in a single administrative domain, for example, a single university, where all users are managed under the same administration. For traits to have a broader usage for services like SIP, which commonly are not bounded by administrative domains, domains that participate in a common authorization scheme must federate with one another. The concept of federation is integral to any trait-based authorization scheme. Domains that federate with one another agree on the syntax and semantics of traits—without this consensus, trait-based authorization schemes would only be useful in an intradomain context. A federation is defined as a set of administrative domains that implement common policies regarding the use and applicability of traits for authorization decisions. Federation necessarily implies a trust relationship, and usually implies some sort of preshared keys or other means of cryptographic assurance that a particular assertion was generated by an authorization service that participates in the federation.

In fact, when trait-based authorization is used, an assertion of attributes can be presented to a UAS instead of the identity of user of the UAC. In many cases, a UAS has no need to know who, exactly, has made a request—knowing the identity is only a means to the end of matching that identity to policies that actually depend on traits independent of identity. This fact allows trait-based authorization to offer a very compelling privacy and anonymity solution. Identity becomes one more attribute of an assertion that may or may not be disclosed to various destinations. Trait-based authorization for SIP depends on authorization services that are trusted by both the UAC and the UAS that wish to share a session. For that reason, the authorization services described in this document are most applicable to clients either in a single domain or in federated domains that have agreed to trust one another's authorization services. This could be common in academic environments, or business partnerships that wish to share attributes of principals with one another. Some trait-based authorization architectures have been proposed to provide single sign-on services across multiple providers. Although trait-based identity offers an alternative to traditional identity architectures, this effort should be considered complementary to the end-to-end cryptographic SIP Identity effort specified in RFC 4474 (see Sections 2.8 and 19.4.8). An authentication service might also act as an authorization service, generating some sort of trait assertion token instead of an authenticated identity body.

19.5.1.2 Trait-Based Authorization Framework

A trait-based authorization architecture entails the existence of an authorization service. Devices must send requests to an authorization service in order to receive an assertion that can be used in the context of a given network request. Different network request types will often necessitate different or additional attributes in assertions from the authorization service. For the purposes of SIP, SIP requests might be supplied to an authorization service to provide the basis for an assertion. It could be the case that a UA will take a particular SIP request, such as an INVITE, for which it wishes to acquire an assertion and forward this to the authorization service (in a manner similar to the way that an authenticated identity body is requested in RFC 4474; see Sections 2.8 and 19.4.8). UAs might also use a separate protocol to request an assertion. In either case, the client will need to authenticate itself to an authorization service before it receives an assertion.

This authentication could use any of the standard mechanisms described in RFC 3261, or use some other means of authentication. Once a SIP UA has an assertion, it will need some way to carry an assertion within a SIP request. It is possible that this assertion could be provided by reference or by value. For example, a SIP UA could include a MIME body within a SIP request that contains the assertion; this would be inclusion by value. Alternatively, content indirection specified in RFC 4483 (see Section 16.6), or some new header, could be used to provide a URI (perhaps an HTTP URL) where interested parties could acquire the assertion; this is inclusion by reference. The basic model is shown in Figure 19.13.

The entity requesting authorization assertions (or the entity that gets some assertions granted) and the entity using these authorization assertions might be colocated in the same host or domain, or they might be entities in different domains that share a federate with one another. The same is true for the entity that grants these assertions to a particular entity and the entity that verifies these assertions. From a protocol point of view, it is worth noting that the process of obtaining some assertions might occur sometime before the usage of these assertions. Furthermore, different protocols might be used and the assertions may have a lifetime that might allow that these assertions are presented to the verifying entity multiple times (during the lifetime of the assertion). Some important design decisions are associated with carrying assertions in a SIP request. If an assertion is carried by value, or uses a MIME-based content-indirection system, then proxy servers will be unable to inspect the assertion themselves. If the assertion were referenced in a header, however, it might be possible for the proxy to acquire and

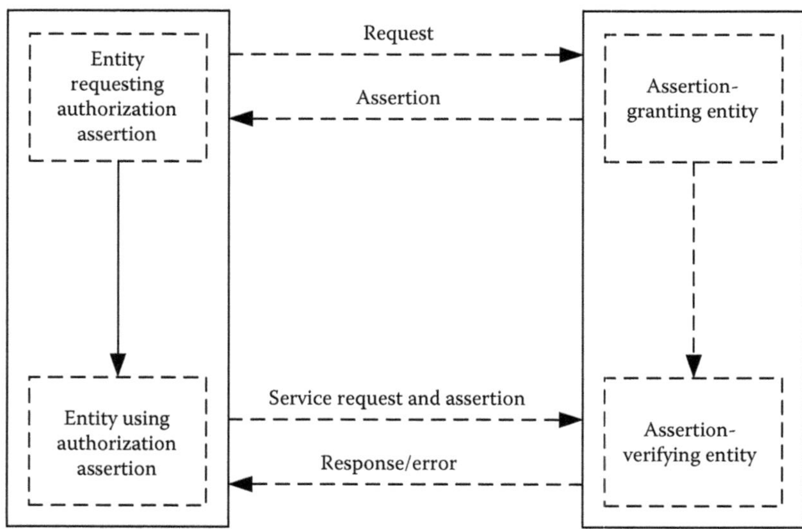

Figure 19.13 Basic trait-based authorization model. (Copyright IETF. Reproduced with permission.)

inspect the assertion itself. There are certainly architectures in which it would be meaningful for proxy servers to apply admission controls based on assertions.

It is also the case that carrying assertions by reference allows versatile access controls to be applied to the assertion itself. For instance, an HTTP URL where an assertion could be acquired could indicate a web server that challenged requests, and only allowed certain authorized sources to inspect the assertion, or that provided different versions of the assertion depending on who is asking. When a SIP UA initiates a request with privacy controls described in RFC 4474 (see Sections 2.8 and 19.4.8), a web server might provide only trait information (faculty, student, or staff) to most queries, but provide more detailed information, including the identity of the originator of the SIP request, to certain privileged askers. The end users that make requests should have some way to inform authorization services of the attributes that should be shared with particular destinations.

Assertions themselves might be scoped to a particular SIP transaction or SIP dialog, or they might have a longer lifetime. The recipient of an assertion associated with a SIP request needs to have some way to verify that the authorization service intended that this assertion could be used for the request in question. However, the format of assertions is not specified by these requirements. Trait assertions for responses to SIP requests are outside the scope of these requirements; it is not clear if there is any need for the recipient of a request to provide authorization data to the requestor. Trait-based authorization has significant applicability to SIP. There are numerous instances in which it is valuable to assert particular facts about a principal other than the principal's identity to aid the recipient of a request in making an authorization policy decision. For example, a telephony service provider might assert that a particular user is a *customer* as a trait. An emergency services network might indicate that a particular user has a privileged status as a caller.

19.5.1.3 Example Use Cases

The following use cases are by no means exhaustive, but provide a few high-level examples of the sorts of services that trait-based authorization might provide. All of the cases below consider interdomain usage of authorization assertions.

19.5.1.3.1 Settlement for Services

When end points in two domains share real-time communications services, sometimes there is a need for the domains to exchange accounting and settlement information in real time. The operators of valuable resources (e.g., PSTN trunking, conference bridges, or the like) in the called domain may wish to settle with the calling domain (either with the operators of the domain or a particular user), and some accounting operations might need to complete before a call is terminated. For example, a caller in one domain might want to access a conference bridge in another domain, and the called domain might wish to settle for the usage of the bridge with the calling domain. Or in a wireless context, a roaming user might want to use services in a visited network, and the visited network might need to understand how to settle with the user's home network for these services.

Assuming that the calling domain constitutes some sort of commercial service capable of exchanging accounting information, the called domain may want to verify that the remote user has a billable account in good standing before allowing a remote user access to valuable resources. Moreover, the called domain may need to discover the network address of an accounting server and some basic information about how to settle with it. An authorization assertion created by the calling domain could provide the called domain with an assurance that a user's account can settle for a particular service. In some cases, no further information may be required to process a transaction; however, if more specific accounting data is needed, traits could also communicate the network address of an accounting server, the settlement protocol that should be used, and so on.

19.5.1.3.2 Associating Gateways with Providers

Imagine a case where a particular telephone service provider has deployed numerous PSTN–SIP gateways. When calls come in from the PSTN, they are eventually proxied to various SIP UAs. Each SIP UAS is interested to know the identity of the PSTN caller, of course, which could be given within SIP messages in any number of ways (in SIP headers, bodies, etc.). However, in order for the recipient to be able to trust the identity (in this instance, the calling party's telephone number) stated in the call, they must first trust that the call originated from the gateway and that the gateway is operated by a known (and trusted) provider.

There are a number of ways that a service provider might try to address this problem. One possibility would be routing all calls from gateways through a recognizable edge proxy server (say, sip.example.com). Accordingly, any SIP entity that received a request via the edge proxy server (assuming the use of hop-by-hop mutual cryptographic authentication) would know the service provider from whom the call originated. However, it is possible that requests from the originating service provider's edge proxy might be proxied again before reaching the destination UAS, and thus in many cases the originating service provider's identity would be known only transitively. Moreover, in many architectures, requests that did not originate from PSTN gateways could be sent through the edge proxy server. In the end analysis, the recipient of the request is less interested in knowing which carrier the request came from than in knowing that the request came from a gateway.

Another possible solution is to issue certificates to every gateway corresponding to the host name of the gateway (gateway1.example.com). Gateways could therefore sign SIP requests directly, and this property could be preserved end-to-end. However, depending on the public key infrastructure, this could become costly for large numbers of gateways, and, moreover, a UAS that receives the request has no direct assurance from a typical certificate that the host is in fact a gateway just because it happens to be named gateway1. Trait-based authorization would enable the trait *is a gateway* to be associated with an assertion that is generated by the service provider (i.e., signed by example.com). Since these assertions would travel end-to-end from the originating service provider to the destination UAS, SIP requests that carry them can pass through any number of intermediaries without discarding cryptographic authentication information. This mechanism also does not rely on host-name conventions to identify what constitutes a gateway and what does not—it relies on an explicit and unambiguous attribute in an assertion.

19.5.1.3.3 Permissions on Constrained Resources

Consider a scenario wherein two universities are making use of a video-conferencing service over a constrained-bandwidth resource. Both universities would like to enforce policies that determine how this constrained bandwidth will be allocated to members of their respective communities. For example, faculty members might have privileges to establish video conferences during the day, while students might not. Faculty might also be able to add students to a particular video conference dynamically, or otherwise moderate the content or attendance of the conference, whereas students might participate only more passively. Trait-based authorization is ideal for managing authorization decisions that are predicated on membership in a group. Rather than basing access on individual users, levels (or roles) could be assigned that would be honored by both universities, since they both participate in the same federation. If the federation honored the traits *faculty*, *staff*, and *student*, they could be leveraged to ensure appropriate use of the network resource between universities participating in the federation. An assertion would then be attached to every request to establish a session that indicated the role of the requestor. Only if the requestor has the appropriate trait would the session request be granted. Ideally, these policies would be enforced by intermediaries (SIP proxy servers) that are capable of inspecting and verifying the assertions.

19.5.1.3.4 Managing Priority and Precedence

There is a significant amount of interest in the Internet telephony community in assigning certain calls a priority based on the identity of the user, with the presumption that prioritized calls will be granted preferential treatment when network resources are scarce. Different domains might have different criteria for assigning priority, and it is unlikely that a domain would correlate the identity of a nonlocal user with the need for priority, even in situations where domains would like to respect one another's prioritization policies. Existing proposals have focused largely on adding a new header field to SIP that might carry a priority indicator. This use case does not challenge this strategy, but merely shows by way of example how this requirement might be met with a trait-based authorization system. As such, the limitations of the header field approach will not be contrasted here with a hypothetical trait-based system. An assertion created by a domain for a particular request might have an associated priority attribute. Recipients of the request could inspect and verify the signature associated with the assertion to determine which domain had authenticated the user and made the priority assessment. If the assertion's creator is trusted by the evaluator, the given priority could be factored into any relevant request processing.

19.5.1.3.5 Linking Different Protocols

Cryptographic computations are expensive, and computing authorization decisions might require a lot of time and multiple messages between the entity enforcing the decisions and the entity computing the authorization decision. Particularly in a mobile environment, these entities are physically separated—or not even in the same administrative domain. Accordingly, the notion of *single sign-on* is another potential application of authorization assertions and trait-based authorization—a user is authenticated and authorized through one protocol, and can reuse the resulting authorization assertion in other, potential unrelated protocol exchanges.

For example, in some environments, it is useful to make the authorization decision for a high-level service (such as a voice call). The authorization for the voice call itself might include authorization for SIP signaling and also for lower-level network functions, for example, a QOS reservation, to improve the performance of real-time media sessions established by SIP. Since the SIP signaling protocol and the QOS reservation protocol are totally separate, it is necessary to link the authorization decisions of the two protocols. The authorization decision might be valid for a number of different protocol exchanges, for different protocols, and for a certain duration or some other attributes.

To enable this mechanism as part of the initial authorization step, an authorization assertion is returned to the end host of the SIP UAC (cryptographically protected). If QOS is necessary, the end host might reuse the returned assertion in the QOS signaling protocol. Any domains in the federation that would honor the assertion generated to authorize the SIP signaling would similarly honor the use of the assertion in the context of QOS. Upon the initial generation of the assertion by an authorization server, traits could be added that specify the desired level of quality that should be granted to the media associated with a SIP session.

19.5.1.4 Trait-Based Authorization Requirements

The following are the constraints and requirements for trait-based authorization in SIP:

- The mechanism must support a way for SIP UAs to embed an authorization assertion in SIP requests. Assertions can be carried either by reference or by value.
- The mechanism must allow SIP UACs to deliver to an authorization service those SIP requests that need to carry an assertion. The mechanism should also provide a way for SIP intermediaries to recognize that an assertion will be needed, and either forward requests to an authorization service themselves or notify the UAC of the need to do so.
- Authorization services must be capable of delivering an assertion to a SIP UAC, either by reference or by value. It may also be possible for an authorization service to add assertions to requests itself, if the user profile permits this, for example, through the use of content indirection as described in RFC 4483 (see Section 16.6).
- Authorization services must have a way to authenticate a SIP UAC.
- The assertions generated by authorization services must be capable of providing a set of values for a particular trait that a principal is entitled to claim.
- The mechanism must provide a way for authorized SIP intermediaries (e.g., authorized proxy servers) to inspect assertions.
- The mechanism must have a single baseline mandatory-to-implement authorization assertion scheme. The mechanism must also allow support of other assertion schemes, which would be optional to implement. One example of an assertion scheme is Security Assertion Markup Language (SAML) [7] and another is RFC 3281 X.509 Attribute Certificates.
- The mechanism must ensure reference integrity between a SIP request and assertion. Reference integrity refers to the relationship between a SIP message and the assertion authorizing the message. For example, a reference integrity check would compare the sender of the message (as expressed in the SIP request, e.g., in the From header field value) with the identity provided by the assertion. Reference integrity is necessary to prevent various sorts of relay and impersonation attacks. Note that reference integrity may apply on a per-message, per-transaction, or per-dialog basis.
- The assertion schemes used for this mechanism must be capable of asserting attributes or traits associated with the identity of the principal originating a SIP request. No specific traits or attributes are required by this specification.
- The mechanism must support a means for end users to specify policies to an authorization service for the distribution of their traits or attributes to various destinations.
- The mechanism must provide a way of preventing unauthorized parties (either intermediaries or end points) from viewing the contents of assertions.
- The assertion schemes must provide a way of selectively sharing the traits or attributes of the principal in question. In other words, it must be possible to show only some of the attributes of a given principal to particular recipients, based on the cryptographically assured identity of the recipient.
- It must be possible to provide an assertion that contains no identity—that is, to present only attributes or traits of the principal making a request, rather than the identity of the principal.
- The manner in which an assertion is distributed MUST permit cryptographic authentication and integrity properties to be applied to the assertion by the authorization service.
- It must be possible for a UAS or proxy server to reject a request that lacks a present and valid authorization assertion, and to inform the sending UAC that it must acquire such an assertion in order to complete the request.
- The recipient of a request containing an assertion must be able to ascertain which authorization service generated the assertion.
- It must be possible for a UAS or proxy server to reject a request containing an assertion that does not provide any attributes or traits that are known to the recipient or that are relevant to the request in question.
- It should be possible for a UAC to attach multiple assertions to a single SIP request, in cases where multiple authorization services must provide assertions in order for a request to complete.

19.5.1.5 SAML Assertion for Role/Trait-Based Authorization in SIP

Earlier in introducing the authentication services in SIP, we described how basic identity information could be asserted (see Section 19.2). However, additional identity information can also be asserted according to the same manner for authorization once authentication is provided. The requirements for asserting additional identity information, referred to as roles or traits, are described above; however, RFC 4484 (see Section 19.5.1) offers only some scenarios for the role or trait-based authorization that will offer scalability, but not any actual solutions in SIP. In this regard, we are describing a method [7] for using the SAML in collaboration with SIP. This scheme defines the SAML assertions in SIP messages for trait-based authorization.

19.5.1.5.1 SIP Authorization System with SAML Assertion

We are considering a SIP authorization system as depicted in Figure 16.31, Section 16.6.1. SIP user profiles that are relevant to the trait-based authentication can be encoded in SAML (e.g., asserting party is making the statement, "Alice has these profile attributes and her domain's certificate is available over there, and I'm making this statement, and here's who I am."). Figure 19.14 shows the call flows of the above SIP authorization system.

In this example, Alice wants to call Bob. The outgoing SIP proxy that acts as the virtual SIP authentication service for asserting identity authenticates Alice (F1–F4 SIP messages) after challenge and response with authentication credentials, and then forwards Alice's SIP INVITE message onto Bob's inbound SIP proxy that serves as the relaying party. This SIP message includes Alice's identity information as blessed by her outgoing proxy, along with a reference to a SAML assertion, which asserts various traits of Alice and points to Alice's domain certificate. If the assertion and domain certificate pass verification by Bob's inbound proxy (relaying party), then the call setup continues.

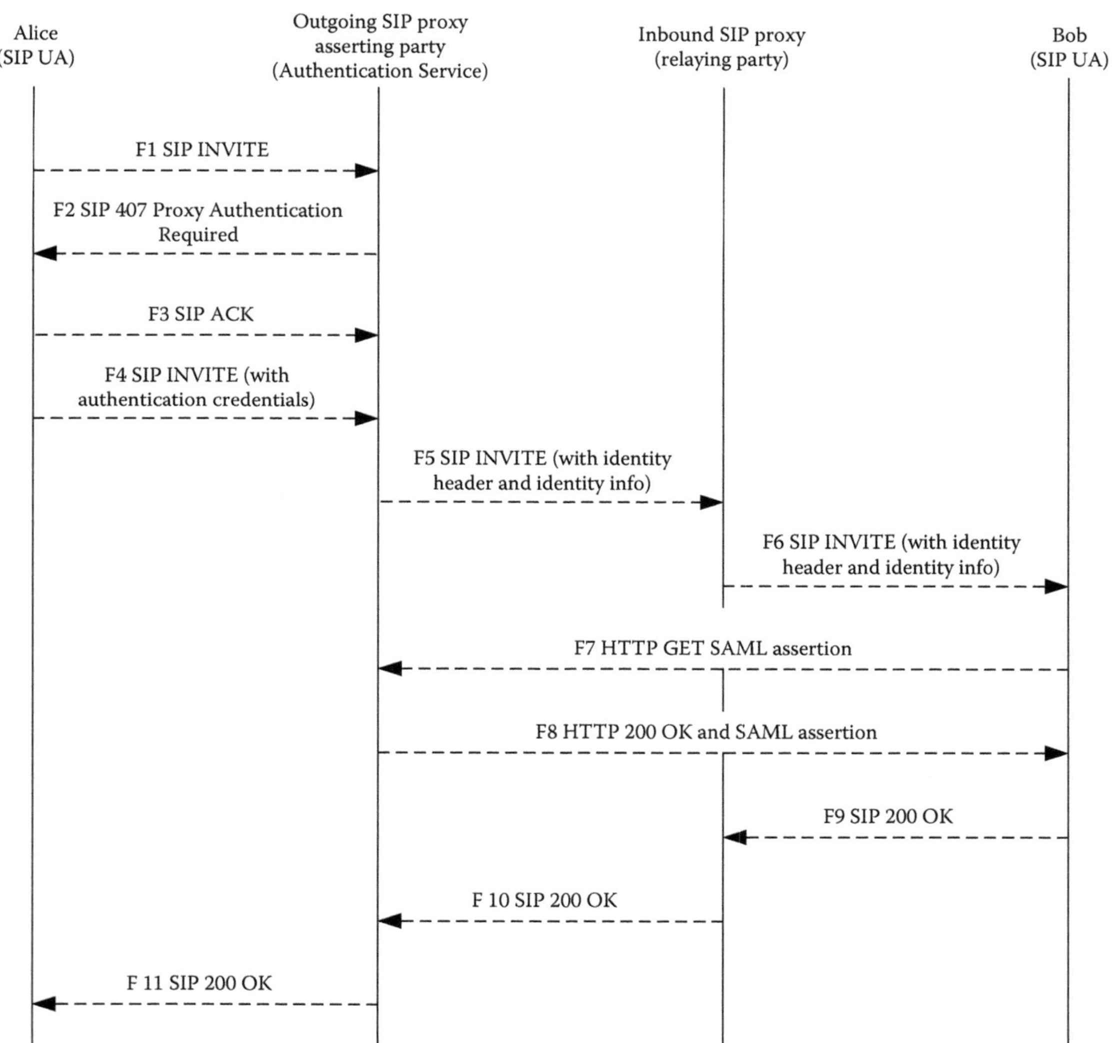

Figure 19.14 Role/trait-based authorization in SIP using SAML. (Copyright IETF. Reproduced with permission.)

- At first, Alice sends an SIP INVITE message (F1) to her outgoing SIP proxy. The outgoing proxy then challenges Alice for her authentication sending SIP 407 Proxy Authorization Required message (F2). Alice sends a SIP ACK message (F3) acknowledging the challenge from the proxy.
- Alice resends a new SIP INVITE message (F4) along with authentication credentials to her outgoing proxy.
- That is, in steps F1 through F4, an authentication and authorization process is executed between Alice's SIP UA and the authentication service, also known as the asserting party. User authorization by the asserting party is important in order to be able to create the SAML assertion and the respective attributes. The SIP UA (Alice) must ensure that the asserting party is genuine.
- The asserting party then verifies the identity information in the SIP INVITE message (F4) with Alice's credentials received from Alice's UA, and generates a SAML assertion attesting to several of Alice's attributes per local security policies. The assertion is held for later retrieval by the relaying party, and the SIP INVITE message (F4) is modified per the processing rules of authenticated identity specified in RFC 4474 (see Sections 2.8 and 19.4.8) and trait-based authorization policies. This includes placing an HTTP URL reference to the aforementioned SAML assertion in the Identity and Identity-Info header field of the SIP INVITE message. The asserting party (Alice's outgoing SIP proxy) send the SIP INVITE message (F5) to the relaying party (Bob's incoming SIP proxy).
- The incoming SIP proxy then relays the SIP INVITE message (F6) to Bob. Bob receives the SIP INVITE message (F6). It extracts the URL from the Identity-Info header field and dereferences it using an HTTP GET message (F7) with SAML assertion to the asserting party.
- The SAML assertion is then returned in the HTTP 200 OK response message (F8). Bob receives it and verifies it, and the domain certifies the assertion references, according to the processing rules of authenticated identity and trait-based authorization policies.
- Finally, if the verification by Bob succeeds, a SIP 200 OK response (F9) that is a success status code is sent to the relaying party. It is then forwarded to the asserting party (F10) and is returned finally to Alice's UA (F11), and the usual call setup proceeds (not shown in Figure 19.14).

19.5.1.5.2 SIP Authorization System Vulnerabilities

SIP messages (e.g., INVITE and others) can pass from the calling party (e.g., SIP UA A: Alice) to the called party (e.g., SIP UA B: Bob) directly or via intermediaries like proxies A and B. The functional entities between the source–destination paths including Bob may not be entirely trustworthy (Figure 19.15). In addition, the INVITE message described above contains an HTTP URL with which one may easily retrieve the associated SAML assertion. Any of the entities residing in the SIP network that handle the SIP message will be able to retrieve the assertion and associated domain certificate.

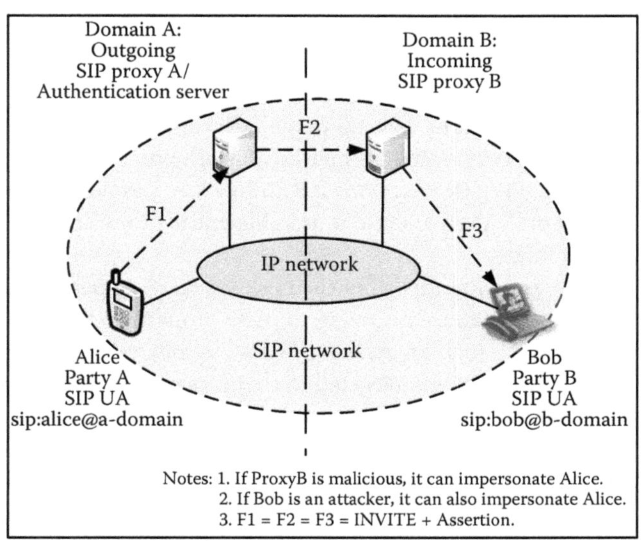

Figure 19.15 Security threats in role/trait-based authorization.

The HTTP-based SAML assertion remains in a web server and the HTTP infrastructure also involves HTTP proxies, and one of those entities could intercept a returned assertion. In this communications environment, it could be conceived that the attacker could then attempt to impersonate (Figure 19.15), for example, by stealing the assertion of, the subject (e.g., Alice) to some SIP-based target entity.

19.5.1.5.3 Vulnerability Mitigations Using SAML Assertion in SIP

Although the SAML assertion can have the public key certificate of a legitimate domain, such an attack is implausible. The main reason is that a message constructed by an impostor using a stolen assertion will not be able to pass the verification stage because the impostor will not have the corresponding private key with which to generate the signed SIP Identity header value. The assertion content stipulated in the SAML assertion profile that the assertion will not be useful to arbitrary parties because of the following:

- The content of the assertion is digitally signed, thus causing any alterations to break its integrity, making them detectable. Because of this, the assertion is to be signed by the same key used to sign the SIP Identity header. This binds the assertion to the subject identity (i.e., the caller's) being asserted by the caller domain's outbound SIP proxy/authentication service.

- The assertion does not contain an authentication statement. It means that no party faithfully implementing the cryptographic authentication scheme specified in RFC 4474 (see Sections 2.8 and 19.4.8) should be relying on SAML assertions as sufficient to allow access to resources.
- The assertion identifies the targeted relaying party and the assertion user. Owing to these properties, an entity receiving such an assertion is able to ascertain whether the assertion was targeted to them, as well as who originated it, and thus make an informed decision whether to proceed with SIP session establishment.
- The assertion explicitly stipulates its validity period. This is simply the well-known and oft-used technique of having security tokens explicitly reflect the time period within which they may be relied upon.
- The assertion contains or refers to the originating user's domain's public key certificate. In addition to all of the above, with this property the assertion refers to (or actually contains) the user's domain public key certificate.

The key is that the above linkage is protected by the signature on the assertion, and the reference to the assertion in the SIP message's Identity-Info header field (as well as several other SIP header fields) is protected via signature. We have seen that there is a verifiable chain from the SIP message to the user's domain public key certificate described above. It is quite possible that any of the links in the chain explained above may not verify in certain circumstances. If this occurs, a relaying party shall not continue with SIP session establishment in view of maintaining the security of the session.

19.5.1.6 Role/Trait-Based Authorization Benefits in SIP

An authorization system for SIP that is not predicated on the distribution of end-users' identities, but rather shares traits of the users, is described here (RFC 4484). The distribution of authorization assertions requires numerous security properties. An authorization service must be able to sign assertions, or provide some similar cryptographic assurance that can provide nonrepudiation for assertions as detailed in RFC 3323 (see Section 20.2). We have described an implementation of role/trait-based authorization scheme using SAML assertion profile in conjunction with SIP for secured SIP session setups satisfying requirements along the line articulated here (RFC 4484). The SAML assertion is extremely flexible and allows for the encoding not only of identity information about the user, but also generic authentication and authorization attributes that provide much richer authorization mechanisms and enable trait-based authorization. The SAML assertion profile based on roles/traits along with identity will make the authorization decision enhance security in SIP. The protection of user privacy in relation to the user's identity, including the asserted identity, is described in RFC 3323 (see Section 20.2).

19.5.2 Authorization through Dialog Identification in SIP

19.5.2.1 Overview

We have defined authorization earlier (see Section 19.1). In addition, authorization is defined in the context of cryptographic authentication (see Section 19.4.8). It appears that authorization is almost tightly related to authentication, and there can be many kinds of policies for providing authorization. However, we solely discuss authorization through dialog identification as specified in RFC 4538. RFC 4538 that is described here defines the Target-Dialog header field for the SIP, and the corresponding option tag, tdialog. This header field is used in requests that create SIP dialogs. It indicates to the recipient that the sender is aware of an existing dialog with the recipient, either because the sender is on the other side of that dialog, or because it has access to the dialog identifiers. The recipient can then authorize the request based on this awareness.

SIP defines the concept of a dialog as a persistent relationship between a pair of UAs. Dialogs provide context, including sequence numbers, proxy routes, and dialog identifiers. Dialogs are established through the transmission of SIP requests with particular methods. Specifically, the INVITE, REFER, and SUBSCRIBE requests all create dialogs. When a UA receives a request that creates a dialog, it needs to decide whether to authorize that request. For some requests, authorization is a function of the identity of the sender, the request method, and so on. However, many situations have been identified in which a UA's authorization decision depends on whether the sender of the request is currently in a dialog with that UA, or whether the sender of the request is aware of a dialog the UA has with another entity.

One such example is call transfer, accomplished through REFER. If UAs A and B are in an INVITE dialog, and UA A wishes to transfer UA B to UA C, UA A needs to send a REFER request to UA B, asking UA B to send an INVITE request to UA C. UA B needs to authorize this REFER. The proper authorization decision is that UA B should accept the request if it came from a user with whom B currently has an INVITE dialog relationship. Current implementations deal with this by sending the REFER on the same dialog as the one in place between UAs A and B. However, this approach has numerous problems as specified in RFC 5057 (see Sections 3.6.5 and 16.2). These problems include difficulties in determining the life cycle of the dialog and its usages, and in determining which messages are associated with each application usage. Instead, a better approach is for UA A to send the REFER request to UA B outside of the dialog. In that case, a means is needed for UA B to authorize the REFER.

Another example is the SIP application interaction framework specified in RFC 5629. In that framework, proxy servers on the path of a SIP INVITE request can place user interface components on the UA that generated or received the request. To do this, the proxy server needs to send a REFER request to the UA, targeted to its GRUU (see Section 4.3), asking the UA to fetch an HTTP resource containing the user interface component. In such a case, a means is needed for the UA to authorize the REFER.

The application interaction framework recommends that the request be authorized if it was sent from an entity on the path of the original dialog. This can be done by including the dialog identifiers in the REFER, which prove that the UA that sent the REFER is aware of those dialog identifiers (this needs to be secured against eavesdroppers through the sips mechanism, of course). Another example is if two UAs share an INVITE dialog, and an element on the path of the INVITE request wishes to track the state of the INVITE. In such a case, it sends a SUBSCRIBE request to the GRUU of the UA, asking for a subscription to the dialog event package. If the SUBSCRIBE request came from an element on the INVITE request path, it should be authorized.

19.5.2.2 Operation

Figure 19.16 shows the basic model of operation. UA A sends an INVITE to UA B, traversing two servers, server A and server B. Both servers act as proxies for this transaction. User B sends a 200 OK response to the INVITE. This 200 OK includes a Supported header field indicating support for this specification (through the presence of the tdialog option tag).

The 200 OK response establishes a dialog between the two UAs. Next, an entity that was present along the request path (e.g., server A) wishes to send a dialog-forming request (such as REFER) to UA A or B (e.g., user B). Thus, the entity

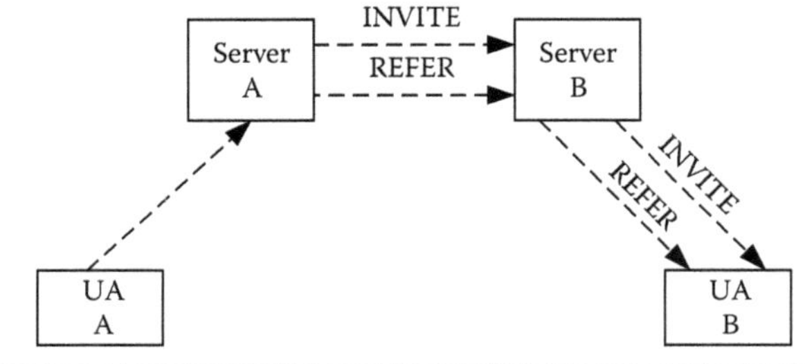

Figure 19.16 Basic operation for authorization through dialog identification.

acts as a UA and sends the request to UA B. This request is addressed to the URI of UA B, which server A learned from inspecting the Contact header field in the 200 OK of the INVITE request. If this URI has the GRUU (see Section 4.3) property (it can be used by any element on the Internet, such as server A, to reach the specific UA instance that generated that 200 OK to the INVITE), then the mechanism will work across NAT boundaries.

The request generated by server A will contain a Target-Dialog header field. This header field contains the dialog identifiers for the INVITE dialog between UAs A and B, composed of the Call-ID, local tag, and remote tag. Server A knew to include the Target-Dialog header field in the REFER request because it knows that UA B supports it. When the request arrives at UA B, it needs to make an authorization decision. Because the INVITE dialog was established using a sips URI, and because the dialog identifiers are cryptographically random (RFC 3261, see Section 3.6), no entity except for UA A or the proxies on the path of the initial INVITE request can know the dialog identifiers. Thus, because the request contains those dialog identifiers, UA B can be certain that the request came from UA A, the two proxies, or an entity to whom the UA or proxies gave the dialog identifiers. As such, it authorizes the request and performs the requested actions.

19.5.2.3 UAC Behavior

A UAC should include a Target-Dialog header field in a request if the following conditions are all true:

- The request is to be sent outside of any existing dialog.
- The UAC believes that the request may not be authorized by the UAS unless the UAC can prove that it is aware of the dialog identifiers for some other dialog. Call this dialog the target dialog.
- The request does not otherwise contain information that indicates that the UAC is aware of those dialog identifiers.
- The UAC knows that the UAS supports the Target-Dialog header field. It can know this if it has seen a request or response from the UAS within the target dialog that contained a Supported header field that included the tdialog option tag.

If the fourth condition is not met, the UAC should not use this specification. Instead, if it is currently within a dialog with the UAS, it should attempt to send the request within the existing target dialog. The following are examples of use cases in which these conditions are met:

- A REFER request is sent according to the principles of RFC 5629. These REFER are sent outside of a dialog and do not contain any other information

that indicates awareness of the target dialog. RFC 5629 also mandates that the REFER be sent only if the UA indicates support for the target dialog specification.
- User A is in separate calls with users B and C. User A decides to start a three-way call, and so morphs into a focus (RFC 4353). User B would like to learn the other participants in the conference. Thus, it sends a SUBSCRIBE request to user A (who is now acting as the focus) for the conference event package (RFC 4575). It is sent outside of the existing dialog between user B and the focus, and it would be authorized by A if user B could prove that it knows the dialog identifiers for its existing dialog with the focus. Thus, the Target-Dialog header field would be included in the SUBSCRIBE.

The following are examples of use cases in which these conditions are not met:

- A server acting as a proxy is a participant in an INVITE dialog that establishes a session. The server would like to use the Keypad Markup Language (KPML) event package (RFC 4730) to find out about keypresses from the originating UA. To do this, it sends a SUBSCRIBE request. However, the Event header field of this SUBSCRIBE contains event parameters that indicate the target dialog of the subscription. As such, the request can be authorized without additional information.
- A server acting as a proxy is a participant in an INVITE dialog that establishes a session. The server would like to use the dialog event package (RFC 4235) to find out about dialogs at the originating UA. To do this, it sends a SUBSCRIBE request. However, the Event header field of this SUBSCRIBE contains event parameters that indicate the target dialog of the subscription. As such, the request can be authorized without additional information.

Specifications that intend to make use of the Target-Dialog header field should discuss specific conditions in which it is to be included. Assuming it is to be included, the value of the callid production in the Target-Dialog header field must be equal to the Call-ID of the target dialog. The remote-tag header field parameter must be present and must contain the tag that would be viewed as the remote tag from the perspective of the recipient of the new request. The local-tag header field parameter must be present and must contain the tag that would be viewed as the local tag from the perspective of the recipient of the new request. The request sent by the UAC should include a Require header field that includes the tdialog option tag. This request should, in principle, never fail with a 420 Bad Extension response, because the UAC would not have sent the request unless it believed the UAS supported the extension. If a Require header field was not included, and the UAS did not support the extension, it would normally reject the request because it was unauthorized, probably with a 403 Forbidden. However, without the Require header field, the UAC would not be able to differentiate between the following:

- A 403 Forbidden that arrived because the UAS did not actually understand the Target-Dialog header field (in which case the client should send the request within the target dialog if it can)
- A 403 Forbidden that arrived because the UAS understood the Target-Dialog header field, but elected not to authorize the request although the UAC proved its awareness of the target dialog (in which case the client should not resend the request within the target dialog, even if it could)

19.5.2.4 UAS Behavior

If a UAS receives a dialog-creating request and wishes to authorize the request, and if that authorization depends on whether or not the sender has knowledge of an existing dialog with the UAS, and information outside of the Target-Dialog header field does not provide proof of this knowledge, the UAS should check the request for the existence of the Target-Dialog header field. If this header field is not present, the UAS may still authorize the request by other means. If the header field is present, and the value of the called production, the remote-tag, and local-tag values match the Call-ID, remote tag, and local tag of an existing dialog, and the dialog that they match was established using a sips URI, the UAS should authorize the request if it would authorize any entity on the path of the request that created that dialog, or any entity trusted by an entity on the path of the request that created that dialog.

If the dialog identifiers match, but they match a dialog not created with a sips URI, the UAS may authorize the request if it would authorize any entity on the path of the request that created that dialog, or any entity trusted by an entity on the path of the request that created that dialog. However, in this case, any eavesdropper on the original dialog path would have access to the dialog identifiers, and thus the authorization is optional. If the dialog identifiers do not match, or if they do not contain both a remote-tag and local-tag parameter, the header field must be ignored, and authorization may be determined by other means.

19.5.2.5 Proxy Behavior

Proxy behavior is unaffected by this specification.

19.5.2.6 Extensibility Considerations

This specification depends on a UAC knowing, ahead of sending a request to a UAS, whether or not that UAS supports the Target-Dialog header field. As discussed earlier, the UAC can know this because it saw a request or response sent by that UAS within the target dialog that contained the Supported header field whose value included the tdialog option tag. Because of this requirement, it is especially important that UAs compliant to this specification include a Supported header field in all dialog-forming requests and responses. Inclusion of the Supported header fields in requests is at *should* strength per RFC 3261 (see Section 2.8). This specification does not alter that requirement. However, implementers should realize that, unless the tdialog option tag is placed in the Supported header field of requests and responses, this extension is not likely to be used, and instead, the request is likely to be re-sent within the existing target dialog (assuming the sender is the UA on the other side of the target dialog). As such, the conditions in which the use of *should* would not be followed would be those rare cases in which the UA does not want to enable usage of this extension.

19.5.2.7 Target-Dialog Header Field Definition

The grammar for the Target-Dialog header field is repeated here for convenience although all header fields are defined in Section 2.4.1:

```
Target-Dialog = "Target-Dialog" HCOLON callid
                *(SEMItd-param);callid from
                RFC 3261
td-param      = remote-param/local-param/
                generic-param
remote-param  = "remote-tag" EQUAL token
local-param   = "local-tag" EQUAL token;token
                and generic-param from RFC
                3261
```

Table 2.5 shows an extension of Tables 2 and 3 in RFC 3261 (see Section 2.8.1) for the Target-Dialog header field.

19.5.2.8 Security Considerations

The Target-Dialog header field is used to authorize requests based on the fact that the sender of the request has access to information that only certain entities have access to. For such an authorization decision to be secure, two conditions have to be met. First, no eavesdroppers can have access to this information. That requires the original SIP dialog to be established using a sips URI, which provides TLS on each hop. With a sips URI, only the UAs and proxies on the request path will be able to know the dialog identifiers. The second condition is that the dialog identifiers be sufficiently cryptographically random that they cannot be guessed. RFC 3261 requires global uniqueness for the Call-ID (see Section 2.8) and 32 bits of cryptographic randomness for each tag (there are two tags for a dialog). Given the short duration of a typical dialog (perhaps as long as a day), this amount of randomness appears adequate for preventing guessing attacks. However, it is important to note that this specification requires true cryptographic randomness as set forth in RFC 4086. Weaker pseudorandom identifiers reduce the probability of collision; however, because they are guessable, they are not sufficient to prevent an attacker from observing a sequence of identifiers, guessing the next one, and then using this specification to launch an attack.

19.5.2.9 Relationship with In-Reply-To

RFC 3261 defines the In-Reply-To header field (see Section 2.8). It provides a list of Call-IDs for calls that the current request references or returns. It was meant to serve a similar purpose as the Reply-To in e-mail: to facilitate the construction of *threads* of conversations in a user interface. Target-Dialog is similar, in that it also references a previous session. Owing to their similarities, it is important to understand the differences, as these two header fields are not substitutes for each other.

First, In-Reply-To is meant for consumption by a human or a user interface widget, for providing the user with a context that allows them to decide what a call is about and whether they should take it. Target-Dialog, on the other hand, is meant for consumption by the UA itself, to facilitate authorization of session requests in specific cases where authorization is not a function of the user, but rather the underlying protocols. A UA will authorize a call containing Target-Dialog based on a correct value of the Target-Dialog header field.

Secondly, Target-Dialog references a specific dialog that must be currently in progress. In-Reply-To references a previous call attempt, most likely one that did not result in a dialog. This is why In-Reply-To uses a Call-ID, and Target-Dialog uses a set of dialog identifiers.

Finally, In-Reply-To implies cause and effect. When In-Reply-To is present, it means that the request is being sent because of the previous request that was delivered. Target-Dialog does not imply cause and effect, but merely awareness for the purposes of authorization.

19.5.2.10 Example Call Flow

In this example, UA A and UA B establish an INVITE-initiated dialog through server A and server B, each of which acts as a proxy for the INVITE. Server B would then like to use the application interaction framework (RFC 5629) to request that UA A fetch an HTML user interface component. To do that, it sends a REFER request to A's URI. The flow for this is shown in Figure 19.17. The conventions of RFC 4475 are used to describe representation of long message lines.

First, the caller sends an INVITE, as shown in message F1.

```
INVITE sips:B@example.com SIP/2.0
Via: SIP/2.0/TLS host.example.com;
branch=z9hG4bK9zz8
From: Caller <sip:A@example.com>;tag=kkaz-
To: Callee <sip:B@example.org>
Call-ID: fa77as7dad8-sd98ajzz@host.example.com
CSeq: 1 INVITE
Max-Forwards: 70
Supported: tdialog
Allow: INVITE, OPTIONS, BYE, CANCEL, ACK,
REFER
Accept: application/sdp, text/html

<allOneLine>
       Contact: <sips:A@example.com;
              gruu;opaque=urn:uuid:f81d4f
              ae-7dec-11d0-a765-
              00a0c91e6bf6;grid=99a>;schemes="
              http,sip,sips"
</allOneLine>

Content-Length:...

Content-Type: application/sdp

--SDP not shown--
```

The INVITE indicates that the caller supports GRUU (note its presence in the Contact header field of the INVITE) and the Target-Dialog header field. This INVITE is forwarded to the callee (messages F2 and F3), which generates a 200 OK response that is forwarded back to the caller (messages F4 and F5). Message F5 might look like

```
SIP/2.0 200 OK
Via: SIP/2.0/TLS host.example.com;
branch=z9hG4bK9zz8
From: Caller <sip:A@example.com>;tag=kkaz-
To: Callee <sip:B@example.org>;tag=6544
Call-ID: fa77as7dad8-sd98ajzz@host.example.com
CSeq: 1 INVITE
Contact: <sips:B@pc.example.org>

Content-Length:...

Content-Type: application/sdp

--SDP not shown--
```

In this case, the called party does not support GRUU or the Target-Dialog header field. The caller generates an ACK (message F7). Server B then decides to send a REFER to user A:

```
<allOneLine>
       REFER sips:A@example.com;
              gruu;opaque=urn:uuid:f81d4f
              ae-7dec-11d0-a765-
              00a0c91e6bf6;grid=99a SIP/2.0
</allOneLine>

Via: SIP/2.0/TLS serverB.example.org;
branch=z9hG4bK9zz10
From: Server B <sip:serverB.example.org>;
tag=mreysh
```

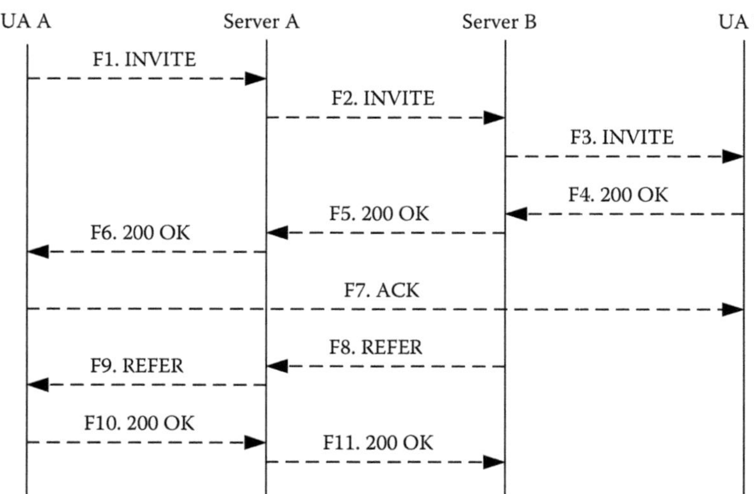

Figure 19.17 Basic call flows for authorization through dialog identification. (Copyright IETF. Reproduced with permission.)

```
<allOneLine>
       To: Caller <sips:A@example.com;
       gruu;opaque=urn:uuid:f81d4f
ae-7dec-11d0-a765-00a0c91e6bf6;grid=99a>
</allOneLine>
Target-Dialog: fa77as7dad8-sd98ajzz@host.
example.com
       ;local-tag=kkaz-
       ;remote-tag=6544
Refer-To: http://serverB.example.org/
ui-component.html
Call-ID: 86d65asfklzll8f7asdr@host.example.
com
CSeq: 1 REFER
Max-Forwards: 70
Require: tdialog
Allow: INVITE, OPTIONS, BYE, CANCEL, ACK,
NOTIFY
Contact: <sips:serverB.example.org>
Content-Length: 0
```

This REFER will be delivered to server A because it was sent to the GRUU. From there, it is forwarded to UA A (message F9) and authorized because of the presence of the Target-Dialog header field.

19.5.3 Media Authorization in SIP

19.5.3.1 Overview

RFC 3313 that is described here defines the P-Media-Authorization header (see Section 2.8), a private extension in SIP, for media authorization that is needed for QOS (see Section 15.4) and media authorization. The P-Media-Authorization header can be used to integrate QOS admission control with call signaling and help guard against DoS attacks. The use of this header is only applicable in administrative domains, or among federations of administrative domains with previously agreed-upon policies, where both the SIP proxy authorizing the QOS, and the policy control of the underlying network providing the QOS, belong to that administrative domain or federation of domains. Furthermore, the mechanism is generally incompatible with end-to-end encryption of message bodies that describe media sessions. This is in contrast with general Internet principles, which separate data transport from applications.

19.5.3.2 Basic Architecture for Media Authorization

In general, QOS provides preferential treatment (see Sections 15.2, 15.3, and 16.11) of one flow, at the expense of another. Consequently, it is important to have policy control over whether a given flow should have access to QOS. This will not only enable fairness in general, but can also prevent DoS attacks. We are concerned with providing QOS for media streams established via the SIP providing appropriate security. We assume an architecture that integrates call signaling with media authorization (see Section 19.5), as illustrated in Figure 19.18. The solid lines (A and B) show interfaces, whereas the dotted line (C) illustrates the QOS-enabled media flow.

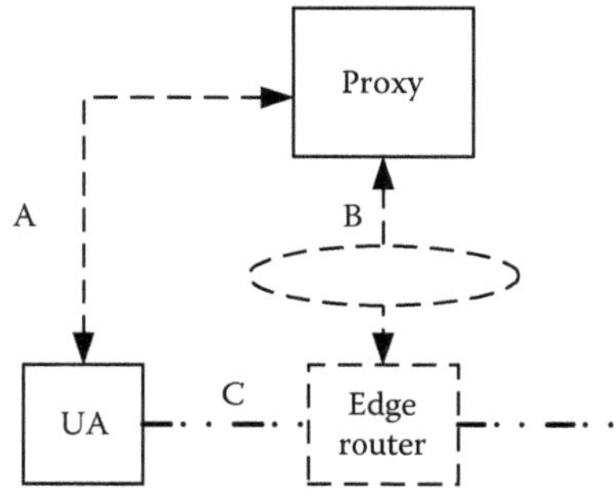

Figure 19.18 Basic architecture for providing media authorization. (Copyright IETF. Reproduced with permission.)

In this architecture, we assume a SIP UA connected to a QOS-enabled network with an edge router acting as a policy enforcement point (PEP) (RFC 2753). We further assume that a SIP UA that wishes to obtain QOS initiates sessions through a proxy that can interface with the QOS policy control for the data network being used. We will refer to such a proxy as a QOS-enabled proxy. We assume that the SIP UA needs to present an authorization token to the network in order to obtain QOS (C). The SIP UA obtains this authorization token via SIP (A) from the QOS-enabled proxy by means of an extension SIP header, defined in this document. The proxy, in turn, communicates either directly with the edge router or with a Policy Decision Point (PDP), not shown in Figure 19.18, in order to obtain a suitable authorization token for the UA.

A session that needs to obtain QOS for the media streams in accordance with our basic architecture described above goes through the following steps. The SIP UA sends an INVITE to the QOS-enabled proxy, which for each resulting dialog includes one or more media authorization tokens in all unreliable provisional responses (except 100), the first reliable 1xx or 2xx response, and all retransmissions of that reliable response for the dialog. When the UA requests QOS, it includes the media authorization tokens with the resource reservation. A SIP UA may also receive an INVITE from its QOS-enabled proxy, which includes one or more media authorization tokens. In that case, when the UA requests QOS, it includes the media authorization tokens with the resource reservation. The resource reservation mechanism is not part of SIP and is not described here.

19.5.3.3 Media Authorization Header Syntax

The P-Media-Authorization header field (see Section 2.8) contains one or more media authorization tokens that are to be included in subsequent resource reservations for the media flows associated with the session, that is, passed to an independent resource reservation mechanism, which is not specified here. The media authorization tokens are used for authorizing QOS for the media stream(s). The P-Media-Authorization header field is described by the following ABNF for convenience, although all SIP ABNF syntaxes are provided in Section 2.4.1:

```
P-Media-Authorization         = "P-Media-
                                Authorization"
                                HCOLON
                                P-Media-
                                Authorization-
                                Token
*(COMMA P-Media-Authorization-Token)
P-Media-Authorization-Token = 1*HEXDIG
```

Note that the P-Media-Authorization header field can be used only in SIP requests or responses that can carry a SIP offer or answer.

19.5.3.4 SIP Procedures for Media Authorization

We are describing SIP procedures for usage in media authorization-compatible systems, from the point of view of the authorizing QOS.

19.5.3.4.1 UAC

The initial SIP INVITE message, mid-call messages that result in network QOS resource changes, and mid-call changes in call destination should be authorized. These SIP messages are sent through the QOS-enabled proxies to receive this authorization. In order to authorize QOS, the QOS-enabled SIP proxy may need to inspect message bodies that describe the media streams (e.g., SDP). Hence, it is recommended that such message bodies not be encrypted end-to-end.

The P-Media-Authorization-Token, which is contained in the P-Media-Authorization header, is included for each dialog in all unreliable provisional responses (except 100), the first reliable 1xx or 2xx response, and all retransmissions of that reliable response for the dialog sent by the QOS-enabled SIP proxy to the UAC. The UAC should use all the P-Media-Authorization-Tokens from the most recent request–response that contained the P-Media-Authorization header when requesting QOS for the associated media stream(s). This applies to both initial and subsequent refresh reservation messages, for example, in a Resource ReSerVation Protocol (RSVP)-based reservation system. A reservation function within the UAC should convert each string of hex digits into binary, and utilize each result as a Policy-Element, as defined in RFC 2750 (excluding Length, but including P-Type, which is included in each token). These Policy-Elements would typically contain the authorizing entity and credentials, and be used in an RSVP request for media data stream QOS resources.

19.5.3.4.2 UAS

The UAS receives the P-Media-Authorization-Token in an INVITE (or other) message from the QOS-enabled SIP proxy. If the response contains a message body that describes media streams for which the UA desires QOS, it is recommended that this message body not be encrypted end-to-end. The UAS should use all the P-Media-Authorization-Tokens from the most recent request–response that contained the P-Media-Authorization header when requesting QOS for the associated media stream(s). This applies both to initial and subsequent refresh reservation messages (e.g., in an RSVP-based reservation system). A reservation function within the UAS should convert each string of hex digits into binary, and utilize each result as a Policy-Element, as defined in RFC 2750 (excluding Length, but including P-Type, which is included in each token). These Policy-Elements would typically contain the authorizing entity and credentials, and be used in an RSVP request for media data stream QOS resources.

19.5.3.4.3 Originating Proxy

When the originating QOS-enabled proxy (OP) receives an INVITE (or other) message from the UAC, the proxy authenticates the caller, and verifies that the caller is authorized to receive QOS. In cooperation with an originating PDP (PDP-o), the OP obtains or generates one or more media authorization tokens. These contain sufficient information for the UAC to get the authorized QOS for the media streams. Each media authorization token is formatted as a Policy-Element, as defined in RFC 2750 (excluding Length, but including P-Type, which is included in each token), and then converted to a string of hex digits to form a P-Media-Authorization-Token. The proxy's resource management function may inspect message bodies that describe the media streams (e.g., SDP), in both requests and responses, in order to decide what QOS to authorize. For each dialog that results from the INVITE (or other) message received from the UAC, the originating proxy must add a P-Media-Authorization header with the P-Media-Authorization-Token in all unreliable provisional responses (except 100), the first reliable 1xx or 2xx response, and all retransmissions of that reliable response the proxy sends to the UAC, if that response may result in network QOS changes. A response with an SDP may result in such changes.

19.5.3.4.4 Destination Proxy

The Destination QOS-Enabled Proxy (DP) verifies that the called party is authorized to receive QOS. In cooperation with a terminating PDP (PDP-t), the DP obtains or generates a media authorization token that contains sufficient information for the UAS to get the authorized QOS for the media streams. The media authorization token is formatted as a Policy-Element, as defined in RFC 2750 (excluding Length, but including P-Type, which is included in each token), and then converted to a string of hex digits to form a P-Media-Authorization-Token. The proxy's resource management function may inspect message bodies that describe the media streams (e.g., SDP), in both requests and responses in order to decide what QOS to authorize. The Destination Proxy must add the P-Media-Authorization header with the P-Media-Authorization-Token in the INVITE (or other) request that it sends to the UAS if that message may result in network QOS changes. A message with an SDP body may result in such changes.

19.5.3.5 Requesting Bandwidth via RSVP Messaging

Below, we provide an example of how the P-Media-Authorization header field can be used in conjunction with the RSVP (RFC 2753). The example assumes that an offer arrives in the initial INVITE and an answer arrives in a reliable provisional response, which contains an SDP description of the media flow.

19.5.3.5.1 UAC Side

Figure 19.19 presents a high-level overview of a basic call flow with media authorization from the viewpoint of the UAC. Some policy interactions have been omitted for brevity. When a user goes off-hook and dials a telephone number, the

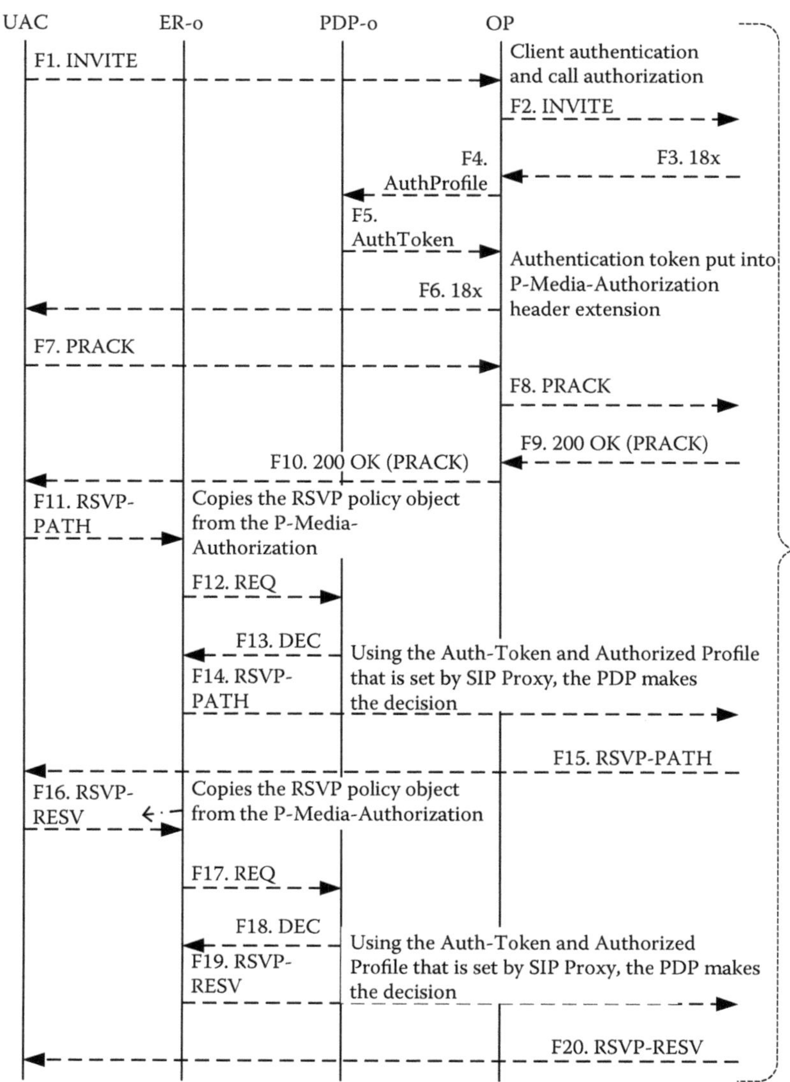

Figure 19.19 Media authorization for a UAC with RSVP. (Copyright IETF. Reproduced with permission.)

UAC collects the dialed digits and sends the initial INVITE message (F1) to the originating SIP proxy. The originating SIP proxy (OP) authenticates the user/UAC and forwards the INVITE message (F2) to the proper SIP proxy. Assuming the call is not forwarded, the terminating end-point sends a 18x response (F3) to the initial INVITE via OP. Included in this response is an indication of the negotiated bandwidth requirement for the connection in the form of an SDP description (see Section 7.7). When OP receives the 18x (F3), it has sufficient information regarding the end points, bandwidth, and characteristics of the media exchange. It initiates a Policy-Setup message to PDP-o, AuthProfile (F4). The PDP-o stores the authorized media description in its local store, generates an authorization token that points to this description, and returns the authorization token to the OP, AuthToken (F5).

The OP includes the authorization token in the P-Media-Authorization header extension of the 18x message (F6). Upon receipt of the 18x message (F6), the UAC stores the media authorization token from the P-Media-Authorization header. Also, the UAC acknowledges the 18x message by sending a PRACK (F7) message, which is responded to with 200 OK (F10). Before sending any media, the UAC requests QOS by sending an RSVP-PATH message (F11), which includes the previously stored P-Media-Authorization-Token as a Policy-Element. ER-o, upon receipt of the RSVP-PATH message (F11), checks the authorization through a PDP-o Common Open Policy Service (COPS) message exchange, REQ (F12). PDP-o checks the authorization using the stored authorized media description that was linked to the authorization token it returned to OP. If authorization is successful, PDP-o returns an *install* Decision, DEC (F13). ER-o checks the admissibility for the request, and if admission succeeds, it forwards the RSVP-PATH message (F14). Once UAC receives the (15) RSVP-PATH message (F15) from UAS, it sends the RSVP-RESV message (F16) to reserve the network resources. ER-o, upon receiving the RSVP-RESV message (F16), checks the authorization through a PDP-o COPS message exchange, REQ (F17). PDP-o checks the authorization using the stored authorized media description that was linked to the authorization token it returned to OP. If authorization is successful, PDP-o returns an install Decision, DEC (F18). ER-o checks the admissibility for the request, and if admission succeeds, it forwards the RSVP-RESV message (F19). Upon receiving the RSVP-RESV message (F20), network resources have been reserved in both directions.

19.5.3.5.2 UAS Side

Figure 19.20 presents a high-level overview of a call flow with media authorization from the viewpoint of the UAS. Some policy interactions have been omitted for brevity. Since the destination SIP proxy (DP) has sufficient information regarding the end points, bandwidth, and characteristics of the media exchange, it initiates a Policy-Setup message to the PDP-t on receipt of the INVITE (F1).

PDP-t stores the authorized media description in its local store, generates an authorization token that points to this description, and returns the authorization token to DP. The token is placed in the INVITE message (F4) and forwarded to the UAS. Assuming that the call is not forwarded, the UAS sends an 18x response (F5) to the initial INVITE message, which is forwarded back to UAC. At the same time, the UAS sends an RSVP-PATH message (F7) that includes the previously stored P-Media-Authorization-Token as a Policy-Element. ER-t, upon receiving the RSVP-PATH message (F7), checks the authorization through a PDP-t COPS message exchange. PDP-t checks the authorization using the stored authorized media description that was linked to the authorization token it returned to DP. If authorization is successful, PDP-t returns an install Decision, DEC (F9). ER-t checks the admissibility for the request, and if admission succeeds, it forwards the RSVP-PATH message (F10). Once the UAS receives the RSVP-PATH message (F11), it sends the RSVP-RESV message (F12) to reserve the network resources. ER-t, upon reception of the RSVP-RESV message (F12), checks the authorization through a PDP-t COPS message exchange. PDP-t checks the authorization using the stored authorized media description that was linked to the authorization token that it returned to DP. If authorization is successful, PDP-t returns an install Decision, DEC (F14). ER-t checks the admissibility for the request and if admission succeeds, it forwards the RSVP-RESV message (F15). Upon receiving the RSVP-RESV message (F16), network resources have been reserved in both directions. For completeness, we show the PRACK message (F5) for the 18x response (F6) and the resulting 200 OK (F19) response acknowledging the PRACK.

19.5.3.6 Advantages of Media Authorization

The use of media authorization makes it possible to control the usage of network resources. In turn, this makes SIP telephony more robust against DoS attacks and various kinds of service frauds. By using the authorization capability, the number of flows and the amount of network resources reserved can be controlled, thereby making the SIP telephony system dependable in the presence of scarce resources.

19.5.3.7 Security Considerations

To control access to QOS, a QOS-enabled proxy should authenticate the UA before providing it with a media authorization token. Both the method and policy associated with such authentication are outside the scope of this document; however, it could, for example, be done by using standard

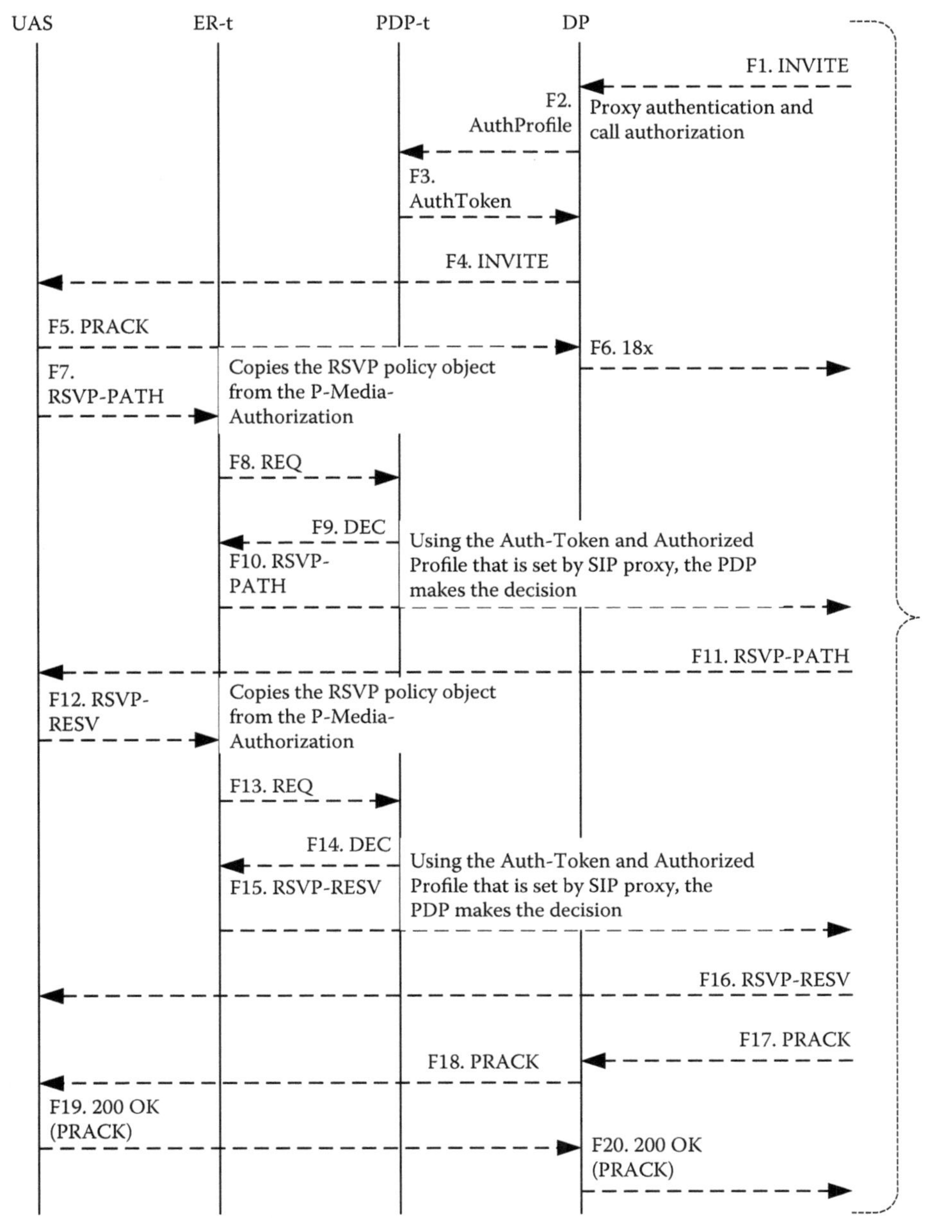

Figure 19.20 Media authorization for UAS with RSVP. (Copyright IETF. Reproduced with permission.)

SIP authentication mechanisms, as described in RFC 3261 (see Section 19.4). Media authorization tokens sent in the P-Media-Authorization header from a QOS-enabled proxy to a UA must be protected from eavesdropping and tampering. This can, for example, be done through a mechanism such as IPSec or TLS. However, this will only provide hop-by-hop security. If there are one or more intermediaries (e.g., proxies) between the UA and the QOS-enabled proxy, these intermediaries will have access to the P-Media-Authorization header field value, thereby compromising confidentiality and integrity. This will enable both theft-of-service and DoS attacks against the UA.

Consequently, the P-Media-Authorization header field must not be available to any untrusted intermediary in the clear or without integrity protection. There is currently no mechanism defined in SIP that would satisfy these requirements. Until such a mechanism exists, proxies must not send P-Media-Authorization headers through untrusted intermediaries, which might reveal or modify the contents of this header. Note that S/MIME-based encryption (see Section 19.6) in SIP is not available to proxy servers, as proxies are not allowed to add message bodies. QOS-enabled proxies may need to inspect message bodies describing media streams (e.g., SDP). Consequently, such message bodies should not be encrypted. In turn, this will prevent end-to-end confidentiality of the said message bodies, which lowers the overall security possible.

SIP messages carry MIME bodies (RFC 3261, see Sections 2.4.2.4 and 3.9), and the MIME standard includes mechanisms for securing MIME contents to ensure both integrity and confidentiality (including the multipart/signed and application/pkcs7-mime MIME types). Implementers should note, however, that there may be rare network intermediaries (not typical proxy servers) that rely on viewing or modifying the bodies of SIP messages (especially SDP), and that secure MIME may prevent these sorts of intermediaries from functioning. This applies particularly to certain types of firewalls. The PGP mechanism for encrypting the header fields and bodies of SIP messages described in RFC 2543 (obsoleted by 3261) has been deprecated.

19.5.4 Early-Media Authorization in SIP

Early media (see Chapter 11), which refers to media such as audio and video, and is exchanged between the callee and the caller before a particular session is accepted by the called party, may need authorization based on policies in certain circumstances. For example, 3GPP's early-media policy prohibits the exchange of early media between end users; it is interconnected with other SIP networks that have unknown, untrusted, or different policies regarding early media; and it has the capability to gate (enable/disable) the flow of early media to/from user equipment. Because of the peculiar behavior of early media, RFC 5009 (see Section 11.5) specifies a private SIP header field specified as P-Early-Media that is used for authorization of early media in SIP. The P-Early-Media header field is used within SIP messages in certain SIP networks to authorize the cut-through of backward or forward early media when permitted by the early-media policies of the networks involved. Within an isolated SIP network, it is possible to gate early media associated with all end points within the network to enforce a desired early-media policy among network end points. However, when a SIP network is interconnected with other SIP networks, only the boundary node connected to the external network can determine which early-media policy to apply to a session established between end points on different sides of the boundary. The P-Early-Media header field provides a means for this boundary node to communicate this early-media policy decision to other nodes within the network.

The use of this extension is only applicable inside a Trust Domain as defined in RFC 3325 (see Sections 2.8, 10.4, and 20.3). Nodes in such a Trust Domain are explicitly trusted by its users and end systems to authorize early-media requests only when allowed by early-media policy within the Trust Domain. This document does not offer a general early-media authorization model suitable for interdomain use or use in the Internet at large. Furthermore, since the early-media requests are not cryptographically certified, they are subject to forgery, replay, and falsification in any architecture that does not meet the requirements of the Trust Domain. An early-media request also lacks an indication of who specifically is making or modifying the request, and so it must be assumed that the Trust Domain is making the request. Therefore, the information is only meaningful when securely received from a node known to be a member of the Trust Domain. Although this extension can be used with parallel forking, it does not improve on the known problems with early media and parallel forking, as described in RFC 3960 (see Section 11.4.8), unless one can assume the use of symmetric RTP. Despite these limitations, there are sufficiently useful specialized deployments that meet the assumptions described above, and can accept the limitations that result, to warrant publication of this mechanism. An example deployment would be a closed network that emulates a traditional circuit switched telephone network.

19.5.5 Framework for Session Setup with Media Authorization

During the session setup (e.g., SIP session establishment), policies may be enforced to ensure that the media streams being requested lie within the bounds of the service profile established for the requesting host. RFC 3521 that is described here specifies such a linkage through use of a token that provides capabilities and of a ticket in the push model specified in authentication, authorization, and accounting framework of RFC 2904. The token is generated by a policy server or a session management server (e.g., SIP proxy) and is transparently relayed through the end host to the edge router where it is used as part of the policy-controlled flow admission process.

In some environments, authorization of media streams can exploit the fact that preestablished relationships exist between elements of the network (e.g., session management servers, edge routers, policy servers, and end hosts). Preestablished relationships assume that the different network elements are configured with the identities of the other network elements and, if necessary, are configured with security keys, and other features required to establish a trust relationship. In other environments, however, such preestablished relationships may not exist either due to the complexity of creating these associations a priori, for example, in a network with many elements, or due to the different business entities involved (e.g., service provider and access provider), or due to the dynamic nature of these associations (e.g., in a mobile environment).

RFC 3521 describes the media authorization concepts using SIP for session signaling, RSVP (RFC 3540) for resource reservation, and COPS (RFCs 2749 and 3084) for interaction with the policy servers. The linkage of a token established during the SIP session setup to the network layer entity such as an IP router for resources reservation for the session maintaining the QOS through a policy server is articulated in this specification. It also facilitates preventing fraud and ensuring accurate billing, but some linkage is required to verify that the resources being used to provide the requested QOS are in line with the media streams requested and authorized for the session. However, no specific standardization, either Informational or Standards Track, for using the token and related objects extending SIP, RSVP, and COPS has been done in RFC 3521 other than some conceptual scenarios for media authorization linking with the session setup.

RFC 3520 defines a session object known as AUTH_SESSION along with many other detailed functional features that represent a session authorization policy element for supporting policy-based per-session authorization and admission control. The host must obtain an AUTH_SESSION element from an authorizing entity via a session signaling protocol such as SIP. The host then inserts the AUTH_SESSION element into the resource reservation message to allow verification of the network resource request. For brevity, this was not described in detail. However, more work is needed to allow use of all those capabilities in this specification integrating with SIP, RSVP, and COPS for interoperability using common standards.

19.6 Integrity and Confidentiality in SIP

19.6.1 S/MIME Certificates

RFC 3261 specifies the use of S/MIME certificates in SIP. The certificates that are used to identify an end user for the purposes of S/MIME differ from those used by servers in one important respect—rather than asserting that the identity of the holder corresponds to a particular host name, these certificates assert that the holder is identified by an end-user address. This address is composed of the concatenation of the userinfo, @, and *domainname* portions of a SIP or SIPS URI (in other words, an e-mail address of the form bob@biloxi.com), most commonly corresponding to a user's AOR. These certificates are also associated with keys that are used to sign or encrypt bodies of SIP messages. Bodies are signed with the private key of the sender (who may include their public key with the message as appropriate); however, bodies are encrypted with the public key of the intended recipient. Obviously, senders must have foreknowledge of the public key of recipients in order to encrypt message bodies. Public keys can be stored within a UA on a virtual keyring.

Each UA that supports S/MIME must contain a keyring specifically for end-user certificates. This keyring should map between AORs and corresponding certificates. Over time, users should use the same certificate when they populate the originating URI of signaling (the From header field) with the same AOR. Any mechanisms depending on the existence of end-user certificates are seriously limited in that there is virtually no consolidated authority today that provides certificates for end-user applications.

However, users should acquire certificates from known public certificate authorities. As an alternative, users may create self-signed certificates. The implications of self-signed certificates are explored further in Section 19.4.8. Implementations may also use preconfigured certificates in deployments in which a previous trust relationship exists between all SIP entities. Above and beyond the problem of acquiring an end-user certificate, there are few well-known centralized directories that distribute end-user certificates. However, the holder of a certificate should publish their certificate in any public directories as appropriate. Similarly, UACs should support a mechanism for importing (manually or automatically) certificates discovered in public directories corresponding to the target URIs of SIP requests.

19.6.2 S/MIME Key Exchange

SIP itself can also be used as a means to distribute public keys in the following manner (RFC 3261). Whenever the CMS SignedData message is used in S/MIME for SIP, it must contain the certificate bearing the public key necessary to verify the signature. When a UAC sends a request containing an S/MIME body that initiates a dialog, or sends a non-INVITE request outside the context of a dialog, the UAC should structure the body as an S/MIME multipart/signed CMS SignedData body. If the desired CMS service is EnvelopedData (and the public key of the target user is known), the UAC should send the EnvelopedData message encapsulated within a SignedData message. When a UAS receives a request containing an S/MIME CMS body that includes a certificate, the UAS should first validate the certificate, if possible, with any available root certificates for certificate authorities. The UAS should also determine the subject of the certificate (for S/MIME, the SubjectAltName will contain the appropriate identity) and compare this value to the From header field of the request. If the certificate cannot be verified, because it is self-signed, or signed by no known authority, or if it is verifiable but its subject does not correspond to the From header field of request, the UAS must notify its user of the status of the certificate (including the subject of the certificate, its signer, and any key fingerprint information) and request explicit permission before proceeding. If the certificate was successfully verified and the subject of the certificate corresponds to the From header field of the SIP request, or if the user (after notification) explicitly authorizes the use of the certificate, the UAS should add this certificate to a local keyring, indexed by the AOR of the holder of the certificate.

When a UAS sends a response containing an S/MIME body that answers the first request in a dialog, or a response to a non-INVITE request outside the context of a dialog, the UAS should structure the body as an S/MIME multipart/signed CMS SignedData body. If the desired CMS service is EnvelopedData, the UAS should send the EnvelopedData message encapsulated within a SignedData message. When a UAC receives a response containing an S/MIME CMS body that includes a certificate, the UAC should first validate the certificate, if possible, with any appropriate root certificate. The UAC should also determine the subject of the certificate and compare this value to the To field of the response; however, the two may very well be different, and this is not necessarily indicative of a security breach. If the certificate cannot be verified because it is self-signed, or signed by no known authority, the UAC must notify its user of the status of the certificate (including the subject of the certificate, its signator, and any key fingerprint information) and request explicit permission before proceeding. If the certificate was successfully verified, and the subject of the certificate corresponds to the To header field in the response, or if the user (after notification) explicitly authorizes the use of the certificate, the UAC should add this certificate to a local keyring, indexed by the AOR of the holder of the certificate.

If the UAC had not transmitted its own certificate to the UAS in any previous transaction, it should use a CMS SignedData body for its next request or response. On future occasions, when the UA receives requests or responses that contain a From header field corresponding to a value in its keyring, the UA should compare the certificate offered in these messages with the existing certificate in its keyring. If there is a discrepancy, the UA must notify its user of a change of the certificate (preferably in terms that indicate that this is a potential security breach) and acquire the user's permission before continuing to process the signaling. If the user authorizes this certificate, it should be added to the keyring alongside any previous value(s) for this AOR.

Note, however, that this key exchange mechanism does not guarantee the secure exchange of keys when self-signed certificates, or certificates signed by an obscure authority, are used—it is vulnerable to well-known attacks. In the opinion of the authors of the RFC, however, the security it provides is better than nothing; it is, in fact, comparable to the widely used SSH application. These limitations are explored in greater detail in Section 19.4.8. If a UA receives an S/MIME body that has been encrypted with a public key unknown to the recipient, it must reject the request with a 493 Undecipherable response. This response should contain a valid certificate for the respondent (corresponding, if possible, to any AOR given in the To header field of the rejected request) within a MIME body with a certs-only smime-type parameter. A 493 Undecipherable sent without any certificate indicates that the respondent cannot or will not utilize S/MIME encrypted messages, though they may still support S/MIME signatures. Note that a UA that receives a request containing an S/MIME body that is not optional (with a Content-Disposition header *handling* parameter of *required*) must reject the request with a 415 Unsupported Media Type response if the MIME type is not understood. A UA that receives such a response when S/MIME is sent should notify its user that the remote device does not support S/MIME, and it may subsequently resend the request without S/MIME, if appropriate; however, this 415 response may constitute a downgrade attack.

If a UA sends an S/MIME body in a request, but receives a response that contains a MIME body that is not secured, the UAC should notify its user that the session could not be secured. However, if a UA that supports S/MIME receives a request with an unsecured body, it should not respond with a secured body; if it expects S/MIME from the sender (e.g., because the sender's From header field value corresponds to an identity on its keychain), the UAS should notify its user that the session could not be secured. A number of conditions that arise in the previous text call for the notification of the user when an anomalous certificate-management event occurs. Users might well ask what they should do under these circumstances.

First and foremost, an unexpected change in a certificate, or an absence of security when security is expected, is a cause for caution but not necessarily an indication that an attack is in progress. Users might abort any connection attempt or refuse a connection request they have received; in telephony parlance, they could hang up and call back. Users may wish to find an alternate means to contact the other party and confirm that their key has legitimately changed. Note that users are sometimes compelled to change their certificates, for example, when they suspect that the secrecy of their private key has been compromised. When their private key is no longer private, users must legitimately generate a new key and reestablish trust with any users that held their old key. Finally, if during the course of a dialog a UA receives a certificate in a CMS SignedData message that does not correspond with the certificates previously exchanged during a dialog, the UA must notify its user of the change, preferably in terms that indicate that this is a potential security breach.

19.6.3 Securing MIME Bodies

Two types of secure MIME bodies are specified to SIP in RFC 3261. The use of these bodies should follow the S/MIME specification (RFC 5751) with a few variations, as follows:

- multipart/signed must be used only with CMS detached signatures. This allows backwards compatibility with non-S/MIME-compliant recipients.
- S/MIME bodies should have a Content-Disposition header field, and the value of the handling parameter should be *required*.
- If a UAC has no certificate on its keyring associated with the AOR to which it wants to send a request, it cannot send an encrypted application/pkcs7-mime MIME message. UACs may send an initial request such as an OPTIONS message with a CMS detached signature in order to solicit the certificate of the remote side (the signature should be over a message/sip body of the type described in Section 19.6.4). Note that future standardization work on S/MIME may define non-certificate-based keys.
- Senders of S/MIME bodies should use the SMIMECapabilities (see Section 2.5.2 of RFC 5751) attribute to express their capabilities and preferences for further communications. Note especially that senders may use the preferSignedData capability to encourage receivers to respond with CMS SignedData messages (e.g., when sending an OPTIONS request as described above).
- S/MIME implementations must at a minimum support SHA1 as a digital signature algorithm, and 3DES as an encryption algorithm. All other signature and encryption algorithms may be supported. Implementations can negotiate support for these algorithms with the SMIMECapabilities attribute.
- Each S/MIME body in a SIP message should be signed with only one certificate. If a UA receives a message with multiple signatures, the outermost signature should be treated as the single certificate for this body. Parallel signatures should not be used.

The following is an example of an encrypted S/MIME SDP body within a SIP message:

```
INVITE sip:bob@biloxi.com SIP/2.0
Via: SIP/2.0/UDP pc33.atlanta.com;
branch=z9hG4bKnashds8
To: Bob <sip:bob@biloxi.com>
From: Alice <sip:alice@atlanta.com>;
tag=1928301774
Call-ID: a84b4c76e66710
CSeq: 314159 INVITE
Max-Forwards: 70
Contact: <sip:alice@pc33.atlanta.com>
Content-Type: application/pkcs7-mime;
smime-type=enveloped-data;
name=smime.p7m
Content-Disposition: attachment;
filename=smime.p7m
handling=required

Content-Type: application/sdp *

v=0 *
o=alice 53655765 2353687637 IN IP4 pc33.
atlanta.com *
s=- *
t=0 0 *
c=IN IP4 pc33.atlanta.com *
m=audio 3456 RTP/AVP 0 1 3 99 *
a=rtpmap:0 PCMU/8000 *
```

19.6.4 SIP Header Confidentiality and Integrity Using S/MIME: Tunneling SIP

RFC 3261, as a means of providing some degree of end-to-end authentication, integrity, or confidentiality for SIP header fields, specifies that S/MIME can encapsulate entire SIP messages within MIME bodies of type message/sip and then apply MIME security to these bodies in the same manner as typical SIP bodies. These encapsulated SIP requests and responses do not constitute a separate dialog or transaction; they are a copy of the outer message that is used to verify integrity or to supply additional information. If a UAS receives a request that contains a tunneled message/sip S/MIME body, it should include a tunneled message/sip body in the response with the same smime-type. Any traditional MIME bodies (such as SDP) should be attached to the inner message so that they can also benefit from S/MIME security. Note that message/sip bodies can be sent as a part of a MIME multipart/mixed body if any unsecured MIME types should also be transmitted in a request.

19.6.4.1 Integrity and Confidentiality Properties of SIP Headers

When the S/MIME integrity or confidentiality mechanisms are used, there may be discrepancies between the values in the inner message and values in the outer message. The rules for handling any such differences for all of the header fields described in this document are given in this section. Note that for the purposes of loose time stamping, all SIP messages that tunnel message/sip should contain a Date header in both the inner and outer headers.

19.6.4.1.1 Integrity

Whenever integrity checks are performed, the integrity of a header field should be determined by matching the value of the header field in the signed body with that in the outer messages using the comparison rules of SIP as described in Section 2.8. Header fields that can be legitimately modified by proxy servers are Request-URI, Via, Record-Route,

Route, Max-Forwards, and Proxy-Authorization. If these header fields are not intact end-to-end, implementations should not consider this a breach of security. Changes to any other header fields defined in this document constitute an integrity violation; users must be notified of a discrepancy.

19.6.4.1.2 Confidentiality

When messages are encrypted, header fields may be included in the encrypted body that are not present in the outer message. Some header fields must always have a plaintext version because they are required header fields in requests and responses—these include To, From, Call-ID, CSeq, and Contact. While it is probably not useful to provide an encrypted alternative for the Call-ID, CSeq, or Contact, providing an alternative to the information in the outer To or From is permitted. Note that the values in an encrypted body are not used for the purposes of identifying transactions or dialogs—they are merely informational. If the From header field in an encrypted body differs from the value in the outer message, the value within the encrypted body should be displayed to the user, but must not be used in the outer header fields of any future messages. Primarily, a UA will want to encrypt header fields that have an end-to-end semantic, including Subject, Reply-To, Organization, Accept, Accept-Encoding, Accept-Language, Alert-Info, Error-Info, Authentication-Info, Expires, In-Reply-To, Require, Supported, Unsupported, Retry-After, User-Agent, Server, and Warning. If any of these header fields are present in an encrypted body, they should be used instead of any outer header fields, whether this entails displaying the header field values to users or setting internal states in the UA. They should not, however, be used in the outer headers of any future messages. If present, the Date header field MUST always be the same in the inner and outer headers.

Since MIME bodies are attached to the inner message, implementations will usually encrypt MIME-specific header fields, including MIME-Version, Content-Type, Content-Length, Content-Language, Content-Encoding, and Content-Disposition. The outer message will have the proper MIME header fields for S/MIME bodies. These header fields (and any MIME bodies they preface) should be treated as normal MIME header fields and bodies received in a SIP message. It is not particularly useful to encrypt the following header fields: Min-Expires, Timestamp, Authorization, Priority, and WWWAuthenticate. This category also includes those header fields that can be changed by proxy servers (described in the preceding section). UAs should never include these in an inner message if they are not included in the outer message. UAs that receive any of these header fields in an encrypted body should ignore the encrypted values. Note that extensions to SIP may define additional header fields; the authors of these extensions should describe the integrity and confidentiality properties of such header fields. If a SIP UA encounters an unknown header field with an integrity violation, it must ignore the header field.

19.6.4.2 Tunneling Integrity and Authentication

Tunneling SIP messages within S/MIME bodies can provide integrity for SIP header fields if the header fields that the sender wishes to secure are replicated in a message/sip MIME body signed with a CMS detached signature. Provided that the message/sip body contains at least the fundamental dialog identifiers (To, From, Call-ID, CSeq), then a signed MIME body can provide limited authentication. At the very least, if the certificate used to sign the body is unknown to the recipient and cannot be verified, the signature can be used to ascertain that a later request in a dialog was transmitted by the same certificate holder that initiated the dialog. If the recipient of the signed MIME body has some stronger incentive to trust the certificate (they were able to validate it, they acquired it from a trusted repository, or they have used it frequently), then the signature can be taken as a stronger assertion of the identity of the subject of the certificate.

To eliminate possible confusion about the addition or subtraction of entire header fields, senders should replicate all header fields from the request within the signed body. Any message bodies that require integrity protection must be attached to the inner message. If a Date header is present in a message with a signed body, the recipient should compare the header field value with its own internal clock, if applicable. If a significant time discrepancy is detected (on the order of an hour or more), the UA should alert the user to the anomaly, and note that it is a potential security breach.

If an integrity violation in a message is detected by its recipient, the message may be rejected with a 403 Forbidden response if it is a request, or any existing dialog may be terminated. UAs should notify users of this circumstance and request explicit guidance on how to proceed. The following is an example of the use of a tunneled message/sip body:

```
INVITE sip:bob@biloxi.com SIP/2.0
Via: SIP/2.0/UDP pc33.atlanta.com;
branch=z9hG4bKnashds8
To: Bob <sip:bob@biloxi.com>
From: Alice <sip:alice@atlanta.com>;
tag=1928301774
Call-ID: a84b4c76e66710
CSeq: 314159 INVITE
Max-Forwards: 70
Date: Thu, 21 Feb 2002 13:02:03 GMT
Contact: <sip:alice@pc33.atlanta.com>
Content-Type: multipart/signed;
```

```
protocol="application/pkcs7-signature";
micalg=sha1; boundary=boundary42
Content-Length: 568

--boundary42

Content-Type: message/sip
INVITE sip:bob@biloxi.com SIP/2.0
Via: SIP/2.0/UDP pc33.atlanta.com;
branch=z9hG4bKnashds8
To: Bob <bob@biloxi.com>
From: Alice <alice@atlanta.com>;
tag=1928301774
Call-ID: a84b4c76e66710
CSeq: 314159 INVITE
Max-Forwards: 70
Date: Thu, 21 Feb 2002 13:02:03 GMT
Contact: <sip:alice@pc33.atlanta.com>
Content-Type: application/sdp
Content-Length: 147
v=0
o=UserA 2890844526 2890844526 IN IP4 here.com
s=Session SDP
c=IN IP4 pc33.atlanta.com
t=0 0
m=audio 49172 RTP/AVP 0
a=rtpmap:0 PCMU/8000

--boundary42

Content-Type: application/pkcs7-signature;
name=smime.p7s
Content-Transfer-Encoding: base64
Content-Disposition: attachment;
filename=smime.p7s;
handling=required
ghyHhHUujhJhjH77n8HHGTrfvbnj756tbB9HG4VQpfyF
467GhIGfHfYT6
4VQpfyF467GhIGfHfYT6jH77n8HHGghyHhHUujhJh756
tbB9HGTrfvbnj
n8HHGTrfvhJhjH776tbB9HG4VQbnj7567GhIGfHfYT6g
hyHhHUujpfyF4
7GhIGfHfYT64VQbnj756

--boundary42-
```

19.6.4.3 Tunneling Encryption

It may also be desirable to use this mechanism to encrypt a message/sip MIME body within a CMS EnvelopedData message S/MIME body; however, in practice, most header fields are of at least some use to the network. The general use of encryption with S/MIME is to secure message bodies like SDP rather than message headers. Some informational header fields, such as Subject or Organization, could perhaps warrant end-to-end security. Headers defined by future SIP applications might also require obfuscation. Another possible application of encrypting header fields is selective anonymity. A request could be constructed with a From header field that contains no personal information (e.g., sip:anonymous @anonymizer.invalid). However, a second From header field containing the genuine AOR of the originator could be encrypted within a message/sip MIME body where it will only be visible to the end points of a dialog.

Note that if this mechanism is used for anonymity, the From header field will no longer be usable by the recipient of a message as an index to their certificate keychain for retrieving the proper S/MIME key to associated with the sender. The message must first be decrypted, and the inner From header field must be used as an index. To provide end-to-end integrity, encrypted message/sip MIME bodies should be signed by the sender. This creates a multipart/signed MIME body that contains an encrypted body and a signature, both of type application/pkcs7-mime. In the following example, of an encrypted and signed message, the text boxed in asterisks ("*") is encrypted:

```
INVITE sip:bob@biloxi.com SIP/2.0
Via: SIP/2.0/UDP pc33.atlanta.com;
branch=z9hG4bKnashds8
To: Bob <sip:bob@biloxi.com>
From: Anonymous <sip:anonymous@atlanta.com>;
tag=1928301774
Call-ID: a84b4c76e66710
CSeq: 314159 INVITE
Max-Forwards: 70
Date: Thu, 21 Feb 2002 13:02:03 GMT
Contact: <sip:pc33.atlanta.com>
Content-Type: multipart/signed;
protocol="application/pkcs7-signature";
micalg=sha1; boundary=boundary42
Content-Length: 568

--boundary42

Content-Type: application/pkcs7-mime;
smime-type=enveloped-data;
name=smime.p7m
Content-Transfer-Encoding: base64
Content-Disposition: attachment;
filename=smime.p7m
handling=required
Content-Length: 231

Content-Type: message/sip *

INVITE sip:bob@biloxi.com SIP/2.0 *
Via: SIP/2.0/UDP pc33.atlanta.com;
branch=z9hG4bKnashds8 *
To: Bob <bob@biloxi.com> *
From: Alice <alice@atlanta.com>;
tag=1928301774 *
Call-ID: a84b4c76e66710 *
CSeq: 314159 INVITE *
Max-Forwards: 70 *
Date: Thu, 21 Feb 2002 13:02:03 GMT *
Contact: <sip:alice@pc33.atlanta.com> *
```

```
Content-Type: application/sdp *

v=0 *
o=alice 53655765 2353687637 IN IP4 pc33.
atlanta.com *
s=Session SDP *
t=0 0 *
c=IN IP4 pc33.atlanta.com *
m=audio 3456 RTP/AVP 0 1 3 99 *
a=rtpmap:0 PCMU/8000 *

--boundary42

Content-Type: application/pkcs7-signature;
name=smime.p7s
Content-Transfer-Encoding: base64
Content-Disposition: attachment;
filename=smime.p7s;
handling=required
ghyHhHUujhJhjH77n8HHGTrfvbnj756tbB9HG4VQpfyF4
67GhIGfHfYT64VQpfyF467GhIGfHfYT6jH77n8HHGghyH
hHUujhJh756tbB9HGTrfvbnjn8HHGTrfvhJhjH776tbB9
HG4VQbnj7567GhIGfHfYT6ghyHhHUujpfyF47GhIGfHfY
T64VQbnj756

--boundary42-
```

19.7 Security for SIP URI-List Services

19.7.1 Objective

Some applications require that, at a given moment, a SIP UA performs a similar transaction with a number of remote UAs. For example, an instant messaging application that needs to send a particular message (e.g., "Hello folks") to *n* receivers needs to send *n* MESSAGE requests—one to each receiver. When the transaction that needs to be repeated consists of a large request, or when the number of recipients is high, or both, the access network of the UA needs to carry a considerable amount of traffic. Completing all the transactions on a low-bandwidth access would require a long time. This is unacceptable for a number of applications. A solution to this problem consists of introducing URI-list services in the network. RFC 5363 that is described here specifies the SIP URI-list services and provides requirements for their invocation. Additionally, it defines a framework for SIP URI-list services, which includes security considerations applicable to these services.

The task of a SIP URI-list service is to receive a request that contains or references a URI list (i.e., a list of one or more URIs) and send a number of similar requests to the destinations in this list. Once the requests are sent, the URI-list service typically informs the UA about their status. Effectively, the URI-list service behaves as a B2BUA. A given URI-list service can take as an input a URI list contained in the SIP request sent by the client or an external URI list (e.g., the Request-URI is a SIP URI that is associated with a URI list at the server). External URI lists are typically set up using out-of-band mechanisms (e.g., XML Configuration Access Protocol [XCAP], RFC 4825). An example of a URI-list service for SUBSCRIBE requests that uses stored URI lists is described in RFC 4662. The remainder of this document provides requirements and a framework for URI-list services using request-contained URI lists, external URI lists, or both.

19.7.2 Requirements

In the following two subsections, we are describing requirements that only apply to URI-list services that use request-contained lists and general requirements that also apply to services using external lists, respectively.

19.7.2.1 URI-List Services Using Request-Contained Lists

- The URI-list service invocation mechanism must allow the invoker to provide a list of destination URIs to the URI-list service.
- The invocation mechanism should not require more than one transaction.

19.7.2.2 URI-List Services Using External Lists

- A URI-list service may include services beyond sending requests to the URIs in the URI list. That is, URI-list services can be modeled as application servers. For example, a URI-list service handling INVITE requests may behave as a conference server and perform media mixing for all the participants.
- The interpretation of the meaning of the URI list sent by the invoker must be at the discretion of the application to which the list is sent.
- It must be possible for the invoker to find out about the result of the operations performed by the URI-list service with the URI list. An invoker may, for instance, be interested in the status of the transactions initiated by the URI-list service.
- URI-list services must not send requests to any destination without authenticating the invoker.

19.7.3 Framework

This framework is not restricted to application servers that only provide request fan-out services. Per the above requirements, this framework also deals with application servers that provide a particular service that includes a request fan-out (e.g., a conference server that INVITEs several participants that are chosen by a UA).

19.7.3.1 Carrying URI Lists in SIP

The requirements related to URI-list services that use request-contained lists identify the need for a mechanism to provide a SIP URI-list service with a URI list in a single transaction. We define a new disposition type (RFC 2183, see Section 2.8.2) for the Content-Disposition header field: recipient-list. Both requests and responses may carry recipient-list bodies. Bodies whose disposition type is recipient-list carry a list of URIs that contains the final recipients of the requests to be generated by a URI-list service. The default format for recipient-list bodies is service specific. Thus, URI-list service specifications must specify a default format for recipient-list bodies used within a particular service. In any case, clients should not include any particular URI more than once in a given URI list. A UAS receiving a request with more than one recipient-list body parts (e.g., each body part using a different URI-list format) must behave as if it had received a single URI list that contains all the URIs present in the different body parts.

A UAS receiving a recipient-list URI list that contains a URI more than once must behave as if that URI appeared in the URI list only once. The UAS uses the comparison rules specific to the URI scheme of each of the URIs in the URI list to determine if there is any URI that appears more than once. Additionally, Section 4 of "Extensible Markup Language (XML) Format Extension for Representing Copy Control Attributes in Resource Lists" (RFC 5364) discusses cases where duplicated URI entries are tagged with different values of the copyControl attribute. Naturally, URI-list services using the copyControl attribute defined in RFC 5364 need to follow the recommendations in RFC 5364 with respect to avoiding sending duplicated requests. The way a UAS interprets a URI list that it has received is service specific, as described in the next section.

19.7.3.2 Processing of URI Lists

According to above general requirements, URI-list services can behave as application servers. That is, taking a URI list as an input, they can provide arbitrary services. Thus, the interpretation of the URI list by the server depends on the service to be provided. For example, for a conference server, the URIs in the list may identify the initial set of participants. On the other hand, for a server dealing with MESSAGEs, the URIs in the list may identify the recipients of an instant message. At the SIP level, this implies that the behavior of application servers receiving requests with URI lists should be specified on a per-service basis. Examples of such specifications are RFC 5366 for INVITE, RFC 5365 (see Sections 6.3.2 and 6.3.3) for MESSAGE, and RFC 5367 for SUBSCRIBE.

19.7.3.3 Results

According to the last general requirement, UAs should have a way to obtain information about the operations performed by the application server. Since these operations are service specific, the way UAs are kept informed is also service specific. For example, a UA establishing an ad hoc conference with an INVITE with a URI list may discover which participants were successfully brought into the conference by using the conference package (RFC 4575).

19.7.4 Security Considerations

Security plays an important role in the implementation of any URI-list service. In fact, it is the most important common area across all types of URI-list services. By definition, a URI-list service takes one request in and sends a potentially large number of them out. Attackers may attempt to use URI-list services as traffic amplifiers to launch DoS attacks. We are proving guidelines to avoid these attacks.

19.7.4.1 List Integrity and Confidentiality

Attackers may attempt to modify URI lists sent from clients to servers. This would cause a different behavior at the server than expected by the client (e.g., requests being sent to different recipients than the ones specified by the client). To prevent this attack, clients should integrity-protect URI lists using end-to-end mechanisms such as S/MIME (see Section 19.6) or, if not available, hop-by-hop mechanisms such as TLS (see Section 3.13). Both S/MIME and TLS can also provide URI-list confidentiality if needed.

19.7.4.2 Amplification Attacks

URI-list services take a request in and send a potentially large number of them out. Given that URI-list services are typically implemented on top of powerful servers with high-bandwidth access links, we should be careful to keep attackers from using them as amplification tools to launch DoS attacks. Attackers may attempt to send a URI list containing URIs whose host parts route to the victims of the DoS attack. These victims do not need to be SIP nodes; they can be non-SIP end points or even routers. If this attack is successful, the result is that an attacker can flood a set of nodes, or a single node, with traffic without needing to generate a high volume of traffic itself. In any case, note that this problem is not specific to SIP URI-list services; it also appears in scenarios that relate to multihoming, where a server needs to contact a set of IP addresses provided by a client. There are several measures that need to be taken to prevent this type of attack. The first one is keeping unauthorized users from using URI-list services.

Thus, URI-list services must not perform any request explosion for an unauthorized user. URI-list services must authenticate users and check whether they are authorized to request the service before performing any request fan-out. Note that the risk of this attack also exists when a client uses stored URI lists. Application servers must use authentication and authorization mechanisms with equivalent security properties when dealing with stored and request-contained URI lists.

Even though the previous rule keeps unauthorized users from using URI-list services, authorized users may still launch attacks using these services. To prevent these attacks, we introduce the concept of opt-in lists. That is, URI-list services should not allow a client to place a user (identified by his or her URI) in a URI list unless the user has previously agreed to be placed in such a URI list. Therefore, URI-list services must not send a request to a destination that has not agreed to receive requests from the URI-list service beforehand. Users can agree to receive requests from a URI-list service in several ways, such as filling a web page, sending an e-mail, signing a contract, or using the consent-based communications in SIP specified in RFC 5360 (see Section 19.8), whose requirements are discussed in RFC 4453 (see Section 19.8.1). Additionally, users must be able to further describe the requests they are willing to receive. For example, a user may only want to receive requests from a particular URI-list service on behalf of a particular user. Effectively, these rules make URI lists that used by URI-list services into opt-in lists. When a URI-list service receives a request with a URI list from a client, the URI-list service checks whether all the destinations have agreed beforehand to receive requests from the service on behalf of this client.

If the URI list has permission to send requests to all of the targets in the request, it does so. If not, it does not send any request at all. RFC 5360 (see Section 19.8) specifies a means for the URI-list service to inform the client that some permissions were missing and how to request them. Note that the mechanism used to obtain permissions should not create opportunities to launch DoS amplification attacks. These attacks would be possible if, for instance, the URI-list service automatically contacted the full set of targets for which it did not have permissions in order to request permissions. The URI-list service would be receiving one SIP request and sending out a number of authorization request messages. The consent-based communications (RFC 5360) avoids this type of attack by having the client generate roughly the same amount of traffic toward the URI-list service as the service generates toward the destinations. To have an interoperable way to meet the requirements related to opt-in lists described in this section, URI-list services MUST implement and should use the consent-based communications (RFC 5360).

19.7.4.3 General Issues

URI-list services may have policies that limit the number of URIs in the lists they accept, as a very long list could be used in a DoS attack to place a large burden on the URI-list service to send a large number of SIP requests. A URI-list service generates a set of requests from a URI list. RFC 3261 (see Section 4.2.1.4) provides recommendations that need to be taken into consideration when forming a request from a URI. Naturally, those recommendations apply to all SIP URI-list services. The general requirement states that URI-list services need to authenticate their clients, and the previous rules are applicable to URI-list services in general. In addition, specifications dealing with individual methods must describe the security issues that relate to each particular method.

19.8 Consent-Based Communications for Enhancing Security in SIP

19.8.1 Objective

The SIP supports communications for several services, including real-time audio, video, text, instant messaging, and presence. This communication is established by the transmission of various SIP requests (such as INVITE and MESSAGE) from an initiator to the recipient with whom communication is desired. Although a recipient of such a SIP request can reject the request, and therefore decline the session, a network of SIP proxy servers will deliver a SIP request to its recipients without their explicit consent. Receipt of these requests without explicit consent can cause a number of problems. These include amplification and DoS attacks. These problems are described in more detail in a companion requirements document (RFC 4453). The consent-based communications specified in RFC 5370 that is described here solves these security problems in SIP meeting the following requirements specified in RFC 4453:

- A relay is defined as any SIP server, be it a proxy, B2BUA, or some hybrid, that receives a request and translates the request URI into one or more next-hop URIs to which it then delivers a request.
- The solution keeps relays from delivering a SIP request to a recipient unless the recipient has explicitly granted permission to the relay using appropriately authenticated messages.
- The solution prevents relays from generating more than one outbound request in response to an inbound request, unless permission to do so has been granted by the resource to whom the outbound request was to be targeted. This mechanism avoids the consent mechanism itself becoming the focus of DoS attacks.

- The permissions are capable of specifying that messages from a specific user, identified by a SIP URI that is an AOR, are permitted.
- Each recipient AOR is able to specify permissions separately for each SIP service that forwards messages to the recipient. For example, Alice may authorize forwarding to her from domain A, but not from domain B.
- It is possible for a user to revoke permissions at any time.
- It is not required for a user or UA to store information in order to be able to revoke permissions that were previously granted for a relay resource.
- The solution works in an interdomain context, without requiring preestablished relationships between domains.
- The solution works for all current and future SIP methods.
- The solution is applicable to forking proxies.
- The solution is applicable to URI-list services, such as resource list servers (RFC 5365, see Sections 6.3.2 and 6.3.3), MESSAGE URI-list services (RFC 5365), and conference servers performing dial-out functions (RFC 5366, see Section 16.7.3).
- In SIP, URI lists can be stored on the URI-list server or provided in a SIP request. The consent framework works in both cases.
- The solution allows anonymous communications, as long as the recipient is willing to accept anonymous communications.
- If the recipient of a request wishes to be anonymous with respect to the original sender, it is possible for the recipient to grant permission for the sender without the original sender learning the recipient's identity.
- The solution prevents attacks that seek to undermine the underlying goal of consent. That is, it is not possible to *fool* the system into delivering a request for which permission was not, in fact, granted.
- The solution does not require the recipient of the communications to be connected to the network at the time communications are attempted.
- The solution does not require the sender of a SIP request to be connected at the time that a recipient provides permission.
- The solution scales to Internet-wide deployment.

19.8.2 Definitions and Terminology

- **Recipient URI:** The Request-URI of an outgoing request sent by an entity (e.g., a UA or a proxy). The sending of such request can have been the result of a translation operation.
- **Relay:** Any SIP server, be it a proxy, B2BUA, or some hybrid, that receives a request, translates its Request-URI into one or more next-hop URIs (i.e., recipient URIs), and delivers the request to those URIs.
- **Target URI:** The Request-URI of an incoming request that arrives to a relay that will perform a translation operation.
- **Translation logic:** The logic that defines a translation operation at a relay. This logic includes the translation's target and recipient URIs.
- **Translation operation:** Operation by which a relay translates the Request-URI of an incoming request (i.e., the target URI) into one or more URIs (i.e., recipient URIs) that are used as the Request-URIs of one or more outgoing requests.

19.8.3 Relays and Translations

Relays play a key role in this framework. A relay is defined as any SIP server, be it a proxy, B2BUA, or some hybrid, that receives a request, translates its Request-URI into one or more next-hop URIs, and delivers the request to those URIs. The Request-URI of the incoming request is referred to as target URI, and the destination URIs of the outgoing requests are referred to as recipient URIs, as shown in Figure 19.21.

Thus, an essential aspect of a relay is that of translation. When a relay receives a request, it translates the Request-URI (target URI) into one or more additional URIs (recipient URIs). Through this translation operation, the relay can create outgoing requests to one or more additional recipient URIs, thus creating the consent problem. The consent problem is created by two types of translations: translations based on local data and translations that involve amplifications. Translation operations based on local policy or local data (such as registrations) are the vehicle by which a request is delivered directly to an end point, when it would not otherwise be possible to.

In other words, if a spammer has the address of a user, sip:user@example.com, it cannot deliver a MESSAGE request to the UA (UA) of that user without having access to the registration data that maps sip:user@example.com to the UA on which that user is present. Thus, it is the usage of this registration data, and more generally, the translation logic, that is expected to be authorized in order to prevent undesired communications. Of course, if the spammer knows the

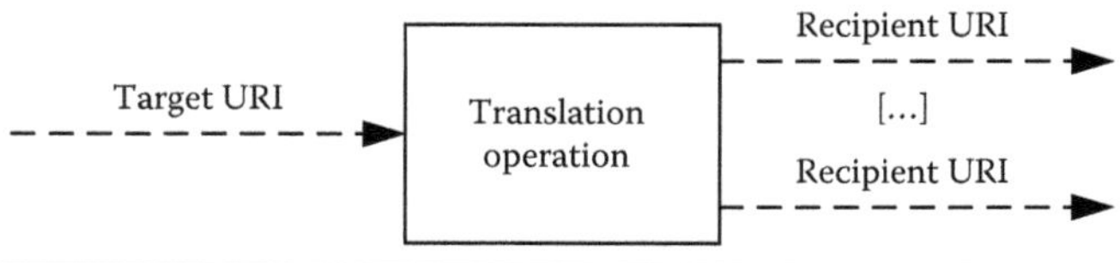

Figure 19.21 Translation operation. (Copyright IETF. Reproduced with permission.)

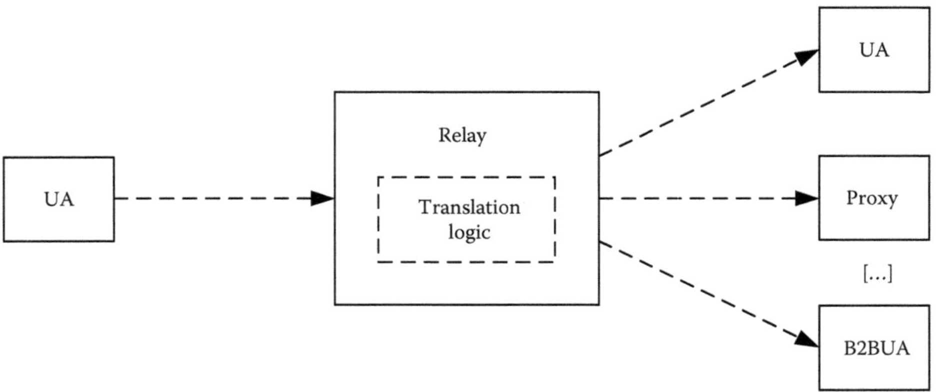

Figure 19.22 Relay performing a translation. (Copyright IETF. Reproduced with permission.)

address of the UA, it will be able to deliver requests directly to it. Translation operations that result in more than one recipient URI are a source of amplification. Servers that do not perform translations, such as outbound proxy servers, do not cause amplification. On the other hand, servers that perform translations (e.g., inbound proxies authoritatively responsible for a SIP domain) may cause amplification if the user can be reached at multiple end points (thereby resulting in multiple recipient URIs).

Figure 19.22 shows a relay that performs translations. The UAC in the figure sends a SIP request to a URI representing a resource in the domain example.com (sip:resource@example.com). This request can pass through a local outbound proxy (not shown), but eventually arrives at a server authoritative for the domain example.com. This server, which acts as a relay, performs a translation operation, translating the target URI into one or more recipient URIs, which can (but need not) belong to the domain example.com. This relay can be, for instance, a proxy server or a URI-list service (RFC 5363, see Section 19.7).

This framework allows potential recipients of a translation to agree to be actual recipients by giving the relay performing the translation permission to send them traffic.

19.8.4 Architecture

Figure 19.23 shows the architectural elements of this framework. The manipulation of a relay's translation logic typically causes the relay to send a permission request, which in turn causes the recipient to grant or deny the relay permissions for the translation. Next we describe the following:

- Role of permissions at a relay
- Actions taken by a relay when its translation logic is manipulated by a client
- Store-and-forward servers and their functionality
- How potential recipients can grant a relay permissions to add them to the relay's translation logic
- Which entities need to implement this specification (RFC 5360) described here

19.8.4.1 Permissions at a Relay

Relays implementing this framework obtain and store permissions associated with their translation logic. These permissions indicate whether or not a particular recipient has agreed to receive traffic at any given time. Recipients that have not given the relay permission to send them traffic are

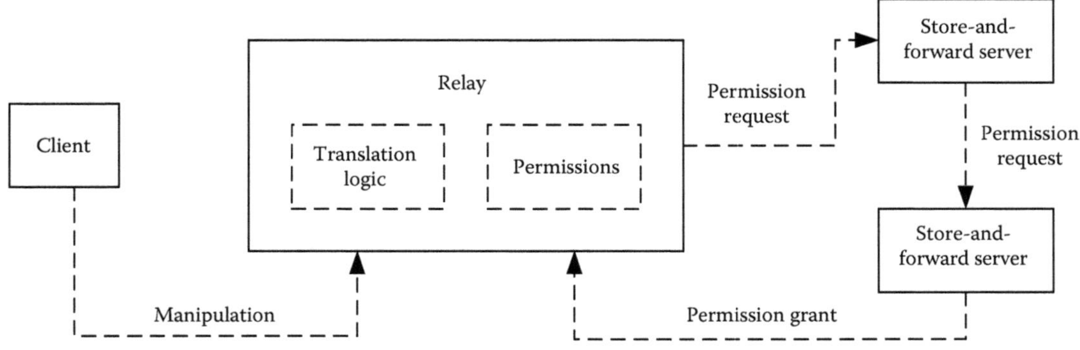

Figure 19.23 Reference architecture. (Copyright IETF. Reproduced with permission.)

simply ignored by the relay when performing a translation. In principle, permissions are valid as long as the context where they were granted is valid, or until they are revoked. For example, the permissions obtained by a URI-list SIP service that distributes MESSAGE requests to a set of recipients will be valid as long as the URI-list SIP service exists or until the permissions are revoked. Additionally, if a recipient is removed from a relay's translation logic, the relay should delete the permissions related to that recipient. For example, if the registration of a contact URI expires or is otherwise terminated, the registrar deletes the permissions related to that contact address.

It is also recommended that relays request recipients to refresh their permissions periodically. If a recipient fails to refresh its permissions for a given period of time, the relay should delete the permissions related to that recipient. This framework does not provide any guidance for the values of the refreshment intervals because different applications can have different requirements to set those values. For example, a relay dealing with recipients that do not implement this framework may choose to use longer intervals between refreshes. The refresh process in such recipients has to be performed manually by their users (since the recipients do not implement this framework), and having too short refresh intervals may become too heavy a burden for those users.

19.8.4.2 Consenting Manipulations on a Relay's Translation Logic

This framework aims to ensure that any particular relay only performs translations toward destinations that have given the relay permission to perform such a translation. Consequently, when the translation logic of a relay is manipulated (e.g., a new recipient URI is added), the relay obtains permission from the new recipient in order to install the new translation logic. Relays ask recipients for permission using MESSAGE requests. For example, the relay hosting the URI-list service at sip:friends@example.com performs a translation from that target URI to a set of recipient URIs. When a client (e.g., the administrator of that URI-list service) adds bob@example.org as a new recipient URI, the relay sends a MESSAGE request to sip:bob@example.org asking whether or not it is OK to perform the translation from sip:friends@example.com to sip:bob@example.org.

The MESSAGE request carries in its message body a permission document that describes the translation for which permissions are being requested and a human-readable part that also describes the translation. If the answer is positive, the new translation logic is installed at the relay. That is, the new recipient URI is added. The human-readable part is included so that UAs that do not understand permission documents can still process the request and display it in a sensible way to the user. The mechanism to be used to manipulate the translation logic of a particular relay depends on the relay. Two existing mechanisms to manipulate translation logic are XCAP (RFC 4825) and REGISTER transactions. Later, we describe a URI-list service whose translation logic is manipulated with XCAP as an example of a translation, in order to specify this framework. We also explain how to apply this consent-based framework to registrations, which are a different type of translation. In any case, relays implementing this framework should have a means to indicate that a particular recipient URI is in the states specified in RFC 5362 (i.e., pending, waiting, error, denied, or granted).

19.8.4.3 Store-and-Forward Servers

When a MESSAGE request with a permission document arrives to the recipient URI to which it was sent by the relay, the receiving user can grant or deny the permission needed to perform the translation. However, the receiving user may not be available when the MESSAGE request arrives, or it may have expressed preferences to block all incoming requests for a certain time period. In such cases, a store-and-forward server can act as a substitute for the user and buffer the incoming MESSAGE requests, which are subsequently delivered to the user when he or she is available again.

There are several mechanisms to implement store-and-forward message services (e.g., with an instant message to e-mail gateway). Any of these mechanisms can be used between a UA and its store-and-forward server as long as they agree on which mechanism to use. Therefore, this framework does not make any provision for the interface between UAs and their store-and-forward servers. Note that the same store-and-forward message service can handle all incoming MESSAGE requests for a user while they are offline, not only those MESSAGE requests with a permission document in their bodies.

Even though store-and-forward servers perform a useful function and they are expected to be deployed in most domains, some domains will not deploy them from the outset. However, UAs and relays in domains without store-and-forward servers can still use this consent framework. When a relay requests permissions from an offline UA that does not have an associated store-and-forward server, the relay will obtain an error response indicating that its MESSAGE request could not be delivered. The client that attempted to add the offline user to the relay's translation logic will be notified about the error, for example, using the Pending Additions event package (RFC 5362). This client may attempt to add the same user at a later point, hopefully when the user is online. Clients can discover whether or not a user is online by using a presence service, for instance.

19.8.4.4 Recipient Grant Permissions

Permission documents generated by a relay include URIs that can be used by the recipient of the document to grant or deny the relay the permission described in the document. Relays always include SIP URIs and can include HTTP (RFCs 7230–7235) URIs for this purpose. Consequently, recipients provide relays with permissions using SIP PUBLISH requests or HTTP GET requests.

19.8.4.5 Entities Implementing This Framework

The goal of this framework is to keep relays from executing translations toward unwilling recipients. Therefore, all relays must implement this framework in order to avoid being used to perform attacks (e.g., amplification attacks). This framework has been designed with backwards compatibility in mind so that legacy UAs (i.e., UAs that do not implement this framework) can act both as clients and recipients with an acceptable level of functionality. However, it is recommended that UAs implement this framework, which includes supporting the Pending Additions event package specified in RFC 5362, the format for permission documents specified in RFC 5361, and the header fields and response code specified in this document, in order to achieve full functionality. The only requirement that this framework places on store-and-forward servers is that they need to be able to deliver encrypted and integrity-protected messages to their UAs, as discussed later. However, this is not a requirement specific to this framework but a general requirement for store-and-forward servers.

19.8.5 Framework Operations

This section specifies this consent framework using an example of the prototypical call flow. The elements described earlier (i.e., relays, translations, and store-and-forward servers) play an essential role in this call flow. Figure 19.24 shows the complete process of adding a recipient URI (sip:B@example.com) to the translation logic of a relay. User A attempts to add sip:B@example.com as a new recipient URI to the translation logic of the relay (F1). User A uses XCAP (RFC 4825) and the XML format for representing resource lists (RFC 4826) to perform this addition. Since the relay does not have permission from sip:B@example.com to perform translations toward that URI, the relay places sip:B@example.com in the pending state, as specified in RFC 5362.

19.8.5.1 Amplification Avoidance

Once sip:B@example.com is in the pending state, the relay needs to ask user B for permission by sending a MESSAGE request to sip:B@example.com. However, the relay needs to ensure that it is not used as an amplifier to launch amplification attacks. In such an attack, the attacker would add a large number of recipient URIs to the translation logic of a relay. The relay would then send a MESSAGE request to each of those recipient URIs. The bandwidth generated by the relay would be much higher than the bandwidth used by the attacker to add those recipient URIs to the translation logic of the relay. This framework uses a credit-based authorization mechanism to avoid the attack just described. It requires users adding new recipient URIs to a translation to generate an amount of bandwidth that is comparable to the bandwidth the relay will generate when sending MESSAGE requests toward those recipient URIs. When XCAP is used, this requirement is met by not allowing clients to add more than one URI per HTTP transaction. When a REGISTER transaction is used, this requirement is met by not allowing clients to register more than one contact per REGISTER transaction.

19.8.5.1.1 Relay's Behavior

Relays implementing this framework must not allow clients to add more than one recipient URI per transaction. If a client using XCAP attempts to add more than one recipient URI in a single HTTP transaction, the XCAP server should return an HTTP 409 Conflict response. The XCAP server should describe the reason for the refusal in an XML body using the `<constraint-failure>` element, as described in RFC 4825. If a client attempts to register more than one contact in a single REGISTER transaction, the registrar should return a SIP 403 Forbidden response and explain the reason for the refusal in its reason phrase (e.g., maximum one contact per registration).

19.8.5.2 Subscription to the Permission Status

Clients need a way to be informed about the status of the operations they requested. Otherwise, users can be waiting for an operation to succeed when it has actually already failed. In particular, if the target of the request for consent was not reachable and did not have an associated store-and-forward server, the client needs to know to retry the request later. The Pending Additions SIP event package (RFC 5362) is a way to provide clients with that information. Clients can use the Pending Additions SIP event package to be informed about the status of the operations they requested. That is, the client will be informed when an operation (e.g., the addition of a recipient URI to a relay's translation logic) is authorized (and thus executed) or rejected. Clients use the target URI of the SIP translation being manipulated to subscribe to the Pending Additions event package. In our example, after receiving the response from the relay (F2), user A subscribes to the Pending Additions event package at the relay (F5). This subscription keeps user A informed about the status of the permissions (e.g., granted or denied) the relay will obtain.

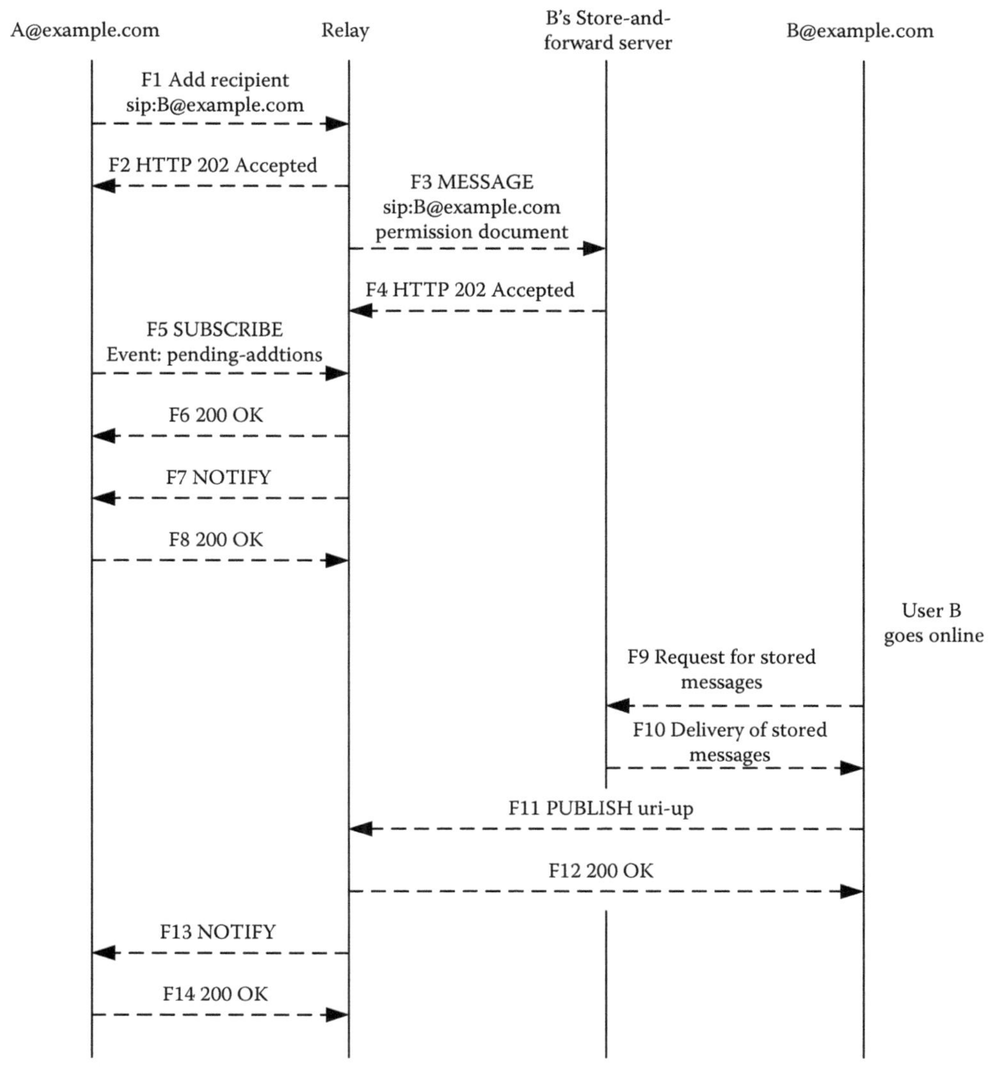

Figure 19.24 Prototypical call flow. (Copyright IETF. Reproduced with permission.)

19.8.5.2.1 Relay's Behavior

Relays should support the Pending Additions SIP event package specified in RFC 5362.

19.8.5.3 Request for Permission

A relay requests permissions from potential recipients to add them to its translation logic using MESSAGE requests. In our example, on receiving the request to add user B to the translation logic of the relay (F1), the relay generates a MESSAGE request (F3) toward sip:B@example.com. This MESSAGE request carries a permission document, which describes the translation that needs to be authorized, and carries a set of URIs to be used by the recipient to grant or to deny the relay permission to perform that translation. Since user B is offline, the MESSAGE request will be buffered by user B's store-and-forward server. User B will later go online and authorize the translation by using one of those URIs, as described later. The MESSAGE request also carries a body part that contains the same information as the permission document but in a human-readable format. When user B uses one of the URIs in the permission document to grant or deny permissions, the relay needs to make sure that it was actually user B using that URI, and not an attacker. The relay can use any of the methods described in Section 19.8.5.6 to authenticate the permission document.

19.8.5.3.1 Relay's Behavior

Relays that implement this framework must obtain permissions from potential recipients before adding them to their translation logic. Relays request permissions from potential recipients using MESSAGE requests. Section 19.8.5.6

describes the methods a relay can use to authenticate those recipients giving the relay permission to perform a particular translation. These methods are SIP Identity (RFC 4474, see Sections 2.8 and 19.4.8), P-Asserted-Identity (RFC 3325, see Sections 2.8, 10.4, and 20.3), a return-routability test, or SIP Digest. Relays that use the method consisting of a return-routability test have to send their MESSAGE requests to a SIPS URI, as specified later.

MESSAGE requests sent to request permissions must include a permission document and should include a human-readable part in their bodies. The human-readable part contains the same information as the permission document (but in a human-readable format), including the URIs to grant and deny permissions. UAs that do not understand permission documents can still process the request and display it in a sensible way to the user, as they would display any other instant message. This way, even if the UA does not implement this framework, the (human) user will be able to manually click on the correct URI in order to grant or deny permissions. The following is an example of a MESSAGE request that carries a human-readable part and a permission document, which follows the format specified in RFC 5361, in its body. Not all header fields are shown for simplicity.

```
MESSAGE sip:bob@example.org SIP/2.0
From: <sip:alices-friends@example.com>;
tag=12345678
To: <sip:bob@example.org>
Content-Type: multipart/
mixed;boundary="boundary1"

--boundary1

Content-Type: text/plain
If you consent to receive traffic sent to
<sip:alices-friends@example.com>, please use
one of the following URIs: <sips:grant-1awdch
5Fasddfce34@example.com> or <https://example.
com/grant-1awdch5Fasddfce34>. Otherwise, use
one of the following URIs: <sips:deny-23rCsdf
gvdT5sdfgye@example.com> or <https://example.
com/deny-23rCsdfgvdT5sdfgye>.
--boundary1

Content-Type: application/auth-policy+xml

<?xml version="1.0" encoding="UTF-8"?>
<cp:ruleset
       xmlns="urn:ietf:params:xml:ns:cons
ent-rules"
       xmlns:cp="urn:ietf:params:xml:ns:com
mon-policy"
       xmlns:xsi="http://www.w3.org/2001/
XMLSchema-instance">
       <cp:rule id="f1">
              <cp:conditions>
                     <cp:identity>
                            <cp:many/>
                     </cp:identity>
                     <recipient>
                            <cp:one id="sip:
                            bob@example.org"/>
                     </recipient>
                     <target>
                            <cp:one id="sip:
                            alices-friends@
                            example.com"/>
                     </target>
              </cp:conditions>
              <cp:actions>
                     <trans-handling
                            perm-uri="sips:
                            grant-1awdch5Fasd
                            dfce34@example.
                            com">
                            grant
                     </trans-handling>
                     <trans-handling
                            perm-uri="https://
                            example.com/grant-
                            1awdch5Fasddfce34">
                            grant
                     </trans-handling>
                     <trans-handling
                            perm-uri="sips:
                            deny-23rCsdfgvdT5sd
                            fgye@example.com">
                            deny
                     </trans-handling>
                     <trans-handling
                            perm-uri="https://
                            example.com/deny-23r
                            CsdfgvdT5sdfgye">
                            deny
                     </trans-handling>
              </cp:actions>
              <cp:transformations/>
       </cp:rule>
</cp:ruleset>

--boundary1--
```

19.8.5.4 Permission Document Structure

A permission document is the representation (e.g., encoded in XML) of a permission. A permission document contains several pieces of data:

Identity of the sender: A URI representing the identity of the sender for whom permissions are granted.

Identity of the original recipient: A URI representing the identity of the original recipient, which is used as the input for the translation operation. This is also called the target URI.

Identity of the final recipient: A URI representing the result of the translation. The permission grants ability for the sender to send requests to the target URI and for a relay receiving those requests to forward them to this URI. This is also called the recipient URI.

URIs to grant permission: URIs that recipients can use to grant the relay permission to perform the translation described in the document. Relays MUST support the use of SIP and SIPS URIs in permission documents and may support the use of HTTP and HTTPS URIs.

URIs to deny permission: URIs that recipients can use to deny the relay permission to perform the translation described in the document. Relays must support the use of SIP and SIPS URIs in permission documents and may support the use of HTTP and HTTPS URIs. Permission documents can contain wildcards. For example, a permission document can request permission for any relay to forward requests coming from a particular sender to a particular recipient.

Such a permission document would apply to any target URI. That is, the field containing the identity of the original recipient would match any URI. However, the recipient URI must not be wildcarded. Entities implementing this framework must support the format for permission documents defined in RFC 5361 and may support other formats. In our example, the permission document in the MESSAGE request (F3) sent by the relay contains the following values:

- Identity of the sender: any sender
- Identity of the original recipient: sip:friends@example .com
- Identity of the final recipient: sip:B@example.com
- URI to grant permission: sips:grant-1awdch5Fasddfce 34@example.com
- URI to grant permission: https://example.com/grant -1awdch5Fasddfce34
- URI to deny permission: sips:deny-23rCsdfgvdT5sdf gye@example.com
- URI to deny permission: https://example.com/deny -23rCsdfgvdT5sdfgye

It is expected that the Sender field often contains a wildcard. However, scenarios involving request-contained URI lists, such as the one described in Section 19.8.5.10, can require permission documents that apply to a specific sender. In cases where the identity of the sender matters, relays must authenticate senders.

19.8.5.5 Permission Requested Notification

On receiving the MESSAGE request (F3), user B's store-and-forward server stores it because user B is offline at that point. When user B goes online, user B fetches all the requests its store-and-forward server has stored (F9).

19.8.5.6 Permission Grant

A recipient gives a relay permission to execute the translation described in a permission document by sending a SIP PUBLISH or an HTTP GET request to one of the URIs to grant permissions contained in the document. Similarly, a recipient denies a relay permission to execute the translation described in a permission document by sending a SIP PUBLISH or an HTTP GET request to one of the URIs to deny permissions contained in the document. Requests to grant or deny permissions contain an empty body. In our example, user B obtains the permission document (1F0) that was received earlier by its store-and-forward server in the MESSAGE request (F3). User B authorizes the translation described in the permission document received by sending a PUBLISH request (F11) to the SIP URI to grant permissions contained in the permission document.

19.8.5.7 Relay's Behavior after Recipient Granting Permission

Relays must ensure that the SIP PUBLISH or the HTTP GET request received was generated by the recipient of the translation and not by an attacker. Relays can use four methods to authenticate those requests: SIP Identity, P-Asserted-Identity (RFC 3325, see Sections 2.8, 10.4, and 20.3), a return-routability test, or SIP Digest. While return-routability tests can be used to authenticate both SIP PUBLISH and HTTP GET requests, SIP Identity, P-Asserted-Identity, and SIP Digest can only be used to authenticate SIP PUBLISH requests. SIP Digest can only be used to authenticate recipients that share a secret with the relay (e.g., recipients that are in the same domain as the relay).

19.8.5.7.1 SIP Identity

The SIP Identity (RFC 4474, see Sections 2.8 and 19.4.8) mechanism can be used to authenticate the sender of a PUBLISH request. The relay MUST check that the originator of the PUBLISH request is the owner of the recipient URI in the permission document. Otherwise, the PUBLISH request should be responded to with a 401 Unauthorized response and must not be processed further.

19.8.5.7.2 P-Asserted-Identity

The P-Asserted-Identity mechanism can also be used to authenticate the sender of a PUBLISH request. However, as discussed in RFC 3325 (see Sections 2.8, 10.4, and 20.3), this mechanism is intended to be used only within networks of trusted SIP servers. That is, the use of this mechanism is only applicable inside an administrative domain with previously agreed-upon policies. The relay must check that the originator of the PUBLISH request is the owner of the recipient URI in the permission document. Otherwise, the PUBLISH request should be responded to with a 401 Unauthorized response and must not be processed further.

19.8.5.7.3 Return Routability

SIP Identity provides a good authentication mechanism for incoming PUBLISH requests. Nevertheless, SIP Identity is not yet widely available on the public Internet. That is why an authentication mechanism that can already be used at this point is needed. Return-routability tests do not provide the same level of security as SIP Identity, but they provide a better-than-nothing security level in architectures where the SIP Identity mechanism is not available (e.g., the current Internet). The relay generates an unguessable URI (i.e., with a cryptographically random user part) and places it in the permission document in the MESSAGE request (F3). The recipient needs to send a SIP PUBLISH request or an HTTP GET request to that URI. Any incoming request sent to that URI should be considered authenticated by the relay.

Note that the return-routability method is the only one that allows the use of HTTP URIs in permission documents. The other methods require the use of SIP URIs. Relays using a return-routability test to perform this authentication MUST send the MESSAGE request with the permission document to a SIPS URI. This ensures that attackers do not get access to the (unguessable) URI. Thus, the only user able to use the (unguessable) URI is the receiver of the MESSAGE request. Similarly, permission documents sent by relays using a return-routability test must only contain secure URIs (i.e., SIPS and HTTPS) to grant and deny permissions. A part of these URIs (e.g., the user part of a SIPS URI) must be cryptographically random with at least 32 bits of randomness. Relays can transition from return-routability tests to SIP Identity by simply requiring the use of SIP Identity for incoming PUBLISH requests. That is, such a relay would reject PUBLISH requests that did not use SIP Identity.

19.8.5.7.4 SIP Digest

The SIP Digest mechanism can be used to authenticate the sender of a PUBLISH request as long as that sender shares a secret with the relay. The relay must check that the originator of the PUBLISH request is the owner of the recipient URI in the permission document. Otherwise, the PUBLISH request should be responded to with a 401 Unauthorized response and must not be processed further.

19.8.5.8 Permission Granted Notification

On receiving the PUBLISH request (F11), the relay sends a NOTIFY request (F13) to inform user A that the permission for the translation has been received and that the translation logic at the relay has been updated. That is, sip:B@example.com has been added as a recipient URI.

19.8.5.9 Permission Revocation

At any time, if a recipient wants to revoke any permission, it uses the URI it received in the permission document to deny the permissions it previously granted. If a recipient loses this URI for some reason, it needs to wait until it receives a new request produced by the translation. Such a request will contain a Trigger-Consent header field with a URI. That Trigger-Consent header field will have a target-uri header field parameter identifying the target URI of the translation. The recipient needs to send a PUBLISH request with an empty body to the URI in the Trigger-Consent header field in order to receive a MESSAGE request from the relay. Such a MESSAGE request will contain a permission document with a URI to revoke the permission that was previously granted.

Figure 19.25 shows an example of how a user that lost the URI to revoke permissions at a relay can obtain a new

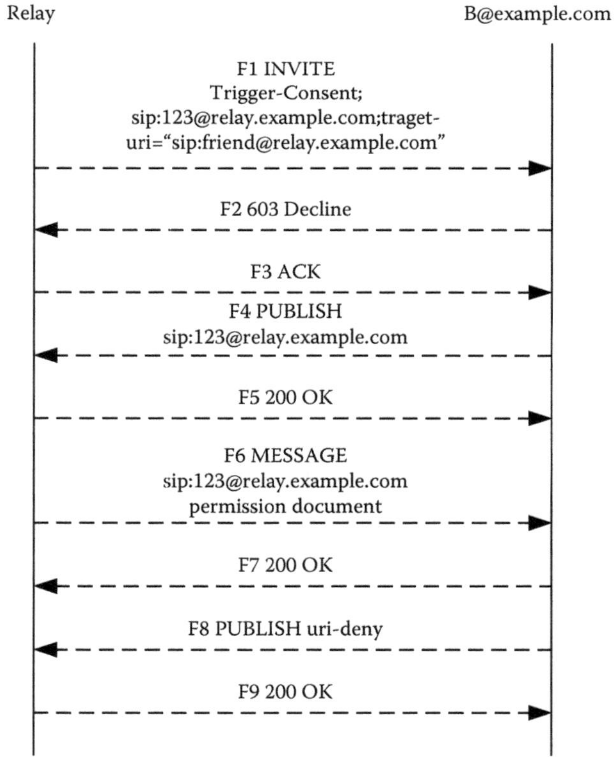

Figure 19.25 Permission revocation. (Copyright IETF. Reproduced with permission.)

URI using the Trigger-Consent header field of an incoming request. The user rejects an incoming INVITE (F1) request, which contains a Trigger-Consent header field. Using the URI in that header field, the user sends a PUBLISH request (F4) to the relay. On receiving the PUBLISH request (F4), the relay generates a MESSAGE request (F6) toward the user. Finally, the user revokes the permissions by sending a PUBLISH request (F8) to the relay.

19.8.5.10 Request-Contained URI Lists

In the scenarios described thus far, a user adds recipient URIs to the translation logic of a relay. However, the relay does not perform translations toward those recipient URIs until permissions are obtained. URI-list services using request-contained URI lists are a special case because the selection of recipient URIs is performed at the same time as the communication attempt. A user places a set of recipient URIs in a request and sends it to a relay so that the relay sends a similar request to all those recipient URIs. Relays implementing this consent framework and providing request-contained URI-list services behave in a slightly different way than the relays described thus far. This type of relay also maintains a list of recipient URIs for which permissions have been received. Clients also manipulate this list using a manipulation mechanism (e.g., XCAP). Nevertheless, this list does not represent the recipient URIs of every translation performed by the relay. This list just represents all the recipient URIs for which permissions have been received—that is, the set of URIs that will be accepted if a request containing a URI list arrives to the relay. This set of URIs is a superset of the recipient URIs of any particular translation the relay performs.

19.8.5.10.1 Relay's Behavior

On receiving a request-contained URI list, the relay checks whether or not it has permissions for all the URIs contained in the incoming URI list. If it does, the relay performs the translation. If it lacks permissions for one or more URIs, the relay must not perform the translation and should return an error response. A relay that receives a request-contained URI list with a URI for which the relay has no permissions should return a 470 Consent Needed response. The relay should add a Permission-Missing header field with the URIs for which the relay has no permissions. Figure 19.26 shows a relay that receives a request (F1) that contains URIs for which the relay does not have permission (the INVITE carries the recipient URIs in its message body). The relay rejects the request with a 470 Consent Needed response (F2). That response contains a Permission-Missing header field with the URIs for which there was no permission.

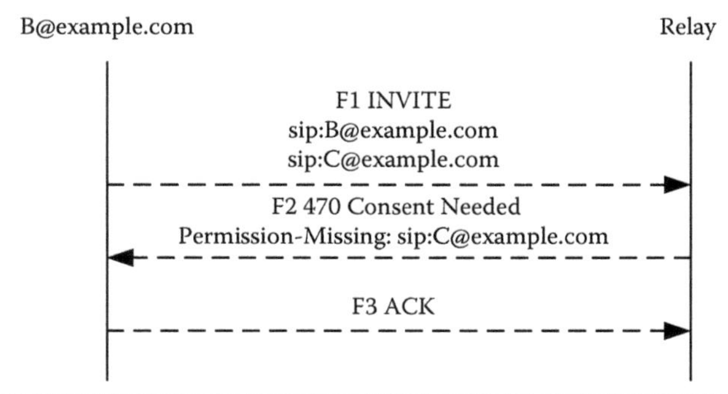

Figure 19.26 INVITE with a URI list in its body. (Copyright IETF. Reproduced with permission.)

19.8.5.10.2 Definition of the 470 Response Code

A 470 Consent Needed response indicates that the request that triggered the response contained a URI list with at least one URI for which the relay had no permissions. A UAS generating a 470 Consent Needed response should include a Permission-Missing header field in it. This header field carries the URI or URIs for which the relay had no permissions. A UAC receiving a 470 Consent Needed response without a Permission-Missing header field needs to use an alternative mechanism (e.g., XCAP) to discover for which URI or URIs there were no permissions. A client receiving a 470 Consent Needed response uses a manipulation mechanism (e.g., XCAP) to add those URIs to the relay's list of URIs. The relay will obtain permissions for those URIs as usual.

19.8.5.10.3 Definition of the Permission-Missing Header Field

Permission-Missing header fields carry URIs for which a relay did not have permissions. The following is the ABNF (RFC 5234) syntax of the Permission-Missing header field for convenience, although the complete BNF for SIP is provided in Section 2.4.1:

```
Permission-Missing  =  "Permission-Missing"
                       HCOLON per-miss-spec
                       *(COMMA per-miss-spec)
per-miss-spec       =  (name-addr/addr-spec)
                       *(SEMI generic-param)
```

The following is an example of a Permission-Missing header field:

```
Permission-Missing: sip:C@example.com
```

19.8.5.11 Registrations

Even though the example used to specify this framework has been a URI-list service, this framework applies to any type of translation (i.e., not only to URI-list services). Registrations are a different type of translations that deserve discussion. Registrations are a special type of translations. The user registering has a trust relationship with the registrar in its home domain. This is not the case when a user gives any type of permissions to a relay in a different domain. Traditionally, REGISTER transactions have performed two operations at the same time: setting up a translation and authorizing the use of that translation. For example, a user registering its current contact URI is giving permission to the registrar to forward traffic sent to the user's AOR to the registered contact URI. This works fine when the entity registering is the same as the one that will be receiving traffic at a later point (e.g., the entity receives traffic over the same connection used for the registration as described in RFC 5626; see Section 13.2). However, this schema creates some potential attacks that relate to third-party registrations.

An attacker binds, via a registration, his or her AOR with the contact URI of a victim. Now the victim will receive unsolicited traffic that was originally addressed to the attacker. The process of authorizing a registration is shown in Figure 19.27. User A performs a third-party registration (F1) and receives a 202 Accepted response (F2). Since the relay does not have permission from sip:a@ws123.example.com to perform translations toward that recipient URI, the relay places sip:a@ws123.example.com in the *pending* state. Once sip:a@ws123.example.com is in the Permission Pending state, the registrar needs to ask sip:a@ws123.example.com for permission by sending a MESSAGE request (F3). After receiving the response from the relay (F2), user A subscribes to the Pending Additions event package at the registrar (F5). This subscription keeps the user informed about the status of the permissions (e.g., granted or denied) the registrar will obtain. The rest of the process is similar to the one described later.

Permission documents generated by registrars are typically very general. For example, in one such document, a registrar can ask a recipient for permission to forward any request from any sender to the recipient's URI. This is the type of granularity that this framework intends to provide for registrations. Users who want to define how incoming requests are treated with a finer granularity (e.g., requests from user A are only accepted between 9:00 and 11:00) will have to use other mechanisms such as CPL (RFC 3880).

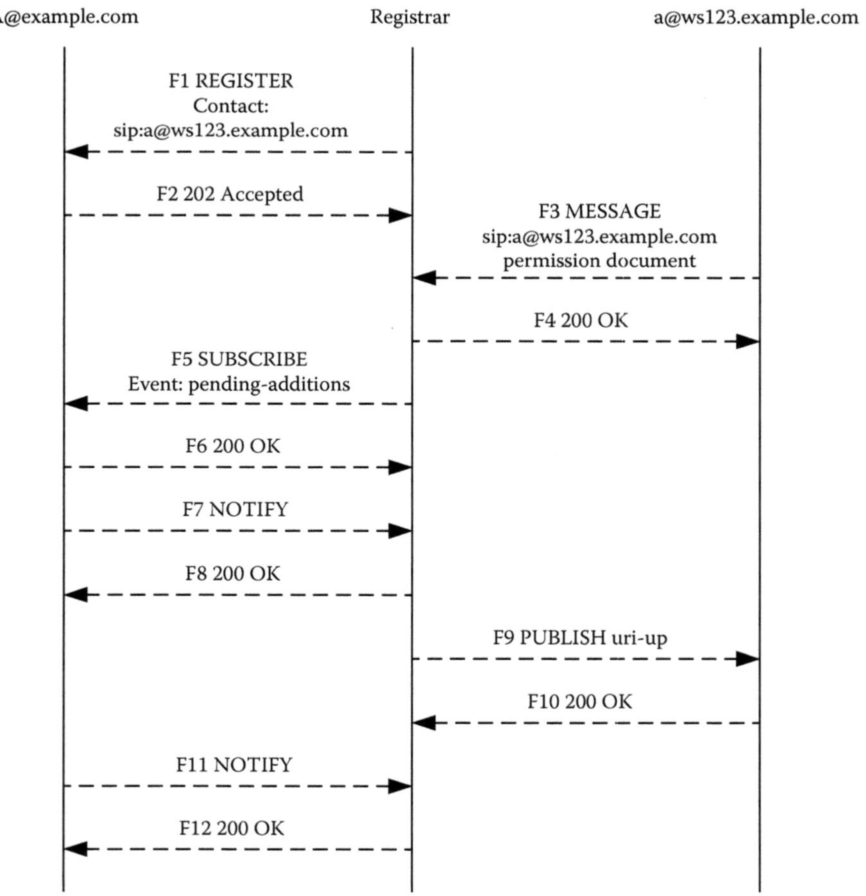

Figure 19.27 Registration. (Copyright IETF. Reproduced with permission.)

Note that, as indicated previously, UAs using the same connection to register and to receive traffic from the registrar, as described in RFC 5626 (see Section 13.2), do not need to use the mechanism described in this section. A UA being registered by a third party can be unable to use the SIP Identity, P-Asserted-Identity, or SIP Digest mechanisms to prove to the registrar that the UA is the owner of the URI being registered (e.g., sip:user@192.0.2.1), which is the recipient URI of the translation. In this case, return routability must be used.

19.8.5.12 Relays Generating Traffic toward Recipients

Relays generating traffic toward recipients need to make sure that those recipients can revoke the permissions they gave at any time. The Trigger-Consent helps achieve this.

19.8.5.12.1 Relay's Behavior

A relay executing a translation that involves sending a request to a URI from which permissions were obtained previously should add a Trigger-Consent header field to the request. The URI in the Trigger-Consent header field MUST have a target-uri header field parameter identifying the target URI of the translation. On receiving a PUBLISH request addressed to the URI that a relay previously placed in a Trigger-Consent header field, the relay should send a MESSAGE request to the corresponding recipient URI with a permission document. Therefore, the relay needs to be able to correlate the URI it places in the Trigger-Consent header field with the recipient URI of the translation.

19.8.5.12.2 Definition of the Trigger-Consent Header Field

The following is the ABNF (RFC 5234) syntax of the Trigger-Consent header field for convenience, although a complete BNF for SIP messages provided in Section 2.4.1:

```
Trigger-Consent     = "Trigger-Consent" HCOLON
                      trigger-cons-spec
                      *(COMMA
                      trigger-cons-spec)
trigger-cons-spec = (SIP-URI/SIPS-URI)
                      *(SEMI trigger-param)
trigger-param       = target-uri/generic-param
target-uri          = "target-uri" EQUAL
                      LDQUOT *(qdtext/quoted-
                      pair) RDQUOT
```

The target-uri header field parameter MUST contain a URI. The following is an example of a Trigger-Consent header field:

```
Trigger-Consent: sip:123@relay.example.com
            ;target-uri="sip:friends@relay.
            example.com"
```

19.8.6 Security Considerations

Security has been discussed throughout the chapter. However, there are some issues that deserve special attention. Relays generally implement several security mechanisms that relate to client authentication and authorization. Clients are typically authenticated before they can manipulate a relay's translation logic. Additionally, clients are typically also authenticated and sometimes need to perform SPAM prevention tasks (RFC 5039) when they send traffic to a relay. It is important that relays implement these types of security mechanisms. However, they fall outside the scope of this framework. Even with these mechanisms in place, there is still a need for relays to implement this framework because the use of these mechanisms does not prevent authorized clients to add recipients to a translation without their consent. Consequently, relays performing translations must implement this framework. Note that, as indicated previously, UAs using the same connection to register and to receive traffic from the registrar, as described in RFC 5626 (see Section 13.2), do not need to use this framework.

Therefore, a registrar that did not accept third-party registrations would not need to implement this framework. As pointed out earlier, when return-routability tests are used to authenticate recipients granting or denying permissions, the URIs used to grant or deny permissions need to be protected from attackers. SIPS URIs provide a good tool to meet this requirement, as described in RFC 5361. When store-and-forward servers are used, the interface between a UA and its store-and-forward server is frequently not based on SIP. In such a case, SIPS cannot be used to secure those URIs. Implementations of store-and-forward servers must provide a mechanism for delivering encrypted and integrity-protected messages to their UAs.

The information provided by the Pending Additions event package can be sensitive. For this reason, relays need to use strong means for authentication and information confidentiality. SIPS URIs are a good mechanism to meet this requirement. Permission documents can reveal sensitive information. Attackers may attempt to modify them in order to have clients grant or deny permissions different from the ones they think they are granting or denying. For this reason, it is recommended that relays use strong means for information integrity protection and confidentiality when sending permission documents to clients. The mechanism used for conveying information to clients should ensure the integrity and confidentially of the information. To achieve these, an end-to-end SIP encryption mechanism, such as S/MIME (see Section 19.6), should be used. If strong end-to-end security means (such as above) are not available, it is recommended that hop-by-hop security based on TLS and SIPS URIs is used.

19.9 SIP Forking Proxy Security

19.9.1 Overview

Interoperability testing uncovered a vulnerability in the behavior of forking SIP proxies. This vulnerability can be leveraged to cause a small number of valid SIP requests to generate an extremely large number of proxy-to-proxy messages. A version of this attack demonstrates fewer than 10 messages stimulating potentially 2^{71} messages. RFC 5393 that is described here specifies normative changes to the SIP protocol to address this vulnerability related to the SIP proxy behavior. This vulnerability enables an attack against SIP networks where a small number of legitimate, even authorized, SIP requests can stimulate massive amounts of proxy-to-proxy traffic.

RFC 5393 strengthens the loop-detection requirements on SIP proxies when they fork requests, that is, forward a request to more than one destination. It also corrects and clarifies the description of the loop-detection algorithm such proxies are required to implement. Additionally, it defines a Max-Breadth mechanism for limiting the number of concurrent branches pursued for any given request. The mechanism only limits concurrency. It does not limit the total number of branches a request can traverse over its lifetime. The mechanisms in this update will protect against variations of the attack described here that use a small number of resources, including most unintentional self-inflicted variations that occur through accidental misconfiguration.

However, an attacker with access to a sufficient number of distinct resources will still be able to stimulate a very large number of messages. The number of concurrent messages will be limited by the Max-Breadth mechanism, so the entire set will be spread out over a long period of time, giving operators better opportunity to detect the attack and take corrective measures outside the protocol. Future protocol work is needed to prevent this form of attack.

19.9.2 Vulnerability: Leveraging Forking to Flood a Network

We are describing setting up an attack with a simplifying assumption: that two accounts on each of two different RFC 3261-compliant proxy/registrar servers that do not perform loop detection are available to an attacker. This assumption is not necessary for the attack but makes representing the scenario simpler. The same attack can be realized with a single account on a single server. Consider two proxy/registrar services, P1 and P2, and four AORs, a@P1, b@P1, a@P2, and b@P2. Using normal REGISTER requests, establish bindings to these AORs as follows (nonessential details elided):

```
REGISTER sip:P1 SIP/2.0
To: <sip:a@P1>
Contact: <sip:a@P2>, sip:b@P2

REGISTER sip:P1 SIP/2.0
To: <sip:b@P1>
Contact: <sip:a@P2>, sip:b@P2

REGISTER sip:P2 SIP/2.0
To: <sip:a@P2>
Contact: <sip:a@P1>, sip:b@P1

REGISTER sip:P2 SIP/2.0
To: <sip:b@P2>
Contact: <sip:a@P1>, <sip:b@P1>
```

With these bindings in place, introduce an INVITE request to any of the four AORs, say a@P1. This request will fork to two requests handled by P2, which will fork to four requests handled by P1, which will fork to eight messages handled by P2, and so on. This message flow is represented in Figure 19.28.

Requests will continue to propagate down this tree until Max-Forwards reaches zero. If the end point and two proxies involved follow RFC 3261 recommendations, the tree will be 70 rows deep, representing $2^{71} - 1$ requests. The actual number of messages may be much larger if the time to process the entire tree's worth of requests is longer than timer C at either proxy. In this case, a storm of 408 responses or a storm of CANCEL requests will also be propagating through the tree along with the INVITE requests. Remember that there are only two proxies involved in this scenario—each having to hold the state for all the transactions it sees (at least 2^{70} simultaneously active transactions near the end of the scenario).

The attack can be simplified to one account at one server if the service can be convinced that contacts with varying attributes (parameters, schemes, embedded headers) are sufficiently distinct, and these parameters are not used as part of AOR comparisons when forwarding a new request. Since RFC 3261 mandates that all URI parameters must be removed from a URI before looking it up in a location service and that the URIs from the Contact header field are compared using URI equality, the following registration should be sufficient to set up this attack using a single REGISTER request to a single account:

```
REGISTER sip:P1 SIP/2.0
To: <sip:a@P1>
Contact: <sip:a@P1;unknown-param=whack>,
<sip:a@P1;unknown-param=thud>
```

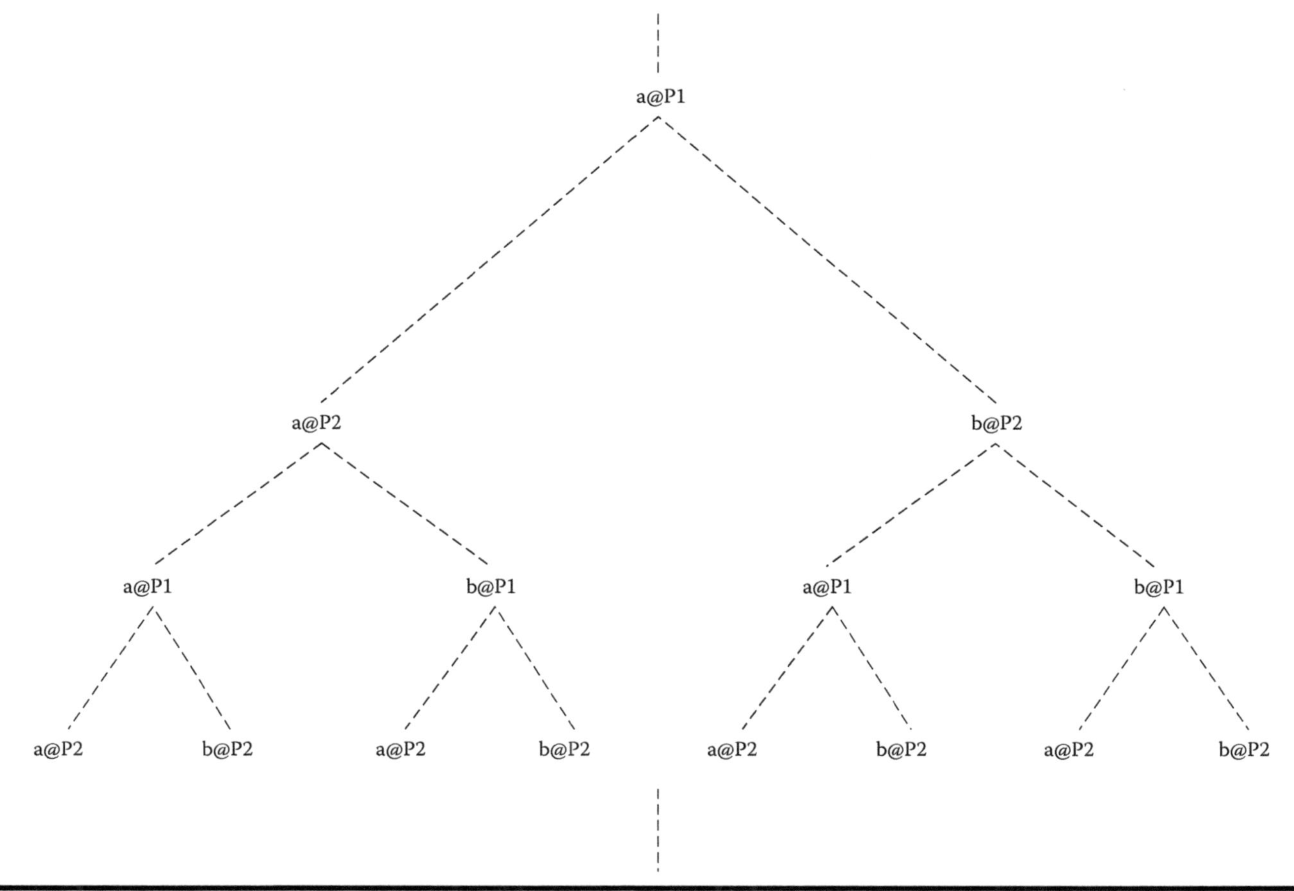

Figure 19.28 Attack request propagation. (Copyright IETF. Reproduced with permission.)

This attack was realized in practice during one of the SIP Interoperability Test (SIPit) sessions. The scenario was extended to include more than two proxies, and the participating proxies all limited Max-Forwards to be no larger than 20. After a handful of messages to construct the attack, the participating proxies began bombarding each other. Extrapolating from the several hours the experiment was allowed to run, the scenario would have completed in just under 10 days. Had the proxies used the RFC 3261-recommended Max-Forwards value of 70, and assuming they performed linearly as the state they held increased, it would have taken 3 trillion years to complete the processing of the single INVITE request that initiated the attack. It is interesting to note that a few proxies rebooted during the scenario and rejoined the attack when they restarted (as long as they maintained registration state across reboots). This points out that if this attack were launched on the Internet at large, it might require coordination among all the affected elements to stop it. Loop detection, as specified in this document, at any of the proxies in the scenarios described thus far, would have stopped the attack immediately. (If all the proxies involved implemented this loop detection, the total number of stimulated messages in the first scenario described would be reduced to 14; in the variation involving one server, the number of stimulated messages would be reduced to 10.)

However, there is a variant of the attack that uses multiple AORs where loop detection alone is insufficient protection. In this variation, each participating AOR forks to all the other participating AORs. For small numbers of participating AORs (e.g., 10), paths through the resulting tree will not loop until very large numbers of messages that have been generated. Acquiring a sufficient number of AORs to launch such an attack on networks currently available is quite feasible. In this scenario, requests will often take many hops to complete a loop, and there are a very large number of different loops that will occur during the attack. In fact, if N is the number of participating AORs, and provided N is less than or equal to Max-Forwards, the amount of traffic generated by the attack is greater than $N!$, even if all proxies involved are performing loop detection. Suppose we have a set of N AORs, all of which are set up to fork to the entire set. For clarity, assume AOR 1 is where the attack begins. Every permutation of the remaining N − 1 AORs will play out, defining $(N - 1)!$ distinct paths, without repeating any AOR. Then, each of these paths will fork N ways one last time, and a loop will be detected on each of these branches. These final

Table 19.1 Forwarded Requests versus Number of Participating AORs

N	*Requests*
1	1
2	4
3	15
4	64
5	325
6	1956
7	13,699
8	109,600
9	986,409
10	9,864,100

branches alone total *N*! requests ((*N* – 1)! paths, with *N* forks at the end of each path; see Table 19.1).

In a network where all proxies are performing loop detection, an attacker is still afforded rapidly increasing returns on the number of AORs they are able to leverage. The Max-Breadth mechanism defined in this document is designed to limit the effectiveness of this variation of the attack. In all of the scenarios, it is important to notice that at each forking proxy, an additional branch could be added pointing to a single victim (that might not even be a SIP-aware element), resulting in a massive amount of traffic being directed toward the victim from potentially as many sources as there are AORs participating in the attack.

19.9.3 Security Considerations

RFC 5393 is entirely about documenting and addressing a vulnerability in SIP proxies as defined by RFC 3261 that can lead to an exponentially growing message exchange attack. The Max-Breadth mechanism defined by RFC 5393 (see Section 9.11.2) does not decrease the aggregate traffic caused by the forking-loop attack. It only serves to spread the traffic caused by the attack over a longer period by limiting the number of concurrent branches that are being processed at the same time. An attacker could pump multiple requests into a network that uses the Max-Breadth mechanism and gradually build traffic to unreasonable levels. Deployments should monitor carefully and react to gradual increases in the number of concurrent outstanding transactions related to a given resource to protect against this possibility. Operators should anticipate being able to temporarily disable any resources identified as being used in such an attack. A rapid increase in outstanding concurrent transactions system-wide may be an indication of the presence of this kind of attack across many resources. Deployments in which it is feasible for an attacker to obtain a very large number of resources are particularly at risk. If detecting and intervening in each instance of the attack is insufficient to reduce the load, overload may occur.

Implementers and operators are encouraged to follow the recommendations being developed for requirements and design for management of overload in SIP handling overload conditions specified in RFCs 5390 (see Section 13.3.9) and 6357, respectively. However, RFC 7339 specifies (see Section 13.3) actual standards extending RFC 3261 for overload control in SIP. Designers of protocol gateways should consider the implications of this kind of attack carefully. As an example, if a message transits from a SIP network into the PSTN and subsequently back into a SIP network, and information about the history of the request on either side of the protocol translation is lost, it becomes possible to construct loops that neither Max-Forwards nor loop detection can protect against.

This, combined with forking amplification on the SIP side of the loop, will result in an attack as described in this document that the mechanisms here will not abate, not even to the point of limiting the number of concurrent messages in the attack. These considerations are particularly important for designers of gateways from SIP to SIP (e.g., as found in B2BUAs). Many existing B2BUA implementations are under some pressure to hide as much information about the two sides communicating with them as possible. Implementers of such implementations may be tempted to remove the data that might be used by the loop-detection, Max-Forwards, or Max-Breadth mechanisms at other points in the network, taking on the responsibility for detecting loops (or forms of this attack). However, if two such implementations are involved in the attack, neither will be able to detect it. In addition, to limit the total number of concurrence branches caused by a forked SIP request, RFC 5393 that is described in this section provides some guidance for intelligent use of the Via header and enhances the loop detection algorithm defined in RFC 3261 (see Sections 3.11.3, 3.11.4, and 9.11).

19.10 Nonrepudiation Services in SIP

Nonrepudiation is a huge necessity in SIP both for private and government domain because of most essential services that are offered using SIP. For example, billing, call/media content tracing/interception, and many other services related to the real-time multimedia applications that are being used by users may demand nonrepudiation services for the business, government, and legal reasons. SIP has a complete set of security mechanisms for both the session and the media level for real-time networked multimedia applications that consist of one or many media such as audio, video, or data applications. SIP/SDP/RTP RFCs such as 3261, 3329, 5379, 3323, 4568, 5029, 5939, 3171, 6191, and others support authentication (see Section 19.4), authorization (see Section 19.5), integrity (see Section 19.6), confidentiality (see Section 19.6), and privacy/anonymity (see Chapter 20), and as described earlier.

We have also illustrated earlier that SIP RFCs like 3261, 4347, and others recommend TLS and DTLS for transport-related security based on which SIP signaling and media traffic are transferred. In addition, S/MIME-based certificates and key exchanges are described earlier in detail (see Section 19.6). In SIP, nonrepudiation that is a value-added service can be built on the top of the basic SIP authentication/authorization, integrity, confidentiality, and privacy (see Chapter 20) standards. RFC 4740 has described how the SIP-based applications can use the DIAMETER protocol for Authentication, Authorization, and Accounting (AAA) services. Thus, we have left it to the implementers as an option to create their own nonrepudiation services.

19.11 Call Flows Explaining SIP Security Features

RFC 3261 provides some call flow examples articulating the security features in SIP. We have included those in the following section often omitting the message body and the corresponding Content-Length and Content-Type header fields for brevity.

19.11.1 Registration

Let us assume Bob registers on start-up. The message flow is shown in Figure 19.29. Note that the authentication usually required for registration is not shown for simplicity. Bob registers his softphone at the registration server (biloxi.com).

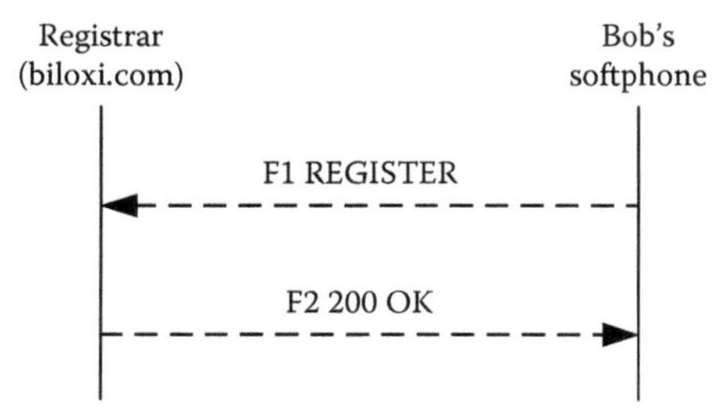

Figure 19.29 SIP registration example.

F1 REGISTER Bob -> Registrar

```
REGISTER sip:registrar.biloxi.com SIP/2.0
Via: SIP/2.0/UDP bobspc.biloxi.com:
5060;branch=z9hG4bKnashds7
Max-Forwards: 70
To: Bob <sip:bob@biloxi.com>
From: Bob <sip:bob@biloxi.com>;tag=456248
Call-ID: 843817637684230@998sdasdh09
CSeq: 1826 REGISTER
Contact: <sip:bob@192.0.2.4>
Expires: 7200
Content-Length: 0
```

The registration expires after 2 hours. The registrar responds with a 200 OK:

F2 200 OK Registrar -> Bob

```
SIP/2.0 200 OK
Via: SIP/2.0/UDP bobspc.biloxi.com:
5060;branch=z9hG4bKnashds7
;received=192.0.2.4
To: Bob <sip:bob@biloxi.com>;tag=2493k59kd
From: Bob <sip:bob@biloxi.com>;tag=456248
Call-ID: 843817637684230@998sdasdh09
CSeq: 1826 REGISTER
Contact: <sip:bob@192.0.2.4>
Expires: 7200
Content-Length: 0
```

19.11.2 Session Setup

This example contains the full details of the example session setup in Section 3.7. The message flow is shown in Figure 3.9 of Section 3.7.1. Note that these flows show the minimum required set of header fields—some other header fields such as Allow and Supported would normally be present.

F1 INVITE Alice -> atlanta.com proxy

```
INVITE sip:bob@biloxi.com SIP/2.0
Via: SIP/2.0/UDP pc33.atlanta.com;
branch=z9hG4bKnashds8
Max-Forwards: 70
To: Bob <sip:bob@biloxi.com>
From: Alice <sip:alice@atlanta.com>;
tag=1928301774
Call-ID: a84b4c76e66710
CSeq: 314159 INVITE
Contact: <sip:alice@pc33.atlanta.com>
Content-Type: application/sdp
Content-Length: 142
(Alice's SDP not shown)
```

F2 100 Trying atlanta.com proxy -> Alice

```
SIP/2.0 100 Trying
Via: SIP/2.0/UDP pc33.atlanta.com;
branch=z9hG4bKnashds8
```

```
;received=192.0.2.1
To: Bob <sip:bob@biloxi.com>
From: Alice <sip:alice@atlanta.com>;
tag=1928301774
Call-ID: a84b4c76e66710
CSeq: 314159 INVITE
Content-Length: 0
```

F3 INVITE atlanta.com proxy -> biloxi.com proxy

```
INVITE sip:bob@biloxi.com SIP/2.0
Via: SIP/2.0/UDP bigbox3.site3.atlanta.com;
branch=z9hG4bK77ef4c2312983.1
Via: SIP/2.0/UDP pc33.atlanta.com;
branch=z9hG4bKnashds8
;received=192.0.2.1
Max-Forwards: 69
To: Bob <sip:bob@biloxi.com>
From: Alice <sip:alice@atlanta.com>;
tag=1928301774
Call-ID: a84b4c76e66710
CSeq: 314159 INVITE
Contact: <sip:alice@pc33.atlanta.com>
Content-Type: application/sdp
Content-Length: 142
(Alice's SDP not shown)
```

F4 100 Trying biloxi.com proxy -> atlanta.com proxy

```
SIP/2.0 100 Trying
Via: SIP/2.0/UDP bigbox3.site3.atlanta.com;
branch=z9hG4bK77ef4c2312983.1
;received=192.0.2.2
Via: SIP/2.0/UDP pc33.atlanta.com;
branch=z9hG4bKnashds8
;received=192.0.2.1
To: Bob <sip:bob@biloxi.com>
From: Alice <sip:alice@atlanta.com>;
tag=1928301774
Call-ID: a84b4c76e66710
CSeq: 314159 INVITE
Content-Length: 0
```

F5 INVITE biloxi.com proxy -> Bob

```
INVITE sip:bob@192.0.2.4 SIP/2.0
Via: SIP/2.0/UDP server10.biloxi.com;
branch=z9hG4bK4b43c2ff8.1
Via: SIP/2.0/UDP bigbox3.site3.atlanta.com;
branch=z9hG4bK77ef4c2312983.1
;received=192.0.2.2
Via: SIP/2.0/UDP pc33.atlanta.com;
branch=z9hG4bKnashds8
;received=192.0.2.1
Max-Forwards: 68
To: Bob <sip:bob@biloxi.com>
From: Alice <sip:alice@atlanta.com>;
tag=1928301774
Call-ID: a84b4c76e66710
CSeq: 314159 INVITE
Contact: <sip:alice@pc33.atlanta.com>
Content-Type: application/sdp
Content-Length: 142
(Alice's SDP not shown)
```

F6 180 Ringing Bob -> biloxi.com proxy

```
SIP/2.0 180 Ringing
Via: SIP/2.0/UDP server10.biloxi.com;
branch=z9hG4bK4b43c2ff8.1
;received=192.0.2.3
Via: SIP/2.0/UDP bigbox3.site3.atlanta.com;
branch=z9hG4bK77ef4c2312983.1
;received=192.0.2.2
Via: SIP/2.0/UDP pc33.atlanta.com;
branch=z9hG4bKnashds8
;received=192.0.2.1
To: Bob <sip:bob@biloxi.com>;tag=a6c85cf
From: Alice <sip:alice@atlanta.com>;
tag=1928301774
Call-ID: a84b4c76e66710
Contact: <sip:bob@192.0.2.4>
CSeq: 314159 INVITE
Content-Length: 0
```

F7 180 Ringing biloxi.com proxy -> atlanta.com proxy

```
SIP/2.0 180 Ringing
Via: SIP/2.0/UDP bigbox3.site3.atlanta.com;
branch=z9hG4bK77ef4c2312983.1
;received=192.0.2.2
Via: SIP/2.0/UDP pc33.atlanta.com;
branch=z9hG4bKnashds8
;received=192.0.2.1
To: Bob <sip:bob@biloxi.com>;tag=a6c85cf
From: Alice <sip:alice@atlanta.com>;
tag=1928301774
Call-ID: a84b4c76e66710
Contact: <sip:bob@192.0.2.4>
CSeq: 314159 INVITE
Content-Length: 0
```

F8 180 Ringing atlanta.com proxy -> Alice

```
SIP/2.0 180 Ringing
Via: SIP/2.0/UDP pc33.atlanta.com;
branch=z9hG4bKnashds8
;received=192.0.2.1
To: Bob <sip:bob@biloxi.com>;tag=a6c85cf
From: Alice <sip:alice@atlanta.com>;
tag=1928301774
Call-ID: a84b4c76e66710
Contact: <sip:bob@192.0.2.4>
CSeq: 314159 INVITE
Content-Length: 0
```

F9 200 OK Bob -> biloxi.com proxy

```
SIP/2.0 200 OK
Via: SIP/2.0/UDP server10.biloxi.com;
branch=z9hG4bK4b43c2ff8.1
;received=192.0.2.3
```

```
Via: SIP/2.0/UDP bigbox3.site3.atlanta.com;
branch=z9hG4bK77ef4c2312983.1
;received=192.0.2.2
Via: SIP/2.0/UDP pc33.atlanta.com;
branch=z9hG4bKnashds8
;received=192.0.2.1
To: Bob <sip:bob@biloxi.com>;tag=a6c85cf
From: Alice <sip:alice@atlanta.com>;
tag=1928301774
Call-ID: a84b4c76e66710
CSeq: 314159 INVITE
Contact: <sip:bob@192.0.2.4>
Content-Type: application/sdp
Content-Length: 131
(Bob's SDP not shown)
```

F10 200 OK biloxi.com proxy -> atlanta.com proxy

```
SIP/2.0 200 OK
Via: SIP/2.0/UDP bigbox3.site3.atlanta.com;
branch=z9hG4bK77ef4c2312983.1
;received=192.0.2.2
Via: SIP/2.0/UDP pc33.atlanta.com;
branch=z9hG4bKnashds8
;received=192.0.2.1
To: Bob <sip:bob@biloxi.com>;tag=a6c85cf
From: Alice <sip:alice@atlanta.com>;
tag=1928301774
Call-ID: a84b4c76e66710
CSeq: 314159 INVITE
Contact: <sip:bob@192.0.2.4>
Content-Type: application/sdp
Content-Length: 131
(Bob's SDP not shown)
```

F11 200 OK atlanta.com proxy -> Alice

```
SIP/2.0 200 OK
Via: SIP/2.0/UDP pc33.atlanta.com;
branch=z9hG4bKnashds8
;received=192.0.2.1
To: Bob <sip:bob@biloxi.com>;tag=a6c85cf
From: Alice <sip:alice@atlanta.com>;
tag=1928301774
Call-ID: a84b4c76e66710
CSeq: 314159 INVITE
Contact: <sip:bob@192.0.2.4>
Content-Type: application/sdp
Content-Length: 131
(Bob's SDP not shown)
```

F12 ACK Alice -> Bob

```
ACK sip:bob@192.0.2.4 SIP/2.0
Via: SIP/2.0/UDP pc33.atlanta.com;
branch=z9hG4bKnashds9
Max-Forwards: 70
To: Bob <sip:bob@biloxi.com>;tag=a6c85cf
From: Alice <sip:alice@atlanta.com>;
tag=1928301774
Call-ID: a84b4c76e66710
CSeq: 314159 ACK
Content-Length: 0
```

The media session between Alice and Bob is now established. Bob hangs up first. Note that Bob's SIP phone maintains its own CSeq numbering space, which, in this example, begins with 231. Since Bob is making the request, the To and From URIs and tags have been swapped.

F13 BYE Bob -> Alice

```
BYE sip:alice@pc33.atlanta.com SIP/2.0
Via: SIP/2.0/UDP 192.0.2.4;branch=z9hG4bKnas
hds10
Max-Forwards: 70
From: Bob <sip:bob@biloxi.com>;tag=a6c85cf
To: Alice <sip:alice@atlanta.com>;
tag=1928301774
Call-ID: a84b4c76e66710
CSeq: 231 BYE
Content-Length: 0
```

F14 200 OK Alice -> Bob

```
SIP/2.0 200 OK
Via: SIP/2.0/UDP 192.0.2.4;branch=z9hG4bKnas
hds10
From: Bob <sip:bob@biloxi.com>;tag=a6c85cf
To: Alice <sip:alice@atlanta.com>;
tag=1928301774
Call-ID: a84b4c76e66710
CSeq: 231 BYE
Content-Length: 0
```

19.12 Threat Model and Security Usage Recommendations in SIP

RFC 3261 explains in great detail that SIP is not an easy protocol to secure. Its use of intermediaries, its multifaceted trust relationships, its expected usage between elements with no trust at all, and its user-to-user operation make security far from trivial. All description of SIP threat model and security recommendation described here is from RFC 3261. Security solutions are needed that are deployable today, without extensive coordination, in a wide variety of environments and usages. To meet these diverse needs, several distinct mechanisms applicable to different aspects and usages of SIP will be required. Note that the security of SIP signaling itself has no bearing on the security of protocols used in concert with SIP such as RTP, or with the security implications of any specific bodies SIP might carry (although MIME security plays a substantial role in securing SIP).

Any media associated with a session can be encrypted end-to-end independently of any associated SIP signaling.

Media encryption is beyond the scope of this chapter. The considerations that follow first examine a set of classic threat models that broadly identify the security needs of SIP. The set of security services required to address these threats is then detailed, followed by an explanation of several security mechanisms that can be used to provide these services. Next, the requirements for implementers of SIP are enumerated, along with exemplary deployments in which these security mechanisms could be used to improve the security of SIP. Some notes on privacy conclude this section.

19.12.1 Attacks and Threat Models

This section details some threats that should be common to most deployments of SIP. These threats have been chosen specifically to illustrate each of the security services that SIP requires. The following examples by no means provide an exhaustive list of the threats against SIP; rather, these are classic threats that demonstrate the need for particular security services that can potentially prevent whole categories of threats. These attacks assume an environment in which attackers can potentially read any packet on the network—it is anticipated that SIP will frequently be used on the public Internet. Attackers on the network may be able to modify packets (perhaps at some compromised intermediary). Attackers may wish to steal services, eavesdrop on communications, or disrupt sessions.

19.12.1.1 Registration Hijacking

The SIP registration mechanism allows a UA to identify itself to a registrar as a device at which a user (designated by an AOR) is located. A registrar assesses the identity asserted in the From header field of a REGISTER message to determine whether this request can modify the contact addresses associated with the AOR in the To header field. While these two fields are frequently the same, there are many valid deployments in which a third-party may register contacts on a user's behalf. The From header field of a SIP request, however, can be modified arbitrarily by the owner of a UA, and this opens the door to malicious registrations. An attacker that successfully impersonates a party authorized to change contacts associated with an AOR could, for example, deregister all existing contacts for a URI and then register their own device as the appropriate contact address, thereby directing all requests for the affected user to the attacker's device.

This threat belongs to a family of threats that rely on the absence of cryptographic assurance of a request's originator. Any SIP UAS that represents a valuable service (e.g., a gateway that interworks SIP requests with traditional telephone calls) might want to control access to its resources by authenticating requests that it receives. Even end-user UAs, for example, SIP phones, have an interest in ascertaining the identities of originators of requests. This threat demonstrates the need for security services that enable SIP entities to authenticate the originators of requests.

19.12.1.2 Impersonating a Server

The domain to which a request is destined is generally specified in the Request-URI. UAs commonly contact a server in this domain directly in order to deliver a request. However, there is always a possibility that an attacker could impersonate the remote server, and that the UA's request could be intercepted by some other party. For example, consider a case in which a redirect server at one domain, chicago.com, impersonates a redirect server at another domain, biloxi.com. A UA sends a request to biloxi.com, but the redirect server at chicago.com answers with a forged response that has appropriate SIP header fields for a response from biloxi.com. The forged contact addresses in the redirection response could direct the originating UA to inappropriate or insecure resources, or simply prevent requests for biloxi.com from succeeding.

This family of threats has a vast membership, many of which are critical. As a converse to the registration hijacking threat, consider the case in which a registration sent to biloxi.com is intercepted by chicago.com, which replies to the intercepted registration with a forged 301 Moved Permanently response. This response might seem to come from biloxi.com yet designate chicago.com as the appropriate registrar. All future REGISTER requests from the originating UA would then go to chicago.com. Prevention of this threat requires a means by which UAs can authenticate the servers to whom they send requests.

19.12.1.3 Tampering with Message Bodies

As a matter of course, SIP UAs route requests through trusted proxy servers. Regardless of how that trust is established (authentication of proxies is discussed elsewhere in this section), a UA may trust a proxy server to route a request, but not to inspect or possibly modify the bodies contained in that request. Consider a UA that is using SIP message bodies to communicate session encryption keys for a media session. Although it trusts the proxy server of the domain it is contacting to deliver signaling properly, it may not want the administrators of that domain to be capable of decrypting any subsequent media session. Worse yet, if the proxy server were actively malicious, it could modify the session key, either acting as an MITM, or perhaps changing the security characteristics requested by the originating UA.

This family of threats applies not only to session keys, but also to most conceivable forms of content carried end-to-end in SIP. These might include MIME bodies that should be rendered to the user, SDP, or encapsulated telephony signals, among others. Attackers might attempt to modify SDP bodies, for example, in order to point RTP media streams to a wiretapping device in order to eavesdrop on subsequent voice communications. Also note that some header fields in SIP are meaningful end-to-end, for example, Subject. UAs might be protective of these header fields as well as bodies (a malicious intermediary changing the Subject header field might make an important request appear to be spam, for example). However, since many header fields are legitimately inspected or altered by proxy servers as a request is routed, not all header fields should be secured end-to-end. For these reasons, the UA might want to secure SIP message bodies, and in some limited cases header fields, end-to-end. The security services required for bodies include confidentiality, integrity, and authentication. These end-to-end services should be independent of the means used to secure interactions with intermediaries such as proxy servers.

19.12.1.4 Tearing Down Sessions

Once a dialog has been established by initial messaging, subsequent requests can be sent that modify the state of the dialog or session. It is critical that principals in a session can be certain that such requests are not forged by attackers. Consider a case in which a third-party attacker captures some initial messages in a dialog shared by two parties in order to learn the parameters of the session (To tag, From tag, and so forth) and then inserts a BYE request into the session. The attacker could opt to forge the request such that it seemed to come from either participant. Once the BYE is received by its target, the session will be torn down prematurely.

Similar midsession threats include the transmission of forged re-INVITEs that alter the session (possibly to reduce session security or redirect media streams as part of a wiretapping attack). The most effective countermeasure to this threat is the authentication of the sender of the BYE. In this instance, the recipient needs only to know that the BYE came from the same party with whom the corresponding dialog was established (as opposed to ascertaining the absolute identity of the sender). Also, if the attacker is unable to learn the parameters of the session due to confidentiality, it would not be possible to forge the BYE. However, some intermediaries (like proxy servers) will need to inspect those parameters as the session is established.

19.12.1.5 DoS and Amplification

DoS attacks focus on rendering a particular network element unavailable, usually by directing an excessive amount of network traffic at its interfaces. A distributed DoS attack allows one network user to cause multiple network hosts to flood a target host with a large amount of network traffic. In many architectures, SIP proxy servers face the public Internet in order to accept requests from worldwide IP end points. SIP creates a number of potential opportunities for distributed DoS attacks that must be recognized and addressed by the implementers and operators of SIP systems.

Attackers can create bogus requests that contain a falsified source IP address and a corresponding Via header field that identify a targeted host as the originator of the request, and then send this request to a large number of SIP network elements, thereby using hapless SIP UAs or proxies to generate DoS traffic aimed at the target. Similarly, attackers might use falsified Route header field values in a request that identify the target host and then send such messages to forking proxies that will amplify messaging sent to the target. Record-Route could be used to a similar effect when the attacker is certain that the SIP dialog initiated by the request will result in numerous transactions originating in the backwards direction.

A number of DoS attacks open up if REGISTER requests are not properly authenticated and authorized by registrars. Attackers could deregister some or all users in an administrative domain, thereby preventing these users from being invited to new sessions. An attacker could also register a large number of contacts designating the same host for a given AOR in order to use the registrar and any associated proxy servers as amplifiers in a DoS attack. Attackers might also attempt to deplete available memory and disk resources of a registrar by registering huge numbers of bindings. The use of multicast to transmit SIP requests can greatly increase the potential for DoS attacks. These problems demonstrate a general need to define architectures that minimize the risks of DoS, and the need to be mindful in recommendations for security mechanisms of this class of attacks.

19.12.2 Security Mechanisms

From the threats described above, we gather that the fundamental security services required for the SIP protocol are as follows: preserving the confidentiality and integrity of messaging, preventing replay attacks or message spoofing, providing for the authentication and privacy of the participants in a session, and preventing DoS attacks. Bodies within SIP messages separately require the security services of confidentiality, integrity, and authentication. Rather than defining new security mechanisms specific to SIP, SIP reuses, wherever possible, existing security models derived from the HTTP and Simple Mail Transfer Protocol (SMTP) space.

Full encryption of messages provides the best means to preserve the confidentiality of signaling—it can also guarantee that messages are not modified by any malicious intermediaries. However, SIP requests and responses cannot be naively encrypted end-to-end in their entirety because message fields such as the Request-URI, Route, and Via need to be visible to proxies in most network architectures so that SIP requests are routed correctly. Note that proxy servers need to modify some features of messages as well (such as adding Via header field values) in order SIP to function. Proxy servers must therefore be trusted, to some degree, by SIP UAs. To this purpose, low-layer security mechanisms for SIP are recommended, which encrypt the entire SIP requests or responses on the wire on a hop-by-hop basis, and that allow end points to verify the identity of proxy servers to whom they send requests.

SIP entities also have a need to identify one another in a secure fashion. When a SIP end point asserts the identity of its user to a peer UA or to a proxy server, that identity should in some way be verifiable. A cryptographic authentication mechanism is provided in SIP to address this requirement. An independent security mechanism for SIP message bodies supplies an alternative means of end-to-end mutual authentication, as well as provides a limit on the degree to which UAs must trust intermediaries.

19.12.2.1 Transport- and Network-Layer Security

Transport- or network-layer security encrypts signaling traffic, guaranteeing message confidentiality and integrity. Oftentimes, certificates are used in the establishment of lower-layer security, and these certificates can also be used to provide a means of authentication in many architectures. Two popular alternatives for providing security at the transport and network layer are, respectively, TLS defined in RFC 4346 and IPSec specified in RFC 4301. IPSec is a set of network-layer protocol tools that collectively can be used as a secure replacement for traditional IP. IPSec is most commonly used in architectures in which a set of hosts or administrative domains have an existing trust relationship with one another. IPSec is usually implemented at the operating system level in a host, or on a security gateway that provides confidentiality and integrity for all traffic it receives from a particular interface as in a virtual private network (VPN) architecture. IPSec can also be used on a hop-by-hop basis.

In many architectures, IPSec does not require integration with SIP applications; IPSec is perhaps best suited to deployments in which adding security directly to SIP hosts would be arduous. UAs that have a preshared keying relationship with their first-hop proxy server are also good candidates to use IPSec. Any deployment of IPSec for SIP would require an IPSec profile describing the protocol tools that would be required to secure SIP. No such profile is given in this document. TLS provides transport-layer security over connection-oriented protocols (for the purposes of this document, TCP); tls (signifying TLS over TCP) can be specified as the desired transport protocol within a Via header field value or a SIP-URI. TLS is most suited to architectures in which hop-by-hop security is required between hosts with no preexisting trust association. For example, Alice trusts her local proxy server, which, after a certificate exchange, decides to trust Bob's local proxy server, which Bob trusts; hence, Bob and Alice can communicate securely.

TLS must be tightly coupled with a SIP application. Note that transport mechanisms are specified on a hop-by-hop basis in SIP; thus, a UA that sends requests over TLS to a proxy server has no assurance that TLS will be used end-to-end. The TLSffRSAffWITHffAESff128ffCBCffSHA ciphersuite defined in RFC 5246 must be supported at a minimum by implementers when TLS is used in a SIP application. For purposes of backwards compatibility, proxy servers, redirect servers, and registrars should support TLSffRSAffWITHff3DESffEDEffCBCffSHA. Implementers may also support any other ciphersuite.

19.12.2.2 SIPS URI Scheme

The SIPS URI scheme adheres to the syntax of the SIP URI (see Section 4.2), although the scheme string is sips rather than sip. The semantics of SIPS are very different from the SIP URI, however. SIPS allows resources to specify that they should be reached securely. A SIPS URI can be used as an AOR for a particular user—the URI by which the user is canonically known (on their business cards, in the From header field of their requests, in the To header field of REGISTER requests). When used as the Request-URI of a request, the SIPS scheme signifies that each hop over which the request is forwarded, until the request reaches the SIP entity responsible for the domain portion of the Request-URI, must be secured with TLS; once it reaches the domain in question, it is handled in accordance with local security and routing policy, quite possibly using TLS for any last hop to a UAS. When used by the originator of a request (as would be the case if they employed a SIPS URI as the AOR of the target), SIPS dictates that the entire request path to the target domain be so secured. The SIPS scheme is applicable to many of the other ways in which SIP URIs are used in SIP today in addition to the Request-URI, including in AORs, contact addresses (the contents of Contact headers, including those of REGISTER methods), and Route headers.

In each instance, the SIPS URI scheme allows these existing fields to designate secure resources. The manner in which a SIPS URI is dereferenced in any of these contexts has its own security properties, which are detailed in RFC 3263 (see Section 8.2.4). The use of

SIPS in particular entails that mutual TLS authentication should be employed, as should the ciphersuite TLSffRSAffWITHffAESff128ffCBCffSHA. Certificates received in the authentication process should be validated with root certificates held by the client; failure to validate a certificate should result in the failure of the request. Note that in the SIPS URI scheme, transport is independent of TLS, and thus sips:alice@atlanta.com;transport=tcp and sips:alice@atlanta.com;transport=sctp are both valid (although note that UDP is not a valid transport for SIPS). The use of transport=tls has consequently been deprecated, partly because it was specific to a single hop of the request. This is a change since RFC 2543 (obsoleted by RFC 3261). Users that distribute a SIPS URI as an AOR may elect to operate devices that refuse requests over insecure transports.

19.12.2.3 HTTP Authentication

SIP provides a challenge capability, based on HTTP authentication that relies on the 401 and 407 response codes as well as header fields for carrying challenges and credentials. Without significant modification, the reuse of the HTTP Digest authentication scheme in SIP allows for replay protection and one-way authentication. The usage of Digest authentication in SIP is detailed Section 19.4.

19.12.2.4 S/MIME

As is discussed above, encrypting entire SIP messages end-to-end for the purpose of confidentiality is not appropriate because network intermediaries (like proxy servers) need to view certain header fields in order to route messages correctly, and if these intermediaries are excluded from security associations, then SIP messages will essentially be nonroutable. However, S/MIME allows SIP UAs to encrypt MIME bodies within SIP, securing these bodies end-to-end without affecting message headers. S/MIME can provide end-to-end confidentiality and integrity for message bodies, as well as mutual authentication. It is also possible to use S/MIME to provide a form of integrity and confidentiality for SIP header fields through SIP message tunneling. The usage of S/MIME in SIP is detailed in Section 19.6.

19.12.3 Implementing Security Mechanisms

19.12.3.1 Requirements for Implementers of SIP

Proxy servers, redirect servers, and registrars must implement TLS, and must support both mutual and one-way authentication. It is strongly recommended that UAs be capable of initiating TLS; UAs may also be capable of acting as a TLS server. Proxy servers, redirect servers, and registrars should possess a site certificate whose subject corresponds to their canonical host name. UAs may have certificates of their own for mutual authentication with TLS; however, no provisions are set forth in this document for their use. All SIP elements that support TLS must have a mechanism for validating certificates received during TLS negotiation; this entails possession of one or more root certificates issued by certificate authorities (preferably well-known distributors of site certificates comparable to those that issue root certificates for web browsers). All SIP elements that support TLS must also support the SIPS URI scheme. Proxy servers, redirect servers, registrars, and UAs may also implement IPSec or other lower-layer security protocols. When a UA attempts to contact a proxy server, redirect server, or registrar, the UAC should initiate a TLS connection over which it will send SIP messages.

In some architectures, UASs may receive requests over such TLS connections as well. Proxy servers, redirect servers, registrars, and UAs must implement Digest Authorization, encompassing all related aspects described in Sections 19.5 and 19.6. Proxy servers, redirect servers, and registrars should be configured with at least one Digest realm, and at least one realm string supported by a given server should correspond to the server's host name or domain name. UAs may support the signing and encrypting of MIME bodies, and transference of credentials with S/MIME as described in Section 19.6. If a UA holds one or more root certificates of certificate authorities in order to validate certificates for TLS or IPSec, it should be capable of reusing these to verify S/MIME certificates, as appropriate. A UA may hold root certificates specifically for validating S/MIME certificates. Note that is it anticipated that future security extensions may upgrade the normative strength associated with S/MIME as S/MIME implementations appear and the problem space becomes better understood.

19.12.3.2 Security Solutions

The operation of these security mechanisms in concert can follow the existing web and e-mail security models to some degree. At a high level, UAs authenticate themselves to servers (proxy servers, redirect servers, and registrars) with a Digest user name and password; servers authenticate themselves to UAs one hop away, or to another server one hop away (and vice versa), with a site certificate delivered by TLS. On a peer-to-peer level, UAs trust the network to authenticate one another ordinarily; however, S/MIME can also be used to provide direct authentication when the network does not, or if the network itself is not trusted. The following is an illustrative example in which these security mechanisms are used by various UAs and servers to prevent the sorts of threats described in Section 19.12.1. While implementers and network administrators may follow the normative guidelines given in the remainder of this section, these are provided only as example implementations.

19.12.3.2.1 Registration

When a UA comes online and registers with its local administrative domain, it should establish a TLS connection with its registrar (see Section 3.3, which describes how the UA reaches its registrar). The registrar should offer a certificate to the UA, and the site identified by the certificate must correspond with the domain in which the UA intends to register; for example, if the UA intends to register the AOR alice@atlanta.com, the site certificate must identify a host within the atlanta.com domain (such as sip.atlanta.com). When it receives the TLS certificate message, the UA should verify the certificate and inspect the site identified by the certificate. If the certificate is invalid, revoked, or if it does not identify the appropriate party, the UA must not send the REGISTER message and otherwise proceed with the registration.

When a valid certificate has been provided by the registrar, the UA knows that the registrar is not an attacker who might redirect the UA, steal passwords, or attempt any similar attacks. The UA then creates a REGISTER request that should be addressed to a Request-URI corresponding to the site certificate received from the registrar. When the UA sends the REGISTER request over the existing TLS connection, the registrar should challenge the request with a 401 Proxy Authentication Required response. The realm parameter within the Proxy-Authenticate header field of the response should correspond to the domain previously given by the site certificate. When the UAC receives the challenge, it should either prompt the user for credentials or take an appropriate credential from a keyring corresponding to the realm parameter in the challenge. The user name of this credential should correspond with the userinfo portion of the URI in the To header field of the REGISTER request.

Once the Digest credentials have been inserted into an appropriate Proxy-Authorization header field, the REGISTER should be resubmitted to the registrar. Since the registrar requires the UA to authenticate itself, it would be difficult for an attacker to forge REGISTER requests for the user's AOR. Also note that since the REGISTER is sent over a confidential TLS connection, attackers will not be able to intercept the REGISTER to record credentials for any possible replay attack. Once the registration has been accepted by the registrar, the UA should leave this TLS connection open provided that the registrar also acts as the proxy server to which requests are sent for users in this administrative domain. The existing TLS connection will be reused to deliver incoming requests to the UA that has just completed registration. Because the UA has already authenticated the server on the other side of the TLS connection, all requests that come over this connection are known to have passed through the proxy server—attackers cannot create spoofed requests that appear to have been sent through that proxy server.

19.12.3.2.2 Interdomain Requests

Now let us say that Alice's UA would like to initiate a session with a user in a remote administrative domain, namely bob@biloxi.com. We will also say that the local administrative domain (atlanta.com) has a local outbound proxy. The proxy server that handles inbound requests for an administrative domain may also act as a local outbound proxy; for simplicity's sake, we will assume this to be the case for atlanta.com (otherwise, the UA would initiate a new TLS connection to a separate server at this point). Assuming that the client has completed the registration process described in the preceding section, it should reuse the TLS connection to the local proxy server when it sends an INVITE request to another user. The UA should reuse cached credentials in the INVITE to avoid prompting the user unnecessarily.

When the local outbound proxy server has validated the credentials presented by the UA in the INVITE, it should inspect the Request-URI to determine how the message should be routed as defined in RFC 3263 (see Section 8.2.4). If the *domainname* portion of the Request-URI had corresponded to the local domain (atlanta.com) rather than biloxi.com, then the proxy server would have consulted its location service to determine how best to reach the requested user. Had alice@atlanta.com been attempting to contact, say, alex@atlanta.com, the local proxy would have proxied to the request to the TLS connection Alex had established with the registrar when he registered. Since Alex would receive this request over his authenticated channel, he would be assured that Alice's request had been authorized by the proxy server of the local administrative domain. However, in this instance the Request-URI designates a remote domain.

The local outbound proxy server at atlanta.com should therefore establish a TLS connection with the remote proxy server at biloxi.com. Since both of the participants in this TLS connection are servers that possess site certificates, mutual TLS authentication should occur. Each side of the connection should verify and inspect the certificate of the other, noting the domain name that appears in the certificate for comparison with the header fields of SIP messages. The atlanta.com proxy server, for example, should verify at this stage that the certificate received from the remote side corresponds with the biloxi.com domain. Once it has done so, and TLS negotiation has completed, resulting in a secure channel between the two proxies, the atlanta.com proxy can forward the INVITE request to biloxi.com.

The proxy server at biloxi.com should inspect the certificate of the proxy server at atlanta.com in turn and compare the domain asserted by the certificate with the *domainname* portion of the From header field in the INVITE request. The biloxi proxy may have a strict security policy that requires it to reject requests that do not match the administrative domain from which they have been proxied. Such security policies could be instituted to prevent the SIP equivalent of SMTP open relays that are frequently exploited to generate spam. This policy, however, only guarantees that the request came from the domain it ascribes to itself; it does not allow biloxi.com to ascertain how atlanta.com authenticated Alice. Only if biloxi.com has some other way of knowing atlanta.com's authentication policies could it possibly ascertain how Alice proved her identity. biloxi.com might then institute an even stricter policy that forbids requests that come from domains that are not known administratively to share a common authentication policy with biloxi.com. Once the INVITE has been approved by the biloxi proxy, the proxy server should identify the existing TLS channel, if any, associated with the user targeted by this request (in this case bob@biloxi.com).

The INVITE should be proxied through this channel to Bob. Since the request is received over a TLS connection that had previously been authenticated as the biloxi proxy, Bob knows that the From header field was not tampered with and that atlanta.com has validated Alice, although not necessarily whether or not to trust Alice's identity. Before they forward the request, both proxy servers should add a Record-Route header field to the request so that all future requests in this dialog will pass through the proxy servers. The proxy servers can thereby continue to provide security services for the lifetime of this dialog. If the proxy servers do not add themselves to the Record-Route, future messages will pass directly end-to-end between Alice and Bob without any security services (unless the two parties agree on some independent end-to-end security such as S/MIME). In this respect, the SIP trapezoid model can provide a good structure where conventions of agreement between the site proxies can provide a reasonably secure channel between Alice and Bob. An attacker preying on this architecture would, for example, be unable to forge a BYE request and insert it into the signaling stream between Bob and Alice because the attacker has no way of ascertaining the parameters of the session and also because the integrity mechanism transitively protects the traffic between Alice and Bob.

19.12.3.2.3 Peer-to-Peer Requests

Alternatively, consider a UA asserting the identity carol@chicago.com that has no local outbound proxy. When Carol wishes to send an INVITE to bob@biloxi.com, her UA should initiate a TLS connection with the biloxi proxy directly (using the mechanism described in RFC 3263 [see Section 8.2.4] to determine how to best to reach the given Request-URI). When her UA receives a certificate from the biloxi proxy, it should be verified normally before she passes her INVITE across the TLS connection. However, Carol has no means of proving her identity to the biloxi proxy, but she does have a CMS-detached signature over a message/sip body in the INVITE. It is unlikely in this instance that Carol would have any credentials in the biloxi.com realm, since she has no formal association with biloxi.com. The biloxi proxy may also have a strict policy that precludes it from even bothering to challenge requests that do not have biloxi.com in the *domainname* portion of the From header field—it treats these users as unauthenticated.

The biloxi proxy has a policy for Bob that all nonauthenticated requests should be redirected to the appropriate contact address registered against bob@biloxi.com, namely <sip:bob@192.0.2.4>. Carol receives the redirection response over the TLS connection she established with the biloxi proxy, so she trusts the veracity of the contact address. Carol should then establish a TCP connection with the designated address and send a new INVITE with a Request-URI containing the received contact address (recomputing the signature in the body as the request is readied). Bob receives this INVITE on an insecure interface, but his UA inspects and, in this instance, recognizes the From header field of the request and subsequently matches a locally cached certificate with the one presented in the signature of the body of the INVITE. He replies in similar fashion, authenticating himself to Carol, and a secure dialog begins. Sometimes, firewalls or network address translators in an administrative domain could preclude the establishment of a direct TCP connection to a UA. In these cases, proxy servers could also potentially relay requests to UAs in a way that has no trust implications (e.g., forgoing an existing TLS connection and forwarding the request over cleartext TCP) as local policy dictates.

19.12.3.2.4 DoS Protection

To minimize the risk of a DoS attack against architectures using these security solutions, implementers should take note of the following guidelines. When the host on which a SIP proxy server is operating is routable from the public Internet, it should be deployed in an administrative domain with defensive operational policies (blocking source-routed traffic, preferably filtering ping traffic). Both TLS and IPSec can also make use of bastion hosts at the edges of administrative domains that participate in the security associations to aggregate secure tunnels and sockets. These bastion hosts can also take the brunt of DoS attacks, ensuring that SIP hosts within the administrative domain are not encumbered with superfluous messaging.

No matter what security solutions are deployed, floods of messages directed at proxy servers can lock up proxy server resources and prevent desirable traffic from reaching its destination. There is a computational expense associated with processing a SIP transaction at a proxy server, and that expense is greater for stateful proxy servers than it is for stateless proxy servers. Therefore, stateful proxies are more susceptible to flooding than stateless proxy servers. UAs and proxy servers should challenge questionable requests with only a single 401 Unauthorized or 407 Proxy Authentication Required, forgoing the normal response retransmission algorithm, and thus behaving statelessly toward unauthenticated requests. Retransmitting the 401 Unauthorized or 407 Proxy Authentication Required status response amplifies the problem of an attacker using a falsified header field value (such as Via) to direct traffic to a third party. In summary, the mutual authentication of proxy servers through mechanisms such as TLS significantly reduces the potential for rogue intermediaries to introduce falsified requests or responses that can deny service. This commensurately makes it harder for attackers to make innocent SIP nodes into agents of amplification.

19.12.4 Limitations

Although these security mechanisms, when applied in a judicious manner, can thwart many threats, there are limitations in the scope of the mechanisms that must be understood by implementers and network operators.

19.12.4.1 HTTP Digest

One of the primary limitations of using HTTP Digest in SIP is that the integrity mechanisms in Digest do not work very well for SIP. Specifically, they offer protection of the Request-URI and the method of a message, but not for any of the header fields that UAs would most likely wish to secure. The existing replay protection mechanisms described in RFC 2617 also have some limitations for SIP. The next-nonce mechanism, for example, does not support pipelined requests. The nonce-count mechanism should be used for replay protection.

Another limitation of HTTP Digest is the scope of realms. Digest is valuable when users want to authenticate themselves to a resource with which they have a preexisting association, like a service provider of which the user is a customer (which is quite a common scenario and thus Digest provides an extremely useful function). By way of contrast, the scope of TLS is interdomain or multirealm, since certificates are often globally verifiable, so that the UA can authenticate the server with no preexisting association.

19.12.4.2 S/MIME

The largest outstanding defect with the S/MIME mechanism is the lack of a prevalent public key infrastructure for end users. If self-signed certificates (or certificates that cannot be verified by one of the participants in a dialog) are used, the SIP-based key exchange mechanism described in Section 19.6 is susceptible to an MITM attack with which an attacker can potentially inspect and modify S/MIME bodies. The attacker needs to intercept the first exchange of keys between the two parties in a dialog, remove the existing CMS-detached signatures from the request and response, and insert a different CMS-detached signature containing a certificate supplied by the attacker (but which seems to be a certificate for the proper AOR). Each party will think they have exchanged keys with the other, when in fact each has the public key of the attacker.

It is important to note that the attacker can only leverage this vulnerability on the first exchange of keys between two parties; on subsequent occasions, the alteration of the key would be noticeable to the UAs. It would also be difficult for the attacker to remain in the path of all future dialogs between the two parties over time (as potentially days, weeks, or years pass). SSH is susceptible to the same MITM attack on the first exchange of keys; however, it is widely acknowledged that while SSH is not perfect, it does improve the security of connections. The use of key fingerprints could provide some assistance to SIP, just as it does for SSH. For example, if two parties use SIP to establish a voice communications session, each could read off the fingerprint of the key they received from the other, which could be compared against the original. It would certainly be more difficult for the MITM to emulate the voices of the participants than their signaling (a practice that was used with the Clipper chip-based secure telephone).

The S/MIME mechanism allows UAs to send encrypted requests without preamble if they possess a certificate for the destination AOR on their keying. However, it is possible that any particular device registered for an AOR will not hold the certificate that has been previously employed by the device's current user, and that it will therefore be unable to process an encrypted request properly, which could lead to some avoidable error signaling. This is especially likely when an encrypted request is forked. The keys associated with S/MIME are most useful when associated with a particular user (an AOR) rather than a device (a UA). When users move between devices, it may be difficult to transport private keys securely between UAs; how such keys might be acquired by a device is outside the scope of this document. Another, more prosaic difficulty with the S/MIME mechanism is that it can result in very large messages, especially when the SIP tunneling mechanism described in Section 19.6.4 is used. For that reason, it is recommended that TCP should be used as a transport protocol when S/MIME tunneling is employed.

19.12.4.3 TLS

The most commonly voiced concern about TLS is that it cannot run over UDP; TLS requires a connection-oriented underlying transport protocol, which for the purposes of this document means TCP. It may also be arduous for a local outbound proxy server or registrar to maintain many simultaneous long-lived TLS connections with numerous UAs. This introduces some valid scalability concerns, especially for intensive ciphersuites. Maintaining redundancy of long-lived TLS connections, especially when a UA is solely responsible for their establishment, could also be cumbersome. TLS only allows SIP entities to authenticate servers to which they are adjacent; TLS offers strictly hop-by-hop security. Neither TLS, nor any other mechanism specified in this document, allows clients to authenticate proxy servers to whom they cannot form a direct TCP connection.

19.12.4.4 SIPS URIs

Actually using TLS on every segment of a request path entails that the terminating UAS must be reachable over TLS (perhaps registering with a SIPS URI as a contact address). This is the preferred use of SIPS. Many valid architectures, however, use TLS to secure part of the request path, but rely on some other mechanism for the final hop to a UAS, for example. Thus, SIPS cannot guarantee that TLS usage will be truly end-to-end. Note that since many UAs will not accept incoming TLS connections, even those UAs that do support TLS may be required to maintain persistent TLS connections, as described in Section 19.12.4.3, in order to receive requests over TLS as a UAS. Location services are not required to provide a SIPS binding for a SIPS Request-URI. Although location services are commonly populated by user registrations (as described in Section 3.3), various other protocols and interfaces could conceivably supply contact addresses for an AOR, and these tools are free to map SIPS URIs to SIP URIs as appropriate. When queried for bindings, a location service returns its contact addresses without regard for whether it received a request with a SIPS Request-URI. If a redirect server is accessing the location service, it is up to the entity that processes the Contact header field of a redirection to determine the propriety of the contact addresses.

Ensuring that TLS will be used for all of the request segments up to the target domain is somewhat complex. It is possible that cryptographically authenticated proxy servers along the way that are noncompliant or compromised may choose to disregard the forwarding rules associated with SIPS (and the general forwarding rules in Section 3.11.6). Such malicious intermediaries could, for example, retarget a request from a SIPS URI to a SIP URI in an attempt to downgrade security.

Alternatively, an intermediary might legitimately retarget a request from a SIP to a SIPS URI. Recipients of a request whose Request-URI uses the SIPS URI scheme thus cannot assume on the basis of the Request-URI alone that SIPS was used for the entire request path (from the client onwards). To address these concerns, it is recommended that recipients of a request whose Request-URI contains a SIP or SIPS URI inspect the To header field value to see if it contains a SIPS URI (however, note that it does not constitute a breach of security if this URI has the same scheme but is not equivalent to the URI in the To header field). Although clients may choose to populate the Request-URI and To header field of a request differently, when SIPS is used this disparity could be interpreted as a possible security violation, and the request could consequently be rejected by its recipient. Recipients may also inspect the Via header chain in order to double-check whether or not TLS was used for the entire request path until the local administrative domain was reached. S/MIME may also be used by the originating UAC to help ensure that the original form of the To header field is carried end-to-end.

If the UAS has reason to believe that the scheme of the Request-URI has been improperly modified in transit, the UA should notify its user of a potential security breach. As a further measure to prevent downgrade attacks, entities that accept only SIPS requests may also refuse connections on insecure ports. End users will undoubtedly discern the difference between SIPS and SIP URIs, and they may manually edit them in response to stimuli. This can either benefit or degrade security. For example, if an attacker corrupts a DNS cache, inserting a fake record set that effectively removes all SIPS records for a proxy server, then any SIPS requests that traverse this proxy server may fail. When a user, however, sees that repeated calls to a SIPS AOR are failing, they could on some devices manually convert the scheme from SIPS to SIP and retry. Of course, there are some safeguards against this (if the destination UA is truly paranoid, it could refuse all non-SIPS requests), but it is a limitation worth noting. On the bright side, users might also divine that SIPS would be valid even when they are presented only with a SIP URI.

19.13 Summary

We have defined the basic security functions authentication, authorization, integrity, confidentiality, and nonrepudiation. The inherent security capabilities that are available in SIP are discussed in this chapter. First, the functionality for negotiating the security mechanisms used between a SIP UA and its next-hop SIP entity at the session level is provided. Second, all security mechanisms of SIP are described in detail. Third, SDP security description is used for negotiation of security context for media security at the media level, after session establishment using SIP signaling messages. Fourth, we have explained the SIP session setup that includes security features using a call flows example. Fifth, we have explained possible security threats that are being faced in the context of SIP that is an application-layer protocol. Finally, the means of mitigating security threats using existing security mechanisms in SIP are provided. In this context, how lower-transport-layer security capabilities complement SIP application-layer security features is discussed. However, a separate chapter is devoted to describing privacy and anonymity in SIP.

PROBLEMS

1. What are the definitions of authentication, authorization, integrity, confidentiality, and nonrepudiation? What are the differences between confidentiality and privacy?
2. Why does SIP need security in both the session and the media level, making security in SIP fundamentally different from other applications? Explain how media-level security depends on session-level security in SIP.
3. Describe with examples how the SDP security features help negotiate security mechanisms to be used for medial-level security. How does the SDP help obtain security features to be used in SRTP and ZRTP?
4. What are the SDP media stream security preconditions that are needed in SIP? How do they ensure media security in delaying the transfer of media? Explain all security preconditions with detailed call flows.
5. Why does SIP need extension with three headers only for making agreement between SIP entities for security mechanisms as specified in RFC 3329? Describe in detail how the security mechanisms are negotiated between SIP entities for client- and server-initiated negotiation.
6. What are the security limitations in negotiating security capabilities as described in RFC 3329? How can we mitigate those limitations?
7. Describe the procedures for authentication in SIP: user-to-user and proxy-to-user.
8. What is digest authentication scheme in SIP? Describe in detail using call flows. How does SIP authentication differ from that of HTTP/1.1?
9. What are the benefits provided by obtaining the domain certificate over TLS for authentication in SIP per procedures defined in RFC 5922? How is the host name resolved in the SIP domain? How should this certificate be used by a SIP service provider? Describe the behavior of SIP entities for the domain certificate.
10. What is AIB? How does it enhance integrity and authentication protection in SIP? Explain with message flows using a third-party conference control where the REFER method is used.
11. How does the cryptographic authentication scheme help authentication in SIP as specified in RFC 4474? Describe the behavior of SIP entities in handling cryptographic authentication. What are the security concerns for this? How can these security holes be mitigated?
12. How are the privacy and security concerns handled in SIP for user identity and the TEL URI scheme in the cryptographic authentication scheme?
13. What is the AKA HTTP digest as specified in RFC 3310? Explain with detailed examples the operation of the digest AKA. What are the security concerns for this scheme? How are the security loopholes mitigated in this scheme?
14. Describe in detail the key-derivation authentication scheme in SIP, including challenge, response, and confirmation. Why is it important for authentication?
15. What has been missing in RFC 3261 for DNS-based authentication for TLS sessions in SIP? How does DNSec enhance security in SIP for TLS sessions? Describe DANS-capable SIP implementation using examples.
16. How does authorization come into picture in SIP? What is role/trait-based authorization? Explain using some use cases and its requirements.
17. What is SAML assertion? How can it be applied in SIP to play the role of authorization? What are the pros and cons of using SAML assertion in SIP? How are the security vulnerabilities taken care of using SAML assertion over the SIP network?
18. How does authorization occur through dialog identification in SIP? Explain the UA and proxy behaviors for this using call flows.
19. Explain media authorization in SIP as defined in RFC 3313 along with bandwidth reservation with an RSVP QOS signaling protocol that is used over the IP network along with UA and proxy behaviors. What are the pros and cons of these procedures of media authorization in SIP from a security point of view?
20. Explain how early-media authorization in SIP can be offered in SIP. Explain the SIP session setup with a media authorization framework as explained in RFC 3521.
21. How do S/MIME certificates help in session-level security? How does the S/MIME key exchange help in securing the SIP session?
22. Explain how the SDP message body of the SIP signaling message secures MIME bodies.
23. How are SIP header integrity and confidentiality protected using S/MIME tunneling? What are the pros

and cons of tunneling SIP headers? Explain using examples.

24. How are the SIP messages' integrity and authentication protected using S/MIME tunneling? What are the pros and cons of tunneling SIP messages? Explain using examples.
25. How is SIP message encryption done using S/MIME tunneling? What are the pros and cons of tunneling encrypted SIP messages? Explain using examples.
26. How do nonrepudiation services work in SIP? Explain with detailed explanations.
27. Develop a SIP network architecture for providing nonrepudiation services in billing using the DIAMETER protocol that offers authentication, authorization, and accounting services in SIP.
28. What are the vulnerabilities in forking by a SIP proxy? Explain with examples. How the suggestions provided in RFC 5393 will mitigate those vulnerabilities of forking in SIP? Write the possible solutions using existing SIP messages, existing other standards, and/or new extensions.
29. What are the requirements for URI-list services using external lists? What are the requirements for URI-list services using Request-Contained lists? Describe the framework specified by RFC 5363 for carrying and processing of URI lists in SIP. What are the security concerns and general issues for carrying URI-list, and how do you mitigate those security loopholes in SIP?
30. What are the security concerns if session invitation, instant messaging, and other requests are sent to a party without its consent in SIP? What requirements do consent-based communications in SIP, specified in RFC 5360, need to meet? What is the content-based communications solution architecture in SIP? Explain with a detailed explanation.
31. How does the relay behave in avoidance of amplification, subscription to permission status, and request for permission for consent-based communications in SIP? How does a relay behave in handling SIP Identity, P-Asserted-Identity, Return Routability, and SIP Digest once the recipient grants permission?
32. How is permission revocation performed for consent-based communications in SIP? Explain the relay behavior related to handling request-contained URI lists. Why are the 470 response code and the Permission-Missing and Trigger-Consent header fields needed in SIP for consent-based communications?
33. Explain the registration scheme for consent-based communications in SIP. Explain the relay behavior in generating the traffic toward the recipient.
34. What are the security concerns in consent-based communications in SIP? How are those security loopholes mitigated?
35. How does this RFC update RFC 3261 for securing forking in SIP? Explain in detail the guidance that is provided by RFC 5393 to implementers for securing forking in SIP. Are these extensions of RFC 3261 mandated by RFC 5393 sufficient to secure a SIP forking proxy? What alternative solution did the authors of this RFC suggest, but was not accepted by the IETF Working Group? Provide your view on this alternative solution for mitigating forking vulnerabilities in SIP.
36. Explain in detail the attacks and threats in SIP at the registration and session levels: registration hijacking, impersonating a server, tampering with message bodies, tearing down sessions, and DoS and amplification.
37. Explain in detail how each of one of these security mechanisms help mitigate particular attacks and threats: SIPS URI scheme, HTTP authentication, S/MIME, and transport- and network-layer security.
38. What are the requirements for implementation of SIP security? What are the security solutions in meeting the requirements for registration, interdomain requests, peer-to-peer requests, and DoS protection?
39. What are the security limitations of HTTP Digest, S/MIME, TLS, and SIPS URIs? Explain in detail with examples.

References

1. Shekh-Yusef, R., "Key-derivation authentication scheme," draft-yusef-sipcore-key-derivation-00 (work in progress), October 2014.
2. Tschofenig, H. et al., "Using SAML to protect the Session Initiation Protocol (SIP)," IEEE Network, September/October 2006.
3. 3rd Generation Partnership Project, "Security architecture (Release 4)," TS 33.102, December 2001.
4. "NIST special publication 800-132—Recommendations for password-based key derivations," December 2010.
5. Finch, T., Miller, M., and Saint-Andre, P., "Using DNS-based Authentication of Named Entities (DANE) TLSA records with SRV records," draft-ietf-dane-srv-07 (work in progress), July 2014.
6. Johansson, O., "TLS sessions in SIP using DNS-based Authentication of Named Entities (DANE) TLSA records," draft-johansson-sipcore-dane-sip-07 (work in progress), October 6, 2014.
7. Kaliski, B., "TWIRL and RSA key size," May 2003.

Chapter 20

Privacy and Anonymity in SIP

Abstract

Besides security, the Session Initiation Protocol (SIP) also needs privacy both at user-session and media level. However, media-level privacy is termed as confidentiality, as described earlier. Session Description Protocol (SDP), which deals with media as part of the SIP signaling message body, may also include user-level information. Here, the message body may need privacy as well. First, we elaborate on the privacy mechanism that needs to be used for the target SIP header and SDP parameters. In this context, nontarget SIP headers and SDP parameters are also described. Second, a variety of privacy types including user- and network-provided privacy in SIP are defined. Accordingly, the construction rules for private messages by SIP user agents (UAs) and the behavior of privacy service are explained. Third, the asserted and connected identity that can be used for privacy in SIP are discussed. Finally, anonymity services along with UA-driven SIP messages related to critical and noncritical privacy-sensitive information are described.

20.1 Introduction

Privacy and anonymity go together because anonymity is enabled through privacy services that can be offered by user agents (UAs) and/or intermediaries located between the source–destination paths. Although the Session Initiation Protocol (SIP) allows anonymous calls as described in Request for Comment (RFC) 3261, extensions to SIP are made by other RFCs described in subsequent sections for providing elaborate privacy services in maintaining the privacy and anonymity of SIP users as desired. We have defined the privacy and anonymity in the context of SIP/Session Description Protocol (SDP), including examples as follows:

Privacy: It is usually applied to the person and the way potential participants are identified and contacted. All information related to the person that remains unknown, including interactions and the methods being used to collect information about the person, are included as a part of privacy. In SIP, privacy may include all personal information about the user's identity, equipment, and workplace such as the To, From, Call-Id, Contact, User-Agent, Sever, or Organization header fields of SIP messages. The location information may consist of Internet Protocol (IP) addresses, ports, used hosts, networks traversed, service providers, or other related information about user's location. SIP message header fields such as Contact, Route, Route-Record, Via, and other fields will carry the user's location information. In addition, SDP message fields carry similar information about the user's location information. The SIP privacy information will include not only the caller or sender, but also the same information about the callee(s), recipient(s), or participant(s).

Anonymity: It represents an "unknown name, user, or person." It means anything related to personal information about the person can be termed as anonymity. Anonymity provides privacy protection by guaranteeing that each released information will not relate to a particular individual even if the information is directly released to the public. In this case, when information (e.g., personal, location, or call information) that relates to privacy as discussed above is kept anonymous, it represents anonymity. For example, an anonymous person participating in a call may speak in a conference, but no one will know the identity of this person if he/she desires to keep his/her identity anonymous. In another case, a person may let his/her identity be known, but will not disclose his location (i.e., anonymous location) while speaking in the conference. SIP has mechanisms for providing anonymity under such circumstances.

RFC 3261 describes how SIP user privacy will be affected by SIP signaling message fields to a great length. For example, SIP messages frequently contain sensitive information about their senders—not only what they have to say, but also with whom they communicate, when they communicate and for how long, and from where they participate in sessions. Many applications and their users require that this kind of private information be hidden from any parties that do not need to know it.

Note that there are also less direct ways in which private information can be divulged. If a user or service chooses to be reachable at an address that is guessable from the person's name and organizational affiliation (which describes most addresses of record [AORs]), the traditional method of ensuring privacy by having an unlisted "phone number" is compromised. A user location service can infringe on the privacy of the recipient of a session invitation by divulging their specific whereabouts to the caller; an implementation consequently should be able to restrict, on a per-user basis, what kind of location and availability information is given out to certain classes of callers. This is a whole class of problem that is expected to be studied further in ongoing SIP work.

In some cases, users may want to conceal personal information in header fields that convey identity. This can apply not only to the From and related headers representing the originator of the request, but also the To—it may not be appropriate to convey to the final destination a speed-dialing nickname, or an unexpanded identifier for a group of targets, either of which would be removed from the Request-URI as the request is routed, but not changed in the To header field if the two were initially identical. Thus, it may be desirable for privacy reasons to create a To header field that differs from the Request-URI. However, how the privacy of the SIP user can be provided has subsequently been described in other RFCs updating RFC 3261.

20.2 Privacy Mechanism in SIP

20.2.1 Background

In SIP, identity is most commonly carried in the form of a SIP Uniform Resource Identifier (URI) and an optional display name. A SIP AOR has a form similar to an e-mail address with a SIP URI scheme (e.g., sip:alice@atlanta.com). A display name is a string containing a name for the identified user (e.g., "Alice"). SIP identities of this form commonly appear in the To and From header fields of SIP requests and responses. A user may have many identities that they use in different contexts. There are numerous other places in SIP messages in which identity-related information can be revealed. For example, the Contact header field contains a SIP URI, one that is commonly as revealing as the AOR in the From header field. In some headers, the originating UA can conceal identity information as a matter of local policy without affecting the operation of the SIP. However, certain headers are used in the routing of subsequent messages in a dialog, and must therefore be populated with functional data.

The privacy problem is further complicated by proxy servers (also referred to in this document as "intermediaries" or "the network") that add headers of their own, such as the Record-Route and Via headers. Information in these headers could inadvertently reveal something about the originator of a message; for example, a Via header might reveal the service provider through whom the user sends requests, which might, in turn, strongly hint at the user's identity to some recipients. For these reasons, the participation of intermediaries is also crucial to providing privacy in SIP.

RFC 3323 that is described here addresses the SIP privacy problems and defines new mechanisms for the SIP in support of privacy. Specifically, UA and privacy service behavior guidelines are provided for the creation of messages that do not divulge personal identity information. In addition, the "privacy service" logical role for intermediaries is defined, meeting privacy requirements that UAs cannot satisfy themselves. Mechanisms are described by which a user can request particular functions from a privacy service. Privacy is defined as the withholding of the identity of a person (and related personal information) from one or more parties in an exchange of communications, specifically a SIP dialog. These parties potentially include the intended destination(s) of messages and/or any intermediaries handling these messages. As identity is defined, withholding the identity of a user will, among other things, render the other parties in the dialog unable to send new SIP requests to the user outside of the context of the current dialog.

Two complementary principles have been used in designing the privacy mechanism in RFC 3323: users are empowered to hide their identity and related personal information when they issue requests; however, intermediaries and designated recipients of requests are entitled to reject requests whose originator cannot be identified. The privacy properties of only those specific headers enumerated in the core SIP specification (RFC 3261), as opposed to headers defined by any existing or planned extension, are discussed in this document—however, the privacy mechanisms described in this document can be extended to support extensions. There are other aspects of the general privacy problem for SIP that are not addressed by RFC 3323. Most significantly, the mechanisms for managing the confidentiality of SIP headers and bodies, as well the security of session traffic, are not reconsidered here. These problems are sufficiently well addressed in the baseline SIP specification and related documents, and no new mechanisms are required.

20.2.2 Varieties of Privacy

A user may possess many identities that are used in various contexts; generally, identities are AORs that are bound to particular registrars (operated by the administrators of a domain) with whom SIP UAs register. The operators of these domains may be employers, service providers, or unaffiliated users themselves. When a user voluntarily asserts an identity in a request, they are claiming that they can receive requests sent to that identity in that domain. Strictly speaking, privacy entails the restriction of the distribution of a specific identity and related personal information from some particular party or parties that are potentially recipients of the message. In particular, there are scenarios in which a party desiring anonymity may send a message and withhold an identity from the final destination(s) while still communicating an identity to one or more intermediaries; send a message and withhold identity from some or all intermediaries, but still communicate an identity end-to-end to the final destination(s); or withhold identity from both intermediaries and final destination(s).

The result of withholding an identity is that the parties in question would be unable, for example, to attempt to initiate a new dialog with the anonymous party at a later time. However, the anonymous party still must be capable of receiving responses and new requests during the dialog in which it is participating. It may be desirable to restrict identity information on both requests and responses. Initially, it might seem unusual to suggest that a response has privacy concerns—presumably, the originator of the request knows who they were attempting to contact, so the identity of the respondent can hardly be confidential. However, some personal information in responses (such as the contact address at which the respondent is currently registered) is subject to privacy concerns and can be addressed by these mechanisms.

20.2.2.1 User Necessity for Privacy

Users may wish for identity information to be withheld from a given party for any number of reasons; for example, users might want to contact a particular party without revealing their identity to impart information with which they would not like to be associated; users might fear that the exposure of their identity or personal information to some networks or destinations will make them a target for unsolicited advertising, legal censure, or other undesirable consequences; or users might want to withhold from participants in a session the identity by which they are known to network intermediaries for the purposes of billing and accounting.

When a UA decides to send a request through a proxy server, it may be difficult for the originator to anticipate the final destination of that message. For that reason, users are advised not to base their estimation of their privacy needs on where they expect a message will go. For example, if a user sends a request to a telephone number, they may believe that the final destination of the request will be a station in the public switched telephone network (PSTN) that is unable to inspect, say, SIP Contact headers, and therefore assume that it is safe to leave such headers in the clear; however, such a request might very well end up being retargeted by the network to a native SIP end point to which Contact headers are quite legible.

RFC 3323 describes three degrees of privacy—one level of user-provided privacy, and two levels of network-provided privacy (header privacy and session privacy). How much privacy does a user need for any given session? Generally, if a user is seeking privacy, they are going to need as much of it as they can get. However, if a user knows of no privacy service, they must be content with user-provided privacy alone. Similarly, if a user knows of an anonymization service that can provide session privacy but is unable to secure session traffic to prevent the anonymizer from possibly eavesdropping on the session, they might judge the loss of session privacy to be the lesser evil. The user might also be aware of exceptional conditions about the architecture in which the UA is deployed that may obviate one or more privacy concerns.

A user may not always be the best judge of when privacy is required even under ideal circumstances, and thus privacy may in some architectures be applied by intermediaries without the user's explicit per-message request. By sending a request through intermediaries that can provide a privacy role, the user tacitly permits privacy functions to be invoked as needed. It is also important that users understand that intermediaries may be unable to provide privacy functions requested by users. Requests for privacy may not be honored due to legal constraints, unimplemented or misconfigured features, or other exceptional conditions.

Note that just as it is the prerogative of users to conceal their identity, so it must also be the prerogative of proxy servers and other users to refuse to process requests from users who they cannot identify. Therefore, users should not just automatically withhold their identity for all requests and responses—inability to ascertain the identity of the originator of the request will frequently be grounds for rejection. Privacy should only be requested when the user has a need for it. Further to this point, withholding some information in signaling might not be necessary for all UAs to ensure privacy. For example, UAs may acquire their IP addresses and host names dynamically, and these dynamic addresses may not reveal any information about the user whatsoever. In these cases, restricting access to host names is unnecessary.

20.2.2.2 User-Provided Privacy

There is a certain amount of privacy that a UA can provide itself. For example, the baseline SIP specification permits a UA to populate the From header field of a request with an anonymous value. Users can take similar steps to avoid revealing any other unnecessary identity information in related SIP headers. A user may have different privacy needs for a message if it traverses intermediaries rather than going directly end-to-end. A user may attempt to conceal things from intermediaries that are not concealed from the final destination, and vice versa. For example, using baseline SIP mechanisms, a UA can encrypt SIP bodies end-to-end to prevent intermediaries from inspecting them. If a SIP message will not pass through intermediaries, however, this step might not be necessary (i.e., lower-layer security, without the addition of security for SIP bodies, could be sufficient). Also note that if a dialog goes directly end-to-end between participants, however, it will not be possible to conceal the network addresses of the participants.

20.2.2.3 Network-Provided Privacy

If a user is sending a request through intermediaries, a UA can conceal its identity to only a limited extent without the intermediaries' cooperation. Also, some information can only be concealed from destination end points if an intermediary is entrusted to remove it. For these reasons, a user must have a way to request privacy from intermediaries, a means that allows users both to signal some indications of the desired privacy services, and to ensure that their call is routed to an intermediary that is capable of providing these services. A user may be aware of a specific third-party anonymizing host, one with which they have a preexisting relationship, or a user may request that their local administrative domain provide privacy services. Intermediaries may also be empowered to apply privacy to a message without any explicit signaling from the originating user, since UAs may not always be cognizant or capable of requesting privacy when it is necessary.

20.2.3 UA Behavior

There are three different ways that a UA can contribute to the privacy of a request—by populating headers with values that reflect privacy requirements, by requesting further privacy services from the network, and by using cryptographic confidentiality to secure headers and bodies. Note that the last of these is outside the scope of this document. The mechanisms provided in this section assume that a UA is sufficiently configurable that a user can select header values and provision privacy preferences (ideally on a per-call basis). If this is not the case, it is possible that a user can route their call through a privacy service that is configured to groom signaling from this UA in order to provide some of the function.

20.2.4 UA Behavior Constructing Private Messages

Privacy starts with the UA. The bulk of the steps that are required to conceal private information about the sender of a message are, appropriately enough, the sender's responsibility. The following SIP headers, when generated by a UA, can directly or indirectly reveal identity information about the originator of a message: From, Contact, Reply-To, Via, Call-Info, User-Agent, Organization, Server, Subject, Call-ID, In-Reply-To, and Warning. Note that the use of an authentication system, such as the SIP Digest authentication method described in RFC 3261 (see Section 19.4), also usually entails revealing identity to one or more parties.

The first and most obvious step is that UAs should not include any optional headers that might divulge personal information; there is certainly no reason for a user seeking privacy to include a Call-Info. Secondly, the user should populate URIs throughout the message in accordance with the guidelines given below. For example, users should create an anonymous From header field for the request. Finally, users may also need to request certain privacy functions from the network, as described in in the subsequent sections. The Call-ID header, which is frequently constructed in a manner that reveals the IP address or host name of the originating client, requires special mention. UAs should substitute for the IP address or host name that is frequently appended to the Call-ID value a suitably long random value (the value used as the "tag" for the From header of the request might even be reused). Note that if the user wants to conceal any of the above headers from intermediaries alone, without withholding them from the final destination of the message, users may also place legitimate values for these headers in encapsulated "message/sip" Secure/Multipurpose Internet Mail Extension (S/MIME) bodies as described in RFC 3261 (see Section 19.6).

20.2.4.1 URIs, Display Names, and Privacy

A certain amount of privacy can be afforded by choosing to populate SIP headers with URIs and display names that do not reveal any identity information. In some of the header fields (e.g., the Reply-To and From headers), URIs are not used in further signaling within the current dialog. In others, like the Contact header, an inaccurate URI will result in a failure to route subsequent requests within the dialog.

20.2.4.1.1 Display Names

It is a relatively common practice in e-mail and other applications to use an assumed name in the display-name component of the From header field. Outside of a business context (especially in applications such as instant messaging or Internet gaming) the use of such aliases is unlikely to provide a cause for distrust. It is recommended that UAs seeking anonymity use a display name of "Anonymous."

20.2.4.1.2 URI User Names

The structure of a URI itself can reveal or conceal a considerable amount of personal information. Consider the difference between sip:jon.peterson@neustar.biz and sip:a0017@anonymous-sip.com. From the former, the full name and employer of the party in question can easily be guessed. From the latter, you learn nothing other than that the party desires anonymity. In some cases, sufficient anonymity can be achieved by selecting an oblique URI. Today, the SIP specification recommends a URI with "anonymous" in the user portion of the From header. In some URIs, such as those that appear in Contact headers, it may also make sense to omit the user name altogether, and provide only a host name, like sip:anonymous-sip.com.

20.2.4.1.3 URI Host Names and IP Addresses

It is assumed by this document that the user that requests privacy wishes to receive future requests and responses within this dialog, but does not wish to reveal an identity that could be used to send new requests to him outside the scope of this dialog. For that reason, a different treatment must be recommended for URIs that are used in the context of routing further requests in the dialog, as opposed to routing new requests outside the context of the dialog. For headers indicating how the user would like to be contacted for future sessions (such as the From header), it might not be immediately obvious why changing the host name would be necessary—if the user name is "anonymous," requests will not be routable to the anonymous user.

Sometimes, merely changing the user name will not be enough to conceal a user's identity. A user's SIP service provider might decisively reveal a user's identity (if it reflected something like a small company or a personal domain). So in this case, even though the URI in the From header would not dereference to the anonymous user, humans might easily guess the user's identity and know the proper form of their AOR. For these reasons, the host name value "anonymous.invalid" should be used for anonymous URIs (see RFC 2606 for more information about the reserved "invalid" Domain Name System [DNS] top-level domain). The full recommended form of the From header for anonymity is (note that this From header, like all others, must contain a valid and unique "tag=" parameter) as follows: From: "Anonymous" <sip:anonymous@anonymous.invalid>;tag=1928301774>. For headers indicating how further requests in the current dialog should be routed (namely the Contact header, Via header, and session information in the SDP), there seems to be little that a user can do to disguise the existing URI, because users must provide a value that will allow them to receive further requests. In some cases, disguising or failing to provide the user name, as described above, may create some level of privacy; however, the host name provides a more significant obstacle. Is there much additional privacy in using an IP address rather than a host name? It does prevent someone who casually inspects a message from gathering information that they might see otherwise.

However, reverse-resolving such addresses is generally trivial, and substituting an IP address for a host name could introduce some complications, for example, due to network address translation and firewall traversal concerns. Headers used in routing may also rely on certain DNS practices to provide services that would be lost if an IP address is used in place of a host name. This document thus recommends that the host portion of URIs that are used in the routing of subsequent requests, such as URIs appearing in the Contact header, should not be altered by the UA owing to privacy considerations. If these headers require anonymization, the user requests that service from an intermediary, namely a privacy service. Note that many of the considerations regarding the Contact header above apply equally well to SIP headers in which a host name, rather than a URI, is used for some routing purpose (namely the Via header).

20.2.5 UA Behavior Expressing Privacy Preferences

There are some headers that a UA cannot conceal itself, because they are used in routing, that could be concealed by an intermediary that subsequently takes responsibility for directing messages to and from the anonymous user. The UA must have some way to request such privacy services from the network. For that purpose, RFC 3323 defines a new SIP header (see Section 2.8), Privacy, that can be used to specify privacy handling for requests and responses. The Privacy header is explained in more detail as stated below:

```
Privacy-hdr  =  "Privacy" HCOLON priv-value
                *(";" priv-value)
priv-value   =  "header"/"session"/"user"/"non
                e"/"critical"/token
```

UAs should include a Privacy header when network-provided privacy is required. Note that some intermediaries may also add the Privacy header to messages, including privacy services. However, such intermediaries should only do so if they are operating at a user's behest, for example, if a user has an administrative arrangement with the operator of the intermediary that it will add such a Privacy header. An intermediary must not modify the Privacy header in any way if the "none" priv-value is already specified. The values of priv-value today are restricted to the above options, although further options can be defined as appropriate, as described in subsequent sections. Each legitimate priv-value can appear zero or one time in a Privacy header. The current values are as follows:

- **header:** The user requests that a privacy service obscure those headers that cannot be completely expunged of identifying information without the assistance of intermediaries (such as Via and Contact). Also, no unnecessary headers should be added by the service that might reveal personal information about the originator of the request.
- **session:** The user requests that a privacy service provide anonymization for the session(s) (described, e.g., in an SDP used in the SIP message body) initiated by this message. This will mask the IP address from which the session traffic would ordinarily appear to originate. When session privacy is requested, UAs must not encrypt SDP bodies in messages. Note that requesting session privacy in the absence of any end-to-end session encryption raises some serious security concerns.
- **user:** This privacy level is usually set only by intermediaries, in order to communicate that user-level privacy functions must be provided by the network, presumably because the UA is unable to provide them. UAs may, however, set this privacy level for REGISTER requests, but should not set "user"-level privacy for other requests.
- **none:** The user requests that a privacy service apply no privacy functions to this message, regardless of any preprovisioned profile for the user or default behavior of the service. UAs can specify this option when they are forced to route a message through a privacy service that will, if no Privacy header is present, apply some privacy functions that the user does not desire for this message. Intermediaries must not remove or alter a Privacy header whose priv-value is "none." UAs must not populate any other priv-values (including "critical") in a Privacy header that contains a value of "none."
- **critical:** The user asserts that the privacy services requested for this message are critical, and that, therefore, if these privacy services cannot be provided by the network, this request should be rejected. Criticality cannot be managed appropriately for responses.

When a Privacy header is constructed, it must consist of either the value "none," or one or more of the values "user," "header," and "session" (each of which must appear at most once), which may, in turn, be followed by the "critical" indicator. The settings for the Privacy header for different SIP methods are described in Section 2.8.

20.2.6 UA Behavior Routing Requests to Privacy Services

The most obvious way for a UA to invoke the privacy function is to direct a request through an intermediary known to act as a privacy service. Doing so traditionally entails the configuration of preloaded Route headers that designate the privacy service. It is recommended that service providers couple the privacy service function with a local outbound proxy. Users can thereby send their messages that request privacy through their usual outbound route. Users should not assume, however, that the administrative domain that is the destination of the request would be willing and able to perform the privacy service function on their behalf. If the originating user wishes to keep their local administrative domain a secret, then they must use a third-party anonymization service outside of any of the principal administrative domains associated with the session.

It is highly recommended that UAs use network or transport layer security, such as TLS, when contacting a privacy service. Ideally, users should establish a direct (i.e., single preloaded Route header) connection to a privacy service; this will both allow the user to inspect a certificate presented by the privacy service, and will provide confidentiality for requests that will reduce the chances that the information that the privacy service will obscure is revealed before a message arrives at the privacy service. By establishing a direct connection to a privacy service, the user also eliminates the possibility that intermediaries could remove requests for privacy. If a direct connection is impossible, users should use a mechanism like SIP Security (SIPS) to guarantee the use of lower-layer security all the way to the privacy service.

If a UA believes that it is sending a request directly to a privacy service, it should include a Proxy-Require header containing a new option tag, "privacy," especially when the "critical" priv-value is present in the Privacy header. That way, in the unlikely event that the UA sends a request to an intermediary that does not support the extensions described in this document, the request will fail. Note that because of special privacy service behavior (described in Section 20.2.8), no subsequent intermediaries in the signaling path of the request will also need to the support the "privacy" option tag—once the privacy service has fulfilled all the required privacy functions, the "privacy" option tag is removed from the Proxy-Require header.

20.2.7 UA Behavior Routing Responses to Privacy Services

Making sure that responses will go through a privacy service is a little bit trickier. The path traversed by SIP responses is the same as the path over which the request traveled. Thus, the responding UA, for example, cannot force a privacy service to be injected in the response path after it has received a request. What a responding UA can do, however, is ensure that the path by which requests reach them traverses their privacy service. In some architectures, the privacy service function will be fulfilled by the same server to which requests for the local administrative domain are sent, and hence it will automatically be in the path of incoming requests. However, if this is not the case, the user will have to ensure that requests are directed through a third-party privacy service.

One way to accomplish this is to procure an "anonymous callback" URI from the third-party service and to distribute this as an AOR. A privacy service provider might offer these anonymous callback URIs to users in the same way that an ordinary SIP service provider grants AORs. The user would then register their normal AOR as a contact address with the third-party service. Alternatively, a UA could send REGISTER requests through a privacy service with a request for "user"-level privacy. This will allow the privacy service to insert anonymous Contact header URIs. Requests sent to the user's conventional AOR would then reach the user's devices without revealing any usable contact addresses.

Finally, a user might generate a Call Processing Language (CPL) script defined in RFC 3880 that will direct requests to an anonymization service. Users are also advised to use transport or network layer security in the response path. This may involve registering a SIPS URI and/or maintaining persistent TLS connections over which their UA receives requests. Privacy services may, in turn, route requests through other privacy services. This may be necessary if a privacy service does not support a particular privacy function but knows of a peer that does. Privacy services may also cluster themselves into networks that exchange session traffic between one another in order to further disguise the participants in a session, although no specific architecture or method for doing so is described in this document.

20.2.8 Privacy Service Behavior

RFC 3323 defines, as indicated earlier, a new SIP logical role called a "privacy service." The privacy service role is instantiated by a network intermediary, frequently by entities that can act as SIP proxy servers. The function of a privacy service is to supply privacy functions for SIP messages that cannot be provided by UAs themselves. When a message arrives at a server that can act as a privacy service, the service should evaluate the level of privacy requested in a Privacy header. Usually, only the services explicitly requested should be applied. However, privacy services may have some means outside SIP of ascertaining the preferences of the user (such as a prearranged user profile), and therefore they may perform such other privacy functions without an explicit Privacy header. Performing even a user-level privacy function in a privacy service could be useful, for example, when a user is sending messages from a legacy client that does support the Privacy header, or a UA that does not allow the user to configure the values of headers that could reveal personal information.

However, if the Privacy header value of "none" is specified in a message, privacy services must not perform any privacy function and must not remove or modify the Privacy header. Privacy services must implement support for the "none" and "critical" privacy tokens, and may implement any of other privacy levels described in Section 20.2.5 as well as any extensions that are not detailed in this document. In some cases, the privacy service will not be capable of fulfilling the requested level of privacy. If the "critical" privacy level is present in the Privacy header of a request, then if the privacy service is incapable of performing all of the levels of privacy specified in the Privacy header, then it MUST fail the request with a 500 Server Error response code.

The reason phrase of the status line of the response should contain appropriate text indicating that there has been a privacy failure as well as an enumeration of the priv-value(s) that were not supported by the privacy service (the reason phrase should also respect any Accept-Language header in the request, if possible). When a privacy service performs one of the functions corresponding to a privacy level listed in the Privacy header, it should remove the corresponding priv-value from the Privacy header—otherwise, any other privacy service involved with routing this message might unnecessarily apply the same function, which in many cases would be undesirable. When the last priv-value (not counting "critical") has been removed from the Privacy header, the entire Privacy header must be removed from a message. When the privacy service removes the entire Privacy header, if the message is a request, the privacy service must also remove any "privacy" option tag from the Proxy-Require header field of the request.

20.2.8.1 Header Privacy

If a privacy level of "header" is requested, then the originating user has asked the privacy service to help to obscure headers that might otherwise reveal information about the originator of the request. However, the values that have been so obscured must be recoverable when further messages in the dialog need to be routed to the originating UA. To provide these functions, the privacy service must frequently act as a transparent back-to-back UA (B2BUA).

First, a request for header privacy entails that the server should not add any headers to the message that reveal any identity or personal information, including the following: Call-Info, Server, and Organization. All of these provide optional information that could reveal facts about the user that has requested anonymity. Privacy services operating on requests should remove all Via headers that have been added to the request before its arrival at the privacy service (a practice referred to as "Via stripping") and then should add a single Via header representing themselves. Note that the bottommost such Via header field value in a request contains an IP address or host name that designates the originating client, and subsequent Via header field values may indicate hosts in the same administrative domain as the client. No Via stripping is required when handling responses.

Contact headers are added by UAs to both requests and responses. A privacy service should replace the value of the Contact header in a message with a URI that does not dereference to the originator of the message such as the anonymous URI. The URI that replaces the existing Contact header field value must dereference to the privacy service. In a manner similar to Via stripping, a privacy service should also strip any Record-Route headers that have been added to a request before it reaches the privacy service—although note that no such headers will be present if there is only one hop between the originating UA and the privacy service, as is recommended above. Such Record-Route headers might also divulge information about the administrative domain of the client.

For the purposes of this document, it is assumed that the privacy service has locally persisted the values of any of the above headers that are so removed, which requires the privacy service to keep a pretty significant amount of state on a per-dialog basis. When further requests or responses associated with the dialog reach the privacy service, it MUST restore values for the Via, Record-Route/Route, or Contact headers that it has previously removed in the interests of privacy. There may be alternative ways (outside the scope of this document) to perform this function that do not require keeping state in the privacy service (usually means that involve encrypting and persisting the values in the signaling somehow).

The following procedures are recommended for handling the Record-Route header field of requests and responses, which provides special challenges to a privacy service:

- When a privacy service is processing (on behalf of the originator) a request that contains one or more Record-Route header field values, the privacy service must strip these values from the request and remember both the dialog identifiers and the ordered Record-Route header field values. As described above, it must also replace the Contact header field with a URI indicating itself. When a response with the same dialog identifiers arrives at the privacy service, the privacy service must reapply any Record-Route header field values to the response in the same order, and it must then add a URI representing itself to the Record-Route header field of the response.
- If the response contains Record-Route header field values of its own, these must also be included (in order) in the Record-Route header field after the URI representing the privacy service. Note that when a privacy service is handling a request and providing privacy on behalf of the destination of the request, providing privacy for Record-Route headers downstream of the privacy service is significantly more complicated. This document recommends no way of statefully restoring those headers if they are stripped.

20.2.8.2 Session Privacy

If a privacy level of "session" is requested, then the user has requested that the privacy service anonymize the session traffic (e.g., for SIP telephony calls, the audio media) associated with this dialog. The SIP specification dictates that intermediaries such as proxy servers cannot inspect and modify message bodies. The privacy service logical role must therefore act as a B2UA to provide media privacy, effectively terminating and reoriginating the messages that initiate a session (although in support of session privacy, the privacy service does not need to alter headers characterizing the originator or destination when the request is reoriginated).

To introduce an anonymizer for session traffic, the privacy service needs to control a middle box (RFC 3303) that can provide an apparent source and sink for session traffic. The details of the implementation of an anonymizer, and the modifications that must be made to the SDP of the SIP message bodies in the messages that initiate a session, are outside the scope of this document. The risk, of course, of using such an anonymizer is that the anonymizer itself is party to your communications. For that reason, requesting session-level privacy without resorting to some sort of end-to-end security for the session traffic with RTP (see Section 7.5) media, for example, Secure Real-time Transmission Protocol (see Section 7.3), is not recommended.

20.2.8.3 Applying User-Level Privacy Functions at a Privacy Service

If a privacy level of "user" is requested, then the originating user has requested that privacy services perform the user-level privacy functions described earlier. Note that the privacy service must remove any nonessential informational headers that have been added by the UA, including the Subject, Call-Info, Organization, User-Agent, Reply-To, and In-Reply-To. Significantly, user-level privacy could entail the modification of the From header, changing it from its original value to an anonymous value. Before the current issue of the SIP specification, the modification of the values of the To and From headers by intermediaries was not permitted, and would result in improper dialog matching by the end points. Currently, dialog matching uses only the tags in the

To and From headers, rather than the whole header fields. Thus, under the new rules, the URI values in the To and From headers themselves could be altered by intermediaries. However, some legacy clients might consider it an error condition if the value of the URI in the From header altered between the request and the response.

Also, performing user-level privacy functions may entail the modification of the Call-ID header, since the Call-ID commonly contains a host name or IP address corresponding to the originating client. This field is essential to dialog matching, and it cannot be altered by intermediaries. Therefore, any time that a privacy service needs to modify any dialog-matching headers for privacy reasons, it should act as a transparent B2BUA, and it must persist the former values of the dialog-matching headers. These values must be restored in any messages that are sent to the originating UA.

20.2.8.4 Network-Asserted Identity Privacy

We have described different types of Network-Asserted Identity (NAI) in Section 10.5. The means by which any privacy requirements in respect of the NAI are determined are outside the scope of this document. It shall be possible to indicate within a message containing a NAI that this NAI is subject to a privacy requirement that prevents it being passed to other users. This indication should not carry any semantics as to the reason for this privacy requirement. It shall be possible to indicate that the user has requested that the NAI not be passed to other users. This is distinct from the above indication, in that it implies specific user intent with respect to the NAI. The mechanism shall support Trust Domain policies where the above two indications are equivalent (i.e., the only possible reason for a privacy requirement is a request from the user), and policies where they are not.

In this case, the NAI specification shall require that the mechanism described earlier shall not be used; that is, a trusted node shall not pass the identity to a node it does not trust. However, the mechanism of "sending of NAI to entities outside a Trust Domain" described earlier may not be used to transfer the identity within the trusted network. Note that "anonymity" requests from users or subscribers may well require functionality in addition to the above handling of NAIs. Such additional functionality is beyond the scope of this document.

20.2.9 Location Information Privacy

RFC 6442 (see Section 9.10), which specifies the target's location information creation and distribution, has described how to maintain the privacy of the target. Location information is considered by most to be highly sensitive information, requiring protection from eavesdropping and altering in transit. RFC 3693 (see Sections 2.8 and 9.10.1) originally articulated rules to be followed by any protocol wishing to be considered a "Using Protocol," specifying how a transport protocol meets those rules. RFC 6280 updates the guidance in RFC 3693 to include subsequently introduced entities and concepts in the geolocation architecture. RFC 5606 (see Section 2.8) explores the difficulties inherent in mapping the GEOPRIV architecture onto SIP elements. In particular, the difficulties of defining and identifying recipients of location information are given in that document, along with guidance provided earlier on the use of location-by-reference mechanisms to preserve confidentiality of location information from unauthorized recipients.

In a SIP deployment, location information may be added by any of several elements, including the originating UA or a proxy server. In all cases, the Rule Maker associated with that location information decides which entity adds location information and what access control rules apply. For example, a SIP UA that does not support the Geolocation header may rely on a proxy server under the direction of the Rule Maker adding a Geolocation header with a reference to location information. The manner in which the Rule Maker operates on these devices is outside the scope of this document. The manner in which SIP implementations honor the Rule Maker's stipulations for access control rules (including retention and retransmission) is application specific and not within the scope of SIP operations. Entities in SIP networks that fulfill the architectural roles of the location server or location recipient treat the privacy rules associated with location information per the guidance provided in RFC 6280. In particular, RFC 4119 (see Section 2.8) gives guidance for handling access control rules; SIP implementations should furthermore consult the recommendations in RFC 5606 (see Section 2.8).

20.2.10 Security Considerations

Messages that request privacy require confidentiality and integrity. Without integrity, the requested privacy functions could be downgraded or eliminated, potentially exposing identity information. Without confidentiality, eavesdroppers on the network (or any intermediaries between the user and the privacy service) could see the very personal information that the user has asked the privacy service to obscure. All of the network-provided privacy functions in this document entail a good deal of trust for the privacy service. Users should only trust privacy services that are somehow accountable to them.

Operators of privacy services should be aware that in the eyes of downstream entities, a privacy service will be the only source to which anonymous messages can be traced. Note that authentication mechanisms, including the Digest authentication method described in the SIP specification, are outside the scope of the privacy considerations in this document. Revealing identity through authentication is highly selective and may not result in the compromise of any private information. Obviously, users that do not wish to reveal their identity to servers that issue authentication challenges may elect not to respond to such challenges.

20.3 Asserted and Preferred Identity for Privacy in SIP

20.3.1 Background

Various providers offering a telephony service over IP networks have selected SIP as a call establishment protocol. Their environments require a way for trusted network elements operated by the service providers (e.g., SIP proxy servers) to communicate the identity of the subscribers to such a service, yet also need to withhold this information from entities that are not trusted when necessary. Such networks typically assume some level of transitive trust among providers and the devices they operate. These networks need to support certain traditional telephony services, and meet basic regulatory and public safety requirements. These include Calling Identity Delivery services, Calling Identity Delivery Blocking, and the ability to trace the originator of a call. While baseline SIP can support each of these services independently, certain combinations cannot be supported without the extensions described in this document. For example, a caller that wants to maintain privacy and consequently provides limited information in the SIP From header field will not be identifiable by recipients of the call unless they rely on some other means to discover the identity of the caller. Masking identity information at the originating UA will prevent certain services, for example, call trace, from working in the PSTN or being performed at intermediaries not privy to the authenticated identity of the user.

Providing privacy in a SIP network is more complicated than in the PSTN. In SIP networks, the participants in a session are typically able to exchange IP traffic directly without involving any SIP service provider. The IP addresses used for these sessions may themselves reveal private information. A general-purpose mechanism for providing privacy in a SIP environment is provided in RFC 3323 (see Section 20.2). This document applies that privacy mechanism to the problem of NAI.

20.3.2 P-Asserted-Identity and P-Preferred-Identity for Privacy

The P-Asserted-Identity defined in SIP (RFC 3325, see Sections 2.8 and 10.4) enables a network of trusted SIP servers to assert the identity of end users or end systems, and to convey indications of end-user requested privacy. The use of this header is only applicable inside a "Trust Domain" as defined in short-term requirements for NAI specified in RFC 3324 (see Section 10.5). Nodes in such a Trust Domain are explicitly trusted by its users and end systems to publicly assert the identity of each party, and to be responsible for withholding that identity outside of the Trust Domain when privacy is requested. The means by which the network determines the identity to assert is outside the scope of this document (although it commonly entails some form of authentication). A key requirement of RFC 3324 is that the behavior of all nodes within a given Trust Domain "T" is known to comply with a certain set of specifications known as "Spec(T)." Spec(T) must specify behavior for the following:

- The manner in which users are authenticated
- The mechanisms used to secure the communication among nodes within the Trust Domain
- The mechanisms used to secure the communication between UAs and nodes within the Trust Domain
- The manner used to determine which hosts are part of the Trust Domain
- The default privacy handling when no Privacy header field is present
- That nodes in the Trust Domain are compliant to SIP (RFC 3261)
- That nodes in the Trust Domain are compliant to this document
- Privacy handling for identity as described in the subsequent section
- Intermediaries including proxy servers within a Trust Domain working as SIP B2BUAs for supporting privacy in SIP as specified in RFC 3323 (see Section 20.2)
- The meanings of the terms Identity, NAI, and Trust Domain defined in RFC 3324 (see Section 10.5)

An example of a suitable Spec(T) is shown here later. This document does not offer a general privacy or identity model suitable for interdomain use or use in the Internet at large. Its assumptions about the trust relationship between the user and the network may not apply in many applications. For example, these extensions do not accommodate a model whereby end users can independently assert their identity by use of the extensions defined here. Furthermore, since the asserted identities are not cryptographically certified, they are subject to forgery, replay, and falsification in any architecture that does not meet the requirements of RFC 3324 (see Section 10.5).

The asserted identities also lack an indication of who specifically is asserting the identity, and so it must be assumed that the Trust Domain is asserting the identity. Therefore, the information is only meaningful when securely received from a node known to be a member of the Trust Domain. Despite these limitations, there are sufficiently useful specialized deployments that meet the assumptions described above, and can accept the limitations that result, to warrant informational publication of this mechanism. An example deployment would be a closed network that emulates a traditional circuit switched telephone network. The mechanism described here relies on a new header field called "P-Asserted-Identity" that contains a URI (commonly a SIP URI) and an optional display name, for example:

```
P-Asserted-Identity: "Brian.Johnson"
sip:bjohnson@network.com
```

A proxy server that handles a message can, after authenticating the originating user in some way (e.g., Digest authentication), insert such a P-Asserted-Identity header field into the message and forward it to other trusted proxies. A proxy that is about to forward a message to a proxy server or UA that it does not trust must remove all the P-Asserted-Identity header field values if the user requested that this information be kept private. Similar is the case for the P-Preferred-Identity header for privacy. Although the syntax for these two headers can be seen in Section 2.4.1, we are again explaining in detail the same two headers later here for convenience.

20.3.3 Proxy Behavior

A proxy in a Trust Domain can receive a message from a node that it trusts or a node that it does not trust. When a proxy receives a message from a node it does not trust and it wishes to add a P-Asserted-Identity header field, the proxy must authenticate the originator of the message, and use the identity that results from this authentication to insert a P-Asserted-Identity header field into the message. If the proxy receives a message (request or response) from a node that it trusts, it can use the information in the P-Asserted-Identity header field, if any, as if it had authenticated the user itself. If there is no P-Asserted-Identity header field present, a proxy may add one containing at most one SIP or SIPS URI, and at most one tel URL. If the proxy received the message from an element that it does not trust and there is a P-Asserted-Identity header present that contains a SIP or SIPS URI, the proxy must replace that SIP or SIPS URI with a single SIP or SIPS URI or remove this header field.

Similarly, if the proxy received the message from an element that it does not trust and there is a P-Asserted-Identity header present that contains a tel URI, the proxy must replace that tel URI with a single tel URI or remove the header field. When a proxy forwards a message to another node, it must first determine if it trusts that node or not. If it trusts the node, the proxy does not remove any P-Asserted-Identity header fields that it generated itself, or that it received from a trusted source. If it does not trust the element, then the proxy must examine the Privacy header field (if present) to determine if the user requested that asserted identity information be kept private.

20.3.4 Hints for Multiple Identities

If a P-Preferred-Identity header field is present in the message that a proxy receives from an entity that it does not trust, the proxy MAY use this information as a hint suggesting which of multiple valid identities for the authenticated user should be asserted. If such a hint does not correspond to any valid identity known to the proxy for that user, the proxy can add a P-Asserted-Identity header of its own construction, or it can reject the request (e.g., with a 403 Forbidden). The proxy MUST remove the user-provided P-Preferred-Identity header from any message it forwards. A UA only sends a P-Preferred-Identity header field to proxy servers in a Trust Domain; UAs must not populate the P-Preferred-Identity header field in a message that is not sent directly to a proxy that is trusted by the UA. Were a UA to send a message containing a P-Preferred-Identity header field to a node outside a Trust Domain, then the hinted identity might not be managed appropriately by the network, which could have negative ramifications for privacy.

20.3.5 Requesting Privacy

Parties who wish to request the removal of P-Asserted-Identity header fields before they are transmitted to an element that is not trusted may add the "id" privacy token defined in this document to the Privacy header field. When a proxy is forwarding the request to an element that is not trusted and there is no Privacy header field, the proxy may include the P-Asserted-Identity header field or it may remove it. This decision is a policy matter of the Trust Domain and must be specified in Spec(T). It is recommended that the P-Asserted-Identity header fields should not be removed unless local privacy policies prevent it, because removal may cause services based on Asserted Identity to fail.

However, it should be noted that unless all users of the Trust Domain have access to appropriate privacy services, forwarding of the P-Asserted-Identity may result in disclosure of information that the user has not requested and cannot prevent. It is therefore strongly recommended that all users have access to privacy services as described in this document. Formal specification of the "id" Privacy header priv-value is described later. Some general guidelines for when users require privacy are given in RFC 3323 (see Section 20.2). If multiple P-Asserted-Identity header field values are present in a message, and privacy of the P-Asserted-Identity header field is requested, then all instances of the header field values must be removed before forwarding the request to an entity that is not trusted.

20.3.6 UAS Behavior

Typically, a UA renders the value of a P-Asserted-Identity header field that it receives to its user. It may consider the identity provided by a Trust Domain to be privileged, or intrinsically more trustworthy than the From header field of a request. However, any specific behavior is specific to implementations or services. This document also does not mandate any UA handling for multiple P-Asserted-Identity header field values that happen to appear in a message (such as a SIP URI alongside a tel URL). However, if a UA server (UAS) receives a message from a previous element that it does not trust, it must not use the P-Asserted-Identity header field in any way. If a UA is part of the Trust Domain from which it received a message containing a P-Asserted-Identity header field, then it can use the value freely but it must ensure that it does not forward the information to any element that is not part of the Trust Domain, if the user has requested that asserted identity information be kept private. If a UA is not part of the Trust Domain from which it received a message containing a P-Asserted-Identity header field, then it can assume this information does not need to be kept private.

20.3.6.1 P-Asserted-Identity Header Syntax

The P-Asserted-Identity header field (see Section 2.8) is used among trusted SIP entities (typically intermediaries) to carry the identity of the user sending a SIP message as it was verified by authentication. A more detail explanation of this header is provided below:

```
PAssertedID        = "P-Asserted-Identity"
                     HCOLON PAssertedID-value
                     *(COMMA PAsserted
                     ID-value)
PAssertedID-value  = name-addr/addr-spec
```

A P-Asserted-Identity header field value MUST consist of exactly one name-addr or addr-spec. There may be one or two P-Asserted-Identity values. If there is one value, it MUST be a sip, sips, or tel URI. If there are two values, one value must be a sip or sips URI and the other must be a tel URI. It is worth noting that proxies can (and will) add and remove this header field. The use of this header by other SIP methods is shown in Table 2.5, Section 2.8.

20.3.6.2 P-Preferred-Identity Header Syntax

The P-Preferred-Identity header field (see Section 2.8) is used from a UA to a trusted proxy to carry the identity the user sending the SIP message wishes to be used for the P-Asserted-Header field value that the trusted element will insert. A more detailed explanation of this header is provided below:

```
PPreferredID        = "P-Preferred-Identity"
                      HCOLON PPreferred
                      ID-value
                      *(COMMA PPreferred
                      ID-value)
PPreferredID-value  = name-addr/addr-spec
```

A P-Preferred-Identity header field value MUST consist of exactly one name-addr or addr-spec. There may be one or two P-Preferred-Identity values. If there is one value, it must be a sip, sips, or tel URI. If there are two values, one value must be a sip or sips URI, and the other must be a tel URI. It is worth noting that proxies can (and will) remove this header field. The use of this header by other SIP methods is shown in Table 2.7, Section 2.8.

20.3.6.3 "id" Privacy Type

This specification adds a new privacy type ("priv-value") to the Privacy header, defined in RFC 3323 (see Section 2.8). The presence of this privacy type in a Privacy header field indicates that the user would like the NAI (see Section 10.5) to be kept private with respect to SIP entities outside the Trust Domain with which the user authenticated. Note that a user requesting multiple types of privacy must include all of the requested privacy types in its Privacy header field value.

```
priv-value="id"
```

Example:

```
Privacy: id
```

20.3.7 Examples

20.3.7.1 NAI Passed to Trusted Gateway

In this example, proxy.network.com creates a P-Asserted-Identity header field from an identity it discovered from SIP Digest authentication. It forwards this information to a trusted proxy, which forwards it to a trusted gateway. Note that these examples consist of partial SIP messages that illustrate only those headers relevant to the authenticated identity problem.

* F1 useragent.network.com -> proxy.network.com

```
INVITE sip:+14085551212@network.com SIP/2.0
Via: SIP/2.0/TCP useragent.network.com;
branch=z9hG4bK-123
To: <sip:+14085551212@network.com>
```

```
From: "Anonymous" <sip:anonymous@anonymous.
invalid>;tag=9802748
Call-ID: 245780247857024504
CSeq: 1 INVITE
Max-Forwards: 70
Privacy: id
```

* F2 proxy.network.com -> useragent.network.com

```
SIP/2.0 407 Proxy Authorization
Via: SIP/2.0/TCP useragent.network.com;
branch=z9hG4bK-123
To: <sip:+14085551212@network.com>;tag=123456
From: "Anonymous" <sip:anonymous@anonymous
.invalid>;tag=9802748
Call-ID: 245780247857024504
CSeq: 1 INVITE
Proxy-Authenticate: .... realm="sip.network
.com"
```

* F3 useragent.network.com -> proxy.network.com

```
INVITE sip:+14085551212@network.com SIP/2.0
Via: SIP/2.0/TCP useragent.network.com;
branch=z9hG4bK-124
To: <sip:+14085551212@network.com>
From: "Anonymous" <sip:anonymous@anonymous
.invalid>;tag=9802748
Call-ID: 245780247857024504
CSeq: 2 INVITE
Max-Forwards: 70
Privacy: id
Proxy-Authorization: .... realm="sip.network
.com" user="bjohnson"
```

* F4 proxy.network.com -> proxy.pstn.net (trusted)

```
INVITE sip:+14085551212@proxy.pstn.net
SIP/2.0
Via: SIP/2.0/TCP useragent.network.com;
branch=z9hG4bK-124
Via: SIP/2.0/TCP proxy.network.com;
branch=z9hG4bK-abc
To: <sip:+14085551212@network.com>
From: "Anonymous" <sip:anonymous@anonymous
.invalid>;tag=9802748
Call-ID: 245780247857024504
CSeq: 2 INVITE
Max-Forwards: 69
P-Asserted-Identity: "" <sip:bjohnson
@network.com>
P-Asserted-Identity: tel:+14085264000
Privacy: id
```

* F5 proxy.pstn.net -> gw.pstn.net (trusted)

```
INVITE sip:+14085551212@gw.pstn.net SIP/2.0
Via: SIP/2.0/TCP useragent.network.com;
branch=z9hG4bK-124
Via: SIP/2.0/TCP proxy.network.com;
branch=z9hG4bK-abc
Via: SIP/2.0/TCP proxy.pstn.net;
branch=z9hG4bK-a1b2
To: <sip:+14085551212@network.com>
From: "Anonymous" <sip:anonymous@anonymous
.invalid>;tag=9802748
Call-ID: 245780247857024504
CSeq: 2 INVITE
Max-Forwards: 68
P-Asserted-Identity: "" <sip:bjohnson
@network.com>
P-Asserted-Identity: tel:+14085264000
Privacy: id
```

20.3.7.2 NAI Withheld

In this example, the UA sends an INVITE that indicates it would prefer the identity sip:bjohnson@network.com to the first proxy, which authenticates this with SIP Digest. The first proxy creates a P-Asserted-Identity header field and forwards it to a trusted proxy (outbound.network.com). The next proxy removes the P-Asserted-Identity header field and the request for Privacy before forwarding this request onward to the biloxi.com proxy server, which it does not trust.

* F1 useragent.network.com -> proxy.network.com

```
INVITE sip:bob@biloxi.com SIP/2.0
Via: SIP/2.0/TCP useragent.network.com;
branch=z9hG4bK-a111
To: <sip:bob@biloxi.com>
From: "Anonymous" <sip:anonymous@anonymous
.invalid>;tag=9802748
Call-ID: 245780247857024504
CSeq: 1 INVITE
Max-Forwards: 70
Privacy: id
P-Preferred-Identity: "" <sip:bjohnson@
network.com>
```

* F2 proxy.network.com -> useragent.network.com

```
SIP/2.0 407 Proxy Authorization
Via: SIP/2.0/TCP useragent.network.com;
branch=z9hG4bK-a111
To: <sip:bob@biloxi.com>;tag=123456
From: "Anonymous" <sip:anonymous@anonymous
.invalid>;tag=9802748
Call-ID: 245780247857024504
CSeq: 1 INVITE
Proxy-Authenticate: .... realm="network.com"
```

* F3 useragent.network.com -> proxy.network.com

```
INVITE sip:bob@biloxi.com SIP/2.0
Via: SIP/2.0/TCP useragent.network.com;
branch=z9hG4bK-a123
To: <sip:bob@biloxi.com>
From: "Anonymous" <sip:anonymous@anonymous
.invalid>;tag=9802748
```

```
Call-ID: 245780247857024504
CSeq: 2 INVITE
Max-Forwards: 70
Privacy: id
P-Preferred-Identity: "" <sip:bjohnson
@network.com>
Proxy-Authorization: .... realm="network.com"
user="bjohnson"
```

* F4 proxy.network.com -> outbound.network.com (trusted)

```
INVITE sip:bob@biloxi SIP/2.0
Via: SIP/2.0/TCP useragent.network.com;
branch=z9hG4bK-a123
Via: SIP/2.0/TCP proxy.network.com;
branch=z9hG4bK-b234
To: <sip:bob@biloxi.com>
From: "Anonymous" <sip:anonymous@anonymous
.invalid>;tag=9802748
Call-ID: 245780247857024504
CSeq: 2 INVITE
Max-Forwards: 69
P-Asserted-Identity: "" <sip:bjohnson@vovida
.org>
Privacy: id
```

* F5 outbound.network.com -> proxy.biloxi.com (not trusted)

```
INVITE sip:bob@biloxi SIP/2.0
Via: SIP/2.0/TCP useragent.network.com;
branch=z9hG4bK-a123
Via: SIP/2.0/TCP proxy.network.com;
branch=z9hG4bK-b234
Via: SIP/2.0/TCP outbound.network.com;
branch=z9hG4bK-c345
To: <sip:bob@biloxi.com>
From: "Anonymous" <sip:anonymous@anonymous
.invalid>;tag=9802748
Call-ID: 245780247857024504
CSeq: 2 INVITE
Max-Forwards: 68
Privacy: id
```

* F6 proxy.biloxi.com -> bobster.biloxi.com

```
INVITE sip:bob@bobster.biloxi.com SIP/2.0
Via: SIP/2.0/TCP useragent.network.com;
branch=z9hG4bK-a123
Via: SIP/2.0/TCP proxy.network.com;
branch=z9hG4bK-b234
Via: SIP/2.0/TCP outbound.network.com;
branch=z9hG4bK-c345
Via: SIP/2.0/TCP proxy.biloxi.com;
branch=z9hG4bK-d456
To: <sip:bob@biloxi.com>
From: "Anonymous" <sip:anonymous@anonymous
.invalid>;tag=9802748
Call-ID: 245780247857024504
CSeq: 2 INVITE
Max-Forwards: 67
Privacy: id
```

20.3.8 Example of Spec(T)

The integrity of the mechanism described in this document relies on one node knowing (through configuration) that all of the nodes in a Trust Domain will behave in a predetermined way. This requires the predetermined behavior to be clearly defined and, for all nodes in the Trust Domain, to be compliant. The specification set that all nodes in a Trust Domain T must comply with is termed "Spec(T)." The remainder of this section presents an example Spec(T), which is not normative in any way.

- Protocol requirements
  The following specifications must be supported:
  - RFC 3261
  - RFC 3325
- Authentication requirements
  Users MUST be authenticated using SIP Digest Authentication.
- Security requirements
  Connections between nodes within the Trust Domain and between UAs and nodes in the Trust Domain MUST use TLS using a cipher suite of RSA_WITH_AES_128_CBC_SHA1. Mutual authentication between nodes in the Trust Domain MUST be performed and confidentiality MUST be negotiated.
- Scope of Trust Domain
  The Trust Domain specified in this agreement consists of hosts that possess a valid certificate
  - That is signed by examplerootca.org
  - Whose subjectAltName ends with one of the following domain names: trusted.div1.carrier-a.net, trusted.div2.carrier-a.net, or sip.carrier-b.com
  - Whose domain name corresponds to the host name in the subjectAltName in the certificate
- Implicit handling when no Privacy header is present
  The elements in the Trust Domain must support the "id" privacy service; therefore, absence of a Privacy header can be assumed to indicate that the user is not requesting any privacy. If no Privacy header field is present in a request, elements in this Trust Domain must act as if no privacy is requested.

20.3.9 Security Considerations

The mechanism provided in this document is a partial consideration of the problem of identity and privacy in SIP. For example, these mechanisms provide no means by which end users can securely share identity information end-to-end without a trusted service provider. Identity information that the user designates as "private" can be inspected by any intermediaries participating in the Trust Domain. This information is secured by transitive trust, which is only as reliable as the weakest link in the chain of trust. When a trusted entity sends a message to any destination with that party's identity in a P-Asserted-Identity header field, the entity must take precautions to protect the identity information from eavesdropping and interception, to protect the confidentiality and integrity of that identity information. The use of transport or network layer hop-by-hop security mechanisms, such as TLS or IPSec with appropriate cipher suites, can satisfy this requirement. Section 10.4 describes in detail the recommended use of the asserted identity.

20.4 Connected Identity for Privacy in SIP

20.4.1 Overview

The SIP (RFC 3261) initiates sessions but also provides information on the identities of the parties at both ends of a session. Users need this information to help determine how to deal with communications initiated by a SIP. The identity of the party who answers a call can differ from that of the initial called party for various reasons, such as call forwarding, call distribution, and call pick-up. Furthermore, once a call has been answered, a party can be replaced by a different party with a different identity for reasons such as call transfer, call-park and retrieval, and other call services. Although, in some cases, there can be reasons for not disclosing these identities, it is desirable to have a mechanism for providing this information. This document extends the use of the From header field to allow it to convey what is commonly called "connected identity" information (the identity of the connected user) in either direction within the context of an existing INVITE-initiated dialog. It can be used to convey

- The callee identity to a caller when a call is answered
- The identity of a potential callee before answer
- The identity of a user that replaces the caller or callee following a call rearrangement such as call transfer carried out within the PSTN or within a B2BUA using third-party call control techniques

Note that the use of standard SIP call transfer techniques, involving the REFER method, leads to the establishment of a new dialog and hence normal mechanisms for caller and callee identity applications. The provision of the identity of the responder in a response (commonly called "response identity") is outside the scope of this document. Note that even if identity were to be conveyed somehow in a response, there would in general be difficulty in authenticating the UAS. Providing identity in a separate request allows normal authentication techniques to be used.

RFC 4916 that is described here provides a means for a SIP UA that receives a dialog-forming request to supply its identity to the peer UA by means of a request in the reverse direction, and for that identity to be signed by an authentication service. Because of retargeting of a dialog-forming request (changing the value of the Request-URI), the UA that receives it (the UAS) can have a different identity from that in the To header field. The same mechanism can be used to indicate a change of identity during a dialog, for example, because of some action in the PSTN behind a gateway. Thereby, RFC 4916 normatively updates RFC 3261 for maintaining the privacy of the identity of the connected user termed as the connected identity.

20.4.2 Terminology

We are repeating the definitions of some terms specifically related to the connected identity for convenience, although these are available in Section 2.2:

- **Caller:** The user of the UA that issues an INVITE request to initiate a call
- **Caller identity:** The identity (AOR) of a caller
- **Callee:** The user of the UA that answers a call by issuing a 2xx response to an INVITE request
- **Callee identity:** The identity (AOR) of a callee
- **Potential callee:** The user of any UA to which an INVITE request is targeted, resulting in the formation of an early dialog; however, because of parallel or serial forking of the request, it is not necessarily the user that answers the call
- **Connected user:** Any user involved in an established call, including the caller, the callee, or any user that replaces the caller or callee following a call rearrangement such as call transfer
- **Connected identity:** The identity (AOR) of a connected user

20.4.3 Overview of Solution

A mid-dialog request is used to provide connected identity. The UA client (UAC) for that request inserts its identity in the From header field of the request. To provide authentication, the Identity header field specified in RFC 4474 (see Sections 2.8 and 19.4.8) is inserted by a suitable authentication service on the path of the mid-dialog request. Unless provided at the UAC, the authentication service is expected to be at a proxy that record-routes and is able to authenticate the UAC. A request in the opposite direction to the INVITE request before or at the time the call is answered can indicate the identity of the potential callee or callee, respectively. A request in the same direction as the INVITE request before answer can indicate a change of caller. A request in either direction after answering can indicate a change of the connected user. In all cases, a dialog (early or confirmed) has to be established before such a request can be sent.

This solution uses the UPDATE method specified in RFC 3311 (see Section 15.4) for the request, or in some circumstances the re-INVITE method. To send the callee identity, the UAS for the INVITE request sends the UPDATE request after sending the 2xx response to the INVITE request and after receiving an ACK request. To send the potential callee identity, RFC 3262 (see Sections 2.5, 2.8.2, and 2.10) is expected to be supported. In this case, the UAS for the INVITE request sends the UPDATE request after receiving and responding to a PRACK request (which occurs after sending a reliable 1xx response to the INVITE request). The UPDATE request could also conceivably be used for other purposes; for example, it could be used during an early dialog to send the potential callee identity at the same time as a SDP offer for early media. To indicate a connected identity change during an established call, either the UPDATE method or the re-INVITE method can be used.

The re-INVITE method would be used if required for other purposes; for example, when a B2BUA performs transfer using third-party call control techniques specified in RFC 3725 (see Section 18.3), it has to issue a re-INVITE request without an SDP offer to solicit an SDP offer from the UA. This solution involves changing the URI (not the tags) in the To and From header fields of mid-dialog requests and their responses, compared with the corresponding values in the dialog-forming request and response. According to RFC 3261, changing the To and From header field URIs is complicated.

RFC 4916, therefore, deprecates mandatory reflection of the original To and From URIs in mid-dialog requests and their responses, which constitutes a change to RFC 3261. RFC 4916 makes no provision for proxies that are unable to tolerate a change of URI, since changing the URI has been expected for a considerable time. To cater for any UAs that are not able to tolerate a change of URI, a new option tag "from-change" is introduced for providing a positive indication of support in the Supported header field. By sending a request with a changed From header field URI only to targets that have indicated support for this option, there is no need to send this option tag in a Require header field. In addition to allowing the From header field URI to change during a dialog to reflect the connected identity, this document also requires a UA that has received a connected identity in the URI of the From header field of a mid-dialog request to use that URI in the To header field of any subsequent mid-dialog request sent by that UA. In the absence of a suitable authentication service on the path of the mid-dialog request, the UAS will receive an unauthenticated connected identity (i.e., without a corresponding Identity header field). The implications of this are discussed in the subsequent section.

20.4.4 UA Behavior outside the Context of an Existing Dialog

20.4.4.1 Issuing an INVITE Request

When issuing an INVITE request, a UA compliant with this specification MUST include the "from-change" option tag in the Supported header field. Note that sending the "from-change" option tag does not guarantee that connected identity will be received in subsequent requests.

20.4.4.2 Receiving an INVITE Request

After receiving an INVITE request, a UA compliant with this specification must include the "from-change" option tag in the Supported header field of any dialog-forming response. Note that sending the "from-change" option tag does not guarantee that connected identity will be received in the event of a change of caller. After an early dialog has been formed, if the "from-change" option tag has been received in a Supported header field, the UA may issue an UPDATE request on the same dialog, subject to having sent a reliable provisional response to the INVITE request and having received and responded to a PRACK request. After a full dialog has been formed (after sending a 2xx final response to the INVITE request), if the "from-change" option tag has been received in a Supported header field and an UPDATE request has not already been sent on the early dialog, the UA must issue an UPDATE request on the same dialog. In either case, the UPDATE request must contain the callee's (or potential callee's) identity in the URI of the From header field (or an anonymous identity if anonymity is required). Note that even if the URI does not differ from that in the To header field URI of the INVITE request, sending a new request allows the authentication service to assert authentication of this identity, and confirms to the peer UA that the connected identity is the same as that in the To header field URI of the INVITE request.

20.4.5 Behavior of a UA Whose Identity Changes

If the "from-change" option tag has been received in a Supported header field during an established INVITE-initiated dialog and if the identity associated with the UA changes (e.g., due to transfer) compared with the last identity indicated in the From header field of a request sent by that UA, the UA must issue a request on the same dialog containing the new identity in the URI of the From header field (or an anonymous identity if anonymity is required). For this purpose, the UA must use the UPDATE method unless for other reasons the re-INVITE method is being used at the same time.

20.4.6 General UA Behavior

20.4.6.1 Sending a Mid-Dialog Request

When sending a mid-dialog request, a UA MUST observe the requirements of RFC 4474 (see Sections 2.8 and 19.4.8) when populating the From header field URI, including provisions for achieving anonymity. This will allow an authentication service on the path of the mid-dialog request to insert an Identity header field. When sending a mid-dialog request, a UA must populate the To header field URI with the current value of the remote URI for that dialog, where this is subject to update in accordance with the rules of Section 20.4.6.2 (Section 4.4.2 of RFC 4916) rather than being fixed at the beginning of the dialog in accordance with RFC 3261. After sending a request with a revised From header field URI (i.e., revised compared with the URI sent in the From header field of the previous request on this dialog or in the To header field of the received dialog-forming INVITE request if no request has been sent), the UA MUST send the same URI in the From header field of any future requests on the same dialog, unless the identity changes again.

Also, the UA must be prepared to receive the revised URI in the To header field of subsequent mid-dialog requests and must also continue to be prepared to receive the old URI at least until a request containing the revised URI in the To header field has been received. The mid-dialog request can be rejected in accordance with RFC 4474 (see Sections 2.8 and 19.4.8) if the UAS does not accept the connected identity. If the UAC receives a 428, 436, 437, or 438 response to a mid-dialog request, it should regard the dialog as terminated in the case of a dialog-terminating request and should take no action in the case of any other request. Any attempt to repeat the request or send any other mid-dialog request is likely to result in the same response, since the UA has no control over actions of the authentication service.

20.4.6.2 Receiving a Mid-Dialog Request

If a UA receives a mid-dialog request from the peer UA, the UA can make use of the identity in the From header field URI (e.g., by indicating to the user). The UA may discriminate between signed and unsigned identities. In the case of a signed identity, the UA should invoke a Verifier, described later, if it cannot rely on the presence of a Verifier on the path of the request. If a UA receives a mid-dialog request from the peer UA in which the From header field URI differs from that received in the previous request on that dialog or that sent in the To header field of the original INVITE request, and if the UA sends a 2xx response, the UA must update the remote URI for this dialog, as defined in RFC 3261 (see Section 3.6). This will cause the new value to be used in the To header field of subsequent requests that the UA sends, in accordance with the rules of Section 20.4.6.1 (Section 4.4.1 of RFC 4916). If any other final response is sent, the UA must not update the remote URI for this dialog.

20.4.7 Authentication Service Behavior

An authentication service must behave in accordance with RFC 4474 (see Sections 2.8 and 19.4.8) when dealing with mid-dialog requests. Note that RFC 4474 is silent on how to behave if the identity in the From header field is not one that the UAC is allowed to assert, and therefore it is a matter for local policy whether to reject the request or forward it without an Identity header field. Policy can be different for a mid-dialog request compared with other requests. Note that when UAs conform with this specification, the authentication service should (subject to the normal rules for authentication) be able to authenticate the sender of a request as being the entity identified in the From header field, and hence will be able provide a signature for this identity. This is in contrast to UAs that do not support this specification, where retargeting and mid-dialog identity changes can render the From header field inaccurate as a means of identifying the sender of the request.

20.4.8 Verifier Behavior

When dealing with mid-dialog requests, an authentication service must behave in accordance with RFC 4474 (see Sections 2.8 and 19.4.8) updated as stated below. RFC 4474 states that it is a matter of policy whether to reject a request with a 428 Use Identity Header response if there is no Identity header field in the request. A UA may adopt a different policy for mid-dialog requests compared with other requests.

20.4.9 Proxy Behavior

A proxy that receives a mid-dialog request must be prepared for the To header field URI and/or the From header field URI to differ from those that appeared in the dialog-forming request and response. A proxy that is able to provide an authentication service for mid-dialog requests must record-route if Supported: from-change is indicated in the dialog-forming request received by the proxy from the UAC.

20.4.10 Examples

In the examples (Figure 20.1) below, several messages contain unfolded lines longer than 72 characters. These are captured between tags. The single unfolded line is reconstructed by directly concatenating all lines appearing between the tags (discarding any line feeds or carriage returns). In the examples, domain example.com is assumed to have the following private key (rendered in Privacy Enhanced Mail format). The private key is used by the authentication service for generating the signature in the Identity header field.


```
-----BEGIN RSA PRIVATE KEY-----
MIICXQIBAAKBgQDPPMBtHVoPkXV+Z6jq1LsgfTELVWpy2
BVUffJMPH06LL0cJSQOaIeVzIojzWtpauB7IylZKlAjB
5f429tRuoUiedCwMLKblWAqZt6eHWpCNZJ7lONcIEwnmh
2nAccKk83Lp/VH3tgAS/43DQoX2sndnYh+g8522Pzwg7E
GWspzzwIDAQABAoGBAK0W3tnEFD7AjVQAnJNXDtx59Aa1
Vu2JEXe6oi+OrkFysJjbZJwsLmKtrgttPXOU8t2mZpi0w
K4hX4tZhntiwGKkUPC3h9Bjp+GerifP341RMyMO+6fPg
jqOzUDw+rPjjMpwD7AkcEcqDgbTrZnWv/QnCSaaF3x
kUGfFkLx5OKcRAkEA7UxnsE8XaT30tP/UUc51gNk2KGKg
xQQTHopBcew9yfeCRFhvdL7jpaGatEi5iZwGGQQDVOVHU
N1H0YLpHQjRowJBAN+R2bvA/Nimq464ZgnelEDPqaEAZW
aD3kOfhS9+vL7oqES+u5E0J7kXb7ZkiSVUg9XU/8Px
MKx/DAz0dUmOL+UCQH8C9ETUMI2uEbqHbBdVUGNk364C
DFcndSxVh+34KqJdjiYSx6VPPv26X9m7S0OydTkSgs3/
4ooPxo8HaMqXm80CQB+rxbB3UlpOohcBwFK9mTrlMB6Cs
9ql66KgwnlL9ukEhHHYozGatdXeoBCyhUsogdSU6/
aSAFcvWEGtj7/vyJECQQCCS1lKgEXoNQPqONalvYhyyMZ
RXFLdD4gbwRPK1uXKYpk3CkfFzOyfjeLcGPxXzq2qzuH
zGTDxZ9PAepwX4RSk
-----END RSA PRIVATE KEY-----
```


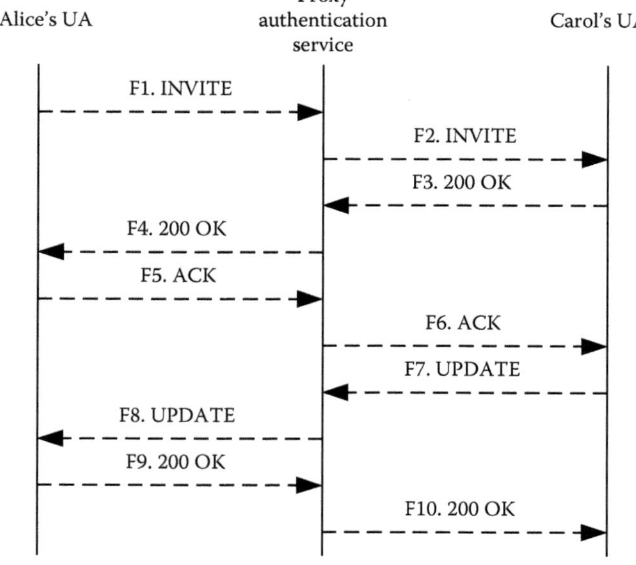

Figure 20.1 Call flows for sending connected identity after answering a call. (Copyright IETF. Reproduced with permission.)

20.4.10.1 Sending Connected Identity after Answering a Call

In this example (Figure 20.1), Carol's UA has been reached by retargeting at the proxy and thus her identity is not equal to that in the To header field of the received INVITE request (Bob). Carol's UA conveys Carol's identity in the From header field of an UPDATE request. The proxy also provides an authentication service and therefore adds Identity and Identity-Info header fields to the UPDATE request.

F1. INVITE:

```
INVITE sip:Bob@example.com SIP/2.0
Via: SIP/2.0/TLS ua1.example.com;
branch=z9hG4bKnashds8
To: Bob <sip:bob@example.com>
From: Alice <sip:alice@example.com>;
tag=13adc987
Call-ID: 12345600@ua1.example.com
CSeq: 1 INVITE
Max-Forwards: 70
Date: Thu, 21 Feb 2002 13:02:03 GMT
Allow: INVITE, ACK, CANCEL, OPTIONS, BYE,
UPDATE
Supported: from-change
Contact: <sip:alice@ua1.example.com>
Content-Type: application/sdp
Content-Length: 154

v=0
o=UserA 2890844526 2890844526 IN IP4 ua1
.example.com
s=Session SDP
c=IN IP4 ua1.example.com
t=0 0
m=audio 49172 RTP/AVP 0
a=rtpmap:0 PCMU/8000
```

F2. INVITE:

```
INVITE sip:Carol@ua2.example.com SIP/2.0
Via: SIP/2.0/TLS proxy.example.
com;branch=z9hG4bK776asdhds
<allOneLine>
       Via: SIP/2.0/TLS ua1.example.com;
       branch=z9hG4bKnashds8;
       received=192.0.2.1
</allOneLine>

To: Bob <sip:bob@example.com>
From: Alice <sip:alice@example.com>;tag=
13adc987
Call-ID: 12345600@ua1.example.com
CSeq: 1 INVITE
Max-Forwards: 69
Date: Thu, 21 Feb 2002 13:02:03 GMT
Allow: INVITE, ACK, CANCEL, OPTIONS, BYE, UPDATE
Supported: from-change
Contact: <sip:alice@ua1.example.com>
Record-Route: <sip:proxy.example.com;lr>
```

```
<allOneLine>
      Identity:
      "xN6gCHR6KxGM+nyiEM13LcWgAFQD3lkni1DPk
      wgadxh4BB7G+VwY13uRv5hbCI2VSvKuZ4LY
      N0JNoe7v8VAzruKMyi4Bi4nUghR/fFGBrpBSjz
      tmfffLTp6SFLxo9XQSVrkm1O4c/4UrKn2ej
      Rz+5BULu9n9kWswzKDNjlYlmmc="
</allOneLine>

Identity-Info: <https://example.com/example
.cer>;alg=rsa-sha1
Content-Type: application/sdp
Content-Length: 154

v=0
o=UserA 2890844526 2890844526 IN IP4 ua1
.example.com
s=Session SDP
c=IN IP4 ua1.example.com
t=0 0
m=audio 49172 RTP/AVP 0
a=rtpmap:0 PCMU/8000
```

F3. 200 OK:

```
SIP/2.0 200 OK

<allOneLine>
      Via: SIP/2.0/TLS proxy.example.com;
      branch=z9hG4bK776asdhds;
      received=192.0.2.2
</allOneLine>

<allOneLine>
      Via: SIP/2.0/TLS ua1.example.com;
      branch=z9hG4bKnashds8;
      received=192.0.2.1
<allOneLine>

To: Bob <sip:bob@example.com>;tag=2ge46ab5
From: Alice <sip:alice@example.com>;
tag=13adc987
Call-ID: 12345600@ua1.example.com
CSeq: 1 INVITE
Allow: INVITE, ACK, CANCEL, OPTIONS, BYE,
UPDATE
Supported: from-change
Contact: <sip:carol@ua2.example.com>
Record-Route: <sip:proxy.example.com;lr>
Content-Type: application/sdp
Content-Length: 154

v=0
o=UserB 2890844536 2890844536 IN IP4 ua2.
example.com
s=Session SDP
c=IN IP4 ua2.example.com
t=0 0
m=audio 49172 RTP/AVP 0
a=rtpmap:0 PCMU/8000
```

F4. 200 OK:

```
SIP/2.0 200 OK

<allOneLine>
      Via: SIP/2.0/TLS ua1.example.com;
      branch=z9hG4bKnashds8;
      received=192.0.2.1
</allOneLine>

To: Bob <sip:bob@example.com>;tag=2ge46ab5
From: Alice <sip:alice@example
.com>;tag=13adc987
Call-ID: 12345600@ua1.example.com
CSeq: 1 INVITE
Allow: INVITE, ACK, CANCEL, OPTIONS, BYE,
UPDATE
Supported: from-change
Contact: <sip:carol@ua2.example.com>
Record-Route: <sip:proxy.example.com;lr>
Content-Type: application/sdp
Content-Length: 154

v=0
o=UserB 2890844536 2890844536 IN IP4 ua2
.example.com
s=Session SDP
c=IN IP4 ua2.example.com
t=0 0
m=audio 49172 RTP/AVP 0
a=rtpmap:0 PCMU/8000
```

F5. ACK:

```
ACK sip:carol@ua2.example.com SIP/2.0
Via: SIP/2.0/TLS ua1.example.com;
branch=z9hG4bKnashds9
From: Alice <sip:Alice@example.com>;
tag=13adc987
To: Bob <sip:Bob@example.com>;tag=2ge46ab5
Call-ID: 12345600@ua1.example.com
CSeq: 1 ACK
Max-Forwards: 70
Route: <sip:proxy.example.com;lr>
Content-Length: 0
```

F6. ACK:

```
ACK sip:carol@ua2.example.com SIP/2.0
Via: SIP/2.0/TLS proxy.example.com;
branch=z9hG4bK776asdhdt

<allOneLine>
Via: SIP/2.0/TLS ua1.example.com;branch=z9hG4
bKnashds9;received=192.0.2.1
</allOneLine>
From: Alice <sip:Alice@example.com>;
tag=13adc987
To: Bob <sip:Bob@example.com>;tag=2ge46ab5
Call-ID: 12345600@ua1.example.com
CSeq: 1 ACK
Max-Forwards: 69
Content-Length: 0
```

F7. UPDATE:

```
UPDATE sip:Alice@ua1.example.com SIP/2.0
```

```
Via: SIP/2.0/TLS ua2.example.com;
branch=z9hG4bKnashdt1
From: Carol <sip:Carol@example.com>;
tag=2ge46ab5
To: Alice <sip:Alice@example.com>;
tag=13adc987
Call-ID: 12345600@ua1.example.com
CSeq: 2 UPDATE
Max-Forwards: 70
Date: Thu, 21 Feb 2002 13:02:15 GMT
Route: <sip:proxy.example.com;lr>
Contact: <sip:Carol@ua2.example.com>
Content-Length: 0
```

Note that the URI in the From header field differs from that in the To header field in the INVITE request–response. However, the tag is the same as that in the INVITE response.

F8. UPDATE:

```
UPDATE sip:Alice@ua1.example.com SIP/2.0
Via: SIP/2.0/TLS proxy.example.com;
branch=z9hG4bK776asdhdu
<allOneLine>
       Via: SIP/2.0/TLS ua2.example.com;
       branch=z9hG4bKnashdt1;
       received=192.0.2.3
</allOneLine>

From: Carol <sip:Carol@example.com>;
tag=2ge46ab5
To: Alice <sip:Alice@example.com>;
tag=13adc987
Call-ID: 12345600@ua1.example.com
CSeq: 2 UPDATE
Max-Forwards: 69
Date: Thu, 21 Feb 2002 13:02:15 GMT
Contact: <sip:Carol@ua2.example.com>

<allOneLine>
       Identity: "g8WJiVEzrbYum+z2lnS3pL+MIhu
       I439gDiMCHm01fwX5D8Ft5Ib9t
       ewLfBT9mDOUSn6wkPSWVQfqdMF/QBPkpsIIROI
       i2sJOYBEMXZpNrhJd8/uboXMl9KRujDFQef
       ZlmXV8dwD6XsPnMgcH8jAcaZ5aS04NyfWadI
       wTnGeuxko="
</allOneLine>

Identity-Info: <https://example.com/
cert>;alg=rsa-sha1
Content-Length: 0
```

F9. 200 OK:

```
SIP/2.0 200 OK

<allOneLine>
       Via: SIP/2.0/TLS proxy.example.com;
       branch=z9hG4bK776asdhdu;
       received=192.0.2.2
</allOneLine>
<allOneLine>
       Via: SIP/2.0/TLS ua2.example.com;
       branch=z9hG4bKnashdt1;
       received=192.0.2.3
</allOneLine>

From: Carol <sip:Carol@example.com>;
tag=2ge46ab5
To: Alice <sip:Alice@example.com>;
tag=13adc987
Call-ID: 12345600@ua1.example.com
CSeq: 2 UPDATE
Contact: <sip:Alice@ua1.example.com>
Content-Length: 0
```

F10. 200 OK:

```
SIP/2.0 200 OK

<allOneLine>
       Via: SIP/2.0/TLS ua2.example.com;
       branch=z9hG4bKnashdt1;
       received=192.0.2.3
</allOneLine>

From: Carol <sip:Carol@example.com>;
tag=2ge46ab5
To: Alice <sip:Alice@example.com>;
tag=13adc987
Call-ID: 12345600@ua1.example.com
CSeq: 2 UPDATE
Contact: <sip:Alice@ua1.example.com>
Content-Length: 0
```

20.4.10.2 Sending Revised Connected Identity during a Call

In this example (Figure 20.2), a call is established between Alice and Bob, where Bob (not shown) lies behind a B2BUA.

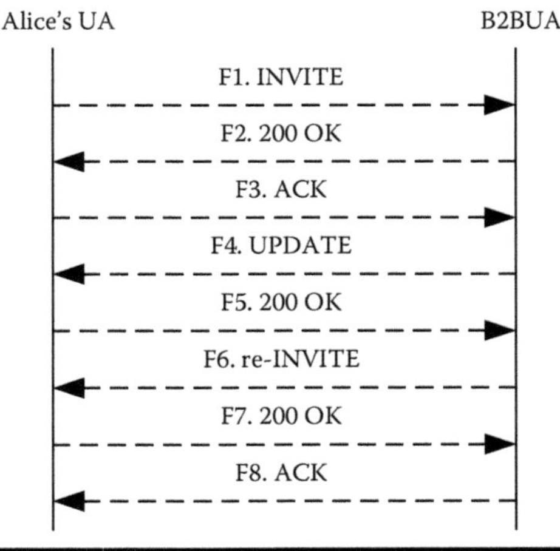

Figure 20.2 Call flows for sending revised connected identity during a call. (Copyright IETF. Reproduced with permission.)

Bob's identity is conveyed by an UPDATE request. Then, the B2BUA executes call transfer using third-party call control techniques as described in RFC 3725 (see Section 18.3) (e.g., under the control of a click-to-dial application). As a result, Alice becomes connected to Carol (also not shown), and a re-INVITE request is issued allowing the session to be renegotiated. The B2BUA provides the authentication service and thus generates the Identity header field in the re-INVITE request to provide authentication of Carol's identity.

F1. INVITE:

```
INVITE sip:Bob@example.com SIP/2.0
Via: SIP/2.0/TLS ua1.example.com;
branch=z9hG4bKnashds8
To: Bob <sip:bob@example.com>
From: Alice <sip:alice@example.com>;
tag=13adc987
Call-ID: 12345600@ua1.example.com
CSeq: 1 INVITE
Max-Forwards: 70
Date: Thu, 21 Feb 2002 13:02:03 GMT
Allow: INVITE, ACK, CANCEL, OPTIONS, BYE,
UPDATE
Supported: from-change
Contact: <sip:alice@ua1.example.com>
Content-Type: application/sdp
Content-Length: 154

v=0
o=UserA 2890844526 2890844526 IN IP4 ua1
.example.com
s=Session SDP
c=IN IP4 ua1.example.com
t=0 0
m=audio 49172 RTP/AVP 0
a=rtpmap:0 PCMU/8000
```

F2. 200 OK:

```
SIP/2.0 200 OK

<allOneLine>
       Via: SIP/2.0/TLS ua1.example.com;
       branch=z9hG4bKnashds8;
       received=192.0.2.1
</allOneLine>

To: Bob <sip:bob@example.com>;tag=2ge46ab5
From: Alice <sip:alice@example.com>;
tag=13adc987
Call-ID: 12345600@ua1.example.com
CSeq: 1 INVITE
Allow: INVITE, ACK, CANCEL, OPTIONS, BYE,
UPDATE
Supported: from-change
Contact: <sip:xyz@b2bua.example.com>
Content-Type: application/sdp
Content-Length: 154

v=0
o=UserB 2890844536 2890844536 IN IP4 ua2
.example.com
s=Session SDP
c=IN IP4 ua2.example.com
t=0 0
m=audio 49172 RTP/AVP 0
a=rtpmap:0 PCMU/8000
```

F3. ACK:

```
ACK sip:xyz@b2bua.example.com SIP/2.0
Via: SIP/2.0/TLS ua1.example.com;
branch=z9hG4bKnashds9
From: Alice <sip:Alice@example.com>;
tag=13adc987
To: Bob <sip:Bob@example.com>;tag=2ge46ab5
Call-ID: 12345600@ua1.example.com
CSeq: 1 ACK
Max-Forwards: 70
Content-Length: 0
```

F4. UPDATE:

```
UPDATE sip:alice@ua1.example.com SIP/2.0
Via: SIP/2.0/TLS b2bua.example.com;
branch=z9hG4bKnashdt1
From: Bob <sip:Bob@example.com>;tag=2ge46ab5
To: Alice <sip:Alice@example.com>;
tag=13adc987
Call-ID: 12345600@ua1.example.com
CSeq: 2 UPDATE
Max-Forwards: 70
Date: Thu, 21 Feb 2002 13:02:12 GMT
Contact: <sip:xyz@b2bua.example.com>

<allOneLine>
       Identity:"AQFLSjCDRhO2eXlWmTajk99612hk
       Jii9giDMWki5uT6qc4BrekywOUuObcwZI3q
       hJReZCN7ybMBNYFZ5yFXWdyet4j3zLNCONU9ma
       +rs8ZOv0+z/Q3Z5cD26HrmitU+OCKWPLOba
       xbkGQry9hQxOmwRmlUgSjkeCEjgnc1iQc3E="
</allOneLine>

Identity-Info: <https://example.com/
cert>;alg=rsa-sha1
Content-Length: 0
```

F5. 200 OK:

```
SIP/2.0 200 OK

<allOneLine>
       Via: SIP/2.0/TLS b2bua.example.com;
       branch=z9hG4bKnashdt1;
       received=192.0.2.2
</allOneLine>

From: Bob <sip:Bob@example.com>;tag=2ge46ab5
To: Alice <sip:Alice@example.
com>;tag=13adc987
```

```
Call-ID: 12345600@ua1.example.com
CSeq: 2 UPDATE
Contact: <sip:Alice@ua1.example.com>
Content-Length: 0
```

F6. re-INVITE:

```
INVITE sip:alice@ua1.example.com SIP/2.0
Via: SIP/2.0/TLS b2bua.example.com;
branch=z9hG4bKnashdxy
From: Carol <sip:Carol@example.com>;
tag=2ge46ab5
To: Alice <sip:Alice@example.com>;
tag=13adc987
Call-ID: 12345600@ua1.example.com
CSeq: 3 INVITE
Max-Forwards: 70
Date: Thu, 21 Feb 2002 13:03:20 GMT
Contact: <sip:xyz@b2bua.example.com>

<allOneLine>
```

```
       Identity:"KCd3YLQHj51SlCQhFMnpQjmP6wHh
       7JGRO8LsB4v5SGEr/Mwu7j6Gpal8ckVM2vd
       1zqH/F4WJXYD1B525uuJm/fN3O1A2xsZ9BxRkh
       4N4U19TL9I2Tok3U3kGg8To/6w1mEXpUQjo
       3OgNYqOBtawHuZI5nrOVaV3IrbQh1b2KgLo="
```

```
</allOneLine>

Identity-Info: <https://example.com/
cert>;alg=rsa-sha1
Content-Length: 0
```

F7. 200 OK:

```
SIP/2.0 200 OK

<allOneLine>
       Via: SIP/2.0/TLS b2bua.example.com;
       branch=z9hG4bKnashdxy;
       received=192.0.2.2
</allOneLine>

From: Carol <sip:Carol@example.com>;
tag=2ge46ab5
To: Alice <sip:Alice@example.com>;
tag=13adc987
Call-ID: 12345600@ua1.example.com
CSeq: 3 INVITE
Contact: <sip:Alice@ua1.example.com>
Content-Length: 154

v=0
o=UserA 2890844526 2890844526 IN IP4 ua1.
example.com
s=Session SDP
c=IN IP4 ua1.example.com
t=0 0
m=audio 49172 RTP/AVP 0
a=rtpmap:0 PCMU/8000
```

F8. ACK:

```
ACK sip:alice@ua1.example.com SIP/2.0
Via: SIP/2.0/TLS b2bua.example.com;
branch=z9hG4bKnashdxz
From: Carol <sip:Carol@example.com>;
tag=2ge46ab5
To: Alice <sip:Alice@example.com>;
tag=13adc987
Call-ID: 12345600@ua1.example.com
CSeq: 3 ACK
Max-Forwards: 70
Content-Length: 154

v=0
o=UserC 2890844546 2890844546 IN IP4 ua3
.example.com
s=Session SDP
c=IN IP4 ua3.example.com
t=0 0
m=audio 49172 RTP/AVP 0
a=rtpmap:0 PCMU/8000
```

20.4.11 Security Considerations

RFC 4474 discusses security considerations relating to the Identity header field in some detail. Those same considerations apply when using the Identity header field to authenticate a connected identity in the From header field URI of a mid-dialog request. A received From header field URI in a mid-dialog request for which no valid Identity header field (or other means of authentication) has been received, either in this request or in an earlier request on this dialog, cannot be trusted (except in very closed environments) and is expected to be treated in a similar way to a From header field in a dialog-initiating request that is not backed up by a valid Identity header field. However, it is recommended not to reject a mid-dialog request on the grounds that the Identity header field is missing (since this would interfere with ongoing operation of the call). The absence of a valid Identity header field can influence the information given to the user. A UA can clear the call if policy or user preference dictates.

A signed connected identity in a mid-dialog request (URI in the From header field accompanied by a valid Identity header field) provides information about the peer UA in a dialog. In the case of the UA that was the UAS in the dialog-forming request, this identity is not necessarily the same as that in the To header field of the dialog-forming request. This is because of retargeting during the routing of the dialog-forming request. A signed connected identity says nothing about the legitimacy of such retargeting, but merely reflects the result of that retargeting. History information specified in RFC 4244 (see Section 2.8) can provide additional hints as to how the connected user has been reached.

Likewise, when a signed connected identity indicates a change of identity during a dialog, it conveys no information about the reason for such a change of identity or its legitimacy. Use of the sips URI scheme can minimize the chances of attacks in which inappropriate connected identity information is sent, either at call establishment time or during a call. Anonymity can be required by the user of a connected UA. For anonymity, the UA is expected to populate the URI in the From header field of a mid-dialog request in the way described in RFC 4474.

20.5 Guidelines for Using Privacy Mechanism in SIP

RFC 5379 provides guidelines for using the privacy mechanism for the SIP that is specified in RFC 3323 (see Section 8.2.4) and subsequently extended in RFCs 3325 (see Sections 2.8 and 20.3) and 4244 (see Section 2.8). It is intended to clarify the handling of the target SIP headers/parameters and the SDP parameters for each of the privacy header values (priv-values). The practical manner of operations of the privacy mechanism is described here as a guideline, and does not change the existing privacy mechanism. In RFC 3323 (see Section 20.2), the semantics of the basic set of priv-values (header, session, user, none, and critical) is defined; however, there are some ambiguities in regards to the target information to be obscured per priv-value, which are not explicitly specified. An ambiguity such as this could result in different interpretations of privacy handling for each of the priv-values defined, both at an entity setting a Privacy header and at an entity processing a Privacy header, which could have an adverse impact on interoperability.

Additional priv-values "id" and "history" are defined in RFCs 3325 (see Sections 2.8 and 20.3) and 4244 (see Section 2.8), respectively. In RFC 4244 (see Section 2.8), the priv-value "history" is defined in order to request privacy for History-Info headers, and the target to be obscured for "history" priv-value is specified as only the History-Info headers. In addition, the RFC clearly describes that History-Info headers are also the target when "header"- and "session"-level privacy are requested. On the other hand, RFC 3325 (see Sections 2.8 and 20.3) defines the P-Asserted-Identity header and a priv-value "id," which is used to request privacy for only the P-Asserted-Identity header, but it does not specify how other priv-values may influence the privacy handling of the P-Asserted-Identity header. Because of this lack of specification, it has been observed that some implementations are suffering from the inability to achieve the intended privacy due to discrepancies in interpretations. This document tries to clarify the SIP headers and SDP parameters to be obscured for each of the priv-values to alleviate the potential interoperability issues already seen due to a lack of explicit text.

20.5.1 Definition

- **priv-value:** Values registered with the Internet Assigned Numbers Authority (IANA) to be used in the Privacy header. Registered priv-values are "header," "session," "user," "none," and "critical" defined in RFC 3323 (see Section 20.2); "id" defined in RFC 3325 (see Sections 2.8 and 20.3); and "history" defined in RFC 4244 (see Section 2.8).
- **privacy service:** A network entity that executes privacy functions before forwarding messages to the next hop. It is sometimes abbreviated to PS in this document.
- **user-level privacy:** Privacy for user-inserted information that can be anonymized by the UA itself.

20.5.2 Semantics of Existing Priv-Values

This section provides the semantics of each priv-value defined in RFCs 3323, 3325, and 4244. The descriptions are taken from the IANA registration (Table 20.1).

20.5.3 Target for Each Priv-Value

Tables in this section show the recommended treatment of SIP headers and SDP parameters per priv-value. SIP headers and SDP parameters not shown in the tables are regarded as

Table 20.1 Semantics of Different Privacy Types

Privacy Type	*Description*	*Reference*
User	Request that privacy services provide a user-level privacy function	RFC 3323
Header	Request that privacy services modify headers that cannot be set arbitrarily	RFC 3323
Session	Request that privacy services provide privacy for session media	RFC 3323
None	Privacy services must not perform any privacy function	RFC 3323
Critical	Privacy service must perform the specified services or fail the request	RFC 3323
Id	Privacy requested for third-party asserted identity	RFC 3325
History	Privacy requested for History-Info header(s)	RFC 4244

Source: Copyright IETF. Reproduced with permission.

nontargets of these priv-values. Some nontarget SIP headers/SDP parameters may carry privacy-sensitive information that may need privacy treatment regardless of the privacy level requested. This is further described later. The way in which SIP headers and SDP parameters listed here are obscured may depend on the implementation and network policy. This document does not prevent different variations that may exist based on local policy but tries to provide recommendations for how a privacy service treats SIP headers and SDP parameters.

20.5.3.1 Target SIP Headers for Each Priv-Value

Table 20.2 shows a recommended treatment of each SIP header for each priv-value. Detailed descriptions of the recommended treatment per SIP header are covered in Section 2.8. The "where" column describes the request and response types in which the header needs the treatment to maintain privacy. Values in this column are

- R: The header needs the treatment when it appears in a request.
- r: The header needs the treatment when it appears in a response.

The next five columns show the recommended treatment for each priv-value:

- **Delete:** The header is recommended to be deleted at a privacy service.
- **Not add:** The header is recommended not to be added at a privacy service.
- **Anonymize:** The header is recommended to be anonymized at a privacy service. How to anonymize the header depends on the header. Details are provided later.
- **Anonymize*:** An asterisk indicates that the involvement of a privacy service and treatment of the relevant header depend on the circumstance. Details are given later.

Any time a privacy service modifies a Call-ID, it must retain the former and modified values as indicated in Section 5.3 of RFC 3323 (see Section 20.2). It must then restore the former value in a Call-ID header and other corresponding headers and parameters (such as In-Reply-To, Replaces, and Target-Dialog) in any messages that are sent using the modified Call-ID to the originating UA. It should also modify a Call-ID header and other corresponding headers/parameters

Table 20.2 Privacy Service Behavior for Each SIP Header

Target Headers	*Where*	*User*	*Header*	*Session*	*Id*	*History*
Call-ID (Note)	R	Anonymize	–	–	–	–
Call-Info	Rr	Delete	Not add	–	–	–
Contact	R	–	Anonymize	–	–	–
From	R	Anonymize	–	–	–	–
History-Info	Rr	–	Delete	Delete	–	Delete
In-Reply-To	R	Delete	–	–	–	–
Organization	Rr	Delete	Not add	–	–	–
P-Asserted-Identity	Rr	–	Delete	–	Delete	–
Record-Route	Rr	–	Anonymize	–	–	–
Referred-By	R	Anonymize*	–	–	–	–
Reply-To	Rr	Delete	–	–	–	–
Server	R	Delete	Not add	–	–	–
Subject	R	Delete	–	–	–	–
User-Agent	R	Delete	–	–	–	–
Via	R	–	Anonymize	–	–	–
Warning	R	Anonymize	–	–	–	–

Source: Copyright IETF. Reproduced with permission.

(such as Target-Dialog and "replaces" parameter) in any further relevant messages that are sent by the originating UA. The detailed behavior for the Call-ID is described later. Identity/Identity-Info, Path, Replaces, Route, Service-Route, and Target-Dialog headers are not targets of these priv-values (and should not be anonymized or modified by a privacy service based on a priv-value in a Privacy header) and are explained further later.

20.5.3.2 Target SDP Parameters for Each Priv-Value

The recommended privacy service behaviors for each SDP parameters are simple. The c, m, o, i, u, e, and p lines in SIP request–response are recommended to be anonymized when user privacy is requested with Privacy:session.

20.5.3.3 Treatment of Priv-Value Not Supported by the Privacy Service

As specified in RFC 3323 (see Section 20.2), if the priv-value of "critical" is present in the Privacy header of a request, and if the privacy service is incapable of performing all of the levels of privacy specified in the Privacy header, it MUST fail the request with a 500 (Server Error) response code as indicated in RFC 3323. Since the protection of privacy is important, even if the priv-value "critical" is not present in the Privacy header, the privacy service should fail the request with a 500 Server Internal Error response code when it is incapable of performing all of the levels of privacy specified in the Privacy header.

20.5.4 Recommended Treatment of User Privacy-Sensitive Information

The following SIP headers and related parameters described below may concern privacy. This section describes what kind of user privacy-sensitive information may be included in each SIP header/parameter, and how to maintain privacy for such information at a UA or a privacy service when the information is indeed privacy sensitive. Note that we have also described all SIP message headers in Section 2.8, but they are explained here for convenience.

20.5.4.1 Target SIP Headers

The privacy considerations and recommended treatment for each SIP header described in subsections may reveal user privacy-sensitive information. This section goes into detail about how each header affects privacy, the desired treatment of the value by the UA and privacy service, and other instructions/additional notes necessary to provide privacy.

20.5.4.1.1 Call-ID

This field frequently contains an IP address or host name of a UAC appended to the Call-ID value. A UA executing a user-level privacy function on its own should substitute for the IP address or host name that is frequently appended to the Call-ID value, a suitably long random value (the value used as the "tag" for the From header of the request might even be reused) as indicated in RFC 3323 (see Sections 2.8 and 20.2). A privacy service may anonymize the Call-ID header when the request contains Privacy:user by substituting for the IP address or host name in the Call-ID a suitably long random value (such as a From tag value) so that it is sufficiently unique as indicated in RFC 3323. Call-ID is essential to dialog matching, so any time a privacy service modifies this field, it must retain the former value and restore it in a Call-ID header in any messages that are sent to/by the originating UA inside the dialog as indicated in RFC 3323.

A privacy service should be prepared to receive a request outside the dialog containing the value of the Call-ID set by the privacy service in other SIP headers (e.g., In-Reply-To/Replaces/Target-Dialog), at least while the dialog state is active for the dialog whose Call-ID was modified by that privacy service. When such a request is received, the Call-ID value contained in the relevant headers indicated above should be replaced by the retained value. Note that this is possible only if the privacy service maintains the state and retains all the information it modified to provide privacy. Some privacy services are known to encrypt information before obfuscation in the Via header, etc. In this case, the privacy service cannot correlate the modified Call-ID value with the original Call-ID. Further challenges are imposed when the privacy service needs to stay on a signaling path to ensure that it receives all the messages targeted toward the caller for which a privacy service provides privacy, especially when the request is out-of-dialog. In-Reply-To, Replaces, and Target-Dialog header/parameter are described below.

20.5.4.1.2 Call-Info

This field contains additional information about the user. A UA executing a user-level privacy function on its own should not add a Call-Info header as indicated in in RFC 3323 (see Sections 2.8 and 20.2). A privacy service must delete a Call-Info header if one exists when user privacy is requested with Privacy:user as indicated in RFC 3323. A privacy service should not add a Call-Info header when user privacy is requested with Privacy:header as indicated in RFC 3323.

20.5.4.1.3 Contact

This field contains a URI used to reach the UA for mid-dialog requests and possibly out-of-dialog requests, such as REFER (see Section 2.5). Since the Contact header is essential for routing further requests to the UA, it must include a functional URI even when it is anonymized. A UA must not anonymize a Contact header, unless it can obtain an IP address or contact address that is functional yet has a characteristic of anonymity as indicated in RFC 3323 (see Sections 2.8 and 20.2). Since RFC 3323 was published, there have been proposals that allow UAs to obtain an IP address or contact address with a characteristic of anonymity. The mechanisms are described in Globally Routable UA URI (GRUU) (see Section 4.3), which provides a functional Contact address with a short life span, making it ideal for privacy-sensitive calls, and TURN (see Section 14.3), through which an IP address of a relay can be obtained for use in a Contact header. A privacy service should anonymize a Contact header by replacing the existing Contact header field value with the URI that dereferences to the privacy service when user privacy is requested with Privacy:header, as indicated in RFC 3323 (see Section 20.2). This is generally done by replacing the IP address or host name with that of the privacy service.

20.5.4.1.4 From

This field contains the identity of the user, such as display name and URI. A UA executing a user-level privacy function on its own should anonymize a From header using an anonymous display name and an anonymous URI as indicated in RFC 3323 (see Sections 2.8 and 20.2). A privacy service should anonymize a From header when user privacy is requested with Privacy:user. Note that this does not prevent a privacy service from anonymizing the From header based on local policy. The anonymous display name and anonymous URI mentioned in this section use the display name "Anonymous," a URI with "anonymous" in the user portion of the From header, and the host name value "anonymous.invalid" as indicated in RFC 3323. The recommended form of the From header for anonymity is

```
From: "Anonymous" <sip:anonymous@anonymous
.invalid>;tag=1928301774
```

The tag value varies from dialog to dialog, but the rest of this header form is recommended as shown.

20.5.4.1.5 History-Info

History-Info specified in RFC 4244 (see Section 2.8) header URIs to which the request was forwarded or retargeted can reveal general routing information. A UA executing a user-level privacy function on its own should not add a History-Info header as indicated in RFC 4244. A privacy service should delete the History-Info headers when user privacy is requested with Privacy:header, Privacy:session, or Privacy:history as indicated in RFC 4244. The privacy could be also expressed for a specific History-Info entry by inserting "privacy=history" in the History-Info header. In such a case, a privacy service should delete the History-Info entry as indicated in RFC 4244. RFC 4244 (see Section 2.8) describes the detailed behavior for dealing with History-Info headers.

20.5.4.1.6 In-Reply-To

The In-Reply-To header contains a Call-ID of the referenced dialog. The replying user may be identified by the Call-ID in an In-Reply-To header.

- `Alice -> INVITE(Call-ID:C1) -> Bob`
- `Bob -> INVITE(In-Reply-To:C1) -> Alice`

In this case, unless the In-Reply-To header is deleted, Alice might notice that the replying user is Bob because Alice's UA knows that the Call-ID relates to Bob. A UA executing a user-level privacy function on its own should not add an In-Reply-To header as implied in RFC 3323 (see Sections 2.8 and 20.2). A privacy service must delete the In-Reply-To header when user privacy is requested with Privacy:user as indicated in RFC (see Sections 2.8 and 20.2). In addition, since an In-Reply-To header contains the Call-ID of the dialog to which it is replying, special attention is required, as described earlier, regardless of the priv-value or presence of a Privacy header. Once a privacy service modifies a Call-ID in the request, a privacy service should restore the former value in an In-Reply-To header, if present in the INVITE request replying to the original request, as long as the privacy service maintains the dialog state.

Example:

- `Alice -> INVITE(Call-ID:C1, Privacy:user) -> PS -> INVITE(Call-ID:C2) -> Bob`
- `Bob -> INVITE(In-Reply-To:C2, Privacy:none) -> PS -> INVITE(In-Reply-To:C1) -> Alice`

Note that this is possible only if the privacy service maintains the state and retains all the information that it modified to provide privacy even after the dialog has been terminated, which is unlikely. Callback is difficult to achieve when a privacy service is involved in forming the dialog to be referenced.

20.5.4.1.7 Organization

This field contains additional information about the user. A UA executing a user-level privacy function on its own should not add an Organization header as implied in RFC 3323 (see Sections 2.8 and 20.2). A privacy service must delete the Organization header if one exists when user privacy is requested with Privacy:user as indicated in RFC 3323. A privacy service should not add an Organization header when user privacy is requested with Privacy: header as indicated in RFC 3323.

20.5.4.1.8 P-Asserted-Identity

This header contains a network-verified and network-asserted identity of the user sending a SIP message. A privacy service must delete the P-Asserted-Identity headers when user privacy is requested with Privacy:id as indicated in RFC 3325 (see Sections 2.8 and 20.3), and should delete the P-Asserted-Identity headers when user privacy is requested with Privacy:header before it forwards the message to an entity that is not trusted. It is recommended for a privacy service to remove the P-Asserted-Identity header if user privacy is requested with Privacy:id or Privacy:header even when forwarding to a trusted entity, unless it can be confident that the message will not be routed to an untrusted entity without going through another privacy service.

20.5.4.1.9 Record-Route

This field may reveal information about the administrative domain of the user. To hide Record-Route headers while keeping routability to the sender, privacy services can execute a practice referred to as *stripping*. Stripping means removing all the Record-Route headers that have been added to the request before its arrival at the privacy service, and then adding a single Record-Route header representing itself. In this case, the privacy service needs to retain the removed headers and restore them in a response. Alternatively, privacy services can remove the Record-Route headers and encrypt them into a single Record-Route header field. In this case, the privacy service needs to decrypt the header and restore the former values in a response.

A privacy service should strip or encrypt any Record-Route headers that have been added to a message before it reaches the privacy service when user privacy is requested with Privacy:header as indicated in RFC 3323 (see Sections 2.8 and 20.2). As in the case of a Call-ID, if a privacy service modifies the Record-Route headers, it must be able to restore Route headers with retained values as indicated in RFC 3323. Some examples where the restoration of the Route headers is necessary and unnecessary are given below. When a UAC (Alice) requires privacy for a request, a privacy service does not have to restore the Route headers in the subsequent request (see Figure 20.3). Figure 20.3 shows that the restoration of route header is unnecessary when UAC requires privacy.

- `Alice -> INVITE(Privacy:header) > P1 -> INVITE(Record-Route:P1, Privacy:header) -> PS -> INVITE(Record-Route:PS) -> P2 -> INVITE(Record-Route:P2,PS) > Bob`
- `Bob -> 200 OK(Record-Route:P2,PS) -> P2 -> PS-> 200 OK(Record-Route:P2,PS,P1) -> P1 -> Alice`

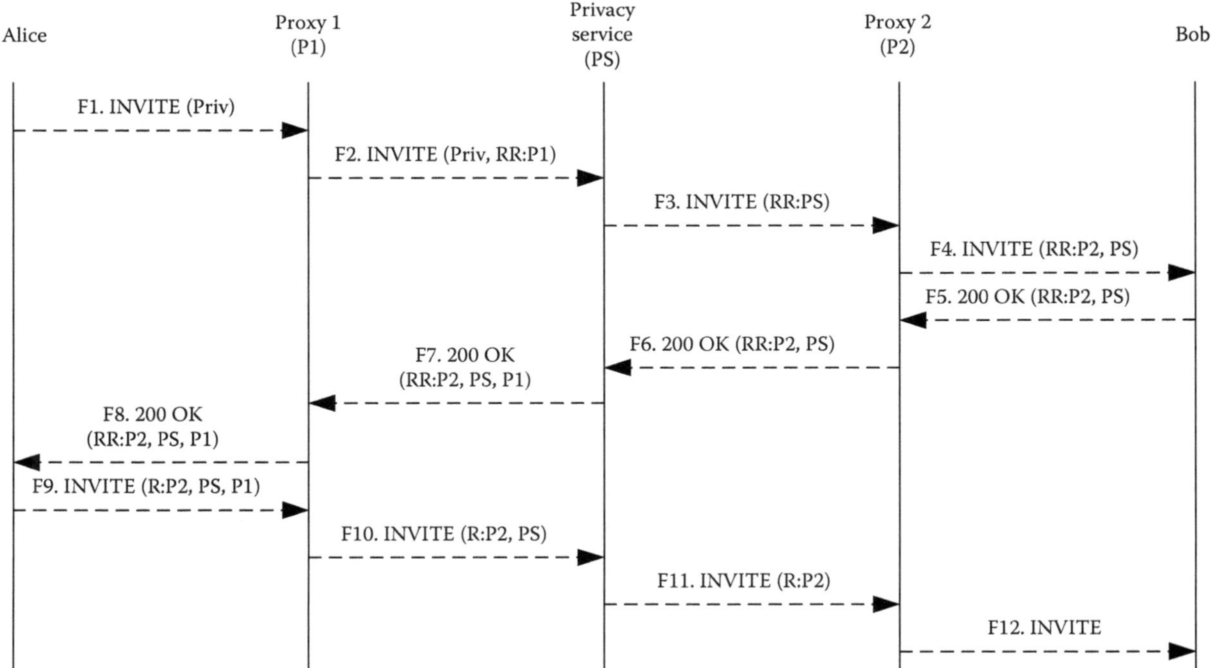

Figure 20.3 Example of when restoration of Route header is unnecessary. (Copyright IETF. Reproduced with permission.)

- Alice -> re-INVITE(Route:P2,PS,P1, Privacy:header) -> P1 -> re-INV(Route:P2,PS, Privacy:header) -> PS-> re-INVITE(Route:P2) -> P2 -> re-INVITE -> Bob

On the other hand, when a UAS (Bob) requires privacy for a response, a privacy service has to restore the Route headers in the subsequent request (see Figure 20.4). Figure 20.4 depicts that the restoration of route header is necessary when UAS requires privacy.

- Alice -> INVITE -> P1 -> INVITE(Record-Route:P1) -> P2 -> INVITE(Record-Route:P2,P1) -> Bob
- Bob -> 200 OK(Record-Route:P2,P1, Privacy: header) -> P2 > PS' -> 200 OK(Record-Route: PS',P1) -> P1 -> Alice
- Alice -> re-INVITE(Route:PS',P1) -> P1 -> re-INVITE(Route:PS') -> PS' -> re-INVITE (Route:P2) -> P2 -> Bob

Note that, in Figures 20.3 and 20.4, Priv means Privacy:header, RR means Record-Route header, and R means Route header.

20.5.4.1.10 Referred-By

The Referred-By specified in RFC 3892 (see Section 2.8) header carries a SIP URI representing the identity of the referrer. The Referred-By header is an anonymization target when the REFER request with the Referred-By header is sent by the user (referrer) whose privacy is requested to be processed in the privacy service. A UA that constructs REFER requests executing a user-level privacy function on its own should anonymize a Referred-By header by using an anonymous URI. A privacy service should anonymize a Referred-By header in a REFER request by using an anonymous URI when user privacy is requested with Privacy:user. On the other hand, the Referred-By header is not an anonymization target when it appears in a request other than REFER (e.g., INVITE) because the URI in the Referred-By header does not represent the sender of the request.

Example 1:
Referrer requests no privacy and referee requests privacy

- Alice -> REFER(Referred-By:Alice) -> Bob
- Bob -> INVITE(Referred-By:Alice, Privacy: user) -> PS -> INVITE(Referred-By:Alice) -> Carol

Example 2:
Referrer requests privacy and referee requests privacy

- Alice -> REFER(Referred-By:Alice, Privacy: user) -> PS > REFER(Referred-By:X) -> Bob
- Bob -> INVITE(Referred-By:X, Privacy:user) -> PS -> INVITE(Referred-By:X) -> Carol

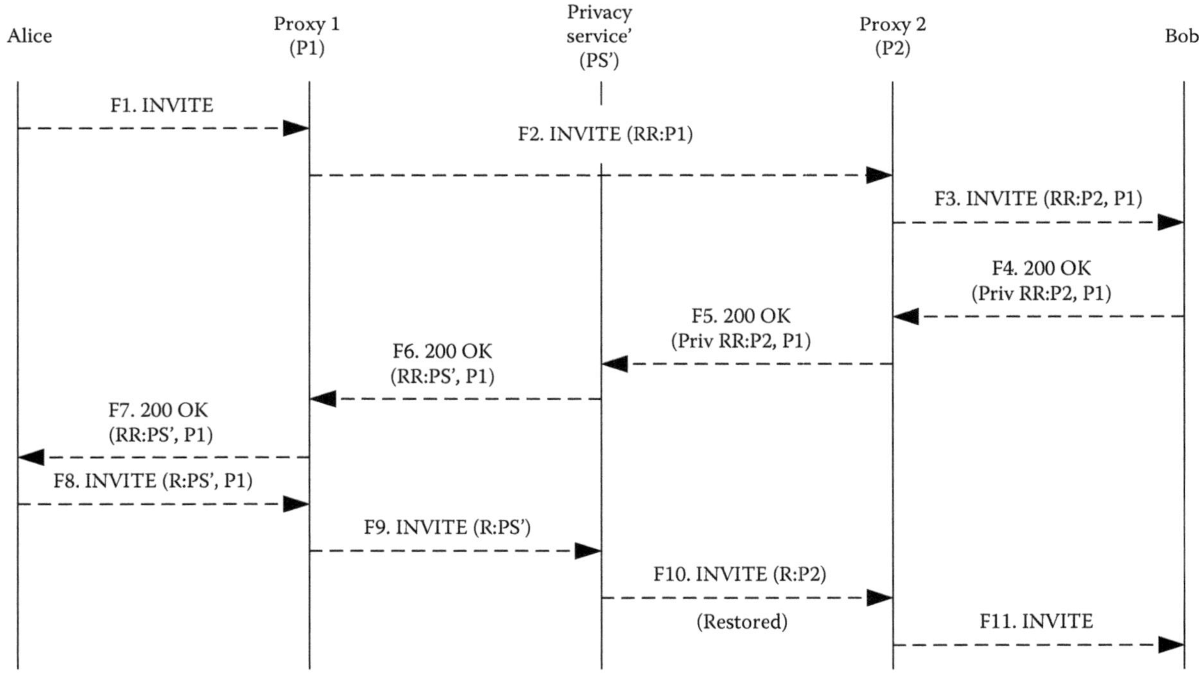

Figure 20.4 Example of when restoration of Route header is necessary. (Copyright IETF. Reproduced with permission.)

20.5.4.1.11 Reply-To

This field contains a URI that can be used to reach the user on subsequent callbacks. A UA executing a user-level privacy function on its own should not add a Reply-To header in the message as implied in RFC 3323 (see Sections 2.8 and 20.2). A privacy service must delete a Reply-To header when user privacy is requested with Privacy:user as indicated in RFC 3323 (see Sections 2.8 and 20.2).

20.5.4.1.12 Server

This field contains information about the software used by the UAS to handle the request. A UA executing a user-level privacy function on its own should not add a Server header in the response as implied in Section 4.1 of RFC 3323. A privacy service must delete a Server header in a response when user privacy is requested with Privacy:user. A privacy service should not add a Server header in a response when user privacy is requested with Privacy:header as indicated in RFC 3323 (see Sections 2.8 and 20.2).

20.5.4.1.13 Subject

This field contains free-form text about the subject of the call. It may include text describing something about the user. A UA executing a user-level privacy function on its own should not include any information identifying the caller in a Subject header. A privacy service must delete a Subject header when user privacy is requested with Privacy:user as indicated in RFC 3323 (see Sections 2.8 and 20.2).

20.5.4.1.14 User-Agent

This field contains the UAC's information. A UA executing a user-level privacy function on its own should not add a User-Agent header as implied in RFC 3323 (see Sections 2.8 and 20.2). A privacy service must delete a User-Agent header when user privacy is requested with Privacy:user as indicated in RFC 3323.

20.5.4.1.15 Via

The bottommost Via header added by a UA contains the IP address and port or host name that are used to reach the UA for responses. Via headers added by proxies may reveal information about the administrative domain of the user. A UA MUST NOT anonymize a Via header as indicated in RFC 3323 (see Sections 2.8 and 20.2), unless it can obtain an IP address that is functional yet has a characteristic of anonymity. This may be possible by obtaining an IP address specifically for this purpose either from the service provider or through features such as TURN (see Section 14.3). A privacy service should strip or encrypt any Via headers that have been added before reaching the privacy service when user privacy is requested with Privacy:header as indicated in in RFC 3323. Refer to the Record-Route header for details of stripping and encryption as described earlier. A privacy service must restore the original values of Via headers when handling a response in order to route the response to the originator as indicated RFC 3323. No Via stripping is required when handling responses.

20.5.4.1.16 Warning

This field may contain the host name of the UAS. A UA executing a user-level privacy function on its own should not include the host name representing its identity in a Warning header. A privacy service should anonymize a Warning header by deleting the host name portion (if it represents a UAS's identity) from the header when user privacy is requested with Privacy:user.

20.5.4.2 Target SDP Parameters

This section describes privacy considerations for each SDP parameter specified in RFC 4566 (see Section 7.7) that may reveal information about the user. When privacy functions for user-inserted information are requested to be executed at a privacy service, UAs must not encrypt SDP bodies in messages as indicated in RFC 3323 (see Sections 2.8 and 20.2).

20.5.4.2.1 c/m Lines

The c and m lines in the SDP body convey the IP address and port for receiving media. A UA must not anonymize the IP address and port in the c and m lines, unless it can obtain an IP address that is functional yet has a characteristic of anonymity as implied in RFC 3323 (see Sections 2.8 and 20.2). This may be possible by obtaining an IP address specifically for this purpose either from the service provider or through features such as TURN (see Section 14.3). A privacy service must anonymize the IP address and port in c and m lines using a functional anonymous IP address and port when user privacy is requested with Privacy:session. This is generally done by replacing the IP address and port present in the SDP with that of a relay server.

20.5.4.2.2 o Line

The user name and IP address in this parameter may reveal information about the user. A UA may anonymize the user name in an o line by setting user name to "-" and anonymize the IP address in the o line by replacing it with a value so that it is sufficiently unique. A privacy service must anonymize the user name and IP address in the o line by setting the user name to "-" and replacing the IP address with a value so that it is sufficiently unique when user privacy is requested with Privacy:session.

20.5.4.2.3 i/u/e/p Lines

These lines may contain information about the user. A UA executing a session-level privacy function on its own should not include user's information in the i, u, e, and p lines. A privacy service should modify the i, u, e, and p lines to delete the user's identity information when user privacy is requested with Privacy:session.

20.5.4.3 Nontarget SIP Headers/Parameters

20.5.4.3.1 Identity/Identity-Info

The Identity header field specified in RFC 4474 (see Sections 2.8 and 19.4.8) contains a signature used for validating the identity. The Identity-Info header field contains a reference to the certificate of the signer of Identity headers. An Identity-Info header may reveal information about the administrative domain of the user. The signature in an Identity header provides integrity protection over the From, To, Call-ID, Cseq, Date, and Contact headers and over the message body. The integrity protection is violated if a privacy service modifies these headers and/or the message body for the purpose of user privacy protection. Once those integrity-protected headers (such as From and Call-ID) are modified, the Identity/Identity-Info header fields are not valid any more. Thus, a privacy service acting on a request for Privacy:user, Privacy:header, or Privacy:session can invalidate integrity protection provided by an upstream authentication service that has inserted Identity/Identity-Info header fields.

The use of such a privacy service should be avoided if integrity protection needs to be retained. Otherwise, if the privacy service invalidates the integrity protection, it should remove the Identity/Identity-Info header fields. An authentication service downstream of the privacy service may add Identity/Identity-Info header fields if the domain name of the From header field URI has not been anonymized (e.g., "sip:anonymous@example.com"), which makes it possible for the service to authenticate the UAC. This authenticated yet anonymous From header means that "this is a known user in my domain that I have authenticated, but I am keeping its identity private" as indicated in RFC 4474. The desired deployment will have a privacy service located before or colocated with the identity service; thus, integrity and privacy can both be provided seamlessly.

20.5.4.3.2 Path

This field may contain information about the administrative domain and/or the visited domain of the UA. However, the Path header is not the target of any priv-values. Given that the Path header (see Section 2.8) only appears in REGISTER requests–responses and is essential for a call to reach the registered UA in the visited domain, it serves no purpose to withhold or hide the information contained in the Path header; rather, it is harmful. The only reason privacy may be considered desirable is if the visited domain wants to withhold its topology from the home domain of the user. In doing so, the domain withholding the topology needs to ensure that it provides sufficient information so that the home domain can route the call to the visited domain, thus reaching the UA. However, anonymization of network privacy-sensitive information is out of scope.

20.5.4.3.3 Replaces Header/Parameter

The Replaces header (see Section 2.8) and the "replaces" parameter contain identifiers of a dialog to be replaced, which are composed of Call-ID, local tag, and remote tag. The sender of the INVITE with a Replaces header is usually not the originating UA or terminating UA of the target dialog to be replaced. Therefore, the Call-ID within the Replaces header is unlikely to be generated by the sender, and thus this header is outside the anonymization target per priv-value. The "replaces" parameter, which appears in a Refer-To header in a REFER request, is not the target of any particular priv-values either. As described in the Call-ID header earlier, regardless of the priv-value or the presence of a Privacy header, once a privacy service modifies a Call-ID in the request, it should monitor headers that may contain Call-ID and restore the portion of the value representing the modified Call-ID to the original Call-ID value in a Replaces header received.

The main challenge for this to function properly is that a privacy service has to be on a signaling path to the originator for every dialog. This is generally not possible and results in REFER requests not functioning at all times. This is a trade-off that is anticipated when privacy is imposed. The privacy requirements mentioned earlier will cause the Replaces header and "replaces" parameter to contain values that will fail the resulting dialog establishment in some situations. This loss of functionality is allowed and/or intended as illustrated above (i.e., it is not the responsibility of a privacy service to ensure that these features always work). The functionality of the Replaces header/parameter when anonymized depends on the circumstances in which it is used. REFER may work or may not work depending on the following three criteria:

- Who generated the Call-ID
- Where the privacy service is on the signaling path
- Who initiates the REFER with the "replaces" parameter

A few examples that explore when the Replaces header/parameter works or fails are given below.

Example 1: Transfer initiated by the originator, privacy service added for first INVITE and REFER

- `Alice -> INVITE(Call-ID:C1, Privacy:user) -> PS -> INVITE(Call-ID:C2) -> Bob`
- `Alice -> REFER(Refer-To:Bob?Replaces=C1, Privacy:user) -> PS -> REFER(Refer-To:Bob?Replaces=C2) -> Carol`
- `Carol -> INVITE(Replaces:C2) -> Bob (Succeed)`

Example 2: Transfer initiated by the originator, privacy service added only for first INV

- `Alice -> INVITE(Call-ID:C1, Privacy:user) -> PS -> INVITE(Call-ID:C2) -> Bob`
- `Alice -> REFER(Refer-To:Bob?Replaces=C1) -> Carol`
- `Carol -> INVITE(Replaces:C1) -> Bob (Fail)`

Note that Example 2 would succeed if the same privacy service (that modifies the Call-ID in the INVITE from Alice) is also added for REFER and modifies the value in the "replaces" parameter from C1 to C2 even if there is no Privacy header in the REFER.

Example 3: Transfer initiated by the originator; privacy service added only for REFER

- `Alice > INVITE(Call-ID:C1) -> INVITE(Call-ID:C1) -> Bob`
- `Alice -> REFER(Refer-To:Bob?Replaces=C1, Privacy:user) -> PS -> REFER(Refer-To:Bob?Replaces=C1) -> Carol`
- `Carol -> INVITE(Replaces:C1, Privacy:user) -> PS' -> INVITE(Replaces:C1) -> Bob (Succeed)`

Example 4: Transfer initiated by the terminating party; privacy service added for both INVITE

- `Alice -> INVITE(Call-ID:C1, Privacy:user) -> PS -> INVITE(Call-ID:C2) -> Bob`
- `Bob -> REFER(Refer-To:Alice?Replaces=C2) -> Carol`
- `Carol -> INV(Replaces:C2) -> PS -> INVITE(Replaces:C1) -> Alice (Succeed)`

Note: Example 4 succeeds because the same privacy service (that modifies the Call-ID in the INVITE from Alice) checks the incoming requests and modifies the value in a Replaces header in the INVITE from Carol to the former value of Call-ID (C1).

Example 5: Hold; privacy service added only for first INVITE

- `Alice -> INVITE(Call-ID:C1, Privacy:user) -> PS -> INVITE(Call-ID:C2) -> Bob`
- `Alice -> REF(Refer-To:Bob?Replaces=C1) -> Music-Server`
- `Music-Server -> INV(Replaces:C1) -> Bob (Fail)`

Note: Example 5 would succeed if the same privacy service (that modifies the Call-ID in the INVITE from Alice) is added for the INVITE from the Music-Server and modifies the value in a Replaces header from C1 to C2.

As the above examples show, in some scenarios, information carried in the Replaces header/parameter would result in failure of the REFER. This will not happen if the Call-ID is not modified at a privacy service.

20.5.4.3.4 Route

This field may contain information about the administrative domain of the UA, but the Route header is not the target of any priv-value. Route headers appear only in SIP requests to force routing through the listed set of proxies. If a privacy service anonymizes the Route header, the routing does not function. Furthermore, there is no risk in revealing the information in the Route headers to further network entities, including the terminating UA, because a proxy removes the value from the Route header when it replaces the value in the Request-URI as defined in RFC 3261 (see Section 4.2). A privacy service that modifies Record-Route headers may need to restore the values in Route headers as necessary. As indicated in RFC 3323 (see Sections 2.8 and 20.2), if a privacy service modifies the Record-Route headers, it must be able to restore Route headers with retained values. Please refer to the Record-Route header as described earlier for further detail and examples.

20.5.4.3.5 Service-Route

The Service-Route header (see Section 2.8) appears only in 200 OK responses to REGISTER requests, and contains information about the registrar. The purpose of the privacy mechanism defined in RFC 3323 (see Sections 2.8 and 20.2) is to secure the user's privacy; thus, the case where a registrar sets a Privacy header is not considered here. Therefore, the Service-Route header is not the target of any priv-values.

20.5.4.3.6 Target-Dialog

The Target-Dialog header (see Section 2.8) faces exactly the same issues as seen for the Replaces header. Please refer to the Replaces header/parameter described earlier for why this is not a target for any particular priv-values, and how a privacy service still needs to evaluate and modify the value contained even if no privacy is requested.

20.6 Anonymity in SIP

20.6.1 Overview

The SIP (RFC 3261) allows users to make anonymous calls. Anonymity may include personal, location, media, and other information. SIP signaling message headers usually contain personal (e.g., UA, organization, From, Call-Id) and location (e.g., Contact, Via, Route, Route-Record) information, while the SDP that contains the media address information such as IP address, port number, and so on, is carried in the SIP signaling message body. The privacy services anonymize all signaling message headers by SIP UA and/or service providers that reside between the source–destination paths related to the personal, location, media, and other information.

However, the privacy services can anonymize different user- and media-related information of the calling and the called party as required. The intermediaries that reside between the source–destination paths need to be able to modify, replace, and add headers of both SIP signaling and message body. In this respect, the intermediaries need to act as the B2BUA to do so rightly as specified in RFC 3323 (see Section 20.2) because a proxy will not be able to do all the functions that are required for providing anonymity/privacy services.

Although SIP RFC 3261 allows users to make anonymous calls by including a From header field whose display name has the value of "Anonymous," greater levels of anonymity can be provided using privacy services with the capabilities subsequently defined in RFC 3323 (see Section 20.2), which introduces the Privacy header field. The Privacy header field allows a requesting UA to ask for various levels of anonymity, including user-level, header-level, and session-level anonymity. In addition, RFC 3325 (see Sections 2.8 and 20.3) defines the P-Asserted-Identity header field, used to contain an asserted identity. RFC 3325 also defined the "id" value for the Privacy header field, which is used to request the network to remove the P-Asserted-Identity header field.

20.6.2 UA-Driven Anonymity

20.6.2.1 Background

RFC 3323 (see Section 20.2) defines a privacy mechanism for the SIP that relies on the use of a separate privacy service to remove privacy-sensitive information from SIP messages sent by a UA before forwarding those messages to the final destination. It does not provide any mechanism for taking control of the privacy services by the UA itself. RFC 5767 that is described here specifies the UA-driven privacy mechanism in SIP by allowing a UA to take control of its privacy, rather than being completely dependent on an external privacy service, enhancing overall privacy services defined in RFC 3323 as well as the usage of RFC 3323 specified in RFC 3325 (see Sections 2.8 and 20.3). The privacy-sensitive information is defined in RFC 5767 more specifically as the information that identifies a user who sends the SIP message, as well as other information that can be used to guess the user's identity. The protection of network privacy (e.g., topology hiding) is not defined in RFC 5767. Privacy-sensitive information includes display name and URI in a From header field that can reveal the user's name and affiliation (e.g., company name), and IP addresses or host names in a Contact header field, a Via header field, a Call-ID header field, or a SDP (see Section 7.7) body that might reveal the location of a UA. RFC 5767 specifies a mechanism for a UA to generate an anonymous SIP message by utilizing mechanisms such as GRUU (see Section 4.3) and TURN (see Section 14.3) without the need for a privacy service.

20.6.2.2 Treatment of Privacy-Sensitive Information

Some fields of a SIP message potentially contain privacy-sensitive information but are not essential for achieving the intended purpose of the message and can be omitted without any side effects. Other fields are essential for achieving the intended purpose of the message and need to contain anonymized values in order to avoid disclosing privacy-sensitive information. Of the privacy-sensitive information listed earlier, URIs, host names, and IP addresses in Contact, Via, and SDP are required to be functional (i.e., suitable for purpose) even when they are anonymized. With the use of GRUU (see Section 4.3) and TURN (see Section 14.3), a UA can obtain URIs and IP addresses for media and signaling that are functional yet anonymous, and do not identify either the UA or the user. How to obtain a functional anonymous URI and IP address is described below. Host names need to be concealed because the user's identity can be guessed from them; however, they are not always regarded as critical privacy-sensitive information. In addition, a UA needs to be careful not to include any information that identifies the user in optional SIP header fields such as Subject and User-Agent.

20.6.2.2.1 Anonymous URI Using the GRUU Mechanism

A UA wanting to obtain a functional anonymous URI must support and utilize the GRUU mechanism unless it is able to obtain a functional anonymous URI through other means outside the scope for this document. By sending a REGISTER request requesting GRUU, the UA can obtain an anonymous

URI, which can later be used for the Contact header field. The detailed process on how a UA obtains a GRUU is described in Section 4.3. To use the GRUU mechanism to obtain a functional anonymous URI, the UA must request GRUU in the REGISTER request. If a "temp-gruu" SIP URI parameter and value are present in the REGISTER response, the UA MUST use the value of the "temp-gruu" as an anonymous URI representing the UA. This means that the UA must use this URI as its local target, and that the UA must place this URI in the Contact header field of subsequent requests and responses that require the local target to be sent.

If there is no "temp-gruu" SIP URI parameter in the 200 OK response to the REGISTER request, a UA should not proceed with its anonymization process, unless something equivalent to "temp-gruu" is provided through some administrative means. It is recommended that the UA consult the user before sending a request without a functional anonymous URI when privacy is requested from the user. Owing to the nature of how GRUU works, the domain name is always revealed when GRUU is used. If revealing the domain name in the Contact header field is a concern, use of a third-party GRUU server is a possible solution; however, this is not specified in RFC 5767.

20.6.2.2.2 Anonymous IP Address Using the TURN Mechanism

A UA that is not provided with a functional anonymous IP address through some administrative means must obtain a relayed address (IP address of a relay) if anonymity is desired for use in SDP and in the Via header field. Such an IP address is to be derived from a STUN (see Section 14.3) relay server through the TURN mechanism, which allows a STUN server to act as a relay. Anonymous IP addresses are needed for two purposes. The first is for use in the Via header field of a SIP request. By obtaining an IP address from a STUN relay server, using that address in the Via header field of the SIP request, and sending the SIP request to the STUN relay server, the IP address of the UA will not be revealed beyond the relay server.

The second is for use in SDP as an address for receiving media. By obtaining an IP address from a STUN relay server and using that address in SDP, media will be received via the relay server. Also, media can be sent via the relay server. In this way, neither SDP nor media packets reveal the IP address of the UA. It is assumed that a UA is either manually or automatically configured through means such as the configuration framework (RFC 6011) with the address of one or more STUN relay servers to obtain an anonymous IP address.

20.6.2.3 UA Behavior

This section describes how to generate an anonymous SIP message at a UA. A UA fully compliant with this document must obscure or conceal all the critical UA-inserted privacy-sensitive information in SIP requests and responses, as described below, when user privacy is requested. In addition, how the UA should conceal the noncritical privacy-sensitive information is described. Furthermore, when a UA uses a relay server to conceal its identity, the UA must send requests to the relay server to ensure that the request and response follow the same signaling path.

20.6.2.4 UA Behavior for Critical Privacy-Sensitive Information

20.6.2.4.1 Contact Header Field

When using this header field in a dialog-forming request or response, or in a mid-dialog request or response, this field contains the local target, that is, a URI used to reach the UA for mid-dialog requests and possibly out-of-dialog requests, such as a REFER request (see Section 2.8). The Contact header field can also contain a display name. Since the Contact header field is used for routing further requests to the UA, the UA must include a functional URI even when it is anonymized. When using this header field in a dialog-forming request or response, or in a mid-dialog request or response, the UA must anonymize the Contact header field using an anonymous URI ("temp-gruu") obtained through the GRUU mechanism, unless an equivalent functional anonymous URI is provided by some other means. For other requests and responses, with the exception of 3xx responses, REGISTER requests, and 200 OK responses to a REGISTER request, the UA must either omit the Contact header field or use an anonymous URI. We have described earlier in detail how to obtain an anonymous URI through GRUU. The UA must omit the display name in a Contact header field or set the display name to "Anonymous."

20.6.2.4.2 From Header Field in Requests

Without privacy considerations, this field contains the identity of the user, such as the display name and URI. RFCs 3261 (see Sections 2.8 and 3.1) and 3323 (see Section 20.2) recommend setting "sip:anonymous@anonymous.invalid" as a SIP URI in a From header field when user privacy is requested. This raises an issue when the SIP-Identity mechanism specified in RFC 4474 (see Sections 2.8 and 19.4.8) is applied to the message, because SIP-Identity requires an actual domain name in the From header field. A UA generating an anonymous SIP message supporting this specification must anonymize the From header field in one of the two ways described below.

Option 1: A UA anonymizes a From header field using an anonymous display name and an anonymous URI following the procedure noted in RFC 3323. The example form of the From header field of option 1 is as follows:

```
From: "Anonymous" <sip:anonymous
@anonymous.invalid>;tag=1928301774
```

Option 2: A UA anonymizes a From header field using an anonymous display name and an anonymous URI with user's valid domain name instead of "anonymous.invalid." The example form of the From header field of option 2 is as follows:

```
From: "Anonymous" <sip:anonymous
@example.com>;tag=1928301774
```

A UA should go with option 1 to conceal its domain name in the From header field. However, SIP-Identity cannot be used with a From header field in accordance with option 1, because the SIP-Identity mechanism uses authentication based on the domain name. If a UA expects the SIP-Identity mechanism to be applied to the request, it is recommended to go with option 2. However, the user's domain name will be revealed from the From header field of option 2. If the user wants both anonymity and strong identity, a solution would be to use a third-party anonymization service that issues an AOR for use in the From header field of a request, and that also provides a SIP-Identity authentication service. Third-party anonymization service is not specified in RFC 5767.

20.6.2.4.3 Via Header Field in Requests

Without privacy considerations, the bottommost Via header field added to a request by a UA contains the IP address and port or host name that are used to reach the UA for responses. A UA generating an anonymous SIP request supporting this specification must anonymize the IP address in the Via header field using an anonymous IP address obtained through the TURN mechanism, unless an equivalent functional anonymous IP address is provided by some other means. The UA should not include a host name in a Via header field.

20.6.2.4.4 IP Addresses in SDP

A UA generating an anonymous SIP message supporting this specification MUST anonymize IP addresses in SDP, if present, using an anonymous IP address obtained through the TURN mechanism, unless an equivalent functional anonymous IP address is provided by some other means. We have described earlier in detail how to obtain an IP address through TURN.

20.6.2.5 UA Behavior for Noncritical Privacy-Sensitive Information

20.6.2.5.1 Host Names in Other SIP Header Fields

A UA generating an anonymous SIP message supporting this specification should conceal host names in any SIP header fields, such as Call-ID and Warning header fields, if considered privacy sensitive.

20.6.2.5.2 Optional SIP Header Fields

Other optional SIP header fields (such as Call-Info, In-Reply-To, Organization, Referred-By, Reply-To, Server, Subject, User-Agent, and Warning) can contain privacy-sensitive information. A UA generating an anonymous SIP message supporting this specification should not include any information that identifies the user in such optional header fields.

20.6.2.6 Security Considerations

This specification uses GRUU and TURN, and inherits any security considerations described in these documents. Furthermore, if the provider of the caller intending to obscure its identity consists of a small number of people (e.g., small enterprise, small office/home office [SOHO]), the domain name alone can reveal the identity of the caller. The same can be true when the provider is large but the receiver of the call only knows a few people from the source of call. There are mainly two places in the message, the From header field and Contact header field, where the domain name is expected to be functional. The domain name in the From header field can be obscured as described earlier, whereas the Contact header field needs to contain a valid domain name at all times in order to function properly.

Note that, in general, a device will not show the contact address to the receiver, but this does not mean that one cannot find the domain name in a message. In fact, as long as this specification is used to obscure identity, the message will always contain a valid domain name as it inherits key characteristics of GRUU. Also, for UAs that use a temporary GRUU, confidentiality does not extend to parties that are permitted to register to the same AOR or are permitted to obtain temporary GRUUs when subscribed to the "reg" event package (RFC 3680, see Section 5.3) for the AOR. To limit this, it is suggested that the authorization policy for the "reg" event package permit only those subscribers authorized to register to the AOR to receive temporary GRUUs. With this policy, the confidentiality of the temporary GRUU will be the same whether or not the "reg" event package is used. If one wants to assure anonymization, it is suggested that the user seek and rely on a third-party anonymization service, which is outside the scope of this document. A third-party anonymization service provides registrar and TURN service that have no affiliation with the caller's provider, allowing the caller to completely withhold its identity.

20.6.3 Rejecting Anonymous Requests

Although users need to be able to make anonymous calls, users that receive such calls retain the right to reject the call because it is anonymous. The SIP does not provide a response code that allows the UAS, or a proxy acting on its behalf, to explicitly indicate that the request was rejected because it was anonymous. The closest response code is 403 Forbidden, which does not convey a specific reason. While it is possible to include a reason phrase in a 403 Forbidden response that indicates to the human user that the call was rejected because it was anonymous, that reason phrase is not useful for automata and cannot be interpreted by callers that speak a different language. An indication that can be understood by an automaton would allow for programmatic handling, including user interface prompts, or conversion to equivalent error codes in the PSTN when the client is a gateway. To remedy this, RFC 5079 that is described here defines the 433 Anonymity Disallowed response code (also see Section 2.6) that indicates that the server refused to fulfill the request because the requestor was anonymous.

20.6.3.1 Server Behavior

A server, generally acting on behalf of the called party, though this need not be the case, may generate a 433 Anonymity Disallowed response when it receives an anonymous request, and the server refuses to fulfill the request because the requestor is anonymous. A request should be considered anonymous when the identity of the originator of the request has been explicitly withheld by the originator. This occurs in any one of the following cases:

- The From header field contains a URI within the anonymous.invalid domain.
- The From header field contains a display name whose value is either "Anonymous" or "anonymous." Note that display names make a poor choice for indicating anonymity, since they are meant to be consumed by humans, not automata. Thus, language variations and even misspelling can cause an automaton to miss a hint in the display name. Despite these problems, a check on the display name is included here because RFC 3261 explicitly calls out the usage of the display name as a way to declare anonymity.
- The request contained a Privacy header field whose value indicates that the user wishes its identity withheld. Values meeting this criteria are "id," specified in RFC 3325 (see Sections 2.8 and 20.3), or "user."
- The From header field contains a URI that has an explicit indication that it is anonymous. One such example of a mechanism that would meet this criteria is [coexistence]. This criterion is true even if the request has a validated Identity header field.
- RFC 4474 (see Sections 2.8 and 19.4.8) can be used in concert with anonymized From header fields.

Lack of an NAI, such as the P-Asserted-Identity header field, in and of itself, should not be considered an indication of anonymity. Even though a Privacy header field value of "id" will cause the removal of an NAI, there is no way to differentiate this case from one in which an NAI was not supported by the originating domain. As a consequence, a request without an NAI is considered anonymous only when there is some other indication of this, such as a From header field with a display name of "Anonymous."

In addition, requests where the identity of the requestor cannot be determined or validated, but it is not a consequence of an explicit action on the part of the requestor, are not considered anonymous. For example, if a request contains a non-anonymous From header field, along with the Identity and Identity-Info header fields (RFC 4474, see Sections 2.8 and 19.4.8), but the certificate could not be obtained from the reference in the Identity-Info header field, it is not considered an anonymous request, and the 433 Anonymity Disallowed response code should not be used.

20.6.3.2 UAC Behavior

A UAC receiving a 433 Anonymity Disallowed must not retry the request without anonymity unless it obtains confirmation from the user that this is desirable. Such confirmation could be obtained through the user interface, or by accessing user-defined policy. If the user has indicated that this is desirable, the UAC may retry the request without requesting anonymity. Note that if the UAC were to automatically retry the request without anonymity in the absence of an indication from the user that this treatment is desirable, then the user's expectations would not be met. Consequently, a user might think it had completed a call anonymously when it is not actually anonymous. Receipt of a 433 Anonymity Disallowed response to a mid-dialog request should not cause the dialog to terminate, and should not cause the specific usage of that dialog to terminate (RFC 5057, see Sections 3.6.5 and 16.2). A UAC that does not understand or care about the specific semantics of the 433 response will treat it as a 400 Bad Request response.

20.7 Summary

We have described in detail privacy in SIP including anonymity services. The variety of privacy types that can be offered in SIP are explained, including when privacy is needed. It is articulated how user- and network-provided privacy services can be offered. In addition, the UA and privacy service behavior are described in constructing SIP messages for maintaining privacy. It is shown that the intermediaries that offer privacy services to users over the SIP network need to behave as SIP B2BUAs. The usual privacy service offered by SIP servers is not UA controlled. The asserted and preferred identity headers enable a network of trusted SIP servers to assert the identity of authenticated users within a given administrative domain. The creation of the Trusted Domain using spec(T) with the NAI is provided in great detail along with examples. In addition, UA-controlled privacy is also specified along with call flows. The detailed description for the recommended treatment of the user privacy-sensitive information is described. The anonymity that is enabled by the SIP privacy service with critical and non-critical privacy-sensitive information, for both UA- and server-controlled privacy, is specified. Finally, the UAC and server behavior for rejecting anonymous calls are discussed.

PROBLEMS

1. What are the differences between privacy, confidentiality, and anonymity? List the user privacy-sensitive information in SIP.
2. What are the varieties of privacy types? Define user- and network-provided privacy. Why do the intermediaries that provide privacy service to SIP users need to act as SIP B2BUAs?
3. How does a UA construct private messages for maintaining privacy in SIP message headers: display names, URI user names, and URI host names and IP addresses?
4. How does a UA express privacy preferences, routing requests to privacy services, and routing responses to privacy services?
5. How does a privacy server provide the following services: header privacy, session privacy, and user-level privacy?
6. What are the security concerns that the privacy service needs to deal with? How are these security loopholes mitigated?
7. How do the P-Asserted-Identity and P-Preferred-Identity headers in SIP used to assert the identity of authenticated users? Why are these headers only applicable to a given administrative domain?
8. What are the specifications for applying the asserted and preferred identity in a given administrative Trust Domain T termed as Spec(T)? Explain using an example.
9. How is the P-Asserted-Identity header in SIP handled by the proxy server under normal conditions, with hints for multiple identities, and with a user requesting privacy?
10. Describe the behavior of the SIP UAS for handling the P-Asserted-Identity header, the P-Preferred-Identity header, and the "id" privacy type.
11. What is NAI in the SIP network? Explain with call flows under the following conditions: NAI passed to trusted gateway and NAI withheld.
12. Provide an example of Spec(T) with detailed explanations.
13. What is connected identity in SIP? How is it used for providing privacy services in SIP?
14. How does a UA handle the connected identity in issuing a request and receiving a response of the INVITE message outside the context of the existing dialog? How does a UA whose identity changes during an established INVITE-initiated dialog handle the connected identity?
15. What are the general behaviors of a SIP UA for sending and receiving a mid-dialog request in relation to the privacy service using the connected identity?
16. Explain the behavior of the following functional entities in the context of offering the privacy service using the connected identity in the SIP network: authentication service, verifier, and proxy.
17. Explain with call flows the privacy service under the following conditions: sending connected identity after answering a call and sending revised connected identity during a call.
18. What are the security concerns in proving the privacy service using the connected identity in the SIP network? How do we mitigate those security holes?
19. Explain the general guidelines for treating the target SIP headers and SDP parameters for each priv-value and treatment of priv-value not supported by the privacy service.
20. Explain the recommended treatment of the user privacy-sensitive information for the privacy service for the target SIP headers, SDP parameters, and nontarget SIP headers/parameters along with their mitigation of security concerns and security holes.
21. Explain in general terms what is meant by anonymity in SIP. How is anonymity and privacy related? Explain with examples.
22. What is user privacy-sensitive information? How does the SIP UA-driven anonymity treat the user privacy-sensitive information?
23. How does a SIP UA handle the UA-driven anonymity of critical and noncritical user privacy-sensitive information?
24. Explain with examples the security concerns and their mitigation for the UA-driven anonymity.
25. How do the UAC and server behave in rejecting anonymous requests? Explain with examples.

Appendix A: ABNF

A.1 Overview

The Session Initiation Protocol (SIP) uses the augmented Backus–Naur Form (ABNF) syntax for its messages. This section provides formal syntaxes and rules for ABNF specified in Request for Comment (RFC) 5234. Internet technical specifications often need to define a formal syntax and are free to employ whatever notation their authors deem useful. Over the years, a modified version of Backus–Naur Form (BNF), called augmented BNF (ABNF), has been popular among many Internet specifications. It balances compactness and simplicity with reasonable representational power. In the early days of the Arpanet, each specification contained its own definition of ABNF. This included the e-mail specifications RFC 733 and then RFC 822, which came to be the common citations for defining ABNF. This appendix/book separates those definitions to permit selective reference.

Predictably, it also provides some modifications and enhancements. The differences between standard BNF and ABNF involve naming rules, repetition, alternatives, order independence, and value ranges. Section A.5 supplies rule definitions and encoding for a core lexical analyzer of the type common to several Internet specifications. It is provided as a convenience and is otherwise separate from the meta language defined in the body of this appendix/book, and separate from its formal status.

A.2 Rule Definition

A.2.1 Rule Naming

The name of a rule is simply the name itself, that is, a sequence of characters, beginning with an alphabetic character, and followed by a combination of alphabetics, digits, and hyphens (dashes).

Note: Rule names are case insensitive.

The names <rulename>, <Rulename>, <RULENAME>, and <rUlENamE> all refer to the same rule. Unlike the original BNF, angle brackets (<, >) are not required. However, angle brackets may be used around a rule name whenever their presence facilitates in discerning the use of a rule name. This is typically restricted to rule name references in free-form prose, or to distinguish partial rules that combine into a string not separated by white space, such as shown in the discussion about repetition below.

A.2.2 Rule Form

A rule is defined by the following sequence:

```
name   =   elements crlf
```

where <name> is the name of the rule, <elements> is one or more rule names or terminal specifications, and <crlf> is the end-of-line indicator (carriage return followed by line feed). The equals sign separates the name from the definition of the rule. The elements form a sequence of one or more rule names or value definitions, combined according to the various operators defined in this appendix/book, such as alternative and repetition. For visual ease, rule definitions are left aligned. When a rule requires multiple lines, the continuation lines are indented. The left alignment and indentation are relative to the first lines of the ABNF rules and need not match the left margin of the document.

A.2.3 Terminal Values

Rules resolve into a string of terminal values, sometimes called characters. In ABNF, a character is merely a non-negative integer. In certain contexts, a specific mapping (encoding) of values into a character set (such as ASCII) will be specified. Terminals are specified by one or more numeric characters, with the base interpretation of those characters indicated explicitly. The following bases are currently defined:

```
b               =       binary
d               =       decimal
x               =       hexadecimal
```

Hence, CR = %d13 and CR = %x0D specify the decimal and hexadecimal representation of US-ASCII for carriage return, respectively. A concatenated string of such values is specified compactly, using a period (.) to indicate a separation of characters within that value. Hence

```
CRLF = %d13.10
```

ABNF permits the specification of literal text strings directly, enclosed in quotation marks. Hence

```
command         =       "command string"
```

Literal text strings are interpreted as a concatenated set of printable characters.

Note: ABNF strings are case insensitive, and the character set for these strings is US-ASCII.

Hence

```
rulename        =       "abc"
```

and

```
rulename        =       "aBc"
```

will match abc, Abc, aBc, abC, ABc, aBC, AbC, and ABC.

To specify a rule that is case sensitive, specify the characters individually.

For example:

```
rulename        =       %d97 %d98 %d99
```

or

```
rulename        =       %d97.98.99
```

will match only the string that comprises only the lowercase characters, abc.

A.2.4 External Encodings

External representations of terminal value characters will vary according to constraints in the storage or transmission environment. Hence, the same ABNF-based grammar may have multiple external encodings, such as one for a 7-bit US-ASCII environment, another for a binary octet environment, and still a different one when 16-bit Unicode is used. Encoding details are beyond the scope of ABNF, although Section A.5 provides definitions for a 7-bit US-ASCII environment as has been common to much of the Internet. By separating external encoding from the syntax, it is intended that alternate encoding environments can be used for the same syntax.

A.3 Operators

A.3.1 Concatenation: Rule1 Rule2

A rule can define a simple, ordered string of values (i.e., a concatenation of contiguous characters) by listing a sequence of rule names. For example,

```
foo             =       %x61 ; a
bar             =       %x62 ; b
mumble          =       foo bar foo
```

so that the rule <mumble> matches the lowercase string *aba*. Linear white space: concatenation is at the core of the ABNF parsing model. A string of contiguous characters (values) is parsed according to the rules defined in ABNF. For Internet specifications, there is some history of permitting linear white space (space and horizontal tab) to be freely and implicitly interspersed around major constructs, such as delimiting special characters or atomic strings.

Note: This specification for ABNF does not provide for implicit specification of linear white space.

Any grammar that wishes to permit linear white space around delimiters or string segments must specify it explicitly. It is often useful to provide for such white space in *core* rules that are then used variously among higher-level rules. The core rules might be formed into a lexical analyzer or simply be part of the main rule set.

A.3.2 Alternatives: Rule1/Rule2

Elements separated by a forward slash (/) are alternatives. Therefore, foo/bar will accept <foo> or <bar>.

Note: A quoted string containing alphabetic characters is a special form for specifying alternative characters and is interpreted as a nonterminal representing the set of combinatorial strings with the contained characters, in the specified order but with any mixture of uppercase and lowercase.

A.3.3 Incremental Alternatives: Rule1 = /Rule2

It is sometimes convenient to specify a list of alternatives in fragments. That is, an initial rule may match one or more alternatives, with later rule definitions adding to the set of alternatives. This is particularly useful for otherwise independent specifications that derive from the same parent rule set, such as often occurs with parameter lists. ABNF permits this incremental definition through the construct

```
oldrule       =      / additional-alternatives
```

so that the rule set

```
ruleset             =       alt1/alt2
ruleset             =       /alt3
ruleset             =       /alt4/alt5
```

is the same as specifying

```
ruleset             =       alt1/alt2/alt3/
                            alt4/alt5
```

A.3.4 Value Range Alternatives: %c##-##

A range of alternative numeric values can be specified compactly, using a dash (-) to indicate the range of alternative values.

Hence

```
DIGIT         =      %x30-39
```

is equivalent to

```
DIGIT         =      "0"/"1"/"2"/"3"/"4"/"5"/
                     "6"/"7"/"8"/"9"
```

Concatenated numeric values and numeric value ranges cannot be specified in the same string. A numeric value may use the dotted notation for concatenation or it may use the dash notation to specify one value range. Hence, to specify one printable character between end-of-line sequences, the specification could be

```
char-line     =      %x0D.0A %x20-7E %x0D.0A
```

A.3.5 Sequence Group: (Rule1 Rule2)

Elements enclosed in parentheses are treated as a single element whose contents are strictly ordered. Thus,

```
elem (foo/bar) blat
```

matches

```
(elem foo blat) or (elem bar blat),
```

and

```
elem foo/bar blat
```

matches

```
(elem foo) or (bar blat).
```

Note: It is strongly advised that grouping notation be used, rather than relying on the proper reading of *bare* alternations, when alternatives consist of multiple rule names or literals. Hence, it is recommended that the following form be used:

```
(elem foo)/(bar blat)
```

This will avoid misinterpretation by casual readers. The sequence group notation is also used within free text to set off an element sequence from the prose.

A.3.6 Variable Repetition: *Rule

The operator "*" preceding an element indicates repetition. The full form is

```
<a>*<b>element
```

where <a> and <b> are optional decimal values, indicating at least <a> and at most <b> occurrences of the element.

Default values are 0 and infinity so that *<element> allows any number, including zero; 1*<element> requires at least one; 3*3<element> allows exactly 3; and 1*2<element> allows one or two.

A.3.7 Specific Repetition: nRule

A rule of the form

```
<n>element
```

is equivalent to

```
<n>*<n>element
```

That is, exactly <n> occurrences of <element>. Thus, 2DIGIT is a two-digit number, and 3ALPHA is a string of three alphabetic characters.

A.3.8 Optional Sequence: [RULE]

Square brackets enclose an optional element sequence:

```
[foo bar]
```

is equivalent to

```
*1(foo bar).
```

A.3.9 Comment: ; Comment

A semicolon starts a comment that continues to the end of line. This is a simple way of including useful notes in parallel with the specifications.

```
                    ; comment or newline
```

A.3.10 Operator Precedence

The various mechanisms described above have the following precedence, from highest (binding tightest) at the top, to lowest (loosest) at the bottom:

Rule name, prose-val, Terminal value
  Comment
  Value range
  Repetition
  Grouping, Optional
  Concatenation
  Alternative

Use of the alternative operator, freely mixed with concatenations, can be confusing. Again, it is recommended that the grouping operator be used to make explicit concatenation groups.

A.4 Definition of ABNF

Notes:

1. This syntax requires a formatting of rules that is relatively strict. Hence, the version of a rule set included in a specification might need preprocessing to ensure that it can be interpreted by an ABNF parser.
2. This syntax uses the rules provided in Section A.5.

```
rulelist      =  1*(rule/(*c-wsp c-nl))

rule          =  rulename defined-as elements
                 c-nl
                 ; continues if next line starts
                 ; with white space

rulename      =  ALPHA *(ALPHA/DIGIT/"-")

defined-as =     *c-wsp (" = "/" = /") *c-wsp
                 ; basic rules definition and
                 ; incremental alternatives

elements      =  alternation *c-wsp

c-wsp         =  WSP/(c-nl WSP)

c-nl          =  comment/CRLF
                 ; comment or newline

comment       =  ";" *(WSP/VCHAR) CRLF

alternation   =     concatenation *(*c-wsp
                    "/" *c-wsp concatenation)

concatenation =     repetition *(1*c-wsp
                    repetition)

repetition =     [repeat] element

repeat        =  1*DIGIT/(*DIGIT "*" *DIGIT)

element       =  rulename/group/option/
                 char-val/num-val/prose-val

group         =  "(" *c-wsp alternation *c-wsp
                 ")"

option        =  "[" *c-wsp alternation *c-wsp
                 "]"

char-val      =  DQUOTE *(%x20-21/%x23-7E)
                 DQUOTE
                 ; quoted string of SP and VCHAR
                 ; without DQUOTE

num-val       =  "%" (bin-val/dec-val/hex-val)

bin-val       =  "b" 1*BIT
                 [1*("." 1*BIT)/("-" 1*BIT)]
                 ; series of concatenated bit
                 values
                 ; or single ONEOF range

dec-val       =  "d" 1*DIGIT
                 [1*("." 1*DIGIT)/("-" 1*DIGIT)]

hex-val       =  "x" 1*HEXDIG
                 [1*("." 1*HEXDIG)/("-"
                 1*HEXDIG)]

prose-val     =  "<" *(%x20-3D/%x3F-7E) ">"
                 ; bracketed string of SP and
                 VCHAR
                 ; without angles
                 ; prose description, to be used
                 as
                 ; last resort
```

A.5 Core ABNF

This section contains some basic rules that are in common use. Basic rules are in uppercase. Note that these rules are only valid for ABNF encoded in 7-bit ASCII or in characters sets that are a superset of 7-bit ASCII.

A.5.1 Core Rules

Certain basic rules are in uppercase, such as SP, HTAB, CRLF, DIGIT, ALPHA, etc.

```
ALPHA   =   %x41-5A/%x61-7A; A-Z/a-z

BIT     =   "0"/"1"

CHAR    =   %x01-7F
            ; any 7-bit US-ASCII character,
            ; excluding NUL
CR      =   %x0D
            ; carriage return

CRLF    =   CR LF
            ; Internet standard newline

CTL     =   %x00-1F/%x7F
            ; controls

DIGIT   =   %x30-39
            ; 0-9
DQUOTE  =   %x22
            ; " (double quote)

HEXDIG  =   DIGIT/"A"/"B"/"C"/"D"/"E"/"F"

HTAB    =   %x09
            ; horizontal tab

LF      =   %x0A
            ; linefeed

LWSP    =   *(WSP/CRLF WSP)
            ; Use of this linear-white-space
            rule
            ; permits lines containing only
            white
            ; space that are no longer legal
            in
            ; mail headers and have caused
            ; interoperability problems in
            other
            ; contexts.
            ; Do not use when defining mail
            ; headers and use with caution
            in
            ; other contexts.

OCTET   =   %x00-FF
            ; 8 bits of data

SP      =   %x20

VCHAR   =   %x21-7E
            ; visible (printing) characters

WSP     =   SP/HTAB
            ; white space
```

A.5.2 Common Encoding

Externally, data are represented as *network virtual ASCII* (namely, 7-bit US-ASCII in an 8-bit field), with the high (8th) bit set to zero. A string of values is in *network byte order*, in which the higher-valued bytes are represented on the left-hand side and are sent over the network first.

Appendix B: Reference RFCs

RFC	Description
0761	DoD standard Transmission Control Protocol. J. Postel. January 1980. (Obsoleted by RFC 0793) (Status: Unknown)
0768	User Datagram Protocol. J. Postel. August 1980. (Also STD 0006) (Status: Internet Standard)
0791	Internet Protocol. J. Postel. September 1981. (Obsoletes RFC 0760) (Updated by RFC 1349, RFC 2474, RFC 6864) (Also STD 0005) (Status: Internet Standard)
0793	0793 Transmission Control Protocol. J. Postel. September 1981. (Obsoletes RFC 0761) (Updated by RFC 1122, RFC 3168, RFC 6093, RFC 6528) (Also STD 0007) (Status: Internet Standard)
1034	Domain Names—Concepts and Facilities. P.V. Mockapetris. November 1987. (Obsoletes RFC 0973, RFC 0882, RFC 0883) (Updated by RFC 1101, RFC 1183, RFC 1348, RFC 1876, RFC 1982, RFC 2065, RFC 2181, RFC 2308, RFC 2535, RFC 4033, RFC 4034, RFC 4035, RFC 4343, RFC 4035, RFC 4592, RFC 5936) (Also STD 0013) (Status: Internet Standard)
1035	Domain Names—Implementation and Specification. P.V. Mockapetris. November 1987. (Obsoletes RFC 0973, RFC 0882, RFC 0883) (Updated by RFC 1101, RFC 1183, RFC 1348, RFC 1876, RFC 1982, RFC 1995, RFC 1996, RFC 2065, RFC 2136, RFC 2181, RFC 2137, RFC 2308, RFC 2535, RFC 2673, RFC 2845, RFC 3425, RFC 3658, RFC 4033, RFC 4034, RFC 4035, RFC 4343, RFC 5936, RFC 5966, RFC 6604) (Also STD 0013) (Status: Internet Standard)
1123	Requirements for Internet Hosts—Application and Support. R. Braden, Ed. October 1989. (Updates RFC 0822, RFC 0952) (Updated by RFC 1349, RFC 2181, RFC 5321, RFC 5966) (Also STD 0003) (Status: Proposed Standard)
1183	New DNS RR Definitions. C.F. Everhart, L.A. Mamakos, R. Ullmann, P.V. Mockapetris. October 1990. (Updates RFC 1034, RFC1035) (Updated by RFC 5395, RFC 5864, RFC 6195, RFC 6895) (Status: Experimental)
1305	Network Time Protocol (Version 3) Specification, Implementation and Analysis. D. Mills. March 1992. (Obsoletes RFC 0958, RFC 1059, RFC 1119) (Obsoleted by RFC 5905) (Status: Draft Standard)
1350	The TFTP Protocol (Revision 2). K. Sollins. July 1992. (Obsoletes RFC 0783) (Updated by RFC 1782, RFC 1783, RFC 1784, RFC 1785, RFC 2347, RFC 2348, RFC 2349) (Also STD 0033) (Status: Internet Standard)
1617	Naming and Structuring Guidelines for X.500 Directory Pilots. P. Barker, S. Kille, T. Lenggenhager. May 1994. (Obsoletes RFC 1384) (Status: Informational)
1876	A Means for Expressing Location Information in the Domain Name System. C. Davis, P. Vixie, T. Goodwin, I. Dickinson. January 1996. (Updates RFC 1034, RFC 1035) (Status: Experimental)
2017	Definition of the URL MIME External-Body Access-Type. N. Freed, K. Moore, A. Cargille. October 1996. (Status: Proposed Standard)
2045	Multipurpose Internet Mail Extensions (MIME) Part One: Format of Internet Message Bodies. N. Freed, N. Borenstein. November 1996. (Obsoletes RFC 1521, RFC 1522, RFC 1590) (Updated by RFC 2184, RFC 2231, RFC 5335, RFC 6532) (Status: Draft Standard)
2046	Multipurpose Internet Mail Extensions (MIME) Part Two: Media Types. N. Freed, N. Borenstein. November 1996. (Obsoletes RFC 1521, RFC 1522, RFC 1590) (Updated by RFC 2646, RFC 3798, RFC 5147, RFC 6657) (Status: Proposed Standard)

2069	An Extension to HTTP: Digest Access Authentication. J. Franks, P. Hallam-Baker, J. Hostetler, P. Leach, A. Luotonen, E. Sink, L. Stewart. January 1997. (Obsoleted by RFC 2617) (Status: Proposed Standard)
2076	Common Internet Message Headers. J. Palme. February 1997. (Status: Informational)
2104	HMAC: Keyed-Hashing for Message Authentication. H. Krawczyk, M. Bellare, R. Canetti. February 1997. (Updated by RFC 6151) (Status: Informational)
2141	2141 URN Syntax. R. Moats. May 1997. (Status: Proposed Standard)
2183	Communicating Presentation Information in Internet Messages: The Content-Disposition Header Field. R. Troost, S. Dorner, K. Moore, Ed. August 1997. (Obsoletes RFC 1806) (Updated by RFC 2184, RFC 2231) (Status: Proposed Standard)
2205	Resource ReSerVation Protocol (RSVP)—Version 1 Functional Specification. R. Braden, Ed., L. Zhang, S. Berson, S. Herzog, S. Jamin. September 1997. (Updated by RFC 2750, RFC 3936, RFC 4495, RFC 5946, RFC 6437, RFC 6780) (Status: Proposed Standard)
2224	NFS URL Scheme. B. Callaghan. October 1997. (Status: Informational)
2277	IETF Policy on Character Sets and Languages. H. Alvestrand. January 1998. (Also BCP 0018) (Status: Best Current Practice)
2326	Real Time Streaming Protocol (RTSP). H. Schulzrinne, A. Rao, R. Lanphier. April 1998. (Status: Proposed Standard)
2327	SDP: Session Description Protocol. M. Handley, V. Jacobson. April 1998. (Obsoleted by RFC 4566) (Updated by RFC 3266) (Status: Proposed Standard)
2387	The MIME Multipart/Related Content-type. E. Levinson. August 1998. (Obsoletes RFC 2112) (Status: Proposed Standard)
2392	Content-ID and Message-ID Uniform Resource Locators. E. Levinson. August 1998. (Obsoletes RFC 2111) (Status: Proposed Standard)
2403	The Use of HMAC-MD5-96 within ESP and AH. C. Madson, R. Glenn. November 1998. (Status: Proposed Standard)
2404	The Use of HMAC-SHA-1-96 within ESP and AH. C. Madson, R. Glenn. November 1998. (Status: Proposed Standard)
2451	The ESP CBC-Mode Cipher Algorithms. R. Pereira, R. Adams. November 1998. (Status: Proposed Standard)
2460	Internet Protocol, Version 6 (IPv6) Specification. S. Deering, R. Hinden. December 1998. (Obsoletes RFC 1883) (Updated by RFC 5095, RFC 5722, RFC 5871, RFC 6437, RFC 6564, RFC 6935, RFC 6946, RFC 7045, RFC 7112) (Status: Draft Standard)
2506	Media Feature Tag Registration Procedure. K. Holtman, A. Mutz, T. Hardie. March 1999. (Also BCP 0031) (Status: Best Current Practice)
2507	IP Header Compression. M. Degermark, B. Nordgren, S. Pink. February 1999. (Status: Proposed Standard)
2508	2508 Compressing IP/UDP/RTP Headers for Low-Speed Serial Links. S. Casner, V. Jacobson. February 1999. (Status: Proposed Standard)
2533	A Syntax for Describing Media Feature Sets. G. Klyne. March 1999. (Updated by RFC 2738, RFC 2938) (Status: Proposed Standard)
2543	SIP: Session Initiation Protocol. M. Handley, H. Schulzrinne, E. Schooler, J. Rosenberg. March 1999. (Obsoleted by RFC 3261, RFC 3262, RFC 3263, RFC 3264, RFC 3265) (Status: Proposed Standard)
2585	Internet X.509 Public Key Infrastructure Operational Protocols: FTP and HTTP. R. Housley, P. Hoffman. May 1999. (Status: Proposed Standard)
2606	2606 Reserved Top Level DNS Names. D. Eastlake 3rd, A. Panitz. June 1999. (Updated by RFC 6761) (Also BCP 0032) (Status: BEST CURRENT PRACTICE)
2617	HTTP Authentication: Basic and Digest Access Authentication. J. Franks, P. Hallam-Baker, J. Hostetler, S. Lawrence, P. Leach, A. Luotonen, L. Stewart. June 1999. (Obsoletes RFC 2069) (Updated by RFC 7235) (Status: Draft Standard)
2671	Extension Mechanisms for DNS (EDNS0). P. Vixie. August 1999. (Obsoleted by RFC 6891) (Status: Proposed Standard)

2672	Non-terminal DNS Name Redirection. M. Crawford. August 1999. (Obsoleted by RFC 6672) (Updated by RFC 4592, RFC 6604) (Status: Proposed Standard)
2703	Protocol-independent Content Negotiation Framework. G. Klyne. September 1999. (Status: Informational)
2738	Corrections to "A Syntax for Describing Media Feature Sets." G. Klyne. December 1999. (Updates RFC 2533) (Status: Proposed Standard)
2749	COPS usage for RSVP. S. Herzog, Ed., J. Boyle, R. Cohen, D. Durham, R. Rajan, A. Sastry. January 2000. (Status: Proposed Standard)
2750	RSVP Extensions for Policy Control. S. Herzog. January 2000. (Updates RFC 2205) (Status: Proposed Standard)
2753	A Framework for Policy-based Admission Control. R. Yavatkar, D. Pendarakis, R. Guerin. January 2000. (Status: Informational)
2778	A Model for Presence and Instant Messaging. M. Day, J. Rosenberg, H. Sugano. February 2000. (Status: Informational)
2782	A DNS RR for Specifying the Location of Services (DNS SRV). A. Gulbrandsen, P. Vixie, L. Esibov. February 2000. (Obsoletes RFC 2052) (Updated by RFC 6335) (Status: Proposed Standard)
2784	Generic Routing Encapsulation (GRE). D. Farinacci, T. Li, S. Hanks, D. Meyer, P. Traina. March 2000. (Updated by RFC 2890) (Status: Proposed Standard)
2818	HTTP Over TLS. E. Rescorla. May 2000. (Updated by RFC 5785, RFC 7230) (Status: Informational)
2822	Internet Message Format. P. Resnick, Ed. April 2001. (Obsoletes RFC 0822) (Obsoleted by RFC 5322) (Updated by RFC 5335, RFC 5336) (Status: Proposed Standard)
2824	Call Processing Language Framework and Requirements. J. Lennox, H. Schulzrinne. May 2000. (Status: Informational)
2827	Network Ingress Filtering: Defeating Denial of Service Attacks which employ IP Source Address Spoofing. P. Ferguson, D. Senie. May 2000. (Obsoletes RFC 2267) (Updated by RFC 3704) (Also BCP 0038) (Status: Best Current Practice)
2848	RFC 2848 The PINT Service Protocol: Extensions to SIP and SDP for IP Access to Telephone Call Services. S. Petrack, L. Conroy. June 2000. (Status: Proposed Standard)
2849	The LDAP Data Interchange Format (LDIF)—Technical Specification. G. Good. June 2000. (Status: Proposed Standard)
2872	Application and Sub Application Identity Policy Element for Use with RSVP. Y. Bernet, R. Pabbati. June 2000. (Status: Proposed Standard)
2904	AAA Authorization Framework. J. Vollbrecht, P. Calhoun, S. Farrell, L. Gommans, G. Gross, B. de Bruijn, C. de Laat, M. Holdrege, D. Spence. August 2000. (Status: Informational)
2914	Congestion Control Principles. S. Floyd. September 2000. (Updated by RFC 7141) (Also BCP 0041) (Status: Best Current Practice)
2931	DNS Request and Transaction Signatures (SIG(0)s). D. Eastlake 3rd. September 2000. (Updates RFC 2535) (Status: Proposed Standard)
2974	Session Announcement Protocol. M. Handley, C. Perkins, E. Whelan. October 2000. (Status: Experimental)
3006	Integrated Services in the Presence of Compressible Flows. B. Davie, C. Iturralde, D. Oran, S. Casner, J. Wroclawski. November 2000. (Status: Proposed Standard)
3043	The Network Solutions Personal Internet Name (PIN): A URN Namespace for People and Organizations. M. Mealling. January 2001. (Status: Informational)
3044	Using the ISSN (International Serial Standard Number) as URN (Uniform Resource Names) within an ISSN-URN Namespace. S. Rozenfeld. January 2001. (Status: Informational)
3050	Common Gateway Interface for SIP. J. Lennox, H. Schulzrinne, J. Rosenberg. January 2001. (Status: Informational)
3084	COPS Usage for Policy Provisioning (COPS-PR). K. Chan, J. Seligson, D. Durham, S. Gai, K. McCloghrie, S. Herzog, F. Reichmeyer, R. Yavatkar, A. Smith. March 2001. (Status: Proposed Standard)
3087	Control of Service Context using SIP Request-URI. B. Campbell, R. Sparks. April 2001. (Status: Informational)

3095	RObust Header Compression (ROHC): Framework and four profiles: RTP, UDP, ESP, and uncompressed. C. Bormann, C. Burmeister, M. Degermark, H. Fukushima, H. Hannu, L.-E. Jonsson, R. Hakenberg, T. Koren, K. Le, Z. Liu, A. Martensson, A. Miyazaki, K. Svanbro, T. Wiebke, T. Yoshimura, H. Zheng. July 2001. (Updated by RFC 3759, RFC 4815) (Status: Proposed Standard)
3108	Conventions for the use of the Session Description Protocol (SDP) for ATM Bearer Connections. R. Kumar, M. Mostafa. May 2001. (Status: Proposed Standard)
3120	A URN Namespace for XML.org. K. Best, N. Walsh. June 2001. (Status: Informational)
3174	US Secure Hash Algorithm 1 (SHA1). D. Eastlake 3rd, P. Jones. September 2001. (Updated by RFC 4634, RFC 6234) (Status: Informational)
3187	Using International Standard Book Numbers as Uniform Resource Names. J. Hakala, H. Walravens. October 2001. (Status: Informational)
3188	Using National Bibliography Numbers as Uniform Resource Names. J. Hakala. October 2001. (Status: Informational)
3204	MIME Media Types for ISUP and QSIG Objects. E. Zimmerer, J. Peterson, A. Vemuri, L. Ong, F. Audet, M. Watson, M. Zonoun. December 2001. (Updated by RFC 3459, RFC 5621) (Status: Proposed Standard)
3219	Telephony Routing over IP (TRIP). J. Rosenberg, H. Salama, M. Squire. January 2002. (Status: Proposed Standard)
3238	IAB Architectural and Policy Considerations for Open Pluggable Edge Services. S. Floyd, L. Daigle. January 2002. (Status: Informational)
3240	Digital Imaging and Communications in Medicine (DICOM)—Application/dicom MIME Sub-type Registration. D. Clunie, E. Cordonnier. February 2002 (Status: Informational)
3261	SIP: Session Initiation Protocol. J. Rosenberg, H. Schulzrinne, G. Camarillo, A. Johnston, J. Peterson, R. Sparks, M. Handley, E. Schooler. June 2002. (Obsoletes RFC 2543) (Updated by RFC 3265, RFC 3853, RFC 4320, RFC 4916, RFC 5393, RFC 5621, RFC 5626, RFC 5630, RFC 5922, RFC 5954, RFC 6026, RFC 6141) (Status: Proposed Standard)
3262	Reliability of Provisional Responses in Session Initiation Protocol (SIP). J. Rosenberg, H. Schulzrinne. June 2002. (Obsoletes RFC 2543) (Status: Proposed Standard)
3263	Session Initiation Protocol (SIP): Locating SIP Servers. J. Rosenberg, H. Schulzrinne. June 2002. (Obsoletes RFC 2543) (Status: Proposed Standard)
3264	An Offer/Answer Model with Session Description Protocol (SDP). J. Rosenberg, H. Schulzrinne. June 2002. (Obsoletes RFC 2543) (Updated by RFC 6157) (Status: Proposed Standard)
3265	Session Initiation Protocol (SIP)-Specific Event Notification. A. B. Roach. June 2002. (Obsoletes RFC 2543) (Updates RFC 3261) (Updated by RFC 5367, RFC 5727) (Status: Proposed Standard)
3274	Compressed Data Content Type for Cryptographic Message Syntax (CMS). P. Gutmann. June 2002. (Status: Proposed Standard)
3303	Middlebox Communication Architecture and Framework. P. Srisuresh, J. Kuthan, J. Rosenberg, A. Molitor, A. Rayhan. August 2002. (Status: Informational)
3311	The Session Initiation Protocol (SIP) UPDATE Method. J. Rosenberg. October 2002. (Status: Proposed Standard)
3312	Integration of Resource Management and Session Initiation Protocol (SIP). G. Camarillo, Ed., W. Marshall, Ed., J. Rosenberg. October 2002. (Updated by RFC 4032, RFC 5027) (Status: Proposed Standard)
3313	Private Session Initiation Protocol (SIP) Extensions for Media Authorization. W. Marshall, Ed. January 2003. (Status: Informational)
3320	Signaling Compression (SigComp). R. Price, C. Bormann, J. Christoffersson, H. Hannu, Z. Liu, J. Rosenberg. January 2003. (Updated by RFC 4896) (Status: Proposed Standard)
3323	A Privacy Mechanism for the Session Initiation Protocol (SIP). J. Peterson. November 2002. (Status: Proposed Standard)
3324	Short Term Requirements for Network Asserted Identity. M. Watson. November 2002. (Status: Informational)

3325	Private Extensions to the Session Initiation Protocol (SIP) for Asserted Identity within Trusted Networks. C. Jennings, J. Peterson, M. Watson. November 2002. (Updated by RFC 5876) (Status: Informational)
3326	The Reason Header Field for the Session Initiation Protocol (SIP). H. Schulzrinne, D. Oran, G. Camarillo. December 2002. (Status: Proposed Standard)
3327	RFC 3327 Session Initiation Protocol (SIP) Extension Header Field for Registering Non-Adjacent Contacts. D. Willis, B. Hoeneisen. December 2002. (Updated by RFC 5626) (Status: Proposed Standard)
3329	Security Mechanism Agreement for the Session Initiation Protocol (SIP). J. Arkko, V. Torvinen, G. Camarillo, A. Niemi, T. Haukka. January 2003. (Status: Proposed Standard)
3351	User Requirements for the Session Initiation Protocol (SIP) in Support of Deaf, Hard of Hearing and Speech-impaired Individuals. N. Charlton, M. Gasson, G. Gybels, M. Spanner, A. van Wijk. August 2002. (Status: Informational)
3361	Dynamic Host Configuration Protocol (DHCP-for-IPv4) Option for Session Initiation Protocol (SIP) Servers. H. Schulzrinne. August 2002. (Status: Proposed Standard)
3362	Real-time Facsimile (T.38)—image/t38 MIME Sub-type Registration. G. Parsons. August 2002. (Status: Proposed Standard)
3370	Cryptographic Message Syntax (CMS) Algorithms. R. Housley. August 2002. (Obsoletes RFC 2630, RFC 3211) (Updated by RFC 5754) (Status: Proposed Standard)
3372	Session Initiation Protocol for Telephones (SIP-T): Context and Architectures. A. Vemuri, J. Peterson. September 2002. (Status: Best Current Practice)
3388	Grouping of Media Lines in the Session Description Protocol (SDP). G. Camarillo, G. Eriksson, J. Holler, H. Schulzrinne. December 2002. (Obsoleted by RFC 5888 (Status: Proposed Standard)
3398	Integrated Services Digital Network (ISDN) User Part (ISUP) to Session Initiation Protocol (SIP) Mapping. G. Camarillo, A.B. Roach, J. Peterson, L. Ong. December 2002. (Status: Proposed Standard)

3401	Dynamic Delegation Discovery System (DDDS) Part One: The Comprehensive DDDS. M. Mealling. October 2002. (Obsoletes RFC 2915, RFC 2168) (Updates RFC 2276) (Status: Informational)
3402	Dynamic Delegation Discovery System (DDDS) Part Two: The Algorithm. M. Mealling. October 2002. (Obsoletes RFC 2915, RFC 2168) (Status: Proposed Standard)
3403	Dynamic Delegation Discovery System (DDDS) Part Three: The Domain Name System (DNS) Database. M. Mealling. October 2002. (Obsoletes RFC 2915, RFC 2168) (Status: Proposed Standard)
3404	Dynamic Delegation Discovery System (DDDS) Part Four: The Uniform Resource Identifiers (URI). M. Mealling. October 2002. (Obsoletes RFC 2915, RFC 2168) (Status: Proposed Standard)
3406	Uniform Resource Names (URN) Namespace Definition Mechanisms. L. Daigle, D. van Gulik, R. Iannella, P. Faltstrom. October 2002. (Obsoletes RFC 2611) (Also BCP 0066) (Status: Best Current Practice)
3420	Internet Media Type message/sipfrag. R. Sparks. November 2002. (Status: Proposed Standard)
3428	Session Initiation Protocol (SIP) Extension for Instant Messaging. B. Campbell, Ed., J. Rosenberg, H. Schulzrinne, C. Huitema, D. Gurle. December 2002. (Status: Proposed Standard)
3459	Critical Content Multi-purpose Internet Mail Extensions (MIME) Parameter. E. Burger. January 2003. (Updates RFC 3204) (Status: Proposed Standard)
3480	Signalling Unnumbered Links in CR-LDP (Constraint-Routing Label Distribution Protocol). K. Kompella, Y. Rekhter, A. Kullberg. February 2003. (Status: Proposed Standard)
3481	TCP over Second (2.5G) and Third (3G) Generation Wireless Networks. H. Inamura, Ed., G. Montenegro, Ed., R. Ludwig, A. Gurtov, F. Khafizov. February 2003. (Also BCP 0071) (Status: Best Current Practice)

3485	The Session Initiation Protocol (SIP) and Session Description Protocol (SDP) Static Dictionary for Signaling Compression (SigComp). M. Garcia-Martin, C. Bormann, J. Ott, R. Price, A.B. Roach. February 2003. (Updated by RFC 4896) (Status: Proposed Standard)
3486	Compressing the Session Initiation Protocol (SIP). G. Camarillo. February 2003. (Updated by RFC 5049) (Status: Proposed Standard)
3487	RFC 3487 Requirements for Resource Priority Mechanisms for the Session Initiation Protocol (SIP). H. Schulzrinne. February 2003. (Status: Informational)
3490	Internationalizing Domain Names in Applications (IDNA). P. Faltstrom, P. Hoffman, A. Costello. March 2003. (Obsoleted by RFC 5890, RFC 5891) (Status: Proposed Standard)
3515	The Session Initiation Protocol (SIP) Refer Method. R. Sparks. April 2003. (Status: Proposed Standard)
3521	Framework for Session Set-up with Media Authorization. L-N. Hamer, B. Gage, H. Shieh. April 2003. (Status: Informational)
3523	Internet Emergency Preparedness (IEPREP) Telephony Topology Terminology. J. Polk. April 2003. (Status: Informational)
3524	Mapping of Media Streams to Resource Reservation Flows. G. Camarillo, A. Monrad. April 2003. (Status: Proposed Standard)
3530	Network File System (NFS) version 4 Protocol. S. Shepler, B. Callaghan, D. Robinson, R. Thurlow, C. Beame, M. Eisler, D. Noveck. April 2003. (Obsoletes RFC 3010) (Obsoleted by RFC 7530) (Status: Proposed Standard)
3540	Robust Explicit Congestion Notification (ECN) Signaling with Nonces. N. Spring, D. Wetherall, D. Ely. June 2003. (Status: Experimental)
3550	RTP: A Transport Protocol for Real-Time Applications. H. Schulzrinne, S. Casner, R. Frederick, V. Jacobson. July 2003. (Obsoletes RFC 1889) (Updated by RFC 5506, RFC 5761, RFC 6051, RFC 6222, RFC 7022, RFC 7160, RFC 7164) (Also STD 0064) (Status: Internet Standard)
3551	RTP Profile for Audio and Video Conferences with Minimal Control. H. Schulzrinne, S. Casner. July 2003. (Obsoletes RFC 1890) (Updated by RFC 5761, RFC 7007) (Also STD 0065) (Status: Internet Standard)
3578	Mapping of Integrated Services Digital Network (ISDN) User Part (ISUP) Overlap Signalling to the Session Initiation Protocol (SIP). G. Camarillo, A.B. Roach, J. Peterson, L. Ong. August 2003. (Status: Proposed Standard)
3581	An Extension to the Session Initiation Protocol (SIP) for Symmetric Response Routing. J. Rosenberg, H. Schulzrinne. August 2003. (Status: Proposed Standard)
3605	3Real Time Control Protocol (RTCP) attribute in Session Description Protocol (SDP). C. Huitema. October 2003. (Status: Proposed Standard)
3608	Session Initiation Protocol (SIP) Extension Header Field for Service Route Discovery During Registration. D. Willis, B. Hoeneisen. October 2003. (Updated by RFC 5630) (Status: Proposed Standard)
3665	Session Initiation Protocol (SIP) Basic Call Flow Examples. A. Johnston, S. Donovan, R. Sparks, C. Cunningham, K. Summers. December 2003. (Status: Best Current Practice)
3666	Session Initiation Protocol (SIP) Public Switched Telephone Network (PSTN) Call Flows. A. Johnston, S. Donovan, R. Sparks, C. Cunningham, K. Summers. December 2003. (Also BCP 0076) (Status: Best Current Practice)
3669	Guidelines for Working Groups on Intellectual Property Issues. S. Brim. February 2004. (Status: Informational)
3680	A Session Initiation Protocol (SIP) Event Package for Registrations. J. Rosenberg. March 2004. (Updated by RFC 6140) (Status: Proposed Standard)
3693	Geopriv Requirements. J. Cuellar, J. Morris, D. Mulligan, J. Peterson, J. Polk. February 2004. (Updated by RFC 6280, RFC 7459) (Status: Informational)
3711	The Secure Real-time Transport Protocol (SRTP). M. Baugher, D. McGrew, M. Naslund, E. Carrara, K. Norrman. March 2004. (Updated by RFC 5506, RFC 6904) (Status: Proposed Standard)

3725	Best Current Practices for Third Party Call Control (3pcc) in the Session Initiation Protocol (SIP). J. Rosenberg, J. Peterson, H. Schulzrinne, G. Camarillo. April 2004. (Status: Best Current Practice)
3735	Guidelines for Extending the Extensible Provisioning Protocol (EPP). S. Hollenbeck. March 2004. (Status: Informational)
3764	Enumservice registration for Session Initiation Protocol (SIP) Addresses-of-Record. J. Peterson. April 2004. (Updated by RFC 6118) (Status: Proposed Standard)
3824	Using E.164 numbers with the Session Initiation Protocol (SIP). J. Peterson, H. Liu, J. Yu, B. Campbell. June 2004. (Status: Informational)
3830	MIKEY: Multimedia Internet KEYing. J. Arkko, E. Carrara, F. Lindholm, M. Naslund, K. Norrman. August 2004. (Updated by RFC 4738, RFC 6309) (Status: Proposed Standard)
3840	Indicating User Agent Capabilities in the Session Initiation Protocol (SIP). J. Rosenberg, H. Schulzrinne, P. Kyzivat. August 2004. (Status: Proposed Standard)
3841	Caller Preferences for the Session Initiation Protocol (SIP). J. Rosenberg, H. Schulzrinne, P. Kyzivat. August 2004. (Status: Proposed Standard)
3842	A Message Summary and Message Waiting Indication Event Package for the Session Initiation Protocol (SIP). R. Mahy. August 2004. (Status: Proposed Standard)
3853	S/MIME Advanced Encryption Standard (AES) Requirement for the Session Initiation Protocol (SIP). J. Peterson. July 2004. (Updates RFC 3261) (Status: Proposed Standard)
3856	A Presence Event Package for the Session Initiation Protocol (SIP). J. Rosenberg. August 2004. (Status: Proposed Standard)
3857	A Watcher Information Event Template-Package for the Session Initiation Protocol (SIP). J. Rosenberg. August 2004. (Status: Proposed Standard)
3858	An Extensible Markup Language (XML) Based Format for Watcher Information. J. Rosenberg. August 2004. (Status: Proposed Standard)
3859	Common Profile for Presence (CPP). J. Peterson. August 2004. (Status: Proposed Standard)
3862	Common Presence and Instant Messaging (CPIM): Message Format. G. Klyne, D. Atkins. August 2004. (Status: Proposed Standard)
3863	Presence Information Data Format (PIDF). H. Sugano, S. Fujimoto, G. Klyne, A. Bateman, W. Carr, J. Peterson. August 2004. (Status: Proposed Standard)
3873	Stream Control Transmission Protocol (SCTP) Management Information Base (MIB). J. Pastor, M. Belinchon. September 2004. (Status: Proposed Standard)
3880	Call Processing Language (CPL): A Language for User Control of Internet Telephony Services. J. Lennox, X. Wu, H. Schulzrinne. October 2004. (Status: Proposed Standard)
3891	The Session Initiation Protocol (SIP) "Replaces" Header. R. Mahy, B. Biggs, R. Dean. September 2004. (Status: Proposed Standard)
3892	The Session Initiation Protocol (SIP) Referred-By Mechanism. R. Sparks. September 2004. (Status: Proposed Standard)
3893	Session Initiation Protocol (SIP) Authenticated Identity Body (AIB) Format. J. Peterson. September 2004. (Status: Proposed Standard)
3903	Session Initiation Protocol (SIP) Extension for Event State Publication. A. Niemi, Ed. October 2004. (Status: Proposed Standard)
3911	The Session Initiation Protocol (SIP) "Join" Header. R. Mahy, D. Petrie. October 2004. (Status: Proposed Standard)
3957	Authentication, Authorization, and Accounting (AAA) Registration Keys for Mobile IPv4. C. Perkins, P. Calhoun. March 2005. (Status: Proposed Standard)
3958	Domain-Based Application Service Location Using SRV RRs and the Dynamic Delegation Discovery Service (DDDS). L. Daigle, A. Newton. January 2005. (Status: Proposed Standard)
3959	The Early Session Disposition Type for the Session Initiation Protocol (SIP). G. Camarillo. December 2004. (Status: Proposed Standard)
3960	Early Media and Ringing Tone Generation in the Session Initiation Protocol (SIP). G. Camarillo, H. Schulzrinne. December 2004. (Status: Informational)

3966	The tel URI for Telephone Numbers. H. Schulzrinne. December 2004. (Status: Proposed Standard) (Obsoletes RFC 2806) (Updated by RFC 5341) (Status: Proposed Standard)
3968	The Internet Assigned Number Authority (IANA) Header Field Parameter Registry for the Session Initiation Protocol (SIP). G. Camarillo. December 2004. (Updates RFC 3427) (Status: Best Current Practice)
3969	The Internet Assigned Number Authority (IANA) Uniform Resource Identifier (URI) Parameter Registry for the Session Initiation Protocol (SIP). G. Camarillo. December 2004. (Updates RFC 3427) (Updated by RFC 5727) (Also BCP 0099) (Status: Best Current Practice)
3986	Uniform Resource Identifier (URI): Generic Syntax. T. Berners-Lee, R. Fielding, L. Masinter. January 2005. (Obsoletes RFC 2732, RFC 2396, RFC 1808) (Updates RFC 1738) (Updated by RFC 6874, RFC 7320) (Also STD 0066) (Status: Internet Standard)
4028	Session Timers in the Session Initiation Protocol (SIP). S. Donovan, J. Rosenberg. April 2005. (Status: Proposed Standard)
4032	Update to the Session Initiation Protocol (SIP) Preconditions Framework. G. Camarillo, P. Kyzivat. March 2005. (Updates RFC 3312) (Status: Proposed Standard)
4033	DNS Security Introduction and Requirements. R. Arends, R. Austein, M. Larson, D. Massey, S. Rose. March 2005. (Obsoletes RFC 2535, RFC 3008, RFC 3090, RFC 3445, RFC 3655, RFC 3658, RFC 3755, RFC 3757, RFC 3845) (Updates RFC 1034, RFC 1035, RFC 2136, RFC 2181, RFC 2308, RFC 3225, RFC 3597, RFC 3226) (Updated by RFC 6014, RFC 6840) (Status: Proposed Standard)
4034	Resource Records for the DNS Security Extensions. R. Arends, R. Austein, M. Larson, D. Massey, S. Rose. March 2005. (Obsoletes RFC 2535, RFC 3008, RFC 3090, RFC 3445, RFC 3655, RFC 3658, RFC 3755, RFC 3757, RFC 3845) (Updates RFC 1034, RFC 1035, RFC 2136, RFC 2181, RFC 2308, RFC 3225, RFC 3597, RFC 3226) (Updated by RFC 4470, RFC 6014, RFC 6840, RFC 6944) (Status: Proposed Standard)
4035	Protocol Modifications for the DNS Security Extensions. R. Arends, R. Austein, M. Larson, D. Massey, S. Rose. March 2005. (Obsoletes RFC 2535, RFC3 008, RFC 3090, RFC 3445, RFC 3655, RFC 3658, RFC 3755, RFC3 757, RFC 3845) (Updates RFC 1034, RFC 1035, RFC 2136, RFC 2181, RFC 2308, RFC 3225, RFC 3597, RFC 3226) (Updated by RFC 4470, RFC 6014, RFC 6840) (Status: Proposed Standard)
4083	Input 3rd-Generation Partnership Project (3GPP) Release 5 Requirements on the Session Initiation Protocol (SIP). M. Garcia-Martin. May 2005. (Status: Informational)
4086	Randomness Requirements for Security. D. Eastlake 3rd, J. Schiller, S. Crocker. June 2005. (Obsoletes RFC 1750) (Also BCP 0106) (Status: Best Current Practice)
4103	RTP Payload for Text Conversation. G. Hellstrom, P. Jones. June 2005. (Obsoletes RFC 2793) (Status: Proposed Standard)
4117	Transcoding Services Invocation in the Session Initiation Protocol (SIP) Using Third Party Call Control (3pcc). G. Camarillo, E. Burger, H. Schulzrinne, A. van Wijk. June 2005. (Status: Informational)
4119	A Presence-based GEOPRIV Location Object Format. J. Peterson. December 2005. (Updated by RFC 5139, RFC 5491, RFC 7459) (Status: Proposed Standard)
4122	A Universally Unique IDentifier (UUID) URN Namespace. P. Leach, M. Mealling, R. Salz. July 2005. (Status: Proposed Standard)
4145	TCP-Based Media Transport in the Session Description Protocol (SDP). D. Yon, G. Camarillo. September 2005. (Updated by RFC 4572) (Status: Proposed Standard)
4149	Definition of Managed Objects for Synthetic Sources for Performance Monitoring Algorithms. C. Kalbfleisch, R. Cole, D. Romascanu. August 2005. (Status: Proposed Standard)
4152	A Uniform Resource Name (URN) Namespace for the Common Language Equipment Identifier (CLEI) Code. K. Tesink, R. Fox. August 2005. (Status: Informational)
4168	The Stream Control Transmission Protocol (SCTP) as a Transport for the Session Initiation Protocol (SIP). J. Rosenberg, H. Schulzrinne, G. Camarillo. October 2005. (Status: Proposed Standard)

4179	Using Universal Content Identifier (UCI) as Uniform Resource Names (URN). S. Kang. October 2005. (Status: Informational)
4195	A Uniform Resource Name (URN) Namespace for the TV-Anytime Forum. W. Kameyama. October 2005. (Status: Informational)
4198	A Uniform Resource Name (URN) Namespace for Federated Content. D. Tessman. November 2005. (Status: Informational)
4234	Augmented BNF for Syntax Specifications: ABNF. D. Crocker, Ed., P. Overell. October 2005. (Obsoletes RFC 2234) (Obsoleted by RFC 5234) (Status: Draft Standard)
4235	An INVITE-Initiated Dialog Event Package for the Session Initiation Protocol (SIP). J. Rosenberg, H. Schulzrinne, R. Mahy, Ed. November 2005. (Status: Proposed Standard)
4240	Basic Network Media Services with SIP. E. Burger, Ed., J. Van Dyke, A. Spitzer. December 2005. (Status: Informational)
4244	An Extension to the Session Initiation Protocol (SIP) for Request History Information. M. Barnes, Ed. November 2005. (Status: Proposed Standard)
4248	The telnet URI Scheme. P. Hoffman. October 2005. (Obsoletes RFC 1738) (Status: Proposed Standard)
4266	The gopher URI Scheme. P. Hoffman. November 2005. (Obsoletes RFC 1738) (Status: Proposed Standard)
4269	The SEED Encryption Algorithm. H.J. Lee, S.J. Lee, J.H. Yoon, D.H. Cheon, J.I. Lee. December 2005. (Obsoletes RFC 4009) (Status: Informational)
4289	Multipurpose Internet Mail Extensions (MIME) Part Four: Registration Procedures. N. Freed, J. Klensin. December 2005. (Obsoletes RFC 2048) (Also BCP 0013) (Status: Best Current Practice)
4301	Security Architecture for the Internet Protocol. S. Kent, K. Seo. December 2005. (Obsoletes RFC 2401) (Updates RFC 3168) (Updated by RFC 6040) (Status: Proposed Standard)
4302	IP Authentication Header. S. Kent. December 2005. (Obsoletes RFC2 402) (Status: Proposed Standard)
4303	IP Encapsulating Security Payload (ESP). S. Kent. December 2005. (Obsoletes RFC 2406) (Status: Proposed Standard)

4305	Cryptographic Algorithm Implementation Requirements for Encapsulating Security Payload (ESP) and Authentication Header (AH). D. Eastlake 3rd. December 2005. (Obsoletes RFC 2402, RFC 2406) (Obsoleted by RFC 4835) (Status: Proposed Standard)
4306	Internet Key Exchange (IKEv2) Protocol. C. Kaufman, Ed. December 2005. (Obsoletes RFC 2407, RFC 2408, RFC 2409) (Obsoleted by RFC 5996) (Updated by RFC 5282) (Status: Proposed Standard)
4313	Requirements for Distributed Control of Automatic Speech Recognition (ASR), Speaker Identification/Speaker Verification (SI/SV), and Text-to-Speech (TTS) Resources. D. Oran. December 2005. (Status: Informational)
4320	Actions Addressing Identified Issues with the Session Initiation Protocol's (SIP) Non-INVITE Transaction. R. Sparks. January 2006. (Updates RFC 3261) (Status: Proposed Standard)
4321	Problems Identified Associated with the Session Initiation Protocol's (SIP) Non-INVITE Transaction. R. Sparks. January 2006. (Status: Informational)
4335	The Secure Shell (SSH) Session Channel Break Extension. J. Galbraith, P. Remaker. January 2006. (Status: Proposed Standard)
4340	Datagram Congestion Control Protocol (DCCP). E. Kohler, M. Handley, S. Floyd. March 2006. (Updated by RFC 5595, RFC 5596, RFC 6335, RFC 6773) (Status: Proposed Standard)
4343	Domain Name System (DNS) Case Insensitivity Clarification. D. Eastlake 3rd. January 2006. (Updates RFC 1034, RFC 1035, RFC 2181) (Status: Proposed Standard)
4346	The Transport Layer Security (TLS) Protocol Version 1.1. T. Dierks, E. Rescorla. April 2006. (Obsoletes RFC 2246) (Obsoleted by RFC 5246) (Updated by RFC 4366, RFC 4680, RFC 4681, RFC 5746, RFC 6176, RFC 7465) (Status: Proposed Standard)
4353	A Framework for Conferencing with the Session Initiation Protocol (SIP). J. Rosenberg. February 2006. (Status: Informational)
4375	Emergency Telecommunications Services (ETS) Requirements for a Single Administrative Domain. K. Carlberg. January 2006. (Status: Informational)

4408	Sender Policy Framework (SPF) for Authorizing Use of Domains in E-Mail, Version 1. M. Wong, W. Schlitt. April 2006. (Obsoleted by RFC 7208) (Updated by RFC 6652) (Status: Experimental)
4411	Extending the Session Initiation Protocol (SIP) Reason Header for Preemption Events. J. Polk. February 2006. (Status: Proposed Standard)
4412	Communications Resource Priority for the Session Initiation Protocol (SIP). H. Schulzrinne, J. Polk. February 2006. (Status: Proposed Standard)
4453	Requirements for Consent-Based Communications in the Session Initiation Protocol (SIP). J. Rosenberg, G. Camarillo, Ed., D. Willis. April 2006. (Status: Informational)
4457	The Session Initiation Protocol (SIP) P-User-Database Private-Header (P-Header). G. Camarillo, G. Blanco. April 2006. (Status: Informational)
4458	Session Initiation Protocol (SIP) URIs for Applications such as Voicemail and Interactive Voice Response (IVR). C. Jennings, F. Audet, J. Elwell. April 2006. (Status: Informational)
4474	Enhancements for Authenticated Identity Management in the Session Initiation Protocol (SIP). J. Peterson, C. Jennings. August 2006. (Status: Proposed Standard)
4475	RFC 4475 Session Initiation Protocol (SIP) Torture Test Messages. R. Sparks, Ed., A. Hawrylyshen, A. Johnston, J. Rosenberg, H. Schulzrinne. May 2006. (Status: Informational)
4479	A Data Model for Presence. J. Rosenberg. July 2006. (Status: Proposed Standard)
4483	A Mechanism for Content Indirection in Session Initiation Protocol (SIP) Messages. E. Burger, Ed. May 2006. (Status: Proposed Standard)
4484	Trait-Based Authorization Requirements for the Session Initiation Protocol (SIP). J. Peterson, J. Polk, D. Sicker, H. Tschofenig. August 2006. (Status: Informational)
4488	Suppression of Session Initiation Protocol (SIP) REFER Method Implicit Subscription. O. Levin. May 2006. (Status: Proposed Standard)
4497	Interworking between the Session Initiation Protocol (SIP) and QSIG. J. Elwell, F. Derks, P. Mourot, O. Rousseau. May 2006. (Status: Best Current Practice)

4504	SIP Telephony Device Requirements and Configuration. H. Sinnreich, Ed., S. Lass, C. Stredicke. May 2006. (Status: Informational)
4508	Conveying Feature Tags with the Session Initiation Protocol (SIP) REFER Method. O. Levin, A. Johnston. May 2006. (Status: Proposed Standard)
4515	Lightweight Directory Access Protocol (LDAP): String Representation of Search Filters. M. Smith, Ed., T. Howes. June 2006. (Obsoletes RFC 2254) (Status: Proposed Standard)
4538	Request Authorization through Dialog Identification in the Session Initiation Protocol (SIP). J. Rosenberg. June 2006. (Status: Proposed Standard)
4542	Implementing an Emergency Telecommunications Service (ETS) for Real-Time Services in the Internet Protocol Suite. F. Baker, J. Polk. May 2006. (Updated by RFC 5865) (Status: Informational)
4566	Session Description Protocol. M. Handley, V. Jacobson, C. Perkins. July 2006. (Obsoletes RFC 2327, RFC 3266) (Status: Proposed Standard)
4567	Key Management Extensions for Session Description Protocol (SDP) and Real Time Streaming Protocol (RTSP). J. Arkko, F. Lindholm, M. Naslund, K. Norrman, E. Carrara. July 2006. (Status: Proposed Standard)
4568	Session Description Protocol (SDP) Security Descriptions for Media Streams. F. Andreasen, M. Baugher, D. Wing. July 2006. (Status: Proposed Standard)
4572	Connection-Oriented Media Transport over the Transport Layer Security (TLS) Protocol in the Session Description Protocol (SDP). J. Lennox. July 2006. (Updates RFC 4145) (Status: Proposed Standard)
4574	The Session Description Protocol (SDP) Label Attribute. O. Levin, G. Camarillo. August 2006. (Status: Proposed Standard)
4575	A Session Initiation Protocol (SIP) Event Package for Conference State. J. Rosenberg, H. Schulzrinne, O. Levin, Ed. August 2006. (Status: Proposed Standard)
4579	Session Initiation Protocol (SIP) Call Control—Conferencing for User Agents. A. Johnston, O. Levin. August 2006. (Status: Best Current Practice)

4582	The Binary Floor Control Protocol (BFCP). G. Camarillo, J. Ott, K. Drage. November 2006. (Status: Proposed Standard)
4583	Session Description Protocol (SDP) Format for Binary Floor Control Protocol (BFCP) Streams. G. Camarillo. November 2006. (Status: Proposed Standard)
4585	Extended RTP Profile for Real-time Transport Control Protocol (RTCP)-Based Feedback (RTP/AVPF). J. Ott, S. Wenger, N. Sato, C. Burmeister, J. Rey. July 2006. (Updated by RFC 5506) (Status: Proposed Standard)
4612	Real-Time Facsimile (T.38)—audio/t38 MIME Sub-type Registration. P. Jones, H. Tamura. August 2006. (Status: Historic)
4628	RTP Payload Format for H.263 Moving RFC 2190 to Historic Status. R. Even. January 2007 (Status: Informational)
4629	RTP Payload Format for ITU-T Rec. H.263 Video. J. Ott, C. Bormann, G. Sullivan, S. Wenger, R. Even, Ed. January 2007. (Obsoletes RFC 2429) (Updates RFC 3555) (Status: Proposed Standard)
4646	Tags for Identifying Languages. A. Phillips, M. Davis. September 2006. (Obsoletes RFC 3066) (Obsoleted by RFC 5646) (Status: Best Current Practice)
4647	Matching of Language Tags. A. Phillips, M. Davis. September 2006. (Obsoletes RFC 3066) (Also BCP 0047) (Status: Best Current Practice)
4648	The Base16, Base32, and Base64 Data Encodings. S. Josefsson. October 2006. (Obsoletes RFC 3548) (Status: Proposed Standard)
4660	Functional Description of Event Notification Filtering. H. Khartabil, E. Leppanen, M. Lonnfors, J. Costa-Requena. September 2006. (Updated by RFC 6665) (Status: Proposed Standard)
4661	An Extensible Markup Language (XML)-Based Format for Event Notification Filtering. H. Khartabil, E. Leppanen, M. Lonnfors, J. Costa-Requena. September 2006. (Status: Proposed Standard)
4662	A Session Initiation Protocol (SIP) Event Notification Extension for Resource Lists. A.B. Roach, B. Campbell, J. Rosenberg. August 2006. (Status: Proposed Standard)

4730	A Session Initiation Protocol (SIP) Event Package for Key Press Stimulus (KPML). E. Burger, M. Dolly. November 2006. (Status: Proposed Standard)
4733	RTP Payload for DTMF Digits, Telephony Tones, and Telephony Signals. H. Schulzrinne, T. Taylor. December 2006 (Obsoletes RFC 2833) (Updated by RFC 4734, RFC 5244) (Status: Proposed Standard)
4734	Definition of Events for Modem, Fax, and Text Telephony Signals. H. Schulzrinne, T. Taylor. December 2006. (Obsoletes RFC 2833) (Updates RFC 4733) (Status: Proposed Standard)
4740	Diameter Session Initiation Protocol (SIP) Application. M. Garcia-Martin, Ed., M. Belinchon, M. Pallares-Lopez, C. Canales-Valenzuela, K. Tammi. November 2006. (Status: Proposed Standard)
4825	The Extensible Markup Language (XML) Configuration Access Protocol (XCAP). J. Rosenberg. May 2007. (Status: Proposed Standard)
4826	Extensible Markup Language (XML) Formats for Representing Resource Lists. J. Rosenberg. May 2007. (Status: Proposed Standard)
4867	RTP Payload Format and File Storage Format for the Adaptive Multi-Rate (AMR) and Adaptive Multi-Rate Wideband (AMR-WB) Audio Codecs. J. Sjoberg, M. Westerlund, A. Lakaniemi, Q. Xie. April 2007. (Obsoletes RFC 3267) (Status: Proposed Standard)
4906	Transport of Layer 2 Frames Over MPLS. L. Martini, Ed., E. Rosen, Ed., N. El-Aawar, Ed. June 2007. (Status: Historic)
4916	Connected Identity in the Session Initiation Protocol (SIP). J. Elwell. June 2007. (Updates RFC 3261) (Status: Proposed Standard)
4919	IPv6 over Low-Power Wireless Personal Area Networks (6LoWPANs): Overview, Assumptions, Problem Statement, and Goals. N. Kushalnagar, G. Montenegro, C. Schumacher. August 2007. (Status: Informational)
4958	A Framework for Supporting Emergency Telecommunications Services (ETS) within a Single Administrative Domain. K. Carlberg. July 2007. (Status: Informational)

4960	Stream Control Transmission Protocol. R. Stewart, Ed. September 2007. (Obsoletes RFC 2960, RFC 3309) (Updated by RFC 6096, RFC 6335, RFC 7053) (Status: Proposed Standard)
4975	The Message Session Relay Protocol (MSRP). B. Campbell, Ed., R. Mahy, Ed., C. Jennings, Ed. September 2007. (Status: Proposed Standard)
4976	Relay Extensions for the Message Sessions Relay Protocol (MSRP). C. Jennings, R. Mahy, A. B. Roach. September 2007. (Status: Proposed Standard)
5002	The Session Initiation Protocol (SIP) P-Profile-Key Private Header (P-Header). G. Camarillo, G. Blanco. August 2007. (Status: Informational)
5009	Private Header (P-Header) Extension to the Session Initiation Protocol (SIP) for Authorization of Early Media. R. Ejza. September 2007. (Status: Informational)
5012	Requirements for Emergency Context Resolution with Internet Technologies. H. Schulzrinne, R. Marshall, Ed. January 2008. (Status: Informational)
5022	Media Server Control Markup Language (MSCML) and Protocol. J. Van Dyke, E. Burger, Ed., A. Spitzer. September 2007. (Obsoletes RFC 4722) (Status: Informational)
5027	Security Preconditions for Session Description Protocol (SDP) Media Streams. F. Andreasen, D. Wing. October 2007. (Updates RFC 3312) (Status: Proposed Standard)
5029	Definition of an IS-IS Link Attribute Sub-TLV. JP. Vasseur, S. Previdi. September 2007. (Status: Proposed Standard)
5031	A Uniform Resource Name (URN) for Emergency and Other Well-Known Services. H. Schulzrinne. January 2008. (Updated by RFC 7163) (Status: Proposed Standard)
5039	The Session Initiation Protocol (SIP) and Spam. J. Rosenberg, C. Jennings. January 2008. (Status: Informational)
5049	Applying Signaling Compression (SigComp) to the Session Initiation Protocol (SIP). C. Bormann, Z. Liu, R. Price, G. Camarillo, Ed. December 2007. (Updates RFC 3486) (Status: Proposed Standard)
5057	Multiple Dialog Usages in the Session Initiation Protocol. R. Sparks. November 2007. (Status: Informational)
5069	Security Threats and Requirements for Emergency Call Marking and Mapping. T. Taylor, Ed., H. Tschofenig, H. Schulzrinne, M. Shanmugam. January 2008. (Status: Informational)
5079	Rejecting Anonymous Requests in the Session Initiation Protocol (SIP). J. Rosenberg. December 2007. (Status: Proposed Standard)
5112	The Presence-Specific Static Dictionary for Signaling Compression (Sigcomp). M. Garcia-Martin. January 2008. (Status: Proposed Standard)
5155	DNS Security (DNSSEC) Hashed Authenticated Denial of Existence. B. Laurie, G. Sisson, R. Arends, D. Blacka. March 2008. (Updated by RFC 6840, RFC 6944) (Status: Proposed Standard)
5168	XML Schema for Media Control. O. Levin, R. Even, P. Hagendorf. March 2008. (Status: Informational)
5196	Session Initiation Protocol (SIP) User Agent Capability Extension to Presence Information Data Format (PIDF). M. Lonnfors, K. Kiss. September 2008.
5226	Guidelines for Writing an IANA Considerations Section in RFCs. T. Narten, H. Alvestrand. May 2008. (Obsoletes RFC 2434) (Also BCP 0026) (Status: Best Current Practice)
5234	Augmented BNF for Syntax Specifications: ABNF. D. Crocker, Ed., P. Overell. January 2008. (Obsoletes RFC 4234) (Updated by RFC 7405) (Also STD 0068) (Status: Internet Standard)
5239	A Framework for Centralized Conferencing. M. Barnes, C. Boulton, O. Levin. June 2008. (Status: Proposed Standard)
5244	Definition of Events for Channel-Oriented Telephony Signalling. H. Schulzrinne, T. Taylor. June 2008. (Updates RFC 4733) (Status: Proposed Standard)
5245	Interactive Connectivity Establishment (ICE): A Protocol for Network Address Translator (NAT) Traversal for Offer/Answer Protocols. J. Rosenberg. April 2010. (Obsoletes RFC 4091, RFC 4092) (Updated by RFC 6336) (Status: Proposed Standard)

5246	The Transport Layer Security (TLS) Protocol Version 1.2. T. Dierks, E. Rescorla. August 2008. (Obsoletes RFC 3268, RFC 4346, RFC 4366) (Updates RFC 4492) (Updated by RFC 5746, RFC 5878, RFC 6176, RFC 7465) (Status: Proposed Standard)
5280	Internet X.509 Public Key Infrastructure Certificate and Certificate Revocation List (CRL) Profile. D. Cooper, S. Santesson, S. Farrell, S. Boeyen, R. Housley, W. Polk. May 2008. (Obsoletes RFC 3280, RFC 4325, RFC 4630) (Updated by RFC 6818) (Status: Proposed Standard)
5318	The Session Initiation Protocol (SIP) P-Refused-URI-List Private-Header (P-Header). J. Hautakorpi, G. Camarillo. December 2008. (Status: Informational)
5322	Internet Message Format. P. Resnick, Ed. October 2008. (Obsoletes RFC 2822) (Updates RFC 4021) (Updated by RFC 6854) (Status: Draft Standard)
5359	Session Initiation Protocol Service Examples. A. Johnston, Ed., R. Sparks, C. Cunningham, S. Donovan, K. Summers. October 2008. (Also BCP 0144) (Status: Best Current Practice)
5360	A Framework for Consent-Based Communications in the Session Initiation Protocol (SIP). J. Rosenberg, G. Camarillo, Ed., D. Willis. October 2008. (Status: Proposed Standard)
5361	A Document Format for Requesting Consent. G. Camarillo. October 2008. (Status: Proposed Standard)
5362	The Session Initiation Protocol (SIP) Pending Additions Event Package. G. Camarillo. October 2008. (Status: Proposed Standard)
5363	Framework and Security Considerations for Session Initiation Protocol (SIP) URI-List Services. G. Camarillo, A.B. Roach. October 2008. (Status: Proposed Standard)
5364	Extensible Markup Language (XML) Format Extension for Representing Copy Control Attributes in Resource Lists. M. Garcia-Martin, G. Camarillo. October 2008. (Status: Proposed Standard)
5365	Multiple-Recipient MESSAGE Requests in the Session Initiation Protocol (SIP). M. Garcia-Martin, G. Camarillo. October 2008. (Status: Proposed Standard)
5366	Conference Establishment Using Request-Contained Lists in the Session Initiation Protocol (SIP). G. Camarillo, A. Johnston. October 2008. (Status: Proposed Standard)
5367	Subscriptions to Request-Contained Resource Lists in the Session Initiation Protocol (SIP). G. Camarillo, A.B. Roach, O. Levin. October 2008. (Updates RFC 3265) (Status: Proposed Standard)
5368	Referring to Multiple Resources in the Session Initiation Protocol (SIP). G. Camarillo, A. Niemi, M. Isomaki, M. Garcia-Martin, H. Khartabil. October 2008. (Status: Proposed Standard)
5369	Framework for Transcoding with the Session Initiation Protocol (SIP). G. Camarillo. October 2008. (Status: Informational)
5370	The Session Initiation Protocol (SIP) Conference Bridge Transcoding Model. G. Camarillo. October 2008. (Status: Proposed Standard)
5373	Requesting Answering Modes for the Session Initiation Protocol (SIP). D. Willis, Ed., A. Allen. November 2008. (Status: Proposed Standard)
5379	Guidelines for Using the Privacy Mechanism for SIP. M. Munakata, S. Schubert, T. Ohba. February 2010. (Status: Informational)
5389	Session Traversal Utilities for NAT (STUN). J. Rosenberg, R. Mahy, P. Matthews, D. Wing. October 2008. (Obsoletes RFC 3489) (Updated by RFC 7350) (Status: Proposed Standard)
5390	Requirements for Management of Overload in the Session Initiation Protocol. J. Rosenberg. December 2008. (Status: Informational)
5393	Addressing an Amplification Vulnerability in Session Initiation Protocol (SIP) Forking Proxies. R. Sparks, Ed., S. Lawrence, A. Hawrylyshen, B. Campen. December 2008. (Updates RFC 3261) (Status: Proposed Standard)
5405	Unicast UDP Usage Guidelines for Application Designers. L. Eggert, G. Fairhurst. November 2008. (Also BCP 0145) (Status: Best Current Practice)
5411	A Hitchhiker's Guide to the Session Initiation Protocol (SIP). J. Rosenberg. February 2009. (Status: Informational)

5432	Quality of Service (QOS) Mechanism Selection in the Session Description Protocol (SDP). J. Polk, S. Dhesikan, G. Camarillo. March 2009. (Status: Proposed Standard)
5483	ENUM Implementation Issues and Experiences. L. Conroy, K. Fujiwara. March 2009. (Status: Informational)
5491	GEOPRIV Presence Information Data Format Location Object (PIDF-LO) Usage Clarification, Considerations, and Recommendations. J. Winterbottom, M. Thomson, H. Tschofenig. March 2009. (Updates RFC 4119) (Updated by RFC 7459) (Status: Proposed Standard)
5502	The SIP P-Served-User Private-Header (P-Header) for the 3GPP IP Multimedia (IM) Core Network (CN) Subsystem. J. van Elburg. April 2009. (Status: Informational)
5506	Support for Reduced-Size Real-Time Transport Control Protocol (RTCP): Opportunities and Consequences. I. Johansson, M. Westerlund. April 2009. (Updates RFC 3550, RFC 3711, RFC 4585) (Status: Proposed Standard)
5547	A Session Description Protocol (SDP) Offer/Answer Mechanism to Enable File Transfer. M. Garcia-Martin, M. Isomaki, G. Camarillo, S. Loreto, P. Kyzivat. May 2009. (Status: Proposed Standard)
5552	SIP Interface to VoiceXML Media Services. D. Burke, M. Scott. May 2009. (Status: Proposed Standard)
5553	Resource Reservation Protocol (RSVP) Extensions for Path Key Support. A. Farrel, Ed., R. Bradford, JP. Vasseur. May 2009. (Status: Proposed Standard)
5583	Signaling Media Decoding Dependency in the Session Description Protocol (SDP). T. Schierl, S. Wenger. July 2009. (Status: Proposed Standard)
5589	RFC 5589 Session Initiation Protocol (SIP) Call Control—Transfer. R. Sparks, A. Johnston, Ed., D. Petrie. June 2009. (Status: Best Current Practice)
5606	Implications of "retransmission-allowed" for SIP Location Conveyance. J. Peterson, T. Hardie, J. Morris. August 2009. (Status: Informational)

5621	Message Body Handling in the Session Initiation Protocol (SIP). G. Camarillo. September 2009. (Updates RFC 3204, RFC 3261, RFC 3459) (Status: Proposed Standard)
5626	Managing Client-Initiated Connections in the Session Initiation Protocol (SIP). C. Jennings, Ed., R. Mahy, Ed., F. Audet, Ed. October 2009. (Updates RFC 3261, RFC 3327) (Status: Proposed Standard)
5627	Obtaining and Using Globally Routable User Agent URIs (GRUUs) in the Session Initiation Protocol (SIP). J. Rosenberg. October 2009. (Status: Proposed Standard)
5628	Registration Event Package Extension for Session Initiation Protocol (SIP) Globally Routable User Agent URIs (GRUUs). P. Kyzivat. October 2009. (Status: Proposed Standard)
5629	A Framework for Application Interaction in the Session Initiation Protocol (SIP). J. Rosenberg. October 2009. (Status: Proposed Standard)
5630	The Use of the SIPS URI Scheme in the Session Initiation Protocol (SIP). F. Audet. October 2009. (Updates RFC 3261, RFC 3608) (Status: Proposed Standard)
5631	Session Initiation Protocol (SIP) Session Mobility. R. Shacham, H. Schulzrinne, S. Thakolsri, W. Kellerer. October 2009. (Status: Informational)
5638	Simple SIP Usage Scenario for Applications in the Endpoints. H. Sinnreich, Ed., A. Johnston, E. Shim, K. Singh. September 2009. (Status: Informational)
5658	Addressing Record-Route Issues in the Session Initiation Protocol (SIP). T. Froment, C. Lebel, B. Bonnaerens. October 2009. (Status: Proposed Standard)
5688	A Session Initiation Protocol (SIP) Media Feature Tag for MIME Application Subtypes. J. Rosenberg. January 2010. (Status: Proposed Standard)
5707	Media Server Markup Language (MSML). A. Saleem, Y. Xin, G. Sharratt. February 2010. (Status: Informational)
5727	Change Process for the Session Initiation Protocol (SIP) and the Real-time Applications and Infrastructure Area. J. Peterson, C. Jennings, R. Sparks. March 2010. (Obsoletes RFC 3427) (Updates RFC 3265, RFC 3969) (Status: Best Current Practice)

5730	Extensible Provisioning Protocol (EPP). S. Hollenbeck. August 2009. (Obsoletes RFC 4930) (Also STD 0069) (Status: Internet Standard)
5751	Secure/Multipurpose Internet Mail Extensions (S/MIME) Version 3.2 Message Specification. B. Ramsdell, S. Turner. January 2010. (Obsoletes RFC 3851) (Status: Proposed Standard)
5761	Multiplexing RTP Data and Control Packets on a Single Port. C. Perkins, M. Westerlund. April 2010. (Updates RFC 3550, RFC 3551) (Status: Proposed Standard)
5764	Datagram Transport Layer Security (DTLS) Extension to Establish Keys for the Secure Real-time Transport Protocol (SRTP). D. McGrew, E. Rescorla. May 2010. (Status: Proposed Standard)
5766	Traversal Using Relays around NAT (TURN): Relay Extensions to Session Traversal Utilities for NAT (STUN). R. Mahy, P. Matthews, J. Rosenberg. April 2010. (Status: Proposed Standard)
5767	User-Agent-Driven Privacy Mechanism for SIP. M. Munakata, S. Schubert, T. Ohba. April 2010. (Status: Informational)
5806	Diversion Indication in SIP. S. Levy, M. Mohali, Ed. March 2010. (Status: Historic)
5839	An Extension to Session Initiation Protocol (SIP) Events for Conditional Event Notification. A. Niemi, D. Willis, Ed. May 2010. (Status: Proposed Standard)
5853	Requirements from Session Initiation Protocol (SIP) Session Border Control (SBC) Deployments. J. Hautakorpi, Ed., G. Camarillo, R. Penfield, A. Hawrylyshen, M. Bhatia. April 2010. (Status: Informational)
5870	A Uniform Resource Identifier for Geographic Locations ("geo" URI). A. Mayrhofer, C. Spanring. June 2010. (Status: Proposed Standard)
5876	Updates to Asserted Identity in the Session Initiation Protocol (SIP). J. Elwell. April 2010. (Updates RFC 3325) (Status: Informational)
5890	Internationalized Domain Names for Applications (IDNA): Definitions and Document Framework. J. Klensin. August 2010. (Obsoletes RFC 3490) (Status: Proposed Standard)
5897	Identification of Communications Services in the Session Initiation Protocol (SIP). J. Rosenberg. June 2010. (Status: Informational)
5910	Domain Name System (DNS) Security Extensions Mapping for the Extensible Provisioning Protocol (EPP). J. Gould, S. Hollenbeck. May 2010. (Obsoletes RFC 4310) (Status: Proposed Standard)
5922	Domain Certificates in the Session Initiation Protocol (SIP). V. Gurbani, S. Lawrence, A. Jeffrey. June 2010. (Updates RFC 3261) (Status: Proposed Standard)
5923	Connection Reuse in the Session Initiation Protocol (SIP). V. Gurbani, Ed., R. Mahy, B. Tate. June 2010. (Status: Proposed Standard)
5924	Extended Key Usage (EKU) for Session Initiation Protocol (SIP) X.509 Certificates. S. Lawrence, V. Gurbani. June 2010. (Status: Experimental)
5939	Session Description Protocol (SDP) Capability Negotiation. F. Andreasen. September 2010. (Updated by RFC 6871) (Status: Proposed Standard)
5947	Requirements for Multiple Address of Record (AOR) Reachability Information in the Session Initiation Protocol (SIP). J. Elwell, H. Kaplan. September 2010. (Status: Informational)
5974	NSIS Signaling Layer Protocol (NSLP) for Quality-of-Service Signaling. J. Manner, G. Karagiannis, A. McDonald. October 2010. (Status: Experimental)
6011	Session Initiation Protocol (SIP) User Agent Configuration. S. Lawrence, Ed., J. Elwell. October 2010. (Status: Informational)
6026	Correct Transaction Handling for 2xx Responses to Session Initiation Protocol (SIP) INVITE Requests. R. Sparks, T. Zourzouvillys. September 2010. (Updates RFC 3261) (Status: Proposed Standard)
6044	Mapping and Interworking of Diversion Information between Diversion and History-Info Headers in the Session Initiation Protocol (SIP). M. Mohali. October 2010. (Status: Informational)
6050	A Session Initiation Protocol (SIP) Extension for the Identification of Services. K. Drage. November 2010. (Status: Informational)

6051	Rapid Synchronisation of RTP Flows. C. Perkins, T. Schierl. November 2010. (Updates RFC 3550) (Status: Proposed Standard)
6061	Uniform Resource Name (URN) Namespace for the National Emergency Number Association (NENA). B. Rosen. January 2011. (Status: Informational)
6066	Transport Layer Security (TLS) Extensions: Extension Definitions. D. Eastlake 3rd. January 2011. (Obsoletes RFC 4366) (Status: Proposed Standard)
6068	The "mailto" URI Scheme. M. Duerst, L. Masinter, J. Zawinski. October 2010. (Obsoletes RFC 2368) (Status: Proposed Standard)
6072	Certificate Management Service for the Session Initiation Protocol (SIP). C. Jennings, J. Fischl, Ed., February 2011. (Status: Proposed Standard)
6076	Basic Telephony SIP End-to-End Performance Metrics. D. Malas, A. Morton. January 2011. (Status: Proposed Standard)
6086	Session Initiation Protocol (SIP) INFO Method and Package Framework. C. Holmberg, E. Burger, H. Kaplan. January 2011. (Obsoletes RFC 2976) (Status: Proposed Standard)
6116	The E.164 to Uniform Resource Identifiers (URI) Dynamic Delegation Discovery System (DDDS) Application (ENUM). S. Bradner, L. Conroy, K. Fujiwara. March 2011. (Obsoletes RFC 3761) (Status: Proposed Standard)
6117	IANA Registration of Enumservices: Guide, Template, and IANA Considerations. B. Hoeneisen, A. Mayrhofer, J. Livingood. March 2011. (Obsoletes RFC 3761) (Status: Proposed Standard)
6140	Registration for Multiple Phone Numbers in the Session Initiation Protocol (SIP). A.B. Roach. March 2011. (Updates RFC 3680) (Status: Proposed Standard)
6141	Re-INVITE and Target-Refresh Request Handling in the Session Initiation Protocol (SIP). G. Camarillo, Ed., C. Holmberg, Y. Gao. March 2011. (Updates RFC 3261) (Status: Proposed Standard)
6157	IPv6 Transition in the Session Initiation Protocol (SIP). G. Camarillo, K. El Malki, V. Gurbani. April 2011. (Updates RFC 3264) (Status: Proposed Standard)
6188	The Use of AES-192 and AES-256 in Secure RTP. D. McGrew. March 2011. (Status: Proposed Standard)
6189	ZRTP: Media Path Key Agreement for Unicast Secure RTP. P. Zimmermann, A. Johnston, Ed., J. Callas. April 2011. (Status: Informational)
6228	Session Initiation Protocol (SIP) Response Code for Indication of Terminated Dialog. C. Holmberg. May 2011. (Status: Proposed Standard)
6280	An Architecture for Location and Location Privacy in Internet Applications. R. Barnes, M. Lepinski, A. Cooper, J. Morris, H. Tschofenig, H. Schulzrinne. July 2011. (Updates RFC 3693, RFC 3694) (Also BCP 0160) (Status: Best Current Practice)
6337	Session Initiation Protocol (SIP) Usage of the Offer/Answer Model. S. Okumura, T. Sawada, P. Kyzivat. August 2011. (Status: Informational)
6350	vCard Format Specification. S. Perreault. August 2011. (Obsoletes RFC 2425, RFC 2426, RFC 4770) (Updates RFC 2739) (Updated by RFC 6868) (Status: Proposed Standard)
6357	Design Considerations for Session Initiation Protocol (SIP) Overload Control. V. Hilt, E. Noel, C. Shen, A. Abdelal. August 2011. (Status: Informational)
6416	RTP Payload Format for MPEG-4 Audio/Visual Streams. M. Schmidt, F. de Bont, S. Doehla, J. Kim. October 2011. (Obsoletes RFC 3016) (Status: Proposed Standard)
6442	Location Conveyance for the Session Initiation Protocol. J. Polk, B. Rosen, J. Peterson. December 2011. (Status: Proposed Standard)
6443	Framework for Emergency Calling Using Internet Multimedia. B. Rosen, H. Schulzrinne, J. Polk, A. Newton. December 2011. (Status: Informational)
6455	The WebSocket Protocol. I. Fette, A. Melnikov. December 2011. (Status: Proposed Standard)
6501	Conference Information Data Model for Centralized Conferencing (XCON). O. Novo, G. Camarillo, D. Morgan, J. Urpalainen. March 2012. (Status: Proposed Standard)
6503	Centralized Conferencing Manipulation Protocol. M. Barnes, C. Boulton, S. Romano, H. Schulzrinne. March 2012. (Status: Proposed Standard)

6505	A Mixer Control Package for the Media Control Channel Framework. S. McGlashan, T. Melanchuk, C. Boulton. March 2012. (Status: Proposed Standard)
6517	Mandatory Features in a Layer 3 Multicast BGP/MPLS VPN Solution. T. Morin, Ed., B. Niven-Jenkins, Ed., Y. Kamite, R. Zhang, N. Leymann, N. Bitar. February 2012. (Status: Informational)
6567	Problem Statement and Requirements for Transporting User-to-User Call Control Information in SIP. A. Johnston, L. Liess. April 2012. (Status: Informational)
6665	SIP-Specific Event Notification. A.B. Roach. July 2012. (Obsoletes RFC 3265) (Updates RFC 3261, RFC 4660) (Status: Proposed Standard)
6698	The DNS-Based Authentication of Named Entities (DANE) Transport Layer Security (TLS) Protocol: TLSA. P. Hoffman, J. Schlyter. August 2012. (Updated by RFC 7218) (Status: Proposed Standard)
6714	Connection Establishment for Media Anchoring (CEMA) for the Message Session Relay Protocol (MSRP). C. Holmberg, S. Blau, E. Burger. August 2012. (Status: Proposed Standard)
6787	Media Resource Control Protocol Version 2 (MRCPv2). D. Burnett, S. Shanmugham. November 2012. (Status: Proposed Standard)
6881	Best Current Practice for Communications Services in Support of Emergency Calling. B. Rosen, J. Polk. March 2013. (Also BCP 0181) (Status: Best Current Practice)
6910	Completion of Calls for the Session Initiation Protocol (SIP). D. Worley, M. Huelsemann, R. Jesske, D. Alexeitsev. April 2013. (Status: Proposed Standard)
6989	Additional Diffie–Hellman Tests for the Internet Key Exchange Protocol Version 2 (IKEv2). Y. Sheffer, S. Fluhrer. July 2013. (Updates RFC 5996) (Status: Proposed Standard)
7022	Guidelines for Choosing RTP Control Protocol (RTCP) Canonical Names (CNAMEs). A. Begen, C. Perkins, D. Wing, E. Rescorla. September 2013. (Obsoletes RFC 6222) (Updates RFC 3550) (Status: Proposed Standard)
7088	Session Initiation Protocol Service Example—Music on Hold. D. Worley. February 2014. (Status: Informational)
7158	The JavaScript Object Notation (JSON) Data Interchange Format. T. Bray, Ed. March 2014. (Obsoleted by RFC 7159) (Status: Proposed Standard)
7203	An Incident Object Description Exchange Format (IODEF) Extension for Structured Cybersecurity Information. T. Takahashi, K. Landfield, Y. Kadobayashi. April 2014. (Status: Proposed Standard)
7230	Hypertext Transfer Protocol (HTTP/1.1): Message Syntax and Routing. R. Fielding, Ed., J. Reschke, Ed. June 2014. (Obsoletes RFC 2145, RFC 2616) (Updates RFC 2817, RFC 2818) (Status: Proposed Standard)
7231	Hypertext Transfer Protocol (HTTP/1.1): Semantics and Content. R. Fielding, Ed., J. Reschke, Ed. June 2014. (Obsoletes RFC 2616) (Updates RFC 2817) (Status: Proposed Standard)
7232	Hypertext Transfer Protocol (HTTP/1.1): Conditional Requests. R. Fielding, Ed., J. Reschke, Ed. June 2014. (Obsoletes RFC 2616) (Status: Proposed Standard)
7233	Hypertext Transfer Protocol (HTTP/1.1): Range Requests. R. Fielding, Ed., Y. Lafon, Ed., J. Reschke, Ed. June 2014. (Obsoletes RFC 2616) (Status: Proposed Standard)
7234	Hypertext Transfer Protocol (HTTP/1.1): Caching. R. Fielding, Ed., M. Nottingham, Ed., J. Reschke, Ed. June 2014. (Obsoletes RFC 2616) (Status: Proposed Standard)
7235	Hypertext Transfer Protocol (HTTP/1.1): Authentication. R. Fielding, Ed., J. Reschke, Ed. June 2014. (Obsoletes RFC 2616) (Updates RFC 2617) (Status: Proposed Standard)
7250	Using Raw Public Keys in Transport Layer Security (TLS) and Datagram Transport Layer Security (DTLS). P. Wouters, Ed., H. Tschofenig, Ed., J. Gilmore, S. Weiler, T. Kivinen. June 2014. (Status: Proposed Standard)
7315	Private Header (P-Header) Extensions to the Session Initiation Protocol (SIP) for the 3GPP. R. Jesske, K. Drage, C. Holmberg. July 2014. (Obsoletes RFC 3455) (Status: Informational)
7339	7 Session Initiation Protocol (SIP) Overload Control. V. Gurbani, Ed., V. Hilt, H. Schulzrinne. September 2014. (Status: Proposed Standard)

7433	A Mechanism for Transporting User-to-User Call Control Information in SIP. A. Johnston, J. Rafferty. January 2015. (Status: Proposed Standard)
7434	Interworking ISDN Call Control User Information with SIP. K. Drage, Ed., A. Johnston. January 2015. (Status: Proposed Standard)
7462	URNs for the Alert-Info Header Field of the Session Initiation Protocol (SIP). L. Liess, Ed., R. Jesske, A. Johnston, D. Worley, P. Kyzivat. March 2015. (Updates RFC 3261) (Status: Proposed Standard)
7463	Shared Appearances of a Session Initiation Protocol (SIP) Address of Record (AOR). A. Johnston, Ed., M. Soroushnejad, Ed., V. Venkataramanan. March 2015. (Updates RFC 3261, RFC 4235) (Status: Proposed Standard)

Index

Page numbers followed by f and t indicate figures and tables, respectively.

B

C

F

G

J

K

L

M

N

Q

R

S

T

U

Milton Keynes UK
Ingram Content Group UK Ltd.
UKHW050440111024
449327UK00045B/2534